LET'S GO

■ THE RESOURCE FOR THE INDEPENDENT TRAVELER

"The guides are aimed not only at young budget travelers but at the independent traveler; a sort of streetwise cookbook for traveling alone."

—*The New York Times*

"Unbeatable; good sight-seeing advice; up-to-date info on restaurants, hotels, and inns; a commitment to money-saving travel; and a wry style that brightens nearly every page."

—*The Washington Post*

"Lighthearted and sophisticated, informative and fun to read. [Let's Go] helps the novice traveler navigate like a knowledgeable old hand."

—*Atlanta Journal-Constitution*

"A world-wise traveling companion—always ready with friendly advice and helpful hints, all sprinkled with a bit of wit."

—*The Philadelphia Inquirer*

■ THE BEST TRAVEL BARGAINS IN YOUR PRICE RANGE

"All the dirt, dirt cheap."

—*People*

"Anything you need to know about budget traveling is detailed in this book."

—*The Chicago Sun-Times*

"Let's Go follows the creed that you don't have to toss your life's savings to the wind to travel—unless you want to."

—*The Salt Lake Tribune*

■ REAL ADVICE FOR REAL EXPERIENCES

"The writers seem to have experienced every rooster-packed bus and lunar-surfaced mattress about which they write."

—*The New York Times*

"Value-packed, unbeatable, accurate, and comprehensive."

—*The Los Angeles Times*

"[Let's Go's] devoted updaters really walk the walk (and thumb the ride, and trek the trail). Learn how to fish, haggle, find work—anywhere."

—*Food & Wine*

LET'S GO PUBLICATIONS

TRAVEL GUIDES

Australia 8th Edition
Austria & Switzerland 12th edition
Brazil 1st edition
Britain & Ireland 2005
California 10th edition
Central America 9th edition
Chile 2nd edition
China 5th edition
Costa Rica 2nd edition
Eastern Europe 2005
Ecuador 1st edition **NEW TITLE**
Egypt 2nd edition
Europe 2005
France 2005
Germany 12th Edition
Greece 2005
Hawaii 3rd edition
India & Nepal 8th edition
Ireland 2005
Israel 4th edition
Italy 2005
Japan 1st edition
Mexico 20th edition
Middle East 4th edition
Peru 1st edition **NEW TITLE**
Puerto Rico 1st edition
South Africa 5th edition
Southeast Asia 9th edition
Spain & Portugal 2005
Thailand 2nd edition
Turkey 5th edition
USA 2005
Vietnam 1st edition **NEW TITLE**
Western Europe 2005

ROADTRIP GUIDE

Roadtripping USA **NEW TITLE**

ADVENTURE GUIDES

Alaska 1st edition
New Zealand **NEW TITLE**
Pacific Northwest **NEW TITLE**
Southwest USA 3rd edition

CITY GUIDES

Amsterdam 3rd edition
Barcelona 3rd edition
Boston 4th edition
London 2005
New York City 15th Edition
Paris 13th Edition
Rome 12th edition
San Francisco 4th edition
Washington, D.C. 13th edition

POCKET CITY GUIDES

Amsterdam
Berlin
Boston
Chicago
London
New York City
Paris
San Francisco
Venice
Washington, D.C.

LET'S GO

AUSTRIA & SWITZERLAND
INCLUDING MUNICH

KATE MCINTYRE EDITOR
VÉRONIQUE HYLAND ASSOCIATE EDITOR

RESEARCHER-WRITERS
PETER A. DODD
TOM MILLER
CATHERINE M. PHILLIPS
BARBARA RICHTER
ANDREA SPILLMANN
GUI WOOLSTON

WILL RIFFELMACHER MAP EDITOR
BRIANA CUMMINGS MANAGING EDITOR

ST. MARTIN'S PRESS ❧ NEW YORK

HELPING LET'S GO. If you want to share your discoveries, suggestions, or corrections, please drop us a line. We read every piece of correspondence, whether a postcard, a 10-page email, or a coconut. **Address mail to:**

Let's Go: Austria & Switzerland
67 Mount Auburn Street
Cambridge, MA 02138
USA

Visit Let's Go at **http://www.letsgo.com,** or send email to:

feedback@letsgo.com
Subject: "Let's Go: Austria & Switzerland"

In addition to the invaluable travel advice our readers share with us, many are kind enough to offer their services as researchers or editors. Unfortunately, our charter enables us to employ only currently enrolled Harvard students.

Maps by David Lindroth copyright © 2005 by St. Martin's Press.

Distributed outside the USA and Canada by Macmillan, an imprint of Pan Macmillan Ltd.
20 New Wharf Road, London N1 9RR
Basingstoke and Oxford
Associated companies throughout the world
www.panmacmillan.com

ISBN: 0-312-33542-3
EAN: 978-0312-33542-7
First edition
10 9 8 7 6 5 4 3 2 1

Let's Go: Austria & Switzerland is written by Let's Go Publications, 67 Mount Auburn Street, Cambridge, MA 02138, USA.

Let's Go® and the LG logo are trademarks of Let's Go, Inc.

ABOUT LET'S GO

GUIDES FOR THE INDEPENDENT TRAVELER

At Let's Go, we see every trip as the chance of a lifetime. If your dream is to grab a machete and forge through the jungles of Brazil, we can take you there. If you'd rather bask in the Riviera sun at a beachside cafe, we'll set you a table. We write for readers who know that there's more to travel than sharing double deckers with tourists and who believe that travel can change both themselves and the world—whether they plan to spend six days in London or six months in Latin America. We'll show you just how far your money can go, and prove that the greatest limitation on your adventures is not your wallet, but your imagination. After all, traveling close to the ground lets you interact more directly with the places and people you've gone to see, making for the most authentic experience.

BEYOND THE TOURIST EXPERIENCE

To help you gain a deeper connection with the places you travel, our researchers give you the heads-up on both world-renowned and off-the-beaten-track attractions, sights, and destinations. They engage with the local culture, writing features on regional cuisine, local festivals, and hot political issues. We've also opened our pages to respected writers and scholars to hear their takes on the countries and regions we cover, and asked travelers who have worked, studied, or volunteered abroad to contribute first-person accounts of their experiences. We've also increased our coverage of responsible travel and expanded each guide's Alternatives to Tourism chapter to share more ideas about how to give back to local communities and learn about the places you travel.

FORTY-FIVE YEARS OF WISDOM

Let's Go got its start in 1960, when a group of creative and well-traveled students compiled their experience and advice into a 20-page mimeographed pamphlet, which they gave to travelers on charter flights to Europe. Four and a half decades later, we've expanded to cover six continents and all kinds of travel—while retaining our founders' adventurous attitude toward the world. Our guides are still researched and written entirely by students on shoestring budgets, experienced travelers who know that train strikes, stolen luggage, food poisoning, and marriage proposals are all part of a day's work. This year, we're expanding our coverage of South America and Southeast Asia, with brand-new *Let's Go: Ecuador*, *Let's Go: Peru*, and *Let's Go: Vietnam*. Our adventure guide series is growing, too, with the addition of *Let's Go: Pacific Northwest Adventure* and *Let's Go: New Zealand Adventure*. And we're immensely excited about our new *Let's Go: Roadtripping USA*—two years, eight routes, and sixteen researchers and editors have put together a travel guide like none other.

THE LET'S GO COMMUNITY

More than just a travel guide company, Let's Go is a community. Our small staff comes together because of our shared passion for travel and our desire to help other travelers see the world. We love it when our readers become part of the Let's Go community as well—when you travel, drop us a postcard (67 Mt. Auburn St., Cambridge, MA 02138, USA) or send us an e-mail (feedback@letsgo.com) to tell us about your adventures and discoveries.

For more information, visit us online: www.letsgo.com.

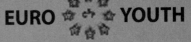

CONTENTS

RESEARCHER-WRITERS

Peter A. Dodd
Salzburger Land, Styria, Tyrol

Peter's route allowed him to savor the opera in Graz and chat up *Privatzimmer* owners in Salzburg. His weekly phone calls were full of colorful stories dramatizing his exploits on the road. Peter has always had a theatrical bent. This past spring, he did more than 200 costume changes during the run of the Hasty Pudding Theatricals drag show. We'll remember him best, though, as the founding member of the Mozart Society Singers and Dancers.

Tom Miller
Italian Switzerland

This was Tom's second time researching for Austria and Switzerland, but his first time bungee-ing off the highest freestanding jump in the world. Luckily, he survived to finish his copybatch. This marathon runner and avid hiker brought energy and stamina to his route. An alum of On Thin Ice, an improv group, Tom was never at a loss for words as he braved language barriers to provide us with the freshest, cleanest copy this side of the Alps.

Catherine M. Phillips
Carinthia, Upper Austria, Lower Austria

Catherine, an Alabama gal, is an old hand at *Let's Go*. She edited *Let's Go: Spain and Portugal 2004* last year, but this was her first time on the road. A modern European history major, she brought a unique understanding of Austria to her writing. When she wasn't sampling Austrian chocolate, she was soaking up the sun at lakes along her route. A guitarist and classical pianist, she delighted in Austria's musical heritage.

Barbara Richter
Vienna, Burgenland

A native Austrian, Barbara brought her encyclopedic knowledge of the region and her chemist's eye for detail to Vienna, her birthplace, only a short trip from her one-time home in Mödling. She used her street smarts to fill the book with great tips and local insights. Her perfect German allowed her to navigate the labyrinthine city with ease. Now that she has completed her route, she will have more time to pursue her passions for snowboarding and rugby.

Andrea Spillmann
German-Speaking Switzerland, Western Austria

Andrea's route covered a wide swath of Switzerland, Liechtenstein, and western Austria, and she collected passport stamps from four countries along the way. Having visited her Swiss grandparents several times growing up, she took to her assignment like a native. This friendly young actress made new friends everywhere she went. Her wild side came out when she tried a new sport for the first time—paragliding.

Gui Woolston
Francophone Switzerland

Gui joined us from the wilds of Connecticut, ready and rarin' to hike his way through Switzerland. His love of the outdoors lent itself to his coverage of extreme sports meccas like Interlaken and the Thunersee. He brought the same clarity of prose to his coverage of larger cities like Geneva, Lausanne, and Bern. An extraordinarily dedicated and conscientious RW, Gui always kept us posted on his adventures.

CONTRIBUTING WRITERS

Alexander Bevilacqua   *Munich*

Alex brought his European flair and appreciation of art to his route, effortlessly blending in with the locals. A student who loves learning about intellectual history, Alex is a world traveler, having spent time in Australia, Italy, Ecuador, Germany, and the United States.

Katherine J. Thompson   *Editor,* Let's Go: Germany

Will B. Payne   *Associate Editor,* Let's Go: Germany

Eric Idsvoog is a PhD candidate in English and American Literature and Language at Harvard University. His areas of expertise include Romanticism and the theory of Romanticism and British, French, and German literature.

Roxana Myrhum is a Social Studies concentrator at Harvard College.

ACKNOWLEDGMENTS

LET'S GO

TEAM A&S THANKS: Will, Brie, and the basement, for your excellent work on maps, your editing prowess, and good times, respectively.

KATE THANKS: Andrea, Barbara, Catherine, Gui, Peter, and Tom. You were a dedicated and fun bunch. Véronique, my AE, for your grace, great sense of humor, and friendship. Will—you rocked those maps. Thanks. Thank you Brie, for your patience and kindness, both as my boss and as my roommate. Christine, thank you for your support and your shopping companionship. I'll miss you dearly. Ben, thanks for bringing the Salina flavor. Andrew, you're the best drinking buddy a girl could have. Clarice, thanks for always being a phone call away. I wish you were even closer. Thanks to Zoila, Kath, and Jess for 3 great years, and to the basement, for a fun summer. Thank you, mom and dad, for your continued love and encouragement.

VÉRONIQUE THANKS: My RWs, for all your hard work and good humor. Kate, for being an amazing editor and friend. Brie, for eagle-eyed edits and keeping me calm. Will, for giving great map. The basement, for 80s playlists and crazy nights out. Yailett, Pragati, Marissa, Laura, Eoghan, Sam J, Matt, Jannie, and Jeff for making my summer in Cambridge so memorable. Alix, for hilarious dispatches from Manhattan. Chris and Johnicka, for keeping up the Yonkers pride. Finally, to my parents, for supporting my decision to take this job and for whisking me away for weekends on Cape Cod.

WILL THANKS: Kate and Veronique for all of their hard work, Elizabeth and the rest of mapland for a chilling summer and my family for all of their support.

Editor
Kate McIntyre
Associate Editor
Véronique Hyland
Managing Editor
Briana Cummings
Map Editor
Will Riffelmacher
Typesetter
Christine Yokoyama

Publishing Director
Emma Nothmann
Editor-in-Chief
Teresa Elsey
Production Manager
Adam R. Perlman
Cartography Manager
Elizabeth Halbert Peterson
Design Manager
Amelia Aos Showalter
Editorial Managers
Briana Cummings, Charlotte Douglas, Ella M. Steim, Joel August Steinhaus, Lauren Truesdell, Christina Zaroulis
Financial Manager
R. Kirkie Maswoswe
Marketing and Publicity Managers
Stef Levner, Leigh Pascavage
Personnel Manager
Jeremy Todd
Low-Season Manager
Clay H. Kaminsky
Production Associate
Victoria Esquivel-Korsiak
IT Director
Matthew DePetro
Web Manager
Rob Dubbin
Associate Web Manager
Patrick Swieskowski
Web Content Manager
Tor Krever
Research and Development Consultant
Jennifer O'Brien
Office Coordinators
Stephanie Brown, Elizabeth Peterson

Director of Advertising Sales
Elizabeth S. Sabin
Senior Advertising Associates
Jesse R. Loffler, Francisco A. Robles, Zoe M. Savitsky
Advertising Graphic Designer
Christa Lee-Chuvala

President
Ryan M. Geraghty
General Manager
Robert B. Rombauer
Assistant General Manager
Anne E. Chisholm

HOW TO USE THIS BOOK

COVERAGE. Welcome to *Let's Go: Austria and Switzerland 2005!* We'll be your guide to all things Austrian and Swiss, from alphorns to the Zillertal. In this book, Austria precedes Switzerland, and each country is broken down into regions that are covered in chapters that move in a clockwise direction geographically. As in real life, Liechtenstein is sandwiched between Austria and Switzerland. Black tabs on the side of each page should help you navigate your way, and an extensive index is always there to fall back upon.

LISTINGS. Unless otherwise noted, our researchers list establishments in order of value from best to worst. Our absolute favorites are awarded the *Let's Go* thumb-pick (🖐). These are also listed "thumbpicks" in the index. Since best value does not always mean cheapest price, we indicate a restaurant or lodging's relative price by means of price ranges ranked ❶ to ❺ (p. xiii).

FEATURES. In addition to providing up-to-date coverage, *Let's Go: Austria and Switzerland 2005* also includes off-the-beaten-track prose detours on items of unique interest to travelers in Austria and Switzerland. Painstakingly compiled by researchers in the field, these features range from information on hidden deals like sleeping in a Swiss barn (see p. 406) to spotlights on local cuisine, such as "Graubunden Grub" (see p. 429) to interviews with vivid locals to the lowdown on regional legends and festivals.

SCHOLARLY ARTICLES. To further aid travelers in understanding the destinations, *Let's Go* solicits experts for in-depth treatments of regional political and cultural issues. This year's article, by literature scholar Eric Idsvoog, examines the role of the Alps in literature.

LANGUAGE ISSUES. Switzerland is a country with four languages and confusing dialects. Though your English may carry you through Vienna and Salzburg, at some point you may be at a loss for words (in a bad way) in Austria as well. To better aid you, this book's appendix (see p. 553) contains a chart of useful phrases in German, French, and Italian. Places that have names in more than one language have all of the names given in the text and maps show the most commonly used name first; when place names differ from their common English names, the English word is listed in parentheses as appropriate. For convenience, common foreign words (like *Altstadt, vieille ville,* and *città vecchia*—all of which mean "old town") are translated when first introduced, and italicized throughout.

SOLO TRAVELERS. Unless otherwise stated, we assume that our reader is a solo traveler. Accommodations and transportation information in this guide is therefore geared toward options for the solo traveler; transportation prices are one-way unless otherwise noted. Nonetheless, we also report on accommodations for travelers in larger groups wherever feasible.

A NOTE TO OUR READERS. The information for this book was gathered by *Let's Go* researchers from May through August of 2004. Each listing is based on one researcher's opinion, formed during his or her visit at a particular time. Those traveling at other times may have different experiences since prices, dates, hours, and conditions are always subject to change. You are urged to check the facts presented in this book beforehand to avoid inconvenience and surprises.

1 2 3 4 5

PRICE RANGES>>AUSTRIA AND SWITZERLAND

Our researchers list establishments in order of value from best to worst; our favorites are denoted by the Let's Go thumbs-up (). Since the best value is not always the cheapest price, however, we have also incorporated a system of price ranges, based on a rough expectation of what you'll spend. For **accommodations,** we base our range on the cheapest price for which a single traveler can stay for one night. For **restaurants** and other dining establishments, we estimate the average amount a traveler will spend. The table tells you what you'll *typically* find in Austria and Switzerland at the corresponding price range; keep in mind that no system can allow for every individual establishment's quirks, and you'll typically get more for your money in larger cities. In other words: expect anything.

ACCOMMODATIONS	RANGE	WHAT YOU'RE *LIKELY* TO FIND
❶	under €15/23SFr	Camping; most HI and university dorm rooms, expect bunk beds and a communal bath; you may have to provide or rent towels and sheets.
❷	€16-25/24-54SFr	Upper-end hostels or small hotels. You may have a private bathroom, or there may be a sink in your room and a communal shower in the hall.
❸	€26-34/55-85SFr	A small room with a private bath. Should have decent amenities, such as phone and TV. Breakfast may be included in the price of the room.
❹	€35-55/86-170SFr	Similar to 3, but may have more amenities or be in a more touristy area.
❺	above €55/170SFr	Large hotels or upscale chains. If it's a 5 and it doesn't have the perks you want, you've paid too much.

FOOD	RANGE	WHAT YOU'RE *LIKELY* TO FIND
❶	under €5/12SFr	Mostly street-corner stands, pizza places, or fast-food joints. Rarely ever a sit-down meal.
❷	€6-10/13-23SFr	Sandwiches, appetizers at a bar, or low-priced entrées. You may have the option of sitting down or getting take-out.
❸	€10-16/24-37SFr	Mid-priced entrées, possibly coming with soup or salad. You'll probably have a waiter, so factor in the tip.
❹	€17-25/38-52SFr	A somewhat fancy restaurant. Few in this range have a dress code, but some may look down on t-shirts and jeans.
❺	above €26/53SFr	Sophisticated food, a stocked wine list, and a swank atmosphere. Dress well; there may be someone in the bathroom to hand you little towels.

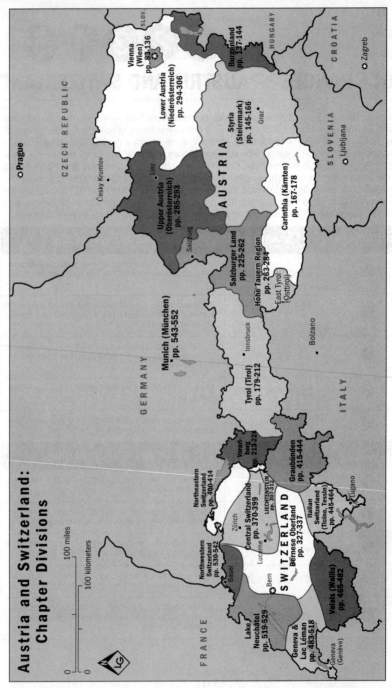

Austria and Switzerland: Chapter Divisions

CZECH REPUBLIC

◊ Prague

Český Krumlov

Vienna (Wien) pp. 83–136 ✦

SLOV

HUNGARY

Burgenland pp. 137–144

CROATIA

◊ Zagreb

GERMANY

Munich (München) pp. 543–552

Linz

Upper Austria (Oberösterreich) pp. 285–293

Lower Austria (Niederösterreich) pp. 294–306

Salzburg

AUSTRIA

Graz

Styria (Steiermark) pp. 145–166

SLOVENIA

◊ Ljubljana

Salzburger Land pp. 225–262

Hohe Tauern Region pp. 263–284

East Tyrol (Osttirol)

Carinthia (Kärnten) pp. 167–178

Innsbruck

Tyrol (Tirol) pp. 179–212

Bolzano

ITALY

Northeastern Switzerland pp. 400–414

Zürich

Vorarl-berg pp. 213–224

LIECHTENSTEIN pp. 307–312

Graubünden pp. 415–444

Northwestern Switzerland pp. 530–542

Basel

Central Switzerland pp. 370–399

Luzern

SWITZERLAND

Bern ✦

Bernese Oberland pp. 327–337

Italian Switzerland (Ticino, Tessin) pp. 445–464

Lugano

FRANCE

Lake Neuchâtel pp. 519–529

Geneva & Lac Léman pp. 483–518

Geneva (Genève)

Valais (Wallis) pp. 465–482

100 miles
100 kilometers
0
0

XIV

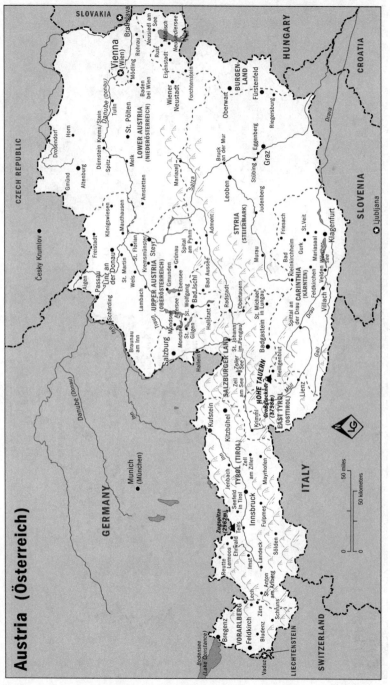

Austria (Österreich)

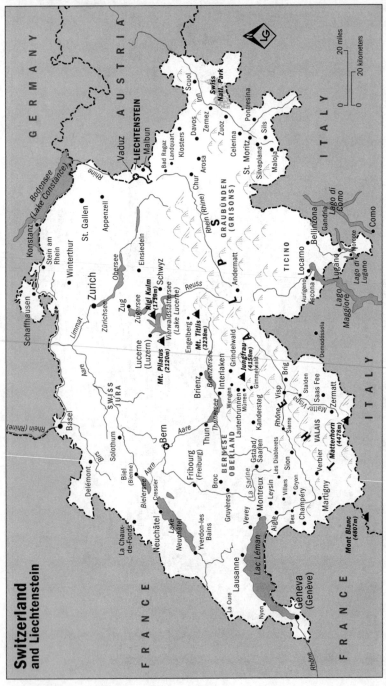

Switzerland
and Liechtenstein

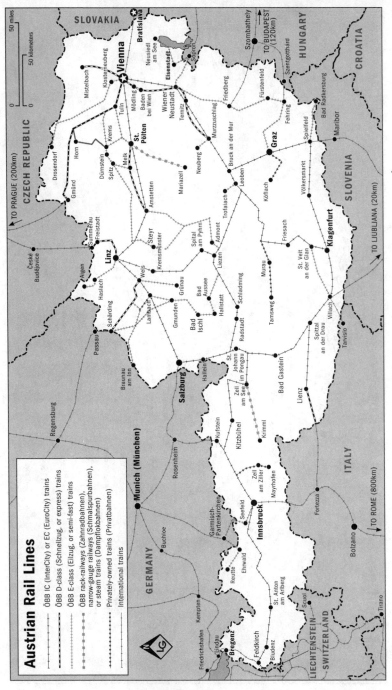

Austrian Rail Lines

- ÖBB IC (InterCity) or EC (EuroCity) trains
- ÖBB D-class (Schnellzug, or express) trains
- ÖBB E-class (Eilzug, or semi-fast) trains
- ÖBB rack-railways (Zahnradbahnen), narrow-gauge railways (Schmalspurbahnen), or steam trains (Dampflokbahnen)
- Privately-owned trains (Privatbahnen)
- International trains

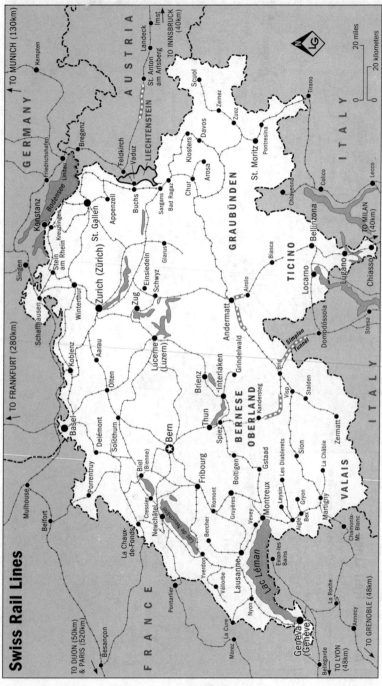

Swiss Rail Lines

DISCOVER
AUSTRIA AND
SWITZERLAND

Austria and Switzerland are an adventurer's paradise, with infinite opportunities for pulse-quickening exploits. Mountain climbing, paragliding, and canyoning, along with unparalleled opportunities for hiking and skiing, provide exposure to an outdoors that has awed visitors for centuries. Though Austria and Switzerland's scenic beauty is ample explanation of why the countries draw millions of tourists each year, it would be wrong to assume that this alone accounts for their popularity. Besides the glorious summits and breathtaking Alpine trails, there are the world-class cities of Vienna, Salzburg, Geneva and Zurich, which showcase many of Europe's most prized artistic, musical, and architectural treasures. Smaller cities like Klagenfurt, Hallstatt, and Lucerne, as well as countless picturesque hamlets, add to the countries' allure with their captivating *Altstädte* (old towns) and quaint charm. Linking everything is a dense network of carefully coordinated trains and well-tended budget accommodations, all of which help thrifty travelers explore on schedule and in comfort.

FACTS AND FIGURES

CAPITAL OF AUSTRIA: Vienna	**CAPITAL OF SWITZERLAND:** Bern
POPULATION: 8,170,000	**POPULATION:** 7,450,000
LIFE EXPECTANCY: men 76, women 82	**LIFE EXPECTANCY:** men 77, women 83
LAND AREA: 83,857km^2 (32,377 mi.^{2})	**LAND AREA:** 41,285 km^2 (15,941 mi.^{2})
LANGUAGE: German	**LANGUAGES:** German, French, Italian, and Romansch
RELIGION: 74% Catholic, 5% Protestant, 4% Muslim, 17% other	**RELIGION:** 46% Catholic, 40% Protestant, 14% other

WHEN TO GO

Everything has its season in Austria and Switzerland, so determine what your primary interests are when deciding when to travel. Outdoor enthusiasts should know that December to March is peak ski season, while July and August are ideal for hiking. In ski country, lodgings are scarcer and more expensive in winter, while cities see increased prices during the summer; rooms can be harder to come by if you don't have a reservation. The cheapest time to go is in the shoulder season (May-June and Sept.-Oct.), when there is the added benefit of milder weather. However, many mountain towns throughout Austria and Switzerland shut down completely in May and June so that the

TOP 10 OFFBEAT FESTIVALS

Since music festivals in Austria and Switzerland are a dime a dozen, the other revelry is often overlooked. Both countries, however, host hundreds of festivals celebrating everything from sheep herding to bacon. Here, a selection of the best:

1. **International Guitar Festival, Fribourg** (p. 528). Late April brings a chance for dozens of performers to show off their chops.
2. **Festival of 1000 Wines, Eisenstadt** (p. 140). Drinking all 1000 might be a bad idea, but this August festival will allow for plenty of sampling.
3. **Schäferwochenende Belalp, Brig** (p. 476). Townspeople herd 2000 sheep from the hills into the heart of Brig the last week in August.
4. **Street Parade, Zurich** (p. 383). Zurichers will be literally dancing in the streets to techno music at this outrageous city-wide rave.
5. **Foire du Lard (Bacon Fair), Martigny** (p. 480). Every December, this Swiss town celebrates this fatty favorite with an outdoor market.
6. **William Tell Shootout, Thun** (p. 303). Aim for the apple at this quirky town event.
7. **Apricot (Marille) Festival, Krems** (p. 299). Savor this delectable fruit in all its forms—including wine—during this summer festival.
8. **Humorfestival, Arosa** (p. 523). Bust a gut at this December celebration of comedy.
9. **Foire du Valais, Martigny** (p. 480). Check out this fair's traditional cowfights.
10. **Festival of Barrel Organs and Ballad Singers, Thun** (p. 341). This folksy festival keeps Thun tuneful in July.

hostel owners can take a break from providing vacations for others. Christmas time is particularly magical in Austria—entire towns are decorated for the holidays and *Christkindlmarkets* selling handmade ornaments, toys, and nutcrackers spring up in the central squares. If you're a classical music or theater fan, be aware that the Vienna State Opera, the Vienna Boys' Choir, and major theaters throughout Austria and Switzerland don't have any performances during July and August, though these months are prime time to frolic in the sun at popular music festivals.

A LEGACY OF CULTURE

Thanks to the imperious Hapsburgs and the smart banking of the savvy Swiss, the two nations have amassed an impressive collection of masterpieces in their museums. **Vienna** has historically reigned supreme as far as paintings are concerned: one of the four largest art collections in the world, collected and commissioned by the Hapsburgs, is now stored in the **Kunsthistorisches Museum** (p. 124). The **Österreichische Galerie** assembles, among other pieces, great works from the Viennese artistic explosion at the beginning of the 20th century, including Klimt's *The Kiss*. The hip, contemporary side of Viennese culture is stored in the **Museums-Quartier,** a massive complex of museums and restaurants that opened its doors to rave reviews in 2001. Housing the **ZOOM Kindermuseum** for the under-12 set, as well as a dance performance center, gardens, and a pedestrian mall, this giant arena explores culture in all directions. To see where art was made—rather than stored—head to **Mozarts Wohnhaus** (p. 240) in **Salzburg.** On the way to Salzburg take a virtual flight at the **Ars Electronica** in **Linz** (p. 289). **Graz**'s recent designation as a cultural capital of Europe illustrates its commitment to the arts. **The Kunsthaus Graz** is a new addition to the museum landscape, added the same year Graz won its cultural capital title.

In Switzerland, don't miss the **Kunsthaus Zürich** (p. 382), which juxtaposes well-known masterpieces with cutting-edge art, or the **Oskar Reinhart Collections** in **Winterthur** (p. 387), where the buildings are as beautiful as the works by Daumier and Picasso within. A trip to **Lausanne** is worthwhile in part because of the haunting works in the **Collection de l'Art Brut** (p. 503), which reveal the unexpected wells of artistic potential locked in the minds of the peasant, the criminal, and the madman. For the young and noisy at heart, the clanging, hands-on, futuristic sculptures in the **Museum Jean Tinguely** are an irresistible draw to **Basel** (p. 537).

RELIVING HISTORY

Centuries of serfdom, feudalism, and imperial power-mongering have left their mark on the landscapes of Austria and Switzerland. Crumbling castles, elaborate palaces, and medieval inner cities will transport you back in time. In Austria, explore the ruins of **Burg Dürnstein** (p. 299), where Richard the Lionheart was held for ransom, or shiver in the Hexenzimmer (Witches' Room) of **Burg Kronegg** in Riegersburg (p. 158), built on a barren cliff of volcanic rock. If you're looking for something a little more ornate, the hulking and yellow **Stift Melk** (p. 301) takes the prize for ecclesiastical Baroque splendor. Vienna and Salzburg hold the lion's share of Austria's palaces—one of the most impressive is **Lustschloß Hellbrunn** (p. 245), which boasts hilarious Wasserspiele (water games) in its gardens.

In Switzerland, the **Château de Chillon** in Montreux (p. 508) is the subject of a famous poem by Lord Byron, while the **Castello di Montebello** in Bellinzona (p. 448) boasts a working drawbridge. The lavishly carved, gilt-wood library of the Benedictine monks in **St. Gallen** (p. 409) is also a masterpiece. To complete the medieval experience, visit the town of **Stein am Rhein** (p. 403), or wander the labyrinthine streets of **Bern** (p. 327).

THE BEATEN PATH...

The backpacker's world is a remarkably small one, concentrated around large hostels in strategic locations throughout Austria and Switzerland. If you want to follow the beaten path and go with the partying crowd, Switzerland's backpacker mecca is **Interlaken** (p. 345), which boasts a dizzying aggregation of hostels and a year-round crowd of young, English-speaking travelers seeking adrenaline rushes of every sort imaginable. Other Swiss hot spots are **Zermatt** (p. 465), **Zurich** (p. 371), **Montreux** (p. 505), and **Geneva** (p. 483). In Austria, nothing can touch **Vienna** and its vast array of accommodations (p. 83) for backpacker-congregating, though **Innsbruck** (p. 179) and **Salzburg** (p. 226) are solid rivals.

...AND THE ROAD LESS TRAVELED

If you didn't come to hang out with the same English-speaking backpackers every night, head for the handful of smaller backpacker resorts/hostels hidden in the hills. Switzerland has a number of these getaways, including the **Swiss Alps Retreat** in Gryon (p. 517), the ultra-friendly **Hiking Sheep Guesthouse** in Leysin, and the adventure-oriented **Swiss Adventure Hostel** in Boltigen. Austria has the **Treehouse** hostel in Grünau (p. 257) and the gorgeous **Schloß Röthelstein** in Admont (p. 159). More comfortable and service-oriented than mainstream hostels, they offer the opportunity to get to know both the owners and the countryside well. *Privatzimmer* are a widespread option for experiencing Austrian and Swiss hospitality away from the crowds of travelers. Try quiet, gorgeous towns like **Sölden** (p. 210) and **Lech** (p. 205) in Austria or **Cressier** (p. 523) in Switzerland for a laid-back glimpse of everyday life in the two countries.

DISCOVER

SUGGESTED ITINERARIES

BEST OF AUSTRIA

BEST OF AUSTRIA (MIN. 2 WEEKS)
For the best nature and culture Austria has to offer, start your journey in **Bregenz** (p. 213), capital city of Vorarlberg. Spend a day in the city, on the shores of Europe's largest freshwater lake. Then spend another day poking around the rolling hills of the Bregenzerwald. Take a train ride through gorgeous Alpine scenery on the way to **Innsbruck** (p. 179). Wander through the old-world charm of the Hapsburg Empire's legacy in the morning and take a daytrip to Schloß Ambras in the afternoon. After that, explore the **Hohe Tauern National Park** from **Zell am See** (p. 273). Take one day to visit the **Krimml Waterfalls,** and another to admire the dramatic mountain scenery on the **Großglockner Hochalpenstraße.** Descend

from the mountains and head north to the hills of Salzburger Land. While it may be crowded with tourists, the **Salzburg** (p. 226) of Maria von Trapp and Mozart is not to be missed. Once one of the most powerful religious centers in Europe, this city boasts an impressive collection of worthy sights that remain from its cultural heyday. **Hallstatt** (p. 247), balanced between cliffs and a lake, is of historical interest as a cradle of European civilization, and is of immediate interest for its stunning hiking and ice caves. Don't forget to sneak down to **Graz** (p. 145), Austria's second-largest city. This vibrant university town hosts a variety of entertainment venues from opera to musical festivals. Don't miss the Schloßberg (castle mountain) for a bird's-eye view of the city. Make your way up to **Melk** (p. 299) for its unmistakable yellow abbey perched high on a hill. Save an afternoon for the Renaissance courtyard, Romanesque fortress, and Gothic chapel at Schloß Schallaburg, only 5km away. The imposing ruins of Schloß Dürnstein loom over the valley as you make your way along the Danube river, past **Krems** and **Stein,** to **Vienna** (p. 83) itself, the former Imperial headquarters. The magic of Strauss's waltzes and the thunder of Beethoven's symphonies reso-

DISCOVER

nate through Vienna's Baroque buildings. From the stately Staatsoper to the glittering Musikverein, the majestic Hofburg to Otto Wagner's simple Kirche am Steinhof, Vienna's attractions provide sensory stimulation galore.

BEST OF SWITZERLAND

BEST OF SWITZERLAND (MIN. 2 WEEKS) Spend your first day or two strolling the quiet squares around John Calvin's Cathédrale de St-Pierre in **Geneva** (p. 483), acquainting yourself with this international city and symbol of diversity for a quadrilingual nation. Make sure to check out the bohemian artist community called Artamis, as well as the UN and WTO buildings on International Head north to lakeside. Stroll through **Lausanne**'s (p. 496) *vieille ville* and visit the must-see Collection de l'Art Brut. Hit up **Neuchâtel** (p. 519), both for its own culinary delights and as a gateway to wine-tasting in tiny **Cressier** (p. 523). Then, step east to **Fribourg,** a refined, multilingual city that provides an easy daytrip to cheese-producing **Gruyères.** Skydive, bungee-jump, and river-raft your way to adrenaline-pumping happiness in **Interlaken** (p. 345), the adventure capital of the world. For quieter thrills, head south into the small mountain towns. Make the expensive but worth it daytrip to the **Jungfraujoch** (p. 352), appropriately dubbed the "top of Europe." To ease off your mountain high, let nearby **Lucerne** (p. 388) intrigue you with its *Altstadt,* museums, clear blue lake, and looming twin peaks. Then take the train to **Zurich** (p. 371) and explore one of the world's most influential banking centers, where Ulrich Zwingli and the Dadaists once tormented revolutions. Then get into hiking mode as you approach **Appenzell,** where down-home Swiss countryside hospitality welcomes you into peaceful forests, flowered meadows, and jagged mountains. To warm up from the crisp mountain air, head for the Mediterranean climate and Italian flair of **Locarno** (p. 448). Take a ferry ride on the calm waters of warm Lago Maggiore, and make a visit to the 500-year-old orange-yellow Franciscan monastery. Now head west to the mighty Alps in **Zermatt** (p. 465), home of the Matterhorn and a number of other towering peaks. The number of hikes and ski trails within walking distance of the town is unparalleled. Time your stay to see the annual Jazz Festival in **Montreux** (p. 505) from late July to early August. The festival attracts headlining acts and street-corner musicians from all over the world, creating an energetic, cosmopolitan atmosphere.

HIKING THE ALPS (MIN. 2 WEEKS) Test out your trail legs on the paths that extend from **Zermatt** (p. 465). The town's most exciting hikes lead to spectacular

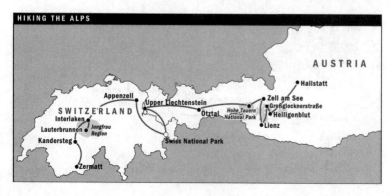

HIKING THE ALPS

views of (or hikes on) the Matterhorn (4199m). In close proximity are several of the highest mountains on the continent. In central Switzerland, unspoiled **Kandersteg** (p. 363) has hikes to glaciers and high-lying glacial lakes like Öschinensee. From there, take a train to **Interlaken** and head into the **Jungfrau region** (p. 352). Cliff-walled valleys allow for both level and extremely steep hikes. **Lauterbrunnen** (p. 356) is near a number of prominent water-falls, and each tiny village affords hikes near the imposing Jungfrau (4158m), Mönch (4099m), and Eiger (3970m), the last of which remains one of the most leg-endary mountaineering challenges in the world. To get away from any hint of a resort, head for rustic **Appenzell** (p. 411), where a network of country guesthouses will warm any hiker's heart (and stomach). Heading south to the wildest canton in the country, Graubünden will bring more splendid isolation in the **Swiss National Park** (p. 430). There is less human pres-ence here than almost anywhere else in the two countries. Nature lovers will appre-ciate the unspoiled wildlife, and hard-core hikers can select between a variety of diffi-cult hikes.

On your way to Austria, make a stop in **Upper Liechtenstein** (p. 311). Above the prince's palace spread craggy peaks on open ridges that afford views into Austria, Switzerland, and Germany.

In Austria, head straight for dramatic scenery in the rugged mountains of the **Ötztal** (p. 210). Trails lead through steep green forests that turn into sweeping Alpine panoramas. Moving eastward, you'll run into the **Hohe Tauern National Park** (p. 263), the largest national park in

Europe. Countless paths lead through meadows and over glaciers beneath tower-ing summits. **Zell am See** to the north and **Lienz** to the south are bases for explora-tion; travel between them on the **Groß-glocknerstraße** (p. 266), arguably the most dramatic mountain road in Europe, if not the world. For the best Hohe Tauern hiking, stay in **Heiligenblut** (p. 268) beneath the Großglockner (3798m), Aus-tria's highest mountain. Finish in **Hallstatt** (p. 247). Hiking here leads past waterfalls and the lush foliage and chalk cliffs of the Dachstein range.

ALPINE SKIING (MIN. 3 WEEKS)

You could land just about anywhere in Switzerland or Austria in the winter and have a fabulous skiing experience. A num-ber of glaciers offer the opportunity for ski-ing year-round, even in August. It's important to differentiate between the fan-cier resorts and simpler ones—discerning travelers will find great skiing for their money *and* the chance to glimpse some famous faces. One good place to start is **Kitzbühel** (p. 195), where downhill skiing was actually invented in 1892—plan care-fully to avoid, view, or participate in the gigantic annual Hahnenkamm World Cup race. On your way west stop in **Mayrhofen** (p. 208), where even August finds skiers on the glacier in **Hintertux**. The next major resort valley to the west is the **Ötztal** (p. 210), which has a more down-to-earth feel, while still providing plenty of high-quality snow and slopes. From there, head into the **Arlberg** region, one of the world's most legendary resort areas. The center of the area is **St. Anton** (p. 203), which hosted

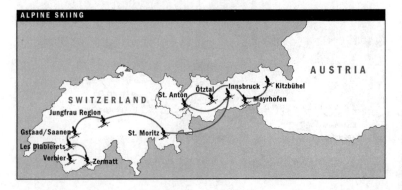

the 2000 World Championships and is usually considered the birthplace of modern skiing. From there, it's an easy train ride to **Innsbruck** (p. 179), home of the 1964 and 1976 Winter Olympics for good reason. Shuttles run to snow-covered mountains, even in summer.

Hopping the border to Switzerland, glitzy **St. Moritz** (p. 441) is a familiar name in any skiing household, particularly the royal families of Britain and Hollywood. From there, head to central Switzerland and the **Jungfrau Region** (p. 352) just south of the mega-resort town of **Interlaken.** The little towns wedged between big mountains provide reasonably priced skiing that will challenge skiers of all levels. Moving to the southwest, you'll run across thriving **Gstaad** and **Saanen** (p. 365), an international resort magnet. Gstaad is covered in movie-star glitz, while Saanen is down-to-earth. Both are especially suited for intermediates. French Switzerland does its best to compete, with **Les Diablerets** (p. 512), where snowboarders and younger crowds flock—even in summer, when glacier skiing draws the crowds. Finally, make sure to take the cog railway up to **Zermatt/Saas Fee** (p. 465), the ski paradise in southwestern Switzerland. Nearby is **Verbier** (p. 480), one of Europe's premier resorts, with more than enough size, snow, and challenge to back up its lofty reputation.

ESSENTIALS

PLANNING YOUR TRIP

ENTRANCE REQUIREMENTS
Passport (p. 9). Required for all foreign visitors.
Visa (p. 11). Required only for a continuous stay of more than three months.
Work Permit (p. 10). Required for all foreigners planning to work in Austria or Switzerland.
Driving Permit (p. 34). Required of all those planning to drive.

EMBASSIES AND CONSULATES

AUSTRIAN CONSULAR SERVICES ABROAD

Australia: 12 Talbot St., Forrest, **Canberra** ACT 2603 (☎00 6295 1533; www.austri-aemb.org.au). Consulates in **Adelaide, Brisbane, Cairns, Melbourne, Perth,** and **Sydney.**

Canada: 445 Wilbrod St., **Ottawa**, ON K1N 6M7 (☎613-789-1444; www.austro.org). Consulates in **Montreal, Toronto, Vancouver, Halifax, Calgary, Regina,** and **Winnipeg.**

Ireland: 15 Ailsesbury Court, 93 Ailesbury Road, **Dublin** 4 (☎01 269 45 77 or 269 14 51; fax 283 08 60; dublin-ob@bmaa.gv.at).

New Zealand: Consulate, Level 2, Willbank House, 57 Willis St., **Wellington** (☎04 499 63 93; fax 499 6392); another consulate in **Auckland.**

UK: 18 Belgrave Mews West, London SW1 X 8HU (☎020 7235 3731; www.austria.org.uk). Consulates in **Birmingham, Edinburgh,** and **Hamilton.**

US: 3524 International Ct. NW, Washington, D.C. 20008-3035 (☎202-895-6700; fax 895-6750; austrianembassy@washington.nu). Consulates in **Chicago, Los Angeles,** and **New York.**

SWISS CONSULAR SERVICES ABROAD

Australia: 7 Melbourne Ave., Forrest, **Canberra** ACT 2603 (☎(06) 6273 3977; fax 6273 3428; vertretung@can.rep.admin.ch). Consulates in **Melbourne** and **Sydney.**

Canada: 5 Marlborough Ave., **Ottawa**, ON K1N 8E6 (☎613-235-1837; fax 563-1394; vertretung@ott.rep.admin.ch). Consulates in **Montreal, Toronto,** and **Vancouver.**

Ireland: 6 Ailesbury Rd., Ballsbridge, Dublin 4 (☎01 353 1218 6382; fax 353 1283; vertretung@dub.rep.admin.ch).

New Zealand: Panama House., 22 Panama St., **Wellington** 6001 (☎04 472 15 93 or 472 15 94; fax 499 63 02); also a consulate in **Auckland**.

UK: 16-18 Montague Pl., London W1H 2BQ (☎020 76 16 60 00; www.eda.admin.ch/london_emb/e/home.html.) Consulates in **Belfast, Edinburgh, Manchester, Guernsey** and **Warwick/Bermuda.**

US: 2900 Cathedral Ave. NW, Washington, D.C. 20008-3499 (☎202-745-7900; www.swissemb.org). Consulates in **Atlanta, Chicago, Houston, Los Angeles, New York,** and **San Francisco.**

CONSULAR SERVICES IN AUSTRIA

All foreign embassies in Austria are located in Vienna.

Australia: IV, Mattiellistr. 2 (☎ 01 506 74; www.australian-embassy.at).

Canada: I, Laurenzerberg 2 (☎01 531 38 30 00; www.kanada.at).

Ireland: I, Hilton Centre, 16th fl., Landstrasse Hauptst. 2A (☎01 715 42 46; fax 713 60 04; irishemb@vienna.at).

UK: III, Jauresg. 10 (☎01 716 13 51 51; www.britishembassy.at).

US: IX, Boltzmanng. 16 (☎01 313 39; www.usembassy-vienna.at).

CONSULAR SERVICES IN SWITZERLAND

Nearly all foreign embassies in Switzerland are located in Bern.

Australia: Consulate: Geneva, Chemin des Fins 2, Case Postale 172, Geneva 1211 (☎022 799 91 00; fax 799 91 78; mission.australia@ties.itu.int).

Canada: Kirchenfeldstr. 88 (☎031 357 32 00; fax 357 32 10; bern@dfait-maeci.gc.ca).

Ireland: Kirchenfeldstr. 68, P.O. Box 3005, (☎031 352 14 42; fax 352 14 55; irlemb@bluewin.ch).

UK: Thunstr. 50 (☎031 359 77 00; www.britain-in-switzerland.ch).

US: Jubiläumstr. 93 (☎031 357 73 11; www.usembassy.ch).

AUSTRIAN NATIONAL TOURIST OFFICES

Australia and New Zealand: 36 Carrington St., 1st fl., **Sydney** NSW 2000 (☎02 9299 3621; fax 9299 3808; info@antosyd.org).

UK and Ireland: 14 Cork St. GB-**London** W13N3 (☎020 76 29 04 61; www.austria.info/uk).

US and Canada: 500 Fifth Ave., Suite 800, P.O. Box 1142, **New York,** NY 10110 (☎212-944-6885; fax 730-4568).

SWISS NATIONAL TOURIST OFFICES

UK: Swiss Centre, 10 Wardour St., **London** W1D 6QF (☎020 7851 1700).

US and Canada: 608 Fifth Ave., **New York,** NY 10020 (☎877-794-8037) International toll free number (☎800-100-200-30; www.myswitzerland.com). Additional offices in **San Francisco** (☎415-362-2260) and **Los Angeles** (☎310-640-8900). In **Canada** call toll free (☎800-002-0030) to be transferred to New York.

DOCUMENTS AND FORMALITIES

PASSPORTS

REQUIREMENTS

Citizens of Australia, Canada, Ireland, New Zealand, the UK, and the US need valid passports to enter Austria or Switzerland and to re-enter their home countries. Austria and Switzerland do not allow entrance if the holder's passport expires in under six months. Returning home with an expired passport is illegal, and may result in a fine.

NEW PASSPORTS

Citizens of Australia, Canada, Ireland, New Zealand, the United Kingdom, and the United States can apply for a passport at any post office, passport office, or court of law. Any new passport or renewal application must be filed well in advance of the departure date, although most passport offices offer rush services for a very steep fee.

PASSPORT MAINTENANCE

ONE EUROPE. European unity has come a long way since 1958, when the European Economic Community (EEC) was created to promote European solidarity and cooperation. Since then, the EEC has become the European Union (EU), a mighty political, legal, and economic institution. On May 1, 2004, ten South, Central, and Eastern European countries—Cyprus, the Czech Republic, Estonia, Hungary, Latvia, Lithuania, Malta, Poland, Slovakia, and Slovenia—were admitted to the EU, joining fifteen other member states: Austria, Belgium, Denmark, Finland, France, Germany, Greece, Ireland, Italy, Luxembourg, the Netherlands, Portugal, Spain, Sweden, and the UK.

What does this have to do with the average non-EU tourist? The EU's policy of **freedom of movement** means that border controls between the first 15 member states (minus Ireland and the UK, but plus Norway and Iceland) have been abolished, and visa policies harmonized. While you're still required to carry a passport (or government-issued ID card for EU citizens) when crossing an internal border, once you've been admitted into one country, you're free to travel to other participating states. Britain and Ireland have also formed a **common travel area,** abolishing passport controls between the UK and the Republic of Ireland.

For more important consequences of the EU for travelers, see **The Euro** (p. 13) and **European Customs** and **EU customs regulations** (p. 12).

Photocopy the page of your passport with your photo, as well as your visas, traveler's check serial numbers, and any other important documents. Carry one set of copies in a safe place, apart from the originals, and leave another set at home. Consulates also recommend that you carry an expired passport or an official copy of your birth certificate in a part of your baggage separate from other documents.

If you lose your passport, immediately notify the local police and the nearest embassy or consulate of your home government. To expedite its replacement, you will need to know all information previously recorded and show ID and proof of citizenship. In some cases, a replacement may take weeks to process, and it may be valid only for a limited time. Any visas stamped in your old passport will be irretrievably lost. In an emergency, ask for immediate temporary traveling papers that will permit you to re-enter your home country.

VISAS, INVITATIONS, AND WORK PERMITS

VISAS

Citizens of Australia, Canada, Ireland, New Zealand, the UK, and the US do not need visas to visit Austria and Switzerland. Austrian visas cost US$43 for a stay up to 90 days. Swiss visas cost US$44 for adults and US$22 for minors and allow you to spend up to a year in Switzerland. Visas can be purchased from the embassies of the two countries.

Double-check entrance requirements at the nearest embassy or consulate of Austria or Switzerland (listed under **Embassies and Consulates Abroad,** on p. 8) for up-to-date info before departure. US citizens can also consult www.pueblo.gsa.gov/cic_text/travel/foreign/foreignentryreqs.html.

WORK PERMITS

Admission to Austria and Switzerland as a visitor does not include the right to work, which is authorized only by a work permit. Studying in either country requires a special visa. For more information on both of these, see **Alternatives to Tourism** (p. 55).

IDENTIFICATION

When you travel, always carry at least two forms of identification on your person, including at least one photo ID. A passport and a driver's license or birth certificate is usually adequate. Never carry all of your IDs together. Split them up in case of theft or loss, and keep photocopies of all of them in your luggage and at home.

STUDENT, TEACHER, AND YOUTH IDENTIFICATION

The **International Student Identity Card (ISIC)**, the most widely accepted form of student ID, provides discounts on some sights, accommodations, food, and transport; access to a 24hr. emergency helpline; and insurance benefits for US cardholders. Applicants must be full-time secondary or post-secondary school students at least 12 years of age. Because of the proliferation of fake ISICs, some services (particularly airlines) require additional proof of student identity.

The **International Teacher Identity Card (ITIC)** offers teachers the same insurance coverage as the ISIC and similar but limited discounts. For travelers who are 25 years old or under but are not students, the **International Youth Travel Card (IYTC)** also offers many of the same benefits as the ISIC.

Each of these identity cards costs US$22 or equivalent. ISIC and ITIC cards are valid through the academic year in which they are issued; IYTC cards are valid for one year from the date of issue. Many student travel agencies (p. 23) issue the cards. For a list of issuing agencies or more information, see the **International Student Travel Confederation (ISTC)** website (www.istc.org).

The **International Student Exchange Card (ISE)** is a similar identification card available to students, faculty, and youth ages 12 to 26. The card provides discounts, medical benefits, access to a 24hr. emergency helpline, and the ability to purchase student airfares. The card costs US$25. Call US ☎ 800-255-8000 for more info, or visit www.isecard.com.

ESSENTIALS

CUSTOMS

Upon entering Austria or Switzerland, you must declare certain items from abroad and pay a duty on the value of those articles if they exceed the allowance established by the customs service of the country you are entering. Note that goods and gifts purchased at **duty-free** shops abroad are not exempt from duty or sales tax: "duty-free" merely means that you need not pay a tax in the country of purchase. Duty-free allowances were abolished for travel between EU member states on July 1, 1999, but still exist for those arriving from outside the EU. Upon returning home, you must likewise declare all articles acquired abroad and pay a duty on the value of articles in excess of your home country's allowance. In order to expedite your return, make a list of any valuables brought from home and register them with customs before traveling abroad, and be sure to keep receipts for all goods acquired abroad.

Austria and Switzerland prohibit or restrict the importation of firearms, explosives, ammunition, fireworks, booby traps, controlled drugs, most plants, lottery tickets, most animals, pornography, and items manufactured from protected species (e.g. ivory or fur). To avoid hassles about prescription drugs, ensure that your bottles are clearly marked and carry a copy of the prescription. No taxes are added to purchases made in Switzerland, though Austria has a value-added tax on certain items. Citizens of non-EU countries can get a refund of this tax for purchases of €75 or more (p. 15).

MONEY

CURRENCY AND EXCHANGE

Austria's unit of currency is the **euro (EUR/€)**, which is divided into 100 cents. Denominations for coins are 1, 2, 5, 10, 20, and 50 cents and 1 and 2 euros, while bills are available in amounts of 5, 10, 20, 50, 100, 200, and 500 euros. In Austria, railroad stations, airports, hotels, and most travel agencies offer exchange services, as do banks and currency exchanges.

The currency chart below is based on August 2004 exchange rates between local currency and Australian dollars (AUS$), Canadian dollars (CDN$), European Union euros (EUR€), New Zealand dollars (NZ$), British pounds (UK£), and US dollars (US$). Check the currency converter on websites like www.xe.com or www.bloomberg.com or a large newspaper for the latest exchange rates.

CURRENCY		
AUS$ = €0.5821		€ = AUS$1.7182
CDN$ = €0.6189		€ = CDN$1.6165
NZ$ = €0.5325		€ = NZ$1.8780
UK£ = €1.4926		€ = UK£0.6698
US$ = €0.8134		€ = US$1.2293

The Swiss monetary unit is the **Swiss franc (SFr)**, which is divided into 100 *centimes* (*Rappen* in German Switzerland). Coins are issued in 5, 10, 20, and 50 centimes and 1, 2, and 5 Swiss francs; bills come in denominations of 10, 20, 50, 100, 500, and 1000 Swiss francs. Currency exchange is easiest at ATMs, train stations, and post offices, where rates are close to bank rates but commissions are smaller.

As a general rule, it's cheaper to convert money in Austria or Switzerland than at home. Bring an ATM card and start your vacation without languishing in lines. Travelers from the US can get foreign currency from the comfort of home: **International Currency Express** (☎888-278-6628) delivers foreign currency or traveler's checks in two days (US$12) at competitive exchange rates.

Currency exchange kiosks and change machines should be your last resort when you need local funds. Most have unfavorable rates and charge hefty commissions. Banks, post offices, and small train stations often have better rates, but ATMs and credit cards are your best bet, since you'll profit from their low corporate rates (p. 13). The only drawback to ATMs is the transaction fee that some banks charge—be sure to check what the fee is with your bank at home. If you need to change cash or traveler's checks, take the time to compare the rates offered by different banks and kiosks (*Wechselstube* in German, *bureau de change* in French, *cambio* in Italian). A good rule of thumb is only to go to banks or kiosks with at most a 5% margin between their buy and sell prices. Since you lose money with each transaction, convert in large sums (unless the rate is unfavorable).

If you use traveler's checks or bills, carry some in small denominations (the equivalent of US$50 or less) for times when you are forced to exchange money at disadvantageous rates, but bring a range of denominations since charges may be levied per check cashed. Store your money in a variety of forms. Ideally, at any given time you will be carrying some cash, some traveler's checks, and an ATM and/or credit card. All travelers should also consider carrying some US dollars (about US$50 worth), which are often preferred by local tellers.

TRAVELER'S CHECKS

THE EURO. The official currency of 12 members of the European Union—Austria, Belgium, Finland, France, Germany, Greece, Ireland, Italy, Luxembourg, the Netherlands, Portugal, and Spain—is now the euro.

The currency has some important—and positive—consequences for travelers hitting more than one euro-zone country. For one thing, money-changers across the euro-zone are obliged to exchange money at the official, fixed rate (see below), and at no commission (though they may still charge a small service fee). Second, euro-denominated traveler's checks allow you to pay for goods and services across the euro-zone, again, at the official rate and commission-free.

At the time of printing, 1€=US$1.23=CA$1.62=NZ$1.88 For more info, check a currency converter (such as www.xe.com) or www.europa.eu.int.

Traveler's checks are one of the safest and least troublesome means of carrying funds. American Express and Visa are the most recognized brands. Many banks and agencies sell them for a small commission. Check issuers provide refunds if the checks are lost or stolen, and many provide additional services, such as toll-free refund hotlines abroad, emergency message services, and stolen credit card assistance. They are readily accepted in major cities in both Austria and Switzerland, but it is more difficult to use them in smaller, less-touristed towns. Ask about toll-free refund hotlines and the location of refund centers when purchasing checks, and always carry emergency cash.

CREDIT, DEBIT, AND ATM CARDS

Where they are accepted, credit cards often offer superior exchange rates, up to 5% better than the retail rate used by banks and other currency exchange establishments. Credit cards may also offer services such as insurance or emergency help, and are sometimes required to reserve hotel rooms or rental cars. **Mastercard** (a.k.a. EuroCard or Access in Europe) and **Visa** (a.k.a. Carte Bleue or Barclaycard) are the most welcomed. **American Express** cards work at some ATMs and at AmEx offices and major airports.

ATM cards are widespread in Austria and Switzerland. Depending on the system that your home bank uses, you can most likely access your personal bank account from abroad. ATMs get the same wholesale exchange rate as credit cards, but there is often a limit on the amount of money you can withdraw per day (usually around US$500). There is typically also a surcharge of around US$5 per withdrawal.

The two major international money networks are **Cirrus** (US ☎800-424-7787; www.mastercard.com) and **Visa/PLUS** (US ☎800-843-7587; www.visa.com). Most ATMs charge a transaction fee that is paid to the bank that owns the ATM.

GETTING MONEY FROM HOME

ATMS AND PINS. To use a cash or credit card to withdraw money from a cash machine (ATM) in Europe, you must have a 4-digit **Personal Identification Number (PIN)**. If your PIN is longer than 4 digits, ask your bank whether you can just use the 1st 4, or whether you'll need a new one. **Credit cards** don't usually come with PINs, so if you intend to hit up ATMs in Europe with a credit card to get cash advances, call your credit card company before leaving to request one.

Travelers with alphabetic, rather than numerical, PINs may also be thrown off by the lack of letters on European cash machines. The following are the corresponding numbers to use: 1=QZ, 2=ABC, 3=DEF, 4=GHI, 5=JKL, 6=MNO, 7=PRS, 8=TUV, and 9=WXY. Note that if you mistakenly punch the wrong code into the machine three times, it will swallow your card for good.

If you run out of money while traveling, the easiest and cheapest solution is to have someone back home make a deposit to the bank account linked to your credit card or ATM card. Failing that, consider one of the following options. The online **International Money Transfer Consumer Guide** (http://international-money-transfer-consumer-guide.info) may also be of help.

WIRING MONEY

It is possible to arrange a **bank money transfer,** which means asking a bank back home to wire money to a bank in Austria or Switzerland. This is the cheapest way to transfer cash, but it's also the slowest, usually taking several days or more. Note that some banks may only release your funds in local currency, potentially sticking you with a poor exchange rate: inquire about this in advance. Money transfer services like **Western Union** are faster and more convenient than bank transfers, but also much pricier. Western Union has many locations worldwide. To find one, visit www.westernunion.com, or call in Australia ☎800 501 500, in Canada 800-235-0000, in the UK 0800 83 38 33, or in the US 800-325-6000. In Austria call 01 514 00 29 86; in Switzerland call the office in Bern at 0800 81 10 99. Money transfer services are also available at **American Express** and **Thomas Cook** offices.

US STATE DEPARTMENT (US CITIZENS ONLY)

In serious emergencies only, the US State Department will forward money within hours to the nearest consular office, which will then disburse it according to instructions for a US$15 fee. If you wish to use this service, you must contact the Overseas Citizens Service division of the US State Department (☎317-472-2328; nights, Sundays, and holidays 202-647-4000).

TIPS FOR SAVING MONEY

Some simpler ways include searching out opportunities for free entertainment, splitting accommodation and food costs with trustworthy fellow travelers, and buying food in supermarkets rather than eating out. Bring a sleepsack (p. 15) to save on sheet charges in European hostels, and do your **laundry** in the sink (unless you're explicitly prohibited from doing so). That said, don't go overboard. Though staying within your budget is important, don't do so at the expense of your health or a great travel experience.

TIPPING

In **Switzerland,** gratuities are already automatically factored into prices. In **Austria,** menus will say whether service is included (*Preise inclusive* or *Bedienung inclusiv*). If it is, you don't have to tip. If it's not, leave a tip up to about 10%. In both countries, however, it is considered polite to round up your bill to the nearest euro or 1 or 2 francs as a nod of approval for good service. Tell the server how much you want back from the money you give: if you just say "*Danke,*" the server will most likely assume that you intend for him or her to keep the change. Don't leave tips on the table. Austrian restaurants expect you to seat yourself. Servers will not bring the bill until you ask them to do so: say "*Zahlen bitte*" (TSAHL-en BIT-uh). Some restaurants charge for each piece of bread eaten during your meal.

TAXES

No taxes are added to purchases made in **Switzerland.** In **Austria,** there is a 10-20% value added tax (VAT) on all books, clothing, souvenir items, art items, jewelry, perfume, cigarettes, alcohol, etc. Tourists must pay this tax at the time of purchase, but may get the tax refunded later if the amount of purchase is €75 (about US$70) or greater at a particular store. To get the refund, fill out the Austrian Form U-34 (the "Global Refund Cheque"), available at most stores, and an ÖAMTC quick refund form to get a check at the airport or train station. Make sure the store affixes their store identification stamp to the forms at the time of purchase. When you leave the country, go to the VAT or customs office (located in the airport or train station) to get your form validated for the amount of the refund, which can be cashed in the airport or station. Unfortunately, only non-EU citizens can claim the VAT refund.

PACKING

Pack lightly: Lay out only what you absolutely need, then take half the clothes and twice the money. The Travelite FAQ (www.travelite.org) is a good resource for tips on traveling light. The online **Universal Packing List** (http://upl.codeq.info) will generate a customized list of suggested items based on your trip length, the expected climate, your planned activities, and other factors. If you plan to do a lot of hiking, also consult **Camping and the Outdoors,** p. 44.

Luggage: If you plan to cover most of your itinerary by foot, a sturdy **frame backpack** is unbeatable. (For the basics on buying a pack, see p. 46.) Toting a **suitcase** or **trunk** is fine if you plan to live in 1 or 2 cities and explore from there, but not a great idea if you plan to move around frequently. In addition to your main piece of luggage, a **daypack** (a small backpack or courier bag) is useful.

Clothing: No matter when you're traveling, it's a good idea to bring a warm jacket or wool sweater, a rain jacket (Gore-Tex® is both waterproof and breathable), sturdy shoes or hiking boots, and thick socks. Flip-flops or waterproof sandals are must-haves for grubby hostel showers. You may also want one outfit for going out, and maybe a nicer pair of shoes. If you plan to visit any religious or cultural sites, remember that you'll need something besides tank tops and shorts to be respectful.

Sleepsack: Some hostels require that you either provide your own linen or rent sheets from them. Save cash by making your own sleepsack: fold a full-size sheet in half the long way, then sew it closed along the long side and one of the short sides.

Converters and adapters: In Austria and Switzerland, electricity is 230 volts AC, enough to fry any 120V North American appliance. Americans and Canadians should buy an adapter (US$20), which changes the shape of the plug, and a converter (US$20), which changes the voltage. Don't make the mistake of using only an adapter, unless appliance instructions explicitly state otherwise. New Zealanders and Australians, who use 230V at home, won't need a converter, but will need a set of adapters to use anything electrical. For more on all things adaptable, see http://kropla.com/electric.htm.

Toiletries: Toothbrushes, towels, cold-water soap, talcum powder (to keep feet dry), deodorant, razors, tampons, and condoms are often available, but may be difficult to find: bring extras. **Contact lenses** are likely to be expensive and difficult to find, so bring enough extra pairs and solution for your entire trip. Also bring your glasses and a copy of your prescription in case you need emergency replacements. If you use heat-disinfection, either switch temporarily to a chemical disinfection system (check first to make sure it's safe with your brand of lenses), or buy a converter to 220/240V.

First-aid kit: For a basic first-aid kit, pack bandages, a pain reliever, antibiotic cream, a thermometer, a Swiss Army knife, tweezers, moleskin, decongestant, motion-sickness remedy, diarrhea or upset-stomach medication (Pepto Bismol or Imodium), an antihistamine, sunscreen, insect repellent, burn ointment, and a syringe for emergencies (get an explanatory letter from your doctor).

Film: Film developing in Austria and Switzerland is extremely expensive, so consider bringing along enough film for your entire trip and developing it at home. Less serious photographers may want to bring a disposable camera or two. Despite disclaimers, airport security X-rays can fog film, so buy a lead-lined pouch at a camera store or ask security to hand-inspect it. Always pack film in your carry-on luggage, since higher-intensity X-rays are used on checked luggage.

Other useful items: For safety purposes, you should bring a **money belt** and small **padlock.** Basic **outdoors equipment** (plastic water bottle, compass, waterproof matches, pocketknife, sunglasses, sunscreen, hat) is also useful. **Quick repairs** of torn garments can be done on the road with a needle and thread; consider bringing electrical tape for patching tears. If you want to do laundry by hand, bring detergent, a small rubber ball to stop up the sink, and string for a makeshift clothesline. **Other things** you're liable to forget are an umbrella; sealable **plastic bags** (for damp clothes, soap, food, shampoo, and other spillables); an **alarm clock;** safety pins; rubber bands; a flashlight; earplugs; garbage bags; and a small **calculator.** A **cell phone** can be a lifesaver (literally) on the road; p. 38 has information on acquiring one that will work at your destination.

Important documents: Don't forget your passport, traveler's checks, ATM and/or credit cards, adequate ID, and photocopies of all of the aforementioned in case these documents are lost or stolen (p. 11). Also check that you have any of the following that might apply to you: a hosteling membership card (p. 41); driver's license (p. 11); travel insurance forms; ISIC card (p. 11), and/or rail or bus pass (p. 26/p. 32).

SAFETY AND HEALTH

GENERAL ADVICE

In any type of crisis situation, the most important thing to do is **stay calm.** Your country's embassy abroad (p. 9) is usually your best resource when things go wrong. Registering with that embassy upon arrival in the country is often a good idea. The government offices listed in the **Travel Advisories** box below can provide information on the services they offer their citizens in case of emergencies abroad.

DRUGS AND ALCOHOL

Marijuana, hashish, cocaine, and narcotics are illegal in Austria and Switzerland, and the penalties for illegal possession of drugs, especially for foreigners, range from stern to severe. It is not unknown for a dealer to increase profits by first selling drugs to tourists and then turning them in to authorities for a reward. The worst thing you can possibly do is carry drugs across an international border: not only could you end up in prison, you could also be hounded by a "Drug Trafficker" stamp on your passport for the rest of your life. Remember that you are subject to the laws of the country in which you travel, not to those of your home country, and it is your responsibility to familiarize yourself with these laws before leaving. Police officers (*Polizei* or *gendarmes)* typically speak little English.

In both Austria and Switzerland you must be 16 to drink legally. Beer is more common than soda, and a lunch without wine or beer is unusual.

SPECIFIC CONCERNS

NATURAL DISASTERS

Those interested in skiing and mountaineering should beware the possibility of avalanches. Hire an experienced guide for dangerous routes and do not venture off marked paths. Avalanches are most common in early and late winter.

TERRORISM

In the wake of the September 11, 2001 attacks on the United States, awareness of terrorist threats has heightened across Europe. Austria and Switzerland are relatively safe, but it is important to remain alert to potential dangers, particularly in major cities and tourist destinations. Follow the Austrian and Swiss news, comply with security measures, and pay attention to travel warnings. Report suspicious persons and unattended luggage or packages to proper authorities. Do not talk about bombs or terrorism in airports, even in jest or casual conversation, as airport security have been instructed to question and detain individuals who do so.

TRAVEL ADVISORIES. The following government offices provide travel information and advisories by telephone, by fax, or via the web:

Australian Department of Foreign Affairs and Trade: ☎ 13 00 555135; faxback service 02 6261 1299; www.dfat.gov.au.

Canadian Department of Foreign Affairs and International Trade (DFAIT): Canada and the US ☎ 800-267-8376, elsewhere call ☎ +1 613-944-4000; www.dfait-maeci.gc.ca. Call for their free booklet, *Bon Voyage...But.*

New Zealand Ministry of Foreign Affairs: ☎ 04 439 8000; fax 494 8506; www.mft.govt.nz/travel/index.html.

United Kingdom Foreign and Commonwealth Office: ☎ 020 7008 0232; fax 7008 0155; www.fco.gov.uk.

US Department of State: ☎ 202-647-5225; fax-back service 202-647-3000; http://travel.state.gov. For *A Safe Trip Abroad,* call ☎ 202-512-1800.

PERSONAL SAFETY

EXPLORING AND TRAVELING

Most safety problems can be avoided by using common sense. The gawking camera-toter is a more obvious target than the low-profile traveler, so try to blend in. Familiarize yourself with your surroundings before setting out. If you must check a map on the street, duck into a café or shop. If you are traveling alone, be sure that someone at home knows your itinerary, and never admit that you're traveling alone. When you arrive in a new city, find out what areas to avoid from the tourist office or the manager of your hostel. When walking at night, stick to busy, well-lit streets and avoid dark alleyways. If you ever feel uncomfortable, leave the area as quickly and directly as you can. Whenever possible, *Let's Go* warns of unsafe neighborhoods and areas, such as drug hangouts. The American Society of Travel Agents provides extensive information at their website (www.astanet.com), including a section on travel safety.

There is no sure-fire way to avoid all the threatening situations you might encounter while traveling, but a good **self-defense course** will give you concrete ways to react to unwanted advances. **Impact, Prepare, and Model Mugging** can refer you to local self-defense courses in the US (☎800-345-5425). Visit the website at www.impactsafety.org for a list of nearby chapters. Workshops (1½-3hr.) start at US$75; full courses (20-25hr.) run US$350-400.

If you are using a **car,** learn local driving signals and wear a seatbelt. Children under 40 lbs. should ride in carseats, available for a small fee from most car rental agencies. Study route maps before you hit the road, and if you plan on spending a lot of time driving, consider bringing spare parts. If your car breaks down, wait for the police to assist you. For long drives in desolate areas, invest in a cellular phone and a roadside assistance program (p. 35). Park your vehicle in a garage or well-traveled area, and use a steering wheel locking device in larger cities. **Sleeping in your car** is one of the most dangerous (and often illegal) ways to get your rest.

Driving in Austria and Switzerland is a pleasant but expensive proposition. Study route maps before you hit the road: depending on the region, some roads have poor (or nonexistent) shoulders, few gas stations, and roaming animals. Twisting mountain roads may be closed in winter, but, when open, require particular caution. Learn the **Alpine honk:** before going blind around an abrupt turn, stop and give the horn a toot before proceeding.

POSSESSIONS AND VALUABLES

Although Austria and Switzerland have low crime rates, thieves are happy to relieve ignorant tourists of their money. Be on the alert, particularly in crowds. Don't keep all your valuables (money, important documents, etc.) in one place. **Photocopies** of important documents allow you to recover them in case they are lost or filched. **Don't carry your wallet or money in your back pocket.** Never count your money in public and carry as little as possible. If you go to ATMs, avoid them in poorly lit or deserted areas and don't go at night. If you carry a purse, buy a sturdy one with a secure clasp, and carry it crosswise on the side away from the street with the clasp against you. Secure packs with small combination padlocks that slip through the two zippers. A **money belt** is the best way to carry cash. You can buy one at most camping supply stores. A nylon zippered pouch with a belt that sits inside the waist of your pants or skirt combines convenience and security. A **neck pouch** is an equally safe way to carry money, though less accessible. Refrain from pulling it out in public. If you must, be very discreet. Avoid keeping anything precious in a waist-pack: your valuables will be highly visible and easy to steal. Keep some money separate from the rest to use for emergencies or in case of theft.

Be particularly careful on **buses** and **trains:** horror stories abound about determined thieves who wait for travelers to fall asleep. Carry your backpack in front of you where you can see it. When traveling with others, sleep in alternate shifts. When alone, use good judgment in selecting a train compartment: never stay in an empty one, and use a lock to secure your pack to the luggage rack. Try to sleep on top bunks with your luggage stored above you (if not in bed with you), and keep important documents and other valuables on your person.

In public, watch your belongings at all times. Beware of con artists and **pickpockets** on the street and on public transportation. On buses and trains, keep your bag close to you. Don't check your baggage on trains, don't trust anyone to "watch your bag for a second," and don't ever put your belongings under your seat in train compartments. If you take a **night train**, either lock your bag to the luggage rack or use it as a pillow. In your hostel, if you can't lock your room, lock your bags in lockers or at the train station (you'll need your own **padlock**).

Be alert in public telephone booths: If you must say your calling card number, do so very quietly. If you punch it in, make sure no one can look over your shoulder.

There are a few steps you can take to minimize the financial risk associated with traveling. First, **bring as little with you as possible.** Second, buy a few combination **padlocks** to secure your belongings either in your pack or in a hostel or train station locker. Third, **carry as little cash as possible.** Keep your traveler's checks and ATM/credit cards in a **money belt**—not a "fanny pack"—along with your passport and ID cards. Fourth, **keep a small cash reserve separate from your primary stash.** This should be about US$50 (US dollars or euros are best) sewn into or stored in your pack, along with your traveler's check numbers and important photocopies.

If you will be traveling with electronic devices, such as a laptop computer or a PDA, check whether your homeowner's insurance covers loss, theft, or damage when you travel. If not, you might consider purchasing a low-cost separate insurance policy. **Safeware** (☎ US 800-800-1492; www.safeware.com) charges $90 for 90-day comprehensive international travel coverage for computers for up to $4000.

PRE-DEPARTURE HEALTH

In your **passport,** write the names of any people you wish to be contacted in case of a medical emergency, and list any allergies or medical conditions. Matching a prescription to a foreign equivalent is not always easy, safe, or possible, so if you take prescription drugs, consider carrying up-to-date, legible prescriptions or a statement from your doctor with the medication's trade name, manufacturer, chemical name, and dosage. While traveling, be sure to keep all medication in your carry-on luggage. For tips on packing a basic **first-aid kit** and other health info, see p. 16.

IMMUNIZATIONS AND PRECAUTIONS

Travelers over two years old should make sure that the following vaccines are up to date: MMR (for measles, mumps, and rubella); DTaP or Td (for diphtheria, tetanus, and pertussis); IPV (for polio); Hib (for *haemophilus* influenza B); and HepB (for Hepatitis B). For recommendations on immunizations and prophylaxis, consult the CDC (see below) in the US or the equivalent in your home country, and check with a doctor for guidance.

USEFUL ORGANIZATIONS AND PUBLICATIONS

The US **Centers for Disease Control and Prevention (CDC;** ☎ 877-FYI-TRIP; www.cdc.gov/travel) maintains an international travelers' hotline and an informative website. The CDC's comprehensive booklet *Health Information for International Travel* (The Yellow Book), an annual rundown of disease, immunization, and general health advice, is free online or US$29-40 via the Public Health Foundation (☎ 877-252-1200; http://bookstore.phf.org). Consult the appropriate government agency of your home country for consular information sheets on health, entry requirements, and other issues for various countries (see the listings in the box on **Travel Advisories, p. 17**). For quick information on health and other travel warnings, call the **Overseas Citizens Services** (M-F 8am-8pm, ☎888-407-4747, after-hours 202-647-4000, from overseas 317-472-2328), or contact a passport agency, embassy, or consulate abroad. For information on medical evacuation services and travel insurance firms, see the US government's website (http://travel.state.gov/medical.html) or the **British Foreign and Commonwealth Office** (www.fco.gov.uk). For general health info, contact the **American Red Cross** (☎800-564-1234; www.redcross.org).

STAYING HEALTHY

Common sense is the simplest prescription for good health while you travel. Drink lots of fluids to prevent dehydration and constipation, and wear sturdy, broken-in shoes and clean socks.

ONCE IN AUSTRIA AND SWITZERLAND

ENVIRONMENTAL HAZARDS

Heat exhaustion and dehydration: Heat exhaustion leads to nausea, excessive thirst, headaches, and dizziness. Avoid it by drinking plenty of fluids, eating salty foods (e.g. crackers), abstaining from dehydrating beverages (e.g., alcohol and caffeinated beverages), and always wearing sunscreen. Continuous heat stress can eventually lead to heatstroke, characterized by a rising temperature, severe headache, delirium, and cessation of sweating. Victims should be cooled off with wet towels and taken to a doctor.

Sunburn: Always wear sunscreen (SPF 30 is good) when spending excessive amounts of time outdoors. If you are planning on spending time near water, in the desert, or in the snow, you are at a higher risk of getting burned, even through clouds. If you get sunburned, drink more fluids than usual and apply an aloe-based lotion. Severe sunburns can lead to sun poisoning, a condition that affects the entire body, causing fever, chills, nausea, and vomiting. Sun poisoning should always be treated by a doctor.

Hypothermia and frostbite: A rapid drop in body temperature is the clearest sign of overexposure to cold. Victims may also shiver, feel exhausted, have poor coordination or slurred speech, hallucinate, or suffer amnesia. *Do not let hypothermia victims fall asleep.* To avoid hypothermia, keep dry, wear layers, and stay out of the wind. When the temperature is below freezing, watch out for frostbite. If skin turns white or blue, waxy, and cold, do not rub the area. Drink warm beverages, stay dry, and slowly warm the area with dry fabric or steady body contact until a doctor can be found.

High altitude: Take care when enjoying Austria and Switzerland's high-altitude hikes and outdoor activities. Allow your body a few days to adjust to less oxygen before exerting yourself. Note that alcohol is more potent and UV rays are stronger at high elevations.

INSECT-BORNE DISEASES

Many diseases are transmitted by insects, especially mosquitoes, fleas, ticks, and lice. Be aware of insects in wet or forested areas, especially while hiking and camping. Wear long pants and long sleeves, tuck your pants into your socks, and use a mosquito net. Use insect repellents such as DEET. **Mosquitoes**—responsible for the spread of malaria, dengue fever, yellow fever, and Japanese encephalitis, among other diseases—can be particularly dangerous in wet, swampy, or wooded areas. **Ticks**, responsible for Lyme and other diseases, can be particularly danger-ous in rural and forested regions, particularly in the Danube delta in Austria and the Winterthur region in Switzerland.

Tick-borne encephalitis: A viral infection of the central nervous system transmitted dur-ing the summer by tick bites (primarily in wooded areas) or by consumption of unpas-teurized dairy products. The risk of contracting the disease is relatively low, especially if precautions are taken against tick bites.

Lyme disease: A bacterial infection carried by ticks and marked by a circular bull's-eye rash of 2 in. or more. Later symptoms include fever, headache, fatigue, and aches and pains. Antibiotics are effective if administered early. Left untreated, Lyme can cause problems in joints, the heart, and the nervous system. If you find a tick attached to your skin, grasp the head with tweezers as close to your skin as possible and apply slow, steady traction. Removing a tick within 24hr. greatly reduces the risk of infection. Do not try to remove ticks with petroleum jelly, nail polish remover, or a hot match. Tick bites usu-ally occur in moist, shaded environments and heavily wooded areas. If you are going to be hiking in these areas, wear long clothes and DEET.

FOOD- AND WATER-BORNE DISEASES

Prevention is the best cure: be sure that your food is properly cooked and the water you drink is clean. Though health regulations in Austrian and Swiss restau-rants impose a high standard, watch out for food from markets or street vendors that may have been cooked in unhygienic conditions. Other potential culprits are raw shellfish, unpasteurized milk, and sauces containing raw eggs. When hiking, resist the temptation to drink from pristine-looking Alpine streams: even glacial runoff can be a home for bacteria. Instead, buy bottled water, or purify your own water by bringing it to a rolling boil or treating it with **iodine tablets.** Note, how-ever, that some parasites such as *giardia* have exteriors that resist iodine treat-ment, so boiling is more reliable. Always wash your hands before eating or bring a quick-drying purifying liquid hand cleaner.

Mad Cow Disease: Bovine spongiform encephalopathy (BSE), better known as Mad Cow Disease, is a chronic degenerative disease affecting the central nervous system of cat-tle that broke out in alarming numbers of cattle in 2001 and 2002. The human variant is called Creutzfeldt-Jakob disease (nvCJD). Both forms involve fatal brain disease. Information on nvCJD is not conclusive, but the disease is supposedly caused by con-suming infected beef. The risk is very small (around 1 case per 10 billion servings of meat). It is believed that consuming milk and milk products does not pose a risk.

Traveler's diarrhea: Results from drinking fecally contaminated water or eating uncooked and contaminated foods. Symptoms include nausea, bloating, and incontinence. Try quick-energy, non-sugary foods with protein and carbohydrates to keep your strength up. Over-the-counter anti-diarrheals (e.g. Imodium) may counteract the problems. The most dangerous side effect is dehydration: drink 8 oz. of water with ½ tsp. of sugar or honey and a pinch of salt, try uncaffeinated soft drinks, or eat salted crackers. If you develop a fever or your symptoms don't go away after 4-5 days, consult a doctor. Consult a doctor immediately for treatment of diarrhea in children.

Hepatitis A: A viral infection of the liver acquired primarily through contaminated water, including through shellfish from contaminated water. Symptoms include fatigue, fever, loss of appetite, nausea, dark urine, jaundice, vomiting, aches and pains, and light stools. The risk is highest in rural areas and the countryside, but it is also present in urban areas. Ask your doctor about the Hepatitis A vaccine (Havrix or Vaqta) or an injec-tion of immune globulin (IG; formerly called gamma globulin).

Giardiasis: Transmitted through parasites (microbes, tapeworms, etc. in contaminated water and food) and acquired by drinking untreated water from streams or lakes. Symptoms include diarrhea, abdominal cramps, bloating, fatigue, weight loss, and nausea. If untreated it can lead to severe dehydration. Giardiasis occurs worldwide.

OTHER INFECTIOUS DISEASES

Rabies: Transmitted through the saliva of infected animals; fatal if untreated. By the time symptoms (thirst and muscle spasms) appear, the disease is in its terminal stage. If you are bitten, wash the wound thoroughly, seek immediate medical care, and try to have the animal located. A rabies vaccine, which consists of 3 shots given over a 21-day period, is available. It is recommended for developing world travel, but is only semi-effective. Rabies is found all over the world, and is often transmitted through dogs.

Hepatitis B: A viral infection of the liver transmitted via blood or other bodily fluids. Symptoms, which may not surface until years after infection, include jaundice, loss of appetite, fever, and joint pain. It is transmitted through activities like unprotected sex, injections of illegal drugs, and unprotected health work. A 3-shot vaccination sequence is recommended for health-care workers, sexually active travelers, and anyone planning to seek medical treatment abroad. It must begin 6 mo. before traveling.

AIDS and HIV: For detailed information on Acquired Immune Deficiency Syndrome (AIDS) in Austria and Switzerland, call the US Centers for Disease Control's 24hr. hotline ☎800-342-2437 or contact the Joint United Nations Programme on HIV/AIDS (UNAIDS), 20, ave. Appia, CH-1211 Geneva 27, Switzerland (☎41 22 791 3666; fax 22 791 4187).

Sexually transmitted diseases (STDs): Gonorrhea, chlamydia, genital warts, syphilis, herpes, and other STDs are more common than HIV and can be just as deadly. **Hepatitis** B and C can also be transmitted sexually. Though condoms may protect you from some STDs, oral or even tactile contact can lead to transmission. If you think you may have contracted an STD, see a doctor immediately.

OTHER HEALTH CONCERNS

MEDICAL CARE ON THE ROAD

Medical care in Austria and Switzerland is generally excellent. Most doctors and pharmacists speak at least some English. If you are concerned about obtaining medical assistance while traveling, you may wish to employ special support services. The *MedPass* from **GlobalCare, Inc.,** 6875 Shiloh Rd. East, Alpharetta, GA 30005, USA (☎800-860-1111; www.globalcare.net) provides 24hr. international medical assistance, support, and medical evacuation resources. The **International Association for Medical Assistance to Travelers** (IAMAT; US ☎716-754-4883, Canada 519-836-0102; www.iamat.org) has free membership, lists English-speaking doctors worldwide, and offers detailed info on immunization requirements and sanitation. If your regular **insurance** policy does not cover travel abroad, you may wish to purchase additional coverage.

Those with medical conditions (such as diabetes, allergies to antibiotics, epilepsy, heart conditions) may want to obtain a **Medic Alert** membership (first year US$35, annually thereafter US$20), which includes a stainless steel ID tag and a 24hr. collect call number, among other benefits. Contact the Medic Alert Foundation, 2323 Colorado Ave, Turlock, CA 95382, USA (☎888-633-4298, outside US 209-668-3333; www.medicalert.org).

WOMEN'S HEALTH

Women traveling in unsanitary conditions are vulnerable to **urinary tract (including bladder and kidney) infections.** Over-the-counter medicines can sometimes alleviate symptoms, but if they persist, see a doctor. **Vaginal yeast infections** may flare up in hot and humid climates. Wearing loosely fitting trousers or a skirt and cotton underwear will help, as will over-the-counter remedies like Monistat or Gynelotrimin. Bring supplies from home if you are prone to infection, as they may be difficult to find on the road. **Tampons, pads,** and reliable **contraceptive devices** are sometimes hard to find and your preferred brand will rarely be available; bring supplies with you.

Abortion is legal in Austria. Switzerland legalized first-trimester abortion in March 2001. Österreichische Gesellschaft für Familienplanung (ÖGF) is a major reproductive health organization in Austria. (☎ 43 1 4785242; www.oegf.at). PLANes, or the Fondation Suisse pour la Santé Sexuelle et Reproductive, serves the same function in Switzerland (☎ 41 21 661 22 33; www.plan-s.ch).

GETTING TO AUSTRIA AND SWITZERLAND

BY PLANE

When it comes to airfare, a little effort can save you a bundle. The key is to hunt around, to be flexible, and to ask persistently about discounts. Students, seniors, and those under 26 should never pay full price for a ticket.

AIRFARES

Airfares to Austria and Switzerland peak between June and August, as well as throughout the winter (particularly around Christmas time). The cheapest times to travel are fall and spring, pre- and post-ski-season. Midweek (M-Th morning) round-trip flights run US$40-50 cheaper than weekend flights, but they are generally more crowded and less likely to permit frequent-flier upgrades. Not fixing a return date ("open return") or arriving in and departing from different cities ("open-jaw") can be pricier than round-trip flights. Patching one-way flights together is the most expensive way to travel. Flights between capitals or regional hubs tend to be cheaper.

If Austria or Switzerland is only one stop on a more extensive globe-hop, consider a round-the-world (RTW) ticket. Tickets usually include at least five stops and are valid for about a year. Prices range US$3400-5000. Try **Northwest Airlines/ KLM** (US ☎ 800-447-4747; www.nwa.com) or **Star Alliance,** a consortium of 22 airlines, including United Airlines (US ☎ 800-241-6522; www.staralliance.com).

Fares from the US to Austria and Switzerland vary tremendously. For a round-trip ticket during peak season, expect to spend anywhere from US $500-1000, versus US$300-500 during off season.

BUDGET AND STUDENT TRAVEL AGENCIES

While knowledgeable agents specializing in flights to Austria and Switzerland can make your life easy and help you save, they may not spend the time to find you the lowest possible fare because they get paid on commission. Travelers holding **ISIC** and **IYTC cards** (p. 11) qualify for big discounts from student travel agencies. Most flights from budget agencies are on major airlines, but in peak season some may sell seats on less reliable chartered aircraft.

> **CTS Travel,** 30 Rathbone Pl., London W1T 1GQ, UK (☎ 0207 209 0630; www.ctstravel.co.uk). A British student travel agent with offices in 39 countries including the US, Empire State Building, 350 Fifth Ave., Ste. 7813, New York, NY 10118 (☎ 877-287-6665; www.ctstravelusa.com).

STA Travel, 5900 Wilshire Blvd., Ste. 900, Los Angeles, CA 90036, USA (24hr. reservations and info ☎800-781-4040; www.sta-travel.com). A student and youth travel organization with over 150 offices worldwide (check their website for a listing of all their offices), including US offices in Boston, Chicago, L.A., New York, San Francisco, Seattle, and Washington, D.C. Ticket booking, travel insurance, railpasses, and more. Walk-in offices are located throughout Australia (☎03 9349 4344), New Zealand (☎09 309 9723), and the UK (☎0870 1 600 599).

Travel CUTS (Canadian Universities Travel Services Limited), 187 College St., Toronto, ON M5T 1P7 (☎416-979-2406; www.travelcuts.com). Offices across Canada and the US including Los Angeles, New York, San Francisco, and Seattle.

USIT, 19-21 Aston Quay, Dublin 2 (☎01 602 1777; www.usitworld.com), Ireland's leading student/budget travel agency, has 22 offices throughout Northern Ireland and the Republic of Ireland. Offers programs to work in North America.

Wasteels, Skoubogade 6, 1158 Copenhagen K. (☎3314 4633; www.wasteels.com). A huge chain with 180 locations across Europe. Sells Wasteels BIJ tickets discounted 30-45% off regular fare, 2nd-class international point-to-point train tickets with unlimited stopovers for those under 26 (sold only in Europe).

✈ **FLIGHT PLANNING ON THE INTERNET.** Many airline sites offer special last-minute deals on the web. Try **Austrian Airlines** (www.austrianair.com/index.html), **Lauda Air** (www.laudaair.com), **Tyrolean Airways** (www.tyrolean.at), and **Swiss International** (www.swiss.com).

STA (www.sta-travel.com) and **StudentUniverse** (www.studentuniverse.com) provide quotes on student tickets, while **Orbitz** (www.orbitz.com), **Opodo** (www.opodo.com), **Expedia** (www.expedia.com), and **Travelocity** (www.travelocity.com) offer full travel services. **Priceline** (www.priceline.com) lets you specify a price, and obligates you to buy any ticket that meets or beats it; **Hotwire** (www.hotwire.com) offers bargain fares, but won't reveal the airline or flight times until you buy. **SideStep** (www.sidestep.com; download required) and **Booking Buddy** (www.bookingbuddy.com) let you enter your trip information once and search multiple sites. Other sites that compile deals for you include www.bestfares.com, www.flights.com, www.onetravel.com and www.travelzoo.com. An indispensable resource on the Internet is the **Air Traveler's Handbook** (www.faqs.org/faqs/travel/air/handbook), a comprehensive listing of links to everything you need to know before you board a plane.

COMMERCIAL AIRLINES

The commercial airlines' lowest regular offer is the **APEX** (Advance Purchase Excursion) fare, which provides confirmed reservations and allows "open-jaw" tickets. Generally, reservations must be made seven to 21 days ahead of departure, with seven- to 14-day minimum-stay and up to 90-day maximum-stay restrictions. These fares carry hefty cancellation and change penalties (fees rise in summer). Book peak-season APEX fares early. Use **Microsoft Expedia** (msn.expedia.com) or **Travelocity** (www.travelocity.com) to get an idea of the lowest published fares, then use the resources outlined here to try to beat those fares. Low-season fares should be appreciably cheaper than the high-season (mid-June to Aug.) ones listed here.

TRAVELING FROM NORTH AMERICA

Standard commercial carriers like **American** (☎800-433-7300; www.aa.com), **United** (☎800-538-2929; www.ual.com), and **Northwest** (☎800-447-4747; www.nwa.com) will probably offer the most convenient flights, but they may not be the cheapest.

Check **Lufthansa** (☎800-399-5838; www.lufthansa.com), **British Airways** (☎800-247-9297; www.britishairways.com), **Air France** (☎800-237-2747; www.airfrance.us), and **Alitalia** (☎800-223-5730; www.alitaliausa.com) for cheap tickets from destinations throughout the US to all over Europe, including destinations in Austria and Switzerland. You might find an even better deal on one of the following airlines, if any of their limited departure points is convenient for you.

Icelandair: ☎800-223-5500; www.icelandair.com. Stopovers in Iceland for no extra cost on most transatlantic flights. New York to Frankfurt May-Sept. US$500-730; Oct.-May US$390-450. For last-minute offers, subscribe to their email Lucky Fares.

Finnair: ☎800-950-5000; www.us.finnair.com. Cheap round-trips to Basel, Bern, Geneva, Vienna, and Zurich; connections throughout Europe.

Martinair: ☎800-627-8462; www.martinair.com. Fly from California or Florida to Amsterdam mid-June to mid-Aug. US$880; mid-Aug. to mid-June US$730.

TRAVELING FROM THE UK AND IRELAND

Because of the many carriers flying from the British Isles to the continent, we only include discount airlines or those with cheap specials here. The **Air Travel Advisory Bureau** in London (☎020 7631 1136; www.atab.co.uk) provides referrals to travel agencies and consolidators that offer discounted airfares out of the UK. **Cheapflights** (www.cheapflights.co.uk) publishes airfare bargains.

Aer Lingus: Ireland ☎0818 365 000; www.aerlingus.ie. Round-trip tickets from Dublin, Cork, Galway, Kerry, and Shannon to Munich and Zurich.

bmibaby: UK ☎0870 264 22 29; www.bmibaby.com. Departures from throughout the UK. Cardiff and Manchester to Geneva.

easyJet: UK ☎0871 750 01 00; www.easyjet.com. Online tickets from London to Zurich and Geneva.

KLM: UK ☎0870 507 40 74; www.klmuk.com. Cheap return tickets from London and elsewhere to Innsbruck, Salzburg, Vienna, and Zurich.

Ryanair: Ireland ☎0818 303 030, UK 087 246 00 00; www.ryanair.com. From Dublin, London, and Glasgow to Graz, Klagenfurt, Salzburg, and Linz.

TRAVELING FROM AUSTRALIA AND NEW ZEALAND

Qantas Air: Australia ☎13 11 31, New Zealand 0800 101 500; www.qantas.com.au. Flights from Australia and New Zealand to Munich, Vienna, and Zurich.

Singapore Air: Australia ☎13 10 11, New Zealand 0800 808 909; www.singaporeair.com. Flies from Auckland, Sydney, Melbourne, and Perth to Zurich.

Thai Airways: Australia ☎1300 65 19 60, New Zealand 09 377 38 86; www.thaiair.com. Auckland, Sydney, and Melbourne to Geneva, Munich, Vienna, and Zurich.

STANDBY FLIGHTS

Traveling standby requires considerable flexibility in arrival and departure dates and cities. Companies dealing in standby flights sell vouchers rather than tickets, along with the promise to get you to your destination (or near your destination) within a certain window of time (typically 1-5 days). You call in before your specific window of time to hear your flight options and the probability that you will be able to board each flight. You can then decide which flights you want to try to make, show up at the airport at the appropriate time, present your voucher, and board if space is available. Vouchers can usually be bought for both one-way and round-trip travel. You may receive a monetary refund only if every available flight within your date range is full; if you opt not to take an available (but perhaps less convenient) flight, you can only get credit toward future travel. Carefully read agreements with any company offering standby flights, as the fine print can leave you in the lurch. To check on a company's service record in the US, call the Better Business Bureau (☎703-276-0100). It is difficult to receive refunds, and clients' vouchers will not be honored when an airline fails to receive payment in time.

GETTING AROUND AUSTRIA AND SWITZERLAND

Fares on all modes of transportation are either **single** (one-way) or **return** (round-trip). "Period returns" require you to return within a specific number of days; "day return" means you must return on the same day. Unless stated otherwise, *Let's Go* always lists single fares. Round-trip fares on trains and buses are usually double the one-way fare.

BY PLANE

The emergence of no-frills airlines has made hopscotching around Europe by air increasingly affordable and convenient. Though these flights often feature inconvenient hours or serve less-popular regional airports, one-way flights average only US$50, making it faster and easier than ever to jet-set across the Continent.

British European: UK ☎01392 366669; www.flybe.com. Flies to Geneva from various European cities.

easyJet: UK ☎0871 750 01 00; www.easyjet.com. Serves 44 destinations in the UK, Spain, France, Portugal, Italy, Switzerland, Germany, the Netherlands, Denmark, the Czech Republic, Slovenia, Hungary, and Greece.

Ryanair: Ireland ☎0818 303 030, UK 087 246 00 00; www.ryanair.com. Serves 84 destinations in the UK, Ireland, Spain, France, Portugal, Italy, Austria, Germany, Belgium, the Netherlands, and Scandinavia.

The Star Alliance European Airpass offers economy class fares as low as US$65 for travel within Europe to more than 200 destinations in 43 countries. The pass is available to transatlantic passengers on Star Alliance carriers, including Air Canada, Austrian Airlines, BMI British Midland, Lufthansa, Mexicana, Scandinavian Airlines System, THAI, United Airlines, and Varig, as well as on certain partner airlines. See www.staralliance.com for more information. In addition, a number of European airlines offer discount coupon packets. Most are only available as tack-ons for transatlantic passengers, but some are stand-alone offers. Most must be purchased before departure, so research in advance.

Europe by Air: ☎888-387-2479; www.europebyair.com. *FlightPass* allows you to country-hop to over 150 European cities, including Innsbruck, Zurich, Bern, Vienna, and Salzburg. US$99 per flight.

Iberia: ☎800-772-4642; www.iberia.com. *Europass* allows Iberia passengers flying from the US to Spain to tack on a minimum of 2 additional destinations in Europe. US$133 each. Destinations include Basel, Vienna, and Zurich.

BY TRAIN

Trains in Austria and Switzerland are generally comfortable, convenient, and reasonably swift. Be sure, however, to lock your compartment door if possible, and keep your valuables on your person at all times. Note that smoking compartments tend to be very smoky. Get your belongings together a few stops before you want to get off, since trains sometimes pause only a few moments before zipping off.

For longer trips, make sure that you are on the correct car, as trains sometimes split at crossroads. Towns in parentheses on schedules require a train switch at the town listed immediately before the parenthesis. You might want to ask if your route requires changing trains, as the schedules are confusing.

The **Österreichische Bundesbahn (ÖBB), Austria's** federal railroad, is one of Europe's most thorough and efficient. The ÖBB prints the yearly *Fahrpläne Kursbuch Bahn-Inland*, a compilation of all rail, ferry, and cable-car schedules in Austria. The massive schedule is available at any large train station, along with its companion guides, the *Kursbuch Bahn-Ausland* for international trains, and the *Internationales Schlafwagenkursbuch* for sleeping cars. Getting around **Switzerland** is also a snap. Federal **(Schweizer Bundesbahn (SBB)** and **Chemins-de-fer fédérales (CFF))** and private railways connect most towns and villages, with trains running frequently. The national 24hr. phone number for **rail information** is ☎ 0900 30 03 00 and has operators who speak English, German, French, and Italian, but it costs 1.19SFr per minute. Check the website for the federal railway system at www.sbb.ch (available in French, German, Italian, and English versions). Be aware that sometimes only private train lines go to remote tourist spots; therefore Eurail and SwissPass may therefore not be valid. Yellow signs announce departure times *(Ausfahrt, départ, partenze)* and platforms *(Gleis, quai, binario)*. White signs are for arrivals *(Ankunft, arrivée, arrivo)*. On major Austrian lines, make reservations at least a few hours in advance.

You can either buy a **railpass,** which allows you unlimited travel within a particular region for a given period of time, or rely on buying individual **point-to-point tickets** as you go. You can purchase individual tickets at every train station in Austria and Switzerland, at Bahn-Total service stations, at the occasional *automat*, most *Tabak* stands, or from the conductor for a small surcharge. Over 130 stations accept major credit cards as well as American Express Traveler's Cheques and Eurocheques. Most ticket validation is based on the honor system, but *Schwarzfahren* (i.e. riding without a ticket) can result in big fines, and playing "dumb tourist" probably won't work.

In Austria, children under six travel free, while children ages six to 12 receive a 50% discount. In Switzerland, travelers under 16 travel free with a parent with the Swiss Family Card. When traveling without a parent, children up to 16 have a 50% discount on all the offers of the Swiss Travel System.

RESERVATIONS. Seat reservations (usually US$3-10) are required only for selected trains (usually on major lines), but you are not guaranteed a seat without one. Strongly consider reserving ahead during peak holiday and tourist seasons (at the very latest, a few hours ahead). You will have to purchase a **supplement** (US$10-50) or special fare for high-speed or high-quality trains such as Germany's ICE and certain French TGVs. InterRail holders must also purchase supplements (US$10-25) for trains like EuroCity, InterCity, Sweden's X2000, and many French TGVs. Supplements are unnecessary for Eurailpass and Europass holders.

OVERNIGHT TRAINS. On night trains, you won't waste valuable daylight hours traveling and you can avoid the hassle and expense of staying at a hotel. The main drawbacks, however, include discomfort, sleepless nights, and the lack of scenery. **Sleeping accommodations** on trains differ from country to country, but typically you can either sleep upright in your seat (for free) or pay for a separate space. **Couchettes** (berths) typically have four to six seats per compartment (about US$20 per person). **Sleepers** (beds) in private sleeping cars offer more privacy and comfort, but are considerably more expensive (US$40-150). If you are using a railpass valid only for a restricted number of days, inspect train schedules to maximize the use of your pass: an overnight train or boat journey uses up only one of your travel days if it departs after 7pm.

SHOULD YOU BUY A RAILPASS? Railpasses were conceived to allow you to jump on any train in Europe, go wherever you want whenever you want, and change your plans at will. In practice, it's not so simple. You still must stand in line to validate your pass, pay for supplements, and fork over cash for seat and couchette reservations. More importantly, railpasses don't always pay off. If you are planning to spend extensive time on trains, hopping between big cities, a railpass will probably be worth it. But in many cases, especially if you are under 26, point-to-point tickets may prove a cheaper option.

MULTINATIONAL RAILPASSES

EURAILPASS. Eurail is valid in most of Western Europe, including Austria and Switzerland. Standard **Eurailpasses,** valid for a consecutive given number of days, are best for those planning on spending extensive time on trains every few days. **Flexipasses,** valid for any 10 or 15 (not necessarily consecutive) days within a two-month period, are more cost-effective for those traveling longer distances less frequently. **Saverpasses** provide first-class travel for travelers in groups of two to five (prices are per person). **Youthpasses** and **Youth Flexipasses** provide parallel second-class perks for those under 26.

EURAILPASSES	15 DAYS	21 DAYS	1 MONTH	2 MONTHS	3 MONTHS
1st-class Eurailpass	US$588	US$762	US$946	US$1338	US$1654
Eurail Saverpass	US$498	US$648	US$804	US$1138	US$1408
Eurail Youthpass	US$414	US$534	US$664	US$938	US$1160

EURAIL FLEXIPASSES	10 DAYS IN 2 MONTHS	15 DAYS IN 2 MONTHS
1st-class Eurail Flexipass	US$694	US$914
Eurail Saver Flexipass	US$592	US$778
Eurail Youth Flexipass	US$488	US$642

Pass holders receive a timetable for major routes and a map with details on possible ferry, steamer, bus, car rental, hotel, and Eurostar discounts. Passholders often also receive reduced fares or free passage on many bus and boat lines.

EURAIL SELECT PASS. The Eurail Select Pass is a slimmed-down version of the Eurailpass: it allows five to 15 days of unlimited travel in any two-month period within three, four, or five bordering countries of the 18 Eurail network countries. **First-class passes** (for individuals) and **Saverpasses** (for people traveling in groups of 2 to 5) range from US$356/304 per person (5 days) to US$794/674 (15 days). **Second-class Youthpasses** for those aged 12-25 cost US$249-556. For a fee, you can add **additional zones** (Austria/Hungary; Belgium/Luxembourg/Netherlands; Greece Plus, including the ADN/HML ferry between Italy and Greece; and/or Portugal). You are entitled to the same **freebies** afforded by the Eurailpass, but only when they are within or between countries that you have purchased.

SHOPPING AROUND FOR A EURAIL. Eurailpasses are designed by the EU itself, and can be bought only by non-Europeans almost exclusively from non-European distributors. These passes must be sold at uniform prices determined by the EU. However, some travel agents tack on a US$10 handling fee, and others offer certain bonuses with purchase, so shop around. Also, keep in mind that pass prices usually go up each year, so if you're planning to travel early in the year, you can save cash by purchasing before January 1 (you have 3 months from the purchase date to validate your pass in Europe).

It is best to buy your Eurail before leaving: only a few places in major European cities sell them, and at a marked-up price. You can get a replacement for a lost pass only if you have purchased insurance on it under the Pass Protection Plan (US$14-17). Eurailpasses are available through travel agents, student travel agencies like STA and Council (p. 23), and **Rail Europe** (Canada ☎ 800-361-7245, UK 08 705 848 848, US 877-257-2887; www.raileurope.com) or **DER Travel Services,** whose services are available at several outfits across the US (☎ 800-782-2424; www.der.com). If your travels will be limited to one area, regional passes are often good values.

OTHER MULTINATIONAL PASSES. For travel in only one area, regional passes are often a good value. The European East Pass covers Austria, the Czech Republic, Hungary, Poland, and Slovakia (5 days in 1 month 2nd-class US $158).

If you have lived for at least six months in one of the European countries where **InterRail Passes** are valid, they are an economical option. There are eight InterRail **zones.** The **InterRail Youthpass** can be purchased by those who are under 26 years of age on the date of purchase. It allows either 21 consecutive days or one month of unlimited travel within one, two, three or all of the eight zones; the cost is determined by the number of zones the pass covers (UK£119-249). A card can also be purchased for 12 days of travel in one zone (£119). The **InterRail Adult Pass** provides the same services as the Under 26 InterRail Card, but at higher prices: UK£169-355. The new **Child Pass** (ages 4-11) offers the same services (UK£85-178). Passholders receive **discounts** on rail travel, Eurostar journeys, and most ferries to Ireland, Scandinavia, and the rest of Europe. Most exclude supplements for high-speed trains. The pass also provides a discount of 50% on about 50 Swiss private trains and buses. For info and ticket sales in Europe contact **Student Travel Centre,** 24 Rupert St., 1st fl., London W1D 6DQ (☎ 020 74 37 81 01; www.student-travel-centre.com). Tickets are also available from travel agents, at major train stations throughout Europe, or through online vendors (www.railpassdirect.co.uk).

DOMESTIC RAILPASSES

If you are planning to spend a significant amount of time within one country or region, a national pass—valid on all rail lines of a country's rail company—may be more cost-effective than a multinational pass. But many national passes are limited and don't provide the free or discounted travel on private railways and ferries that Eurail does. Some of these passes can be bought only in Europe, some only outside of Europe; check with a railpass agent or with national tourist offices.

NATIONAL RAILPASSES. The domestic analogs of the Eurailpass (p. 28), national railpasses are valid either for a given number of consecutive days or for a specific number of days within a given time period. National railpasses are the way to go if you're going to be covering long distances within Austria or Switzerland. Usually, they must be purchased before you leave. Though they will usually save frequent travelers some money, in some cases you may find that they are actually a more expensive alternative to point-to-point tickets. For more information on national railpasses, check out http://raileurope.com/us/rail/passes/single_country_index.htm.

Austrian Railpass: Sold worldwide, this pass is valid for 3 days of unlimited train travel in a 15-day period on all federal lines, state, and private rail lines in Austria. Also grants a 40% discount on bicycle rental in over 130 railway stations and 50% discount on DDSG steamers between Passau and Linz and 20% on steamers between Melk, Krems, and Vienna. You can purchase up to 5 additional rail days. 2nd-class $107, each additional day $15. Travelers ages 6-12 travel at half-price. The card itself has no photo, so you must carry a valid ID in case of inspections.

France and Switzerland Pass: Allows travel on France's national railways and the Swiss SBB system. The **France and Switzerland Youthpass** offers the same benefits, but at a discounted rate for travelers under 26.

Swiss Card: Same round-trip as the Swiss Transfer Ticket, plus 50% off unlimited rail and bus tickets within the month period between your entry and departure. 2nd-class $116.

Swiss Flexipass: Entitles you to 3, 4, 5, 6, or 8 days of unlimited rail travel within a 1-month period, 1st- or 2nd-class, with the same benefits as the SwissPass. 2nd-class adult passes for 3 days start at US$156, 4 days at $184, 5 days at $212, 6 days at $240, 8 days at $282.

SwissPass: Offers unlimited rail travel for a certain number of consecutive days: choose between 4, 8, 15, 22 days, or 1 month, 1st- or 2nd-class. It also permits unlimited urban transportation in 36 cities, unlimited travel on some private railways and lake steamers, and 25% discounts on excursions to most mountaintops. 2nd-class 4-day passes start at US$160, 8 days at $225, 15 days at $270, 21 days at $315, and 1 month at $350.

Swiss Saver Flexipass: Offers the same benefits as the Swiss Flexipass at a 15% discount for groups of 2 or more adults traveling together.

Swiss Saver Pass: Offers the same benefits as the SwissPass at a 15% discount for groups of 2-5 adults traveling together.

Swiss Transfer Ticket: Good for one round-trip to and from any entry point (airport or border crossing) to any single destination within Switzerland. Both ways must be a single day of travel, no more than a month apart. 2nd-class US$80.

Switzerland and Austria Pass: Allows travel on Austria's national railways and the Swiss SBB system. The **Switzerland and Austria Saverpass** provides a discount for two travelers. **Switzerland and Austria Youthpass** offers a discount for travelers under 26.

VORTEILScard <26: For students under 26, offers similar benefits as the VORTEILScard Senior. Good in Austria for 1 year. €18.10. Requires a photo and ISIC card for non-Austrian students. Call ☎(01) 93 00 03 64 57 for more information. Operators speak German.

VORTEILScard Behinderte: For disabled travelers, offers similar benefits as the VORTEILScard Senior. Good in Austria for 1 year. €18.10. Requires ID and proof of disability. Call ☎(01) 93 00 03 64 57 for information. Operators speak German only.

VORTEILScard Senior: The ÖBB offers a discount card for women over 60 and men over 65 called the VORTEILScard Senior, available in train stations and most travel agencies. Holders get 45% off train fares, 50% if booked on the web (www.oebb.at), at ticket vending machines, or by phone (☎05 17 17). The card is also valid for 25% off selected steamers, currency exchange at half the charge, and various other benefits. Good in Austria for 1 year. €25.44. Requires a photo and proof of age. Call ☎01 93 00 03 83 57 for more information. Operators speak German only.

EURO DOMINO. Like the Interrail Pass, the Euro Domino pass is available to anyone who has lived in Europe for at least six months; however, it is only valid in one country (which you designate upon buying the pass). Reservations must still be paid for separately. **Supplements** are included for many high-speed trains (e.g., German ICE). The pass must be bought within your country of residence. Prices vary by country. Inquire with your national rail company for more information.

EURO-DOMINO PASS (SWITZ.)	3 DAYS	5 DAYS	8 DAYS
2nd-Class	€101	€123	€156
2nd-Class Youth (under 26)	€80	€100	€130

EURO-DOMINO PASS (AUSTRIA)	3 DAYS	5 DAYS	8 DAYS
2nd-Class	€104	€130	€169
2nd-Class Youth (under 26)	€76	€94	€112

ESSENTIALS

RAIL-AND-DRIVE PASSES. In addition to simple railpasses, many countries (as well as Europass and Eurail) offer rail-and-drive passes, which combine car rental with rail travel—a good option for travelers who wish both to visit cities accessible by rail and to make side trips into surrounding areas. Per-person prices range from $371-509, depending on the type of car. Children under the age of 11 cost $165, and to add more days costs $49-89 per day (see **Getting Around Austria and Switzerland: By Car**, p. 33).

DISCOUNTED TICKETS

For travelers under 26, **BIJ** tickets (Billets Internationals de Jeunesse; operated by **Wasteels**) are a great alternative to railpasses. Available for international trips within Europe as well as most ferry services, they knock 20-40% off first- and second-class fares. Tickets are good for two months after purchase and allow stopovers along the normal direct route of the train journey. Issued for a specific international route between two points, they must be used in the direction and order of the designated route and must be bought in Europe. The equivalent for those over 26, **BIGT** tickets provide a 20-30% discount on first- and second-class international tickets. Both types of tickets are available from European travel agents, at Wasteels offices (usually in or near train stations), or directly at the ticket counter in some nations. For more info, contact **Wasteels Switzerland** (www.wasteels.ch) or **Wasteels Austria** (www.wasteelsaustria.com).

> **FURTHER READING AND RESOURCES ON TRAIN TRAVEL**
>
> *Thomas Cook European Timetable,* updated monthly, covers all major and most minor train routes in Europe. In the US, order it from Forsyth Travel Library (US$28; ☎800-367-7984; www.forsyth.com). In Europe, find it at any Thomas Cook Money Exchange Center. Alternatively, buy directly from Thomas Cook (www.thomascook.com).
>
> *Guide to European Railpasses,* by Rick Steves. Available online and by mail. (US ☎425-771-8303; www.ricksteves.com). Free; delivery $5-6.
>
> *On the Rails Around Europe: A Comprehensive Guide to Travel by Train,* by Melissa Shales. Thomas Cook Ltd. (US$19).
>
> *Europe By Eurail 2000,* by Laverne Ferguson-Kosinski. Globe Pequot Press (US$18).
>
> On the web: Info on rail travel and railpasses (www.raileurope.com) and point-to-point fares and schedules (www.raileurope.com/us/rail/fares_schedules/index.htm.) allows you to calculate whether buying a railpass would save you money. European railway server with links to rail servers throughout Europe (http://mercurio.iet.unipi.it/home.html).

BY BUS

Like the railroads, the bus networks of Austria and Switzerland are extensive, efficient, and comfortable. It may be difficult to negotiate the route you need, but short-haul buses can reach rural areas inaccessible by train. Bus stations are usually adjacent to the train station. The efficient **Austrian system** consists mainly of orange BundesBuses that serve mountain areas inaccessible by train. Buy tickets at the station or from the driver. For buses in heavily touristed areas during high season (such as the Großglocknerstraße in summer), you should probably make reservations. Anyone can buy discounted tickets, valid for one week, for any particular route. Trips can be interrupted under certain conditions, depending on your ticket—be sure to ask. Small, regional bus schedules are available for free at most post offices. For more bus information, call ☎ 0222 711 01 within Austria (from outside Austria dial 1 instead of 0222) 7am-8pm Austrian time.

In **Switzerland,** PTT Post Buses connect rural villages and towns. SwissPasses are valid on many buses. Eurailpasses are not. Even with the SwissPass, you might have to pay extra (5-10SFr) if you're riding one of the direct, faster buses. In cities, public buses transport commuters and shoppers alike to outlying areas. Buy tickets in advance at automatic machines, found at most bus stops. The system works on an honor code and inspections are infrequent, but expect to be hit for 50-60SFr if you're caught riding without a valid ticket. *Tageskarten*, valid for 24hr. of free travel, run around 7.50SFr.

Eurolines, 4 Vicarage Rd., Edgbaston, Birmingham B15 3ES (☎ 08705 808080; www.eurolines.com or www.eurolines.co.uk). The largest operator of Europe-wide coach services. Unlimited 15-day high-season UK£174, under 26 and over 60 UK£145; low-season UK£135/113. 30-day high season UK£259/209; low-season UK£189/153). 60-day high season UK£299/229; low-season UK£239/189 travel passes that offer unlimited transit between 31 major European cities.

Busabout, 258 Vauxhall Bridge Rd., London SW1V 1BS (☎ 207 950 1661; www.busabout.com). Offers 5 interconnecting bus circuits covering 60 cities and towns in Europe. Consecutive Day Passes, Flexi Passes, and Add-On Passes are available. Consecutive Day Standard/student passes are valid for 2 weeks (UK£239/219), 4 weeks (UK£389/339), 6 weeks (UK£479/429), 8 weeks (UK£569/499), 12 weeks (UK£699/619), or for the season (UK£819/729).

BY CAR

ON THE ROAD

The **speed limit** in Austria is 50kph (31mph) within cities unless otherwise indicated, 130kph (81mph) on highways, and 100kph (62mph) on all other roads. In Switzerland, the speed limits are 50kph in cities, 80kph on open roads, and 120kph on highways. In both countries, all people must wear **seatbelts** or face heavy fines. Children under 12 may not sit in the front passenger seat unless a child's seatbelt or a special seat is installed. Driving under the influence of alcohol is a serious offense: fines begin at €400 and violators may also lose their licenses.

The **Association for Safe International Road Travel (ASIRT),** 11769 Gainsborough Rd., Potomac, MD 20854, USA (☎ 301-983-5252; www.asirt.org), can provide more specific information about road conditions. ASIRT considers road travel (by car or bus) to be relatively safe in both Austria and Switzerland. With armies of mechanized road crews ready to remove snow at a moment's notice, roads at altitudes of up to 1500m generally remain open throughout winter. (Mountain driving does present special challenges, however: see p. 34). Many small Austrian and Swiss towns, however, forbid cars entirely. Others forbid only visitors' cars, require special permits, or restrict driving hours. EU citizens driving in Austria and Switzerland don't need special documentation. Registration and license will suffice. All cars must carry a first-aid kit and a red emergency triangle. Emergency phones are located along all major highways. The **Austrian Automobile, Motorcycle, and Touring Club (ÖAMTC;** ☎ 01 71 19 90) provides an English-language service and sells a set of eight detailed road maps, far superior to the tourist office maps. The **Swiss Touring Club,** 4 Chemin de Blandonnet, 1214 Vernier, Case Postale 820 (☎ (022) 417 2727; www.tcs.ch) operates road patrols to assist motorists in need.

ESSENTIALS

DRIVING PERMITS AND CAR INSURANCE

! **DRIVING PRECAUTIONS.** In the summer, bring substantial amounts of water (5 liters of **water** per person per day) for drinking and for the radiator. For long drives to unpopulated areas, register with police before setting out and again upon arrival. Check with the local automobile club for details. When traveling for long distances, make sure tires are in good repair and have enough air, and get good maps. A **compass** and a **car manual** can also be very useful. You should always carry a **spare tire** and **jack, jumper cables, extra oil, flares, a flashlight (torch),** and **heavy blankets** (in case your car breaks down at night or in the winter). If you don't know how to **change a tire,** learn before heading out, especially if you are planning on traveling in deserted areas. Blowouts on dirt roads are exceedingly common. If you do have a breakdown, **stay with your car:** if you wander off, there's less likelihood trackers will find you.

INTERNATIONAL DRIVING PERMIT (IDP)

If you plan to drive a car while in Austria or Switzerland you must be at least 18. If you plan to drive a car while in **Austria**, and are not a citizen of an EU country, you must have an International Driving Permit (IDP) in addition to your driver's license. Most car rental agencies in **Switzerland** don't require the permit, but it may be a good idea to get one anyway, in case you're in a situation (e.g., an accident or stranded in a small town) where the police do not know English: information on IDPs are printed in ten languages, including German, French, and Italian.

Your IDP, valid for one year, must be issued in your own country before you depart. An application for an IDP usually requires one or two photos, a current local license, an additional form of identification, and a fee. To apply, contact your home country's automobile association. Be careful when purchasing an IDP online or anywhere other than your home automobile association. Many vendors sell permits of questionable legitimacy for higher prices.

CAR INSURANCE

Most credit cards cover standard insurance. If you rent, lease, or borrow a car, you will need a **green card,** or **International Insurance Certificate,** to certify that you have liability insurance and that it applies abroad. Green cards can be obtained at car rental agencies, car dealers (for those leasing cars), some travel agents, and some border crossings. Rental agencies may require you to purchase theft insurance in countries that they consider to have a high risk of auto theft.

RENTING A CAR

To rent a car in **Austria,** you must be at least 21 for most companies (and 23 or 25 for others) and carry both an International Driver's Permit and a valid driver's license that you have had for at least one year (p. 34). Most Austrian companies restrict travel into Hungary, the Czech Republic, Poland, and Slovakia. Rental taxes are high (21%). In **Switzerland,** the minimum rental age is 21 but also varies by company. You must possess a valid driver's license that you have had for at least one year (foreign licenses are generally valid). In both countries, drivers under 25 must often pay a daily surcharge. Rates for all cars rented in Switzerland and Austria include an obligatory annual road toll, called a *vignette* (40SFr per year in Switzerland, €7.60 per ten days; €72.60 per year in Austria).

It is much less expensive to reserve a car from the US than from Europe. Ask airlines about special fly-and-drive packages: you may get up to a week of free or discounted rental. Expect to pay US$200-400 per week, plus tax, for a very small car.

Reserve ahead and pay in advance if at all possible. Always check if prices quoted include tax and collision insurance. Some credit card companies provide insurance, allowing their customers to decline the collision damage waiver. Ask about discounts and check the terms of insurance, particularly the size of the deductible.

Auto Europe, US and Canada ☎888-223-5555 or 207-842-2000; www.autoeurope.com.

Avis, Australia ☎136 333, Canada 800-272-5871, New Zealand 0800 65 51 11, UK 0870 606 0100, US 800-230-4898; www.avis.com.

Budget, Canada ☎800-268-8900, UK 1344 484 100, US 800-527-0700; www.budgetrentacar.com.

Europe by Car, US ☎800-223-1516 or 212-581-3040; www.europebycar.com.

Europcar International, 3 avenue du Centre, 78 881 Saint Quentin en Yvelines Cedex, France (☎30 44 90 00, US 877-940-6900; www.europcar.com).

Hertz, Australia ☎9698 2555, Canada 800-263-0600, UK 0990 99 66 99, US 800-654-3131; www.hertz.com.

Kemwel, US ☎877-820-0668; www.kemwel.com.

LEASING A CAR

For longer than 17 days, leasing can be cheaper than renting. It is often the only option for those ages 18 to 21. The cheapest leases are agreements to buy the car and then sell it back to the manufacturer at a prearranged price. As far as you're concerned, though, it's a lease and doesn't entail enormous financial transactions. Leases generally include insurance coverage and are not taxed. The most affordable ones usually originate in Belgium, France, or Germany. Expect to pay around US$1100-1800 (depending on size of car) for 60 days. Contact **Auto Europe, Europe by Car,** or **Kemwel** (see above) before you go.

 ROADSIDE ASSISTANCE.
In **Austria**, call ☎ **120.** In **Switzerland**, call ☎ **140.**

BY BICYCLE

With a mountain bike, you can do some serious natural sightseeing. Many airlines will count your bike as your second free piece of luggage; a few charge extra (US$60-110 one-way). Bikes must be packed in a cardboard box with the pedals and front wheel detached; many airlines sell bike boxes at the airport (US$10). Most ferries let you take your bike for free or for a nominal fee, and you can always ship your bike on trains and buses so long as there is extra room (for busy travel days, consider reserving a spot in advance.) In Switzerland, train stations rent bikes and often allow you to drop them off elsewhere.

If you're planning on doing long-distance touring, you'll need **paniers** to hold your luggage, a good **helmet** (US$25-50), and a good U-shaped **Citadel or Kryptonite lock** (from US$30). For equipment, **Bike Nashbar,** 6103 State Rte. 446, Youngstown, OH 44406 (US ☎877-688-8600; www.nashbar.com), beats all competitors' offers and ships anywhere in the US or Canada. Good resources include *Europe by Bike*, by Karen and Terry Whitehall (US$15) and **Mountaineers Books,** 1001 S.W. Klickitat Way, Suite 201, Seattle, WA 98134 (☎800-553-4453; www.mountaineersbooks.org). Know how to change a tire; bring a few simple tools and bike manual.

Blue Marble Travel (Canada ☎519-624-2494. France 42 36 02 34, US 215-923-3788; www.bluemarble.org) offers bike tours for small groups ages 20-49 through Austria and Switzerland. **CBT Tours,** 2506 N. Clark St. #150, Chicago, IL 60614 (☎800-736-2453; www.cbttours.com), offers full-package biking, mountain biking, hiking, and multisport tours (US$1500-2500) to Switzerland.

BY MOPED AND MOTORCYCLE

Mopeds can be put on trains and ferries, and are a good compromise between costly car travel and the limited range of bicycles. However, they're uncomfortable for long distances, dangerous in the rain, and unpredictable on rough roads. If you've never been on a **moped** before, twisting Alpine roads are not the place to start. Always wear a helmet, and never ride with a backpack. Expect to pay about US$20-35 per day. Look for a moped at auto repair shops, and remember to bargain. **Motorcycles** are more expensive and normally require a license, but are better for long distances. **Bosenberg Motorcycle Excursions,** Mainzer Str. 54, 55545 Bad Kreuznach, Germany (☎49 67 16 73 12; www.bosenberg.com), arranges tours in Austria and Switzerland and rents motorcycles (Apr.-Oct.). They have gateways in Zurich and Bern (contact the German office.). Before renting, ask if the price includes tax and insurance, or you may be hit with an unexpected fee. Avoid handing your passport over as a deposit: if you have an accident or mechanical failure you may not get it back until you cover all repairs, so pay ahead of time instead. *Europe by Motorcycle*, by Gregory Frazier (Arrowstar Publishing; US$20), is helpful for planning your itinerary and making arrangements.

KEEPING IN TOUCH

BY MAIL

The postal systems of Austria and Switzerland are quick and efficient. Mark all letters and packages "mit Flugpost" or "par avion." In all cases, include the postal code if you know it; those of Swiss cities begin with "CH," Austrian with "A."

SENDING MAIL HOME FROM AUSTRIA AND SWITZERLAND

For airmail transit times, see **Sending Mail to Austria and Switzerland** (p. 36). To send a postcard or letter under 20g from Switzerland to an international destination within Europe costs 1.10SFr first ("A") class and 0.90SFr second ("B") class, and to any other international destination via airmail costs 1.80SFr for A and 1.10SFr for B. Domestically, postcards require 0.90SFr for A and 0.70SFr for B. To send a postcard from Austria to any destination costs €0.55. A letter under 50g within Austria costs €0.75. A letter under 50g to another European country costs €1.10 (priority) or €1.00 (economy), to any other international destination costs €1.75/€1.25. Aerogrammes, printed sheets that fold into envelopes and travel via airmail, are available at post offices. Make sure to mark international mail with "Luftpost," although it's usually assumed unless otherwise specified.

SENDING MAIL TO AUSTRIA AND SWITZERLAND

To ensure timely delivery, mark envelopes "airmail," "par avion," or "Luftpost." In addition to the standard postage system whose rates are listed below, **Federal Express** (www.fedex.com; Australia ☎ 13 26 10; Canada and US 800-463-3339; Ireland 1800 535 800; New Zealand 0800 733 339; UK 0800 123 800) handles express mail services from most countries to Austria and Switzerland.

RECEIVING MAIL IN AUSTRIA AND SWITZERLAND

General Delivery: Mail can be sent to Austria and Switzerland through **Poste Restante** (the international phrase for General Delivery; in German **Postlagernde Briefe**) to almost any city or town with a post office. Address letters as in the following example: Napoleon BONAPARTE, *Postlagernde Briefe,* A-1010 Vienna, Austria. In Switzerland use the same formula, but have the postal code be preceded by a CH. The mail will go to a special desk in the central post office, unless you specify a post office by street address or postal code. As a rule, it is best to use the largest post office in the area, as mail may be sorted there anyway. When picking up your mail, bring a form of photo ID, preferably a passport. There is generally no surcharge; if there is a charge, it usually does not exceed the cost of domestic postage. If the clerks insist that there is nothing for you, have them check under your first name as well. *Let's Go* lists post offices and postal codes in the **Practical Information** section for each city and most towns.

American Express: AmEx's travel offices throughout the world offer a free **Client Letter Service** (mail held up to 30 days and forwarded upon request) for cardholders who contact them in advance. Address the letter in the way shown above. Some offices will offer these services to non-cardholders (especially AmEx Traveler's Cheque holders), but call ahead to make sure. *Let's Go* lists AmEx office locations for most large cities in **Practical Information** sections; for a complete, free list, call US ☎ 800-528-4800.

BY TELEPHONE

CALLNG HOME FROM AUSTRIA OR SWITZERLAND

A **calling card** is probably your cheapest bet. Calls are billed collect or to your account. You can frequently call collect without even possessing a company's calling card just by calling their access number and following the instructions. **To obtain a calling card** from your national telecommunications service before leaving home, contact the appropriate company listed below (using the numbers in the first column). To **call home with a calling card,** contact the operator for your service provider in Austria and Switzerland by dialing the appropriate toll-free access number (listed below in the second column). Before settling on a calling card plan, be sure to research your options in order to pick the one that best fits both your needs and your destination.

COMPANY	TO OBTAIN A CARD, DIAL:	TO CALL ABROAD, DIAL:
AT&T (US)	800-361-4470	0800 225 5288
Canada Direct	800-561-8868	0800 888 0014
MCI (US)	800-777-5000	0800 888 8000
Telstra Australia	13 22 00	0800 800 061

CALLING WITHIN AUSTRIA AND SWITZERLAND

The simplest way to call within the country is to use a pay phone. Most pay phones in Austria and Switzerland accept only **prepaid phone cards,** not coins. Phone cards are available at kiosks, post offices, or train stations. Rates are highest in the morning, lower in the evening, and lowest on Sunday and late at night. Dial the city code (refer to the phone code box in each city's **Practical Information**) before each number when calling from outside the city; within the city, dial only the number.

ESSENTIALS

PLACING INTERNATIONAL CALLS. To call Austria or Switzerland from home or to call home from Austria or Switzerland, dial:

1. The **international dialing prefix.** To call from **Australia**, dial 0011; **Canada** or the **US**, 011; **Ireland, New Zealand**, the **UK, Austria,** and **Switzerland,** 00.
2. The **country code** of the country you want to call. To call **Australia**, dial 61; **Canada** or the **US**, 1; **Ireland,** 353; **New Zealand,** 64; the **UK,** 44; **Austria,** 43; and **Switzerland** 41.
3. The **city/area code.** *Let's Go* lists the city/area codes for cities and towns in Austria and Switzerland opposite the city or town name, next to a ☎. If the first digit is a zero (e.g., 020 for London), omit the zero when calling from abroad (e.g., dial 20 from Canada to reach London).
4. The **local number.**

CELLULAR PHONES

Cell phones are quite common in Austria and Switzerland. Locals sport the latest models and text messaging is a popular form of communication.

The international standard for cell phones is GSM, a system that began in Europe and has spread to much of the rest of the world. To make and receive calls in Austria or Switzerland you will need a **GSM-compatible phone** and a **SIM (subscriber identity module) card,** a country-specific, thumbnail-sized chip that gives you a local phone number and plugs you into the local network. Many SIM cards are **prepaid,** meaning that they come with calling time included and don't require that you sign up for a monthly service plan. Incoming calls are frequently free. When you use up the prepaid time, you can buy additional cards or vouchers (usually available at convenience stores) to get more. For more information on GSM phones, check out www.telestial.com, www.vodafone.com, www.orange.co.uk, www.roadpost.com, www.t-mobile.com, or www.planetomni.com. Companies like **Cellular Abroad** (www.cellularabroad.com) rent cell phones that work in a variety of destinations around the world, providing a simpler option than picking up a phone in-country. Servers in Austria and Switzerland include Mobilkom Austria (www.mobilkomaustria.com), T-Mobile (www.t-mobile.at), Tele.Ring (www.telering.at), Orange (www.orange.ch), and TDC/Sunrise (www.sunrise.ch).

GSM PHONES. Just having a GSM phone doesn't mean you're necessarily good to go when you travel abroad. The majority of GSM phones sold in the United States operate on a different **frequency** (1900) than international phones (900/1800) and will not work abroad. Tri-band phones work on all three frequencies (900/1800/1900) and will operate through most of the world. As well, some GSM phones are **SIM-locked** and will only accept SIM cards from a single carrier. You'll need a **SIM-unlocked** phone to use a SIM card from a local carrier when you travel.

BY EMAIL AND INTERNET

Internet access is widespread in Austria and Switzerland. You can check your email from cybercafés, which *Let's Go* lists in the **Practical Information** section for each city, and sometimes from universities, libraries, and hostels. Though limited free access is sometimes available in bookstores and libraries, regular Internet

access isn't cheap. There is no standard price, but it tends to range from 10 to 15SFr per hour in Switzerland and €2-5 per hour in Austria. For a complete listing of cybercafés in Austria and Switzerland, visit www.netcafeguide.com.

Increasingly, travelers find that taking their **laptop computers** on the road with them can be a convenient option for staying connected. Laptop users can call an Internet service provider via a modem using long-distance phone cards specifically intended for such calls. They may also find Internet cafés that allow them to connect their laptops to the Internet. Most excitingly, travelers with wireless-enabled computers may be able to take advantage of an increasing number of Internet "hotspots," where they can get online for free or for a small fee. Newer computers can detect these hotspots automatically; otherwise, websites like www.jiwire.com, www.wi-fihotspotlist.com, and www.locfinder.net can help you find them. For information on insuring your laptop while traveling, see p. 19.

ACCOMMODATIONS

HOSTELS

Many hostels are laid out dorm-style, often with large single-sex rooms and bunk beds, although private rooms that sleep two to four are becoming more common. They sometimes have kitchens and utensils for your use, bike or moped rentals, storage areas, transportation to airports, breakfast and other meals, laundry facilities, and Internet access. There can be drawbacks: some hostels close during certain daytime "lockout" hours, have a curfew, don't accept reservations, impose a maximum stay, or, less frequently, require that you do chores. In Austria and Switzerland, a dorm bed in a hostel averages around US$12-20.

A HOSTELER'S BILL OF RIGHTS. There are certain standard features that we do not include in our hostel listings. Unless we state otherwise, you can expect that every hostel has no lockout, no curfew, a kitchen, free hot showers, some system of secure luggage storage, and no key deposit.

HOSTELLING INTERNATIONAL

Joining the youth hostel association in your own country (listed below) automatically grants you membership privileges in **Hostelling International (HI)**, a federation of national hosteling associations. Non-HI members may be allowed to stay in some hostels, but will have to pay extra to do so. HI hostels are scattered throughout Austria and Switzerland, and are typically less expensive than private hostels. HI's umbrella organization's website (www.hihostels.com), which lists the web addresses and phone numbers of all national associations, are a great place to begin researching hostelling in a specific region. Other comprehensive hostelling websites include www.hostels.com and www.hostelplanet.com.

Most HI hostels also honor guest memberships—you'll get a blank card with space for six validation stamps. Each night you'll pay a nonmember supplement (one-sixth the membership fee) and earn one guest stamp. Get six stamps, and you're a member. This system works well in most of Western Europe, but in some countries you may need to remind the hostel reception. A new membership benefit is the FreeNites program, which allows hostelers to gain points toward free rooms. Most student travel agencies (p. 23) sell HI cards, as do all of the national hosteling organizations listed below. All prices listed below are valid for **one-year memberships** unless otherwise noted.

Australian Youth Hostels Association (AYHA), 422 Kent St., Sydney, NSW 200 (☎02 9261 1111; www.yha.com.au). AUS$52, under 18 AUS$19.

Hostelling International-Canada (HI-C), 205 Catherine St. #400, Ottawa, ON K2P 1C3 (☎613-237-7884; www.hihostels.ca). CDN$35, under 18 free.

An Óige (Irish Youth Hostel Association), 61 Mountjoy St., Dublin 7 (☎830 4555; www.irelandyha.org). €20, under 18 €10.

Hostelling International Northern Ireland (HINI), 22 Donegall Rd., Belfast BT12 5JN (☎02890 31 54 35; www.hini.org.uk). UK£13, under 18 UK£6.

Youth Hostels Association of New Zealand (YHANZ), Level 1, Moorhouse City, 166 Moorhouse Ave., P.O. Box 436, Christchurch (☎0800 278 299 (NZ only) or 03 379 9970; www.yha.org.nz). NZ$40, under 18 free.

Scottish Youth Hostels Association (SYHA), 7 Glebe Cres., Stirling FK8 2JA (☎01786 89 14 00; www.syha.org.uk). UK£6, under 17 £2.50.

Youth Hostels Association (England and Wales), Trevelyan House, Dimple Rd., Matlock, Derbyshire DE4 3YH, UK (☎0870 770 8868; www.yha.org.uk). UK£13.50, under 18 UK£6.75.

Hostelling International-USA, 8401 Colesville Rd., Ste. 600, Silver Spring, MD 20910 (☎301-495-1240; www.hiayh.org). US$28, under 18 free.

BOOKING HOSTELS ONLINE. One of the easiest ways to ensure you've got a bed for the night is by reserving online. Click to the **Hostelworld** booking engine through **www.letsgo.com,** and you'll have access to bargain accommodations from Argentina to Zimbabwe with no added commission.

ESSENTIALS

OTHER TYPES OF ACCOMMODATIONS

HOTELS, GUESTHOUSES, AND PENSIONS

Hotel singles in Austria cost about €40-100 per night, doubles €70-250; in Switzerland, the prices range 50-75 SFr for a single, and 80-150SFr for a double. You'll typically share a hall bathroom; a private bathroom will cost extra. Some hotels offer "full pension" (all meals) and "half pension" (no lunch). Smaller guesthouses and pensions are often cheaper than hotels. If you make reservations in writing, indicate your night of arrival and the number of nights you plan to stay. The hotel will send you a confirmation and may request payment for the first night. Often it is easiest to make reservations over the phone with a credit card.

PRIVATE ROOMS AND PENSIONS

Renting a **private room** (*Privatzimmer*) in a family home is an inexpensive and friendly way to house yourself. Such rooms generally include a sink and use of a toilet and shower. Many places rent private rooms only for longer stays, or they may levy a surcharge (10-20%) for stays of less than three nights. *Privatzimmer* start at 25-60SFr per person in Switzerland. In Austria, rooms range from €18-30 a night. Slightly more expensive, **pensions** (*Pensionen*) are similar to the American and British notion of a bed-and-breakfast. Generally, finding rooms for only one person might be difficult, especially for one-night stays, as most lodgings have rooms with double beds (*Doppelzimmer*); single travelers can get these rooms if they pay a bit more. Continental breakfast is *de rigueur*; in classier places, meat, cheese, and an egg will grace your plate and palate. Contact the local tourist office for a list of private rooms and *Pensionen*.

UNIVERSITY DORMS

Some **colleges and universities** (see **Vienna: Accommodations,** p. 96) open their residence halls to travelers when school is not in session. Some do so even during term-time. Rates tend to be low, and many offer free local calls. *Let's Go* lists colleges that rent dorm rooms among the accommodations for appropriate cities. College dorms are popular with many travelers, especially those looking for long-term lodging, so reserve ahead.

HOME EXCHANGES AND HOSPITALITY CLUBS

Home exchange offers the traveler various types of homes (houses, apartments, condominiums, villas, even castles in some cases), plus the opportunity to live like a native and to cut down on accommodation fees. For more information, contact HomeExchange.Com, P.O. Box 787, Hermosa Beach, CA 90254 USA (☎800-877-8723; www.homeexchange.com), or Intervac International Home Exchange (☎04 232 38 38 in Austria, in Switzerland 0 719 44 27 79; www.intervac.com).

Hospitality clubs link their members with individuals or families abroad who are willing to host travelers for free or for a small fee to promote cultural exchange and general good karma. In exchange, members usually must be willing to host travelers in their own homes. A small membership fee may also be required. **GlobalFreeloaders.com** (www.globalfreeloaders.com) and **The Hospitality Club** (www.hospitalityclub.org) are good places to start. **Servas** (www.servas.org) is an established, more formal, peace-based organization, and requires a fee and an interview to join. An Internet search will find many similar organizations, some of which cater to special interests (e.g., women, gay and lesbian travelers, or members of certain professions.) As always, use common sense when planning to stay with or host someone you do not know.

ESSENTIALS

CAMPING AND THE OUTDOORS

CAMPING

Camping is an inexpensive way to tour Austria and Switzerland. Be prepared, though, as most campsites are not isolated areas: they are large plots more often filled with RVs than tents. Camping in Austria and Switzerland is less about getting into nature and more about having a cheap place to sleep. Almost all campsites are in valleys near towns, although many are perched underneath impressive mountains. Most sites are open in the summer only, but some sites are specifically set aside for winter camping. In Switzerland, prices average 6-9SFr per person, and 4-10SFr per tent site. In Austria, prices run €4-6 per person and €4-8 per tent (plus tax if you're over 15), making camping only sometimes cheaper than hosteling.

Unlike in the United States, camping outside of established campsites in the backcountry is almost never allowed; violators may be subject to steep fines. Backcountry hikers and mountaineers can resort to the well-maintained system of mountain huts *(Hütten)*, which are strategically positioned throughout the Alps to serve all needs outside of an emergency high-mountain bivouac *(Biwak)*. Huts in Austria range from spartan, high-altitude shelters to sprawling affairs with full-service restaurants. A bed generally costs no more than €20, or €10 with ÖAV membership, and often can be substantially cheaper, especially if you are willing to sacrifice a bit of comfort. In Switzerland huts are listed from those in *Kategorie 1* (large huts with many amenities) to *Kategorie 3* (primitive structures or bivy shelters). Swiss huts run about 30SFr for adults, with discounts for SAC members, children, and young adults. Many huts in both countries offer meals in an in-house restaurant. Travelers can choose to pay for meals separately, or pay one price for half-board *(Halbpension)*, including bed, breakfast, and dinner.

HIKING

Austria and Switzerland are renowned for their hiking, with paths ranging from simple hikes in the Swiss Jura and the wine valleys of eastern Austria to ice-axe-wielding expeditions over glaciers to the towering peaks of the Berner Oberland, Valais, and the Hohe Tauern. Nearly every town and city in the two countries has a series of trails in its vicinity shown on maps available at the local tourist office.

Free hiking **maps** are available from even the most basic tourist office, but for lengthy hikes every hiker should have a topographic map of no more than 1:50,000 scale. In Austria and Switzerland two companies make these maps: **Freytag-Berndt** and **Kümmerly-Frey** (maps about US$10). They are available in kiosks, bookstores, and tourist offices, and from **Pacific Travellers Supply**, 12 W. Anapamu St., Santa Barbara CA 93101, USA (☎805-963-4438; www.pactrav.com).

Hiking trails are marked by signs indicating the estimated time to nearby destinations. ("Std." is short for *Stunden*, or hours.) Usually trails will also be marked with either a red-white-red marker, or a blue-white-blue marker. The blue marker, or any trail marked *"Für Geübte,"* means that mountaineering equipment is needed, while the red markers line paths that require no more than sturdy boots and hiking poles. Most mountain hiking trails (unless you have specialized equipment) and mountain huts are open only late June to early September because of snow cover that lasts into the summer.

Österreichischer Alpenverein (ÖAV), (Willhelm-Greil-Str. 15, A-6010 Innsbruck (☎(0512) 595 47; www.oeav.at). Maintains most mountain huts across Tyrol and Austria. Third-party insurance, accident provision, travel discounts, and a wealth of maps and mountain information are included with membership. €41; students 27 and under, juniors age 19-25, seniors 61 and over €30; children 18 and under €14.

BACKCOUNTRY USE IN AUSTRIA AND SWITZERLAND. Be aware that backcountry camping is prohibited in public areas in both countries. Travelers planning **overnight hikes** must stay in the Alpine huts described above. Sleeping in one of these huts helps to preserve the fragile Alpine ecosystem, and it is generally safer for you: when you leave, you are expected to list your next destination in the hut book, thus alerting search-and-rescue teams if a problem should occur.

Schweizer Alpen-Club/Club Alpin Suisse (SAC-CAS), Sektion Bern, Monbijoustr. 61, CH 3007, Bern (☎ 031 370 18 18; fax 370 18 00). Maintains a large number of the Alpine huts in Switzerland. As a federation of smaller clubs, membership is through a particular town or region's branch; cost and member privileges vary by branch.

Naturfreunde (Austria ☎ 01 892 35 34; www.naturfreunde.at; Switzerland ☎ 031 306 67 68; www.naturfreunde.ch)) also maintains a number of huts and coordinates activities in a wide range of outdoor sports.

FURTHER READING: HIKING.
100 Hikes in the Alps, by Vicky Spring (US$15).
Walking Austria's Alps: Hut to Hut, by Jonathan Hurdle (US$11).
Walking Switzerland the Swiss Way, by Marcia and Philip Lieberman (US$13). The "Swiss Way" refers to hiking hut-to-hut.
Walking in the Alps, by Kev Reynolds (US$23). A comprehensive reference for more serious hikers not intended as a travel guide.
Swiss-Bernese Oberland, by Philip and Loretta Alspach (US$17).
Walking Easy in the Austrian Alps and *Walking Easy in the Swiss Alps,* by Chet and Carolee Lipton (US$15).

The **Great Outdoor Recreation Pages** (www.gorp.com) provides excellent general information for travelers planning on camping or spending time in the outdoors.

LEAVE NO TRACE. Let's Go encourages travelers to embrace the "Leave No Trace" ethic, minimizing their impact on natural environments and protecting them for future generations. Trekkers and wilderness enthusiasts should set up camp on durable surfaces, use cookstoves instead of campfires, bury human waste away from water supplies, bag trash and carry it out with them, and respect wildlife and natural objects. For more detailed information, contact the **Leave No Trace Center for Outdoor Ethics,** P.O. Box 997, Boulder, CO 80306, USA (☎ 800-332-4100 or 303-442-8222; www.lnt.org).

USEFUL PUBLICATIONS AND RESOURCES

A variety of publishing companies offer hiking guidebooks to meet the educational needs of novice or expert. For information about camping, hiking, and biking, write or call the publishers listed below to receive a free catalog. Campers heading to Europe should consider buying an International Camping Carnet. Similar to a hostel membership card, it's required at a few campgrounds and provides discounts at others. It is available in North America from the Family Campers and RVers Association and in the UK from The Caravan Club (see below).

Automobile Association, Contact Centre, Carr Ellison House, William Armstrong Drive, Newcastle-upon-Tyne NE4 7YA, UK (☎ 0870 600 0371; www.theAA.com). Publishes **Caravan and Camping Europe** (UK£8) as well as Big Road Atlases for Europe.

The Caravan Club, East Grinstead House, East Grinstead, West Sussex, RH19 1UA, UK (☎44 01342 326 944; www.caravanclub.co.uk). For UK£30, members receive travel equipment discounts, maps, and a monthly magazine.

Sierra Club Books, 85 Second St., 2nd fl., San Francisco, CA 94105, USA (☎415-977-5500; www.sierraclub.org). Publishes general resource books on hiking and camping.

The Mountaineers Books, 1001 SW Klickitat Way, Ste. 201, Seattle, WA 98134, USA (☎206-223-6303; www.mountaineersbooks.org). Boasts over 600 titles on hiking, biking, mountaineering, natural history, and conservation.

NATIONAL PARKS

Austria and Switzerland have one national park each. Austria's, the Hohe Tauern National Park, is the largest national park in Europe. It encompasses 29 towns within its boundaries and offers dramatic views of the Alps. The more adventurous can hike up these peaks. Those looking for a less exhausting way to a good vantage point can take a scenic ride on the Großglocknerstraße, which runs between Zell am See and Lienz, two of the towns in the park (p. 273).

The Swiss National Park is much smaller than the Austrian one, and the hikes are not as intense nor as varied, but it is still a beautiful place to explore the Swiss landscape, wildlife, and flora. Both parks have strict rules about preservation, and neither allows camping within its borders.

WILDERNESS SAFETY

THE GREAT OUTDOORS

Staying **warm, dry, and well-hydrated** is key to a happy and safe wilderness experience. For any hike, prepare yourself for an emergency by packing a first-aid kit, a reflector, a whistle, high-energy food, extra water, raingear, a hat, and mittens. For warmth, wear wool or insulating synthetic materials designed for the outdoors. Cotton is a bad choice since it dries painfully slowly.

Check **weather forecasts** often and pay attention to the skies when hiking, as weather patterns can change suddenly. Always let someone, either a friend, your hostel, a park ranger, or a local hiking organization, know when and where you are hiking. Know your limits and do not attempt a hike beyond your ability. See **Safety and Health,** p. 16, for information on outdoor ailments and medical concerns.

CAMPING AND HIKING EQUIPMENT

WHAT TO BUY

Good camping equipment is both sturdy and light. North American suppliers tend to offer the most competitive prices.

Sleeping bags: Most sleeping bags are rated by season: "summer" means 30-40°F (around 0°C) at night; "four-season" or "winter" often means below 0°F (-17°C). Bags are made of **down** (warm and light, but expensive, and miserable when wet) or of **synthetic** material (heavy, durable, and warm when wet). Prices range US$50-250 for a summer synthetic to US$200-300 for a good down winter bag. **Sleeping bag pads** include foam pads (US$10-30), air mattresses (US$15-50), and self-inflating mats (US$30-120). Bring a **stuff sack** to store your bag and keep it dry.

Tents: The best tents are free-standing (with their own frames and suspension systems), set up quickly, and only require staking in high winds. Low-profile dome tents are the best all-around. Worthy 2-person tents start at US$100, 4-person at US$160. Make sure your tent has a rain fly, and seal its seams with waterproofer. Other useful accessories include a **battery-operated lantern,** a plastic **groundcloth,** and a nylon **tarp.**

Backpacks: Internal-frame packs mold well to your back, keep a lower center of gravity, and flex adequately to allow you to hike difficult trails, while **external-frame packs** are more comfortable for long hikes over even terrain, as they carry weight higher and distribute it more evenly. Make sure your pack has a strong, padded hip-belt to transfer weight to your legs. There are models designed specifically for women. Any serious backpacking requires a pack of at least 4000 in.^{3} (16,000cc), plus 500 in.^{3} for sleeping bags in internal-frame packs. Sturdy backpacks cost anywhere from US$125 to 420—your pack is an area where it doesn't pay to economize. On your hunt for the perfect pack, fill up prospective models with something heavy, strap it on correctly, and walk around the store to get a sense of how the model distributes weight. Either buy a **rain cover** (US$10-20) or store all of your belongings in plastic bags inside your pack.

Boots: Be sure to wear hiking boots with good **ankle support.** They should fit snugly and comfortably over 1-2 pairs of **wool socks** and a pair of thin **liner socks.** Break in boots over several weeks before you go to spare yourself blisters.

Other necessities: Synthetic layers, like those made of polypropylene or polyester, and a pile jacket will keep you warm even when wet. A **space blanket** (US$5-15) will help you to retain body heat and doubles as a groundcloth. Plastic **water bottles** are vital. Look for shatter- and leak-resistant models. Carry **water-purification tablets** for when you can't boil water. Although most campgrounds provide campfire sites, you may want to bring a small **metal grate** or grill. For those places (including virtually every organized campground in Europe) that forbid fires or the gathering of firewood, you'll need a **camp stove** (the classic Coleman starts at US$50) and a propane-filled **fuel bottle** to operate it. Also bring a **first-aid kit, pocketknife, insect repellent,** and **waterproof matches** or a **lighter.**

SKIING

The fact that four Winter Olympics (St. Moritz 1928 and 1948, Innsbruck 1964 and 1972) have been held in Austria and Switzerland is no accident—the skiing in these two countries is easily among the best in the world. An Austrian, Matthias Zdarsky, wrote the world's first instructional book on skiing in 1897 and organized the world's first slalom race in Lilienfeld in 1905. St. Anton, where the world's first ski club was founded in 1901, is often credited as the "birthplace of modern skiing." Kitzbühel is home to what is probably the world's most famous ski race, the Hahnenkamm. Swiss resorts such as Verbier and Zermatt are meccas to diehard skiers because of their challenging runs, wild vertical drop, and overall vastness.

Skiing in the Alps deserves its excellent reputation for a number of reasons. Many travelers are drawn to the old-school charm of the small Alpine villages that predate accompanying resorts by centuries. Vertical drop is higher in the Alps than at almost any resort in North America, and the weather is often both more consistent and gentler. Expert skiers can find some of the most difficult terrain anywhere in the world, along with the freedom to explore at will. Off-trail skiing still only exists in its true form in Europe, where resorts allow people to ski wherever they please as long as they take responsibility for their actions (and foot the bill for rescue, if necessary). Most Alpine skiing is above the timber line, so even the not-so-adventurous can ski thousands of vertical feet without ever leaving sight of sweeping 180-degree panoramas. In addition, a number of resorts offer year-round skiing on glaciers. In Austria, these include Stubai (near Innsbruck), Hintertux (near Mayrhofen), and Obergurgl (in the Ötztal). In Switzerland, summer glacier skiing exists in Zermatt, Saas Fee, and Les Diablerets.

ORGANIZED ADVENTURE TRIPS

Organized adventure tours offer another way of exploring the wild. Activities include hiking, biking, skiing, canoeing, kayaking, rafting, climbing, photo safaris, and archaeological digs. Tourism bureaus often can suggest parks, trails, and outfitters. Organizations that specialize in camping and outdoor equipment like REI and EMS (see above) also are good source for info. **Specialty Travel Index** (US ☎ 800-442-4922, elsewhere 415-459-4900; www.specialtytravel.com) is another source.

SPECIFIC CONCERNS

SUSTAINABLE TRAVEL

As the number of travelers on the road continues to rise, the detrimental effect they can have on natural environments becomes an increasing concern. Through a sensitivity to issues of ecology and sustainability, today's travelers can be a powerful force in preserving and restoring the places they visit.

Ecotourism, a rising trend in sustainable travel, focuses on the conservation of natural habitats and using them to build up the economy without exploitation or overdevelopment. Travelers can make a difference by doing advance research and by supporting organizations and establishments that pay attention to their impact on their natural surroundings and strive to be environmentally friendly.

ECOTOURISM RESOURCES. For more information on environmentally responsible tourism, contact one of the organizations below:
The Centre for Environmentally Responsible Tourism (www.c-e-r-t.org).
Earthwatch, 3 Clock Tower Place, Ste. 100, Box 75, Maynard, MA 01754, USA (☎800-776-0188 or 978-461-0081; www.earthwatch.org).
International Ecotourism Society, 733 15th St. NW, Washington, D.C. 20005, USA (☎202-347-9203; www.ecotourism.org).

RESPONSIBLE TRAVEL

Travelers should become aware of the social and cultural implications of the choices they make when they travel. **Community-based tourism** aims to channel tourist money into the local economy by emphasizing tours and cultural programs that are run by members of the host community and that often benefit disadvantaged groups. An excellent resource for general information on community-based travel is *The Good Alternative Travel Guide* (UK£10), a project of **Tourism Concern** (☎020 7133 3330; www.tourismconcern.org.uk).

TRAVELING ALONE

Traveling alone can facilitate independence and interaction with locals, but it makes one more vulnerable to harassment and street theft. As a lone traveler, try not to stand out as a tourist and be careful in deserted or very crowded areas. Do not admit that you are traveling alone. Maintain regular contact with someone at home who knows your itinerary. For more tips, read *Traveling Solo* by Eleanor Berman (Globe Pequot Press, US$18), visit www.travelaloneandloveit.com, or subscribe to **Connecting: Solo Travel Network,** 689 Park Rd., Unit 6, Gibsons, BC V0N 1V7, Canada (☎604-886-9099; www.cstn.org; membership US$28-45).

SENIOR TRAVELERS

Seniors often qualify for hotel and restaurant discounts as well as discounted admission to many tourist attractions. If you don't see a senior citizen price listed, ask and you may be pleasantly surprised. In general for Switzerland, women over 62 and men over 65 qualify as seniors; in Austria, it's women over 60 and men over 65. A **Seniorenausweis** (Senior Citizen Identification Card) entitles holders to a 50% discount on all Austrian federal trains and BundesBuses and works as an ID for discounted museum admissions. The card costs €25.40, requires a passport photo and proof of age, and is valid for one calendar year. It is available in Austria at railroad stations. Both National Tourist Offices offer guides for senior citizens. Many discounts require proof of status, so prepare to be carded.

WOMEN TRAVELERS

Women travelers will likely feel safer in Austria and Switzerland than just about anywhere in the world: violent crime is rare and civility is a deeply ingrained cultural standard. It's easy to be adventurous without taking undue risks. If you are concerned, consider staying in hostels which offer single rooms that lock from the inside or in religious organizations with rooms for women only. Some travelers report that carrying pictures of a "husband" or "children" is extremely useful to help document marital status.

Always carry extra money for a phone call, bus, or taxi. **Hitchhiking** is never safe for lone women, or even for two women traveling together. Look as if you know where you're going and approach older women or couples for directions if you're lost or uncomfortable.

Your best answer to verbal harassment is no answer at all: feigning deafness, sitting motionless, and staring straight ahead at nothing in particular can be very effective strategies. The extremely persistent can sometimes be dissuaded by a firm, loud, and very public "Go away!" in the appropriate language (see **Appendix**, p. 557). Seek out a police officer or a passerby if you are being harassed. Memorize the emergency numbers in places you visit, and consider carrying a whistle on your keychain. A self-defense course will both prepare you for a potential attack and raise your level of awareness of your surroundings (see p. 18).

GLBT TRAVELERS

Austria and Switzerland are relatively conservative countries. In the rural countryside especially, public displays of homosexuality may be unwelcome. However, more cosmopolitan and tolerant cities such as Geneva, Zurich, and Vienna have a wide variety of homosexual organizations and establishments, from biker and Christian groups to bars and barber shops. The German adjective for gay is *schwul* (sh-VOOL); for lesbian, *lesbisch* (LEZ-bisch). The collective nouns are *Schwul* and *Lesbe*. Bisexual is *bisexual* or simply *bi* (bee). In French, *homosexuelle* can be used for both men and women, but the preferred terms are *gai* (geh) and *lesbienne* (les-BYENN).

Homosexuelle Initiative (HOSI; www.hosi.at) is a nationwide organization with offices in most cities that provides information on gay and lesbian establishments, resources, and supports as well as publishing warnings about aggressively intolerant areas and establishments. HOSI Wien, II, Novarag. 40, Vienna (☎/fax (01) 216 66 04; www.hosiwien.at), publishes Austria's leading gay and lesbian quarterly magazine, the *Lambda-Nachrichten*. The age of consent for everyone in **Switzerland** is 16. **The Pink Cross** (www.pinkcross.ch) hosts Switzerland's nationwide lesbian, gay, and bisexual information hotline.

Rainbowline (☎084 880 50 80) is in German, French, English, and Italian. **Dialogai,** headquartered in Geneva at 11-13 r. de la Navigation (mailing address Case Postale 69, 1211, Geneva 21; ☎022 906 40 40; www.dialogai.org), provides gay and lesbian information for French-speaking Switzerland.

Listed below are contact organizations, mail-order bookstores, and publishers that offer materials addressing some specific concerns. **Out and About** (www.planetout.com) offers a bi-weekly newsletter addressing travel concerns and a comprehensive site addressing gay travel concerns. The online newspaper **365gay.com** also has a travel section (www.365gay.com/travel/travelchannel.htm).

Gay's the Word, 66 Marchmont St., London WC1N 1AB, UK (☎44 20 7278 7654; www.gaystheword.co.uk). The largest gay and lesbian bookshop in the UK, with both fiction and non-fiction titles. Mail-order service available.

Giovanni's Room, 1145 Pine St., Philadelphia, PA 19107, USA (☎215-923-2960; www.queerbooks.com). An international lesbian/feminist and gay bookstore with mail-order service (carries many of the publications listed below).

International Lesbian and Gay Association (ILGA), 81 rue Marché-au-Charbon, B-1000 Brussels, Belgium (☎32 2 502 2471; www.ilga.org). Provides political information, such as homosexuality laws of individual countries.

▼ **FURTHER READING: GLBT TRAVEL**

Spartacus 2004/2005: International Gay Guide. Bruno Gmunder Verlag (US$33).

Ferrari Guides' Gay Travel A to Z, Ferrari Guides' Men's Travel in Your Pocket, Ferrari Guides' Women's Travel in Your Pocket, and *Ferrari Guides' Inn Places.* Ferrari Publications (US$16-20).

TRAVELERS WITH DISABILITIES

Austria and Switzerland are relatively accessible to travelers with disabilities *(behinderte Reisende).* Disabled visitors to **Austria** may want to contact the Vienna Tourist Board, Obere Augartenstr. 40, A-1025 Vienna (☎01 211 14; www.info.wien.at), which offers booklets on accessible Vienna hotels and a guide for the disabled. The Austrian National Tourist Offices in New York and Vienna offer listings for wheelchair-accessible sights, museums, and lodgings in Vienna. With three days' notice, the Austrian railways will provide a wheelchair for the train. The international wheelchair icon indicates access. In **Switzerland,** disabled travelers can contact **Mobility International Schweiz,** Frogurbstr. 4, 4600 Olten (☎062 206 88 35; www.mis-infothek.ch). Most Swiss buildings and restrooms have ramps. The Swiss Federal Railways have wheelchair access for most of their cars. Inter-City and long-distance express trains have wheelchair compartments.

Those with disabilities should inform airlines and hotels of their disabilities when making reservations: some time may be needed to prepare special accommodations. Call ahead to restaurants, museums, and other facilities to find out if they are handicapped-accessible. **Guide dog owners** should inquire about the quarantine policies of each destination country.

Rail is probably the most convenient form of travel for disabled travelers in Europe. Many stations have ramps, and some trains have wheelchair lifts, special seating areas, and specially equipped toilets. In Switzerland all IC, most EC, and some regional trains are handicapped-accessible. For those who wish to rent cars, some major **car rental** agencies (Hertz, Avis, and National) offer hand-controlled vehicles.

USEFUL ORGANIZATIONS

Access Abroad (www.umabroad.umn.edu/access). A website devoted to making study abroad available to students with disabilities. The site is maintained by Disability Services Research and Training, University of Minnesota, University Gateway, Ste. 180, 200 Oak St. SE, Minneapolis, MN 55455, USA (☎612-626-1333).

Accessible Journeys, 35 West Sellers Ave., Ridley Park, PA 19078, USA (☎800-846-4537; www.disabilitytravel.com). Designs tours for wheelchair users and slow walkers. The site has tips and forums for all travelers.

Directions Unlimited, 123 Green Ln., Bedford Hills, NY 10507, USA (☎800-533-5343). Books individual vacations for the physically disabled. Not an info service.

Flying Wheels, 143 W. Bridge St., P.O. Box 382, Owatonna, MN 55060, USA (☎507-451-5005; www.flyingwheelstravel.com). Specializes in escorted trips to Europe for people with physical disabilities. Plans custom accessible trips worldwide.

Mobility International USA (MIUSA), P.O. Box 10767, Eugene, OR 97440, USA (☎541-343-1284; www.miusa.org). Provides a variety of books and other publications containing information for travelers with disabilities.

Society for Accessible Travel and Hospitality (SATH), 347 Fifth Ave., Ste. 610, New York, NY 10016, USA (☎212-447-7284; www.sath.org). Advocacy group. Publishes free online travel info and the travel magazine *OPEN WORLD* (annual subscription US$13, free for members). Annual membership US$45, students and seniors US$30.

MINORITY TRAVELERS

Although Austria and Switzerland are predominantly white, they are, as a general rule, tolerant of minority travelers. Most minority travelers will not have difficulty, though the farther you venture into the countryside, the more likely it is that you will encounter the occasional odd stare. Villagers are notoriously curious, so don't be surprised or offended if old women linger in their windows to catch a glimpse of you. In recent years, a growing population of foreign workers (particularly Turks) has felt the sting of Swiss anxiety about economic recession, but physical confrontations are rare. Anti-Semitism is not a large problem in either country.

RELIGIOUS CONCERNS

While the predominance of Catholics and Protestant churches make it simple for anyone of those faiths to find a place to worship, the same task can be challenging for those of other faiths.

Buddhist communities have centers in **Vienna** (Fleischmarkt 16, 1st fl., A-1010 Vienna; ☎01 513 38 80; bodhidharma.zendo@blackbox.at); **Innsbruck** (An der Furt 18, II., A-6020 Innsbruck; ☎/fax 0512 36 71 13; aldo.deutsch@uibk.ac.at); and **Salzburg** (Schloßstr. 38, A-5020 Salzburg; ☎/fax 62 74 75 16; sunyata@magnet.at).

Jehovah's Witnesses can check www.watchtower.org for more information.

Jewish visitors to Vienna can contact **The Jewish Welcome Service** (☎(01) 533 27 30). **The Jewish Community Center** Seitenstetteng. 4, Postfach 145, A-1010 Vienna (☎(01) 53 10 40; fax 533 15 17), is a good resource for information elsewhere in Austria. Open M-Th 8am-5pm, F 8am-2pm. Switzerland has its own version, the **Federation of Swiss Jewish Communities,** Gotthardstr. 65, 8002 Zurich (☎01 201 55 83; fax 01 202 16 72). Or consult *The Jewish Travel Guide,* which lists synagogues, kosher restaurants, and Jewish institutions in over 100 countries, available in Europe from Vallentine

Mitchell Publishers, Crown House, 47 Chase Side, Southgate, London N14 5BP, UK (☎020 89 20 21 00; fax 020 844 85 48) and in the US ($20.95) from ISBS, 5824 NE Hassallo St., Portland, OR 97213 (☎800-944-6190).

Mormons in Switzerland can visit the temple in Zollikofen, near Bern (Templestr. 2, CH-3052 Zollikofen; ☎031 915-5252). For Austria, www.ettl.co.at/mormon/english.

Muslims can turn to www.islam.ch (available in German, French, or Italian) for information and addresses throughout Switzerland.

DIETARY CONCERNS

Vegans will likely have difficulty outside of large cities, but **ovo-lacto vegetarians** can enjoy many traditional meatless dishes. The travel section of the Vegetarian Resource Group's website (www.vrg.org/travel) has a comprehensive list of organizations and websites that help vegetarians and vegans traveling abroad. For more information, visit your local bookstore or health food store and consult *The Vegetarian Traveler: Where to Stay if You're Vegetarian, Vegan, Environmentally Sensitive,* by Jed and Susan Civic (Larson Publications; US$16).

Vegetarians will also find numerous resources on the web. Try www.vegdining.com and www.happycow.net for starters. Sites like www.vegetarismus.ch (Switzerland) and http://netbase.t0.or.at/~ivi/rests.htm (Austria) offer more specific listings for those countries.

Travelers who keep **kosher** should contact synagogues in larger cities for information on kosher restaurants. Your own synagogue or college Hillel should have access to lists of Jewish institutions across the nation. The Swiss National Tourist Office distributes the pamphlet *The Jewish City Guide to Basel.* Also see **Religious Concerns,** p. 52. **Diabetic travelers** can pick up *The Diabetic Traveler* by Davida F. Kruger. (American Diabetes Association, $14.95).

THE ART OF TRAVEL

WWW.LETSGO.COM Our freshly redesigned website features extensive content from our guides; community forums where travelers can connect with each other and ask questions or advice—as well as share stories and tips; and expanded resources to help you plan your trip. Visit us soon to browse by destination, find information about ordering our titles, and sign up for our e-newsletter!

Backpacker's Ultimate Guide: www.bugeurope.com. Tips on packing, transportation, and where to go. Also tons of country-specific travel information.

BootsnAll.com: www.bootsnall.com. Numerous resources for independent travelers, from planning your trip to reporting on it when you get back.

How to See the World: www.artoftravel.com. A compendium of great travel tips, from cheap flights to self defense to interacting with local culture.

Travel Intelligence: www.travelintelligence.net. A large collection of travel writing by distinguished travel writers.

Travel Library: www.travel-library.com. A fantastic set of links for general information and personal travelogues.

World Hum: www.worldhum.com. An independently produced collection of "travel dispatches from a shrinking planet."

INFO ON AUSTRIA AND SWITZERLAND

Atevo Travel: www.atevo.com/guides/destinations. Detailed introductions, travel tips, and suggested itineraries.

Austrian Introduction: www.austria.org. Official American website for Austria with information on visas, tourism, business, and culture.

CIA World Factbook: www.odci.gov/cia/publications/factbook/index.html. Vital statistics on the geography, government, economy, and people of Austria and Switzerland.

Geographia: www.geographia.com. Culture and people of Austria and Switzerland.

PlanetRider: www.planetrider.com. A subjective list of links to the "best" websites covering the culture and tourist attractions of Austria and Switzerland.

Swiss Introduction: www.myswitzerland.com. Tourism highlights, including virtual tours, hotel booking, and weather report in Switzerland.

World Travel Guide: www.travel-guides.com. Helpful practical info.

Youth Hostel Listings: The official hostel websites for Austria (www.oejhv.or.at/e-choose.htm) and Switzerland (www.jugendherberge.ch).

ALTERNATIVES TO TOURISM

A PHILOSOPHY FOR TRAVELERS

Let's Go believes that the connection between travelers and their destinations is an important one. We know that many travelers care passionately about the communities and environments they explore—but we also know that even conscientious tourists can inadvertently damage natural wonders and harm cultural environments. With this chapter, *Let's Go* hopes to promote a deeper understanding of Austria and Switzerland and enhance your experience there.

There are several options for those who seek alternatives to tourism. As a **volunteer** in Austria or Switzerland, you can participate in projects ranging from archaeological digs to youth theater camps, either on a short-term basis or as the main component of your trip. Later in this section, we recommend organizations that can help you find the opportunities that best suit your interests, whether you're looking to pitch in for a day or a year.

Studying at a college or language program is another option. The rich history and landscape of the area make it an appealing place to study anything from music in Vienna to geology in the Swiss Alps.

Many travelers also structure their trips by the **work** that they can do along the way, either odd jobs as they go or full-time stints in cities where they plan to stay for some time. Cities are the best places to find long-term work, while short-term positions are available in both urban and rural areas.

> Start your search at **www.beyondtourism.com,** Let's Go's brand-new searchable database of Alternatives to Tourism, where you can find exciting feature articles and helpful program listings divided by country, continent, and program type.

VOLUNTEERING

Volunteering can be one of the most fulfilling experiences you have in life, especially if you combine it with the thrill of traveling in a new place. It allows you to improve the locations you visit rather than contribute to the strain on the infrastructure, the private lives of the local residents, and the ecosystem.

>
> **VISA INFORMATION.** Generally, visas in Austria and Switzerland are not a problem for volunteering placements. Existing programs usually have special arrangements and take care of the necessary paperwork or at least assist in the process. If not, it will be necessary to obtain a residence permit for either country if you are staying for longer than 3 months. See Essentials: Visas, Invitations, and Work Permits, p. 10.

Despite the benefits of volunteerism, such opportunities in both Austria and Switzerland are limited. Both countries cater more to tourism than volunteering. Austria especially has strict rules about the role of foreign volunteers. If you are not a citizen of the EU, it is virtually impossible to volunteer in either country without the help of a placement organization or service. Foreign volunteers in Austria and Switzerland tend to work directly for organizations that have set up programs to use short-term volunteers to complete (usually) unskilled work for them. These organizations arrange everything, typically including procurement of a visa and work permit if necessary. The trade-off for this is almost invariably a big participation fee. However, the cost can be worth it for many people, because the fee usually covers airfare, living expenses, and logistical details, and because placement organizations can provide a group environment and support system.

Your best bet when considering volunteering options is to do your homework. A first-pass search often will not unveil some of the most reputable, worthy opportunities to be found. There is a dizzying variety of web resources available, including search engines, databases, and websites that list volunteer opportunities. There are two main types of organizations, religious and nonsectarian, although there are rarely restrictions on participation for either. For an incredibly comprehensive and well-chosen bibliography of volunteerism-related reading, download the PDF files at **World Volunteer Web:** www.worldvolunteerweb.org/research/bibliography.

GENERAL VOLUNTEERING

AFS International, 71 West 23rd St., 17th fl., New York, NY 10010, USA (☎212-807-8686; www.afs.org). Programs in both Austria and Switzerland. Placements with host families for students (16-18 years old) to attend schools abroad for a year, for young adults 18+ in volunteer assignments, and for teachers in volunteer educator posts.

English Language Teaching Assistant Program (ELTAP), Division of Education, University of Minnesota, Morris, MN 56267, USA (☎320-589-6400; www.eltap.org). Assigns students and adults to posts as English teaching assistants at schools in Switzerland. Application fee US$300; program fee US$2553 includes room, board, and social and cultural activities. Participants earn UMN course credit for their work or a certificate that can be listed on resumés.

International Cultural Youth Exchange (ICYE), Große Hamburger Str. 30, D-10115 Berlin, Germany (☎0049 30 28 39 05 50; www.icye.org). Volunteer work placements for youths ages 16-30. Limited posting for Austria, but a wide variety in Switzerland. Lists both short- and long-term assignments.

Service Civil International/International Voluntary Service (SCI-IVS), 5474 Walnut Level Rd., Crozet, VA 22932 (☎/fax 206-350-6585; www.sci-ivs.org). Arranges placement in summer volunteer work camps and middle- and long-term volunteering assignments in Austria and Switzerland. Registration fee US$175.

Volunteers for Peace (VFP), 1034 Tiffany Rd., Belmont, VT 05730, USA (☎ 802-259-2759; www.vfp.org). 2-3 week community service projects with international volunteers 18+ (some 15+). May-Sept., US$200 registration fee.

ECOTOURISM

ATG Oxford, 69-71 Banbury Rd., Oxford, England, OX2 6PJ (☎44 0 1865 315 678; www.atg-oxford.co.uk/contact.php), offers walking-based tours of Salzburg. It focuses on conservation and sustainable tourism.

Bergwald Projekt/Mountain Forest Project, Hauptstr. 24, 7014 Trin, Switzerland (☎011 41 81 630 4145; www.bergwaldprojekt.ch), organizes week-long conservation projects in Austria, Switzerland, and Germany.

AGRICULTURE AND RURAL DEVELOPMENT

Landdienst-Zentralstelle, Mühleg. 13, Postfach 2826, CH-8021 Zurich, Switzerland (☎41 (0)1 261 44 88; www.landdiest.ch).

Workcamp Switzerland, Bastionweg 15, 4500 Solothurn, Switzerland (☎41 (0) 32 621 50 37; www.workcamp.ch). Offers 2-week long sessions in which volunteers live in a group environment and work on a common community service project.

WWOOF (Willing Workers On Organic Farms) Switzerland, Postfach 59, 8124 Maur, Switzerland (www.welcome.to/wwoof). Matches short-term workers with organic farms in Switzerland. Also offers programs in Austria.

YOUTH AND THE COMMUNITY

Concordia, Heversham House, 2nd fl. 20-22 Boundary Rd., Hove, BN3 4ET (☎01273 422218; www.concordia-iye.co.uk). UK volunteer organization that includes community projects in Austria, such as renovating historic buildings and parks, directing a youth drama project, and creating hiking paths.

UNA Exchange, Cathays Park, Cardiff, Wales CF10 3AP (☎029 2022 3088; www.unaexchange.org). Message boards advertise volunteer exchanges in Austria.

Youth Action for Peace, 8 Golden Ridge, Freshwater, Isle of Wight PO40 9LE (☎08701 657 927; www.yap-uk.org). Organizes youth exchanges and workcamps.

HISTORICAL RESTORATION

The **Archaeological Institute of America** (☎617-353-9361; www.archaeological.org) lists archaeological fieldwork projects worldwide, including Western Europe.

STUDYING

Study abroad programs range from basic language and culture courses to semester-long study at a university, often for credit. In order to choose a program that best fits your needs, research as much as you can before making your decision. Determine costs and duration, as well as what kind of students participate in the program and what sort of accommodations are provided.

In programs that have large groups of students who speak your language, you may feel more comfortable, but you will not have the same opportunity to practice a foreign language or to befriend other international students. For accommodations, dorm life provides a better opportunity to mingle with fellow students, but there is less of a chance to experience the local scene. If you live with a family, there is a potential to build lifelong friendships with natives and to experience day-to-day life in more depth, though conditions can vary greatly from family to family.

UNIVERSITIES

Most university-level study abroad programs are conducted in German, French, or Italian, though many programs offer classes in English and beginner- and lower-level language courses. Those relatively fluent in German may find it cheaper to enroll directly in a university abroad, although getting college credit may be more difficult. You can search **www.studyabroad.com** for various semester-abroad pro-

VISA INFORMATION. Study in **Austria** requires a residence permit (*Aufenhaltserlebnis*). If you are a citizen of a country normally allowed free entry (see **Essentials,** p. 10), you can pick this up from the government once you arrive. Otherwise, you must apply in advance with the Austrian embassy in your country. To view the list of documents necessary for the permit, visit the "Entry & Residence" section of the Austrian Exchange Service's website (www.oead.at).

Study in **Switzerland** for less than 3 months may not require a visa or residence permit if you are a citizen of a country normally allowed free entry. If you are not, or your period of study is longer, you must apply for a residence permit from the Swiss embassy in your country. To obtain a permit, you must submit 3 copies of the permit application (available through the Swiss embassy), a copy of your passport, 3 passport-sized photos, and proof of your acceptance into a program of study at a Swiss institution.

In some cases, your host institution will take care of visa and residence permit applications, but usually you will have to apply yourself or at least pay the necessary fees. Especially in Switzerland, the application process can drag on, often for several months, so plan far in advance. Ask your host institution for their specific policy and for advice on entry and residence requirements.

grams that meet your criteria, including your desired location and focus of study. Another particularly good resource for finding programs that cater to your interests is the **Institute of International Education** (www.iiepassport.org/webapp/controller/PassportSearchForm), which provides a searchable database with copious numbers of respectable, well-developed programs. The following is a list of organizations that can help place students in university programs abroad or that have their own branch in Austria or Switzerland.

AMERICAN PROGRAMS

American Institute for Foreign Study, College Division, River Plaza, 9 West Broad St., Stamford, CT 06902, USA (☎800-727-2437; www.aifsabroad.com). Runs year-long, semester-long, and summer programs at the University of Salzburg for college students.

Central College Abroad, Box 1040, 812 University, Pella, IA 50219, USA (☎800-831-3629; www.central.edu/abroad). Offers internships, as well as summer, semester-, and year-long programs in Vienna. Application fee US$30.

College Consortium for International Studies (CCIS), 2000 P St. NW, Ste. 503, Washington, D.C. 20036, USA (☎800-453-6956; www.ccisabroad.org). Runs programs at Franklin College in Lugano, Switzerland and Salzburg College in Austria. Offers courses in the humanities, social sciences, and business. Summer and semester-long programs.

Global Campus, University of Minnesota, 230 Heller Hall, 271 19th Ave. South, Minneapolis, MN 55455, USA (☎612-626-9000; www.umabroad.umn.edu). Run through the UMN Office of International Programs, Global Campus sponsors a large number of study abroad opportunities (for course credit, depending on your home institution).

Institute for the International Education of Students (IES), 33 N. LaSalle St., 15th fl., Chicago, IL 60602, USA (☎800-995-2300; www.IESabroad.org). Offers year-long and semester programs in Vienna. Summer music program. Internship opportunities. US$50 application fee. Scholarships available.

International Association for the Exchange of Students for Technical Experience (IAESTE), 10400 Little Patuxent Pkwy., Ste. 250, Columbia, MD 21044, USA (☎410-997-2200; www.aieste.org). Offers 8- to 12-week programs in Austria for college students who have completed 2 years of technical study. Application fee US$25.

International Student Exchange Program (ISEP), 1616 P Street NW, Ste. 150, Washington, D.C. 20036, USA (☎202-667-8027; www.isep.org). Provides student exchanges from hundreds of schools in the US and a handful of institutions in Australia, Canada, and Great Britain to 3 universities in Switzerland and 3 universities in Austria.

Kentucky Institute for International Studies (KIIS), Murray State University, P.O. Box 9, Murray, KY 42071-0009, USA (☎270-762-3091; www.kiis.org). Offers summer and semester-long enrollment at their school in Bregenz; environmental and cultural course offerings. Course credit given through Murray State University. Application fee US$150.

School for International Training, Admissions, Kipling Rd., P.O. Box 676, Brattleboro, VT 05302, USA (☎800-336-1616 or 802-257-7751; www.sit.edu/studyabroad/europe/swiss.html). Semester- and year-long programs in Switzerland for the International Studies, Organizations, and Social Justice Program run US$16,045. Fee includes tuition, room, board, personal expenses, and travel cost. Also runs the **Experiment in International Living** (☎800-345-2929; www.usexperiment.org), 3- to 5-week summer programs that offer high school students local homestays and travel opportunities in Geneva and its environs. Tuition $4700.

AUSTRIAN AND SWISS PROGRAMS

To find colleges and universities in Austria and Switzerland, head to **General Education Online** (www.findaschool.org).

Eidgenössische Technische Hochschule (ETH; Swiss Federal Institute of Technology), Student Exchange Office, ETH Zentrum, CH-8092 Zurich, Switzerland (www.mobilitaet.ethz.ch). ETH, a member of the Trans-Atlantic Science Student Exchange Program (TASSEP), arranges study abroad for students at specific institutions in the US, Canada, and the EU. Also runs bilateral exchange agreements with schools in Australia, Canada, Singapore, the UK, USA. Study exchanges with participating schools are generally cheap; ask your Study Abroad Office or Chemistry Department if your school participates in the program.

European University Center for Peace Studies (EPU), Rochusplatz 1, A-7461 Stadtschlaining, Austria (☎33 55 24 98; www.aspr.ac.at/welcome.htm). Winner of the 1995 UNESCO Prize for Peace Education, EPU offers masters degrees and certificates in Peace and Conflict Transformation.

Swiss School of Hotel and Tourism Management, Comercialstraße 19, 7007 Chur, Switzerland (☎0041 812 57 06 64; www.ssh.ch/index2.html). Offers MBAs, BSs, and Swiss diplomas in tourist industry related fields. Students must be at least 18 years old, have a high school diploma, and speak fluent English. Tuition 19,500SFr per semester.

University of Fribourg, American College Program (ACP), American College Program, Admissions, Av. de Beauregard 13, Case postale 102, CH-1701 Fribourg, Switzerland (☎026 300 81 90; www.unifr.ch/acp). Available at over 100 colleges and universities in the US, the ACP allows students to take a full slate of courses at the University of Fribourg. Students can choose between semester and full-year options.

Webster University, Study Abroad Office, Webster University, 470 E. Lockwood, St. Louis, MO 63119, USA (☎800-984-6857 or 314-968-6900; www.webster.edu/worldwide_locations.html). Students from around the world can study at Webster University's Geneva and Vienna campuses. Both locations offer full-degree programs or summer and semester sessions. All courses are taught in English and fully accredited.

LANGUAGE SCHOOLS

Language schools can be independently run international or local organizations or divisions of foreign universities. They rarely offer college credit. They are a good alternative to university study if you desire a deeper focus on the language or a slightly less rigorous courseload. These programs are also good for younger high school students who might not feel comfortable with older students in a university program. There are a number of excellent online databases to aid in your search, including **Campus Austria** (www.campus-austria.at) and the **Institute of International Education** (www.iiepassport.org/webapp/controller/PassportSearchForm). Some good programs include:

ASC International House, 72 rue de Lausanne, 1202 Geneva (☎ 022 731 85 20; www.asc-ih.ch). Language programs in Switzerland, with German and French courses.

Eurocentres, 101 N. Union St., Ste. 300, Alexandria, VA 22314, USA (☎ 703-684-1494; www.eurocentres.com) or in Europe: Head Office, Seestr. 247, CH-8038 Zurich, Switzerland (☎ 41 1 485 50 40). French language programs (with homestays) for beginning to advanced students for learning at several locations in Switzerland.

National Center for Study Abroad (☎ 414-278-7410; www.nrcsa.com). Pre-registers students for 6 schools/programs in Austria and 1 school in Switzerland (see the listing for Eurocentres, above). Austrian programs are largely centered around language classes, but some include topics such as Austrian culture and history, music, and ski instructor certification. Prices and dates vary by program.

Wiener Internationale Hochschulkurse, Ebendorserstr. 10, A-1010 Vienna, Austria (www.univie.ac.at/wihok). Offers beginner- and advanced-level German courses.

WORKING

As with volunteering, work opportunities tend to fall into two categories. Some travelers want long-term jobs that allow them to get to know another part of the world as a member of the community, while other travelers seek out short-term jobs to finance the next leg of their travels.

With the economic freedom resulting from the formation of the European Union and the widespread proliferation of the Internet, it is becoming both easier and more common for job markets to be international, and for employers and employees to find one another from different countries. Along with many other countries, Austria and Switzerland have seen a rise in the number of opportunities for foreign workers to find jobs within their countries.

Perhaps the easiest way to find work in Austria or Switzerland is through enrollment in a pre-designed work abroad program, similar in feel to study abroad and overseas volunteer placements. In return for rather substantial participation fees, such programs generally handle work permit paperwork, provide employees with housing and sometimes meals, and afford a ready-made social network of others who have traveled from home to work in a foreign country. For many people, especially those whose emphasis is more on short-term travel experience rather than professional advancement, these programs can be attractive options.

However, those whose primary goal is to acquire an in-depth understanding of Swiss or Austrian culture may want to look elsewhere. With the possible exception of direct enrollment in a university, no possible form of sustainable travel comes close to providing the level of cultural integration and understanding that comes with setting up your own independent work experience. In contrast to working abroad, volunteer and study programs inevitably involve some insulation from the local culture. As a resident working and living alongside native-born citizens, it is tough to avoid some degree of cultural immersion, which brings with it the kind of local sensitivity that sustainable travel tries to bring about.

In Austria and Switzerland, people who want to work long-term should look for jobs in banking or the hotel or sales industries. Short-term work is often available at hotels, ski resorts, and farms. Sites like www.emploi.ch have searchable databases of available jobs.

A Forum in the Alps

Experiencing European intellectual culture does not require sitting in uncomfortable café chairs and drinking intolerably strong coffee while learning how to say *post-structuralism* in a variety of languages (although all of that is fun, too). For scholarly travelers, the Alpbach European Forum is a welcome alternative to both high-commitment study abroad programs and to wandering aimlessly around the Parisian Left Bank in the hopes of seeing Sartre's ghost. In 2003 I visited Alpbach, located near Innsbruck, in the Tyrolean countryside, as a scholarship student. For two weeks I joined dozens of other participants in exhausting treks up steep Alpine roads to exchange perspectives on issues ranging from the ethics of evolutionary psychology to the paradoxes presented by quantum mechanics. The climb was definitely worth it.

In the tumultuous years after WWII Otto Molden and Simon Moser founded the Alpbach European Forum with some lofty goals in mind. The scholars wanted to create a place where the damage caused by the war could be repaired with thought—a kind of thought that would not be constrained by academic disciplines or international boundaries. In a bold and romantic move, they located the conference in a small, isolated Alpine village, a perfect setting for open discussion and deep contemplation. Since then the forum has grown to attract participants from all over Europe and the world. People gather there for a variety of programs, some of which are focused on cutting-edge questions in technology, some of which look to apply traditional philosophy to modern ethical questions.

The people you meet at Alpbach will be the highlight of your experience there. Some, such as philosopher Hans Albert, have been attending the conference since its inaugural years. Seek out Hans and other long-term Alpbach groupies to make early 20th century European thought come alive: Hans loves to buy bright-eyed students a drink and share memories of his friends, the philosophers Karl Popper, Martin Heidegger, and Max Horkheimer. Of course, there is plenty of young blood at Alpbach as well. In my two weeks there I encountered people from all over the globe who, probably because of the open and friendly setting of the conference, often shared with me their views on American culture and the US's recent world behavior, among other things. Nowhere else in my European travels had people been so interested in my worldview and accepted me as a participant rather than a tourist. I learned so much about European culture and history--not only from my classes but also from informal discussions held at beautiful wood-paneled pubs with young E.U. bureaucrats who had seen and helped create momentous political changes across the continent.

Alpbach is a rather expensive skiing location during the winter months, and seeing the beautiful countryside in the summer for a fraction of that cost is part of the fun of the conference. Many participants go on walking hikes early in the morning before class, and people frequently take a "day off" when the call of the wild starts to drown out their discussion of shifting patterns of immigration. The landscape? Think *The Sound of Music*, only with steeper mountains, more cows, and stricter zoning laws (e.g., "all houses must have flower boxes"). You may even see the town band pass by, dressed in their *Lederhosen* and feathered caps. *Wunderbar!* Just in case you're not the outdoorsy type, there is also a discotheque on the mountain, where you can express your political views on EU expansion by getting down with a cute Hungarian or Czech.

If you're interested in any facet of European politics, culture, or academia, visiting Alpbach is a wonderful alternative to tourism. From the people, to the beautiful setting, to the knowledge you'll gain, the conference is an experience you'll never forget. It can be easily included as a stopover in a larger trip across Austria or Europe—after the conference, Italy beckoned me from the south and I drove there (through the Alps!) for a little vacation. So be adventurous! The Alpbach European Forum is definitely one of the brightest gems that Austria has to offer its travelers, and I guarantee that your time there will be rewarding, inspiring, and—most importantly—fun!

Applications to the program are available online at www.alpbach.org.

Roxana Myrhum is a Social Studies concentrator at Harvard College

LONG-TERM WORK

If you're planning on spending a substantial amount of time (more than three months) working in Austria or Switzerland, search for a job well in advance. International placement agencies are often the easiest way to find employment abroad, especially for teaching English. **Internships,** usually for college students, are a good way to segue into working abroad, although they are often unpaid or poorly paid (many say the experience, however, is well worth it). Be wary of advertisements or companies that claim the ability to get you a job abroad for a fee: often the same listings are available online or in newspapers, or are even out-of-date. Some reputable organizations include:

Association for International Practical Training (AIPT), 10400 Little Patuxent Pkwy. Ste. 250, Colombia, MD 21044, USA (☎410-997-2200; www.aipt.org). Provides cultural and career exchanges for students, professionals, and companies. Its longest running program is the International Association for the Exchange of Students for Technical Experience (IAESTE) which provides internships for students. Also helps in international job searches, and runs a service that secures work permits for US\$250-400.

CDS International, 871 United Nations Plaza, New York, NY 10017-1814, USA (☎212-497-3500; www.cdsintl.org). Established non-profit providing international career development support, including a work abroad program in Switzerland for US citizens 30 and under. The program provides assistance in finding an employer and support in work authorization for a US\$400 fee. Also offers internships, such as the Culinary Arts and Hospitality Management Internship Program. (www.cdsintl.org/capsintro.html. Participation fee US\$700. Open to US citizens ages 21-30.) CDS also provides general resources for international work experience.

StepStone, StepStone ASA, 2 Bell Ct., Leapale Ln., Guildford, Surrey GU1 4LY, England (☎44 14 83 73 94 50; www.stepstone.com). An online database covering international employment openings for most of Europe, including Austria and Switzerland. Several search options and a constantly changing list of openings.

TEACHING ENGLISH

While English teachers are almost always in demand in Austria and Switzerland, they are rarely well paid, except in some elite private American schools. In most cases, you must have at least a bachelor's degree to be a full-fledged teacher, although undergraduates can get summer positions teaching or tutoring.

Many schools require teachers to have a **Teaching English as a Foreign Language (TEFL)** certificate. Not having this certification does not necessarily exclude you from finding a teaching job, but having it may help you find a higher-paying one. Native English speakers working in private schools are most often hired for English-immersion classrooms where no German, French, or Italian is spoken.

Placement agencies or university fellowship programs are the best resources for finding teaching jobs in Austria and Switzerland. The alternative is to make contact directly with schools or just to try your luck once you get there. If you try the latter, the best time to look is several weeks before the start of the school year. The following organizations place teachers in Austria and Switzerland.

International Schools Services (ISS), 15 Roszel Rd., Box 5910, Princeton, NJ 08543-5910, USA (☎609-452-0990; www.iss.edu). Hires teachers for more than 200 overseas schools, including schools in Switzerland. Candidates should have experience teaching or with international affairs; 2-year commitment expected.

Office of Overseas Schools, US Department of State, Rm. H328, SA-1, Washington, D.C. 20522, USA (☎202-261-8200; www.state.gov/m/a/os/c6776.htm). Maintains a list of schools and agencies that arrange placement for Americans to teach abroad.

SHORT-TERM WORK ■ 63

AU PAIR WORK

Au pairs are typically women ages 18-27 who work as live-in nannies, caring for children and doing light housework in exchange for room, board, and a small spending allowance or stipend. Most former au pairs speak favorably of their experience. One perk of the job is that it allows you to get to know the country without the high expenses of traveling. Drawbacks, however, often include long hours of being on duty and somewhat mediocre pay. In Austria and Switzerland, wages range €75-120 per week. Much of the au pair experience depends on the family you're placed with. The agencies below are a good starting point for looking for employment as an au pair.

Au Pair Austria, Mariahilferstraße, Vienna A-1060, Austria (☎/fax 43 19 20 38 42 or 43 15 95 57 45; www.aupairaustria.com).

Au Pair in Europe, P.O. Box 68056, Blakely Postal Outlet, Hamilton, Ontario L8M 3M7, Canada (☎905-545-6305; www.princeent.com).

AupairConnect, Max Global, Inc., 8370 W. Cheyenne Avenue #76, Las Vegas, NV 89129, USA (www.aupairconnect.com).

Childcare International, Ltd., Trafalgar House, Grenville Pl., London NW7 3SA, England (☎44 020 8906-3116; www.childint.co.uk).

SHORT-TERM WORK

Traveling for long periods of time can get expensive. Therefore, many travelers try their hand at odd jobs for a few weeks at a time to help finance another month or two of touring around.

The most prevalent short-term jobs can be found in ski instruction, farm work, the hospitality industry, and camp counseling. Short-term work is most easily found through established programs, although it can be managed independently as

ALTERNATIVES TO TOURISM

LET'S GO

well. In Austria and Switzerland, short-term work is common in the tourism and hospitality industries. If you have ski instructor certification (usually PSIA or CSIA), you can probably find work as an instructor at a ski resort, especially if you are proficient in German or French.

Another popular option is to work several hours a day at a hostel in exchange for free or discounted room and/or board. Most often, these short-term jobs are found by word of mouth, or simply by talking to the owner of a hostel or restaurant. Due to the high turnover in the tourism industry, many places are eager for help, even if it is only temporary. *Let's Go* tries to list temporary jobs like these whenever possible: look in the **Practical Information** sections of larger cities or check out the list below for the available short-term jobs in popular destinations.

Hotel Career, Benzenbergstr. 39-47, D-40219 Düsseldorf, Germany (☎49 211 938 89 70; www.hotel-career.com). A great source for finding jobs in the hotel and accommodations industry worldwide, including many listings in Austria and especially Switzerland. Its great search engine can lead you to a wide array of seasonal, year-long, and longer career-building positions. Positions suitable for a broad variety of people, from those with no experience to those with several years of experience.

International Cooperative Education, 15 Spiros Way, Menlo Park, CA, 94025, USA (☎650-323-4944; www.icemenlo.com). Finds summer jobs for students in Switzerland. Costs include a US$200 application fee and a US$600 fee for placement.

Village Camps, Personnel Office, Dept. 1000, CH-1260 Nyon, Switzerland (☎229 90 94 05; www.villagecamps.com/personnel/about.htm). These summer camps in Leysin, Switzerland and Zell am See, Austria, for 7- to 18-year-olds offer a number of jobs to English-speaking foreign workers. Many positions for citizens of Australia, Canada, the EU, NZ, Switzerland, and the US.

FOR FURTHER READING ON ALTERNATIVES TO TOURISM

Alternatives to the Peace Corps: A Directory of Third World and U.S. Volunteer Opportunities, by Joan Powell. Food First Books, 2000 (US$10).

How to Get a Job in Europe, by Sanborn and Matherly. Surrey Books, 1999 (US$22).

How to Live Your Dream of Volunteering Overseas, by Collins, DeZerega, and Heckscher. Penguin Books, 2002 (US$17).

International Directory of Volunteer Work, by Whetter and Pybus. Peterson's Guides and Vacation Work, 2000 (US$16).

International Jobs, by Kocher and Segal. Perseus Books, 1999 (US$18).

Overseas Summer Jobs 2002, by Collier and Woodworth. Peterson's Guides and Vacation Work, 2002 (US$18).

Work Abroad: The Complete Guide to Finding a Job Overseas, by Hubbs, Griffith, and Nolting. Transitions Abroad Publishing, 2000 (US$16).

Work Your Way Around the World, by Susan Griffith. Worldview Publishing Services, 2001 (US$18).

Invest Yourself: The Catalogue of Volunteer Opportunities, published by the Commission of Voluntary Service and Action (☎718-638-8487).

AUSTRIA

The shape and size of Austria (*Österreich*) have changed so many times in its history that Oskar Bender once said, "To be Austrian is not a geographical concept but a spiritual idea." At the peak of Hapsburg megalomania, the Austrian Empire was one of the largest in history, encompassing much of Europe, from Poland and Hungary in the east to the Netherlands in the west. Today it is approximately the size of Maine. Although the mighty empire crumbled during World War I, Austria remains a complex, multi-ethnic country with a unique political and cultural history. The wide range of identities within the empire continues today in the diversity of the nine provinces, (*Bundesländer*), of present-day Austria. Clockwise from the northeast, Austria's provinces are Vienna (*Wien*), Burgenland, Styria (*Steiermark*), Carinthia (*Kärnten*), Tyrol (*Tirol*), Vorarlberg, Salzburg, Upper Austria (*Oberösterreich*), and Lower Austria (*Niederösterreich*). At one time each province was an independent region but later became part of the Hapsburg lands by marriage, treaty, or trade.

Today, each province retains a deep-rooted character and unique dialect. The mention of Austria evokes images of onion-domed churches set against snow-capped alpine peaks, castles rising from lush meadows of golden flowers, and 10th-century monasteries towering over the majestic Danube. The mountains attract tourists year-round: alpine sports dominate the winter scene, while visitors flock to the mountain lakes in the warmer months.

LAND

Austria is a landlocked nation that shares its borders with eight countries. It has long been a crucial cog in the machine of European commerce, thanks to the navigable Danube, the only major European river that flows east. The blue-green river has also been central to Austrian aristocracy: both ruling families of early Austria, the Babenbergs and the Hapsburgs, set up residences on its shores. Today, river cruises showcase these ruined castles as well as the vineyards whose fruit sweetened the Middle Ages. The Danube's trade capabilities were enhanced in 1992 with the completion of a canal connecting the Danube to the Rhine and Main rivers, allowing the movement of barges from the North Sea to the Black Sea.

Forests and meadows cover two-thirds of Austria's total land area, and much of the country is studded with mountains. The Alps span the southern and western regions of the country, while the flatter north and east are home to most of the population. The highest point—the *Großglockner*—looms at 3798m (12,457 ft.) in the central Alps, drawing sightseers and adventure seekers. The mining of salt from vast underground deposits has also proved a valuable industry. To the Celts in 500 BC as well to as many contemporary towns today, this "white gold" has been an invaluable resource.

FLORA AND FAUNA

Since much of Austria remains densely forested, you won't have to go far off the beaten path to discover the rich woodland life. The flowers aren't going anywhere, but wildlife tends to be shy, so keep voices low when you walk or hike. Though you're unlikely to see **ibex** or **marmots** unless you're hiking at high elevations, **red deer, roe deer, hare, foxes, badgers, marten,** and **pheasants** are common to the country and to Central Europe in general. A small bear population lives in the southern mountainous and deeply wooded regions. Lake Neusiedl, Austria's only steppe lake, hosts hundreds of bird species on reed-fringed waters. Austria's national parks, which comprise 3% of the land, are good places to spot protected wildlife.

Oak, beech, and birch trees predominate in Austria's vast forests, with fir trees at higher elevations and stone pines in the mountain regions. Colorful and delicate alpine flora, including **Edelweiss, primrose, buttercups,** and **blue gentian** (on the back of the Austrian five-cent euro piece), blanket meadows and mountains alike.

HISTORY

IN THE BEGINNING

The first prehistoric tourists descended on Austria in the form of nomadic hunter-gatherers in about 80,000 BC, initiating the region as a popular destination. As the nomads settled and began mining salt, farming, and domesticating livestock, 6km-thick glaciers crawled north, carving out the Alpine valleys of postcard fame today and making room for greater habitation of Austrian lands. The 25,000-year-old carved-stone fertility goddess Venus of Willendorf (so valuable that the Natural History Museum in Vienna displays only a copy) reflects the artistry of this early civilization. By 6000 BC, even the remotest areas of Austria were part of a vigorous commercial network that linked mining centers and agricultural communities, as the recent discovery of the 5300-year-old hunter-trader Ötzi proved.

As economic opportunities moved beyond salt, aggressive peoples fought for a share of wealth. In 500 BC, the **Celts** took control of the salt mines and established the kingdom of **Noricum,** which developed a relatively affluent economy based on a thriving salt and iron trade. In turn, the **Romans** conquered their Austrian neighbors to secure the Danube frontier against marauding Germanic tribes in 15 BC. One of the first Roman military posts was Vindobona, present-day Vienna.

Germanic raids finally forced the Romans to retreat from Noricum in the 5th century. Over the next three centuries, various peoples, including the Huns, Ostrogoths, and Lombards, roamed through the Austrian territories, but none established a lasting settlement. Eventually, three groups divided the region, with **Slavs** in the southwest, **Bavarians** in the north, and **Alemanni** in the south. Bavarian nobles converted peasants to Christianity in an attempt to establish law and order and create a power base. The Archbishopric of Salzburg, created through their efforts, has remained Austria's ecclesiastical center.

HOLY ROMANS AND HAPSBURGS (800-1740)

Charlemagne was the first to make Austria the barrier and meeting point between Eastern and Western Europe by conquering Bavaria in 787. After his death, the German King Otto regained control of the Holy Roman Empire, naming Margrave Liutpoldus (a.k.a. **Leopold of Babenberg**) Duke of the Empire's eastern territories in 976. Leopold, a Bavarian lord, was the first ruler Austria called its own. During his reign, Austria gained its name: *Ostarrichi* (Old High German for *Österreich*), which meant "Eastern Realm" of the Empire.

The **Babenbergs,** who served as the Dukes of the Eastern Realm for the next 270 years, claimed Vienna as their home, extending their protectorate through strategic marriages. The Babenburgs made a tidy profit off of international bargains. For instance, when Duke Leopold V captured **Richard the Lionheart** on his way home from the Crusades, he chose not to give Richard over to the Holy Roman Emperor, who had put a price on the head of the English king, and instead returned Richard to England for cold, hard cash.

To the detriment of the dynasty, the last Babenberg died childless, leaving the country fragmented for 19 years. Bohemian King Ottokar II, the new Holy Roman Emperor, and the Swiss nobleman **Rudolf of Hapsburg** emerged as the major contenders for control of the Austrian lands. Rudolf had only a small plot of land in Switzerland before he beat out Ottokar in the Battle of Marchfeld in 1278, thereby claiming all of Austria and laying the foundation for six centuries of Hapsburg rule. Like their Babenberg predecessors, the Hapsburgs made every effort to increase their property through treaties and marriages, with memorable success (though they lost their original Swiss holdings after a farmers' revolution). Gradually, the Hapsburgs accumulated the regions that make up modern Austria plus a few others. Friedrich expanded the direct claims of the Hapsburg family by strategically betrothing his son, **Maximilian I,** to the heiress of the powerful Burgundian kingdom, giving the Hapsburgs control of much of western Europe.

Maximilian was the living embodiment of the adaptation of Ovid's couplet: *Bella gerant alii, tu felix Austria nube* ("Let other nations go to war; you, lucky Austria, marry"). Maximilian's son **Philip** married into the Spanish royal house, endowing his son, **Charles V,** with a vast empire that encompassed Austria, the Netherlands, Spain, Burgundy, Spanish America, and Italian and Mediterranean possessions. It was during Charles's reign that the Hapsburg Empire reached its height of power. However, it appears that the power was too much for Charles, who gave the Austrian empire and crown to his brother **Ferdinand** (and the Spanish possessions to his son Philip) before retiring to the woods to become a monk in 1556. Thanks to another marriage planned earlier by Maximilian, Ferdinand managed (despite not knowing German, Czech, or Hungarian) to add Bohemia and Hungary to the Hapsburg possessions, The Imperial Crown was passed down through the Hapsburg line until the collapse of the empire in the 19th century.

PROTESTING CHANGE

The Hapsburg ship hit rough waters in the 16th and 17th centuries, when Martin Luther's Protestant Reformation swept through the Empire. By the time Ferdinand II assumed control of the Hapsburg empire in 1619, nearly nine-tenths of the population of Austria had been converted to Protestantism. Ferdinand II, inspired by his Jesuit education, made Austria the first battleground of the Catholic Counter-Reformation. Resistance by Protestant Bohemian nobles in Prague to Ferdinand's plans sparked the **Thirty Years' War** (1618-1648). Austrian imperial troops promptly (and forcibly) converted most of the peasants back to Catholicism and chased Protestants in the upper classes off to Protestant Germany. This victory was followed by a greater setback at the end of the war, the **Treaty of Westphalia,** in which the Hapsburgs forfeited vast tracts of territory. While Austria recuperated, the Ottoman Turks repeatedly besieged Vienna until French Prince Franz Eugene drove them out with a Christian relief army. In thanks for his assistance, Eugene was given **Schloß Belvedere** (p. 121). Eugene again came through for the Hapsburgs when he led their troops to victory over the French in the **War of Spanish Succession,** which ended with a treaty giving Belgium, Sardinia, and parts of Italy to the Hapsburgs.

CASTLES CRUMBLE (1740-1900)

What the Hapsburgs gained in land they sacrificed in stability. Lacking a dominant ethnic group and having had a series of foreign leaders, the empire began to crumble in the 18th century. When **Maria Theresia** ascended to the throne in 1740, her neighbor, King Friedrich the Great of Prussia, seized Silesia (now southwest Poland); she spent the rest of her life unsuccessfully maneuvering to reclaim it. In the **War of Austrian Succession** (1740-1748), Maria Theresia came to be known as

Landesmutter (mother of the people). She married her daughter **Marie Antoinette** to the French Prince Louis XVI, a marriage that ended under the guillotine during the French Revolution. The French revolutionaries who killed Maria Theresia's daughter soon declared war on her son, **Joseph II,** who by 1792 was ruling Austria. Under the military genius of young General **Napoleon Bonaparte,** the Republic of France wrested Belgium and most of Austria's remaining Italian territories from the Hapsburgs. His troops even invaded Vienna, where Napoleon took up residence in Maria Theresia's favorite palace, Schönbrunn (p. 120).

Napoleon's success led to the establishment of a consolidated Hapsburg empire. In 1804, **Franz II** renounced his claim to the now-defunct Holy Roman crown and proclaimed himself Franz I, Emperor of Austria. During the Congress of Vienna, which redrew the map of Europe after Napoleon's defeat, Austrian Chancellor **Clemens Wenzel Lothar von Metternich** masterfully re-unified Austrian power. For the rest of the century, Metternich's foreign policy was dictated by a desire to maintain monarchical stability throughout Europe. Metternich feared the crumbling of the Ottoman Empire to the south and the resulting creation of new independent Slavic states in the Balkans, rightly believing that the independence of these states would encourage the Slavic people who comprised half the population of the Hapsburg Empire to fight for their own independence. In order to maintain stability within Austria, Metternich introduced harshly repressive social policies.

Like much of Europe in the first half of the 19th century, however, Austria is remembered more during this period for technological progress. This progress led to the rise of a stereotypically uninspired middle class, satirized in the character Papa Biedermeier in the poems of Ludwig Eichrocht. The term **Biedermeier** came to label the bourgeois domestic culture that flourished in this time (p. 74).

As the Ottoman Empire disintegrated, domestic resistance to Austria's repressive social policies increased, precisely what Metternich had feared. In 1848, students and workers built barricades, took control of the imperial palace, and demanded a constitution and freedom of the press. The revolutionary forces were divided and the government was able to suppress the workers' revolution and a Hungarian rebellion. Epileptic emperor **Ferdinand I,** however, was pressured to abdicate in favor of his nephew, **Franz Josef I,** who ruled for 68 years.

Under **Otto von Bismarck,** Prussia dominated European politics and defeated Austria in 1866. The Austrian fall from power continued in 1867, when the Hungarian parliament voted to end the Austrian Empire and form the dual **Austro-Hungarian Empire,** over which Franz Josef was a figurehead. Still, non-German speakers were marginalized within the new empire until 1907, when the government ceded basic civil rights to all peoples in the Empire and accepted universal male suffrage. These concessions to the Slavic peoples of the Empire came too late. Burgeoning nationalist sentiments, especially among the Serbia-inspired South Slavs, led to severe divisions within the multinational Austro-Hungarian Empire.

THE RISE OF THE REPUBLIC

The now-free Slavic states of the Ottoman Empire—particularly Serbia—agitated the Slavic elements within the Austro-Hungarian Empire. When Franz Ferdinand, heir to the imperial throne, and his wife, Sophie, were assassinated by a young Serbian nationalist in Sarajevo in 1914, Franz Josef finally had an excuse to attack the Serbs. Austria's declaration of war set the dominos falling, and Europe tumbled into **World War I.** Franz Josef died in 1916, leaving the throne to his reluctant grandnephew Charles I. Despite his valiant efforts and those of the army, declarations of independence by the Empire's non-German peoples and the desperate maneuvering of Viennese intellectuals ensured the demise of the monarchy. On November 11, 1918, Charles finally got the peace he had striven for, but only after liberals declared the first **Republic of Austria,** ending the 640-year-old Hapsburg dynasty.

Between 1918 and 1938, Austria had its first bitter taste of parliamentary democracy. After the Treaty of Versailles that ended the first World War forbade a unified *Deutsch-Österreich,* the **First Republic** suffered massive inflation and unemployment. By the mid-1920s the Austrian government had stabilized the currency and established economic relations with neighboring states, but violent internal strife between political parties weakened the Republic's already shaky democratic foundation. In 1933, the weak coalition government gave way to **Engelbert Dollfuss's** declaration of martial law. In order to protect Austria from Hitler, Dollfuss entered an alliance with fascist Italy. Two years later, just as Mussolini and Hitler made peace, Austrian Nazis assassinated Dollfuss. His successor, **Kurt Schuschnigg,** was also unable to maintain Austrian independence in the face of Nazi pressure.

WORLD WAR II AND THE SECOND REPUBLIC

The First Republic ended with the Nazi annexation of Austria. On March 9, 1938, hoping to stave off a Nazi invasion, Schuschnigg called a referendum against unity with Germany, but Hitler demanded Schuschnigg's resignation. On March 12, the new Nazi chancellor of Austria invited German troops into the country, where they met with no resistance. Many Austrians believed the *Anschluß* (union with Germany) would improve their future. When the Nazis marched into Vienna on March 14, thousands cheered them on. Austria lost both its name (it became the *Ostmark,* merely the "alpine district") and its self-respect. With the exception of individual resistance fighters, cooperation with the Nazis and anti-Semitism (long an Austrian tradition) became the rule, and a failing Austrian economy began to prosper. While **WWII** raged, Austrian and German Nazis directed the construction of Mauthausen, Austria's main concentration camp, and its 49 sub-camps. An estimated 150,000 Jews, along with leading intellectuals, dissidents, handicapped persons, Gypsies, and homosexuals, were systematically tortured and murdered. One-third of the Jewish population was purged, and most others fled the country.

After Soviet troops brutally "liberated" Vienna in 1945, Allied troops divided Austria into four zones of occupation to re-establish an Austrian government. By April 1945, a provisional government was established with 75-year-old **Karl Renner** as president. In November, the National Assembly declared Austria's independence from Germany. Despite Russian plundering and severe famines in the late 1940s, the Marshall Plan helped to jump-start the Austrian economy, laying the foundation for Austria's present prosperity. In 1955, after **Joseph Stalin** died, Austria signed the State Treaty, under which the four powers granted Austria complete sovereignty on the condition that it remain neutral.

The State Treaty, along with the Federal Constitution of the First Republic, which was restored in 1945, formed the basis of the **Second Republic.** These documents provide for a president (head of state) who is elected to a six-year term; a chancellor (head of government), usually the leader of the strongest party; a bicameral parliamentary legislature, and powerful provincial governments. Until recently the government has been dominated by two parties, the Social Democratic Party (SPÖ), and the People's Party (ÖVP). The two parties have built up one of the world's most successful industrial economies, with enviably low unemployment and inflation rates as well as a generous, progressive welfare state.

During the 1990s, Austria moved toward closer European integration. In 1994 **Thomas Klestil** was elected President on a platform of integration. In 1995 the country was accepted into the **European Union (EU),** and the Austrians accepted mem-

AUSTRIA

bership through a national referendum. Unlike some EU countries, Austria also joined the **Economic and Monetary Union (EMU),** and replaced its currency, the Austrian Schilling, with the euro in 2002.

TODAY

HAIDER AND AUSTRIA'S SWING TO THE RIGHT

Austria has recently been plastered over front pages internationally, thanks to the gains made by the far-right **Freedom Party** in 1999's elections. This party is infamous for its leader **Jörg Haider,** who assumed the reins of the then-powerless party in 1986. Haider is known for his anti-immigrant stance and for making remarks that were sympathetic to the Nazis. He demanded a complete ban on immigration, playing off Austrian fears of the influx of immigrants from Eastern Europe. In the November 1999 elections, Haider's party claimed 27% of the vote, second among all parties, effectively breaking up the traditional two-party lock that the Social Democratic Party and People's Party had held on the country's politics since WWII. The Social Democratic Party, which has ruled the country for decades, came in first with 33% of the vote but refused to form a coalition with Haider's party; consequently, Haider's Freedom Party formed a coalition government with the conservative People's Party in February 2000. **Wolfgang Schlüssel** of the People's Party became the chancellor of the new government, while six of the government's 12 cabinet posts were held by Freedom Party members. In Vienna, 100,000 protestors turned out on the day that the Freedom Party government was sworn in. At the same time, the 14 other nations of the **European Union** simultaneously levied unprecedented political sanctions against Austria that essentially cut off official political contact; the United States recalled its ambassador for "consultation," while the Belgian Foreign Minister called traveling to Austria "immoral." Still, when the new government was entering office, Haider and Schlüssel signed the declaration "Responsibility for Austria," which stated that the new government would work "for an Austria in which xenophobia, anti-Semitism, and racism have no place." Haider resigned from his post as president of the Freedom Party three weeks after the new government took power in February to dispel questions about his role in the government, though many have called this a purely political move.

As a result of these developments, other European nations dropped their sanctions against Austria in September 2000. Many critics have claimed that the sanctions were only pushed through in the first place because the liberal Social Democratic parties that rule in a majority of the European nations wanted to protect themselves from challenges by right-wing parties in their own countries.

Haider is now beginning his second term as governor of the province of Carinthia. After Haider's departure and the resignation of its leader, vice chancellor Susanne Riess-Passer, the Freedom Party's popularity has waned, having lost 4 out of its 5 seats in the 2004 elections. After the death of Thomas Klestil in July 2004, **Heinz Fischer** has become Austria's president.

PEOPLE

DEMOGRAPHICS

Austrians are fiercely proud of their culture, history, and principles. Following the longevity pattern established by Emperor Franz Joseph, Austrians enjoy a life expectancy of 78 years. Social welfare is comprehensive, and unemployment hovers at around 4%. Ethnically, the Austrian people embody the idea of the "melting pot," for although 98% of its 8 million people call themselves German, nearly every Austrian has genealogical ties to at least one of the many other ethnic groups once within the Hapsburg empire. As befits the erstwhile stronghold of the Counter-Reformation, 78% of Austrians are Roman Catholic, 5% are Protestant, and 17% belong to Muslim, Jewish, Baptist, and other religious denominations.

LANGUAGE

Although German is the official language of Austria, common borders with the Czech Republic, Slovakia, Hungary, Italy, Slovenia, Liechtenstein, and Switzerland make multilingualism imperative for most Austrians. Even non-Austrian German speakers sometimes have difficulty understanding Austrians, as the German spoken in Austria differs by accent and vocabulary from other German-speaking countries. Tourists eager to try out their *Deutsch* don't need to be too worried about being understood, as nearly all Austrians understand High German, but it is helpful to know some general peculiarities of Austrian German. As a result of the Hapsburg Empire's international connections, many French, Italian, Czech, Hebrew, and Hungarian words have slipped into the language (e.g. *Babuschka* for old woman). Austrians don't greet each other with the standard *Guten Tag*, opting instead for *Servus* or *Grüss Gott*. One way to recognize familiar words in Austrian German is to remember that Austrians add a diminutive *"erl"* (instead of the High German *"chen"* or *"lein"*) to a lot of words: store clerks may ask if you want a *Sackerl* (a small bag), waiters might inquire if you would like a *Bisserl* (a little bit) more of this or that, and a young girl is called a *Mäderl*. Many vegetables have unique names in Austrian German: the German *Kartoffel* (potato) becomes *Erdapfel*, tomatoes are *Paradeiser*, corn is not *Mais* but *Kukuruz*, and green beans are *Fisoln*. Austrians mean "this year" when they say *heuer* and January when they say *Jänner*. If you get to know an Austrian well, chances are they'll say *Ferti!* or *Servus!* for goodbye.

CULTURE

FOOD AND DRINK

Just as the Austrians and their language are ethnically intermixed, many of the most famous Austrian dishes are foreign in origin: *Gulasch* (stewed meat and vegetables with paprika) is Hungarian; *Knödel* (dumplings) are Bohemian; and the archetypal Austrian dish, wiener schnitzel, probably originated in Milan. Immigrants continue to influence Austrian cooking; Turkish dishes like *Dönerkebab* are on their way to becoming an integral part of Austrian cuisine. In addition, each region of Austria contributes its own particular traditional dishes, such as Carinthian *Kasnudeln* (large cheese- or meat-filled pasta squares) or Salzburger *Nockerl* (a mountain of sweetened, baked egg whites).

Loaded with fat, salt, and cholesterol, traditional Austrian cuisine is a cardiologist's nightmare but a delight to everyone else. **Staple foods** are simple and hearty, centering around *Schweinefleisch* (pork), *Kalbsfleisch* (veal), *Wurst* (sausage), *Eier* (eggs), *Käse* (cheese), *Brot* (bread), and *Kartoffeln* or *Erdapfeln* (potatoes). Austria's most renowned dish, wiener schnitzel, is a meat cutlet (usually veal or pork) fried in butter with bread crumbs and often served with french fries. Although schnitzel is Austria's most famous meat dish, its most scrumptious variety is *Tafelspitz*, a delicious boiled beef. Soups are also an Austrian speciality. Try *Gulaschsuppe* (goulash soup) and *Frittatensuppe* (pancake strips in broth).

Most of Austria's culinary inventions appear on the **dessert** cart. Tortes commonly contain *Erdbeeren* (strawberries) and *Himbeeren* (raspberries). Don't miss *Marillen Palatschinken*, a crêpe with apricot jam, or *Kaiserschmarrn*, the Kaiser's favorite (pancake bits with a plum compote). Austrians adore the sweet dessert *Knödeln*, especially *Marillenknödel* (sweet dumplings with a whole apricot in the middle), though the typical street-stand dessert is the *Krapfn*, a holeless doughnut usually filled with jam. The pinnacles of Austrian baking, however, are the twin delights of *Sacher Torte* (a rich chocolate cake layered with marmalade) and *Linzer Torte* (a light yellow cake with currant jam).

Recently, **vegetarianism** has gained popularity in Vienna, and even meaty dishes are showing the influence of a lighter, vegetable-reliant style. Vegetarians should look for *Spätzle* (a homemade noodle often served with melted cheese), *Steinpilze* (enormous mushrooms native to the area), *Eierschwammerl* (tiny yellow mushrooms), or anything with the word *Vegi* in it. Supermarket connoisseurs will have a blast with Austrian staples: yogurt (rich, almost dessert-like), the cult favorite Nutella (a chocolate-hazelnut spread), *Almdudler* (a lemonade-like soft drink), *Semmeln* (very cheap, fresh rolls), the original *Müsli* (granola on steroids), and all kinds of chocolate, including Milka and Ritter Sport.

In the afternoon, Austrians flock to *Café-Konditoreien* (café-confectioners) to nurse the national sweet tooth with *Kaffee und Kuchen* (coffee and cake). While drinking a *Mélange*, the classic Viennese coffee with frothy cream and a hint of cinnamon, nibble on a heavenly *Mohr im Hemd*, a chocolate sponge cake topped with hot whipped chocolate.

To wash it all down, try any variety of Austrian alcoholic beverage. The most famous Austrian **wine** is probably *Gumpoldskirchen* from Lower Austria, the largest wine-producing province. *Klosterneuburger*, named for the district near Vienna where it's produced, is dry and reasonably priced. Austrian **beers** are outstanding. *Ottakringer* and *Gold Fassl* flow from Vienna's taps, *Stiegl Bier* and *Augustiner Bräu* from Salzburg's, *Zipfer Bier* from Upper Austria's, and *Gösser Bier* from Styria's. Austria imports a great deal of Budweiser beer, but theirs is *Budvar*—the original Bohemian variety, not the chintzy American imitation. If you're looking for something to keep you up rather than put you to sleep, try a Red Bull in its country of origin.

CUSTOMS AND ETIQUETTE

In general, following good manners from your own country will take you far in German-speaking ones. The rules aren't too different in Austria, although there are a few ways you can disguise your status as a tourist and impress the locals. For instance, most Germans and Austrians hold their fork in their left hand and knife in their right, but don't switch them after cutting. While forking left-handed is hard, it can impress the locals (unless your schnitzel lands in your lap). Elbows on the table is fine; in fact, they'll look at you a little funny if you have your hands under the table or in your lap. Seat yourself in cafés and most restaurants. Meals in Europe are paced a bit slower, so take in the atmosphere and take your time.

THE ARTS

Ever since the wealth of the Hapsburg Empire made extensive patronage possible, Austria has maintained an impressively rich artistic tradition. Living in a country of Alpine splendor, Austrians have long sought to create beauty, challenge thought, and recreate life through personal expression. Classical music has evolved with every new wave of fresh talent in Vienna over the past three centuries. Austria's span of architectural advancements, from Romanesque ruins to Hapsburg decadence to the postmodern Haas House, is a continual reminder of the local innovation that has long characterized the region.

HISTORY

Landlocked in the middle of Europe and rolling with cash, the Hapsburgs married into power and bought into art. In keeping with the cosmopolitan nature of their empire, the family pursued a cultural policy that favored foreign artists over their native sons and daughters. Building on the popularity of Baroque palaces and churches in the 17th and 18th centuries, the Empire's artists began to develop a distinct architectural style that still dominates the old centers of former Hapsburg towns across Central and Eastern Europe. Around the turn of the 20th century, Austrian artists finally got fed up with traditionalism and foreign decadence and decided to stir up the coals a bit.

ARCHITECTURE

GOLDEN ARCHES. Austria's past as an outpost of the Roman empire is visible in the ruins of **Carnuntum** and **Vindobona** (Vienna). The influence of such classical remains can be seen in the Romanesque art and architecture of the early Middle Ages throughout Austria: for example, in the *Riesentor* of Vienna's **Stephansdom** (p. 109) and the cycle of frescoes in **Nonnberg Abbey** near Salzburg (p. 240). Ordinarily this influence takes the form of semi-circular arches, columns, and delicate metalwork, but the builders of the 8th-century **Martinskirche** of Linz actually "borrowed" Roman tombstones to fill in the walls (p. 289). The elaborate enamel **Verduner Altar,** by the master Nicholas of Verdun, at Stift Klosterneuburg (p. 134), is evidence of the richness of art under the Babenburgs. If it isn't rich enough for your blood, check out the 10th-century **Imperial Crown** of the Holy Roman Emperor, encrusted with cabochons and gold filigree, its shape reminiscent of Roman arches.

GOTHIC TRANSCENDENCE. The invention of flying buttresses, pointed arches, and groin vaults that came with the French Gothic style all meant that walls could be thinner, vaults could be higher, and windows could flood the whole space with light. The 14th-century additions to the **Stephansdom** in Vienna also show the delicate tracery and stained glass work typical of the period. Sculpture reached new heights with the intricate carvings of **Anton Pilgram** (p. 109) and the altarpieces of **Albrecht Altdorfer** (p. 291). Don't miss Austria's castles: these magnificent fortress-palaces, exemplified by **Festung Hohensalzburg** (p. 237), combined the medieval desire for imposing beauty with the practical goal of imposing power.

BAROQUE EXTRAVAGANCE. Austria's preeminent Baroque architects were Johann Bernhard Fischer von Erlach, Lukas von Hildebrandt, and Johann Prandtauer. **Von Erlach,** born in Graz to a sculptor father, drew up the plans for Vienna's Schönbrunn and Hofburg palaces (p. 120 and p. 118). His best works, however, were ecclesiastical, including the ornate **Karlskirche** in Vienna. **Von Hildebrandt** shaped Austria's more secular side. His penchant for theatricality shows up in the palace's succession of pavilions and grand views of Vienna. Stone sphinxes dotting his ornamental gardens allude to Eugene's victory over the Ottomans. **Prandtauer** was a favorite of the Church. His yellow Benedictine abbey at **Melk** peers over the Danube. After beating the Turks, Prince Eugene of Savoy (p. 66) got Prandtauer to revamp the **Schloß Belvedere** (p. 121).

JUGENDSTIL. The early 20th century saw more streamlined ornamentations, and a new ethic of function over form gripped Vienna's artistic elite. Vienna's guru of architectural modernism, **Otto Wagner,** cured the city of its "artistic hangover." His

Kirche am Steinhof (p. 117) and Postsparkasse (p. 115) enclose fluid *Jugendstil* interiors within stark, delineated structures. Wagner frequently collaborated with his student **Josef Maria Olbrich**, notably on the Majolicahaus (p. 116) and the Karlspl. Stadtbahn (p. 116). Wagner's admirer **Josef Hoffmann** founded the **Wiener Werkstätte** in 1903, drawing on Ruskin's English arts and crafts movement and Vienna's new brand of streamlined simplicity. Its influence later resonated in the **Bauhaus** style of Weimar Germany. **Adolf Loos**, Hoffmann's principal antagonist, strongly opposed such attention to luxury. Loos once said, "Ornamentation is a crime," setting himself against the Baroque grandeur that Imperial Vienna supported. Few examples of his work reside in his native city, but his notorious **Goldman and Salatsch building** (1909-1911) in the Michaelerpl. went beyond aesthetics toward a more starkly functional architecture.

URBAN SOCIALISM. In the 1920s and early 1930s, the **Social Democratic** administration built thousands of apartments in large **municipal projects,** their style reflecting the newfound assertiveness of the workers' movement. The most outstanding project of the era is the **Karl-Marx-Hof** (p. 117). The huge structure, completed in 1930, extends over 1km and consists of 1600 apartments clustered around several courtyards. The Austrian Socialist party fought a pitched battle with rightist rioters in this apartment complex before the outbreak of World War II.

The structures created by American-trained architect **Hans Hollein** recall the sprawling abandon of his training ground while maintaining the Secessionists' (p. 74) attention to craftsmanship and elegant detail. His exemplary contribution to Viennese **postmodern** architecture is the **Haas House** (p. 109), completed in 1990. Controversy has surrounded the building ever since sketches were published in the mid-80s, mainly because it stands opposite Vienna's landmark, Stephansdom. Examples of modern interior design include the **Restaurant Salzamt** (I, Ruprechtspl. 1) and **Kleines Café** (p. 105), both by Hermann Czech.

FINE ARTS

BIEDERMEIER. Between the era of Napoleon and the foundation of the Republic, Austria developed a large, restless middle class. Since political expression and social critique were virtually impossible during this era, artistic expression was funneled into a narrow channel of naturalistic and applied art centered around the family circle and domestic ideals, dominated by genre, landscape, and portrait painting. The *Biedermeier* period (p. 67) is remembered today primarily as a furniture style, but it was also an artistic movement with limited crossover into literature, characterized by a predilection for symmetry, naturalism, and harmonious detail. *Biedermeier* architecture is exemplified by the well-ordered dignity of the **Dreimäderlhaus** at Schreyvogelg. 10 in Vienna. The best of the period's furniture is on view in the **Biedermeier Room** of the Österreichisches Museum für Angewandte Kunst (p. 126).

ART NOUVEAU AND THE VIENNESE SECESSION. In 1897, the "young" artists split from the "old," as proponents of *Jugendstil* modernism took issue with the Viennese Academy's rigid conservatism and traditional symbolism. The idea was to leave the prevailing artistic conventions behind and formulate a new way of seeing the world. **Gustav Klimt** (1862-1918) and his followers founded what is known as the **Secession** movement. They aimed to provide the nascent Viennese avant-garde with a forum in which to show their work and to make contact with foreign artists. In their revolt against the old-guard Künstlerhaus, Secessionists sought to create space and appreciation for new artistic styles, particularly their own trademark style, Art Nouveau. The effect of this freedom is apparent in Klimt's own later paintings (such as *The Kiss*), which integrate naturalistic portraits into abstractly patterned backgrounds.

EXPRESSIONISM. Oskar Kokoschka and **Egon Schiele** revolted against art in the early 20th century, taking as their themes frailty, neuroses, and sexual energy. Kokoschka is often considered the founder of Viennese **Expressionism.** A renowned portraitist, he was known to scratch the canvas with his fingernails in efforts to capture the "essence" of his subjects. Schiele painted with a feverish intensity of line and color. His paintings are controversial even today for their depictions of tortured figures seemingly destroyed by their own bodies or by debilitating sexuality. His figures are twisted, gnarled, and oddly erotic.

MUSIC

THE CLASSICAL ERA. Toward the end of the 18th century, Vienna was a musical colony. Composers hung out in salons, making fun of each other and listening to themselves play music they wrote. The popular style, now described as "Viennese Classicism," fed on itself: the more music was written, the more people wanted to write music. The first master composer of Viennese Classicism was **Josef Haydn** (1732-1809). Working for the princes of Esterhazy, Haydn created a variety of new musical forms that led to the shaping of the sonata and the symphony, structures that dominated music throughout the 19th century. Fifty-two piano sonatas, 24 piano and organ concertos, 104 symphonies, and 83 string quartets provide rich and abundant proof of his pioneering productivity. He wrote the imperial anthem, *Gott erhalte Franz den Kaiser*, in order to rouse patriotic feeling during the Napoleonic wars. After WWI, Germany adopted the melody as its national anthem.

The work of **Wolfgang Amadeus Mozart** (1756-1791) represents the pinnacle of Viennese Classicism. Born in Salzburg, Mozart was a child prodigy, playing violin and piano by age four, composing simple pieces by five, and performing at Europe's imperial courts by age six. In 1781 the *Wunderkind* left Salzburg for Vienna, where he produced his first mature concerti, his best-known Italian operas (including *Don Giovanni* and *La Nozze di Figaro*), and the beloved string showpiece, *Eine kleine Nachtmusik*. Throughout his life, Mozart wrote with unprecedented speed, creating 626 works of all kinds during his 35 years, always jotting down music without preliminary sketches or revisions. Unfortunately, what he produced didn't always sell. Mozart's overwhelming emotional power found full expression in his final work, the (unfinished) *Requiem*, which he continued composing until the last hours before his death, fulfilling his bitter aside to favorite student Franz Süssmayr: "You see, I *have* been writing this Requiem for myself." He was buried in an unmarked pauper's grave. Within a few decades of his death, however, Mozart was recognized once more as a master, who in Tchaikovsky's words was "the culmination of all beauty in music."

Only **Ludwig van Beethoven** (1770-1827) could compete with Mozart for the devotion of the Viennese. Born into a family of Flemish musicians in Bonn, he lived and died in Vienna. Beethoven's gifts were manifest in his piano sonatas, string quartets, overtures, and concertos, but shone most intensely in his nine symphonies, today at the core of the orchestral repertoire. His *Ninth Symphony* had an enormous cultural impact, in part because of his introduction of singers to the symphonic form—a chorus and four soloists sing the text to Friedrich Schiller's *Ode to Joy*. Beethoven's *Fidelio*, which premiered May 23, 1814, at the Kärntnertortheater in Vienna, is regarded as one of the greatest German operas. Due to increasing deafness, the composer could maintain contact with the world only through a series of conversational notebooks, which provide an extremely thorough, though one-sided, record of his conversations (including his famous emotional outpouring, the *Heiligenstadt Testament*, written in Vienna's 19th district). Music historians place Beethoven between Viennese Classicism and Romanticism.

THE ROMANTIC ERA AND LATE NINETEENTH CENTURY. The music of **Franz Schubert** (1797-1828) is the lifeblood of Romanticism, a movement characterized by swelling emotion, larger orchestras, interest in the natural world, and storytelling. Born in the Viennese suburb of Lichtenthal in 1797, Schubert began his career as a chorister in the imperial Hofkapelle and later made his living teaching music. Mainly self-taught, he composed the *Unfinished Symphony* and the *Symphony in C Major*, which are now considered masterpieces but were virtually unknown during his lifetime. His lyrical genius was more readily recognized in his *Lieder*, a musical setting of poems by Goethe, Schiller, and Heine. These great song cycles were made famous during musical soirées called *Schubertiaden*, which spawned a new trend of social gatherings in *Biedermeier* Vienna, featuring chamber music, readings, and alcohol. This burst of creativity was cut short by his early death from syphilis at the age of 32. Schubert's gift for pure melody lived on and was a catalyst for later musical innovations.

Like Beethoven, **Johannes Brahms** (1833-1897) straddled musical traditions. In his home near the Karlskirche in Vienna, Brahms composed his Hungarian Dances, piano concerti, and numerous symphonies, all of which were first performed by the Vienna Philharmonic. Despite his own Romantic compositions, Brahms is often regarded as a Classicist who used his status and position in the Viennese *Musikverein* to oppose Romanticism and the musical experiments of his arch-rival, **Richard Wagner.** His artistic credo, "If we cannot compose as beautifully as Mozart or Haydn, let us at least try to compose as purely," emphasized his devotion to the classical style and his disinterest in modern music.

Orchestral music had mass appeal as well. Beginning with **Johann Strauss the Elder** (1804-1849), the Strauss family kept Vienna dancing for much of the 19th century. Johann Sr. composed mostly waltzes and showy pieces, including the famous *Radetzkymarsch*, which is still played every New Year by the Vienna Philharmonic. Largely responsible for the "Viennese Waltz," **Johann Strauss the Younger** (1825-1899) shone in his youth as a brilliant violinist and savvy cultural entrepreneur. The waltz became popular during the Congress of Vienna, offering a fresh exhilaration that broke free from older, more stiffly formal dances. Richard Wagner, Strauss's most famous rival, noted admiringly on a visit to the city that Viennese waltzing was "more potent than alcohol." Sensing the trend, Strauss became its master, eventually writing the *Blue Danube* and *Tales from the Vienna Woods*, two of the most recognized waltzes of all time, thereby earning the title "King of the Waltz." In his spare time he managed to produce some popular operas as well, *Die Fledermaus* being his most celebrated.

Gustav Mahler's (1860-1911) music, as a direct precursor to the Second Viennese experiments of Arnold Schönberg, incorporates fragments and deliberately inconclusive musical segments. Like modern literature, these compositions read like nostalgic remnants of a once certain and orderly world. Mahler employed unusual instrumentation and startling harmonic juxtapositions. His Eighth Symphony, called *Symphony of a Thousand*, requires an orchestra and two full choruses. Mahler's music hides formalist experimentation beneath a rich emotional beauty. His works form an integral part of the fin de siècle Viennese avant-garde.

THE MODERN ERA. While Mahler destabilized the conventions of composition, **Arnold Schönberg** (1874-1951) broke away from traditional harmony altogether. Originally a devotee of Richard Wagner, Schönberg rejected compositional rules that require music to be set in a tonal key and, with his 12-tone system, pursued what is generally called atonality. Some of Schönberg's most famous works are *Pierre Lunaire* and the string piece *Verklärte Nacht*. **Anton von Webern** (1883-1945) studied under Schönberg, eventually adopting and expanding his 12-tone system in music that is incredibly sparse, a sharp contrast to the lush, opulent, often overwritten music of his contemporaries. Webern drifted into obscurity and depression as the Nazis took over. While fleeing the Nazis, he was accidentally shot by US troops in Salzburg. **Alban Berg** (1885-1935), another student of Schönberg's who used a modified version of the 12-tone system, completed few works because of his obsession with ideal expression. Like Schönberg and Webern, he suffered under the Nazis as a creator of "degenerate art" and died young, in 1935.

LITERATURE

EARLY EXAMPLES. A collection of poetry dating from around 1150 and preserved in the abbey of Vorau in Styria marks the earliest known Austrian literature in German. Apart from sacred poetry, the courtly style known as *Minnesang* developed in the 12th and 13th centuries and culminated in the lyrical works of minstrel **Walther von der Vogelweide.** On a more epic scale, the **Nibelungenlied,** which dates from around 1200, is one of the most impressive heroic epics in German (also the primary source for Richard Wagner's *Ring of the Nibelungen* opera cycle). **Emperor Maximilian I** (1459-1519), nicknamed "The Last Knight," provided special support for theater and the dramatic arts during his reign. Splendid operas and pageants frequently involved the whole imperial court and led to popular religious drama that has survived in the form of rural **Passionspiele** (passion plays).

THE CLASSICAL WRITERS. Born in Vienna in 1801, **Johann Nestroy** wrote biting comedies and satires lampooning social follies. Although his name is not readily recognized by Anglophones, Nestroy is one of the canonical figures of German drama, famous for such plays as *Der Talisman* and *Liebesgeschichten und Heiratssachen*, as well as the *Tannhäuser*, on which Wagner based his famous opera. Often called Austria's greatest novelist, **Adalbert Stifter** wrote around the same time period as Nestroy but concerned himself much more with classical *Bildungsroman* themes and descriptions of nature. Many of his short stories and novels, such as *Der Condor* (1840), *Die Mappe meines Urgroßvaters* (1841), and *Der Nachsommer* (1857), are classics in the canon of German literature.

A Classicist with a more lyrical style, **Franz Grillparzer** penned plays about the conflict between a life of thought and a life of action. Grillparzer worked as a clerk in the Austrian bureaucracy and wrote some of his most critically acclaimed plays, such as *Des Meeres und Der Liebe Wellen* (1831), in his spare time. Most of Grillparzer's fame came posthumously, when interest grew in his published work and the beautifully composed *Der arme Spielmann* was discovered.

FIN DE SIÈCLE. Around 1890, Austrian literature rapidly transformed in the heat of the "merry apocalypse" atmosphere that permeated society. The satires of **Karl Kraus** tried to awaken the collapsing empire's conscience, while **Sigmund Freud** analyzed its dreams. **Arthur Schnitzler** heated up the Empire's stage with bedroom scenes, while **Hugo von Hofmannsthal** staged its death by rethinking medieval and Baroque tragedies. At the Café Griensteidl, lyric poet, critic, and one-time director of the *Burgtheater* **Hermann Bahr** loosely presided over a pioneer group known as **Jung Wien** (Young Vienna), aimed at capturing the subtlest nuances of the Viennese atmosphere. Hofmannsthal walked a tightrope between Impressionism and verbal decadence, creating such exquisite pieces of drama as *Yesterday* (1891) and *Everyman* (1911), while at the same time collaborating with Richard Strauss to write librettos for, among other things, *Der Rosenkavalier*. Schnitzler, a playwright and colleague of Freud, was the first German to write stream-of-consciousness prose. He skewered Viennese decadence in dramas and essays, and shocked contemporaries by portraying the complexities of erotic relationships in many of his plays, including his famous *Merry-Go-Round* (1897).

Many of Austria's literary titans, such as **Marie von Ebner-Eschenbach** and **Franz Kafka,** lived within the Hapsburg protectorate of Bohemia. Ebner-Eschenbach is often called the greatest female Austrian writer, known for her vivid individual portraits and defense of women's rights. Kafka often traveled to Vienna to drink coffee at the Herrenhof Café and swap ideas with other writers. No one else could master the surrealism of Kafka's writing, however, most famously demonstrated in *Die Verwandlung (The Metamorphosis),* a bizarre, disorienting tale in which the narrator comes to terms with his unexpected transformation into a beetle.

The collapse of the Austro-Hungarian monarchy marked a major turning point in the intellectual and literary life of Austria. Novelists **Robert Musil** and **Joseph Roth** concerned themselves with the consequences of the empire's breakdown. Roth's novels, *Radetzkymarsch* and *Die Kapuzinergruft,* romanticize the former empire. Musil is most famous for his unfinished work in three volumes, *Der Mann Ohne Eigenschaften (The Man Without Qualities).*

THE 20TH CENTURY. **Georg Trakl's** Expressionist works epitomize the early 20th-century fascination with death and dissolution; "all roads empty into black putrefaction" is his most frequently quoted line. Other Prague-born greats such as **Franz Werfel** and **Rainer Maria Rilke** shaped Austrian literature between the wars. Werfel's works investigate the dark side of the human psyche. In addition to his essays and stories, Rilke is most famous for his lyric poetry cycles the *Duino Elegies* and *Sonnets to Orpheus.* After WWII, Rilke's poetry and Kafka's oppressive parables of a cold world became models for a new generation of writers. These artistic movements owe their fascination with the unconscious to the new science of psychoanalysis launched by **Sigmund Freud.** Freud is best known for his theories of sexual repression, particularly applicable to bourgeois society, and his theories of the unconscious, which recast the literary world forever.

Contemporary Austrian literature is still affected and informed by its dark, dramatic literary tradition, but there is plenty of modern innovation as well. **Ingeborg Bachman's** stories and novels left an important legacy for Austrian feminism. One of the stalwarts of modern Austrian writing, **Thomas Bernhard** wrote *Holzfäller* (Woodcutters) and *Wittgenstein's Nephew.* **Peter Handke** has written many experimental novels and co-wrote the screenplay for Wim Wenders' film *Wings of Desire.*

FILM

While most English speakers might not be able to name more than one Austrian actor (Arnold Schwarzenegger is easy), national filmmaking has endured a rocky tradition, alternatively thriving and waning. Emperor Franz Josef himself attended a screening in April 1896 of a short film created by the French Lumière brothers in Vienna. Inspired by Cecil B. DeMille in the U.S., the **Kolowrat** created the massive *Sodom und Gomorrha* in 1922. The addition of sound to movies preceded **W. Forst's** 1933 invention of the Viennese musical film in *Leise flehen meine Lieder. Anschluß* in 1938 brought about the end of independent domestic film production and the consolidation of filmmakers under the Wien-Film corporation. Wien-Film was confiscated by Allied forces in 1945 and the cinematic tradition was reborn in 1946. Austrian films moved in a variety of directions, from the "woods and mountain" genre of films like *Echo der Berge* to operettas and works addressing contemporary social problems. Beginning in 1954, the illustrious *Goldene Feder* (Golden Feather) has been bestowed upon the director of the year's "Best Film."

SPORTS AND RECREATION

Austrians take their recreation seriously; provisions for athletic funding are even written into the national constitution. This has been especially true in the intrepid spirit of mountain adventure that flows through the veins of many towns in Salzburger Land, Carinthia, and especially Tyrol, East Tyrol, and Vorarlberg. Over 450,000 Austrians belong to the *Österreichische Alpenverein* (ÖAV; Austrian Alpine Union), the national organization for mountain recreation and preservation. More than perhaps any other country in the world, Austria is known for its charming mountain villages, which are home to some of the world's oldest and most famous ski resorts. Its celebrated and extensive system of mountain huts has been emulated by mountain organizations in many other parts of the world. Beyond mountains, Austria is a nation of sports and fitness enthusiasts; biking, soccer, cycling, auto racing, curling, and tennis are popular pastimes.The *Österreichisher Fußball-Bund* (ÖFB; Austrian Soccer Federation) boasts 2317 clubs and 373,300 members. National fitness campaigns are not uncommon, and the Fitness March and Fitness Run are part of the Austrian National Day.

Austrian athletes have also met with success on the world stage. **Thomas Muster** was the top-ranked tennis player in the world in 1996. **Jochen Rindt** was crowned Formula One champion in 1970. Austrians also take extensive *Wanderungen* (hikes): they enjoy their country's natural beauty just as much as tourists do.

SKIING

The fact that two Winter Olympics (Innsbruck 1964 and 1972) have been held in Austria is no accident: its skiing is easily among the best in the world. Destinations like the Arlberg region, Innsbruck, the Zillertal, and the Ötztal have long attracted skiers from around the globe. **Kitzbühel** is home to the world's most famous and notoriously difficult ski race, the **Hahnenkamm**. Skiing is possible in summer on eight glaciers, including those near **Hintertux, Obergurgl, Zell am See,** and **Innsbruck.**

EARLY HISTORY. Austria has a long and storied skiing history. **Matthias Zdarsky** wrote the world's first instructional book on skiing in 1897 and organized the world's first slalom race in Lilienfeld in 1905. St. Anton is often credited as the "birthplace of modern skiing," since it is the site of one of the world's first ski clubs in 1901. **Hannes Schneider** was a young ski instructor with St. Anton's Hotel Post when he developed the "Arlberg Technique" of alpine skiing, which is still the skiing technique taught in ski schools today. He was also instrumental in pioneering North American skiing through his work with Mt. Cranmore in New Hampshire, and teamed up with German Arnold Fanck to write 1925's *Wunder des Schneeschuhs* (The Wonders of Skiing), which is still the best-selling ski book of all time. In 1930, **Rudolph Lettner** made a major contribution to ski technology with the invention of the metal edge for better grip and carving. Since then, the Austrians have held a reputation as the best ski engineers in the world, and much of the best ski equipment in the world, from skis to ski lifts, is still crafted in Austria.

PIONEERS ABROAD. Students of Schneider's went on to advance the sport of skiing both in Europe and North America. Their efforts produced the first ski school resort in America. In addition to teaching skiing, Austrians awed Americans with their ability and fearlessness on the slopes. More than almost anyone else, **Toni Matt** will forever be a ski legend in America. He came to New Hampshire in the 1930s to teach for the Hannes Schneider ski school at Mt. Cranmore and in 1939 decided to compete in the well-known American Inferno race on Mt. Washington. Virtually unknown as a racer, Matt amazed everyone by completing the summit-to-base run (over 4000 vertical feet) in only 6 minutes 30 seconds, cutting the previous course record in half. The feat included a legendary descent down the near-vertical slopes of Tuckerman Ravine. Matt skied the head wall without making a single turn, achieving an estimated velocity of nearly 90mph.

AUSTRIA'S NATIONAL PASTIME. Austrian skiers have excelled on the slopes ever since the first races were organized (also by Austrians). Mostly Austrians populate Vienna's **Straße der Sieger** (Street of Winners), where the world's most legendary skiers are honored with bronze handprints. Much like soccer in Great Britain and baseball and basketball in America, skiing in Austria has long held the country's fascination. Generations of Austrians have grown up practicing their turns, with dreams of one day being a superstar like **Toni Sailer** ("The Blitz from Kitz"). In 1956 he became the first of only two Olympic skiers in history to win gold medals in each of the three major alpine skiing categories. Most impressive were his margins of victory, the narrowest of which was a full 3½ seconds. Among many other Austrian Olympic champions, few stand out so much as **Franz Klammer** ("Kaiser Franz," "The Klammer Express"). Winner of an Olympic gold in Innsbruck in front of 60,000 adoring countrymen, he was also a five-time World Cup champion in the 1970s and 80s and World Champion in St. Moritz in 1974. In the last decade, **Hermann Maier** ("The Herminator") has become an international ski icon, winning two World Championships and nine World Cup titles, as well as two gold medals at the 1998 Olympics in Nagano, Japan. He also survived one of the most spectacularly memorable crashes in downhill racing. Even more recently, **Stephan Eberharter** has emerged as Austria's big skiing star, with gold medals at the 2002 Olympics and the 2003 World Championships.

Austrian women have fared just as well on the international stage as the men. **Annemarie Moser-Pröll** won gold in the downhill at Lake Placid in 1980, and has 61 World Cup wins to her credit, more than any other woman in history. A close rival for "best female skier ever" is **Petra Kronberger,** who is the only skier (male or female) ever to win World Cup races in five different categories in a single season. Today, no Austrian woman's star burns quite as brightly as that of **Alexandra Meissnitzer,** who won in two categories at the 1999 World Championships, and took home two medals from the 1998 Olympics. She narrowly missed medals in Salt Lake City in 2002, but rebounded by winning a giant slalom at the 2004 World Cup.

SNOWBOARDING. Although Austrians have dominated the skiing world for almost a century, they have begun to change with the times. As snowboarding has increased in popularity in America, Austrians have also taken to it as a new form of winter recreation. Although the sport is still on the rise, remarkable young talent has already surfaced in Austria. Nicknamed "The Dominator," **Martin Freinademetz** has been at or near the top of the snowboarding slalom circuit for over a decade, with two World Championships and two World Cup titles to his credit. On the freestyle side of the sport, **Stefan Gimpl** is one of the best riders in the world, consistently defeating North American and European opponents in big air events.

MOUNTAINEERING

The longstanding Austrian passion for the outdoors is understandable given the country's topography. The Austrians are enthusiastically proud of their *Dreitausender* (3000m. peaks, something like Colorado's "fourteeners"). For Austrians, love of the mountains is inherently an active pursuit, especially in the high Alpine ranges in the south and west. The **Hohe Tauern National Park** straddles the border of the provinces of Carinthia, Salzburger Land, East Tyrol, and Tyrol, and encloses rugged chains such as the Glocknergruppe and the Goldberggruppe. Extreme mountaineering challenges are present on peaks like the **Großglockner** (Austria's highest mountain), whose northeast face presents a number of long and daunting icy climbs. Other ranges to the west in Tyrol, including the Stubaier Alpen, Zillertaler Alpen, and Ötztaler Alpen, include high peaks with rocky pillars, serrated ridges, snow-covered peaks, and big-mountain challenges to keep even world-class mountaineers busy.

Despite the large array of mountains at home, Austrians have long been known for pioneering climbing worldwide. In nearby Switzerland, the imposing *Eiger Nordwand* (North Face of the Eiger) was one of the world's great mountaineering challenges until it was climbed by Austrians **Anderl Heckmair, Ludwig Vörg, Heinrich Harrer,** and **Fritz Kasparek** in under four days in 1938. Today, the world's most celebrated mountaineer is without a doubt **Reinhold Messner,** born in South Tyrol (technically in Italy but culturally still very Austrian). After completing a number of the most difficult climbs in the Alps by his early twenties, Messner was invited on a 1970 expedition to the Rupal Face of Pakistan's Nanga Parbat (8125m). The route has still not been repeated. He later became the first person to climb all fourteen of the world's 8000m peaks, and the second person to climb the highest peak on each continent. In 1980, without the aid of supplemental oxygen, he successfully climbed Mt. Everest alone on an extremely difficult, previously unclimbed route. Messner described the high-altitude experience as feeling as if "I am nothing more than a single narrow gasping lung, floating over the mists and summits."

Perhaps Messner's biggest achievement, however, is his role, along with Mayrhofen native **Peter Habeler,** in the development of **alpine-style climbing** on the world's highest peaks. Previously, all Himalayan climbs were attempted expedition-style, using scores of porters, weeks of time, and large amounts of money. But Messner and Habeler completed the second ascent of Pakistan's Gasherbrum I (8068m) in only three days, using a minimum of gear and food. Then, in 1978, they used the same fast-attack technique to make the first ascent of Mt. Everest (8848m) without the aid of supplemental oxygen. A flurry of media attention followed, fueling a fierce debate in mountaineering circles as to the wisdom and safety of Alpine-style ascents. Today, although still somewhat controversial, Alpine-style is the preferred form for many important routes, and the only way in which many climbs are even feasible.

A number of other Austrians are responsible for important first ascents. Well before Habeler and Messner popularized Alpine-style climbing, **Kurt Diemberger** used the approach to become the only mountaineer in the world with two first ascents of 8000m summits, climbing Broad Peak (8047m) in 1957 and Dhaulagiri (8167m) in 1960. Also on the Broad Peak team were three other Austrians, including **Hermann Buhl,** who in 1953 completed the epic first ascent of Nanga Parbat (8215m). While others on the expedition turned around due to the threat of bad weather, Buhl pushed alone to the summit and was forced to spend a night above 8000m without a tent or sleeping bag. The next day, hallucinating from the thin air and unable to eat or drink, he amazed his teammates by descending back to Camp V, alive after almost 48hr. alone at high altitude.

HOLIDAYS AND FESTIVALS

Shops and businesses are closed on national and most religious holidays, which in 2005 include New Year's Day (January 1) and Epiphany (January 6), Good Friday (March 25), Easter Monday (March 28), Labor Day (May 1), Ascension Day (May 5), Whitmonday (May 16), Corpus Christi (June 10), Assumption Day (August 15), National Day (October 26), All Saint's Day (November 1), Immaculate Conception (December 8), Christmas (December 25), and Boxing Day (December 26). As Austria is a Catholic country, Catholic religious holidays are observed nearly everywhere, and towns and cities essentially shut down. Below are a list of festivals you'll want to participate in if you're in the neighborhood.

AUSTRIAN FESTIVALS

DATE	NAME AND LOCATION	DESCRIPTION
February	Fasching, Vienna	"Carnival Season" brings waltzes, parties, and a parade the day before Lent.
mid-April to mid-May	Danube Best (Donaufestival): Krems and Korneuburg	A celebration of art, music, and theater along the Danube (Donau) River.
mid-May to mid-June	Vienna Festival (Fest-Wochen)	Thousands descend upon the city for a celebration with theater, exhibits, and renowned orchestras.
early July	Love Parade, Vienna	Begun after the fall of the Berlin Wall, the annual festive parade celebrates love, respect, and tolerance for all.
late July to late Aug.	Salzburg Music Festival	A summer series of concerts by the Vienna Philharmonic and others.
August	Eisenstadt Fest	Freeflowing music and wine. What could be better?
Oct. 26	Austrian National Day	Commemorates formation of Austria as new independent nation after WWII.
mid-Nov. to Dec. 24	Vienna Christmas Market (also in Salzburg)	Festive cabin-like booths are erected in front of the baroque cathedral.
December 6	Krampus (everywhere, especially small towns)	Watch out as St. Nicholas and his mischievous companion Krampus wander the streets.
December 31	New Year's Eve, everywhere	The top draw is Vienna for the annual performance of *Die Fledermaus* at the opera.

ADDITIONAL RESOURCES

CULTURE AND HISTORY

Vienna and its Jews: The Tragedy of Success, 1880s-1980s (1988). George E. Berkley.

The Classic Art of Viennese Pastry (1997). Christine Berl.

The Fall of the House of Hapsburg (1963). Edward Crankshaw.

Fin-de-Siècle Vienna (1961). Carl Schorske.

FICTION

The World of Yesterday (Die Welt von Gestern; 1943). Stefan Zweig.

The Metamorphosis (Die Verwandlung; 1915). Franz Kafka.

The Confusions of Young Törless (Die Verwirrungen des Zöglings Törless; 1906). Robert Musil.

Eyes Wide Shut (Die Traumspiele; 1900). Arthur Schnitzler.

TRAVEL BOOKS

German Survival Guide: The Language and Culture You Need to Travel With Confidence in Germany and Austria (2001). Elizabeth Bingham.

The Wines of Austria (2000). Philip Blom.

Karen Brown's Austria: Charming Inns & Itineraries (2004). Karen Brown.

VIENNA (WIEN)

Occupying a pivotal position between Eastern and Western Europe, Vienna is a living monument to nearly two millennia of rich history. From humble origins as a Roman camp, to Baroque glory days under the Hapsburg dynasty, to the gaslit "merry apocalypse" of its bohemian fin de siècle café culture, Vienna has often rivaled Paris, London, and Berlin in cultural and political significance. Here Freud grappled with the human psyche, Mozart found inspiration for his symphonies, Musil wrote the sprawling *Man Without Qualities*, and Maximilian I and Maria Theresia altered the shape of European politics. Although the darker ghosts of Austria's past still lurk in the Judenplatz, location of a war-time Jewish ghetto, Austria's politicians have worked to redefine Vienna's position as that of an international mediator. The city's atmosphere is becoming increasingly cosmopolitan and open-minded, and the MuseumsQuartier, an ultra-modern venue for architecture, film, theater, and dance, vies with a burgeoning club scene in proving that Vienna is a city still writing its own dynamic brand of history.

SUGGESTED ITINERARIES

ONE DAY. Wake yourself up with fresh coffee and a pastry at **Café Central** (p. 105), then hit the *Innenstadt,* starting with a climb up the tower of **Stephansdom** (p. 109) in the center of the city. Take tram 1 or 2 along the **Ringstraße** (p. 114), which circles Vienna's medieval district. It showcases architectural triumphs such as Wagner's Jugendstil *Postsparkasse, the Burgtheater, and the* **Hofburg** (p. 118) and **public gardens** (p. 121). Indulge in afternoon dessert at **Demel** (p. 105), before heading to the **Spittelbergmarkt** to view local artwork and shop for gifts. Refuel near **Naschmarkt** (p. 116) before catching an opera or concert at night.

THREE DAYS. Spend your first day as above, then discover how art was "made and unmade" in Vienna's world-class **art museums,** especially the **Kunsthistorisches Museum** (p. 124) or the brand-new **Liechtenstein Museum** and **MuseumsQuartier** (p. 125). Eat a bite-sized lunch at Kafka's favorite restaurant, **Trzesniewski** (p. 102). Then explore outside the Ring: tour **Schloß Belvedere** (p. 121) and linger in yet another café (trust us). Spend the evening tasting new wine in the *Heurigen* (wine gardens; p. 107) nestled in the suburbs of Vienna before visiting the Bermuda Dreieck. Spend another day at **Schloß Schönnbrunn** and its amazing gardens. On your last evening, watch Vienna sparkle from the **Donauturm** (p. 122), and then walk down to the hopping boardwalk of the Danube and **Donauinsel** to dance and drink among hip Austrians in the clubs that line the river.

FIVE DAYS. Tackle three of your days as above, but take time to explore different neighborhoods within the Ring. Seek out the Vienna of the past near Judenplatz, Am Hof, and Freyung (p. 111). If it's Sunday, enjoy a mass sung by the **Vienna Boys' Choir** (p. 129). Then daytrip along the **Danube** between Krems and Melk (p. 295). Back in Vienna, (window) shop the upscale "Kaiserlich und Königlich" stores in **Kohlmarkt** (p. 110) or along Kärtnerstr. and Mariahilferstr. As a final fling, return to the heart of Vienna for the spectacular evening tour of the **Stephansdom.**

✈ INTERCITY TRANSPORTATION

BY PLANE. Vienna's airport is the **Wien-Schwechat Flughafen** (☎7007 0), home of **Austrian Airlines.** (☎05 1789; www.aua.com. Open M-F 7am-10pm, Sa-Su 8am-8pm.) Daily flights to and from New York and Washington, D.C. and frequent flights to Berlin, London, and Rome, among other places, are available. Travelers under 25 and students under 27 qualify for discounts on select routes.

The city center is far from the airport (18km), but easily accessible by public transportation. The cheapest way to reach the city is to take train S7 "Flughafen/ Wolfsthal," which stops at **Wien Mitte** and **Wien Nord** (approximately every 30min. 4:55am-10:40pm; €3, Eurail not valid). The heart of the city, Stephanspl., is a short metro ride from Wien Mitte on the U3 (orange) line.

The **City Airport Train (CAT;** ☎ 25 250; www.cityairporttrain.com) takes only 16min. to reach **Wien Mitte** every 30min. 6:06am-11:36pm (€9, round-trip €16, children under 15 free when traveling with an adult, Eurail not valid). Buy tickets at the machines at the airport rather than on the train to avoid paying a surcharge. Alternatively, take the **Vienna Airport Lines Shuttle Bus,** (http://english.viennaairport.com/bus.html), which follows two different routes. The first route serves the **Südbahnhof,** the **Südtirolerplatz,** and the **Westbahnhof** (approximately every 30min. 6:05am-12:05am; €6, round-trip €11, children under age 6 free, Eurail not valid). The second route services the **Schwedenplatz** (approximately every 30min. 6:20am-12:20am; €6, round-trip €11, children under age 6 free, Eurail not valid).

By far the easiest (though most expensive) way to and from the airport is by a private airport shuttle, such as **JetBus** (☎ 700 73 87 78), located just outside the baggage claim. Shuttles deliver passengers to any address in the city for staggered, though always substantial, sums of money (to Wien Mitte €22 per taxi car). Call a day in advance to arrange pickup for a return trip.

BY TRAIN. Vienna has two main train stations with international departures. The Westbahnhof is accessible by the U3 (orange) line, the U6 (brown) line, or the S7; the Südbahnhof is accessible by the U1 (red) line with a connection on the S60 or S7. For general train information (throughout Austria), call ☎ 05 17 17 (24hr.) or check www.oebb.at. Note that fares regularly change and that special prices may be available at certain times, so check ahead.

Westbahnhof, XV, Mariahilferstr. 132 (☎ 89 23 39 2). Trains from here run primarily west. Domestically to: **Bregenz** (8hr., 5 per day, €57); **Innsbruck** (5-6hr., every 2hr., €48.50); **Linz** (2hr., every hr., €23.50); **Salzburg** (3hr., every hr., €36.50). Internationally to: **Amsterdam** (14hr., 8:28pm, must switch trains in Frankfurt, €152.30); **Berlin** (11hr., 9:28pm, €108); **Budapest** (3-4hr., 6 per day, €37.60); **Hamburg** (9hr.; 10:45am, 7:50pm; €124.60); **Munich** (4hr., 5 per day, €63.10); **Paris** (14hr., 8:34pm, €155.70); **Zurich** (9hr., 3 per day, €77.70). The **information counter** is open M-F 7:30am-9:20pm, Sa 7:30am-8:50pm, Su and holidays 8am-8:50pm.

Südbahnhof, X, Wiener Gürtel 1a. Trains leave for destinations to the **south** and **east.** Domestically to: **Graz** (2½hr., every hr., €26.90) and **Villach (5hr., every hr.,** €40). Internationally to: **Berlin** (9½hr., 10:34am, €87.90); **Bratislava** (1hr., 19 per day, €15.40); **Krakow** (7-8hr., 4 per day, €45.30); **Prague** (4hr., 5 per day, €40.70); **Rome** (14hr., 7:29pm, €110.60); **Venice** (9-10hr., 2 per day, €71.80); and other European cities. The information counter is open daily 7am-8pm.

3 stations handle mostly commuter trains. The largest is **Franz-Josefs Bahnhof,** IX, Althamstr. 10, on the tram 5. The other 2 stations are **Bahnhof Wien Mitte,** in the center of town, and **Bahnhof Wien Nord,** by the Praterstern on the north side of the Danube Canal. Bahnhof Wien Nord is the main S-Bahn and U-Bahn link for trains heading north, but most Bundesbahn trains go through the other stations. Some regional trains (Krems, for example) also leave from **Spittelau,** on the U4 and U6 subway lines.

BY BUS AND BOAT. Travel by bus in Austria is seldom cheaper than travel by train. Compare prices before buying a ticket. City bus terminals are located at Wien Mitte/Landstr., Hütteldorf, Heiligenstadt, Floridsdorf, Kagran, Erdberg, and Reumannpl. (Open 7am-10pm.) Domestic **BundesBuses** (☎ 711 01) run from these stations to local and international destinations. Purchase tickets on the bus.

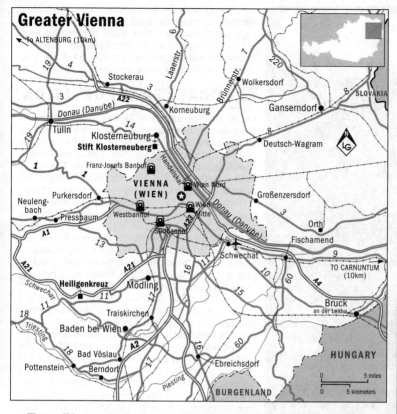

Greater Vienna

The well-known **Donau Dampfschifffahrtsgesellschaft Donaureisen (DDSG)**, I, Friedrichstr. 7 (☎58 88 00; www.ddsg-blue-danube.at), organizes cruises on the Danube, stopping at Melk, Spitz, Dürnstein, and Krems/Stein (see p. 295). The DDSG also operates hydrofoils to Bratislava (1½hr.; June-Aug. daily 9:30am; Apr. and Sept.-Oct. W-Su 9am; May W-Su 9:30am; €22, round-trip €33.50) and Budapest. (5½hr.; May-July 8am; Aug.-Sept. 8am and 1pm; Apr. and Oct.-Nov. 9am; €75, round-trip €99; ISIC holders €59/€84. Eurail and ISIC holders get 20% off within Austria, ages 10-15 half-price, under age 10 free when accompanied by an adult.)

BY CAR. From the **west,** take A1, which runs from Vienna to Salzburg via Linz. From the **south,** take A2, which runs directly into the city. From the **east,** take A4. From the **north,** take A22, which runs along the Danube. A number of much smaller highways lead to Vienna, including Rtes. 7 and 8 from the north and Rte. 10 from the south. An economical but less predictable alternative to the train is **ride-sharing. Mitfahrzentrale Wien** pairs drivers and riders over the phone. Call to see which rides are available. (☎408 22 10; www.mfz.at. Open M-Sa 7am-noon.) A ride to Salzburg costs €18.50, to Prague €19.90. Reservations two days in advance are recommended.

VIENNA

Although *Let's Go* does not recommend hitching, **hitchhikers** headed for Salzburg have been seen taking U4 to "Hütteldorf," from which the highway leading to the *Autobahn* is 10km farther. Hitchers traveling south often ride tram #67 to the last stop and wait at the rotary near Laaerberg.

⬛ LOCAL TRANSPORTATION

Public transportation in Vienna is extensive and dependable. The **subway** (U-Bahn), **tram** (Straßenbahn), **commuter train** (S-Bahn), and **bus** systems operate under one ticket system. Vienna and the surrounding regions are divided into zones. The city of Vienna forms a single zone. Therefore a single fare ticket is sufficient to travel anywhere within the city. A single fare is €2 if purchased from a machine on a bus, or €1.50 if purchased in advance from a machine in a station, ticket office, or tobacco shop (*Tabak* or *Trafik*). This ticket permits you to switch from bus to U-Bahn to tram to S-Bahn, as long as your travel is uninterrupted. To validate a ticket, punch it in the machine immediately upon entering the first vehicle. Do not stamp the ticket again when you switch trains. A ticket stamped twice or not stamped at all is invalid, and plainclothes inspectors may fine you €60 plus the ticket price. Other ticket options (available at the same places as pre-purchased single tickets) are a **24hr. pass** (€5), a **72hr. pass** (€12), a **7-day pass** (€12.50; valid M midnight to M 9am), or an **8-day pass** (€24; valid any 8 days, not necessarily consecutive; valid also for several people traveling together). The **Vienna Card** (€16.90) offers free travel for 72hr., as well as substantial discounts at museums, sights, and events, and is especially useful for non-students. If you are traveling with a child over 6, a bicycle, or a dog, you must also buy a half-price ticket (single fare €0.80, double fare €1.50). Children under 6 always ride free, as does anyone under 15 on Sundays and school holidays. (The pocket map available at tourist offices lists official holidays.) You can take bicycles on all underground trains; each train restricts bikes to certain cars, marked with a bicycle symbol.

Regular trams and subway cars stop running between midnight and 5am. Beginning around 12:30am, a **NightLine** runs along most tram, subway, and major bus routes. (Buses come every 30min.) In major hubs like Schottentor, some buses leave from slightly different areas than the daytime buses. "N" signs with yellow cat eyes designate NightLine stops. A complete schedule is available at bus counters in U-Bahn stations. (Single fare €1.50; day transport passes also valid.)

The **public transportation information line** has live operators who give directions to any point in the city. (☎790 91 00. M-F 6am-10pm, Sa-Su 8:30am-4:30pm.) **Information stands** (marked with an "i") in many stations can also provide detailed instructions on how to purchase tickets, as well as an indispensable free pocket map of the U-Bahn and S-Bahn systems. Stands in the U-Bahn at Karlspl., Stephanspl., and the Westbahnhof are also open on weekends and holidays. (Open M-F 6:30am-6:30pm, Sa-Su and holidays 8:30am-4pm.) Other stands are located at Praterstern, Philadelphiabrücke, Landstr., Floridsdorf, Spittelau, and Volkstheater. (Open M-F 6:30am-6:30pm.)

Taxis: ☎313 00, 401 00, 601 60, or 814 00. Stands at Westbahnhof, Südbahnhof, Karlspl. in the city center, and by the Bermuda Dreieck for late-night revelers. Accredited taxis have yellow and black signs on the roof. Base rate €2.50, €0.20 per 0.2km; slightly more expensive on holidays and at night (11pm-6am).

Car Rental: Avis, I, Opernring 3-5 (☎587 62 41). Open M-F 7am-6pm, Sa 8am-2pm, Su 8am-1pm. **Hertz** (☎70 07 32 661), at the airport. Open M-F 7am-11pm, Sa 8am-8pm, Su 8am-11pm.

Auto Repairs: Call **ÖAMTC** (☎120) or **ARBÖ** (☎123).

Parking: In District I street parking is allowed M-F 9am-7pm for 1½hr. In districts II-IX and XX, street parking is allowed M-F 9am-8pm for 2hr. Parking permits/vouchers are available from banks, railway stations, Vienna Line ticket offices, and *Tabaks* (€0.40 per 30min.). Parking at other hours and outside the Gürtel is free. Handicapped visitors can park for an unlimited period of time in short-term parking with a valid handicap permit. 24hr. garages are open in the aforementioned districts (www.parkeninwien.at). However, it is easiest to find parking in the garages that line the Ringstr., including 2 by the Opera House, 1 at Franz-Josef-Kai, and 1 at the Marek-Garage at Messepalast (€2.70 per day, €13.30 per week). Parking illegally risks a €25-150 fine.

Bike Rental: Rentals generally average €5 per hr. **Pedal Power,** II, Ausstellungsstr. 3 (☎729 72 34; www.pedalpower.at). €17 per 4hr., €32 for 24hr., additional fee for delivery. They also offer bike tours of the city (€19-23). Discounts for students and Vienna Card holders. Open Mar.-Oct. 8am-7pm. Check Wombats Hostel for cheap bike and in-line skate rentals. Pick up *Vienna By Bike* at the tourist office for details on the bicycle scene, including city bike information.

■ ORIENTATION

Vienna is divided into 23 **districts** *(Bezirke)*. The first is the *Innenstadt*, (city center), and the others spiral out clockwise. Street signs indicate the district number before the street and address. Postal codes correspond to the district number: 1010 for the first district, 1020 for the second, 1110 for the eleventh, etc. *Let's Go* includes district numbers for establishments before the street address.

Almost all of Vienna's major attractions are densely concentrated within or immediately outside of **District I** *(the Innenstadt)*, which is defined by the Ringstraße on three sides and the Danube Canal *(Donaukanal)* on the fourth. The **Ringstraße** (or "Ring") consists of various segments: Franz-Joseph-Kai, Stubenring, Parkring, Schubertring, Kärntner Ring, Opernring, Burgring, Dr.-Karl-Renner-Ring, Dr.-Karl-Lüger-Ring, and Schottenring. The **tourist office** is near the intersection of the Opernring, Kärntner Ring, and Kärntnerstr., by the Karlspl. U-Bahn stop. The *Innenstadt* contains many of the museums, palaces, churches, parks, cafés, restaurants, and much of the nightlife for which Vienna is known.

Unfortunately, because of this impressive concentration of attractions, District I contains almost no affordable accommodations options. Excellent alternatives can be found in the districts surrounding the *Innenstadt*. District II is directly

VIENNA

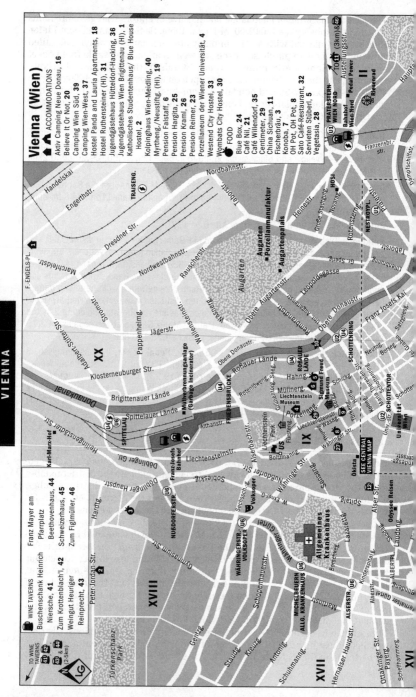

Vienna (Wien)

ACCOMMODATIONS
Aktiv Camping Neue Donau, 16
Believe It Or Not, 20
Camping Wien Süd, 39
Camping Wien-West, 37
Hostel Panda and Lauria Apartments, 18
Hostel Ruthensteiner (HI), 31
Jugendgästehaus Hütteldorf-Hacking, 36
Jugendgästehaus Wien Brigittenau (HI), 1
Katholisches Studentenhaus/ Blue House
Hostel, 2
Kolpinghaus Wien-Meidling, 40
Mytheng./Neustiftg. (HI), 19
Pension Falstaff, 6
Pension Hargita, 25
Pension Kraml, 26
Pension Reimer, 23
Porzellaneum der Wiener Universität, 4
Westend City Hostel, 33
Wombats City Hostel, 30

FOOD
Blue Box, 24
Café Nil, 21
Café Willendorf, 35
Centimeter, 29
China Sichuan, 11
Fischerbräu, 3
Konoba, 7
OH Pot, OH Pot, 8
Sato Café-Restaurant, 32
Servieten Stüberl, 5
Vegetasia, 28

WINE TAVERNS
Buschenschank Heinrich
  Niersche, 41
Zum Krottenblach'l, 42
Weingut Heuriger
  Reinprecht, 43
Franz Mayer am
  Pfarrplatz
Beethovenhaus, 44
Schweizerhaus, 45
Zum Figlmüller, 46

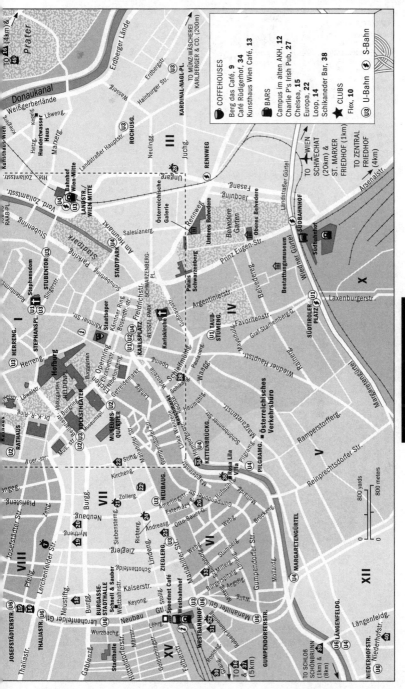

VIENNA

COFFEEHOUSES
Berg das Café, 9
Café Rüdigerhof, 34
Kunsthaus Wien Café, 13

BARS
Campus im alten AKH, 12
Charlie P's Irish Pub, 27
Chelsea, 15
Europa, 22
Loop, 14
Schikaneder Bar, 38

CLUBS
Flex, 10

(U3) U-Bahn   (S) S-Bahn

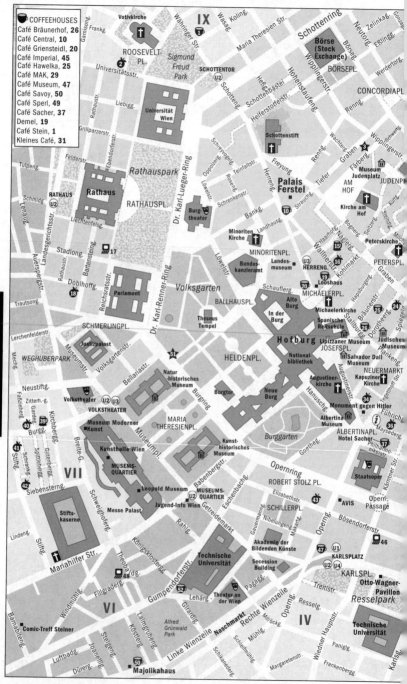

COFFEEHOUSES
Café Bräunerhof, 26
Café Central, 10
Café Griensteidl, 20
Café Imperial, 45
Café Hawelka, 25
Café MAK, 29
Café Museum, 47
Café Savoy, 50
Café Sperl, 49
Café Sacher, 37
Demel, 19
Café Stein, 1
Kleines Café, 31

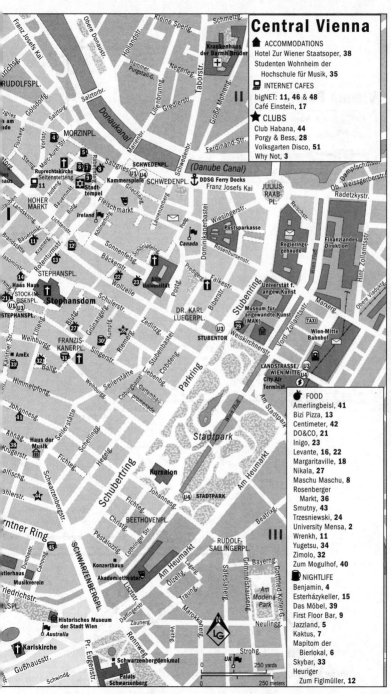

Central Vienna

🏠 ACCOMMODATIONS
Hotel Zur Wiener Staatsoper, **38**
Studenten Wohnheim der
  Hochschule für Musik, **35**

🖥 INTERNET CAFES
bigNET: **11, 46 & 48**
Café Einstein, **17**

⭐ CLUBS
Club Habana, **44**
Porgy & Bess, **28**
Volksgarten Disco, **51**
Why Not, **3**

🍴 FOOD
Amerlingbeisl, **41**
Bizi Pizza, **13**
Centimeter, **42**
DO&CO, **21**
Inigo, **23**
Levante, **16, 22**
Margaritaville, **18**
Nikala, **27**
Rosenberger
  Markt, **36**
Smutny, **43**
Trzesniewski, **24**
University Mensa, **2**
Wrenkh, **11**
Yugetsu, **34**
Zimolo, **32**
Zum Mogulhof, **40**

🍺 NIGHTLIFE
Benjamin, **4**
Esterházykeller, **15**
Das Möbel, **39**
First Floor Bar, **9**
Jazzland, **5**
Kaktus, **7**
Mapitom der
  Bierlokal, **6**
Skybar, **33**
Heuriger
  Zum Figlmüller, **12**

VIENNA

VIENNA

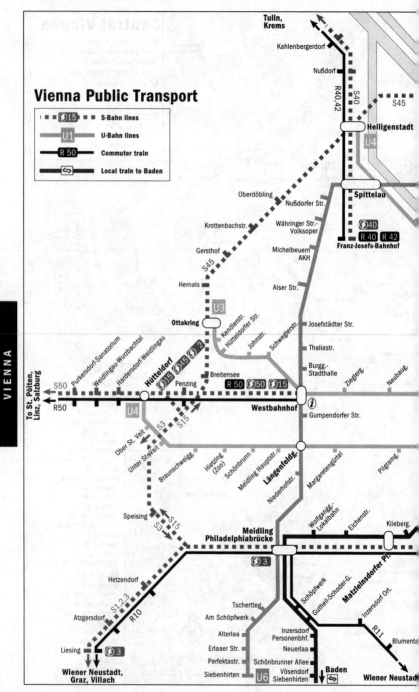

Vienna Public Transport

■ ■ ⑤15 ■ ■	S-Bahn lines
U1	U-Bahn lines
R 50	Commuter train
⇆	Local train to Baden

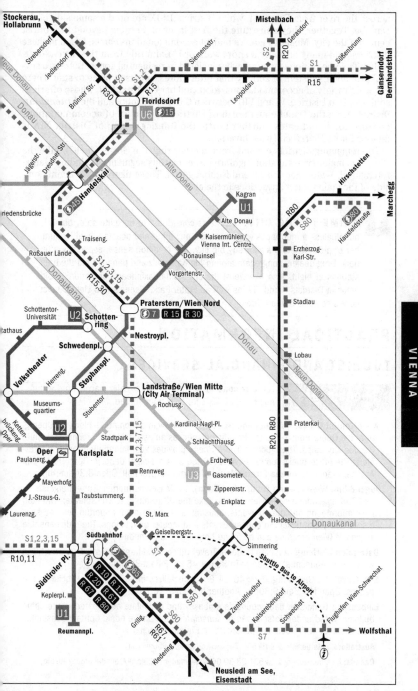

across the river from District I, while Districts III-IX are on the same side of the Danube. Together, they constitute the first layer of districts beyond the tourist center of the city. Most of Vienna's budget accommodations can be found in these districts, and many are only a short walk or U-Bahn ride from the *Innenstadt*. Although some options are somewhat isolated in residential zones, there are several prominent clusters of activity that offer more than just a place to stay. There is a wide variety of accommodations, food, and bars in **District VII**, whose offerings spill over into Districts VI and VIII, between the Westbahnhof and the *Innenstadt*. **District IX,** on the Danube just north of District I, has a lot of accommodations options, food, and cafés. Farther north, the **Grinzing** region of District XIX is famous for its *Heurigen* (wine taverns).

The remaining districts expand from another ring, the Gürtel ("belt"). Like the Ring, this major two-way thoroughfare has numerous segments, including Margaretengürtel, Währinger Gürtel, and Neubaugürtel. These districts are mainly outside of the main tourist attractions in the city.

CRIME IN THE CITY. Vienna is considered to be quite safe, but it is nonetheless a metropolis with crime like any other and boasts a healthy number of pickpockets. As with any big city, use common sense, especially after dark. Drug dealers congregate around the Karlsplatz and hang around the train stations at night. Also beware of the city's small skinhead population. Avoid areas in Districts X and XIV, as well as Prater Park. Vienna's Red Light District covers sections of the Gürtel.

PRACTICAL INFORMATION

TOURIST AND FINANCIAL SERVICES

PHONE CODES The **city code** for Vienna is 01 for calls placed from within Austria, 011 43 1 for calls from abroad.

Main Tourist Office: I, Albertinapl. (☎211 14 0; www.info.wien.at). 1 block up Operng. from the Opera House. The tourist office dispenses an assortment of brochures, including free city maps. The brochure *Youth Scene* provides vital information for young travelers. The office books rooms for a €2.90 fee plus a 1-night deposit. Open 9am-7pm. Another branch at **Vienna International Airport,** in arrival hall. Open 8:30am-9pm.

Jugend-Info Wien (Vienna Youth Information), VII, MuseumsQuartier/Babenbergerstr. 1. (☎1799; jugendinfowien@wienXtra.at). Take the U3 (orange) to Volkstheater. Hip staff have information on cultural events, housing, and employment opportunities and sells discounted youth tickets to concert events and theater productions. The indispensable *Jugend in Wien* brochure can be found here. Open M-Sa noon-7pm.

Österreich Werbung (Austrian National Travel Office), IV, Margaretenstr. 1 (☎588 66 0; www.austria-tourism.at). Open M-Th 8am-4:45pm, F 8am-3:30pm.

STA Travel, IX, Garnisong. 7 (☎40 14 80), specializes in student travel, tickets, and passes. Open M-F 9am-5:30pm. Another **branch** at IX, Türkenstr. 6.

Embassies: Generally, each country's embassy and consulate are located in the same building, listed under *Botschaften* or *Konsulate* in the phone book. Contact consulates for assistance with visas and passports and in emergencies.

Australia: IV, Mattiellistr. 2-4 (☎506 74; www.australian-embassy.at).

Canada: I, Laurenzerberg 2 (☎531 38 30 00; www.dfait-maeci.gc.ca/canadaeurope/austria).

Ireland: I, Rotenturmstr. 16-18, 5th fl. (☎71 54 24 6; vienna@iveath.irlgov.ie).

New Zealand: Consulate, XIX, Karl-Tornay-g. 34 (☎318 85 05; psunley@aon.at).

UK: III, Jauresg. 10 (☎716 13 51 51; www.britishembassy.at).

US: IX, Boltzmanng. 16 (☎313 39 0; www.usembassy.at).

Currency Exchange: ATMs are your best bet. Nearly all accept Cirrus, MC, and V. **Banks** and **airport exchanges** use the same official rates. Most are open M-W and F 8am-12:30pm and 1:30-3pm, Th 8am-12:30pm and 1:30-5:30pm. **Train station** exchanges offer long hours (daily 7am-10pm at the Westbahnhof) and a minimum fee of €6 for the first 3 checks (€300 max.). Stay away from the 24hr. bill-exchange machines in the *Innenstadt*, as they generally charge outrageous prices.

American Express: I, Kärntnerstr. 21-23 (☎515 40), down the street from Stephwanspl., cashes AmEx checks for free, and Thomas Cook and Visa checks and money exchange for sums under €100 (commission €7). Sells theater, concert, and other tickets, and holds mail for 4 weeks for AmEx members. Open M-F 9am-5:30pm, Sa 9am-noon. For 24hr. refund service, call ☎0800 20 68 40.

LOCAL SERVICES

Luggage Storage: Small lockers are €2 per day at all train stations.

Lost Property: Fundbüro, XVIII, Bastieng. 36 (☎400 080 91). For items lost on public transportation, call ☎790 94 35 00. Open daily 6am-10pm. For the Vienna lost and found office call ☎9300 880 22222.

Bookstores: Shakespeare & Company, I, Bezirksterng. 2 (☎535 50 53). Eclectic and intelligent. International magazine selection. Open M-Sa 9am-7pm. The **British Bookshop,** I, Weihburgg. 24 (☎512 19 45; www.britishbookshop.at), has an extensive travel section. Open M-F 9:30am-6:30pm, Sa 9:30am-5pm. MC/V. New **branch** at VI, Mariahilferstr. 4 (☎522 67 30). **Comic-Treff Steiner,** VI, Barnabiteng. 12 (☎504 32 94). One of Vienna's best comic book stores. Open M-F 9:30am-6:30pm, Sa 9:30am-1pm.

Radio: FM4, 103.8FM. Alternative music with news updates every hr. until 7pm in English, French, and German, including the BBC World Service. **Radio Ö3,** 99.9FM. Pop and rock. **Energy** (104.2FM) and **88.6FM** both play mainstream pop. **Radio Wien,** 89.9FM, plays oldies and Austro pop.

GLBT Organizations: The bisexual, gay, and lesbian community in Vienna is more integrated than in other Austrian cities. For the gay goings-on about town, pick up the *Vienna Gay Guide* (www.gayguide.at) from the tourist office, the monthly Viennese magazine *Extra Connect* (in German), or the free monthly publication *Bussi* at any gay bar, café, or club. *Falter* newspaper lists gay events in a special heading. The following organizations also sponsor events and offer help in Vienna:

 Rosa-Lila-Tip, VI, Linke Wienzeile 102 (☎585 4343), is a popular resource and social center for gays and lesbians, whether native to Vienna or just visiting. Friendly staff speak English and provide counseling, information, a library, and nightclub listings (see **Nightlife,** p. 132). Open M-W 5-8pm.

 Homosexuelle Initiative Wien (HOSI), II, Novarag. 40 (☎216 66 04; www.hosiwien.at). Lesbian group and phone network W 7pm. Prints *Lambda Nachrichten*. Open Tu-F 7-10pm (includes phone counseling). Youth counseling Th 7pm.

 Lesbischwul und Transgender Referat (☎588 01 49511 588). Gay student counseling group. F 1-3:30pm.

Laundromat: Most hostels offer laundry service for €4. **Schnell und Sauber,** VII, Westbahnhofstr. 60 (☎524 64 60). From Westbahnhof, take tram #18 to "Urban-Loritzpl." 6kg wash €4.50, dry €1 per 20min. Soap included. Open 24hr. **Münz-wäscherei Karlberger & Co.,** III, Schlachthausg. 19 (☎798 81 91). 6kg wash €7, dry €2. Soap €1. Open M-F 7:30am-6:30pm, Sa 7:30am-1pm.

VIENNA

Public Showers and Toilets: At Westbahnhof, there are well-maintained showers and toilets. 30min. shower €3. Shampoo and towel €1 each. Showers and baths also available at the airport and at **Jörgerbad** XVII, Jörgerstr. 42-44 (U6 to Alser Str., then tram 43 dir: Neuwaldegg. to Palffyg.; walk 1 block. Closed M-Tu). Cheap pay toilets (€0.50) are in most U-bahn stations; a special *Jugendstil* toilet is in Graben (9am-7pm, €0.50).

Snow Reports: In German. For Vienna, Lower Austria, and Styria ☎15 83; for Salzburg, Upper Austria, and Carinthia ☎15 84; for Tyrol and Vorarlberg ☎15 85.

EMERGENCY AND COMMUNICATION

Emergencies: Police ☎133. **Ambulance** ☎144. **Fire** ☎122.

Poison Control: ☎406 43 43. 24hr.

Crisis Hotlines: All hotlines have English-speaking employees. **Rape Crisis Hotline:** ☎523 22 22. M and Th 1-6pm, Tu and F 10am-3pm. **24hr. immediate help for women:** ☎717 19.

Medical Assistance: Allgemeines Krankenhaus, IX, Währinger Gürtel 18-20 (☎404 00 0). **Emergency care** ☎141. **24hr. pharmacy** ☎15 50. Consulates offer lists of English-speaking physicians.

Internet Access: bigNET.internet.cafe, I, Kärntnerstr. 61 (☎503 98 44); I, Hoher markt 8-9 (☎533 29 39); and the largest Internet café in Austria, Mariahilferstr. 27 (☎205 06 21), with an English-speaking staff. €3.70 for 30min.; €5.90 per hr. **Café Stein,** IX, Währingerstr. 6-8 (☎31 97 24 19). €4 per 30min. **Café Einstein,** VIII, Rathauspl. 4 (☎405 26 26). €1 per 15min. Open M-F 7am-2am, Sa 9am-2am, Su 9am-midnight. **Speednet Café** (www.speednet-cafe.com), in Westbahnhof. €1.30 for 10min., €5.80 per hr. Open M-Sa 7am-midnight, Su and holidays 8am-midnight.

Post Offices: Hauptpostamt, I, Fleischmarkt 19. Vast structure contains phone, fax, and mail services. Open 24hr. Address *Poste Restante* to "LAST NAME, First Name; *Postlagernde Briefe;* Hauptpostamt; Fleischmarkt 19; A-1010 Wien." Branches throughout the city and at the train stations; look for yellow signs with the trumpet logo.

Postal Codes: 1st district A-1010, 2nd A-1020, 3rd A-1030, etc., to the 23rd A-1230.

⌂⌂ ACCOMMODATIONS AND CAMPING

Hunting for cheap rooms in Vienna during peak tourist season (June-Sept.) can be unpleasant; write or call for reservations at least five days in advance. Otherwise, plan on calling from the train station early in the morning to put your name down for a reservation. If there are no vacancies, ask to be put on a waiting list, and inquire about alternative lodgings. Those unable to find a hostel bed should consider a *Pension*. Institutional hostels tend to offer smaller rooms and more privacy, although some are further removed from the city center. Many accommodations include breakfast or offer it for a small fee (around €4). One-star establishments are usually adequate and are most common in districts VII, VIII, and IX; singles start around €30, doubles €40.

For longer stays, try **Odyssee Reisen und Mitwohnzentrale,** VIII, Laudong. 18. Odyssee's staff find rooms that cost approximately €25 per person per night and apartments for 1-2 people for about €65 per night. For one-month stays, rooms go for €300 per person plus commission, and apartments start at €450 plus commission. (☎402 60 61; www.mwz.at. Bring your passport to register. Open M-F 10am-2pm and 3-6pm.) **Arwag** offers similar services via the web (www.arwag.at) or through a 24hr. hotline (☎79 70 00). Alternatively, visit either **Österreichische Hochschülerschaft** at Rooseveltpl. 5 or the bulletin boards on the first floor of the **Neues Institut Gebäude** (NIG building) on Universitätstr. 7 near the Votivkirche.

ACCOMMODATIONS BY LOCATION

HOSTELS AND DORMITORIES

▨ **Hostel Ruthensteiner (HI)**, XV, Robert-Hamerlingg. 24 (☎ 893 42 02; www.hostelruthensteiner.com). Exit Westbahnhof at the main entrance and turn right onto Mariahilferstr.; turn left on Haidmannsg. Take the 1st right on Robert-Hamerlingg. and continue to the middle of the block. This top-notch hostel boasts an extremely knowledgeable, English-speaking staff and a friendly atmosphere. Spotless rooms, sunny, rose-filled courtyard featuring an oversized chess set, and free use of a small kitchenette with a fridge. Breakfast €2.50. Showers, sheets (except for 10-bed rooms, with one-time rental payment of €2), and lockers included. **Internet** €2 for 25min. Laundry €6. 4-night max. stay. Reception 24hr. Reserve 2-3 weeks in advance in summer. 32-bed "Outback" summer dorm €11.50; 4- to 10-bed dorms €11.50-13; singles, doubles, and triples €14-25. AmEx/MC/V (€0.40 extra for using credit card). ❷

Wombats City Hostel, XV, Grang. 6 (☎ 897 23 36; www.wombats-hostels.com). From Westbahnhof, take the main exit and turn right onto Mariahilferstr. Continue until 152 (on the corner of Rosinag.). Turn right onto Rosinag. and continue until Grang. (2nd left). Although near the train tracks and a number of auto-body shops, this superb modern hostel compensates with colorful, clean rooms, a pub (summer 6pm-2am; winter 7pm-2am) and various perks, including free movie screenings. Breakfast €3.50. Shower and lockers in each room. Towels €3. Laundry €4.50. **Internet** €1 per 12min. In-line skate rental €8 per day. Bike rental €13 per day. 3- to 6-bed rooms €16; doubles €42. ❷

Westend City Hostel, VI, Fügerg. 3 (☎ 597 67 29; www.westendcityhostel.at). Located right near Westbahnhof. Exit "Äussere Mariahilfstr." and cross the large intersection, make a right on Millerg. and a left on Fügerg. Look for the white building with vibrant purple accents. This large new hostel has comfortable beds and an ideal location. **Internet** €2.60 per 30min., bigNet Internet cards accepted. Breakfast and sheets included. Laundry, detergent, and drying €6. Reception 24hr. Check-out 10:30am. Quiet hours 10pm-7am, but the common room is still open. 12-bed dorms €16.80; 6- to 8-bed dorms €17.80; 4-bed €19; singles €40.50; doubles €48.60. Rates are slightly cheaper Nov.-Feb. except around New Year's. ❷

VIENNA

Myrthengasse (HI), VII, Myrtheng. 7, across the street from Believe It or Not, and **Neustiftgasse (HI),** VII, Neustiftg. 85 (☎523 63 16; www.jugendherberge.at.). These simple but clean and modern hostels, both under the same management, are a 20min. walk from the *Innenstadt.* A small lounge and dining room make them perfect for meeting other travelers. Breakfast, lockers (but no locks), and sheets included. Dinner €5.50. Bring your own lock or purchase one for €3.65. Laundry €3.50. **Internet** access €4.36 per 30min. 6-night max. stay. Reception at Myrtheng. 24hr. Lockout 9am-2pm. Rooms separated by sex (except for families). Reservations recommended; arrive by 4pm. 2- to 6-bed dorms with shower and sink, but 2-bed rooms cannot be reserved ahead of time. €14.50-17.50. Non-members add €3.50. Wheelchair accessible. AmEx/MC/V. ❷

Believe It Or Not, VII, Myrtheng. 10, Apt. #14 (☎526 46 58). From Westbahnhof, take U6 (brown; dir: Floridsdorf) to "Burgg./Stadthalle," then bus #48A (dir: Ring) to "Neubaug." Walk back on Burgg. 1 block and take the 1st right on Myrtheng. Ring the bell. A converted 2nd-floor apartment, this cute hostel has a kitchen and 16 beds squeezed into 2 co-ed bunkrooms. Sheets and lockers included. Reception 8am-1pm. Check-in until 11pm. Lockout 10am-12:30pm. Reservations recommended. Ages 18-30. Big dorms €13, small dorms €15. ❷

Kolpinghaus Wien-Meidling, XIII, Bendlg. 10-12 (☎813 54 87; www.kolpinghaus-wien12.at). Take U6 (brown) to "Niederhofstr." Head right on Niederhofstr. and take the 4th right onto Bendlg. This institutional hostel has 184 beds and is conveniently near the U-Bahn. Some rooms have balconies. Breakfast and sheets included. Showers in all rooms. Reception 24hr. Lounge, TV, and foosball tables. Check-out 9am. 2-bed rooms €22.50-25.20; 4- or- 6-bed rooms €17.50-18.50. AmEx/MC/V. ❷

Hostel Panda, VII, Kaiserstr. 77, 3rd fl. (☎522 25 55; www.lauria-vienna.at/panda). From Westbahnhof take U6 (brown; dir: Floridsdorf.) to "Burg/Stadthalle." Take 2nd left on Kaiserstrab. From Südbahnhof, take tram #18 to "Westbahnhof," and follow directions from Westbahnhof. On the 3rd fl. of an old-fashioned, semi-*Jugendstil* Austrian apartment building, this eclectic hostel has 19 mattresses packed into 2 co-ed dorms. While cramped, the rooms have access to kitchen and TV. **Internet** access and laundry available at nearby businesses. Bring lock for lockers. Generally, 2-night min. stay. Check-in until midnight. Lockout 10am-2pm. Ages 17-30. Dorms €13. ❷

Jugendgästehaus Wien Brigittenau (HI), XX, Friedrich-Engels-Pl. 24 (☎33 28 294; oejhv-wien-jgh-brigittenau@oejhv.or.at). Take U1 (red) or U4 (green) to "Schwedenpl.," then tram N to "Floridsdorferbrücke/Friedrich-Engels-Pl." Follow the signs through the underpass. This roomy hostel, while not centrally located, is close to the *Donauinsel* and only a 20min. tram ride from the city center. Lounge with pool table, foosball, and TV. Breakfast and sheets included. Safe available at reception. Lunch and dinner €5.50 each. **Internet** €2.60 for 20min. 5-night max. stay. Reception 24hr. No lockout. Reservations recommended. Wheelchair accessible. 24-bed dorms (men only) €13.50-14.50; 2- to 6-bed rooms with washbasin €14.50-15.50, with bath €16.50-17.50. Non-members add €3.50. AmEx/MC/V. ❷

Jugendgästehaus Hütteldorf-Hacking (HI), XIII, Schloßbergg. 8 (☎877 02 63; fax 87 70 26 32). From Karlspl., take U4 (green) to "Hütteldorf," take the Hadikg. exit, cross the foot bridge, and follow signs to the hostel (10min.). Or take bus #53B from the side of the foot bridge opposite the station. From Westbahnhof, take S50 to "Hütteldorf" and follow directions above. This secluded hostel has a large yard with Heuriger-style tables, free parking, simple 2- to 8-bed rooms, some with private showers, and one 32-bed dorm room. Breakfast and sheets included. Free luggage storage. Reception 7am-11:45pm. Lockout 9:30am-3pm. Curfew 11:45pm unless you buy a keycard (€2). Reservations recommended, especially for groups. €12.50-15. Add €2.70-3 per person for 4-bed rooms; €3.70-4 for 3-bed rooms; €11-14 for singles; €5.50-6 for doubles. Non-members add €3.50. Discounts for groups of 21 or more. AmEx/MC/V. ❷

HOTELS AND PENSIONS

When it comes to hotels, the prices are higher, but you pay for convenient reception hours, no curfews, and no lockouts.

Pension Kraml, VI, Brauerg. 5 (☎587 85 88; www.pensionkraml.at). Take U3 (orange) to "Zierierg.," exit onto Otto-Bauerg., take the 1st left onto Köenigsegg, then 1st right. From Südbahnhof, take bus #13A to Esterhazyg. and walk up Brauerg. Near the *Innenstadt* and the *Naschmarkt*, Kraml has large, elegant rooms and a lounge with cable TV. Breakfast included. 38 beds. Reserve 2-3 weeks in advance. Singles €28; doubles €48, with shower €58, with bath €68; triples €68, with shower €75. Apartment with bath for 3-5 people €90-120. V. ❸

Pension Hargita, VII, Andreasg. (☎526 19 28; fax 04 92). Take U3 (orange) to "Zieglerg." and take Andreasg. exit. Small rooms equipped with sink and TV are serene with hardwood floors, seafoam walls, and cozy beds. Breakfast €3. Reception 8am-10pm. Check-out 10am. Reserve ahead during high season. Singles €35, with shower €40; doubles €48, with shower €55, with bath €63-70; triples €70-76. MC/V. ❹

Lauria Apartments, VII, Kaiserstr. 77, Apt. #8 (☎522 25 55). From Westbahnhof, take tram #5 to "Burgg." Small but comfortable cluster of apartments. Kitchen with hot plates. Sheets, lockers, and TV included. 2-night min. stay. Reception 8am-2pm. Lockout 10am-2pm. Doubles €46; triples €63; quads €80. MC/V for bills over €100. ❷

Pension Reimer, VII, Kircheng. 18 (☎523 61 62; pension.reimer@aon.at), is centrally located and has huge, comfortable rooms with tables and sinks. Individualized breakfast included. Singles €31-41; doubles €52-70, depending on season and whether or not room contains private bath. MC/V for long stays only. ❹

Pension Falstaff, IX, Müllnerg. 5 (☎317 91 27; fax 31 79 18 64). Take U4 (green) to "Roßauer Lände." Cross Roßauer Lände, head down Grünentorg., and take the 3rd left onto Müllnerg. Reception is on the 1st floor. Medium-sized rooms in a quiet location. Breakfast included. Reception 7:30am-9pm. Singles €35, with shower €42; doubles €53-67. Additional bed €20. ❹

Hotel Zur Wiener Staatsoper, I, Krugerstr. 11 (☎513 12 74 75; www.zurweinerstaatsoper.at). From Karlspl., exit Oper, follow Kärntnerstr. towards the city center, and turn right on Krugerstr. This simple, elegant hotel offers a prime downtown location. All rooms come with shower. Buffet breakfast included. Safety deposit box €4. Singles €76-95; doubles €109-140; triples €131-160 (prices rise Apr.-June, Sept.-Oct., and on holidays). AmEx/MC/V. ❺

UNIVERSITY DORMITORIES

Porzellaneum der Wiener Universität, IX, Porzellang. 30 (☎317 72 82; fax 317 72 82 30). From the Südbahnhof, take tram D (dir: Nußdorf) to "Seeg." From Westbahnhof, take tram #5 to "Franz-Josefs Bahnhof," then tram D (dir: Südbahnhof) to "Seeg." A dormitory during the year, the Porzellaneum rents rooms to travelers July-Sept. The small but clean rooms contain a bed, dresser, and desk. No lockers, but reception may be able to keep luggage for 1 day or store valuables. Reception 24hr. Reserve 1 week in advance by phone or email. Singles €18-20; doubles €34-38; quads €64-72, depending on whether or not towels and sheets are included. ❸

Katholisches Studentenhaus/Blue House Hostel, XIX, Peter-Jordanstr. 29 (☎369 55 85; fax 369 55 85 12; bluehousehostel@gmx.at). From Westbahnhof, take U6 (brown; dir: Heiligenstadt) to "Nußdorferstr.," then bus #35A or tram #38 to "Hardtg." and turn left; walk approximately 5min. up Peter-Jordanstr. From Südbahnhof, take tram D to "Schottentor," then tram #38 to "Hardtg." Open July to mid-Sept.. Set in a quiet, residential neighborhood, this friendly hostel offers free **Internet,** a community room with TV, table tennis and foosball, and a small yard. Kitchen and fridge space available. Reception 24hr. Dorms €20, 1-month stay €250; doubles €34/€420. ❸

Studentenwohnheim der Hochschule für Musik, I, Johannesg. 8 (☎514 84 7700; www.johannesgasse8.at). Head 3 blocks down Kärntnerstr. from Stephansdom and turn left onto Johannesg. Although there are families and backpackers, much of the clientele consists of music students; the former monastery has 23 practice rooms with grand pianos (€5 per hr.; call in advance to reserve the concert halls). Breakfast included. Reception 24hr. Reserve well in advance. Singles €33-39; doubles €58-70; triples €66; quads €80; quints €100. Apartment (includes 2 double rooms, bathroom, kitchen, living room) €28.50 per person, entire apartment €90. Discounts for groups larger than 20. ❸

CAMPING

Wien-West, Hütelbergstr. 80 (☎914 23 14; www.wiencamping.at). Take U4 (green) to "Hütteldorf," then bus #14B or 152 (dir: Campingpl.) to "Wien West II" for reception. This campground, 8km from the city center, is crowded but very clean. The campground is only 20min. from the city center and 2min. from a seemingly endless network of hiking paths through the Vienna Woods. Laundry, grocery stores, wireless **Internet,** showers, and cooking facilities. Reception 7:30am-9:30pm. Open Mar.-Jan. July-Aug. and New Year's €6.50 per person, €5 per tent; Sept.-June €5.50/€4; €3.50-4 per child ages 4-15. 2- and 4-person bungalows €23-27; 4-person €33-37. Electricity €3. Wheelchair accessible. ❶

Wien Süd, Breitenfurterstr. 269 (☎867 36 49; www.wiencamping.at). Take the U6 (brown; dir: Siebenhirten) to "Philadelphiabrücke" and take bus #62A to "Campingplatz Wien Süd." Located on the southwestern side of the city, this former imperial park encompasses vast expanses of woods and meadows. Laundry services, a café, small playground, a supermarket, and kitchen. Open May-Sept. €5.50-6.50 per person, €4-5 per tent, €7-8 per camper. Electricity €3.50-4. Wheelchair accessible. ❶

Aktiv Camping Neue Donau, XXII, Am Kleehäufel 119 (☎/fax 202 40 10; www.wiencamping.at), 4km from the city center and adjacent to Neue Donau beaches; take U1 (red) to "VIC/UNO-City" then bus #91a to "Kleehäufel." Located right along the Danube, this camping site offers wireless **Internet,** beach volleyball, tennis courts, waterskiing, and boat and bike rentals. Laundry, supermarket, and kitchen. Open Apr.-Sept. €5.50-6.50 per adult, €3.50-4 per child, €4-5 per tent, €7-8 per camper. Showers included. Wheelchair accessible. ❶

◨ FOOD

For the Viennese, food is not mere fuel for the body: it is a multi-faceted traditional experience that begins when you wish someone *"Mahlzeit"* (roughly, *"bon appétit"*) and ends with one of the city's renowned pastries. Be aware that Viennese pastries are not only unbelievably rich, but are also priced for patrons who are likewise blessed. Unless you buy your sin wholesale at a local bakery, *Sacher Torte, Imperial Torte,* and even *Apfelstrudel* can cost up to €5.

Vienna's restaurants are as varied as its cuisine. *Gästehäuser, Imbiße* (food stands), and *Beisln* (small taverns or restaurants) serve inexpensive meals that stick to your ribs and are best washed down with copious amounts of beer. *Würstelstände,* found on almost every corner, provide a quick, cheap lunch (a sausage runs €2.50). The restaurants downtown near **Graben** and **Kärntnerstraße** are generally expensive. A cheaper bet is the neighborhood north of the university, and near the Votivkirche (take the U2/purple to "Schottentor"), where **Universitätsstraße** and **Währingerstraße** meet. Cafés with cheap meals also line **Burggasse** in District VI. The area radiating from the **Rechte** and **Linke Wienzeile** near Naschmarkt (take U4/green to "Kettenbrückeg.") houses cheap restaurants, and the **Naschmarkt** contains open-air stands where you can purchase fresh fruits and vegetables, bread, and a variety of ethnic food.

TIP Most places close earlier on Saturday afternoons and all day Sunday. In general, restaurants stop serving after 11pm. Some supermarkets, however, are open daily; if you're stuck without food on a Sunday, head to the one in the Westbahnhof, though prices will be slightly higher.

At Christmastime, **Christkindlmarkt** offers hot food and potent punch amid vendors of ornaments and candles. From late June to July, the **Festwochen** film festival brings international foodstuffs to the stands behind the seats (stands open daily 11am-11pm). The open-air **Brunnenmarkt** is inexpensive, and has a Turkish-style flair (take U6/brown to "Josefstädterstr.," then walk up Veronikag. 1 block and turn right). *Bäckereien* (bakeries) are everywhere (chains include **Anker** and **Der Mann**). To combat the summer heat, hit one of the ubiquitous gelato shops.

As for grocery stores, the lowest prices are on the shelves of **Billa, Zielpunkt, Hofer,** and **SPAR**. More pricey chains include **Ledi, Mondo,** and **Renner**. Kosher groceries are available at **Kosher Supermarkt**, II, Hollandstr. 10 (☎216 96 75).

FOOD BY TYPE

AUSTRIAN
🏮 Smutny (102)	I ❸
🏮 Trzesniewski (77)	I, III, VI ❷
Centimeter (103)	VII, VIII, IX ❷
Plachutta (79)	I ❺
Amerlingbeisl (103)	VII ❷
Konoba (104)	VIII ❸
Fischerbräu (103)	XIX ❷
Servieten Stüberl (80)	IX ❷
University Mensa (80)	IX ❸

FRENCH
🏮 Nikala (102)	I ❷

VEGETARIAN
Wrenkh (79)	I ❷
Inigo (78)	I ❶
Rosenberger Markt (78)	I ❶
Café Willendorf (104)	VI ❸
Blue Box (104)	VII ❷
Amerlingbeisl (103)	VII ❷

ASIAN AND INDIAN
Yugetsu (103)	I ❹
Vegetasia (103)	III ❷
Zum Mogulhof (104)	VII ❸
China Sichuan (104)	XXII ❸

FUSION
🏮 DO&CO (102)	I ❺
Margaritaville (103)	I ❸
Wrenkh (79)	I ❷
Inigo (102)	I ❷
Vegetasia (103)	III ❷
Café Willendorf (104)	VI ❸
Blue Box (104)	VII ❷
🏮 OH Pot, OH Pot (103)	IX ❷

ITALIAN
Bizi Pizza (78)	I ❷
Zimolo (78)	I ❸

GREEK, TURKISH, AND MIDDLE EASTERN
🏮 Sato Café-Restaurant (103)	XV ❶
Levante (78)	I, VIII ❷
Maschu Maschu (103)	I, VIII ❶
Café Nil (104)	VII ❷

CAFÉS
🏮 Kleines Café (81)	I
🏮 Café Central (81)	I
🏮 Demel (82)	I
Café MAK (81)	I
Café Hawelka (81)	I
Café Bräunerhof (82)	I
Café Museum (82)	I
Café Sacher (82)	I
Café Griensteidl (82)	I
Café Imperial (82)	I
Kunsthaus Wien Café (106)	III
🏮 Café Sperl (106)	VI
Café Savoy (106)	VI
Café Rüdigerhof (107)	VI
Berg das Café (106)	IX
Café Stein (82)	IX

HEURIGEN
🏮 Buschenschank Heinrich Niersche (107)	XIX
🏮 Zum Krottenbach'l (107)	XIX
Weingut Heuriger Reinprecht (108)	XIX
Franz Mayer am Pfarrplatz Beethovenhaus (108)	XIX

VIENNA

RESTAURANTS

Inexpensive student cafeterias include **Vienna Technical University,** IV, Wiedner Hauptstr. 8-10 (☎586 65 02; open for school term M-F 1-5:30pm) and **Afro-Asia Mensa,** IX, Türkenstr. 3, near the Schottentor. (Around €4.50. Open M-Sa 11:30am-2:30pm.)

INSIDE THE RING

▨ **Nikala,** I, Grünanger. 10 (☎512 56 87), off Singerstr. near Stephanspl. The building has had many incarnations, including a burlesque theater. Sexy lighting combined with decorations retained from previous eras make this eatery captivating enough for even Al Capone (a former customer). The sensual decor complements scrumptious crêpes (€4-15). Other French entrées €6-19. Wheelchair accessible. Open M-F 4pm-midnight, Sa-Su 11am-midnight. AmEx/MC/V. ❷

▨ **Trzesniewski,** I, Dorotheerg. 1 (☎512 32 91; www.speckmitei.at), 3 blocks down the Graben from the Stephansdom. With its famous stand-up buffet, this unpronounceable establishment has been serving open-faced mini-sandwiches for over 100 years. These sandwiches come in 21 varieties and cost €0.80. Favorite toppings include salmon, onion, paprika, and egg. A mini-beer, called *Pfiff* (0.125L, €0.70), goes well with the sandwiches. Open M-F 8:30am-7:30pm, Sa 9am-5pm. **Branches** at VI, Mariahilferstr. 95 (☎596 42 91), and III, Hauptstr. 97 (☎712 99 64) in Galleria. ❷

▨ **Smutny,** I, Elisabethstr. 8 (☎587 13 56; www.smutny.com). Exit Karlspl. onto Elizabethstr.; Smutny is directly on the right. Vienna's oldest Budweiser Budvar restaurant, Smutny serves traditional Austrian cuisine. Dishes include *schnitzel* and *Gulasch* (around €10) and a €6 *Menü.* Open 10am-midnight. AmEx/MC/V. ❸

Plachutta, I, Wollzeile 38 (☎512 15 77; www.plachutta.at). Take the U3 to "Stubentor" and walk down Wollzeile. This restaurant serves Vienna's best *Tafelspitz* (€20). Other entrées €12-24. Open daily 11:30am-11:15pm. ❺

DO&CO, I, Stephanspl. 12, 7th fl. (☎535 39 69). Set above the Stephanspl. cathedral in the Haas Haus, this gourmet restaurant offers both traditional Austrian and international specialties like Thai noodles and Uruguay beef. Prices are high, but so is the quality. The restaurant has an amazing view of the *Innenstadt.* Reservations recommended. Entrées €18-23.50. Open daily noon-3pm and 6pm-1am. V. ❺

Levante, I, Wallnerstr. 2 (☎533 23 26; www.levante.at). Walk down Graben away from the Stephansdom, turn left onto Kohlmarkt, and right onto Wallnerstr. This Turkish franchise features street-side dining with some vegetarian dishes. Entrées €7.20-12.40. Sandwiches €3.60. Pizza €5.10-7.50. **Branches** at I, Wollzeilestr. 19 (off Rotenturm, take U3 or U1 to "Stephanspl."); I, Wallnerstr. 2; VII, Mariahilferstr. 88a; and VIII, Josefstädterstr. 14 (take U2 to "Rathaus"). All open daily 11am-11:30pm. MC/V. ❷

Bizi Pizza, I, Rotenturmstr. 4 (☎513 37 05). 1 block up Rotenturmstr. from Stephanspl. One of the best deals in the city center, this self-serve restaurant whips up fresh, affordable pizza and *antipasti.* Pasta €5-6. Whole pizza €5-7, huge slices €2.40. Open daily 10am-11:30pm. **Branches** with same hours: I, Franz-Josefs-Kai 21 (☎535 79 13); Mariahilferstr. 22-24 (☎523 16 58); and X, Favoritenstr. 105 (☎600 50 10). ❷

Zimolo, I, Ballg. 5 (☎513 17 54; fax 99 78), near Stephanspl. off Weihburgg. A 2min. walk down Weiburgg. (somewhat hidden; walk down the lane to get to the restaurant). This sexy café has candlelit tables and friendly staff. Serves delicious Italian dishes, fish specialties in particular, and an Italian wine selection. Entrées average €7-19. Wheelchair accessible. Open M-Sa noon-3pm and 6pm-midnight. AmEx/MC/V. ❸

Inigo, I, Bäckerstr. 18 (☎512 74 51). This popular dining spot, across from Vienna's Jesuit church, was founded by a Jesuit priest as part of a socioeconomic reintegration program. It provides employment, training, and social work for 17 people who are long-term unemployed. Serves a diversity of international dishes and vegetarian options (€5-10) and a salad bar (€3-7). Wheelchair accessible. Open July-Aug. M-F 10:30am-midnight; Sept.-June also Sa 10:30am-midnight and Su 10am-4pm. AmEx/MC/V. ❷

Rosenberger Markt, I, Mayserderg. 2 (☎512 34 58; www.rosenberger.cc), off Kärntnerstr. The upstairs bistro serves sandwiches (€3), cakes, and freshly-squeezed juices. The downstairs self-serve restaurant offers a large selection of salad, fruit salad, waffle, antipasto, potato, and pasta bars. You pay by the size of your plate, not by weight, so pile high. Salads €3-7. Waffles €4-4.40. *Antipasti* €4-7. Wheelchair accessible. Bistro open 7:30am-11pm. Restaurant open 10:30am-11pm. AmEx/MC/V. ❶

Margaritaville, I, Bartensteing. 3 (☎405 47 86). Take U2 (purple) to "Rathaus." Walk down Landesgerichtsstr. and make a left onto Stadiong., then right onto Bartensteing. Authentic Mexican food in a decidedly Latin atmosphere. Entrées €6.20-20.40. Open M-Sa 4pm-2am, Su 4pm-midnight. AmEx/MC/V. ❸

Wrenkh, I, Bauernmarkt 10 (☎533 15 26). This predominantly vegetarian restaurant has an incredible drink selection with everything from fresh fruit juices to original, specially designed mixed drinks (€3-8). Delicious and creative cuisine is served in a relaxed, classy atmosphere. Vegetarian entrées €9.80-16.50. Lunch *Menü* also available (small €7.70, large €9.40). Open daily 11am-midnight. AmEx/MC/V. ❷

Maschu Maschu, I, Rabensteig 8 (☎533 29 04). In the Bermuda Dreiecke, right next to the Danube. This tiny eatery serves cheap, filling Middle Eastern falafel and shawarma (€3 each). Open M-W 11:30am-midnight, Th-Sa 11:30am-3am. ❶

Yugetsu, I, Führichg. 10 (☎512 27 20). A 2min. walk from Kärntnerstr., this restaurant serves sushi galore. While the prices are high for entrées and *Menüs* (€11.30-63), individual sushi rolls run €1.95-18.90. Serves Teppan-Yaki upstairs (starting at €28.70 à la carte). Open daily noon-3pm and 6pm-midnight. AmEx/V/MC. ❹

OUTSIDE THE RING

▨ **Centimeter,** IX, Liechtensteinstr. 42 (☎319 84 04; www.centimeter.at). Take tram D to "Bauernfeldpl." This chain offers cold (€0.10 per cm) and warm sandwiches (€0.15 per cm) by the centimeter in addition to huge portions of greasy Austrian fare (€4.60-11) and some vegetarian options. Beer is available by the *Seiderl* (0.3L; €2.20), *Krügerl* (0.5L; €3), *Maß* (1L; €6), or *Meter* (2.67L; €18). Other **branches** at VIII, Lenaug. 11 (☎405 78 08); VII, Stiftg. 4 (☎524 33 29); VII, Zieglerg. 42 (☎526 41 11); and IV, Schleifmühlg. 7 (☎941 43 35). Open M-Th 10am-1am, F 10am-2am, Sa 11am-2am, Su 11am-midnight. AmEx/MC/V. ❷

▨ **OH Pot, OH Pot,** IX, Währingerstr. 22 (☎319 42 59; www.ohpot.at). Take U2 (purple) to "Schottentor." This joint serves amazing fusion fare that draws on cuisines from Chilean to Ethiopian. Try their filling "pots", stew-like concoctions that come in veggie and meat varieties (€8.20). Open M-F 11am-midnight, Sa-Su 6pm-midnight. AmEx/MC/V. ❷

▨ **Sato Café-Restaurant,** XV, Mariahilferstr. 151 (☎897 54 97). Take U3 (orange) or U6 (brown) to "Westbahnhof." Conveniently located near the Ruthensteiner and Wombats hostels, this family-run restaurant offers excellent Turkish fare, including vegetarian dishes. Entrées (€5-9). Delicious breakfast omelettes €3-4. Lunch sandwiches €2-3. English menu and take-out available. Open daily 8am-midnight. ❶

Amerlingbeisl, VII, Stiftg. 8 (☎526 16 60). Take U3 (orange) to "Neubaug." and take the "Stiftg." exit. The grapevine-covered courtyard resembles a *Heuriger*. Its laid-back atmosphere attracts a young crowd. Occasional live music. Entrées average €5-9. Late breakfast (until 3pm) €4-9.50. Open daily 9am-2am (hot food served until 1am). V. ❷

Fischerbräu, XIX, Billrothstr. 17 (☎369 59 41). Take U6 (brown) to "Nußdorfer Str.," follow the exit sign to Währinger Gürtel. Continue until Döblinger Hauptpl., turn left, and left again onto Billrothstr. At Fischerbräu, young and middle-aged locals enjoy home-brewed beer (0.3L €2.30, 0.5L €3) and various breads (€3.40-4.80), among other Austrian dishes, in a large, tree-covered courtyard. Live Jazz music Sept.-May Su 11am-3pm. Open July-Aug. daily 4pm-1am; Sept.-June M-Sa 4pm-1am, Su 11am-1am. ❷

Vegetasia, III, Ungarg. 57 (☎713 83 32; www.vegetasia.at). Take the O tram to "Neulingg." Recently renovated, this Taiwanese restaurant offers an elegant setting in which to enjoy vegetarian specialties, including tofu, *seitan*, and plenty of other soy delights.

Lunch buffet M-Sa €6.80. Open M and W-Su 11:30am-3pm and 5:30-11pm. Another **branch** at VII, Kaiserstr. 45 (☎523 10 91). Open Tu-Su 11:30am-3pm and 5:30-11pm. Branch in III closed Tu evenings, branch in VII closed M evenings. AmEx/MC/V. ❷

Servieten Stüberl, IX. Servieteng. 7 (☎317 53 36; www.servietenstueberl.at). Take U4 to Rossauer Lände, walk down Grünentorg. and make right onto Servieteng. With a courtyard overlooking the Servientenkirche, this family-run restaurant serves its own wine and Austrian entrées (€7-14). Open M-F 10am-midnight. MC/V.

Café Nil, VII, Siebensterng. 39 (☎526 61 65). Take tram #49 from the Volksgarten to Siebensterng. This low-key Middle Eastern café serves pork-free dishes and some vegetarian dishes (€5-11). Breakfast until 3pm. Open daily 10am-midnight. ❷

Blue Box, VII, Richterg. 8 (☎523 26 82; www.bluebox.at). Take U3 (orange) to "Neubaug.," turn onto Neubaug., and take your first left onto Richterg. At Blue Box restaurant meets club. During the day, Blue Box serves original Viennese, French, or vegetarian cuisine (entrées €4.70-7.90) and late breakfast (until 5pm). At night, this hip hangout draws a 20- to 40-year-old crowd, and features an orange-filtered chandelier, black leather couches, and a distinct lack of light, while DJs spin the latest trance and trip-hop. Open M 6pm-2am, Tu-Th 10am-2am, F-Sa 10am-4am, Su 10am-2am. V. ❷

University Mensa, IX, Universitätsstr. 7 (☎42 77 29, ext. 841; www.mensa.at), on the 7th fl. of the university building, between U2 (purple) stops "Rathaus" and "Schottentor." Typical cafeteria meals €4. Mensa open Sept.-June M-F 11am-2pm. Adjoining snack bar open July-Aug. 8am-3pm; Sept.-June 8am-6pm. ❸

Café Willendorf, VI, Linke Wienzeile 102 (☎587 17 89). Take U4 (green) to "Pilgramg." and enter the big pink building, which also houses the Rosa Lila Villa, the mecca of Vienna's queer scene. This artsy café, bar, and restaurant with a vine-covered outdoor terrace serves creative vegetarian fare (€7-10). Meat dishes €9-13. Relaxed atmosphere, largely gay and lesbian crowd. Meals until midnight. Open daily 6pm-2am. ❸

Zum Mogulhof, VII, Burgg. 12 (☎526 28 64). Delicious Indian food served by candlelight—indulgence that won't strain your wallet. Vegetarian and meat dishes €8-12. Open daily 11:30am-2:30pm and 6-11:30pm. AmEx/MC/V. ❸

Konoba, VIII, Lerchenfelder Str., 66-88 (☎929 41 11; www.konoba.at). From Dr.-Karl-Renner Ring take tram #46 to Strozzig. Continue walking for a few blocks. This seafood eatery serves a succulent variety of fresh fish and vegetables. Entrées €6-18. Open Su-F 11am-2pm and 6pm-midnight, Sa 6pm-midnight. MC/V. ❸

China Sichuan, XXII, Arbeiterstrandbadstr. 122 (☎263 37 13; www.sichuan.at). Take the U1 (red) to "Alte Donau." Restaurant is a 10min. walk from the station. Serving delicious Chinese dishes in an authentic Oriental ambiance (every stone was actually moved from China), this is the perfect destination after a day swimming and sunning on the Danube. Lunch *Menü* €7-9. Dim sum €3-4. Entrées €9-24. Plenty of vegetarian options. Open M-F 11:30am-2:30pm and 5:30-11pm, Sa-Su from 11:30am-11pm. AmEx/MC/V. ❸

█ CAFÉS

"Who's going to start a revolution? Herr Trotsky from Café Central?"
—Austrian general quoted on the eve of the Russian Revolution

In Vienna, the coffeehouse is not simply the place to resolve your midday caffeine deficit. For years these establishments were havens for artists, writers, and thinkers, who flocked to the brooding interiors to exchange ideas and jabs at each other's work. Surrounded by dark wood and dusty velvet, they drank coffee and stayed late into the night composing operettas, writing books, and shaping modern thought. The bourgeoisie followed suit, and the coffeehouse became the city's living room, giving rise to a grand culture. Peter Altenberg, "the café writer," scribbled lines, while exiles Lenin and Trotsky played chess. Theodor Herzl made plans for a Zionist Israel, and Kafka came to visit the Herrenhof.

The original literary café was **Café Griensteidl**, but after it was demolished in 1897 the torch passed to **Café Central** and then to **Café Herrenhof**. Cafés still exist under all these names, but only Café Central looks as it did in imperial times; today, however, it is mainly frequented by tourists.

The quintessential Viennese coffee is the *Mélange*, and you can order every kind of coffee as a *Kleiner* (small) or *Grosser* (large), *Brauner* (brown, with a little milk) or *Schwarzer* (black). Whipped cream is *Schlagobers*; if you don't like it, say *"ohne Schlag, bitte."* Choosing your coffee in Vienna requires careful study (see **"One More Cup Of Coffee..."** below). Decadent pastries complete the picture: *Apfelstrudl*, cheesecakes, tortes, *Buchteln* (warm cake with jam in the middle), *Palatschinken*, *Krapfen*, and *Mohr im Hemd*, and of course the famous *Sachertorte* have all helped place Vienna on the culinary map. The *Konditoreien*, no less traditional, focus their attention on delectables rather than coffee. To see a menu, ask for a *Speisekarte*.

> **🔲 TIP**
>
> **ONE MORE CUP OF COFFEE...** Here is a quick reference guide to some of the most tempting Viennese coffees:
>
> *Mélange:* espresso-like coffee with hot milk, and whipped cream or cinnamon
> *Mokka:* strong black coffee, much like espresso
> *Kapuziner: Mokka* with cream, sprinkled with cocoa, chocolate, or cinnamon
> *Verlängerte:* weak coffee with cream
> *Fiaker:* black coffee with rum
> *Pharisär:* black coffee with rum, sugar, and whipped cream
> *Wiener Eiskaffee:* chilled black coffee and vanilla ice cream, with whipped cream
> *Maria Theresia:* black coffee with orange liqueur and whipped cream

INSIDE THE RING

Kleines Café, I, Franziskanerpl. 3. Turn off Kärntnerstr. onto Weihburg. The café is located in the courtyard of the Franziskanerkirche, featuring green paneling, a low, vaulted ceiling, nightclub posters, and a few tables in the courtyard. The sandwiches (€2.80-4) are the café's specialty, but there are also excellent salads in the summer (around €6.50). *Mélange* €2.70. Open daily 10am-2am.

Café Central, I (☎533 37 63 24), inside Palais Ferstel at the corner of Herreng. and Strauchg. Take U3 to Herreng. and walk up a few blocks. Café Central has surrendered to tourists because of its fame, but this mecca of the café world, with its arched ceilings and wall frescoes, is definitely worth a visit. Piano music M-F 3:30-6:30pm. Live music daily 6:30-9:30pm. Open M-Sa 8am-10pm, Su 10am-6pm. AmEx/MC/V.

Café Hawelka, I, Dorotheerg. 6 (☎512 82 30), off Graben, 3 blocks down from the Stephansdom. Dusty wallpaper, dark wood, and old red-striped velvet sofas make the café both down-to-earth and glorious. The Hawelkas put this legendary café on the map in 1939. Today, at 91 years and 93 years respectively, Josephine and Leopold still work in the café alongside their son and now also their grandson. *Buchteln* (a Bohemian doughnut, fresh from the oven at 10pm) €1.20. *Mélange* €2.80. Open M and W-Sa 8am-2am, Su and holidays 4pm-2am.

Café MAK, I, Stubenring 3-5 (☎714 01 21), inside the Museum für Angewandte Kunst. Take tram #1 or 2 to "Stubenring." This modern café, outfitted with funky *Bauhaus* furniture, offers a diverse menu ranging from Italian to Mexican. Dine outside in a beautiful courtyard. Students crowd the café after 10pm. Hot food €8-15. Open Tu-Su 10am-midnight.

Demel, I, Kohlmarkt 14 (☎535 17 17 0; www.demel.at), 5min. from the Stephansdom. Walk down Graben and make a left onto Kohlmarkt. The most lavish Viennese *Konditorei*, Demel was confectioner to the imperial court until the Empire dissolved. All of the chocolate is made fresh every morning. A fantasy of mirrored rooms, cream walls, and legendary desserts. *Mélange* €3.80. Wheelchair accessible. Open daily 10am-7pm. AmEx/MC/V.

VIENNA

Café Griensteidl, I, Michaelerpl. 2 (☎535 26 92). Down the street from Café Central toward the Hofburg, right in the heart of downtown. As Vienna's first literary café, Griensteidl was a meeting place for many Austrian writers, philosophers, and artists; today, it provides a relaxed café atmosphere for locals and tourists alike. Sample a wide array of ice cream, such as Griensteidl *Eiszauber* (vanilla ice cream with walnuts, apricots, chocolate, and gingerbread spices; €5.50), while scanning the selection of international newspapers. Open daily 8am-11:30pm. AmEx/MC/V.

Café Imperial, I, Kärntner Ring 16 (☎501 10 313; fax 50 11 03 55). From the Opera, turn left onto the Ring and walk 5min. This elegant café is well decorated, with chandeliers and a lovely courtyard. Serves its own insignia-stamped, marzipan-filled *Imperial Torte* (€4). The *Imperial Torte* was originally made only for the Kaiser, but is now available to everyone. Wheelchair accessible. Open daily 7am-11pm. AmEx/MC/V.

Café Sacher, I, Philharmonikerstr. 4 (☎514 560; www.sacher.com), behind the opera house. This historic establishment has served world-famous *Sacher Torte* (€4.50) in stunning red style for years. While it remains elegant, casual clothing is fine. Wheelchair accessible. Café open 8am-11:30pm. Bakery open 9am-11:30pm. Next to the café is the **Sacher Eck,** a wine bar that also serves Sacher desserts. The gift shop at the Sacher Eck sells whole *Sacher Torten* (€9.20-34, depending on size). AmEx/MC/V. (Also see **Sights: Hotel Sacher,** p. 113.)

Café Bräunerhof, I, Stallburgg. 2 (☎512 38 93). Walk down Bräunerstr., make a left onto Stallburgg. Located in a small alley near the Hofburg. Great selection of newspapers, including English and French papers. You can order *Gulasch* and *Käse und Schinken* (cheese and cold cuts). *Mélange* €2.90. Open M-F 8am-8:30pm, Sa 8am-6:30pm, Su 10am-6:30pm. V.

Café Museum, I, Operng. 7 (☎586 52 02; www.cafe-museum.at), near the Opera. Head away from the *Innenstadt* to the corner of Operng. and Friedrichstr. Built in 1899 by Adolf Loos, in a plain, spacious style with striking curves, this café attracts a mixed bag of artists, lawyers, students, and chess players. Typical Austrian coffees €2.10-5.40. Also carries tea specials. Open daily 8am-midnight.

OUTSIDE THE RING

Café Sperl, VI, Gumpendorferstr. 11 (☎586 41 58). Take U2 (purple) to "Museumsquartier," exit to Mariahilferstr., walk 1 block on Getreidemarkt, and turn right onto Gumpendorferstr. Built in 1880, Sperl is one of Vienna's oldest and most elegant cafés. Renovations have removed a few of the original trappings, but the fin de siècle atmosphere remains, complimented by modern billiards tables. Coffee €2-4.50. Cake €1.67-2.54. Live piano music Sept.-June Su 3-6:30pm. Open M-Sa 7am-11pm, Su 3-8pm. July-Aug. closed Su. AmEx/MC/V.

Café Savoy, VI, Linke Wienzeile 36 (☎586 73 48), is a gorgeous café with dark wood and decaying gold trim. A large gay and lesbian crowd makes this a lively nightspot on weekends. *Mélange* €2.50. Open M-F 5pm-2am, Sa 9am-2am, holidays 8pm-2am.

Café Stein, IX, Währingerstr. 6 (☎31 97 24 1; www.cafe-stein.com). Take U2 to Schottentor. Chrome seats outside (allowing you to see and be seen) and clustered tables in the smoky red-brown and metallic interior. Intimate, lively, and hip, at night it transforms into **Stein's Diner** (open M-Sa 7pm-1am). Occasionally hosts special events such as poetry slams. **Internet** access €3.50 per 30min. 5-11pm. Breakfast until 8pm. Open M-Sa 7am-1am, Su 9am-1am.

Kunsthaus Wien Café, III, Untere Weißgerberstr. 13 (☎712 04 97). Take tram N from Schwedenpl. to Radetzkypl. In a verdant courtyard of Hundertwasser's Kunsthaus museum (p. 117), this café with a typical Hundertwasser wavy floor serves local and vegetarian fare (€3.40-13.80). *Mélange* €2.60. Open daily 10am-11pm. MC.

Berg das Café, IX, Bergg. 8 (☎319 57 20). Take U2 (purple) to "Schottentor" and take a right off Währingerstr. onto Bergg. Austria's first gay and lesbian daytime café. Today, this hip and modern hangout is frequented by a mixed crowd. Always crowded, Berg offers wonderful food, desserts, and music in a relaxed atmosphere. *Mélange* €2.50.

Lunch menu €7. Open daily 10am-1am. MC/V. Berg has merged with nearby gay/lesbian bookstore **Das Löwenherz** (☎317 29 82), which carries plenty of English titles. Open M-Th 10am-7pm, F 10am-8pm, Sa 10am-6pm. MC/V.

Café Rüdigerhof, V, Hamburgerstr. 20 (☎586 31 38). Take U4 to "Kettenbrückeng."; Hamburgerstr. branches off from Rechte Wienzeile. In a 1902 building designed by Oskar Mamorek, a student of Otto Wagner, this *Jugendstil* café is adorned with floral patterns and leather couches (a gift from King Hussein to the owner) and has a large, leaf-covered garden overlooking the Wien River. Traditional Austrian dishes €5.10-7.10. *Mélange* €2.30. Open daily 10am-2am. AmEx/MC/V.

▨ HEURIGEN (WINE TAVERNS)

The *Heurigen*, marked by a hanging branch of evergreen at the door, are the best places to learn about Austrian *Gemütlichkeit* while enjoying home-grown wine and savoring Austrian buffet-style delicacies. The wine, also called *Heuriger*, is from the most recent harvest and at a real *Heuriger* must be typically grown and pressed by the owner. Good *Heuriger* wine is generally white, fruity, and full of body. *Grüner Veltliner* is a good representative of the variety; avoid reds. *Heuriger* is ordered by the *Achtel* or the *Viertel* (eighth- or quarter- liter, respectively; about €2 per *Viertel*). *G'spritzer* (wine and soda water, served separately, then mixed) is a popular way of enjoying *Heuriger*. Half of the pleasure of visiting a *Heuriger*, however, comes from the atmosphere. Worn picnic benches and old shade trees provide an ideal spot in which to converse or listen to *Schrammelmusik* (sentimental folk songs played by elderly musicians who inhabit *Heurigen*). A *Heuriger* generally serves simple buffets (grilled chicken and pork, cabbage or corn, and pickles) that make for inexpensive meals. Order your food inside and sit down outside; a waitress will come around to serve the wine. Those looking for some traditional fare should order *Bratenfett*, gravy from a *Schweinsbraten* (pig), or *Liptauer*, a bread spread made from farmer's cheese, paprika, and herbs, and served on *Schwarzbrot* (black bread).

Open during summer, *Heurigen* cluster together in the northern, western, and southern Viennese suburbs, where the grapes grow. The most famous region, **Grinzing**, in District XIX, produces a uniquely strong wine. Unfortunately, those in Grinzing (incidentally Beethoven's favorite neighborhood) are well known to tour bus operators. You'll find better atmosphere and prices among the hills of **Sievering, Neustift am Walde** (both in District XIX), and **Neuwaldegg** (XVII). Authentic, charming, and jolly *Heurigen* abound on Hochstr. in **Perchtoldsdorf**, just southwest of the city. To reach Perchtoldsdorf, take U4 (green) to "Hietzing" and tram #6 to "Rodaun." Walk down Ketzerg. until Hochstr. and continue for a few minutes to reach the *Heurigen* area. True *Heuriger* devotees should make the trip to **Gumpoldskirchen**, a celebrated vineyard village that hosts an annual wine festival during the end of June or the beginning of July. Gumpoldskirchen can be reached by S1 (dir: Wiener Neustadt) from Wien Meidling or from the Südbahnhof. Most vineyard taverns are open daily from 4pm to midnight, making them a particularly good option for a Sunday afternoon when everything else is closed.

▨ **Buschenschank Heinrich Niersche**, XIX, Strehlg. 21 (☎440 21 46). Take U6 (brown) to "Währingerstr./Volksoper" then tram #41 to "Pötzleing." and connect to bus #41A until "Pötzleindorfer Friedhof." Take 1st right onto Strehlg. On the left side of the street, hidden from tourists in the backyard of a house, this beautiful garden overlooks the fields of Grinzing. The friendly owners serve excellent wines. 0.25L *Weißer G'spritzer* (white wine spritzer) €1.60. 0.25L white wine €2.20. 0.25L red wine €2.40. Open M and Th-Su 3pm-midnight.

▨ **Zum Krottenbach'l**, XIX, Krottenbachstr. 148 (☎440 12 40). Take U6 (brown) to "Nußdorferstr." then bus #35A (dir: Salmannsdorf) for approximately 15min. to "Kleingartenverein/Hackenberg." Stretching across a sequence of terraced gardens, this *Heuriger* offers a comfortable spot for savoring the fruit of the vine in a very traditional atmosphere in which everything (including the light fixtures) is made of gnarled wood. Larger but more touristy and family-oriented than Buschenschank Niersche. 0.25L of wine about €2. Open daily winter 3pm-midnight; summer 4:30pm-midnight.

Weingut Heuriger Reinprecht, XIX, Cobenzlg. 22 (☎32 01 47 10; www.weingut-reinprecht.at). Take U4 (green) to "Heiligenstadt," then bus #38A to "Grinzing." Walk up Sandg. and keep right onto Cobenzlg. when road splits. Once a convent, this place now fits the *Heuriger* stereotype on a larger scale, with endless picnic tables under an ivy-laden trellis, and *Schrammel* musicians strolling from table to table. 0.25L white wine €2.30. Open Mar.-Nov. daily 3:30pm-midnight. MC/V.

Franz Mayer am Pfarrplatz Beethovenhaus, XIX, Pfarrpl. 2 (☎370 12 87; www.mayer.pfarrplatz.at). Take U4 (green) to "Heiligenstadt," then bus #38A to "Fernsprechamt/Heiligenstadt." Walk uphill and head right onto Nestelbachg. Beethoven used to stay here back when it offered guest quarters. Traditional *Heuriger* food in grapevine-covered courtyard. Pricey food (€12.40 per person for a mixed plate), but excellent wines at a reasonable price (0.25L €2.30). Wheelchair accessible. Live music 7pm-midnight. Open M-F 4pm-midnight, Su and holidays 11am-midnight. MC/V.

Zum Figlmüller, I, Wollzeile 5 (☎512 61 77; www.figlmueller.at). From Stephanspl. walk up Schönlaterng. to Wollzeile. This Weinstube serves an excellent, large *Schnitzel* that drips over the edges of the plate (€11.50). Open daily 11am-10:30am. Another **branch:** I, Bäckerstr. 6. Open daily noon-midnight. AmEx/MC/V.

Schweizerhaus, Prater 116 (☎728 01 52 13; www.schweizerhaus.at). This beer garden directly in the Prater serves traditional Austrian specialities, but is most famous for its *Stelze* (leg of pork; €14 per kg). 0.5L draught beer €3.20. Open when Prater is daily 11am-11pm.

◎ SIGHTS

Vienna's streets are by turns stately, residential, and decaying. Expect contrasts around every corner: the expanse of the Ringstraße and the narrow confines of a cobblestone courtyard, the curling flourishes of a Baroque palace and the spare lines of Socialist public housing. Grab the brochure *Vienna from A to Z* (discount €3.60, with Vienna Card) at the tourist office. Don't miss the **Hofburg, Schloß Schönbrunn, Schloß Belvedere,** or any of the buildings along the **Ringstraße.** Those ensnared by the flowing tendrils of *Jugendstil* architecture can find many examples of it in Vienna. Ask the tourist office for the *Architecture in Vienna* pamphlet, which contains photos and addresses of *Jugendstil* treasures all over town.

The range of available **tours** is overwhelming—walking tours, ship tours, bike tours, tram tours, jogging tours, and more. There are 50 themed walking tours alone, (some, however, given only in German) detailed in the brochure *Walks in Vienna* (☎774 89 01; www.wienguide.at; free at the tourist office). Tours cost €11, but some require additional admission fees to sites. Topics range from "Unknown Underground Vienna," which explores crypts, excavation, and medieval cellars, to "Hollywood Goes Vienna—Vienna Goes Hollywood." Tours on fin de siècle "old-timer" **trams** run May to October. (☎7909 100. 1hr. Departs from Karlspl. near the Otto Wagner Pavilion Sa 11:30am and 1:30pm, Su and holidays 9:30, 11:30am, 1:30pm. €15.) The drivers of legendary **Fiaker** (horse-drawn carriages; www.fiaker.at) are happy to taxi you wherever your heart desires, but be sure to agree on the price before you set out (usually €30-40 per 20min.). There are official *Fiaker* stands in Stephanspl., Albertinapl., Heldenpl., and at the corner of Graben and Kohlmarkt. **Pedal Power,** II, Ausstellungsstr. 3, rents bikes and conducts guided tours (☎729 72 34; www.pedalpower.at). For more information on sports in Vienna pick up the "Sports & Nature in Vienna" brochure, free at the tourist office. **Bus tours** are given by **Vienna Sightseeing Tours,** IV, Graf Starhemberg G. 25 (☎712 46 83 0; www.viennasightseeing.at) and **Cityrama,** I, Börgeg. 1 (☎534 13 0). Tours start at €30. For a do-it-yourself tour, take tram #1 or 2 around the Ring.

INSIDE THE RING

District I, the *Innenstadt* or *innere Stadt* (Inner city), is Vienna's epicenter, enclosed on three sides by the sweeping arc of the Ringstraße and on the northern side by the **Danube Canal.** With its Romanesque arches, Gothic portals, *Jugenstil* apartments, and modern Haas Haus, the *Innenstadt* is a perfect for sightseeing.

STEPHANSPLATZ

Take U1 (red) or U3 (orange) to "Stephansplatz."

As the heart of Vienna, Stephansplatz teems with activity in the shadow of the massive **Stephansdom.** Shops and cafés abound, providing ample opportunity for people-watching: suited professionals, political demonstrators, and camera-toting tourists all converge on the square, while students in period costumes sell tickets to Strauss or Mozart concerts.

STEPHANSDOM. Affectionately known as *"Der Steffl,"* Stephansdom (St. Stephen's Cathedral) is Vienna's most sacred landmark, with its Gothic sculptural program and 450-ft. **South Tower.** The **North Tower** was never completed; the architect met an unfortunate demise. *(Open M-Sa 6am-10pm, Su 7am-10pm. Free. English mass Sa 7pm.)* Take the elevator up the North Tower to see the *Pummerin*, the Steffl's famous bell. *(Open Jul.-Aug. 9am-6:30pm; Apr.-June and Nov.-Oct. 9am-6pm; Nov.-Mar. 8:30am-5pm. Elevator ride €4.)* Or climb the 343 steps of the South Tower for a 360° view of Vienna and close encounters with gargoyles. *(Open 9am-5:30pm. €3.)*

Notable exhibits inside the cathedral include the early 14th-century Albertine choir and the Gothic organ loft by **Anton Pilgram,** so delicate in its construction that Pilgram's contemporaries warned him it would never bear the organ's weight. Pilgram replied that he would hold it up himself and carved a self-portrait at the bottom, bearing the entire burden on his back. The **high altarpiece** of the *Stoning of St. Stephen* is just as stunning. *(Cathedral tours M-Sa 10:30am and 3pm, Su and holidays 3pm; in English Apr.-Oct. daily 3:45pm. €4. Fantastic 90min. evening tour June-Sept. Sa 7pm; €10. Meet at the entrance to the south tower.)*

Downstairs, skeletons of thousands of plague victims fill the **catacombs.** The **Gruft** (vault) stores all of the Hapsburg "innards." *(Tours M-Sa 10-11:30am and 1:30-4:30pm every 30min., Su and holidays 1:30-4:30pm every 30min. €4.)* Everyone wanted a piece of the rulers—the Stephansdom got the entrails, the Augustinerkirche got the hearts, and the Kapuzinergruft (on Neuer Markt) got the remainder. In the North Tower hangs *the Pummerin*, the **bell** of the Stephansdom, and the world's heaviest free-ringing bell (the whole bell moves, not just the clapper). The original bell, cast in 1711 from the metal of captured Turkish cannons, was smashed during WWII, to the dismay of the Viennese. A series of photographs inside chronicles the process of reconstruction. The new bell has rung in every New Year since 1957.

HAAS HAUS. This controversial modern building, opposite the cathedral at Stephanspl. 12, reflects the Stephansdom in its postmodern glass and marble façade. The view is even better from inside the Haus, which houses the restaurant DO&CO on the top floor. Primarily a shopping center, the Haus opened in 1990 amid rumors of bureaucratic bribery and is considered to be something of an eyesore by most Viennese.

NEAR PETERSPLATZ

From Stephanspl., walk down Graben from Stephansdom; Peterspl. is on the right.

GRABEN. Now closed to all traffic except feet and hooves, this boulevard was once a moat surrounding the Roman camp that became Vienna. The landscape of Graben today shows the debris of Baroque, *Biedermeier*, and *Jugendstil* efforts, which include **Ankerhaus** (#10) and the red-marble **Grabenhof** by Otto Wagner. One of the most

JUGENDSTIL SITES IN VIENNA

Around 1900, Vienna was home to a prominent *Jugendstil* movement, led by Otto Wagner. *Jugendstil* architecture attempts to merge art with function in everyday life and often incorporates flowing lines and designs from nature.

1. Karlsplatz Stadtbahn Pavillion (p. 116), in Karlspl. This tram station was designed by Otto Wagner in 1899.

2. Majolicahaus (p. 116). A spiral staircase sets apart this apartment building, (Linke Wienzeile 40), a joint project by Wagner and his student Joseph Maria Olbrich.

3. Jugendstil toilets (p. 110) An underground public toilet complex on the Graben conceived by Adolf Loos.

4. Dr.-Karl-Lueger Gedächniskirche (p. 117), Max Hegele's creation, this church stands in the approximate center of the Zentralfriedhof.

5. Postsparkasse (p. 115). Designed by Wagner, this post office/savings bank sits by the *Schubertring*.

6. Stadtbahn-Hofpavillon (p. 130). Another Wagner design, the pavilion is located on Schönbrun-

interesting sights is the underground *Jugendstil* public toilet complex, designed by Adolf Loos. The **Pestsaüle** (Plague Column) in the square was built in 1693 by Leopold I, to celebrate the passing of the Black Death.

PETERSKIRCHE. Construction on the church began in the 12th century, but the vast majority of Peterskirche was completed in 1733. A classic Baroque interior, stunning frescoes (especially in the dome), and religious martyrs encased in glass make this a sight worth seeing. The church still holds Latin masses on Sundays at 11:15am. *(Open daily 7am-6pm. Free.)*

KOHLMARKT. Once a wood and charcoal market, this second leg of the *Fußgängerzone* starts at the end of Graben, just past Peterskirche. It's lined with upscale shops marked "K.U.K." *(Kaiserlich und Königlich)*, indicating that they once earned the Hapsburg seal of approval.

HOHER MARKT, RUPRECHTSPLATZ, MORINPLATZ

From Stephanspl., walk down Rotenturmstr. and turn left onto Lichtensteg, which runs into Hoher Markt. Judeng. runs from Hoher Markt to Ruprechtspl. and Morzinpl.

These three squares lie just north of Peterspl. Hoher Markt is the oldest square in town, mainly offering historical attractions, while Ruprechtspl. is home to Vienna's oldest church as well as a slew of cafés and bars in Vienna's hottest nightlife district, known as the **Bermuda Dreiecke** (see **Nightlife,** p. 132). Morzinpl. is a rather run-down plot of land along the Danube with a dark past.

HOHER MARKT. Both a market and execution site during medieval times, Hoher Markt was the center of the Roman encampment Vindobona. Roman ruins lie beneath the shopping arcade directly across from the fountain. *(Open Tu-Su 9am-12:15pm and 1-4:30pm. €2, students €1.)* Fischer von Erlach's *Vermählungsbrunnen* (Marriage Fountain), depicting the union of Mary and Joseph, is the square's focal point. But the biggest draw is the corporate-sponsored *Jugendstil Ankeruhr* (clock). Built in 1914 by Franz Matsch, the bronze and copper timepiece has 12 3m-tall historical figures, ranging from Emperor Marcus Aurelius to Joseph Haydn. One of the statues rotates past the Viennese coat of arms each hour, accompanied by music from its era. At noon, all the figures appear. Under the walkway with the *Ankeruhr* is a sculptural relief depicting the signs of the Zodiac.

RUPRECHTSKIRCHE. Overlooking the Danube on Ruprechtspl., the Romanesque 11th-century Ruprechtskirche is the oldest church in Vienna, built on the site of a Carolingian church from AD 740. Maria Theresia donated the well-clad skeleton of an early Christian martyr, which still lives in a glass case in the corner. *(Open M-W and F 10am-noon, Th 3-5pm.)*

STADTTEMPEL. Hidden away in Ruprechtspl. at Seitenstetteng. 2-4, the Stadttempel (City Temple) was built in 1826 following an imperial regulation that Jewish and Protestant places of worship could not have conspicuous street fronts. A sign of intolerance at the time, the regulation saved the synagogue from greater persecution. Of Vienna's 94 synagogues, only the Stadttempel escaped Nazi destruction during *Kristallnacht* in November 1938. It was spared because it stood on a residential block, concealed from the street. The torching of neighboring buildings damaged the synagogue, but it has been restored in Neoclassical style. Today, an armed guard patrols the synagogue as a precaution against repeats of a 1983 terrorist attack. *(Bring your passport. Open M-Th 10am-4pm. €2, students €1.)*

MORZINPLATZ. This largely residential area once held the Hotel Metropole, headquarters of the Gestapo, where numerous Viennese were tortured for speaking out against the *Anschluß*. The hotel was demolished in 1945; **The Monument to the Victims of Fascism** now stands in its place. Although the history of this monument is significant, travelers should be wary of traveling here, especially after dark.

NEAR JUDENPLATZ

From Stephanspl., walk down Graben. When Graben ends, go right and continue in the same direction on Bognerg. Turn right onto Seitzerg. and continue in the same direction on Kurrentg. Or, from Hoher Markt, walk down Wipplingerstr. and turn left onto Jordang.

Wipplingerstr., which runs east-west along the square's north side, offers a number of architectural sights. The peaceful calm of the square creates an atmosphere conducive to appreciation of its sobering history.

JUDENPLATZ. Once the Jewish ghetto of Vienna, this square's focus is Rachel Whiteread's **Memorial to the Victims of the Holocaust.** Over 65,000 Austrian Jews were killed between 1938 and 1945. The memorial, a giant inverted library made of concrete, was unveiled in October 2000. Also in the square is a statue of Jewish playwright Gotthold Ephraim Lessing (1729-81). Originally erected in 1935, the statue was torn down by the Nazis; a new model was returned to the spot in 1982. The **Museum Judenplatz,** directly behind the memorial, documents the remarkable and tragic history of European Jews, with an emphasis on WWII. It also displays excavations of a synagogue built in

ner Schloßstr. next to the Schönbrunner Schloßpark near today's Hietzing U-Bahn stop.

7. Secession Building (p. 126). Nicknamed "The Golden Cabbage" because of its unusually shaped dome, this museum was designed by Joseph Maria Olbrich.

8. Looshaus (p. 113). The Kaiser detested this house, designed by Adolf Loos, so much that he referred to it as "the house without eyebrows."

9. Kirche am Steinhof (p. 117). Another of Wagner's masterworks, this church belongs to a state mental hospital.

10. Ankeruhr am Hohen Markt. (p. 110). Each hour, larger-than-life-sized historical figures emerge to ring in the time on this whimsical clock, a 1914 design by Franz Matsch.

1294, which was burned down in the Jewish purge of 1421. (☎535 04 31; www.jmw.at. *Wheelchair accessible. Open M-Th and Su 10am-6pm, F 10am-2pm. €3, students €1.50.)* House #2, **Zum Grossen Jordan,** bears a 16th-century relief and inscription, which at the time was meant to celebrate the medieval diaspora of Vienna's Jews.

MARIA AM GESTADE. This narrow, long church's cramped position on the very edge of the old medieval town caused the nave to curve toward the south. The steep steps from the west door leading to **Tiefergraben,** a former tributary of the Danube, explain the phrase *am Gestade* ("by the riverbank"). Maria is worthy of a complete visit, so make an appointment ahead of time in order to walk around the canopied Gothic choir of the church. *(Salvatorg. 12. Walk down Schwertg., right off Wipplingerstr., passing Judenpl. on the left. ☎533 95 94. Open daily 7am-6pm. Free.)*

ALTES RATHAUS. The *Altes Rathaus* (Old Town Hall), Wipplingerstr. 8, was occupied from 1316 to 1885, when the government moved to the Ringstr after the city was expanded beyond the ring. The building is graced by a Donner fountain depicting the myth of Andromeda and Perseus. The *Altes Rathaus* is also home to the tiny **Austrian Resistance Museum,** chronicling anti-Nazi activity during WWII, and temporary exhibits. *(☎534 36 90 319; www.doew.at. Displays in German. Open M and W-Th 9am-5pm. Archive/library open M-Th 9am-5pm. Tours by appointment. Free.)*

AM HOF, FREYUNG, MINORITENPLATZ

From Stephanspl., walk down Graben. When Graben ends, turn right onto Bognerg. Am Hof will be on the right, Freyung straight ahead, and Minoritenpl. to the left (take Strauchg. off Freyung). Or, from Judenpl., take Drahtg., which runs into Am Hof.

AM HOF. *Am Hof* literally means "at the court," referencing the Babenberg residence that once existed here. It later became a medieval jousting square and now houses the **Kirche am Hof** (Church of the Nine Choirs of Angels; built 1386-1403 in Gothic style; Baroque renovations in 17th century) and the black **Mariensäule** (Column to Mary). The latter was erected by Emperor Ferdinand III in gratitude to the Virgin Mary for her protection of Vienna (from the Protestant Swedes) during the Thirty Years' War. A **Roman stronghold** and the **Collalto Palace** (where Mozart first performed publicly at the age of 12) surround the square. Am Hof also hosts an eclectic weekend **market.** *(Open Sa-Su 11am-1pm. Free.)*

FREYUNG. Just west of Am Hof, Freyung's center is the **Austriabrunnen** (Austria fountain). The name *Freyung* ("sanctuary") comes from the **Schottenstift** (Monastery of the Scots) just behind the fountain, where medieval fugitives could claim asylum. Freyung was also used for public executions in the Middle Ages; now the annual **Christkindlmarkt** blots out such unpleasant memories with the charm of performances, gifts, and baked goods. *(Open daily late Nov. to Dec. 23 9am-9pm; Christmas Eve 9am-5pm. Music and choir performances daily 9:30am-7:30pm.)* Three art galleries flank Freyung: the **Schottenstift Museum,** the **Kunstforum,** and **Palais Harrach.** A glass-roofed passage (adorned with chic shops) leads to the Italianate **Palais Ferstel,** housing one of Vienna's most cherished coffeehouses, **Café Central** (p. 105).

MINORITENPLATZ. Go down Herreng. from Freyung and take a right onto Landhausg. The square contains the 14th-century **Minoritenkirche,** whose tower was destroyed during the Turkish siege of Vienna in 1529. A mosaic copy of da Vinci's *Last Supper*, commissioned by Napoleon and purchased by Franz I, adorns the north wall of the church. *(☎533 41 62. Open daily 8am-6pm. Free.)* On the south side of the square stands the **Bundeskanzleramt** (Federal Chancery), where the Congress of Vienna met in 1815, and where Chancellor Engelbert Dollfuss was assassinated by Nazis in 1934. The Bundeskanzleramt is closed to the public.

MICHAELERPLATZ

Take U3 (orange) to "Herreng." Take a left onto Herreng., which leads into Michaelerpl. Or, from Minoritenpl., go back up Landhausg. and take a right onto Herreng.

Herreng., Kohlmarkt, and Schauflerg. all intersect in this prominent square, which is dominated by the Neo-Baroque, half-moon-shaped **Michaelertor,** the spectacular main gate of the Hofburg (p. 118). In the middle of Michaelerpl. lie remnants of the wall of the *Paradeislgarten* (Imperial Gardens) and excavated foundations of the Roman military camp **Vindobona,** where Marcus Aurelius penned his *Meditations.*

MICHAELERKIRCHE. Michaelerpl. is named after this church, which occupies the block between Kohlmarkt and Hapsburgerg. The church's Romanesque foundation dates back to the early 13th century, but construction continued until 1792: note the Baroque statues over the Neoclassical doorway. Vienna's largest Baroque organ dominates the interior, while the **crypt** has a number of open coffins containing corpses from the 17th and 18th centuries. To see some of the approximately 250 coffins in the crypt, you must take a tour. (☎0699 104 74 828. Open May-Oct. M-F 6:30am-5pm. Tours in both German and English Easter to Nov. 11am, 1, 3pm; for tours during the rest of the year check for posting on church door or call ahead. €4, children €2.50.)

LOOSHAUS. On the corner of Kohlmarkt and Herreng. stands the Looshaus (now home to the Raiffeisenbank), constructed by Adolf Loos in 1910-11. Emperor Franz Josef branded it "the house without eyebrows," because of what he perceived to be a shocking lack of the customary Viennese window pediments. Offended by the building's modernity, the emperor never again used the Michaelerpl. entrance to the Hofburg. (Open M-W and F 8am-3pm, Th 8am-5:30pm. Free.)

NEAR NEUER MARKT

Take U1 (red) or U3 (orange) to "Stephanspl." Walk down Kärntnerstr., away from the Stephansdom. Turn right on Donnerg., which leads into Neuer Markt. Or, from Albertina, walk down Tegetthoffstr., which runs into Neuer Markt.

Neuer Markt centers around George Raphael Donner's replica of the **Donnerbrunnen,** a graceful personification of the Danube, surrounded by the four gods who represent her tributaries. The streets radiating from it lead to some of the most famous sights in Vienna. Parallel to Neuer Markt and running south toward the **Staatsoper** on Ringstraße, **Kärntnerstraße** is one of Vienna's largest pedestrian zones, lined with tourist shops and outdoor cafés.

KAPUZINERKIRCHE (CHURCH OF THE CAPUCHIN FRIARS). On the southwest corner of Neuer Markt. Behind its pale orange 17th-century façade lies the **Kaisergruft** (Imperial Vault), a series of subterranean rooms filled with coffins, including remains (minus heart and entrails: see **Augustinerkirche,** p. 120, and **Stephansdom,** p. 109), of all Hapsburg rulers since 1633. Empress Maria Theresia rests next to husband Franz Stephan of Lorraine in a Rococo sepulcher surrounded by angels. (☎512 68 53. Open daily 9:30am-4pm; entrance until 3:40pm. Imperial Vault €4, students and seniors €3.)

HOTEL SACHER. At the end of Kärntnerstr., across from the rear of the Opera, stands the legendary Hotel Sacher. The hotel once served as a meeting place for the social and political elite to discuss affairs of state, while its *chambres separées* provided discreet locations for affairs of another sort. John Lennon and Yoko Ono awed the public by holding a press conference in one of the Sacher's suites while lying naked in bed—all, of course, in the name of peace. Today, most tourists come for the hotel's renowned *Sacher Torte* (€4.50).

MONUMENT GEGEN KRIEG UND FASCHISMUS. Located behind Hotel Sacher on Albertinapl. where the residential Philipphof stood before being destroyed by bombs in WWII, this "Memorial against War and Fascism" was unveiled in 1988 to commemorate the suffering caused by WWII.

THE RINGSTRAßE

Trams #1 runs along the Ringstr. clockwise, whereas tram #2 runs counterclockwise; the U-bahn's endpoints at U2 (purple) stop "Schottentor" and U3 (orange) stop "Stubentor." From Neuer Markt, take Donnerg. out of the Markt and turn right onto Kärntnerstr., which leads roughly to the middle of the Ring.

The Ringstraße defines the boundaries of the inner city and is an historical attraction itself. After the last siege by the Ottoman Turks in 1683, city fortifications were installed around the city for protection. Then in 1857, nine years after a revolution, the military demanded that District I be surrounded by new fortifications, but the emerging bourgeoisie wanted the removal of all formal barriers and open space within the city. Imperial designers reached a compromise: the walls would be razed to make way for the 57m-wide, 4km-long Ringstraße. It would be both a pleasant, tree-studded spread of boulevard and a sweeping circle of road designed for the efficient transport of troops. Urban planners from all over Europe put together a group of monuments dedicated to aspects of Western culture: religion, scholarship, commerce, politics, and art. In total, 12 giant public buildings were erected along the Ring. Counterclockwise from Schottenring, they are the **Börse**, the **Votivkirche**, the **Universität**, the **Neues Rathaus**, the **Burgtheater**, the **Parliament**, the **Kunsthistorisches Museum** and **Naturhistorisches Museum**, the **Staatsoper**, the **Museum für Angewandte Kunst**, and the **Postsparkasse**.

SCHOTTENRING. The first stretch of the Ring extending out from the Danube Canal, Schottenring leads past the Italianate Börse (stock exchange) to Schottentor, which is surrounded by university cafés, bookstores, and bars. Across Universitätsstr. rise the twin spires of the Votivkirche, a white Neo-Gothic cathedral completed in 1879. It was commissioned by Franz Josef's brother Maximilian after the Emperor survived an assassination attempt at that spot in 1853. The interior pays homage to a number of Austria's military heroes. *(Open Tu-Sa 9am-1pm and 4-6:30pm, Su 9am-1pm.)*

DR.-KARL-LÜGER RING. The next stretch of the Ring runs from the university to Rathauspl. **Universität Wien** was founded in 1365, but by the 19th century, the original building had become far too small. A massive new building was built in the Italian Renaissance style to celebrate the beginning of the "Golden Age" of science. The professors, however, had hoped for a more modern building that would suggest the continuance of their own Golden Age. Inside the university is a tranquil courtyard lined with busts of famous departed professors.

DR.-KARL-RENNER RING. Rathauspl. and Parliament mark this section of the Ring. The **Neues Rathaus** (town hall), honors the Flemish burghers who pioneered the idea of town halls and civic government in Europe. A broad walkway lined with statues partitions the *Rathaus* Park in two. Opera buffs will enjoy the free nightly **Music Film Festival** (p. 130) in July and August (film screenings at 9pm). *(Free tours M, W, F 1pm; meet at the blue Information booth outside.)* Across the street from the *Rathaus* is the **Burgtheater** (Imperial Court Theater), which has seen the premieres of some of the most famous operas and plays by Austrians, including Mozart's *La Nozze di Figaro* (The Marriage of Figaro). Inside are frescoes by Gustav Klimt, his brother, and his partner Matsch. *(☎514 44 4140. Performance season Sept.-June. If a show is not sold out, students can get tickets for €7 at the box office in the theater 30min. prior to the start of the show. Tours in English July-Aug. daily 2, 3pm; tours in German only Sept.-June daily M-Sa 3pm, Su 11am. €4.50, students €2.)* Next to Rathauspl. is the **Parliament.** Decked out with winged chariots, a grand ramp leading to its columned façade, and an imposing statue of wise Athena, the Parliament invokes the great democracies of ancient Greece. *(☎40 11 00. Tours M and W 10 and 11am, Tu and Th 2 and 3pm, F 11am, 1, 2, and 3pm, as long as Parliament is not in session. €3, students €2.)*

BURGRING. On Burgring, opposite the Hofburg on either side of Maria-Theresien-Pl., stand two of Vienna's largest and most comprehensive museums, the **Kunsthistorisches Museum** (Museum of Art History; p. 124) and the **Naturhistorisches Museum** (Museum of Natural History; p. 127). When construction was complete, the builders realized with horror that Apollo, patron deity of art, stood atop the Naturhistorisches Museum, and Athena, goddess of science, atop the Kunsthistorisches Museum. Also note the statue of Empress Maria Theresia, surrounded by key statesmen and advisers. She holds the Pragmatic Sanction, which granted women the right to succeed to the throne.

OPERNRING/KÄRNTNERRING. Opernring runs from the Burggarten (see **Gardens and Parks,** p. 121) to Schwarzenbergstr., marked by an equestrian statue, the Schwarzenberg Denkmal. The largest feature of Opernring is the **Staatsoper** (State Opera; p. 127). Built in 1869 by and for the opera-adoring public, the Staatsoper had first priority during the construction of the Ringstraße. After its destruction by Allied bombs in 1945, Vienna meticulously restored the exterior and re-opened the building in 1955. Today, the Staatsoper is still at the heart of Viennese culture. You can tour the gold, crystal, and red velvet interior, but seeing an opera can be cheaper. (☎ 514 44 26056. Tours €4.50, students €2. Call ahead for times.)

SCHUBERTRING/STUBENRING. From Schwarzenbergstr. to the Danube Canal, Schubertring borders the **Stadtpark** (see **Gardens and Parks,** p. 121). The **Postsparkasse** (Post Office Savings Bank), near the end of Stubenring, is Otto Wagner's greatest triumph of function over form and the most contemporary of the Ringstraße monuments. The building raises formerly concealed elements of construction (like the thousands of metallic bolts) to the level of modernist art. The interior, now a bank but still decorated in Art Nouveau style, is open during banking hours. (George-Coch-Pl. 2. Open M-W and F 8am-3pm, Th 8am-5:30pm.)

OUTSIDE THE RING

As the city expands beyond the Ring in all directions, the distance between notable sights also expands. But what the area outside the Ring gives up in accessibility, it makes up for in its varied attractions. Some of Vienna's most famous modern architecture is outside the Ring, where 20th-century designers found more space to build. At the same time, this modern sprawl is also home to a number of startlingly beautiful Baroque palaces and parks that were once beyond the city limits.

NEAR KARLSPLATZ

Take U1 (red), U2 (purple), or U4 (green) to "Karlspl." Or, from the Staatsoper walk 2 blocks down Kärntnerstr. away from the city center, and turn left after Rechte Wienzeile.

Once a central gathering place for the Viennese, Karlspl. is now isolated behind a major traffic artery. Nonetheless, it's home to Vienna's most impressive Baroque church, the **Karlskirche,** and is surrounded by the **Musikverein** and several major museums, including the **Secession Building,** the **Künstlerhaus,** and the **Kunsthalle.**

KARLSKIRCHE. Situated in the center of the gardens, the Karlskirche is an eclectic architectural masterpiece, combining a Neoclassical portico with a Baroque dome and towers on either side. Two massive columns, covered with spiraling reliefs depicting the life of St. Carlo Borromeo ("Karl"), frame the central portion of the church. The interior is beautiful, with colorful ceiling frescoes and a golden sunburst altar. Designed by Fischer von Ehrlach and completed by his son, Johann Michael, this imposing edifice was constructed in 1793 to fulfill the promise Emperor Charles VI made to the Viennese during a plague epidemic in 1713. (www.karls-kirche.at. Open M-Sa 9am-12:30pm and 1-6pm, Su 1-6pm. €4, students €2; price includes admission to small museum. An additional €2 to take the elevator up.)

VIENNA

RESSELPARK. The park opposite Karlskirche, named for Josef Ressel (Czech-born inventor of the propeller), is tranquil and tree-shaded. The **Historisches Museum der Stadt Wien** is to the left of the Karlskirche (see **Museums**, p. 124), while the yellow and blue **Kunsthalle** stands out at the opposite end of the park. Across the park along Karlspl., a terrace links to the *Jugendstil* **Karlsplatz Stadtbahn Pavilions,** designed in 1899 by Otto Wagner.

SECESSION BUILDING. Northwest of Resselpark, across Friedrichstr. at #12, is the Secession Building. Its white walls, subtle decoration, and gilded dome (hence the nickname "The Golden Cabbage") are meant to clash with the Historicist Ringstraße. Otto Wagner's pupil Josef Olbrich built this fin de siècle monument to accommodate artists who broke with the rigid, state-sponsored Künstlerhaus. The inscription above the door reads, *Der Zeit, ihre Kunst; der Kunst, ihre Freiheit,* ("To every age its art; to art, its freedom.") The Secession exhibits of 1898-1903 were led by Gustav Klimt and drew cutting-edge European artists. The exhibitions remain firmly dedicated to avant-garde art (see **Museums**, p. 124).

MAJOLICAHAUS. This colorful section of the Wagner Apartments, Linke Wienzeile 40, is at the "Kettenbrücken." (U4/green) station, and a 15min. walk from Karlspl. From the Secession Building, head away from Karlspl. down Friedrichstr., which runs into Linke Wienzeile. This acclaimed *Jugendstil* apartment building was a collaborative effort by Wagner and Olbrich. The wrought-iron spiral staircase is by Josef Hoffmann, founder of the Wiener Werkstätte, a communal arts-and-crafts workshop and key force in the momentum of the style. The Majolicahaus's gilded neighbor, the **Goldammer** building, is another Wagnerian mecca.

NASCHMARKT. West of Karlspl., along Linke Wienzeile, is the beginning of the Naschmarkt, a colorful food bazaar that moved from Karlspl. to its present location in the 1890s. During the week, the Naschmarkt, which derives its name from the German verb *naschen* (to nibble), presents a smorgasbord of fruits and vegetables laid out in front of bakeries, cafés, *Wurst* vendors, and cheese and spice shops. On Saturdays, it becomes a giant **flea market,** selling anything from loose junk to traditional Austrian clothing. *(Open M-F 6am-6:30pm, Sa 6am-2pm.)*

THEATER AN DER WIEN. Farther down Linke Wienzeile, opposite the Naschmarkt, stands the theater that hosted the premiere of Mozart's *Die Zauberflöte* (The Magic Flute, p. 129). The names of the street and the theater commemorate the Wien river, which used to flow freely through Vienna, but is now partly buried under city streets. *(☎588 300; www.musicalvienna.at. Open for performances only.)*

MUSIKVEREIN. Step across Lothringerstr. opposite Karlspl. to view the Musikverein, home of the Wiener Philharmoniker. The building's modest exterior conceals the sublime **Grosser Saal,** where the crème de la crème of the international music scene perform. Standing-room tickets offer an inexpensive way to admire both the music and the golden caryatids that line the hall (p. 128). *(☎505 81 90; www.musikverein.at. Open only for performances; call ahead for prices and concert information.)*

SCHWARZENBERGPLATZ

Take tram #1, 2, D, or 71 to "Schwarzenbergpl." From Karlspl., walk down Lothringerstr. and make a left onto Schwarzenbergstr.

Schwarzenbergpl., marked by the illuminated **Hochstrahlbrunnen** (Tall Fountain), is an elongated square with a rather infamous military history. During the Nazi era, the occupied city renamed the square *"Hitlerplatz;"* when the Russians brutally liberated Vienna, they renamed it *"Stalinplatz"* and erected an enormous **Russen Heldendenkmal** (Russian Heroes' Monument), a concrete colonnade behind a column bearing the figure of a Russian soldier, with a quotation from Stalin inscribed in the base. The Viennese have attempted to destroy the monstrosity three times, but the product of sturdy Soviet engineering refuses to be demolished.

PALAIS SCHWARZENBERG. Its location on a traffic island behind the Hochstrahl-brunnen makes it hard to believe that Palais Schwarzenberg, designed in 1697 by architect Fischer von Erlach's rival, Lukas von Hildebrandt, was once the center of a neighborhood preferred by Vienna's nobility. Redesigned by von Erlach, the palace (off-limits to the public) is part swank hotel, part Swedish Embassy.

ALONG THE DONAUKANAL

The Danube Canal cuts a semi-circle into the city south of the river, extending beyond the Inn-enstadt. Much of the area inside of the semi-circle is now taken up by parks (see Gardens and Parks, p. 121), but the outside edge of the canal provided building space for some of Vienna's great 20th-century architects to experiment with populist architecture.

HUNDERTWASSER HAUS. Fantastic Realist and environmental activist Frieden-sreich Hundertwasser (1928-2000) designed Hundertwasser Haus in opposition to the aesthetic of *Rot Wien* (see **Karl-Marx-Hof,** p. 117. Completed in 1986, it is a multi-colored building with 50 apartments. Hundertwasser included trees and grass in the undulating balconies as a means of bringing life back to the urban desert the city had become; oblique tile columns and free-form color patterns also contribute to this flamboyant rejection of architectural orthodoxy. Despite hordes of visitors, Hundertwasser Haus remains a private residence. *(At the corner of Löweng. and Kegelg. Take tram N from Schwedenpl. to "Hetzg." www.hundertwasserhaus.at.)*

KUNST HAUS WIEN. Three blocks away, at Untere Weißgerberstr. 13, is another Hundertwasser project, in this case an art museum (see **Museums,** p. 124). A café is inside (see **Cafés,** p. 104). *(From Schwedenpl. take tram N to Radetzkypl. From Wien-Mitte take tram O to Radetzkypl. www.kunsthauswien.at.)*

MÜLLVERBRENNUNGSANLAGE (GARBAGE INCINERATOR). Behind the "Spittelau" U-Bahn station. Hundertwasser fans will enjoy his jack-in-the-box of a trash dump. It features a smokestack topped by a golden disco ball. Hundertwasser also designed a ferry that cruises the Danube for the DDSG (p. 84).

KARL-MARX-HOF. The most famous example of public housing built during the interwar years, Karl-Marx-Hof, designed by Karl Ehn, illustrates the ideology and aesthetic of *Rot Wien* (Red Vienna; the socialist republic from 1918 until the *Anschluß*). The "palace for the people" stretches out for a full kilometer, with more than 1600 identical orange-and-pink apartments still inhabited today. The Social Democrats used this structure as their stronghold during the civil war of 1934, until army artillery shelled the place and broke down the resistance. *(Heiligen-stadterstr. 82-92. Take U4/green to "Heiligenstadt.")*

OTHER SIGHTS

KIRCHE AM STEINHOF. XIV, Baumgartner Höhe 1. Commissioned for the inmates of the state mental hospital in 1907, this unique *Jugendstil* church unites streamlined symmetry and Wagner's signature functionalism. The white walls are tiled for easy cleaning, the holy water in the basins by the door runs continuously for maximum hygiene, all corners are rounded to avoid injuries, and the pews are widely spaced to give nurses easy access to patients. The stained-glass windows were designed by Koloman Moser, a vanguard member of the Secession. *(Take U2/purple or U3/orange to "Volkstheater," then bus #48A to "Otto Wagner-Spital/Psychi-atriches Zentrum."* ☎ *91 06 01 12 04. The inside is closed until the beginning of 2006 due to restorations and the outside may be covered by scaffolding.)*

THE ZENTRALFRIEDHOF. The Viennese like to describe the **Zentralfriedhof** (Central Cemetery) as half the size of Geneva but twice as lively (2,500,000 people are buried here). The first interfaith cemetery, its opening in 1874 sparked heavy debate. Located beyond the main entrance at **Tor II,** which is the main entrance

VIENNA

gate designed in *Jugendstil* by Max Hegele, are the celebrity graves, built to draw visitors to the cemetery. Here lie Beethoven, Wolf, Strauss, Schönberg, and Moser. The real person does not necessarily lie underneath each gravestone. For instance, beyond Tor II also stands an honorary monument to Mozart, but the great composer's true resting place is an unmarked pauper's grave in the **Cemetery of St. Marx,** III, Leberstr. 6-8. St. Marx's deserves a visit not just for sheltering Mozart's dust, but also for its *Biedermeier* tombstones and the wild profusion of lilac blossoms that festoon it for two weeks in spring.

Tor I leads to the **Jewish Cemetery.** Sadly, the state of the Jewish Cemetery mirrors the fate of Vienna's Jewish population—many of the headstones are cracked, broken, lying prone, or neglected because the families of most of the dead are gone from Austria. Various structures throughout this portion of the burial grounds memorialize the millions murdered in Nazi death camps.

Tor IV leads to the Protestant section, while **Tor V** leads to the new Jewish cemetery. Also worth a visit is the *Jugendstil* **Dr.-Karl-Lüger Chapel** located behind the crypt for deceased Austrian presidents of the Second Republic. To the east of the Zentralfriedhof is the melancholy **Friedhof der Namenlosen** on Alberner Hafen, where the nameless corpses of people fished out of the Danube are buried. *(Tor II, the main entrance, is at XI, Simmeringer Hauptstr. 234. Take tram #71 from Schwarzenbergpl., or tram #72 from Schlachthausg. The tram stops by Tor I and by Tor II. Bus #6A also serves the other gates. You can also take S7 to "Zentralfriedhof," which stops along the southwest wall of the cemetery. A map of the cemetery is available at Tor II. Open May-Aug. 7am-7pm; Mar.-Apr. and Sept. 7am-6pm; Nov.-Feb. 8am-5pm. Free.)*

⊙ HAPSBURG PALACES

HOFBURG

Take tram #1 or 2 anywhere on the Ringstr. to Heldenpl., or enter from Michaelerpl.

A massive reminder of the Hapsburgs' 700-year reign, the sprawling **Hofburg** was the imperial family's winter residence. Construction on the original fortress began in 1275, but it didn't become the official dynastic seat until the mid-16th century. As few Hapsburgs were willing to live in their predecessors' quarters, hodgepodge additions and renovations continued until the end of the family's reign in 1918. Today, the complex houses several museums as well as the **Österreichische Nationalbibliothek** (Austrian National Library), the performance halls of the **Lipizzaner stallions** and the **Vienna Boys' Choir,** a convention center, and the offices of the Austrian President. It also includes the **Burggarten** and the **Volksgarten** (see **Gardens and Parks,** p. 121). The Hofburg is divided into several sections, including **In der Burg,** the **Alte Burg, Heldenplatz,** the **Neue Burg, Stallburg, Josefsplatz,** and **Albertina.** The museums, libraries, and apartments within the Hofburg may suit some people's tastes, but the best way to see this palatial cluster is to walk around and look up.

IN DER BURG

If you come through the Michaelertor, you'll first enter the courtyard called In der Burg (within the fortress). A monument to Emperor Franz II sits in the center opposite the red- and black-striped **Schweizertor** (Swiss Gate), erected in 1552 and named for the Swiss mercenaries who guarded it under Empress Maria Theresia. Street musicians take advantage of the wonderful acoustics here to play melodies from the old Empire. This section of the Hofburg contains the entrances to the **Kaiserappartements,** the **Silberkammer,** and the new **Sisi Museum.** *(Open daily 9am-5pm. Combined admission €7.50, students €5.90. Audioguide included in admission.)*

KAISERAPPARTEMENTS (IMPERIAL APARTMENTS). Once the private quarters of Emperor Franz Josef (1830-1916) and Empress Elisabeth (1838-1898), neither one spent much time in the Hofburg (or with each other, for that matter). Amid all the Baroque trappings, the two most personal items seem painfully out of place: Emperor Franz Josef's military field bed and Empress Elisabeth's wooden gym are a silent testimony to their lonely lives. *(Entrance on the right side of the Michaelertor.)*

SILBERKAMMER. On the ground floor opposite the ticket office. This vast collection of silver and porcelain once adorned the imperial table; it includes a 100-ft.-long gilded candelabra and the impressive **Laxemburg Goblet,** ca. 1821.

SISI MUSEUM. This exhibit explores the myth and reality behind the life of Empress Elisabeth. It includes some of her portraits, jewelry, and poetry.

ALTE BURG

Behind the Schweizertor lies the **Schweizerhof,** the inner courtyard of the Alte Burg (Old Fortress), which stands on the same site as the original 13th-century palace. The Alte Burg houses the **Burgkapelle** and the **Weltliche und Geistliche Schatzkammer** (Secular and Sacred Treasury).

BURGKAPELLE. From the Schweizertor, make a right at the top of the stairs. This Gothic chapel is where the heavenly voices of the **Wiener Sängerknaben** (Vienna Boys' Choir) harmonize on Sundays and religious holidays. *(☎ 533 99 27. Open M-Th 11am-3pm, F 11am-1pm. €1.50. Choir performs mid-Sept. to early June; call ahead to reserve a ticket; see p. 129.)*

WELTLICHE UND GEISTLICHE SCHATZKAMMER. Entrance beneath the steps to Burgkapelle, through the Schweizertor and to the right. This room contains the Hapsburg jewels, the crowns of the Holy Roman and Austrian Empires, imperial christening robes, and a gorgeous, gold-painted cradle, which Maria Louisa (Napoleon's wife) gave to her infant son. The treasury also houses a "horn of a unicorn" (really an 8-ft.-long narwahl's horn), a tooth reported to have belonged to John the Baptist, and numerous pictures and sculptures of saints. *(Open M and W-Su 10am-6pm. €8, seniors and students €6. Free audioguide available in English.)*

NEUE BURG

Built between 1881 and 1913, the Neue Burg (New Fortress) is the youngest wing of the palace, built as a last attempt on the part of the Hapsburgs to assert their imperial power. The double-headed golden eagle crowning the roof symbolized the double empire of Austria-Hungary. Planned in 1869, the intended (but never fully realized) design called for twin palaces across Heldenpl., both connected to the Kunsthistorisches Museum and Naturhistorisches Museum by arches spanning the Ringstr. Today, the Neue Burg **houses** Austria's largest library, the **Österreichische Nationalbibliothek** (Austrian National Library), the fantastic **Völkerkunde Museum,** and three branches of the **Kunsthistorisches Museum** (p. 124).

ÖSTERREICHISCHE NATIONALBIBLIOTHEK. The Austrian National Library holds millions of books and an interesting little museum filled with ancient books written on papyrus, as well as scriptures and musical manuscripts. A reading room is open to the public; in-library use of books is allowed with picture ID. *(Entrance on Heldenpl. ☎ 53 41 02 52; www.onb.ac.at. Open Oct.-June M-F 9am-9pm, Sa 9am-12:45pm; July-Sept. M-F 9am-4pm, Sa 9am-12:45pm. Closed Sept. 1-7. Free. Museum ☎ 53 41 03 23. Open M, W, F Oct.-June 10am-5pm; July-Sept. 10am-4pm. €3, students €2.)*

REICHSKANZLEITRAKT (STATE CHANCELLERY WING). This building is notable for its architecture, especially the buff statues on the exterior (representing the labors of Hercules), said to have inspired the 11-year-old Arnold Schwarzenegger, then on his first visit to Vienna, to pump up. *(Standing with your back facing the red Schweizertor, the Reichskanzleitrakt is the building spanning the right length of the square.)*

OTHER HOFBURG SIGHTS

HELDENPLATZ. From the Michaelertor, walk past the red Schweizertor and continue straight through the three-arched passageway. On March 15, 1938, the enormous Heldenpl. (Heroes' Square) was filled with a jubilant crowd cheering Adolf

Hitler's proclamation of the *Anschluß* (the unification of Germany and Austria). The equestrian statues facing each other (both by Anton Fenkhorn) depict two of Austria's great military commanders: Prince Eugène of Savoy and Archduke Charles, whose horse rears triumphantly on its hind legs with no other support— a feat of sculpting never again duplicated. Poor Fenkhorn later went insane, supposedly due to his inability to recreate the effect.

STALLBURG (PALACE STABLES). Attached to the northeast side of the Alte Burg (to the left of the Michaelertor, when facing it from the outside) is the Renaissance Stallburg, the home of the Royal Lipizzaner stallions and the **Spanische Reitschule** (Spanish Riding School). The cheapest way to catch a glimpse of the famous steeds is to watch them train. *(Mid-Feb. to June and late Aug. to early Nov. Tu-F. Check ahead for exact dates and times. Tickets sold at the door at Josefspl., Gate 2, from about 8:30am. Approximately €20.)* For a more impressive (and expensive) display, you can attend a **Reitschule performance,** which requires ticket reservations in writing months in advance. *(☎ 533 903 113; www.srs.at. Write to: Spanische Reitschule, Michaelerpl. 1, A-1010 Wien. Check ahead for exact time and date. If you reserve through a travel agency, expect a surcharge. Reservations only; no money accepted by mail. Tickets €40-160, standing-room €24-28.)* You can also learn about Lipizzaner history and training at the **Lipizzaner Museum** (p. 127).

JOSEFSPLATZ. Just south of Stallburg, this courtyard is named after the statue of Emperor Josef II in the center. The square contains the ticket entrance for the Stallburg and the entrance to the **Prunksaal** (State Hall). Dating to 1723, the Prunksaal glitters with gilded wood and marble pillars, and is the secular counterpart of Fischer von Erlach's magnificent Karlskirche (p. 115). A segment of the National-bibliothek, this is the largest Baroque library in Europe. Wander through the floor-to-ceiling bookcases that house over 200,000 leather-bound books (with a collection of over 2.6 million books total) and pay your respects to the 16 marble statues of various Hapsburg rulers, including Charles VI, the library's founder. *(☎ 53 41 0 397; www.onb.ac.at. Prunksaal open May-Oct. M-W and F-Su 10am-4pm, Th 10am-7pm; Oct.-May M-W and F-Su 10am-2pm, Th 10am-7pm. €5, students €3.)*

AUGUSTINERKIRCHE. High mass is held each Sunday in this 14th-century Gothic church, located in a wing attached to the Prunksaal's south side, on Josefspl. Eighteenth-century renovations (and Napoleonic flourishes) have somewhat altered the original interior. The Augustinerkirche saw the wedding of Hapsburgs Maria Theresia and Franz Stephan, and the church's **Herzgrüftel** (Little Heart Crypt) became their final resting place. *(Church open M-Sa 8am-5pm, Su 11am-6pm. Free.)*

ALBERTINA. Originally part Augustinian monastery, part 18th-century palace, the Albertina has undergone renovations, including a restoration of the building's original façade (damaged during WWII). Today the Albertina displays temporary exhibits. Past exhibits have included Rembrandt and Pop Art. *(☎ 53 48 30; www.albertina.at. Open M-Tu and Th-Su 10am-6pm, W 10am-9pm. €9, students €6.50.)*

SCHLOß SCHÖNBRUNN

Take U4 (green) to "Schönbrunn." www.schoenbrunn.at. Wheelchair accessible. Apartments open daily Apr.-June and Sept.-Oct. 8:30am-5pm; Nov.-Mar. 8:30am-4:30pm; July-Aug. 8:30am-6pm. Imperial tour €8, students €7.40; grand tour €10.50/€8.60. Audioguides in English included.

Named after a "beautiful brook" on the property, Schönbrunn had humble beginnings as a hunting lodge. Two earlier versions were destroyed before architect Fischer von Erlach conceived a plan for a palace befitting an emperor. Construction began in 1696, but the high costs slowed the project considerably until Maria Theresia inherited it in 1740. Under her rule, the Rococo palace that would become her favorite residence was finally completed. Its unique mustard-yellow color has been named *Maria Theresien gelb*, which can be seen throughout Austria. When Napoleon conquered Vienna, he acquired a fondness for the place and promptly made it his headquarters. The Imperial Tour passes through the **Great Gallery,** where the Congress of Vienna danced the night away after a day of dividing up the continent and where years later in 1961 Kennedy would meet Krushchev. Also included is the **Hall of Mirrors,** where the six-year-old Mozart played. If you take the shorter Imperial Tour, you'll miss sumptuous pleasures of the palace, such as the Oriental art and rosewood paneling in the **Millions Room.** The Hapsburgs' suites are exquisite, trimmed in gold and silver. Schönbrunn also hosts Mozart and Strauss concerts in the **Orangerie** *(☎812 500 40; daily 8:30pm; €36-50),* and the **Marionettentheater Schloß Schönbrunn** performs famous operas with wooden marionettes. *(☎817 32 47. Tickets €7-28. www.marionettentheater.at.)*

THE GARDENS. Equally impressive as the palace are its Imperial gardens. Designed by Emperor Joseph II, the gardens extend nearly four times the length of the palace. They include a wide range of themes, from neatly ordered forests to geometric flower designs. Also featured is the massive stone **Neptunbrunnen** (Neptune Fountain), with Romanesque sculptures. *(Open daily 6am-dusk. Free.)*

On the East side of the garden is the **Palmenhaus,** Europe's largest greenhouse of tropical plants. *(Open daily May-Sept. 9:30am-6pm; Oct.-Apr. 9:30am-5pm. €3.30, students €2.90.)* Desert plants and animals can be seen in the Wüstenhaus (Desert Experience House which was originally commissioned by Emperor Franz Joseph I. *(Open daily summer 9am-6pm; winter 9am-5pm. €4, students €2.50.)* There is also a **maze** in whose center stands two stones that were activated by a master of Feng Shui and are said to radiate energy and harmony. *(€3, students €2.50.)* The sprawling complex is crowned by the **Gloriette,** an ornamental temple perched on a hill with a beautiful view of the gardens. In the summer, open-air opera is performed in the park. Built to amuse Maria Theresia's husband in 1752, the **Schönbrunn Tiergarten** (zoo) is the world's oldest menagerie, but it is basically just a side diversion within the gardens. *(Zoo open daily Apr.-Sept. 9am-6:30pm; Mar. and Oct. 9am-5:30pm; Feb. 9am-5pm; Nov.-Jan. 9am-4:30pm. €12, students €5.)*

SCHLOß BELVEDERE

Take tram D or tram #71 one stop past Schwarzenbergpl., or walk up Prinz-Eugen-Str. from Südbahnhof. Walking southeast from Schwarzenbergpl. (away from the city center), you'll find Belvedere just beyond the Schwarzenberggarten. www.belvedere.at.

Originally the summer residence of Prince Eugène of Savoy, one of Austria's great military heroes, the Belvedere has played a large role in the imperial history of Vienna. After Eugène's heirless death in 1736, his cousin sold off his possessions and Empress Maria Theresia snatched up the palace as a showroom for the Hapsburgs' art collection, opening the extensive gardens to the public. Though the imperial art moved to the Kunsthistorisches Museum in the 1890s, Archduke Franz Ferdinand lived in the Belvedere until his 1914 assassination. The grounds of the Belvedere, stretching from the Palais Schwarzenberg to the Südbahnhof, now contain three sphinx-filled gardens (p. 121) and the Österreichische Gallerie (p. 124).

⚠ GARDENS AND PARKS

The Viennese have gone to great lengths to brighten the urban landscape with parks. The Hapsburgs opened the city's public gardens and have maintained them for centuries, until WWI, after which they became public property. There are several parks along the Ring (including the **Stadtpark, Resselpark, Burggarten,** and **Volksgarten**), as well as many in the suburbs. The gardens of **Schloß Schönbrunn, Schloß Belvedere** (p. 121), and the **Palais Liechtenstein** are particularly beautiful.

ALONG THE RING. Established in 1862, the **Stadtpark** (City Park) was the first municipal park outside the former city walls. One of Vienna's oft-photographed monuments, the gilded **Johann-Strauss-Denkmal** occupies **the center of the park and** sometimes acts as a backdrop for the Vienna Boys' Choir. *(Take U4/green to "Stadtpark.")*

Clockwise up the Ring, past the Staatsoper, lies the **Burggarten** (Palace Garden), a quiet park with gorgeous greenhouses. It also contains monuments to such Austrian notables as Mozart, Emperor Franz Josef, and Emperor Franz I (Maria Theresia's husband). The **Babenberger Passage** leads from the Ring to the marble **Mozart Denkmal** (1896). Reserved for the imperial family and members of the court until 1918, the Burggarten is now a favorite destination for local residents of all ages.

The Burggarten borders Heldenpl., across from the Kunsthistorisches Museum and behind the Hofburg, which abuts the **Volksgarten** (People's Garden). Once the site of a defensive bastion destroyed by Napoleon's troops, this park now brims with roses in all colors. In the center of the park is the **Temple of Theseus**, while at the north end a stark, white statue of Empress Elisabeth rests on a throne. Erected after her assassination, the plaque at the base of the statue reads: "The people of Austria erected this monument to their unforgettable Empress Elisabeth in steadfast love and loyalty." There are plenty of places to sit in the park and watch the sun set over the *Rathaus*.

AUGARTEN. The Augarten, on Obere Augartenstr., northeast of downtown Vienna in Leopoldstadt, is Vienna's oldest public park. Originally a formal French garden, the Augarten was given a Baroque face-lift and opened to the public by Kaiser Josef II in 1775. Today, the Augarten is no longer as fashionable as it was in the days of Mozart and Strauss, due primarily to the ominous WWII **Flaktürme** (concrete anti-aircraft towers) that dominate the center of the park. Buildings located within the Augarten include the **Augartenpalais,** now a boarding school for the Vienna Boys' Choir and the headquarters for the **Augarten Porzelle** (Augarten China Factory), founded in 1718. The Augarten store sells fine china. *(Obere Augartenstr. 1. ☎211 24 18; www.augarten.at. Open M-F 9:30am-6pm. To reach the park, take tram #31 up from Schottenring or tram N to "Obere Augartenstr." and head left down Taborstr.)*

PRATER. Extending southeast from the Wien Nord Bahnhof/Praterstern, this park was a private game reserve for the Imperial Family until 1766 and the site of the World Expo in 1873. Situated in the woodlands between the Donaukanal and the river proper, the park is surrounded by ponds, meadows, and stretches of forest. The Prater is most famous for its old-school amusement park, with the stately wooden 65m-tall **Riesenrad.** *(Giant Ferris Wheel; 10min. ride and admission into a historical exhibit €7.50.)* Locals cherish this wheel of fortune, and when it was destroyed in WWII the city built an exact replica, which has been turning since 1947. The area near U1 (red): "Praterstern" is the actual amusement park, which contains rides, arcades, restaurants, and casinos. Entry to the complex is free, but each attraction charges admission. The kitschy thrill rides and wonderfully campy spook-houses are packed with children during the day, but the Prater becomes less wholesome after sundown due to the proliferation of peep shows. *(☎728 0516; www.prater.at. Official season runs mid-Mar. to Oct., but park is open all year. 24hr daily. Rides open approximately 10am-1am.)*

ON THE DANUBE. The Danube's spring floods were problematic once settlers moved outside the city walls, so the Viennese stretch of the Danube was diverted into canals from 1870 to 1875 and again from 1972 to 1987. One of the side benefits of this restructuring was the creation of new recreational areas, ranging from new tributaries, including the **Alte Donau** and the **Donaukanal,** to the **Donauinsel,** a narrow island stretching for kilometers. Filled with in-line skaters and bikers, the Donauinsel is devoted to soccer fields, swimming areas, boats, summer restaurants, bars, and clubs. The northern shore of the island, along the Alte Donau, is lined with beaches and bathing areas. *(Take U1/red (dir: Kagran) to "Donauinsel" or "Alte Donau." www.donauinsel.at. Open May-Sept. M-F 9am-8pm, Sa-Su 8am-8pm. Beach admission roughly €4.)* To catch a view of Vienna at its best, go after sundown to **Donaupark** and take the elevator up to the revolving restaurant in the **Donauturm** (Danube Tower), near the UN complex. *(Take the U1/red to "Kaisermühlen/Vienna International Center," exit towards Schüttaustr., and follow signs to the park. Tower open daily 10am-midnight. €5.20, students €4.10.)* On select days, the brave can also bungee-jump from the 150m tower. *(Jochen-Schweizer. ☎ 269 62 47; www.jochen-schweizer.at. Open select days (mainly Su) mid-Apr. to mid-Nov. 10am-8pm. Starting at €99. Call ahead to reserve a time.)* The area celebrates during the annual open-air **Donauinsel Fest** *(www.donauinselfest.at),* which stages jazz and rock concerts, fireworks displays, and recreational activities in late June. (See **Festivals,** p. 130.)

IN THE SUBURBS. Nearly every district in Vienna has public gardens tucked away somewhere, like the **Türkenschanz Park** in district XVIII. The garden is famous for its Turkish fountain, its pools, and its peacocks. In summer, feed the ducks or walk past the water lilies. In winter, come for sledding or ice skating. *(Take bus #40A or 10A, and enter the park anywhere along Gregor-Mendel-Str., Hasenauerstr., or Max-Emmanuelstr.)*

West of District XIII is the **Lainzer Tiergarten** (Lainz Game Preserve). Once exclusive hunting ground for the royals, this enclosed park has been a nature preserve since 1941. Along with paths, restaurants, and spectacular vistas, the park holds the **Hermes Villa,** a gift of Emperor Franz Joseph to his wife Empress Elisabeth. It now houses exhibitions by the Historical Museum of Vienna, most recently one about women's fashion in the 20th century. *(Take U4/green; (dir: Hütteldorf) to "Hietzing;" change to streetcar #60A to "Hermesstr." At the intersection, take a sharp right and walk 1 block to the bus stop. Take bus #60B to "Lainzer Tor." ☎804 13 24; www.wienmuseum.at. Open Tu-Su and holidays Apr.-Sept. 10am-6pm; Oct.-Mar. 9am-4:30pm. Villa €4, students and seniors €2, family €6. F mornings free.)*

Districts XIV, XVII, XIX, and XX fade into well-tended forests that are attractive hiking destinations. The **Pötzleindorfer Park,** at the end of tram line #41 (dir: Pötzleindorfer Höhe) from Schottentor, overlaps the lower end of the Wienerwald.

WIENERWALD. Far to the north and west of Vienna sprawl the forested hills of the Wienerwald (Vienna Woods), which extends past Baden bei Wien to the first foothills of the Alps. The woods are known for their excellent *Heurigen* and delicious white wines (p. 107). One of the most famous and easily accessible routes into the Wienerwald is via **Kahlenberg** and **Leopoldsberg,** hills north of Vienna that provide great views of the city and direct entrance to the woods. **Kahlenberg** (484m) is the highest point of the rolling forest, with spectacular views of Vienna, the Danube, and the Alps in the distance. The Turks besieged Vienna from here in 1683, and Polish king Jan Sobieski celebrated his liberation of the city from Saracen infidels in the small **Church of St. Joseph.** *(Open daily 10am-noon and 2-5pm).* For a good outlook point, climb the Stephaniewarte on the Kahlenberg, part of the valley's old fortifications. *(Just off the central square of Kahlenberg. Open May-Oct. Sa noon-6pm, Su and holidays 10am-6pm.)* The area around Kahlenberg, Cobenzl, and Leopoldstadt is criss-crossed by hiking paths marked with blazes. You can follow in an early Pope's footsteps with a hike to the Leopoldskirche, a renowned pilgrimage site, located 1km east of Kahlenberg on Leopoldsberg (425m). It is on the site of a Babenberg fortress destroyed by the Turks in 1529. The Kahlenberg and Leopoldsberg are a 11km hike from Nußdorf, which can be accessed by tram D. Alternatively, take bus 38A to Kahlenberg and Leopoldsberg. For more information on hiking in the area, call ☎4000 97 947.

Another interesting hike leads to **Klosterneuburg,** a Baroque monastery founded by Leopold (p. 134), which is a 1½hr. walk from Leopoldsberg.

VIENNA

A PRINCELY GIFT

What may be the world's most significant private art collection s now, after a 66-year hiatus, gain open to the public. On March 29, 2004, Prince Hans-Adam II of Liechtenstein opened he Liechtenstein Museum in Vienna's 9th district.

Hans-Adam II and his predecessors have acquired a collection that today consists of some 600 pictures ranging in style rom early Renaissance to Austrian Romanticism. The history of he collection can be retraced to Prince Karl I of Liechtenstein 1569-1627). An avid collector, Karl I also commissioned artwork, ncluding two pieces by Adrian de Fries. Prince Karl's heirs continued what became a Liechtenstein radition of art collecting. From 807 to 1938 Liechtenstein's private collection was displayed in he Garden Palace in the Rossau.

World War II brought financial roubles for the royal family. In 938 the museum in Vienna was closed and some of the artwork was sold. However, after Hans-Adam II restructured the family's inances, the art collection once gain became a priority. In 1985-5, the Liechtenstein collection was temporarily exhibited at the New York Metropolitan Museum of Art, but the collection only eturned to its former and permanent home in the Garden Palace n Vienna in 2004.

The museum opened after a enovation of the Garden Palace

🏛 MUSEUMS

All museums run by the city of Vienna are **free Friday before noon** (except public holidays) **and all day Sundays;** they are marked in the tourist office's free *Museums* brochure with a red and white coat of arms. Individual museum tickets usually cost €1.50-10—slightly less with the **Vienna Card,** though student or senior discounts are generally even larger. If you're in town for a long time, invest in the **Museum Card** (issued through the Verein der Museumsfreunde) to save on entrance fees (ask for the card at a museum ticket window). The most recent addition to the museum circuit is the collection at the Liechtenstein Museum (p. 128). Also fairly new is the **MuseumsQuartier** (☎523 58 81; www.mqw.at). Originally the imperial barracks, the **Messepalast,** Museumspl., was transformed in 2001 into the **MuseumsQuartier** (p. 125), a modern complex combining several collections.

ART MUSEUMS

▨ **Österreichische Galerie** (Austrian Gallery), III, Prinz-Eugen-Str. 27 (☎79 557 134; www.belvedere.at), in the Belvedere Palace behind Schwarzenbergpl. (p. 121). Walk up from the Südbahnhof, take tram D to "Schloß Belvedere," or tram #71 to "Unteres Belvedere." The collection is in 2 parts. The **Upper Belvedere** (built in 1721-22) houses Austrian and European art of the 19th and 20th centuries. The highlight of the Upper Belvedere is, without a doubt, the Gustav Klimt collection, which includes his masterpiece *The Embrace.* However, the remainder of the exhibits are equally as impressive and include masterpieces by Egon Schiele, van Gogh, Manet, and Kokoschka. Also notable is the Marble Hall, which contains a fresco by Carlo Carlone. The **Lower Belvedere** contains the **Austrian Museum of Baroque Art,** which showcases an extensive collection of sculptures by Donner and Maulbertsch, as well as Messerschmidt's comical busts. David's majestic portrait of Napoleon on horseback is here, as is the **Museum of Medieval Austrian Art,** which boasts an impressive collection of Romanesque and Gothic sculptures and altarpieces. Wheelchair accessible. Both Belvederes open Tu-Su 10am-6pm. Last admission 30min. before closing. €7.50, students €5 (price includes both Upper and Lower Belvederes and Atelier Augarten). Audioguide in Upper Belvedere €4.

Kunsthistorisches Museum (Museum of Fine Arts), I (☎525 240; www.khm.at). Take U2 (purple) to "Museumsquartier," U2 (purple)/U3 (orange) to "Volkstheater," or tram 1, 2, D, or J. Across from the Burgring and Heldenpl. on Maria Theresia's right. Houses the world's 4th-largest art collection, including vast numbers of 15th- to 18th-century Venetian and Flemish paintings. Must-sees include Vermeer's *Art of Painting* (room 24) and Raphael's *Madonna* *in the Meadow* (room 4). In addition to the picture gallery, the Kunsthistorisches Museum also houses a collection of Greek and Roman Antiquities, a Collection of Sculpture and Decorative Arts, an Egyptian and Near Eastern Collection, and special exhibits. Open Tu-Su 10am-6pm. Picture gallery also open Th until 9pm. €10, students and seniors €7.50. Audioguides €2 (1st audioguide is free, but there is a separate audioguide for each exhibit).

Exhibits at Neue Burg, I (☎525 24 484; www.khm.at). Entrance at Heldenpl. **Ephesos Museum** exhibits the extensive findings of the Austrian excavation of classical ruins from Ephesus in Turkey, including an ancient Greek temple. **Hofjagd- und Rustkammer** (Arms and Armor Collection) is the world's 2nd-largest such collection. **Sammlung alter Musikinstrumente** (Ancient Musical Instrument Collection) includes Beethoven's harpsichord, Mozart's piano, and a wide array of Renaissance instruments. Open M and W-Su 10am-6pm. €8, students €6; includes 1 audioguide.

MuseumsQuartier (☎523 58 81; www.mqw.at) is one of the 10 largest art districts in the world. Take U2 (purple) to "Museumsquartier," or U2/U3 (orange) or tram 1, 2, D, or J to "Volkstheater." Uniting Baroque architecture with ultramodern film, visual art, and performance spaces, this area offers a smattering of large museums, including:

Leopold Museum (☎52 57 00; www.leopoldmuseum.org). The world's largest Schiele collection, plus works by Klimt, Kokoschka, Gerstl, and Egger-Lienz. Open M, W, F-Su 10am-7pm, Th 10am-9pm. €9, students €5.50. Check www.cafe-leopold.at for music events (in particular eclectic hip-hop) at night.

Kunsthalle Wien (☎521 89 33; www.kunsthallewien.at). Themed exhibits of international contemporary artists, from sculptors to filmmakers. Open M-Tu and F-Su 10am-7pm, Th 10am-10pm. Exhibition Hall 1 €7.50, students €6; Exhibition Hall 2 €6/€4.50; both €10.50/€8.50.

Museum Moderner Kunst (Museum of Modern Art; ☎525 00; www.mumok.at). Holds Central Europe's largest collection of modern art in a brand-new building made from basalt lava. Highlights include Classical Modernism, Pop Art, Photo Realism, Fluxus, and Viennese Actionism. 20th-century masters include Magritte, Motherwell, Picasso, Miró, Kandinsky, Pollock, Warhol, and Klee. Open Tu-Su 10am-7pm, Th until 9pm. €8, students €6.50. Audioguide €2.

Kunst Haus Wien, III, Untere Weißgerberstr. 13 (☎712 04; www.kunsthauswien.com; see p. 117). Take U1 (red) or U4 (green) to "Schwedenpl.," then tram N to "Hetzg." This museum, designed by Hundertwasser, displays much of his work, as well as exhibits of contemporary art from around the world. A Bettina Rheims exhibit will take place Jan.-Apr. 2005. Open daily 10am-7pm. Each exhibit €9, students €7; both exhibits €12/€9; M half-price (except holidays).

and the adjoining gardens. A particularly impressive part of the palace is Vienna's largest secular Baroque room, the Hercules Hall, which contains an extraordinary ceiling fresco by Andrea Pozzo. In addition to a strikingly beautiful French state coach, the museum contains masterpieces by Raphael, Peter Paul Rubens, Rembrandt, Franz Xaver Messerschmidt, and many others.

Most Viennese were excited about the reopening of the Liechteinstein Museum in the Garden Palace. However, some citizens of Liechtenstein worried that the move of the princely collection to Vienna coincided with a move of other interests of the princely family from Vaduz to Vienna. Hans-Adam II negated these fears. He is still considering plans to open another art gallery in Vaduz. After all, only 300 of the 1600 pieces were moved to Vienna. The rest remain in storage in Vaduz.

The Lichtenstein Museum is open M and W-Su 9am-8pm. Tickets are €10, for students €5. For more information, see Museums, p. 124.

Österreichisches Museum für Angewandte Kunst (MAK; Austrian Museum of Applied Art), I, Stubenring 5 (☎71 13 60; www.mak.at). Take U3 (orange), or trams 1 or 2 to "Stubentor." A museum dedicated to the beauty of design, from the smooth curves of Thonet bentwood chairs to the intricate detail of Venetian glass. For Klimt enthusiasts, *The Kiss* is a special highlight. Recent exhibits have included photography and film by Dennis Hopper and an Andy Warhol retrospective. Open Tu 10am-midnight, W-Su 10am-6pm. €7.90, students €4, Sa free. Tours by appointment ☎71 13 62 98; €9.90.

Akademie der Bildenden Kunst (Academy of Fine Arts), I, Schillerpl. 3 (☎588 162 25; www.akbild.ac.at). From Karlspl. turn left onto Friedrichstr., right onto Operng., and left on Nibelungeng. This building houses the art academy famous for having rejected Hitler's application. In addition, the Academy offers an excellent collection, including several works by Peter Paul Rubens and Hieronymus Bosch's *The Last Judgment*. Wheelchair accessible. Open Tu-Su and holidays 10am-6pm. €5, students €3. Call ahead for guided tours in English. Audioguides €2.

Secession Building, I, Friedrichstr. 12 (☎587 53 07; www.secession.at), on the western side of Karlspl. (p. 116), easily distinguished by its dome of 3000 gilt laurel leaves (once derisively nicknamed the "head of cabbage"). Primarily devoted to exhibits of contemporary art, although the main attraction is almost 100 years old: Klimt's controversial *Beethoven Frieze,* a 30m-long visual interpretation of Beethoven's Ninth Symphony. Pick up an English brochure for an explanation of the work's symbolism. Wheelchair accessible. Open Tu-Su and holidays 10am-6pm, Th until 8pm. €6, students €3.50; exhibit only €4.50/€3.

Salvador-Dali-Palais Surreal, I, Josefspl. 5 (☎512 25 49; www.dali-wien.at). By the Hofburg; take U3 (orange) to "Herreng." The Baroque palace of the Pallavicini family now houses a renowned collection of sculptures by Dalí, including one called *Space Elephant*. Open daily 10am-6pm. €6.50, students and seniors €3.60. AmEx/MC/V.

OTHER MUSEUMS

▨ **Haus der Musik,** I, Seilerstatte 30 (☎516 48; www.hdm.at). Near the Opera House and the Musikverein, this new, interactive science-meets-music museum will capture the imagination of people of all ages. Spanning 4 floors, the exhibits help you experience the physics of sound, learn about famous Viennese composers (each has his own room), and play with a neat invention called the Brain Opera. Admission includes the Philharmonic exhibit, where the virtual conductor allows you to conduct the Vienna Philharmonic yourself and where you can compose your own waltz by rolling dice. Open daily 10am-10pm. €10, students €8.50.

Historisches Museum der Stadt Wien (Historical Museum of Vienna), IV, Karlspl. (☎50 58 74 70; www.wienmuseum.at), to the left of the Karlskirche (p. 115). Historical artifacts and paintings document Vienna's evolution from a Roman encampment through the Turkish siege of Vienna to the subsequent 640 years of Hapsburg rule. Don't miss the Loos room, the fin de siècle art, or the 19th-century *Biedermeier* exhibits. Open Tu-Su 9am-6pm. Permanent and temporary exhibits each €4, students €2; combo ticket €5/€2.50. All exhibits on F morning and the permanent exhibit on Su are free.

Jüdisches Museum (Jewish Museum), I, Dorotheerg. 11 (☎535 04 31; www.jmw.at). From Stephanspl., off Graben. Jewish culture and history, including fragments of text stamped into the walls, holograms, and more traditional displays. Temporary exhibits focus on prominent Jewish figures and contemporary Jewish art. Wheelchair accessible. Open M-W, F, Su 10am-6pm, Th and Sa 10am-8pm. €5, students €2.90.

Bestattungsmuseum (Undertaker's Museum), IV, Goldegg. 19 (☎501 95 0). Take tram D to "Schloß Belvedere" or U1 to "Südtirolerpl." Displays a morbidly fascinating collection, including coffins with alarms (should the body decide to rejoin the living) and Josef II's proposed reusable coffin. Open M-F noon-3pm; phone for an appointment. Free.

Freud Museum, IX, Bergg. 19 (☎319 15 96; www.freud-museum.at). Take U2 (purple) to "Schottentor," then walk up Währingerstr. to Bergg or take tram D to "Schlickg." Ring bell for entrance on 2nd floor. This small museum is situated in the house where Freud lived and worked until his exile to England. The famed couch is not here, but there is a small exhibit with artifacts such as the young Freud's report cards and circumcision certificate. Open daily July-Sept. 9am-6pm; Oct.-June 9am-4pm. €5, students €3. Free written guide in English (must be returned). Audioguides €1.50.

Lipizzaner Museum, I, Reitschulg. 2 (☎525 24 583; www.lipizzaner.at). Originally built as the residence of Archduke Maximillian and formerly the imperial pharmacy, the Lipizzaner is now a museum dedicated to the imperial horses, featuring paintings, harnesses, and video clips. Open daily 9am-6pm. €5, students €3.60. Tours €2 Sa noon in both German and English; or call ahead (☎524 24 416) to arrange a tour in English.

Naturhistorisches Museum (Natural History Museum), I (☎52 17 70), opposite the Kunsthistorisches Museum; accessible via U2 (purple)/U3 (orange) to "Volkstheater." A substantial collection of dinosaur skeletons, meteorites, and giant South American beetles. 2 of its star attractions are man-made: a spectacular floral bouquet comprised of gemstones and a miniaturized replica of the Stone Age beauty *Venus of Willendorf* (the original is locked in a vault). Open M and Th-Su 9am-6:30pm, W 9am-9pm. Last admission 30min. before closing. €8, students €3.50.

🎵 ENTERTAINMENT

While Vienna offers standard entertainment in the way of theater, film, and festivals, the heart of the city beats to music. All but a few of classical music's marquee names lived, composed, and performed in Vienna. Mozart, Beethoven, and Haydn wrote their greatest masterpieces in Vienna, creating the **First Viennese School;** a century later, Schönberg, Webern, and Berg teamed up to form the **Second Viennese School.** The Vienna **Konservatorium** and **Hochschule** are world-renowned conservatories. Also not to be missed are the various modern and classical dance groups of Vienna, in particular, the **Vienna Staatsoper Ballet.** Vienna has performances ranging from the above average to the sublime all year long, and many are affordable to the budget traveler.

> 🎵 **TO EVERYTHING THERE IS A SEASON.** Be aware that Vienna's biggest cultural draws, the **Staatsoper** (State Opera), the **Wiener Philharmoniker** (Vienna Philharmonic), the **Wiener Sängerknaben** (Vienna Boys' Choir), and the **Lipizzaner Stallions** don't perform in Vienna during July and August.

OPERA

Staatsoper, Opernring 2 (www.wiener-staatsoper.at), Vienna's premier opera, performs about 300 times per year, nearly every night Sept.-June. To get tickets:

Standing-room tickets: The cheapest way to enjoy the opera. 567 standing-room tickets are available for every performance, though you can only buy 1 or 2 per person, right before the performance. While the box office opens 80min. before curtain, those with the desire (and the stamina) should start lining up at least 1½hr. before curtain (2-3hr. in tourist season and for more popular productions) in order to get orchestra tickets. The standing line forms inside the side door on the side of the Opera by Operng. After procuring your precious ticket, hurry to a space on the rail and tie a scarf around it to reserve your spot. Casual dress is tolerated, but no shorts or sneakers are permitted. Parterre €3.50, balcony €2, gallery €2.

Box office tickets in advance: The more secure ticket option is to purchase tickets through the official ticket offices by fax or phone or in person; they charge no fees above the ticket price. The main ticket office is the Bundestheaterkasse, I, Hanuschg. 3, around the corner from the opera. There is also a ticket office inside the Staatsoper with the same hours (though closed Su and holidays). Tickets may be purchased 1 month before performance. Seats €5-254, depending on location and show. ☎514 44 78 80; fax 514 44 3318. Open M-F 8am-6pm, Sa-Su 9am-noon; Sa during Advent 9am-5pm. Students can get cheap tickets (€5-18) for shows that are not sold out 30min. prior to start of the show at the Staatsoper ticket office.

Internet: The Bundestheaterkasse maintains a multilingual website (www.bundestheater.at, also www.culturall.com) that allows you to purchase tickets in advance, view the seating plan, and check out the season schedule. However, the web is probably better used as a source of information than as a means of buying your tickets, because it charges a hefty commission.

Volksoper, IX, Währingerstr. 78 (☎513 1 513; www.volksoper.at), specializes in lighter comedic opera, operettas, and musicals. As the Staatsoper was once for royalty, the "people's opera" is for the commoners. While the theater is less elaborate, the music is fantastic and the diversity of performances makes it a lively arts center. Arrive 45min. before the show to get the best seats in the house for €7. Repertoire is diverse and includes modern operas, musicals, and dance troupes such as Alvin Ailey. Tickets are available at the box office (open Sept.-June M-F 8-6pm, Sa-Su 9am-noon) and through Bundestheaterkasse and its website (www.culturall.com). Tickets range €7-250, depending on performance and location.

Wiener Kammeroper (Chamber Opera), I, Fleischmarkt 24 (☎513 60 72; www.wienerkammeroper.at). Performs everything from classical operas to modern parodies in an open-air theater. Standing tickets €5-8, seats €14-54, students 30% off when there is a play M-F. Noon-7:30pm. Reserve tickets online or purchase them at the theater (M-F noon-6pm; until 7:30pm and Sa 4pm-7:30pm). Mozart's operas are staged in the Schönbrunner Schloßpark during the summer as part of the **Klangbogen** festival (information ☎427 17; pick up a brochure at the tourist office).

Liechtenstein Museum, IX, Fürsteng. 1 (☎319 57 67 252; www.liechtensteinmuseum.at). Take tram D to Bauernfeldpl. or bus 40A from Schottentor., to Bauernfeldpl. One of the world's largest private collections, the Liechtenstein Museum includes works by Raphael, Rubens, Rembrandt, all belonging to Prince Hans-Adam II of Liechtenstein. This baroque exhibit is housed in the newly restored Gartenpalais Liechtenstein, beyond which extend beautiful gardens. Open M and W-Su 9am-8pm. €10, students €5.

ORCHESTRAS

Wiener Philharmoniker (Vienna Philharmonic; www.musikverein.at). Performances in the **Musikverein,** Bösendorferstr. 12, on the northeast side of Karlspl. The Musikverein is Austria's—perhaps the world's—premier concert hall. Constructed in 1867, the building allows for unmatched acoustic perfection. The Philharmoniker's program is essentially conservative, although it occasionally includes contemporary classical music. Tickets to Philharmoniker concerts are mostly on a subscription basis and tend to sell out well in advance, but there are 3 ways to get them (it's worth it):

Musikverein box office tickets in advance: Contact the box office of the Musikverein in person or by letter. Ask about special concerts for teenagers. **Standing-room tickets** are available from the Musikverein, but even they must be bought in advance. Open Sept.-June M-F 9am-8pm, Sa 9am-1pm. Write to Gesellschaft der Musikfreunde, Bösendorferstr. 12, A-1010 Wien for more info.

Bundestheaterkasse tickets in advance: As with the Staatsoper, tickets to the Philharmoniker are offered through the Bundestheaterkasse (see **Staatsoper,** p. 115).

Internet: The Philharmoniker maintains its own website (www.wienerphilharmoniker.at), which provides a full schedule, sells tickets, and provides links to sites selling tickets to Philharmoniker performances on tour and at festivals throughout the country. As always, beware of commissions.

Wiener Symphoniker (Vienna Symphony Orchestra), Vienna's second fiddle is frequently on tour, but plays some concerts at the late-19th-century Konzerthaus, III, Lothringerstr. 20, and at the Musikverein (p. 116). The orchestra focuses on 20th-century classical music, including some experimental works. The season runs Sept.-June. Get tickets and information from the Konzerthaus and Musikverein box offices. (Open early Sept. to early June M-F 9am-7:45pm, Sa 9am-1pm; early June to early Sept. M-F 9am-1pm. Tickets €15-100. ☎24 20 02; www.wiener-symphoniker.at, www.konzerthaus.at.)

CHORAL MUSIC

Wiener Sängerknaben (Vienna Boys' Choir). Main showcase is mass every Su at 9:15am (mid-Sept. to late June only) in the **Hofburgkapelle** (U3/orange "Herreng."). Contact HMK@aon.at for info; for more on the singers, see www.wsk.at. To get tickets:

Reserve tickets (€6-30) at least 2 months in advance; write to Hofmusikkapelle, Hofburg, A-1010 Wien, but do not enclose money. You will be sent a slip and can pick up tickets at the Burgkapelle on the F before mass 11am-1pm or 3-5pm, or before Su mass 8:15-9am.

Unreserved seats are sold in small quantity the F before mass 11am-1pm and 3-5pm (get in line 30-60min. early). Max. 2 per person. Some tickets sold early Su morning.

Standing room is free, despite rumors to the contrary, but arrive before 8am on Su.

Online. Follow link for concert dates at www.wsk.at and email appropriate address.

The lads also perform every Friday at 3:30pm at the **Konzerthaus** (see **Wiener Symphoniker,** p. 128). May-June and Sept.-Oct. For tickets (€28.50-32), contact Reisebüro Mondial, Faulmanng. 4, A-1040 Wien (☎58 80 41 41; ticket@mondial.at).

Sunday High Masses occur in the major churches of the city (Augustinerkirche, Michaelerkirche, Stephansdom) and, while they don't include the Boys' Choir, they are glorious, free musical experiences. Services begin at 10 or 11am, year-round.

Wiener Singakademie bills itself as the oldest concert choir in Europe. Brahms was their director for the 1863-1864 season. The choir worked with some of the greatest conductors of choral music, including Mahler, Strauss, Solti, Furtwängler, and Gardiner. They perform in the Konzerthaus. See **Wiener Symphoniker,** p. 128, for ticket info.

THEATER

In the past few years, Vienna has become a city of musicals, with productions of Broadway favorites. 2005 will feature *Romeo und Julia*. A recent fad has been interpretations of famous Austrians' lives, including *Elisabeth, Mozart*, and the "cyber show" *Falco*. Take U1 (red), U2 (purple), or U4 (green) to "Karlspl." to find the **Theater an der Wien,** VI, Linke Wienzeile 6, Vienna's top venue for musicals. The nearby **Raimund Theater** shows popular musicals. Buy tickets at the box office or by phone. (☎58 885; www.musicalvienna.at. Box office at Theater an der Wien open daily 10am-7pm, at Raimund Theater open daily 10am-1pm and 2-6pm. €10-180. Last-minute student tickets available 1hr before start; €11. Standing room tickets also available 1hr. before start at theater; €2.50). **Vienna's English Theatre,** VIII, Josefsg. 12, presents drama in English. (☎40 21 26 00; www.englishtheatre.at. Box office M-F 10am-7:30pm. Tickets €13.50-35.50, student rush €9.) The **International Theatre,** IX, Porzellang. 8, is also an English-language venue. (☎319 62 72. Closed July-Aug. Tickets €20-22, under 26 €11.) **WUK,** IX, Währingerstr. 59 (☎40 12 10), is a center for dance and concerts. Two German-language theaters are **Burgtheater** and **Akademietheater** (tickets at the **Bundestheaterkasse;** see **Opera,** p. 127).

FILM

Though not on the same level as that of Berlin or Paris, Vienna's film scene has much to offer. Serious *cinéastes* should check out the new arenas for experimental film at the MuseumsQuartier. **Films** in English usually play at **Burgkino,** I, Opernring 19 (☎587 84 06; www.burgkino.at; last show around 9:15pm, Sa around 11pm); **Top Kino,** VI, Rahlg. 1 (☎208 30 00; www.topkino.at; films 5:30-10pm), at the intersection of Gumpendorferstr.; and **Haydnkino,** VI, Mariahilferstr. 57, near the U3/orange stop "Neubaug." (☎587 22 62; www.haydnkino.at. Last show usually around 9:30pm.) In the newspaper, films listed with "OF" after the title are shown in the original language; films listed as "OmU" are shown in the original language with subtitles. **Votivkino,** IX,

THE LOCAL STORY

THE CURSE OF THE LIMOUSINE

The story begins in the year 1914, when Archduke Franz Ferdinand, heir to the struggling Hapsburg throne, received an open-topped limousine as a gift from his family. Shortly thereafter, while on an official visit to Sarajevo, the Archduke and his wife were assassinated while riding through the streets in the limo, setting off the nationalistic fervor that started WWI.

After the assassination of the Ferdinands, the limousine passed into the hands of General Potiorek, a commander in the Austrian Army. Right at the beginning of the War, Potiorek suffered a humiliating defeat by the feeble and highly disorganized Serbian Army. His reputation in tatters, Potiorek returned to Vienna only to die impoverished and alone in an insane asylum. The next in line to receive the limousine was a member of Potiorek's personal staff, who owned the car for only two weeks before he lost control of the limo, ran down two peasants, and then swerved into a tree. He died instantly.

The limousine remained ownerless until the end of WWI, at which point it was purchased by a governor of Yugoslavia. After restoring the limo, the governor survived a series of accidents, the last of which cost him one of his arms. He immediately sold the limousine to a doctor.

The doctor enjoyed the limo for

Währingerstr. 12 (☎ 317 35 71; www.votivkino.at), near Schottentor, is an art house popular with students and shows all films in the original language with German subtitles. **Artis Kino, Filmcasino,** and **Stadtkino** also show subtitled art and foreign films. **Künstlerhauskino,** I, Karlspl. 5 (☎ 505 43 28; www.k-haus.at/kino), hosts arthouse film festivals (except in July). Movie tickets cost €5-10; ask about student discounts. In most Austrian cinemas you pay for an assigned seat. In summer, there are several **open-air cinemas** in the Augarten park. (Take tram #31 to "Obere Augartenstr." Shows 9:30pm. €7.50.) Ask at the tourist office for details on occasional free movies in the Volksgarten. While Vienna hosts a full-sized film festival in August (see **Festivals,** below), the rest of the year the Austrian **Filmmuseum,** I, Augustinerstr. 1 (☎ 533 70 54), shows a program of classic and avant-garde films.

FESTIVALS

Vienna hosts an array of annual festivals. The **Vienna Festival** (www.festwochen.at), mid-May to mid-June, has a diverse program of exhibitions, plays, and concerts. The Staatsoper, Volkstheater, and various other establishments host the annual **Jazzfest Wien** during the first weeks of July, featuring many famous acts. For information, contact Jazzfest Wien (www.viennajazz.org). In addition, on the first weekend in June, most clubs and bars in Vienna host bands and DJs for **Lange Nacht der Musik.** (Entrance to all events €15. Tickets can be purchased at any participating location or at www.events.ORF.at/langenachtdermusik.) Vienna has held the **Klangbogen** (☎ 427 17; www.klangbogen.at) every summer from mid-July to mid-August since 1952. It features excellent concerts throughout Vienna, including **Wiener Kammeroper** (Chamber Opera; ☎/fax 513 60 72; www.wienerkammeroper.at), and performances of Mozart's operas in an open-air theater in the Schönbrunner Schloßpark. Pick up a brochure at the tourist office. From mid-July to mid-August, the **Im-Puls Dance Festival** (☎ 523 55 58; www.impulstanz.com) attracts the world's great dance troupes and offers seminars to enthusiasts. Some of Vienna's best parties are thrown by the parties (political, that is). The Social Democrats host the late-June **Danube Island Festival** (www.donauinselfest.at), which draws millions of party-goers annually, while the Communist Party holds a **Volkstimme Festival** in mid-August. Both cater to impressionable youngsters with free rock, jazz, and folk concerts. In mid-October, the annual city-wide film festival **Viennale** kicks off. (Get tickets at www.viennale.at.) In past years, the program has featured over 150 movies from 25 countries. Finally, Vienna's **Rathausplatz Music Film**

Festival, in the Rathauspl. at dusk July-August, is actually in part a display of culinary treats from all around the world. Meanwhile, a huge screen broadcasts operas, ballets, and concerts from around the world. Past years have included *Die Fledermaus, Carmen,* and a New Year's Concert by the Vienna Philharmonic. Also of interest are two colorful parades in summer. During the last weekend of June is the **Regenbogenparade**—a predominantly gay and lesbian celebration of free love. The following weekend is another **Love Parade,** modeled after the one in Berlin, in which more than 400,000 people gather around the Prater and Donau to hear over 20 DJs spin everything from techno to trance. People are literally dancing in the streets—with clothing, without clothing, and everywhere in between.

WINTER FESTIVITIES

The Viennese don't let long winter nights go to waste. Christmas festivities begin in December with **Krampus** parties. Krampus (Black Peter) is a hairy devil that accompanies St. Nicholas on his rounds and gives bad children coal and sticks. On December 5, people in Krampus suits lurk everywhere, rattling their chains and chasing passersby, while small children nibble marzipan Krampus effigies.

As the weather gets sharper, huts of professional *Maroni* (chestnut) roasters and *Bratkartoffeln* (potato pancake) toasters pop up everywhere. Cider, punch, red noses, and *Glühwein* (a hot, spicy mulled wine) become ubiquitous. **Christmas markets** *(Christkindlmärkte)* open around the city. The best-known Christmas market is probably the somewhat tacky **Rathausplatz Christkindlmarkt,** which offers, among other things, excellent *Lebkuchen* (a soft gingerbread-like cookie), *Langos* (a Hungarian round bread soaked in hot oil, garlic, and onions), and beeswax candles. (Open daily 9am-9pm.) **Schloß Schönbrunn's** *Weihnachtsmarkt* offers old-fashioned Christmas decorations. (Open M-F noon-8pm, Sa-Su 10am-8pm.) Visit the happy **Spittelberg** market, where artists and university kids hawk offbeat creations (open M-F 2-9pm, Sa-Su and holidays 10am-9pm), or the **Weihnachtsdorf im Unicampus,** (at the university campus. Open daily 1-10pm.) The **Trachtenmarkt** shop in Schotteng. near Schottentor offers festive-ambience-soaked Christmas shopping. Most theaters, opera houses, and concert halls have Christmas programs (p. 131). The city also turns Rathauspl. into an enormous outdoor skating rink in January and February.

The climax of the New Year's season is the **Neujahrskonzert** (New Year's concert) by the Viennese Philharmonic, broadcast worldwide. The refrain of

six months before he was found trapped under the car in a ditch, crushed to death. The limousine was given to a family member of the doctor, a diamond dealer, who owned the car for a year without incident. He later committed suicide.

The next victim to claim ownership of the limousine was a Swiss racecar driver—he met his demise when he crashed into a stone wall. He was thrown out of the car and over the wall, falling to his death.

At this point, now both an urban legend and an item of significant historical value, the limousine was purchased by a Serbian farmer for an astronomical sum. One day, unable to start the limo, the farmer attempted to tow the car with a horse and buggy. However, having forgotten to turn off the ignition, the limousine mysteriously started, pitched forward, and overturned the buggy, killing the farmer.

The last fatality occurred on the way to a wedding—the limousine had come into the possession of a garage owner who repaired the car to look as it did during Archduke Ferdinand's era. Trying to get to the wedding on time, the limo spun out of control on the highway, crushing most of its passengers.

Today, the limousine resides in Vienna's military history museum—no one has been brave enough to take it out for a spin.

the *Radetzkymarsch* by Strauss signals that the new year has truly begun. New Year's also brings a famously flashy **Imperial Ball** in the Hofburg. For those lacking seven-digit incomes, the City of Vienna organizes a huge chain of *Silvester* (New Year's) parties in the *Innenstadt*. Follow the **Silvesterpfad,** marked by lights hung over the street, for outdoor karaoke, sidewalk waltzing, firecrackers, and hundreds of people drinking champagne in the streets. At midnight, the *Pummerin*, St. Stephan's giant bell, rings across the country, broadcast by public radio stations. Also on New Year's, a huge snowboard ramp is erected before the Riesenrad for **Soul City.** Famous snowboarders perform tricks while DJs spin.

New Year's is barely over before **Fasching** (Carnival season) arrives in February and spins the city into bubbly bedlam. These are the weeks of the Viennese waltzes, the most famous of which, the **Wiener Opernball** (Viennese Opera Ball), draws the glitterati. Tickets must be reserved years in advance. For a free *Fasching* celebration, join the **carnival parade** that winds its way around the Ring, stopping traffic before Lent.

▨ NIGHTLIFE

Vienna has one of the highest bar-to-cobblestone ratios in the world. The *Heurigen* provide an old-world Austrian way to spend an evening (p. 107), but for a more urban night, head downtown. Take the subway (U1/red or U4/green) to "Schwedenpl.," within blocks of the **Bermuda Dreieck** (Bermuda Triangle), so called both for the three-block triangle it covers and for the tipsy revelers who never make it home. Or, head down **Rotenturmstraße** toward Stephansdom, or walk around the areas bounded by the Jewish synagogue and Ruprechtskirche. Another good zone for nightlife in the inner city is the **Bäckerstraße,** with its cellar bars. Slightly outside the Ring, the streets off Burgg. and Stiftg. in District VII and the university quarter (Districts XIII and IX) have loud, hip bars. Along the Ring underneath the U6 tracks sit various bars, many of them also offering space to dance. Along the Danube is the **Donauinsel,** a boardwalk filled with cafés and clubs. In the summer, check out the Palmenhaus in the Imperial Gardens at Schönbrunn.

Vienna's kinetic club scene rages every night of the week, later than most bars. DJs spin until dawn, and some clubs keep it going until 11am the next morning. One fact of Viennese nightlife: it starts late. Don't arrive until after 11pm. The best nights are Friday and Saturday, beginning around 1am or so. For the scoop on raves, concerts, and parties, grab the fliers at swank cafés like **MAK** (p. 105) or **Berg das Café** (p. 106), or pick up a copy of the indispensable *Falter* (€2)—it lists concerts, updates on the gay and lesbian scenes, and places that have sprung up too recently for *Let's Go* to review. Keep in mind that Vienna's club turnover is incredibly rapid, and various establishments' crowds change pretty regularly. A good clubbing strategy is to ask around and try multiple places until you find what you're looking for. Also, grab a schedule for the **Nightbus** system (p. 86), which runs across Vienna all night after regular public transportation stops.

BARS

INSIDE THE RING

Mapitom der Bierlokal, I, Seitenstetteng. 1 (☎535 43 13). Located right in the center of the Bermuda Triangle, this cozy bar has large tables with candles. Beer on tap (0.3L €2.40, 1.5L €9.20). A great place to chat after work on F nights. Open daily 5pm-3am, F-Sa 5pm-4am.

Kaktus, I, Seitenstetteng. 5 (☎0676 67 04 496), in the heart of the Bermuda Triangle. Packed with beautiful 20-somethings and dripping with freely flowing alcohol, this bar offers mainstream music and attractive bartenders. Dress to impress. Beer on tap (0.5L) €3.40. Happy hour (all drinks half-price) M-Th 7-10pm. Sexy service (topless bartenders) F-Sa. Open Su-Th 7pm-3am, F-Sa 7pm-4am.

Skybar, I, Kärntnerstr. 18 (☎513 17 12 0; www.skybox.at). From Stephanspl. walk down Kärntnerstr. Take outside elevator by Steffl sign up to 6th fl., then follow sign. Possibly Vienna's fanciest bar, Skybar offers a great view of two-thirds of Vienna. Live music Tu and Th. Business casual. Cocktails €7.50-12.50. Reservations recommended. Sky-restaurant is next door. Open M-Sa 11:30am-4am, Su 6pm-3am. AmEx, MC, V.

Esterházykeller, I, Haarhofg. 1 (☎533 34 82). Take U3 (green) to "Herreng.," off Naglerg. One of Vienna's least expensive, most relaxed *Weinkeller*. Classy without being snobby. *Grüner Veltliner* wine is €2.20 for 0.25L. Open summer M-F 4-11pm; winter M-F 11am-11pm, Sa-Su 4-11pm.

Jazzland, I, Franz-Josefs-Kai 29 (☎533 25 75). Near U1 (red)/U4 (green) "Schwedenpl." Excellent live jazz of all styles wafts through the bricked interior, appealing to a slightly older clientele. Music 9pm-1am. Cover starting at €11. Open Tu-Sa 7pm-2am.

Benjamin, I, Salzgries 11-13. Outside the Triangle area, down the steps from Ruprechtskirche, left onto Josefs Kai, and left onto Salzgries. Dark and loud, this is a rocker's heaven. Tequila shots €2.70. Free foosball M-W. Open M-F 7pm-2am, Sa-Su until 4am.

First Floor Bar, I, Seitstentteng. 5 (☎535 41 06); enter the big wooden door and walk upstairs. Somewhat hidden in the Bermuda Triangle, this swank upstairs bar plays jazz music and offers an array of mixed cocktails (€7-9), including 8 different kinds of martinis. Great selection of Cuban cigars (€4-20). Open M-Sa 7pm-4am, Su 7pm-3am. AmEx/MC/V.

OUTSIDE THE RING

Das Möbel, VII, Burgg. 10 (☎524 94 97; www.dasmoebel.at). U2 (purple)/U3 (orange) to "Volkstheater." Das Möbel ("The Furniture") functions as a showcase for furniture designers. The metal couches, car-seat chairs, and Swiss-army tables rotate every 3 months and are used (and purchased) by an artsy crowd. Assortment of international newspapers. *Mélange* €2.30. Open daily 10am-1am. MC/V only for furniture purchase.

Chelsea, VIII, Lerchenfeldergürtel U-Bahnbögen 29-30 (☎407 93 09; www.chelsea.co.at). Under the U-Bahn, between Thaliastr. and Josefstädterstr. 3-4 times per week (fewer in July-Aug.) bands from all over rock this underground bar/club. A mixed crowd dances to bands or DJ in a techno-pop atmosphere. Cover €7-11 if a band is playing. Beer (0.5L) €3.10, wine (0.13L) €1.50. Open daily 6pm-4am.

Schikaneder Bar, IV, Margaretenstr., 22-24 (☎585 58 88; www.schikaneder.at). Take U1, U2, or U4 (green) to "Karlspl." Exit onto Wiedener Hauptstr. and head slightly right onto Margaretenstr. (5min.). For a laid-back, unpretentious atmosphere, Schikaneder is the place to go. This artsy bar offers good conversation and plenty of beverages (beer starting at €2, wine by the glass €2.30). The place is packed by 9pm, so be sure to get there early. Open daily 5:30pm-4am. Next door is an alternative movie theater that frequently shows movies in English. (€6. Call ☎585 58 88 for information.)

Charlie P's Irish Pub, IX, Währingerstr. 3 (☎409 79 23; www.charlieps-irishpub.at). Take U2 to Schottentor and walk up Währingerstr. A local crowd composed of many students orders its pints in English here. 0.5L of Guinness is €4.80. Open M-Th 4pm-2am, F 4pm-3am, Sa noon-3am, Su noon-1am.

Loop, VII, Lerchenfeldergürtel 26-27 (☎402 41 95; www.loop.co.at). Under the U-Bahn, down the street from Chelsea. While slightly more expensive, this modern, sleek lounge/bar offers a polished atmosphere bathed in the sounds of soul, funk, house, and new jazz. Cocktails €6-9. Happy hour Su-Th midnight-1am all cocktails €4.80. Open M-W and Su 7pm-2am, Th-Sa 7pm-4am.

Campus im alten AKH, IX, Alserstr. 4. Take U2 (purple) to "Schottentor," then tram 43 or 44 to "Lange G." and backtrack about 200 ft. A park with playgrounds fills the courtyard of this university building, while the sides are lined with 2 *Biergarten* (Universitäts Bräuhaus and Stiegl's Ambulanz), a *Heuriger* (Bierheuriger zum Gangl), and a café (Salittl). Drinks €2-3. Meals around €5. Open daily 9am-2am.

Europa, VII, Zollerg. 8 (☎526 33 83; www.hinterzimmer.at). Concert posters cover the red and blue walls. A hip and attractive 20-something crowd hangs out late. *Mai Tai* €7. *Mélange* €2. Open daily 9am-5am. Kitchen open until 4am. V.

DISCOS AND DANCE CLUBS

Flyers advertise "Clubbings"—huge, organized parties throughout the city. They're a bit like raves, only more widely attended. More information is listed in *Falter*.

Volksgarten Disco, I, Volksgarten (☎533 05 18; www.volksgarten.at). Take U2 (purple) or U3 (orange) to "Volkstheater." Hip-hop/R&B and a teenage crowd on F nights; house and a somewhat older crowd Sa. A mellower option is the adjoining Volksgarten Pavillon, a garden bar with trip-hop, trance, lounge, or house, depending on DJ and night. Cover €6-13. Open Th-Su 10pm-5am. Pavillion open daily in summer; usually no cover.

Flex, I, Donaulände/Augartenbrücke (☎533 75 25; www.flex.at), around the corner from the Schottenring U-Bahn station. Head toward the river and down a narrow staircase. This on-the-water club is a paradise for those tired of the Bermuda Triangle crowd. Dance, get a beer (€4), and grab a spot in the local scene. Benches and tables by the river provide a more relaxed atmosphere. Cover starts at €4. Free after 3:30am. DJs start spinning at 11pm. Open daily 8pm-4am and even earlier in the summer.

Club Habana, I, Mahlerstr. 11 (☎513 20 75; www.clubhabana.at). This basement salsa fest will put the rumba and Latin fire into pretty much anyone. Dancers of all levels are welcome—professionals hit center stage and amateurs line the exterior. Check the Internet for listings of salsa lessons before the clubbing starts. Delicious Brazilian cocktails €8. Cuban cigars €6-26. 18+. Open Th-Sa 9pm-6am, Su-W 9pm-4am. AmEx/MC/V.

Porgy & Bess, I, Riemerg. 11 (☎512 88 11; www.porgy.at). Take U1 (red) to "Stubentor," or tram 1A to "Riemerg." Unequivocally the best jazz club in Vienna, Porgy & Bess draws both Austrian and international musicians to perform within its tastefully decorated walls. While jazz is the primary focus of the club, electronica occasionally spices up the program. Mixed crowd primarily composed of locals, with plenty of room to sit or dance. Shows generally around €15. Mixed drinks €6.80-11.50. Open M-Th and Su 8pm-2am, F-Sa 8pm-4am. MC/V.

Why Not, I, Tiefer Graben 22 (☎925 30 24). This newly renovated gay bar/disco offers both a meeting and greeting venue and a subterranean black-box dance floor. Drinks start at €3. F features 60s-80s music; house and pop rock on Sa nights. Cover €8 (includes €2 drink tickets). Open F-Sa and nights before holidays 10pm-6am.

◪ DAYTRIPS FROM VIENNA

STIFT KLOSTERNEUBURG

Take S-40 from Heiligenstadt (U4/green) or Spittelau (U4, U6/red) to "Klosterneuburg-Kierling" (15min., every 30min., €2.60), or walk 1½hr. from Leopoldsberg. Exit the station, make a left and follow the signs to the Rathaus. The monastery is at the top of the hill (¼ mi.)

Founded by the Babenberg Leopold III in AD 1114, this *Chorherrenstift* (monastery) put the small town of Klosterneuburg on the map as the center of medieval Austrian art and culture. Expanded in 1730 by Emperor Karl IV, the current site boasts not only the palace he built (only two of nine planned domes were completed), but also a museum and a magnificently ornate church. Today, 20 *Augustiner-Chorherren* (Augustinian monks) still reside in the *Stift*. A tour traces the monastery's architectural transition from Romanesque to Baroque and includes the gold-enameled, 51-plaque Verduner Altar, Klosterneuburg's "most precious artwork." (☎02243 411 212; fax 02243 411 31. Tours every hr. M-Su 10am-5pm. €5.50, seniors €4.80, students €3.20. Tours in English Su 2pm or by advanced booking.)

Klosterneuburg's **Stiftsmuseum** offers an impressive collection of paintings, sculpture, tapestries, and relics from medieval and modern times. The museum connects to the **Kaiserzimmer** (Imperial Rooms), which served as the residence of Emperor Charles VI. The high ceilings, porcelain candelabras, and intricate woodwork evoke Austria's former imperial glory. The Stiftsmuseum and the Kaiserzimmer can be viewed without a tour. (Open May to mid-Nov. Tu-Su 10am-5pm. €4.80, seniors €5.90, students €2.90.) Tour and museum combo tickets are also available (€6.90, seniors €5.90, students €3.90.) Check ahead for special exhibitions at Stift Klosterneuburg (☎ 02243 411 251; www.stift-klosterneuburg.at).

STIFT ALTENBURG

Stift Altenburg can be reached via the small town of Horn, which is accessible by train from Franz-Josefs Bahnhof (1½hr.; every hr., but none of the trains are direct; €17.20). Local bus (dir: Franzen or Zwettl) in Horn leaves for the Stift from the Hauptpl. (1.5km from train station, every 1½hr., €1.90). Alternatively, if weather permits, walk the picturesque 6km path from Horn to the Stift (follow the green signs).

Built in 1144 by order of the countess Hildburg von Poigen-Rebgau, this Benedictine monastery stands out as one of Austria's prime examples of Baroque architecture. Originally Gothic in style, the abbey was regularly attacked by Hussites and Swedes during the Thirty Years' War. Most of what is visible now was built after Swedish soldiers sacked the monastery in 1645. Altenburg's subsequent reconstruction stands as a masterpiece of Baroque architecture, with highlights including pastel and gold frescoes of Biblical scenes. Particularly interesting is the **Bibliothek** (library), which contains frescoes with biblical pictures containing themes from philosophy, medicine, and law. The monastery also contains a **crypt** and an ornate ceremonial staircase. Religious artifacts dating back to the 12th century (which somehow survived the Swedes) are also on display. To see the crypt and library, you must take a tour. Information boards describe the *Stift* in German and Czech. Ask at the Klosterladen for information pamphlets in English. Tours are only available for groups and must be arranged in advance. (☎ 02982 3451; www.stift-altenburg.at. Open daily mid-June to Aug. 10am-6pm; Apr. to mid-June and Sept.-Nov. 10am-5pm; last admission 1hr. before closing. €7, students €6.)

The region surrounding the *Stift* is also noteworthy for various rustic goods: high-quality honey, spices, tea, sheep's milk, and wool. To purchase these items, visit the *Stift*'s **Klosterladen.** (☎ 02982 3451 21; info@stift-altenburg.at. Open daily Palm Sunday to early Nov. 9am-noon and 12:45-5pm.) For a taste of the local wines, tour the **Altenburger Stiftskeller,** one of Austria's largest wine cellars. Tours are available only to groups with advance reservations and lasts 20-30min. (€3.50, includes 0.13L of wine.) The abbey also hosts annual art exhibits and summer concerts given by the **Stift Altenburger Musikakademie.** (For tickets and information call ☎ 02982 3451 or email kultur.tourismus@stift-altenburg.at.)

CARNUNTUM

Get to Petronell-Carnuntum by S7 from Wien Nord (Praterstern) or Wien Mitte (dir: Wolfstahl; 1hr., every hr., €8.40). Walk down Brukerstr. (5min.), make a left onto Hauptstr., and continue walking for another 3 blocks; the park/info center is on the right. By car from Vienna: take highway A4, exit at Fischamend, and follow road B9 to Petronell-Carnuntum (30-45min.).

Once the largest Roman outpost in the region, Carnuntum played a vital role in the Imperial defense of its Danube frontier until being conquered by Germanic tribes in the 3rd century. It's now the largest archeological site in Austria. The **Archäologischer Park Carnuntum** showcases a reconstructed temple dedicated to the goddess Diana, the remains of houses, a highly advanced sewer system, and public baths, all dating from the 1st-3rd centuries AD. (Open mid-Mar. to mid-Nov. daily

9am-5pm. Tours July-Aug. M-F 10am, noon, 2pm; Sa 11am; Su 2pm.) Situated about 2.5km away, the **Amphitheater Bad Deutsch-Altenburg** boasts the remnants of an ancient military camp. (Open mid-Mar. to mid-Nov. daily 9am-5pm. Tours Sa 3:30pm.) Another 1km from the military camp lies the **Museum Carnuntum,** which displays Austria's most extensive collection of Roman artifacts, from jewelry to religious objects. (Open mid-Mar. to mid-Nov. M noon-5pm, Tu-Su 10am-5pm, Sa-Su 11am-5pm. Single entrance to all three sites valid for one season €7; students, children, and seniors €5; families €14. Tours Su 3:30pm. €3, families €6, children ages 6-18 €2.) Carnuntum also hosts an annual **gladiator show** and a **Roman Christmas market.** For information visit www.carnuntum.co.at or call ☎ 02163 33770.

TULLN

Tulln can be reached by train from Spittelau (40min.; approx. every 20min. Mar.-Oct. Tu-Su 1-6pm; €3, students and seniors €7). Walk approximately 1km north on Frauentorg. (which turns into Bahnhofstr.) from the train station to reach the Hauptpl.

Located on the Danube, Tulln's sights include ruins from a Roman settlement and beautiful churches. The first Roman military settlement in Rome was founded approximately AD 45-100. A fresco providing proof of the Roman settlement in AD 104 is on display at the **Römermuseum,** Marc Aurel-Parc 1b. (Open Mar.-Oct. Tu-Su 1-6pm. €3, students and seniors €2.) (Directly east of the museum is the excavation of the **porta principalis dextra,** which served as the eastern entrance to the Roman camp (free). In addition, the **Salzturm,** a tower from the Roman city wall, remains intact. (At the corner of Nibelungeng. and Donaulände. Free). The former prison now hosts the **Egon Schiele-Museum** on Fischerg. Egon Schiele, the famous painter born in Tulln in 1890, spent time in this prison. The small but interesting museum displays some of Schiele's work and a reconstruction of his cell. (Open Mar.-Oct. Tu-Su 1-6 pm. €3.50, students and seniors €2.50.) Tulln also contains two churches, the **Minoritenkirche** on Minoritenpl., dating to 1225 (open 8am-7pm; free) and the **Stadtpfarrkirche** on Wienerstr. and Kircheng., dating to AD 1014. (Open summer 7:30am-7:30pm; winter 7:30am-5pm. Free.) Rebuilt in the 18th century, the Minoritenkirche is one of Austria's most beautiful Baroque churches. The Stadtpfarrkirche contains Romanesque, Gothic, Baroque, and Rococo elements. Next to the Stadtpfarrkirche is the late-Romanesque **Karner,** a cemetery chapel. (Open summer 7:30am-7:30pm. Free.) Part of the city walls and the **city tower** remain from the 13th century (free). In addition, Tulln hosts a **Naschmarkt** every Friday 10am-6pm in the Hauptplatz where many local farmers sell fresh produce.

BURGENLAND

Just southeast of Vienna lies Burgenland, a vast expanse of sunflowers, vineyards, and wheat fields with a history as rich as its soil. Cradled by rolling hills and dense forests in the west, the Neusiedlersee in the northeast, and the peaks of the Rosaliengebirge on the present southeastern border, the region still retains much of its Hungarian heritage. In fact, it owes its name to three castles that now lie across the Hungarian border. Not surprisingly, the province has Hungarian-influenced cuisine and pockets of Hungarian speakers in its more rural parts. Burgenland's gentle hills and lush river valleys give it the rich wines and *Heurigen* (cozy, vine-covered taverns) that make it world-famous. Wine connoisseurs will want to drive or bike the clearly-marked Weinroute Burgenland. Because of the seasonal nature of many of its delights, it's best to coordinate your visit to Burgenland with one of the many festivals that enliven the sleepy towns.

HIGHLIGHTS OF BURGENLAND

Walk in Haydn's footsteps through the sumptuous apartments of the Hungarian Esterházy family in **Eisenstadt** (p. 140).

Sample rich, new, privately produced wines in the vineyards of **Rust** (p. 142).

Windsurf on the Neusiedlersee, then catch the *Stadtfest* in **Neusiedl am See** (p. 141)

EISENSTADT   ☎ 02682

Where I wish to live and die.
　—Josef Haydn

Haydn, *Heurigen*, and Huns are the three cultural pillars of Burgenland's tiny provincial capital (pop. 13,500). As court composer for the Esterházy princes, Haydn composed some of his greatest melodies here, and the town still basks in his glory. The Esterházys, powerful Hungarian landholders claiming descent from Attila the Hun, are to this day one of the wealthiest families in Europe, and still occupy their ancestral home. They first settled in Eisenstadt when it was part of Hungary and decided to remain there despite the shifting borders. Today the family owns many of the region's famed vineyards, whose wines rival those from Bordeaux.

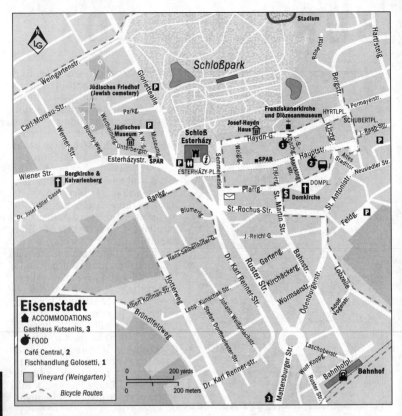

Eisenstadt

▲ ACCOMMODATIONS

Gasthaus Kutsenits, **3**

♦ FOOD

Café Central, **2**
Fischhandlung Golosetti, **1**

▢ Vineyard (Weingarten)

- - - Bicycle Routes

TRANSPORTATION

The easiest way to get to Eisenstadt from Vienna is by **bus** from Südtirolerpl. (U1/red; 1½hr.; every 30min. 6am-8:45pm, fewer on weekends; €6). **Buses** run from Eisenstadt to Rust, Mörbisch, and Wiener Neustadt. The bus stop is at the far end of Dompl. near the cathedral. The bus back to Vienna stops near the Doner Kebap stand. Buy your ticket on the bus and tell the driver where you're going. Getting there by **train** is complicated: from the Südbahnhof, take a Regionalzug toward Deutschkreutz and change trains in Wulkaprodersdorf (1¼hr., 2 per hr., €8). Another option is to take the S-bahn from the Südbahnhof (1½hr., every hr., €8) and switch trains in Neusiedl am See. Board the last train car, since the train splits on its way to Eisenstadt; one section heads to Hungary. To get to Eisenstadt by **car,** take *Autobahn* A3 south from Vienna (50km). From Wiener Neustadt, take Bundesstr. 53 or *Autobahn* S4 east. There is a parking garage beneath the Esterházy Palace. (€0.50 per 30min. Max. 3hr. Open M-F 7am-6pm, Sa 7am-noon.)

ORIENTATION AND PRACTICAL INFORMATION

Eisenstadt is centered around Hauptstr., the city's *Fußgängerzone* (pedestrian zone). Follow Bahnstr. (which becomes St. Martinstr. and then Fanny Eißler.) through the rotary to Rusterstr. to get there from the train station. From the bus stop, walk half a block to the church. With your back to the church, cross Pfarrg. and walk down tiny Marckingstr. to Hauptstr. Turn left and walk to the end, where Schloß Esterházy is on your right. The **tourist office** is in the right wing of the castle. The English-speaking staff has information on accommodations, musical events, guided tours, and *Heurigen* in the Eisenstadt area. (☎67 390; tourism@eisenstadt.co.at. Open 9am-5pm.) **Bank Austria Creditanstalt,** on the corner of St. Martinstr. and Dompl., offers **currency exchange** for up to US$1,000 for a €23 fee. (Open M-W 8am-12:30pm and 1:30-3pm, Th 8am-12:30pm and 1:30-5:30pm.) **Public bathrooms** are at Dompl. and Esterházy Palace. The **post office,** on the corner of Pfarrg. and Semmelweise, has a Western Union. (☎622 71. Open M-F 7am-6pm, Sa 8am-12:30pm.) **Postal Code:** A-7000.

■ ❏ ACCOMMODATIONS AND FOOD

With no youth hostel in the vicinity, *Privatzimmer* are the only budget option. Most are on the outer city limits and rent only during July and August. The hostels in **Vienna** (p. 96) and **Neusiedl am See** (p. 141) are cheaper and only 1hr. away. What accommodations do exist are packed in July and August; reservations are a must. At **Gasthaus Kutsenits ❸,** Mattersburgerstr. 30, a clean room is yours at a reasonable price if you're willing to walk 2km down a busy four-lane highway. From Schloß Esterházy, head back down Rusterstr. to the rotary and take a right onto Mattersburgerstr. (☎635 11. Breakfast included. Rooms €23-40.)

The many **Heurigen** in Eisenstadt offer cheap, modest meals with their wines. Or, just wander along Hauptstr. and follow your nose. **Café Central ❶,** Hauptstr. 40, is a popular lunch spot offering delicious baguette sandwiches (€1.20-3.60) and strudel (€1.80) in a cool, shady enclave. (☎752 34. Open M-Th 7am-midnight, F-Sa 7am-2am, Su 9am-midnight.) **Fischhandlung Golosetti ❶,** Joseph-Stanislaus-Albachg. 4, off Hauptpl., sells big, cheap *Schnitzelsemmeln* and other meat sandwiches for €4-5. (☎629 37. Open Tu-Th 8am-6pm, F 7:30am-6pm, Sa 8am-1pm.)

SPAR Markts are at Esterhazystr. 38 (open M-F 6:30am-12:30pm and 2:30-6pm, Sa 6:30am-noon) and Hauptstr. 13 (open M-F 7:30am-6:30pm, Sa 7:30am-5pm).

◎ ♫ SIGHTS AND ENTERTAINMENT

SCHLOß ESTERHÁZY. Built on the foundations of the Kanizsai family's 14th-century fortress, the castle-turned-palace now known as Schloß Esterházy is still owned by the family whose name it bears. Recently, the palace was actually rented out by the Austrian provincial government, which according to rumor paid millions for maintenance of the splendid **Red Salon** during the lease. The castle has its share of history too: in the **Haydnsaal** (Haydn Hall), the famous composer conducted the court orchestra almost every night from 1761 to 1790. Since the government removed the marble floor and replaced it with a wooden one, the room is so acoustically perfect that every seat provides the same quality of sound. The room is a visual symphony of red velvet, gold leaf, frescoes, and woodwork. (*At the end of Hauptstr.* ☎719 30 00; www.schloss-esterhazy.at. *50min. mandatory tours in German with English text Apr.-Oct. daily every hr. on the hr. 9am-5pm; Nov.-Mar. M-F 10am and 2pm. €5, students and seniors €4, family ticket €11; combined ticket for palace and Haydn-Haus €6.*)

HAYDN EVENTS. Catering to the town's Haydnmania, **Haydnmatinees** feature revolving groups of chamber musicians playing 50min. of his music. (*In the palace.* ☎719 30 00. *Late June to early Sept. W-F 11am. €8, students €5.50, family ticket €17.*) The palace also hosts **Haydnkonzerte.** (*July-Aug. Th 8pm; May-June and Sept.-Oct. Sa 7:30pm. €17-21.*) True Haydn enthusiasts can wait for The Big One: the **Internationale Haydn-**

tage comes to town September 9-19. Held outdoors near the Schloß, it features concerts, operas, and large free video screenings of past concerts. *(Festival office ☎ 618 660; www.haydnfestival.at. Tickets €17-80.)*

THE OLD TOWN. The *Kapellmeister* had a short commute to the concert hall each day: he lived just around the corner. His modest residence is now the **Josef Haydn-Haus**, Haydng. 21, which exhibits original manuscripts, period instruments, and an amazing music stand designed for octet performances. Don't miss the rotating yearly exhibits focusing on particular aspects of the composer. *(☎ 719 39 00; www.haydn-haus.at. Open early Apr. to early Nov. daily 9am-5pm. Guided tours Nov.-Mar. only by appointment €3.50, students €2.50.)*

The *maestro* lies buried in the **Bergkirche**. Haydn's remains were placed there in 1932 after phrenologists removed his head to search for signs of musical genius on the skull's surface. After being displayed at the Vienna Music Museum for years, Haydn's head was reunited with his body in 1954. Entrance to the Bergkirche includes admission to the **Kalvarienberg**, a pilgrimage annex to the church, which illustrates the 14 Stations of the Cross with hand-carved biblical figures. The rooftop stations provide a view of Burgenland. *(From the palace, make a right on to Esterházystr. and walk 2 blocks. ☎ 626 38. Open Easter to Oct. daily 9am-noon and 1-5pm. €2.50, seniors €2, students €1.)*

JEWISH MUSEUM. Eisenstadt's **Jüdisches Museum** covers the history of Jewish life in Eisenstadt and the Burgenland region. The Esterházys were known for their hospitality toward Jews, who played a major part in their rise to power. The exhibits are arranged according to Jewish holidays and contain religious items dating from the 17th century. The building contains an original private synagogue with a beautiful ark in the style of Empress Josephine, as well as Gothic and Oriental murals from the early 1800s. *(Unterbergstr. 6. From the palace, make a right and then another right onto Glorietteallee, then take the 1st left to Unterbergstr. ☎ 651 45; www.ojm.at. Open May-Oct. Tu-Su 10am-5pm; Nov.-Apr. reservations mandatory. €4, students €3, under age 8 free.)* Around the corner on Wertheimerstr., near the hospital, is a **Jewish cemetery** dating back several centuries.

FESTIVALS. Leaving Eisenstadt without sampling the wine would be like leaving Vienna without tasting *Sacher Torte*. From June 26 to July 5 the **Winzerkirtag Kleinhöflein** floods Hauptpl. with kegs, flasks, and bottles as local wineries showcase their goods. From August 20 to 30 is the **Festival of 1000 Wines,** when wineries from all over Burgenland crowd the palace's *Orangerie.* If you like music with your wine, visit May 22-23 when the free outdoor **Eisenstadt Fest** provides all kinds of music. At any other time of the year, fresh wine is available straight from the wineries themselves. Most are small and aren't allowed to open for more than three weeks per year to sell their wine. But fear not—the wineries stagger their opening times so that wine is always available. Ask the tourist office for a schedule. Most of the *Buschenschenken* (wine taverns) are on Kleinhöfler-Hauptstr.

THE NEUSIEDLERSEE REGION

Burgenland's major lake, the Neusiedlersee, is but a vestige (320 km^2) of the water that once blanketed the whole Pannonian Plain. It's large enough that you can barely see the opposite shore, but amazingly never gets deeper than 2m. The shoreline recedes periodically, exposing thousands of square meters of dry land; from 1868 to 1872, the lake dried up entirely. Warm and salty, the See is a haven for more than 250 species of waterfowl. The tall marsh reeds surrounding the lake

BURGENLAND

shelter many rare plants and animals, including bugs, which can make it unpleasant to swim anywhere other than designated areas. **Storks** thrive here, and a glance of their chimney-nests is believed to bring good luck. In 1992, the lake and marsh area were incorporated into the **Neusiedlersee-Seewinkel** national park. (☎021 75 34 42; www.nationalpark-neusiedlersee.org.) **Cruises** (*Schifffahrt*) on the Neusiedlersee allow travel between Rust, Illmitz, and Mörbisch. For more information about the region, contact the **Neusiedlersee Tourismus verbund** at Hauptpl. 1, A-7100 Neusiedl am See (☎22 29; www.neusiedlersee.at).

NEUSIEDL AM SEE ☎02167

Less than 1hr. from Vienna by train, Neusiedl am See is the gateway to the Neusiedlersee region. The principal attraction is the lake, not the town, so consider Neusiedl a day at the beach. Pack a picnic and escape the bustle of Vienna to sail, windsurf, or float along the shallow rippling shores of the See. The Neusiedlersee Card, available at the tourist office and at the lake, gives you admission to the lake as well as discounts on museum entrances throughout the region.

ⓔⓗ TRANSPORTATION AND PRACTICAL INFORMATION. Trains from Vienna (Südbahnhof; €6) and Eisenstadt (€1.50) arrive at Neusiedl am See's **Hauptbahnhof.** (Information and ticket window open 5am-9pm.) To town, head left, veering onto Bahnstr. Turn right onto busy Eisenstädterstr. (which becomes Obere Hauptstr.), following it for 20min. into Hauptpl. Or, take the Bundesbus from the train station parking lot (first bus runs at 4:50am). By **car** from Vienna, take A4, exit 3. From Eisenstadt, take Rte. B50 north and Rte. B51 east. Hail a **taxi** by calling ☎20909, 1718, 5959, or 2245.

The **tourist office** is in the *Rathaus* at Hauptpl. 1. (☎22 29; www.neusiedlamsee.at. Open July-Aug. M-F 8am-6pm, Sa 10am-noon and 2-6pm, Su 4-7pm; May-June and Sept. M-Th 7:30am-noon and 1-4:30pm, F 7:30am-1pm; Oct.-Apr. M-Th 8am-noon and 1-4:30pm, F 8am-1pm.) **Raiffeisenbank,** Untere Hauptstr. 3, has currency exchange. (☎25 64. Open M-Th 8am-12:30pm and 1:30-4pm, F 8am-12:30pm and 1:30-4:30pm.) The train station offers **luggage storage** (€2). For emergency help, call ☎144. The friendly owner of Café Rendez-Vous, Untere Hauptstr. 70, provides **Internet** access. (€1 for 15min., €1.95 for 30min, €3.90 per hr.) The **post office,** Untere Hauptstr. 53, is on the corner of Untere Hauptstr. and Lisztg. (Open M-F 8am-5:30pm.) **Postal Code:** A-7100.

ⓘⓒ ACCOMMODATIONS AND FOOD. Hordes of Austrian families escaping Vienna will be your competition for accommodations, so call ahead. **Jugendherberge Neusiedl am See (HI) ❷,** Herbergg. 1, sports 86 beds in 21 quads and one double. Follow Wienerstr. and turn left onto Goldbergg. The hostel is on the corner at Herbergg. Sitting atop one of Austria's highest peaks, the hostel boasts immaculate pastel rooms with lockers. Amenities include a pool table, foosball, outdoor basketball court, and TV. There are showers for every two rooms, but bathrooms are in the hall. (☎/fax 22 52. Breakfast included. Sheets €1.80. Reception 8am-2pm and 5-8pm. Open Mar.-Oct. Under 19 €11.50, over 19 €12.80.)

The cordial staff at **Gasthof zur Traube ❸,** Hauptpl. 9, will lead you to delightful rooms and an upstairs lounge area, complete with plush, olive green couches. Ask for a room with a patio. (☎24 23; www.zur-traube.at. Breakfast included. All rooms have bath. Singles €36; doubles €56; triples €72.)

Weinlaubengasthof Rathausstüberl ❸, around the corner from the *Rathaus* on Kircheng. 2, is a sunny *Pension* with two singles and 13 doubles. (☎28 83; www.rathausstueberl.at. Breakfast buffet and Neusiedlersee Card included. All rooms with shower, bath, and cable TV. Reservations recommended. €28-€58 per person.) The *Pension* also has a restaurant with a lovely shaded courtyard, great wine, and plenty of fresh fish and vegetarian dishes. The *Menü*, which includes soup and an entrée, costs around €6. (Open Mar.-Dec. daily 10am-10pm.)

Rauchkuchl ❷, Obere Hauptstr. 57, offers *Blaufränker* red wine and other homemade specialties as well as the opportunity to hear local dialect. (☎25 85. Open Tu-Sa 5-11pm.) Towards Rauchkuchl at Obere Hauptstr. 9-11 is the small wine cellar **Weinbau Mullner** (☎/fax 33 95), with a cheap and wide selection, including the famous sweet **Eiswein** (€9 per bottle), made from frozen grapes. It's a bit difficult to find; go up the driveway and knock. If the weather's nice, grab a picnic lunch for the lake at the **Billa** grocery store on Seestr. (Open M-W 8am-7pm, Th 7:30am-7pm, F 7:30am-7:30pm, Sa 7:30am-5pm.)

⚠️🔦 OUTDOOR ACTIVITIES AND ENTERTAINMENT. To get to the **Seebad** (lake area), go to the end of Seestr. (1km), or catch a bus at the *Hauptbahnhof* or in Hauptpl. (2:45, 3:45, 4:40, 5:45, 6:45, 7:45pm; schedules posted at each bus stop; €2.) The lakeshore is rocky, but pleasant. (Lake entrance only with purchase of Neusiedlersee Card: €2.80, ages 14-18 €2.20, under 14 €1.90.)

The **Segelschule Neusiedl am See** (☎34 00 44; www.segelschule-neusiedl.at), at the docks on the far right, rents **dinghies** (3- to 4-person boat €15 per hr., €45 per half-day, €73 per day), **sailboards** €11/€33/€55), or standard **surfboards** (from €11 per hr. The Segelschule is open daily 8:30am-6pm. Paddleboats, rowboats, and electric boats are also for rent nearby.

On the first Saturday in August, Neusiedl hosts a **Stadtfest.** The *Fußgängerzone* (pedestrian zone) comes to life with food booths and music. Admission is free; contact the festival office for more information. (☎32 93; www.impulse-neus-iedl.at. Open W and F 10am-noon.)

RUST   ☎ 02685

Tiny Rust is a summertime haven for tourists looking to enjoy a day at the lake and some of Burgenland's best wines. Known for its sweet dessert wines *(Ausbruch)*, nesting storks, and prime location on the Neusiedlersee, Rust is the perfect weekend destination for students and families alike.

📧🔦 TRANSPORTATION AND PRACTICAL INFORMATION. Rust lies 14km east of Eisenstadt on the Neusiedlersee. It does not have a train station, but **Post-Buses** run from Eisenstadt (30min., several per day, €3) and from platform 24 at the Vienna Südtirolerpl. (1½hr.; 7, 9:55, 11:55am, 3:55, and 6:25pm; last bus back to Vienna leaves Rust at 8:10pm. €9.) You will need to change buses in Eisenstadt; wait where the bus stops and get on the next bus marked Mörbisch. The **bus stop** is located at the post office at Franz-Josef-Pl. 14. By **car** from Vienna, take *Autobahn* A3 to Eisenstadt and then Bundesstr. 52 straight into Rust. A wall map one block left from the front door of the post office will help with orientation.

The **tourist office,** in the Rathaus at Conradpl. 1, hands out maps, plans bicycle tours, and gives information on wine tastings, the lake, and *Privatzimmer*. From the front door of the post office, head left and take a left when you see the church and flagpoles. (☎502; www.rust.at. Open July-Aug. M-F 9am-noon and 1-6pm, Sa 9am-noon and 1-4pm, Su 9am-noon; May-June, and Sept. M-F 9am-noon and 1-5pm, Sa-Su 9am-noon; Oct. M-F 9am-noon and 1-4pm. Nov.-Mar. M-Th 9am-noon and 1-4pm, F 9am-noon; Apr. M-F 9am-noon and 1-4pm, Sa 9am-noon.) The **Raiffeisenbank Freistadt,** Rathauspl. 5, is the best place to **exchange money.** It also has a 24hr. **ATM.** (☎607 05. Open M-F 8am-noon and 1:30-4pm. €1 per check plus a

1.5% commission.) **Bike rental** is available at **Fahrrad Verleih,** Hauptstr. 4. Go through the archway of the Rathaus and into the floral patio to the left. (☎68 36. Open 7am-7pm in summer. €7 per day.)

█ █ ACCOMMODATIONS AND FOOD. If you want to stay in Rust, a *Privatzimmer* is the way to go. There is a free phone available in the archway of the Rathaus to reserve rooms. A lovely, flower-filled patio leads to brown-themed rooms at **Gasthof-Pension Marsoner ❸,** Schubertg. 3. Enjoy your breakfast in the cozy dining area in the adjacent building. From the front door of the post office, follow Eisenstadtstr. right. (☎234. Breakfast included. Singles €26; doubles €42.) Rust's new **Jugendgästehaus ❷,** located at Ruster Bucht 2, sits on the lakefront near tennis courts and bike paths. The streamlined new dorms and sunny breakfast rooms sparkle. From Conradpl., take a right onto Hauptstr., then take a left on Am Seekanal. Take a right onto Seestr. and follow it to the end (10min.); the *Jugendgästehaus* is past Storchencamp near the marina on the right. (☎591; www.tiscover.com/jugendgasthaus.rust. Neusiedlersee Card for entrance to the lakeshore included. Reception until 8pm. Dorms €14.50-16.50. Discounts for stays longer than 3 days.) A pricier option is the four-star **Austria Trend—Seehotel Rust ❹,** Am Seekanal 2-4, which will see to your every need while maintaining a beach-and-country feel. (☎38 10; www.austria-trend.at/rus. Singles €90-100; doubles €75-93.50. Early Jan. to mid-July and late Aug. to early Dec. €87-98; €72-91.50.)

For hostel prices within a 2min. walk of the lake, try **Storchencamp Rust Jugendherberge ❷,** which has clean rooms but no place to lock your belongings. From the beginning of April through October, the hostel also offers camping at the attached **Ruster Camping Platz Freizeitcenter ❶,** which has showers, laundry, a game room, a playground, and a grocery store. (☎595 55 38 in winter; www.gmeiner.co.at. Sheets €2.60. Reception 7:30am-10pm. Wheelchair accessible. Rooms €11.70-24.80, with shower and bath €13.50-26.80. Camping €4.40-5.10 per adult, €2-2.60 per child. €3.20-4 per tent. Neusiedlersee Card for entrance to the shore and showers included. 10% discount on electric and paddle boats.)

Vineyard-restaurants called *Buschenschenken* offer cheap snacks and superb wine; the tourist office has a list. Many are only open in the evenings. Good eats line Rathausstr., though the ravenous should seek out **Zum Alten Haus ❷,** on the corner of Feldg. and Franz-Josef-Pl., which serves up enormous portions of schnitzel and salad for only €9. From the front of the post office, head right. (☎230. Open Tu-Su 9am-10pm.) **Alte Schmiede ❸,** Seezeile 24, festooned with grapevines, serves traditional Austrian food with a Hungarian twist in a lively, friendly atmosphere. (☎64 18. Live traditional music lunch and dinner. Reservations recommended. Open daily 10am-3pm and after 5pm.) The **ADEG Markt** is at Oggauerstr. 3. (☎66 39. Open M-F 7am-noon and 3-6pm, Sa 7am-noon.)

◙ █ SIGHTS AND OUTDOOR ACTIVITIES. Rust is home to the **Weinakademie Osterreich,** Austria's only Wine Academy, in the Seehof at Hauptstr. 31. The institution offers courses ranging from wine cultivation to basic bartending, and holds wine tours and tastings. Inquire at the tourist office. (☎68 53 or 64 51; info@weinakademie.at. Open for wine tastings Sept. daily 2-6pm; Oct.-Aug. F-Su 2-6pm. €11 for 10 tastes.) Many vintners *(Weinbauern)* offer wine tastings and tours of their own cellars, as is the case at **Rudolf Beilschmidt,** Turnerweg 6 (☎326; weinbau.beilschmidt@gmx.at; May-Sept. F 5pm) and **Weingut Marienhof,** Weinbergg. 16. (☎251. 2½hr. tours May-Oct. Tu 6pm. €10; price varies according to number of wines tasted.)

Around the corner from the tourist office, the **Fischerkirche** is the oldest church in Burgenland, dating back to the 12th century. In the 13th century, Queen Mary of Hungary donated the Marienkapelle (Mary's Chapel) after fishermen rescued her

BURGENLAND

from the Mongols; her chapel contains lovely 15th-century sculptures of the Madonna. Romanesque and Gothic sections have also survived the Baroque remodeling fervor. *(Open May-Sept. M-Sa 10am-noon and 2:30-5pm, Su 11am-noon and 2-5pm.; Oct.-Apr. M-Sa 11am-noon and 2-3pm, Su 11am-noon and 2-4pm. Tours by appointment €1; call ☎ 067 69 70 33 16.)*

Sun worshippers can enjoy the **public lake** on the south shore of the Neusiedlersee (www.seenadrust.at). From Conradpl., walk down Hauptstr., take a left onto Am Seekanal, then right onto Seestr., which cuts through the 7km of marsh lands surrounding the lake. Don't be scared off by the lake's cloudy water—the muddy color comes from the shallow, easily disturbed clay bottom. The lakeshore area has a chlorine pool, showers, lockers, restrooms, phones, water slide, and a snack bar. Keep your entrance card to exit the park. *(☎ 591. €4, after 11am €3, after 4pm €2.)*

Rent a **boat** from the *Bootsverleih* attached to the *Jugendgästehaus.* *(Paddleboats €6 for 30min., €8 for 1hr., €21 for 3hr., €30 for 5hr.; electric boats €8/€11/€30/€45, 4-person minimum.)* **Schiffrundfahrten** (boat tours) depart to Podersdorf, on the opposite shore, from the docks to the right of the *Jugendgästehaus.* *(☎ 6893. Boats leave Rust Apr.-Oct. Sa-Su, and holidays 10am and 4pm and return from Podersdorf 11:30am and 5:30pm. €6 per person.)* The area is loaded with **bike trails,** covering a total of 170km. Many follow the circumference of the lake shore; others wind between towns on the Austro-Hungarian border. There are also two designated bike paths leading to Podersdorf and Breitenburg that cross the lake.

STYRIA (STEIERMARK)

Styria, promoted by tourist offices as "the Green Heart of Austria," is the country's second largest province. Styria has been spared the brunt of the tourist invasion prevalent elsewhere, which has allowed for the preservation of its folk traditions and ancient forests. Even its largest city, Graz, remains relatively untarnished by tourists. The crumbling medieval strongholds and farm for the Lipizzaner stallions are among the region's notable attractions. The province is also famous for its wine: Styrian vineyards are essential to any wine tour of Europe.

HIGHLIGHTS OF STYRIA

Peruse the collected treasures of **Graz's** Landesmuseum Joanneum (p. 152).

Marvel at a glass-blowing demonstration in **Bärnbach** (p. 155).

Discover hidden staircases in **Admont's** Benediktinerstift (p. 159).

GRAZ ☎ 0316

Locals treat this bustling metropolis like they would a goddess. She is adored, well maintained, and decorated in nothing but the best. Visitors mingle with the stylish natives on the shop-laden Herrengasse or on the narrow cobblestone Sporgasse, and street musicians play late into warm starry nights. Each summer the ancient churches, charming squares, and romantic Renaissance courtyards become venues for musical festivals including the regional favorite *Styriate*. This, among many other traditions, earned Graz the title of European Cultural Capital in 2003. During that exciting year, a slew of international architects and artists, known as the Grazer School, descended upon the open-minded city and built breathtaking modern pieces like the amorphous green-plated Kunsthaus, an island in the middle of the Mur River shaped like two seashells. Two towers rising from the small mountain in the center of town commemorate a mighty

fortress that withstood centuries of attacks. The mountain continued to be a refuge during war in the 20th century: the citizens of Graz hid in the air-raid tunnels deep inside. The eastern slope of the mountain leads down into the calm *Stadtpark*, full of sunbathers and frisbee-throwers. In the evening, the areas around the park become a center for hip nightlife, thanks to the 42,000 students at nearby Karl-Franzens University.

✖ INTERCITY TRANSPORTATION

Flights: Flughafen Graz, Flughafenstr. 51 (☎290 20), 9km from the city center. Take bus #630 or #631 from the airport into town (20min., 19 per day 5am-11pm, €1.70). Taxis into town cost €15-20, depending on your destination.

Trains: Trains arrive at the **Hauptbahnhof,** on Europapl., west of city center. (☎05 17 17. Open 6am-10pm.) To: **Innsbruck** (5-6hr., 7 per day 6:42am-10pm, €43.50); **Linz** (3½hr., every 2hr. 6:42am-6:42pm, €29.50); **Munich** via Salzburg (6¼hr., €63.10); **Salzburg** (4¼hr., 8 per day 6:42am-8pm, €36.50); **Vienna Südbahnhof** (2½hr., 19 per day 5:30am-9:23pm, €26.90); **Zurich** (10hr.; 8:42am, 10pm; €74.30); **Venice** (9hr.; 10:23am, 8:23pm; €65).

Buses: Graz-Köflach Bus (GKB), Köflacherg. 35-41 (☎59 87; www.busbahnbim.at). Buses run 24hr. Buses leave from Griespl. for western Styria. **Post Bus** office, Andreas-Hofer-Pl. 17 (☎72 810). Open M-F 7am-3pm. **Bundesbus** Hohensdanferg. 6 (☎80 21 48 29). Lines depart from Europapl. 5 (by the train station) and from Andreas-Hofer-Pl.

✖ ORIENTATION

Graz spreads across the Mur River in the southeast corner of Austria. Two-thirds of Graz consists of beautiful parks, earning it the nickname "Garden City." **Hauptplatz** is the city center. **Jakominiplatz,** 5min. from Hauptpl., is the hub of the city's bus and streetcar system. **Herrengasse,** a pedestrian street lined with cafés and boutiques, connects Hauptpl. to Jakominipl., forming the heart of the *Fußgängerzone*. The **Universität** is past the Stadtpark, in Graz's northeast corner. The **Hauptbahnhof** lies on the other side of the river, a short ride from Hauptpl. on tram #3 or 6. To get to the city center from the train station, hop on the #3 or 6 tram to the Hauptpl. stop.

▐ LOCAL TRANSPORTATION

Public Transportation: For information on all local buses, trams, and trains, call or visit **Mobil Zentral,** Schönaug. 6 (☎82 06 06). The staff is informative and English-speaking. Open M-F 9am-6pm, Sa 9am-1pm. Purchase single tickets (€1.70) and 24hr. tickets (€3.40) from the driver, and booklets of 10 tickets (€13) or week-tickets (€8.20) from any *Tabak*. Children under 15 half-price. Tickets are valid for all trams, buses, and the cable car and elevator that ascend the Schloßberg. Validate them at the orange stamp box on the buses. Most trams and buses go until 11:30pm, but a Night Owl program runs 11:30pm-2:30am on the weekends.

Taxi: Funktaxi, ☎983. **City-Funk,** ☎878.

Car Rental: Budget, Europapl. 12 (☎72 20 74, airport 290 23 42).

Automobile Clubs: ÖAMTC, Conrad-von-Hötzendorf-str. 127 (☎50 40). **ARBÖ,** Kappellenstr. 45 (☎27 16 00).

Bicycle Rental: Bicycle Graz, Körösistr. 5 (☎82 13 57 0). 7-speed bikes €9 per day, trekking bikes €7.50, mountain bikes €11. Open M-F 7am-1pm and 2-6pm.

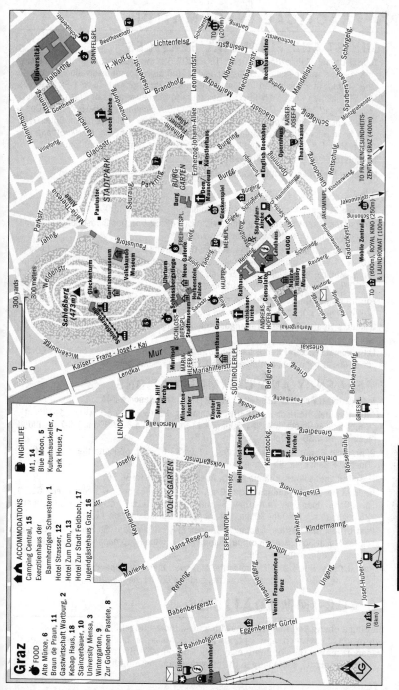

⁊ PRACTICAL INFORMATION

TOURIST AND FINANCIAL SERVICES

Tourist Office: Main office, Herreng. 16 (☎807 50; www.visitgraz.com), has free city maps and a walking guide. English-speaking staff makes room reservations. **Tours** of the *Altstadt* in English start in front of the office (2hr.; Apr.-Oct. Tu-W, F-Su 2:30pm; €7.50, children ages 6-15 €3.75). Bus tours to the newer parts of Graz and Schloß Eggenberg (2½hr.; Apr.-Oct. M, Th 2:30pm; €11.50, children ages 6-15 €5.75). Open June-Sept. M-F 9am-7pm, Sa 9am-6pm, Su 10am-6pm, holidays 10am-6pm; Oct.-May M-Sa 9am-6pm, Su 10am-6pm. **Branch office,** ☎807 50, in the *Hauptbahnhof.* Open M-W, F 8:30am-1pm and 2-5:30pm, Th 8:30am-1pm and 2-6:30pm.

Consulates: UK, Schmiedg. 10 (☎82 61 05).

Currency Exchange: Most banks open M-F 8am-noon and 2-4pm.

LOCAL SERVICES

Luggage Storage: At the Hauptbanhof. Small bag €2, large €3.50. 24hr.

Bookstores: English Bookshop, Tummelpl. 7 (☎82 62 66), has 2 vast floors of fiction and nonfiction. Open M-F 9am-6pm, Sa 9am-noon.

GLBT Organizations: Verein Frauenservice Graz (Women's Information Center), Idlhofg. 20 (☎71 60 22; office@frauenservice.at). Office open M-F 9:30am-2:30pm, Tu 9am-5pm. Medical help available W 5-7pm. Pick up the *Genuine Gay Guide* to Styria at LOGO (see below) or at the tourist office.

Youth Organizations: Jugend Informationsservice "LOGO," Schmiedg. 23a (☎81 60 74; www.logo.at), offers free brochures and advice for youths. Open M-F noon-5pm.

Women's Health Center: Frauengesundheitszentrum Graz, Joanneumring 3, 3rd fl. (☎83 79 98; www.fgz.co.at).

Laundromat: Putzerei Rupp, Jakoministr. 34 (☎82 11 83). 5kg load €6, soap €0.50, dryer €0.30 per 3min., centrifuge €0.50. Open M-F 8am-5pm.

EMERGENCY AND COMMUNICATIONS

Emergencies: Police ☎133 (office 888 27 75), **Ambulance** ☎144.

AIDS Hotline: Steirische AIDS-Hilfe, Schmiedg. 38 (☎81 50 50; www.aids-hilfe.at). Counseling available Tu 4:30-7:30pm, W 11am-1pm, Th 4:30-7:30pm, F 5-7pm. Blood tests Tu, Th 4:30-7:30pm.

Pharmacy: Bären Apotheke, Herreng. 11 (☎83 02 67), opposite the tourist office. Open M-F 8am-6pm, Sa 8am-noon. AmEx/MC/V.

Hospital: Landeskrankenhaus (LKH), Auenbruggerpl. 1 (☎38 50).

Internet Access: Jugendgästehaus Graz, Idlhofg. 74 (see below). 3 computers. €1.50 per 20min. Open daily 7am-10pm. **Sit,** Hans-Sach-g. 10 (☎81 45 65; www.sitnsurf.at). 25 computers. €2.60 for 30min., €4.50 per hr. Open daily 8am-11pm.

Post Office: Main office, Neutorg. 46. Open M-F 7:30am-8pm, Sa 8am-noon. Cashier closes M-F at 5pm. **Branch office,** Europapl. 10, in the *Hauptbahnhof.* Open M-F 7am-11pm, Sa 8am-8pm, Su 1-8pm.

Postal Code: Since Graz straddles the Mur river, there are separate postal codes for each side: A-8010 for the *Altstadt* side, and A-8020 for the *Hauptbahnhof* side.

⌂ ACCOMMODATIONS

Finding a cheap bed in Graz is hard because most budget hotels and *Pensionen* run from €25, with cheaper options in the boondocks. Luckily, the web of local transport makes the commute easy. Ask the tourist office about *Privatzimmer* (€15-30 per night), especially in the crowded summer months.

Jugendgästehaus Graz (HI), Idlhofg. 74 (☎ 48 76; jgh.graz@jgh.at), 20min. from the train station. Exit the station, cross the street, head right on Eggenberger Gürtel, left on Josef-Huber-G. (after the car dealership), and take a right at Idlhofg. The hostel is through a parking lot on the right. Buses #31 and 32 run from Jakominipl. (last bus around midnight). This brand-new hostel has a café, TV room, and **Internet** access (€1.50 per 20min.). Breakfast buffet included. Laundry €2, soap included; dryer €2. Night key available (€20 deposit). Reception 7am-11pm. 4-bed dorms €17; singles €24; doubles €40. All rooms with bath. €3 surcharge for stays of less than 3 nights. Those looking for an even better deal can stay in the *Notlager*, (basement rooms with hall bath), for €16.80 for the first night and €14.20 for subsequent nights. MC/V. ❸

Hotel Strasser, Eggenberger Gürtel 11 (☎ 71 39 77; fax 71 68 56), 5min. from the train station. Exit the station, cross the street, and head right on Eggenberger Gürtel; the hotel is on the left, across from the car repair shop. Airy rooms with sky-high ceilings are clean, comfortable, and colorful. Modern art throughout the stylish rooms and halls. Breakfast included. Free parking. Singles €29, with shower €36; doubles €45/€54; triples with shower €65. AmEx/DC/MC/V. ❸

Hotel Zur Stadt Feldbach, Conrad-von-Hötzendorf-Str. 58 (☎ 82 94 68; fax 82 94 68 15), 15min. walk down Jakominipl. Take tram #4 (dir: Liebnau) or 5 (dir: Puntigam) to "Jakominigürtel." The hotel is on the right. Rooms are plain, clean, and spacious. Hall bathrooms. Breakfast €5. 24hr. reception on 2nd fl. Singles €26, with shower €33; doubles €40/€51; triples with shower €65. ❸

Exerzitienhaus der Barmherzigen Schwestern, Marieng. 6a (☎ 71 60 20; fax 77 59 11 17). Walk straight out of the train station onto Keplerstr., then take a left onto Marieng. The convent is on your right (10min.). The Marienpl. stop of bus #53 drops you off to the right of the convent gates. Ring the bell marked *Exerzitienhaus*. As you might expect from a convent, the rooms are plain and very clean. The grounds of the hostel provide a quiet area in a noisy town; guests are encouraged to relax and enjoy the absence of city sounds. Breakfast €5. Dorms €16, with shower €19; singles €23/€27. ❷

Hotel Zum Dom, Burgerg. 14 (☎ 82 48 00; fax 82 38 00 8; www.domhotel.co.at). From the tourist office turn right then left onto H-Sachs-G., and then left again onto Burgerg. The hotel will be on your left. This stylish palace-turned-hotel in the old city brings luxury up-to-date—the red carpets and chandeliers are integrated into a hip, colorful atmosphere. Each of the spacious rooms has a name, is uniquely decorated, and has a different kind of marble in each bathroom. Breakfast included. Singles €90; doubles €165, come with either a shower or jacuzzi. ❺

Camping Central, Martinhofstr. 3 (☎ 067 63 78 51 02; guenther_walter@utanet.at). Take bus #32 from Jakomininpl. to "Bad Straßgang" (15min.). Follow signs, taking the next right at the Mondo supermarket, and walk up the road. This conveniently-located campground includes admission to a public swimming pool. Laundry €3, dryer €3. Reception 7am-10pm. Open Apr.-Oct. €13 per person, includes tent site and shower; car or camper €24 for 2 people, includes shower and electricity; additional adults €7, children ages 4-15 €5. Additional tax of €0.75 per person per night. ❶

◧ FOOD

Graz's student and tourist communities sustain a bonanza of cheap eateries. On Hauptpl., concession stands sell *Wurst*, ice cream, and other fast food (€1.50-3) until late. Low-priced student hangouts also line Zinzendorfg. near the university. Note that most salads come dressed in the local dark pumpkin-seed oil. At **farmers' markets** on Kaiser-Josef-Pl. and Lendpl. (M-Sa 7am-12:30pm), and *Standl* on Hauptpl. and on Jakominipl. (M-F 7am-6pm, Sa 7am-12:30pm), vendors hawk various goods. There's a **SPAR** grocery store inside the train station (open daily 6am-9pm), and numerous Billas and SPARs around town.

STYRIA

ON THE MENU

STYRIAN FOOD CHEAT SHEET

Set in a fertile valley, Graz offers fresh and delicious local cuisine unique to the Styrian region. Styrian (Steier) food is German, with Mediterranean and Eastern influences. Local dishes of note are *Backhenderl* (crispy fried chicken), *Sterz* (polenta) and *Wurzelfleisch* (cooked pork and vegetables). Mushrooms (*Pilze* or *Schwarmel*) are a particular specialty of the region.

Southeastern Austria is also famous for wines from the countryside. Locally produced whites—*Welschreisling, Weissburgunder, Chardonnay*, and *Sauvingnon blanc*, as well as the West Styrian *Rosé-schilcher*, are all popular selections. While in the countryside eat at a *Buschenschank* (restaurant associated with one of the wineries) to sample the cuisine outdoors, often with a beautiful view. With your wine, try ordering the local classic *Brettljause*, a cold plate with ham, sausage, pickles, cheese, and other cold fixings.

If staying in the city, there are a number of sidewalk cafés and restaurants that take advantage of the well-preserved Renaissance architecture to provide ambiance. On any given night if you wander up the alleyways in the *Altstadt* you're bound to find crowded courtyards with live music—wonderful spots to experience local flavor, in the atmosphere and on your dinner plate.

Braun de Praun, Morellenfeldg. 32 (☎32 20 03). With over 30 menu options (€10-18) and just as many daily specials, Braun de Praun is an Austrian restaurant unafraid of a little culinary experimentation. Main dishes include curry pork with glazed banana and almond-raisin rice (€12.50) and pork "mexicano" (€12.50), but the numerous Styrian dishes, hordes of locals, and *Biergarten* atmosphere keep it firmly rooted in Graz. Open M-Sa 8am-2am. Kitchen closes at 1:30am. AmEx/MC/V. ❸

Alte Münze, Schloßbergpl. 8 (☎82 91 51). *Gasthaus* Alte Münze serves scrumptious Styrian specialties in a traditional setting. Located directly under the beautiful and steep Russian Steps leading up to the clocktower, this historic house was the mint of Graz under Empress Maria Teresia (The basement has minting scenes and old coins on display). Excellent *Kasspatzln* (cheese dumplings) are €6.90 with salad. Try the local dessert *Besoffene Liesl* (*Gugelhopf* cake in apple wine; €3.40). Daily *Menü* €6.90-9.50. Open Tu-Sa 8am-11pm. ❷

Zur Goldenen Pastete, Sporg. 28 (☎82 34 16), just up the street from the Hauptpl. This charming deep red *Gasthaus* is the oldest in the city, built in 1575. It serves large helpings of Austrian classics on the spacious patio and in the ornate dining room. Viennese pork cutlet €9. Most entrées cost €9-12. Open daily 11am-midnight. AmEx/MC/V. ❸

Wintergarten, Sackstr. 3-5 (☎81 16 16), in the atrium of the luxurious Erzherzog Johann Hotel, offers gourmet entrées (€14-20) that change every week. Try their 7-course daily *Menü* (€50). Open W-Su 11:30am-2pm and 6pm-midnight. AmEx/MC/V. ❺

Stainzerbauer, Burgerg. 4 (☎82 11 06), specializes in Styrian food. Delicious dishes include a cooked beef called *Tafelspitz* (€16.50) and roasted calf's liver with apple pieces, bacon, and polenta (€13.80), all served in the traditional and cozy indoor dining room or in the elegant atmosphere of the Renaissance courtyard decked out with fresh flowers and ivy. Open M-Sa 11am-midnight. DC/MC/V. ❹

Gastwirtschaft Wartburg, Halbärthg. 4 (☎32 65 20). This smoky bar resembles an Irish pub. Filling dishes satisfy the student crowd and keep 3 large rooms and both bars full. Lunch specials €5.70, entrées €4-9. Open M-F 10am-4am, Sa 5pm-2am. ❷

Kebap Haus, Jakoministr. 16 (☎81 10 06), just south of Jakominipl. A superior Turkish restaurant with falafel or lamb sandwiches (take-out €2.70-3, sit-down €3.10-3.90), and delicious pizzas (€5.70-6). Lunch specials (around €5.50) include soup, entrée, and salad. Open M-Sa 11am-midnight. AmEx/MC/V. ❷

University Mensa, Sonnenfelspl. 1 (☎32 33 62; fax 32 33 62 75), just east of the Stadtpark at the intersection of Zinzendorfg. and Leechg. Take bus #39 or 63 to "Uni/Mensa" for the best deal in town. Simple, satisfying *Menüs* (€3.30-4.90) include schnitzel, fries, and a Coke. Large a la carte selection. Open M-F 9am-2:30pm. ❶

◎ SIGHTS

THE OLD TOWN. For an entertaining and cheap way to explore Graz, try using the tourist office's free walking tour brochure, *Sights and Attractions in Graz*. If you are into architecture, ask about the New Graz Architecture brochure. The tourist office, a sight in and of itself, is in the **Landhaus,** the seat of the provincial government. In 1557, the building was remodeled in Lombard style by architect Domenico dell'Allio. Through the arch to the right is a striking Renaissance arcaded courtyard, where *Classics in the City* is held every summer (see p. 154).

PROVINCIAL ARSENAL. Anton Solar built the Landeszeughaus between 1642 and 1644 to house the weapons that would defend Styria from the Ottoman Turkish invaders. The first-floor cannon room contains an exhibit called "For the Protection of the Country" detailing the history of the arsenal (with English translations). In 1749, after the Turks had packed up their cannon and gone home, the armory was to be dismantled, until an eloquent protest by Styrian nobles convinced Empress Maria Theresia to preserve it. The building served as a firehouse until it opened as a museum in 1882. Today, the four-story collection includes enough spears, muskets, and armor to outfit 28,000 burly mercenaries. *(Herreng. 16, next to the tourist office. ☎80 17 98 10. Tours in German, French, English at 11am, 3pm, or by appointment. Open Apr.-Oct. Tu-Su 10am-6pm, Th 10am-8pm; Nov.-Mar. Tu-Su 10am-3pm. €1.40. Admission with Joanneum ticket, otherwise adults €4.50, children €3.)*

CHURCHES. The yellow Gothic **Stadtpfarrkirche** was the Abbey Church for the Dominican Order in the 16th century, and suffered severe damage in WWII. The new stained-glass windows installed in 1953 made headlines around the world; the left panel behind the high altar portrays the scourging of Christ, silently watched over by two figures bearing a resemblance to Hitler and Mussolini. The church holds **organ concerts.** *(Herreng. 23. Concerts mid-May to early Aug. Th 11:45am. Schedule available at tourism office or church. Free.)*

Nearby stands Graz's **Dom** (cathedral), built in 15th-century Gothic style by Emperor Friedrich III. In 1485, the church mounted a picture on the south side of the building in remembrance of the "Scourges of God:" the plague, Ottoman invasions, and locusts—holy terrors that had wiped out 80% of the population only five years prior. *(On Hofg., opposite the Burggarten and Burgtor. Open 8am-8pm. Impromptu organ music 11am-noon.)* Next door is the solemn 17th-century Hapsburg **Mausoleum,** an elaborate domed tomb that holds the remains of Ferdinand II. Cryptic English signs are pasted to the stone walls. Master architect Fischer von Erlach (responsible for much of Vienna's Baroque grandeur, including the lush Shonbrunn) designed the beautiful frescoes upstairs. *(Around the corner from the Dom, on Burgg. Free.)*

The 13th-century Gothic **Leechkirche** is the city's oldest structure, having been built (1202), destroyed (1250), and rebuilt (1275-1283). While less popular than its younger counterparts, it deserves a visit from those interested in Gothic architecture. *(Zinzendorfg. 5, between Stadtpark and the university.)*

SCHLOßBERG. The wooded **Schloßberg** rises 123m above Graz. The hill is named for a castle which stood on it from 1125 until 1809, when it was destroyed by Napoleon's troops. Though the castle is mostly gone, the Schloßberg remains a beautiful city park. From Schloßbergpl., visitors can climb the zigzagging stone steps of the **Schloßbergstiege,** built by Russian prisoners during WWI and known as the

Russenstiege (Russian steps) or the *Kriegstiege* (war steps). The path continues through the terraced Herberstein Gardens, a lush park with sweeping views surveying the vast Styrian plain surrounding Graz. The **Glockenturm** (bell-tower), built in 1588, is one of the few castle structures still standing, having been spared by the little emperor in return for a sizeable ransom from Graz's citizens. *(Tower open only with Schloßberg tour, see below.)* Its enormous bell (Liesl) draws a crowd with its 101 clangings (supposedly because it was forged from 101 Turkish cannon balls) thrice daily at 7am, noon, and 7pm. Next to Liesl, you'll find the **Freilichtbühne in den Kasematten,** an outdoor theater built into the ruins of the castle foreman's massive basement. The nearby **Uhrturm** (clock tower), whose clockworks date from 1712, was originally constructed in 1265 and then rebuilt in 1569. *(North of Herreng. and Hauptpl. ☎ 831 17 87. Tours in German or English Apr. to mid-Oct. daily every hr. on the hour 9am-5pm; meet at Glockenturm. €2.15, students and children €1.05.)*

From Schloßbergpl., the **Schloßberg Passage** burrows into the *Berg.* A network of tunnels was blasted into the hill during WWII to serve as a bomb shelter for up to 50,000 civilians. Visitors may walk through the cool, dark main passage and peer down spooky side tunnels. The largest side tunnel opens up into a large modern chamber, the **Dom im Berg,** which is now a popular venue for all sorts of events. *(The quickest way to the top of the Schloßberg is the Lift im Berg, which takes you up 77m; enter from Schloßbergpl. Or take the historic Schloßbergbahn, in operation since 1894. Both are open daily Apr.-Sept. 9am-11pm; Oct.-Mar. 10am-10pm; fare is a valid public transportation ticket or €1.60, children €0.80. Dom im Berg open 8am-8pm, free.)*

PARKS AND GARDENS. Down the hill on the eastern side near the *Uhrturm* and through the Paulustor arch is the **Stadtpark.** Graz acquired the ornate central fountain, whose eight mermaids struggle with huge spitting fish, at the 1873 Vienna World's Fair. South of the fountain is the **Burggarten,** a bit of carefully pruned greenery complementing what remains of Emperor Friedrich III's 15th-century *Burg.* His cryptic wall inscription "A.E.I.O.U." remains a mystery, varyingly interpreted as *"Austria Erit In Orbe Ultima,"* (Austria will be the Ultimate on Earth) or *"Alles Erdreich Ist Österreich Untertan"* (All on Earth is Under Austria).

OTHER SIGHTS. The newest floating addition to the Graz riverscape (completed in 2003) is the **Murinsel,** shaped like a mussel shell. New York architect Vito Acconci designed the piece to house a chic café, open-air theater, and children's playground. Feel free to walk through this island from the bridges on either side. The magnificent **Opernhaus** was built in less than two years by Viennese architects Fellner and Helmer. *(At Opernring and Burgg., down the street from the mausoleum. ☎ 80 08.)*

🏛 MUSEUMS

The tourist office offers a handy pamphlet describing all of Graz's museums and galleries along with their locations, contact information, and prices.

LANDESMUSEUM JOANNEUM. Graz's state museum is Austria's oldest public museum. The holdings are so vast that officials have been forced to keep portions in museums scattered throughout the city. One ticket, purchased at any location, is valid for the Garrisonsmuseum, the Natural History museum, and most art museums in the city. *(For information contact Landesmuseum Joanneum, Rauberg. 10. ☎ 80 17 96 60; www.museum-joanneum.et. €4.30, students and seniors €2.90.)*

KUNSTHAUS GRAZ. The newest addition to the Landesmuseum, completed in the fall of 2003, the Kunsthaus "really does stand out like an alien from another planet" according to co-architect Colin Fournier. The "alien" has "needles," "nozzles," and a sea-green "skin" complete with 900 neon lights that can display giant messages on the east façade—and that's just the outside. Inside, the Kunsthaus specializes in the last 40 years of modern art created in a plethora of different mediums (design, multimedia, film, photography, and architecture). The museum housed exhibits by 20th-century minimalist Sol LeWitt and experimental photographer Vera Luther in its inaugural year. Check at the Kunsthaus or tourism office for an exhibit schedule. *(Lendkai 1. ☎ 8017-9200; www.kunsthausgraz.at. Open Tu-Su 10am-2pm, Th 10am-8pm. Guided tours Tu-Su 11am and 4pm, Th 11am, and 6:30pm; €2.50. Admission €6, students and children €2.50.)*

ART MUSEUMS. The **Joanneum** includes the **Neue Galerie,** housed in the elegant Palais Herberstein, which showcases offbeat, avant-garde 19th- and 20th-century works and paintings. *(Sackstr. 16, at the foot of the Schloßberg. ☎ 82 91 55; fax 81 54 01. Open Tu-Su 10am-6pm, Th 10am-8pm. Tours in German or English Tu, Th, Su 11am, 3pm, or by appointment; €1.50. Admission with Joanneum ticket.)* Its counterpart, located three streets behind the tourist office, is the **Alte Galerie.** This gallery presents a mid-sized collection of medieval and Baroque art, mostly of Styrian origin. Notable holdings include Lucas Cranach's *Judgment of Paris* and Jan Brueghel's copy of his father's gruesome *Triumph of Death.* *(Neutorg. 45. ☎ 80 17 97 70; fax 80 17 98 47. Open Tu-Su 10am-6pm. Tours by appointment. Admission with Joanneum ticket.)* The **Künstlerhaus,** an independent museum in the *Stadtpark,* hosts small exhibitions ranging from Tibetan artifacts to Secessionist paintings by Klimt. *(Open M-Sa 9am-6pm, Su 9am-noon. €1.60, students and children free.)*

HISTORY AND SCIENCE MUSEUMS. At the city museum, or **Stadtmuseum,** temporary exhibits complement the permanent display, which features 19th-century drawings of the city alongside modern photographs and a large-scale model of the city c.1800. Another exhibit is the "Museumsapotheke," which is a reconstructed pharmacy of the Biedermaier period. *(Sackstr. 18, next to the Neue Galerie at western foot of the Schloßberg. ☎ 82 25 80. Open Tu 10am-9pm, W-Sa 10am-6pm, Su 10am-1pm. €7, students and children €1.50.)* On the Schloßberg, the **Garrisonsmuseum** exhibits a modest collection of military uniforms and feathered helmets. *(☎ 82 73 48. Open Tu-Su 10am-5pm. Admission with Joanneum ticket, otherwise €1.60, students €0.85, children €0.40.)* The Joanneum's scientific wing is the **Natural History Museum.** The museum has a specimen of the largest beetle species in the world, an Ichthysaur (fish lizard) fossil, and a dinosaur egg. From the geology gallery, you can leave through the secret exit of the coal mine, the "Schaubergwerk." *(Rauberg. 10. ☎ 80 17 97 30. Open Tu-Su 9am-4pm. Admission with Joanneum ticket, otherwise adults €4.50, children and students €3.)*

ENTERTAINMENT

The tourist office is a great place to find out what is going on in Graz. Ask for a free copy of the magazine *Was ist Wo?* (in German), which details current events with prices and locations. The staff can also help you track down tickets to events and suggest fun free (or cheap) alternatives.

OPERA, THEATER, AND DANCE

For professional music and dance performances, Graz's neo-Baroque **Opernhaus,** at Opernring and Burgg. (☎ 80 08), sells standing-room tickets 1hr. before curtain call. The program includes operas and ballets of worldwide repute. For many young hopefuls, Graz is considered a stepping stone to an international career. One big dance show comes each July while the regular companies are on vacation. Tickets cost €10-100, but standing-room slots start at €2, and student rush tickets (26 and under) cost €5. The **Schauspielhaus** (☎ 80 00), the theater on Freiheitspl. (entrance on Hofg.), sells bargain seats just before

THE HIDDEN DEAL

RUSH, RUSH, RUSH

Any operagoer worth his salt investigates rush ticket options early and often. Wheeling and dealing to get premium seats for the minimum price has become an art form. In Graz, however, one need not pledge their first-born to end up with the best seats in the house.

Why is the Graz Opera so special? For one thing, Graz's shows are groundbreaking. It is often unfairly compared to its more famous cousin in Vienna. Without the burden of a strictly classical repertoire or overpaid "stars" that plague the capital city, the Graz Opera enjoys the freedom to create stunning sets and to mix experimental works with old favorites. Even the classics here are less than sacred; the 2003 season closed with Igor Stravinsky's *The Rake's Progress* as a dystopian 1950's British sitcom complete with a fiery sheet-metal hell and a giant subway map of London looming over the stage!

The Opera is also a breeding ground for fresh talent. The Opernghaus has nurtured some of the most famous performers and conductors in Austrian history. It is known for its youthful, starry-eyed, energetic company. Divas need not apply.

Tickets are a steal at €2 (or less depending on the show!). While there is standing room in the back, often these rush tickets correspond to the best seats in the house—the first three rows!

showtime (daily ticket sales 10am-4pm). All tickets and performance schedules are available at the **Theaterkasse,** Kaiser-Josef-Pl. 10, at the tram stop (☎80 00; open M-F 8am-6:30pm, Sa 8am-1pm), and the central ticket office or **Zentralkartenbüro,** Herreng. 7, on the left inside the passage. (☎83 02 55; www.zkb.at. Open M-F 9am-6pm, Sa 9am-noon.)

FESTIVALS

Since 1985, the city has hosted its own summer festival, **Styriarte.** Concerts, mostly classical, are held daily from late June to late July in the gardens of Schloß Eggenberg, the large halls of Graz Convention Center, and the squares and churches of the old city. Tickets are available at Palais Attems, Sackstr. 17. (☎82 50 00; fax 82 50 00 15; www.styriarte.com. Open M-F 9am-noon and 2-5pm.) Every summer between July and August, the **American Institute of Musical Studies** moves to Graz. Students perform works from Broadway to Schönberg. Ask for a schedule at the tourist office. Tickets are available through the Zentralkartenburo or AIMS itself. (Elisabethstr. 93. ☎32 70 66; www.aimsgraz.com. Tickets €9-37.) From July to mid-August, **organ concerts** are held once a week at the Stadtpfarrkirche (generally Wednesdays at 8pm but dates vary: check at the tourism office; €8, students and children €5). July and August also bring **Jazz-Sommer Graz,** a festival of free concerts. Previous years have seen jazz legends like Dave Brubek, Slide Hampton, and Dizzy Gillespie. (Contact the tourist office. Concerts Th-Sa 8:30pm at Maria Hilferpl.) From late July to early August, Graz surrenders its streets to **La Strada,** the international festival of puppet and street theatre (www.lastrada.at). From late September to October, the **Steirischer Herbst** (Styrian Autumn) festival, Sackstr. 17 (☎81 60 70; www.steirischerst.at.), celebrates avant-garde art with a month of films, performances, art installations, and parties.

FILM

International award-winning movies play in the **Rechbauerkino** theater, Rechbauerstr. 6 (☎83 05 08; www.filmzentrum.com). It occasionally screens un-dubbed arthouse films in English (€6.50, children €5, matinees €5). The **Royal Kino,** Conrad-von-Hötzendorfstr. 10 (☎82 61 33), a few blocks south of Jakominipl., shows new releases in English or their original languages, without subtitles (€7.20, if you sit in one of the first 3 rows €6.20, M-W all features €5, Th-Su before 5:45pm €6.20; students Th-F €5.40, Sa-Su €6.70).

◙ NIGHTLIFE

After-hours activity in Graz can be found in the **Bermuda Dreieck** (Bermuda triangle), in the old city behind Hauptpl. and bordered by Mehlpl., Färberg., and Prokopig. Locals quip that whoever steps into the Bermuda triangle at night never leaves. Dozens of beer gardens and bars are packed all night, every night. Standard procedure is to sit outdoors until about 11pm, when ordinance requires festivities move indoors. Most university students prefer to down their beers in the pubs lining Zinzendorfg. and Halbärthg. on the other side of the Stadtpark.

Kulturhauskeller, Elisabethstr. 30, underneath the *Literaturhaus*. From the Stadtpark, head straight down Elisabethstr. A young hip crowd frequents this subterranean hot spot. 3 back-lit bars serve *Weißbier* for €2.80. Slow mellow beats precede the loud, throbbing dance music. The partying doesn't really get rolling until midnight on weekends. 19+. Obligatory security fee €2. Open Tu-Sa from 9pm until the party dies.

Park House (☎82 74 34, www.parkhouse.at), in the Stadtpark. From the Künstlerhaus, cross Erzherzog-Jonann-Allee and follow the stream 70m. This mellow jazz, blues, and techno music from bar is heard before the enclosed pavilion is seen. The large outdoor bar area is packed with 18- to 30-year-olds night and day. In-house DJs nightly. Drinks €2.30-6.50. Open daily spring to fall 11am-5am; winter 5pm-5am.

Blue Moon, Sackstr. 40 (☎82 97 56, www.bluemoon.graz.com). Set back 50ft. from the street, this local hangout just south of the *Schloßbergbahn* attracts a crowd of artists, musicians, and gays. The black-lit dance floor and small diagonal bar bookend a series of wicker tables and chairs. Check out its cool architecture—the low curved ceilings aren't just for ambience: the bar is actually built back inside the mountain along a tunnel dug as an air raid shelter in WWII. Beer €3, cocktails €6-10. Open M-Sa 8pm-3am.

M1, Forberpl. 1. The view from this ultra-mod bar is hands down the best in town. 3 stories above the Bermuda triangle, M1 serves drinks from 2 different bars and on 3 levels jutting off of a spiral staircase. The terrace on the top floor overlooks the *Altstadt* and hundreds of its red tile roof tops while speakers below play smooth jazz late into the night. Drinks €2.50-7. Cocktail bar Friday and Saturday. Open daily 10am-2am.

> **◪TIP** **GOOD, BETTER, GÖSSER.** Styrian guesthouses and bars proudly flaunt their regional brew. Gösser Brauerie, which can be found just south of Leoben on the same grounds as the Stiff Göss, the oldest abbey in Austria, has been creating an authentic Austrian beer for hundreds of years. Any bar in Styria will sell a large frothy glass for 20-30 cents less than any other brew.

◪ DAYTRIPS FROM GRAZ

BÄRNBACH AND THE STÖLZE GLAS-CENTER

Take the train from Graz to Köflach (50min., 8 per day 6:38am-5:40pm, €5.40), then take the bus to the Hauptpl. in Bämbach. Buses leave after the arrival of every train, and the bus trip is included in the train ticket if your total trip time does not exceed 2hr. From the Hauptpl., head straight on Voitsbergerstr. The Glas-Center will be on your left (3min.). By car, take A2 to Mooskirchen and follow the signs toward Voitsberg and then Bärnbach.

The sleek glass façade of the Stölze Glas-Center, Hochregisterstr. 1-3, is one of many examples of the beautiful glass produced here. The center houses a **glass museum** which traces the development of glass through history and displays many interesting glass pieces, from ancient beads to modern art. A section is devoted to work produced in Bärnbach itself, including perfume bottles, lamps, and a special hand-blown 135L bottle of Almdudler. The showroom in the center has items for sale, ranging from simple ashtrays to elegant vases. Morning tours (specific times depend on demand) showcase **glass-blowing** demonstrations. (☎03142 629 50; glascenter@stoelze.com. Open M-F 9am-5pm, Sa 9am-1pm; May-Oct. M-F 9am-5pm, Sa-Su 9am-1pm. €5.50, children €3.) The Bärnbach **tourist office** is located inside the glass center, but there is also a branch by the **Hundertwasser Church.** (☎031 42 62 00 03 39 06. Open M-F 9am-5pm, Sa-Su 9am-noon.) Free **public toilets** are on the Hauptpl. and by the church. The **post office** is on the right just up Hauptstr. from the Hauptpl. (☎629 49 13. Open M-F 8am-noon and 2-6pm.) **Postal Code:** A-85.

SCHLOß EGGENBERG

Take tram #1 (dir: Eggenberg) to "Schloß Eggenberg" (5am-midnight). Cross the street and backtrack ¼ block, taking the 1st right onto Schloßstr. (10 min.) ☎58 32 64. Exhibits open Apr.-Nov. Tu-Su 9am-4pm. Tours in German and English Apr.-Oct. Tu-Su every hr. 10am-noon and 2-4pm. €6; children, students, and seniors €4.50; Prunkräume (state rooms) tour included. Gardens open daily Apr.-Sept. 8am-7pm; Oct.-Mar. 8am-5pm. €1; free with castle entrance.

West of Graz, the grandiose **Schloß Eggenberg**, Eggenberger Allee 90, contrasts sharply with its plain suburban surroundings. Built for Prince Ulrich of Eggenberg, this multi-towered palace now holds an exquisite historical coin museum, an exhibition of artifacts from antiquity, and a prehistoric museum (all open Feb.-Nov. Tu-Su 9am-5pm). The resonating bird calls and wandering peacocks give it an exotic feel. Incidentally, the last knights' tournament in Styria took place here in 1777; knights took sides based on the answer to the question "Which are prettier, blondes or brunettes?" (Really.) The guided tour of the elegant **Prunkräume**—filled with 17th-century frescoes, tile ovens, and ornate chandeliers—reveals the palace's convoluted design as a microcosm of time. Four towers symbolize the seasons, 12 gates the months, and 365 windows the days. The **Planetensaal**, or Planet Hall, is decorated with illustrations of the days as gods, who bear a suspicious resemblance to the Eggenberger family.

ÖSTERREICHISCHES FREILICHTMUSEUM

The most convenient way to get to the museum is a bus that runs from Lendpl. in Graz (dir: Gratwein; M-Sa 9am, 12:30pm) straight to the museum (return 1:23, 4:35pm; €3.20.) Trains run to Stübing from Graz every hr. (€3.20); from the Stübing train station, turn onto the main road and walk 25min. to the museum. Drivers should take A9 north and then follow the signs to the museum.

The **Österreichisches Freilichtmuseum** (Open-Air Museum), in the nearby town of **Stübing**, recreates 19th-century Austrian farm life in a quiet wooded valley. The museum consists of 90 farmhouses, barns, mills, and storehouses from all over Austria, transported plank by plank and lovingly restored in small villages by their region of origin. Especially interesting are the displays detailing how grain is farmed, how cheese is made, and how bees are kept. Sturdy shoes are best because the walk is long and steep. You can also observe the practice of traditional crafts such as wood carving and lace making. A snack bar at the midpoint of the tour serves slices of bread with various spreads, pastries, and apple wine (€1 each), all fresh from the farm. (☎03124 537 00. Open June-Aug. Tu-Su 9am-6:30pm, no entrance after 5pm; Apr.-May and Sept.-Oct. Tu-Su 9am-5pm, no entrance after 4pm. Exhibits in German. English guidebook €2.20. 2hr. tour in English or German upon request with a group of 5 or more; €2.20. Admission €7, students €4.50, children €3.50.)

LIPIZZANER GESTÜT PIBER (STUD FARM)

The stud farm is 1km outside of the town of Köflach. Take the train from Graz (50min., 8 per day 5:26am-1:40pm, €5.40), then the bus to Piber. Buses leave after the arrival of every train. By car from Graz, take A2 and exit Mooskirchen, then drive through Voitsberg and Bärnbach to Piber. Signing up for the tour from the tourist office in Graz will eliminate any transportation hassles and guarantee an English tour (leaves Sa 2pm from the Graz tourist office, Herreng. 16; €24, children €9).

The **Gestüt Piber (Piber Stud Farm)** is the home of the world-famous **Lipizzaner** horses, whose delicate footwork and snow-white coats are the pride of the Spanish Riding School in Vienna. Born either solid black or brown, they become progressively paler, reaching a pure white color some time between the ages of five and ten. The rolling green hills of Piber are home to the mares, their foals, and trained stallions in retirement. On a 1hr. tour of the stud farm, you can see the horses up close in the stables and visit the carriage house and the Lipizzaner museum in the 300-year-old Piber castle. (☎ 031 44 33 23; www.piber.com. Open Apr.-Oct. daily 9am-5:30pm. €11, students and children €6. Tours available hourly. Call beforehand for English tours.)

STYRIAN WINE COUNTRY

Dominating the Austrian market and competitive throughout Europe, Styrian wine is known for its light, fruity bouquet. Try some local varieties in Deutschlandsberg and then visit the *Weinbauschulen*, where the wine is produced.

DEUTSCHLANDSBERG   ☎ 03462

Deutschlandsberg (pop. 8,000) is a resort town tucked in the rolling hills of southern Styria. Its blooming flowers and freely flowing wine make it a great place to unwind. It's small enough to be quaint but large enough to offer a wealth of dining and drinking options. Sample the local *Schilcher* wine, a dry blush specialty. The main sight in town is the **Burg Deutschlandsberg**, Burgstr. 19, a 12th-century fortress that now houses the ritzy *Burghotel* and the *Burg* museum. From the tourist office, go down the Hauptpl., take a right up Burgstr., and follow the signs. Take the stairs up to the top of the bastion for great views of the town. (☎ 56 02; burgmuseum@deutschlandsberg.at. Open Mar. to mid-Nov. daily 9:30am-5pm; last entry 4pm. Museum €9, students €8, children €6.) From the castle, head back to town along the Schloßstr., where a number of wineries provide refreshments.

The best places to eat (and drink) are the *Buschenschanken* (wine taverns) along Schloßweg, which runs from the castle to the train station. At the top of the hill is **Stöcklpeter ❷**, Schloßweg 53. A sunny terrace with bright red tablecloths and green and yellow umbrellas offers views of the valley and castle. Traditional food (grill plate €8.40) is best with a glass of *Schilcher* (0.25L €2.60). (☎ 28 89. Open Tu-Sa 9am-10pm, Su 9am-9pm. MC/V.) A cheap and convenient option in town is **China Restaurant Peking ❷**, Hauptpl. 39, which offers fast two filling lunch *Menüs* for €4.80-5.80. (☎ 26 40. Open Su-M and Th-Sa 11:30am-2:30pm and 5-11pm.) Turn left from the train station and walk a block to find a **Merkur** market, on Frauental-erstr. (Open M-Th 8am-7pm, F 7:30am-7:30pm, Sa 7am-5pm.) A good accommodations choice is **Buschenschank Kästenbauer ❸**, Schloßweg 21a, situated atop a sloping vineyard. From the train station, turn right, then right again onto Villenstr., cross the tracks, and go left up the footpath (20min.). Some of these large newly renovated rooms have balconies, and all have TV, shower, and toilet. (☎/fax 29 13. Singles €32; doubles €50. MC/V.) **Trains** run from Graz to Deutschlandsberg (dir:

Wies-Eibiswald; 15 per day 5:26am-8:40pm, €7). **Buses** also run directly to Deutschlandsberg from Graz Griespl. for the same price (8 per day 6:20am-10:35pm). **By car** from Graz, take A2 to Leiboch, and from there B76 through Stainz toward Weis/Eibiswald. To get to the **tourist office**, Hauptpl. 34, from the train station, walk straight down the stairs and turn right onto Frauentalerstr. At the rotary turn left onto Fabrinkstr. and continue past the post office to the next intersection where you turn right onto Hauptpl.; the office is on your right. (20min.) The staff provides a hiking and biking map for western Styria (€7) and a free map of the Deutschlandsberg area. (☎75 20; tourismus.deutschlandsberg@uta-net.at. Open Apr.-Oct. M-Tu and Th-F 9am-noon and 3-6pm, W 9am-3pm, Sa 10am-1pm; Nov.-Mar. M-F 9am-3pm, Sa 9am-noon.) The **post office** is at the corner of Fabrikstr. and Frauentalerstr. on the way from the station to the tourist office. (☎46 55 21. Open M-F 8am-12:30pm and 2-5:30pm.) **Postal Code:** A-8530.

RIEGERSBURG
☎03153

This sleepy town, buried in the rolling green hill country east of Graz, might go unnoticed if not for its impressive castle, the **Burg Kronegg**, which balances on the edge of a steep cliff over vast farmland and misty hills. Reach it using the steep, stone-paved path to the castle (30min.), or you can simply turn left from the bus stop, walk up the road to the edge of town, and pay €2 to be lifted to the top by the *Seilbahn.* Lush vineyards clothe the castle slopes, while cypresses peek out in the distance. Take a good look at the elaborate iron pattern covering the well in the castle's second courtyard—it's said that any woman who can spot a horseshoe within the design will find her knight in shining armor within a year. In the shadow of the castle stands the **Greifvogelwarte Riegersburg**, which showcases birds of prey. (☎73 90. Shows in German M-Sa 11am, 3pm, Su 11am, 2, 4pm. Entrance 30min. before the show. €6, children €4.) The castle houses two museums, which are connected thematically as well as physically. The **Hexenmuseum** (Witch Museum) spreads over eight of the rooms, with an exhibit on Feldbach's witch trial (1673-1675), the biggest in Styria's history. The **Burgmuseum** showcases 16 of the castle's rooms with a fascinating exhibit called "Legendary Riegersburg—Legendary Women." The **Weiße Saal** (White Hall), with its stucco ceiling flourishes and crystal chandeliers, serves as a projection surface for the museum's video of waltzing dancers in decolleté gowns in one of several impressive multimedia displays. (☎83 13 1. Open Apr.-Oct. daily 9am-5pm. Su tours of Burgmuseum July and Aug. only 10am, 12:30pm, 3pm; Hexenmuseum 11am, 1:30pm. English tours and guide sheets available upon request. €9.50, students and children €7.)

Lasslhof ❸, at the Riegersburg bus stop, is a yellow hotel with a popular bar/restaurant. Eat some wiener schnitzel with potatoes and salad (€6.50) at the restaurant downstairs or snack on *Frankfurter mit Gulaschsaft* for €3.80. (☎82 01. Breakfast included. Restaurant open 7am-10pm. Reception 7am-10pm. €16.50 per person, with bath and TV €23. €4 fee for 1-night stays; €4 extra for a single.) Stock up on groceries at **SPAR,** just downhill from Lasslhof on the main road. (Open M-F 6:30am-6pm, Sa 6:30am-noon.) Riegersburg is most accessible during the week. A train runs from Graz to Feldbach (1hr., approximately every hr. 6:18am-10:43pm, €8), where a bus to Riegersburg leaves the bus depot near the train station (15min.; 7 per day M-F 6:30am-6:30pm, Sa 9:30 am). An alternative to the train from Graz is the bus from Jakminipl., which runs during the week (M-F 5:30pm, Sa 12:35pm); however the return bus runs only at pre-dawn hours (5:40am). If you are in Riegersburg and do not want to wait for the bus back to Feldbach, Mobile Taxi can take you back to the train station (☎432 13 62). **By car,** Riegersburg is an easy 55km trip from Graz. Take A-2 and get off at the Ilz Exit, then follow the signs. The main **tourist office** is at the beginning of the trail to the castle. To reach it, turn right after the Sparkasse across the Lasslhof. (☎86 70; www.riegersburg.com. Open Apr.-Oct. M-F 11am-5pm.) If you are in Riegersburg when the tourist office is closed, pick up brochures and information at Hexenladen, the wine store next door. **Postal Code:** A-8333.

ADMONT   ☎ 03613

Admont (pop. 2800), gateway to the Gesäuse Alpine region, lies on the border of Styria and Upper Austria, along the Enns River. The rural town is most famous for the **Benediktinerstift** (Benedictine abbey), founded in 1088 and currently staffed by 26 monks. It contains the largest monastic library in the world, containing over 200,000 volumes, including some that date back to the 8th century. Housed within the same complex is a fine arts museum, natural history museum, and collection of religious artifacts. The monastery combines church history with modern art and exciting multimedia exhibits. One spectacular room shows a video that explains the role of the monks in the 21st century and is reflected on the seemingly endless wall of mirrored tiles. To get there, head to the church, then take a right to the courtyard behind it. (☎231 26 01. Open Apr.-Oct. daily 10am-5pm; Dec.-Mar. F-Su 10am-1pm. Guided tours 11am, 3pm; available in English if you call ahead. English info sheets €0.40. €8, students €4. Tours €1.80.)

While in Admont, try one of the leisurely hikes around the valley. An easy walk starting from the train station heads past the swimming pool and down the **Kajetan-Promenade** to the nature park **Eichelau** (15min.). For a longer excursion, try the 1½hr. hike on the bike path running along the river, which has good views of the nearby mountains. To get to the path, head down Hauptstr. until you reach the Fleischerei. Turn right and follow signs for the R7 bike path, which eventually loops back to the beginning. The **Naturbad,** less than a 5min. walk from the train station, is a great place to swim outdoors. The non-chlorinated pool is refreshingly cool, and includes a diving board, shallow area for kids, and volleyball courts. To get there from the train station, face away from the tracks, turn left, then go right into Friedhofsweg cemetery and follow the signs. (Open 9am-7pm in good weather. €2.90.) Normally one of the best places to stay in Admont is **Schloß Röthelstein,** the youth hostel located nearby in a 330-year-old castle. However, the hostel will be closed until June of 2005 for renovations. Check with the tourist office for more information. As an alternative, try the lovely and well-kept **Frühstückspension Mafalda ❸,** Bachpromenade 75. At the post office, turn left and cross the train tracks, then take two rights and cross the tracks again. Mafalda is right under the tracks, only a few minutes from the town center. (☎21 88. Breakfast, TV, and hall showers included. €20 per person; €21.80 for one-night stays.)

To get to the restaurant in the **Gasthaus Kamper ❷,** head down Hauptstr. for several blocks; it will be on your right. Kamper offers good service, a local crowd, and large portions. (Salad bar buffet €2.30-4.50; entrées €8-12. Open Tu-Su 11am-9pm. AmEx/MC/V.) **Stiftskeller ❸,** in the monastery, is a modern restaurant on the higher end of the price spectrum. (☎33 54; www.stiftskeller-admont.at. 3-course *Menü* €15-20. AmEx/MC/V.) For groceries, head to **ADEG,** across from the church. (Open M-F 7:30am-6pm, Sa 7am-noon.) The Admont **train station** desk is open M-F 7am-2:40pm and 4:15-8:40pm, Sa 7am-2:40pm and 4:35-7:30pm, Su 8:30am-2:40pm and 4:25-8:40pm. **Trains** run from **Selzthal,** the regional hub, to Admont (15min., 7:18am-8:18pm, €3.50). Get to Selzthal from Linz (2hr., 6:15am-4:17pm, €16.20) or Bruck an der Mur (switch trains in Leoben, trains from there are 5 per day 7:27am-3:27pm, €3.10). **Buses** to Linz depart from the post office and marketplace (riding the bus requires many changes). To reach the **tourist office** from the train station, head left down Bahnhofstr., then turn right onto Haupstr. The office will be on your left after the church. Staff finds rooms free of charge and offers activity information, comprehensive regional information, and free maps of Admont. (☎21 64; fax 36 48; www.xeis.at. Open M-F 8am-6pm and Sa-Su 9am-noon.) To reach the **post office,** head left from the train station. It's at the corner of Haupstr. on the way to the tourist office. (☎22 41. Open M-F 8am-noon and 2:30-5:30pm, exchange closes at 5pm.) **Postal Code:** A-8911.

LEOBEN ☎03842

Leoben (pop. 30,000) is the proud little town that miners built—quite successful miners. Their legacy is as clear in the city center (the Hauptplatz mining houses) as it is in the present day mining operations just outside of town. Economic prosperity has made it an attractive city and desirable stop on any trip. There's an ancient church, the Gösser beer brewery, and an idyllic city park, Am Glacis. The large town square is ringed with both elaborate old buildings and sleek modern ones. Leoben hosts the international business community at its giant convention center, and all of Styria watches when the tennis matches take place in the massive Donnawitz Stadium. Beyond the narrow city streets, forest trails lead into the green countryside that gave the town its name: Liubina, or "lovely region."

🖥🔊 TRANSPORTATION AND PRACTICAL INFORMATION. The train station information counter. (☎425 45, ext. 390) is open M-F 9am-6pm. **Trains** arrive from: Graz (1hr., every 2hr. 6:42am-8pm, €9.50); Klagenfurt (2hr., every hr. 1:48am-8:30pm, €21); Salzburg (3½hr., 3:45am-8:19pm, €28), and Vienna Sudbahnhof (2hr., every 2hr. 6:57am-10:45pm, €22.50). From smaller towns such as Mariazell, take the **bus** to Bruck an der Mur and then the train to Leoben (15min., 1 per hr. 6:12am-12:55pm, €3.20). For local connections, the main **bus station** in Leoben is a 10min. walk from the train station; turn right onto Parkstr. from Franz-Josef-Str. just before Hauptpl. Since this station does not have an information counter, check the schedules posted by each stop or ask a bus driver for more info. Leoben is minutes from *Autobahn* A9, which runs south to Graz and northwest to Steyr and Linz. Head straight out of the train station and cross the Mur river, and you'll be on **Franz-Josef-Straße,** the main traffic artery of Leoben. Continue straight and you'll reach the center of town, the **Hauptplatz.** The **tourist office** is on the right. (☎440 18; www.leoben.gv.at. Open M 7am-5pm, Tu-F 7am-6:30pm, Sa 9am-12:30pm.) Other services include: **ATMs** at the post office and Raiffeisenbank, Hauptpl. 15 (open M-Th 8am-noon and 2-4:30pm, F 8am-noon and 2-3:30pm); a **parking garage** under Hauptpl. with an entrance on Langg. (turn left off Franz-Josef-Str. onto Dominikanerg; €1.50 per hr., €13.50 per day); **lockers** in the train station (€2); free **public restroom** in the parking garage, accessible from the elevator in the center of Hauptpl. (open M-Sa 7am-8pm, Su 8am-6pm); **taxis** at a stand by the train station (☎17 18); and a **hospital** (☎401). The **post office** is at Erzherzog-Johann-Str. 17, the last right off Franz Josef Str. before Hauptpl. (☎42 47 40. Open M-F 8am-7pm, Sa 8-10am.) **Postal Code:** A-8701.

🛏 ACCOMMODATIONS. In Leoben, there are not many budget rooms. The **Schulverein der Berg-und-Hüttenschule Leoben ❸,** Max-Tendlerstr. 3, rents 48 double rooms, some of which can be rented as singles. Head away from the train station down Franz Josef-Str., then turn right down Max Tendler-Str., which will run into the hostel (10min.). Rooms are large and plain with a bed, desk, and dresser. Call ahead. (☎448 88; fax 44 88 83. Reception M-Sa 7am-4pm. Breakfast included, excluding Su. Singles €18.30; doubles €32.) **Gasthof Altmann ❸,** Südbahnhofstr. 32, has 12 doubles and a three-lane bowling alley. Exiting the train station, facing

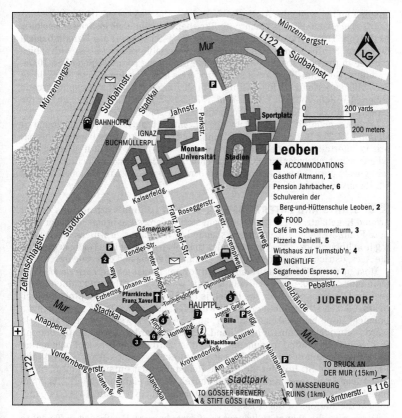

Leoben

▲ ACCOMMODATIONS

Gasthof Altmann, **1**
Pension Jahrbacher, **6**
Schulverein der
  Berg-und-Hüttenschule Leoben, **2**

🍴 FOOD

Café im Schwammerlturm, **3**
Pizzeria Danielli, **5**
Wirtshaus zur Turmstub'n, **4**

🎵 NIGHTLIFE

Segafreedo Espresso, **7**

away from the tracks, turn left and walk down Südbahnhofstr. for 10min.; Altmann is the large green house on the right. Private TVs and showers make Altmann more luxurious than most hotels in this price range. The bowling alley and restaurant (meals €6.50-14.50) fill with locals. (☎/fax 422 16. **Bowling alley** open Tu-Sa 10am-midnight, Su 10am-3pm; €1 for 12min. Free parking. Breakfast €4. Closed late July. Singles €28; doubles €48. MC/V.) **Pension Jahrbacher ❹**, Kirchg. 14, offers bright spacious rooms on the Mur river, just next to the Schwammerlturm: turn right at the street just before tourist information on Hauptpl. and you will see the tower. The newly remodeled rooms come with chic decorations, bathrooms, TVs, and refrigerators. Watch out for the sloping walls and ceilings in some rooms. (☎436 00; jahrbacher.gmbh@gmx.at. Breakfast €4. Singles €38; doubles €70.)

🎵🍴 **FOOD AND NIGHTLIFE.** Kirchg. is home to a number of cheap restaurants. Alternatively, you could grab a bite, perhaps an extravagant *Eis* (-cream) creation, at one of the numerous outdoor cafés crowding the Hauptpl. **Wirsthaus zur Turmstub'n ❷**, Kirchg. 7-9, serves reasonably priced local fare in an Austrian setting, and features dishes like the Miner's plate, a mixed heap of meat to satisfy any appetite (except a vegetarian one!). Enjoy vegetarian meals (€6.50-6.90) and salads (€3-6), if you can stand a little smoke. (☎426 49; www.turmstubn.at. Open M 10am-2pm, Tu-F 10am-10pm, Sa-Su 10am-5pm.

STYRIA

English menu available. AmEx/MC/V.) Climb the glass steps of the *Schwammerlturm* (named for its mushroom-like shape) to find **Café im Schwarmmelturm** at the top. They serve only drinks. (Open M, W-Su 10am-1am.) **Pizzeria Danielli ❷**, Langg. 8, offers great Italian meals at reasonable prices (€5-8) with tables outside in the pedestrian zone and inside the dining room. (Open M-Sa 10am-midnight, Su 10am-10pm.) Get some groceries at the **markets** along Franz-Josef Str.; **Billa** supermarket, Josef-Grafg. 6, in the basement of the shopping arcade (open M-W 8am-7pm, Th 7:30am-7pm, F 7:30am-7:30pm, Sa 7:30am-5pm); or the **farmers' market** on Kirchpl. (open Tu and F 7am-1pm).

Leoben's nightlife is defined by the **Segafredo Espresso Bar,** easily found at Hauptpl. 22. The throngs of hip and fashionable young adults that populate this bar are as entertaining as the drum n' bass music that pours out of it. Closing only when the last customer leaves, this bar's fun movie theme and projection TV entertain guests until the wee hours of the morning. (www.segafredo-leoben.at. Beer €2.10; mixed drinks €2-5. M-Sa 9am-late.)

◨ ▣ SIGHTS AND ENTERTAINMENT. Most of Leoben's attractions center around **Hauptplatz,** 10min. from the train station (cross the bridge and bear right onto Franz-Josef-Str.). Sights are designated by a square sign with an ostrich eating iron horseshoes. The symbol alludes to Leoben's robust iron trade: in the Middle Ages, ostriches were thought to be capable of eating and digesting iron.

Most of the buildings on Hauptpl. are former homes of the *Hammerherren* (hammer men), the men who made their wealth from the iron mines in the region. The most ornate of the bunch is the 1660 **Hacklhaus,** Hauptpl. 9, which bears a dozen statues on its red-and-white façade. Justice holds a sword and a balance, Hope brandishes an anchor, and Wisdom views the world—all backwards—through the mirror in his hand. Standing guard at the center of Hauptpl. is a beautifully crafted monument erected to ward off the fires and plague that devastated much of Styria in the early 18th century. Look for St. Florian the Fire-Proof and St. Rosalia the Plague-Resistant. Just outside Hauptpl. is **Pfarrkirche Franz Xaver,** a rust-colored church whose elaborate interior is dominated by black-and-gold decorations. Go through the Kreuzgang to see 14 paintings of the stations of the cross.

Don't miss the chance to inspect the **Gösser brewery,** Brauhausg. 1. To get to Göss, take bus G or GL from the Bus Banhof, or walk south down Gösser Str. along the Mur in the sun (45min.). The brewery's slogan, plastered throughout Austria, is "Gut, Besser, Gösser" ("Good, Better, Gösser"). Examine antique brewing machinery and swill down a free stein of fresh brew. (☎20 90 58 02. Museum open Apr.-Oct. Sa-Su 10am-6pm. Tours 11am, 1, 3pm and whenever a crowd arrives. €4, students €2.) A few feet away from the beer museum in Göss is Styria's oldest abbey, the **Stift Göss,** founded in 1000. (☎221 48. Open 8am-noon. Call ahead for tours.) The **Stadttheater,** Homanng. 5, is the oldest functioning theater in Austria, completed in 1790. (☎406 23 02. Advance tickets at Zentralkartenbüro, or 1hr. before performances at box office. Theater closed June-Sept.) June and July bring the **Leobener Kultursommer,** a program of theater, concerts, literary readings, and treasure hunts. Tickets at the Zentralkartenbüro in the tourist office. (Open M 9:30am-12:30pm and 3-5pm, Tu-F 9am-12:30pm and 3-6:30pm, Sa 9am-12:30pm.)

To wander away from Leoben, use hiking maps from the tourist office. A 30min. hike begins at the Stadtpark and leads to the **Massenburg ruins.** The castle was torn down in 1820, but its 13th-century gate building still stands. For a longer excursion, try the relatively easy 3hr. **hike** from the Massenburg Ruins East to the Hans Prost Haus, which offers a wonderful view of the valley.

⬛ DAYTRIP FROM LEOBEN

EISENERZ ☎ 03848

Take bus #820 from Leoben (1 hr., 16 per day 6:25am-8:40pm, €5.40). By car, take 146 from Liezen or 115 from Leoben.

The skyline of the strip-mining town Eisenerz is dominated by the astounding *Erzberg*, an orange and maroon tower of stone that looks like a misplaced Aztec pyramid. According to legend, the iron ore in the area around Eisenerz was a gift from a merman who lived in a grotto not far from town. The villagers formed a clever plot to capture him, and as exchange for his release he offered them 10 years of silver, 100 of gold, or iron forever. The men chose iron, and that was the beginning of the prosperous mining center.

The **tourist office,** Theodorkornerplatz, is located in a new building on the main square. (☎37 00; www.eisenerz-heute.at. Open May-Oct. M-F 9am-1pm and 3-5pm; Nov.-Apr. M-F 10:30am-noon and 3-5pm.) A free **public toilet** is next to the fountain in the Bergmannpl. A youth hostel, **Jugend und Familiengastedorf Eisenerz ❸,** is located 5km from the city center. It is a large complex and offers 2- to 6- person suites with toilet and shower in the rooms. Also available is a sauna, café and free parking for guests. (☎43 316 / 70 83; www.jgh.at. €18.50 per person.)

The pyramid of the **Erzberg** is a powerful monument to mining. From the tourist office, head straight out across Freiheitspl., turn left onto Hieflauerstr., then left again up to Bergmannpl. Continue across the square to the street branching off at the upper right, make the next right to the Erzberg, and follow the pointing tridents of the merman signs (15min.). After donning a yellow helmet and slicker, you'll be ready for action on two possible tours. The **Schaubergwerk Erlebniswelt** takes you on a train deep inside the mountain where there is a demonstration of how dynamite is used in mining and a Miner's Chapel dedicated to St. Barbara. You'll also see mining at the entrance to the tunnels, where rock is ground in a huge mortar. The other tour is the **Hauly Abenteuerfahrt,** in which you ride up the mountain in a huge dump truck designed to transport tons of stone from the mines. A ride in one of the "largest taxis in the world" certainly provides a unique way to see Eisenerz. (☎32 00; www.abenteuer-erzberg.at. Open daily May to late Oct. Tours 10am-3pm. German-language tours of the Schaubergwerk 10am, 12:30, 3pm. English guides are available upon request. Calling ahead for either tour is recommended. 1½hr. tour of Schaubergwerk or the 1hr. Hauly ride €13, students and children €6.50; combined ticket €22/€11.)

There are a number of **hikes** and **mountain biking** trails from Eisenerz into the mountains. Either pick up a map at the tourist office or head straight down the road from the bus stop to a parking lot just past the hospital. In about 2½hr., you can hike from the parking lot to the Urlaubskreuz and then descend to the Leopoldsteiner See. From there you can either take the bus back to Eisenerz or return the way you came. In winter time the Präblich **ski area** and its eight lifts come to life. Take the bus toward Leoben; there is a shop right at the base of the main lift. Ski rental and ski courses available from the base. (☎0 38 49 or 60 600.)

MARIAZELL ☎ 03882

The little town of Mariazell, extravagantly subtitled *Gnadenzentrum Europas* (Europe's Center of Mercy), is both a resort and a pilgrimage site. While many come for lazy walks, hikes, skiing in the Bürgeralpe, or a dip in the nearby Erlaufsee, the faithful and needy come to pay homage to a shrine, the miracle-working Madonna carved out of linden wood.

STYRIA

THE LOCAL STORY

LEGEND OF MARIAZELL

In the year 1157, a monk named Magnus was sent to convert the natives of the region. Magnus rode north through Styria for days without seeing a soul. The only possessions he brought were his horse and a carved wooden statue of the Virgin Mary. Magnus rode for several days through precarious mountain passes and over dangerous hills without seeing a soul. When Magnus finally encountered other travelers, he was at first overjoyed, but later dismayed to find they were thieves. Just past midnight, he had a vision of the Virgin Mary sitting on the crescent moon holding the infant Jesus. She warned that he must go immediately and take the statue of her with him.

He raced down the mountain with the robbers hot on his heels, only to be stopped by a wall of stone. Magnus quickly and desperately pulled out the statue of Maria, closed his eyes, and prayed. A thunderous crash made him open his eyes and, to his amazement, the rock had opened enough for him to squeeze through to safety! He emerged in a lovely green valley populated by friendly woodsmen and decided to place the miraculous statue on a tree trunk. Thus was the beginning of Mariazell as a center of mercy.

▐ TRANSPORTATION

It takes some determination and patience to get to Mariazell. The town is accessible from St. Pölten by the mountain **train** Mariazellerbahn (2½hr., 5 per day 7:25am-3:22pm, €11.50). However, the **train station** is actually in the neighboring St. Sebastian. From the station, face away from the tracks, turn right down Erlaufseestr., and uphill onto Wiener Str., to the town center, Hauptpl. (20min). Buses stop right near the center of town and connect Mariazell to: Bruck an der Mur (1¾hr., 5 per day 5:15am-6:15pm, €8.20); Graz (3hr., 4 per day 5:45am-6:10pm, €15); Vienna (4hr.; 5:53am, 4pm; €15.20). The **bus station** is down the steps from the post office. For bus information check the listings posted in the waiting area or ask waiting bus drivers for times and rates. To reach Mariazell **by car** from Graz, take Rte. S35 north to Bruck an der Mur, then Rte. S6 to Rte. 20 north over Aflenz-Kurort and Seeberg-Sattel. From Vienna, take *Autobahn* A1 west to St. Pölten, and exit onto Rte. 20 south (1hr.), over Lilienberg and Annaberg.

▄▐ ORIENTATION AND PRACTICAL INFORMATION

The **tourist office** is at Hauptpl. 13, just uphill from the basilica (5min.). To get there from the bus stop, face away from the station and head left on Ludwig-Leber-Str., then left again on Grazer Str., and you'll get to the Hauptpl. (☎23 66; www.mariazell.at. Open May-Sept. M-F 9am-5:30pm, Sa 9am-4pm, Su 9am-noon; Oct.-Apr. M-F 9am-5pm, Sa 9am-4pm.) The **train station** is at Erlaufseestr. 19. (☎22 30. Open daily 7:30am-6:20pm.) Other services include: **currency exchange** and **ATM** at the Raiffeisenbank (turn right from Wienerstr. at Hauptpl.; open M-F 8am-noon and 2-4pm, Sa 8-11am); **pharmacy** Apotheke zur Gnadenmutter at Hauptpl. 4 (☎21 02; open M-F 8am-noon and 2-6pm, Sa 8am-noon, Su 9:30am-12:30pm); St. Sebastian **Hospital**, Spitalg. 4 (☎22 22); **emergency assistance** (☎144); and smoky **Internet-Café** with two computers, Hauptpl. 8 (☎37 13; open M-Tu and Th-Sa 9am-11pm, Su noon-11pm; €1.50 for 15min., €2.50 for 30min., €4 per hr.) The **post office** is downhill from the tourist office; turn right in front of Xing Long and head downhill. (☎26 31. Open M-F 8am-12:30pm and 1:30pm-5pm.) **Postal Code:** A-8630.

▐ ACCOMMODATIONS

Haus Zach, Wiener Neustädter Str. 29 (☎22 72), on the edge of Mariazell, is slightly more authentic than other hostels in the area. A 20min. walk past the tourist office down Wiener Neustädter Str. leads to this large white house with red window boxes in a cow pasture, on the left. Large, comfortable rooms with matching painted furniture and balconies with views of the valley create a peaceful atmosphere. Breakfast and TV included. Hall bathrooms. €16.50 per person, €2.50 fee for 1-night stays. ❸

Pension Zechner, Wienerstr. 25 (☎60 40; fax 60 40 20). Head downhill from the tourist office and to the right. Cozy rooms with large windows overlook the busy Wienerstrasse. All of the rooms have a bathroom, and many of them have a balcony for taking in the view. Common room with TV and small video library. Breakfast included. Call first so the cheery Frau can open the door. Singles €22.30; doubles €44. In winter €23.13/€46.13. ❸

Sportzentrum-Jugend und Familiengästedorf (HI), Erlaufseestr. 49 (☎/fax 34 543; www.jgh.at). From the train station, face away from the tracks, turn left, and walk about 5min. (30-40min total from Mariazell). Colorful modern apartment-style rooms and lots of amenities make the walk worthwhile. Amenities include **Internet** (coin operated), restaurant (8am-11pm), **climbing wall,** sauna (€8), steam bath (€5.80), squash (M-F €4.35 per 30min., Sa-Su €5.45) and tennis courts (M-F €8.70 per hr.; rackets €2), bike rental (€3.50 per half-day, €7 per day), and a fitness studio (€4.35). 2- to 4-bed rooms €23 per person; singles €29. Under 3 nights €2.50 fee. MC/V. ❸

◨ FOOD

There is a **Billa** Supermarket on Wienerstr. 4. (Open M-W 8am-7pm, Th 7:30am-7pm, F 7:30am-7:30pm, Sa 7:30am-6pm, Su 8am-4pm.)

Wirtshaus Brauerei, Wienerstr. 5 (☎25 23), occupying the oldest building in town, the Wirsthaus served its first home-brewed beer in 1673 and is still quenching the thirst and hunger of pilgrims with its beer (large €3, small €2.40) and large pretzels (€1.40). Main dishes of schnitzel and sausage €9. Tours available M-W and F-Su; no groups on weekends. Open M-Sa 10am-midnight, Su 10am-2pm. MC/V. ❷

Goldenes Kreuz, Wienerstr. 7 (☎23 09), boasts simple, elegant decor including white tablecloths in the candle-lit interior. Enjoy fresh fish entrées, vegetarian fare (€7-9), and traditional dishes (€7-14). Open daily 11am-2pm and 6-11pm. ❸

Hotel Goldener Löwe, Hauptpl. 1a (☎24 44), just downhill from the tourist office, lets you sit on the terrace overlooking Hauptpl. while sipping homemade *Met* (mead; €1.50), nectar of the gods. Serves Italian and Austrian dishes and fancy *Eis* concoctions, but the real reason to visit is the **1st-fl. bathrooms.** A rock- and plant-filled waterfall runs on the wall, a map of constellations lights up as you enter, and each stall is equipped with a 15min. hourglass. Open Tu-Sa 9am-7pm. ❸

Radlwirt, Wiener Neustädter Str. 6 (☎27 31), just up Wiener Neustädter Str. from the tourist office. Offers live music by the owner, whose keyboard is set up in the corner. Austrian dishes €7-9. Open 8am-10pm; hours may vary in winter. ❷

◉ ◭ SIGHTS AND OUTDOOR ACTIVITIES

▧ **BASILIKA MARIAZELL.** Over the years, this town has welcomed millions of devout Christians who come to see the Madonna within the basilica. The building's black spires are visible from anywhere in town. Empress Maria Theresia took her first communion in Mariazell and donated the silver and gold grille that encloses the Gnadenaltar (Mercy Altar) with the Madonna. There are 10-15 services per day for the flocks of pilgrims from Austria and eastern Europe. (*Kardinal-Tisserant-Pl. 1.* ☎*259 50; www.basilika-mariazell.at. Open daily 6am-8pm. Free tours at 8, 10, 11:15am, 6:30pm in German.*) The church's amazing *Schatzkammer* (treasure chamber) overflows with the gifts of former pilgrims, ranging from paintings and

STYRIA

embroidery from the grateful cured to a pearl rosary given by Pope John Paul II upon his pilgrimage to Mariazell in 1983. Behind the church you'll find the *Kerzengrotte* (candle grotto), where you can buy a candle for €0.75. *(Open May to late Oct. Tu-Sa 10am-3pm, Su 11am-3pm. €3, students €1.50, children €1.)*

OUTDOOR ACTIVITIES. A cable car at Wienerstr. 24 zips to the top of the Bürgeralpe. *(☎ 25 55. Every 20min. Jan.-Mar. 8am-5pm; May to late Oct. 9am-5pm; Dec. 8am-4pm. Ascent €6.80, round-trip €9.90; children €5/€6.)* Four ski lifts provide access to the nearby ski slopes and hiking trails. *(Open Dec.-Mar. 8am-5pm. 1-day pass €23, children €11.50; 2-day €43/€21.50.)* For ski information, call the Mariazell tourist office or contact the **Ski- und Snowboardschule,** Hauptpl. 12. *(☎ 27 20. Courses M-Sa 10am-noon and 1:30-3:30pm. 1-day course €28.)* In warmer weather, wander Mariazell's hiking trails. Two types of maps *(€2.18 and €4.20)* are available from the tourist office. You might also consider taking a swim in the crystal clear **Erlaufsee,** a tiny lake surrounded by a white pebble beach. *(From the town center, take the Hans Wertnek Promenade (5km), or catch the city bus from the Postampt to the "Erlaufsee Herrenhaus" stop. 10min., 4 per day July-Aug. 8am-4:45pm, €0.80.)*

CARINTHIA (KÄRNTEN)

Jutting between East Tyrol and Salzburger Land in the west and reaching into the Hohe Tauern National Park and the Glocknergruppe mountain range is Austria's southernmost province, Carinthia. Natives consider Carinthia a vacation paradise, thanks to its warm lakesides. There are nearly 200 lakes in the region, including the **Wörthersee, Ossiachersee, Faakersee,** and **Millstättersee.** In addition to the lakes, abbeys and castles dot the hillsides. If you'll be in Carinthia for a while, consider investing in a **Kärnten Card,** good for two or five weeks of unlimited local transportation, free admission to over 100 area sights and museums, and discounts on many cable cars, cruises, toll roads, stores, and restaurants. (2 weeks €32, ages 7-16 €13, ages 6 and under free; 5 weeks €45/€22/free.)

HIGHLIGHTS OF CARINTHIA

Escape to **Velden,** on the warm, sunny shores of the **Wörthersee** (p. 173).

Travel the (mini) world in Klagenfurt's **Minimundus** amusement park (p. 172).

Admire the view from the impressive medieval castle in **Hochosterwitz** (p. 173).

KLAGENFURT
☎ 0463

On the eastern edge of the emerald Wörthersee, Klagenfurt (pop. 92,000) is a summer destination for Austrian travelers. Austria's southernmost provincial capital attracts thousands of German tourists, who unwind in its lakefront suburbs. The Wörthersee is the warmest lake in the Alps, and serves as Europe's largest skating arena in winter. Renaissance courtyards and espressos in outdoor cafés characterize the leisurely quality of life in and around the town.

Carinthia (Kärnten)

CARINTHIA

▐ TRANSPORTATION

Trains: Hauptbahnhof (☎ 05 17 17), at the intersection of Südbahngürtel and Bahnhofstr. Open daily 5:15am-7:30pm; after-hours use the fare machine. To: **Graz** via Bruck an der Mur (3hr., 11 per day every 2hr. 4:40am-8:30pm, €27.70); **Launsdorf** (dir: Bruck and der Mur; at 10 and 50min. past alternating hours 1:50am-7:35pm, €6); **Lienz** (2hr., 6:21 and 11:09am, €19.40); **Salzburg** (3½hr.; 5:25, 7:26, 9:36, 11:26am, 1:26, 3:36, 5:26, 7:36pm; €27.70); **Vienna Südbahnhof** (4hr., 13 per day 1:48am-8:30pm, €37.30); **Vienna Westbahnhof** (7hr.; 7:26, 11:26am, 3:36pm, €38.50); **Villach** (25min., 2-3 per hr. 12:16am-11:55pm, €6); **Innsbruck** (5hr.; 7:26, 9:36, 11:26am, 1:26, 3:36, 5:36pm; €38.50). Trains also head to: **Florence** (6¾hr.; 11:47pm, 12:16, 12:32am); **Rome** (9¼hr., 11:47pm); and **Venice** (5½hr., 3:06am and 1:09pm).

Buses: Autobusbahnhof (☎ 05 17 17, Central Bus info 38 22 00; www.oebb.at). Buses depart from the Autobusbahnhof to most destinations in Carinthia, including **Graz** (2½hr.; 7:45am, 4:05, 5:05pm; €16.30). Ticket window open M-F 7:30-11am and 11:30am-3:30pm. You can also buy tickets aboard the bus.

By Car: Klagenfurt lies on A2 from the west, Rte. 91 from the south, Rte. 70 from the east, and Rte. 317 from the north. From **Vienna** or **Graz,** take A2 south to Rte. 70 west.

Public Transportation: Klagenfurt's **bus** system is punctual and comprehensive. The tourist office distributes *Fahrpläne* (schedules). The central bus station is at Heiligengeistpl. (☎ 521 534). Buy single tickets (€1.60, children €0.90; 24hr. passes €4/€2.80 or weekly passes (€13/€7) from the driver. *Tabak* kiosks sell cut-rate blocks of tickets. Illegal riders risk a €60 fine. City bus lines #40-42 leave from the train station and go through Neuerpl.

Car Rental: Hertz, St. Ruprechterstr. 12 (☎ 561 47). Open M-F 8am-5pm, Sa 9am-noon. **Avis,** Villacherstr. 1c (☎ 559 38; www.avis.at). Open M-F 7:30am-4:30pm, Sa 9-11am.

Bike Rental: Impulse has 25 affiliates in Carinthia, including the headquarters at Pischeldorferstr. 20. (☎ 516 310; www.impulse.co.at; open Apr.-Sept. M-F 8am-6pm; Oct.-Mar. M-Th 8am-5pm, F 8am-12:30pm), Neuer Pl. 8 (☎ 537 22 23; open M-F 8am-8pm, Sa-Su 10am-5pm), and Campingpl. See. (☎ 211 69. Open M-Sa 9am-9pm.) €5 per 5hr., €9 per day; mountain bikes €10/€16. Helmets €1-2. Children 40% off. The tourist office distributes the pamphlet "Bicycle-Touring," which details local bike paths ranging 10-34km, past castles and monasteries.

▰◢ ▱ ORIENTATION AND PRACTICAL INFORMATION

Alterplatz, Neuer Platz, and **Heiligengeistplatz** comprise the heart of the city and the center of tourist and commercial activity. They lie within the **Ring,** the inner district of Klagenfurt, bordered by St.-Veiter-Ring, Völkermarkter Ring, Viktringer Ring, and Villacher Ring. **Villacherstraße** runs along the **Lendkanal,** a canal that stretches 3.5km from the city center to the Wörthersee.

Tourist Office: Gäste Information (☎ 537 22 23; www.info.klagenfurt.at) is on the 1st fl. of the *Rathaus* at Neuer Pl. 1 . The staff organizes daily tours of the *Altstadt* in German. (1½hr., July-Aug. 10am.) Call 2 weeks in advance to arrange a tour in English, or pick up the "A Walk Through the Old Town" pamphlet and guide yourself. Open May-Sept. M-F 8am-8pm, Sa-Su 10am-5pm; Oct.-Apr. M-F 8am-6pm.

Currency Exchange: At all post offices (exchange machine 24hr.). The post office on Dr. Hermann Str. 4 also has a **Western Union.**

Luggage Storage: Lockers (€2.50-3.50) at the train station require exact change.

Pharmacy: Landschafts-Apotheke, Alterpl. 32. (☎ 550 77). Open M-F 8am-6pm, Sa 8am-noon. AmEx/MC/V. Check any pharmacy window to find the **24hr. pharmacy** on call that night.

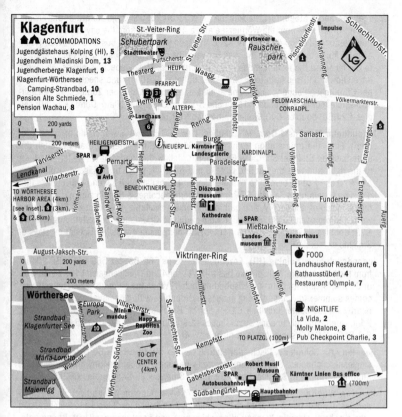

Klagenfurt

▲▲ ACCOMMODATIONS
Jugendgästehaus Kolping (HI), **5**
Jugendheim Mladinski Dom, **13**
Jugendherberge Klagenfurt, **9**
Klagenfurt-Wörthersee
  Camping-Strandbad, **10**
Pension Alte Schmiede, **1**
Pension Wachau, **8**

🍴 FOOD
Landhaushof Restaurant, **6**
Rathausstüberl, **4**
Restaurant Olympia, **7**

🍺 NIGHTLIFE
La Vida, **2**
Molly Malone, **8**
Pub Checkpoint Charlie, **3**

Hospital: Klagenfurt Landeskrankenhaus, St.-Veiter-Str. 47 (☎538).

Emergencies: Police ☎133 or 53 33. **Ambulance** ☎144. **Medical Emergency** ☎141. **Poison** ☎01 406 43430.

GLBT Organizations: Queer Klagenfurt, Postfach 146 (☎50 46 90). Hotline W 7-9pm.

Counseling Services: The knowledgeable staff at the **Jugend Info** office, Fleischbankg. 4 (☎17 99), advise on academic, social, and legal issues. Open M-Th 7:30am-4pm, F 7am-12:30pm. **AIDS-Hilfe Kärnten,** Bahnhofstr. 22 (☎551 28; www.hiv.at). Open M-Tu and Th 5-7pm.

Internet Access: Internet Café, (☎302 45), inside the Sparkasse bank on Neuerpl. €1.46 per 30min. Open M-F 8am-6pm. **Sir Magic's Internet Pub,** Waagg. 10 (☎59 45 94; www.internet-cafe.at). €1 per 15min. Open daily 10am-2am. AmEx.

Post Office: Dr. Hermann Str. 4, (☎55 65 50). Off Neuer Pl. (Open M-F 7:30am-6pm, Sa 7:30am-11pm.)

Postal Code: A-9010.

🏠🏠 ACCOMMODATIONS AND CAMPING

For budget stays, two student dorms serve as overflow accommodations for youth hostels during July and August, usually at the same rates as the primary hostel. The tourist office distributes the English-language "Rooms," a pamphlet that lists all *Privatzimmer*, hostels, and campgrounds.

■ **Jugendherberge Klagenfurt,** Neckheimg. 6 (☎23 00 20; www.oejhv.or.at), at Universität-str., a 20min. walk from the Wörthersee and a 45min. walk from the city center. From the train station, take bus #40, 41, or 42 to "Heiligengeistpl.," then bus #10 or 11 to "Neck-heimg." from stand #2. Take the road between the car dealerships. The hostel's proximity to the lake and the local nightlife make it worthwhile. Mostly spacious quads. All rooms have shower and separate toilet. Breakfast buffet (7-8:30am) and sheets included. Din-ner €6. Kitchen, laundry, and sauna available. **Internet** €2.60 per 20min. 2 wheelchair-accessible rooms. Reception 7-11am and 5-10pm. Check-out 10am. Dorms €17.50; sin-gles €24.50; doubles €40. Non-members add €3.50. ❸

Jugendheim Mladinski Dom, Mikschallee 4 (☎356 51; www.web.chello.at/mladinski-dom). From the train station, turn right on Südbahngürtel, then right and through the underpass on St.-Peter-Str. Cross Ebentalerstr., follow the road that curves left and then to the right, and take the 1st left. Or take bus #40, 41, or 42 to "Heiligengeistpl.," then bus #70 or 71 (dir: Ebental) to "Windischkaserne" from stand #13, and walk in the same direction (bus runs M-Sa until 6:57pm). This dorm becomes a B&B in summer, with large rooms including shower, TV, and bathroom. Parking available. Breakfast €2.50. Laundry: wash and dry each €2.80. Reception 6am-midnight. Open early July to late Aug. Singles €22; doubles €37. Under age 13 €10. €1.50 per person per night discount for stays of 3 nights or more. ❸

Jugendgästehaus Kolping (HI), Enzenbergstr. 26 (☎569 65; fax 569 656 32). 20min. from the train station. Walk or take bus #40, 41, or 42 to "Heiligengeistpl." and then #60 or 61 (dir: Steing. for both) to "Elisabethankirche." When the students leave, Kolping wel-comes summer travelers, offering singles and doubles with gleaming bathrooms. Use of nearby fitness center facilities €1.50 per hr. Breakfast included. Reception July-Aug. 24hr. Open early July to early Sept. Singles €29; doubles €46. Ages 10-15 €20-40; ages 6-9 €16/€16. €3 surcharge for 1-night stay. ❸

Pension Alte Schmiede, Pischeldorferstr. 8 (☎/fax 59 35 59 or 0664 1003787). Airy, singles and doubles. One apartment with living room, couch, balcony, and satellite TV. All rooms with bath. Breakfast until 9am, €3. Singles €27-34; doubles €52-64. ❸

Pension Wachau, Wilfriedg. 19 (☎217 17; www.pension-wachau.at). From Heili-gengeistpl., take bus #10 or 11 to Neckheimg., then walk back 2 blocks to Wilfriedg. and take a right. Residential Wachau offers shiny pine and floral rooms, all with TV and bath. Parking available. Breakfast included. Reservations recommended. Singles €42-44; dou-bles €70-74. AmEx/DC/MC/V. ❹

Klagenfurt-Wörthersee Camping-Strandbad (☎211 69; www.tiscover.at/camping-klagenfurt), on Metnitzstrand off Universitätsstr. From the train station, take bus #40, 41, or 42 to "Heiligengeistpl.," then bus #12 to "Strandbad Klagenfurter See." Turn left and walk 2min. The busy yet comfortable campsite is on the left, across the street from the Wörthersee. On-site grocery store. Beach access. Hot showers included. Mid-June to mid-Aug. €7.30 per adult, €4.20 per child ages 3-14. Early May to mid-June and mid-Aug. to late Sept. €4.50/€2.30. Large caravan site €8.40, small site €4.20. Tax €1.34 per per-son per night. AmEx/MC/V. ❶

🍴 FOOD

With a few exceptions, restaurants in Klagenfurt are closed on Sundays. The tour-ist office's *Sonntagsbraten* lists addresses and hours of cafés, restaurants, and bars that are open on Sundays. Every Thursday and Saturday 8am-noon, the com-pact **Benediktinerplatz** on the lower west side of the *Altstadt* welcomes a fruit and vegetable market. There is a **SPAR** on the corner of Bahnhofstr. and Miesstalerstr. (Open Tu-F 6:50am-6:30pm, Sa 6:50am-1pm, Su 8am-noon and 5-7pm), and one near Heiligengeistpl. (Open M-F 8:30am-6:30pm, Sa 8:30am-5pm.)

▧ **Restaurant Olympia,** Stauderpl. 1, just west of Heiligengeistpl. Greek food prepared by Greek owners can't be beat. Meals fit for heros include tzatziki (€3.10), pita (€2.10), and gyro platters (€10-12). Wash it all down with Metaxa or ouzo (€1.90). And in case you just can't stop yourself, there's always wiener schnitzel (€7.40). Midday buffets M-F 11:30am-2pm, €6.90. Open daily 11:30am-3pm and 5:30pm-midnight. ❷

Landhaushof Restaurant (☎ 50 23 63; fax 75 17), inside the courtyard of the Landhaus on Ursulineng. Savor tastefully presented meals in the courtyard in front of the Landhaus, or eat in the stylish dining rooms. Lunch *Menü* €6. Wiener schnitzel €10. Open daily 11am-midnight, kitchen open until 11pm (Su 10pm). AmEx/DC/MC/V. ❷

Rathausstüberl, Pfarrpl. 8 (☎573 47), on a cobblestone street near the Pfarrkirche, serves fresh Carinthian specialties like *Marillen-* and *Zweschgenknödeln* (apricots and plums baked into a shell covered in brown sugar and butter; €6.50-7.30) alongside favorites like *Spätzel* (€6.50). Enjoy beer (0.3L €2.20, 0.5L €2.70) and a full meal with the sociable local crowd. Open M-Sa 11am-10pm. ❷

🅖 SIGHTS

Klagenfurt and its suburbs are home to no fewer than 23 castles and mansions: the tourist office's English brochure *"From Castle to Castle"* gives a suggested itinerary. Another brochure, the German-language *"Museumswandern,"* gives addresses and hours for the city's 17 art galleries, 18 museums, and other attractions.

THE OLD TOWN. The *Altstadt* buildings display an amalgam of architectural styles: *Biedermeier,* Italian Renaissance, Mannerist, Baroque, and *Jugendstil.* At the edge of Alterpl. stands the 16th-century **Landhaus,** originally an arsenal and later the seat of the provincial council. The symmetrical towers, staircases, and flanking projections create an elegant courtyard. Inside, 665 brilliant coats of arms blanket the walls of the *Wappensaal.* Artist Johann Ferdinand Fromiller took 20 years to complete these pieces. Guided tours in English last 20-30min. from 10am-4pm on the hour. (☎57 75 72 15. Open Apr.-Oct. daily 9am-5pm. €3, students and seniors €2, free with Kärnten Card.)

A stroll through Kramerg., one of the oldest streets in Klagenfurt, leads past the bronze statue of the legendary **Wörther-See Manndl,** whose little keg incessantly spills water into the pool below. Continue on Kramerg. directly to **Neuer Platz,** a torrent of motion and activity. Empress Maria Theresia gazes regally over the eastern end, while opposite her a 60-ton copper half-lizard, half-serpent creature spits water defiantly at his conqueror, a moustached Hercules. The fountain represents the slaying of the **Lindwurm,** Klagenfurt's heraldic beast.

CATHEDRAL. Rebuilt after Allied bombing in 1944, the modern exterior of the **Kathedrale** renders it almost indistinguishable from its surroundings on **Domplatz.** Inside, however, it is awash with high arches, crystal chandeliers, pink and white floral stucco, and a brilliant gold altar. The tiny **Diözesanmuseum** next door displays pre-war ecclesiastical treasures, including the *Holleiner Kreuz,* dating from 1170, as well as the oldest existing stained-glass window in Austria—an 800-year-old sliver portraying Mary Magdalene. (Lidmanskyg. 10. ☎57770 1064. Cathedral open daily 6:30am-7pm. Free. Museum open M-Sa early to mid-June. 10am-noon; mid-June to mid-Sept. 10am-noon; mid-June to mid-Sept. 10am-noon and 3-5pm; mid-Sept. to mid-Oct. 10am-noon. €2.30, seniors €1.50, students and children under 10 €1.20.)

LANDESMUSEUM. Critters stare blankly from behind glass as natural history exhibits lead visitors to the *Lindwurmschädel,* the fossilized rhino skull discovered in 1335 that inspired the *Lindwurm* statue at Neuer Pl. Upstairs are 18th-century musical instruments, minerals and crystals, and a shoemaker's shop. The museum's Roman-era collection culminates in a fully-preserved 3rd-century floor mosaic of a young shepherd. (Museumg. 2. ☎53 63 05 52; www.landesmuseum-ktn.at. Open Apr.-Oct. Tu-W and F-Su 10am-6pm, Th 10am-8pm; Nov.-Mar. Tu-W and F-Su 10am-4pm, Th 10am-10pm. €5, seniors and students €3, family €11.50. Free entry with Kärnten Card.)

MINIMUNDUS. Don't miss Klagenfurt's most shameless concession to tourist kitsch, the **Minimundus** park, only minutes from the Wörthersee. During the audioguide tour, Louis Armstrong belts "It's a Wonderful World" as you go around the world in 45 minutes. Artists have cut over 170 world-famous buildings and sights down to size, creating intricate models, all on a 1:25 scale. You'll be at eye level with the Parthenon, Big Ben, the Taj Mahal, and many more. Some of the models took over three years to build. *(Villacherstr. 241. From the train station, take bus #40, 41, or 42 to "Heiligengeistpl.," then switch to bus #10, 11, 20, 21, or 22 (dir: Strandbad) to "Minimundus." ☎ 21 19 40; www.minimundus.at. Open daily Apr.-Oct. 9am-5pm; May-June and Sept. 9am-6pm; July-Aug. 9am-9pm. €11, students and seniors €10, ages 6-15 €6, family €25. English guidebook €4, audioguide €2. Price includes admission to nearby Planetarium. Half-off with Kärnten Card.)*

HAPP'S REPTILIEN ZOO. To prevent the persecution of the *Lindwurm's* descendants, Happ's exhibits reptiles in their natural environments. A loose definition of "reptile" encompasses spiders, scorpions, guinea pigs, and a 10,000-gallon aquarium with finned friends from the *Wörthersee*. If it's dangerous, it's here. The accident-prone should avoid Saturday's 3pm piranha and crocodile feeding. *(Villacherstr. 237, next door to Minimundus. ☎ 234 25; fax 234 25 14. Open daily May-Oct. 8am-6pm; Dec.-Apr. 9am-5pm. €8.50, students and seniors €7.50, children 4-15 €4.50.)*

🔩 NIGHTLIFE AND ENTERTAINMENT

The best of Klagenfurt's nightlife rages in the pubs of **Pfarrplatz** and **Herrengasse**, within 5min. of each other. For the latest, scan the tourist office's *Veranstaltung-Kalender* (calendar of events), available in English, and their brochures listing concerts, gallery shows, museum exhibits, and plays. Get tickets from **Reisebüro Springer**, Neuerpl. 2 (☎ 387 00; www.springerreisen.at. Open M-F 9am-6pm, Sa 9am-noon.) The *Jugendstil* **Stadttheater** is Klagenfurt's main venue for operas and plays: everything from Christopher Marlowe to Broadway musicals. (Box office ☎ 540 64. Open from mid-Sept. to mid-June Tu-Sa 9am-noon and 4-6pm. €3-40, students and seniors half-price.) For dancing, try Pfarrpl.'s bar/lounge **Scotch**, Pfarrpl. 20, an after-9pm establishment that attracts a cross-section of ages.

Herreng.'s nightlife is around **La Vida**, Herreng. 5 (☎ 780 31 31), a tequileria-cocktail bar with an outdoor garden a few steps away from the indoor bar, where you can get your Latin groove on. Next door, **Pub Checkpoint Charlie**, Herreng. 3, has a mix of young and middle-aged patrons. (☎ 412 47 65. Open M-Sa 5pm-2am). To avoid the stumbling crowds and pulsing beats, stake out a booth in **Molly Malone**, the Irish pub at Theaterg. 7, for all the Guinness you can handle (☎ 57 200. Open M-W 5pm-1am, Th-Sa 5pm-2am, Su 6pm-midnight. MC/V).

🔼 OUTDOOR ACTIVITIES

On hot spring and summer days, crowds bask in the sun and loll in the clear water of the Wörthersee. This water-sport haven is Carinthia's largest and most popular lake. The two **beaches** closest to Klagenfurt are **Strandbad Klagenfurter See** (www.happy-net.at/stw/strandbad.htm; open 8am-8pm; locker key deposit €5) and **Strandbad Maria-Loretto**. (Open in good weather daily June-Aug. 9am-7pm; May and Sept. 9am-6pm. Day fishing license €11.) Both are easily reached by public transportation. From the train station, take bus #40, 41, or 42 to "Heiligengeistpl.," then bus #10, 11, or 12 to "Strandbad Klagenfurter See." To get to the quieter Maria-Loretto on the lake's southern shores, head left down Metnitz Strand, when facing Strandbad Klagenfurter See. Walk past the campground 700m and turn onto Lorettoweg. There are no lifeguards: swim at your own risk. (Each beach €3.20, children €1.50; after 3pm €1.90/€0.80; family €6.80.)

To enjoy the water without getting (too) wet, rent a **rowboat** (€2.10 per 30min.), **paddle boat** (€3.50), or **motorboat** (€6 from **STW Bootsverleih** near Strandbad Klagenfurter See. A *Radwandern* brochure, free at the tourist office, suggests **bike** tours, including one along a castle-church circuit. The Karawanken mountains to the south, including **Hochobir** (2139m), provide good **hiking,** but many are accessible only by car. Ask at the tourist office for details. Stock up on camping and outdoor supplies at **Northland Sportswear,** Volkermarkter Ring 3. (Open M-F 9am-6pm, Sa 8am-noon.)

■ DAYTRIPS FROM KLAGENFURT

BURG HOCHOSTERWITZ

Hochosterwitz is just outside the town of Launsdorf, northeast of Klagenfurt and 10km east of St. Veit. Trains run to Launsdorf from Klagenfurt (dir: St. Veit/Bruck an der Mur; 30min., M-F 10 per day at 10 and 50min. after the hr., fewer on Sa-Su). Follow the road behind the train station to the right for 25min. to the base of Hochosterwitz (you can't miss it) and the main parking lot and entrance kiosk. Drivers take Rte. 83 from Klagenfurt to St. Veit and switch to the district road to Hochosterwitz.

Dominating the countryside from atop a steep hill, **Burg Hochosterwitz** is a testament to the wealth and power of Carinthian nobility. This is the stuff that medieval dreams are made of—a fortified wall winds around the hillside, protecting a stocky castle with turrets and towers. The castle's elevation above pastures and crop fields make it even more imposing. Carinthian governor Georg von Khevenhüller bought the property in 1571 and made extensive renovations. Irked by marauding Ottoman Turks, he constructed 14 massive towers, each equipped with its own nickname and keyhole-shaped shooting apertures, to guard the road up to the castle. The path to the top commands postcard-worthy views at every turn, taking in town, country, and mountains beyond. (Open daily May-Sept. 8am-6pm; Apr. and Oct. 9am-5pm. €7, seniors €5, ages 6-15 €4, under 6 free. Groups of 10 or more €6. English brochure €3. 10% discount with Kärnten Card.)

A steep, winding 20min. walk through gates and across drawbridges leads to the castle proper. Or, take the **funicular** (€3 round-trip). Part of the castle has been converted into a **museum** filled with royal portraits and a collection of remarkably well-preserved medieval weaponry. Don't miss the letter congratulating Phillip II of Spain on his victory against the Turks at Lepanto. (Tours in German every 45min. Open same hours as castle. Free with castle admission.)

VELDEN   ☎ 4274

Trains run from Klagenfurt to Velden (dir: Spittal-Milstattersee; 20min., 1-2 per hr., round-trip €9). To reach the town center from the train station (☎ 1717), head slightly right on leaving the station, take the little path straight down, and head left on Bahnhofstr. in the opposite direction of the sign pointing left to "Zum See."

Dubbed the "Austrian Riviera," tiny Velden attracts loads of Austrian, Italian, and German tourists heading for the Wörthersee in summer. In mid-July, the town's main street rumbles with race cars, and nightly firework shows light up the sky, set to music from Beethoven to the Beatles. Public and private docks heavy with sunbathers fill every crevice of the shore not occupied by cafés and marinas. The turn-of-the-century architecture and relaxing pace combine with every modern amenity to make an ideal stop on a contemporary European tour.

For the **tourist office,** Villacherstr. 19, turn right at the end of Bahnhofstr. into Am Corso, then right at the intersection onto Villacherstr. It's on the left side of the road, in a concrete and glass building. A free 24hr. accommodations phone is outside. (☎ 21 03; www.velden.at. Open July-Aug. M-Th 8am-8pm, F-Sa 8am-10pm, Su 9am-5pm; May-June and Sept. M-Th 8am-6pm, F-Sa 8am-8pm, Su 9am-5pm; Nov.-Apr. M-F 8am-5pm, Sa 9am-5pm.)

Though it's a resort town replete with casino and castles, Velden does have several budget accommodations options. To get to **Jugend- und Familiengästehaus Cap Wörth ❸,** Seecorso 37-39, take bus #5310 from the Bahnhof to "Cap Worth"

CARINTHIA

(6:40am, 2:20, 5:25pm) or take Bahnhofstr. down and head right onto Am Corso; then take a sharp left onto Seecorso and follow it 15min. until it intersects Süduferstr. This spa-type hostel is directly on the Wörthersee, with indoor and outdoor swimming, a large dining room, volleyball field, small restaurant and bar, and expansive wooded campus. The rooms have lockers (keys provided), sliding wooden beds, and reading lamps. (☎26 46; www.oejhv.or.at. Reception 7am-11pm. Wheelchair-accessible rooms. Dorm beds €21.90; singles with private bath €28.90; doubles €50.80.) You can rent bikes from the Impulse shop affiliated with the *Gästehaus* (☎2426). To reach **Pension Teppan** ❸, Sternbergstr. 7, from the train station, follow Bahnhofstr. to the end and turn right onto Am Corso. Turn right again onto Kirchenstr. across from the casino and head left through Casinopl. Pension Teppan is three to four blocks uphill, at the intersection of Kirchenstr. and Sternbergstr. (15min.) The *Pension* has comfy rooms on a hill above the town center. (☎31 69. Breakfast included. Call ahead. Open Apr.-Sept. €26. Slight discount for stays of more than 2 nights.)

Camping Kofler ❶, Klagenfurterstr. 62, is located on the water's edge, a 15min. walk from Velden. Or, take bus #5179 toward Klagenfurt from the Bahnhof (8:46, 10:26am, 12:53, 2:43, 4:11, 5:11, 6:10pm) and watch for the Restaurant Kolfer sign on the right. The campground offers both RV and tent space, water sports, a restaurant, showers and toilets, and occasional live music from American musicians. (☎31 93. Reception opens at 8am early July to late Aug. €15 per adult, €11 per child ages 14-16, €8 per child under 14; mid-June to early July and early to mid-Sept. €12/€8/€7; mid-Sept. to mid-June €9 per adult, children free. Includes campsite, parking, warm water, lake entrance, and tax.)

After swimming, refuel at the trendy **Restaurant Aqua** ❷, Seecorso 3, with three levels of outdoor seating and meals like pasta (€9.80-13.90), salad (€3.90-9.80), and a Sunday buffet (€14.25). Head straight through the rotary and the end of Am Corso and go to the right of the pink Apotheke. Its lakefront location encourages a very casual dress code. (☎517 71. Open daily 9am-1am. AmEx/DC/MC/V.)

Beaches line Seepromenade and Seecorso, most of which are limited to hotel guests. Crowds congregate at **Strandclub** at the tip of the lake. (☎511 01. Rowboats €11 per hr., motorboats €14.) Public beaches include **Strandbad Leopold**, to the right past the golden Schloß on Seecorso (☎26 32; €3.30, children €2.60, deck chair or umbrella €2.60), and the more secluded **Strandbad Wrann**, behind Seehotel Europa. From Bahnhofstr. go straight between the Escada boutique and the Fashion Corner, or head left up Klagenfurterstr. for 3min. (☎27 70. Open daily 8am-9pm. €5.50, children €3.20. Rowboats €3, motorboats €14.)

Windsurfing, waterskiing, and **sailing** are also available to the adventurous; ask at the tourist office for particular venues. Lakeside activities include volleyball, ping pong, and mini-golf, depending on the *Strandbad*. The water-shy can bike along the lake for beautiful views. Ask inside the Agip gas station at Villacherstr. 21 to the right of the tourist office for **bike rental** from **Impulse** (☎04274 24 82), or rent from the Impulse location at the Jugend- und Familiengästehaus.

THE DRAUTAL

The moderate climate and plentiful lakes in central Carinthia's Drautal (Drau Valley) lend it a decidedly un-Teutonic atmosphere. The winding **Drau** makes water sports a major industry, and Mediterranean cultural influences abound, though the region's proximity to the Villacher and Gailtaler Alps provides ample opportunity for Alpine activities like skiing and hiking. The extensive Villach Highway Interchange provides easy access to the Drautal's major lakes, the **Millstättersee, Ossiachersee,** and **Faakersee,** whose waters glisten due to a unique mineral and metallic makeup that reflects startling blues, aquas, and greens.

VILLACH
☎ 04242

Villach (pop. 58,000) is a lively city that quickly gives way to grassy, tree-lined suburbs. Italian and Slavic influences make the city multicultural and vibrant, catering to many different types of visitors. An important transportation hub to its southern neighbors, Villach is a pleasant place from which to spend a day exploring the nearby **Gerlitzen** (1911m) and **Dobratsch** (2166m) peaks, or as a base for trips to **Berg Landskron** castle and lakes **Ossiachersee** and **Faakersee**.

TRANSPORTATION

Trains run to: Graz (3¼hr., 13 per day 4:15am-8:05pm, €31.50); Klagenfurt (25min., 37 per day 1:21am-11:55pm, €6); Spittal (25min., 6am-10pm, €6); Vienna Südbahnhof (5-5½hr., 19 per day 1:21am-8:05pm, €40). A **free city bus** travels a circuit covering most of Villach. (Every 20min. M-F 8:40am-6:20pm, Sa 8:40am-12:20pm.) **Ferries** chug up and down the Drau. (☎ 580 71; www.schifffahrt.at/drau. Free with the Kärnten Card.) **Tour boats** cruise from Villach's Congress Center to Wernberg by Faakersee on the Drau or from one of nine ports in the Ossiachersee. (2-day round-trip €16, 2½hr. round-trip €10.50, 1hr. one-way €6.50, €2 for bicycle transport.) Find **taxis** at the train station. (☎ 288 88, 53366, or 55555.) Rent bike at Das Radl, Italienerstr. 25. (☎ 269 54. €12 per day.)

ORIENTATION AND PRACTICAL INFORM

Villach sprawls on both sides of the Drau River. Bahnhofstr. stre___ m the station down over a 9th-century bridge into **Hauptplatz**, the comm___ art of the city. The towering St. Jakob's church punctuates the far end ___ e Drau marks the entrance. Several narrow streets and alleys branch off of H___tpl. leading to clubs, restaurants, and museums.

To get to Villach's **tourist office**, Rathauspl. 1, from the station, take ___nhofstr. straight over the bridge and go all the way down Hauptpl. to Rathauspl. ___he office is on the left. (☎ 205 29 00; www.villach.at. Open high-season M-F 9a___-6pm, Sa 9am-noon; low-season M-F 9am-12:30pm and 1:30-5pm.) The **regional to___ ist office** (☎ 420 00; fax 420 00 42) in St. Ruprecht offers up-to-date ski informat___n. Other services include: **ATMs** throughout the city; 24hr. electronic **lockers** at t___e station (€2-3.50; exact change only); the local **hospital** (☎ 20 80) on Dreschnidstr.; **police** (☎ 203 30) at Tralteng. 34.; and **Internet** access at Ken-i-di, Ledererg. 16. (☎ 213 22. €0.10 per min. Open M-Th 6pm-midnight, F-Sa 6pm-2am.) The main **post office** at the train station **exchanges currency** and has a Western Union. (Open M-F 7:30am-7pm, Sa 8am-noon.) **Postal Code:** A-9500.

ACCOMMODATIONS

Jugendgästehaus Villach (HI), Dinzlweg 34 (☎ 563 68; jgh.villach@oejhv.or.at). From the train station, walk down Bahnhofstr., over the bridge, and through Hauptpl. Turn right on Postg., walk through Hans-Gasser-Pl., which merges into Tirolerstr. after you cross the little bridge at the busy highway, and bear right at St. Martinerstr. Dinzlweg is the 1st street on the left. (30min.) The hostel is the lemon stucco building down an unmarked path to the right past the tennis courts. 140 beds in spacious 5-bed dorms, each with its own shower and toilet. Sauna, foosball, and table tennis. Email access via pre-paid card (€2.60 for 20min.). Breakfast and sheets included. Lunch or dinner €6. Key available with ID. Reception 7-10am and 5-11pm. Check-in 5-11pm. Check-out by 10am. Dorms €16.80; singles €23.80 MC/V. ❷

Hotel Goldenes Lamm, Hauptpl. 1 (☎ 241 05; www.goldeneslamm.at), offers unbeatable location for reasonable prices. Simple, country-style rooms replete with satellite TV and phone. Breakfast €7 per person per day extra. June-Sept. and late Dec. to early Jan. Singles €53; doubles €80; triples €99; quads €116. Early Jan. to May €48/€69/€86/€103. Oct. to late Dec. €49/€70/€88/€105. AmEx/MC/V. ❹

Gasthof Bacchus, Khevenhüllerg. 13 (☎219 33 or 06 99 12 49 67 54; www.bacchus24.at). From Rathauspl. and the tourist office, go through the Volksbank archway to the left and head slightly right. Bacchus is the large pink building with a turret 1 block to the right. Conveniently in the middle of town, the hotel doubles as a *Weinstübe* and restaurant. Breakfast included. Singles €30-40; doubles €60-80. ❹

🔲 🎵 FOOD AND ENTERTAINMENT

Lederergasse overflows with small, cheap eateries, while **Hauptplatz** and **Kaiser-Josef-Platz** seat swankier patrons. There is a **Billa** supermarket on the left in Hauptpl. and a **farmers' market** on Burgpl. (W and Sa mornings). Villach's nightlife is clustered in several different locations, particularly near **Salud,** Seilerg. 1, down pub street Ledererg. on the right after crossing the bridge into town, and in Kaiser-Josef-Pl. near **Stern** (see **Food,** p. 170). For a college-age crowd and alternative music, head to tiny **Café-Bar Pelikan,** Rathausg. 3 (☎06 76 35 38 51 53), literally right around the corner from Salud. **Per Du,** Ledererg. 29, serves an array of international wines in a more sedate area all the way at the end of Ledererg. (☎226 23. Open M-Sa 6pm-1:30am.) In the heart of the *Fußgangerzone,* **Barsoho,** Freihausg. 13, attempts to conjure American-British trendiness. From the tourist office, head through the Volksbank archway and to the left on Freihausg. (☎247 55. Open daily 9pm-2am. AmEx/MC/V.)

Trattoria Pizzeria Trastevere, Widmanng. 30 (☎21 56 65; www.trastevere.co.at), serves fine Italian cuisine in an enclosed courtyard to professionals and families, many of whom are Italian visitors. Take a right immediately in front of St. Jakob-Kirche. Menu M-F 11:30am-2pm (€8). Open daily 11am-2am. Kitchen open 11:30am-midnight. ❷

Park Café, Moritzstr. 2 (☎27 77 01), across from the post office branch at the very end of Hauptpl. Enjoy a glass of wine or lunch on the patio, or in a charming 1930s-style smoking room. Wine and beer €2.40-4. Sandwiches €2.90. Sunday brunch €10. Café open M-Sa 7am-midnight, Su 9am-10pm. AmEx/MC/V. ❶

Stern, Kaiser-Josef Pl. 5 (☎247 55). Take a right off Hauptpl. onto Rathausg. and then right into Kaiser-Josep-Pl. Hip restaurant-bar with leather couches and a comfortable atmosphere for indulging in a hookah or two. Appetizers €7-9. Entrées €9-14. Open M-F 7am-midnight, Sa 9am-2am. Kitchen open until 11pm. AmEx/DC/MC/V. ❸

Salud, Seilerg. 1 (☎269 35; www.salud.at). Turn right off Hauptpl. before the trinity column. Salud offers Mexican dishes for about €8. Happy hour daily 11pm-1am. Mojitos €5 on Th. Open M-Sa 5pm-2am. Kitchen open until midnight. ❷

Konditorei-Restaurant Rainer, Oberer Kirchenpl. 5 (☎243 77; www.rainer-villach.at), is a 140-year-old Villach tradition under the shadow of St. Jakob-Kirche. Exquisite sugar figurines, mounds of truffles, and glistening fruit tarts under glass. 50 dessert options (€2-5.95). Open M-Sa 7am-7pm, Su 10am-7pm. ❶

👁 🏔 SIGHTS AND OUTDOOR ACTIVITIES

DOWNTOWN. Any tour of Villach traverses **Hauptplatz,** the city's 800-year-old commercial center. The far end of the square lives in the shadow of the **St. Jakob-Kirche,** right across from the tourist office. Raised on a stone terrace, this 12th-century church became Austria's first Protestant chapel in 1526. An ascent up the church's **Stadtpfar-**

rturm, the tallest steeple in Carinthia (94m), provides a view of Villach and its environs. (☎ 205 25 40. *Open June-Sept. M-Sa 10am-6pm, Su noon-5pm; May and Oct. M-Sa 10am-4pm. €1.80, students €1, free with Kärnten Card. Free organ concerts in the church June-Aug. Th 8pm.*) The **Stadtmuseum,** Widmanng. 38 has archaeological displays spanning six millennia, as well as art from the Middle Ages and the original Villach coat of arms from 1240. There is a huge 3-D model of Carinthia's landscape. (*Turn right up Weissbriachg. near the church. Turn left at Trastevere.* ☎ 205 35 35 or 205 35 00; www.villach.at. *Open early May to late Oct. M-Sa 10am-4:30pm. €2.50, students €1.80, under 8 free; discount with Kärnten Card.*) Across from the museum, a glass **Holocaust Memorial** is almost hidden by shrubs.

Tierpark Rosegg, 5km away near Velden, protects more than 350 species of animals, including bison and white wolves, on lush grounds near a castle. (*☎ 04274 523 57. Open daily July-Aug. 9am-6pm; Apr.-June and Sept.-Nov. 9am-5pm.*) Built for Madame Lucrezia (Mozart's Italian lover), **Schloß Rosegg** challenges visitors with a kilometer of hedges comprising Austria's largest labyrinth. Wax figures round out the castle's offerings. (*☎ 04274 30 09; www.rosegg.at. Open May-Oct. Tu-Su 10am-6pm. Labyrinth closed during inclement weather.*)

OTHER SIGHTS AND FESTIVALS. The twin pink towers of **Heilig-Kreuz-Kirche** are framed by mountains on the left as you cross the bridge into Hauptpl. Car enthusiasts can refuel at the **Villacher Fahrzeugmuseum,** Draupromenade 12, to the right before crossing the bridge. Two rooms crammed with vehicles salvaged from showrooms nationwide give you a look at over 185 vintage rides. (*☎ 255 30 or 224 40; www.oldtimermuseum.at. Open daily mid-June to mid-Sept. 9am-5pm; mid-Sept. to mid-June 10am-noon and 2-4pm. €5.50, ages 6-15 €3.50, discount with Kärnten Card.*) On the first Sa in August, the **Villacher Kirchtag** (Church Day), helps the town celebrate its "birthday" with raucous revelry. (*Admission €6.*)

OUTDOOR ACTIVITIES. Villach lies in a valley between lovely **Ossiachersee** (8km from Villach) and the placid **Faakersee** (10km) both of which have nearby winter resorts. The nearby terrain is ideal for **swimming, boating,** and **cycling.** Peaks near Villach are ideal for **hiking** and **skiing.** The Drei-Ländereck lifts on the Slovenian border offer additional slopes. (1-day ticket €25, ages 15 and under €15.)

SPITTAL AN DER DRAU
☎ 4762

At the foot of the Goldeck Mountain, by the Drau river, sits the small city once known for its *Spittal* (hospital). People came from far and wide to find cures for their ailments. They still do, only now laughter is the best medicine at the *Komödienspiele* (comedy play festival) held at Schloß Porcia every July and August. The self-proclaimed *Komödienstadt* ("City of Comedy"), Spittal has seen its share of tragedy too, as the ghost at Schloß Porcia will attest. Along with its mascot, the tragicomic clown Pierrot, Spittal embodies a healthy mixture of Mediterranean gaiety and Central European melancholy.

⚏▪ TRANSPORTATION AND PRACTICAL INFORMATION. Trains run frequently to Spittal from: **Klagenfurt** (1-1½hr., every hr. 6:32am-8:51pm, €12); **Lienz** (45-60min., every hr. 6:20am-9:17pm, €10); **Villach** (30min., 1-2 per hr. 5:20am-11:18pm, €6). **Lockers** are available at the train station (€2). To reach the town center from the train station, walk down Bahnhofstr. 5min. and cut diagonally across the park to the right. The creamy white Schloß Porcia is at the end of the park and houses the **tourist office,** Burgpl. 1. (☎ 56 60; www.spittal-drau.at. *Open July-Aug. M-F 9am-8pm, Sa 9am-noon; Sept.-June M-F 9am-6pm, Sa 9am-noon.*)

▪▫ ACCOMMODATIONS AND FOOD. The **Jugendherberge Spittal (HI) ❷,** Zur Seilbahn 2, is at the base of Goldeck Mountain. From the train station turn right and walk past the post office. Cross the bridge over the road and take an immediate right onto the ramp leading under the bridge (Ortenburgerstr.), walk under the train tracks, and make the second right onto Wiesenweg. Take a left through the parking lot and follow the signs to "Goldeck" that lead around an ice rink and a sporting complex (20min.). New doubles and quads with skylights are upstairs from the bar and tennis courts. (☎32 52. Breakfast included. Reception 8am-midnight in the café-bar. Call ahead. Dorms €18.) **Jugendherberge Goldeck (HI)** ❷, 1640m up the mountain, is a hostel with a view. Follow directions for the first hostel and take the cable car to "Mittelstation." (Cable car runs every 15min. Last ascent 5pm. Last descent 5:20pm. €10.) Exit out the back of the cable car station and head straight down the gravel path to the four-way path "intersection." Take the path to the right, pass the cows (beware of the dog), and pass the Alpengasthof. The hostel is the next building on the left. The proprietress organizes hiking expeditions during the summer, as well as handicraft classes. (☎27 01. Breakfast included. Reception 8am-10pm. Call ahead. Open Christmas-Easter and late June to late Sept. Dorms €16.)

Eat like a countess at **Schloß Café** ❸, Burgpl. 1, where a piece of Spittaler Torte runs €2.50. For a meal, try the handmade personal pizzas (€3.90) or *Kärtner Nudel*. Light lunch entrées are about €7; daily specials are €4.50-8. **Internet** access inside costs €1.50 per 30min. (☎47 07. Open Sept.-June M-F 7:30am-11pm, Sa 8:30am-9pm, Su 2-8pm; July-Aug. daily until midnight.) Hungrier folks will enjoy the filling food and expansive beer garden at **Das Gösserbrau** ❷, Villacherstr. 5, just on the other side of the river from the center of town. From the tourist office, head down the street and through the red-arched building. (☎23 83; fax 333 31. Wiener schnitzel with salad and fries €9, *Topfenstrudel* €2.50. Open daily 10am-midnight. Kitchen open 11am-10:30pm, Su 9am-10pm.) (☎351 21. Open daily 11:30am-2:30pm and 5:30-10pm.) Buy groceries at **SPAR** supermarket inside the Gerngroß store, Neuerpl. 1. (Open M-F 8:30am-6pm, Sa 9am-5pm. AmEx/DC/MC/V.)

◪ **SIGHTS.** The plain façade of **Schloß Porcia** fails to prepare the eye for the delicate beauty of the Florentine Renaissance courtyard within. The arcades serve as a backdrop for laughter at Spittal's *Komödienspiele* in summer (see **Entertainment**, p. 178). The castle also houses the less funny **Museum für Volkskultur** (Museum of Folk Culture). Creative displays, including a reconstructed 1900 classroom and rooms devoted to local mining and mountaineering, recreate Carinthian daily life, with explanations in English. Check out the collection of carnival masks and *Bartl* costumes: in Carinthia, he's Santa's little helper, only he dresses like a devil, wears a sheepskin and carries a switch to hit bad kids. (☎28 90. Open midMay to late Oct. daily 9am-6pm; early Nov. to mid-May M-Th 1-4pm. €4.50, students and seniors €2.25. Discount with Kärnten Card.)

🎭 🎿 **ENTERTAINMENT AND OUTDOOR ACTIVITIES.** During July and August, the annual ◪**Komödienspiele** (Comedy Festival) fills Schloß Porcia's courtyard with laughter. Europe's greatest comedies are performed by the actors of Spittal's own *Komödienschule*. (Box office in Schloß Porcia open every performance day 9am-7pm. Tickets €22-29, standing room €6. Students 40% off.) On the last weekend in June of every odd-numbered year, Spittal celebrates **Salamancafest.** Sixteenth-century garb is standard, drawing the town back to the time of the aristocratic Salamancas who built Schloß Porcia. Food and drink stalls swarm the town center and street musicians add to the merriment. The highlight of the festivities, however, isn't so merry. The gruesome death of Countess Katherina's son is reenacted in an attempt to appease her ghost. If you're not content to stay on level ground, take the **Goldbergbahn** past the hostel all the way to the mountain peak. Spittal's ski lift transports skiers and thrill-seekers slowly and swingingly up all 2900m, where ten ski trails of varying difficulty await. (Every 15 min. early June to late Sept. daily 9am-5:20pm; €14.50 round-trip, free with Kärnten Card.)

TYROL (TIROL)

The Hapsburgs fell in love with Tyrol, and it's not hard to see why. Few other regions so effortlessly blend culture, natural spectacle, and world-class athletics. Craggy summits rising in the north and south cradle four-star resorts and untouched valleys like the Ötztal and Zillertal. In the center of it all, stylish Innsbruck flaunts Baroque façades and bronze statues before an appreciative audience of foreigners. The architecture blends seamlessly with impressive Alpine backgrounds, showcasing why Tyrol has become one of the world's most celebrated mountain playgrounds.

HIGHLIGHTS OF TYROL

Gape at the world's largest jewel in **Innsbruck** (p. 187).

Relive your Olympic dreams on the slopes in **Seefeld** (p. 192).

Use **Sölden** as a base for exploring the dramatic **Ötztal Arena** (p. 210).

INNSBRUCK   ☎ 0512

Although the 1964 and 1976 Winter Olympics brought Innsbruck (pop. 128,000) international recognition, the mountain city has too rich a history to be relegated to ski-resort status. Beginning with Maximilian I, many Hapsburgs called Innsbruck home; numerous intricate Baroque façades are the legacy of their prolonged stay here. Though the family is gone, the beauty that drew them here remains: the jagged ridge of the Nordkette peaks loom almost directly above the

Tyrol (Tirol)

TYROL

Altstadt's cobblestone streets. If the natural beauty, history, and skiing aren't tempting enough, several quiet mountain suburbs offer the opportunity to enjoy the area around Innsbruck away from the normal city bustle.

⬛ INTERCITY TRANSPORTATION

Flights: The airport, **Flughafen Innsbruck**, Fürstenweg 180 (☎225 25), is 4km from town. Shuttles to and from the main train station from the airport F 6-11pm, with service at 15min. intervals 6:51-8:30pm (€1.70). **Austrian Airlines** has offices in Innsbruck. Call the airport info number and they will transfer you. **Tyrolean Airways** (☎222 20) offers regional flights.

Trains: Hauptbahnhof, Südtirolerpl. (☎05 17 17). At least 1 ticket counter open M-Sa 6am-9:30pm, Su 6:30am-9:30pm. After-hours purchase is by machines (English and other languages available on touch-screen display). Trains to: **Munich** (2hr., 20 per day, €31.80); **Salzburg** (2½hr., 21 per day, €29.50); **Vienna Westbahnhof** (5½-7hr., 23 per day, €48.50); **Zurich** (4hr., 15 per day, €43.70). The **Innsbruck Westbahnhof** and **Bahnhof Hötting** are cargo stations.

Buses: BundesBuses (☎05 17 17) and **PostBuses** (☎58 51 55) leave from the station on Sterzingerstr., immediately behind and to the left of the *Hauptbahnhof.* (☎53 07) for Innsbruck buses, (☎56 16 16) for destinations in Tyrol but outside of Innsbruck.

By Car: From the east or west take *Autobahn* A12. From Vienna, take A1 west to Salzburg, then A8 (in Germany) west to A93, which becomes A12 again in Austria. From the south, take A13 north. From Germany and the north, take A95 to Bundesstr. 2 east, which becomes Bundesstr. 177 east in Austria.

🄴 LOCAL TRANSPORTATION

Public Transportation: Head to the **IVB** Office at Stainerstr. 2, off Burggraben Maria-Theresien-Str., to pick up a local bus schedule. (☎53 07; fax 217. Open M-F 7:30am-6pm.) The main **bus station** is in front of the main entrance to the train station. Single-ride 1-zone tickets €1.60, 24hr. tickets €3.40, 4-ride tickets €5.10, week-long passes €10.70, from the office or any *Tabak.* Validate your ticket when you board the bus or risk a €55 fine. Most buses stop running around 11:30pm; check each line for specifics. 2 Nachtbus lines run after-hours every night; NL1, NL2, and NL3 joins them on the weekends and they all go through Maria-Theresien-Str. and Marktpl. (every 30min. 11:39pm-5:09am) on their way to the *Hauptbahnhof* and beyond.

Taxis: Lined up at the *Hauptbahnhof,* or call ☎53 11, 17 18, 56 17 17, or 29 29 15. Approximately €10 from the airport to the *Altstadt.* Base fare €4.80; Su, holidays, and M-Sa 10pm-6am €5.10. €0.15 per km, after 1st 1.3km.

Car Rental: Avis, Salurnerstr. 15. (☎57 17 54; mobile 0664 134 54 38). Open M-F 7:30am-6pm. **Hertz,** Südtirolerpl. 1 (☎58 09 01; fax 09 01 17). Open M-F 7:30am-6pm, Sa 8am-1pm. AmEx/DC/MC/V. **Denzel Drive** offers 3-day weekend summer specials for €98 including taxes (☎58 20 60; www.denzeldrive.at). Open M-F 8am-6pm. DC/MC/V.

Auto Repairs: ARBÖ (☎123). **ÖAMTC** (☎120).

Bike Rental: Sport Neuner, Maximilianstr. 23 (☎56 15 01). Mountain bikes and helmets €20 per day, €16 per half-day. Also has a shop for bike maintenance. Open M-F 9am-6pm, Sa 9am-noon.

Hitchhiking: While *Let's Go* doesn't recommend hitching, thumbers have been known to take bus C to "Geyrstr." and cross the parking lot of DEZ mall to the Shell gas station.

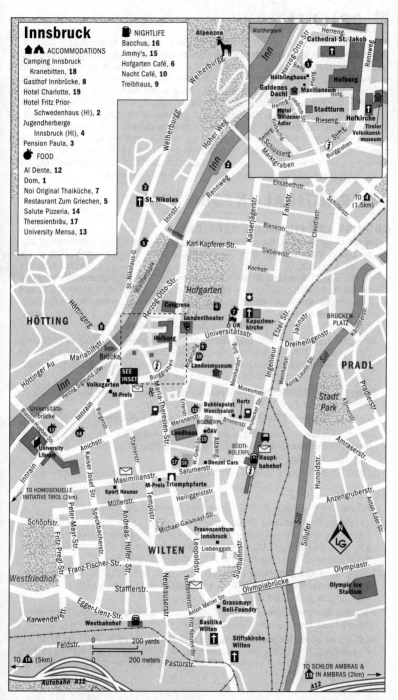

Innsbruck

🏠🏡 ACCOMMODATIONS

Camping Innsbruck
Kranebitten, **18**
Gasthof Innbrücke, **8**
Hotel Charlotte, **19**
Hotel Fritz Prior-
Schwedenhaus (HI), **2**
Jugendherberge
Innsbruck (HI), **4**
Pension Paula, **3**

🍴 FOOD

Al Dente, **12**
Dom, **1**
Noi Original Thaiküche, **7**
Restaurant Zum Griechen, **5**
Salute Pizzeria, **14**
Theresienbräu, **17**
University Mensa, **13**

🍸 NIGHTLIFE
Bacchus, **16**
Jimmy's, **15**
Hofgarten Café, **6**
Nacht Café, **10**
Treibhaus, **9**

TYROL

⊞ ORIENTATION

Most of Innsbruck lies between the **Inn River** to the west and the train tracks to the east. The main street is **Maria-Theresien-Straße,** running north-south, at times parallel to both the river and the train tracks. Open only to taxis, buses, and trams, and crowded with tourists and cafés, Maria-Theresien-Str. runs between the *Altstadt* and Maximilianstr., another big street. Take tram #3 or bus A to "Maria-Theresien-Str." to get to the *Altstadt* from the *Hauptbahnhof;* or exit the station, turn right onto Südtirolpl. and later Bruneckerstr., then left onto Museumstr. and continue straight ahead for 10min. Most sights are near the *Altstadt.* To reach the **university district,** near Innrain, continue down Museumstr. toward the river, curving left onto Burggraben, across Maria-Theresien-Str., and onto Marktgraben. The university itself is to the left down Innrain. Though Innsbruck is not particularly confusing (for an old, imperial European city), a color map available at the train station or at tourist offices is useful.

⊞ PRACTICAL INFORMATION

TOURIST AND FINANCIAL SERVICES

Innsbruck Information, Burggraben 3 on the ground fl. (☎53 56; www.tiscover.com/innsbruck), is on the edge of the *Altstadt* just off the end of Museumstr. Tons of brochures, a city map (€1), and a helpful staff. Open daily 9am-6pm. Currency exchange closes 5:30pm. **Branches** at the train station and major motor exits. **Jugendwarteraum** or "The Pool" (☎58 63 62), in the *Hauptbahnhof* near the lockers, is primarily a waiting room loaded with games and other free fun stuff for young people and backpackers. Free **Internet** available. They also hand out free maps, and hostel and skiing information. Open mid-Sept. to June M-F 11am-7pm, Sa 10am-1pm.

Hiking Information and Insurance: Österreichischer Alpenverein (ÖAV), Wilhelm-Greil-Str. 15 (☎595 47; www.alpenverein-ibk.at). The Austrian Alpine Union's Innsbruck area office provides fantastic advice and information on huts and hiking opportunities. Membership €58, students and seniors €47, children ages 6-18 €16.50.

Budget Travel: Tiroler Landesreisebüro, Boznerpl. 7, (☎59 88 50; fax 57 54 07), by Wilhelm-Greil-Str. Open M-F 9am-6pm. AmEx/DC/MC/V.

Consulate: UK, Kaiserjägerstr. 1 (☎58 83 20). Open M-F 9am-noon.

Currency Exchange: Good rates at the train station **post office** (see p. 183) and **Innsbruck-Information** (see above). Most **banks** are open M-Th 7:45am-12:30pm and 2:15-4pm, F 7:45am-3pm.

ATMs: Outside the train station, post office, and in front of banks throughout the city.

LOCAL SERVICES

Lockers: at the train station. €2-3.50 for 24hr. Electronic lockers.

Bookstores: Buchhandlung Tirolia, Maria-Theresien-Str. 15 (☎596 11; fax 58 20 50). 19 shelves of English-language classics and a large table with bestsellers. Open M-F 9am-6pm, Sa 9am-5pm. **Wagner'sche,** Museumstr. 4 (☎59 50 50; fax 595 05 38). Some bestsellers and classics. Open M-F 9am-6pm, Sa 9am-5pm.

Library: Innsbruck Universität Bibliothek, Innrain 50 (☎507 24 31), where it crosses Blasius-Heuber-Str. Take bus O, R, or F to "Klinik." Reading room open July-Aug. M-F 8am-2pm; Sept.-June M-F 8am-8pm, Sa 8am-6pm.

Religious Services: Catholic Mass in English at the Jesuit church in Karl-Rahnerpl. on Universitätstr. every Sa 6pm. List of services in other languages outside of St. Jakob.

GLBT Organizations: Homosexuelle Initiative Tirol, Innrain 100 (☎56 24 03; fax 57 45 06). All meetings 8:30-11:30pm. Mixed younger crowd M, lesbian night Tu, gay night Th, transgender night every other F. Call ahead to check about meetings. To attend the monthly party, call for information on location and time. **Frauenzentrum Innsbruck** (Women's Center), Liebeneggstr. 15 (☎58 08 39), runs a women's-only café for lesbians and straights M, W, F 8pm-midnight, and hosts discotheques and poetry readings. Office hours Tu 10am-1pm, Th 2-5pm.

Laundromat: Bubblepoint Waschsalon (☎56 50 07 14; www.bubblepoint.com), 2 snazzy locations full of English-speakers at Brixnerstr. 1, and Andreas-Hofer-Str. at the corner of Franz-Fischer-Str. Wash €4 for 7kg, dryer €1 per 10min. Soap included. **Internet** access €0.50 per 10min. Open M-F 8am-10pm, Sa-Su 8am-8pm.

EMERGENCY AND COMMUNICATIONS

Emergencies: Police ☎133, headquarters at Kaiserjägerstr. 8 (☎590 00). **Ambulance** ☎144 or 142. **Fire** ☎122. **Mountain Rescue** ☎140.

Pharmacy: Apotheke St. Anna, Maria-Theresien-Str. 4 (☎58 58 47; fax 15 67). Open M-F 8am-6pm, Sa 8am-noon. DC/MC/V.

Medical Assistance: Universitätsklink, Anichstr. 35 (☎50 40).

Internet Access: International Telephone Discount, Bruneckstr. 12 (☎59 42 72 61). Turn right from the *Hauptbahnhof;* it's on the left just past the end of Südtirolerpl. €0.90 per min. Reduced rates on international phone calls. Open daily 9am-11pm.

Post Office: Maximilianstr. 2 (☎500 79 00). Open M-F 7am-9pm, Sa 7am-3pm, Su 10am-8pm. Address *Poste Restante* to: Postlagernde Briefe, Hauptpostamt, Maximilianstr. 2, A-6010 Innsbruck. Additional branch in the train station. Open daily 7am-7:30pm; currency exchange until 5pm.

Postal Code: A-6020.

ACCOMMODATIONS

Although 9000 beds are available most of the year in Innsbruck, the only hostel open in June is Jugendherberge Innsbruck. The opening of student dorms to backpackers in July and August alleviates the crush somewhat. Book in advance. Visitors should join the free **Club Innsbruck** by registering at any Innsbruck accommodation. Membership gives discounts on skiing and ski buses (mid-Dec. to mid-Apr.), bike tours, and the club's hiking program (June-Sept.).

Hostel Fritz Prior-Schwedenhaus (HI), Rennweg 17b (☎58 58 14; www.tirol.com/youth-hostel). Take bus #4 to "Handelsakademie," continue to the end of the street and straight across Rennweg to the river's edge. This 95-bed hostel located in a cul de sac adjacent to the Inn River offers clean, spacious rooms. On summer weekdays, luggage may be stored at the front desk. Private shower and bathroom included. No door locks but rooms come with lockers for valuables. Breakfast €4. Sheets €2.10. Laundry €5.40, soap included. **Internet** €0.50 per min. Keys with ID deposit. Reception 7-9:30am and 5-10:30pm. Check-in before 6pm. Curfew 10:30pm, but with a key guests can stay out later. Open July-Aug. and late Dec. to early Jan. Dorms €10; doubles €28; triples €41.25. Wheelchair accessible. ❷

Jugendherberge Innsbruck (HI), Reichenauer Str. 147 (☎34 61 79; www.youth-hostel-innsbruck.at). Take bus R to "Landesmuseum" from the train station (2min.) then bus O to "Jugendherberge" (12min.). With 70s glass-and-concrete architecture and sliding doors, this 178-bed hostel, tiered like an Aztec pyramid, resembles a high-powered corporation. Bare-bones rooms with locking closets and shelves for belongings make for cramped quarters. 2 TV rooms. Bike rental €11 per day. Breakfast (7-8am), hall showers, and sheets included. **Internet** access €0.10 per min., after 9pm €0.05 per min. Laundry (€3.30) until 10pm. Reception July-Aug. 3-10pm; Sept.-June 5-10pm. Check-in 5-10pm. Lockout 10am-5pm. Curfew 11pm, but a guard is available for night owls. Quiet time from 10pm. 6-bed dorms €14.50 1st night, €11.95 thereafter; 4-bed dorms €17.20/€14.65; singles with shower €28; doubles with shower €40.80. Non-members add €3. ❸

Gasthof Innbrücke, Instr. 1 (☎28 19 34; www.innsbruck.nethotels.com/innsbruecke). From the *Altstadt,* cross the river at Innsbrücke; the Gasthof is at the corner. This 575-year-old inn has both a river and mountain view: an unbeatable combination of price and location. Head downstairs for a drink at the *Innkellner* (beer €2.40-3.20). Breakfast included. Parking €5. Reception 24 hr. Singles €28, with shower and toilet €36; doubles €47/€62; triples €70/€90; quads with shower and toilet €110. MC/V. ❸

Pension Paula, Weiherburgg. 15 (☎29 22 62; fax 29 30 17; www.pensionpaula.at). Take bus D to "Schmelzerg." and head uphill. Ask for one of the large, well-furnished balcony rooms for a stunning view of the town below. Breakfast, sinks, and TVs included. Singles €27, with shower and toilet €34; doubles €47/€56; triples with shower and toilet €73; quads with shower and toilet €84. ❸

Hotel Charlotte, Phillipine-Welser-Str. 88a (☎34 12 70; www.tirol.com/hotel-charlotte-ibk). Take the #3 bus to "Amras," then walk onto the main road and follow the signs. A farm facing the hotel and the single-family houses nestled nearby lend a country feel to the surroundings, despite the proximity to the train tracks. TV, shower, and toilet in every room, semi-private and shared balconies, outdoor swimming pool, and parking lot. Breakfast included. Singles €52; doubles €76. MC/V. ❹

Camping Innsbruck Kranebitten, Kranebitter Allee 214 (☎/fax 28 41 80; www.camping-inginnsbruck.com). Take bus O from the "Landesmuseum" stop (near the train station on Museumstr.) to "Technik" and then bus LK to "Klammstr." Walk downhill to the right, and follow the road. These pleasant grounds in the shadow of a snow-capped mountain include a playground for the young at heart. Restaurant with **Internet** access (€3 per 30min.) open 8-11am and 4pm-midnight. Showers included. 24hr. shuttle service to Innsbruck. Laundry €4.50. Reception Sept.-June 8am-9pm; July-Aug. 8am-11pm. If reception is closed, find a site and check in the next morning. €5.50 per adult, €3.50 per child under age 15, €3 per tent, €3 per car. Tent rental €8. Electricity €3. Bike rental €7.50 per day. ❶

◨ FOOD

Gawking at the overpriced delis and *Konditoreien* on glamorous Maria-Theresien-Str. won't fill your stomach, so escape the *Altstadt* and its profiteers by crossing the river to Innstr., in the university district, where ethnic restaurants and cheap pizzerias proliferate. Those looking for inexpensive late-night eats may find themselves pleasantly surprised (and filled) by the cheap, large kebab and pizza portions served in and around the *Hauptbahnhof.* A few more late-night pizza digs are near the station on Ingenieur-Etzol-Str.

▨ **Theresianbräu,** Maria-Theresien-Str. 51 (☎58 75 80), bills itself as the oldest private brewery. Its blacklit bar is built around 2 giant copper brewing kettles. The microbrew, a pleasant dark lager, is available in 0.1-2.4L glasses (.5L stein €3.30) alongside traditional meals such as *Käsespätzl* (homemade dumplings with cheese; €6.80) and several types of *Gröstl* (roast potato, beef, and fried egg; €5.70-6.50). Chocolate fondue for 2 or more is available after 6pm (€6.50 per person). Frequent live music entertains a diverse crowd of locals, students, and tourists. Open M-W 10:30am-1am, Th-Sa 10:30am-2am, Su 10:30am-midnight. MC/V. ❷

▨ **Noi Original Thaiküche,** Kaiserjägerstr. 1 (☎58 97 77), cooks up a vast array of Thai soups (€4.20-9), and deliciously spiced dishes from the wok (€8.50-10), ranging from mild to flaming. Most tables are outside and come with umbrellas and pistachio-green chairs. Inhale the sweet aroma drifting out of the kitchen while enjoying your meal. Open M-F 11:30am-3pm and 6-11pm, Sa 5-11pm. ❷

Salute Pizzeria, Innrain 35 (☎58 58 18), on the side of the street farthest from the river. A popular student hangout with black-and-white pictures on the wall and what appears to be a tree growing in the middle of the floor. Walk up to the counter to order, then sit back and wait for some of the least expensive pizza in town. Make sure to get a seat quickly, though: Salute's is never empty for very long. Pizza €4.50-9. Pasta €5-7. Salads €3-6. Open 11am-midnight. ❷

Dom, Pfarrg. 3 (☎23 85 51; www.domcafe.at). Located in the heart of the *Altstadt* and diagonally across from the cathedral, this restaurant-café offers light fare, such as soups (€3.10), salads (€3.50-7.50), sandwiches (€2.40-5), and a wide selection of ice cream desserts (€2-4.30). The arched ceilings and red interior give this place the feel of a wine cellar, but in the summer most prefer to sit outside facing the *Dom*. **Internet** access €0.14 per min. Open daily 11am-2am. AmEx/MC/V. ❶

Al Dente, Meraner Str. 7 (☎58 49 47), offers a wide variety of original dishes with a hip Italian flair. The food is prepared right before your eyes. The lively crowd makes this a great place to relax between sightseeing stops. Scrumptious pasta €6.40-10.60. Open daily 11am-10:30pm. AmEx/DC/MC/V. ❷

Restaurant zum Griechen, Innstr. 28 (☎29 15 37) is not to be confused with a mere kebab place: both the restaurant and the portions are huge. Gyros (€8.50) are on the menu, but souvlaki dishes—grilled meat with tomato sauce, rice, and vegetables—steal the show. *Fasoulada* soup (navy bean and tomato; €3.50) and grilled fish (€8-13) round out the menu. Open daily 11am-2:30pm and 5pm-midnight. ❷

University Mensa, Herz. Siegm Ufer 15. On the 2nd fl. Cheaper eats in Innsbruck are hard to come by. This student cafeteria serves 2 daily *Menüs* (soup, entrée, and salad €3.30-4.90). Open during the term (mid-Aug. to mid-July) M-F 9am-2:30pm. Hot lunch 11am-1:30pm. ❶

MARKETS

M-Preis Supermarket has branches inside the train station, at Museumstr. 34, Innrain 15, Maximilianstr. by the arch, and across from the train station on the corner of Salurnerstr. and Sterzingerstr. Generally open M-F 7:30am-6:30pm, Sa 7:30am-5pm.

Farmers' Markets at Franziskanerpl. (Th 9am-2pm), Sparkassenpl. (F 8:30am-2:30pm), St. Nikolaus-Brunnenpl. (Sa 8:30-11am), and the *Markthalle* near the river at Innrain and Marktgraben. Food, flowers, fungi, and fun, though the prices on some organically grown produce may cause shoppers to scramble back to the supermarket. Open M-F 7am-6:30pm, Sa 7am-1pm.

◉ 🏛 SIGHTS AND MUSEUMS

Visiting all that Innsbruck has to offer in a short period is cheapest with the Innsbruck Card, available at museums, cable cars, and the tourist office. It allows entry into all museums, cable cars, buses, and trains (24hr. €21, 48hr. €26, 72hr. €31). It also includes rides on the Sightseer, a bright red mini-bus that comes complete with air-conditioning and headphones that share interesting (though brief) historical tidbits throughout the ride. For the duration of your Innsbruck Card, you can hop on or off at any one of the bus stops with cartoonish red "Sightseer" signs. A 2hr. bus tour, including the Altstadt and a visit to the ski jump, leaves from the train station. (June-Sept. noon and 2pm; Oct.-May noon. €13, children €6.)

THE OLD TOWN. The *Altstadt*, a cobbled mix of ornate old buildings, churches, and museums on the river Inn, is often crowded with tourists. Its centerpiece is the Goldenes Dachl (Golden Roof) on Herzog Friedrichstr., a shiny, gold-shingled balcony (2657 gold shingles to be exact.) built to commemorate the marriage of Emperor Maximilian I and Bianca Maria Sforza. Facing the Dachl, turn around to the left to see the cream façade of the 15th-century Helbinghaus, blanketed with a pale green, 18th-century floral detail and intricate pink stucco work. For a panoramic view of the medieval *Altstadt*, climb the 148 steps in the graffiti-lined staircase of the 15th-century Stadtturm (city tower), across from Helbinghaus. (☎512

56 15 00. Open daily June-Sept. 10am-8pm; Oct.-May 10am-5pm. €3.50, students and seniors €2, under age 15 €1.) The 15th-century Hotel Goldener Adler (Golden Eagle Inn) is a few buildings to the left of the Stadturn. A marble slate testifies that Goethe, Heine, Sartre, Mozart, Wagner, Camus, and Maximilian were once guests there.

Innsbruck's most exciting street is Maria-Theresien-Straße, which begins at the edge of the *Altstadt* and runs south. The street, lined by pastel-colored Baroque buildings housing expensive shops, gives a clear view of the snow-capped Nordkette mountains. At the end of the street (away from the *Altstadt*) stands the Triumphpforte (Triumphal Arch), built in 1765 to commemorate the betrothal of Emperor Leopold II. Up the street, the delicate Annasäule (Anna Column), carved from pink granite, commemorates the Tyroleans' victory on St. Anne's Day (July 26, 1703) after a bloody and unsuccessful Bavarian invasion during the War of Spanish Succession.

MAXIMILIANEUM. Given its ideal location, this small museum is always chock-full of tourists. It commemorates Innsbruck's favorite emperor, Maximilian I. The Maximilianeum provides a solid introduction to local history. A 20min. video (in 6 languages, including English) details Maximilian's conquest of Europe from Portugal to Hungary, which shaped the future of Innsbruck and Tyrol. *(Inside the building under the Goldenes Dachl. Open May-Sept. daily 10am-6pm; Oct.-Apr. Tu-Su 10am-5pm. €3.60, students €1.80, seniors €2.90, families €7.20; headphones for commentary included.)*

CATHEDRAL ST. JAKOB. The drab gray façade of the Dom St. Jakob (remodeled in 1717-1724) conceals a riot of pink and white High Baroque ornamentation within. Trompe l'oeil ceiling murals depict the life of St. James. The cathedral's prized possession is the (small) altar painting of Our Lady of Succor by Lukas Cranach the Elder. A 1944 air raid destroyed much of the church, but renovations have restored it to its former grandeur. *(1 block behind the Goldenes Dachl. Open daily Apr.-Sept. 7:30am-7:30pm; Oct.-Mar. 8am-6:30pm. Free.)*

HOFBURG. The Hofburg (Imperial Palace) was built in 1460 and remodeled between 1754 and 1770 under the direction of Maria Theresia. Imposing furniture, large portraits, and elaborate chandeliers fill the 25 sumptuously decorated rooms. The biggest room is the Giants' Hall, a gigantic, two-story ballroom featuring huge paintings of Maria Theresia, Francis I, and their 16 children. The White Room contains the portrait of Maria's youngest daughter, Marie Antoinette of France (with head, without cake). Don't miss the gilded "Augusta Family" tableau in the Audience Room, depicting the whole Hapsburg gang in big, round, gold medallions. *(Behind the Dom St. Jakob to the right. Entrance in the arch on Hofg. ☎58 71 86; www.tirol.com/hofburg-ibk. Open daily 9am-5pm. Last entrance 4:30pm. Call ahead for English tours. Group tours (limit 35 people) €29.07. English guidebook €1.82. €5.45, students €3.63, seniors €4, children ages 6-14 €1.09.)*

TIROLER VOLKSKUNSTMUSEUM. Built between 1553 and 1563 as the "New Abbey," the Tiroler Volkskunstmuseum (Handicrafts Museum) was converted into a school in 1785 and then a museum in 1929. The exhaustive collection of home and farm implements, peasant costumes, and period rooms provides a dusty introduction to Tyrolean culture from the past few centuries. Included are butter churns, playing cards, and the *Brotgrammeln* tools used to break bread. Downstairs is a collection of incredibly detailed *Krippen* (nativity scenes). *(www.tiroler-volkskunstmuseum.at Universitätsstr. 2. At the head of Rennweg. ☎58 43 02; fax 58 43 02 70. Open M-Sa 9am-5pm, Su 9am-noon. €5, students and children €1.50.)*

HOFKIRCHE. The 16th-century Hofkirche (Imperial Church) houses an intricate sarcophagus decorated with alabaster scenes from Maximilian I's life and the *Schwarze Mander*. Twenty-eight bronze statues of Hapsburg saints and Roman emperors line the nave. Dürer designed the statues of King Arthur, Theodoric the

Ostrogoth, and Count Albrecht of Hapsburg, who pay their last respects to the emperor. Oddly, Maximilian's resting place is not in the Hofkirche, but in Wiener Neustadt, near Vienna. The elegant Silver Chapel holds the corpse of Archduke Ferdinand II instead. *(In the same building as the Volkskunstmuseum. Open July-Aug. daily 9am-5:30pm; Sept.-June M-Sa 9am-5pm; Su noon-5pm.)*

HOFGARTEN (IMPERIAL GARDEN). Walk through the manicured grounds of the Hofgarten and admire the ponds, elaborate flowerbeds, and concert pavilion. A crowd sometimes shouts advice to chess players moving the 1m-tall pieces. Walk farther for a lovely spot to escape the crowds of the *Altstadt*. Unfortunately, the grass is for your visual pleasure only: signs and grounds keepers constantly remind tourists to park it on the benches. *(Walk down Museumstr. toward the river, turning right onto Burggraben and continuing as it becomes Rennweg. Open daily 6am-10:30pm. Free.)*

LANDESMUSEUM. Originally opened in 1823, the recently renovated Landesmuseum (Regional Museum) boasts collections from prehistory through the Middle Ages. Romanesque, Gothic, and modern arts and crafts form a high point of the gallery's display. Special exhibits on larger-than-life historical figures like infamous Italian-turned-Austrian banking princess Claudia di Medici in the summer of 2004. *(Museumstr. 15. ☎ 594 89, ext. 9; fax, ext. 109; www.tiroler-landesmuseum.at. Open June-Sept. M-W F-Sa 10am-6pm, Th 10am-9pm; Oct.-May Tu-Su 10am-6pm. Library open Tu-F 10am-5pm. €8, seniors and groups €6, children €4. Audioguide €2.)*

ALPENZOO. The Alpenzoo (Alpine Zoo) is the highest-altitude zoo in Europe and houses every vertebrate species indigenous to the Alps, including bears and golden eagles. Also of note is the bearded vulture in the zoo: with a 3m wingspan, its largest bird species of the Alps. Don't miss the word's largest cold-water aquarium. *(Weherfurgg. 37, near Schwedenhaus hostel, across the covered bridge: follow signs uphill 15min. ☎ 29 23 23; www.alpenzoo.at. The Sightseer stops at the zoo every 30min. 9am-5pm, and a bus to the zoo leaves from in front of the Landestheater every hr. 10am-5pm in summer. €1.50, students and children €1; round-trip €2.60/€1.60. Open daily Apr.-Sept. 9am-6pm; Oct.-Mar. 9am-5pm. €7, students and seniors €5, ages 6-15 €3.50.)*

CRYSTAL MUSEUM. For those weary of never-ending museums and luxurious mansions, the bizarre and entertaining **Swarovski Kristallwelten** is a breath of fresh air, with its oddly named rooms like "Floating Poem," "Giant's Belongings," and "Global Networks." The only consistent theme to this massive "ice" palace is that every room is dripping with crystals. While the impressive jewelry on display may seem like a shameless plug for the decorative figurines made in the nearby factory (the gift shop is nearly as large as the exhibits), the Chamber of Wonders makes it clear that the Swarovskis have artistic as well as capitalistic ambitions. Make sure to go through the hand-shaped hedge maze in the park. *(Take the train from Innsbruck Hauptbhanhof to Wattens (20min., 15 per day 6:34am-8:34pm, round-trip €6.20). From the train station, cross the bridge and follow the brown signs for 20min. Take bus #4125 from the bus station to "Wattens Kristallwelten," then walk a little farther and take a left. Bus 35min., every 30min. 7:45am-8:22pm, round-trip €6.10. ☎ 05224 510 80; www.swarovski.com/crystalworld. Open daily 9am-6pm. €8, groups €7, under age 12 free.)*

☒ OUTDOOR ACTIVITIES

HIKING. A ☒**Club Innsbruck** membership lets you in on one of the best deals in Austria (see **Accommodations,** p. 183). The club's excellent **hiking** program provides guides, transportation, and equipment (including boots) free to hikers of all ages. Participants meet in front of the Congress Center (June-Sept. daily at 9am), board a bus, and return from the mountains by 4 or 5pm. The hike isn't strenuous, the

EXTREME SLEIGHING

For thrill-seekers still standing after carving Innsbruck's grueling Alpine slopes, hiking to impossible heights, and biking the unforgiving off-road paths this side of the Atlantic, one more breathtaking experience remains. Bobsledding (in German, *bobsleighing*) reached a younger generation with the 1993 flick "Cool Runnings," which chronicled the adventures of the Jamaican racing team. For 95 euro anyone (Jamaican or otherwise) can shuttle down all 1,270m of the Olympic ice chute.

This track has a dramatic past and present. In 1976, four German athletes rode into the Olympic record books on a four-man racing sled. They shot down the brand new Igls bobsled run in a staggering 51 seconds. In recent years, the Igls track has been used for several world and European championships. To document his own triumph, each rider receives a diploma after he opens his eyes and is pried out of his seat. (60 seconds and 14 curves after he started.)

For more information and to make reservations (which are required), visit www.olympia-innsbruck.at or call 37 75 25. Sleds run from Jan-Feb every Tuesday morning from 10am-noon and Thursday at 7pm.

views are phenomenal, and the English-speaking guides are qualified and friendly. There are a total of 40 different hikes, so many return the next day for new adventures. Free nighttime lantern hikes leave Tuesday at 7:45pm. The 30min. hike near Igls culminates in a party with traditional Austrian song and dance. Everyone ends up taking part (willing or not).

If you want to hike on your own, there are several options. For easier hikes, take the J-line bus to "Patscherkofel Seilbahnen" (20min.). The lift provides access to moderate 1½-5hr. hikes near the bald summit of the *Patscherkofel*, offering vistas of neighboring mountains, Innsbruck, and other towns far below. (☎377 234; fax 377 234 15. Open 9am-4pm in winter and until 5pm in summer. Round-trip €15, ages 16-18 €12, ages 7-15 €8, dogs €1.50).

For more challenging hikes, head to the lifts ferrying passengers up to the **Nordkette** mountains. The first lift, a short hike from the river and the Schwedenhaus, can also be reached by taking the J bus to "Hungerbergbahn." From here, a second lift leads to the Seegrube, just below the rocky walls of the peaks above. A third and final lift leads to the very top, at the Hafelekarspitze. From both the Seegrube and Hafelekarspitze, several hikes lead up and along the jagged ridges of the Nordkette, but be prepared: they are neither easy, nor particularly well-marked. Even if you don't go hiking, the trip up is worth it for the views. For those more interested in flying down mountains than climbing up them, Innsbruck-Information has a €95 **paragliding** package, including transport, equipment, and photos (or call **MountainFly,** ☎37 84 88).

WINTER ACTIVITIES. Club Innsbruck membership significantly simplifies winter **ski excursions.** Hop on the complimentary club ski shuttle (schedules at the tourist office) to any suburban cable car (mid-Dec. to mid-Apr.). Membership provides discounts on ski passes. The **Innsbruck Gletscher Ski Pass** (available at all cable cars and at Innsbruck-Information offices) is valid for all 60 lifts in the region (3 days with Club Innsbruck card €87, teens and seniors €69.50, children €52.50; 6 days €150/€120/€90). The tourist office **rents ski equipment** for the Intersport shop on the mountain (downhill €17 per day, children €9; cross-country €9/€9; snowboarding €18 per day). The bus to the **Stubaier Gletscherbahn** for **summer skiing** leaves at 7:20 and 8:30am (☎05226 81 41; www.stubaier-gletscher.com). Take the earlier bus: summer snow is slushy by noon. In winter, buses leave at 9:45am and 5min. past every hr. 11am-5pm (1½hr., last bus back 4:30pm, round-trip €13.80). One day of winter glacier skiing costs €33.50 (summer

€23.50, ages 16-19 €21.80, ages 10-15 €16.80, under 10 free). Both branches of **Innsbruck-Information** offer summer ski packages (bus, lift, and rental €49). For a 1min. thrill, summer and winter **bobsled** rides are available at the Olympic bobsled run in Igls (Bus J to "Patscherkofelbahn;" follow the signs). (May-Sept. ☎ 0664 357 86 07; fax 37 88 43. Rides Th-F after 4pm; the sled has wheels rather than runners. €22. Late Dec. to late Feb. ☎ 37 75 25; fax 33 83 89. Rides Tu 10am-noon, Th 7pm. €30. Professionals pilot the 4-person sleds. Reservations required.)

🎭 ENTERTAINMENT

At a corner of the Hofgarten, the **Congress Center** and **Tiroler Landestheater** (☎ 520 74) host various festivals and concert series in Innsbruck. In August, the **Festival of Early Music** features concerts by some of the world's leading soloists on period instruments at Schloß Ambras, Congress Center, and Hofkirche. (☎ 56 15 61; www.altemusik.at. Tickets €9-127.) The **Landestheater** presents plays, operas, and dance most nights of the year. Recent productions include Henry Mancini's *Victor/Victoria* and Johann Strauss' *Der Zigeunerbaron*. (☎ 52 07 44; www.landestheater.at. Concerts €6-49, standing room €6; plays €8, standing room €6. Rush tickets available 30min. before the show to anyone under 21 and students under 27 for a 40% discount.)

The **Tyrol Symphony Orchestra of Innsbruck** plays Mozart, Beethoven, Stravinsky and more in the Congress Center from October to May. (☎ 58 00 23. Tickets for symphony concerts €25-39, master concerts €33-85; children and students under 27 30% off.) **Chamber music concerts** (€16-24) are held in the concert hall of the Tyrol Conservatory. (☎ 58 34 47. Same discounts apply.) The Spanish Hall at Schloß Ambras holds **classical music concerts** most Tuesday nights in summer (€10-44; same discounts apply). In late June and mid-July world-renowned dancers—everyone from the Boris Eiffman Ballet to the African Dance Company Momboye—come to the **International Dance Summer** in the Congress Center to perform. Workshops are also conducted throughout the three-week festival. (☎ 57 76 77; www.tanzsommer.at. International Dance Packages include accommodation with concert admission and the Innsbruck Card; 1 night €59, 2 nights €121. Tickets for productions at Innsbruck-Information, Burggraben 3; €20-68.) If you're looking for something a little more dicey, check out **Casino Innsbruck.** In a massive complex in the Innsbruck Hilton, by Landhauspl. (☎ 593 50; www.casinos.at. Semi-formal dress. Open daily from 3pm. AmEx/DC/MC/V.)

IN RECENT NEWS

FLYING HIGH ABOVE INNSBRUCK

On January 4th 2002, the first skier of the famed Four Jump Tournament, the German Sven Hannawald, flew from the sparkling new Bergisel ski jump in a world-record-breaking 134.5m. Designers had put their finishing touches on the daringly modern jump just before the competition.

The new jump rises like the head of a metallic snake out of the trees. Its multipurpose design not only created one of the most advanced jumps in the world, it also left room for a café and observation deck so guests can take in the stunning 360-degree view of the Nordkette mountains.

Credit for this architectural feat goes to Iraqi architect Zaha Hadid. While she lives and works in London, she has received international acclaim and designed buildings in Tokyo, Cincinnati, and even an extension to the Reina Sofia Museum in Madrid. Her artistic designs elegantly fuse function and nature. In fact, she has received her second commission from the city of Innsbruck (in 2004) to design the new Nordkettebahn tram, which will travel from the city up 2,269 m to the Hafelekarspitze Peak.

, I WANT TO RIDE THE GIANT VAT OF BEER!

There is more than enough home-brew in Zell am Ziller to keep every resident sauced for months. The town is home to the Zillertal Bier factory; every year its inhabitants pay homage to their local brewery with a weekend of drunken festivities in May. The Braumeister's vats, Tyrol's oldest, concoct the beloved and potent Gauderbock especially for the occasion. The celebration even has its own jingle: *Gauderwurst und G'selchts mit Kraut / hai, wia aut dosmunden / und 10 Halbe Bockbier dauf / mehr braucht's nit zum G'sundsein!* ("Gauder sausage and smoked pork with sauerkraut / hey, how good it tastes / and 10 pints of beer to go with it / what more could you need for your health!")

One of the festival's highlights is the Ranggein, a type of traditional wrestling cheered on by an excited, and somewhat sloshed, crowd. Wrestlers used to challenge animals like pigs, sheep, and goats—now they only pick on animals of their own species.

On Sunday, the entire town dons their best lederhosen and most colorful dresses—called "trachten"— for the concluding parade, the Trachtenumzug. Everyone marches behind "Gaudl" the spirit of the Gauderfest clad in the traditional (electric pink and blue) duds. Gaudl rides in style high atop a giant vat of Zillertal Beer.

⚑ NIGHTLIFE

Most visitors collapse after a full day of Alpine adventure, but there's action aplenty to keep partygoers from their pillows. Nightlife revolves around Maria Theresien-Str. between the casino and the *Altstadt*. For the very latest club events, stop by Treibhaus (see below) and pick up one of the fliers by the door.

Hofgarten Café (☎58 88 71; www.hofgarten.at), inside the Hofgarten park. Follow Burggraben under the Hoffburg and past the *Landestheater*, enter the park through the gate on the right and walk straight until you hear the crowd. Giant white umbrellas shade the daytime crowd from the sun in the sprawling garden. At night all 4 bars work simultaneously to keep the drinks coming to the tables of 20- and 30-somethings. In summer, live music most Th. Snacks €2.50-10. Beer 0.2L €2, 0.3L €2.40, 0.5L €3.20. Open daily 10am-4am, kitchen open until midnight.

Treibhaus, Angerzellg. 8 (☎57 20 00; www.treibhaus.at). From the *Altstadt* on Museumstr. turn left onto Angerzellg., and right again into the alley next to China Restaurant. Innsbruck's favorite place for everyone from jazz-inspired adults to teenage students, Treibhaus boasts a ground-floor café sandwiched between 2 enormous performance spaces: a rock n' roll hall in the basement and a jazz theater on the 2nd fl. (both 500+ capacity). Live music 5 nights per week during the school year (Sept.-June). Food €3.60-6.80. Beer €1.80-3. Open M-Sa 10am-1am, Su and holidays 4pm-midnight.

Bacchus, 18 Salurnerstr. (☎94 02 10). Diagonally across from the casino. Enter from the side of the building's driveway. This underwater-themed bar and disco, largely gay and lesbian, is situated beneath a popular café-bar. Mixed in ages, sexual orientation, and gender, the discotheque really gets going with dancing around 2am, and caters to students, local *Innsbruckers*, and tourists alike. A friendly place with lots of lively conversation. Beer €2.60-4. Open M-Th 9pm-4am, F-Sa 9pm-6am.

Jimmy's, Wilhelm-Greil-Str. 17 (☎57 04 73), by Landhauspl. East meets West beneath the all-seeing eyes of the 4 fluorescent Buddhas (hanging on the wall). Not a nook left un-hip in this trippy world of brushed steel and rough-hewn stone. 2 bars and an eclectic menu, sporting dishes from Asia and Italy. Try the Rudolf Valentino *ciabatta* (filled bread pocket; €4). Mixed drinks €4-6.60. Beer €1.80-3.30. Open M-F 11am-2am, Sa 8pm-2am. Kitchen daily 11am-2pm and 6-11pm. DC/MC/V.

Nacht Café, Museumstr. 5 (☎57 68 26), near the tourist office. For the night owls who can never get enough partying, the Nacht Café offers throbbing techno/dance music. The café's flashy green and blue lights reflect off the metallic surfaces all night, long after everywhere else is closed. Every night has its own special drink. 2hr. Happy hour 10pm-midnight. Beer €2.80-3.60. Snacks €3.50-12. Open 10pm-6am, but really stays open until everyone leaves. AmEx/DC/MC/V.

⚡ DAYTRIPS FROM INNSBRUCK

SCHLOß AMBRAS

The castle stands southeast of Innsbruck, at Schloßstr. 20. The easiest way to get to Ambras is to take the Sightseer Bus which runs from the Arch on Maria-Theresien-Str. to the Schloß (20min., €1.60). You can also take tram #6 (dir: Igls) to "Tummelpl./Schloß Ambras" (20min., €1.60), or tram #3 from Maria-Theresien-Str., which leaves every 7½min., to the last station, "Ambras." Follow signs from the stops. Walk from the city only with a map from the tourism office, as the trail is poorly marked (40-60min.).

One of Innsbruck's most impressive edifices and museums is **Schloß Ambras,** a Renaissance castle built in the 16th century by Archduke Ferdinand II of Tyrol, who acquired vast collections of art, weapons, and trinkets—from Roman busts to the armor of Japanese shoguns.

The museum's inner courtyard includes a manicured garden and an outdoor café. Around the courtyard is the Hochschloß, which houses the famous Spanischer Saal (Spanish Room), with Hapsburg coats-of-arms and intricate mythological paintings. Upstairs from the Spanish Room are the three floors of the Hapsburg Portrait Gallery (open June-Aug.), showcasing an assortment of famous rulers, including several popes, Hapsburg Kaisers, Napoleon Bonaparte, Catherine the Great, and Louis XVI and Marie Antoinette. Be sure to see the rare two-horned rabbit. The highlight of a trip to Ambras is the Curiosity and Wonders chamber which features armor for giants, paintings of wolf-people, and the portrait that inspired Bram Stoker's novel *Dracula*. (☎34 84 46; www.khm.at/ambras. Open Apr.-Oct. daily 10am-5pm; Dec.-Mar. M and W-Su 10am-5pm. Tours €2; reservations required for English tour. €8; students, seniors and children ages 7-18 €6.) After touring the castle, emerge and take a break in the gardens outside, which include manicured shrubs, modern sculptures, and shady, forested hillsides. Keep an eye out for the peacocks.

STAMS ☎5262

Frequent regional trains that head west towards Landeck stop in Stams (35min., €5.85). By car, take Autobahn A12/E60 or Hwy. 171 directly to the abbey. To reach the basilica itself, you only need to look from the train station in the direction of the town; the giant yellow and cream façade is unmistakable–walk towards it.

Stift Stams is a magnificent onion-domed monastery 40km west of Innsbruck. Founded by the Tyrolean Duke Meinhard II in 1273, the cloisters were completely restyled in the 18th century. The 26 Cistercian monks who reside there allow several guided tours per day through the majestic **Basilika** and the heavily frescoed **Fürstensaal.** The basilica, restored for its 700th anniversary in 1974, features the masterwork of local artist Andreas Thamasch. Twelve of his gilded wooden statues line the walls of the basement **crypt** where Duke Meinhard and his wife are buried. Stift Stams contains many examples of stunning artwork, but travelers should note that it is the only tourist site in Stams. It is rather far from Innsbruck for those without a special interest in Rococo buildings or monasteries. (☎5263 56 97; www.tirol.com/stif-stams. Entrance to the cloisters only with the tour. Tours July-

TYROL

Aug. M-Sa every 30min. 9-11am and 1-5pm; every hr. June and Sept. M-Sa 9-11am and 1-5pm; Jan.-Apr. and Oct.-Dec. M-Sa 9-11am and 2-4pm; May 9-11am and 2-5pm. Tours Su only in the afternoon. €3.50, seniors €3, students and children €2.) A **museum** (☎ 05263 62 42), also within the monastery, has a small collection of religious paraphernalia, including golden monstrances, crosiers and reliquaries. (One contains the teeth of saints.) Open mid-June to Sept. Tu-Su 10-11:30am and 1:30-5pm. €4, seniors €3, students and children €2.)

SEEFELD IN TIROL   ☎ 05212

After Innsbruck borrowed its smaller neighbor's terrain for skiing events during the 1964 and 1976 Winter Olympics, Seefeld became famous enough to lure celebrities and charge high prices for its snowy slopes. Some cities don't even have one five-star hotel, so Seefeld's 5 five-star hotels alongside its 26 four-star hotels are unique for the region, and indicative of the town's price levels.

■✸🚺 **ORIENTATION AND PRACTICAL INFORMATION.** To reach Seefeld, high in the Nordkette Mountains, take the train from the Innsbruck *Hauptbahnhof* to Munich and get off at the Seefeld stop (40min., 15 per day 6:35am-8:35pm, €4.80). To get to the town center, go from the train station down Bahnhofstr., which becomes Klosterstr. Dorfpl., Seefeld's main square, and Innsbruckerstr. are on your left coming from the train station; to the right, Münchenstr. forms the other arm of the *Fußgängerzone* (pedestrian zone). The **tourist office,** Klosterstr. 43, provides a list of accommodations. If you need **luggage storage** for an hour or so, the tourist office is your best chance. (☎ 23 13; www.seefeld.at. Open mid-June to mid-Sept. and mid-Dec. to Mar. M-Sa 8:30am-6:30pm; mid-Sept. to mid-Dec. and Apr. to mid-June M-Sa 8:30am-12:15pm and 3-6pm.) For a **snow report,** call ☎ 37 90. **Internet** access is available at Hotel Bergland, Innsbruckerstr. 3, (€0.14 per min.). An **ATM** at Sparkasse Bank across from the station. The **post office** is on Klosterstr. one block past the tourist office. (Open M-F 8am-noon and 2-5pm). **Postal Code:** 6100.

🚼⊡ **ACCOMMODATIONS AND FOOD.** Seefeld has no hostel, making *Pensionen* and *Privatzimmer* the best budget options. Prices per person average €24-40 in the winter, €17-36 in the summer. Make reservations in advance through the tourism office in the tourist-packed winter months. Accommodation and price lists are available at the tourism office.

The entire *Fußgängerzone* is stocked with rows of pricey restaurants, outdoor cafés, and bars, but there are a very few reasonably cheap establishments. Try **Sportcafé Sailer ❷,** Innsbruckerstr. 12. This centrally located restaurant offers traditional Tyrolean specialties such as *Gröstl* (potatoes, bacon and eggs) averaging €10-12, and soups for €3.80. While the menus are seasonal, the food is always served in a festive atmosphere. In summer, outdoor seating is available at the beginning of the *Fußgängerzone*. (☎ 200 51; www.sportcafésailer.at. Open summer and winter daily 11:30am-10pm; low-season 11:30am-2pm and 6-10pm.) The **SPAR,** Innsbruckstr. 24, is across from Sport Sailer just off Dorfpl. (Open M-Sa 8am-6:30pm, Su 10am-noon.)

🌄 **OUTDOOR ACTIVITIES.** The tourist office distributes *Seefeld A-Z,* a listing of services and season-specific activity calendars. It runs an excellent summer **hiking** program of 5-7hr. hikes that wind through the surrounding countryside, too. (Hikes leave mid-June to mid-Sept. Tu and F 9:30am, W 8:30am. Register by 5pm the day before. €5 with free guest card from hotels.) To wander on your own, pick up hiking or biking maps (€5/€4.50) at the tourist office. For an impressive hike with several tricky ascents and less uphill hiking than you might expect, try the trails that leave from the **Roßhütte** (1760m) area, accessible with the **Roßhütte Bergbahnen,** including a funicular leading to the hut. Two gondolas climb still higher, to the **Seefelder Joch** (2064m) and the **Härmelekopf** (2045m). To get there, turn right out of the train station, and right again following the sign to "Roßhütte." (15min. walk. For all 3 gondolas buy the *Topkarte:* €16, youth €14, children €10. Funicular and 2 gondolas €16/€14/€10. Add up to €2 for visitors not staying in Seefeld. Open late May to mid-Oct. 9am-5pm with rides every 30min. except 12:30pm.) From the *Seefelder Joch,* it's a 30min. hike to the **Seefelder Spitze** (2220m), with dazzling panoramas on both sides. Continuing farther down the mountain for about 45min., a narrow trail leads through tight switchbacks and hugs precipitous limestone cliffs before slowly climbing to the arm below the **Reither Spitze** (2373m), the highest mountain in the area. From here, finish the loop back down to the lifts, or undertake another 30min. scramble over steep and tricky terrain to the peak, where an unobstructed 360° view of the Tyrolean Alps awaits. Often the "trail" is just a scramble over rock walls with red blazes painted on them. From the summit, there are two options: brave the path a second time or take the trail to the *Nördlinger Hütte* back towards the lifts. Views of the valley on the second route are tamer, but so is the path (4-5hr.).

Seefeld offers winter tourists two money-saving ski passes. The **Seefeld Card** is valid for Seefeld, Reith, Mösern, and Neuleutasch. (1-day pass €30, ages 16-17 €27, ages 5-15 €18.) The **Happy Ski Pass** is valid at Seefeld, Reith, Mösern, Neuleutasch, Mittenwald, Garmisch-Zugspitze, Ehrwald, Lermoos, Biberwier, Bichlbach, Berwang, and Heiterwang. (Pass available for 3-20 days. For 7-day passes and up, a photograph is required. 3 days €83, ages 16-17 €76, ages 5-15 €50.) Twelve different **sports equipment rental** shops lease alpine and cross-country skis, snowboards, and toboggans at standard rates. (Downhill skis with poles and boots €10-€26, snowboards €13-25.) A free **ski bus** runs between town and the **Roßhütte** and **Gschwandtkopf** ski areas (daily, every 20min. 9:20am-4:40pm). For those who prefer their skiing on the level, choose from the 100km of *Langlauf* (cross-country) trails (map available at the tourist office). Toboggan rental from any ski shop is €4 per day.

EHRWALD ☎ 05673

Ehrwald (pop. 2300) located in Austria's *Wetterstein* area, lies on the Austrian side of the *Zugspitze* (2964m), which is Germany's highest mountain and Ehrwald's prize attraction. The village seems unfazed by this tourist magnet, however, retaining a decidedly small-town charm.

🖪🖬 TRANSPORTATION AND PRACTICAL INFORMATION. All trains to and from Ehrwald pass through Garmisch-Partenkirchen in Germany. **Trains** run from Garmisch-Partenkirchen to: Ehrwald (26min., 5:46am-7:59pm, €2.80) and Innsbruck (2hr., 5:45am-6:57pm, €9.70). By **car,** *Autobahn* A12 follows the Inn from Innsbruck to Mötz. Bundesstr. 314 runs north from Mötz to Ehrwald, close to Germany and Garmisch-Partenkirchen. Bundesstr. 198 runs along the Loisach river. The **tourist office,** Kirchpl. 1, is in the town center, a few steps beyond the church. From the train station, follow Bahnhofstr. to Haupstr. and continue for about 15min., turning left at the town center, following signs pointing toward the church. (☎ 23 95; www.ehrwald.com. Open July-Sept. and Dec.-Mar. M-F 8:30am-6pm, Sa 9am-noon; Oct.-Nov. and Apr.-June M-F only.) A 24hr. automated kiosk and phone service in the lobby provides access to accommodations with vacancies. Other services include: **currency exchange** at banks (open M-F 8am-noon and 2-4:30pm) and the post office; **ATM** at the **Raiffeisenbank,**

TYROL

between the church and tourist office; a **pharmacy**, on Haupstr. 8 (☎22 74; open M-F 8am-noon and 1-6:30pm, Sa 8:30am-noon, Su 10am-noon and 5-6pm); 24hr. **taxi service** with Patis Taxi (☎06 64; www.patis-taxi.at); and **bike rental** at **Zweirad Zirknitzer**, Zugspitzstr. 16, across the tracks and up the hill. (☎32 19. €20 per day, children €14. Open M-F 8am-noon and 1-5:30pm, F 8am-noon and 1-3pm, Sa 10am-noon.) **Intersport Leitner**, in Kirchpl., is a slightly better deal. (☎23 71; www. intersport-leitner.com. €14 per day, full-suspension bikes €20.) **Internet** access is available at **Musikcafe/Zugspitaal**, on Haupstr. set back from the street in the Hallenbad complex, about 150m before the center of town. (☎32 32; www.musikcafe.at. Open W-Th 10pm to late, F-Su 5pm to late.) The **post office**, Hauptstr. 5, is on the right about 100m before the town center coming from the train station. It sells phone cards and has a Western Union service. (Open M-F 7:30am-noon and 2-5pm.) **Postal Code:** A-6632.

⚏⚏ ACCOMMODATIONS AND FOOD. Ehrwald is filled with inexpensive guest houses, many of which are close to the train station on Bahnhofstr. Pick up a **guest card** at the tourist office for discounts. **Gästehaus Konrad ❸**, Kirweg 10, is about 20min. from the train station but only a few from the town center. Proceed as if going towards the tourist office, but instead of heading left toward the church, take the first right onto Kirweg. This quaint house with balconies offers a peaceful spot from which to enjoy the scenery. (Rooms €20 per person.) Camping is available at **Camping Dr. Lauth ❶**, Zugspitzstr. 34, if you're willing to walk about 25min. uphill. (Not exactly scaling Mt. Everest, but it's a steady incline nonetheless.) Head left out of the train station and turn left immediately. Take the right-hand fork past Zweirad Zirknitzer and continue uphill (ignore the "Leaving Ehrwald" sign). After the road curves left at the Thörleweg intersection, the well-marked campground is on the right. Pitch your tent in the shadow of the *Zugspitze* in a clean, inexpensive campground. Amenities include an Italian restaurant (open 8am-midnight), a beer garden with a grill (open from 5pm), a playground for children, a game room complete with darts and foosball, and a bathroom with showers. (☎26 66; www.camping-ehrwald.at. Reception 8am-midnight. Laundry €3.60 for wash and dry. May-Oct. €5.75 per person, €4.50 per child, €1.10 tax per person; Nov.-Apr. €6/ €4.80/€1.40, €4.40 per tent. Electricity €0.65 per kilowatt.)

Enjoy a varied and relatively inexpensive menu amidst the magic of an enchanted forest at **▥Restaurant Mooswirt ❸**, Haupstr. 21, in the Hallenbad building. Vines wind over a stone fence and log cabin façade, while witches and goblins fly over the bar. A glass pane overlooking the beautiful swimming pool comprises one wall, while a mural of the Alps covers another. Grilled steaks start at €10.60, while fish entrees range from €9.60 to €14.50, including a grilled salmon filet for €11.60. Vegetarian options include *Spätzle* with a four-cheese sauce and salad, and range in price from €7.80 to €8.80. (☎27 66. "Super Salads" €7.80-13.30. Beer from €2.40. Wine from €3.90. Open daily 10am-11pm. Kitchen open 11:30am-2pm and 5-9pm.)

The **Metzgerei Restaurant ❷**, Hauptstr. 15, has a surprising number of casual tables beyond its storefront meat counter. Sit down for a traditional entree (€7.30-9.10) or any one of a variety of grilled *Wursts* (€4.70-6.40). For even cheaper meals, consider ordering from the take-out menu, with options including wiener schnitzel for €3.50. (☎23 41. Open M-Sa 11:30am-8pm.) **Al Castagno ❸** is an outdoor café with cheery yellow tablecloths and an exhaustive menu. (Pizza €6.50-9.50. Fish €18-21.50. Steak €13-22. Kitchen open M and W-Su 11:30am-2pm and 6-11pm.) If you're planning a picnic, try the **SPAR supermarket**, Hauptstr. 1, next to the post office. (Open M-F 7am-7pm, Sa 7:30am-5pm.)

⚑ OUTDOOR ACTIVITIES. The **Tiroler Zugspitzbahn** is Ehrwald's leading tourist attraction and an astounding feat of engineering. This cable car climbs to the 2964m summit of the *Zugspitze* in 7min. In fair weather, the observation station at the ride's end has a breathtaking view, and various hiking and biking trails ranging from 30min. to 6hr. leave from the top. Special full-moon cable car rides run on the appropriate day June to September. Check with the tourist office or www.zugspitze.at for a list of dates and times. Bring a sweater, even in summer. (☎23 09. Trains run mid-May to late Oct. and late Nov. to early Mar. daily every 20min. 8:40am-4:40pm. €32, ages 16-17 €24.50, ages 6-15 €18.50.) The **Ehrwalder Almbahn** doesn't climb as high (1510m), but neither do the prices. (☎24 68. Mid-May to mid-Oct. and mid-Dec. to late Mar. 8:30am-4:45pm. €11, ages 16-17 €9:50, ages 6-16 €6.50.) Buses leave from Kirchpl. for the *Zugspitzbahn* (10min., 8 per day 8:20am-6:20pm, €1.50) and the *Ehrwalder Almbahn* (10min.). Try Bergsport-Total, across the street from the tourist office. (☎056 73; www.bergsport-total.at. Hikes €10-19, bike tours €14-18, climbing €100-130, rafting from €35.) The tourist office also sells hiking maps for €6.50 and provides information on outdoor activities as well as a pamphlet listing mountain huts and giving hiking times to each (most between 30min. and 3hr. from various cable car and bus stops).

For winter guests, Ehrwald offers the **Happy Ski Pass,** the only lift ticket good for three days or more. It gives access to 143 lifts, 200km of ski runs, 100km of cross-country trails, and several winter sports arenas (see **Seefeld,** p. 192; 3-day pass €83, youth €76, children €50.) For shorter ski trips, one- and two-day tickets are available for the Zugspitzarena, the mountains by Ehrwald. (1-day pass €31, ages 16-17 €28.50, ages 5-15 €18.50; after 11am €28/€25.50/€17; 2-day €57.50/€52.50/€34) Shops in the main square and at lift stations rent ski equipment (€19-27 per day, €99-119 per week).

KITZBÜHEL ☎ 05356

When Franz Reischer arrived in Kitzbühel in 1892, his 2m snowshoes and wild ideas about sliding down mountains stirred up a fair amount of skepticism. Two years later, the town held its first ski championship, and the six peaks surrounding Kitzbühel were named "the Ski-Circus." Now the annual **International Hahnenkamm Race** (Jan. 21-23, 2005), considered "the Wimbledon of World Cup Skiing," attracts thousands of spectators to watch the world's finest get knocked over by the infamous first turn, known as the *Mäusefalle* (Mousetrap). When the snow melts, outdoorsy locals and tourists alike revel in the ample hiking and cycling trails climbing the towering peaks. Meanwhile, those looking for some town action find posh designer stores and kitschy souvenir kiosks lining the streets. For many the fun just begins at nightfall, when the music plays and the alcohol flows in the bars filling Kitzbühel.

▐ TRANSPORTATION

Kitzbühel has two **train stations:** the **Hauptbahnhof,** Bahnhofpl. 2 (☎64 05 53 85 13), and the **Hahnenkamm Bahnhof.** All **buses** stop at the *Hauptbahnhof* and a few stop at the Hahnenkamm station. Kitzbühel lies on Bundesstr. 161 and is the east terminus of Bundesstr. 170. By **car** from Innsbruck, take *Autobahn* A12 east to Wörgl and switch to Bundesstr. 170. From Salzburg, take Bundesstr. 21 south to 305 and then to 178; at St. Johann in Tirol, switch to 161 south, which leads straight to Kitzbühel.

TYROL

Trains: Trains leave to: **Innsbruck** (1hr., every 2hr., €12); **Salzburg** (2½hr., 9 per day, €27.70 via Kufstein or €20.80 via Zell am See); **Vienna** (6hr.; 4:55-7:30am; €41.50, or €44.50 via Zell am See); **Zell am See** (45min., every 2hr., €8.70).

Buses: All depart regularly from the **Hauptbahnhof;** some buses also depart (less frequently) from the **Hahnenkamm** station. Destinations include Lienz, Kufstein, and Wörgl; for a complete listing of train and bus routes (bus schedule available until sold out only), pick up the free *Fahrpläne Bus und Bahn* from the tourist office. A *Stadtbus* local line (€1.50 per ride) serves the city.

Taxis: In front of the *Hauptbahnhof*, or call ☎ 67 200.

Car Rental: Hertz, Josef-Pirchlstr. 24 (☎ 648 00; fax 721 44), at the traffic light on the way into town from the main station. Open M-F 9am-6pm, Sa 9am-noon. 20% discount with valid guest card. AmEx/DC/MC/V.

Bike Rental: Mountain bikes at **Stanger Radsport,** Josef-Pirchlstr. 42. €22 per day 8am-6pm, €16 per half-day noon-6pm; standard bikes €16/€10. Open M-F 8am-noon and 1:30-6pm, Sa 9am-noon. DC/MC/V. Also at nearly any **Intersport** in town; ask for their 2005 rates.

Parking: There are 4 lots in Kitzbühel: **Griesgasse, Pfarrau, Hahnenkamm,** and **Kitzbüheler Horn.** The latter 2 are next to the major ski lifts. In winter a free park-and-ride service operates between the lots and lifts. Free parking at Kitzbüheler Horn and Pfarrau. 50% of the spaces are free at Griesg. Pay parking at Hahnenkamm is €3 per day or overnight, €20 per week, €130 for the season.

■ 🛈 ORIENTATION AND PRACTICAL INFORMATION

Kitzbühel lies on the hilly banks of the Kitzbüheler Ache (river), at the foot of several peaks, including the Kitzbüheler Horn (2000m) and the Steinbergkogel (1971m). The train stations are on opposite sides of the town. To reach the *Fußgängerzone* from the *Hauptbahnhof*, head straight out the front door, down Bahnhofstr., and turn left at the main road. At the traffic light, turn right and follow the road uphill. The city center is maze-like; look for the occasional *Zentrum* (center) signs to point you back to the middle. A free map from the tourist office proves invaluable for navigating the streets.

Tourist Office: Hinterstadt 18 (☎ 62 15 50; www.kitzbuehel.com), near the *Rathaus* in the *Fußgängerzone*. Make sure to pick up a Kitzbühel guest card, which is free upon request and provides discounts to many shops and services in town. **Guided hikes** (2½-6hr.; June-Oct. M-F 8:45am and Sa-Su on request; free with guest card) in the country surrounding the city and **guided informative tours** start at the office. Both are available in English. Open July-Aug. and Christmas to mid-Mar. M-F 8:30am-6pm, Sa 9am-6pm, Su 10am-6pm; Nov. to Christmas and mid-Mar. to June M-F 8:30am-12:30pm and 2:30-6pm, Sa 8:30am-noon.

Budget Travel: Reisebüro Eurotours, Jochbergstr. 18 (☎/fax 6060 or 6066; www.eurotours.at), exchanges currency. Open M-F 8:30am-12:30pm and 3-6pm, Sa 8:30am-12:30pm.

Currency Exchange: At banks, travel agencies, and the post office. The post office and most banks have **ATMs** outside.

Lost and Found: ☎ 662 33 or 621 61; www.fundinfo.at or www.fundamt.gv.at. In the *Rathaus,* next to the tourist office. Open daily 8am-noon and 1:30-7pm.

Lockers: At the *Hauptbahnhof.* €2.50-3.50 for 24hr. Open 5am-1am.

Police: ☎ 133. **Fire:** ☎ 122. **Medical Emergencies:** ☎ 144. **Auto Repair:** ☎ 123. **Mountain Rescue:** ☎ 140.

Ski Conditions: ☎ 62 15 50 (in English or German). **Road Conditions:** ☎ 15 86.

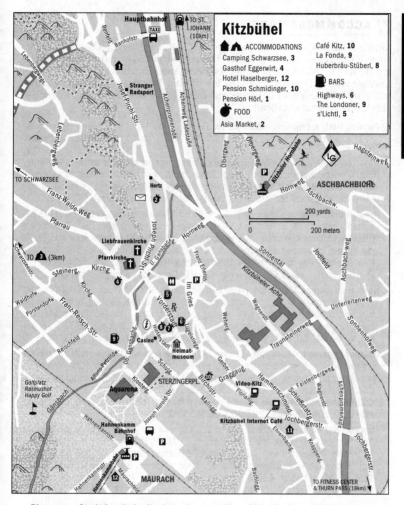

Kitzbühel

ACCOMMODATIONS
Camping Schwarzsee, **3**
Gasthof Eggerwirt, **4**
Hotel Haselberger, **12**
Pension Schmidinger, **10**
Pension Hörl, **1**

FOOD
Asia Market, **2**

Café Kitz, **10**
La Fonda, **9**
Huberbräu-Stüberl, **8**

BARS
Highways, **6**
The Londoner, **9**
s'Lichtl, **5**

Pharmacy: Stadt-Apotheke Vogl, Vorderstadt 15. ☎634 15; Open M-F 8am-noon and 2:30-6:15pm, Sa 8am-noon.

Internet Access: Video-Kitz, Schloßerg. 10 (☎724 27; kitzvideo@kitz.net). On Jochberg-erstr., head down the stairs in front to Schloßerg. They also rent videos. Internet €0.10 per min., €2.50 per 30min. Open M-Sa 11am-9pm, Su 11am-5pm. **Kitzbühel Internet-café,** Jochbergerstr. 3 (☎0664 497 1204), about 1min. farther down from Video-Kitz, offers additional computers as well as laptop plug-ins and wireless Internet. €0.10 per min. Open M-Sa 10am-8pm (sometimes 9pm, depending on crowds), Su 11am-5pm.

Post Office: Josef-Pirchlstr. 11 (☎627 12), between the stoplight and the *Fußgänger-zone*. Fax and copier (€0.20) inside. Open M-F 8am-noon and 2-6pm. **Currency exchange** open M-F 8am-noon and 4-5pm.

Postal Code: A-6370.

▌ ACCOMMODATIONS

Kitzbühel has almost as many guest beds (7678) as inhabitants (8625), but the only youth hostel is restricted to groups. Prices are as much as €8 more during the winter. Be sure to call ahead in winter, as the ski races create a huge bed shortage. Cheaper lodging is also available by bus or train 6km away in **Kirchberg** (tourist office ☎ 05357 20 00), or in homes and farms in the country around Kitzbühel; check with the tourist office.

Pension Hörl, Joseph-Schmidlstr. 60 (☎ 631 44). From Hotel Kaiser, turn left onto the main street (Joseph-Schmidlstr.). Pension Hörl will be about 1min. farther on the left. The only down-side to this convenient location is a bit of noise from passing cars. Cozy down comforters and comfy beds usually win out over the drone of traffic, lulling weary hikers, skiers, and shoppers to sleep. Some rooms have balconies. Shared toilet and bath/shower. Breakfast included, and the friendly English-speaking owner will gladly boil water for guests' tea throughout the day. Reception all day. Singles €20-25.

Pension Schmidinger, Ehrenbachg. 13 (☎ 631 34; www.schmidinger.cc). From the *Innenstadt*, head south on Bichlerstr., which merges with Ehrenbachg. The 17 rooms are clean, have local craftsman-style woodwork, and are furnished with desk and TV. All rooms have newly tiled showers. Almost all are doubles, but if there is space lone travelers can have one to themselves. Breakfast included. Reception about 8am-8pm. Call ahead. Summer rooms €25-30; winter €32-35. Discounts for longer stays. ❸

Hotel Haselberger, Maurachfeld 4 (☎ 628 66; www.haselsberger.com). Just 1min. from the bottom station of the *Hahnenkammerbahn,* with cables passing inches from the windows. A full-service hotel with hunting lodge decor, Haselberger offers rooms with cable TV, phone, and bath. Parking and breakfast included. Summer €35-38 per person; winter €42-50. Children under age 6 50% off, ages 6-14 25% off. AmEx/MC/V. ❹

Gasthof Eggerwirt, Gänsbachg. 12 (☎ 624 55; www.eggerwirt-kitzbuehel.at). Approaching town center from the station on Josef-Pirchl-Str., head down the stairs onto Gänsbachg. Mostly doubles; all with TV, phone, safe, and bath. Internet terminal for guests. On-site restaurant. Breakfast and parking included. Summer €35-44 per person; winter €52-68. Add €5 for singles and €4 per night for stays shorter than 3 nights. Children ages 3-12 50% off, ages 12-15 30% off. MC/V. ❹

Camping Schwarzsee, Reitherstr. 24 (☎ 628 06; www.bruggerhof-camping.at). Take the *Stadtbus* (€1.50) from the train stations (7:20am-6:22pm, only 1 bus 8:07am-12:22pm). Restaurant with *Menüs* from €7.50. Playground, sauna, and a free "Tentfest" Fridays at 7pm. Showers included. Tents welcome. Reception 8am-5pm. May-Sept. €8.50 per adult, €5.90 per child ages 2-12. Dec.-Mar. €8.40-€9.10/€6. Tax €0.55/€0.71. Electricity €0.80 per kilowatt hr. AmEx/MC/V. ❶

▐ FOOD

Local specialties include *Tiroler Speckknödel* (bacon-fat dumplings), served either *zu Wasser* (in broth) or *zu Lande* (dry, with salad or sauerkraut), and *Gröstl* (meat and potato hash topped with a fried egg). There is a **SPAR Markt** on the corner of Ehrenbachg. and Bichlstr. (Open M-F 7:30am-6:30pm, F 7:30am-7pm and 8am-7pm, Sa 7:30am-1pm, Su 7:30am-5pm.)

Huberbräu-Stüberl, Vorderstadt 18 (☎ 656 77). In the center of town with a terrace that overlooks the street, Huberbräu offers a whole variety of schnitzels (€7.80-13.50) and Tyrolian *Gröstl* (€6.50). Or wash down a *Blutwurst* (blood sausage) with a Huberbräu and get change back from a ten. Hearty soups with bread €2-4. Closed late May and early June. Open M-Sa 8am-midnight, Su and holidays 9am-midnight. ❷

Asia Markt, on Joseph-Pirchlstr. across from the post office. A limited but delicious selection of wok specialties fills this Asian grocery store with the aroma of spices. Crisp veggies with tofu (€4.50) or chicken (€5) served with a heaping scoop of rice at the 4 tables in the front of the store or to-go. Open daily noon-2pm and 3-6pm. ❶

La Fonda, Hinterstadt 13 (☎736 73). Straw hats, orange stucco walls, and Garth Brooks on the stereo: it's Tex-Mex done Austrian-style. Taco €4.70. Chips with a whole variety of dips €3.80. Spare ribs €5.90-11.70. Burgers €6.30-6.70. Salads €3.10-6.90. Sandwiches €5.70-7.90. Despite crowds, La Fonda maintains a laid-back atmosphere. Take-out on request. Open daily June-Sept. 11am-2am; Dec.-Mar. 4pm-2am. ❷

Café Kitz, Bichlstr. 7 (☎753 26). This small café boasts excellent *Tiroler Speckbrettl* (bacon, cheese, and pepper platter) and wiener schnitzel (€9.50). Enjoy friendly, prompt service while dining on the terrace in the shopping district along Graggaug. Most entrees €7-10, with a few others, such as grilled perch-fish, running €13-16. Open M-F 8:30am-noon and 2-6pm, Sa 8:30am-12:30pm. DC/MC/V. ❷

🔆 🎵 SIGHTS AND ENTERTAINMENT

Kitzbühel's church steeples define the skyline. The ornate **Pfarrkirche** (parish church) and the **Liebfrauenkirche** (Church of Our Lady), covered with multi-colored marble and baroque ornamentation, are two of the most impressive. Between the churches stands the **Ölberg Chapel,** dating from 1450, with frescoes from the late 1500s. The local **Heimatmuseum** (Regional Museum), Kirchg. 2, celebrates the town's longevity with artifacts in Kitzbühel's oldest house, dating from the 12th century. Bronze-age pottery, medieval mining equipment, old farm equipment and household tools, and winter sporting equipment of all sorts trace the town's industries and life through the centuries. (☎672 74. Open mid-June to mid-Sept. daily 10am-6pm; mid-Sept. to early Dec. Tu-Sa 10am-1pm; early Dec. to mid-Jan. daily except for Christmas and New Year's Day 10am-1pm and 3-6pm; mid-Jan. to mid-June Tu-Sa 10am-1pm. Adults €4, with guest card €3; children ages 6-18 €3; under age 6 free; groups €3.)

At the free **concerts** in the center of town, you might find anything from folk harpists to Sousa bands. Scheduled events include a March 2005 Jazz Festival and San Pellegrino Star Cup and, in April 2005, a *Bridge-Turnier.* Current events listings are available at tourist office. **Casino Kitzbühel** is near the tourist office. (☎623 00; www.casinos.at. W ladies' night: €25 worth of chips for €21, free long drink and raffle ticket. Semi-formal. 18+. No cover. Open July-Sept. 7pm-late.) At the end of July, the **Austrian Open** Men's Tennis Championship (Generali Open) comes to town, drawing such athletes as Austria's own Thomas Muster to the Kitzbühel Tennis Club. Ask about Ladies' Day, with free admission for women. (☎720 76; www.generaliopen.at. Tickets ☎633 25.)

🍸 NIGHTLIFE

During the high tourist season (roughly mid-Dec. to Mar. and July-Sept.), Kitzbühel nightlife becomes a hopping scene. Particularly during special events like the *Hahnenkamm* race in January and the Generali Open (July 23-31, 2005), tourists pack the streets, looking for a place to party. With more than 30 bars in town, Kitzbühel is up to the challenge.

⧉ The Londoner, Franz-Reichstr. 4 (☎714 28). A staple for 27 years, The Londoner is the place to be. The bar has a huge list of specialties for €3, including the Slippery Nipple, Flugerl, and Kamikazi. Tartan covers the walls, and the liveliness of both staff (all English speakers) and guests makes for an unbeatable party, complete with juicy gos-

TYROL

sip and flying beer by the end of the night. During the famous Hahnenkamm race, the men's downhill stars take off their shirts and dance on the bar. Beers on tap from €2.60. Dec.-Apr. live bands all week; May-Nov. 2 times per week. Open Dec.-Apr. daily noon-4am; May-Nov. Su-Th 7pm-2am, F-Sa 7pm-3am.

Highways, Im Gries 20 (☎753 50), is aptly named, filled with Route 66 memorabilia and a Cadillac convertible with a table and benches inside. From the tourist office, turn right and exit under the arch onto Bichlstr., left onto Graggaug., walk 2 blocks and turn left onto Im Gries. Home to crowds of teenagers in summer and tourists in winter, Highways serves burgers (€3.70-4), pizza (€5.10-7), and sandwiches (€3.70-4), and offers an extensive drink menu (cocktails €7, beer from €2). Their loud music consists of 60s-90s hits, soul, and rock 'n' roll, interspersed with occasional live acts and karaoke Tu nights in the winter. Open daily May-Oct. 9pm-3am; Nov.-Apr. 8pm-3am.

s'Lichtl, Vorderstadt 9. Hits from the 50s on up to today spill out from s'Lichtl onto the pedestrian zone below, inviting a mixed crowd to a disco ball- and glass bubble-decorated wooden bar. Live DJ. Beer €3. Drinks €5. W 60s night. Open June-Mar. daily 9pm-1 or 2am (whenever the crowd thins).

⚠ OUTDOOR ACTIVITIES

Few visitors to Kitzbühel remain at ground level for long. The Kitzbühel **ski area,** the "Ski Circus," is one of the finest in the world. Every winter since 1931, Kitzbühel has hosted the **Hahnenkamm Ski Competition,** part of the annual World Cup and considered one of the world's most difficult runs. It turns the town into a rollicking seven-day party. (☎735 55 for tickets. €4-15 per day.) For summer visitors, three- or six-day vacation passes can save a bundle of money. They're good for free lifts and the *Aquarena* swimming pool (see below). They are available at all lifts. (3-day pass €35, children €19.50; 6-day €48/€26.50.)

SKIING. The best deal is the **Kitzbüheler Alpen Ski Pass,** which gives access to 260 lifts and 680km of skiing trails. (Valid any 6 days of the season. €176, children €96. 1-day ski pass €35, mid-Mar. to late Dec. €30.50; children €17.50. Passes grant access on 64 lifts and shuttle buses that connect them. Lift ticket prices drop for 2- to 14-day purchases.) Tickets for individual lifts, such as the **Gaisberg, Maierl I,** and **Obergaisberg,** are also available. Purchase passes at any of the lifts or at the **Kurhaus Aquarena,** which offers a pool, as well as a sauna and solarium at extra fees. (☎643 85; www.bergbahn-kitzbuehel.at. Open daily 9am-8pm. €8, children €5; with guest card €6.80/€4.50; half-price in winter with ski pass.)

Rent skis at the Hahnenkamm lift or from a sports shop in the area. Try **SportHütte Winkler,** across from Hahnenkammbahn. (☎747 28. Skis €19-29 per day, youth €6, children €5; boots €8-10, children €4; snowboard €22-25. Open M-Sa 8:30am-6pm; call for Su and holiday hours. AmEx/MC/V.) Other options include **Kitzsport Schlechter,** at Jochbergerstr. 7 (☎625 04; www.horsthoerl@kitzsport.at), **Skiport Flori** (☎725 13; m.resch.kitz@aon.at), or **Skiverleih.** (☎654 96; josef-dagn@skischule-reith.at. Hours generally M-F 8:30am-noon and 2:30-6pm, Sa 8:30am-12:30pm.) One-day group lessons cost around €35. Ask at the tourist office about **ski packages**—special low-season deals on lodging, ski passes, and instruction. Week-long packages without instruction start at €280 per person.

HIKING. More than 70 **hiking trails** snake up the mountains surrounding Kitzbühel. Among these are a variety of pleasurable day hikes, covering a wide range of difficulty levels. Pick up a free *Hiking Trail Map* at the tourist office, which details trailheads, estimated hiking times, and difficulty ratings.

Hausbergweg: (5km; 5-6hr. round-trip). Follow the signs to "Hahnenkamm" the whole way up. Good for relatively advanced hikers. The Hausbergweg is a consistently steep trail that tracks straight up the spine of the Hahnenkamm, at times right on the famed slope itself.

Grand views almost the entire way, particularly toward the top, make this trail well worth all the sweat. If you go, leave time for some reasonably priced, hearty Tyrolean cuisine at **Gasthaus Seidlalm ❷**, on the side of the trail. (☎631 35. Open May-Oct. and Dec. to Easter daily 9am-6pm.) The hike finishes at the top of the Hahnenkammbahn (below) and provides access to other trails that go even farther and higher.

Seidlalmweg: (about 10km; 2-5hr. round-trip). Somewhat less difficult than the Hausbergweg. There are a number of ways to hike this trail without going the whole 10km. The lower parts of the trail generally go through the forest, while the higher part that cuts across the mountains has the best scenery. Starting points are at the Hahnenkammbahn parking lot and the parking lot near the Streifalm chair lift.

Schwarzseerundgang: (3.2km; 1½hr. round-trip). A great choice for those who don't want to climb a mountain (or even part of one). A generally level, enjoyable hike from Pfarrauparkpl. along the lake on the outskirts of Kitzbühel.

For those with a bit more cash, cable cars do the climbing for you and provide the same open vistas. You can take the **Hahnenkammbahn** to the top of its namesake. During the summer the starting gate is open 11am-3:30pm, allowing free access to the course, albeit without the snow. (☎69 51. Open daily 8:30am-5pm. Ascent or round-trip €14.50, with guest card €13.50; children €8, accompanied by an adult €4. 3-day pass €35, children €19.50; 6-day €48/€26.50; all summer €113. The *Summerhit* special includes a 3-course lunch and a ride on the Hahnenkamm for €21.) At the top of the Hahnenkammbahn is the **Bergbahn Museum Hahnenkamm,** which gives a history of winter sports in the area, and includes a larger-than-life ski simulator. (☎69 57. Open daily 10am-4pm. Free.) The **Kitzbüheler Hornbahn lift** ascends to the **Alpenblumengarten,** where more than 120 different types of flowers blossom each spring. (Open late May to mid-Oct. 8:30am-5pm. Same prices as Hahnenkammerlift. Free tours July-Aug. 10am, 1:30pm.) The smaller **Gaisberg, Resterhöhe,** and **Bichlalm** lifts also run in summer. (€6.50, with guest card €6; children €3.50, accompanied by adult €2.)

Guest card holders can take advantage of the tourist office's **hiking program.** Daily 3-5hr. hikes cover over 100 routes and are easy or moderate. (Mid-May to mid-Oct. M-F 8:45am; call ahead for weekend hikes. Free with guest card, but doesn't include cable cars and taxi.) **Kontact³**, Wieseneggw. 7 (☎0664 1000 580; www.kizt-adventure.at), offers paragliding (from €98), canyoning (from €50), rafting (call for prices), and more. **Mountain Bike Tours** are available from the Hotel Tyrol, Josef-Pirchlst. 14. (☎0650 720 3500; www.mountainedge.co.uk. €34 per day including bike rental and guide, €14 for a 1½hr. "quick blast" including rental and guide. Passport deposit. Book at least a day ahead of time. Tours leave 10am from Hotel Tyrol.)

The **Schwarzsee,** 2.5km from Kitzbühel, is famed for its healing mud baths. Float in the water and gaze at the mountains. (See directions to Camping Schwarzsee; last bus back at 6pm. ☎623 81. Open 8am-6pm. €3, children €1; after noon €2/€1; after 4pm €1/€0.50. Electric boat rental 8:30am-6pm. €7 per 30min. Rowboat rental €3.70.)

▟ DAYTRIP FROM KITZBÜHEL

KUFSTEIN   ☎ 05372

Trains run from Kitzbühel (1hr., 2 per hr. 4:56am-9:29pm, €7.50), and from Innsbruck (1hr., 2 per hr., €10.50). The station is on the west bank of the Inn river. Ticket office open M-F 6am-7:30pm, Su and holidays 7:45am-noon and 12:45-7:30pm.

A sleepy village along the swift-flowing Inn River, Kufstein retains the small-town atmosphere that some of its bigger and glitzier neighbors lack. The impressive 12th-century *Festung* (fortress) on a hill in the middle of town and the mountainous backdrop provide good reasons for a daytrip. The **tourist office**, Unterer Stadtpl. 8, across the river from the train station, distributes free hiking, biking, and skiing maps, and a list of accommodations and restaurants. (☎622 07; www.kufstein.at. Open high-season M-F 8:30am-6pm, Sa 9am-noon; low-season M-F 8:30am-noon and 2-5pm.) **Erste** bank, Hans Reischstr. 12, left from Unterer Stadtpl., offers **money exchange**. (Open M-W 8am-noon and 2-4pm, Th 8am-noon and 2-6pm, F 8am-noon and 1-4pm.) **Sparkasse 24hr. ATM** is also left from Unterer Stadtpl., about 50m down Hans Reischstr.

The **Pension Striede ❸**, Mittendorfstr. 20, is tucked away in a quiet tree-lined street about a 10min. walk from the town's center. From the station, cross the bridge and go straight through Unterer Stadtpl. and then right onto Kinkstr.; after 5min. left onto Weissachstr. and then almost immediately a left onto Mittendorf-str., in front of the large Red Cross building. Bear left again when the road forks and continue for about 3min. until you see the *Pension* on your right. Pension Striede offers 15 rooms equipped with TV and bath, many with balconies. (☎623 16. Parking available. €23-26 per person.)

Restaurants fill the Untere Stadtpl., serving up relatively inexpensive food. Kebab stands on either side of the bridge offer especially cheap meals. **Asia Wok Restaurant ❷**, on Arkadenpl. 6, offers a tasty change from typical Austrian fare. Turn right onto Kinkstr. and, just in front of the *Festung*, left into Ark-adenpl. Amiable waiters serve stir-fry dishes, soups, salads, and sushi to a background of Asian pop music. Vegetarian meals include tofu chop suey (€7.90), while a wide variety of fish dishes cost around €9.50-17.90. (☎720 55. Chicken, pork, and beef dishes €7.50-10.90. All-you-can-eat lunch buffet €5.80, children €3.20. (Open daily 11am-3pm and 5:30-11:30pm.) A **SPAR** grocery store about 50m past the tourist office includes a bakery and tiny café. (Open M-F 7:30am-6:30pm, Sa 7am-5pm.) **Martin Reformhaus** is a large health-food store on Kaisbergerstr. at Franz Josephpl., left from Untere Stadtpl. (Open M-F 8:30am-1pm and 2-6pm, Sa 8:30am-1pm. MC/V.)

Kufstein's main attraction is the **Festung** (fortress), which towers over the rest of the city. Climb to the fortress grounds via a wooden *Gangsteig* (covered staircase) or take a short cable car ride. Once within the *Festung*, you're free to walk around the stone ramparts and grassy knolls, many of which provide excellent views of the river valley below. At the top of the fortress, the **Heimat-museum** (Regional Museum) features an assortment of prehistoric and early modern artifacts, rooms devoted to the lifestyles of locals in previous centuries, and a room with a model of the *Festung* and a history of its construction. Above the Heimatmuseum is a tower containing the restored former city jail. (☎60 23 50. Open Palm Sunday to mid-Nov. 9am-5pm; mid-Nov. to the F before Palm Sunday 10am-4pm. Entrance to fortress, museum, and cable-car ride summer €8, students €4.40; winter €7/€4. 1hr. tours in summer upon request €1.50.) The *Festung* also houses the 4037 pipes of the **Heldenorgel** (Heroes' Organ), the world's largest open-air organ, constructed in 1931 in honor of Austrian soldiers who died in WWI. An exhibit in the fortress near the pipes contains WWI artifacts including uniforms and grenades. The organ is played every day at noon, and during July and August again at 6pm. (€0.80 for auditorium seat; or stand a bit outside and hear the pipes nearly as well.)

For hiking, take the **Kaiserlift** into the mountains. Turn left at the end of Unterer Stadtpl., walk a few blocks, and follow the signs to the chairlift parking lot. The first lift goes to Duxeralm, the second to Brentenjoch. (Open daily 9am-4:30pm. Duxeralm ascent €4.35, children €1.35; round-trip €5.45/€2.90. Bren-tenjoch ascent €7.25/€2.90, round-trip €10.15/€4.35; 10% discount for children up to 15 or for visitors with a guest card.) There are myriad mid-level **hiking trails** on the mountain. After Unterer Stadtpl., take Georg-Pirmoserstr. to

Bachg. (turns into Schutzerstr.) to the trailheads. At the top near the Brenten-joch, the trails open up to breathtaking vistas. The back of Mt. Kaiser is visible above Duxeralm—just follow the signs to Berghaus Aschenbrenner and climb from there (4-5hr. total hiking time without any chairlifts). The Inn cycling route from Landeck to Passau runs through Kufstein and is popular with bikers. The tarmac path has gentle slopes but doesn't get too steep.

ST. ANTON AM ARLBERG ☎ 05446

One of the world's premier ski towns, St. Anton captured the world's attention in 2001 when it hosted the world skiing championships. In anticipation of the event, town officials moved the train station to the other side of the valley and con-structed a glistening new conference center and sports complex. What has been constant both before and after this facelift is the yearly winter influx of tourists looking to hit the world-class slopes.

■ **TRANSPORTATION.** St. Anton lies at the bottom of a steep, narrow valley, with neighboring **St. Jakob** and **St. Christoph** (both technically part of St. Anton) each a few minutes away. Several **train** routes run from St. Anton to: Feldkirch (45min., every 2hr. 5:15am-11:59pm, €6.60); Innsbruck (1¼hr., every 2hr. 6:13am-12:45am, €12.80); Vienna Westbahnhof (6½-8½hr., 8 per day 6:13am-11:18pm, €52.50); Zurich (2½-3½hr., 7 per day 5:28am-7:59pm, €32.80). A shuttle bus runs from the Zurich airport to St. Anton. (☎ 05582 226. 3hr.; 4 per day 10am-6:30pm; €45, children under age 12 half-price.) From late June to September and December to April, **PostBuses** (☎ 05442 644 22) run from the *Hauptbahnhof* to: Lech (30min., June-Sept. 5 per day 8am-5pm); St. Christoph (10min., June-Sept. 5 per day 8am-5pm, €1.80); St. Jakob (5min., June-Sept. 12 per day 6:21am-6:35pm, €1.80). A **free town bus** leaves from the post office every 10min. past the hour 7:10am-6:10pm. Call for a winter bus schedule. Buses stop at the train station and the "Westterminal," the parking lot by the highway on the east side of town. A sign with a black eagle denotes the free city bus stops. **Bike rental** is available at Intersport Alberg, in the pedestrian zone. (☎ 34 53; info@intersport-arl-berg.com. €20-28 per day, €99-139 per week. Open M-F 9am-noon and 1-6pm, Sa 9am-noon.) For a **taxi**, call ☎ 231 15 or 22 75.

■ ■ **ORIENTATION AND PRACTICAL INFORMATION.** St. Anton's main road runs the length of the *Fußgängerzone*. The **tourist office,** across from the train station, provides information on St. Anton and the Arlberg region. Ask about the **St. Anton Pluscard,** which offers discounts throughout the town. Outside is a 24hr. accommodations board. (☎ 226 90; www.stantonamarlberg.com. Open May to late Nov. M-F 8am-6pm, Sa-Su 9am-noon; Dec.-Apr. M-F 8:30am-6:30pm, Sa 9am-noon and 1-6pm, Su 10am-noon and 3-6pm.) Other services include: **currency exchange** at banks (M-F 8am-noon and 2-5pm); **Internet** access at **Mailbox,** near SportCafé Schneider (open July-Oct. noon-5pm; Nov.-Apr. 9am-9pm; €0.13 per min.); 24hr. **lockers** (including some sized for skis) at the station (€2-3.50); **snow report** (☎ 25 65); **ski rescue service** (☎ 235 22 23); **police** (☎ 133, town police ☎ 23 62 13 or 22 37); and **ambulance** (☎ 144). To find the **post office,** exit the tourist office, turn right down the main road, right again opposite Hotel Schwarzer Adler, and then take a quick right after the bend to the left. (☎ 33 800. Open M-F 8am-noon and 2-5:30pm.) **Postal Code:** A-6580.

■ ■ **ACCOMMODATIONS AND FOOD.** During the ski season, prices double and rooms fill up well in advance, so make reservations early. Your best bet for an affordable winter lodging may be in **St. Jakob** (5min. by free city bus); check

TYROL

with the St. Anton tourist office. To get to **Pension Pepi Eiter ❸,** turn left from the tourist office and head uphill; after 300m, a green sign points the way, a sharp right turn before Haus Elizabeth. The grandfatherly owner shows guests to their pine-panelled rooms, complete with comfy beds and TV. A sauna is also available upon request. (☎25 50 or 23 19. Breakfast and parking included. June-Sept. €18-20 per person; mid-Dec. to Apr. €36.) **Hotel Arlberg ❺,** Dorfstr. 90, about 15min. from the tourist office, offers a taste of luxury, complete with sauna, whirlpool, and indoor swimming pool. There is cable TV, bath/shower, toilet, hair dryer, safe, direct telephone, and radio in every room. (☎221 00; www.hotelarlberg.com. Breakfast buffet and 4-course dinner included. Reception open summer 7:30am-10pm, winter 7am-11pm. Singles €57-65; doubles €100-116, with separate sitting area and fridge €116-136; suites €64-74 per person. Children ages 3-7 in parents' room 50% off, ages 8-14 25% off. Sept.-May prices rise as much as €40-100 per person. AmEx/MC/V.)

Pasta-lovers rejoice: heaven awaits amidst the red velvet chairs of **Pizzeria Ristorante Dolce Vita ❸,** Dorfstr. 61, in the Versalia Galerie. The nearly 60 different pasta dishes include tortellini, tagliatelle, gnocchi, and more (€5.50-8.90). The menu also features 20 different types of pizza starting at €5, while fish, steak, and pork options round out the menu for between €11.50 and €19.40. (☎302 79. Open daily 6-11pm. MC/V.) The restaurant in the luxurious **Hotel Post ❹,** in the *Fußgängerzone,* satisfies the gourmet in everyone at an affordable price. Elegant presentation of the mouth-watering seasonal specials includes even the smallest detail; the freshly-made berry sorbet (€1.50 per scoop) is served atop an ice- and flower-petal-filled custard dish. Menu options and prices fluctuate, but main courses typically range from €12 to €21 and include a variety of vegetarian, fish, and meat options. A three-course "surprise" *Menü* costs €22. (☎221 30. Hot food served 11:30am-2pm and 6:30-9pm.)

For a great meal at a low price, head to **Restaurant Grieswirt ❸,** between the *Fußgängerzone* and the post office. Hearty entrees (€6.50-19.30) and two daily *Menüs* including soup, entrée, and dessert (€12-13.50) will leave you fully satisfied. (☎29 65; fax 200 56. Open daily June-Sept. 9am-9pm; Dec. to mid-Apr. 11am-10:30pm.) **SportCafé Schneider ❷,** Dorfstr. 19, is to the right down the *Fußgängerzone* from the tourist office. A cross between an *Imbiß* and a restaurant, SportCafé is perfect for a quick lunch or late dinner. They serve a small selection of soups and sandwiches (€3-5.20), spaghetti Bolognese (€6.90), and ice cream desserts for €3-4.70. (☎25 48. Open daily 9am-midnight.) The local **SPAR Markt,** Dorfstr. 62, is down the main road, 10min. away from the tourist office, just past the *Fußgängerzone.* (Open M-F 7am-7pm, Sa 7am-5pm.)

▓ OUTDOOR ACTIVITIES. A century after the Ski Club Arlberg was founded, St. Anton's main draw is still its exceptional slopes. Some 262 trails cover the area, divided into 260km of groomed trails and 185km of ungroomed ("deep snow") runs, all accessed by over 80 cable cars and lifts. **Ski passes** for the Arlberg region are sold at the ski lift stations (Galzigbahn, Rendlbahn, St. Christophbahn, and Nasserein-bahn), or at the ticket office in the *Fußgängerzone* behind the Hotel Post. (Half-day pass €29.50, ages 16-19 €27, ages 7-15 €17.50; 1-day pass €39/€35.50/€23.50; 7-day pass €208/€1798/€125. Further discounts apply outside of peak season.) Those interested in St. Anton's free 4.3km **toboggan run** should call ☎235 20. There are two **ski schools** in St. Anton: **Ski School Arlberg** (☎33 11; www.skischool-arlberg.com. Open Su-F 8:30am-4:30pm, Sa 9am-noon and 1-5pm; 1-day group lessons €53, 1-day private lessons €209) and **Ski and Snowboard School St. Anton.** (☎35 63; www.skistanton.com. Open Su-F 8:30am-4:30pm, Sa 8am-5pm. 1-day group lessons €53; 4hr. private lessons €209; 3-day snowboarding lessons €60, 3-day €137.)

In the summer, St. Anton is a hiker's heaven. Trails lead through the hills around town and the tourist office dispenses free maps and directions and sells more detailed hiking maps for €4 and €6.50. Once a week in July, the tourist office sponsors **wildflower hikes**. The easy **Rosannaschlucht hike** (3hr. loop) leads through the Rosanna gorge between St. Anton and Ferwall to the west, out to the emerald-green Ferwall See, and back on the hills on the other side of the river. Walk left from the tourist office on the highway leaving St. Anton towards Lech, and look for the Rendl cable car on the left side of the road, where the trail begins. From there, the **Leutkircher Hütte** mountain hut is a moderate 3hr. hike. (☎ 05448 82 07. Open early July to late Sept.) For a great view from the roof of the Arlberg, take the series of three Galzigbahn lifts starting in St. Anton to the top of the 2811m Valluga. (Lifts in summer daily 9am-4:15pm. Round-trip €19.) A number of wonderful hikes through high Alpine country can be found in the neighboring resort towns of **Lech** and **Zürs**. Try the strenuous hike around the **Madloch** between the two towns, or the **Gipslöcher Naturlehrpfad**, which wanders through the strange landscape of natural sinkholes on the mountainside above Lech. Inquire at the St. Anton tourist offices for bus schedules, and at the Lech tourist office for hikes. (☎ 05583 22 45; www.lech-zuers.at.) **Biking** in the Arlberg is arduous but rewarding; 150km of marked mountain bike paths await, including the popular Ferwall Valley and Moostal trails. **H2O Adventure** (☎ 05446 39; www.events-more.at) offers rafting (€26-56), canyoning (€45-87), tubing (€30-35), paragliding (from €90) and mountain bike excursions (full day €43, downhill €40, half-day €25).

THE ZILLERTAL

When the fog descends on the small villages of the Zillertal (Ziller Valley), they might as well be cut off from the rest of the world. Squeezed between three mountain ranges, the area is remote and peaceful year-round. Boasting more trails than roads and a larger ski patrol than police force, the Zillertal is a great place for skiing and hiking. In March 2001 the province of Tyrol listed three of the region's valleys as protected areas, and classified the region as the Alps High-Mountain Nature Park.

⌐ TRANSPORTATION

Trains: The Zillertal can be reached by train from the north through Jenbach, at the head of the valley. Trains leave the Jenbach station (☎ 05244 62 54 63 85) for: **Innsbruck** (20-35min., 2-3 per hr. 4:31am-10:38pm, €5.30); **Vienna** (4½-6½hrs., 7per day 5:19am-7:50pm, €46.50); **Wörgl** (20min., 2-3 per hr. 5:19am-12:06am, €4.60). For travel to within the valley contact the **Zillertalbahn (Z-bahn)** (☎ 05244 60 60; www.zillertalbahn.at), an efficient network of private buses and trains connecting the villages. The Z-bahn has 2 types of trains, the Dampfzug and the Triebwagen. The Dampfzug is an historic red steam train targeted at tourists; it costs extra and moves more slowly. The Triebwagen is a normal train, and has the same rates as the Z-bahn Autobus. One of either the Triebwagen or Autobus leaves daily every hr. 6am-9pm. Beyond Mayrhofen, travel is by bus only. Those planning to stay in the region for several days should consider the **Zillertal card (Z-card),** which covers all train and bus lines from Jenbach to Hintertux (except the Dampfzug). In the summer the card also includes mountain lifts other than the upper gondolas of the Hintertux Glacier.

Buses: If possible, travel to or from the Zillertal over the Gerlos Pass on A165 to Zell am Ziller. The road offers awe-inspiring vistas, curves, and creeks not to be missed. Transit through the valley this way is available by Zillertalbus (☎ 05282 22 11) from Zell am

TYROL

Ziller to **Königsleiten** (departs Zell 8:52, 11:10am, 1:30, 4:10pm; €4), and then a connection with the **Postbus** from Königsleiten to **Krimml** (☎0250 856 23 52; 9:50am, 5:05pm; €4). The road is also open to **cars** and **bikes.**

⚠️⛷️ HIKING AND SKIING

The **Z-card** is valid on all summer lifts in the Zillertal, including those in Zell am Ziller, Fügen, Mayrhofen, Gerlos, and Hintertux. Passes are available at tourist offices, lifts, or railway stations in Zell am Ziller and Mayrhofen, and may be used only once per day at each lift. (6-day pass €39.80, children €19.90. €2 deposit.) Hiking without cable cars is also possible throughout the valley. The Zell am Ziller **ski area**, recently connected to the Gerlos and Königsleiten ski areas, is the largest ski zone in Tyrol. The **Zillertal Super Skipass** covers lifts for the entire region, and is available at any valley lift station. (☎716 50; www.zillertalski.at. 4-day Super Skipasses including the Hintertux Glacier €118, ages 15-18 €94.50, children €59.)

ZELL AM ZILLER ☎05282

Zell am Ziller (pop. 4,000), 25km south of Jenbach, embodies picture-book images of Austrian mountain villages, with fields of tall grass and taller mountains embracing clusters of wood-shuttered Alpine houses. Founded by monks in the late 8th century (hence the *Zell*, or chapel), Zell surrendered to materialism in the 1600s when it flourished as a gold-mining town. Today, this idyllic and unassuming village offers skiing and hiking without resort-town hype.

▐ **TRANSPORTATION.** Zell is at the north-central end of the Zillertal, between Jenbach and Mayrhofen. Those taking **ÖBB trains** should get off at **Jenbach** and switch to the **Zillertalbahn** (**Z-bahn;** p. 205), which leaves from the front of the train station. Z-bahn trains and buses leave at least once per hr. 6am-9pm for Jenbach or Mayrhofen. Get to Zell am Ziller by **car** from the Inntalautobahn, taking the Wiesing/Zillertal exit and driving 24km on Zillertal-Bundesstr. 109.

▐▐ **ORIENTATION AND PRACTICAL INFORMATION.** The center of town is **Dorfplatz.** Straight out of the train station down Bahnhofstr., Dorfpl. intersects both of Zell's main streets, Unterdorf next to the river, and Gerlosstr. by the train tracks. From the station, head right on Bahnhofstr., and turn right at the end to get to the **tourist office,** Dorfpl. 3a. Pick up a map, hiking maps (€4.80-7.95), skiing information, and accommodations listings. There's a free reservations phone on the side of the office. (☎22 81; www.zell.at. Open May-June and Oct.-Nov. M-F 8:30am-12:30pm and 2:30-6pm; July-Sept. also Sa 9am-noon and 4-6pm; Dec.-Apr. also Su 4-6pm. Other services include: **taxis** (☎26 25, 23 45, or 22 55), **bike rental** at the train station (€12, children €7.20), **mountain rescue** or **police** (☎133) and **ambulance** (☎144). The **post office** at Unterdorf 2 has an **ATM** in front. (☎23 33. Open M-F 8am-noon and 2-6pm.) The **postal code** is A-6280.

▐▐ **ACCOMMODATIONS AND CAMPING.** Many places offer decent rates, and good accommodations can be found without trekking too far from the town center. To reach **Haus Huditz ❷**, Karl-Platzer-Weg 1, cross the train tracks by the tourist office and continue onto Gerlosstr. Bear left onto Gauderg. at the Mode Journal building and look for Karl-Platzer-Weg on the left at the next fork in the road (10min.). The warm and friendly owner provides beverages, TV, down comforters, and balconies with mountain views. (☎22 28; huditz.bern-hard@gutanet.at. Breakfast included. Shower €1. €15.50, in winter €17.) **Hotel Rosengarten**

❸, Rosengartenweg 14, has window boxes with geraniums and marigolds. It offers spacious rooms, all with balcony, shower, and satellite TV. On-site sauna and café. (☎24 43; fax 244 34. Doubles with shower Apr.-Oct. €32, Dec.-Mar. €35.) **Camping Hofer ❶**, Gerlosstr. 33, is only a few blocks from the town center. Free weekly hikes, a swimming pool, and a playground are all provided. There's a grocery store across the street. "Duo Knightfights," the house band, performs in the bar adjacent to reception W nights. Showers included. (☎22 48; office@campinghofer.at. Laundry €7. Reception mid-Dec. to early Jan. and July to mid-Aug. 8am-10pm; May-June and Sept.-Oct. 9am-noon and 3-8pm. €4.50-6 per adult, €5.50-6.50 per campsite, €1 tax per person per night. Also offers rooms: doubles with shower €18-22, winter €20-24.)

◻ **FOOD.** Regional specialties include *Käsespätzle* (baked noodles with cheese and onions, and sometimes *Wurst* or eggs), *Zillertaler Krapfen* (crispy fried shells filled with potatoes and cheese), and *Tiroler Gröstl* (fried potatoes, onions and bacon with a fried egg on top). **SB Restaurant Zeller Stuben ❷**, Unterdorf 11, the cheapest place around, serves big buffet-style portions. The restaurant upstairs features six to eight daily *Menüs* including soup, entrée, and dessert for €8-14. (☎22 71. Children's and vegetarian menus available. Spaghetti €5.50, *Gulaschsuppe* €3. Both restaurants open July-Oct. and late Dec. to mid-Apr. daily 11am-9pm.) Cross the river for **Pizza Café Reiter ❷**, Zelbergr. 4. Stay outdoors by the river or sit inside and watch continuous videos of paragliders. The chef serves pizza (€5-10), calzones (€7), and pasta. (☎22 89. Open daily 11am-midnight.) Put the cherry on your night at **Café-Konditorei Gredler ❶**, Unterdorf 10, near SB restaurant. Former Confectioner of the Year Tobias Gredler whips up desserts for patrons to enjoy on the riverside patio. The banana chocolate torte actually looks like a banana, thanks to the yellow sugar and chocolate shell; the other 14 tortes (€2.50) are no less intricate or delectable. (☎248 90; www.torten.net. Open daily June-Oct. 10am-11pm; mid-Dec. to May 10am-6pm.) **Billa Supermarket** is on Bahnhofstr. on the way to the tourism office. (Open M-F 7:30am-6:30pm and Sa 7:30am-noon.)

▨ **OUTDOOR ACTIVITIES.** For skiing, Zell sells single-day passes valid on the **Kreuzjoch-Rosenalm Königsleiten** and **Gerlosplatte**, 155km of slopes served by 55 ski lifts (1 day €33, ages 15-19 €26.50, under age 15 €16.50; 3 days €90/€72/€45) and Super Skipasses for longer visits, including access to the **Hintertux** glacier (€118/ €94.50.) Single-ride tickets are available for non-skiers who tag along to watch (€5.50, round-trip €9; children €2.80/€4.50). Obtain passes at the **Kreuzjoch** (☎71 65), **Gerlosstein** (☎22 75), or **Ramsberg** (☎27 20) cable car stations. (All 3 lifts open 8:30am-5pm.) Get info from the snowphone (☎71 65 26; www.zillertalarena.com). **Rent skis** at any of Zell's sporting goods stores. Try **Pendl Sport** at Gerlosstr. 6. (☎22 87; fax 39 17. Open Easter to Nov. M-F 8am-noon and 2:30-6:30pm, Sa 8am-noon; Dec. to Easter also Sa 2-6pm. DC/MC/V.) Prices average €16-20 for skiing gear and €24 for snowboards. Rent **toboggans** at the Gerlossteinbahn. (Open M-Sa 7:45am-9:15pm, Su 8:30am-4:30pm.)

Summer activities include **Nordic walking**. Early birds can join the "Sunrise Experience" (5am start), among other tours. (July-Sept. M-F. Prices depend on the length and type of walk but average around €10.) Much hiking around Zell am Ziller is lift-assisted. Two of the three ski lifts in Zell's vicinity offer **Alpine hiking**: the **Kreuzjochbahn** and **Gerlossteinbahn** (**Kreuzjochbahn** ☎716 50. Open 8:40am-12:30pm and 1-5:10pm. Round-trip without guest card €14.60, with guest card €13.20; to Rosenalm €9.80/€8.80. **Gerlossteinbahn** ☎22 75 11. Open 8:30am-12:15pm and 1-5pm. Round-trip €8.80/€9.80.) The Karspitz (2264m) provides an ideal hiking goal; on sunny days you can see the entire valley and the waterfalls on the opposite ridge. From the Kreuzjochbahn top station, turn right and follow path #10. At Grindalm, you have the option of heading straight towards Kreuzwiesienalm (a small, refreshing *Gasthaus*), and farther to the peak. Take path #11 back to the lift.

Those preferring air travel to hiking on the ground should head to **Pizza Air**, the self-proclaimed "World's Smallest Airline." (☎22 89. Offers tandem flights of 5-25min. for €70-110.) For a down-to-earth look at Zell's history, take a tour of the nearby **gold mine.** The journey begins at a petting zoo and adjacent cheese factory before moving on to a 45min. hike to the mine entrance. (☎48 20; fax 32 72. 2hr. tours every hr. May-Sept. daily 9am-6pm. €10, ages 3-16 €5.)

MAYRHOFEN   ☎ 05285

At the southernmost end of the Zillertal, Mayrhofen draws flocks of travelers from afar who have come to see the Alps. The polished town is the center of tourist activity for the Zillertal, and therefore also the center for food, mountain schools, and nightlife. Four separate valleys (the **Zillergrund, Stillupgrund, Zemmtal,** and **Tuxertal**) converge on the town, providing endless opportunities for hikers and skiers. Mayrhofen residents walk the walk: native Peter Habeler and fellow Tyrolean Reinhold Messner completed the first oxygen-unaided ascent of Mt. Everest in 1978. Habeler now runs the town's alpine school.

🖪🎿 TRANSPORTATION AND PRACTICAL INFORMATION. Mayrhofen is accessible via the **trains** and **buses** of the Z-Bahn from Jenbach (50-60min., 20 per day 6:05am-9:05pm, €5.60) and Zell am Ziller (15min., 27 per day 6:43am-9:52pm, €2). The **train station** lies slightly northwest of town; to reach the center from the station, take a left onto the Umfahrungsstr. and turn right at the intersection. (☎623 62. Open daily 7am-7:30pm.) **Taxis** (☎638 40 or 622 60) take you anywhere in town for less than €5. The **tourist office,** Dursterstr. 225, is in the upper end of town. From the train station, turn left onto Umfahrungsstr., then right onto Dursterstr. The office is on the left. The office leads free **guided hikes and tours,** from valley tours to 5hr. hikes; transportation costs (€5-15) not included. A 24hr. accommodations board is outside. Tours June-Oct. M-F; call ahead for details. (☎67 60; info@mayrhofen.at. Open M-F 8am-6pm, Sa 9am-noon, Su 10am-noon; July-Aug. also Sa 2-6pm.) Other services include an **ATM** at Hypo-Tirol bank at the corner of Einfahrt Mitte and Hauptstr.; **luggage storage** at the train station (open daily 7am-6:30pm, €2.50 per piece); **bike rental** at the train station (€12 per day, €7.20 for a half-day after 1pm); **police** (☎133); **fire** (☎122); **mountain rescue** (☎140); **ambulance** ☎144. The **post office,** Einfahrt Mitte 434, is on your right on the way into town. (☎62 35 10. Open M-F 8am-noon and 2-6pm.) The **Postal Code:** A-6290.

🖪🍴 ACCOMMODATIONS AND FOOD. Accommodations fill up quickly in Mayrhofen, so it's best to make reservations in advance. To get to **Haus Woldrich ❸**, Brandbergstr. 355, from the tourism office, head back towards the Bahnhof and take a left onto Siegeleger. which turns into Brandbergstr. The house will be on the left (5min.). The guest house offers spacious rooms, some with balconies. (☎/fax 623 25. Breakfast included. Singles Apr.-Oct. €16, with shower €22-24; Dec. to Easter €18-22.) **Haus Andreas ❸**, Sportplatzstr. 317, is a 5min. walk past the tourist office. Turn right onto Sportplatzstr. It offers eight beds in blue-and-white-decorated doubles and triples, all with balconies. (☎/fax 638 45. Breakfast buffet included. Closed in May. €20-26.) **Hotel Pension Sieglerhof ❸**, Dursterstr. 226, across the street from the tourist office, provides a dark wood interior and TV in each room. Bar serves drinks after 5pm. (☎62

493; fax 62 49 37. Apr.-Nov. €20-23 per person, with bath €31-33; Dec.-Mar. €23-25/€31-33.) For **Camping Mayrhofen** ❶, Laubichl 125, head left from the station and away from town. At the first intersection turn right, then take an immediate left onto Gemeindestr.; the campground is 700m ahead on the right. Amenities include a pool and children's play area. (☎625 80; www.alpenparadies.com. Meals at the on-site restaurant around €8. Solarium €5, sauna €6. No vehicles can enter 10:30pm-6:30am. Open year-round, but limited service in Nov. Summer €6.50 per person, winter €5. Tax €0.65. Cars €2.50; tents and RVs €3.30.) **Mo's Esscafé and Musikroom** ❶, Hauptstr. 417. This New Orleans jazz café seems a bit out of place in the Austrian Alps, but its cheery multi-lingual staff doesn't seem to notice. The Mo burger (€4.30) and succulent seasoned fries (€1.20), will fuel your belly. There's live music on weekends. (☎634 35; fax 63 43 54. Open Easter to Dec. M-Sa noon-1am; Dec. to Easter Tu-Sa noon-1am, Su-M 4pm-1am.) **Restaurant Manni** ❷, Hauptstr. 439, offers weekly specials (€8-12.50) like baked potatoes filled with sour cream and chicken strips and veggies, along with pizza (€13) and other standards. (☎633 01. Open daily 11am-midnight. AmEx/MC/V.) **Café Dengg** ❷, Hauptstr. 412, serves well-prepared dishes beneath an awning just down Hauptstr. (☎648 66. Spaghetti €6.80. Pizzas €7-8. Open M-Sa 9am-11pm.) There's a **BILLA,** Am Marienpl. 346, left from Europahaus and then an immediate right onto Seigler (☎634 24), and a **SPAR Markt** on Hauptstr., right from Einfahrt Mitte. (☎639 10. Open M-F 7:30am-6:30pm, Sa 7:30am-6pm, Su 8am-noon.)

☒ OUTDOOR ACTIVITIES. Mayrhofen offers ample opportunities for hiking. The **Z-Card** (see p. 205) can be a great deal for those who prefer to ride lifts up into the mountains rather than hike. The **Penkenbahn** gondola passes directly over the town on its way to the 1850m Penkenberg. (☎622 77. Open end of May to mid-Oct. daily 9am-5pm. €14.40, with guest card €12.90, children €7.70.) From there, follow path #23 uphill to the **Penkenjoch** (1½hr.) for panoramic views of the valley. The **Ahornbahn** lift takes passengers to the vicinity of both easy and difficult hikes. (☎626 33. Mid-June to mid-Oct., every 30min. 8:30am-noon and 12:30-5pm. Same prices as the Penkenbahn.) For the easy **Edelhütte hike** (1½-2hr.), exit the Ahornbahn, head left, and look for trail #42. Winding through meadows before reaching the hut (2238m), the hike offers views of neighboring mountains.

In winter, **skiers** and **snowboarders** flock to the Ahorn, Penken, and Horberg ski areas. All three are covered by the **Ski Zillertal 3000** pass, along with neighboring villages Finkenberg and Tux. (1-day pass €32.50, ages 14-19 €26, ages 7-13 €16.50, under 7 free; 3-day pass €90/€72/€45.) The pass includes transit on local ski buses. The **Zillertal Super Skipass** covers the whole valley (see p. 206). **Ski rental** at **Intersport,** Hauptstr. 415. (☎624 00; fax 624 00 15. Open M-F 8:30am-12:30pm and 2-6:30pm, Sa 8:30am-6pm, Su 8:30am-noon and 3-6pm.)

The **Cultural Countryside Walking Tour** leads uphill to a scenic location with two historic sites. Pick up a walking map from the tourist office for Steinerkogl and Emberg., and take the Postbus to Brandberg. Follow the map to Emberg's Bauernhof Hanserhof, a 500-year-old farm still in operation, and the *Schrofen-mühle*, where a water-powered mill grinds grain the old-fashioned way. From this vantage point on the ridge you see the entire valley beneath, including Mayrhofen and the *Ahornspitze* (2973m). **A bicycle path** runs along the length of the valley. Bike maps are available at the tourist office.

Catch winds with paragliders in surrounding valleys, or take a tandem flight with instructors at **Flugtaxi Mayrhofen,** Sportplatzstr. 300 (☎0664 205 50 11; from €55), or **Stocky-Air,** in the yellow gondola right next to the Penkenbahn lift. (☎0664 340 79 76. 7-8min. flight €55, 20-30min. €110.) Other adventure activities including rafting (from €29) and canyoning (from €27) can be found at

Action Club Zillertal, Hauptstr. 458 (☎629 77; www.action-club-zillertal.com). Similar prices and activities can also be had next door at **Mountain Sports Zillertal,** Hauptstr. 456 (☎312 02 66; www.mountain-sportszillertal.com).

⬛ **NIGHTLIFE.** For après-ski action, head left from the tourist office and take the first right, stay left at the fork, and look for signs to **Scotland Yard,** Schellingstr. 372. The bar is a popular hangout for skiers and snowboarders . Get there by 10:30pm in the winter, when this English-speaking establishment sometimes doesn't even have standing room. (☎623 39; www.scotlandyard.at. Beer about €3. Open daily 7pm-3am. MC/V.)

THE ÖTZTAL

Bending its way between hundreds of 3000m peaks south to the Italian border, the Ötztal (Ötz valley) offers some of the wildest and most impressive scenery in the Tyrolean Alps. Tiny farms cling impossibly to mountainsides while rivulets carve through the rocks to create picturesque waterfalls and a silt-gray river. The 1991 discovery of a frozen man who lived 5000 years ago (nicknamed Ötzi), proves that visitors have been enjoying the breathtaking views for millennia. The area known as the Ötztal Arena is Austria's largest skiing and snowboarding center. There is glacier skiing in summer, as well as some of the most difficult (and rewarding) hiking outside of the Hohe Tauern. Bahnhof Ötztal sends **trains** to Innsbruck (30-45min., 5:27am-1:31am, €7.50) and St. Anton (1hr., 4:14am-11:01am, €8.40). **Buses** go through the Ötztal's main town of Sölden before forking into the narrow Gurgler and Venter ranges. Buses to more remote towns run on reduced hours in summer and fall.

SÖLDEN ☎ 05254

Wedged in the Ötztal valley 36km south of Bahnhof Ötztal, Sölden is ideal for exploring the razor-sharp, snow-streaked mountains on either side of the valley. Numerous area ski lifts serve eager skiers throughout the winter, when the town becomes a ski resort. In the summer, these mountains provide fantastic hiking as well as glacier skiing up high near all the 3000m peaks.

⬛ **TRANSPORTATION AND PRACTICAL INFORMATION.** There are several bus stops in town but the PostBus only stops at the centrally-located "Postamt" unless otherwise requested. **PostBuses** arrive from Bahnhof Ötztal (1hr., every hr. 7:05am-7:15pm, €6.90) before departing for Vent (30min., 5 per day 8:03am-4:40pm, €4.40) and Obergurgl (25min., every hr. 8:05am-7:15pm, €2.60). From the "Post Office" bus stop, turn right and walk a few hundred feet back the way the bus came, cross the bridge past the little hospital, and keep walking straight to the **tourist office,** which has two **Internet** terminals. (☎510; www.soelden.com. €0.10 per min. Open M-Sa 8am-6pm, Su 3-6pm; winter also Su 9am-6pm.) A 24hr. accommodations board and telephone is across from the "Shell Tankstelle" bus stop. **E. T.'s Internet Café,** Hof 430 (☎24 89) at the "Hotel Huberttus" bus stop, charges €0.10 per min. (Open daily noon-10pm.) **Rent bikes** at any one of the five sports shops in town (€16-18 per day, €25-28 for weekend). The **post office** is at Hof 439. (☎22 66. Open M-F 8am-noon and 2-6pm; mid-Jan. to Apr. also Sa 9-11am.) **Postal Code:** A-6450.

⬛ **ACCOMMODATIONS AND FOOD.** Be aware that lodging prices rise significantly in winter. Luckily, nearly every house in this sleepy village becomes a winter guesthouse to hold the throngs of skiers. To get to **Haus Alpenrose** ❸,

Santel 166b, take the first right after the "Shell Tankstelle" bus stop. Proprietor Reinhard Schöpf has long been a local mountain guide and ski instructor—he can tell you where the best skiing and hiking can be found. All rooms come with TV, shower, and a balcony. (☎23 33. Mid-Dec. to Apr. €25-35 per person; July-Sept. €20; Oct. to mid-Dec. €25.) For a down-home family experience, try **Haus Wachter ❸**. Get off the bus at "Schmiedhofbrücke," cross the bridge, and turn right. If the Wachters and their two children don't charm you, the gigantic breakfast buffet will. Rooms include TV, balcony, and private bath. (☎ 24 23; fax 24 34. Dec.-May €40; June-Nov. €30.) To get to **IDEAL ❸**, Rainstadl 736, cross the bridge in front of Tyrolerhof and make a left in front of the tourist office, take the second right and walk to the mountain's base. This newly built house offers expansive views and large furnished rooms with foyers and private bathrooms. (☎/fax 304 13; ideal@soelden.at. Summer €13-20; winter €32-42; fall €30-35; children 20-60% discount.)

There are several restaurants in town. Many close in summer. **Hotel Stefan ❷** is located 30m from the Hochsölden chairlift, diagonally across from the SPAR. First, you'll notice the restaurant's quiet, romantic rooms with wood paneling; and then, once the food arrives, some of the most flavorful traditional dishes in all of Tyrol. Try the *Schlutzkrapfen* (mushrooms, sauce, and breaded chicken; €7.50) or ask for the daily special for €6-10. (☎22 37; fax 22 37 25. Open daily 11:30am-2:30pm and 6-10:30pm. AmEx/MC/V.) **Restaurant-Pizzeria Corso ❷**, across the bridge from the Hotel Liebe Sonne, serves pizza (€6.70-12.20) and pasta (€7.30-10.80) in an elegant, candle-lit atmosphere, with a large glass-enclosed terrace overlooking the Ötztaler Ache river. (☎24 98; fax 29 80. Open June-Apr. Tu-Su noon-midnight.) If the blaring oom-pah music and rustic agricultural implements at **Törggele Stub'n ❷** don't scream "Tyrol," then the menu will. Cheese dumpling soup (€4.50) and traditional Tyrolean *Käsespätzle* (€8.50) will satisfy your hunger. As you are walking in (or out) check out the stuffed raccoons and ferrets engaged in a high stakes poker game. (Cross the bridge toward the tourist office; Törggele is on your right. ☎35 35. Open daily 11am-11:30pm.) Turn left from the post office for the **SPAR Supermarkt**. (Open M-Sa 8:30am-12:30pm and 2:30-6pm.)

◪ OUTDOOR ACTIVITIES. The high altitude of Sölden's skiing areas (1377-3058m) guarantees snow even in the summer. The **Gaislachkoglbahn**, whisking passengers up the 3058m Gaislachkogl in a twin-cable gondola is, according to Sölden's advertisements, "the largest and most modern continuous bi-cable overhead ropeway in the world." (Open late June to mid-Sept. and Dec.-Apr. Round-trip for non-skiers in winter and hikers in summer €19, ages 8-16 €10.) **Lift tickets** for the 32 cable cars and lifts that serve Sölden's slopes are sold at the Gaislachkoglbahn booth at the southern end of town. (Mid-Dec. to Apr. €39, ages 15-18 €30, under 15 €24.) There are ski and snowboard schools in and around Sölden, including **Sölden/Hochsölden** (☎23 64; www.ski-soelden.com; 4hr. group lessons €46) and **Yellow power** (☎220 35 00; www.yellowpower.at; 4hr. group lesson €47-52). Ask at the tourist office about the 5km toboggan run, which has lighting for the evenings.

The steep hillside above Sölden between **Hochsölden** and the **Rettenbachalm** is excellent for hiking. To get to Hochsölden, the best bet is to use the **Sesselift Hochsölden,** in the parking lot behind the Intersport down the road from the post office. (Open end of June to mid-Sept. daily 9am-noon and 1-4:15pm. Round-trip €7, ages 8-14 €4.) If you want to start on the Rettenbachalm side, a moderate trailhead is on the right of the post office (about 2hr. one-way).

VORARLBERG

Austria's westernmost regi[...] the intersection of four nat[...] two currencies, making for a diverse and vibrant province. A broad representation of Vorarlberg can be found in cities like Feldkirch, which retains its medieval influences; Bregenz, an international magnet for the arts; and Dornbirn, the state's economic center and gateway to the pastoral Bregenzerwald region. A number of hiking and skiing options exist, especially in the higher parts of the province. From the tranquil Bodensee in the west, Vorarlberg's elevation increases as you move south and east, rising through rolling hills to the imposing Arlberg range (passable only through the 10km Arlberg Tunnel) on the boundary with Tyrol.

HIGHLIGHTS OF VORARLBERG

Watch world-class performers at the **Bregenzer Festspiele** (p. 218).

See evidence of Vorarlberg's medieval past in **Feldkirch** (p. 219).

Admire the works of painter Angelika Kaufmann in **Schwarzenberg** (p. 223).

BREGENZ
☎ 05574

Bregenz, the capital city of Vorarlberg, spreads along the eastern coast of the Bodensee. The city's prime location made it popular with guests from around the world long before the days of Eurail. First came the Celts, and then the Romans, who established a camp called Brigitania on the site of the present-day city. Later the Irish missionaries Gallus and Columban dropped by and dubbed the shining lake surrounded by mountains "The Golden Bowl." Bregenz now plays host to travelers strolling along the lakeside, exploring the winding cobblestoned streets of the historic **Oberstadt**, or taking in one of their world-renowned performances.

▉ TRANSPORTATION

Trains: Bahnhofstr. (☎675 50, 232 or 1810, information 05 17 17). To: **Feldkirch** (30-45min., 2-4 per day 5am-11:42pm, €4.50); **Innsbruck** (2¼hr., 8 per day 5am-9:45pm, €25.10); **Munich** (2½hr., 4 per day 9:20am-7:20pm, €34.20); **St. Gallen** (45min., 4 per day 10:40am-8:40pm, €10.30); **Vienna** (8-10hr., 5 per day 5am-9:45pm, €57); **Zurich** (1¾hr., 4 per day 10:40am-8:40pm, €25.70).

Regional Buses: BundesBuses leave from the train station to: **Dornbirn** (30min., every 30min. 4:55am-6:55pm, €2.10); **Egg** (1hr., 1-2 per hr. 6:51am-6:51pm, €3.30); and other regional destinations.

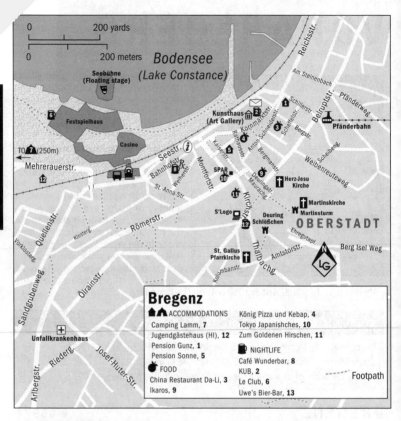

Bregenz

▲▲ ACCOMMODATIONS
Camping Lamm, **7**
Jugendgästehaus (HI) **12**
Pension Gunz, **1**
Pension Sonne, **5**

● FOOD
China Restaurant Da-Li, **3**
Ikaros, **9**

König Pizza und Kebap, **4**
Tokyo Japanishches, **10**
Zum Goldenen Hirschen **11**

● NIGHTLIFE
Café Wunderbar, **8**
KUB, **2**
Le Club, **6**
Uwe's Bier-Bar, **13**

- - - - - Footpath

Public Transportation: 4 bus lines run through the city. Day pass €2.

Taxis: ☎ 650 00, 866 88, or 718 00.

Parking: By the *Festspielhaus*. Open 8am-noon and 1-6pm. €0.50 per hr., €3.60 per day; 6pm-midnight €2.20 per hr. Hours are typically 8am-noon and 1:30-6pm.

ⓘ PRACTICAL INFORMATION

Tourist Office: Bregenz Tourismus und Stadtmarketing, Bahnhofstr. 14 (☎ 495 90; www.bregenz.at). Exit the train station toward the town, face away from the lake, and turn left; it's the glass building on the right with the green "i" sign. The staff makes hotel reservations (€2.50), has *Privatzimmer* lists, gives out hiking and city maps, and provides concert info and free **Internet** access. Open M-F 9am-noon and 1-5pm, Sa 9am-noon; during the *Festspiele* M-Sa 9am-7pm.

Consulate: UK, Bundesstr. 110 (☎ 785 86), in neighboring **Lauterach.**

ATM: At the train station.

Lockers: At the train station. €2.50-3.50. Open 6:45am-9:40pm.

English-Language Bookstore: H. Lingenhöle & Co, Kaisterstr. 1, in the same complex as SPAR market (☎ 424 38; info@lingenhoele.com). Open M-F 9am-6pm, Sa 8:30am-4pm.

Pharmacy: Bahnhofstr. 25. M-Th 8am-12:30pm and 2-6pm, F 8am-6pm, Sa 8am-12:30pm.

Internet Access: S'Logo, Kirchstr. 47 (☎441 91). €0.08 per min. Open daily 5pm-1am.

Post Office: Seestr. 5 (☎437 007), on Seestr. across from the harbor. Open M-F 8am-7pm (cashier closes at 5pm), Sa 8am-noon.

Postal Code: A-6900.

ACCOMMODATIONS AND CAMPING

With six four-star hotels and lower-priced *Pensionen*, Bregenz accommodates both backpackers and affluent vacationers. When the *Festspiele* comes to town in midsummer, prices rise and advance reservations become absolutely necessary.

Jugendgästehaus (HI), Mehrerauerstr. 5 (☎428 67; www.jgh.at). Cross the bridge that goes out of the train station and over the tracks toward the lake. Facing away from the tracks, walk left through the parking lot; it's the big, yellow-brick building straight ahead when you come out onto the street. This well-staffed hostel in an old factory offers spic-and-span bunks in 2- to 6-person rooms, all with bathroom and shower, and some with their own lofts. Light sleepers should ask for a room on the opposite side of the train tracks. **Internet** access in café €1.50 per 20min. Breakfast buffet and sheets included. Dinner €6, lunch and dinner together €10.50. Free bike and luggage storage. Reception 7am-10pm. Lockout 11pm, open every 30min. until 1am, and at 2am and 3am; keycard available from front desk opens back door at all hours. Check-out 10am. Dorms Apr.-Oct. €17.50; Nov.-Mar. €16.20. For singles add €7, for doubles €5. Tax May-Sept. €1.24; Oct.-Apr. €0.51. For 1- or 2-night stays, add €3. DC/MC/V. ❷

Pension Sonne, Kaiserstr. 8 (☎425 72; www.bbu.at). Exit station towards the town ("zum Stadt") and, with your back to the lake, make a left on Bahnhofstr., then right on Kaiserstr. Rooms with wood floors and sink, located in the heart of the *Fußgängerzone*. The hallways' colorful rugs give the place an inviting atmosphere. Breakfast included. Reception 7:30am-7pm. Check-in after noon. Singles €32-39, with shower and toilet €38-44; doubles €60-74; triples €81-99; quads €128. Add €5-6 per person for rooms with bath. ❷

Pension Gunz, Anton-Schneider-Str. 38 (☎/fax 236 57), located 2 blocks behind the post office. This homey *Pension* offers rooms with private showers above a small pastry shop/restaurant. Hall bathroom. Breakfast included. Restaurant serves fresh fish from the Bodensee, daily *Menüs* for €5-10, and light meals and vegetarian options for €3-7.80. Restaurant and reception 8am-8pm. €30-35 per person. AmEx/MC/V. ❷

Camping Lamm, Mehrerauerstr. 50-51 (☎717 01 or 745; fax 71 74 54), is 10min. past the youth hostel. Small, economical campground with adjoining restaurant/*Pension*. Their small, grassy plot houses tents and campers. Lamm has its own stables and will let kids ride the ponies. Moderate traffic noise. Reception 8-10am and 5-8pm, or inquire within restaurant. €3.50 per person, €1.75 per child ages 6-14, €2.60-3.30 per tent, €2.60 per car, €4.40-5.50 per RV, €3-3.60 per camper. Electricity €2.60. ❶

FOOD

Markets fill Kornmarktstr. with fresh vegetables, breads, flowers, cheeses, and more Tu and F. There's a **farmers' market** Sa 8am-noon. **SPAR** supermarket is open M-Th 8am-7pm, F 8am-7:30pm, Sa 8am-5pm.

Ikaros, Deuringstr. 5 (☎529 54). Look for the blue-and-white-striped awning at the edge of Leutbühel in the *Fußgängerzone*. This exceptional café offers a little taste of the Mediterranean with a wide variety of Greek dishes, including lunch *Menüs* (€6 for appetizer and entrée), salads, and main dishes (€3.80-9.20) served indoors to Greek music or outdoors amidst potted palms. A plate of assorted appetizers (€6.80) includes everything from a stuffed grape leaf to sundried tomatoes, olives, a variety of dips, and more. Open M-F 10am-2pm and 5pm-1am, Sa 10am-1am. ❶

YOWSA! THAT'S A NICE SUPPER

In Austria, the biggest meal of the day takes place in the middle. Lunch is a sacred time when schools and businesses empty and droves of people return home to eat their schnitzel, strudel, or tafilspitz. The ubiquitous sign "geschlossen 12-14" means closed for lunch.

A humbler, distinctly Austrian meal takes place in the evening. *Jause* (pronounced Yow-sa) is a delightful little snack for the discerning palate that is easy to make, particularly because it does not involve cooking! It is popular on the weekends (when work and other activities do not interfere).

Jause is a meat, cheese, and vegetable buffet. Trays of several different types of meat—salami, ham, bologna, and wurst—share the table with baskets of bread. An oil-and-vinegar dressing is poured over a simple tomato and mozzarella salad. Many varieties of cheese are also served.

These ingredients and dishes are not always required. Substitutions are not only possible, they are encouraged. Hard-boiled eggs, carrots, or other vegetables—especially for vegetarians!—make fine supplements. Feel free to individualize the meal and make it your own. Stay away from the onions though, or your guests will shout "yowsa!" for another reason.

Tokyo Japanisches Restaurant, Römerstr. 2 (☎589 78) in the same shopping center as SPAR market, features a menu filled with sushi (€1.60-2.20 per piece, €7.80-18.90 for a mixed plate), wok stir-fries (€5.90-15.90) and other Japanese specialties. Or, sit beside the long conveyor belt that runs the length of the bright and airy dining room; just pluck off whichever tiny servings of sushi and appetizers you want. Soups, salads, and appetizers €2.10-4.90; vegetarian choices abound. Open daily 11am-11pm.

Zum Goldenen Hirschen, Kirchstr. 8 (☎428 15), near the *Fußgängerzone.* Dark furniture, small stained-glass windows, and a half-timbered-style interior give an authentic feel to a place that has brewed its own beer and served local favorites like *Schweinenbraten* with *Sauerkraut* and *Knödel* (€7.50) for over 300 years. Vegetarian menu available. Open M and W-Su 10am-midnight. AmEx/DC/MC/V. ❷

China Restaurant Da-Li, Anton-Schneider-Str. 34 (☎534 14), near *Pension* Gunz, serves typical Chinese fare. Stop by weekday afternoons for some great deals: the *Mittagsmenü* with rice, spring roll, and main dish (€5), or the lunch buffet (€7). Nice atmosphere with Chinese music and a plant-filled interior. Your reward for finishing your meal is a free shot of warm peach schnapps. Entrées (€6.70-16) include vegetarian options, fried rice and noodles, and lots of meat and fish stir-fries. Soups and appetizers €2.30-4. Open daily 11:30am-2:30pm and 5:30-11:30pm. MC/V. ❶

König Pizza und Kebap, Rathausstr. 6 (☎538 81), is open late, late, late. Serves some of the cheapest food in town in a squeaky-clean eatery with extensive bar options. Eat-in or take-out pizzas (€4-7.20), *Dönerkebaps* and veggie kebabs (€2.60-5.50). Open M-Th 11am-3am, F-Sa 11am-4am, Su noon-4am. ❶

⬮ SIGHTS

On the hill above Bregenz looms the **Oberstadt,** or "upper city," a once-fortified settlement that contains many of the city's oldest and most attractive buildings. A short hike up Maurachg. from the *Fußgängerzone* transports visitors into another world, complete with towering walls and rows of pastel-painted, wood-beamed houses, many of them hundreds of years old. Some of the homes have incorporated fragments of the old city walls into their construction; others have extensive rose gardens or are painted with murals. The major landmark of the Oberstadt is the wooden **Martinsturm,** dating from the 13th century, which supports Europe's largest onion dome. The second and third floors of the tower house the **Vorarlberg Militärmuseum,** which chronicles in German every war the Vorarlbergers ever fought. The third floor, overlooking the Bodensee and beyond, is not to be missed. *(☎466 32; www.members.aon/martinsturm. Open mid-Apr. to mid-Oct. Tu-Su 9am-6:30pm. €1, ages 6-14 €0.50.)* Next door is the **Martinskirche,** filled with frescoes dating back to the early 14th century. Particularly noteworthy are the depictions of St. Christopher, the Holy Symbol of Grief, and the 18th-century Stations of the Cross. Across Ehregutapl. (with the fountain) from the Martinsturm is **Deuring Schlößchen,** a 17th-century castle that houses a decidedly non-budget hotel.

The narrow stone *Meißnersteige* walkway leads down from the left corner of the castle. Cross Thalbachg. and hike 3min. up Schloßbergstr., taking a sharp left when the road forks and heading up the stone steps to reach **St. Gallus Pfarrkirche.** The white-stucco sanctuary of the 11th-century church, reputedly founded by the medieval Irish missionaries St. Gallus and St. Columba, glows with lavish gold ornamentation and a detailed ceiling fresco that dates from 1738. The shepherdess in the altar painting has the face of Maria Theresia, who donated 1500 guilders to the church in 1740. On the opposite side of the *Oberstadt* at the corner of Am Brand and Bergmannstr., the twin steeples of the **Herz-Jesu Kirche** seem to breach the heavens. Its soaring arches are cleverly painted to look like brick and stone, while the Expressionist stained-glass windows glow with brilliant colors.

Walking from the tourist office through the *Fußgängerzone* and away from the train station, you'll come across a large, imposing building covered with translucent gray tiles: the **Kunsthaus Bregenz.** The spooky, stark concrete interior, with its gleaming floor and dim sunlight fighting its way through milky glass windows, makes a perfect home for avant-garde art displays. Exhibits rotate approximately every two months. 2005 will feature local and artists and, in the summer, Roy Liechtenstein. *(☎48 59 40; www.kunsthaus-bregenz.at. Open Tu-W and F-Su 10am-6pm, Th 10am-9pm., during the Festspiele daily 10am-9pm. €6, students €4.50, family card €10.)*

🔼 OUTDOOR ACTIVITIES

There's no better place to stretch your legs than the **Strandweg** and **Seepromenade,** which follow the curve of the Bodensee from one end of town to the other. All along the waterfront, groomed paths, rose gardens, and strategically placed ice cream stands surround playgrounds, and a mini-golf course. For would-be mariners who like to steer themselves, **paddle-** and **motorboat rentals** are available from the "Bootsmeiten" stand near Wirtshaus am See, next to the harbor. (Open daily 10am-twilight. Motorboats €11-19 per 30min., paddle boats €6.50 per 30 min.) Several companies run 🔲**sightseeing cruises** on the Bodensee from the Bregenz Hafen (harbor), Seestr. 4 (☎428 68; www.bodenseeschifffahrt.at), opposite the post office. Ferries run the 3½hr. length of the shimmering lake to the **Blumen Insel Mainau** (Mainau Flower Isle) on the German side, which features a Baroque castle and church, an indoor tropical palm house, a butterfly house, and gardens rife with orchids, tulips, dahlias, and 400 kinds of roses. (Ferries leave Bregenz Apr.-June 9:10, 10:20, 11am; July to early Oct. also at 8am. Return 2:50, 4:15, and 4:28pm; July to early Oct. also 4:55pm. Admission to the island Mar.-Oct. €11, seniors €9.60, students €5.40, children 6-15 €3, family card for parents and children up to 15 €21; mid-Oct. to mid-Mar. €6, students €3, children under 15 free. Round-trip ferry and admission €29.50.) An alternative 2hr. cruise will take you to the **Zeppelin-Museum** in Friedrichshafen, Germany, former home base of round-the-world Zeppelin flights. Along with a mock-up of the Hindenberg's passenger cabin, it has a large exhibit of oil paintings and sculpture dating to the 15th century. (☎49

07541 380 10; www.zeppelin-museum.de. €7.50, seniors €6.50, students and children under 16 €3. Open May-Oct. Tu-Su 10am-6pm; Nov.-Apr. Tu-Su 10am-5pm. Ferries leave Bregenz Apr.-June Tu-F 9:10, 10:20am, 2:35pm; July-Oct. also 8am, 12:25pm. Return Apr.-June 3:05, 4:25, 5:53pm; July-Oct. also 12:23, 6:34pm. Round-trip including museum entrance €25.70.)

The **Pfänderbahn** cable car leaves from the top of Schillerstr., uphill from the post office, and swings up the **Pfänderspitze** (1064m) for a panorama that stretches all the way to Germany's Black Forest. (☎42 16 00; www.pfaenderbahn.at. Every 30min. 9am-7pm. One-way €5.70, round-trip €9.80; seniors €5.10/€8.80; youth 16-19 €4.50/€7.80; children 6-15 €2.80/€4.90; family-card including adults and children to 19 years €11.40/€17.60.) At the top of Pfänderspitze, there are nature trails in the free **Alpine Wildlife Park,** which pass enclosures housing native animals. A 10min. walk from the top of the lift is the "Greifvogel," a 40min. **bird flight show,** which sends birds of prey swooping across the mountainside. (May-Oct. daily 11am and 2:30pm. €4.10, children under 16 €2.10.)

🎵 🎭 ENTERTAINMENT AND NIGHTLIFE

Walking along the Promenade, it's impossible to miss the huge **Seebühne,** Europe's largest floating stage and the centerpiece for the annual **Bregenzer Festspiele.** Every year from mid-July to mid-August, the Vienna Symphony Orchestra and other opera, theater, and chamber music groups come to town, bringing over 200,000 tourists with them. As the sun sets over the lake, the lights rise on stage. The main events are performances on the floating stage, drawing capacity crowds of 6800. In 2005, the festival will run from July 20 to August 21. Verdi's *Der Troubadour* will occupy the main stage, while the Festspielhaus will feature such performances as Carl Nielsen's comic opera Maskerade and concerts by the Vienna Symphony Orchestra, Danish National Orchestra, and Vorarlberg Symphony-Orchestra. Dozens of other opera, music, and dance shows play throughout the *Festspiele.* For in-demand shows (usually weekend or high-profile productions), reserve tickets months in advance. Weekday performances, however, rarely sell out more than a few days before the show. (Ticket sales begin in Oct. Write to: Postfach 311, A-6901 Bregenz. ☎40 76; www.bregenzerfestspiele.com. Seebühne seats €26-125; *Festspielhaus* €40-135; concerts €12-75. Students under 26 25% off, except for premieres. Standing-room tickets available.)

Le Club, in the *Festspielhaus*, is the place to be after the show. A fashionable theatre crowd lounges on block furniture framed by plush red walls and high, high ceilings. As the wine glasses empty, the dance floor fills, and cast members have been known to show off their moves alongside everyone else. Drinks in this chic lounge are surprisingly cheap; wine starts at €2.60, and sweet or sour spritzers are €3.20-3.60. (Open during the *Festspiele* Th-Sa 11:30pm until the wee hours of the morning.) There are several late-night student hangouts on and around Kirchstr. **Uwe's Bier-Bar,** Kirchstr. 25, is a popular bar with a young, lively crowd. (Beer €2.60-4. Open Su-Th 7pm-1am, F-Sa 7pm-2am.) The outdoor tables at **Café Wunderbar,** Bahnhofstr. 4 (www.wunderbar.at), prove the perfect spot for people-watching or chilling with friends in the heart of Bregenz's bustling night-life. Primarily young people congregate here, and occasional live music beginning at 10pm features everything from hip hop and funk to Latin to techno or disco. **KUB,** the Kunstmuseum's own café and bar, serves light food by day and an extensive line of drinks by night. A mixed crowd fill the numerous outdoor tables or the few tables inside the chic glass building. (☎485 940. Open daily 10am-1pm.)

FELDKIRCH ☎ 05522

Just minutes from the borders of Switzerland and Liechtenstein, Feldkirch (pop. 30,000) has served as a trade and transportation hub for centuries. More than any other city in Vorarlberg, Feldkirch's history remains vivid today—the triangular *Altstadt* is a maze of pastel Baroque buildings and medieval towers, lined by arcades that shelter shops and fruit stands. The city itself is compact, quickly fading into shady suburbs with cliffs and mountains rising nearby.

⬛ TRANSPORTATION. Trains depart from Feldkirch to: Bregenz (45min., 1-2 per hr. 5am-midnight, €4.60); Innsbruck (2hr., 5:25am-12:21am, €20.80); Salzburg (4¼hr., 7 per day 5:25am-12:21am, €41); Zurich (1½-2½hr., 6 per day 4:45am-9:04pm, €24.50). The Liechtenstein **bus** system runs to Schaan, near Vaduz (30min., every 30min. 6:05am-11:05pm, €1.40), with connections to Buchs and Sargans in Switzerland. Get bus info at the tourist office or at ☎739 74 or 42 32 37 66 99. (Open M-Th 8am-12:30pm and 2-4:30pm, F 8am-noon.) **City buses** connect Feldkirch's subdivisions (€1.10, day pass €2.20). Buses stop at the train station and at the main bus stop, which can be reached by exiting the train station, walking away from the tracks, and turning left at the intersection. **Car Rental** available from **Hertz** (☎277 06) or **Autoverleih Kopf**, Koningshofstr. 14 (☎734 18). **Taxis** line up outside the train station, or call ☎17 18 or 842 00. Many shops give out coins for free **parking;** check with a salesclerk.

◼ 🛈 ORIENTATION AND PRACTICAL INFORMATION. Primary locations of interest in Feldkirch are clustered on the Ill river in the old city, a confusing warren of streets that necessitates a map (free at the tourist office). To reach the city center, turn left from the station and walk past the cemetery, cross the main busy intersection at Schloßgraben, and after one block make a right onto Neustadt and a left at the main Cathedral. The **tourist office,** Schloßerg. 8, is in Palais Liechtenstein at the beginning of the city center, and distributes free walking-tour maps, sells hiking maps for €5.75, and provides info about the city and its events. (☎734 67; www.tiscover.at/feldkirch. Open May-Sept. M-F 9am-6pm, Sa 9am-noon; Oct.-Apr. M-F 8am-noon and 1-5pm, Sa 9am-noon.) **Currency exchange** is available at any bank during the week or at the train station on the weekends (Sa-Su 6:35am-11:30pm). Lockers also available at the train station (€2-2.50). The **Sparkasse** just down the street from the tourist office has a popular computer kiosk on the first floor providing free **Internet** access; be prepared to wait. (Open M-Th 8am-noon and 2-4pm, F 8am-4pm.) The **hospital** is on Carinag. (☎303-0). **Police** (☎304 12 22) and **lost and found** (☎304 12 35) are located in the *Rathaus,* Schmiedg. 1-3. An **ATM** and the **post office,** Bahnhofstr. 31, are across from the station. (☎34 00. Open M-F 7am-7pm, Sa 7am-noon.) **Postal Code:** A-6800.

📷 📷 ACCOMMODATIONS AND CAMPING. Feldkirch's tourist office maintains a short list of *Privatzimmer.* **Jugendherberge "Altes Siechenhaus" (HI) ❷,** Reichstr. 111, Feldkirch's lone hostel, can be reached by Bus #2 and 60 to Götzis or by walking out of the station onto the main road, Bahnhofstr. (which becomes Reichstr.). Turn right and walk 15-20min. The hostel may well be the most historic spot on your visit—it's a white 700-year-old brick-and-wood building that served as an infirmary during several plague epidemics. Today, it is preserved as a family-oriented hostel complete with a picnic-table-filled backyard and comfortable sitting and TV rooms. The breakfast buffet (€4.60) features bacon, hard-boiled eggs, and pickles. (☎731 81; fax 793 99. Sheets included; €1.50 discount if you bring your own. Laundry €3. Free **Internet.** Reception M-Sa 7am-10pm, Su 7-10am and 7-10pm. Hostel key available for

€1.60 plus €20 deposit or ID. Wheelchair accessible. Oct.-Apr. dorms with bunk beds €17.47, in a basement room with mattresses on the floor €13.43; children 5-15 €12.43; children under 5 €7. May-Sept. €2 less. Guest tax €0.87.) Or try **Gasthof Löwen Tosters ❸**, Egelseestr. 20. Take bus #1 or 3 (dir: Tosters) to "Burgweg," a leafy suburb of Feldkirch. From the stop, walk back; it's on the right at the first intersection. Breakfast, shower, and TV included. Restaurant meals €9-14 (Tu-Su only). Parking available. (☎728 68; members.aon.at/loewen. Reception M 6:30am-noon, 3-5pm, 8-11pm; Tu-Su 6:30am-noon and 3-11pm. Singles €40-41; doubles €56-58.) For **Waldcamping Feldkirch ❶**, Stadionstr, take bus #1 (dir: Gisingen) to "Milchhof," and follow the signs. Nicer than most, this campground offers camping under the pines, right next to the sprawling town swimming pool. (☎743 08; www.waldcamping.at. Laundry available. Kiosk 7:30-10am and 5-9pm. Reception 8am-noon and 2-10pm. July-Aug. €5.25 per person, €3.05 per child ages 6-14, €3-4.50 per tent, €3.70 per car. Sept.-June €4.40/€2.15/€2.70/€2.35-3.70. MC/V.)

🚩 **FOOD.** Eateries line the streets of the *Fußgängerzone*, and with the convenient location comes high prices. A few budget establishments are just outside the pedestrian area. Try **Pizzeria-Trattoria La Taverna ❷**, Vorstadtstr. 18, a busy restaurant near the river, offering an extensive menu with plenty of pizza (€5.10-7.20) and many varieties of pasta (€5.50-9.10), all in a candlelit, wine-cellar interior. (☎792 93. Open daily 11:30am-2pm and 5pm-midnight.) **Haus Leone 12 ❶**, Leonhardspl. 4, attracts tourists and shoppers looking for a light lunch or afternoon pick-me-up. Specialty coffee drinks fill the menu, while loose-leaf tea arrives on a small tray with an hourglass to ensure the perfect brewing time (€2.20). (☎849 50. Open M-Th 8am-midnight, F-Sa 8am-2am.) For a taste of something different, **Sangam ❷**, Reichstr 171, about 50m from the train station at the intersection of Reichstr. and Banhofstr., offers Indian and Chinese specialties. Chinese entrées range from €7.63 for rice and noodle stir-fries to €11.26 for meat specialties. Typical Indian curries and tandooris range from €9.50 for vegetarian stews to €39.50 for a full menu for two (vegetarian menu for 1 from €12.20). (☎735 14; www.sangam.at. Open daily 11:30am-2pm and 5:30-10pm. V.) A giant **Inter-SPAR** with a self-service restaurant is on Neustadt, near the Schatterburg, in the same complex as the Holiday Inn. (Open M-F 8:05am-7:30pm, Sa 8am-5pm.) Marktpl. hosts an **outdoor market** every Saturday morning March to November.

🎭 📷 **SIGHTS AND ENTERTAINMENT.** Feldkirch's Gothic cathedral, the **St. Nikolaus Kirche**, forms one edge of the *Altstadt*. The cathedral received a face-lift in 1478 after a series of devastating fires. Frescoes of Feldkirch history and the coats of arms of local potentates adorn the 15th-century **Rathaus** on Schmiedg. At nearby Schloßerg. 8 stands the **Palais Liechtenstein,** completed in 1697. The palace once supported the royal seat of the Prince of Liechtenstein (p. 307) but now houses the town library, tourist office, and city archives.

At the edges of the *Altstadt*, three towers of the original city wall remain: the **Katzenturm**, the **Pulverturm**, and the **Wasserturm**. Outside the *Altstadt*, one block toward the station on Bahnhofstr., lies the **Kapuzinerkloster** (Capuchin monastery), built in 1605. For a fantastic view of the *Altstadt*, hike up the staircase on Burgg. to reach the **Schattenburg**, Feldkirch's most impressive structure, dating from 1260. (Castle and café open Tu-Su 10am-midnight.) From the early 1200s until 1390, the castle was the seat of the Counts of Montfort, who dominated the Vorarlberg region. The town purchased the castle in 1825 to save it from demolition and a private group converted it into the **Feldkirch Heimatmuseum,** which showcases the region's history, including an 800-year-old fresco, carved wooden furniture, coins from AD 69, and an armory full of old weapons. (☎/fax 719 82. Open Tu-Su Mar.-Oct. 9am-noon and 1-5pm; Dec.-Feb. 11am-4pm. Closed Nov. €2.50, ages 12-18 and students under 26 €1.50, ages 6-12 €1.)

Feldkirch schedules a number of festivals and special events. Perhaps the biggest is the **Feldkirch Festival,** a music celebration that features opera and theater by such composers as Strauss, Haydn, and Mozart. (June 2-12, 2005; contact the Palais Liechtenstein, Schloßerg. 8. ☎ 829 43; www.feldkirchfestival.at.) The **Wine festival** takes place July 8-10, 2005 and the **Gaukler festival** fills the Markpl. with theatre, music, clowns, jugglers, acrobats, magicians, and other entertainers from across the globe July 29-30 2005. The annual **Christmas bazaar** brings crafts, candy canes, and carols November 25 to December 24, 2005.

BREGENZERWALD

Spreading out to the south and east of Bregenz, the Bregenzerwald is home to many small towns that preserve the rustic flavor of Vorarlberg's past. Steep mountains rise sharply around the villages, cradling pastures, pine forests, and lush meadows. Explore the Bregenzerwald by taking daytrips into the region from Bregenz or Dornbirn, or by staying in the charming, rural towns of the *Wald* itself.

⬛ TRANSPORTATION

Bregenz and Dornbirn both serve as transportation hubs for the Bregenzerwald. Bundesstr. 200 heads generally southeast from Dornbirn. Public transportation in the Bregenzerwald is based around a regional network of **buses (Netz);** train service between towns is limited. A **Tageskarte Euregio Bodensee** allows for unlimited travel by bus and train in the region. (1 day for 2 zones €20, for all zones €26; ages 6-15 €10/€13; family of up to 2 adults and 4 children €40/€46.)

⬛ ACCOMMODATIONS

Staying in the Bregenzerwald on the cheap is possible in most small towns. Huts dot the mountains; their telephone numbers are available at the tourist office and in the *Kumpass* Bregenzerwald/Westallgäu map/handbook available at newsstands as well as in the booklet distributed by Vorarlberg tourist offices.

DORNBIRN   ☎ 05572

Dornbirn (pop. 45,000), not technically in the Bregenzerwald but nearby nonetheless, is considerably larger and more industrial than its tiny woodland neighbors. Home of the Vorarlberg Institute for Architecture and influential in the acceptance of new architectural designs, the city is making its mark artistically and culturally. Natural wonders just outside town include a steep cave-like gully with a waterfall.

⬛ TRANSPORTATION AND PRACTICAL INFORMATION. Trains   to:
Bregenz (10-15min., 3-4 per hr. 5:28am-1:08am, €2.10); Feldkirch (20-30min., 2-3 per hr. 5:09am-12:18am, €3.30); Innsbruck (2¼hr., 7 per day 5:09am-9:52pm, €23.50); Lindau (20min., 11 per day 5:28am-7:07pm, €3.30); St. Anton am Arlberg (1hr., 7 per day 5:09am-9:52pm, €6.60). The station has **lockers** (€2) and **luggage storage** (€2.10; M-Sa 6:30am-8:50pm, Su 7:30am-8:50pm). Regional **buses** depart from the parking lot at the train station and across the street. Line #38 runs to Schwarzenberg (7:20am-10:05pm; Su last train at 6:10pm); line #47 to Ebnit (8:42am-6:20pm, Sa last bus at 4:42, Su and holidays 6:20pm); and line #40 to Schoppennau via Egg (7:32am-9:35pm). Both stop in front of the post

office, next to the Bahnhof. Day pass for all Dornbirn city buses €2.10. For information, call the Town Bus Buro at ☎323 00 or the Land Bus Buro at ☎313 00. Exit the station and walk straight on Bahnhofstr. to reach the town center. **Taxis** are available at the train station or by calling the free hotline (☎0800 226 450). The **tourist office,** Rathauspl. 1, is through Marktpl., across Stadtstr., and then about 50m to the left. It has a list of accommodations pasted on the window and sells hiking maps for €6. (☎221 88; www.dornbirn.info. Open M-F 9am-noon and 1-6pm, Sa 9am-noon.) Other services include: a **pharmacy** in the center of town on Markstr. 3. (☎228 52; open M-F 8am-6pm, Sa 8am-1pm; AmEx/MC/V); **lost and found** in the Rathaus (☎306 26 02); **Internet** access at **Netgate,** Bahnhofstr. 26, on the way to the town center (€1.40 per 15min.; open M-Sa 9am-midnight, Su 2-10pm); **ATM** at the post office and across from the tourist office at **Raiffeisenbank,** which also **exchanges currency** for about €2 per US$100. (Open M-Th 7:45am-noon and 1:45-4pm, F 8am-noon and 1:45-4:30pm.) The **post office** is next to the train station. (Open M-F 8am-7pm, Sa 8am-noon; exchange until 5pm.) **Postal Code:** A-6850.

⌐⌐ ACCOMMODATIONS AND FOOD. Most budget accommodations in Dornbirn are a fair distance from town. Try **Haus Ottowitz ❸,** Im Winkel 15. From Riedg., take bus #7 (dir: Oberdorf.) to "Bürgleg." (1-2 per hr. 6:20am-6:20pm, Sa 7:20am-6:35pm), walk uphill, and turn left onto Im Winkel. Tucked away on a quiet residential street and surrounded by towering trees, this "hotel" is actually a private house with a down-home feel, complete with friendly dogs and family. Reasonably-priced singles and doubles include TV, balcony, and views of Dornbirn and the Bodensee. (☎330 25; angelika.ottowitz@vol.at. Breakfast included. €22 per person.) If you'd rather be closer to Dornbirn, try **Gasthof Bären ❹,** 17 Dr. Anton-Schneiderstr. Turn left from the train and follow Dr. Anton-Schneiderstr. for 15min., or take bus #13 or 20 (dir: Bregenz) to Eigenheim, and walk 2min. farther. The large, yellow building just past SPAR market boasts affordable rooms with hall toilet, and a crowd of regulars who down Mohrenbraus in the adjoining *Biergarten.* (Breakfast included. All rooms with shower and TV. Singles €35; doubles €56.)

While *Menüs* are generally cheap and tasty, **⬛Extrablatt ❷,** the self-proclaimed café-bar at 4 Bahnhofstr. (on the way to Marktpl.) has turned them into an art form, serving full meals including soup, salad, and entrée for €6.20. The house pizza is crammed full of ham, pepperoni, corn, green peppers, and onions on a thin, chewy crust (€7.20). Sit with the lunchtime and late-night crowds on the geranium-laden terrace or sip on an elaborate mixed drink (€3.80-6.60) while listening to classic American rock and pop in the smoky, art-nouveau interior. (☎255 68. Open daily 8am-1am.) For tasty, if slightly more expensive Tex-Mex, mosey on over to **Sloppy Joe's ❸,** Riedg. 11. From the train station, head left onto F-M-Felderstr. and right onto Riedg. This brightly decorated restaurant and bar one floor above the street plays peppy Latin beats and is filled with the aroma of ribs (€11.50-12), chicken wings (€8-8.50), fajitas (€11-14), chili (€11-11.50), steaks (€13.50-17) and more. For a cheaper meal, consider a large bowl of steaming soup (€3.50-7.50). The breath-killing "Sopa de Ajo" garlic broth has a fried egg floating in it and a freshly-toasted roll on the side. (☎349 60. Open daily 11am-2pm and 5pm-midnight.) If your stomach has any space left after your Mexican meal, head downstairs to **Eissalon Ricardo 4D** for out-of-this-world ice cream concoctions or a simple scoop of creamy gelato (€0.87). The huge **EuroSPAR** market, behind the church on Mozartstr., sells everything from bananas to flip-flops, while the restaurant upstairs serves meals from €4.80. (Open M-F 7:40am-7pm, Sa 7:40am-5pm.)

MUSEUMS. Take city bus #5 to Gütle (1-2 per hr. M-F 6:15am-6:50pm, Sa 7:15am-7:05pm, Su 9:05am-5:05pm) to get to the **Rolls-Royce Museum,** Gütle 11a, which houses three floors filled with Rolls-Royce cars, engines, and memorabilia from as early as 1925. After exploring the museum, guests can check out the elegant tea room on the top floor. The museum is at the same bus stop as the Rappenlochschlucht and two stops from the Karrenseilbahn (see **Hiking,** p. 223); the three sites together make for a good day. (☎526 52; www.rolls-royce-museum.at. Open Tu-Su Apr.-Oct. 10am-6pm; Nov.-Mar. 10am-5pm. €8, seniors €7, children €4.) The **Stadt Museum,** across from the church in the town center, has rotating exhibits on its first floor and historical artifacts on the floors above, dating from 800 BC to the 20th century. (☎330 77; www.dornbirn.at. Open Tu-Su 10am-noon and 2-5pm. €2.50, students and children €1.) **Inatura** is a nature museum inside Dornbirn's city garden. Follow Schulg. (behind St. Martin's Church) in the opposite direction from the train station, turn right onto Realschulstr. and immediately left onto Jahng. The garden will be on your right. It's about 10min. from the tourist office. (☎232 35; www.inatura.at. Open M-W and F-Su 10am-6pm, Th 10am-9pm. €8, students and seniors €5.50, children €4.)

HIKING. The hills and forest surrounding Dornbirn are chock-full of great hiking trails. Be sure to pick up a map from the tourist office, as trails often cross over one another and it is easy to follow the wrong one. Take the bus to the last stop on the #5 bus (dir: Gütle) for the 1½hr. hike to the **Rappenlochschlucht,** which is a steep gaping cleft through a mountain ridge where a small waterfall reflects amazing sunrises and sunsets. For a pleasant view of the town, the valley, and the Bodensee, hop on the **Karrenseilbahn** cable car, which takes riders nearly 1km (976m) above sea level. (Take bus #5, dir: Gütle. Open summer Su-Th 9am-11pm, F-Sa 9am-midnight. Round-trip €8.30, youth and seniors €6.60, children €4.20; after 6pm €5.40/€4.30/€2.70.) From there, numerous hikes spread out over the countryside. One particularly nice hike circumnavigates the Staufenberg, offering views of the mountains and waterfalls from the shade of a pine forest. The highlight is crossing the cow pasture near Schuttanen, which can set off quite a bovine ruckus if you're not polite. From Karren, follow signs to Kuhberg (10min.), then to Staufenberg and Schuttanen. Exit the pasture through the turnstile, then keep right and follow signs to the Karrenseilbahn. (2½hr., moderate.)

SCHWARZENBERG ☎05512

You'll get the impression that not much has changed in Schwarzenberg (pop. 1750) in the last few centuries. Cradled by a ring of mountains, it exemplifies the charms of the Bregenzerwald, with many of the houses built of wood from nearby forests. The **Pfarrkirche** is an airy church with wrought-iron gravestones, unstained carved wood columns, and an altar painting by the town's most famous (sometime) resident, Angelika Kauffmann (1741-1807). Kauffmann was one of the few wealthy female painters of her age, and her work received great acclaim in England and Italy. The **Angelika Kauffmann Museum,** a 300-year-old wooden lodge a few minutes up the main road, houses a small collection of the artist's paintings and memorabilia. (☎29 67 or 20 84. Open May-Sept. Tu, Th, Sa-Su 2-4pm; Oct. Tu and Sa 2-4pm. €3, with guest card €2.50, ages 6-14 €1.) This year, Schwarzenberg will host its 11th annual **Schubertiade,** a celebration of the composer's works and the creative spirit of local talents, spread over several weekends during the year. Such weekends see multiple performances, from chamber concerts to poetry readings. Purchase same-day tickets at the **Angelika-Kauffmann Saal** near the tourist office. (☎05576 729 01;

www.schubertiade.at.) Signs in the town center, across from the church, point the way to several well-marked hikes and walks. If you have 3hr. to spare, try the simple loop up to the **Lustenauer Hütte** (☎49 13. Open May-Oct.). When you come to the hillside town of Klausberg, bear right at each fork in the dirt road, and you'll be at the hut within 25min. From there, continue on the other side of the loop back to Schwarzenberg.

There are dozens of guest houses in Schwarzenberg and the outlying regions. The tourist office can find inexpensive private accommodations. **Haus Feuerstein ❸**, Hof 20, behind the church near the town square, provides private rooms in a charming wood-panelled house, parts of which are over 200 years old. (☎20 39. Breakfast included. €25-26 per person. For stays longer than 3 nights singles €20; all other rooms €18 per person.) For a warm meal, head 50m downhill from the town square to **Mesner Stüble ❷**, which serves pasta and Gasthof-style dishes costing €6.90-16.20 and soups for €2.90-3.20. (☎20 02. Open Dec.-Oct. M-Sa 3pm-midnight, Su 10am-midnight.) Stock up on groceries at the local **SPAR,** downhill from the town square. (Open M-Th 7am-noon and 2:30-6pm, F 7am-6pm, Sa 7am-noon.)

SALZBURGER LAND

The Salzburger Land derives its name from the German *Salz* (salt). It was this "white gold" that drew Roman Emperor Claudius's attention to the region in the first century, inciting him to unite it with his Empire for the first time. Although tourism displaced the salt trade long ago, images of St. Barbara, the patron saint of miners, are everywhere. The province encompasses the shining lakes and rolling hills of the Salzkammergut, where Salzburg and Hallstatt are among the more enticing destinations. Though mostly in the province of Upper Austria, the Salzkammergut is accessible primarily through Salzburg.

HIGHLIGHTS OF SALZBURGER LAND

Satiate your sweet tooth with **Mozartkugeln** (see p. 234).

Hobnob with upper echelon musicians at the **Salzburger Festspiele** (see p. 242).

Get in touch with your animal instincts at the **Hellbrunn Zoo** (see p. 246).

SALZBURG ☎ 0662

Salzburg resonates with sound. Tourists whistle ditties, street musicians play medieval (and pop) ballads, and sopranos belt arias in one of the largest and grandest opera houses in Europe. Set against a backdrop of mountains and graced with Baroque artistic and musical wonders, Salzburg is overflowing with fascinating stories waiting to be heard. In the 17th and 18th centuries it was the ecclesiastical center of Austria and was governed by a series of Prince-Archbishops: men who were both secular and religious rulers. This Golden Age produced architectural masterpieces and fostered a rich musical culture. The city's love for homegrown genius Mozart reaches a dizzying climax every summer during the Salzburger *Festspiele* (see p. 242), when admirers the world over come to pay their respects. The *Festspiele* lasts five weeks, during which time hundreds of operas, concerts, plays, and open-air performances dazzle the crowds. Salzburg's appeal comes not only from its architectural aesthetics or its musical past, but also from its deserved reputation as an impeccably clean and very safe city. Tourists and locals mingle harmoniously in this, a city not just of sound, but of music.

◪ INTERCITY TRANSPORTATION

Flights: Flughafen Salzburg (☎ 858 00; www.salzburg-airport.com), 4km west of the city center, has frequent connections to **Amsterdam, Innsbruck, Paris, Vienna,** and other major European cities. It is considerably cheaper, however, to fly into **Munich** (see p. 543) and take the train from there. If you do fly into or out of Salzburg, bus #2 (dir: Bahnhof from the airport, dir: Walserfeld from the train station) circles between the train station and the airport (15min., every 5-10 min. 5:32am-11pm, €1.70). A taxi from the airport to the train station should cost roughly €11.

Trains: There are 2 train stations in Salzburg. The main passenger hub, the **Hauptbahnhof** on Südtirolerpl., is the first Salzburg stop for trains coming from Vienna, while the Salzburg Süd Bahnhof (the first stop when coming from Innsbruck) is primarily a cargo station. For reservations dial ☎ 05 17 17. Ticket office open 24hr. Trains from Hauptbahnhof to: **Graz** (4hr., 8 per day 5:24am-5:18pm, €36.50); **Innsbruck** (2hr., 11 per day 6:23am-12:45am, €29.50); **Klagenfurt** (3hr., 8per day 7:13am-9:18am, €26.10); **Munich** (2hr., 30 per day 4:27am-11:57pm, €25.80); **Vienna** (3½hr., 26 per day 2:18am-9:35pm, €36.50); **Zell am See** (1½-2hr., 17 per day 4:51am-9:18pm, €11.30); **Zurich** (6hr., 7 per day 6:23am-12:45am, €65.20).

Buses: Leave from the bus depot in front of the train station. Get information at the Reisebüro am Bahnhof in the train station (☎ 05 17 17; M-F 9am-6pm). **Bundes-Buses** to **Mondsee** (1hr., every hr. 6:35am-10:20pm, €4.50); **St. Wolfgang** (1½hr., every hr. 5:50am-7:15pm, €7.60); **Bad Ischl** (1½-2hr., every hr. 5:50am-9:15pm, €8.30); and throughout Salzburger Land.

By Car: From Vienna, exit at any of the Salzburg-West exits off *Autobahn* A1. Of these exits, the Salzburg-Nord exit is near Itzling and Kasern, and the Salzburg-Süd exit lies south of the city near Schloß Hellbrunn and Untersberg. A8 and E52 lead from the west of Salzburg into Rosenheim and then branch off to Munich and Innsbruck. A10 heads north from Hallein to Salzburg. From the Salzkammergut area, take Grazer Bundesstr. #158. Since public transportation is efficient within the city limits, consider the **Park and Ride**—park for free off the highway and take the bus into town. The most convenient lot is **Alpensiedlung Süd** on Alpenstr. (exit: Salzburg-Süd), but a bigger and closer lot is open July-Aug. at the **Salzburger Ausstellungszentrum** and costs €1 per hr. (exit: Salzburg-Mitte).

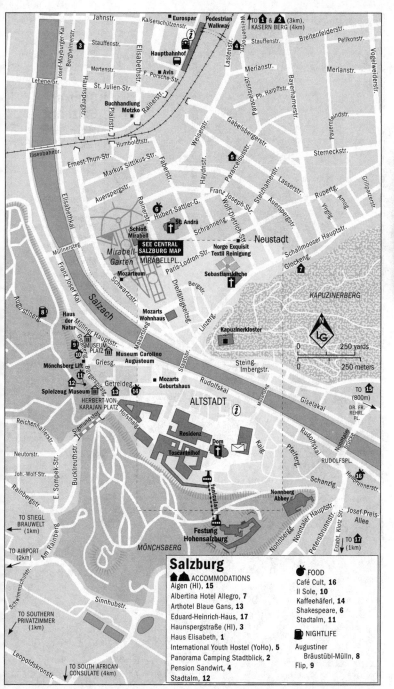

Salzburg

🏔 ACCOMMODATIONS

Aigen (HI), **15**
Albertina Hotel Allegro, **7**
Arthotel Blaue Gans, **13**
Eduard-Heinrich-Haus, **17**
Haunspergstraße (HI), **3**
Haus Elisabeth, **1**
International Youth Hostel (YoHo), **5**
Panorama Camping Stadtblick, **2**
Pension Sandwirt, **4**
Stadtalm, **12**

🍎 FOOD

Café Cult, **16**
Il Sole, **10**
Kaffeehäferl, **14**
Shakespeare, **6**
Stadtalm, **11**

🍺 NIGHTLIFE

Augustiner
Bräustübl-Mülln, **8**
Flip, **9**

SALZBURGER LAND

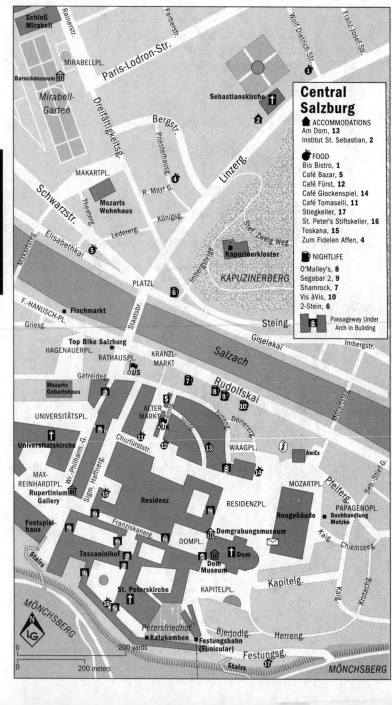

Central Salzburg

🏠 ACCOMMODATIONS
Am Dom, **13**
Institut St. Sebastian, **2**

🍴 FOOD
Bio Bistro, **1**
Café Bazar, **5**
Café Fürst, **12**
Café Glockenspiel, **14**
Café Tomaselli, **11**
Stiegkeller, **17**
St. Peter's Stiftskeller, **16**
Toskana, **15**
Zum Fidelen Affen, **4**

🍷 NIGHTLIFE
O'Malley's, **8**
Segabar 2, **9**
Shamrock, **7**
Vis àVis, **10**
2-Stein, **6**

Passageway Under
Arch in Building

✈ ORIENTATION

Salzburg, just a few kilometers from the German border, covers both banks of the **Salzach River.** Two of Salzburg's three hills loom on the skyline near the river: the **Mönchsberg** over the **Altstadt** (old city) on the south side and the **Kapuzinerberg** by the **Neustadt** (new city) on the north side. The third hill, the **Rainberg**, is hidden by the Mönchsberg on the southwest side of the city. The Hauptbahnhof is on the northern side of town beyond the *Neustadt*; buses #1, 3, 5, and 6 connect it to downtown. From the bus, disembark at "Mirabellplatz" in the *Neustadt* or "Mozartsteg," a footbridge that leads to Mozartpl. in the *Altstadt*. On foot, from the train station to the *Neustadt*, turn left out of the station onto Rainerstr., follow it all the way (under the tunnel) to Mirabellpl., and continue walking until you reach the footbridge that leads to the *Altstadt*.

⊟ LOCAL TRANSPORTATION

Public Transportation: Get information at the **Lokalbahnhof** (☎44 80 61 66), next to the train station (when you exit the train station, turn left and after a few steps enter the doors on your left and head down the stairs). Twenty **bus** lines cut through the city, with central hubs at Hanuschpl. in the *Altstadt*, Mirabellpl., Äußerer Stein, and the Hauptbahnhof in the *Neustadt*. Single tickets (€1.70) are available at machines or from the drivers; books of 5 (€7) are available at *Tabak* (newsstand/tobacco shops) and at the Lokalbahnhof ticket office. *Tageskarte* (€3.20) or *Wochenkarte* (€10) allow travel on buses within the city for a full day or week, and are available at machines, the ticket office, or *Tabak* shops. Punch your ticket when you board or risk a €36 fine. Buses make their last run from downtown at 10:30-11:30pm, earlier for less-frequented routes. **BusTaxi** fills in when the public buses stop running. Meet it at the stop at Hanuschpl. or Theaterg. and tell the driver your destination. (Su-Th 11:30pm-1:30am, F-Sa 11:30pm-3am. €3 for anywhere within the city limits.)

Parking: Consider the "Park and Ride" option (see **Intercity Transportation: By Car,** p. 226). Otherwise, try **Altstadt-Garage** inside the Mönchsberg (open 24hr.; €2.40 per hr., €14 per day); **Mirabell-Congress-Garage** in Mirabellpl. (open 7am-midnight; €3.20 per hr., €15 per day); or **Parkgarage Linzer Gasse** at Glockeng. off Linzerg. (open 7am-10pm; €1.80 per hr., €14.40 per day). Other lots are at the airport, Hellbrunn, and Hauptbahnhof.

Taxis: (☎81 11). Stands at Hanuschpl., Residenzpl., and the train station.

Car Rental: Avis, Ferdinand-Porsche-Str. 7 (☎87 72 78; www.avis.at).

Bike Rental: Top Bike Salzburg, (☎062 72 or 45 56; www.topbike.at). At the train station and the Staatsbrücke. €13 per day, €41 per week. 10% off with Salzburg Card, 20% off at the train station with valid train ticket. Open daily Apr.-June, Sept., Oct. 10am-5pm; July-Aug. 9am-7pm. Closed in bad weather.

Hitchhiking: While *Let's Go* does not recommend hitching, hitchers headed to Innsbruck, Munich, or Italy have been seen on bus #2 to the German border. Those bound for Vienna have been known to take bus #4 (dir: Langwied) to the *Autobahn* at "Schmiedlingerstr." or #15 (dir: Bergheim) to the *Autobahn* at "Grüner Wald."

🛈 PRACTICAL INFORMATION

TOURIST AND FINANCIAL SERVICES

Tourist Office, Mozartpl. 5 (☎88 98 73 30; www.salzburg.info), in the *Altstadt*. From the train station, take bus #3, 5, 6, or 55 to "Mozartsteg," head away from the river and curve to your right around the building into Mozartpl. On foot from the train station, turn left on Rainerstr., cross Staatsbrücke, and continue along the river's south bank to Mozartsteg (20min.). The staff has free hotel maps, lists available rooms, and offers the **Salzburg Card** (see p. 237). Reservation service is €2.20, for 3 or more people €4.40, plus a 10% deposit deductible from the 1st night's stay. Guided tours of the city leave daily at 12:15pm (€8, in German and English). Open daily 9am-8pm. Extended hours during *Festspiele*. Another **branch** at **train station** platform #2a (☎88 98 73 40). Generally open daily 9:15am-8pm, though hours may vary.

Consulates: UK, Alter Markt 4 (☎84 81 33; fax 84 55 63). Open M-F 9am-noon. **US,** Alter Markt 1/3 (☎84 87 76; fax 84 97 77), in the *Altstadt*. Open M, W, Th 9am-noon.

Currency Exchange: Banks offer better rates for cash than AmEx offices but often charge higher commissions. Banking hours M-F 8am-12:30pm and 2-4:30pm. **Rieger Bank,** Alter Markt 15, has extended exchange hours. Open daily 10am-2:30pm and 3-8pm. The **train station's** exchange is open 7am-9pm. **Panorama Tours** offers bank rates with no commission; available only to guests taking their tour (see p. 240).

American Express: Mozartpl. 5, A-5020 (☎80 80; fax 808 01 78), near the tourist office. Provides all banking services and charges no commission on AmEx cheques. Holds mail for check- or card-holders and books tours. Open M-F 9am-5:30pm. Open Sa 9am-noon only for money or traveler's check exchange.

LOCAL SERVICES

Luggage Storage: At the train station, on the lower level. 24hr. small lockers €2, medium €2.50, large €3.50. At the tourist office on Mozartpl. €1, with a €5 key deposit.

Bookstores: Buchhandlung Motzko (Platz der Bucher), has 2 stores with English-language sections. Elisabethstr. 1 (☎883 31 10), near the train station, has a shelf of English books. Kaig. 11 (☎88 33 11 50), in the *Altstadt,* has a small selection of best-sellers. Both stores open M-F 9am-6:30pm, Sa 9am-5pm. **Buchhandlung Höllrigl,** 10 Sigmund Haffnerg., just beyond Café Tomaselli, is the oldest bookstore in Austria (opened in 1594). There's an English-language section on the 2nd floor.

GLBT Organizations: Homosexual Initiative of Salzburg (HOSI), Müllner Hauptstr. 11 (☎43 59 27; www.hosi.at), hosts regular workshops and meetings, and publishes a list of bars, cafes, and restaurants available at the main tourist office. Other resources include a library and a transgender group.

Laundromat: Norge Exquisit Textil Reinigung, Paris-Lodronstr. 16 (☎87 63 81), on the corner of Wolf-Dietrich-Str. Self-serve wash and dry €10 (including their soap, which patrons must use). Full-serve €14.20; clothes ready by 5pm if you bring them in early in the morning; otherwise, pick up next day. Open M-F 7:30am-6pm, Sa 8am-noon.

Public Toilets: Look for the green WC signs located at most tourist sites. In the Festungsbahn lobby, the Hanuschpl. fish market, and the *Altstadt* under the archway between Kapitelpl. and Dompl. Although these restrooms are free, it is polite to tip the attendant.

EMERGENCIES AND COMMUNICATIONS

Emergencies: Police ☎133. Headquarters at Alpenstr. 90 (non-emergency ☎63 83). **Ambulance** ☎144. **Fire** ☎122.

Rape Hotline: Frauennotruf (☎88 11 00). Ask for Dr. Andrea Laher.

AIDS Hotline: (☎88 14 88).

Women's Emergencies: Frauenhilfe Salzburg (☎84 09 00 or 84 42 69). Ask for Annemarie Schobesberger, Ulli Huber, Dr. Gertraud Hess, or Ulrike Klingeis.

Pharmacies: Elisabeth-Apotheke, Elisabethstr. 1a (☎87 14 84; fax 87 14 844), a few blocks south of the train station. Pharmacies in the city center are open M-F 8am-6pm, Sa 8am-noon; outside the center M-F 8am-12:30pm and 2:30-6pm, Sa 8am-noon. There are always 3 pharmacies open; check the door of any closed pharmacy for info.

Medical Assistance: Call the hospital, **St. Johannspital Landeskrankenanstalten Salzburg,** Müllner Hauptstr. 48 (☎44 820; a.burger@lks.at).

Internet Access:

Internet Café, Mozartpl. 5 (☎84 48 22; www.cybar.at). 20 workstations. €0.15 per min. Open daily Sept.-June 10am-11pm; July-Aug. 9am-midnight.

BIGnet.café, Judeng. 5-7 (☎84 14 70). Snack bar, funky music, and a total of 33 workstations make for great surfing. 10min. €1.50, 30min. €3.70, 1hr. €5.90. Open daily 9am-10pm.

Piterfun Internetc@fe, Ferdinand-Porsche-Str. 7 (office@piterfun.at). Bright colors and loud techno give a rave ambience. 18 workstations directly across from the train station. 15min. €1.80, 30min. €2.90, 1hr. €5. Open daily 10am-10pm.

Post Office: (☎88 30 30), at the Hauptbahnhof. Address Poste Restante mail with the specific postal code 5021 and it will be held at the post office for 3 weeks. Open M-F 7am-8:30pm (counter closes at 6pm), Sa 8am-2pm, Su 1-6pm.

Postal Code: A-5020.

ACCOMMODATIONS

HOSTELS AND DORMITORIES

Stadtalm, Mönchsberg 19c (☎84 17 29; www.stadtalm.com), towers over the *Altstadt* from atop the Mönchsberg Peak. Take bus #1 (dir: Europark) to "Mönchsbergaufzug", then walk down the street a few steps and through the stone arch on the left to the Mönchsberglift (elevator), which takes you to the top of the mountain (9am-9pm; one-way €1.50, round-trip €2.40, free with the Salzburg card (see p. 237). At the top, climb the steps and follow signs for "Stadtalm." Or climb the stairs in Toscaninihof after the end of Wiener-Philharmoniker-G., turn right at the top, and look for the "Stadtalm" sign. Get a princely view on a pauper's budget at the most scenic hostel in Salzburg. Holds 26 in simple 2- to 6-bed rooms. Showers and toilets off of the main hallway. Hot water 7am-10am and 7pm-10pm. Breakfast included. Reception 9am-9pm. Curfew 1am. Open Apr.-Sept. Dorms €13. AmEx/DC/MC/V. ❷

Institut St. Sebastian, Linzerg. 41 (☎87 13 86; www.st-sebastian-salzburg.at). From the station, take bus #1, 3, 5, or 6 to Mirabellpl. Cross the street and continue in same direction. Turn left onto Bergstr. and left at the end onto Linzerg. Facing St. Sebastian Church, the hostel is through the arch on the left. Smack in the middle of the *Neustadt* on the church grounds, the buildings are dorms for female students during the school year but accept travelers of either gender year-round. Rooftop terrace with postcard views of the city. Breakfast, kitchen, and lockers included. Laundry €3, €4 for both laundry and soap. Reception 8am-noon and 4-9pm. No curfew. Dorms €15, with sheets €17. Singles €21, with shower €33; doubles €40/€54; triples €60/€69; quads €72/€84. MC/V accepted with stay of more than one night but cash is preferred. ❸

Haunspergstraße (HI), Haunspergstr. 27 (☎87 96 49; fax 88 34 77), near the train station. Take bus #1 (dir: Messezentrum) or #2 (dir: Walserfeld) one stop to Jahnstr. Walk in the same direction as the bus to the corner and the hostel is directly across the street. If it is a nice day, walk on Kaiserschützenstr., which becomes Jahnstr. Take the 3rd left onto Haunspergstr. and walk 1 block to the hostel. It will be on the right-hand side on the corner of Stauffernstr. This student dorm becomes a hostel when school ends in early July. Houses 90 in spacious 2- to 4-bed rooms. Breakfast and sheets included. All rooms either have a private shower or share it with 1 other room. Reception 7am-2pm and 5pm-midnight. Open early July to early Aug. 4-person dorms €18; 2-person dorms €21. MC/V. ❷

Eduard-Heinrich-Haus (HI), Eduard-Heinrich-Str. 2 (☎62 59 76; hostel.eduard-heinrich@salzburg.co.at). Take bus #3 (dir: Salzburg-Süd) or bus #8 (dir: Alpensiedlung) to "Polizeidirektion." Cross over Alpenstr., then continue down Billrothstr. past a brilliantly colorful apartment complex (think electric blue), turn left on Robert-Stolz-Promenade footpath, walk 200m, and take 1st right; the hostel is the big pink and salmon building up the driveway on the left. Near the Salzach Forest, with enormous 6-bed rooms and lobbies on each floor with leather couches and a TV. Each room has a private bathroom. Breakfast and lockers included. **Internet** access: 20min. €2.60, 40min. €4.40, 75min. €7.30. Reception M-F 7am-midnight, Sa-Su 7-10am and 5pm-midnight. No curfew—the room key lets you into the building after hours. Rooms of 5-6 people €15.42, 3-4 people €18.42, 1-2 people €21.42. MC/V, but cash is preferred. ❸

Aigen (HI), Aignerstr. 34 (☎62 32 48; hostel.aigen@salzburg.co.at). From the station, bus #3, 5, or 6 to "Mozartsteg.," then bus #7 (dir: Alpensiedlung) to "Finanzamt." Walk 5min. in the same direction as the bus. Aigen's large yellow gates are there to welcome you on the right behind the hedges. Large hostel with clean, spacious, and simple 2-, 4-, and 6-bed dorms. Breakfast, shower, locker, and sheets included. Reception 7-10am and 5-11pm. No curfew. 6-person dorms €14.42, 4-person €17.42, 2-person €20.24. Singles €27.31. MC/V. ❸

International Youth Hotel (YoHo), Paracelsußtr. 9 (☎87 96 49 or 834 60; www.yoho.at). Facing away from the train station, go left down Rainerstr. and then turn left again onto Gabelsbergerstr. through the tunnel. Take the 2nd right onto Paracelsus-str. (7min.). *The Sound of Music* is screened daily at 10:30am and at the request of tourists. Filled with beer-sipping postcard writers, this hostel is a no-frills place to crash. Thin walls make the jukebox, which plays until around 2am, to wake even the soundest sleeper. (Earplugs are a must!) Lockers in the hall €1. Happy Hour in bar 6-7pm with 0.5L Stiegl €1.50, other brews €2.50. Breakfast €3-4. Dinner entrées (including veggie options) €5-6. Sheets €5 deposit. Front door locks at 1am, but you can ring the bell anytime and an attendant will let you in. 6- to 8- bed dorms €15; 4-bed dorms €17; 2-bed dorms €20. €3 more for shower in room. MC/V. ❸

PRIVATZIMMER AND PENSIONEN

Privatzimmer and *Pensionen* in the center of the city can be quite expensive, but better quality and lower prices await on the outskirts, minutes from downtown Salzburg by train. Rooms on the little hill called **Kasern Berg** are officially outside of Salzburg, which means the tourist office can't recommend them, but the clean, comfortable rooms and bargain prices make these *Privatzimmer* a terrific housing option. However, keep in mind that these rooms amid quiet, rolling fields are not in the city and require reliance on public transportation. Stays include a home-made Austrian breakfast of rolls, meat, cheese, homemade jam, and eggs. The *Privatzimmer* owners care about all of their guests and cook, clean, and live with a local Austrian flair that you won't find in a hotel. The best way to reach the Berg is by train. All northbound regional trains run to Kasern Berg (generally 4min., every 30min. 6:17am-11:17pm, €1.60; Wochenkarte and Eurail valid). Get off at the first stop, "Salzburg-Maria Plain," and take the only road up the long hill, or call from the Hauptbahnhof and your host will pick you up at Maria Plain. All the Kasern Berg Pensionen are along this road, whose position on a hill above the city affords marvelous views of the valley below. By car, exit A1 on "Salzburg Nord."

Haus Lindner, Panoramaweg 5 (☎/fax 45 66 81; www.haus-linder.at). Head 5min. up the road from the train station and take a left at the top of the hill onto Panoramaweg. In her charming house at the top of the hill, friendly owner Matilda offers homey rooms, some with balconies for mountain views. The entire house is warmly decorated with lots of sunflowers in vases. Capacity of 15 people makes it the biggest in Kasern Berg. Families welcome. Breakfast served on a sunny terrace and in a room with satellite TV, available for guests' use during the day. Make reservations at least 24hr. in advance. €15-17 per person. Credit cards accepted, but cash preferred. ❷

Haus Moser, Turnerbühel 1 (☎ 45 66 76). Walk 100 yards past the Moser driveway to find the steep hidden stairs on the right side of Kasern Berg road across from Germana Kapeller. If you have a heavy backpack, try the long and winding driveway entrance at beginning of Kasern Berg road. Charming, elderly couple warmly welcomes you into their home, offering comfortable rooms in this cozy, dark-timbered, antler-decorated home. 2 rooms have a balcony. Free drinks, breakfast, shower, and laundry included. No curfew. €15 for 1 night, €14.50 for longer stays. ❷

Haus Christine, Panoramaweg 3 (☎/fax 45 67 73; haus.christine@gmx.at). The house before Haus Lindner. Haus Christine has spacious, clean triples and quads with a country motif. Breakfast served on a lovely glass-enclosed patio overlooking the countryside—the best view on the block. 1st night €15, subsequent nights €14. Credit cards accepted, but cash preferred. ❷

Germana Kapeller, Kasern Bergstr. 64 (☎ 45 66 71; www.germana.at). Lively, gregarious hostess Germana maintains impeccably decorated rooms with pleasant, vibrant colors. Some rooms have hand-carved furniture, and others have balconies. 2 terraces for lounging overlook the valley. Reservations, made in advance by telephone or email, are preferred. €15-17. Cash only. ❷

Haus Seigmann, Kasern Bergstr. 66 (☎ 45 00 01). 3 clean bright rooms, some with balconies overlooking the valley, as well as 2 patios on the hillside where afternoon tea is served. Relax on the lounge chairs outside, in the TV room downstairs, or curled up in bed under a snug comforter. Small kitchen available for guests' use upon request. Rosmarie is a talkative, charming hostess. No curfew. Reservations required. €16, subsequent nights €15. MC. ❷

The following *Privatzimmer* are on the southern edge of Salzburg but are easily accessible by car and by public transportation. Take bus #1 to "Moosstrasse," continue to the corner and take a left onto Moostrasse, then hop on bus #16 heading south. For Haus Ballwein, get off at "Gsengerweg" and for Haus Bankhammer get off at the next stop, "Marienbad."

⌘ Haus Ballwein, Moostr. 69a (☎/fax 82 40 29; www.privatvermieter.com/haus-ballwein). Spacious rooms with balconies looking out onto fields and distant mountains in 2 remodeled barns make this the perfect reprieve from city life. Breakfast room with teapot collection hanging from ceiling. Rooms come with shower (in the hall for singles) and satellite TV. Bicycle rental €7 per day. Singles €22; doubles €38-50. Cash only. ❸

Haus Bankhammer, Moostr. 77 (☎/fax 83 00 67; bankhammer@anon.at). This house has simple, spacious rooms with carved wooden beds and armoires. Doubles with bath. Breakfast of homemade strawberry-rhubarb jam and fresh milk from the dairy. Owner Helga will do laundry for guests. Rooms €23-26 per person. MC/V. ❸

The following *Privatzimmer* are located in other parts of Salzburg.

Haus Elisabeth, Rauchenbichlerstr. 18 (☎/fax 45 07 03; info@haus-elizabeth.net). Take bus #3 to "Itzling-Pflanzmann," turn around and walk about 50m back, then head right onto Rauchenbichlerstr., over the footbridge, and continue along the gravel path sloping uphill to your right. Spacious rooms have TV, balcony, and sweeping city view. Breakfast buffet included. Refrigerators available for guest use. Singles with shower €26; doubles €44-50; one quad €80. ❸

Pension Sandwirt, Lastenstr. 6a (☎/fax 87 43 51). Exit the train station from the platform #13 staircase, turn right on the footbridge, right again at the bottom onto Lastenstr., and go behind the building with the "Post" sign (3min.). The hosts of this bed-and-breakfast (not a private home) speak excellent English and will let you do laundry for free. All rooms are somewhat cramped but have TV. Breakfast included. Surprise: the shower is actually in the bedroom. Singles €24; doubles €38, with shower €45.50; triples €53.50; quads €65. ❸

HOTELS

Am Dom, Goldg. 17 (☎84 27 65; bach@salzburg.co.at). This historic wood-panelled hotel is great if you are looking for clean, quiet accommodations in a wonderful location in the heart of the *Altstadt*. As its name implies, it is located just across the square from the Dom cathedral. Make sure to reserve a room ahead of time in the summer—this small hotel of only 14 rooms fills up fast. Singles €68; doubles €94. AmEx/MC/V. ❹

Arthotel Blaue Gans, Getreideg. 41-43 (☎84 24 91; www.blauegans.at). Take bus #1 directly to the back door of the hotel at Herbert-v-Karajan Pl., or from Hanauer Pl. take a left on Getreideg. The hotel is on the left. The Blaue Gans dates back hundreds of years, even if its decor does not. Each room in this cosmopolitan hotel has sleek furniture and a unique piece of modern art, as well as a TV. The hotel is home to minimalist sculpture and elaborate wall paintings. Check out the elevator for a cool surprise. Singles €99-119; doubles €109-195. AmEx/MC/V. ❺

Albertina Hotel Allegro, Glockeng. 4b (☎889 60; www.albertina-hotels.at). Turn off Schallmooser Hauptstr. at the sign for the "Parkgarage Linzer Gasse" and turn right into Glockeng. Hidden behind a row of traditional Salzburg buildings, this stylish blue building without a first floor is a delightfully modern departure from the classical architecture surrounding it. The interior is well lit and decorated in swaths of bright color. Open July-Sept. Singles €46; doubles €72. ❹

CAMPING

Panorama Camping Stadtblick, Rauchenbichlerstr. 21 (☎45 06 52; www.panorama-camping.at). Next to Haus Elisabeth (p. 233) and run by the same family. By car, take exit "Salzburg-Nord" off A1. It's bring-your-own-tent (or RV) in this peaceful green yard with a view of the city. Ideal location is only minutes away from the city center (20min. walking and 5min. on the bus from Hauptbahnhof). On-site convenience store. Laundry €5. Shower included. Open late Mar. to early Nov. €6.20 per person, *Let's Go* readers €5.30; 2-person RV with fridge and stove €25; 4-person €36. Lots with parking and tent (including electricity) €3.50. ❶

🔂 FOOD AND DRINK

With countless beer gardens and pastry-shop patios, Salzburg is a great place to eat outdoors. The local specialty is **Salzburger Nockerl,** a large soufflé of egg whites, sugar, and raspberry filling baked into three mounds to represent the three hills of Salzburg. If you order one be prepared to wait 20-30min. and pay around €10-12. Also make sure you have a friend to share it with—it's huge. Another regional favorite is **Knoblauchsuppe,** a rich cream soup loaded with croutons and pungent garlic—a potent weapon against unwanted admirers. During the first two weeks of September, local cafés dispense **Stürm,** a delicious, cloudy cider (reminiscent, aptly enough, of a storm) that hasn't quite finished fermenting.

There are probably more world-famous **Mozartkugeln** ("Mozart balls"), hazelnuts covered with marzipan and nougat and dipped in chocolate, lining café windows than there are notes in all Mozart's works combined. A Salzburg confectioner invented the treats in 1890, but mass production inevitably took over. Although mass-produced *Kugeln* wrapped in gold and red are technically *echt* (authentic), try to find the handmade ones wrapped in blue and silver. Reasonably priced *Kugeln* are sold at the **Holzmayr** confectioners (€0.50 for gold, €0.75 for silver) or at Konditorei **Fürst** (€0.80 for silver), both on Alter Markt.

In most cases, markets are open weekdays 8am-7pm and Saturday 8am-noon. Salzburg has many supermarkets on the Mirabellpl. side of the river but few in the *Altstadt*. **SPAR** is widespread, and a giant **EuroSpar** sprawls next to the train station and bus terminal at Sudtirolerp. 11. (Open M-F 8am-7pm, Sa 7:30am-5pm.) **Open-air markets** are held on Universitätpl. (M-F 6am-7pm, Sa 6am-1pm) and Mirabellpl. down into Hubert-Sattlerg. (Th 5am-noon).

RESTAURANTS

Zum Fidelen Affen, Priesterhausg. 8 (☎87 73 61), off Linzerg. This wood-paneled restaurant is popular with locals. Hearty, honest Austrian food keeps everyone coming back "To the Faithful Ape." Try the toasted black bread with various toppings, the farmer's salad (€10), or the "Monkey Steak," (a roasted pork dish). The Ape has vegetarian options like spinach dumplings (€10). Open M-Sa 5pm-midnight. MC/V. ❸

Stadtalm, Mönchsberg 19c (☎84 17 29). Even if you aren't staying in the Stadtalm youth hostel, consider making a trip to the Mönchsberg lift to eat at the delightful café of the same name. This casual spot features picnic tables with large sun umbrellas. Enjoy chicken cordon bleu (€10), Greek salad (€6), or a glass of Stiegl (€3) while soaking up a view of the *Altstadt*. Open Mar.-Oct. daily 10am-10pm. ❸

St. Peter's Stiftskeller, St.-Peter-Bezirk 1/4 (☎84 12 680; www.haslauer.at). From Dompl., pass through the arch that leads to Franziskanerg. and take the first left. Tucked in a courtyard at the foot of the cliffs, St. Peter's Stiftskeller is considered the oldest restaurant in Central Europe: when construction on the fortress Hohensalzburg began in 1077, this restaurant had already been in business for over 200 years. Traditional Austrian food and old-fashioned decor. Most entrées €18-20. Asparagus risotto (€13). Open daily 11am-midnight; during the *Festspiele* until 1am. MC/V. ❹

Stiegkeller, Festungsg. 10 (☎84 26 81). A short walk up the Festungsg. from the bottom of the Festungsbahn. A Salzburg tradition since 1492. With seating for 1600, there's plenty of room in this restaurant, both outside under shady trees and inside under imposing antlers. Dinner options include the good old standby *Schweinsbraten* (roast pork with sauerkraut and dumpling; €9.90), as well as perch fillet (€14.60) and salad with strips of roast turkey (€8.50). Open May-Sept. daily 11am-11pm. MC/V. ❸

Shakespeare, Hubert-Sattlerg. 3 (☎87 91 06; www.shakespeare.at), off Mirabellpl. This eclectic spot serves a variety of foods, from Italian to Austrian to Chinese dishes. Spicy Szechuan pork €10, spaghetti alla carbonara €7. Art exhibitions bimonthly in the back rooms. **Free Internet.** Open daily 8am-2am. Kitchen open until 11pm. D/MC/V. ❷

ON THE MENU

GOULASH, RECONSIDERED

A dish called "Goulash" does not automatically conjure images of sugar, spice and everything nice. In Austria, however, this dish is a staple of the modern diet. This reporter decided it was time to face his fears and uncover the truth behind this mysterious meal.

Myth #1: Goulash is a grayish-brown goop. Goulash, or *Rindsgulyas* in German, can hardly be called a soup—or the more offensive "goop"! It is an concoction of steak tips, potatoes, and bread dumplings. A beef and paprika sauce rounds out the meal as a slightly and surprisingly tangy garnish.

Myth #2: Goulash is served only in winter. Restaurants throughout Austria serve steaming hot goulash year-round. But it does not grace the menus of touristy chain diners—appropriately so. Rindsgulyas is particularly popular in western areas around Salzburg and Innsbruck, the locals know where to find it.

Myth #3: Goulash is gross! The meal satisfies even the most skeptical patrons with its surprisingly succulent sauce. The marinated beef hardly requires cutting and all of the elements come together to make a delicious Austrian specialty. One should not expect to find only beef goulash here; it comes in many forms including beef, pork, sausage, potato or even hard-boiled egg.

Il Sole, Gstätteng. 15 (☎84 32 84), just to the right of the bottom of the Mönchsberg lift. The wonderful aroma of fresh-cooked pizza (€6-9) greets you as you enter this lovely Italian restaurant. Enjoy lasagna (€6.50), or one of the many pasta dishes. Open daily 11:30am-2:30pm and 5:30pm-midnight. Closed Tu in spring and fall. AmEx/MC/V. ❷

Bio Bistro, Wolf-Dietrich-Str. 1 (☎87 07 12). Walk down Linzerg. from the *Altstadt.* Turn left onto Wolf-Dietrich. Inside this organic eatery and spice store you will find a world of aromas and a new vegetarian lunch *Menü* each day (€6), with soup (€3) and 3 kinds of salad (€4-6). Dinner *Menü* includes appetizer, main course, and dessert (€10). Open M-Sa 9am-9pm, Su 11am-9pm. ❷

Toskana, Sigmund Haffnerg. 11 (☎80 44 69 009), through the iron fence and on the right. This college cafeteria is a good deal for penny-pinchers, with 2 hot entrées (€4-6), served in a beautiful smoky courtyard just within the university grounds. Get there early, before ravenous students deplete the food supply. Open July-Aug. daily 9am-3pm; Sept.-June M-Th 8:30am-5pm, F 8:30am-3pm. ❶

CAFÉS

The Salzburg cafés explode with life on spring and summer days. Tourists catching their breath from whirlwind tours of popular churches and stately rooms quickly realize that a Salzburg café is an authentic Austrian experience in the midst of hundreds of years of history. Locals frequent their favorites on breaks from work to catch up on the news over strudel and espresso. Before running to the next event or exhibit, spend a few minutes inside one of the many cafes or bask in the sun at an outdoor table.

Café Bazar, Schwarzstr. 3 (☎87 42 78; www.cafe-bazar.at). From the *Altstadt,* cross the Makart bridge and turn left onto the foot path. The terrace in back provides a peaceful way to escape the crowds along the tree-shaded riverbank of the Salzach. Enjoy a light lunch (€5), or indulge in a dessert such as raspberry yogurt, *Sachertorte,* or *Mozarttorte* (around €2.75). Open M-Sa 7:30am-midnight.

Café Tomaselli, Alter Markt 9 (☎80 84 44 88), has been a favorite haunt for wealthier *Salzburger* since 1705. The interior glows with the light of the crystal chandeliers reflecting off the warm wood paneling and gold trim. Try the hot chocolate with rum (€4), guaranteed to warm your belly. Cakes about €3 on a mobile dessert counter. Sample the *Glühwein* (€4), *Grog* (€4), or *Tomaselliums Café,* a decadent concoction of mocha, Mozart liqueur, whipped cream, and almond slivers (€6). Newspapers available for perusal. Open M-Sa 7am-9pm, Su 8am-9pm; during the *Festspiele* until midnight.

Café Fürst, Brodg. 13 (☎84 37 59). On Alter Markt, right across from Café Tomaselli. Savor a *Mozartkugel* (€0.80), or any one of a vast selection of candies (try the marzipan potato), pastries, *Torte,* strudels, and cakes (around €2). Branch in Mirabellpl. Open daily June-Sept. 8am-9pm; Oct.-May. 8am-8pm. AmEx/DC/MC/V.

Café Cult, Hellbrunnerstr. 3 (☎84 56 01). Go into the Kunstlerhaus building and around to the back on the ground floor. This Mediterranean café in the back of a local art gallery is popular with the artistic set of Salzburg. Eat on the glass terrace by the river or on the trendy orange furniture. Meals €6-9. Open M-F 9am-11pm, Sa 9am-3pm.

Café Glockenspiel, Mozartpl. 1 (☎84 14 03). Near the tourist office, this place serves ice cream concoctions (€4.40-5.80) and cakes (€3.10). The restaurant ❸ upstairs serves good typical Austrian fare, ranging from *Bratwurst* (€6.60) to duck (€15.90). Vegetarian specials include tortellini and *Spinatspätzle.* Sit at a table on the square and listen to free concerts of light classical music each evening in July and Aug., or watch the flocks of tourists parade past the Mozart statue. Open daily Easter.-Aug. 9am-11pm; Sept.-Easter 9am-7pm; during the *Festspiele* until midnight. AmEx/DC/MC/V.

Kaffeehäferl, Getreideg. 25 (☎84 32 49), from Hagenauerpl. facing Mozarts Geburtshaus turn right down Getreidg. Walk 25m and turn left into the passage across from McDonald's. Unpretentious courtyard café provides an oasis from the rush of Getreideg. Coffee around €3, Johannis juice €2.10. Open M-Sa 9am-7pm, Su noon-7pm.

◎ SIGHTS

Salzburg is a relatively small town with a disproportionate number of *Sehenswürdigkeiten* (points of interest). Whether you're into flower gardens or centuries-old fortresses, Salzburg's got it. The tourist office sells the **Salzburg Card,** which grants admission to all museums and sights as well as unlimited use of public transportation, but it's a good deal only if you cram lots of sightseeing into a short time period. (Mid-Jan. to mid-June and mid-Sept. to late Dec.: 24hr. card €19., 48hr. €26, 72hr. €32; ages 7-15 half-price. Mid-June to mid-Sept.: €21/€28/€34.)

FESTUNG HOHENSALZBURG ←

☎84 24 30. Grounds open daily mid-June to mid-Sept. 9am-7pm; mid-Sept. to mid-Mar. 9am-5pm; mid-Mar. to mid-June 9:30am-6pm. If you walk up, entrance to fortress is €3.60, ages 6-15 €2, which allows only access to the perimeter of the castle; combo ticket includes fortress, castle interiors, and museums €7.20/€4.

Built between 1077 and 1681 by the ruling prince-archbishops, **Festung Hohensalzburg** was used as a refuge during religious and class wars. Looming over Salzburg from atop Mönchsberg, it has never been successfully attacked, making it the largest completely preserved castle in Europe. Nowadays, penetrating the castle walls is just a matter of a few euros.

FESTUNGSBAHN. The trail up to the fortress and the *Festungsbahn* (funicular) can be found at the far end of Kapitelpl. on Festungsg. The stairs require about 20min. of uphill walking. Because the ride ends inside the fortress walls, funicular tickets include entrance. *(☎84 97 50. Every 10min. May-Sept. 9am-9pm; Oct.-Apr. 9am-5pm. Round-trip €8.50, children €4.50. MC/V.)*

FÜRSTENZIMMER. The inner depths of the castle contain formidable Gothic state rooms, the fortress organ (nicknamed the "Bull of Salzburg" for its off-key snorting), a torture chamber and an impregnable watchtower that affords an unmatched view of the city and a 360-degree view of the surrounding mountains.

BURGMUSEUM. Inside the fortress, this museum exhibits findings from 16th-century excavations, stick figures displaying weapons used between 1300 and 1700, and a series of side-by-side timelines depicting the history of the Festung, Salzburg, and the world at large. Also notable are the music samples in the section on Turkish music from Austria.

RAINER MUSEUM. Exhibits here include objects of war from the 17th century to the present, including uniforms, books, weapons, and paintings. Don't miss the life-size model of an Austrian soldier in Alpine uniform, complete with ice pick, hiking boots, and knee-length pants. The fortress also has a marionette museum.

OTHER SIGHTS. From the fortress, many footpaths spread out over the Mönchsberg, providing bird's-eye views of the city below. At times, the paths are framed by damp stone walls, many of which were originally parts of the city wall, dating back to the 13th century. From these trails, hikers can descend back to the *Altstadt* via the stairs or the **Mönchsberglift** (an elevator built into the mountain), which opens onto Gstätteng. 13. *(Operates daily 9am-9pm. €1.60, round-trip €2.60; children half-price. Included in the price of a Salzburg Card.)* Down the hill and to the right of

THE LOCAL STORY

THE FORGOTTEN FRESCOES

Frauscher Hermann works for the Festival Houses of Salzburg. This building contains three of the largest opera stages in Austria and is home to the Festpiele every summer. It also contains a half-decorated lobby and is missing several large frescoes, which should adorn its walls.

In the lobby of the Festival Halls there are frescoes depicting themes from the Bible, mythology and even the first play performed at the Salzburg Festival, *Jedermann*. The pictures have been here since the opening of the house in 1926. But during World War II these pictures were not to be seen on these walls.

They were controversial because they represented the political view of the Christdemocrats, the ruling party in Salzburg in the 1920's. They were the opposite of the Nazi ideology at the time. In 1938, the Nazis decided to destroy the pictures completely. This was "art which is not to be seen."

One painter in the house knew a technique to preserve the frescos from the walls. He copied them onto linen and saved them during the years of World War II. But some of the images got lost during the bombing of Salzburg. Others were destroyed by storage in humid cellars. But most of them could be saved and after the war, they were reinstalled on the walls so we can see them today.

the fortress, **Nonnberg Abbey** (where the real Maria von Trapp lived) is still a private monastic complex and is closed to the public. Visitors can opt to tour the dimly lit church in the complex and see the Romanesque wall paintings at no charge.

THE ALTSTADT

THE CITY CENTER. In the shadow of the hilltop fortress, arcade passages open up into tiny courtyards filled with geraniums and creeping ivy that lead, in turn, to the tourist-jammed Getreidegasse. The buildings here are the oldest in the city, some dating back to the 12th century. Many of the shops have wrought-iron signs dating from the Middle Ages, when the illiterate needed pictorial aids.

RESIDENZ (ARCHBISHOP'S RESIDENCE). The square on the far side of the cathedral is Residenzplatz, named for the magnificent *Residenz* of Salzburg's powerful prince-archbishops. The ecclesiastical elite of Austria have resided here, in the heart of the *Altstadt*, since 1595. Mozart conducted symphonies within. An audioguide offers commentary on the Baroque *Prunkräume*, massive state rooms decorated with immense ceiling frescoes and stucco work, gilded furniture, and 17th-century Flemish tapestries. The *Residenz* also houses a gallery (see p. 241). Outside the palace, dead-center in Residenzpl. is the largest Baroque fountain in the world, featuring amphibious horses charging through the water. Appropriately, *Fiaker* (horse-drawn carriages) congregate in the square. *(For more information on the Residenz call ☎ 80 42 26 90. Open late Mar. to mid-Apr. daily 10am-5pm. €7.30, students €5.50, children €2.50, audioguide included. Carriage rides €33 for 30min.)*

MOZARTS GEBURTSHAUS (MOZART'S BIRTHPLACE). The long red and white flag suspended from the roof of the **Mozarts Geburtshaus** is a beacon for music pilgrims worldwide. Although Mozart eventually settled in Vienna, his birthplace holds the most impressive collection of the child genius's belongings: his first viola and violin, a pair of keyboard instruments, and buttons from his coat. Several rooms also recreate life in Salzburg and Austria during Mozart's time, as well as what Mozart's young years as a traveling virtuoso must have been like. Come before 11am to avoid the tourists who crowd around the exhibits, blocking the prodigy's relics from all but the most persistent. *(On the 2nd floor of Getreideg. 9. ☎84 43 13. Open daily July-Aug. 9am-7pm; Sept.-June 9am-5:30pm. Last entrance 30min. before closing. €5.50, students and seniors €4.50, children €1.50.)*

UNIVERSITY CHURCH. Behind Mozart's birthplace is the *Universitätskirche*, one of the largest Baroque chapels in Europe, and designer Fischer von Erlach's masterpiece. Its distinctive dome stands watch over Universitätspl. and the daily farmer's market. Sculpted clouds coat the nave, while pudgy cherubim (lit by pale natural light from the dome) frolic all over the church's immense apse. *(Hours vary, though generally open daily 9am-5pm. Free.)*

FESTSPIELHAUS. The *Festspielhaus*, once the riding school for the archbishops' horses, now houses many of the big-name events of the annual *Festspiele*. It has three performance spaces: the large Opera House, the small Opera House, and an open-air performance space. *(☎ 84 90 97. Down Wiener-Philharmonikerg. from Universitätspl. Tours daily July-Aug. 9:30am, 2pm, 3:30pm; June and Sept. 2pm, 3:30pm; Oct.-May 2pm. €5, ages 12 and under €2.90.)* Opposite the *Festspielhaus*, the **Rupertinum Gallery** hosts temporary exhibits of modern painting, sculpture, and photography. *(☎ 80 42 25 41. Open mid-July to Sept. Tu and Th 9am-5pm, W 10am-9pm; Oct. to mid-July Tu, Th-Su 10am-5pm, W 10am-9pm. €8, students €4.50.)*

ST. PETER'S. The **Toscaninihof,** the courtyard of **St. Peter's Monastery,** hides the stone steps leading up the Mönchsberg cliffs. The monastery itself, which was already standing when St. Rupert arrived in Salzburg in AD 696, is the oldest monastery north of the Alps. The **Stiftskirche St. Peter,** within the monastery, began as a Romanesque basilica in the 1100s and still features a marble portal from 1244. In the 18th century, the building was remodeled in Rococo style, with green and pink moldings curling delicately across the graceful ceiling and gilded cherubim blowing golden trumpets. *(Open 9am-12:15pm and 2:30-6:30pm. Free.)*

PETERSFRIEDHOF (CEMETERY). *Petersfriedhof* is one of the most peaceful places in Salzburg, partly because large tour groups are denied entry. Some of the tiny cemetery's flower-covered graves date back to the 1600s. In the middle is St. Margaret's Chapel, built between 1485 and 1491. *(Continue through the arch to the right of the Stiftskirche St. Peter. Open daily Apr.-Sept. 6:30am-7pm; Oct.-Mar. 6:30am-6pm.)*

KATAKOMBEN (CATACOMBS). Near the far end of the cemetery, against the Mönchsberg, lie the medieval catacombs. The part open to visitors consists of two rooms built into the rock wall above the cemetery. The old stone passageways will make you feel like a medieval monk, minus the robes. In the lower room (St. Gertrude's Chapel), a fresco commemorates the martyrdom of Thomas à Beckett. *(Near the far end of the cemetery, against the Mönchsberg. ☎ 78 47 435. Open May-Sept. Su, Tu-Sa 10:30am-5pm; Oct.-Apr. W-Th 10:30am-3:30pm. €1, students and ages 6-18 €0.60.)*

DOM (CATHEDRAL). Archbishop Wolf Dietrich's successor, Markus Sittikus, commissioned the baroque *Dom* in 1628. Mozart was christened here in 1756 and later worked at the cathedral as *Konzertmeister* and court organist. The cathedral boasts five organs which, when all played at once, create a phenomenal surround-sound experience. The original cupola was destroyed during WWII, but was restored in 1959 to its previous condition. The square leading out of the cathedral, Domplatz, features a statue of the Virgin Mary. Around her swarm four lead figures representing Wisdom, Faith, the Church, and the Devil. *(Across the square from Residenzpl., the cathedral is the large building with green domes. Free.)*

MOZARTPLATZ. Mozartplatz is dominated by the **Neugebäude,** seat of the city government's bureaucracy. A 35-bell **Glockenspiel** atop the building rings out a Mozart tune (posted on the corner of the *Residenz*) every day at 7am, 11am, and 6pm. The Hohensalzburg fortress's organ bellows a response. *(To the northwest of Residenzpl.)*

SALZBURGER LAND

SALZBURGER LAND

THE NEUSTADT

SCHLOß MIRABELL AND GARDENS. On the bus and walking route into town, Mirabellpl. holds the marvelous Schloß Mirabell. The supposedly celibate Archbishop Wolf Dietrich had his own place in the Residenz (see p. 238), but he also had this Renaissance beauty built in 1606 for his mistress Salome Alt and their 10 children. He named the palace *Altenau* in her honor, but when the new archbishop, Markus Sittikus, imprisoned Wolf Dietrich for arson, he seized the palace and changed its name to *Mirabell*. The castle is now the seat of the city government, and some of the mayor's offices are open for public viewing. The palace hosts classical concerts in the evening, and fans swear that the *Marmorsaal* (Marble Hall) is one of the best concert halls in Europe. *(Open M-F 8am-4pm. Free.)*

Behind the palace, the delicately cultivated **Mirabellgarten** is a maze of flower beds and groomed shrubs. On the left side is a gigantic fountain with four sculptures representing Greek myths, including the rape of Helen and Pluto's abduction of Proserpina. Walk up the staircase by the smaller fountain directly in front of Schloß Mirabell to the **Dwarf Garden,** named for the vertically challenged statues that share the space with playful Salzburg toddlers. The statues' grotesque marble faces were supposedly modeled after the archbishop's court jesters.

From one of the hedge-enclosed clearings in the Mirabellgarten, you can see a tiny wooden shack called the **Zauberflötenhäuschen,** where Mozart supposedly composed *The Magic Flute* in just five months. It was transplanted from Vienna as a gift to Salzburg's conservatory for young musicians, the **Mozarteum,** which borders the gardens on Schwartzstr. 26-28. The Mozarteum was built for the Salzburg Academy of Music and Performing Arts. There are regular performances in its concert hall (p. 240). It is also known for its enormous **Mozart Archives.** *(☎88 94 013; fax 88 24 19. Open M-F 9am-noon and 2-5pm. Free.)*

MOZARTS WOHNHAUS (MOZART'S RESIDENCE). Mozart moved to the **Wohnhaus** at age 17 with his family from their house in the *Altstadt*, staying from 1773 to 1780. An audioguide plays selections from Mozart's work as an accompaniment to the displays, which feature some original scores from the maestro and old pianos he once played. *(Makartpl. 8. ☎87 42 27 40; fax 87 29 24. Open daily July-Aug. 9am-6:30pm; Sept.-June 9am-5:30pm. €5.50, students €4.50; audioguide included.)*

KAPUZINBERG AND SEBASTIANSKIRCHE. At Kapuzinerberg's crest stands the simple *Kapuzinerkloster* (Capuchin Monastery) that Wolf Dietrich built in the late 16th century. Stations of the cross are represented by dioramas behind iron gates on the path from town. The outlook point alongside the path offers a scenic view of the city from the north. *(From Mirabellpl., follow Dreifaltigkeitg. south to its intersection with Linzerg.; head under the stone arch on the right side of Linzerg. 14 and follow the stone staircase up to the monastery.)* Farther down Linzerg. is the 18th-century *Sebastianskirche*. On the far side of the church is the entrance to an Italian-style cemetery, with overgrown graves and fir trees. In the center, framed by arched walkways, stands the mausoleum of Archbishop Dietrich, which has skylights in the dome that reflect light off the ceramic wall tiles. The tombs of Mozart's wife, Constanze, and father, Leopold, are also here, on the path leading to the mausoleum.

THE SOUND OF MUSIC

In 1964, Julie Andrews, Christopher Plummer, and a squad of 20th Century Fox crew members arrived in Salzburg to film *The Sound of Music*, based on the true story of the von Trapp family. Salzburg has never been the same. The city feeds off the increased tourism derived from the film's popularity, although many Salzburgers themselves have never seen the film, and most who have dislike it. Three companies run **Sound of Music Tours** in Salzburg, and many hostels and pensions work with one of them to offer discounts to guests. **Salzburg Sightseeing Tours** (☎88 16 16; fax 87 87 76) and **Panorama Tours** (☎87 40 29; fax 87 16 18) operate rival kiosks on Mirabellpl. and run similar programs. (€33, children €17. Tours leave from Mirabellpl. 9:30am and 2pm.) The alternative, **Bob's Special Tours,** Rudolfskai 38, has no kiosk, but they do have minibuses. The smaller vehicles enable visitors to tour *Altstadt* locations that the big tour buses can't reach. (☎84 95 11; www.bobs-tours.com. Tours in summer daily 9am and 2pm; in winter 10am. €35, students €32.) All three companies offer free pick-up from your hotel or hostel. Tours last 4hr. and are generally worth the money if you're a big *Sound of Music* fan or if you want an overview of the area. Another option is **Fraülein Maria's Bicycle Tours**, which start at the entrance to the Mirabellgarten behind the Hotel Bristol and cost only €22 for a 3hr. trip, including the bike rental. Riders need not be very fit to complete the relatively flat trail. (☎34 26 297. Mid-May to late Aug. daily 9:30am.)

You can save money and get closer to the sights by renting a bike and doing the tour on your own. Though Maria, the main character in the film, was a nun-apprentice at **Nonnberg Abbey,** in reality she merely taught there, high above the city near the Festung (p. 237), which serves as a backdrop for the number in which a gaggle of nuns sing "How Do You Solve A Problem Like Maria?" The gazebo where Liesl and Rolf unleashed their youthful passion is on the grounds of **Schloß Hellbrunn** (p. 245). From the Hellbrun parking lot, head down Hellbrunner Allee. On the way, you'll pass the yellow castle used for the exterior of the von Trapp home (Maria sang "I Have Confidence" in front of the long yellow wall). It's now a dorm for music students at the Mozarteum. Continue along Hellbrunner Allee until it turns into Freisaalweg. At the end of Freisaalweg, turn right on Akadamiestr., which ends at Alpenstr. and the river. The river footpath leads all the way back to Mozartsteg. and Staatsbrücke (1hr.). The back of the von Trapp house (where Maria and the children fell into the water after romping in the city) was filmed at the **Schloß Leopoldskron** behind the Mönchsberg, now a center for academic studies. Visitors are not permitted on the grounds, but to get a glimpse of the house, take bus #25 to "Pensionistenheim Nonntal," turn left on Sunnhubstr., and left again up Leopoldskroner Allee to the castle. Other filming locations scattered throughout Salzburg include the **Mirabellgarten** (p. 240) and the **Festspielhaus** (p. 239). Although the von Trapps were married in the church at Nonnberg Abbey, the scene was filmed in **Mondsee** (p. 260) instead. The sightseeing tours allow guests to stop in Mondsee for 45min., but the town is really worth a whole daytrip for its pastry shops and beautiful lake. **Buses** leave the Salzburg train station from the main bus depot (45min., every hr., €5.40).

To squeeze the last few euros out of starry-eyed tourists, the Sternbräu hosts a **Sound of Music Dinner Show.** Performers sing your favorite film songs while servers ply you with food. (☎82 66 17. May-Oct. Dinner at 7:30pm; show at 8:30pm. Dinner, show and a drink €29.)

🏛 MUSEUMS

Although Salzburg's museums often get lost in the shadow of the *Festung, The Sound of Music,* and the *Festspiele,* they are worthwhile attractions. There are also galleries on Sigmund-Haffnerg. that allow budget art viewing.

ART MUSEUMS. Museum Carolino Augusteum, named after Emperor Franz I's widow, Caroline Augusta, houses Roman and Celtic artifacts, including mosaics and burial remains, naturally preserved by the region's salt. The upper floors feature Gothic and Baroque art. (☎62 08 08; www.smca.at. *From Hanuschpl., walk down Griesg. and turn right onto Museumpl. Open daily 9am-5pm. €3.50, students €1.10.)* The **Resi-**

denz Gallery (*www.residenzgalerie.at*), in the *Residenz*, displays 16th- to 19th-century art. (*Residenzpl. 1.* ☎ *84 04 51. Open daily 10am-5pm, but closed most Mondays. €5, students €4.*) The **Barockmuseum** (*www.barockmuseum.at*), in the Orangerie of the Mirabellgarten, pays tribute to the art of 17th- and 18th-century Europe. (☎ *87 74 32. Open Tu-Sa 9am-noon and 2-5pm, Su 9am-noon. €3.00; students, seniors, and ages 6-14 €1.50.*)

BEER MUSEUM. Stiegl Brauwelt (Brew World) is attached to the Stiegl brewery, close to downtown. Three floors showcase the history of beer-making and modern beer culture. Don't miss the *Brauwelt*, a two-story bottle pyramid. Two glasses of Stiegl beer, a *Brezel* (pretzel), and a souvenir beer glass cap the tour. (*Brauhausstr. 9. Take bus #1 to "Brauhaus" and walk up the street to the giant yellow building.* ☎ *83 87 14 92; www.stiegl.co.at. Open Su-W 10am-4pm. €9.20, students €8.30.*)

OTHER MUSEUMS. The **Haus der Natur,** opposite the Carolino Augusteum, is an enormous child-friendly natural history museum (80 rooms) with everything from alligators and giant snakes to huge rock crystals and spinning planets. (*Museumpl. 5.* ☎ *84 26 53 or 84 79 05. Open 9am-5pm. Reptile zoo open 10am-5pm. €4.50, students and children €2.50.*) Inside the main entrance to the *Dom*, the **Dom Museum** houses an unusual collection called the **Kunst- und Wunderkammer** (Art and Curiosity Chamber) that includes jewel-encrusted cups, gilded prayer books, and a golden dove made in the 13th century. In the main museum, the giant *Rupertskreuz*, a statue of St. Rupert, who built the first cathedral in Salzburg, guards the back room. (☎ *84 41 89; www.kirchen.net/dommuseum. Open mid-May to mid-Oct. M-Sa 10am-5pm, Su 1-6pm. €4.50, students €1.50. Guided tours Sa 10:30am, €1.45.*) Between Residenzpl. and Dompl., the **Domgrabungsmuseum** displays excavations of Roman ruins, some dating back to the 2nd century AD. (☎ *84 52 95. Open May-Oct. W-Su 9am-5pm. €1.80, students €1.45.*) The **Spielzeug Museum,** near the *Festspielhaus*, features three floors of puppets, dolls, electric trains, and nifty pre-Lego blocks from 1921. (*Bürgerspitalg. 2.* ☎ *620 80 83 00. Open daily 9am-5pm. Puppet show Tu-W 3pm. €2.70, students €0.80.*)

🎭 ENTERTAINMENT

SALZBURGER FESTSPIELE

Max Reinhardt, Richard Strauss, and Hugo von Hofmannsthal founded the renowned **Salzburger Festspiele** (Festival) in 1920. Every year since, Salzburg has become a mecca for opera-lovers from late July to the end of August. A few weeks before the festival, visitors strolling along Getreideg. may bump into world-class stars taking a break from rehearsal. Last year's headliners included Placido Domingo, Jessye Norman, and Thomas Hampson. On the eve of the festival's opening, over 100 dancers don regional costumes, accessorize with torches, and perform a *Fackeltanz* (torch dance) on Residenzpl. During the festivities themselves, operas, plays, films, concerts, and tourists overrun every available public space.

TICKETS. Information and tickets for *Festspiele* events are available through the *Festspiele Kartenbüro* (ticket office) and *Tageskasse* (daily box office) in Karajanpl. 1, against the mountain and next to the tunnel. (Open late July to late Aug. M-F 9:30am-6:30pm; early to mid-July M-Sa 9:30-5pm; Sept.-June 9:30am-3pm. The festival prints a program that lists concert locations and dates and is available at any tourist office (€1.50). The summer season is presented each November and fans snap up the best seats months before the festival begins. To order tickets, contact Kartenbüro der Salzburger Festspiele, Postfach 140, A-5010 Salzburg (☎ 804 55 00; www.salzburgfestival.at), no later than the beginning of January. After that, the office publishes a list of remaining seats, which generally includes some cheap tickets to the operas, concerts, and plays, as well as standing-room places. These, however, are snapped up quickly by subscribers or student groups, leaving only very expensive tickets and seats at avant-garde music concerts. Middle-man ticket distributors sell marked-up cheap tickets, a legal form of scalping—try AmEx or Panorama Tours. Those 26 or younger can try for cheap subscription tickets by writing before March to Direktion der Salzburger Festspiele, Attn: Claudia Reisecker and Elfi Schweiser, Postfach 140, A-5010 Salzburg.

FREE EVENTS. The powers that be have discontinued hawking last-minute tickets for dress rehearsals to the general public. As an alternative, consider taking in the **Fest zur Eröffungsfest** (Opening Day Festival), when concerts, shows, and films are free. Tickets for these events are available on a first-come, first-serve basis at the box office in the *Großes Festspielhaus* on Hofstallg. The only other event visitors can always attend without advance tickets is *Jedermann,* the city's staging of Hugo von Hofmannsthal's modern morality play. The production occurs every year in front of the cathedral. At the end, people placed in strategic locations throughout the city cry out the eerie word *Jedermann* (everyman) which echoes all over town. Shouting contests determine which locals win the opportunity to be one of the ghostly criers. Standing-room tickets for shows are available at the *Festspielhaus.*

CONCERTS

Even when the *Festspiele* is not on, Salzburg hosts many other concerts. The **Salzburg Academy of Music and Performing Arts** performs on a rotating schedule in the **Mozarteum** (p. 240). The school often dedicates one cycle of concerts to students at a reduced or waived ticket price. (For tickets to any of these concerts, contact Kartenbüro Mozarteum, Postfach 156, Theaterg. 2, A-5024 Salzburg. ☎87 31 54; www.mozarteum.at. Open M-Th 9am-2pm, F 9am-4pm.) The **Dom** also has a concert program in July and August. Five separate organs in the cathedral create a powerful effect. (Times vary—check the main cathedral door for upcoming programs. €8.80, students €7.37, children free.)

For an enchanting (and expensive) evening, attend a **Festungskonzert** (Fortress Concert) in the fortress's ornate *Fürstenzimmer* (Prince's chamber) or *Goldener Saal* (Golden Hall). Concerts are mostly on Fridays and Saturdays year-round and daily June to September and include dinner at the fortress restaurant for a slight surcharge. Reservations are required for concerts. (For more information, contact Festungskonzerte, Anton-Adlgasserweg

THE FLORAL FLOTILLA

Hallstatters are not afraid to forgo serenity for religion. They fill the Hallstatter See with all types of boats, brightly colored flowers and church music once every year to celebrate the Feast of Corpus Christi, a Catholic celebration sixty days after Easter. On this day, Catholics remember and honor the body of Christ (*Corpus Christi* in Latin). It is by no means unique to Hallstatt; in fact, it is a National Holiday in Austria much like Christmas and Easter.

Hallstatt's is an exceptional celebration because of its storied past and the ornate floating ritual itself. The rites begin at dawn in Hallstatt's elaborate 15th century *kirche* before hundreds of villagers dressed in their best. Toddlers and schoolchildren reverently spread flower petals over the altar and throughout the church symbolizing the arrival of spring and life anew. After the service, a band leads the clergy and the choir out of the church through the picturesque streets of Hallstatt to the dock.

There the rest of the town waits in boats strewn with flowers. The angelic voices of a girls' choir herald the beginning of this short trip across the lake to Obertraun. The priest leads the floral flotilla and many boats of various shapes and sizes disturb the tranquility and serenity of the See to symbolize the spreading of Christianity.

22, A-5020 Salzburg. ☎82 58 58; www.mozartfestival.at. Open daily 9am-9pm. Tickets €29-36, students €20; with dinner €44-48/€33.) A less tourist-oriented activity is the year-round **Salzburger Schloßkonzerte** in Schloß Mirabell. The box office is in Mozarts Wohnhaus, Theaterg. 2. (☎84 85 86; www.salzburgerschlosskonzerte.at. Open M-F 9am-5:30pm.)

In July and August, **outdoor opera** rings out from the historical hedge-theater of Mirabellgarten. Tickets are available from the box office in Schloß Mirabell. (☎84 85 86; fax 84 47 47. Open M-F 9am-5:30pm. Free.) In addition, from May through August there are **outdoor performances,** including concerts, folk-singing, and dancing. The tourist office has leaflets on scheduled events. Mozartpl. and Kapitelpl. are also popular stops for talented street musicians and touring school bands, and the thickly postered Aicher Passage next to Mirabellpl. is a great source of information for other upcoming musical events.

While it is possible to get tickets from each of the above venues at their own box offices, one convenient way of finding and getting tickets to a concert is to visit the *Altstadt* tourist office on Mozartpl. The Salzburg Ticket Service available there allows you to purchase tickets to numerous performing arts productions. (☎84 03 10; www.salzburgticket.com.)

THEATER, MOVIES, AND GAMBLING

Next to Mirabellgarten, at the **Salzburger Marionettentheater** (☎87 24 06; www.marionetten.at), handmade marionettes perform to recorded *Festspiele* operas. For information, contact Marionettentheater, Schwarzstr. 24, A-5020 Salzburg. (Box office open M-Sa 9am-1pm and 2hr. before curtain. €18-35. AmEx/MC/V.) Win enough money to pay your concert ticket debt at **Casino Salzburg** in Schloß Klesssheim. Slot machines, blackjack, roulette, and poker await. Ask at the tourist office about the free shuttle service from the city center. (☎85 44 55 or 85 48 58. Open starting at 3pm. 19+. Minimum of €20 to play. Semi-formal attire required.)

⚠ OUTDOORS

If you're overwhelmed by Salzburg's indoor culture, set your sights on one of the city's many outdoor excursions. Try an adventure tour with **Crocodile Sports,** Gaisbergstr. 34a (☎64 29 07; www.crocodile-sports.com)—they pick you up from your hostel for a day (or multiple days) you'll never forget. Adventures include **canyoning** (€45-132), **canoeing** (€36-210), **paragliding** (€115), and **rafting** (€36-124). The lower prices are generally for day or half-day trips; the higher prices correspond to those that are multi-day and include food and accommodations of some kind. Call ahead. You can now also take a 40-50min. boat trip with **Salzburg City Cruise Line** leaving from the Makart Bridge. The cruise, which runs up the Salzach past the city center and back, is a relaxing way to admire Salzburg's skyline. (☎82 57 69 12; www.salzburgschifffahrt.at. Open Apr.-May and Sept. 10am-5pm, June-Aug. 9:30am-7pm. Boats depart about every hr. €10, children €7.)

⛲ NIGHTLIFE

Salzburg's daytime charm becomes nighttime boogie in its lively and varied nightlife scene. The more boisterous stick to the section of Rudolfskai between the Staatsbrücke and Mozartsteg, where a youthful crowd congregates in the street. Elsewhere, especially along Chiemseeg. and around Anton-Neumayr-Pl., you can throw back a few drinks in a more reserved *Beisl* (bar/lounge). More refined cocktail lounges can be found along Steing. and Giselakai on the other side of the river.

Augustiner Bräustübl-Mülln, Augustinerg. 4 (☎43 12 46). From the *Altstadt,* follow the footpath from Hanuschpl. downstream along the river. After the next bridge (the Müllnersteg), take the stairs going up to your left. Cross the street, then continue to your right along the Müllner Hauptstr. Turn left when you get to Augustinerg., and head up under the archway. The entrance will be on your right. Serving home-brewed beer since 1621 in the halls of a former monastery, this gigantic complex seats 2800, split evenly between an outdoor *Biergarten* and 4 gigantic indoor halls. Beer €2.40-€2.70. To save a bit of cash, give your stein directly to the *Biermeister* standing by the barrels. The stands outside the beer halls sell snacks. Open M-F 3-11pm, Sa-Su 2:30-11pm.

2-Stein, Giselakai 9 (☎87 71 79). The place to come for Salzburg's gay and lesbian scene. Heteros are welcome and frequent this hip bar. On weekends, the two-floor club draws a fashionable crowd. Drinks around €5-6. Open M-W 6pm-4am, Th-Su 6pm-5am.

O'Malley's, Rudolfskai 16 (☎84 92 63; www.omalleyssalzburg.com). Two bars ensure that you always have a drink (generally €3-5), while the wall decorations and music evoke the Emerald Isle. Happy Hour 6-8pm, all beer half-price. Open June-Aug. Su-Th 6pm-2:30am, F-Sa 6pm-4am; Sept.-May Su-Th 7pm-2:30am, F-Sa 7pm-4am.

Shamrock, Rudolfskai 11 (☎84 16 10; www.shamrock.at). Built around part of the old city wall, this relaxed Irish pub has plenty of room—just keep going until you find a spot you like, or stay by the dance area in front to take in the nightly live folk music. Also shows sporting events. Most drinks €2-5. Open Su noon-2am, M-Th 3pm-4am, F-Sa noon-4am. AmEX/D/MC/V.

Vis à Vis, Rudolfskai 24 (☎84 12 90). Designed as a tunnel under the *Altstadt,* with blacklight and blue neon. A sharply dressed crowd packs every nook around the couches and chairs. Open M-F 3-11pm, Sa-Su 2:30-11pm.

Flip, Gstätteng. 17 (☎84 36 43). Away from the hectic scene on Rudolfskai, this bar helps keep the Gstätteng. corner of Salzburg alive. The sloping stone roof in the back creates cave-like surroundings while you sip your cocktail (most around €4-6). Side corners, small round tables and U-shaped booths allow for greater intimacy. Open Su-Th 7pm-4am, F-Sa 7pm-5am. AmEx/D/MC/V.

Segabar 2, Rudolfskai 18 (☎84 68 98). This busy bar along the strip on Rudolfskai packs in a young, lively, mostly teenage crowd on weekends with blasting music and TV, creating a crowded party scene. Drinks €1.10. Open M-W 8pm-4am, Th-Su 8pm-5am.

DAYTRIPS FROM SALZBURG

HELLBRUNN AND UNTERSBERG

To reach Hellbrunn, take bus #25 (dir: Hellbrunn) to "Hellbrunn" from the train station, Mirabellpl., or Mozartsteg. 30min. down tree-lined Hellbrunner Allee (see p. 240).

LUSTSCHLOß HELLBRUNN. Just south of Salzburg, this estate was built between 1613 and 1615 at the behest of Archbishop Markus Sittikus. The sprawling complex includes a palace, fish ponds, flower gardens, and tree-lined footpaths. An audio tour leads through the small palace, which includes a "fish room" and a "bird room" devoted to paintings of the rare and exotic animals the Archbishop had collected at Hellbrunn as a sign of his power. Don't be surprised if you hear screams of surprised laughter from outside; Archbishop Markus amused himself by creating water-powered figurines and a booby-trapped table that could spout water on his guests. The tour of these *Wasserspiele* (water games) is a delight on a warm day. Prepare yourself for a much wetter-than-average walk in the park, with sights including a small crown suspended high in the air on a stream of water and a mechanical demon spouting water from his nose. *(www. hellbrunn.at. Open daily July-*

Aug. 9am-6pm; May-June and Sept. 9am-5:30pm; Apr. and Oct. 9am-4:30pm. Castle tour, gardens, Wasserspiele, and Volkskundemuseum €7.50, students €5.50. In July and Aug. there are evening tours of the Wasserspiele at 7, 8, 9, and 10pm; €7, students €3.50.)

VOLKSKUNDEMUSEUM (FOLKLORE MUSEUM). On the hill above the manicured grounds sits the tiny hunting lodge Monats-schlössl (Little Month Castle), which was built when the Archbishop won a bet that he couldn't build a castle in a month. The castle now houses three floors of exhibits, including several *Salzburger Schönperchten*, traditional 2m-tall hats worn to scare away the demons of winter. *(☎82 03 72 49 21. Open Apr.-Oct. daily 9am-5pm.)*

STEINTHEATER AND HELLBRUNN ZOO. Continue past the Monats-schlössl to the Steintheater, where the first opera performance in the German-speaking world took place here in 1616. Near the castle lies the Hellbrunn Zoo, the modern-day descendant of the Archbishop's exotic animal collections. Residents include leopards, red pandas, and cranes. The zoo prides itself on not caging animals: instead, they put them behind fences with cliffs at their backs. *(☎82 01 76; www.salzburg-zoo.at. Open daily June-Sept. 8:30am-6:30pm; Dec. to mid-Feb. until 4:30pm; mid-Feb. to May until 5:30pm. €7, students €5, children €3.50.)*

UNTERSBERG PEAK. Bus #25 continues south from Hellbrunn (catch the bus at the main road) to the **Untersberg peak** (last stop: "St. Leonhard"), where **Charlemagne** supposedly rests beneath the ground. A **cable car** glides for 15 min. over the rocky cliffs to the summit. From there, the 30min. hike over the alpine ridge out to the Salzburger *Hochthron* provides unbelievable mountain scenery. *(☎062 46 87 12 17. Cable cars leave every 30 min. Open daily July-Sept. 8:30am-6:30pm; Dec.-Feb. 9am-4pm; Mar.-June and Oct. 8:30am-5pm. Roundtrip €17, €15 with Salzburg Card.)*

THE SALZKAMMERGUT

Historically, the Viennese art community, including Klimt, Brahms, Schiele, and Strauss, summered in the Salzkammergut. Today, tourists, bands of Austrian schoolchildren, and groups of elderly Europeans travel to its smooth crystal lakes and towering mountains. Though the region takes its name from the salt mines that once financed Salzburg's architectural treasures, today the idyllic lakes in the summer and the fresh snow in winter support the area. Salzburg is the hub for all transportation in the area. If your trip allows only one stop in the Salzkammergut, make it Hallstatt, whose strikingly beautiful locale makes it worth more than a day's visit. After Hallstatt, the desirability of other destinations will depend on what you're seeking: you can find everything from posh spas to rustic hostels. For all the best bargains, pick up the ▓**Salzkammergut Card,** which provides 30% discounts on countless local sights and attractions (€4.90; available at local tourist offices). For information on the region, contact the Hotel Destination Salzkammergut, Wirerstr. 10, A-4820 Bad Ischl (☎613 22 69 09; info@salzkammergut.at).

▐ **TRANSPORTATION.** The Salzkammergut is easily navigable, with 2000km of footpaths, dozens of cable cars and chairlifts, and numerous hostels. Within the region, there is a dense network of **buses** that are the most efficient and reliable method of travel into and through the lake region, since much of the mountainous area is bare of rail tracks. When traveling by bus, be sure to plan your route in advance, as some connections run infrequently (dial ☎05 17 17 from Salzburg for complete schedule information). *Let's Go* does not recommend hitchhiking, but **hitchers** from Salzburg have been seen taking bus #29 to Gnigl and coming into the Salzkammergut at Bad Ischl. **Bikers** should check out the 280km **Salzkammergut bike path** winding through many towns in the region. (Contact the Salzkammergut regional tourist office for information, or consult www.radtouren.at/english.) **Hikers** can capitalize on dozens of **cable cars** in the area before setting out on their own, though hiking from the base is almost always an option. Ask for hiking maps at any tourist office. Reasonably priced **ferries** service each of the larger lakes (railpass discounts available on the **Wolfgangsee, Attersee,** and **Traunsee** lines).

 ACCOMMODATIONS. Hostels are common throughout the area, but you can often find far superior rooms in private homes and *Pensionen* at just above hostel prices. **Campgrounds** dot the region, although for a higher-altitude experience, the many **alpine huts** accessible from hikes are a better bet. Contact the **Österreichischer Alpenverein** (Austrian Alpine Club; ☎ 051 25 95 47) for info.

> **SALZKAMMERGUT PAY-PER-VIEW.** Anyone who stays in a Salzkammergut hotel will notice a curious trait: room prices vary depending on their view of the lake rather than their size or comfort level. Unless you want to splurge, ask for a room without a view.

HALLSTATT ☎ 06134

On the banks of the Hallstättersee, in a valley surrounded by the sheer cliffs of the Dachstein mountains, Hallstatt is easily the most striking lakeside village in the Salzkammergut. Hallstatt's perch on a mountainside ensures that the lake dominates the horizon from nearly every vantage point. Hallstatt's salt-rich earth has helped preserve its archeological treasures, which are so extensive that one era in Celtic studies (800-400 BC) is dubbed "the Hallstatt era."

⌐ TRANSPORTATION

From Salzburg, the **bus** (€15) is the cheapest way to get to Hallstatt, but it requires layovers in both Bad Ischl and Gosaumühle. Buses depart from Bad Ischl every hour 6:50am-6:50pm. The **bus stop** is at the edge of downtown on Lahnstr., across from the Konsum market. The **train station** is on the other side of the lake, but there is no staffed office to help travelers. Follow the sign to *"Shiffstation"* to catch the **ferry**. The ferry shuttles passengers between the town and the station before and after each train (15min., 6:50am-6:29pm, €1.90). Trains stop at "Hallstatt" through the night, but after the last ferry leaves, any passengers that get off the train will be stranded at the station, across the lake from the town. All trains come from Attnang-Puchheim in the north or Stainach-Irdning in the south. Outbound trains run to: Attnang-Puchheim (1½hr., every hr., €10); Bad Ischl (30min., €2.90); Salzburg via Attnang-Puchheim (2½hr., €17); Stainach-Irding (50min., every 2hr., €7.40). **By car** from Salzburg or the Salzkammergut towns, take Rte. B-158 to Bad Ischl onto Rte. B-145 to Gosaumühle, then B-166 to Hallstatt. Automobile access to Hallstatt is limited to the town's overnight guests May-October. Ample day **parking** lots are available near the tunnels leading into town (free for guests staying in town overnight: inquire at your hotel).

⊞ ⚡ ORIENTATION AND PRACTICAL INFORMATION

Hallstatt is on the Hallstättersee, a shimmering oasis at the southern tip of the Salzkammergut. To get to the **tourist office** from the ferry stop, face away from the lake and turn left, walking past the Gemeindeamt until you see the office on your right at Seestr. 169 (4min.). From the bus stop, face away from the lake and turn right, walking on the lake along Seestr. for 5min. The office will be on your left, and provides free maps and finds rooms. (☎ 82 08; www.tis-cover.com/hallstatt. Open July-Aug. M-F 9am-5pm, Sa 10am-5pm; Nov.-May M-F 9am-noon and 2-5pm.) When the office is closed, you can always consult the tourist computer at the bus station, which has information on activities and accommodations, as well as a free reservations phone. Other services include an **ATM** next to the post office; **laundry** at Hotel Grüner Baum, 104 Marktpl. (€11 for washing and drying service; inquire at reception) and Camp Kausner-Höll, Lahnstr. 201 (€8; inquire at reception); **public bathrooms** next to the tourist office and bus stop; and a **doctor** with an in-house **pharmacy** at Baderpl. 108. (Dr. Sonja Gapp ☎ 84 01. Walk-in hours M-Tu 8am-noon, Th 5-7pm, F-Sa 8-11am.) **Internet** access (€5 per 20min.) and **bike rental** (€6 per half-day, €11 per day) are available at Hotel Grüner Baum. The **post office**, Seestr. 160 (☎ 82 01), is below the tourist office. (Open M-Tu and Th-F 8am-noon and 1:30-5:30pm, W 8am-noon.) **Postal Code:** A-4830.

▮ ACCOMMODATIONS AND CAMPING

Frühstückspension Seethaler, Dr.-F.-Mortonweg 22 (☎ 84 21; pension-seetha-ler@ann.at). Turn uphill next to the tourist office and follow the signs; it will be on your right. This pension has melded 4 houses into one and created an interesting interior design in the process. All rooms have balconies, most with amazing lake views. Breakfast in an antler-studded room included. Shower €1 per 8min. 4-bed dorms €20, with in-room shower and toilet €28; 2- to 4-person apartment with kitchen €26. ❸

Seehotel Grüner Baum, Marktpl. 104 (☎ 82 63; www.hallstatt.net/gruenerbaum). If you're tired of "water closets" that actually are closets, it's time for a soak in the tub in one of the enormous bathrooms at the Hotel Grüner Baum. This hotel has the best location in town: on the lake steps away from the old market square. The building was once a salt trader's house and retains much of its historic feel with old-fashioned furniture and decorations from Hallstatt's salt mining heyday. Pets welcome. Breakfast included. Closed Nov. to mid-Apr. Singles €50-85; doubles €100-170. AmEx/D/MC/V. ❹

Gästehaus Zur Mühle, Kirchenweg 36 (☎/fax 83 18; toeroe.f@magnet.at). Walk uphill to the right of the tourist office, toward the short tunnel at the upper right corner of the square. The hostel is at the end of the tunnel, by the waterfall. Close to the city center with homey, wood-paneled 3- to 20-bed dorms. Breakfast €2.50. Lunch and dinner available at the restaurant downstairs; see p. 249. Showers included. Locker with €20 deposit. Reception 10am-2pm and 4-10pm. Closed in Nov. Dorms €10. MC/V. ❷

Frühstückspension Sarstein, Gosaumühlstr. 83 (☎ 82 17). From the ferry landing, turn right on Seestr. and walk for 10min.; it will be on the right. Although the bathrooms show signs of wear, Frau Fischer's *Pension* offers glorious vistas of the lake and village as well as a beachside lawn for sunning and swimming. Frau Fisher is like the sweet Austrian grandmother you never had; communication comes naturally even though she does not speak English. Breakfast included in quaint lakeside room. Hall bathrooms and showers (showers €1 per 10min.). Singles and doubles €18 per person, with balcony €20-22; doubles with shower, bathroom, and balcony €28. ❸

Camping Klausner-Höll, Lahnstr. 201. (☎ 832 24; camping.klausner@magnet.at.) From the tourist office, walk past the bus stop on Seestr. for 10min. to this clean campground at the base of the mountains. Laundry €8. Gate closed daily noon-3pm and 10pm-7:30am. Open mid-Apr. to mid-Oct. €5.80 per adult, €3 per child ages 6-14, €3.70 per tent, €2.90 per car, €4.50 per camper, €5.80 per trailer. Electricity €2.90. MC/V. ❶

SALZBURGER LAND

▶ FOOD

While rooming in Hallstatt isn't pricey, eating is. The cheapest food is at the **Konsum** supermarket across from the bus stop. (Open M-Tu and Th-F 7:30am-noon and 3-6pm, W 7:30am-12:30pm, Sa 7:30am-noon.)

Bräugasthof, at Seestr. 120 (☎200 12). From the tourist office, turn right and head down Seestr. for 3min. Nice weather merits a splurge on a Bräugasthof fresh fish entrée, appropriate for its serene lakeside location. The chef cooks up lunch dishes for €9-13 and dinner for €10-16, including *Reinake* fresh from the Hallstättersee (€14). Open daily 11:30am-3pm and 6-9pm. MC/V accepted in the evening. ❸

Gästehaus zum Weißen Lamm, Dr.-F.-Mortonweg 166 (☎83 11). Uphill behind the tourist office. Head downstairs to the "mountaineer's cellar" or to their outdoor patio for 2 daily *Menüs* (€8-9) for lunch and dinner including soup, entrée, and dessert. Open daily 10am-10pm; closed Tu in winter. Kitchen open 11am-3pm and 5-10pm. ❷

Gästehaus Zur Mühle (see p. 248; ☎/fax 83 18). Nibble on pizza (€5.80-7.30), salad (€2.20-6.80), and pasta (€5.80-6.90) at the pizzeria in the hostel. Sit out on the ivy-covered terrace and enjoy the view of the lake and the quiet of Hallstatt's back streets. Open Dec.-Oct. M and W-Su 11am-2pm and 5-9:30pm. MC/V. ❷

Bar Zimmermann, Marktpl. 59. For a late-night snack, try homemade pastries, savory treats (around €3), and, of course, beer (€3) at this bar on Markpl. Open 9am-2am. ❶

▶ SIGHTS AND MUSEUMS

Hallstatt packs a surprising number of attractions into a very small space. The tourist office sells an English cultural guide (€3.90), but strolling the steep, twisting streets requires no plan. Be sure to get a guest card at your accommodation for discounts on many attractions, as well as discounted entrance to the town by car.

CHURCH AND CHARNEL HOUSE. The **Pfarrkirche** is the starting point of Hallstatt's most ornate religious festival: the Corpus Christi celebration. The charnel house in the church graveyard offers a fascinating (if slightly macabre) insight into the burial scene in Hallstatt. Within the parish charnel house (*Beinhaus* in German, literally "bone-house") rest the bones of villagers from the 16th century onward, the latest added in 1995. The Celts buried their dead high in the mountains, but Christians wanted to rest in the churchyard. Unfortunately, space on the steep hillside soon ran out, so the skulls and bones of the long deceased were transferred after 10 or 20 years to the charnel house. Each of 610 skulls was decorated with a wreath of flowers (for females) or ivy (for males) and inscribed with the name of the deceased and the date of death. The skulls were then stacked neatly on a shelf supported by leg bones. *(From the ferry dock, follow the signs reading "K. Kirche." Open daily June-Sept. 10am-6pm; May and Oct. 10am- 4pm; Nov.-Apr. call ☎82 79 for an appointment. €1, students €0.40.)*

MUSEUMS. In the mid-19th century, archeologists in Hallstatt unearthed a collection of artifacts, a pauper's grave, and the crypts of the ruling class (circa 1000-500 BC) all incredibly well-preserved. The Prähistorisches Museum and Heimatmuseum, across from the tourist office, exhibit some of these treasures, including coiled copper jewelry from the tombs and mines, costumes of the region, modern mining equipment, and local art. Renovations done in 2002 add entertaining (and sometimes shocking) multimedia effects, such as a floor-shaking earthquake to simulate the cause of the landslide of AD 350 and the sound of burning wood and collapsing buildings to recreate the fire of 1750. (☎ 82 80 15; fax 82 80 12. Open July-Aug. daily 10am-7pm; Apr.-June and Sept.-Oct. daily 9am-6pm; Nov.-Feb. Su-Tu 10am-4pm. €6, students and children €3. AmEx/MC/V.)

SALT MINES. The 2500-year-old Salzbergwerke are the oldest saltworks in the world. Fascinating guided tours (1hr., in English and German) include a zip down a wooden mining slide, a visit to an eerie lake deep inside the mountain, and a ride on a miner's train. Ask for a salt rock as a souvenir, or pick up the photo taken of you as you speed down the slide. (☎ 200 24 00; fax 031 22. Open daily May-Sept. 9:30am-4:30pm; Oct. 9:30am-3pm. €14.50, students €8.70, children €7.25-€8.70, seniors €13.50. Reach the salt mines via either the cable car or the 1hr. hike (see below). To get to the cable car, turn right at the bus circle and follow the "Salzbergwerk" signs to Salzbergbahn. From the top of the cable cars it's a 15min. walk uphill. Trains run daily May-Sept. 9am-6pm; Oct. 9am-4:30pm. For the last tour, take the 4pm train; in Oct. 2:30pm. Tours every 15min. €4.70, round-trip €7.90; children under 15 €2.80/€4.70. Combination train and tour €19.90, students €11.95, children €9.95-€11.95, seniors €7.90, children 4 and under not allowed.)

▲ OUTDOORS

HIKING. Hallstatt offers some of the most spectacular day hikes in the Salzkammergut. They lead through forests where drops of water cling to the pine needles year-round, thanks to a climate very close to that of a temperate rainforest. The tourist office offers bike trail maps (€7.20) and an excellent Dachstein hiking guide, describing 38 hikes in the area (€5.80, available in English). Hike to nearby mountain huts (using the Dachstein hiking guide) or try one of the following hikes:

Salt mine (Salzbergwerk) hike (1hr.). Walk to the Salzbergbahn (see directions and info above) and head up on the road to the right, turning at the black and yellow "Salzwelten" sign. The steep, well-paved hike leads to the salt mine tour, with increasingly elevated and astonishing views of the *Hallstätter See*. Halfway up, look for an entrance to the stone tunnel of the old mine named after Emperor Franz Joseph. The stairs to your left lead to an archaeological memorial path that provides information (in German) about the history of the burial field discovered there.

Waldbachstrub waterfall hike (1½-2hr.). From the bus station, follow the signs heading away from the lake for a light walk along a stream that leads to a clear, cold waterfall. For 40min. the path follows the sound of the rushing river along the *Malerweg*. When you come to a sign reading "Waldbachstrub" make a detour (if you have sturdy shoes) to the *Gletschergarten* to see a fantastic array of riverbed formations created by glaciers during the last Ice Age. From the main trail, continue by following the "Waldbachstrub" signs for 10min. to the magnificent double waterfall. To get back to Hallstatt, retrace your steps or turn left when you get to the bridge and make your way to the bus station.

Gangsteig (45min.-1½hr.), for experienced hikers only, is a primitive stairway carved into the side of the cliff. Completing the trail will take hiking shoes and a strong will to climb, but the work is worth it for the relatively light traffic and beautiful vistas of the valley. Follow the Waldbachstrub hike until 2min. before the falls, where "Gangsteig" is marked on the right. It's about another hour to the top.

WATER SPORTS AND SKIING. For a view of the mountains from below rather than above, try a scenic boat trip around the lake with **Schiffrundfarten Hemetsberger.** Ferries leave from both ferry landings in town. (☎ 82 28. 50min.; May to late Sept. in good weather 11am, 1, 2, 3pm or by appointment; €7.) **Boat rental** for two people costs €6 per 30min. for an electric boat, €5 for a paddleboat, and €4 for a rowboat from **Hallstatt Schmuck** near the ferry landing by the Marktpl. **Swimming** ir the lake is free, but watch out—the water's cold. The best place to swim in the lake is the public park, which can be reached from the bus stop by heading away from town along the Seelände, the road closest to the water's edge.

Winter visitors can take advantage of Hallstatt's **ski bus** (free with snow gear rental, contact the tourist office for info), which runs to the Krippenstein and Dachstein-West ski areas several times per day. Dachstein's **lifts** (3 cable cars and 6 lifts) run from mid-December to April. Lift tickets cost €26 for adults, €15 for children, and €24 for seniors. The *Inneres Salzkammergut* also provides 116km of cross-country ski trails. The tourist office gives out ski maps.

◤ DAYTRIP FROM HALLSTATT

OBERTRAUN AND THE DACHSTEIN CAVES ☎ 06131

To reach Obertraun from Hallstatt, take the bus from the Lahn bus station, on the lake near the Salzbergbahn at the western end of town. (7 per day, 12 per day in peak season, 8:50am-4:50pm , €1.90.) Stop at the cable car station "Dachstein" for the caves. Ride the cable car up 1350m to "Schönbergalm" for the ice and mammoth caves (every 15min. 8:40am-5:30pm, last trip for a tour at 4:15pm; round-trip €13.40, children €7.90). The Koppenbrüller cave is a 15min. walk from the bus stop in Obertraun. For cave tours, wear sturdy shoes and warm clothing: the caves hover near freezing all year.

The frigid beauty of the **Dachstein Caves** is as breathtaking as the caves are immense. The **Rieseneishöhlen** (Giant Ice Caves) are the primary attraction. Their brilliant blue ice formations not only last year-round, but continue to grow, even in the summer. Tour guides control the lighting panels illuminating the structures throughout the cave. If there is any place in Austria that will bring out your inner geologist, this is it. The **Mammuthöhlen** (Mammoth Caves) are up on the mountain along with the ice caves. As the name implies, they have an explored length of over 60km. Tours, offered in German (ask tour guide for an English translation), are required and last 50min. You'll be assigned to a group at the Schönbergalm station. From the station there is a 45min. scenic hike to the entrance of the cave. (☎84 00. *Open May to mid-Oct. 9am-5pm. Admission to each cave €8.20, children €5; for both caves €12.70/€7.20.*) The **Koppenbrüllerhöhle**, a giant spring, is in the valley near the village of Obertraun. This cave is more romantic than gigantic, and can be reached without cable car from the Obertraun bus or Koppenbrüllerhöhle train stops. (*Tours May-Sept. every hr. 9am-4pm €7, children €4.20.*)

For a panoramic **hike**, try the **Karstlehrpfad** (*3-4hr., accessible from late June to the first snowfall*), beginning from **Krippenstein,** the top station of the Dachstein lift. From there, follow the path below the Schutzhaus restaurant and go left at the split. From the peak, you will be able to see the entire Dachstein plateau. The finish is at the bottom of the **Gjaidalm lift,** which returns to the Dachsteinbahn. (*Open daily 9am-5pm. Ticket for both lifts €18.90, children €11.80.*)

Obertraun is a 1hr. walk from the caves. Buses are infrequent; check the schedule. The Obertraun **tourist office** is in the Gemeindeamt, Obertraun 180. From the train station, turn right onto the main road and follow signs. (☎351; fax 342 22. *Open July-Aug. M-F 8:30am-noon and 2-5:30pm, Sa 9-11am; Sept.-June M-F 8am-noon and 2-5pm.*) An **ATM** is at the Volksbank next to the tourist office. The **Post office,** Obertraun 94, is inside the Konsum market. (☎382. *Open M-Tu and Th-F 8am-noon and 2-5pm, W 8am-noon.*) Buy groceries at **Konsum market,** at the turn-off for the tourist office. (*Open M, W, F 7:30am-noon and 3-6pm, Tu and Th 7:30am-noon, Sa 7am-noon.*)

BAD ISCHL
☎ 06132

Bad Ischl, in the heart of the Salzkammergut, has been the vacation spot for the Who's Who of Hapsburg royalty for 200 years—even the Kaiser came here to relax. It was a salt-mining town for centuries, until Dr. Franz Wirer arrived in 1821 to study the curative properties of the area's heated brine baths. He began to prescribe brine bath vacations in Bad Ischl for his patients. Seeking a cure for their infertility, Archduke Francis Charles and Archduchess Sophia journeyed to Bad Ischl and produced three sons, the so-called **Salt Princes.** Today the baths still exist, and a lively community has grown around them.

⌸ TRANSPORTATION

Only one **train** comes through the train station (☎ 24 40 70; desk open M-F 6:30am-6:35pm, Sa 8:05am-5:15pm), running between Attnang-Puchheim in the north (1hr., 5:05am-8:15pm, €6.50) and Hallstatt in the south (40min., 6:15am-6:05pm, €2.90). Trains go through these towns to Linz (€11.60) and Vienna (4hr., €30.50). **Buses** leave the station (☎ 231 13; desk open M-F 8am-4pm) for Salzburg (1½hr., every hr. 5:50am-10:50pm, €7.27) and St. Wolfgang (40min., every hr. 6:42am-6:15pm, €3.10). By **car,** Bad Ischl lies on Rte. 158 and 145. From Innsbruck or Munich, take A1 East past Salzburg and exit onto Rte. 158 near Thalgau. From Salzburg, take Rte. 158 through St. Gilgen and Fuschl. From Vienna, take A1 West to Rte. 145 at Regau.

◪ ◨ ORIENTATION AND PRACTICAL INFORMATION

Though one of the only towns in the Salzkammergut not on a lake, Bad Ischl lies at the junction of the **Traun** and **Ischl** rivers, which form a horseshoe around the city. The **tourist office** is on Bahnhofstr. 6. From the station, turn left on Bahnhofstr. The office has lists of *Pensionen* and *Privatzimmer* and an excellent free map, as well as a free phone to call hotels. Also available are free guided tours (1hr.), leaving from the Trinkhalle on Sundays at 10am and Thursdays at 4pm. (☎ 277 57. Open mid-June to Sept. M-F 9am-6pm, Sa 9am-3pm, Su 10am-1pm; Oct. to mid-June M-F 9am-5pm, Sa 9am-noon.) **Salzkammergut-Touristik,** Götzstr. 12, the regional tourist office, is also a great resource for information, places to stay, and bike rental (mountain bike €13 per day, city bike €10 per day). From the station, turn right down Bahnhofstr. and turn left onto Götzstr., just before you get to the river. (☎ 24 00 00. **Internet** access 1€ for 10min. Open daily 9am-8pm.) Other services include: an **ATM** at Oberbank on Franz Josef Str.; **lockers** at the train station (€1.50-2.50); **public restrooms** at the train station; **Kurapotheke** pharmacy, Kreuzpl. 18. (☎ 232 05. Open 8am-noon, 2-6pm, and for emergencies.) The **post office,** down Bahnhofstr., is on the corner of Auböckpl. by the Trinkhalle. (**Internet** access €2.50 for 35min., €4.50 per hr. Open M-F 8am-6pm, Sa 9am-noon.) **Postal Code:** A-4820.

⌂ ACCOMMODATIONS

Every guest who stays the night in Bad Ischl pays a *Kurtax,* which entitles you to a guest card (June to mid-Sept. €1.50 per person per night; Oct.-May €1). The card lists sights that grant reductions for cardholders, like the Lehar Museum and the Fotomuseum of Kaiserina Elisabeth.

Jugendgästehaus (HI), Am Rechensteg 5 (☎ 265 77; fax 265 77 75). From the tourist office, walk left on Bahnhofstr., turn right on Franz Josef Str., and keep going until you see the "*Jugendgästehaus*" sign to the left, after the bend to the right. Minutes from the

Kaiser's summer residence, this clean, dorm-style hostel offers mostly quads, each with its own bathroom. Its location next to a water park can be a curse or a blessing in the summer months, when the gleeful squeals of children pour through the open windows. Breakfast is included and served early in the morning (7:30-8:30am). Reception 8am-1pm and 5-7pm. Quiet hour 10pm. Check-out 9am. Reservations recommended. 4-bed dorms €13; doubles €19; singles €26.50. HI membership required. MC/V. ❸

Villa Dachstein, Rettenbachweg (☎23 151; www.villadachstein.at) Five minutes from the train station, take a right on Bahnhofstr. and head straight. On the other side of the river, take a right onto the footpath, which heads steeply uphill after going under the railroad bridge. For a restful stay, this villa not only has great views of Bad Ischl, but also offers spacious rooms. The charming breakfast room complete with two antique stoves lends the place lots of character. Breakfast included. €32-35 per person. ❹

Hotel Stadt Salzburg, Salzburger Str. 25 (☎235 64; stadt-salzburg@eunet.at). From the train station, head left down Bahnhofstr., right on Franz Josef Str., and then left through Kreuzpl. to Salzburger Str. At the higher end of the price spectrum, this 3-star hotel offers such luxuries as a sauna and terrace. TV, bar, and safe in each room. Catering to the fish-loving demographic, the hotel offers special fly-fishing programs. Breakfast included. Singles €42; doubles €70. MC/V. ❹

Haus Stadt Prag, Eglmoosg. 9 (☎/fax 236 16). From the train station, go left on Bahnhofstr., right on Franz Josef Str., and left on Kreuzpl. until it becomes Salzburgerstr.; follow the signs from there. This bright pension provides comfortable and spacious rooms with balconies, which are alive with plantlife. Breakfast included. All rooms with bath and TV. Singles €30; doubles €56. MC/V. ❸

SALZBURGER LAND

❂ FOOD

Restaurants are not difficult to find, and *Eis* (ice cream) stands are practically more numerous than people. As an alternative to eating out, the **Konsum grocery store** is conveniently located at Auböckpl. 12, behind the Trinkhalle. (Open M-F 7:30am-6:30pm, Sa 7:30am-5pm.) Browse the **open-air market** held every Friday morning on Salinenpl. and Sunday on the Esplanade of the Traun River.

Konditorei Zauner, Pfarrg. 7 (☎235 22). This crowded eatery is almost as famous as the Kaiser himself. Established in 1832, Zauner has an international reputation for heavenly sweets and *Tortes*. Enjoy the royal treatment in the pink-walled sitting room, complete with marble floors and brass chandeliers, and treat yourself to their extravagant desserts (most around €2.80) and *Eis* creations. Open 8:30am-6pm. MC/V. ❷

Bistro Oriental, Kreuzpl. 13. At the turn-off, look to your left behind the building on Franz Josef Str. This modern café serves fresh and flavorful kebabs (€3.30) and has several vegetarian delights. Open daily 10am-10pm. ❷

China Restaurant Happy Dragon, Pfarrg. 2 (☎234 32), just off of the intersection of Pfarrg. and Wirestr. on the river side, is one of the most pleasant places to eat along the river. Chinese standards like sweet-and-sour pork go for around €7-8. Dinners €10-13. Open daily 11:30am-3pm and 6-11pm. MC/V. ❷

Gasthaus zu Bürgerstub'n, Kreuzpl. 7 (☎235 68), just up the street from Bistro Oriental. The restaurant, secluded from the main street in a courtyard, offers traditional Austrian dishes in a relaxed setting. Try the house specialty featuring 3 different types of fish fillet (€12). Open M-W and Sa 10am-3pm, Th-F 10am-3pm and 6-10pm. MC/V. ❷

Gasthaus Sandwirt, Eglmoosg. 4 (☎264 03), just up the street from Haus Stadt Prag. For good deals on a sit-down meal, come to this local bar/restaurant hidden in a residential neighborhood at the edge of town. The extensive menu offers both Austrian and Italian dishes (€4-20). For dessert, join in Bad Ischl's love for Kaiserin Elizabeth by ordering her favorite dish, *Coupe Sisi*, a sundae with vanilla, chocolate, and hazelnut ice cream doused in chocolate liqueur (€4.30). Live Austrian music Th-Su 10-11:30 pm. Open M-W and F-Su 11am-1:30pm and 5-9pm, Th 11am-1:30pm. MC/V. ❷

🔍 SIGHTS

Other than the baths, Bad Ischl's main attractions are the Hapsburgs' cultural and architectural legacies, including the Kaiservilla and Pfarrkirche. For those eager to engage the outdoors, the Siriuskogl hike (30min.) lets you see it all from above.

VILLAS. In 1854, Austria's last empress received the **Kaiservilla** as a wedding present from her mother-in-law. Though she didn't care for the place, her husband Emperor Franz Josef designated it as his family's summer getaway. Enjoy strolling the beautifully groomed grounds. Inside the villa is the desk where Franz Josef signed the declaration of war against Serbia that led to WWI. In addition, his vast collection of mounted chamois horns (over 2000) still graces the walls in his wing of the house. Entrance is allowed only through a guided tour in German, with text available in English and 10 other languages. *(Just off Franz Josef Str.* ☎ *232 41. Open May to mid-Oct. daily 9-11:45am and 1-5:15pm. Tickets can be bought at the entrance to the park. €9.50, students €4.50, children €4.)* Also within the Kaiserpark, you'll find the ivy-covered **Marmorschlößl**, which houses a Photo Museum of Hapsburg family photos and temporary exhibitions. *(*☎ *244 22. Open Apr.-Oct. daily 9:30am-5pm. €1.50, children €0.70, family card €3.)* The **Lehár Villa,** Lehárkai 8, former summer home of Franz Lehár, longtime Bad Ischl resident and composer of *The Merry Widow*, is worth a visit. From Bahnhofstr., continue straight until you hit the river and esplanade, then take Grazerstr. across the river and turn left. *(*☎ *269 92. Open May-Sept. 10am-5pm. Obligatory tour in German and English €4.50, students and children €2.)*

PARISH CHURCH AND ORGAN. The **Stadtpfarrkirche** houses gorgeous wall paintings and the magnificent late-Baroque **Kaiserjubiläumsorgel** (Emperor's Jubilee Organ). To get there, turn left out of the tourist office, then right onto Franz Josef Str.; the church will be on your left. Empress Maria Theresia had it built in place of the original Gothic building, whose tower still stands behind the church. Don't miss the ceiling frescoes depicting the life of St. Nicholas. Its open, light-flooded interior and acoustics are equally breathtaking. Check in front of the church for organ performance times (free).

SALT BATHS. Whether or not the **brine baths** that Dr. Wirer promoted really have curative powers, they certainly relieve stress. The bath facilities are mostly in the posh **Kaiser Therme,** a resort across from the tourist office on Bahnhofstr. 1. Children can play in the large heated indoor/outdoor pool and watch the television projected on the white wall. (Note that there is no lifeguard on duty.) Splash around in the heated salt baths with whirlpools or relax in the spacious **sauna.** Massages, mud baths, and other services are more expensive, but are sure to soothe both body and soul. *(*☎ *23 32 40. Baths with whirlpool open 9am-10pm; €10, children €6. Sauna open Su-Tu 1:30-10pm; Tu men only, Th women only; 3hr. €14, children €8. Massages, etc. M-Sa 8am-noon or by appointment.)*

🏔 OUTDOOR ACTIVITIES

For hiking and biking, pick up free maps of local paths from the *Salzkammergut* tourist office, though a more detailed biking map is available for €10.80. For a good place to start hiking, head to the summit of nearby **Mt. Katrin**

(1544m). Get to the **Katrinseilbahn** cable car (☎237 88; 12min.; 1 per hr. mid-May to Oct. daily 9am-5pm; ascent €12, children €8) by taking a city bus (€2.90) from the train station (€1.30, day pass €2.20, family day pass €2.90) or by walking 30min. on the extension of Bahnhofstr. along the Esplanade, Kaltenbachstr., and Dumbastr. For a shorter Bad Ischl-based hike, try the **Siriuskogl hike** (20-30min.), which requires no cable car and rewards hikers with a wondrous, panoramic view of Bad Ischl and its environs. To begin, exit the tourist office to the right, walk toward the train station, walk right across the river, and continue over the bridge on the right onto Grazerstr. Turn left onto Siriuskoglg., and follow the sign "Zum Siriuskogl." After passing through the outskirts of Bad Ischl, stick to the main trail to the top, about 30min. from the base. For refreshments, **Gasthaus Siriuskogl** is situated on the summit. It's a small restaurant that serves primarily cold dishes. (☎258 36. Open May-Oct. daily 10am-10pm.) In winter, Bad Ischl maintains an extensive network of **cross-country ski** trails (free maps at the tourist office). The bus to the Katrinseilbahn also leads to trails around the Kaltenbach. Rettenbach, a cross-country ski area that is not accessible by bus, is 7km northwest of town.

🎵 ENTERTAINMENT

For the most up-to-date information on Bad Ischl performing arts events, pick up the brochure *Bad Ischl Events* from the tourist office. Free outdoor **Kurkonzerte** take place twice per day (10am and 4pm) between May and October at the *Kurpark* along Wienerstr. or in the *Trinkhalle*, depending on the weather. The exact program of performances by the 20-piece *Kurorchestra* or quartet is posted weekly on kiosks, in the hotels, and at the *Kurhaus* itself. Every year in mid-August, the **Bad Ischler Stadtfest** brings a weekend of music—classical, pop, jazz, boogie-woogie, and oompah. Immediately after the Stadtfest on August 18, the Bad Ischlers celebrate Franz Josef's birthday with live music on the Esplanade. In July and August, the **Bad Ischl Operetten Festspiele** celebrates the musical talent of composer Franz Lehár with regular performances of several operettas. Tickets are available from the Büro der Operettengemeinde Festspiele, Kurhausstr. 8, A-4820 Bad Ischl. (☎238 39; www.operette.badischl.at. Open daily July 9am-6pm; Aug.-June 9am-3pm.) From May to October a **flea market** comes to the Esplanade on the first Saturday morning of the month. At Christmastime, Bad Ischl indulges in all sorts of Yuletide festivities, including a **Christkindlmarkt** (Christmas market), Advent caroling in the *Kurhaus*, tours of elaborate **Weihnachtskrippen** (nativity scenes) in the area, and horse-drawn sleigh rides *(Pferdeschliffen)*.

🔅 DAYTRIP FROM BAD ISCHL

GMUNDEN ☎07612

Only 1 train goes through Gmunden, running from Attnang-Pucheim in the north to Stainach-Irding in the south. The town is best done as a day (or slightly longer) trip from Bad Ischl (€5) or Hallstatt (€7.40). Within the city, the streetcar line runs from the train station to the lake (Franz Josef Pl.), with a stop at the ceramics factory. Due to renovations, in 2005 the streetcar may follow only ½ its route. If the car stops before the lake, follow the driver and other passengers to the bus that will continue to the center of town. By car from Salzburg, take A1 east and exit onto 145 at Regau. From Vienna, take A1 west and exit onto 144 at Steyermuhl.

Situated at the edge of the clean and cold Traunsee, Gmunden is well known for its castles, green-and-white ceramics, and beautiful mountain scenery. The city began as a Celtic settlement, and records of it date back to the year AD 909. The **ceramics factory** itself, known as the Gmunden Keramik Manufacture, is the best place to buy its work and offers guided tours. *(Keramikstr. 24. Take the streetcar to "Keramik."* ☎ *786 39. Tours M-Th 9am-2:30pm, F 9-11am; €3. Store open M-F 9am-6pm, Sa 9am-1pm.)* Ceramic creations dotting the town include the bells hanging in the town hall and the fountain in Rinnholz Square. The best place to see true masterpieces, however, is the **Galerie Schloß Weyer,** a museum dedicated to Meissner porcelain (Gmunden's specialty) situated inside a small Renaissance castle. It has seven rooms of delicate figurines, elaborate table services, and opulent Oriental rugs. Head to the Grünberg *Seilbahn* and then continue on Freyg. for 300m. *(Freyg. 27.* ☎ *650 18; fax 656 05 31. Open Tu-F 10am-noon and 2-5:30pm, Sa 10am-1pm. €7.50.)* The picturesque **Seeschloß Ort** is worth a visit for its location out in the waters of the Traunsee. Walk down the Promenade away from the river, take the first street left, then follow the signs. Don't be surprised the scores of German tourists: this castle is the location of popular German TV show "Schloßhotel Ort." Unfortunately, the castle is not in fact a hotel, and you can't go inside any of its rooms.

The **Museum of Historical Sanitary Objects** offers a remarkable collection of sinks, toilets, and tubs. Highlights include a collapsible travel bidet and the bidet that belonged to Empress Elizabeth. The museum feeds into the **Volkskundemuseum,** a small exhibit of historical objects like umbrellas, pipes, and waffle irons. *(From Franz Josef Pl. continue in the direction of the streetcar and make a sharp left heading uphill before crossing the bridge. The museum will be on your right.* ☎ *79 44 25. Open May-Oct. Tu-Sa 10am-noon and 2-5pm, Su 10am-noon. €4, students under 18 €1, family ticket €3.)*

There are several places to rent **boats** along the Promenade, including F. Berger Bootverleih or Oberleitner. *(Electric boat €6 for 30min., €10.50 per hr.; pedal boat €4.50/€7.50; rowboat €3/€5.)* Visitors can take a ride on Europe's oldest paddle-driven **steamer,** *Gisela.* *(Tours leave from in front of the Rathaus, just beyond Franz Josef Pl. 50min. tours €7.50, children €5.50; 2½hr. €13.50/€10.50.)*

Gmunden's *Seilbahn* (cable car station) serves as a point of departure for several **hikes.** To get the cable car, head from Franz Josef Pl. past the *Rathaus* and across the bridge. When the road branches, head to the right and continue for 10min. on this street, making a left onto Freyg. The *Seilbahn* will be on the right. From the Grünberg, numerous trails branch off and lead throughout the nature preserve toward neighboring towns. Pick up a hiking map for free at the tourist office (only available in German), or purchase a more detailed one for €2.20 at the gondola. *(Gondola open daily July-Aug. 8:30am-6pm; May-June and Sept.-Oct. 8:30am-5pm. €7.20, children €4.20; round-trip €16/€6.)* For a day hike, consider heading from the Grünberg down to Laudachsee and then back through the woods and fields to Gmunden via Franzl im Holz. This 2-3hr. hike offers you a wonderful view of the valley as well as a peaceful resting point at the Laudachsee. The trail is well-marked and mostly flat or downhill.

To get to the **tourist office** from the train station, take the streetcar to the end of the line. Backtrack along the streetcar's route away from the bustling town center along the lake for 10min. The office will be on the left. The new tourist office opened in March of 2004 and can be found at Toscana Parkplatz 1. The staff is informative and speaks English. (☎ 643 05; www.traunsee.at. **Internet** available. Open July-Aug. M-F 8am-9pm, Sa-Su 10am-8pm; May-June and Sept.-Oct. M-F 8am-6pm, Sa 9am-1pm, Su 10am-3pm; Nov.-Apr. M-Th 8am-1pm and 2-6pm, F 8am-1pm and 2-5pm, Sa 9am-1pm.) There is a secondary tourist office located in the city center in the *Rathaus* (town hall; ☎ 21 33). Both offices have a computer outside that contains useful accommodation, restaurant, and historical information.

For overnight stays, pick up a list of *Privatzimmer* at the tourist office. One good option is **Haus Reier ❷**, Freyg. 20. Walk to the Grünberg *Seilbahn* and then continue 100m along Freyg. The house is on the right. (☎/fax 724 25. Singles €25. Discounts available for longer stays.)

GRÜNAU   ☎07616

Sitting in the middle of the **Totes Gebirge** (Dead Mountains), Grünau is a tiny community in a rugged outdoor environment ideal for hiking, skiing, boating, fishing, swimming, and relaxing.

The town is best experienced from **The Treehouse ❷**, Schindlbachstr. 525, a backpacker's dream resort. Each room has its own bathroom with private shower and goose-down blankets. Call ahead to have one of the staff pick you up at the train station free of charge—otherwise it is more than a 1hr. walk left down Schindlbachstr. from the town center. Manager Gerhard and his wife encourage you to make yourself at home and take advantage of its facilities: TV room with hundreds of recently released English-language movies, sauna, basketball court, pool tables, and tennis courts (all free of charge, equipment provided), plus two bars for nighttime revelry. (☎84 99; www.treehousehostel.net. **Internet** access €0.10 per min. **Mountain bike** rental €8 per day. Breakfast buffet included. 3-course dinner €7. 6-bed dorm €14.50; doubles €37; triples €52.50; quads €66. AmEx/MC/V.)

To help its guests enjoy the mountains, the Treehouse staff organizes adventure tours, including **canyoning** (€50, not in winter, 8 people min.), **bungee jumping** (€95, only on weekends), and **horseback riding** (€10 per hr.). For **hiking,** a free map available at the tourist office or the Treehouse helps to navigate the mountains and three lakes in the vicinity. For a day hike, walk to the Kasberg (1500m, round-trip, 7hr.) or for a half-day to the Spitzplaneck (1617m, 4-5hr.). The more adventurous may try the longer hike to Große Priel (2515m), which can also be a two-day trek with a mountain hut stay (€10; ask the Treehouse staff for info).

In Grünau, there are 40km of **ski** slopes accessed by 14 lifts. The new cable car, a 5min. walk from the hostel, makes reaching the 44 slopes quick and easy. The Treehouse loans snow apparel (jackets, snowsuits, gloves, etc.) to its guests for free. Day ski-lift passes are €21 (for Treehouse guests), while ski and snowboard rental from the base runs €13. A ski school charges €37 per day for skiing lessons and €44 for snowboarding. (☎/fax 89 01. Open daily Oct.-Apr. 9am-4pm.)

A small regional **train** runs to Grünau from Wels (1hr.; 5:47am-8:48pm; €6.50, discounts available for groups) which can be reached via Salzburg, Linz, or Vienna. A **bus** runs frequently from Rathauspl. in Gmunden to the Grünau town center and train station (45min.; M-F 8 per day, Sa-Su 3 per day 5:35am-5:20pm; €3.60). The **tourist office** is on the right, across the street from the town center's bus stop. The staff hands out free maps of Grünau and lists of *Pensions* in the area. (Open M-F 9am-noon and 2-5pm, Sa 9am-noon.)

ST. WOLFGANG   ☎06138

This cozy lakeside village, once the site of mass pilgrimage, is now the definition of a resort town. Bishop Wolfgang of Regensburg built a celebrated church here on the Abersee (now the Wolfgangsee) in AD 976. After his canonization, the church he built became a medieval pilgrimage site. Today the town welcomes present-day pilgrims of the camcorder- and fannypack-toting variety. Many vacationers spend a week or longer relaxing in lakeside hotels. During the summer months, some 2000 visitors pass through St. Wolfgang, admiring the bright blue waters and striking mountain scenery, as well as the winding cobblestone streets and excitement of the **Schafbergbahn** (steam engine station).

SALZBURGER LAND

▛ TRANSPORTATION

The town has no train station, but **buses** run every hour to and from Bad Ischl (40min.; M-F 5:05am-8:13pm, Sa 6:02am-8:13pm, Su 9:13am-8:13pm; €3) and from there you can catch a bus to Salzburg. The Wolfgangsee **ferry** (☎223 20) runs to nearby St. Gilgen (45min., 9:15am-3:15pm, €5) and Strobl (30min.; 8:20am-7pm; €4, children half-price, Eurail valid). From Vienna by **car,** take A1 West to Mondsee and head south through St. Lorenz and Scharfling. From Salzburg, take Rte. 158 east through Hof, Fuschl, and St. Gilgen.

▛ ▛ ORIENTATION AND PRACTICAL INFORMATION

St. Wolfgang is a lovely place to get lost in, which is fortunate, since street names are difficult to find and maps are as rare as they are indecipherable. Nature itself comes in handy. The lake and the mountain on either side of St. Wolfgang form natural boundaries to the south and north respectively. The town is basically one long strip of buildings running from east to west. Along this strip, there are three bus stops: "St. Wolfgang Au," "St. Wolfgang Markt," and "St. Wolfgang Schafbergbahn." For the town center, get off at "St. Wolfgang Markt" and walk uphill, staying to the right at Pilgerstr. as you go around the bend. For those arriving via ferry, disembark at the "St. Wolfgang Markt" bus stop and head up the Promenade to the left for the town center. The main **tourist office,** Au 140, is a few steps away from the "St. Wolfgang Au" stop, but to get there from town walk 5min. uphill from the church on M. Pacher Str. (☎80 03; www.wolfgangsee.at. Open June-Sept. M-F 9am-7pm, Sa 9am-noon; Oct.-May M-F 9am-noon and 1-6pm, Sa 9am-noon.) Services include: **ATMs** in the tourist office; **public bathrooms** near the bus stop "St. Wolfgang Markt" (€0.50); and **pharmacy** Apotheke Zum Hl Wolfgang near Hotel Peter on M. Pacher Str. (☎33 37. Open M-F 8am-12:30pm and 2:30-6pm, Sa 8am-noon, Su 9-11am, and for emergencies.) For the **post office,** turn left from the church toward the Schafbergbahn. The post office will be on the right. (☎22 01. Open June-Sept. M-F 8am-noon and 2-5pm; Oct.-May M-Tu and Th-F 8am-noon and 2-5pm, W 8am-noon.) **Postal Code:** A-5360.

▛ ACCOMMODATIONS AND CAMPING

With so many tourists passing through town, finding a bed can be tough. Between June and September, calling ahead is crucial. The tourist office provides a brochure listing hotels, *Pensionen*, and *Privatzimmer.* Many private homes open to tourists in the summer months; look for the red and white "Zimmer Frei" flags signaling a spare bed.

Haus am See, M. Pacher Str. 98 (☎22 24), across the street from the tourist office, behind a cluster of large trees. 40 beds in a sprawling old house 150 ft. above the lake. The rooms are clean and the view is fantastic (most rooms have balconies). The house itself is charmingly masculine with deer antlers adorning the foyer. Breakfast included. Hall showers. Parking available. Open June-Sept. Prices depend on balcony and view. Boathouse at the lake's edge sleeps 12 at €20 per person. 5-person dorms €11; singles €15-20; doubles €30-44; quads €59-88. Surcharge for 1-night stays. ❷

Strandhotel Margaretha, Margarethenstr. 67 (☎23 79; hotelf@wolfgangsee.com). Just beyond the Schafbergbahn outside of town, this perfectly placed hotel offers wonderful opportunities to enjoy the idyllic scenery, including a lakeside deck and free use of the hotel's rowboat and bicycles. Doubles €50-80. Singles available on request for about €60. All rates depend on duration of stay, view, and time of year. AmEx/MC/V. ❹

Haus Reif, Sternalle 143 (☎/fax 22 15; www.tiscover.at/gaestehaus.reif). From the bus stop "St. Wolfgang Markt," head downhill and take the 1st right at the flashing light. Haus Reif will be on your right. The black and white home literally blooms with color—its manicured lawn and the verse painted above the front door make it easy to spot. Head up the marble staircase to large rooms, all with toilet and balcony. Breakfast included. Singles €25-27; doubles €30-35. ❸

Pension Raudaschl, Deschbühel Au 41 (☎25 61). From the tourist office, walk toward town past the parking lot and turn uphill at Hotel Peter heading toward the cluster of black and white houses. This smaller *Pension,* on the way to the major hiking paths, offers 7 rooms, many with private wooden balconies and baths. Breakfast included. Open May-Oct. Singles €22; doubles €44. Add 20% for 1-night stays. ❸

Camping Appesbach, Au 99 (☎22 06; fax 22 06 03). From the tourist office, walk down M. Pacher Str. away from town for about 1km and then turn left onto Au. For the appropriately equipped, this lakeside field is ideal. Parking available. Use of the beach and warm showers included. Open May-Oct. €5 per adult, €3 per child, €4 per space. ❶

SALZBURGER LAND

🍴 FOOD

Most of St. Wolfgang's restaurants and *Imbiße* (little cafés) are rather expensive. Snack shacks selling sausages and fries (€2-5) line M. Pacher Str. Sit down at **Gasthof Franz Josef ❷**, at the St. Wolfgang Markt ferry landing (at the church, head downhill to the left), for vegetarian entrées, which run €5.50-6.50. (Open Easter-Sept. 11am-9pm. MC/V.) In any direction along M. Pacher Str. within a 5min. walk of the church are restaurants to appease all appetites. *Konditoreien* (cake shops) serve up local specialty *Schafbergkugeln,* also known as *Mozartkugeln* (about €1.70), a tennis-ball-sized hunk of milk chocolate filled with cream, spongecake, nuts, and marzipan. Pick one up at **Bäckerei Gandl,** Im Stöckl 84, across from the post office. (☎22 94. Open M-Sa 6:30am-6pm, Su 7am-1pm.) The **SPAR** on Pilgerstr. sells standard groceries. At the church, turn right toward the Schafbergspitze. (Open M-Tu and Th-F 7:30am-noon and 2-6pm, W 7am-noon, Sa 7am-6pm.)

👁 SIGHTS

WALLFAHRTSKIRCHE (PILGRIMAGE CHURCH). St. Wolfgang's main attraction, the Wallfahrtskirche, is in the Marktpl. The church's interior is unbelievably ornate. The masterful altarpiece, completed by Michael Pacher in 1480 after a decade of fine crafting and detailing, opens like a heavenly portal to reveal the coronation of Mary, complete with trumpeting angels. The golden Gothic spires extending above the coronation scene cleverly direct the viewer's awe, either to the newly-crowned Mary or the heavens. The Baroque Schwanthaler Altar, installed in the center of the nave in 1676, was originally made to replace Pacher's, but the sculptor Thomas Schwanthaler bravely persuaded the abbot to leave Pacher's masterpiece alone. Together the altars almost overwhelm the church—don't miss smaller treasures like Schwanthaler's *Rosenkranzaltar* (Rose Garland Altar) or the St. Wolfgang memorial room. To see the breadth of St. Wolfgang's attractions in under 30min., take a carriage ride (25min., €19) from the church. *(Turn right out of the tourist office and head straight down the road, M. Pacher Str.)*

SCHAFBERGBAHN. St. Wolfgang's other major attraction is the **Schafbergbahn,** a romantic steam engine that slowly ascends to the summit of Schafberg 1734m above sea level. The railway was built in 1892, and Hollywood found it charming enough to merit a cameo in *The Sound of Music.* From the top, dozens of trails wind down the mountain, leading to nearby towns St. Gilgen, Ried, and Falkenstein. Tickets for the 40min. ride run as steep as the mountain. (☎ 223 20; www.schafbergbahn.at. May-Oct. every hr. 9am-6pm; ascent €13, half-way €10, round-trip €22; children 6-15 half-price. Eurail valid.) If you pay full price, you might as well take advantage of the deal offered by the ▨ **Berghotel Schafberg- spitze ❹** (☎ 35 42; fax 354 24), a lovely mountain inn peeking over the Schaf- berg's steepest face. For €48 per person, you get a round-trip ticket on the railway, a room (with shower), and breakfast. Reserve in advance and pay at the Schafbergbahn station.

🔦 🎵 OUTDOORS AND ENTERTAINMENT

The clear *Wolfgangsee* is great for water sports. Facing the church, turn right and walk 5min. down Pilgerstr. for **public lake** access. **Waterskiing** is available through **Stadler** on the *Seepromenade* near the Schafbergbahn. (☎ 066 44 01 75 36; €10 per circuit.) Rent **boats** in town at the landing near Marktpl. and at the *Seepromenade*. (Motor boats €8 per 30min., €14 per hr.; pedal boats €8 per hr.) **Hiking** trails are clearly marked from town; maps from the tourist office cost €1.20-6.40. Try **Vormauerweg** ("C," marked near Pension Raudaschl, about a 90min. walk) to **Vormauerstein**, a 1450m peak overlooking the lake. Return over Aschau by Sommerauweg 28 to make a complete loop (4-4½hr.). **Bike rent- als** are available from **Pro Travel Agency** by the *Markt* ferry landing. (☎ 252 50. Open daily 9am-6pm. €9 per day. Lock and helmet included.) On a weekend evening in St. Wolfgang, catch a production of Ralph Benatzky's *Im Weißen Rössl* (White Horse Inn) at Michael-Pacher-Haus, the city theater. (☎ 80 03. Performed in German late May to mid-Sept. F 8:30pm. Tickets at the White Horse Inn, or from box office; €14, children €8.)

MONDSEE ☎ 06232

This colorful one-street town's position on the Salzkammergut's warmest lake makes it a relaxing getaway from the bustle of Salzburg. Mondsee (named "moon lake" after its crescent-shaped body of water) offers numerous hiking and biking opportunities as well as less strenuous amusement in the Schloßgalerie's art exhibits. The newly renovated Alpenseebad (beach), where you can fly down the giant waterslide or laze on the sandy beach, is situated against a lovely backdrop.

▐ TRANSPORTATION. Mondsee has no train station but is accessible by **bus** from Salzburg's Hauptbahnhof (50min., 1-2 per hr. 6:40am-8:30pm, €4.60) and from Vienna, Wien-Mitte (4hr., Apr.-Oct. M-Sa 7:30am, Nov.-Mar. M-F 7:30am). Buses run to St. Gilgen on the Wolfgangsee (20min., M-F 6:25, 8:40, 11:50am, 6:55, and 7:15pm, Sa 11:50am; €2.60). By **car**, take *Autobahn* A1 or the more scenic Rte. 158 from Salzburg to St. Gilgen and then Rte. 154 along the lake to Mondsee.

▧ ▐ ORIENTATION AND PRACTICAL INFORMATION. To reach the **tourist office,** Dr.-Franz-Müllerstr. 3, head up the road from the bus stop, turn right onto Rainerstr., and continue to Marktpl. Turn right again; the office is on the left. A box in front of the office contains maps of Mondsee. (☎ 22 70; info@mondsee.at.org. Open July-Aug. daily 8am-7pm; June and Sept. M-F 8am-noon and 1-5pm, Sa 9am- noon and 3-6pm; Oct.-May M-F 8am-noon and 1-5pm.) **ATMs** are at the Volksbank by the tourist office, at the Raiffeisenbank on Rainerstr., and at the Salzburger Sparkasse on Marktpl. The **post office,** on Franz-Kreuzbergerstr., is across from the bus station. (☎ 266 50. Open M-Th 8am-noon and 2-5:30pm, F 8am-12:30pm and 2-5:30pm; exchange closes at 5pm.) **Postal code:** A-5310.

⚑ ACCOMMODATIONS. *Gasthöfe* and hotels crowd the area near Marktpl., and *Privatzimmer* hang *Zimmer Frei* signs. The tourist office lists available rooms.

Pension Klimesch, M. Guggenbichler-str. 13 (☎25 63). Walk toward the lake from the bus station, take a left onto Atterseestr., then a right onto Guggenbichler-str.; it will be to the left. This well-kept Pension, close to the lake, has 15 cheery rooms up a steep flight of stairs, a common room with a TV, and feather comforters. The friendly hostess offers a generous breakfast on her back patio, weather permitting. Breakfast included. Singles from €24-28; doubles €52. ❸

Jugendgästehaus (HI), Krankenhausstr. 9, (☎24 18; jgh.mondsee@oejhv.or.at). Go up Kreuzbergerstr. from the bus station, right on Rainerstr., and left onto Steinerbachstr. After 150m, where the street branches, follow Krankenhausstr. around the bend to the left; the hostel is hidden off a driveway to the left. Slightly off the main drag, you can find a place to crash in this retro-style hostel, with wood paneling and orange and brown decor. The hostel serves lunch and dinner (€5) and has reading corners with newspapers and games. Often filled with groups, so call ahead. Breakfast buffet included. Reception M-F 8am-1pm and 5-7pm, Sa-Su 5-7pm. Check-in 5-10pm, check-out by 9am. Closed Jan. 15-Feb. 15. Dorms €13.80; singles with bath €27.30; doubles €31-€38.20; quads €56-€66.40. Non-members pay €3.50 surcharge. MC/V. ❸

Hotel Leitnerbräu, Steinerbachstr. 6 (☎65 00; www.leitnerbraeu.at). Heading up Rainerstr., turn left onto Steinbachstr. A typical mint-on-the-pillow, all-the-corners-tucked-in-perfectly kind of place. The friendly staff, soothing pale green decor, and unlimited use of a fitness room, sauna, and steam bath make a stay here truly relaxing. Breakfast and **Internet access** included. Parking €8 per day. Whirlpool €8.90. Singles €70-85; doubles €115-160. AmEx/MC/V/D. ❸

⟁ FOOD. Marktpl. is full of restaurants and *Gasthöfe* serving Austrian and Italian fare. The **Konsum,** across from Rainerstr. 15, sells groceries. (Open M-F 7:30am-7pm, Sa 7:30am-5pm.) A **farmers' market** comes to Marktpl. Saturdays May-Sept.

Jedermanns, Marktpl. 9. Serves regional specialties such as *Kaiserschmarren* (similar to French toast) as well as salads and pasta. Try the salmon fillet (€13.50). *Rindsgulyas* €6-8. Open Tu-Su 9am-11pm. Closed Nov. MC/V/D. ❷

Blaue Traube, Marktpl. 1 (☎22 37), specializes in Austrian cuisine. Most entrées €6-10; prices remain the same for the lunch menu, with a wide selection including dishes like *Mondseer Kasspatzen* with caramelized onion (€5.96). Open 9am-11pm. ❸

Krone Restaurant, Rainerstr. 1, directly across from the tourist office. The patio is ideal for a leisurely summer meal. Offers local and international food. Fillet of pork with vegetable risotto (€12.40) and Swiss-style sausage salad (€3.60). Open daily 11am-11pm; full menu 11am-2pm and 5pm-11pm, lunch menu 2-5:30pm. AmEx/MC/V. ❸

◧ ⚞ ⟐ SIGHTS, OUTDOOR ACTIVITIES, AND ENTERTAINMENT. Mondsee is the lake resort closest to Salzburg and has remained one of the least touristy, despite tour buses that roll in to see the local **Pfarrkirche,** on Markatpl., site of the wedding scene in *The Sound of Music*. The church connects to the remains of a Benedictine monastery from AD 748, over which the *Schloß* (castle) was built. The completely-renovated *Schloß* houses businesses, bars, and the **Schloßgalerie,** which displays temporary exhibits. (☎77 44. Open daily 11am-7pm. Free.) The open-air **Freilichtmuseum,** on Hilfbergstr., features a 500-year-old smokehouse, dairy, and farmhouse. (*Behind the church and uphill to the left. Open May-Aug. Su-Tu 10am-6pm; Sept.-Oct. Su-Tu 10am-5pm; Apr. and late Oct. Sa-Su only 10am-5pm. €2.20, children and students €1.10, seniors €1.90.*)

In summer, the *Mondsee* buzzes with activity, but not motor boats—motors are heavily restricted to protect wildlife. The newly renovated **Alpenseebad,** down Kreutzbergerstr. from the bus station, is the main **public beach.** (☎ *22 91. Open in fair weather May-Sept. 9am-6pm. €4.40, children and students €1.80.)* For waterskiers or wakeboarders, the **Wasserskizentrum** is inside the Seebad. (☎ *066 41 60 52 10. Rafting €12 per circuit, 2-person rafting same price; waterskiing €10 per circuit.)* Rent a **bike** at **Velofant,** next to the Seebad. *(Open May-Sept. daily 9:30am-7pm. Mountain bike €18 per day; road bike €13 per day).* Or, rent a **boat** from Peter Hemetsberger, owner of the **Kaipromenade**—just head down to the dock. (☎ *24 60. Rowboats and paddleboats €6 per 30min.; electric boats €8 per 30min.)* He also offers *Mondsee Schifffahrten,* boat rides around the lake. *(1hr.; 10:45am, 12:15, 1, 2, 3:30, 4:30, 5:30pm, or as requested. €6.90, children half price.)* You can pick up an extensive guide of day **hikes** at the tourist office. There's a 2hr. hike around the Mondseeberg: start behind the Pfarrkirche to the right, at the sign for "Hochalm-Oberwang."

Mondsee holds the **Mondseetage,** an annual classical music festival, September 3rd to 11th *(tickets range from €8-36 depending on seating).* Tickets can be ordered via the Mondseetage Bestellbüro (☎ *35 44; www.mondseetage.com).* Every year **Hugo von Hofmannsthal's** 1922 morality play, *Jedermann,* is performed (in German) at the open-air **Freilichtbühne** theater. (☎ *066 43 38 74 97. Performances mid-July to mid-Aug. Sa 8:30pm. Tickets start at €11-13; advance tickets available at Foto Schwaighofer, Rainerstr. 12.)*

HOHE TAUERN REGION

The enormous **Hohe Tauern** range extends well into Carinthia, Salzburg, Tyrol, and East Tyrol. Part of the Austrian Central Alps, it boasts 246 glaciers and 304 mountains over 3000m in height. Between 1958 and 1964, large tracts of mountain land in Salzburg and Carinthia were declared preserves. An agreement signed by the governing heads of Tyrol, Salzburg, and Carinthia on October 21, 1971, made **Hohe Tauern National Park** the largest national park in all of Europe. Officially, the park encloses 29 towns and 60,000 residents, though most of the territory is uninhabited. One of the park's main goals is preservation, so there are no large campgrounds or recreation areas within its borders. The best way to take advantage of this rare circumstance is by hiking one of the numerous trails, which range from pleasant ambles to mighty summit climbs attempted only by world-class mountaineers. The brochure *Natur Erlebnis* ("An Experience in Nature"), available at any park office and most area tourist offices, plots 84 different hikes and ascents on a map of the park and provides short descriptions of each hike. Appropriately, the founding papers for the park were signed in **Heiligenblut,** the most central town for visitors. **Zell am See** and **Lienz,** on either end of the **Großglocknerstraße,** are two of the larger towns, while tiny **Krimml** offers famous waterfalls.

HIGHLIGHTS OF THE HOHE TAUERN REGION

Make the trip between Lienz and Zell am See on the **Großglocknerstraße,** the world's most exciting highway (p. 266).

Sleep in the shadow of Austria's mightiest mountain, the Großglockner, in the tiny mountain town of **Heiligenblut** (p. 268).

Go skiing in August on the glacier above **Zell am See** (p. 273).

HOHE TAUERN NATIONAL PARK

Unlike national parks in other countries, the Hohe Tauern National Park is owned not by the government, but by a consortium of private farmers and members of the **Österreichischer Alpenverein** (**ÖAV;** Austrian Alpine Union). In

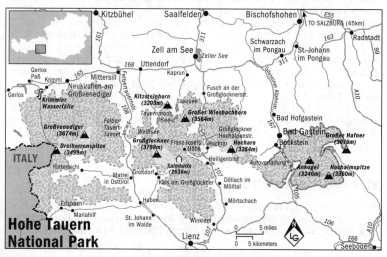

1914, the land enclosing the **Glockengruppe range** was actually for sale. Just as it was about to be sold to an individual who wanted to turn it into a private hunting ground, wealthy industrialist Albert Wirt bought it instead and donated it to ÖAV so that it could be enjoyed by all. The land remains privately owned and, with the exception of the park's mountainous center, many of its meadows and valleys are used for raising cattle or cutting timber. Farmers still herd their cattle over the same 2500m *Tauern* (ice-free mountain paths) once trod by Celts and Romans. The Glockergruppe, in the heart of the park, contains Austria's highest peak, the **Großglockner** (3798m), and many lakes and glaciers. The park is home to dozens of species of endangered alpine flowers (like the fiery *Almsrauch*, or "meadow smoke") and armies of marmots. The *Bartgeir* (bearded vulture) and the lyre-horned ibex were recently reintroduced after near extinction. A hair-raising drive—or a vigorous bike ride—down the Großglocknerstraße offers a beautiful, if summary, look at the peaks and valleys of the park. Rest stops dot the highway, providing vistas of valleys that can be explored only by foot.

ORIENTATION

The center of the park and BundesBus hub, above Heiligenblut, is **Franz-Josefs-Höhe** and the **Pasterze glacier** (p. 266). Aside from the skiing and hiking opportunities on these mammoths, the main attractions in the park are the **Krimml Waterfalls** (p. 278), just west of Zell am See, and the **Großglocknerstraße** (p. 266), a spectacular high mountain road that runs north-south through the center of the park, between Zell am See and Lienz, through the Franz-Josefs-Höhe.

TRANSPORTATION

Two **train** lines service towns near the park: one runs west from Zell am See along the northern border of the park, ending in Krimml (1½hr., 19 per day 6:06am-10:56pm, €6.80); another runs south from Salzburg to Bad Gastein in the southwest corner (1¾hr., 15 per day 7:13am-9:13pm, €11.10). The park itself is criss-crossed by **bus** lines, with some buses running infrequently and others changing schedules in early summer. Pick up a schedule in one of the tourist offices, then be sure to confirm with your driver when the next bus to your destination departs. Bus routes go through the center of the park at Franz-Josefs-Höhe. Buses run to Franz-Josefs-Höhe from Lienz via Heiligenblut (1½hr., €7.20 total fare), and from Zell am See (2hr., 2 per day 9:20am-12:20pm, €10). Return trips run to: Heiligenblut (30min.; 4 per day 9:30am-5:45pm, return 5 per day 9:30am-5:10pm; last trains for each trip M-F only; €3.60); Lienz (1½hr., 6-8 per day 6:19am-5:15pm, €7.20); Zell am See (2hr., 2 per day 11:45am-3:50pm, €10). It's either an 8km walk to Heiligenblut or an expensive cab ride if you miss the last bus. By **car** from Kitzbühel, take Bundesstr. 161 south to 108, which goes through the park. From Lienz, take Bundesstr. 107 or 108 north into the park. From Zell am See, take Bundesstr. 311 south to 107. In case of **breakdown,** call the ÖAMTC (☎120).

PARK INFORMATION

Because the park is distributed over three different provinces, the network of tourist information is decentralized. Check www.hohetauern.org, or talk to the park service branch closest to you. The **Kärnten (Carinthia) Park Office** is located at

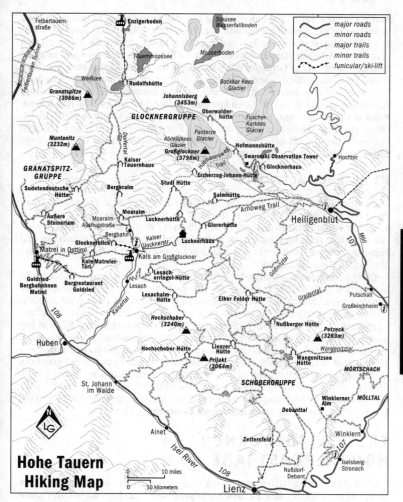

Hohe Tauern Hiking Map

Döllach 14 in Großkirchheim (☎ 048 25 61 61; fax 61 61 16), the **Tyrol office** is on Kirchpl. 2 in Matrei (☎ 04875 51 61; npht@tirol.gv.at), and the **Salzburg office** is on Grossvenediger 306 in Neukirchen (☎ 06565 65 58; fax 65 58 18).

ACCOMMODATIONS

Given that camping is forbidden in the park, visitors can either operate out of a nearby town or stay in any of numerous huts throughout the park. Zell am See and Lienz make good bases for exploring the park; Krimml, on the park's northern border, and Heiligenblut, smack in the middle, are smaller and closer. Bad Gastein provides both a central location close to the park and a rail line, making it especially convenient. Mountain huts are excellent places to rest, usually offering private rooms and dorms. A *Hauswirt* (caretaker) provides food. Bringing your own is frowned upon; if you do, make sure it's consumed elsewhere. A few *Hütten* are within a day's hike of Heiligenblut and provide intimate views of the Großglockner, including the **Salmhütte** (2644m, 6hr. hike from Heiligenblut or 2-3hr. hike from Glocknerhaus; accessible by car. (☎ 04824 20 89. Open mid-June to Sept.), and the **Glorerhütte** (2642m, 2hr. from Salmhütte. ☎ 0664 303 22 00. Open late June to late Sept.). The **Erzherzog-Johann-Hütte** is the highest and nearest to the Großglockner. (3454m. ☎ 04876 85 00. Open late June to late Sept.; by guide only.) For a list of huts pick up a *Hüttenführer* at any tourist office, and for more info, contact the ÖAV in Lienz (p. 279). Camping in the park is prohibited.

⚔ OUTDOOR ACTIVITIES

The best **cycling** in the area is on the **Tauernweg** from Krimml to Zell am See (then on to Salzburg), giving glimpses of the Hohe Tauern to the south. Tourist offices and www.tauernradweg.com have more info on the route. Every town has at least one store that rents bicycles; check with the local tourist office. Cyclists can also ride the grueling Großglocknerstraße, but be aware that bikes are not always allowed off the main highway.

Hiking trails head into isolated valleys from every road and town. With over 50 mountain huts in or near the park offering overnight stays, serious backpackers can lose themselves in the park for weeks at a time. To do so, pick up the *Hüttenführer* guide at any park office. The park's "An Experience in Nature" brochure suggests good hikes. Also essential are trail maps, which cost around €7.50 at any park office and give descriptions of popular hikes and cultural attractions along the trails. The park also leads daily guided tours along various trails (usually €6-10) detailed in the brochure. The program changes each summer, but generally includes hikes along the Geotrail Tauernfenster, the Pasterze glacier, and a wildlife trek. For Anglophones there is a good description of hikes on the park's website, but the best idea is to purchase a topographic map of the area and talk to the tourist office. For hiking safety advice, see **Essentials,** p. 44.

THE GROßGLOCKNER HOCHALPENSTRAßE

Each day more than 3000 visitors pack cars, motorcycles, and buses for a ride along the breathtaking **Großglockner Hochalpenstraße** ("Großglocknerstraße"), one of the most beautiful highways in the world. Skirting Austria's loftiest mountains, the Großglocknerstraße winds for 48km amid silent valleys, meadows of wildflowers, powerful waterfalls, and giant glaciers, between Heiligenblut and Bruck an der Großglockner. **Bundesstraßen 311** and **197** connect the official parts of the road to the larger towns of Zell am See and Lienz, respectively. These two highways are often unofficially considered part of the Großglocknerstraße, and are generally included in bus tours, along with a stop at Franz-Josefs-Höhe.

Although the entire length of the road is thrilling, there are several highlights. The climb as you approach the Hochtor (2505m, highest point on the Großglocknerstraße) takes you from abundant Alpine flora and fauna to chilly environments that are under 10ºC (50ºF) at night. On a clear day, time is best spent at **Franz-Josefs-Höhe,** enjoying the magnificent views. Don't miss the 1.2km Edelweißestraße spur, which runs by the **Edelweißspitze** (2571m).

Many visitors traverse the Großglocknerstraße in **tour buses** or **rental cars,** neither of which is recommended for those with light wallets or weak stomachs. **Public buses,** with their giant windows, serve as excellent tour buses at much lower prices, although their schedules can be inconvenient. If you only have one day, resist the urge to disembark at any of the smaller stops along the way—buses come so infrequently that you may be stuck for hours.

The full trip on Großglockner Hochalpenstraße, with scenic rest stops along the way, lasts about 2hr. (1hr. round-trip driving time). Between Lienz and Zell am See, it's about 4hr. (3hr. total driving time). Drivers must pay **tolls** at Ferleiten on the Zell am See side, or Roßbach on the Heiligenblut side (1-day pass €26, 1 month €32; motorcycles €17/€22). Parking at Franz-Josefs-Höhe is free upon entry. There are also parking and scenic pull-off areas along the road.

Be aware that the road is open only 5am-10pm mid-June to mid-September and 6am-8:30pm in May and June, with last entry 45min. before close. Snowfalls dumping up to 4m of heavy snow on the road force the Großglocknerstraße to close entirely from October to April. For info on **road conditions** call the Großglockner Hochalpenstraßen Aktiengesellschaft (GROHAG; ☎ 0662 873 67 30; www.grossglockner.at). Großglocknerstraße is not part of the National Park, nor under its auspices. Be aware of this when asking park volunteers about the road, or road officers about the park.

> **! DRIVING SAFETY TIPS.** Many first-time drivers of the Großglocknerstraße are tempted to lean heavily on the brakes, which can lead to brake failure and overheating. Instead, shift to low gear, drive slowly, and never, ever pass anyone.

⚠ ACTIVITIES ALONG THE GROßGLOCKNERSTRAßE

KAISER FRANZ-JOSEFS-HÖHE. Buses to Großglockner Hochalpenstraße from Zell am See, Lienz, and Heiligenblut finish their routes at Kaiser Franz-Josefs-Höhe, a large observation center stationed above the **Pasterze glacier.** Located on Gletscherstraße, an 8km spur off the Großglocknerstraße, the Kaiser Franz-Josefs-Höhe is packed with tour buses and camera-toting visitors spread over two levels of parking lots (with a free bus running between them every 10min.), but even they can't detract from the sight of the glacier's icy tongue extending down the valley. Unless it's shrouded in clouds, you can glimpse the towering summit of the Großglockner (3797m) on the left wall of the valley. Franz-Josefs-Höhe has its own **park office** at the beginning of the parking area, with a free mini-museum and Hohe Tauern information center. The staff also answers questions about availability and opening times of mountain huts in the vicinity. (☎ 04824 27 27. Open daily mid-May to mid-Oct. 10am-4pm.)

GLACIER FUNICULAR AND OBSERVATION CENTER. The **visitor center,** near the parking lots, has three floors devoted to the first ascent of the Großglockner, the geology of the mountain, free educational films, and panoramic views with labels on each mountain. (Open daily 10am-4pm. Free.) Take the elevator next to the visitor center or the winding road to the **Swarovski Observation Center** for an even better view, as well as brief but fun exhibits on park wildlife and glacier formation. Binoculars are available for viewing the surrounding terrain. If you're lucky, you might see some ibex chewing the grass on the mountain behind you. (Open daily 10am-4pm. Free.) The nearby **Gletscherbahn funicular** ferries you down from Franz-Josefs-Höhe close to the glacier. (☎ 04824 25 02. Runs mid-May to late Sept. daily 9am-4pm. Round-trip €7, children €5.50.) Or, hike down yourself (see **Hiking,** below). Catch the glacier while you can—it is receding an average of 20m per year.

HIKING. On any hike in the park, make sure to dress in layers–you should be prepared for rapid temperature changes (as much as 20°F in an hour). Information on more difficult hikes can be obtained from the park office; make sure to purchase a detailed trail map of the area *(ÖAV Map #40; €7.19).* **Guides** are available for hiking, climbing, or ski touring. *(Heiligenblut park office ☎ 04824 27 00; Heiligenblut Bergführerverein ☎ 04824 27 00.)* For a moderate hike, try the ▨**Gletscherweg** (3hr.). Heading down to the glacier (or coming up from it), follow the "Gletscherweg" sign. This varied trail leads away from the Pasterze glacier through an area that in decades past was covered in ice. The large piles of rock and dust—debris left behind by the glacier—will make you feel like you're walking on the moon. Later highlights include a glacier-fashioned sand lake and the reservoir where runoff from the icy mass still collects. The whole Hohe Tauern panorama comes into view on the descent to the reservoir. The final hour is a stiff climb back to Franz-Josefs-Höhe, so be sure to rest every few minutes and drink plenty of water.

HEILIGENBLUT ☎04824

Convenient accommodations for those wishing to explore Franz-Josefs-Höhe and the Hohe Tauern region are in Heiligenblut (pop. 1250), in the middle of the Großglocknerstraße. As the town closest to the highest mountain in Austria, Heiligenblut is a great starting point for hikes. Mountains rise sharply on each side of the valley, wedging Heiligenblut into a narrow corridor that looks northward to the Großglockner. The town's name, which means "holy blood," derives from a legend about a Byzantine general named Briccius who died nearby in a snowstorm. He carried with him a vial supposedly containing a few drops of Christ's blood, now kept in a reliquary in the town church.

▣▨ TRANSPORTATION AND PRACTICAL INFORMATION. Buses run to Heiligenblut from Franz-Josefs-Höhe (30min.; July-Sept. 4 per day 9:30am-5:45pm, May and Oct. 1 per day 4pm; €3.60); Lienz (1hr., 2-6 per day 6:19am-5:15pm, €5.90); and Zell am See (2½hr., 3 per day 9:20am-12:20pm, €11) via various connecting towns, depending on the time. Check with bus driver. The bus stop is in front of Hotel Glocknerhof. **"Friendly-Taxi"** service is available by calling ☎ 0664 371 79 85. The **Kärnten tourist office,** Hof 4, up the street from the bus stop, dispenses information about accommodations, hiking, sporting activities, and park transportation. (☎ 20 01 21; www.heiligenblut.at. Open July-Aug. M-F 9am-6pm, Sa 9am-noon and 4-6pm; Sept.-June M-F 9am-noon and 2-6pm, Sa 9am-noon and 4-6pm.) The **National Park tourist office,** behind Intersport, provides detailed information about hiking trails, maps, and mountain accommodations. (Open daily July-Aug. daily 10am-6pm; June 2-5pm.) An **ATM** is next to the tourist office at **Raiffeisenbank. Police** can be reached at ☎ 22 33, or, in an emergency ☎ 133. **Internet** is available at the **Post Hotel** (30min. card €3) and **Glocknerhof Hotel** (€2 per 10min.) The **post office** with **currency exchange** is below the center of town at the bottom of the hill. Follow the main road past the chair lift. (☎ 22 01. Open M-F 8am-noon and 2-4:30pm. Exchange closes 4pm.)

▨▧ ACCOMMODATIONS AND FOOD. To reach the **Jugendgästehaus Heiligenblut (HI) ❷,** Hof 36, take the path down from the wall behind the bus stop parking lot. Large rooms, some with baths and showers, await you. (☎ 22 59; www.oejhv.or.at. Breakfast included, 8am. Dinner and lunch €6 each. Reception July-Aug. 7-11am and 5-10pm; Sept.-June 7-10am and 5-9pm. Lockout 10am-4pm. Curfew 10pm. €16.50 per person. **HI members** only; exceptions made depending on space.) **Pension Bergkristall ❸,** Hof 71 is on the uphill side of a U-curve on the street behind the tourist office. Turn right from the tourist office and follow the street, making a sharp right at the chairlift and continuing uphill, one block from the cable lift. The pension's rooms have balconies and TV. Some suites include living room, kitchen, and shower or bath. (☎20 05; fax 20 05 33. Breakfast included. Easter to Nov. €24; slightly higher in winter.) **Nationalpark Camping-Großglockner ❶**, Haderg. 11, across the Möll river. offers scenic campgrounds and a restaurant. Follow directions to the *Jugendgästehaus*, continuing down the hill and over the river, then turn right and continue for another 5-10min. (☎20 48; www.heiligenblut.at/nationalpark-camping. Laundry €3.70. Reception 8am-midnight. €5.90 per adult in summer, €6.60 in winter; €3 per child; €2.20 per car, caravan, or motorcycle. Electricity €2.20.)

Cheap eats are rare in the center of town, as most restaurants are run by the big hotels. For affordable grub, follow directions toward Camping, but turn left after the river (15-20min.) to reach **Gasthof Sonnblick ❷**, Hof 21. Nestled in a wildflower-filled meadow with mountains rising on all sides, this restaurant offers cheap meals, fantastic views, and eclectic decor, including a pastiche of some 200 badges from fire departments around the world. Pizza €6.50-7.50. Spinatkrapfen €6.20. Wiener schnitzel €8.20. Gröstl and spaghetti each €7.50. Salads €3.20-9.50. (☎213 10; fax 213 15. Open daily 8am-9pm.) Lodged between the souvenir stores in the square in the center of town is **Dorfstüberl ❸**, Hof 4 (☎22 14), an outdoor café that serves pizzas (€7-9.20) alongside hearty meat entrées for €9-11. (☎20 19. Open daily 8:30am-midnight.) There is an **ADEG**, Hof 46, just a short ways up the road from the tourist office and across from the start of the Großglockner Hochalpenstraße. (☎22 14. Open summer M-F 8am-6:30pm, Sa 8am-6pm, Su 8:30am-6pm; winter M-Sa 8am-6pm, Su 9am-6pm.)

🏔 **HIKING.** The Heiligenblut hiker is a happy one, as almost any hike in the area brings amazing scenery. Before heading out, familiarize yourself with a hiking map, available at the Heiligenblut National Park office, the tourist office, or from many shops nearby. Hohe Tauern National Park officially exists only on the western side of Heiligenblut, across the Möll River from the church and tourist office. To get there, take the road out of Heiligenblut and descend the hill. Turn right, cross the river, and turn right again. Walk until you see hiking information signs on the left, or walk a bit farther to the parking lot for trails at the end of the road. The **National Park Office,** Hof 8, behind Intersport, can suggest routes and offer advice; they also have a small exhibit on wildlife and geology that will make your hike that much more educational. (Open in summer daily 10am-6pm.)

🥾 **Wirtsbauer Alm hike** (4hr. round-trip; moderate to difficult). From the parking lot, take the main trail past the signs to the Gössnitzfall. After some steady uphill climbing, the path leads to a meadow and a trail leading up the mountain on the left. Past the initial climb on this trail, the hike is mostly flat, cruising along wooded cliffs above the churning Gössnitz River. The Wirtsbauer Alm boasts magnificent views of the entire Alpine valley and all the peaks nearby. The hike to **Elberfelderhütte** (☎22 85) is 4½hr. farther and is entirely above the tree line on a path that often skirts the cliff's edge, passing the 3 Langtal Lakes. Both the Wirtsbauer Alm and the Elberfelderhütte accommodate overnight stays (roughly July to mid-Sept.). Call ahead or ask the park office in Heiligenblut.

Salmhütte hike (day hike; moderate to strenuous). This is as close as you can get to the Großglockner peak without a professional guide. Hop on the bus toward Franz-Josef-Hohe to Glocknerhaus. Proceed downhill, cross the dams across Margaritze Lake, then follow the signs to Salmhütte along trail 741, the "Viennese Highway." The path climbs steadily for the next 1½-2hr. before leveling off at around 2450m, ¼ mi. above the valley floor. The 3 "sword peaks" tower over you; to the left is the fantastically green Leiterbach valley. You'll eventually reach the Salmhütte, which was built in 1799 by the first expedition up Großglockner and was, in fact, where most of them quit walking and went home. If you're more determined, continue another hour over increasingly rugged, difficult terrain past the ruins of the expedition's stone hut, following the cairns uphill to the **Hohenwirt glacier.** This is where you turn around and let the professionals continue on to Erzherzog Johann Hütte (it will take them about 2hr. to cover a ¼ mi.). Return to the Salmhütte, then take the low road, trail 702b, back to Heiligenblut and enjoy close-ups of the valley and the marmots you towered above on the way out. (Glockneraus to Salmhütte 3hr.; round-trip to glacier 2hr.; return to Heiligenblut 4hr.) ÖAV map #40 (Großglocknergruppe) is extremely useful.

Gössnitzfall hike (1hr.; moderate). Hike begins shortly after the parking lot and continues off the main path, following the sign for "Aussichtspunkt Gössnitzfall." After 10-15min. of steep climbing, an 80m-high waterfall appears. Continue to the top of the trail, where you can see the gushing beast in all its glory. The gorge surrounding it is twice as high and just as steep as the waterfall itself. The mist coming off the falls will cool you down, a fitting reward for your effort.

Großglockner (various times; extreme). The king of the Hohe Tauern (3798m) is only to be ascended from Heiligenblut after late July through the Leitertal and should only be attempted by experienced hikers in the company of a guide. Inquire at the mountain hiking office. Generally speaking, Großglockner ascents are done in 1 of 2 ways:

Fürstbischof Salm Weg via **Salmhütte** (1½ days). The classic way to the top, passing over the Hofmannskees and the Meletzkigrat. Guides charge around €105 per person for 4-person groups, €125 for 3 people, €165 for 2 people, and €260 for a single person.

Fürstibischof Salm Weg over the Pasterze glacier. Prices per person: €110 for 4 people, €135 for 3, €175 for 2, €285 for 1 person.

Ⅺ OTHER OUTDOOR ACTIVITIES. Two skiing mountains, **Schareck** and **Hochfleiß**, rise from the valley's main station (☎ 022 88 18), middle station (☎ 022 88 24), and Tauernberg station (☎ 22 88 15), and offer 13 ski lifts, challenging runs and open-bowl skiing. Passes available at the Seilbahn lift station past the tourist office. (www.skiheiligenblut.at. Access to ski areas in Ost Tyrol and Carinthia with the Gold pass, 1½-day min. Adults €46, ages 15-18 €37, children under 15 €23.) **Bike** and **ski rental** are available at Intersport Pichler, Hof 6-7, across from the tourist office. (☎ 22 56 45, intersport@pichler.at. Bikes €18 per day, €28 per weekend, €64 per week; skis and snowboards €14-26 per day. Open May-June and Sept.-Nov. M-F 9am-6pm, Sa 9am-4pm; July-Aug. M-F 9am-6pm, Sa 9am-4pm, Su 10am-4pm; Dec.-Apr. M-Sa 9am-12:30pm and 2:30-6pm, Su 9am-noon and 3-6pm.)

BAD GASTEIN ☎ 06432

Close to the border of the National Park and serviced by both train and bus lines, Bad Gastein (pop. 5,500) proves a convenient starting location for hikes, bike trips, skiing, and other voyages into the mountains of the Hohe Tauern region. The town, famous for its thermal baths and the huge waterfall crashing through its center, has attracted royalty for centuries. Luxurious resorts fill the town's skyline, while hostels make it an affordable option for all.

⊡ TRANSPORTATION. Trains run to Salzburg (6 per day 9:15am-9:42pm); Munich (3 per day 11:15am-7:18pm); Mallnitz-Obervillach (15min., every 1-2 hr. 5:03am-10:45pm); Bad Hofgastein (10min., 1 per hr. 12:09am-9:15pm). Post Buses connect Bad Gastein with neighboring towns, including Böckstein and Bad Hofgastein. Check with tourist office or train ticket office for schedules.

⬛🛈 ORIENTATION AND PRACTICAL INFORMATION. Bad Gastein is centered around the waterfalls, with the train station located uphill, 5-10min. by foot along a steep path that cuts through the many hotels and restaurants filling the town. Cross the street from the train and turn left. Signs immediately point the way downhill to the waterfalls. The **tourist office** is at Mozart Platz, Kaiser-Franz-Josefstr 27. From the train station, turn left onto Banhoflpl. Follow the road downhill (it will turn into Kaiser-Franz-Josefstr.) for 15min. The office offers information on hotels, attractions, skiing, hiking, and biking. Their free "Wander Lift & Bike Information" map offers hiking suggestions. Beware, however, that distances on the map can be misleading. To get to the center of town from the tourist office, turn right onto Kaiser-Franz-Josephstr. and walk downhill for about 10min. (☎ 339 35 60; info@badgastein.at. Open July-Aug. and Dec. to mid-Mar. M-F 8am-6pm, Sa 9am-3pm, Su 9am-noon; Sept.-Nov. and mid-Mar. to June M-F 8am-6pm, Sa 9am-noon.) The **train station** sells tickets and has a **Western Union** service. (Open M-F 7-11:30am and 12:15-4:45pm, Sa 7-11:20am, Su and holidays 9am-2:45pm.) **Rent bikes** from Hervis, uphill from the train station on Pykerhöhenstr. 1. (☎ 64 24. Mountain bike €12 per day, €8 per 3hr.; city bike €10/€6; kid's bike €8/€4.) Euro Youth Hostel and Jugendherberge Badgastein also offer bike rental for €10 per day. There is a **pharmacy** in the center of town on Kongresspl. (☎ 85 000. Open M-F 8am-noon and 2:30-6:30pm, Sa 8:30am-noon.) The **post office** is next to the train station. (☎ 0664 624 21 50. Open M-F 8am-noon and 2-6pm, Sa 8-10pm.) **Postal Code:** 5640.

▌▐ ACCOMMODATIONS AND FOOD. The best bet for those on a budget is the **Euro Youth Hostel ❸,** 100m from both the train station (turn right and walk until you see it on the left side of the road, before SPAR market) and the Stubnerkogel ski lift/cable-car. Located in what was, until recently, the four-star Hotel Krone, this backpacker's paradise still has the original marble-and-wrought-iron staircase and elegant dining room. The knowledgeable and enthusiastic staff go out of their way to help guests, offering hiking and biking suggestions (they've done all the paths themselves), booking paragliding, rafting, and canyoning adventures, and recommending restaurants and sights in town. A sunny patio and comfortable sitting/TV room (with a full selection of English DVDs) await those looking for a more relaxing day, while an in-house restaurant/bar offers up delicious meals and great fun. **Internet** €1 per 20min., 24 hr. daily. **Bike rental** €10 per day. Laundry available. Buffet breakfast included. Sheets included. (☎ 233 00; www.euro-youth-hotel.com. All rooms have shower, toilet, phone, and balcony, while the large dorm rooms have spacious and modern bathrooms on the hall. Dorms €15.50; singles €29; doubles €48; triples €69.) **Jugendherberge Badgastein,** Ederpl 2, offers another option for inexpensive accommodations about 15min. from the train station and about 25min. from town. To get there, turn right from the station onto Bahnhofpl. and follow the road past Euro-SPAR as it curves under the railroad bridge. After that, take the second right, following the road as it curves around to Ederpl. Make another right in front of the Bayr Stübl, and the hostel will be immediately on your left. A plain concrete building, it has a TV room, sauna, fitness room, barbecue grill, and game room. Doubles and 4-bed rooms include shower and toilet. (☎ 20 80; fax 506 88; badgastein@jungehotels.at. Dinner and lunch €5 each. Reception 8am-1:30pm and 4-10pm. Dorms €14 in summer, €19 in winter. Doubles €32/€21. Add €3 for a single and €2.50 for stays shorter than 3 nights. Tourist tax €1.24 for ages 16 and up. Children ages 3-6 50% off, ages 6-12 30% off.)

HOHE TAUERN

Hotel-restaurants and upscale cafés fill the center of town, while the area around the train station tends to offer cheaper meals. The restaurant in the **Euro Youth Hostel** attracts locals as well as guests with some of the cheapest food in the area. Hearty salads with seared turkey or sautéed local mushrooms cost €6, while full daily menus, including salad and dessert, are €8. Vegetarian options (€6-7) include spinach and ricotta tortellini or fried camembert with salad, while grilled salmon with croquettes and veggies is €9. (For contact info, see Euro Youth Hostel, p. 271.) English menu available. Kitchen open Tu-Su 11:30am-2pm and 5:30-9:30pm.) In the center of town, **Gastein Restaurant-Café**, Kaiser-Franz-Josefstr 4, offers 17 varieties of pizzas and four calzones for €4.50-8.40. Full-meal salads are €7-10, while a salad from the large buffet is €4. Pasta options start at €6.80, while meat and fish choices range from €9.70 to €17.30. Traditional dishes, including *knödel*, range from €6.50-7 and include a buffet salad. Head down the path from the train station, and the Café will be directly across the street from where it lets out. (☎50 97. English menu. Children's playroom. Open daily 11am-9pm.) The giant **Euro-SPAR** market is next to the Euro Youth Hostel and boasts a convenience store upstairs and a grocery store downstairs. (Open M-Th 8am-7pm, F 8am-7:30pm, Sa 7:30am-5pm.)

⊞ SIGHTS AND ENTERTAINMENT. Bad Gastein's thundering waterfall ⌐ been one of its main attractions for centuries, and for good reason. The ⌐m torrent crashes right through the center of town, spraying passers-by ⌐en the wind is just right. To reach it, turn right onto Kaiser-Franz-Josefstr. ⌐at the base of the path down from the train station, and continue for 5min. to a bridge about halfway up the falls. Follow the street downhill and take any number of paths off to the left for closer views from the base. About halfway from the path to the fall is the **Gasteiner Museum.** Located upstairs in the Congress building, it comprises a few rooms filled with random collections of paintings, stuffed birds and wildlife, and tourism posters and memorabilia. One room is devoted to royalty in Bad Gastein. (☎34 88. Open June to mid-Oct. daily 10:30am-noon and 3:30-6pm.)

A 30- to 40min. stroll along the river on the Elizabeth promenade leads straight to the historic mining village of Böckstein. (Turn right from the train station and continue straight, turning right just past the SPAR market onto the promenade.) A small cluster of 18th century industrial buildings awaits at the end of the path. Among them lie the beautiful oval **Maria zum Guten Rat** church, with a frescoed ceiling, and the tiny **Montan Museum,** which features displays about Bad Gastein's mining industry and medieval gold rush. (☎54 14. Open mid-May to mid-Oct. M-Sa 10am-noon and 3-5:30pm. €2.20, children and students €1; gold-panning from mid-June, W and F from 10am; €3.)

Bad Gastein's **casino,** located halfway between the tourist office and the town center on Kaiser-Franz-Josephstr. 14, tempts guests to try their luck at poker, blackjack, American and French roulette, and slot machines. Thursday is Ladies' Night, where women get one glass of Sekt and €25 worth of chips for €21. (☎24 65. Free parking for guests in the APCOA garage. Open daily from 7pm.)

Packed with skiers during the winter months, bars tend to empty out during the summer. **Tanzbar Weinfassl,** on Kongresspl., has live music, darts, and seating inside huge wine barrels. Mostly older people fill the dance floor until 10pm, when a younger crowd takes over. The club plays oldies, country, contemporary hits, and more. Beer €3.10, hamburger €4. (☎2403 33. Open 7pm-1am). **Bergfex**, in the center of town in the Arcotel Elisabethpark, serves dinner from 6-10pm and typical Austrian drinks (and international favorites) after that. Peach walls, wooden tables and dim lighting provide a backdrop for a primarily middle-aged crowd in the summer, with a few people in their 20s and

30s thrown in. Winter brings a younger crowd, from 20 on up. (☎25 51 0. Beer €3.20. Open late May to Oct. 7pm-1am officially, although people often stay until 4 or 6am; Dec.-Apr. 6pm until everyone leaves. Special theme parties, including Mexican night, every W.)

🏃 OUTDOOR ACTIVITIES.

HIKING. Surrounded by peaks stretching more than 2500m into the sky, Bad Gastein is a paradise for skiers, hikers, bikers, and outdoor enthusiasts in general. For those who want to enjoy the sights without a strenuous hike up, the Gasteiner Bergbahnen services Stubnerkogel and Graukogel. (☎64 55. €13.50 to the top, with guest card €12, children 6-15 €7; descent €7/€7/€3; round-trip €15.50/€14/8.) The Stubnerkogel lift climbs to 2230m (open daily mid-May to mid-Oct., 1 per hr. 8:30am-4pm, last descent 4:15pm). The Graukogel lift reaches 1961m and is open daily July-Sept. 8:30am-4pm (last descent 4:45pm.) Most hikes lead through cow pastures. To avoid being chased by an angry farmer, be sure to close any gates you open. One of the easiest routes takes hikers from the top of the **Stubnerkogel cable car** to **Angertal bus stop.** The walk takes about 4hr. and is all downhill along a narrow, curving path offering spectacular views. The **Böcksteiner Hohenweg,** of about medium difficulty, takes 3hr. and starts from the Stubnerkogel middle station (€8, with guest card €6.50, children €4). Follow the signs uphill to Zittrauer Hochalm. The path continues steeply downhill to Böckfeldalm, and then continues through the forest to Altböckstein, offering views over the entire valley. A trek from the **Stubnerkogel mountain station** to the Bockhartsee to Sportgastein takes 5-6hr. and should be attempted only by experienced hikers. From the top station, follow signs towards Zittrauertisch. A short descent to the right leads to Miesbicht Scharte, getting very steep toward the end. From there, it leads directly down to Unteren Bockhartsee, an artificially-created lake. From there, hikers have the option of continuing another hour to Oberen Bockhartsee, a natural lake, or taking the bus from Sportgastein back to Bad Gastein. For a pleasant stroll, follow the level **Elisabeth Promenade** along the river. This wide gravel path is also popular with bicyclists.

SKIING. The area surrounding Bad Ga͟͟͟͟͟͟ ͟͟͟͟͟ers from across the globe with 250km of slopes and 53 lifts. The **Ski** ͟ ͟ grants access to all of these plus those in Salzburger Sportwelt, Großark ͟ ͟dadming-Dachstein Tauern and Hochkönig's Winterreich, making it Austria's largest ski alliance. (www.ski-made.com. 2 day pass €67, youth €62.50, child €33.50. Any five days within a seven day period €159/€148/€79.50. Five consecutive days €144/€134.50/€72.) Be sure to catch the 8km slope stretching from the Stubnerkogel to Angertal, the longest in the region. Shops renting gear fill the town, and ski schools abound.

ZELL AM SEE ☎06542

Surrounded by a ring of snow-capped mountains cradling a broad turquoise lake, Zell am See (pop. 9700) functions as a year-round resort for mountain-happy European tourists. It also proves a base from which to explore the 30 surrounding peaks of the Hohe Tauern range, many of which rise more than 3000m above sea level. Hiking trails and ski slopes lure tourists into the heights, while the lake calls just as enticingly to those who desire a relaxing day of boating, fishing, swimming, or sunbathing. Meanwhile, visitors to the cobblestoned town center wind through shops and cafés during the day and bars and dance clubs at night.

HOHE TAUERN

▢ TRANSPORTATION

Zell am See lies at the intersection of Bundesstr. 311 from the north and Bundesstr. 168 from the west. It's also accessible by Bundesstr. 107 from the south, which runs into Bundesstr. 311 north. From **Salzburg,** take Bundesstr. 21 south to 305 and then to 178; at **Lofer,** switch to 311 south.

Trains: The station (☎ 73 21 43 57) is at the intersection of Bahnhofstr. and Salzmannstr. Ticket counter open M-Sa 6:10am-7:30pm, Su and holidays 7:10am-7:45pm. Trains arrive from: **Innsbruck** (1½-2hr., 3:45am-9:27pm, €19.60); **Kitzbühel** (45min., 7:17am-9:27pm, €8.70); **Vienna** (5hr., 10:40am-10:56pm, €41) via **Salzburg** (1½hr., 1-2 per hr., €11.30).

Buses: **BundesBus** station on Postpl., behind the post office and facing the corner of Gartenstr. and Schulstr. Buy tickets from the driver or call (☎ 54 44). Open M-F 7:30am-1:30pm. Buses run to a variety of local destinations, including: **Krimml** (1½hr., 5:48am-8:49pm, €7.60); **Salzburg** (2hr., 5:35am-8:50pm, €9.90); **Franz-Josefs-Höhe** (mid-June to Sept.; 7:20am, 10:45, 12:20pm; one-way €11.90, round-trip €17.10).

Taxis: At the train station, or call ☎ 727 22.

Car Rental: Europcar, Salzachtal Bundesstr. 1-3 (☎ 573 48 12); **Trike und Car Center,** Brucker Bundesstr. 114 (☎ 0664 253 03 81); or **Jet-Tankstelle,** Loferer Bundesstr. 11 (☎ 732 25).

Bike Rental: From **Sport Olympia,** Kircheng 1 (☎ 722 27); **Adventure Service,** Steinerg. 9 (☎ 735 25); **Sport Achleitner,** Postpl. 2 (☎ 735 81); and **Intersport,** Bahnhofstr. 13 in the *Fußgängerzone* or at the *Schmittenhöhe Talstation* (☎ 726 06). Mountain bikes €18-20 per day, €84 for 6 days; city bikes €10/€55 for 6 days; children €5-8 per day.

Parking: On Brucker-Bundersstr. between the tourist office and the post office; on Magazinerstr. at the Bahnhof; between Saalfeldnerstr. and Lofer Bundesstr.; by the *Hallenbad;* and underground at the post office. Above-ground parking €1.50 per hr., 3hr. max €2.50. Underground €1.40 per hr., €11.20 per day. Open 24hr.

▰ ❼ ORIENTATION AND PRACTICAL INFORMATION

Zell am See is one of several towns clustered on or near the lake and connected by bus or bike path. The closest town, Schüttdorf, is only a 15min. walk. Zell am See's pedestrian zone lies to the right and up the hill from the train station.

Tourist Office: Brucker Bundesstr. 1a (☎ 770; www.europasportregion.info/en). From the station, turn right, take the left fork, go around the corner, and turn right again. Open July to mid-Sept. and mid-Dec. to Mar. M-F 8am-6pm, Sa 9am-noon and 4-6pm, Su 10am-noon; Apr.-June and Sept. to mid-Dec. closed Su.

Currency Exchange: At banks or the post office. Almost every bank has an **ATM.** Open M-F 8:30am-12:30pm and 2-4:30pm.

Luggage Storage: At the train station, in the office next to the ticket window. €2.10 per piece. Open M-Sa 6:10am-7:30pm, Su 7:10am-7:45pm. 24hr. electronic luggage or ski lockers €2.50.

Lost and Found: In the Town Hall, on Brucker Bundesstr. 2 (☎ 06542 766 17).

Weather Conditions and Cable Car Report: ☎ 736 94 for *Schmittenhöhe* only. Regional conditions posted daily in English at the tourist information office.

Emergencies: Police ☎ 133 (non-emergency 737 010). **Fire** ☎ 122. **Medical Emergency** ☎ 141. **Ambulance** ☎ 144. **Mountain rescue** ☎ 140.

Internet: Café Estl, Bahnhofstr. 1 (☎726 10; www.icak.at), has computers downstairs from the café. €1 per 10min. Open M-F 7:30am-10pm, Sa 9am-10pm, Su 10am-10pm. **Schloß Rosenberg's** reading room, Brucker Bundesstr. 2 (☎065 427 6652). Open M 2-6pm, Tu-Th 10am-noon and 2-6pm, F 10am-noon.

Post Office: Postpl. 4 (☎73 79 10). Open early July to mid-Sept. and Christmas to Easter. M-F 7:30am-5:30pm, Sa 8-11am; mid-Sept. to Christmas and Easter to early July M-F 7:30am-5:30pm, Sa 8-10am.

Postal Code: A-5700.

ACCOMMODATIONS

Zell am See has more than its share of four-star hotels (and prices), but it has not forgotten the budget traveler. Ask at your accommodation for a free **guest card**, which provides numerous discounts on activities throughout the city.

Pensione Sinilill (Andi's Inn), Thumersbacherstr. 65 (☎735 23). Take the BundesBus (dir: Thumersbach) to "Krankenhaus" (€1.45, last bus 7:15pm). Turn left after exiting the bus, walk about 200m, and look for an old wooden sign on the left side of the street. If you call ahead, Andi will pick you up. On the north shore of the lake, this *Pension* features simple furniture and an easy-going environment. The lived-in feel of the house gives it a charm most *Pensionen* lack. Andi, reared in Zell am See, knows everything about the town and can tell you what's worthwhile. Big breakfast included. Hall bathrooms and shower. Singles €15; doubles, some with balcony, €30. ❷

Haus der Jugend (HI), Seespitzstr. 13 (☎571 85; fax 57 18 54). Exit the station facing the lake ("Zum See"), turn right, and walk along the footpath beside the lake. When the footpath ends, take a left onto Seespitzstr. (15min.). The footpath is deserted at night and dark in spots. You can also take the Stadtbus to "Alpenblick" (€1.50, last bus 7:45pm). A lawn and terrace right on the lake, perfect for swimming or sunbathing and with fantastic views, make this a popular spot for families and groups. Other amenities include TV room with VCR, foosball table, and snack shop. Breakfast included. Lunch and dinner €5.50 each; outdoor BBQ once per week in summer. €1 deposit for locking wardrobes in some rooms. Reception 7-9am and 4-10pm. Check-out 9am. Lockout noon-4pm. Curfew 10pm, although 24hr. access keys are available. Reservations recommended. 6-bed dorms €17; 4-bed dorms €19; doubles €21. Children ages 4-6 50% off, ages 7-12 30% off. MC/V. ❷

Pension Herzog, Saalfeldnerstr. 20 (☎725 03; www.members.aon.at/pension.herzog). From the Bahnhof, turn right and go uphill, through and out of the *Fußgängerzone*, past Hotel Grüner Baum. This well-kept pension with flower-filled wooden balconies sits near the lake and a babbling brook. All rooms have a private sink. Breakfast included (7:30-9:30am). Reception 7am-8pm. Check-out 10am. Rooms with private toilet and shower €25-28, private shower with shared toilet €19-22, shared toilet and shower €15-17; singles €5 extra. €1.50 extra for stays of 1-2 nights. Children 3-15 staying in parents' room 50% off, ages 15 and up 30% off. ❷

Camping Seecamp, Thumersbacherstr. 34 (☎721 15; www.see-camp.at), in Zell am See/Prielau, can be reached by BundesBus (dir: Thumersbach) to "Seecamp" (last bus 7:15pm, €1.40). Lakefront campground with restaurant, outdoor café, grocery, playroom complete with ball-pit and Nintendo, showers, and laundry (from €4, iron included). Kayaking, sailing, surfing, and bike rental. The winter ski shuttle stops here. Showers included. Reception M-Sa 8-11am and 4-6pm, Su 9-11am and 4-6pm. Check-out 11am. Car lockout noon-2pm and 10pm-7am. €7.40 per person, €4 per child ages 5-15, €4 per tent, €2.50 per car, €1.50 per motorbike. €0.90 tax per person. Electricity, TV, and gas €2.20 each. Sept.-Dec. and May-June 20% off. AmEx/MC/V. ❶

HOHE TAUERN (sidebar)

◘ FOOD

Zell am See lies in the Pinzgau region, where food is prepared to sustain the strenuous labors of farmers. Try the *Brezensuppe* (a clear soup with cheese cubes) as an appetizer and then *Pinzgauer Käsnocken* (homemade noodles and cheese, onions, and chives). Top it all off with *Lebkuchen Parfait* (spice cake), *Blattlkrapfen* (deep-fried stuffed pancakes), or *Germknödeln* (a steamed sweet roll served with poppy seeds, butter, and sugar). The **SPAR** is at Brucker Bundesstr. 4. (Open M-Th 7:30am-6:30pm, F 7:30am-7pm, Sa 7:30am-5pm.)

Ristorante Pizzeria Giuseppe, Kircheng. 1 (☎723 73), in the *Fußgängerzone.* From the station, walk past the church and go straight. Subdued lighting and tasteful decoration give this place a pleasant ambience. Plenty of vegetarian options and an extensive wine list. Pasta dishes €5.80-9.70. Pizza €5.90-9.30. Salads €6.90-7.90. Open Tu-Su 11:30am-11pm. DC/MC/V with €20 min. order. ❷

Fischrestaurant "Moby Dick," Kreuzg. 16 (☎733 20). This fish-store/restaurant certainly smells, well, fishy—but no matter. Try a double fishburger with potatoes and salad (€7.50), single fishburger (€1.90), or pick your own 200g filet and have it grilled or fried with your choice of veggies (€9.80). Main dishes occasionally feature fish straight from the lake. Open M-F 9am-6pm, Sa 9am-1pm. V. ❶

Kupferkessel, Brucker-Bundesstr. 18 (☎727 68; fax 72 76 86). As you exit the Bahnhof, turn left and follow the road as it curves uphill and dead-ends at the Kupferkessel. A converted gas station, different parts of the restaurant have different atmospheres, from California-kitchen-style (with seating surrounding the chefs) to an outdoor patio and bar draped in vines and flowers. The menu features pizza (€5.50-8.80 for a small), steak (€9.20-14.90), and salad (€4.60-8.10). Open M-Sa 11am-2am, Su 5pm-2am. AmEx/DC/MC/V. ❷

◉ ⚑ OUTDOOR ACTIVITIES AND SIGHTS

HIKING AND ADVENTURE SPORTS. Though expensive, the **Schmittenhöhebahn** leads to many hikes. The BundesBus (dir: Schmittenhöhebahn/Sonnenalmbahn Talstation; 7min., 7:20am-5:50pm, €1.70 from post office) goes to the lift, about 2km north of town on Schmittenstr. (Lift runs mid-May to late Oct. daily 8:15am-6pm. Ascent €15.20, with guest card €13.60, children €7.60; descent €11.30/€10.20/€5.65. Round-trip €19.30/€17.30/€9.65; only 1st child in family pays.) The lift station provides several brochures (with English translations) detailing hikes ranging from strolls to treks. In the former category, the **Erlebnisweg Höhenpromenade** connects the top stations of the Schmittenhöhe and Sonnkogel lifts. Displays on history, nature, and ecology line the way. Guided hikes, free with a lift ticket, leave from the lower stations and have a variety of themes, including botanical hikes, forest walks, and children's hikes (1hr., July-Oct. M-F). Contact the Schmittenhöhebahn Aktiengesellschaft (☎78 92 12) for details.

Independent of the downtown park, the Zell am See area provides many opportunities to work those calf muscles. Consider the **Pinzgauer Spaziergang,** which begins at the upper terminal of the *Schmittenhöhebahn* and is marked "Alpenvereinsweg" #19 or 719. It dips and climbs a bit at the beginning, but levels off high in the Kitzbüheler Alps. While the shortest trail from here leads to Rohrentörl (2½hr.), most people take an entire day to hike along this trail, eventually taking a side trail leading to one of the valley towns west of Zell am

See. From there you can take the bus back. For a shorter hike, walk up Mozart-str. until it ends, and follow the hiking trail. The **Kohlergrabenweg** is a 1hr. hike that gradually ascends through the forest to the *Schmittenhohebahn* lower station. For **rafting** (€41), **canyoning** (€69), **paragliding** (€100, excluding lift ticket), and **mountain bike** (tours €22-29) information, contact **Adventure Service,** Steinerg. 9 (☎735 25; fax 742 80).

SKIING. The **Zell/Kaprun Ski Pass** covers both Zell am See and nearby Kaprun; a free bus runs between the two every 30-45min. from late December to late March, as well as every 30min. between Zell am See and the Schmittenhöhe-bahn from late December to late April. (2-day pass €64, ages 16-18 €57.50, ages 7-15 €32, under 7 free when accompanied by an adult.) Get a report on ski conditions in the Schmittenhöhe area (☎789 in English) or the Kitzsteinhorn-Kaprun area (☎06547 86 21). The **Kitzsteinhorn** (3203m) and its glacier in Kaprun offer **summer skiing;** get there early to avoid skiing in slush. (Day passes late June to mid-Oct €27, ages 16-18 €24.50, ages 7-15 €13.50; mid-Oct. to mid-Dec. and mid-Apr. to May €34.50/€31/€17.) Renting snowboarding or skiing gear costs €21-29 per day, available at **Intersport Bründl** on the glacier. (☎06547 83 88. Open M-F 8am-noon and 2:30-6:30pm, Sa 8am-6pm, Su 9am-11am and 3-6pm.) Intersport also has several other shops open in winter, as well as one near the top of Kitzsteinhorn.

OTHER ACTIVITIES. Zell's buildings are clustered in the valley of the *Zellersee*. Stroll around the lake or get wet at one of the **beaches: Strandbad Zell am See,** on the Esplanade near the center of town (walk down Franz-Josef-Str.), complete with platform diving, a heated pool, and a waterslide (☎726 50); **Strandbad Seespitz,** by the Haus der Jugend (☎551 25); or **Thumersbacher Strandbad,** almost directly opposite downtown on the shore's other side (☎723 55). (Round-trip boat passage from the downtown park €4.10, children €2. Beaches open June to early Sept. 9am-7pm. €5.30 with guest card, ages 6-16 €3.20, under 6 free.) **Boat tours** depart from the Zell Esplanade, off Salzmannstr. (40min.; 13 per day 9:30am-5:30pm; €7.40, ages 6-14 €3.70.) Visit Strandbad Thumersbach Kurpark or Zeller Strandbad for **water skiing** (€8, parachute €37, wakeboard €10.50). **Boat rental** is available on the north shore of the lake. (Follow directions to campsite Seecamp. Sailboat €10 per hr. or €30 per day; windsurfer €8/€24; paddleboat €4 per 30min., €6 per hr.)

Amidst the cafés and shops in the middle of Zell's *Fußgängerzone* stands the *Vogtturm*, Kreuzg. 2, a medieval tower that has housed the quirky **Heimatmuseum** since 1985. The museum overflows with exhibits on everything from the toilet that Franz Joseph used at the Hotel Schmittenhöhe to stuffed birds and a history of coinage in the *Pinzgau*. (☎0664 586 27 06. Open May to mid-Oct. and mid-Dec. M-F 1:30-5:30pm. €2.20, with guest card €2, children 6-15 €1.10.) On Wednesday nights during the summer, the pedestrian zone comes alive with vendors, street performers, and music starting at 7pm for the **Zeller Sommer Nachtsfest.**

◪ NIGHTLIFE

Those who want to get really hammered should try the local drinking game **Nageln,** in which drinkers compete to see who can drive a nail into a tree stump first—with the head of a hammer. Somehow, you end up drunk.

Pinzgauer Diele, Kircheng. 3 (☎21 64), has 2 bars and a small disco-ball-lit dance area guaranteed to get you moving. Mostly an over-25 crowd during the week, Pinzgauer gets its share of teenagers on the weekends. Live DJs play whatever appeals to the tourists filling the floor, spinning everything from oldies to hip-hop, pop, and R&B. Mixed drinks €3.50-5.20. Beer from €3.10. During the summer, it doubles as a restaurant, open daily 11am-10pm, with the disco beginning M-Th at 9pm and F-Su at 10pm. Winter months it is only for après-ski, open daily 4pm-4am. Closed mid-Apr. to mid-May.

B17 Hangar, Salzmannstr. 2 (☎474 24; www.b17-hangar.at). Turn right from train station; at the fork, take the right hand road for about 5min. A mixed crowd sits at the bar amidst airplane parts and stainless steel in what feels like, as the name suggests, an airplane hangar. A 2nd bar and rooftop patio transport patrons into a tropical paradise, complete with giant hibiscus flowers. Young and old alike enjoy cocktails (€7-7.30) to the background rock and occasional pop or Latin tune. Open M-Sa 6pm-1am.

Bierstad'l, Kircheng. 1. (☎72 36 33), under Pizzeria Ristorante Giuseppe. Everyone from young teens on up gathers in this cozy, dimly bit bar to sample the 33 different brews in stock. Mainly rock and jazz play, with the occasional live band to spice things up. Beer on tap from €2.90, while cocktails and mixes run €4.60-8.20. Open daily 8:30pm-4am. Closed Apr. to mid-May and mid-Sept. to Nov.

Crazy Daisy's Bar, Brucker Bundesstr. 10-12 (☎725 16 59), across from the tourist office, is a fun though touristy joint featuring wacky, irreverent t-shirts and the aforementioned hammer-in-stump game. Beer from €2.40. "Cocks and Tails" €5.80-6.80. Happy hour summer 8-10pm; winter 4-6pm. Open summer 8pm-1am; winter 4pm-1am. MC/V.

▶ DAYTRIP FROM ZELL AM SEE

KRIMML ☎06564

*The Pinzgauer Lokalbahn **train** comes only westward from Zell am See (1¾hr., 5:48am-6:49pm, €6.90.) A steam train July to mid-Sept. (Su; €6.90, Eurail valid, children ages 6-15 50% off.) **Bundesbus** lines run from Zell am See (1½hr., 11 per day 5:47am-8:55pm, €7.60) and Zell am Ziller (1½hr.; 8:52am, 1:32pm; €5.60) to the start of the falls (bus stop: "Maustelle Ort"). Paid parking at the entrance of the waterfall can be avoided; Krimml offers free parking within walking distance. Ask the tourist office for details. Entrance to the falls costs €1.50 (children €0.50) 8am-6pm. The **OAV/National Park Information** stand (☎72 12), next to the ticket booth, offers maps, pamphlets, and German guides for €3.30-14. Open May-Oct. M-Sa 11am-4pm.*

Each year, over 400,000 visitors charge up the sloping path near Krimml to the Krimml Waterfalls, a set of three roaring cascades that were incorporated into the Hohe Tauern National Park in 1983. Dropping a total of 380m, the Krimml waterfalls, taken together, are the largest series of falls in Europe. The Krimml Kees (glacier), 20km up the valley, feeds the falls. The wide, upward-sloping **Wasserfallweg** (4km) hiking path starts past the entrance booth and is filled with tourist kiosks and snack stands for the first few hundred meters before cutting through forest and moss-covered rock. The first set of falls are accessible almost directly from the entrance. It's 30min. from there to the second cascade, and an additional 30min. to the third, with the path getting progressively steeper as you continue. Alternatively, a **taxi service** transports paying customers to the second and third cascades. (☎72 28. €5.60 per person from the base to the third waterfall, including park entry; ask about special group fares.) The first and most powerful cascade (65m) is visible almost immediately after the entrance; it kicks up a huge skirt of spray that douses rocks, plants, and those tourists who just have to get a liiiittle closer for the perfect picture. The second falls drop from a precipice named **Jagasprung** (Hunter's Leap). As legend has it, a poacher once jumped from here to the other side of the falls to elude his pursuers. Tourists gather on the rocks surrounding the base of this middle fall to wade in the small pools, hopping from rock to rock. The third set of falls (60m) is the most scenic—one long cascade from the upper river valley. The trail continues through the upper Ache valley; a further 30min. walk provides views of the towering **Dreiherrenspitze** (3499m) near the source of the waterfalls. Near the main parking lot before the entrance to the waterfalls lies **WasserWunderWelt**, a new water museum/park with two floors of fun facts about water, including the Krimml waterfalls. The Aqua-Park outside has games, including a gauntlet that blasts tourists with water when they step on the wrong tiles. (☎201 13; www.wawuwe.at. Open May-Oct. daily 10am-5pm; mid-Jan. to mid-Apr. noon-9pm. €7, children €3.50.)

The **tourist office**, Oberkrimml 37, is 2min. from the "Krimml Ort" bus stop; follow the road by the stop, then turn right down the hill in front of the church. (☎723 90; www.krimmls.at. Free 24hr. accommodation phone and computer. Open M-F 8am-noon and 2:30-5:30pm, Sa 8:30-10:30am.) There is an **ATM** at Raiffeisenbank across from the church. The **post office** next door to the tourist office offers good **currency exchange** rates. (☎72 01. Open M-Tu and Th-F 8am-noon and 2-5pm, W 8am-noon.)

Haus Mühlegg ❸, Oberkrimmlstr. 24, is 5min. downhill along the road past ADEG and the sport shop: when the road turns right downhill, stay to the left. Signs point to this brown farmhouse with flowers on every terrace and chickens in the yard. Cowbells lull guests to sleep, while mountain views and a fresh breakfast greet them in the morning. The large rooms have homey, folk-art-painted furniture; most have balconies and private showers, but a shared toilet. (☎74 59 or 73 38. Singles €18; doubles €36.) **Gasthof Post ❸** is located across from the ADEG. The hotel is complete with a restaurant, sauna (daily 3-9:30pm), solarium (€6.50 per 30min.), whirlpool, darts, billiards, fitness room, children's playroom and playground, and live music on Mondays during the high season. A breakfast buffet (7:30-10am) is included. (☎73 58; www.salzburgerland.com/post. Reception 7am-1pm and 3-10pm. May-Oct. €29-32 per person; Dec.-Apr. €40-50, €60 over the Christmas/New Year holidays; ages 5-12 50% discount, ages 12-14 20%.) Buy groceries at **ADEG**, up the hill from the tourist office on Oberkrimmlstr. (☎74 59. Open M-F 7am-noon and 2-6pm, Sa 7am-noon.)

LIENZ ☎04852

Lienz is the primary city of East Tyrol (Osttirol), despite a population of only 12,000. The center bustles with businesses and cafés, but walk away from it for 5min. and you'd swear you were in a small mountain village. Walk 15min. out of town, and you'll find yourself in a valley surrounded by the Dolomites and the

be done cheaply with an Osttiroler Card, available at the tourist offi—

⌐ TRANSPORTATION

Trains: Hauptbahnhof, Bahnhofpl. (☎05 17 17). Information booth open M 4:45am-6:55pm, Tu-F 7:20am-6:55pm, Sa 6:20am-6:55pm, Su and holidays 8:30am-6:55pm. Trains to: **Innsbruck** (3hr., 5 per day 4:42am-6:54pm, €17.60); **Spittal-Millstättersee** (Spittal an der Drau; 1hr., 17 per day 5:20am-8:19pm, €10); **Vienna** (7hr.; 5:20am, 12:14, 3:04pm; €44.50); **Villach** (2hr., 6 per day 5:20am-7:23pm, €12.)

Buses: BundesBus (☎649 44; fax 623 57). Buses leave from the Hauptbahnhof for destinations throughout the region. Lienz ticketing open M-F 8am-noon and 2-4pm, closed Sa-Su and holidays. Buses to: **Franz-Josefs-Höhe** (1½hr., 3-4 per day 8am-4:10pm); **Heiligenblut** (1hr., 2-12 per day 8am-7:15pm, €7); **Kitzbühel** (2hr., 1-2 per day 5:45am-5:15pm, €12.40); **Zell am See** via Franz-Josefs-Höhe (2 daily 10am, 2pm). A **free Stadtbus** circles the city, making 14 stops before returning to station parking lot (early July to late Aug. every hr. 8am-7pm).

By Car: Lienz lies at the junction of Bundesstr. 108 from the northwest, 106 and 107 from the northeast, and 100, which runs east-west. From Innsbruck, take *Autobahn* A12 E to 169 south. At Zell am Ziller, switch to 165 E, and at Mittersill take 108 S to Lienz. From Salzburg, take *Autobahn* A10 S to 311, and, just before Zell am See, switch to 107 S to Lienz.

Taxis: ☎638 63, 640 64, 636 90, or 653 65.

Parking: At Europapl. €0.50 per hr., max. 3hr.

Bike Rental: Trend Sport Wibmer, Egger-Lienz Pl. 1 (☎ 690 98). €15 per day. **Papin Sport** (☎0474/91 34 50), in the train station parking lot. Pick-up in Lienz with a return elsewhere €3 extra. Mountain bike €18 per day, children €12; half day €10.

✳ 🛈 ORIENTATION AND PRACTICAL INFORMATION

The Isel River, which feeds into the Drau, splits Lienz. The Dolomites spread south into Italy, while peaks to the north rise toward the Hohe Tauern range. From the train station, Hauptpl. and the *Altstadt* are across Tiroler Str. and to the left past Bozenerpl.

Tourist Office: Europapl. 1 (☎652 65; www.lienz-tourismus.at). From the station, turn left on Tiroler Str. and right on Europapl. **City tours** in German M and F 10am; call ahead for English. Open M-F 8am-6pm, Sa 9am-noon and 5-7pm, Su 10am-noon. (€30, children 6-14 €15, under 6 free). **Iselsberg-Stronach Information Center** (☎641 17) has info on **national park tours.** Open early July to mid-Sept. M-Sa 8am-noon and 3-7pm, Su 9am-noon and 4-7pm.

Currency Exchange: Best rates are in the **post office,** which has an **ATM** in front. Exchange open M-F 8am-7pm. **ATM**s also at the train station and banks.

Luggage Storage: In the train station. Small lockers €2.50, large €3, ski lockers €4. Open daily 6am-9:30pm.

Hospital: Emanuel-von-Hibler-Str. 5 (☎60 60).

Emergencies: Police, Hauptpl. 5 (☎133), **Fire** ☎ 122, **Mountain Rescue** ☎140, **Ambulance and Water Rescue** ☎144, **Road service** ☎120.

Internet Access: At the **Bücherei** (public library; ☎639 72), inside the Franziskanerkloster at Mucharg. 4. €2 per hr. Open Tu 9am-noon and 3-7pm, W-F 9am-noon and 3-6pm, Sa 9am-noon. Also **Odin's Café,** Schweizerg. 3 (☎635 97). €0.10 per min., €3.80 per hr. Open M-Sa 4pm-2am, Su 7pm-7am.

Post Office: Bozenerpl. 1, at the beginning of Hauptpl. across from the train station. Open M-F 7:30am-6:30pm, Sa 8-11am.

Postal Code: A-9900.

📌 ACCOMMODATIONS AND CAMPING

Though every other building in the Altstadt is a red-carpeted, cheery-stuccoed *Gastehaus* or hotel, it can be surprisingly difficult to find rooms in town, particularly during the street festival. Try to call ahead.

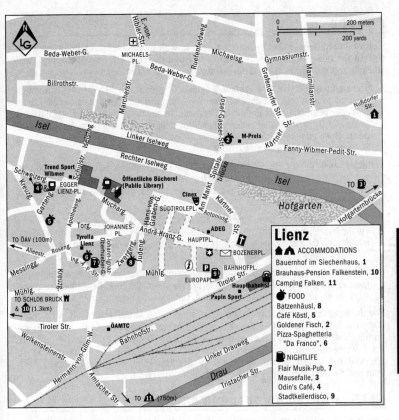

Lienz

▲▲ ACCOMMODATIONS
Bauernhof im Siechenhaus, **1**
Brauhaus-Pension Falkenstein, **10**
Camping Falken, **11**

🍴 FOOD
Batzenhäusl, **8**
Café Köstl, **5**
Goldener Fisch, **2**
Pizza-Spaghetteria "Da Franco", **6**

🍸 NIGHTLIFE
Flair Musik-Pub, **7**
Mausefalle, **3**
Odin's Café, **4**
Stadtkellerdisco, **9**

HOHE TAUERN

Bauernhof im Siechenhaus, Kärntnerstr. 39 (☎ 621 88). From the station, turn right onto Tiroler Str. and walk across the Isel; take the 1st left and then an immediate right. Walk 1 block to Kärntnerstr. and turn left. This wood-beamed farmhouse was a home for the sick during the Middle Ages and now offers large rooms decorated with jigsaw puzzles. All rooms with radio, most with shower. Doubles €32; triples €47. ❷

Brauhaus-Pension Falkenstein, Pustertalerstr. 40 (☎ 622 70; fax 704), is run by the same folks who own the Gössler brewery next door, so expect fresh beer at the restaurant/Biergarten downstairs. Take the Lienz-Arnbach bus from the train station to Falken-

Camping Falken, Eichholz 7 (☎ 640 22; camping.falken@tirol.com), is across the Drau River. From the station, turn left onto Tiroler Str. and left at the ÖAMTC garage, then pass through the tunnel and over the Drau. Continue past the stadium, then turn left down the asphalt footpath (15min.). This site, encircled by fields and mountains, has a ping-pong table, soccer field, mini-playground, and store. Laundry €3. Car lockout 1-3pm and 10pm-7am in the bigger lot. Reception 8-10am and 4-8pm. Reservations recommended. July-Aug. €6 per adult, €4 per child, €7.50 per tent site, €9.50 per caravan site. Sept.-June prices €0.50 less. Showers €1. ❶

◗ FOOD

Calorie-laden delis, bakeries, and cafés lie in wait in Hauptpl. and along Schweizerg. in the heart of the city. A venture through the side streets off Hauptpl. will unearth more options, from tapas to sushi.

Pizzeria-Spaghetteria "Da Franco," Ägidius Peggerstr. (☎699 69). Head through Hauptpl. to Johannespl., turn left at Zwergerg., and continue down the small alley, then gradually bear right up onto Ägidius Peggerstr. Try terrific stone-oven pizza (€6-9) and pasta (€7-9) in this restaurant established by Italians who decided to make it big up north. Open summer 11:30am-2:30pm and 5pm-midnight; winter 11:30am-2pm and 5:30pm-midnight. AmEx/DC/MC/V. ❷

Batzenhäusl, Zwergg. 1a. Offers great deals, like the wiener schnitzel platter (€6.50), but the real attraction is the outdoor *Gastgarten* next to the old city wall. On weekends, the Batzbar fills with a diverse crowd and frequently has live music. Daily *Menü* €8.50. Open M-Sa 10am-2am. ❷

Goldener Fisch, Kärntnerstr. 9 (☎621 32; www.tiscover.at/goldener-fisch). Formerly a *Versteigerungsmarkt* (cattle market), this restaurant offers excellent *Tomaten-Mozzarella Nudel* (€7.80) and daily *Menüs* (€6.80-11.30) in a popular outdoor patio environment with occasional live music. Open daily 7:30am-10pm. AmEx/DC/MC/V. ❸

Café Köstl, Kreuzg. 4 (☎620 12). In the *Altstadt,* this diner-style restaurant/bakery is good for a light lunch. Ham and eggs or *Bratwurst* run €2.50-4. Delectable ice cream sundaes are around €4. Take-out available. Open M-F 7am-8pm, Sa 7am-12:30pm. ❶

For those attempting to stay on a budget, there is an **ADEG Aktiv Markt** in Hauptpl. (Open M-F 8am-6pm, Sa 8am-noon) and an **M-Preis** right behind Goldener Fisch with an entrance through the parking lot. (☎72 66 70. Open M 7:30am-6:30pm, Tu-Th 7:30am-6:30pm, F 7:30am-7:30pm, Sa 7:30am-5pm.) The **Bauernmarkt** on Südtirolerpl. (open Sa 9am-1pm) and the **Stadtmarkt** on Messingg. (open F 2:30-7pm and Sa 9am-1pm) offer fresh local fruits and vegetables.

◉ ⚠ SIGHTS AND OUTDOOR ACTIVITIES

On a hill above Lienz, Schloß Bruck houses the **Museum der Stadt Lienz.** From the tourist office, turn right on Tiroler Str., following it as it becomes Albin-Eggerstr. and then Iseltalerstr. (20min.). The castle was built in the mid-13th century as the Count of Gorz's home and includes a small chapel whose walls and ceiling are adorned with frescoes. It now serves as a museum with rotating exhibits and a permanent exhibit on hometown impressionist painter Albin Egger-Lienz (whose scenes of farmers at work have been popular in the area for 70 years). Heavy hitters Klimt and Rodin round out the collection, complemented by Roman and pre-historic artifacts. Climb the castle's tower for a regal view. (☎625 80 83; www.museum-schlossbruck.at. Open daily late May to mid-Sept. 10am-6pm; mid-Sept. to late Oct. Tu-Sa 10am-5pm. €6, children €4.50, students €2, family €12.)

HIKING. The Dolomites around Lienz make for excellent hikes. For information on hikes and huts in both the Dolomites and the Hohe Tauern National Park, contact either the tourist office or Lienz's chapter of the **Österreichischer Alpenverein (ÖAV),** Franz-von-Defreggerstr. 11. Take Alleestr. all the way to the end; it's on the righthand corner. (☎721 05. Open M 9-11am, F 3-6pm.) Various day hikes leave from **Schloß Bruck.** (1-7hr. round-trip) Signs on the trail to the castle give hiking information.

Hochsteinhütte (4hr. to the hut, 7hr. round-trip). From Schloß Bruck, follow signs to "Hochsteinhütte" and keep going. This well-marked hike to the ÖAV-maintained hut is moderately steep and suitable for intermediate or seasoned hikers. The climb to the hut (2057m) gives the best views of all, with gorgeous panoramas of the Dolomites to the south and the Hohe Tauern range extending northward. Head for the hut's terrace, sit back, and enjoy the elevation with a glass of beer.

Böses Weibele (1½-2hr. out, 3hr. round-trip). Those with a bit more fortitude can continue past the Hochsteinhütte and head toward this peak, the highest around (2521m). Getting to the "Evil Wench" requires a mostly uphill trek completely above the tree line, making you feel like you're on top of the world. Depending on how late in the summer it is, you may have to ford a few streams of snow. Not for the faint of heart.

Waldehrpfad Hike (45min.). Follow the "Waldehrpfad-Leisach" signs near Schloß Bruck. A level, leisurely forest hike past a number of signs (in German) offering fun facts about the forest and species of flora along the way. Most of the hike stays in the woods, but there are occasional views across the valley. Follow the white-and-red blazes and avoid trails that plunge downward. Eventually a sign for "Lienz" appears: follow this path, which ends 20min. out of the town center (otherwise the hike continues, depositing you in nearby Leisach). From the bottom of the path, take a left onto the road, then a right onto Bundesstr. 100, and walk 15min. back to Lienz.

SKIING. Lienz is a great place from which to attack the ski trails of the Dolomites. The **Lienzer Bergbahnen** (☎ 639 75; www.lienzer-bergbahnen.at) offers two passes: the **Lienzer Pass** for main peaks Hochstein and Zettersfeld, and the **Silver Pass,** for the entire region. (Card deposit €5. Silver pass 1½ day minimum €53, ages 15-18 and over 66 €43, children 7-15 €27. Lienzer Pass €29.50/€23.50/€15.) The **Skischule Lienzer Dolomiten** offers instruction in skiing from their base on Zettersfeld; take the Bergbahn to get there. (☎ 656 90; fax 672 62. €39 per hr., €9 for each additional person; private snowboard lessons €24 per hr.) **Joachim's Ski Shop** rents **skis** and **snowboards.** (☎ 685 41; fax 642 03. Complete downhill equipment from €18-30 per day, children €8; snowboard €24/€16.)

OTHER ACTIVITIES. Swimming is at the **Dolomitenbad** waterpark, across the Drau on the way to the campground. (☎ 638 20. Open M noon-9pm, Tu-F 9:30am-9pm, Sa-Su 9:30am-8pm. €4.50; students €3.30; seniors, children, and the disabled €2.) Rookie **paragliders** can call Bruno Girstmair, Beda Weberg. 4 (☎/fax 655 39; www.girstmair.com), for tandem flights from the nearby peaks.

🎵 📷 ENTERTAINMENT AND NIGHTLIFE

For a mixed crowd of 17- to 50-year-old locals, students, and tourists, head to the **Mausefalle,** Großglocknerstr. 4, in Nußdorf, the town adjacent to Lienz.

including reggae, jazz, blues, and folk. (☎ 698 35. Beer €2. Open M-W 5pm-1am, Th-Sa noon-whenever, Su noon-9pm.) Disco-lovers should like the **Stadtkeller-disco,** Tiroler Str. 30, near Europapl., where two bars and a dance floor beckon. (☎ 62 85 24. W 9-11pm all drinks €1.60. Cover €3.50 includes 1 drink. Open daily 9pm-4am.) **Odin's Café,** Schweizerg. 3, hops to loud rock and rap. There are lots of young locals, special events (including a boat-burning on the river), and **Internet** access (€0.10 per min.). (Beer and wine €1.50-3. Open M-Sa 4pm-

2am, Su 7pm-7am.) **Cinex Lienz,** Am Markt 2 (☎67 111), in the town center, shows mostly recently-released American **films** dubbed into German. (Shows 3pm-midnight. Tickets €5.50-8.)

The third week of July brings out the street artists—musicians, actors, and the finest chalk artists in the world—for the **Straßentheater Festival** in the city center. This includes five nights of free performances. During the second weekend of August, Lienz's annual **Stadtfest** calls all the local *Musiktappelle* to bring out their horns and play the polka from 2pm to 2am, while everyone else makes merry and drinks like crazy. (Admission to town center €4.) The summer months also witness the reaffirmation of Tyrolean culture in a series of *Musiktanzabende*r (music and dance evenings). Watch as local men dust off their old *Lederhosen* and perform the acclaimed *Schuhplattler*—the age-old shoe-slapping dance. (June-Aug. occasionally F 8pm. Free.)

UPPER AUSTRIA (OBERÖSTERREICH)

The province of Oberösterreich is comprised of three regions: the **Mühlviertel** in the northeast; the **Innviertel**, covering the western half; and the **Salzkammergut** in the southwest, which encompasses the popular resort area. The charming streets of the provincial capital **Linz** wind through the city's industrial soul; it is a major center of iron, steel, and chemical production, and home to many Danube port installations. Cyclists of all levels flock to Upper Austria's relatively flat terrain for **bike tours** along the well-paved paths that wind through the entire province.

HIGHLIGHTS OF UPPER AUSTRIA

Savor a jam-saturated **Linzer Torte** while relaxing in a garden café (p. 288).
Study the sobering horrors of history at **KZ-Mauthausen** (p. 291).

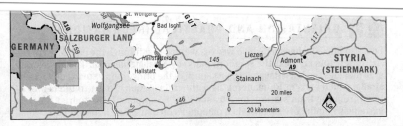

LINZ AN DER DONAU ☎ 0732

As a stopover between Vienna to the east and Salzburg to the west, Linz (pop. 183,500) is often overlooked. The third-largest city in the country, Linz was once home to Kepler, Mozart, Beethoven, Bruckner, and Hitler. Technologically, it surpasses Austria's other cities. Linz's industrial outskirts are not particularly scenic, but the wealth generated by the factories has been used to modernize and gentrify the central city, with interesting shops, modern art galleries, cybercafés, and state-of-the-art museums. The city's annual festivals—the classy Brucknerfest and the tomfoolery of the *Pflasterspektakel* (street performers' fair)—draw artists and spectators from all over the world.

▐ TRANSPORTATION

Trains connect to Austrian and European cities. **Buses** and trains leave from the **Hauptbahnhof,** which is undergoing a €45 million renovation in 2004-2005. The bus depot is outside the main exit of the train station and to the left. (Open M-F 7:50am-3:30pm, Sa 7am-1:20pm.) **Motorists** arrive via *Autobahn* West (A1 or E16).

Trains: Hauptbahnhof, Bahnhofpl. (☎517 17). To: **Innsbruck** (3¼hr., 13min. past the hr. 12:20am-11:23pm, €38); **Klagenfurt** (5hr., 5:10am-7:33pm, €36.50); **Munich** (3hr., every 1-2hr. 1:35am-10:33pm, €45.70); **Prague** (5½hr; 6:15, 7:35, 9:35am, 1:35, 6:35pm; €31.50); **Salzburg** (1½hr., 13 and 33min. after the hr. 1:35am-11:22pm, €17.70); **Vienna** (2¼hr., 32 and 52min. after the hr. 3:43am-10:57pm, €23.50). Not all international trains run daily, so it's better to change trains in Vienna.

Ferries: Wurm & Köck operates boats in **Krems** and **Linz** (Untere Donaulände 1; ☎78 36 07; www.donauschiffarht.de), and **Passau** (☎0851 92 92 92; fax 355 18). To **Passau** (5-7hr.; late Apr. to late Oct. 8am; €21, round-trip €24) and **Krems** (early July to early Sept. W 9am, early May to early Oct. Sa 9am; €37, round-trip €46). Boats dock in Linz at the **Donau Schiffstation,** and stop at a number of Austrian and Bavarian towns along the way. Children under age 15 and seniors half-price.

Public Transportation: Linz's public transport system runs to all corners of the city. Pick up an indispensible *Verkehrslinienplan* from the tourist office. Trams start at the Hauptbahnhof and run north through the city along Landstr. through Hauptpl. and across Nibelungenbrücke. Several buses traverse Linz, and nearly all pass through **Blumauerplatz,** down the block and to the right from the train station. A hub closer to the city center is **Taubenmarkt,** below Hauptpl. on Landstr. A ticket for 4 stops or fewer ("Mini") costs €0.70; more than 4 ("Midi") €1.50; and a day ticket ("Maxi") €3. Buy tickets from a *Tabak,* or the orange machines at bus or streetcar stops, or face a €40 fine. The tourist office sells a combination ticket that includes a day ticket for tram #3 and a round-trip cable car ride to **Pöstlingberg** (€5, children €2.50).

Taxis: At Hauptbahnhof, Blumauerpl., Schillerpl., and Hauptpl. (☎69 69, 606 606, or 17 18).

Parking: Free parking at **Urfahrmarkt** and at Stadion Parkpl. Ziegeleistr., beginning directly west from the train station. Limited parking zones are marked by blue lines; €0.50 per 30min. Garages are located throughout the city (outside the *Altstadt*). Prices range €10-23 per day.

▐▐ ▐ ORIENTATION AND PRACTICAL INFORMATION

Linz straddles the **Danube,** which weaves west to east through the city. Most of the *Altstadt* sights are near the southern bank, by **Nibelungenbrücke.** This pedestrian area includes the huge **Hauptplatz,** just south of the bridge, and extends down **Landstraße,** which ends in Blumauerpl. near the train station. To get to the center of town from the train station, take tram #3 to "Hauptplatz." The tourist office is extremely helpful, offering detailed pamphlets on dining and hotels in Linz.

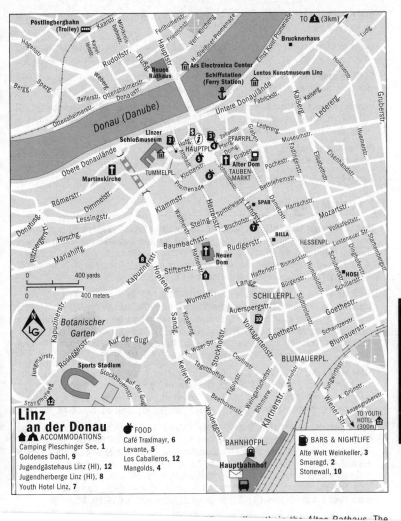

Linz an der Donau

ACCOMMODATIONS
Camping Pleschinger See, 1
Goldenes Dachl, 9
Jugendgästehaus Linz (HI), 12
Jugendherberge Linz (HI), 8
Youth Hotel Linz, 7

FOOD
Café Traxlmayr, 6
Levante, 5
Los Caballeros, 12
Mangolds, 4

BARS & NIGHTLIFE
Alte Welt Weinkeller, 3
Smaragd, 2
Stonewall, 10

UPPER AUSTRIA

the city, including a voucher for a meal up to €10 at selected restaurants and a free ride on the Linz City Express mini-train. Open May-Oct. M-F 8am-7pm, Sa 10am-7pm, Su 10am-7pm; Nov.-Apr. M-F 8am-6pm, Sa-Su 10am-6pm.

Currency Exchange: Banks open M-W 8am-noon and 2-4:30pm, Th 8am-noon and 2-5:30pm, F 8am-2pm. **24hr. exchange machine** at the train station. **Bank Austria Creditanstalt,** Hauptpl. 32, also exchanges currency. (Open M-W 8:30am-noon and 2-4pm, Th 8:30am-noon and 2-5:30pm, F 8:30am-2pm.) **Western Union** operates out of the Bahnhof.

American Express: Bürgerstr. (☎66 90 13). Only acts as tourist agency; doesn't handle traveler's checks. Open M-F 9am-5:30pm.

Luggage Storage: In coin-operated **lockers** to the left past the glass doors of the tourist office. €1 (accepts only €1 coins). Also to the left as you exit the train station (€2-3.50).

GLBT Organizations: Homosexuelle Initiative Linz (HOSI), Schubertstr. 36 (☎60 98 98; www.hosilinz.at). Open M-F 4-10pm. Counseling M 8-10pm, Th 6:30-10pm.

Internet Access: BIGnet.internet.cafe, Graben 17 (☎70 79 68 20 10; www.bignet.at). €1.50 per 10min., students €1.20; €3.70/€2.80 per 30min. Open daily 10am-midnight. Also **free** at the **Ars Electronica Museum** (p. 289).

Post Office: Bahnhofpl. 11, between the train and bus stations. Open M-F 7am-6pm, Sa 9am-6pm, Su 9am-1pm. 2nd office at Domg. 1. Open M-F 8am-6pm.

Postal Code: A-4020, 2nd branch A-4010.

ACCOMMODATIONS

Jugendherberge Linz (HI), Kapuzinerstr. 14 (☎699 12831412). From the train station, take tram #3 to "Taubenmarkt" and walk, or take bus #27 (dir: Chemie) from Tauben Markt and get off at Hopfeng. This friendly, no-frills hostel offers the cheapest 4- and 6-bed rooms in town. Showers and sheets included. Reception 8-10am and 6-8pm. Reservations recommended. Dorms €13.

Youth Hotel Linz, Wankmullerhofstr. 39 (☎070 34 23 61; fax 070 34 23 61 75). From Hauptpl., take tram #1 (dir: Auwiesen) or #2 (dir: Hillerstr.) to "WIFI." Then take a left on Wolfgang-Pauli Str. slightly behind you, and a right onto Wankmullerhofstr. A new budget option with private bath, shower, and TV. Pleasant reception staff. Breakfast buffet included with price. 103 rooms. Reception open from 10am. Parking available. Singles from €26.50; doubles from €39.50. MC/V. ❸

Goldenes Dachl, Hafnerstr. 27 (☎0676 5152215 or 77 58 97; fax 77 58 97). From the train station, take bus #45 (dir: Stieglbauernstr.) or #46 (dir: Hafen) to "Auerspergpl." The family-run hotel has large, sunny rooms in a great location. Courtyard dining area. Breakfast included. Call ahead. Singles €22.20; doubles €46.40. ❸

Jugendgästehaus Linz (HI), Stanglhofweg 3 (☎66 44 34; jgh.linz@oejhv.or.at). From the train station or Tauben Markt, take bus #27 (dir: Chemie) to "Botanischer Gardens" Walk about 50m and take a left onto Stanglhofweg. Caution: #27 stops running up the hill at 7:42pm on weekdays. Take bus #17 or #19 afterwards. Parking available. Breakfast and sheets included. Ask for key to hall locker. Private bathrooms. Reception M-F 7am-3pm and 5-9pm, Sa-Su 8-10am and 6-9pm. Curfew midnight. Call ahead for stays more than 1 night. Dorms €15.58; singles €27.08; doubles €39.16. MC/V. ❸

Camping Pleschinger See (☎30 53 14; camping-linz@utanet.at). Take tram #1 or 3 to Rudolfstr. and then bus #33 to "Pleschinger See." On the Linz-Vienna biking path on Pleschinger Lake. Plenty of room to sunbathe and swim, with great views of the countryside. Open May-Nov. €4 per adult, €2.35 per child. ❶

FOOD

Duck into the alleyway restaurants off Hauptpl. and Landstr. to avoid inflated prices, or seek out the supermarkets: **Billa,** Landstr. 44 (open M-W 8am-7pm, Th 7:30am-7pm, F 7:30am-7:30pm, Sa 7:30am-5pm) or **SPAR Markt,** Passage City Center, farther down Landstr. (Open M-F 7:30am-7pm.) Linz's rich namesake dessert, the **Linzer Torte,** is worth the price (usually €3). It's unique for its dry ingredients—lots of flour and absolutely no cream. The secret is in the red-currant jam filling, which seeps through and moisturizes the crumbly crust.

Mangolds, Hauptpl. 3 (☎78 56 88), is a vegetarian paradise in a pleasant outdoor space. This cafeteria-style restaurant uses only the freshest ingredients in its fruit and vegetable drinks (€2.90) and extravagant salad bar with 15 different kinds of salad (€1.16 per 100g). 30% discount after 6pm. Open M-F 11am-8pm, Sa 11am-5pm. ❶

Café Traxlmayr, Promenadestr. 16 (☎77 33 53). Chandeliers and marble tables adorn both the elegant interior of this Viennese-style café and its sprawling outdoor patio. For €4.50 you can nibble on rolls and jam, sip coffee from your own pot, and watch people play chess, cards, and billiards through the afternoon. Try the *Palatschinken* (sweet crêpe filled with jam; €1.90) or the *Linzer Torten* (€2.20). Open M-Sa 8am-10pm. ❶

Los Caballeros, Landstr. 32 (☎77 89 70; www.caballeros.at). A Mexican restaurant and bar with a large tequila selection and an excellent all-you-can-eat lunch *Menü* (€6.40). Enjoy a Corona (€4.20) indoors or in the courtyard. Daily specials after 10pm (€7.50). Ribs, wings, fajitas, and steak tacos €10-16. Open daily 11am-2am. MC/V. ❷

Levante, Hauptpl. 13 (☎79 34 30; www.levante.at), has outdoor seating on Hauptpl. and authentic Turkish and Greek food at low prices. €4 sandwiches are a great deal. *Menü* €6. Entrées €8-12. Falafel €7. Open daily 11:30am-11:30pm. AmEx/MC/V. ❷

🔆 SIGHTS

THE OLD TOWN. Start your exploration of Linz at **Hauptplatz,** where the green Pöstlingberg looms from across the Danube. The plaza grew in the 14th and 15th centuries in proportion to the taxes collected on salt and iron passing downstream. The marble **Trinity Column** commemorates the city's escape from the horrors of war, famine, and plague. An octagonal tower and astronomical clock crown the Baroque **Rathaus.** To date, only two people have ever addressed the public from its balcony: Adolf Hitler and Pope John Paul II. Free-spirited stargazer **Johannes Kepler** (who explained the elliptical orbits of the planets) completed his major work, *Rudolph Tables,* while living around the corner at Rathausg. 5. In 1745 Linz's first print shop opened there; today it houses a pub.

CHURCHES. On nearby Domg. stands Linz's dual-spired **Alter Dom** (Old Cathedral), where symphonic composer Anton Bruckner played during his stint as a church organist. *(Open daily 7am-7pm.)* To the south, the neo-Gothic **Neuer Dom** (New Cathedral) is the largest church in Austria. Its tower could have been the highest in the country, but regulation decreed no tower could outdo Vienna's Stephansdom. *(Open daily 7am-7pm.)* **Martinskirche** is the oldest church in Austria. The central structure was erected during the late 8th century using debris from Roman ruins

3D room that sends you even higher to explore the outer reaches of space. Free Internet access with entrance. *(Hauptstr. 2. ☎727 20; www.aec.at. Open W-Th 9am-5pm, F 9am-9pm, Sa-Su 10am-6pm. €6, students and seniors €3. MC/V.)* The sleek architecture of the newly opened **Lentos Kunstmuseum Linz** nearly rivals its collections. The symmetrical, glass-encased building features 1500 works, focusing on contemporary work of native Austrian artists, including Kokoschka and

Klimt. *(Ernst-Koref-Promenade 1. Call ahead for guided tours. ☎ 70 70 36 00; www.lentos.at. Open M, W, F-Su 10am-6pm, Th 10am-10pm. Wheelchair accessible. €6.50; seniors, students, and children €4.50; families €13. Audioguides in English €3.)* The **Linzer Schloßmuseum** presents an eclectic collection of objects from the Middle Ages to the 20th century, including one of Beethoven's pianos and a lock of Nietzsche's hair. Special exhibits are on the ground floor. *(Tummelpl. 10. ☎ 774 419; www.schlossmuseum.at. Open Tu-F 9am-5pm, Sa-Su 10am-4pm. €3, students and seniors €1.70, families €7. 2nd fl. (with Beethoven's piano) closed for renovation 2004-2005; call ahead. English brochure available, but all displays in German.)*

BOTANICAL GARDEN. For sheer olfactory ecstasy, visit the cactus and orchid garden. Take bus #27 (dir: Chemie) from Taubenmarkt to "Botanischer Garten." *(Rosegerstr. 20-22. ☎ 70 70 18 72. Open daily May-Aug. 7:30am-7:30pm; Apr. and Sept. 8am-7pm; Mar. and Oct. 8am-6pm; Nov.-Feb. 8am-5pm. €2; students, children, and seniors €1.)*

URFAHR AND PÖSTLINGBERG. Across Nibelungenbrücke on the left bank of the Danube is the area known as **Urfahr,** a separate city until Linz swallowed it up in the early 20th century. It boasts some of the city's oldest buildings and a view of Linz from the apex of the **Pöstlingberg** (537m). To reach the summit, take tram #3 to "Bergbahnhof Urfahr," then either hike 500m up Hagenstr. (off Rudolphstr., which is off Hauptstr. near the bridge) or hop aboard the **Pöstlingbergbahn,** a century-old trolley that ascends the summit. *(☎ 34 00 75 06. 17min. Every 20min. M-Sa 5:20am-8pm, Su 7:15-am-8pm. €2.20, round-trip €3.50; children €1.10/€1.70.)* The dual-spired **Pöstlingbergkirche** stands guard on the crest of the hill. The "magic dragon" train **(Grottenbahn),** into the fairy-tale caves of Pöstlingberg appeals to children. *(☎ 78 01 75 06; www.linzag.at. Open daily Apr.-Oct. 10am-6pm. €4, under age 15 €2.)*

🎵 ENTERTAINMENT

From mid-Sept. to mid-Oct., the **Brucknerfest** brings a rush of concerts paying homage to native son Anton Bruckner at the **Brucknerhaus** concert hall. The opening concerts (the second week in Sept.), billed as *Klangwolken* (sound-clouds), include spectacular outdoor lasers, a children's show, and a classical evening with Bruckner's 7th Symphony broadcast live into the surrounding Donaupark for 50,000 fans. *(☎ 77 52 30; www.brucknerhaus.at. Tickets €16-80, standing room about €8. Contact Brucknerhaus-kasse, Untere Donaulände 7, A-4010 Linz.)* During July, the city hosts **Pflasterspektakel,** a free, three-day street performers' festival. Every few steps down Landstr. and Hauptpl., international artists perform Houdini acts, fire-eating, outdoor theater, bongo concerts, and punk rock.

🎭 NIGHTLIFE

The pulse of Linzer nightlife is the **Bermuda Dreiecke** (Bermuda Triangle), behind the west side of Hauptpl. (head down Hofg. or follow the crowds of pub crawlers).

Alte Welt Weinkeller, Hauptpl. 4 (☎ 77 00 53). A Renaissance-era "wine and culture cellar" where patrons soak up wine (€3-6) and enjoy Latin music. Tasty salads (€3-7) and polenta (€7). Open M-F 11:30am-2:30pm and 5:30pm-2am, Sa 5:30pm-2am. ❶

Smaragd, Altstadt 2 (☎ 79 40 60; www.smaragd.cc). This café, bar, club, and performance complex draws eclectic locals seeking late-night revelry under the moon and stars painted on its walls. Have a bowl of chili con carne (€4.20) and wash it down with a Desperado (tequila beer; €4). The student crowd really cranks up the party around 2am. Tu-W live music, Th Fiesta Latina, F-Sa disco and DJs. Open daily 8pm-6am. ❶

Stonewall, Rainerstr. 22 (☎60 04 38; www.stonewall.at), is a bar during the week and a disco on the weekends. Attracts a largely gay and lesbian crowd, some of whom arrive in drag to dance among the miniature Greek statues and life-size armor. Drinks €4-9. Disco F-Sa 11pm-4am. Open M-Sa 8pm-4am, Su 6am-2pm. MC/V. ❷

🔁 DAYTRIPS FROM LINZ

MAUTHAUSEN

From Linz, take a train to St. Valentin (includes most Vienna-bound trains; 20min., 4:43am-11:01pm, €3.90). Transfer at St. Valentin to Mauthausen (9min.; 53min. past every hr. 5:18am-7:53pm; €1.90). Return trains from St. Valentin to Linz run every 30min. 5:26am-10:15pm. Mauthausen's train station is 6km from the camp. Bus #360 will take you from the station to Mauthausen proper, but not all the way to the camp. Instead, consider taking a cab (☎2439; €1.50-2.50 per km) or take the road leading straight back away from the station and follow the green arrow signs to "Ehem. KZ-Mauthausen" through town (70min.). Maps available from the tourist office in town. By car, take Autobahn A1 (Vienna-Linz) at Enns. (www.mauthausen-memorial.gv.at. Camp open daily Apr.- Sept. 8am-6pm; Oct. to mid-Dec. and Feb.-Mar. 8am-4pm. Admission until 45min. before closing. €2, students and seniors €1.)

The meadows and farms down the Danube from Linz disguise Mauthausen, where the preserved remains of a Nazi *Konzentrationslager* (KZ; concentration camp) stand in silent vigil. Built by Dachau prisoners in 1938, Mauthausen was the central camp for all of Austria and administered 49 subcamps throughout the country. More than 200,000 prisoners passed through its towered gates, mainly Russian, Italian, and Polish POWs, along with Austrian homosexuals and political criminals, Hungarian and Dutch Jews, gypsies, Spanish anti-fascists, and Communists. Mauthausen's infamous **Todesstiege** (Staircase of Death) led to the stone quarry where inmates were forced to work to exhaustion. One of the former barracks has been converted into a **museum** (☎07238 22 69) covering the camp's history, accompanied by haunting photographs of the overcrowded camps. Just outside the walls, a memorial park stands as stirring testimony to international remembrance. A free brochure or audio tour (in English) walks you through the central camp. Video documentaries (45min.) in several languages screen daily.

ST. FLORIAN'S ABBEY

To reach the abbey from Linz Hauptbahnhof, take the Post Bus from stand A (dir: St. Florian Stift; 25min., 6:10am-10:35pm, €2.20). The tourist office has info about the abbey and accommodation (Marktpl. 3; ☎/fax 07224 56 90). The abbey gives daily tours (1¼hr.) in German with an English brochure. ☎07224 89 020. Abbey open Apr.-Oct. €5.30, students €4.50, children €2. Tours 10, 11am, noon, 2, 3, 4pm. 20min. concerts May-Oct. Su-M and W-F 2:30pm; €2.40. Tour and concert together €6.80.

who began his career here first as a choirboy, then as a teacher, and finally as an organist and composer. His body is interred beneath the organ inside the spectacular, recently renovated church, allowing him to vibrate in perpetuity to the sound of his dearly-beloved pipes. The abbey also possesses the world's largest collection of works by Albrecht Altdorfer of Regensburg, an Old Master of the Danube school. Note that Altdorfer paints some of Christ's tormentors as Turks, the sworn enemies of the Austrian Empire. The 14 **Kaiserzimmer** (imperial rooms), built in

case of an imperial visit, overwhelm visitors with their Baroque splendor and their amazing success at covering every inch of the room in the same color fabric. The (literally) cool crypt contains the neatly-stacked remains of 6000 early Christians. Those who prefer the living should check out the lovely roses in the courtyard and the fat fish swimming in Florian's saintly moat.

THE MÜHLVIERTEL

Stretching north and west from Linz, the Mühlviertel's shaded woodland paths and pastures entice adventurers and hikers from all over the world. The region was once the stomping ground of the Celts, but in the Middle Ages Christians constructed churches out of supposedly Celt-proof local granite. This same granite filters the region's curative mineral-rich waters and hot springs.

Several ancient paths traverse the Mühlviertel. Along the old **Mühlviertel Weberstraße** (Weaver's Road), textile-oriented towns display their methods of linen preparation. The **Gotischestraße** winds past numerous examples of High Gothic architecture, and the **Museumstraße** sports numerous **Freilichtmuseen** (open-air museums). Poppies *(Mohn)* are another of the Mühlviertel's big selling points: (legal) products range from poppy seed oil to mouth-watering poppy seed strudels. Throughout this pastoral countryside, *Bauernhöfe* (farmhouses) open their doors to world-weary travelers. Contact the **Mühlviertel Tourist Office** for brochures detailing trails and *Bauernhöfe*. (Blütenstr. 8, Linz. ☎ 0732 73 50 20; www.tiscover.com/muehlviertel.)

FREISTADT   ☎ 07942

Freistadt, the largest town in the Mühlviertel, is an idyllic village at the juncture of the **Jaunitz** and **Feldaist** rivers. Due to its location on the Pferdeeisenbahn route, which connected the Babenberg and Hapsburg lands, Freistadt was the crossroads for the medieval salt and iron trades. Freistadt's pride and joy, the community-owned **Freistädter Brauerei**, Promenade 7, is still in operation and open to the public. (☎ 75 777. Open M-Th 7am-4:30pm, F 7am-noon. Call ahead for a tour.)

☎▼ TRANSPORTATION AND PRACTICAL INFORMATION. Freistadt is accessible from Linz. The **Post Bus** leaves from Linz's main train station (1hr.; 6:20, 8, 8:45, 9:35, 11:35am, 12:20, 12:30, 12:55, 1:30, 1:50, 2:15, 4:15, 4:25, 5:25, 6:15, 7:45, 8:15pm; €6) and arrives at Böhmertor in Freistadt, just outside the old city walls. **Trains** also run from Linz (dir: Sommerau; 1hr., 5:59am-6:59pm, €6.70), but they arrive 4km outside of town at the Bahnhof; either follow the signs to "Zentrum" or call a taxi (☎ 72 354; €10).

The tiny **tourist office**, Hauptpl. 14, has a free reservation service and provides info about nearby villages. (☎757 00; fax 757 00 20. Open May-Sept. M-F 9am-7pm, Sa 9am-noon; Oct.-Apr. M-F 9am-5pm.) The **post office** is located on Promenade 11 at St. Peterstr. (Open M-Th 8am-noon and 2-5:30pm, F 8am-5:30pm, Sa 8-10:30am.) **Postal Code:** A-4240.

☎☐ ACCOMMODATIONS AND FOOD. Crash for the night at **Camping Freistadt**, Eglsee 12. Follow the highway out of the Altstadt toward Prague and turn right at the rotary toward Gmund. Forty year-round plots and amenities await campers and caravaners. (☎725 70; www.freistadt.at/ffc. AmEx/MC/V.)

There are plenty of inexpensive meals in this budget-friendly town. **Café Vis à Vis ❷**, Salzg. 13, offers the local *Mühlviertel Bauernsalat* (farmer's salad; €6), and local *Freistädter* beer (€3.20). (☎742 96. Open M-F 9am-2am, Sa 5pm-2am.) Food is easy to find on Hauptpl. as well. The best ice cream in Freistadt is at **Café Lubinger ❶**, Hauptpl. 10. (Soft-serve €1. Scoops €0.70, less for each additional scoop. Open M and W-Sa 8am-7pm, Su 9am-7pm.) From the bus stop, the most convenient grocery store is **ADEG**, Untere Hafnerzeile 3. (Open M-F 6:30am-noon and 2:30-6pm, Sa 6:30am-noon.) You will pass a **Billa** and a **Euro SPAR** on your way into town from the train station.

☑ SIGHTS. Wander around Freistadt's inner and outer fortifications and scan the horizon from its watchtower. The moat is gradually being drained and filled with grass to form a belt-like park around the town. Pick up *A Walk Through the*

tour. (☎ 722 14; www.museumssuuu...........

5pm. €2.40, students and seniors €1.60, under 6 €0.80, family €4.80.)

LOWER AUSTRIA
(NIEDERÖSTERREICH)

Surrounding Vienna, the province of Niederösterreich accounts for a quarter of Austria's land mass and 60% of its wine production. Castle ruins lie in the hills above medieval towns, and hikers and bikers enjoy the varied terrain on daytrips from Vienna. The region's food is delicious: one local specialty, the Wienerwald cream strudel, is a sinful mixture of flaky crust, curds, raisins, and lemon peel.

HIGHLIGHTS OF LOWER AUSTRIA

Climb up to the ruins of Richard the Lionheart's prison, **Schloß Dürnstein** (p. 299).

Marvel at the buttery stucco of **Melk's** Benedictine abbey (p. 299).

Smell the roses, all 20,000 of them, in **Baden bei Wien's** rosarium (p. 305).

Lower Austria
(Niederösterreich)

DANUBE VALLEY (DONAUTAL)

The "Blue Danube" may be largely the invention of Johann Strauss's imagination, but the valley of this shallow, muddy-green river inspired him to create music for good reason. Ride a ferry or bike along its shores to experience the beauty of Austria's most famous river. The **Wachau** region holds the most exemplary bends of the river—be sure to catch those between Melk and Krems. **Donau Dampfschifffahrts-Gesellschaft (DDSG)** ships sail daily from Vienna and within the Wachau valley along the Danube from early April to late October. (☎58 88 00; www.ddsg-blue-danube.at.) These trips, complete with commentary, run from Reichsbrücke in Vienna to **Durnstein** via **Tulln** and **Krems,** and to **Melk** via **Krems.** (Departs Vienna 8:45am, returns 5pm. Reservations required. €19, round-trip €25.)

If you're not coming from Vienna, you can simply take the DDSG daily ferries between the most beautiful towns in the Wachau valley. **Boats** leave Krems for Melk at 10:15am, 1, and 3:45pm, docking at Dürnstein and Spitz on the way. (3hr.; €15.80, round-trip €20.50; bike transport free, but call ahead.) **Rail/ferry combinations** (€39.20) are available in Vienna, including train fare to the Wachau region, the ferry within the Wachau valley between Krems and Melk, and entrance to a site of your choice, including the Benedictine abbey of Melk, Schloß Schallaburg, or the Kunsthalle Krems. ISIC holders 20% discount, seniors 20% discount M-F; children ages 10-15 half-price with parent, under age 10 free with parent.) Contact the DDSG or tourist offices for special ship/bus ticket combinations. Specialty tours include the *Nibelungen,* which sails through areas described in the ancient saga, and a *Heurigen* ride with a live *Liederabend* (evening song) trio.

Cyclists should take advantage of the **Danube Cycle Path** (Donauradweg). This 382km riverside bike trail threads its way from Bratislava in the Czech Republic, through the Wachau Valley, Linz, and Vienna, to Passau, on the German border. It links the Danube villages and offers captivating views of crumbling castles, latticed vineyards, and medieval towns. Area tourist offices carry the route map and information on bike rental. There is also information on the route at www.radtouren.at/english. One of the most dramatic fortresses on the ride is the 13th-century **Burg Aggstein-Gastein,** formerly inhabited by Scheck von Wald, a robber baron known to fearful sailors as **Schreckenwalder** (the Terror of the Woods).

KREMS AND STEIN   ☎02732

At the head of the Wachau region, the neighboring towns of Krems and Stein are surrounded by lush, green hills covered with terraced vineyards. Historically, Krems and Stein have shared a mayor to coordinate trade and military strategy on the Danube trading route, and through the years the towns have

Krems holds most of the sights, from art exhibits to sporting events, Stein has a gorgeous *Altstadt.* Its crooked, narrow, cobblestone passages twist and wind back on themselves, giving it an old-world feel. In the valley around the towns, vineyards produce 120 different wines. Head for Steiner Kellerg., the high street in Stein, where *Heurigen* offer the local wines and great views of the Stift Göttweig (abbey) across the Danube. Tour buses often block the entrance to this street leading to the *Heurigen*—rich wine and the impressive panorama of the valley make it worthwhile for every tourist.

▐ TRANSPORTATION

Many visitors arrive on bicycles, but the **train station** (☎ 82536 345) is a 5min. walk from Krems's *Fußgängerzone*. Regional trains connect Krems to Vienna's Spittelau station (€11.50, 5:05am-10:05pm) via Tulln. A **bus depot** (☎ 82536 390) is in front of the station. Both buses and trains leave every 30min. for Melk and St. Pölten. Krems lies along the **DDSG ferry** route from Passau through Linz and Melk to Vienna (p. 299.) Ferries go to: Melk (early Apr. to Oct. 10:15am, late Apr. to late Sept. 1, 3:45pm; one-way €15.80, round-trip €20.50); Vienna (5pm; one-way €19, round-trip €25); and Durnstein (10:50am). The ferry station is on the riverbank close to Stein and the ÖAMTC campground, near the intersection of Donaulände and Dr.-Karl-Dorreck-Str. To reach Krems from the landing, walk down Steiner Donaulände, which becomes Ringstr., then left onto Utzstr. To reach Stein, follow Dr.-Karl-Dorreck-Str. and then take a left onto Steiner Landstr.

▐ ORIENTATION AND PRACTICAL INFORMATION

A long *Fußgängerzone* connects the two towns: starting in Krems and heading into Stein are Untere Landstr., Obere Landstr., Schillerstr., Undstr., and Steiner Landstr. These streets are a couple of blocks up from, and run generally parallel to, busy Ringstr., which turns into Steiner Donaulände. To get to the *Fußgängerzone*, exit through the front door of the train station, cross Ringstr., and follow Dinstlstr. uphill. Head left to get to Stein. The **tourist office** is housed in the Kloster Und at Undstr. 6. From the train station, take a left on Ringstr. and continue 15min. before taking a right onto Meyereck-Str. The staff has information on accommodations, sports, and entertainment, as well as the indispensable *Heurigen Kalender*, which lists the opening times of regional wine taverns. Self-guided walking tours with discmen (€6) and group guided walking tours in several languages leave for Krems or Stein. (1½hr.; €56 per group or €2.80 per person for groups larger than 20.) They also book hotel rooms. (☎ 826 76; www.tiscover.com/krems. Open Easter to Oct. M-F 8:30am-6pm, Sa 10am-noon and 1-5pm, Su 10am-noon and 1-4pm; Nov. to Easter M-F 9am-6pm.) **Internet** access available at one computer at Café Collage, Untere Landstr. 40. (Access free with purchase at café. Open M-F until 7pm, Sa-Su until 6pm.) **ATMs** are along shopping streets. **Lockers** (€2-3.50) are at the train station.

R&R, Steiner Landstr. 103, rents **bikes**. Go a little past the shop and through the archway to the left; the entrance is in back. From the ferry landing, cross the street straight ahead and look for the tent. (☎ 710 71. Open M-F 9am-noon and 1-6pm. €13 per day, €7 per half-day.) The Adler Apotheke **pharmacy** at Obere Landstr. 3 has been in Krems since 1528. (Open M-F 7:30am-noon and 2:30-6pm, Sa 7:30am-noon.) Other services include: **public toilets** at the train station, tourist office, and in the Stadtpark; **ambulances** at ☎ 822 44 and **police** at ☎ 133. **Currency exchange** and **Western Union** are at the **post office** in Krems right off Ringstr. on Brandströmstr. (☎ 826 06. Open M-F 8am-6pm.) The **post office** in Stein is at Steiner Landstr. 68. (☎ 822 81. Open M-F 8am-noon and 1:30-5pm.) **Postal Code** in Krems: A-3500, in Stein: A-3504.

▐ ACCOMMODATIONS

No matter where you stay, ask your hosts for a **guest card** for a number of discounts. *Privatzimmer* are available on Steiner Landstr. and throughout town.

Radfahrjugendherberge (HI), Ringstr. 77 (☎ 834 52 and 0043 664 6530615; oejhv.noe.krems@aon.at). Walk away from the tourist office back down Meyereckstr. and make a left onto Ringstr. The hostel is clean and accommodates 52 in comfortable

4- and 6-bed rooms. Bikers welcome. Breakfast, lockers, sheets, and bicycle storage included. Reception 7-9:30am and 5-8pm. For advance bookings, call the central office in Vienna (☎533 53 53; fax 535 08 61). Open Apr.-Oct. Dorms €12.20. Non-members pay €3.50 extra. €2.20 surcharge on stays less than 3 nights. Tax included. ❷

Hotel-Restaurant "Alte Post," Obere Landstr. 32 (☎822 76; fax 843 96). Krems's oldest guest house (dating from the 1500s) will host you amid its dark velvet couches, embroidered curtains, and garden café. Rooms are medium-sized. Breakfast included. Singles €26-42; doubles €50-70. ❹

ÖAMTC Donaupark Camping, Wiedeng. 7 (☎844 55), is on the grassy Danube riverbank near the highway. Follow Ringstr. left from the train station and past the tourist office, around the rotary toward Spitz. Turn left at the 2nd rotary and follow the signs. The campground is on the right. Tennis courts, swimming pools, and a lake nearby. Showers included. Special facilities for disabled guests. Reception 7:30-10am and 4:30-7pm. Open Apr.-Oct. €3.65 per adult plus €0.77 tax, €2.54 per child ages 5-14, €3.65 per car. Tent spots €2.20-4.36; bring your own tent. Electricity €1.82. ❶

🍴 FOOD

Krems's *Fußgängerzone* overflows with restaurants and cafés. There are two **SPAR** markets: one a block from the train station on Sparkasseng. and another at Obere Landstr. 15. (Open M-Th 7:30am-6:30pm, F 7:30am-7pm, Sa 9:30am-5pm.)

Heuriger Hamböck, Steiner Kellerg. 31 (☎845 68), has a leafy terrace with a view of the town's spires and a restaurant decorated with old *Fässchen* (kegs), presses, and harvesting paraphernalia. The owner gives free tours of the cellar, including a wine tasting. For a fragrant experience, try the sweet apricot and raspberry wine (€1). Snacks €2.80-4. Open daily 3pm until everyone leaves. ❶

Café-Konditorei Hagmann, Untere Landstr. 8 (☎831

€0.80) for the road. Truffles €0.50. Exquisite sugar figurines from €0.35. Open M-F 7am-6:30pm, Sa 7am-5pm, Su 1:30-6pm. ❶

Schwarze Kuchl (☎831 28), right next door to Hagmann, offers a salad buffet (small €2.76, large €4) and assorted goulashes (€4-7) in a pleasant, homey interior decorated with kitchen utensils. Open M-F 8:30am-7:30pm, Sa 8:30am-5pm. ❷

THE LOCAL STORY

HOW MANY GREEKS DOES IT TAKE TO KILL A RHINOCEROS?

Once upon a time, Klagenfurt was harassed by a winged, virgin-consuming lizard, the *Lindwurm* (dragon). This awful monster terrorized the area, preventing settlers from draining the marshes, not to mention decimating the eligible young maiden population. Enter Hercules, who arrived all the way from Greece to quickly dispatch the beast and save the village. Centuries later, the "skull" of the slain beast was found, proving many an old wives' tale about the heroic defeat of the town's scaly scourge. The townspeople commissioned sculptor Ulrich Vogelsang to recreate the monster using the skull as his model. The bronze fountain-statue of the *Lindwurm* on Neuer Platz became the town's symbol, despite the fact that, in 1840, scientists proved the skull belonged not to the beast, but to a prehistoric rhino. *Lindwurm* or not, the skull now rests proudly in the *Landesmuseum*. Klagenfurt's collective heart broke in 1945 when an Allied soldier climbed onto the

Lindwurm once again drools spitefully in Hercules' direction.

🄲 SIGHTS AND ENTERTAINMENT

THE OLD TOWNS. Krems's *Fußgängerzone*, the center of mercantile activity, consists of Obere and Untere Landstr. Take Marketg. where Obere Landstr. becomes Untere Landstr. to arrive in **Pfarr Platz,** home of the Renaissance **Rathaus** and the **Pfarrkirche,** with its piecemeal Romanesque, Gothic, and Baroque architecture. Once there, go behind the church and up the stairs to Piaristen Stiege to the **Piaristenkirche,** surrounded by life-sized depictions of Jesus' crucifixion. Keep following Obere Landstr. and take a right onto Schmidg. to enter Körnermarkt and Dominikanerpl., home of the **Dominikanerkirche,** now the Weinstadt Museum (below). At the end of the pedestrian zone stands the **Simandlbrunnen,** a statue depicting a husband kneeling in front of his stern wife. The statue commemorates the power and influence of women in Krems during the Renaissance, when they succeeded in shutting down the Simandl brotherhood, a fraternity of carousing and late-night debauchery. At the end of Obere Landstr. is the Kremser Tor, a remnant of the town's medieval ramparts. Following straight ahead past the Kunsthalle Krems brings you into Stein, where medieval buildings line **Steiner Landstraße,** and stone steps tucked between houses lead to impressive views of the town and valley. This section of town is a great place to meander past the city's architectural treasures.

KUNSTHALLE KREMS. This art museum on the border of Krems and Stein is one in a series of museums known as the *Kunstmeile,* which is spread out along Steiner Landstr. The enormous exhibition hall has fascinating cultural and historical exhibits on rotation, often about postmodern or non-European art. *(Franz-Zeller-Pl. 3. ☎90 80 10; www.kunsthalle.at. Wheelchair accessible. Open daily 10am-6pm. €8, students and seniors €7, under age 6 €3.50.)* The Karikatur Museum is across the parking lot to the left and displays high-art political and social satire. *(Steiner Landstr. 3a. ☎90 80 20; www.karikaturmuseum.at. Wheelchair accessible. Open daily 10am-6pm. €8, students and seniors €7, under age 6 €3.50, combination ticket for both museums €10.)*

WEINSTADT MUSEUM. Built in the Dominikanerkloster, this excellent museum in Krems features paintings by the world-renowned Baroque artist Martin Johann Schmidt and, in the cloister cellars, archaeological treasures from the Paleolithic Era through the Middle Ages. Changing exhibits cover subjects ranging from local folklore to apocalyptic art. *(Körnermarkt 14. ☎801 567 or 801 572; www.weinstadtmuseum.at. Open Mar.-Nov. Tu-Su 10am-6pm. €3.60, students and seniors €2.50.)*

WINE CELLARS AND APRICOT DISTILLERY. The **Heurigen** (wine cellars) are not to be missed. Plan carefully: they are only allowed to stay open for three weeks every two months from April to October. If you don't have time for *Heurigen,* stop by the city-owned **Weingut Stadt Krems.** The winery offers free tours of the cellar and bottling center. Tastings after the tour usually seduce visitors into buying wine. *(Stadtgraben 11. Go left to the end of Obere Landstr., through the clock tower archway, and to the right. Go past #26 all the way to the end of the street. ☎80 14 40; www.weingutstadtkrems.at. Open for tours M-Sa 9am-noon and 1-5pm.)* For all things apricot, head to Steiner Landstr. 100-102, where the **Bailoni distillery** massages apricots into booze for the entire Wachau region; ask for a free sample of apricot brandy or schnapps. (Open M-W 7am-noon and 1-5pm, F 7am-noon.)

FESTIVALS. Krems loves to throw a party, even for something as humble as the *Marille* (apricot) Check with the tourist office for exhaustive info. Each year the **Donaufestival,** from mid-June to early July, brings open-air music and dancing, kicking off a summer of cultural activities including theater, circus, symposia, folk music, and even Korean drumming. From July 15 to August 15, Krems hosts a

Musikfest, featuring a number of organ, piano, and quartet concerts in the Kunsthalle and various churches. Tickets are available at the tourist office. From late August to early November, Krems hosts the **Weinherbst,** which features wine tastings, culinary specialties, presentations, and folklore.

▶ DAYTRIP FROM KREMS

DÜRNSTEIN

Trains connect Dürnstein to Krems (10min., every hr. 6am-7pm, €1.90) and Vienna's Franz Josef Bahnhof (1¼hr., every 2hr., €10.68). To reach town, descend the hill, turn right, and pass through the underground walkway (5min.). Boats dock at the DDSG ferry station on the Donaupromenade, a riverside road with beaches and bike paths. To reach town, turn right on Donaupromenade, left on Anzugg., and left on Hauptstr.

Down the Danube from Krems, this medieval village thrills tourists and locals alike with its mythical charm. The high-security prison back in Stein is no match for the ruined fortress of the Kuenrings, where **Richard the Lionheart** was imprisoned after his capture on the way back from the Third Crusade in 1192. Only the sure-footed should attempt the path up to castle, which at times has 45° inclines.

Although Richard's capture was the last hurrah for the local Kuenringer dynasty, they continued to prosper on their home turf, building **Stift Dürnstein.** This Baroque abbey, commissioned by the daughter of the penultimate heir to the throne in 1372, was dedicated to the Virgin Mary. Joseph II dissolved it at the same time that he dismantled most of Austria's ecclesiastical institutions, but it has been well maintained nevertheless. Two richly robed skeletons lie in state in the chapel. (Apr.-Oct. ☎ 02711 375, Nov.-Mar. 02711 227; fax 02711 432. Open Apr.-Oct. daily 9am-6pm. €2.40, students and children €1.50; with tour €3.85/€2.90.)

The **tourist office** is next to the Nah & Frisch grocery store. From the station turn right at the bottom of the hill; the green "i" is on the right. The office and the *Rathaus* (take a right halfway down

NO WORK, ALL PLAY

HOW DO YOU SOLVE A PROBLEM LIKE MARILLE?

By baking a 50m-long strudel, of course.

During the *Alles Marille* ("Everything Apricot") festival in Krems, held the third Friday and Saturday in July, the fuzzy fruit appears in every form imaginable, from apricot schnapps to apricot ice cream to apricot dumplings to apricot spritzer. The pièce de résistance, however, is Café Hagmann's 50m-long *Marillenstrudel,* which stretches down Taglisher Markt street. Everyone in town can literally get a piece of the action from this perpetual pastry, laden with fluffy apricot cream and sugared almonds (30cm for €3). A folk band in traditional dress serenades the town with Austrian favorites from under an awning festooned with apricot balloons, while revelers sun themselves and imbibe all things apricot. All of Krems turns out for the fun, including the mayor himself. Young and old alike stroll amid cafés and vendors, creating the closest thing to traffic Krems gets. To top it all off, Saturday ends with a huge party down by the milk and honey. So as you bike, drive, or walk along the Danube and see the trees laden with their precious golden goods, drop into Krems and indulge with the locals in a truly lavish fruit fetish.

MELK   ☎ 02752

Melk's yellow-trimmed monastery looming over the countryside is one of the most striking sights in Austria. The Babenburgs built a fortress and parish here in AD 960, which eventually became the Benedictine monastery around which Melk formed. The monas-

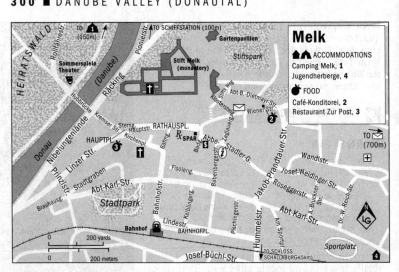

tery was renowned in the medieval world for its monumental library and learned monks. Today it is one of few ecclesiastical institutions that report directly to the Pope, with no bishop as middle-man. Below the abbey, the tiny town is a jumble of Renaissance houses, narrow pedestrian zones, cobblestone streets, old towers, and remnants of the medieval city wall.

TRANSPORTATION AND PRACTICAL INFORMATION

Trains link Melk to Vienna's Westbahnhof (1½hr., €12) and Krems (€6) via St. Pölten (17min., 15min. and 40min. past every hr., €6). Just outside the station's main entrance is the **bus depot.** Bus #1451 runs from Melk to Krems (2hr., 6:15am, €6). Melk is at the end of the **DDSG ferry** route between Vienna and Passau (from Krems €15.50, round-trip €20.50; p. 299). The **tourist office,** Babenbergstr. 1, has large **lockers** (€1) and **bike racks,** and makes free room reservations. (☎52307 410; www.tidiscover.com/melk. Open July-Aug. M-Sa 9am-7pm, Su 10am-noon and 5-7pm; May and June M-F 9am-noon and 2-6pm, Sa-Su 10am-noon and 4-6pm; Sept. M-F 9am-noon and 2-6pm, Sa-Su 10am-noon and 4-6pm; Oct. M-F 9am-noon and 2-5pm, Sa 10am-noon.) Services include: **currency exchange** at Raiffisenbank, Abbe Stadlerg. 6, (☎527 270; open M-Th 8am-noon and 1-4pm, F 8am-4:30pm, Sa 8-11am); **luggage storage** (€2-3.50) at the train station; and **bike rental** at Hotel zur Post, Linzerstr. 1. (☎523 45. €7 after 3pm, €10 per day, €18 for 2 days.) The **pharmacy** Landschaftsapotheke, Rathauspl. 10, is next to the town hall. (☎235 15. Open M-F 8am-noon and 2-6pm, Sa 8am-noon.) The **post office** is no longer in the town proper: use yellow mailboxes or save your big packages for the next town. **Postal Code:** A-3390.

ACCOMMODATIONS AND FOOD

To soak up the cozy atmosphere of Melk, stay in a *Pension* or *Privatzimmer,* or on a country farm (generally €15-26). The tourist office has a complete list. Brush up on your table tennis skills at the **Jugendherberge ❷,** Abt-Karl-Str. 42, 10min. from the station. This clean hostel offers 104 beds in quads with private showers and hall toilets. No lockers are available, but the front desk will keep valuables in a safe. (☎526 81; www.noejhw.at. Breakfast and bicycle storage included. Reception 8-10am and 5-9pm. Open early Mar. to late Oct. Dorms €15.70, ages 19 and under €12.20. €2 surcharge per night for stays less than 3 nights.) **Farhaus Familie Jensch/Camping Melk ❶** has camping plots overlooking the Danube next to the ferry landing. Walk down Rollfährestr. for 15min. (☎/fax 532 91. Reception 8am-midnight. €3 per person, €3 per tent, €2 per car. Showers €1.10. Tax €0.80.) The vast majority of restaurants and cafés are located on Rathauspl. **Restaurant Zur Post ❸**, Linzer Str. 1, whose bright yellow outdoor patio is full of relaxed locals, tempts the tastebuds with regional specialties like Wachau turkey stew (€8), apricot dumplings (€2), and roast beef with onions (€14). (☎523 45. Open daily 10am-11pm.) **Café-Konditorei Backerei Teufner,** Wiener Str. 36, will prepare you for the monastery tour. Teufner delights customers with tiramisu, enticing freshly-baked breads, coffee, and ice cream. (Open M-F 6:30am-6pm, Sa 6:30am-noon, Su 7:30-10am.) Stock up on food at **SPAR Markt,** Rathauspl. 9. (Open M-F 7am-6pm, Sa 7am-5pm.) There's an open-air **market** every W 8am-4pm on Rathauspl.

👁 🎵 SIGHTS AND ENTERTAINMENT

STIFT MELK. Melk's prime attraction is the impressive **Stift** (Benedictine abbey). The monastery is huge—the secular wing alone was large enough to house Maria Theresia and her coterie of 300 on visits from Vienna. Today, this wing is filled with eerily lighted exhibits (mostly in German) and various Baroque optical tricks, including a portrait of Leopold II, whose eyes follow you around the room, and a flat ceiling that appears to be a dome when viewed from directly beneath its center. The stunning library in the opposite wing brims with sacred and secular texts painstakingly hand-copied by monks. The two highest shelves in the gallery are fake—in typical Baroque fashion, the monks sketched book spines onto the wood to make the collection appear even more impressive. However, the Rule of St. Benedict, Virgil texts, and work by the Venerable Bede are not fake. The church itself, maintained by 20 monks, is a Baroque masterpiece. Maria Theresia donated the skeleton that adorns the side altar of St. John. He and his counterpart across the aisle are unknown refugees from the catacombs of Rome, lounging in jeweled, embroidered outfits with thin veils over their gaping sockets. The greatest treasure of the monastery is the 1362 Melker Kreuz (Melk Cross), decorated with gold and jewels. The monks curate temporary exhibits of contemporary art and commissioned artist Peter Bischof to paint new murals over weather-ruined frescoes in the interior of the main courtyard. You can also visit the monastery's small garden with its delicate pavilion containing fanciful frescoes of colonial encounters. (☎555 232; www.stiftmelk.at. Open daily May-Sept. 9am-6pm; Oct.-Apr. 9am-5pm; 11am-2pm only with guided tour. Last entry 1hr. before closing. English guide book €3.50-6.90. Guided tours daily in German every hr. 10am-4pm; call ahead to arrange tour in English. €7, students €4.20, tour €1.60 extra. Garden open May-Oct. €3, students €2, children €1; free with Stift ticket.)

LOWER AUSTRIA

17 498 05; www.schallaburg.at. Open May-Oct. M-F 9am-5pm; Sa-Su and holidays 9am-6pm. €7, students €3, seniors €5, family €14. Call ahead for a tour.) The castle doubles as the **International Exhibition Center of Lower Austria.** In 2005, the main exhibit will focus on Austria's return to a republic in 1955. There is also a display on 100 years of Austrian radio, and a small toy exhibit. (Shuttle vans leave Melk's train station daily 9:50, 10am, 1:15, 1:30, 4:20, 4:30pm. Return shuttles run 10, 10:15am, 1:30, 1:40, 1:50, 4:30, 4:45pm. Each way 15min.; €2.50, students €1.50. ☎2754 63 17. Exhibits in German.)

OUTDOOR ACTIVITIES. A network of **hiking** trails winds through the wooded groves of the Wachau region. The tourist office provides a map that lists sights, paths, and information on the 10km Leo Böck trail, 6km Seniorenweg, and 15km Schallburggrundweg. **Cyclists** follow the Danube toward Willendorf on a former canal-towing path. The 30,000-year-old **Venus of Willendorf,** a voluptuous 11cm stone figure and one of the world's most famous fertility symbols, was discovered there in 1908. The more sedentary may prefer a **ferry** across the Danube to **Spitz** and **Dürnstein,** for the local *Jause* (an Austrian version of British high tea). The returning ferry passes the **Heiratswald** (Marriage Woods)—Melk awards couples who marry here with a young sapling tree.

SOMMERSPIELE. The **Sommerspiele Melk** (Melk Summer Festival) comes to town from mid-July through mid-August. An open-air stage across the Danube provides the perfect setting for enjoying world-class theater (in German) on summer nights. Tickets are available at the Melk tourist office. (www.sommerspiele-melk.at. Performances Th-Sa 8:30pm. Tickets €17-35.)

ST. PÖLTEN ☎ 02742

If the intricacy and splendor of Baroque churches and the peaceful charm of medieval towns have ceased to impress, head to St. Pölten (pop. 50,030) for a jolt of 21st-century austerity. With avant-garde theater, dance performances, and a minimalist expanse of bureaucratic buildings only a government could devise, this capital city of Lower Austria satisfies the postmodernist in everyone. St. Pölten does not have a youth hostel and works well as a daytrip from Krems, Melk, or Vienna.

⊟⁊ TRANSPORTATION AND PRACTICAL INFORMATION. The **train station** connects St. Pölten with Vienna's Westbahnhof (45min., 3 per hr., €8), Krems (45min.; 11:05am, 5pm; €12), Linz (1¾hr.; 10:13, 11:27am, 12:13, 1:13, 2:13, 3:01, 4:43, 5:01, 5:21, 6:13, 9:15, 11:05pm; €16.70), and Melk (17min.; on the hr. until 10:35pm, last train back to Melk leaves at 12:10am; €4).

The **tourist office** provides a list of accommodations, leads 1hr. **tours** of the inner city in English (reserve up to a week ahead), and rents **cassette tours** in several languages for €1.45. (☎353 354; www.st-poelten.gv.at. Open Apr.-Oct. M-F 8am-5pm, Sa 9am-5pm, Su and holidays 10am-5pm; Nov.-Mar. M-F 8am-5pm.) There is a free reservation phone just across Rathausg. from the tourist office. Other services include: **currency exchange** at Bank Austria, Rathauspl. 2 (☎050505 92300; open M-F 8am-12:30pm and 2-4pm); **bike rental** at the tourist office (€9.45 per day); and 24hr. **lockers** at the train station (€2-3.50). **Post offices** are at the left end of the Bahnhof (open M-F 7am-6pm, Sa 8am-noon) and at 12 Wiener-Str. (Open M-F 8am-noon and 2-6pm.) **Postal Code:** Bahnhof office 3101, Wiener-Str. office 3102.

⊓⊡ ACCOMMODATIONS AND FOOD. The tourist office has lists of *Pensionen* and *Privatzimmer.* Most are outside the city limits, but for a little more cash you can stay closer to the *Altstadt.* Don't be dismayed by the large beer ad painted onto the side of the pink and blue **Mariazellerhof ❸,** Mariazellerstr. 6: clean, green rooms with private bath await within. Guests are encouraged to use the kitchen available on every floor. (☎769 95; fax 769 98. Breakfast included. Reception M-Th 7am-9pm, F-Su 7-10am and 4-9pm. Singles €35; doubles €58.) The green-trimmed Art Nouveau **Stadthotel Hauser-Eck ❹,** Schulg. 2, offers spacious rooms with floor-to-ceiling curtains, TVs, minibars, and sofas. (☎733 36; www.hausereck.at. Breakfast included. Singles €35-45; doubles €60-74. V.) The

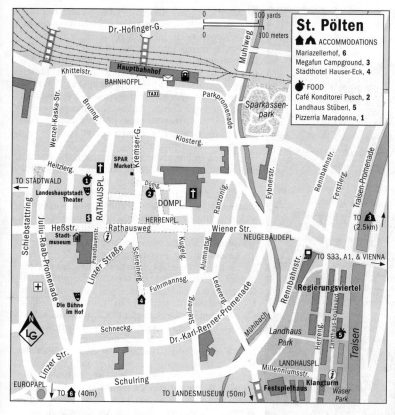

St. Pölten

▲▲ ACCOMMODATIONS

Mariazellerhof, 6
Megafun Campground, 3
Stadthotel Hauser-Eck, 4

🍴 FOOD

Café Konditorei Pusch, 2
Landhaus Stüberl, 5
Pizzerria Maradonna, 1

campsite **Megafun ❸**, Am Ratzersdorfer See, is on a small lake northeast of town. Take bus #4, across the street from the train station, to "Unterratzersdorf Schule" (15min., every 30min. 5:45am-6:45pm, €1.80). Go down Ratzersdorfer Hauptstr., and take a left onto Fritschstr. As it curves to the left, take a right onto E.-Werk-Weg, continue until you cross the stream, then turn left onto Bimbo-Binder-Promenade. The campground is on your right. (10min.) (☎251 510; fax 251 510 118. Reception 6am-midnight. €5.75 per person, €2.75 per child, €3.25 per tent, €2.75 per car, €6.25 per RV.)

St. Pölten's local specialties include oysters, fried black pudding, and savory Wachau wine. **Pizzeria Maradonna ❷**, Heitzlerlerg. 1, serves a wide variety of pasta (€6), seafood (€10 and up), and pizza (€6), while shielding diners from

schiff from its outdoor patio, and serves paella (€7.30), tacos (€6), and Greek salad (€6). (☎24 24; www.landhausstueberl.at. Open M-F 8am-8pm, Sa 9am-3pm.) **Café Konditorei Pusch ❶**, Domg. 8, features fruit frappes (€3) and decadent pastries (€2-3). Eat a Viennese breakfast (€4) in the popular outdoor seating area. (☎352 322. Open M-F 7am-7pm, Sa 7am-6pm. MC/V.) **SPAR Gourmet** supermarket is on Kremserg. 21. (Open M-F 7:15am-6:30pm, Sa 7:15am-5pm.)

A KODAK MOMENT

Being the savvy, cosmopolitan traveler that I am, I decided to foil the airport's high-intensity security scanners by having my film developed in Austria before heading home. A friendly man took my three rolls of memories and promised to have them back to me the same afternoon. When I returned to recoup the fruits of his labor, all three rolls were perfectly developed. I smiled and reached into my bag for my wallet. The cash register made a series of *ka-ching* noises and came up with the total: €59.70. My jaw and my bank account dropped. My hand changed directions, going from the cash stash to the Visa. "I'm sorry. No *kredit karten*," the man informed me. I mumbled something about a *Bancomat* and stumbled out into the blinding sunshine to withdraw the hefty sum from a nearby ATM. Cash-poor but picture-rich, I hurried away from the shop, cynically repeating the old adage, "these pictures are worth a thousand dollars."

Morals of the story: don't have your film developed on a major plaza in any town. Don't forget to ask how much it will cost per roll, since many places won't post prices exactly because they want to quote different prices to foreigners. Lastly, get a digital camera, and avoid this situation entirely.

-Catherine Phillips

◼ SIGHTS. The 13th-century **Rathausplatz**, in the heart of St. Pölten, sits atop the site of a second-century Roman settlement. A Neoclassical bust of Romantic genius Franz Schubert watches over the **Schubert Haus** at Rathausg. 2, site of the composer's frequent 19th-century sojourns. Josef Maria Olbrich designed the only *Jugendstil* **synagogue** in Lower Austria, along with a few other *Jugendstil* buildings in the *Altstadt*. The centuries of rumormongering witnessed in **Herrenplatz** at St. Pölten's daily market inspired the *Gossiping Women* sculpture.

Narrow alleys just after Wienerstr. 29 and Herrenpl. lead to **Domplatz**. The remains of the Roman settlement of Aelium Cetium were discovered here when sewer installers tripped over Roman hypocausts (ancient floor heating systems). The **Dom** (cathedral) is intact and features gilded accents, added to transform the original Roman basilica into a Baroque masterpiece. (Open daily until 6pm. Free.)

Visitors of all ages will enjoy still-life and real life at the **Landesmuseum**, Franz-Schubert-Platz 5. Fascinating displays from sculpture to terrariums deal with the history, art, and nature of Lower Austria. (☎908 09 01 00; www.landesmuseum.net. Open Tu-Sa 10am-6pm. €2. Call ahead for tours in English, €2. Audioguide €2.50. Admission €8, students €7, children €3.50, families €16. Kombitickets for any combination of the *Landesmuseum*, Schloss Schallaburg, and Kunsthalle Krems €10-20, families €20-40.) The **Stadtmuseum**, Prandtauerstr. 2, has a thorough collection detailing St. Pölten's history, from Roman times to the present. Its noteworthy *Jugendstilgalerie* features nudes and pastoral scenes by husband-and-wife duo Ferdinand Andri and Charlotte Andri-Hampel. Don't miss the hall of personalized bookplates upstairs. (Open Tu-Sa 10am-5pm. €1.60, students €0.80.)

The **Regierungsviertel** (government quarter) is a futuristic collection of minimalist buildings. Its centerpiece is the Landtagschiff, a semi-circular building on the Traisen River. The lofty **Klangturm** (sound tower) was intended to provide contrast to the horizontal sweep of the other buildings (tower elevator closed 2004-2005). The **Festspielhaus** theater and the outdoor modern scupltures give the area a lively atmosphere. Facing the solid rear wall of building 1a is Hans Kupelwieser's *Hohlkopfwand*, an array of several dozen identical silver heads stacked in rows.

◼ ENTERTAINMENT. Die Bühne im Hof, Linzerstr. 18, hosts modern theater and dance; the 2004-2005 season includes Brazilian dance and chant music. (☎211 30 and 35 22 91; www.bih.at. Office open M-Tu and Th-F 9am-5pm, Sa 9am-noon. Tickets €41-200, under 6 free.) **The Stadttheater,** Rathauspl. 11, stages traditional opera and ballet; Mozart's *The Magic Flute* (Dec.) and the ballet *Hamlet* (May) will take center stage in 2005. (☎/fax 352 026 19; www.stadttheater.info. Office open M-F 9am-5pm. Tickets €12-32; box office sells a few standing-room tickets for €11 on performance evenings.) Neither theater has performances from June to August. The **Festspielhaus,** Franz-Schubert-Pl. 2, stages classical music and modern dance concerts. (☎90 80 80 222; www.festspielhaus.at. Buy tickets at Die Buhne im Hof for 2005 concerts featuring the Vienna Philharmonic, in March, and Hollywood in Music, in May. Tickets €41-200. Students and seniors 50% off.) Ballet enthusiasts should check out the **Ballettkonservatorium St. Pölten,** the classical ballet school and training ground for the prestigious **Ballett St. Pölten.**

Seasonal festivities include the **St. Pöltner Festwoche,** which brings all kinds of events to local theaters and museums from mid-May to mid-June. In early July, the **St. Pöltner Hauptstadtfest** raises its tents, and locals cut loose to opera, musicals, and ballet. From mid-July to late August, the **International Culture and Film Festival** screens free flicks. (www.filmfestivals.at, or call the tourist office at ☎353 354.)

BADEN BEI WIEN ☎02252

Surrounded by vineyards, dense woodlands, and sulfur springs, Baden is a great weekend spot for anyone looking to relax. Although primarily a day spa devoted to therapeutic massage and thermal bath treatments, Baden also offers fishing, bowling, tennis, golf, ice skating, and horseback riding. The city's expansive flower-filled Rosarium, its Casino (the largest in Europe), and the nearby Wienerwald (Vienna Woods) make Baden a veritable playground for people of all ages. Higher summer prices make traveling to Baden as a daytrip a good idea.

TRANSPORTATION AND PRACTICAL INFORMATION. The easiest way to get to Baden is by the **Badener Bahn,** a tram that runs from Vienna's Karlspl., beneath the Opera House, to Baden's Josefspl. (1hr., every 15min. 5am-10:30pm, €3.50.) In Karlspl., go straight past the information office into the round foyer and take a right to the escalator marked Kartnerstr. The blue-and-white Badener Bahn will pick up right in front of you. If you get on a tram marked "Wolfganggasse," ride it to that station and then take the next tram marked "Baden." **Trains** also travel frequently between Vienna's **Südbahnhof** and Josefpl. (outbound from Vienna 4:40am-11:15pm, inbound 4:16am-11pm; €5.) By **car** from the west, take *Autobahn* West to Bundesstr. 210 at "Alland-Baden-Mödling." From Vienna, take *Autobahn* South (Süd) and exit at "Baden." Baden's **tourist office** is at Brusattipl. 3 in the Leopoldsbad building. (Open M-Sa 9am-6pm, Su and holidays 10am-1pm.) Bear right toward the fountain and follow Erzherzog-Rainer-Ring to Brusattipl. The tourist office is at the end of the street. In summer, they offer **free tours** of the *Altstadt* in English, German, French, and Italian (1½hr.; M 3:30pm, Sa 10am), the wine region (2hr.; W 3pm, make appointments in advance), and guided **hiking** tours (Tu and Sa 2pm). (☎22 60 06 00; www.baden.at. Open May-Oct. M-Sa 9am-6pm, Su and holidays 10am-1pm; Nov.-Apr. M-F 9am-5pm.) Other services include clean, free **public toilets** at Brusattipl., the Rosarium, and the train station; **police** at ☎133; and **medical emergency** at ☎144. **Internet** access is available at Videowelt, Voslauerstr. 11-13. (Open M-Sa 9am...

ACCOMMODATIONS AND FOOD. The tourist office can give you a list of lodgings in Baden with prices and descriptions. **Pension Steinkellner ❸,** Am Hang 1, offers reasonably priced rooms in a typical Austrian *Gästehaus* decorated with African and South American souvenirs. The small lounge with a fireplace leads out onto an upstairs patio, which is open throughout the year. It's 10min. from the center of town, but the proprietors will pick you up if you call ahead. From Josefspl., head up Vöslauerstr. and cross the street and head left at the rotary. Take a right onto Albrechtsg. (☎862 26; www.baden-bei-wien.at/steinkeller. Breakfast included. Singles €26; doubles €50.) Closer to the *Altstadt* are the plain but sturdy rooms at **Pension Wienerstub'n ❸**, Weilburgstr. 19. Walk around behind the tourist office, through the grounds of the Romertherme, and take a right on *Gutenbrunnerstr.* (☎481 02; www.hotel-artner.at. Breakfast included. Singles with shower and bath €20; doubles €27.50-35.)

Locals crowd **Café Damals ❷**, Rathausg. 3, to dine with a cardboard Franz Joseph in a cool, ivy-covered courtyard. A satisfying lunch with a host of colorful characters runs only €6. (☎426 86. Wheelchair accessible. Open M-F 10am-midnight, Sa 10am-5pm, Su 10am-7pm. AmEx/MC/V.) There are plenty of cafés along Hauptpl. and Pfarrg. For a side of history with your *Tafelspitz* (boiled beef), head to **Gasthaus zum Reichsapfel ❷**, Spiegelg. 2. From Hauptpl., follow Theresieng. and take a right on Pfarrg., which becomes Antong. Spiegelg. will be on the left. The oldest guesthouse in Baden, it has served hungry wayfarers since the 13th century. (☎482 05. Dishes €6-10. Wheelchair accessible. Open M and W-F 5pm-11:30pm, Sa-Su 11am-2pm and 5-11pm. AmEx/MC/V.) **Billa**, off Hauptpl. at Wasserg. 14 (open M-W 8am-7pm, Th 7:30am-7pm, F 7:30am-7:30pm, Sa 7:30am-5pm), and **SPAR Gourmet**, Rathausg. 7 (open M-F 7:30am-6:30pm, Sa 7:30am-5pm), are grocery stores in the *Fußgängerzone*. There is also a **farmer's market** on Brusattipl. (Open M-F 8am-6pm, Sa 8am-1pm.)

🄶 **SIGHTS.** To reach Baden's lovely **Fußgängerzone** from the tourist office, head left and take a right onto Erzherzog-Rainer-Ringstr., then take a left onto Rathausg. Hauptpl., at the heart of the *Fußgängerzone*, features the striking **Dreifaltigkeitsäule** (Trinity Column), erected in 1718. The thermal baths that were Baden's biggest attraction in the days of Caesar Augustus are still the focal point of the city. The **Thermalstrand bad Baden,** Helenenstr. 19-21, lets you simmer in a hot sulfur thermal bath and cool off in room-temperature chlorinated pools. Children can play on the huge waterslide and in the sand. (☎486 70. Open M-F 8:30am-7:30pm, Sa-Su 8am-6:30pm. M-F €5.60, after 1pm €4.80; Sa-Su €6.80/€5.60; students €2.90.) The **Kurdirektion** itself, Brusattipl. 4 (☎445 31; www.kurhausbaden.at), is the center of curative spa treatments, housing a thermal pool open to all visitors (€8.60). The spa has water-jet massage therapy (€23.40), sulfur mudpacks (€19.50), and massages (15min. €11.60, 50min. €37.10). A giant new spa complex, the **Römertherme Baden,** right behind the tourist office at Brusattipl. 4, offers soothing luxuries all year long. (☎450 30; www.roemertherme.at. Open May-Sept. M-F 9am-9:30pm, Sa-Su and holidays 10am-7pm; Oct.-Apr. M-F 9am-9:30pm. 2hr. soak €8.50, students €6.60. 25min. massage €23.40.) The **Kurpark** lies north of Hauptpl. via Maria-Theresien-G. On the southeastern edge of the Wienerwald, this carefully landscaped garden is studded with statues and temples commemorating famous Austrian musicians. To the left, past the gazebo, is the **Theresiengarten,** laid out in 1792, with a flower clock that has been ticking since 1929.

The **Kaiser Franz-Josef Museum,** Hochstr. 51, sits atop the Badener Berg at the far end of the park. Take the "Arenaweg" path behind the Sommerarena and follow the brown signs 40min. uphill; when you get to a fork in the road with signs pointing to the museum in both directions, take the middle path straight ahead and keep going up past the railing. Follow signs for Kneipp Rundwanderweg and follow the blue marks on trees. The museum hosts exhibitions of folk art, weapons, religious memorabilia, and photography. (☎411 00. Open Apr.-Oct. Tu-Su 2-6pm. €2.50, seniors €1.50, students and children €1.) The **Beethovenhaus,** at Rathausg. 10, is where the composer spent summers while composing the *Missa Solemnis* and much of his *Ninth Symphony*. The museum features his death mask and locks of his hair. (Open Tu-F 4-6pm, Sa-Su and holidays 9-11am and 4-6pm. €2.70; children, students, and seniors €1.20.) Gaming aficionados can live out their James Bond fantasies at the posh **Casino,** outside the Kurpark at Kaiser-Franz-Ring 1. (☎444 96; www.ccb.at. 19+. Semi-formal dress required. Opens daily at 3pm.)

LIECHTENSTEIN

FACTS AND FIGURES

CAPITAL: Vaduz

CURRENCY: Swiss franc (SFr)

POPULATION: 33,863

MAJOR EXPORTS: dental products

FORM OF GOVERNMENT: hereditary constitutional monarchy

LAND AREA: 160 km²

LANGUAGE: German

RELIGION: 80% Catholic, 7.4% Protestant, 12.6% other

GEOGRAPHY: flat, river valley in west with two largest towns (Vaduz and Schaan); mountainous terrain in east

PHONE CODE | Country code 423. **International dialing prefix** 00.

EMERGENCIES | Police ☎ 117. **Mountain Rescue** ☎ 1414. **Fire** ☎ 118. **Medical emergency** and **Ambulance** ☎ 144. **Roadside assistance** ☎ 140.

Liechtenstein

A recent Liechtenstein tourist brochure unfortunately mislabeled the already tiny 160 km² country as an even tinier 160 m². Ironically, this is often how much most people see of the world's only German-speaking monarchy, as travelers usually pause only long enough in the capital city of Vaduz to buy the obligatory postage stamp and hastily record their visit in a passport. Most miss the Alpine beauty of this tiny country altogether. Its ruling monarch, Prince Hans Adam II, is the first ruler to actually live in Liechtenstein since the present dynasty came to power in 1699. Liechtenstein's ties to Switzerland were established in 1924 with a customs and monetary union, replacing a similar agreement with the Austro-Hungarian empire from 1852 to 1919.

The lack of an army and independent foreign representation does not mean the Principality *(Fürstenturm)* of Liechtenstein is weak; the booming industries of dental manufacturing, banking, and tourism have brought considerable wealth. Nonetheless, many locals remain down-

A SIX-HOUR TOUR

Let's Go *Researcher-Writer Tom Miller volunteered to supplement his job by going for a run—a long one. No stranger to marathons, Tom (having completed the 2001 Bay State marathon in 3hr. 13min. and the 2002 Boston marathon in 3hr. 40min.) was up for the challenge. Though he found it a fantastic way to see the countryside,* Let's Go *does not necessarily recommend this mode of sightseeing for everyone.*

Though we joke about being able to see all of Liechtenstein in a day, it's actually possible to see the entire nation in a little under six hours. The LGT-Alpin marathon runs 42km from Bendern (outside of Schaan) to Malbun, in the southeastern corner of the country. My editor and I rearranged my entire schedule so I could run it.

It was worth it.

The course began in the relatively flat farmland near the Rhine. It was an unseasonably warm day—well over 80°F at 9:30am—and the smell of cow manure was overwhelming at times as we ran past farmers harvesting hay. Beginning in the capital city of Vaduz, the next 11km were entirely uphill, rising over 1000m. Most of us slowed to a walk early on, but the enthusiastic Liechtensteiners were out in force chanting, "Haub, haub, haub! Bravo!" as we lumbered past.

The course finally flattened out at about km 22, in the mountain-

to-earth; old-fashioned huts in the more isolated regions are built at the same rate as ultra-modern buildings in Vaduz. Above the valley towns, cliff-hanging roads are gateways to what's truly worth visiting—the mountains above offer hiking and skiing without a touristy atmosphere.

VADUZ AND LOWER LIECHTENSTEIN

Liechtenstein's capital is a town of tourists traveling in packs, scrambling to find something worthy of a photo opportunity. Often they find nothing but the *Schloß* towering above and the high prices looming in town. A handful of museums await here, but that's about it; Vaduz rarely requires more than one day. While campers and bikers might enjoy the surrounding countryside of Lower Liechtenstein ("lower" referring to the region's 500m elevation), others should consider heading for the hills in Upper Liechtenstein, particularly Malbun.

🚃 TRANSPORTATION. Although trains from Austria and Switzerland pass through the country, Liechtenstein itself has no rail system. Instead, it has a cheap, efficient **Post Bus** system. (Short trips 2.40SFr, longer trips 3.60SFr; students, retirees, and children ages 16 and under half-price. SwissPass valid. Free with Erlebnisspass.) A one-week bus ticket (10SFr; students, seniors, and children ages 16 and under 5SFr) covers all of Liechtenstein, as well as buses to Swiss and Austrian border towns. If you're planning on taking more than two rides, it's the best deal in the country. The principality is a 20-30min. bus ride from **Sargans** or **Buchs** in Switzerland and **Feldkirch** in Austria (3.60SFr). For a **taxi,** call ☎373 29 52 or 392 22 22.

📋 PRACTICAL INFORMATION. Liechtenstein's **national tourist office,** Städtle 37, one block up the hill from the Vaduz Post Bus stop, will stamp your passport with Liechtenstein's bi-colored seal (2SFr, free with Erlebnispass). It also gives advice on hiking, cycling, and skiing in the area, sells hiking maps (in German only) for 8-15.50SFr and offers walking tours of the old town. (☎239 63 00; www.tourismus.li. Open May-Oct. daily 9am-noon and 1:30-5pm, Nov.-Apr. M-F only.) For **currency exchange,** try the **Liechtenstein Landesbank** next to the post office, or the **post office** in Schaan. The *Erlebnispass,* available at the tourist office and at some hotels and attractions, offers a variety of free and reduced entrance fares and fees on museums, transportation, and various activities. (2 days 19SFr, children

13SFr; 6 days 39SFr/26SFr.) **Free Internet** is available at Telecom-Shop, Austr. 77. Take bus #1 (dir: Sargans) to "Rütti" from "Schaan/Vaduz." (Also at Rathauspl. in Vaduz. ☎237 74 74. Open M 10am-6:30pm, Tu-F 8am-6:30pm, Sa 8am-4pm.) Rent **bicycles** at Bike-Garage in nearby Triesen. (☎390 03 90. 35SFr per day. Open M-F 8am-noon and 1:30-6pm, Sa 8am-2pm.) **Parking** is available on Aulerstr. across from the Old Castle Inn (1SFr per hr. M-F 7am-noon and 2-5pm, 3hr. max.) and also by the theater. For Liechtenstein's **hospital**, dial ☎235 44 11. Schloß Apotheke is a full-service **pharmacy** on Äulestr. 10, a few yards from the bus stop. (Open M-F 8am-6:30pm, Sa 8am-3pm, Su 10-11:30am. AmEx/MC/V.) The main **post office** near the tourist office, on Städtle 38, sells tickets for the opera, theater, and sporting events. It also offers **Internet** for 5SFr per 15min. Monday through Saturday from 8am to closing. (☎239 63 63. Open M-F 7:45am-6pm, Sa 8-11am.) **Postal Code:** FL-9490.

⌐⌐ ACCOMMODATIONS AND FOOD. Budget

housing options in Vaduz are few and far between. Liechtenstein's sole **Jugendherberge (HI) ❷**, Untere Rüttig. 6, is in neighboring Schaan. From Vaduz, take bus #1 (dir: Schaan) to "Mühleholz," walk toward the intersection with traffic lights, and turn left down Marianumstr. Walk 4-5min. and follow signs to this spotless pink hostel on the edge of a farm. Clean rooms, a large breakfast buffet, and a game room with Nintendo make this a great place to stay. (☎232 50 22; www.youthhostel.ch. Dinner 12.50SFr (6:30-7:30pm). **Internet** 2SFr per 10min. Laundry: wash 3-3.20SFr, dry 3.20-3.40SFr. Towel 2SFr. Fridge, lockers, and biking information in the basement. Reception 7-10am and 5-10pm. Check-out 10am. Curfew 10pm; key code available for late entry. Quiet hours 10pm-7am. Open Feb.-Oct. Dorms 30SFr; doubles 40SFr.) **Landgasthof Au ❹**, Austr. 2, offers simple but comfortable rooms close to town. From the Vaduz Post Bus stop, walk straight out of town for 10min. The hotel is on the right immediately past the second traffic circle. (The road will change names from Äulestr. to Heiligkreuz to Austr.) Alternatively, take the #1 bus to "Au;" the hotel is about 25m from the stop; you can see it. (☎232 11 17; fax 232 11 68. Breakfast included. Hall shower unless otherwise noted. Private parking. Reception in restaurant below, 8am to around 11pm. Singles 60SFr; doubles 95SFr, with shower/bath 120SFr; triples 145SFr/155SFr.) For convenience, budget-friendly **Hotel Post ❸**, Bahnhofstr. 14, is right by the Schaan Post Bus stop and train station, which can be a downside for light sleepers. Rooms are large, carpeted, and rea-

sabove Gaflei. Coming around the corner I heard the sound of dozens of bells tolling and wondered if a local church had decided to ring its bells for us. As I came around a hairpin turn, I found about 400 cows, all wearing bells. To my left I had a perfect view of the yellow-green rolling hills in the Rhine valley below and of the snow-covered peaks of the Alps straight ahead. A paraglider chose this moment to fly overhead, and I wondered if I hadn't stumbled into a picture postcard by mistake.

The euphoria wore off in km 31-35, which were again steep uphills, this time over narrow, rocky paths. As one Liechtensteinian runner stumbled past me, he yelled out, "Hey Meester Meeler!" I had my name written across the back of my shirt, but couldn't figure out how he knew I was American. When I asked him in German how he knew, he said, "Because no one spells Miller with an 'i' around here."

The final 8km were all downhill as we circled the valley that contains Malbun at reckless speeds, hurtling our way toward the finish line on paths that would have alarmed even downhill skiers. I finished in 5 hr. 40min. and 40s, about 2½hr. behind the winner, having crossed the entire country and ascended 1800m in the process. I think the mountain goats were proud of us—they've been doing the same thing for years.
—Tom Miller

sonably priced. (☎232 17 18. Breakfast included at the restaurant downstairs. Reception 8am-11pm. 50-60SFr.) For a night under the stars, try **Camping Mittagspitze ❶**. Take bus #1 (dir: Sargans) to "Säga," cross the street, and walk toward the mountains on the street near the bus stop, following the signs. This country campground has great scenery and its own swimming pool, TV/lounge room, laundry, playground, and self-service store. Reception is just past the two brooks. (☎392 26 86. Shower included. Laundry 4.50SFr. Reception June-Aug. 8-11:30am and 5-8:30pm; Sept.-May 7-8am and 5-6pm. 8.50SFr per person, 4SFr per child, 5-8SFr per tent, 4SFr per car, 8-10SFr per trailer or caravan. Electricity 5.5SFr. Tax 0.60SFr per person.)

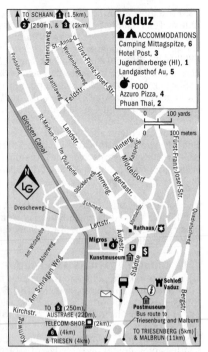

Eating cheaply in Liechtenstein is challenging, as most meals in the center of town will easily run 25-30SFr. **Azzuro Pizza ❷**, Aulestr. 20, sells pizzas to eat there or take out for 7.50-10.50SFr and kebabs for 9.50SFr. (☎232 48 18. Open M-F 8am-7pm, Sa 8am-6pm, Su 10am-6pm.) **Phuan Thai ❷**, 11 Landesstr. (bus #1, dir: Falknis), offers duck curry, pad thai and other Asian meals served on bright sunflower tablecloths or to go for 10-12SFr. Groceries are available at **Migros**, Aulestr. 20, across from the tour bus parking lot in Vaduz. (Open M-F 8am-1pm and 1:30-7pm, Sa 8am-6pm.)

⬛ SIGHTS. The 12th-century Schloß Vaduz, regal home of Hans Adam II, Prince of Liechtenstein, presides over the town. You can hike up to the castle for a closer look; the 20min. trail begins down the street from the tourist office, heading away from the post office. The signs along the path offer lessons on Liechtensteinian government in German, French, and English. The interior of the ruler's residence is off-limits to the masses, except for a select group of rich politicians, retirees, and university students with excellent grades, who are all invited annually to visit the Prince, usually on New Year's Day. Across the street from the tourist office is the large modern building housing the **Kunstmuseum Liechtenstein,** Städtle 32. The museum shows modern art, and some rotating special exhibits. The modern art exhibits, the bulk of the collection, are a mixed bag (including a few huge installation pieces like a giant white marble ball enclosed in glass). A new exhibit by Favio Marcaccio will begin in Oct. 2004, and a multi-year exhibit of older masterpieces from the private Fürsten collection will be installed in Fall 2004. (☎235 03 00; www.kunstmuseum.li. Open Tu-W and F-Su 10am-5pm, Th 10am-8pm. 8SFr; students, seniors, and ages 10-16 5SFr. Special exhibits occasionally cost extra. Free with Erlebnispass.) Reproductions of the royal art collection often end up on postage stamps displayed in the small **Postmuseum**, Städtle 37, upstairs from the tourist office. (☎236 61 05; fax 236 61 09. Open daily Apr.-Oct. 10am-noon and 1:30-5:30pm; Nov.-Mar. 10am-noon and 1:30-5pm. Free.)

UPPER LIECHTENSTEIN

Just when it seems that the roads cannot possibly become any narrower or steeper, they do—welcome to Upper Liechtenstein. Even if you're only in the country for one day, take the short bus trip to **Triesenberg** or **Malbun** (30min. from Vaduz) for spectacular views of the Rhine valley below.

TRIESENBERG

Spanning a series of switchbacks and foothills 800m above the Rhine, the first town up the mountain (serviced by bus #10) is Triesenberg (pop. 2600). Founded in the 13th century by Swiss immigrants forced to flee Valais due to religious intolerance, the town has a **Heimatmuseum** chronicling the history of these intrepid people and of the region. With hundreds of artifacts, from cowbells to a weaving loom to whimsical carvings in tree roots, it's worth a look. (Facing uphill from the bus stop, head to the left. ☎262 19 26; fax 19 22. Open Sept.-May Tu-F 1:30-5:30pm, Sa 1:30-5pm; June-Aug. also Su 2-5pm. 2SFr, children 1SFr.) The **tourist office** is in the same building as the museum and has the same hours, phone, and fax.

For great hiking, take bus #34 to "Gaflei" (20min., every hr.). Stunning views of the Rhine Valley await on a 1½hr., relatively flat hike through Alpine meadows and forests. (From the parking lot exit, head toward the gravel path on the left toward "Silum" and then "Ob. Tunnel, Steg." At the end, walk through the tunnel, then down the road to Steg, where bus #10 runs to Vaduz or Schaan every hr.) Follow the signs for the "Drei Schwestern" (Three Sisters) for a challenging hike (5½-6hr.). The trail climbs up from Gaflei, up a couple of ladders, and across the craggy peaks that grace postcards in every kiosk in the country. From Drei Schwestern, head toward Sarojasattel and Planken, and take the bus back to Vaduz or Schaan. Other, shorter hikes (15-60min.) are also marked from Gaflei.

MALBUN

A peninsula of green farmland surrounded by mountains, the village of Malbun sits high in an Alpine valley in the southeastern corner of Liechtenstein. It is one of the most picturesque locations in the principality, at the end of a long mountain road full of hairpin turns. The **tourist office** is inside Malbun Sports. (☎263 65 77; www.malbun.li. Open June-Oct. and mid-Dec. to mid-Apr. M-Sa 9am-noon and 1:30-5pm.) A **Falcon Show** entertains guests during the summer in the Hotel Galina, two doors left from Malbun Sports. (☎263 34 24; www.galina.li. Tu-Su 3pm.) In winter, two chairlifts, four T-bars, and one ski school provide access to the slopes. (2004 day pass prices 37SFr, youths and seniors 31SFr, children 25SFr; 6-day pass 155SFr/127SFr/98SFr; low-season 136SFr/110SFr/84SFr. Check with tourist office for 2005 prices.) Right in the middle of town, **Malbun A.G.** (☎263 97 70 or 262 19 15; www.schneesports-chule.li) offers one-day ski lessons (70SFr, children 60SFr), three-day classes (160SFr/130SFr), and private lessons (1 day 230SFr). **Malbun Sport** (☎/fax 263 37 55) rents **skis** and **snowboards.** (35SFr, children 13-18SFr. Cross-country skis 28SFr. Open M-F 8am-6pm, Sa-Su 9am-5pm. AmEx/MC/V.) **Cross-country skiing** is available 2km away in Steg.

During the summer, the #10 bus from Vaduz (30min., every hr., 3.60SFr) takes hikers to Malbun. The most worthwhile hike is round-trip to **Pfälzerhütte** (5hr.), the starting point of which is the top of the only chairlift open in the summer, the **Sareiserjoch.** (One-way 7.50SFr, round-trip 11.70SFr; ages 5-16 4.30SFr/6.40SFr. Open daily in good weather 8-11:50am and 1-4:50pm.) At the beginning of June, there is snow on one side of the trail, wildflowers on the other, and *Murmeltiere* (marmots) throughout. Cross the rocky final ascent to the peak of

Augustenberg (2359m), Liechtenstein's second highest mountain, then descend a few hundred meters to the Pfälzerhütte (mountain hut). To get home, head toward Gritsch and then Tälihöhi, completing a near-circuit of the valley that encloses Malbun. Numerous bike paths in the area provide great opportunities to see wildlife. For some excitement, climb up and then ride back down on the steep, narrow road from Triesenberg to Malbun. For an easy but rewarding ride, try the **Fürstenweg** loop between Vaduz and Schaan. Start at the Alte Rhein bridge in Vaduz and follow the river. When you get to where the train tracks cross the river in Schaan, head right and away from the river. The route heads to the Kloster Dux (Dux chapel), then through the woods and up to Schloß Vaduz, and then back down to Vaduz.

The best place to stay for hiking and skiing access is **Hotel Alpen ❸**, near the bus stop and tourist office. The hotel has a restaurant, swimming pool, and a large common room with TV. Some rooms have cable TV, phone, and a stocked fridge, but you'll pay extra for the luxury. (☎ 263 11 81; www.alpenhotel.li. Reception 8am-10pm. Open mid-May to Oct. and mid-Dec. to Apr. Winter 60SFr per person, with shower 70SFr, with bath, toilet, and TV 80SFr. Summer 10SFr less.)

SWITZERLAND

Right in the middle of Europe, yet isolated by the Alps (crucial to the nation's much vaunted neutrality), Switzerland is a nation of dramatic cultural variety. Divided into German-, French-, and Italian-speaking regions, Switzerland retains much of the customs and cuisines of the nations it borders, yet recreates and combines them with a flavor that is uniquely Swiss.

Switzerland has an amazing wealth of natural beauty. From the forests of the Jura to the mountain peaks of the Alps, hikers, skiers, bikers, and paragliders from all over the globe travel to the nation to take advantage of its winding trails, challenging slopes, and jagged summits. The country's urban centers are as fascinating to explore as the Alps that surround them. Besides being international hubs of commerce, trade, and diplomacy, cities such as Zurich, Geneva, and Lucerne are also cultural centers home to world-class concert halls, museums, and cathedrals.

Comfortable and calm, Switzerland is a delightful country in which to travel. Food and accommodations are of consistently high quality, and the country's efficient public transportation system makes it an ideal destination for independent visitors. Though Switzerland is not known for being affordable, budget travelers can generally find bargains, especially since many of the best attractions (like sunsets over mountain peaks) cost nothing.

LAND

Switzerland is a mountainous country. Although only one-seventh of the Alps lie within Switzerland's borders, no other country is as geographically defined by them. Nor does any other country contain as many of the range's highest peaks: eight of the 10 tallest peaks in the Alps are either on Switzerland's borders or wholly within them. Accounting for 60% of Switzerland's total surface area, the Alps rise in central and southern Switzerland to form high, jagged peaks with steep, narrow river valleys. Thousands of years ago, glaciers swept over the area, carving out the sharp ridges, chutes, cirques, and waterfalls that have made the Alps famous for rugged beauty. The glaciers also passed through the valleys surrounding the Alps and the Jura, creating Switzerland's major lakes: Lac Léman, the Bodensee, Neuchâtel, Lucerne, Lago Maggiore, the Thunersee, and the Obersee.

Northern Switzerland is characterized by the Jura (Celtic for wood), the subalpine region comprised primarily of woodlands on limestone hills. The Jura once saw extensive ore mining and metal processing, but has more recently been promoted as a tourist destination with hiking, riding, and cross-country skiing. The renowned Swiss watchmaking industry originated in the Jura region.

FLORA AND FAUNA

PLANTS

Switzerland's varied regions allow many different types of trees to flourish. While beech and oak trees predominate in the deciduous woods of the Swiss midland and at lower elevations in the Alpine valleys, spruce and fir occupy areas of higher altitudes. In the southern and eastern Alpine interiors, forests of pine and larch contrast starkly with the palm trees along the shores of Lake Lugano.

A SAINTLY BREED

In AD 1050, the Archdeacon Bernard de Menthon founded a hospice in a mountain pass in the Jungfrau region and brought with him a breed of large, furry dogs of Gallic origin. In addition to providing shelter for passing merchants, Bernard and the monks working under him would venture into blizzards in search of stranded travelers. Though it is uncertain whether or not the dogs accompanied the monks on their rescue missions—early accounts relate that dogs were used to run an exercise wheel that turned a cooking spit—by the time of Bernard's canonization, dogs bearing his name had become famous and regularly patrolled the pass (now also named after Bernard).

Gifted with a fine sense of smell, a thick coat, an amiable attitude, and a neck just made to tie a barrel of brandy to, the St. Bernards made a name for themselves by saving over 2000 lives over several hundred years. In the 1810s, a single dog named Barry saved 40 lost travelers. Today, few St. Bernards still work as rescue dogs—smaller, lighter breeds less liable to sink in the snow have taken their place. The St. Bernard is now a popular household pet, and though it has entered the popular imagination through films like *Cujo* and the *Beethoven* movies, it will always have dignity as the Alpine fixture it once was.

Floral diversity abounds even in the harshest and rockiest areas of the Alps, with several species of wildflowers thriving in the midst of snowy conditions. **Edelweiss,** famous for its elusiveness (and for the *Sound of Music* song), has wooly stems and leaves and white, star-shaped blossoms. The **lady's slipper** is slightly iris-like in appearance, with a yellow bulb and maroon tendrils coming out all around it. More conventional flowers like **daisies, buttercups, bellflowers,** and **dandelions** also flourish. Wildflowers appear in late April and fade by the end of October.

ANIMALS

Many of Switzerland's fauna are of the familiar barnyard and wildlife variety with an Alpine twist. **Black squirrels** are plentiful, and **red foxes** and **hedgehogs** make an occasional appearance. Less recognizable animals include the **marmot,** a furry, cat-sized rodent that inhabits the Schilt and upper Sefinen valleys, and **tächis,** large black birds common around Mürren and Schilthorn. In the Bernese Oberland, normal deer thrive alongside Switzerland's own variation, the **Gemse,** which tend to be smaller, with miniscule horns. The extinction of many of these animal populations was prevented by the creation of the Swiss National Park in Lower Engadine.

The cow is an institution in Switzerland: one or more bovine encounters during a trip through the Alps is almost guaranteed. Often a herd of them will pass you as you are hiking; simply stand still and let them go by so that they don't start heading in the wrong direction. Swiss cows can be of the Simmentaler (light brown and white), Brown Swiss (solid gray-brown), or Holstein (black and white) varieties.

HISTORY

FROM CAVE MEN TO CELTS

The early Swiss established settlements only 30,000 years ago, after the end of the last glacial period. By 750 BC, the Celts dominated Switzerland. The artistic and warlike **Helvetians,** whose land extended across the alpine valleys of central Switzerland, gained notoriety for their (largely unsuccessful) attempts to invade Roman Italy, first in 222 BC, and again as allies of Carthage between 218 and 203 BC (when they assisted Hannibal and his elephants in their famous crossing of the Alps). Julius Caesar halted the Helvetian attempts to advance into Gaul in 58 BC by crushing their tribes and colonizing their lands.

As Roman influence waned in the 5th century, the tribes settled permanently. **Burgundians** filled the west, merging peacefully with the Romanized Celts and absorbing their culture and language. The more aggressive **Alemanni,** a Germanic tribe, forced their culture on the Celts of central and northern Switzerland, eventually pushing the Burgundians west to the Sarine River (which now stands as the border between German- and French-speaking Switzerland). Slightly less numerous, the **Rhätians,** an Etruscan people, populated eastern Switzerland (now Graubünden), and their language, **Rhäto-Romansch,** a combination of Roman Latin and the Rhätian Tuscan dialect, is still spoken today.

ALEMANNI LEGACY (1000-1519)

The nonconformist Alemanni set the stage for centuries of Swiss individualism and decentralized rule. Without strong Roman imperial control, the patchwork of states enjoyed de facto political autonomy. The descendents of the Alemanni therefore clashed with Holy Roman Emperor **Rudolf of Hapsburg** when he attempted to take three of their communities (Uri, Schwyz, and Unterwalden—the "Forest Cantons") under his direct control in the late 13th century. In a secret pact, the three Forest Cantons decided to rebel and signed the **Everlasting Alliance** in 1291, an agreement that obligated the cantons to defend each other from outside attack. In 1315, the Swiss and the Hapsburgs met at the Battle of Morgarten, resulting in Hapsburg defeat. The Swiss consider the Everlasting Alliance to be the beginning of the Swiss Confederation. It also signaled the beginning of 350 years of struggle against the **Hapsburg Empire.**

Despite conflict between the Swiss and the Hapsburg emperors, the three-canton core of Switzerland expanded over the next several centuries to include Bern, Lucerne, Zurich, Glarus, and Zug. Zurich allied with Hapsburg emperor Frederick II, but the other cantons compelled Zurich to renounce its alliance and rejoin the Confederation by force of arms. In another attempt to conquer the Swiss, the Hapsburgs enlisted the help of the "Swabian League," a group of Southern German cities whose motto became "the Swiss, too, must have a master." The Swabian War (1499-1500) lasted less than nine months, but strong Swiss efforts helped to establish independence from the Holy Roman Empire.

REFORMATION TO REVOLUTION (1519-1815)

The lack of a strong central government to settle disputes between cantons of different faiths caused problems for the Swiss during the **Protestant Reformation.** As Lutheranism swept Northern Europe, radical theologian **Ulrich Zwingli** of Zurich spearheaded his own brand of Protestantism that stressed both the importance of laypeople reading scripture and a rejection of the symbols and rituals of Catholicism. In 1523, the city government of Zurich sanctioned Zwingli's proposed *Theses* and strengthened Zwingli's influence by banning Anabaptism and harshly punishing its followers. Meanwhile, in Geneva, French-born lawyer and priest **John Calvin** preached a doctrine of predestination: neither God's grace nor good works could get you into heaven, but leading a good life was an indication that you were destined for it. For a time he exercised a theocratic sway over Geneva and instituted moral reforms, turning the city into a shining example of Protestant social control.

While Zurich and Geneva became strongholds of the Protestant movement, the Forest Cantons remained loyal to the Catholic Church. Religious differences, combined with tensions between urban and rural cantons, resulted in armed conflict, culminating in the defeat of the Protestants at Kappel in 1531 and the death of Zwingli. In the mid-16th century the Confederation finally interceded, granting Protestants certain freedoms, but prohibiting them from imposing their faith on others. The Confederation managed to remain neutral during the **Thirty Years' War.** In 1648 the **Peace of Westphalia** granted the Swiss official neutrality and a recognition of their independence from the Austrian Hapsburg empire.

After two centuries of relative quiet, Swiss independence was challenged in 1789, when Napoleon's troops invaded Switzerland and established the **Helvetic Republic.** Rebelling against the French puppet government, the Swiss overthrew the regime in 1803. Napoleon's **Mediation Act** settled the anarchy that ensued and established Switzerland as a confederation of 19 cantons. After Napoleon's defeat at Waterloo, the Congress of Vienna added Geneva, Neuchâtel, and the Valais to the Confederation and (again) officially recognized Swiss neutrality.

DIPLOMACY: 1815 TO THE 20TH CENTURY

The establishment of neutrality meant Switzerland could turn its attention to domestic issues. Industrial growth brought material prosperity, but the era was far from golden. The **Federal Pact** of 1815 that replaced Napoleon's decrees again made Switzerland a confederation of sovereign states united only for common defense, making united foreign policy still impossible. Because of logistical barriers (each canton had its own laws, currency, postal service, weights, measures, and army—not to mention language and religion), the inhabitants of different cantons regarded each other as foreigners.

In 1846, continuing religious differences led to the formation of a separatist defense league of Catholic cantons known as the **Sonderbund.** In July 1847, the **Diet,** a parliamentary body representing the other cantons, declared the Sonderbund incompatible with the Federal Pact and demanded its dissolution. A civil war broke out, ending with Protestant victory 25 days later. In 1848, the winning cantons wrote a new constitution, modeled after that of the United States, which guaranteed republican and democratic cantonal constitutions and set up the first federal executive body. The central government then established a free-trade zone and unified postal, currency, and railway systems across all the cantons.

Now internally stable, Switzerland began to resolve international conflicts. The **Geneva Convention of 1864** established international laws for conduct during war. Geneva also became the **International Red Cross** headquarters. Swiss neutrality was tested in both the **Franco-Prussian War** and **World War I** because French-speaking and German-speaking Switzerland had different loyalties. In 1920, Geneva became the headquarters of the ill-fated **League of Nations,** solidifying Switzerland's reputation as the center for international diplomacy. At the onset of **World War II,** Switzerland mobilized 20% of its population for a defensive army. Fortunately, Hitler's plan to invade Switzerland was thwarted by Allied landings, distractions on the North African front, and the protective Alpine border. The Swiss government, in order not to incur Germany's wrath, officially impeded passage through its territory, while Jews, escaping Allied prisoners, and other refugees from Nazi Germany found secret asylum in Switzerland. Aside from some accidental bombings in 1940, 1944, and 1945, Switzerland survived the war unscathed.

As the rest of Europe cleaned up the rubble of two world wars, Switzerland nurtured its sturdy economy. Zurich emerged as a banking and insurance center, while Geneva housed international organizations. Although Geneva became the focal point of international diplomacy, Switzerland remained independent in its diplomatic relationships, continually declining offers of membership to the United Nations, NATO, and the European Economic Community.

TODAY

THE PEOPLE'S PARTY AND IMMIGRATION

While Austria made international headlines when its far-right, anti-immigrant political party made gains in October 1999 elections, no one seemed to notice when a similar thing happened in Switzerland two weeks later. The far-right **Swiss**

People's Party (*Schweizerische Volkspartei*) captured 23% of the vote, catapulting from fourth to second among the country's four main parties. The party is strongly anti-immigrant: its members rallied behind the cry "Stop Asylum Abuse," a reaction to the influx of refugees pouring into Switzerland from Eastern Europe. After the People's Party's victory in the election, Jörg Haider of Austria was one of the first to congratulate its leader, fellow business maverick and fast-talking far-right political-leader **Christoph Blocher,** the leader of the People's Party.

The People's Party's jump of 7.9 percentage points since the 1995 elections is astounding, given that the percentage of the vote received by one party has almost never changed more than 1-2% between consecutive elections. It demonstrates the Swiss fear that Eastern European refugees are taking their jobs. One in every five people living in Switzerland is foreign, and immigrants were blamed when unemployment rose in the recent recession. The Swiss panicked when the unemployment rate hit a high of around 5% in the mid-1990s, a rate still low by most other countries' standards. Recently, Switzerland accepted more Kosovar refugees proportional to its population than any other country. The Swiss have never been thrilled with immigration, and the recent influx has heightened such concerns.

SWITZERLAND'S INTERNATIONAL TIES

Switzerland has historically resisted international organizations primarily because they threaten the Swiss people's fierce sense of independence from outside entanglements. In March 2002, however, Switzerland finally joined the **United Nations,** in an initiative supported by both the people and cantons.

During the Cold War, Switzerland's independence and stability were economically advantageous, helping its people attain one of the highest standards of living in the world. But as the rest of Europe has become more stable and integrated, Switzerland's independence has become isolating and has frequently excluded the nation from trade deals. The government, therefore, offered the people the opportunity to join the **European Economic Area (EEA),** the economic forerunner to the EU, in 1992. The people rejected the government's plan through a referendum in which 80 percent of the people turned out to vote (usual turnout for referenda is 35 percent). This vote precluded the chance to vote on EU membership.

After the 1992 vote, the government initiated bilateral negotiations with the EU to create closer ties and to eventually move Switzerland toward

IN RECENT NEWS

THE UNION FOREVER?

Switzerland has always been a proud little country, fiercely guarding its independence. This attitude influences the majority of its political decisions, including its choice to remain a tiny island in the sea of the European Union. In 1993 and again in 2001 the country refused proposals to join the collective, and today its citizens have passionate views on the subject.

Some maintain that, since Switzerland is in the middle of Europe, there is no reason for it not to join. Utterly bemused by what appears to be a stubborn inflexibility on the part of the government and their fellow citizens, these Swiss cite the problems facing those seeking jobs in other European countries as well as the strain on trade and the economy that isolation has put on Switzerland. Already, produce and other imports from outside the country cost half as much as that from local farmers.

Others, however, worry that joining the EU will destroy the Swiss economy. They worry that quality and price standards will compromise Swiss products and force people to change their trades and lifestyles. If Switzerland loses its uniqueness, the tourism trade, a major source of capital in this relatively resource-poor country, will suffer.

With both sides offering valid and passionate views, this issue will likely remain a source of contention.

membership. The People's Party was the only political party that did not endorse the new bilateral negotiations. The fear that Switzerland was moving toward isolationism was calmed, however, when in May 2000 two-thirds of the people voted to accept the bilateral negotiations between the EU and the Swiss government in a referendum.

The People's Party remains an active force in Swiss politics, and the 2003 election results have threatened to shake up the careful political system of consensus that has developed over the last 50 years. The People's Party received 26.6% of the vote, the most of any of the Swiss parties, leading them to request a second seat on the seven-seat Federal Council, the cabinet-like board that is the most powerful political body in the country. For the last 50 years the People's Party has held one seat, while the other three parties have each held two seats, a political arrangement known as the **magic formula.** This formula was carefully crafted so that the Federal Council fairly represented three major languages and two major religions.

PEOPLE

DEMOGRAPHICS

Switzerland is a culturally diverse nation, with people of German origin making up 65% of the population, French origin 18%, Italian 10%, and Romansch 1%. Other minorities, including mostly foreign workers from Eastern Europe, make up the other 6% of the population. Though heterogeneous in culture, the Swiss are rather homogeneous in character, generally described as gracious, proper, and hard-working. Most Swiss are active people, tempted to venture outdoors by the alluring mountain landscape. Skiing and hiking are national pastimes, with more than 40% of the population regularly wandering through the countryside, which perhaps accounts for the 80-year life expectancy rate. In general, the Swiss enjoy an incredibly high standard of living and a low unemployment rate of 3.7% due to a strong market economy. Literacy is virtually 100%.

LANGUAGE

When in Switzerland, try to speak as the Swiss do (whatever the language happens to be). Fewer people speak English in Switzerland than in many other European countries because of the number of languages that must be learned to get by within Switzerland. Thus, while many do speak English, you're always better off trying one of Switzerland's official federal languages first: German, French, Italian, or Romansch. Each language spans a particular geographic region: **German** is spoken by 64% of the population, throughout central and eastern Switzerland; in western Switzerland, **French** is the language of choice for 19% of the Swiss; 8% speak **Italian,** primarily in the southern Ticino region. **Romansch** is spoken by less than 1% of the population, but it has historical and ethnic significance, having survived for hundreds of years in the isolated mountain valleys of Graubünden (p. 415).

German speakers beware: **Swiss German** (*Schwyzertüütsch*) is unlike any of the dialects spoken in Germany and Austria, nearly unintelligible to a speaker of High German (*Hochdeutsch*). Linguistically, Swiss German more closely resembles Middle High German, spoken in Germany 500 years ago. Geographic isolation led to the development of highly disparate dialects in each Swiss region. *Wallisertütsch*, spoken in the southern Valais region, is one of the oldest Swiss German dialects and hence one of the least comprehensible, even to

German-speaking Swiss. On the other hand, *Bärntütsch* and *Züritüütsch*, spoken around Bern and Zurich respectively, are more easily decipherable, though there is no written standard of Swiss German. Although words like *chääschüchli* (cheesecake) and *chuchichäschtli* (kitchen cabinets) may sound harsh to Anglophone ears, most German Swiss prefer their dialect to High German. If you want to pick it up, start with basic practical terms that are nearly the same in all dialects, such as the days of the week: *Mäntig, Zyschtig, Mittwuche, Donschtig, Frytig, Samschtig, Sunntig*. The Swiss will appreciate any effort you make to speak their language, so take a breath and practice saying *Grüezi* (hello).

RELIGION

When the dust settled after the Protestant Reformation, Switzerland ended up almost evenly divided between Catholics (46%) and Protestants (40%), though Protestantism has been in slight decline since World War II. Other religious groups (primarily Jews and Muslims) and agnostics make up the remaining poplation. Switzerland has been a welcoming home to many religious minorities. Geneva, the "City of Peace," houses various international religious organizations representing 130 faiths, such as the World Council of Churches, the Baha'i International Community, the Lutheran World Federation, the Quaker UN Office, the Christian Children's Fund, and the World Jewish Congress.

CULTURE

FOOD AND DRINK

Switzerland is not for the lactose intolerant. The Swiss are serious about dairy products, from rich and varied **cheeses** to decadent milk chocolate. Even the major Swiss soft drink is a dairy-based beverage, *rivella*. These divine bovine goodies are always available at local Migros or Co-op supermarkets. As far as **chocolate** goes, the Swiss have earned bragging rights for their expertise: with the invention of milk chocolate in 1875, Switzerland was poised to rule the world. Today the country is home to some of the world's largest producers: **Lindt, Suchard,** and **Nestlé.** Visit the Lindt factory in Zurich or the Nestlé factory near Bulle to load up on free samples. **Toblerone,** manufactured in Bern, is an international favorite famous for the bits of nougat in creamy milk chocolate, packaged in a nifty triangular box.

IN RECENT NEWS

NEW SWISS MISSES AND MISTERS

Always a safe haven in a war-torn world, Switzerland has recently found itself in the midst of a new wave of immigration. Refugees from Kosovo, Turkey, and other Eastern European countries have been pouring into the country to escape the turmoil in their homes. The Swiss aren't entirely pleased with this influx, however. In a proud country with strong social mores and an inflexible view of what is and is not culturally acceptable, immigrants have trouble gaining acceptance. Part of the problem is that they rarely speak the language when they enter the country and some of them never learn it at all. Most also cling strongly to the traditions of their country. Their foreign ways of life unsettle many Swiss, who have trouble understanding why immigrants cannot adapt to the ways of their new land. Thus, while there is no major violence on the surface, tension between locals and the newest inhabitants lies just below the surface of many interactions.

The government, meanwhile, has been trying to adjust policies to deal with immigration and naturalization, but it is often split. In May of 2004, current policies were reviewed and amended, but the attitude of the citizens has remained the same, and the tension merely increases with the number of immigrants.

Cheese and chocolate cravings satiated, one might desire a more substantial entrée. Not surprisingly, Swiss dishes vary from region to region, and what your waiter brings you is most likely related to the language he is speaking. An array of "typical" Swiss dishes might include the Zurich speciality *Geschnetzeltes* (strips of veal stewed in a thick cream sauce), *Luzerner Chugelipastete* (pâté in a pastry shell), *Papet Vaudois* (leeks with sausage from Vaud), *Churer Fleischtorte* (meat pie from Chur), and Bernese salmon. Each region or town usually has its own specific bread: ask for it by name at the local market or bakery (e.g. when in St. Gallen, ask for *St. Galler-brot*) .

Switzerland's hearty peasant cooking will keep you warm through those frigid Alpine winters. Bernese **Rösti,** a plateful of hashbrown potatoes skilleted and occasionally flavored with bacon or cheese, is as prevalent in the German regions as **fondue** (from the French *fondre*, "to melt") is in the French. Usually a blend of Emmentaler and Gruyère cheeses, white wine, *kirsch*, and spices, fondue is eaten by dunking small cubes of white bread into a *caquelon* (a one-handled pot) kept hot by a small flame. Valaisian **raclette** is made by cutting a wheel of Raclette cheese in half and heating it until the top layer melts; the melted cheese is then scraped onto baked potatoes and garnished with meat or vegetables.

While the words **Swiss cheese** may conjure up images of lunch-box sandwiches filled with a hard, oily, holey cheese, Switzerland actually produces innumerable varieties, each made from a particular type of milk. Nearly every canton and many towns have specialty cheeses. Cheese with holes is usually *Emmentaler*, from the valley of the same name near Bern. *Gruyère* is a stronger version of *Emmentaler*. *Appenzeller* is a hard cheese with a sharp tang. *Tome* is a generic term for a soft, uncooked cheese similar to French *chèvre*. In the Italian regions, cheese often resembles the *Parmigiano* from Italy more than the mountain cheeses of the Alpine regions. As Swiss cheese standards are regulated by law, cheese in Switzerland is always of superb quality.

The Swiss are adept at the art of **confectionery.** Among the most tempting cakes are the *Baseler Leckerli* (a kind of gingerbread), *Zuger Kirschtorte* (cherry cake), Engadine nutcakes, the *bagnolet crème* of the Jura (eaten with raspberries and anise seed biscuits), soda rolls, *rissoles* (pear tarts), and the nougat and pralines of Geneva. *Vermicelli* (not the Italian pasta, but a dessert made of chestnut mousse) is popular all over Switzerland.

The Romans introduced **wine** to the region, but it was not until the 9th century that the beer-drinking laity pried it away from the clergy. Because today there is very little land available for grape growing, Swiss wines are in short supply and are thus more expensive than most imports. Both whites and reds are very good; the red Dole and the white Aigle are especially fine. A wine statute in 1953 imposed rigorous quality controls, helping Swiss wine to retained its excellent reputation.

Each canton has its own local **beer,** a popular beverage in German-speaking Switzerland. Beer is relatively cheap, often less expensive than Coca-Cola. Some notable brands include the dry, moderate-tasting *Original Quöllfrische*, an organic lager from the Brauerei Locher in Appenzell (formerly the beer of choice on Swiss Air flights), the subtly licorice-flavored *Dunkel Lagerbier*, from Stadt Bühler in Gossau, and *Chambière*, a mix of beer and sweet wine from Lucerne.

CUSTOMS AND ETIQUETTE

When in Switzerland be punctual and mind your manners. Remember to say hello and goodbye to shopkeepers and proprietors of bars and cafés, and always shake hands when being introduced. Though not uniform across the entire country, it is customary to greet friends or even acquaintances with a kiss on the cheek. At mealtimes, keep both hands above the table at all times. Lay down your knife and fork "open" (apart from one another), unless you are completely finished with your meal. When dining in public, leave your fork and knife crossed in an "X" on your plate if you need to get up and do not want the server to clear your plate; when finished, place the knife and fork together in the lower right hand corner of your plate, pointing towards the center.

THE ARTS

While Switzerland is not known for creating great monuments in the artistic canon, it does have a lively arts scene today. This scene is particularly visible in contemporary works by young Swiss artists at Zurich's cutting-edge **Kunsthaus** (p. 382) or during a night spent prowling the city's underground music scene.

ARCHITECTURE

Switzerland is home to impressive examples of various European styles, from Romanesque to Gothic to Baroque. The varying climate and distinctive building materials (stone, wood, clay) have engendered distinctive Swiss styles such as the Bernese farmhouse, the Engadine house, and the Ticino *rustico*. In recent years world-renowned architects such as Le Corbusier, Peter Zumthor, Maro Botta, and Herzog and de Meuron have given Swiss towns and cities a modern face.

PAINTING AND SCULPTURE

Early greats among Swiss painters include **Urs Graf** (ca. 1485-1529), a swashbuckling soldier-artist-poet skilled in court portraiture, and **Ferdinand Hodler** (1853-1918), a Symbolist painter who used Swiss landscapes to convey metaphysical messages. In the 20th century, Switzerland has been a primary space for liberal experimentation, exemplified by the work of **Paul Klee,** a member of the Bauhaus faculty, and by the school of *der Blaue Reiter* (The Blue Rider) led by Kandinsky. Klee's delicate watercolors and paintings helped pioneer abstract art forms by calling dominant modes of artistic expression into question.

During the World Wars, Switzerland's art scene was energized by an influx of talented refugees, including **Jean Arp, Richard Hülsenbeck, Janco, Tristan Tzara,** and **Hugo Ball,** some of whom produced the **Dada** explosion in Zurich in 1916. Together they founded the "Cabaret Voltaire" and "Galerie Dada," short-lived centers of Dada activity. The Dada creed championed the irrational, mocking order with chaos. Marginal participants in the Zurich Dada scene later developed into artists in their own right. **Jean Tinguely** created kinetic, mechanized Dada fantasies that celebrated the beauty (and craziness) of motion.

Between and after the wars, Switzerland continued to attract liberal artistic thinkers. The **Zurich School of Concrete Art,** which operated primarily between wars, combined elements of Surrealism with ideas from Russian Constructivism in an attempt to work with objects and environments to explore interactions between humans and space. The school included Paul Klee and **Meret Oppenheim** (a Surrealist famous for her *Fur Teacup*), and its philosophy led sculptor **Alberto Giacometti** to play with spatial realities in his creations of the 1930s. Later, Giacometti rejected the fantastical, abstract elements of Surrealism in order to concentrate on a deep representationalism, creating small, exaggerated, slender figures like *Man Pointing*. After sitting out WWII in London and spending time in Prague, Austrian Expressionist painter **Oskar Kokoschka** moved to Switzerland in 1953, settling in Villeneuve. When Kokoschka died in 1980, his widow Olda found herself with an overabundance of pictures and subsequently founded the Foundation Oskar Kokoschka in the Musée Jenisch in Vevey (p. 511).

I met dozens of people, imaginative and unimaginative, cultivated and uncultivated, who had come from far countries and roamed through the Swiss Alps year after year—they could not explain why.

Mark Twain, *A Tramp Abroad*, ch. 30 (1879)

Well over a century after Twain, the mountains of Switzerland and Austria are still alive with the sound of enthusiastic tourists. This hasn't always been the case. Our attraction to the mountains, whether ineffable or simply inarticulate, marks us as the heirs of a change in taste that began in the eighteenth century.

For the heroine of Daniel Defoe's 1724 novel *Roxana*, the Alps are "those frightful mountains," half of an unpleasant paragraph between Paris and Venice in which she gets out of a carriage and onto a mule with nary a word about the scenery. Her reaction is typical of centuries of European travelers who wanted to go through rather than to the Alps. But a confluence of changes in science, politics and the arts turned the mountains into a destination rather than an obstacle by century's end, a place where the terror and discomfort felt by earlier generations would be transformed into the exhilarating experience of the sublime.

While writers throughout Europe both reflected and furthered this change in taste, the most important of them was surely Jean-Jacques Rousseau. Born in Geneva, he chose the villages and countryside around nearby Vevey as the setting for his enormously popular and influential novel *Julie; or, the New Eloise* (1760). The Alpine landscapes of Rousseau's novel mingle with the beauty of his heroine and with the simple virtues of the Swiss people and their republican government, forcibly contrasted with the decadence of Paris under monarchy. After the Swiss people had begun to burn his books, Rousseau numbered this idealization among the errors he confessed in his autobiography: "How mistaken I was, and yet how naturally! I thought I saw all this in my native land, because I carried it in my heart."

The potential for similar errors continued to haunt and inspire writers of the next century as they roamed this newly literary landscape – "classic ground," wrote Mary Shelley in 1816 with Rousseau firmly in mind, "peopled with tender and glorious imaginations of the present and the past." Her tour of the Alps resulted in the publication of *Frankenstein* the following year. Victor Frankenstein, who like Rousseau is born in Geneva, sees beauty in the surrounding mountains but also, in their inaccessible peaks, "the habitations of another race of beings." The novel offers this deadly Alpine landscape as a powerful analogy for Victor's monster, and for the place in his heart that created and abandoned it.

William Wordsworth's account of his passage through the Alps on a walking tour of 1790, when hopes were still high for the nascent French Revolution, may be the greatest passage of English poetry written about the experience of the mountains. Placed at the center of his autobiographical epic *The Prelude*, the episode recounts Wordsworth's anticlimactic journey through the Simplon Pass. Slightly lost but moving forward in tense expectation of the moment when he will cross the Alps, Wordsworth encounters a local who informs him that – he already has. Recalling his disappointment nearly 15 years later, though – disappointment in the crossing and ultimately in the Revolution that has likewise gone awry – leads Wordsworth's older self to recognize the place of "Imagination" in his hopeful experience of a landscape at once remembered and visionary, natural and divine.

Returning to the Simplon thirty years later, Wordsworth would remark how improved roads and ever increasing numbers of "pilgrims of fashion" had altered the landscape of his youth. The same sentiment occasionally rose to a pitch of fury in John Ruskin, the Victorian art critic for whom a childhood spent reading Wordsworth and an early encounter with the Alps led to a veneration of mountain beauty. Ruskin writes from Vevey in 1869: "I know what the Swiss lakes were; no pool of Alpine fountain at its source was clearer. This morning, on the Lake of Geneva, at half a mile from the beach, I could scarcely see my oar-blade a fathom deep. The light, the air, the waters, all defiled!" A decade later, Twain will gleefully recount to America how he scaled the mountains of Switzerland with the help of servants, carriages, telescopes – even, on occasion, his own two feet.

But if the Alps seem to be fully mapped territory by the latter half of the 19th century, we can nevertheless see them anew through the consummately literary but still original eyes of Henry James and his first great character, Daisy Miller. James stages the first encounter between his naïve heroine, fresh from Schenectady, and her highly cultured and cynical suitor, Winterbourne, in a partially Americanized Vevey where "the entertainment of tourists is the business of the place." Trying to make small talk, Winterbourne asks her how she'll be traveling to Italy: "And are you – a – thinking of the Simplon?' 'I don't know,' she said. 'I suppose it's some mountain.' Ignorant? Perhaps – but Daisy's palpable want of culture also promises a chance, not so much to discover the Alps as to experience them anew. If only Winterbourne would, or could, take the chance.

Eric Idsvoog is a PhD candidate in English and American Literature and Language at Harvard University. His areas of expertise include Romanticism and the theory of Romanticism and British, French, and German literature.

LITERATURE

Though not renowned for its literary tradition, Switzerland has been home to many famous writers. **Jean-Jacques Rousseau,** best known for his *Social Contract* (inspiration for the French Revolution) was born in Geneva in 1712. Rousseau always proudly acknowledged his Swiss background, despite the fact that he spent most of his time outside the country and that the Swiss burned his books. Long-term Swiss resident **Jacob Burckhardt** promoted a new history of culture and art from his Basel home in the late 19th century. His works include *History of the Italian Renaissance* and *Cicerone: A Guide to the Enjoyment of Italian Art.*

The age of Romanticism found **J.J. Bodmer** and **J.J. Breitinger's** advocacy of literature in Swiss German in conflict with many of their German contemporaries who strove to standardize German through literature. The Swiss-born **Madame de Staël** (born Germaine Necker) was an important writer in her own right as well as the driving force behind Romanticism's spread from Germany to France. Switzerland also produced several Realist authors, most notably **Gottfried Keller,** who penned a classic 19th-century German *Bildungsroman* entitled *Der Grüne Heinrich.* **Conrad Ferdinand Meyer** was another highly influential Swiss writer who is best known for his historical novellas.

Only in the 20th century has Swiss literature come into its own with such greats as **Hermann Hesse,** who wrote the masterpiece *Siddhartha* and received the Nobel Prize for literature in 1946. Hesse's works, including *Steppenwolf* and *Narcissus and Goldmund,* explore the duality of spirit and nature and the protagonist's journey to inner self. **Blaise Cendrars,** an early 20th-century avant-garde author who wrote in French, retains a small devoted following today due to his novels' lively, modern feel. Writer and psychologist **Carl Gustav Jung** began as an acolyte of Freud but split off by 1915, when he wrote *Symbols of Transformation.* Later he set up a flourishing psychoanalytic practice in Zurich. Critics laud **Max Frisch** for his Brechtian style and thoughtful treatment of Nazi Germany. His most widely known works are the play *Andorra* and the novel *Homo Faber,* which was made into a film in the early 1990s. **Friedrich Dürrenmatt** has written a number of dark, humorous plays, most notably *Der Besuch der Alten Dame* (The Visit of the Old Lady) and *Die Physiker* (The Physicists). Both Dürrenmatt and Frisch are critical of, but loyal to, their home country.

Switzerland also has a long tradition of hosting writers from other countries. Ever since **Voltaire** came to Geneva in 1755 to do some heavy-duty philosophizing, Switzerland has been the promised land for intellectuals, artists, and soon-to-be-famous personalities. George Gordon, otherwise known as the opium-smoking Romantic poet **Lord Byron,** quit England in 1816 for Switzerland. Byron wrote "Sonnet on Chillon" while brooding on Lake Geneva. His contemporary **Percy Shelley** crafted "Hymn to Beauty" and "Mont Blanc" in the vale of Chamonix. Shelley's wife **Mary Wollstonecraft Shelley** came across some ghost stories while in Switzerland, which, heightened by Switzerland's eternal mist and craggy Alps, inspired *Frankenstein.* Speaking of ghosts, such geniuses as **Nikolai Gogol, Fyodor Dostoyevsky, Victor Hugo, Ernest Hemingway,** and **F. Scott Fitzgerald** still haunt the Geneva countryside where they wrote when they were in more tangible form. **James Joyce** fled to Zurich during WWI and stayed to scribble the greater part of *Ulysses* between 1915 and 1919.

Other great minds came from Germany, Austria, and Italy. **Johann Wolfgang von Goethe** caught his first distant view of Italy from the top of St. Gotthard Pass in the Swiss Alps. **Friedrich Schiller** wrote about the massive church bell in Schaffhausen before penning *Wilhelm Tell.* While on holiday in the Engadine Valley, **Friedrich Nietzsche** went nuts and produced his mountaintop tome *Thus Spake Zarathustra.* **Richard Wagner** composed most of his major operas during his years with Nietzsche in verdant Switzerland. **Thomas Mann** also found refuge in Switzerland; his novel *The Magic Mountain* was set in the Swiss Alps. More recently, Switzerland has harbored writers and scientists from the former Eastern bloc, notably Russian author **Alexander Solzhenitsyn** and Czech novelist **Milan Kundera.**

MUSIC

The subversive artistic spirit of the late 20th and early 21st centuries has generated Swiss bands no longer confined by the limits of genre. Jazz musicians fuse their style with techno or hip hop, traditional Swiss French music gets a modern make-over, and rock bands experiment with electronic music. Catch a sampling of these style fusions at the festivals that heat up summer nights throughout Switzerland.

A sampling of popular bands might feature **Chitty Chitty Bang Bang,** a Franco-Swiss rock foursome that has released four CDs. **Der Klang** has invented a French *chanson* style which has led them far past the limits of the genre. Popular not only in Switzerland but also in Germany and Japan, **Gotthard**'s raw, bluesy vocals, hard-rock rhythms and plentiful solos recall the sound of Bon Jovi. A rock band with folk roots, Geneva's **Polar** has performed with the likes of Massive Attack and Fiona Apple. The phrase "Swiss hip-hop" may cause some snickers, but Switzerland does hold its own with a handful of groups, including **Wrecked Mob** from Lucerne, **Def Cut,** who recently released his first album in the US, and **Sens Unik,** one of the most famous and well-established Swiss hip-hop outfits. Crossing several genres is the jazz musician **Erik Truffaz,** who learned his trumpet skills from the famed Miles Davis. His sound combines jazz with hip hop and techno.

FILM

As in Austria, the Swiss government subsidizes many film projects in order to encourage the growth of a domestic film industry. A handful of Swiss films have garnered recognition at various international film festivals. Its own annual **Locarno Film Festival,** attended by over 4000 film professionals representing 20 countries, is considered to be among the top six film festivals in the world.

The Swiss have also made their mark on American film industry. **Emil Jannings** won the first Academy Awards for Best Actor for his work in *The Way of All Flesh* (1927) and *The Last Commandment* (1928). Swiss American and Academy Award winner **William Wyler** directed numerous noteworthy pictures including *Ben Hur* and *Roman Holiday.* More recently, **H.R. Giger** served as art director and set designer for the intense and gripping films *Alien* and *Species,* and **Xavier Koller's** film about Turkish refugees traveling to Switzerland, *Journey of Hope,* won an Academy Award for best foreign language film in 1991.

SPORTS AND RECREATION

The active Swiss spend much of their leisure time doing athletics. Thus, it came as no surprise when in 1972 a federal law ensured government financial support for the promotion of sports. Exercise and sports are regarded as integral parts of life and there are numerous sports organizations throughout the country. Even the headquarters of the **International Olympic Committee (IOC)** are located in Lausanne.

With more than 50,000km of designated footpaths, **hiking** remains one of the most popular recreational activities. **Skiing** is also extremely popular: Switzerland is known for having some of the best slopes in the world. Two sports unique to the country are **Hornussen** and **Schwingen. Hornussen** involves an offensive team that uses long metal rods with wooden handles to knock a disc called the *hornuss* as far as possible down the field, while the defensive team uses a wooden shield to prevent the advance of the disc. If the disc lands on the field without being inter-cepted, the defense loses a point; if the defense knocks it down, they gain a point. **Schwingen** (p. 384) is a type of Swiss wrestling in which each participant grabs the waistband of his opponent with his right hand and a band on his opponent's leg with his left hand in an attempt to throw him down and hold his back to the ground. The match is over once the wrestler loses both hand-holds or has both shoulder blades touching the ground.

HOLIDAYS AND FESTIVALS

National holidays in Switzerland are almost all of Christian origin. Expect most establishments to be closed on Easter (March 27 in 2005), Christmas (December 25), New Year's Eve (December 31), and Good Friday (March 25), in some areas.

SWITZERLAND'S HOLIDAYS

DATE	NAME & LOCATION	DESCRIPTION
January 1	New Year's Day	Celebration of the new year
March 1	*Unabhängigkeitstag;* Neu-châtel	Independence Day
April 30	Walpurgis Nacht	Night before May 1, when witches dance on the Blocksberg in the German Harz mountain range
August 1	Swiss National Day	Commemoration of the agreement made at the beginning of August 1291 between Uri, Schwyz, and Unterwalden
October 24	United Nations Day	Commemoration of the ratification of the UN charter in 1994
December 31	Restoration	Celebration of the restoration of the oligarchic Republic after brief French domination

ADDITIONAL RESOURCES

GENERAL HISTORY

Switzerland: A Village History (2000). David Birmingham.

Target Switzerland: Swiss Armed Neutrality in World War II (2000). Stephen P. Halbrook.

Swiss Banks and Jewish Souls (1999). Gregg J. Rickman.

Why Switzerland? (1996). Jonathan Steinberg.

FICTION

Siddhartha (1922) and *Steppenwolf* (1927). Hermann Hesse.

Daisy Miller (1878). Henry James.

The Magic Mountain (1924). Thomas Mann.

Frankenstein (1818). Mary Shelley.

A Tramp Abroad (1879). Mark Twain.

TRAVEL BOOKS

The German Way: Aspects of Behavior, Attitudes, and Customs in the German-Speaking World (1996). Hyde Flippo.

Living and Working in Switzerland: A Survival Handbook (2003). David Hampshire.

Trekking and Climbing in the Western Alps (2002). Hilary Sharp.

SWITZERLAND

FESTIVAL FEVER. Back in the 70s, a handful of Swiss hipsters put a new spin on the time-worn tradition of celebrating the harvest or honoring a religious holiday with a rip-roaring raucous festival. What started as a small movement has grown to encompass more than a dozen festivals in nearly every part of the Swiss countryside. Thousands of people migrate from festival to festival all summer long, following the sounds of jazz, blues, folk, rock, pop, soul, funk, hip-hop, drum 'n' bass, house, and techno. Many of the festivals offer free campsites for all comers and have cheap tickets. Listed below are the festivals not to be missed.

Bern, *Gurtenfestival*. This 3-day festival in mid-July attracts 15,000 visitors per day to the Gurten hill above Bern (5min. from town center). Features 2 stages and 3 dance tents. (www.gurtenfestival.ch.)

Winterthur, *Winterthurer Musikfestwochen*. This 17-day festival in late Aug. exhibits over 100 acts of many genres. Open-air festival the last weekend. (☎(052) 212 61 16; www.winterthur.musikfestwochen.ch.)

Nyon (near Geneva), *Paléo Festival Nyon*. Switzerland's largest open-air music festival in late July wins the prize for diversity of acts, ranging from hip hop and reggae to electronic grooves to ska, as well as rock, pop, and even traditional French *chanson*. A free campsite offers accommodations for thousands of festival-goers. (☎(022) 365 10 10; www.paleo.ch.)

Le Lausanne/Pulley for Noise. An alternative to alternative music festivals, this 3-day fest in early Aug. focuses on up-and-coming groups as well as better-known bands like Sneaker Pimps and The Good Life. (www.fornoise.ch.)

St. Gallen, *Open-Air St. Gallen*. This weekend festival in early July combines crowd-pleasing favorites like Ben Harper and the Black Eyed Peas with many less mainstream bands. (☎(071) 388 78 08; www.openairsg.ch.)

Zurich, *Streetparade*. For one day in early Aug., more than 400,000 house and techno fans congregate on the streets of Zurich and stay to party afterwards. No tickets necessary. (www.street-parade.ch.)

Gampel (near Sion), is growing in popularity, attracting 30,000+ visitors each year because of appearances by big names such as Pink and The Cure. (☎(027) 932 50 13; www.openairgampel.ch.)

BERNESE OBERLAND

The Swiss are fiercely proud of the Bernese Oberland. When WWII threatened to engulf the country, the Swiss army resolved to defend the area to the death and were aided in their endeavor by the natural fortress of mountains. The jutting peaks now shelter a pristine wilderness that lends itself to discovery through scenic hikes up the mountains and around the twin lakes, the Thunersee and Brienzersee. Not surprisingly, the area's opportunities for paragliding, mountaineering, and white-water rafting are unparalleled. North of the mountains and lakes lies exuberant Bern, Switzerland's capital and the metropolitan heartbeat of the region. Bern's wide streets buzz with activity, while hills in the background hint at the wilderness to the south.

The Bernese Oberland is great for hiking, but plan your trips wisely: cable cars are expensive. Whenever possible, *Let's Go* lists hikes which are possible without mechanical assistance. If you must rely on the cable cars, consider saving money by taking them up the mountain and walking down. Try to use a town or village as a hub from which to explore the surrounding area, or buy a regional pass. The 15-day **Berner Oberland Regional Pass** (265SFr; with SwissPass or half-fare card 212SFr) grants five days of unlimited free regional travel and a 50% discount on the other 10. A seven-day pass (220SFr, with SwissPass 176SFr) includes three days of unlimited travel and a 50% discount on the other four days. Both are available at train station.

HIGHLIGHTS OF THE BERNESE OBERLAND

Climb the Münster for the best view in **Bern** (p. 335).
Ski surrounded by natural grandeur on the **Jungfraujoch** (p. 352).
Scream, soar, and hold onto your lunch as you paraglide over **Interlaken** (p. 350).

BERN ☎031

Though it borders the French-speaking part of the country, Bern belongs to German-speaking Switzerland. The Duke of Zähringen founded Bern in 1191, naming it for his mascot, the bear. Today, the legacy of that choice defines the city: bears are found in the pits outside the city and their pictures adorn countless fountains and flags. Bern's been the capital since 1848, but don't expect power politics and men in black. Bern prefers to focus on the finer things in life. Arcade-lined streets house numerous shops and *Weinstubes*, inspiring the adage, "Venice is built on water, Bern on wine." The Rosengarten (Rose Garden) peers over the city, giving fantastic views of Bern's red-tiled roofs, and the lush green banks of the swiftly moving Aare provide a respite for laid-back locals. Rebuilt in 1405 after a devastating fire, Bern's sandstone and mahogany buildings are dominated by the Bundeshaus (Parliament Building) and the Gothic Münster's spire. Such architectural marvels caused UNESCO to name the city a world treasure in 1983.

✈ INTERCITY TRANSPORTATION

Flights: Bern-Belpmoos Airport (☎960 21 11), 20min. from central Bern and served by Air Engadina (☎08 48 84 83 28). Direct flights daily to **Amsterdam, Basel, Brussels, London, Lugano, Munich, Paris, Rome,** and **Vienna.** 50min. before each flight, an airport bus that guarantees you'll make it leaves from the train station in front of the tourist office (10min., 14SFr). Check at the tourist office for a current bus schedule.

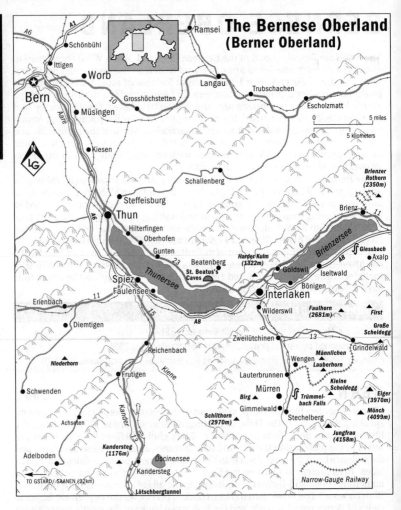

The Bernese Oberland (Berner Oberland)

Trains: In the station, the **domestic ticket counter** is upstairs (open daily 5:30am-9:45pm); **international tickets** can be bought at the ticket office upstairs (open M-F 7:30am-6:50pm, Sa 7:30am-4:50pm), or, if it's closed, at the domestic counter for trips in the next 48hr. To: **Basel** (1¼hr., 4 per hr. 4:33am-11:52pm, 34SFr); **Berlin** (8hr., 14 per day 5:49am-11:17pm, 184SFr); **Geneva** (2hr., 3 per hr. 4:26am-11:24pm, 47SFr); **Interlaken** (50min., every hr. 6:52am-11:26pm, 23SFr); **Lausanne** (1¼hr., every 30min. 4:26am-11:24pm, 30SFr); **Lucerne** (1½hr., every 30min. 5:04am-11:21pm, 30SFr); **Milan** (3½hr., 10 per day 6:19am-6:22pm, 73SFr); **Munich** (6½hr., every hr. 5:16am-10:13pm, 120SFr); **Paris** (6hr., almost every hr. 5:49am-11:24pm, 111SFr); **Salzburg** (7¼hr., 2 per day 5:47am-9:49pm, 133SFr); **Vienna** (12hr., every hr., 5:47am-11:17pm, 152SFr); **Zurich** (1¼hr., every 30min. 5:04am-11:52pm, 45SFr). 25% off on all international fares for ages 26 and under.

By car: From **Basel** or the **north,** take A2 south to A1. From **Lucerne** or the **east,** take 10 west. From **Geneva** or **Lausanne,** take E62 east to E27/A12 north. From **Thun** or the **southeast,** take A6 north.

◆ ORIENTATION

Medieval Bern lies in front of the train station and along the Aare River, which cuts in and out of the city. The Kornhausbr. leads across the river to the north to the newer side of town. Staying to the south and venturing along the river walkways near Marzilibr. and Helvetiapl. is a favorite pastime of locals. Bern is worth touring even on a rainy day, thanks to the 6km of arcades that cover the streets. For a fantastic view, head to the Rosengarten, on the far side to the Aare. **Warning:** Like many cities, Bern has a drug community; it tends to congregate around the Parliament park and Münster terraces, and, at night, in the stairways around the train station.

▢ LOCAL TRANSPORTATION

Public Transportation: Bernmobil, Bubenbergpl. 5 (☎321 86 41 or 321 86 31; infotel 321 84 84; info@bernmobil.ch). A **visitor's card** from the Jurahaus ticket office entitles the holder to unlimited travel on Bernmobil routes. 24hr. pass 7.50SFr; 48hr. 11SFr; 72hr. 15SFr. This pass is cheaper than the day pass alone (9SFr), which is dispensed at vending machines along with one-way tickets (1-6 stops 1.70SFr, 7 or more stops 2.60SFr; children always 1.70SFr; SwissPass valid). Buses run roughly 5:45am-midnight. **Nightbuses** called "Moonliners" leave the train station at 12:45am Th-Sa nights, also regularly 2-3:15am F-Sa nights, covering major bus and tram lines (5-20SFr; no reductions). The Bernmobil office has maps and timetables. Open M-W and F 6:30am-7:30pm, Th 6:30am-9pm, Sa-Su 7:30am-6:30pm.

Taxis: Bären-Taxi (☎371 11 11). **NovaTaxi** (☎331 33 13; www.novataxi.ch). Stands: Bahnhofpl., Waisenhauspl., and Casinopl. 6.80SFr base; 3.10SFr per km. 8pm-6am, Su and holidays 3.40SFr per km.

Car Rental: Avis AG, Wabernstr. 41 (☎378 15 15). **Hertz AG,** Kocherg. 1, Casinopl. (☎318 21 60). **Europcar,** Laupenstr. 22 (☎381 75 55).

Parking: At the **Bahnhof,** entrance at Schanzenbr. or Stadtbachstr., at **Parking Casino,** Kocherg. and **Metro,** on Waisenhauspl., as well as **City West,** Belpstr., runs 1.80-3.60SFr per hr. Day-permit parking discs available at the tourist office. Parking permits (9SFr) available at machines at tram stops. Note: all decks are underground; well-placed road signs throughout the city report how many free spaces remain and point the way toward the various decks. Many parking locations have spots on the first level that are well-lit and reserved only for single women (*Frauenplätze*).

Bike Rental: The small blue **Bernrollt Kiosk** outside the train station and another at Kornhauspl. lends bikes for **free.** 20SFr deposit plus ID required. Bikes must be returned on the same day. Open daily May-Oct. 7:30am-9:30pm. Also try the luggage counter at the **train station.** (☎05 12 20 23 74. Open daily 7am-9pm. 30SFr per day.)

▢ PRACTICAL INFORMATION

TOURIST AND FINANCIAL SERVICES

Tourist Office: (☎328 12 12; www.bernetourism.ch), on the street level of the station. Distributes city maps (1SFr) and *Bern Aktuell,* a bi-monthly guide to events in the city, and makes free room reservations. Pick up the restaurant guide which has a small, free version of the bulky map sold by the tourist office. The free blue-and-yel-

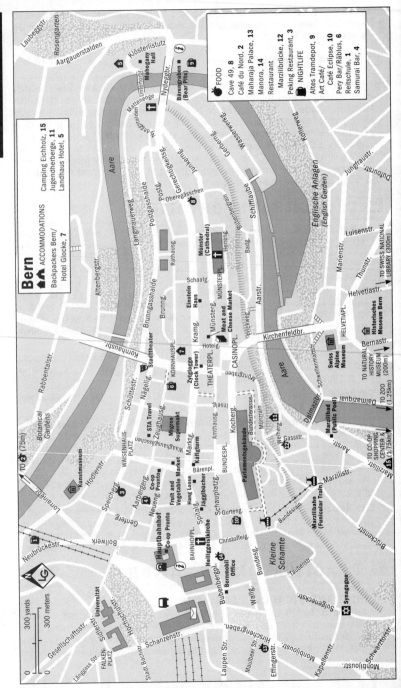

Bern

ACCOMMODATIONS
Backpackers Bern/
Hotel Glocke, **7**

Camping Eichholz, **15**
Jugendherberge, **11**
Landhaus Hotel, **5**

FOOD
Cave 49, **8**
Café du Nord, **2**
Maharaja Palace, **13**
Manora, **14**
Restaurant
Marziliibrücke, **12**
Peking Restaurant, **3**

NIGHTLIFE
Altes Tramdepot, **9**
Art Café/
Café Eclipse, **10**
Pery Bar/Räblus, **6**
Reitschule, **1**
Samurai Bar, **4**

> **🎯 TIP** **FÜSSGÄNGER FRIENDLY.** The wide cobblestone streets of Bern unequivocally belong to the *Füssgänger* (pedestrian). Even in the sections of the *Altstadt* that do allow motor vehicles, most are forced to a slow crawl by the crowds of diners and merrymakers who own the streets. Bern motorists have more obstacles: the city's ubiquitous 16th-century fountains. The stone fountains have been restored repeatedly since the mid-1500s to maintain their gaudy color schemes. Highlights include the *Gerechtigkeitsbrunnen* on Gerechtigkeitsg., in which Justice stomps on the Pope, Emperor, Sultan, and Mayor; and the *Kindlifresserbrunnen* ("Child-Devourer Fountain") at Kornhauspl., tastefully translated as "Ogre Fountain."

low *Bern: Plan/Map mit sofortiger Übersicht* is an excellent larger map that even includes bus routes. 24hr. accommodations board and a free phone line to hotels. **City tours** available by bus (May-Nov. daily 11am; Nov. also Sa 11am; 29SFr 10SFr children), on foot (Apr. Su-F 11am; May-Oct. 2:30pm), or by raft (20-45SFr). Open June-Sept. daily 9am-8:30pm; Oct.-May M-Sa 9am-6:30pm, Su 10am-5pm. **Branch office** at the bear pits (p. 335) open daily June-Sept. 9am-6pm; Jan. and Mar. 10am-4pm; Nov. and Feb. 11am-4pm. The branch office shows a mildly entertaining movie detailing Bern's history every 20min., alternately in French and German. Free.

Budget Travel: STA, Zeughausg. 18 (☎312 07 24; www.statravel.ch). Sells ISICs. Open M-W and F 9:30am-6pm, Th 9:30am-7pm, Sa 10am-4pm. **Hang Loose,** Spitalg. 4 (☎313 18 18; www.hangloose.ch), has student airfares and ISICs. Open M-F 9am-6pm, Th 9am-8pm, Sa 9am-noon.

Embassies and Consulates: Nearly all foreign embassies in Switzerland are in Bern, southeast of the Kirchenfeldbr. A complete list of consular services can be found in the **Essentials** section (p. 8).

Currency Exchange: Downstairs in the station. No commission on traveler's checks. Cash advances on DC/MC/V. **Western Union** transfers M-F 9am-7pm, Sa-Su 8am-5pm. Exchange open daily 6:30am-9pm. Automatic **24hr. currency exchange machines** at UBS across from the station at Bubenbergpl. 3, and at the Migros Bank, Aarbergerg. 20.

ATM: At the train station or at **Credit Suisse** (Kornhauspl. 7, M-F 8am-6pm; Bundespl. 2, M-F 8:30am-4:30pm, Th until 6pm) and **UBS** (Bubenbergpl. 3, Bärenpl. 8, M-W and F 9am-6:30pm, Th until 6pm).

LOCAL SERVICES

Luggage Storage: Downstairs in the train station. 24hr. lockers 4-8SFr. **Luggage watch** at the Fly-Gepäck counter upstairs 7SFr. Open daily 7:30am-10pm.

Lost Property: Downstairs in station (open M-F 8am-6pm) and at Zeughausg. 18 (☎220 23 37; open M-F 8am-noon and 2-6pm).

Bookstore: JäggiBücher, Spitalg. on Bubenbergpl. 47-51 (☎320 20 20), in Loeb dept. store. 2 floors of books including English bestsellers and travel guides. Open M-W and F 9am-6:30pm, Th 9am-9pm, Sa 8am-4pm.

Libraries: Stadtbibliothek (Municipal and University Library), Münsterg. 61 (☎320 32 11), stacks books for the central library of the University of Bern and the city's public library. Open M-F 10am-6pm. *Medienraum* (on 2nd floor) with **Internet** and general work spaces open M-Tu and Th-F 10am-9pm, W noon-9pm, Sa 8am-noon. **Swiss National Library,** Hallwylstr. 15 (☎332 89 11). Lending library and catalog room open M-Tu and Th-F 9am-6pm, W 9am-8pm, Sa 9am-2pm. Reading room open M-Tu and Th-F 8am-6pm, W 8am-8pm, Sa 9am-4pm.

GLBT Organizations: Homosexuelle Arbeitsgruppe die Schweiz-HACH (Gay Association of Switzerland), c/o Anderland, Mühlenpl. 11, CH-3011 Bern; www.haz.ch. Headquarters of Switzerland's largest gay organization. **Homosexuelle Arbeitsgruppe Bern (HAB)**, Mühlenpl. 11, Case Postal 312, CH-3000 Bern 13 (☎311 63 53) in Marzilibad, along the Aare. Hosts meet-ups W evenings with beverages and library access. **Schlub** (Gay Students' Organization of the University of Bern), c/o Studentinnenschaft, Lercheweg 32, CH-3000 Bern 9; ☎371 00 87; http://subwww.unibe.ch/grp/schlub).

Laundromat: Jet Wasch, Dammweg 43 (☎078 743 92 09). Take bus #20 (dir: Wyler) to "Lorraine." Wash 8kg for 6SFr, 5kg 4SFr; dry 4SFr for 1hr. Soap 0.80-1.20SFr. Open M-Sa 7am-9pm, Su 9am-6pm.

Public Toilets and Showers: McClean, at train station. 1-2SFr for toilets, 12SFr for towels, shampoo, and 20min. showers. Open daily 6am-midnight.

EMERGENCY AND COMMUNICATIONS

Emergency: Police ☎117 and downstairs in the station. **Ambulance** ☎144. **Doctor** ☎311 22 11. **Rape Crisis Hotline** ☎332 14 14. **Mental Health Hotline** ☎ 143.

Pharmacy: In the station. Open daily 6:30am-10pm. **Bären Apotheke,** at the clock tower. Open M 1:45-6:30pm, Tu-W and F 7:45am-6:30pm, Th 7:45am-9pm, Sa 8am-4pm. AmEx/DC/MC/V. In the **Co-op Shopping Center** near Camping Eichholz. Open M-F 8am-6:30pm, Sa 8am-4pm. **24hr. pharmacy** call ☎311 22 11.

Internet Access: Stadtbibliothek, Münsterg. 63, offers Internet access for 4SFr per hr. in the *Medienraum* 1 floor up from the street. 2 terminals offer 10min. free surfing. Open M-Tu and Th-F 10am-9pm, W noon-9pm, Sa 8am-noon. **JäggiBücher,** Spitalg. on Bubenbergpl. 47-51 (☎320 20 20), in Loeb dept. store. 2 computers allow max. 20min. free, 4 more computers cost 5SFr per 30min. Open M-W and F 9am-6:30pm, Th 9am-9pm, Sa 8am-4pm.

Post Office: Schanzenpost 1, a block from the train station. *Poste Restante* to Postlagernde Briefe, Schanzenpost 3000, Bern 1. Open M-F 7:30am-9pm, Sa 8am-4pm, Su 5-9pm. At Bärenpl., open M-F 7:30am-6:30pm, Sa 8am-noon. On Senftigenstr. near Camping Eichholz, open M-F 7:30am-noon and 1:45-6pm, Sa 8:30am-noon.

Postal Codes: CH-3000 to CH-3030.

🛏🛏 ACCOMMODATIONS AND CAMPING

🛏 **Backpackers Bern/Hotel Glocke,** Rathausg. 75 (☎311 37 71; www.bernbackpackers.com). From the train station, cross the tram lines, turn left onto Spitalg., continuing through Bärenpl. and the Käfigturm onto Marktg. Turn left at Kornhauspl., pass the Zytglogge clock tower, and then turn right on Rathausg. The hostel is immediately on your right. A backpacker's dream—clean, new, and ideally located. Crowds of social English-speaking backpackers fill the TV/lounge area. Windows overlook the *Altstadt*. **Internet** (2SFr for 15min.) and free kitchen access. Laundry 6SFr to wash and dry. Sheets included. Reception 8-11am and 3-10pm. Strict 10am check-out. Doors lock after 10:30pm 24hr. keycard access. 4- to 6-bed dorms 29-31SFr; 2-bed single-sex dorms 39SFr; singles 60-75SFr; doubles 100-120SFr, with shower 130-150SFr. AmEx/DC/MC/V, 35SFr minimum for credit card. ❷

Jugendherberge (HI), Weiherg. 4 (☎311 63 16; www.jugibern.ch). From the station, cross the tram lines and go down Christoffelg. Take the stairs to the left of the park entrance gates and go down the slope, then turn left onto Weiherg., following the hostel signs. A friendly European and American crowd of backpackers and families use this hostel near the river and restaurants and clubs. Large common areas. Wheelchair accessible. **Internet** 0.50SFr per min., half-price midnight-7am. Breakfast, lockers, and sheets included. Lunch M-F 13SFr; dinner 12SFr. Laundry wash 4SFr, dry 1SFr per 15min. Reception June-Sept. 7-10am and 3pm-midnight; Oct.-May 7-10am and 5pm-midnight. 24-hour key card access. Check-out 10am. Reservations by fax and e-mail only. Closed 2nd and 3rd weeks in Jan. Dorms 31.30-36.30SFr. Singles from 49.30SFr; doubles from 79.40SFr (reserve far in advance). Non-members add 6SFr. MC/V. ❷

Landhaus Hotel, Altenbergstr. 4-6 (☎331 41 66; landhaus@spectraweb.ch). From the train station, turn left on Spitalg. and follow it all the way to Nydegg Kirche. Take the stairs down to the church, walk down the hill on Nydeggstalden, cross Untertorbr., and the hotel will be on your left. Though not entirely in the town, near the bear pits, *Rosengarten*, and the Altes Tramdepot. Partitioned bunks providing more privacy than most dorms. Located above a stylish restaurant and bar along the Aare that provides cheap take-out. Internet 1.60SFr plus time used (ask at reception). Free kitchen access. Breakfast 7SFr for dorms; included in other rooms. Sheets 5SFr in the dorms; included in other rooms. Reception daily 9am-10pm. Partitioned 6-bed dorms 30SFr, 35SFr with pillow; singles with sink 75-105SFr; doubles with linens and breakfast 95-135SFr, with bath 140-160SFr; triples 130SFr; 4-bed family room 140-160SFr. Towels 3SFr in dorms, included in other rooms. AmEx/DC/MC/V. ❷

Camping Eichholz, Strandweg 49 (☎961 26 02; www.campingeichholz.ch). Take tram #9 to "Wabern," backtrack 50m, and take the 1st right. Walk down Eichholzstr.; signs point the way (10min.). A convenient riverside location means that the site is often filled with penny-saving backpackers. On-site restaurant. Shopping center nearby with post office, pharmacy, and grocery store (see Local Services above and Food below). Parking 2-3.20SFr. Laundry 5SFr. Reserve ahead. Reception 7am-10pm. Open late Apr. to Sept. 6.90SFr per person, students 5.50SFr, children under 16 3SFr, tents 5-8.50SFr. Cars 12SFr. Bungalow with very simple singles 21.90SFr; doubles 30SFr; triples 68SFr. Electricity 3SFr. Showers 1SFr for 5 min. MC/V. ❶

◪ FOOD

Die Front (the Front), a row of restaurants along Bärenpl., fills up with locals and tourists at night, when restaurant owners spread an ocean of tables and chairs across the entire street. Food along *Die Front* is moderately priced, but nothing too special—the locale is perhaps better suited for people-watching. Wherever you are, try one of the city's hearty specialties: *Gschnätzlets* (fried veal, beef, or pork), *Suurchabis* (a sauerkraut), or *Gschwellti* (steamed potatoes).

◪ **Café du Nord,** Lorrainestr. 2 (☎332 23 38, fax 23 00), take Lorrainebr. (after crossing river, the restaurant is directly on the right), or take the #20 bus to "Gewerbeschule." A relaxed atmosphere where a diverse, alternative crowd smokes and socializes. Turtle-neck-clad poets sit next to guitar-strumming hippies in the outdoor seating draped with vines and Christmas lights. Spacious bar inside. Meat entrees 22-32SFr. Pasta plates from 17SFr. Special seasonal menus. Su night Indian specials. Beer from 4SFr. Open M-F 8am-12:30am, Sa 9am-12:30am; kitchen open M-Sa 11:30am-2pm and 6:30-10pm, Su 4-11:30pm. MC/V. ❸

Manora, Bubenbergplatz 5a (☎382 64 64), across the plaza from the station, is a dream come true for budget travelers and vegetarians. Buffet meals include mountains of fresh fruits, fish, salads, and desserts, all at reasonable prices. Sandwiches, meats, and smoothies also excellent. Crowded but friendly. Open daily 6:30am-11pm; food service ends at 10:30pm; hot food served after 10am. ❷

Peking Restaurant, Speicherg. 27 (☎312 14 28, fax 311 69 94). From the station, head left on Bollwerk and turn right on Speicherg. The restaurant is on the right. One of the best budget options in Bern: get a box of hot, tasty Chinese food and a cold canned drink to take away for 9.90SFr. Eat in the clean, brightly-decorated restaurant for a bit more (12-15SFr). Open daily 11am-2:30pm, 6-11:30pm. ❷

Maharaja Palace, Effingerstrasse 4, (☎382 64 64). From the station, head across the plaza past the church onto Christoffelg. Turn right onto Bundesg. and walk two blocks. This small Indian restaurant is an excellent value. Lunch buffets (15SFr, 12SFr vegetarian. Served M-F 11:45am-2pm.) or pricier dinner entrées like lamb curry (28.50SFr) or yogurt chicken (30SFr). Open M-F 11am-2:30pm, 5:30-11pm, Sa-Su 5:30-11pm. ❸

Restaurant Marzilibrücke, Gassstr. 8 (☎311 27 80). Turn right from the Jugendherberge onto Aarstr. and then again onto Gasstr. From the center of town, take the winding path down the hill below the Parliament building and take your first right. Head around the corner onto Gasstr. Divided into a stylish restaurant and a more casual pizzeria, this classy joint overflows with couples, families, and small groups looking to enjoy the outdoor seating just steps from the Aare. Gourmet pizzas (15.50-25.50SFr) and a quality wine list (4.20-6.70SFr per glass). Most other dinner options 20-30SFr. Reservations recommended. Open M-Th 11:30am-11:30pm, F 11:30am-12:30am, Sa 4pm-12:30am, Su 10am-11:30pm. Pizzeria open M-F 5:30-11pm, Sa-Su 4-11pm; kitchen open daily until 10pm, pizza available daily until 11pm. AmEx/DC/MC/V. ❸

Cave 49, Gerechtigkeitsg. 49 (☎377 30 91). From the clock tower, head away from the station on Kramg. After the road bends slightly to the right, the stairs for Cave 49 will be on the right. A cross between a restaurant and a bar, Cave 49 is what the name implies: a sort of cave underneath the sidewalk. This Spanish tavern is frequented by both a boisterous local crowd and well-dressed businessmen. Enjoy tortellini with parmesan (15SFr) or *chorizo* (paprika sausage; 6.50SFr). Beers from 3SFr, wine from 4SFr. Open Tu-Su 10am-12:30am; kitchen open 11am-2pm and 6-10pm. V. ❷

MARKETS

Co-op Pronto, in the train station, stocks basic groceries. Wheelchair accessible. Open M-F 7am-10pm, Sa-Su 7:30am-10pm. MC/V. **Branch** on the corner of Neueng. and Bärenpl. Open M-Th 6am-7pm, F 6am-9:30pm, Sa 6am-4pm, Su 6am-6pm. MC/V.

Co-op Shopping Center, near Camping Eichholz after Dorfstr. on Seftigenstr. From the campsite, head away from the river on Strandweg., and turn right onto Eichholz St. 24-hr. ATM, Swisscom payphones, and anything else you need. Wheelchair accessible. Open M-Th 8am-7pm, F 8am-9pm, Sa 7:30am-4pm. MC/V.

Migros Supermarkt, Marktg. 46, sells food, toiletries, clothing, and stationery. Also has a restaurant and take-out counters, including one with 5SFr sandwiches and a daily *Menü* (10-12SFr). Wheelchair accessible. Open M 9am-6:30pm, Tu-W and F 8am-6:30pm, Th 8am-9pm, Sa 7am-4pm.

Fruit and vegetable markets sell fresh produce daily on Bärenpl. (May-Oct. M-F 6am-6pm, Sa 6am-4pm) and every Tu and Sa 7am-noon on Bundespl. A **meat and cheese market** fills Münsterg. every Sa 7am-noon. The off-the-wall **onion market,** which takes the city by storm every 4th M of Nov., is Bern's best-known festival.

👁 🏛 SIGHTS AND MUSEUMS

Bern is a walkable city, with major sights stretching out from the Parliament. Museums ring **Helvetiaplatz** near Kirchenfeldbr. (take tram #3, 5 or 19). If you are in town in late March, check out the annual **Museum Night Bern,** when area museums stay open from 6pm-2am and host bands, bars, and restaurants.

THE OLD TOWN. The medieval architecture of Bern's *Altstadt* glows red with Swiss flags and geraniums. Behind church spires and government domes, the hills along the Aare river create a majestic backdrop—on a clear day, you can see snowy peaks in the distance. The huge **Bundeshaus,** center of the Swiss government, dominates the Aare and glows at sundown. Free tours of the **Parlamentsgebäude** (Parliament building) are available. *(☎322 85 22. Wheelchair accessible. 45min. tour every hr. M-Sa 9-11am and 2-4pm, except on holidays and during special parliamentary proceedings. English tours at 11am, 2pm. Call the afternoon before to confirm as places fill quickly. Free.)*

From the state house, Kockerg. and Herreng. lead to the 15th-century Protestant **Münster** (cathedral). Although many of its treasures were destroyed during the Reformation, some remain. The late Gothic structure's highlight is the sculpture above the main entrance, which depicts punished sinners. None of the buttresses along the church's sides are identical. Real detectives might find the stone inscription, made without an architect's approval by one of the church's construction workers, that reads: "We did the best we could." Climb the spiral stairs of its 100m spire, one of the tallest in Switzerland, for amazing views. *(☎312 04 62. Open Easter-Oct. Tu-Su 10am-5pm; Nov.-Easter Tu-F 10am-noon and 2-4pm, Sa 10am-noon and 2-5pm, Su 11am-2pm. Tower closes 30min. before the church. 3SFr, children under 16 1SFr. Church service Su 10-11:30am.)*

From the Bundeshaus, turn left off Kocherg. at Theaterpl. to reach the 13th-century **Zytglogge** (clock tower). At 4min. before the hour, figures on the tower creak to life with highly uneventful clanging and a couple of weak rooster squawks; the oohs and aahs of gathered tourists are more fervent, but quickly die down. *(Tours of the interior May-Oct. daily 4:30pm, also July-Aug. 11:30am 8SFr.)*

BEAR PITS. Across the Nydeggbr. on the right lie the **Bärengraben** (bear pits.) Descendants of the original Bern bear lounge lazily in stone-lined pits that date back to the 15th century. Tour groups and screaming kids provide the bears with hours of amusement and annoyance. The bears have grown so complacent that they will only eat food thrown directly within reach of their mouths. During Easter, newborn cubs are publicly displayed for the first time. *(Open daily June-Sept. 9am-5:30pm; Oct.-May 10am-4pm. 3SFr to feed the bears.)* The tourist office at the pits presents **The Bern Show,** a slick multimedia recap of Bernese history that ends with an overly indulgent photo-montage. *(Every 20min. Alternately in German and English. Free.)* The path snaking up the hill to the left leads to the ■**Rosengarten;** sit among the blossoms and admire a stellar view of the red tile roofs of Bern's Altstadt and the spires of the cathedral. The garden, the fountains and flora of which are maintained by the city of Bern, is always open. Save your legs and take the #10 bus (dir: Ostermundigen) to "Rosengarten" or follow signs from the tourist office (10 min. walk straight uphill).

KUNSTMUSEUM. Bern's largest art museum sprawls over three floors and boasts an impressive collection dating to the Renaissance, with special focus on Swiss masterpieces. Works by current artists are displayed next to those of artists who inspired them. A smattering of big names are upstairs: Picasso, Giacometti, Ernst Kirchner, Pollock, and some Dada works by Hans Arp. The museum also has a chic café and screens art films. Although the museum was once known as the home of much Paul Klee's work, these paintings and watercolors are moving to Bern's new Klee Center, opening summer 2005; see www.paulkleezentrum.ch for details. *(Hodlerstr. 8-12, near Lorrainebrücke. ☎328 09 44, café ☎328 09 28; www.kunstmuseumbern.ch. Information available in English. Open Tu 10am-9pm, W-Su 10am-5pm. Mandatory bag-check 2SFr deposit. Permanent collection 7SFr, students and seniors 5SFr. Entire collection, including special exhibits, is usually 18SFr. Under 16 free. Extra fees for temporary exhibitions.)*

RIVER AARE. Several walkways lead steeply down from the Bundeshaus to the Aare; a cable car assists passengers on the way up (Wheelchair accessible; 6:30am-9pm; 1.10SFr). The riverbank is ideal for shady walks. On hot days, locals dive lemming-style from the bridges and ride its swift currents. Only experienced swimmers should join in, especially if starting farther upstream at Eichholz. For a more languid afternoon, the **Marzilibad public pool** lies on the river 3min. to the right of the Jugendherberge. (*Open May-Aug. M-F 8:30am-8pm, Sa-Su 8:30am-7pm; Sept. M-F 8:30am-7pm, Sa-Su 8:30am-6pm. Safe 2SFr; lockers and showers available.*)

GARDENS AND ZOO. The **Botanical Gardens** of the University of Bern sprawl along the river at Lorrainebrücke. Exotic plants thrive alongside native Alpine greenery. Check out the platter-sized lily pads in the tropical greenhouse. (*Take bus #20 to "Gewerbeschule."* ☎ 631 49 45. *Wheelchair accessible. Park open daily Mar.-Sept. 8am-5:30pm; Oct.-Feb. 8am-5pm. Greenhouse open daily 8am-5pm. Free.*) **Dählhölzli Städtischer Tierpark** (Zoo), next to the river and across from the campgrounds, gives you the chance to see horses, chickens, and llamas. The enclosures are small and mainly for young children. (*Tierparkweg 1. Walk south along the Aare or take bus #19 to "Tierpark."* ☎ 357 15 15. *Open daily summer 8am-6:30pm; low-season 9am-5pm. 7SFr, students 5SFr. Parking available.*)

BERNISCHESHISTORISCHES MUSEUM. This collection jams a wealth of artifacts and displays into the five floors of the former castle. Bern's lengthy history is on display, from technology to religious art to 15th-century sculptural finds. The collection of oversized Burgundian tapestries is one of the museum's prized possessions. (*Helvetiapl. 5.* ☎ 350 77 11. *Tours in German, French, English. Wheelchair accessible. Open Tu and Th-Su 10am-5pm, W 10am-8pm. 13SFr, students 8SFr, school groups and children under 16 4SFr. 2SFr locker deposit.*)

SWISS ALPINE MUSEUM. For those interested in geography, maps, and moutaineering, this museum is worth a visit. Intricate models of the most famous peaks in the Alps give a history of Swiss cartography and of Alpine exploration. The main floor is an array of topographical models of the country and offers info-stations with innumerable slides. The second-floor exhibit includes devil masks used to protect against threats from the other world. (*Helvetiapl. 4.* ☎ 351 04 34; *www.alpinesmuseum.ch. Signs in German, French, Italian, and English. Wheelchair accessible. Open M 2-5pm, Tu-Su 10am-5pm. 11SFr, students and seniors 5SFr. Add 1SFr for temporary exhibits.*)

MUSEUM OF NATURAL HISTORY. Most people come to this bright, colorful museum to see Barry, the now-stuffed St. Bernard who saved over 40 people in his lifetime. Other hits include an enormous pulsating ant farm and hyper-realistic dioramas of hyenas feeding on zebra corpses. Very family- and school group-friendly. (*Bernastr. 15, off Helvetiapl.* ☎ 350 71 11. *Open M 2-5pm, Tu and Th-F 9am-5pm, W 9am-6pm, Sa-Su 10am-5pm. 7SFr, students 5SFr, under 16 free. Extra for temporary exhibits.*)

ALBERT EINSTEIN'S HOUSE. The humble home in which Einstein lived while developing his theory of special relativity is now a mecca for physics lovers. Old pictures, letters, and even a copy of his school records line the walls. (*Kramg. 49.* ☎ 312 00 91. *Open Feb.-Nov. Tu-F 10am-5pm, Sa 10am-4pm. 3SFr, students and children 2SFr.*)

🎭 ENTERTAINMENT

Bern's cultural tastes run the gamut from classical music concerts to late-night café bands. Events are well publicized on kiosks and bulletin boards. Publications like *Non-Stopp* and *Berner Woche* (the "Going Out" sections of two Bern newspapers) and *Gay Agenda* are available at the tourist office, along with the most informative and complete guide, the monthly **Bewegungsmelder,** which contains concert schedules and maps pointing out all event locations.

Operas and ballets are performed at the **Stadttheater,** Kornhauspl. 20. (☎311 07 77. Summer season runs from July to late August but there are performances all year; for ticket info, contact Theaterkasse, Kornhauspl. 18, CH-3000 Bern 7. ☎329 51 15, theaterkass@stadttheaterbern.ch. Open M-F 10am-6:30pm, Sa 10am-4pm.) Bern's **Symphony Orchestra** plays in the fall and winter at the Konservatorium für Musik, Kramg. 36. (Tickets ☎311 62 21; www.bernersymphonieorchester.ch.) July's **Gurten Festival** has attracted such luminaries as Bob Dylan, Elvis Costello, Björk, and Sinead O'Connor. (www.gurtenfestival.ch. 1-day ticket 65SFr, 2-day 95SFr, 3-day 135SFr. Tickets ☎0900 800 800.) Jazz-lovers arrive in early May for the **International Jazz Festival.** Past performers include B.B. King and Hank Jones. (Tickets at any Bankverein Swiss branch; www.jazzfestivalbern.ch. About 16SFr.) Other festivals include the Bernese Easter-egg market in late March and the notorious **Onion Market** on the fourth Monday in November. The orange grove at Stadtgärtnerei Elfnau (take tram #19 to "Elfnau") has free Sunday concerts in summer. Additionally, **Mahogany Hall,** Klösterlistutz 18, (☎244 75 77, www.mahogany.ch), by the bear pits, is a popular venue for jazz, bluegrass, and folk on Thursday through Saturday evenings. Tickets 18-25SFr. The **Bern Carnival** (www.baernerfasnacht.ch) is held for three days in March prior to Lent. It all begins when a bear held captive in the Prison Tower is released. The Bernese respond by donning bear masks and taking to the streets where there are street performers, a parade, and partying well into the night.

From mid-July to mid-August, **OrangeCinema** (www.orangecinema.ch) screens recently released films, including many American ones, in the open air. Buy tickets at the tourist office in the train station or at the Orange Shop at Spitalg. 14.

▣ NIGHTLIFE

The fashionable folk linger in the *Altstadt*'s bars and cafés at night. An alternative crowd gathers under the gargoyles and graffiti of the Lorrainebr., behind and to the right of the station down Bollwerk. Grab the map in Bewegungsmelder, or check out www.cityhunter.ch for DJ schedules and to plan your evening.

Pery Bar/Räblus and **Kornhausplatz,** Schmiedenpl. 3 (☎311 59 08), off Kornhauspl. The area around the Kornhaus and this "see-and-be-seen" bar floods with a 20+ crowd and the local hockey team on weekends. Disco music spins inside, but everyone chats it up outside. Weeknights bring an older, more mellow clientele. The Räblus Restaurant serves lunch and dinner. Beers from 4.90SFr; wines from 5SFr. Bar open M-W 5pm-1:30am, Th 5pm-2:30am, F-Sa 5pm-3:30am.

Art Café and **Café Eclipse,** Gurteng. 6 (☎318 20 70). A café by day and a smoky bar by night. Casually trendy decor is overshadowed by neighboring pophouse, Café Eclipse. A raucous 20+ crowd fills the bars on weekend nights. Occasional live acts and DJs. Beers from 5SFr. Open M-W 7pm-12:30am, Th-F 7pm-3:30am, Sa 8pm-3:30am.

Reitschule, Neubrückstr. 8 (☎302 83 72). From the station, head down Bollwerk and turn right underneath the overpass. This big, rambling nightclub is revered by left-wing locals and virtually legendary for its activist, alternative culture and laid-back atmosphere. Kick back on the patio with a beer and listen to the DJ spin hip-hop and who knows what. A seedier population emerges at night, so go with a group if you aren't comfortable clubbing alone. Beers from 3.50SFr. *Menüs* 5SFr. Open daily 8pm-late.

Altes Tramdepot (☎368 14 15, www.altestramdepot.ch) across Nydeggbr. to the right of the bear pits. Although hordes of tourists wander through the bar looking for the toilets downstairs, Altes retains something of a local feel. The Tramdepot has a laid-back air for early evening beers and conversation. Brews on tap 4-4.30SFr. Most dinner dishes around 20SFr; vegetarian options available. Open daily summer 10am-12:30am; winter 11am-12:30am; restaurant closes at 11:30pm.

Samurai Bar, Aarbergerg. 35 (☎311 88 03, www.samurai-bar.ch), is a hub of Bern's limited gay clubbing scene. Dance the night away to DJs Th-Sa. Open M-Th and Su 8pm-2:30am, F-Sa 8pm-3:30am.

THE THUNERSEE

From the Thunersee, the forests, sheer rock faces, and peaks off the Jungfrau seem deceptively accessible. Though the lake is smaller than it looks, and the Jungfrau's proximity is a trick of proportion, the region boasts larger-than-life charms of its own: the area is dotted with castles, and the local mountains are often snowy. The Thunersee's three significant towns, **Thun, Spiez,** and **Interlaken,** all lie on the main Bern-Interlaken-Lucerne rail line. **Boats** operated by the BLS shipping company (☎334 52 11; www.bls.ch) putter to the smaller villages between the Thun and Interlaken West railway stations (2hr., late June to late Sept. every hr. 8:10am-11:35pm, evening cruises available June-Dec.; Eurail, SwissPass, and Berner Oberland pass valid). A ferry day-pass good as far as **Brienz** (on the Brienzersee) is 6.60SFr.

THUN   ☎033

Known as the "Gateway to the Bernese Oberland," Thun (pop. 38,000) lies on the banks of the Aare River and the Thunersee. Ringed by castles of every imaginable size and color, this quiet town caused Johannes Brahms to observe that "relaxing in Thun is delightful, and one day will not be enough." Though picturesque and historic, Thun is not stodgy. The Selve area offers everything from crowded discothèques and bars to a roller skating rink and an indoor racetrack.

◪ TRANSPORTATION

Trains to: Bern (every 30min. 5:12am-11:20pm, 13.40SFr); Interlaken East (every hr. 7:17am-11:47pm, 15.20SFr); Interlaken West (every hr. 6:43am-11:47pm, 14.20SFr); and Spiez (every 30min. 6:43am-12:52am, 6.60SFr). There is a rail information desk (open M-F 9am-6:30pm, Sa 9am-4pm). Boat landing (☎223 53 80) across the street and to the right of the station. **Boats** depart for: Faulensee (11SFr); Hilterfingen (5.60SFr); Interlaken West (20SFr); Oberhofen (6.60SFr); and Spiez (10.20SFr).

◪◪ ORIENTATION AND PRACTICAL INFORMATION

Thun is split by outflow of the Thunersee, and its *Altstadt* is situated on an island surrounded by the roaring waters of the Innare Aure and the Aussare Aure. Thun's main street, the tree-lined boulevard Bälliz, changes to Einkaufstr. halfway down the length of the island. The oldest squares and the castle are situated across the river from the train station on the Aare's north bank. On the south bank lie Thun's transportation centers, the train station and ferry. Thun's gritty and exciting nightlife is along the Scheibenstr. Thun's **tourist office,** Seestr. 2, is outside the station. (☎222 23 40; fax 83 23. Open July-Aug. M-F 8am-7pm, Sa 9am-noon and 1-4pm; Sept.-June M-F 8am-noon and 1-6pm, Sa 9am-noon.) The

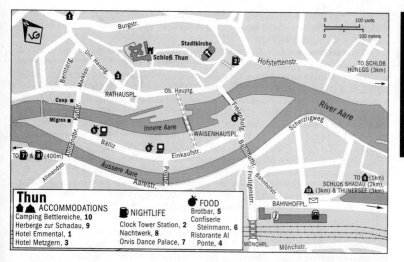

Thun

▲▲ ACCOMMODATIONS	♪ NIGHTLIFE	● FOOD
Camping Bettlereiche, 10	Clock Tower Station, 2	Brotbar, 5
Herberge zur Schadau, 9	Nachtwerk, 8	Confiserie
Hotel Emmental, 1	Orvis Dance Palace, 7	Steinmann, 6
Hotel Metzgern, 3		Ristorante Al
		Ponte, 4

office organizes **guided tours** of the city and the castle on the first and second Saturdays of the month. (May-Oct. Reservations required. 18SFr.) Services include: **currency exchange** (open M-Sa 6am-8pm, Su 6:30am-8pm) and **bike rental** (open M-Sa 8:30am-8pm; 30SFr per day). **Lockers** (4-6SFr) are at the station. **Free bike rental** at Waisenhauspl. next to the post office (open May-Oct. 7:30am-9:30pm; ID and 20SFr deposit required. Bikes must be returned on the same day.) **Taxis** usually outside the station, or call ☎22 22 for pickup. **Parking** is available at the Parkhaus Aarestr. on Aarestr. (☎222 78 26; 1.50SFr per hr.; half-price nights and weekends.) Get **Internet** access at the Cipper Club (Bälliz 25. Open M-F 4-11:30pm, Sa 11am-11pm. 10SFr per hr.) or at Space Gate (on Bälliz, toward the station; 6SFr per 30 min.) The **post office** is at Panaromastr. 1a, by the station. (Open M-F 7:30am-7pm, Sa 8am-noon.) **Postal Code:** CH-3601.

ACCOMMODATIONS AND FOOD

Hotel Metzgern ❸, Untere Hauptg. 2, has simple but sunny sink-equipped rooms above the restaurant downstairs. From the station, veer left on Bahnhofstr. and go straight over two bridges. Signs lead the way. (☎222 21 41; fax 21 82. Breakfast included. Reception Tu-Th and Su 8am-11:30pm, F-Sa 8am-12:30am. Singles, doubles, triples 62SFr per person; 55SFr for stays of more than 1 night; 50SFr for more than 1 week. Children 7 and under half-price. MC/V.) The **Herberge zur Schadau ❾** is right next to the train tracks. Exit the train station, turn right, and walk 10min. down Seestr. The hostel, a large blue building, is on the right. It packs 30 beds into five rooms. (☎222 52 22. Breakfast included. Reception 8-10am, 2-7pm, quiet hours 11pm-7am. 45SFr per person.) Spacious and modern rooms with sparkling private bathrooms are hidden within the unique exterior of **Hotel Emmental ❹**, Bernstr. 2. (☎222 01 20. Breakfast and sheets included. Reception 7am-2pm and 4pm-midnight. Apr.-Oct. 80SFr per person. Nov.-Mar. singles 70SFr, doubles 120SFr.)

Campers should head to **Camping Bettlereiche ❶**. Take bus #1 to "Camping" or turn right from the station and walk 45min. down Seestr., which veers sharply left and becomes Gwattstr. The campsite is near water and surrounded by hills. (☎336 40 67; fax 40 17. Showers included. Reception 8:30am-noon and 2-

7:30pm, until 8:30pm in July-Aug. July-Aug. 10.70SFr per person, children 5SFr, 9-11SFr per tent; Apr.-June and Sept.-Oct. 8.70SFr per person, children 4SFr, 7-9SFr per tent. AmEx/MC/V.)

Unlike hotel rooms, food in Thun is cheap. Affordable restaurants and take-out pizza and kebab stands line Bahnhofstr. The **Brotbar ❶**, Bälliz 11, is equal parts corner bakery and swanky café. Cross the river at Allmendbr. and turn right onto Bälliz. Order from a health-conscious menu while sipping exotic teas (3.60SFr), or a creamy smoothie (2.50-3SFr) made from homemade yogurt and fresh fruit. (☎222 22 21. Open M-W 7am-6:30pm, Th-Sa 7am-12:30am. Wheelchair accessible.) Dine and feed the waterfowl at **Ristorante Al Ponte ❸**, Freienhofg. 16, at the foot of the Sinnebr. beside the river. Prices here are mostly in the teens; the *gnocchi al Arrabiata* is a good choice at (14.50SFr) as is the large risotto menu (18.80SFr). (Hours variable. Outside tables wheelchair accessible.) For delectable chocolates, pastries and sandwiches in a comfy corner tea room, try **Confiserie Steinmann ❶**, Bälliz 37, just past Brotbar. Enjoy mouth-watering *Thuner Leckerli* made from honey, lemon rind, and nuts (5 pieces 6SFr) or strawberry tarts for 3.50SFr. (☎222 20 47. Wheelchair accessible. Open M 8am-6:30pm, Tu-Th 6:45am-6:30pm, F 6:45am-9pm, Sa 6:45am-4pm.)

Both **Migros** and **Co-op** have markets and restaurants on Allmendstr. straddling the Kuhbr. (Both open M-W and F 8am-6:30pm, Th 8am-9pm, Sa 7:30am-4pm.) At the **open-air market** in the *Altstadt*, across the river from the train station, vendors hawk souvenirs, clothes, and produce (Sa 8am-noon). A **food market** covers Bälliz on Wednesdays and Saturdays 8am-2pm.

👁 SIGHTS

SCHLOß THUN. This 12th-century castle looks down on the town from the top of the *Altstadt*. The one-time residence of the barons, governors, and mayors of Thun, the castle now houses a museum which shows off a collection of vicious weaponry, old folk instruments (including Alphorns), accordions, and even a hammered dulcimer. The tower was the site of a gruesome fratricide in 1322, when Eberhard of Kyburg unsportingly defenestrated his brother Hartmann. Downstairs in the *Rittersaal* (Knight's Hall) the castle hosts classical music concerts in June. (☎223 20 01; www.schlossthun.ch. *From the station, bear left down Bahnhofstr. and go over 2 bridges, turn right onto Obere Hauptg., and then left up the Risgässli steps, and left again at the top; follow the signs to Schloß/Museum. Open Apr.-Oct. daily 10am-5pm; Feb.-Mar. daily 1-4pm. Open Sundays in winter from 1-4pm. 6SFr, students 4SFr, children 2SFr, children under 6 free, families 12SFr. For concert tickets call ☎223 25 30 or contact the tourist office; tickets 30-50SFr.)*

SCHLOß SCHADAU. The pastel pink Schloß Schadau, in the peaceful Walter Hansen Schadaupark on the shores of the Thunersee, was built in 1850 in the style of castles in France's Loire Valley. The castle houses a large gastronomy book collection and a fabulous **restaurant.** Hidden by the foliage, the nearby **Wocher Panorama** recreates the lake and its environs with a room-sized painting of the area. Surrounding the castle are well-manicured flower gardens and an expanse of grass that is perfect for sunbathing. (*Seestr. 45; from the station, turn right and walk about 15min. Or, take bus #1 to "Scherzligen."* ☎223 24 62. *Panorama open May-Oct. daily 10am-5pm. 4SFr, students 3SFr, under 17 free. Gastronomy Museum open Tu-Th 2-5pm.* ☎223 13 32. *3SFr. Restaurant open May-Oct. Tu-Sa 10am-10pm, Nov.-Apr. W-Su 10am-10pm.* ☎222 25 00.)

SCHLOß HÜNEGG. Located in the wooded hills of Hilterfingen, Hünegg, the most elaborate of the Thunersee castles, houses displays of well-preserved and lavish *fin de siècle* furnishings along with a mid-eighteenth century drinking hall. Built between 1861 and 1863 for a Prussian baron, the castle has been unchanged since 1900. The castle is very much in use today—it even hosts the occasional birthday party. *(Bus #21 runs to Hilterfingen. Walk 100m back towards Thun; castle will be on the right.* ☎ *243 19 82. Open mid-May to mid-Oct. M-Sa 2-5pm, Su 10am-noon and 2-5pm. 8SFr, students 7SFr, children 1.50SFr.)*

⚠ OUTDOOR ACTIVITIES

The popular local half-day **hike** up **Heilingenschwendi,** the hillside above Thun on the lake's north shore, provides a view of the distant Jungfrau mountains. Past the casino and the village of Seematten, turn left, cross the river, and head up through the wooded ridge. Continue farther to the **Dreiländeregg** and **Niesenbänkli** for a panoramic view (3hr.). If you push on to the village of **Schwendi,** near the top, continue hiking a little farther to **Schloß Oberhofen** (see above), where you can catch bus #21 back to town. If the *Schlößer* stifle you, hit the water. There are numerous places to jump in, but the turquoise water is a little cold, so be prepared. The tourist office has information on **sailing, wind-surfing, river-rafting,** and **boat rental.**

🎵 🎭 ENTERTAINMENT AND NIGHTLIFE

Bälliz is lined with pricey drinking spots, most with outdoor seating. For a lower-key, cheaper evening, head to **Clock Tower Station,** Obere Hauptg. 89, just past the Risgässli steps that lead to Schloß Thun. Everyone will feel at home in this small, Canada-themed sports bar, though the crowd is mainly composed of a loyal group of Thun locals. Grilled food served until 2am. (☎ 223 57 96. Open Tu-Sa 6pm-3:30am.)

The *Selvereal* provides more lively entertainment and an energetic crowd. From the train station, go down Bahnhofstr., turn left on Aarestr. and keep going until it turns into Schiebenstr. and veers left. Sandwiched between train tracks and the electric company, this hip section of town comes to life after dark. Although you'll find the occasional small bar, warehouse-like clubs with graffiti murals dominate the scene here. This strip is home to the **Thun Indoor Karting,** Scheibenstr. 37, an indoor racetrack where you can rent a car, safety equipment, and the track for an exhilirating race. (☎ 222 83 44. Open M 5-10pm, Tu 4-10pm, W-Th 4-11pm, F 4pm-1am, Sa 2pm-1am, Su 2-8pm. All equipment 25SFr, students who arrive before 8pm 17SFr.)

Many bars and clubs lie on the same street, including the very fashionable **Orvis Dance Palace,** Scheibenstr. 8, which features stages for dancing and DJs spinning techno and house. A separate room has billiards. (☎ 222 27 55. 20+. Cover Th 5SFr, F-Sa 10SFr. Open Th 9pm-2:30am, F-Sa 9pm-3:30am.) Next door, **Nachtwerk** has a DJ on each floor: techno on the first, hip-hop on the second, and Top 40 on the third.

Thun's outdoor **festivals** juxtapose folk music and gunplay. Traditional festivals include the **Ausschiesset** (shootout) among military cadets on the last Monday and Tuesday in September and the William Tell shoot honoring whoever takes the best shot at a model of Gessler. The *Altstadt* rocks with merry music in the **Festival of Barrel Organs and Ballad Singers** every July. The end of July features an open-air **Film Festival** (www.thunerfilmopenair.ch).

🚩 DAYTRIP FROM THUN: SPIEZ

Trains every hr. to: Bern (30min., 17.20SFr); Thun (10min., 6.60SFr); Interlaken West (20min., 9.20SFr). Boats to Thun (8.40SFr every hr.) and Interlaken (11.40SFr every hr.).

Schloß Spiez, the most famous attraction in Spiez, is a medieval fortress with Romanesque, Gothic, and Renaissance flourishes. To see the castle, bear left on Bahnhofstr. from the station, turn right onto Thunstr., then left onto Seestr. Stroll through the lovely lakeside rose gardens and visit the placid chapel for free. Inside the fortress is a museum which features a banquet hall dating from 1614, a room of weapons, medieval graffiti, and an exquisite view of the lake. (☎/fax 654 15 06. Open Easter to mid-Oct. M 2-5pm, Tu-Su 10am-6pm. The castle hosts classical music concerts May to June and live theater in August (☎654 70 18).

The mountain piercing the sky above Spiez is the **Niesenberg** (2363m). Hikes on the mountain, while not for beginners, are accessible and wind through the neighboring towns of Niesen, Kulm, and Schwandegg. Pick up hiking maps at tourist offices in Interlaken, Thun, or Spiez, or at any train station kiosk. Hiking all the way up or down the mountain is tough, but a **funicular** chugs to the top, and the **Lötschberg train** towards Reichenbach from Spiez (every hr., round-trip 7.20SFr) connects with the funicular at Mülenen. (June-Nov. 8am-5pm; round-trip 43SFr, with Swisspass 32.30SFr, after 4pm half-price.) The funicular's builders pushed the frontiers of human achievement by constructing steps alongside the track, which became the **longest flight of steps in the world.** Unfortunately, only professional maintenance teams are allowed to use the steps (all 11,674 of them).

The **tourist office,** to the left as you exit the train station, sells hiking maps and helps find cheap rooms. **Internet access** is 1SFr per 5min. (☎654 20 20; fax 21 92. Open July-Aug. M-F 8am-6:30pm, Sa 9am-noon and 2-4pm; Sept. M-F 8am-noon and 2-6pm, Sa 9am-noon; Oct.-Apr. M-F 8am-noon and 2-6pm; May M-F 8am-noon and 1-6pm; June M-F 8am-6:30pm and Sa 9am-noon.) If you're not staying in Thun, try the ▓Swiss Adventure Hostel (p. 347) in tiny Boltigen, 35min. from Spiez by train (dir: Zweissimen). Eat at the elaborate **Migros** market and restaurant by the station. (Open M-Th 8am-6:30pm, F 8am-9pm, Sa 7:30am-4pm.)

BRIENZ AND THE ROTHORN ☎033

Switzerland's oldest cog railway, a parkful of traditional Swiss dwellings, and a reputation for wood-carving excellence draw visitors to Brienz. The opaque green waters of the bordering **Brienzersee** move slowly below sharp cliffs and dense forests. More relaxed than Interlaken or Thun, Brienz attracts a somewhat older crowd.

☐⊿ TRANSPORTATION AND PRACTICAL INFORMATION. Brienz makes an ideal daytrip from Interlaken by **train** (20min., every hr. 6:36am-10:35pm, 6.60SFr) or **boat** (1¼hr., every hr. 8:20am-5:32pm, 15.20SFr). Brienzersee cruises leave Interlaken's Ostbahnhof (June-Sept. every hr. 8:31am-5:40pm, Apr.-May and late Sept.-Oct. 4 per day 9:31am-2:31pm; 25.80SFr. Eurail and SwissPass valid). The station, dock and Rothorn cog railway terminus are on the right boundary of the town, flanked on Hauptstr. by the post office, banks, and a supermarket. The Brienz-Dorf wharf bookends the town on the west end. A tiny river flows through the middle of town. The hostel and campsites lie a short walk along the lake east of the town proper. Brienz's **tourist office,** Hauptstr. 143, is across from and left of the train station. (☎952 80 80; fax 80 88. Open M-F 8am-noon and 2-6pm, Sa 9am-noon and 4:30-6pm; July-Aug. M-F 8am-noon and 1-6pm, Sa 9am-12:30pm and 4:30-6pm, Su 4:30-6pm.) The tourist office sells passes for 3 days of free travel on any of the region's trains, buses, or mountain transport and 4 days of half-price travel. (Adults 98SFr, children ages 6-16 78SFr, children under 6 free.) The train station **exchanges currency** and has **lockers** (3-5SFr; both open daily 6:30am-9pm). **Police ☎** 117; **ambulance ☎**144; **Rotbahn Apotheke** across from Walz Tea Room. (Open M-F 8am-12:15pm and 1:30-6:30pm; Sa 8am-4pm. MC/V.) **24hr. emergency ☎**951 15 29. **Park** at the **Parkhaus**

Co-op behind the Co-op on Hauptg. (1½hr. limit M-F 7am-7pm, Sa 7am-4pm; unlimited parking M-F 7pm-7am, Sa 4pm-7am.) The **post office** is next to the train station. (☎951 25 05. Open M-F 7:45-11:45am, 1:45-6pm; Sa 8:30-11am.) **Postal Code:** CH-3855.

♫♪ ACCOMMODATIONS AND FOOD. The **Brienz Jugendherberge (HI)** ❷, Strandweg 10, 400m left from the train station as you're facing the lake, offers crowded summer-camp-style bunks with doorstep access to the lake and a great view. (☎951 11 52; www.youthhostel.ch/brienz. Breakfast included. Dinner 11.50SFr. Kitchen facilities. Wheelchair accessible. Reception 7:30-10am and 5-10pm. Open mid-Apr. to mid-Oct. Dorms 25.90-27.50SFr; doubles 62SFr.) **Hotel Garni Walz** ❹, Hauptstr. 102, to the left from the station on the main road just past the river, offers centrally located rooms overlooking the lake, each situated atop a tea room. (☎951 14 59; www.firstweb.ch/walz-brienz. Breakfast included. High-season singles 95SFr; doubles 130SFr; triples 195SFr. Low-season singles 80SFr; doubles 106SFr; triples 135SFr. AmEx/MC/V.) For a luxurious getaway at a reasonable price, head further down the street to **Seehotel Bären Brienz** ❹. Wide hallways decorated with old jazz posters lead the way to spacious rooms complete with fluffy comforters, telephones, and balconies overlooking the river. The top floor houses massage rooms and a comfortable deck. (Breakfast included. Dinner 15SFr. Wheelchair accessible. Reception 7:30am-9pm. Check-out 11am. Singles 65SFr (84SFr high season), with shower 124SFr/138SFr; doubles same price per person, also available with small foreroom. AmEx/DC/MC/V.) Two campgrounds lie past the hostel on the waterfront. **Camping Aaregg** ❶ past the other campsite, has an on-site restaurant. (☎951 18 43; www.aaregg.ch. Reception 8am-noon and 2-8pm. **Bikes** 30SFr per day, 15SFr per half day. Laundry 8SFr. Open Apr.-Oct. 9SFr per adult; 4.50SFr per child; 14.20SFr per tent.) **Camping Seegärtli** ❶ is more secluded and slightly closer to town. It offers free lake swimming and fresh bread at 8am. (☎951 13 51. Parking 3SFr. Reception 8am-7pm. Open Apr.-Oct. 7.50SFr per adult plus 2.60SFr tax; 4SFr per child plus 1SFr tax.)

Both the Seehotel Bären and Hotel Walz have good restaurants. In a quiet dining room or peaceful terrace, the **Bären** ❹ offers a vegetarian menu (19.50-25SFr), fish options (23.50-36.50SFr), and house specialities such as lamb filet for 32.50-38.50SFr. (Wheelchair accessible. Open daily 7:30am-midnight. AmEx/DC/MC/V.) **Walz Tea Room** ❸ has a covered terrace with a view of the lake and the Axalphorn. The welcoming café offers a wide variety of salad (14.90-26SFr), omelettes (14-16.50SFr), and pasta (10.50-18.50SFr). The *Apfelstrudel* (2SFr) from the attached bakery is to die for. During evenings in July, bands from the Montreaux Jazz Festival perform at the café. **Internet** access is also available for 5SFr per 15min. (☎951 14 59. Open daily 8am-10pm. AmEx/MC/V.) **Restaurant Steinbock** ❸, on Hauptstr. next to the river, provides outside tables and a warm wooden interior. The restaurant boasts an English-speaking staff and English menus. Options include Swiss-style macaroni with apple sauce (18SFr). (☎951 40 55. Wheelchair accessible. Open daily 8:30am-11:30pm. AmEx/DC/MC/V.) The **Co-op** is on Hauptg. facing the station. (Open M-Th 7:45am-6:30pm, F 7:45am-8pm, Sa 7:45am-4pm.) A **Migros** is located at the western end of town. (Open M-F 8am-6:30pm, Sa 8am-4pm.)

▥ MUSEUMS. The **Freilichtmuseum Ballenberg** (Open-Air Museum; www.ballenberg.ch), on Lauenenstr. in the nearby town of Ballenberg, is an 80-hectare country park dedicated to the preservation of Swiss heritage and culture. Authentic rural Swiss houses are clumped by geographical region into 13 villages; most were transplanted from their original locations. Many have live exhibitions of traditional trades, such as iron-smithing or cheese-making. 250 native farm animals and a friendly staff make this museum a major attraction. A new addition to the *Schokoladerei* provides **chocolate demonstrations** and **taste-testing**. The museum is worth at least a whole day's visit, so plan accordingly. *(☎ 952 10 30 or 952 10 40. Open from mid-Apr. to Oct. 10am-5pm. 16SFr, with visitors' card 10% off; children 8SFr; 2-day pass 28/14SFr. Family ticket 25SFr. The park is a 1hr. walk from the train station, but a bus also connects the 2 every hr. 6:45am-5pm, round-trip 6SFr.)*

Brienz is also the center of various cantonal wood-carving schools. The **Kantonale Schnitzlerschule** (Wood-Carving School; ☎951 17 51) and the **Geigenbauschule** (Violin-Making School; ☎952 18 61; www.geigenbauschule.ch.) both provide galleries that display their craft. From the station, turn right onto the Hauptst. Follow it for 10 min., and turn right onto Schleeg. The schools will be to the right. Home to 10 students, the *Geigenbauschule* houses a collection of antique instruments and a showroom of finished violins for a mere 5000SFr each. *(Wood-carving school open M-Th 8-11:30am and 2-5pm, F 8-11:30am and 2-4:15pm; July to mid-Aug. and mid-Sept. to mid-Oct. M-F 8-11:15am. Violin-making school open Sept.-May M-F 8-11am and 2-5pm; June-Aug. call for opening hours. Both free.)*

The **Jobins Living Woodcarving Museum** lets visitors learn about the history of wood-carving, watch artisans at work, and try their hands at a work-in-progress public display. Bring your wallet if you're really interested—barely a museum, it is more a gallery and a store. The tiny museum has signs in German and offers guided tours in English, French, and German. *(On the Hauptst. From the station, walk past the river. The museum is after the Bank Brienz Oberhasli, on the right. ☎952 13 00; www.jobin.ch. Open May-Oct. daily 8-11:30am and 2-5pm for individual visits, 8am-7pm for guided tours. Nov.-Apr. M-Sa 8-11:30am and 1:30-5pm for individual visits, 8am-6pm for guided tours. Admission 5SFr, guided tour 15SFr. AmEx/DC/MC/V.)* Many local wood-carvers also let tourists watch them work; contact the tourist office for a list.

■ **HIKING.** Though superior hikes can be found around the Jungfrau, Brienz does offer several good options. The **Rothorn** (2350m) is the most accessible peak near Brienz thanks to the **Brienz Rothorn Bahn.** In operation for 109 years, the Rothorn Bahn is the oldest cog steam railway in Switzerland. *(☎952 22 22; www.brienz-rothorn-bahn.ch. 1hr.; June-Oct. every hr. 7:39am-4:10pm, last descent 5:30pm; 46SFr, round-trip 72SFr; with Bernese Oberland pass 22SFr/34SFr; with SwissPass 33SFr/57SFr.)* Getting off at **Planalp,** halfway up the mountain, allows medium-range hikes back down. Follow the railway down, turning left below Planalp to head through Baalen and Schwanden (3½hr.). From the summit, head east toward the lake and turn right at the Eiseesaltel, continuing down to Hofstetten, Schwanden, and Brienz (4hr.). Shelter is available at the **Hotel Rothorn ❸** on the summit (2350m). *(☎951 12 21; fax 12 51. Breakfast included. Reception 8-11am and 2-5:30pm. Dorms 34SFr; singles 90SFr; doubles 140SFr. Open during the summer only. AmEx/V.)*

A bus from the station climbs to **Axalp** (8:15am-4:15pm, 9.20SFr) where you can hike to the **Axalphorn** (2321m) on the opposite side of the lake from Brienz by walking along either the east or west ridge (800m, half-day). As both trails are occasionally hard to make out, a map is a necessity (check the tourist office at Brienz).

Brienzersee's south shore is accessible by various boat services (check the tourist office). **Giessbach Falls,** with 14 cascades, is a 10min. ride from Brienz (6.60SFr) and a 1hr. ride from Interlaken. The walk to the falls passes a palatial hotel (15min.) which is also accessible by cable car from the dock (4.50SFr, round-trip 6SFr). From the hotel, a bridge traverses the river to the falls. A path to the left, along the streams, offers a view of all the waterfalls. At the top, a ridge walk leads to the right over the lake, and then down to the breezy lakeside village **Iseltwald** where a ferry travels to Brienz. (Mid-June to mid-Sept. every hr. 9:09am-6:12pm; mid-Sept. to Oct. 4 per day 11:40am-4:40pm. 14SFr.) Alternatively, for a low-key walk, turn right from the train station and take the steep and well-traveled footpath to the left toward the **Wildpark** and discover where the wood-carvers get their inspiration. (Always open. Free.)

INTERLAKEN

☎ **033**

In AD 1130, two literal-minded Augustinian monks named the land between the **Thunersee** and the **Brienzersee** "Interlaken," or "between lakes." That land has grown from a collection of small medieval villages to a booming modern city devoted to tourism. Geographically, Interlaken lies at the foot of some of the most famous mountains in Switzerland (the **Eiger, Mönch,** and **Jungfrau**), providing easy access to several natural playgrounds. Beneath the enchanting sight of the Jungfrau (4158m), the town spreads out around a large central green, the **Höhematte,** a popular landing pad for the hundreds of paragliders that drift down from the skies each day. Thanks to its mild climate and natural wonders, Interlaken has earned a well-deserved place as one of Switzerland's prime tourist attractions and as its top outdoor adventure spot.

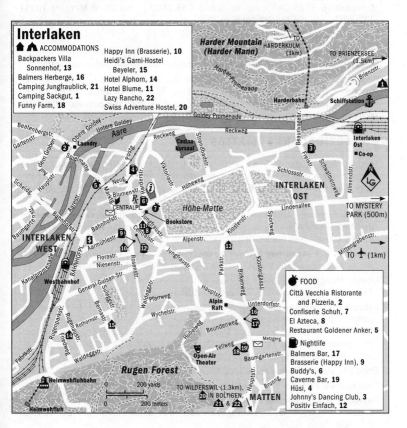

Interlaken

▲ 🏠 ACCOMMODATIONS
Backpackers Villa
 Sonnenhof, **13**
Balmers Herberge, **16**
Camping Jungfraublick, **21**
Camping Sackgut, **1**
Funny Farm, **18**
Happy Inn (Brasserie), **10**
Heidi's Garni-Hostel
 Beyeler, **15**
Hotel Alphorn, **14**
Hotel Blume, **11**
Lazy Rancho, **22**
Swiss Adventure Hostel, **20**

🍴 FOOD
Città Vecchia Ristorante
 and Pizzeria, **2**
Confiserie Schuh, **7**
El Azteca, **8**
Restaurant Goldener Anker, **5**

🍺 Nightlife
Balmers Bar, **17**
Brasserie (Happy Inn), **9**
Buddy's, **6**
Caverne Bar, **19**
Hüsi, **4**
Johnny's Dancing Club, **3**
Positiv Einfach, **12**

BERNESE OBERLAND

⌐ TRANSPORTATION

By **car,** Interlaken lies on A6. The city has two train stations. The **Westbahnhof** stands in the center of town bordering the Thunersee, near most shops and hotels. Trains to Bern, Basel, and other western towns stop here. The **Ostbahnhof,** on the Brienzersee 1km from the town center, is cheaper for connecting to eastern towns. Both stations post hotel prices and offer courtesy phones for reservations.

Trains: The **Westbahnhof** (☎826 47 50) and **Ostbahnhof** (☎828 73 19) have trains every hr. to: **Bern** (6:01am-10:34pm, 24SFr); **Basel** (5:32am-10:34pm, 56SFr); **Geneva** (5:33am-9:35pm, 63SFr); **Lucerne** (5:33am-8:39pm, 26SFr); **Lugano/ Locarno** (5:33am-4:37pm, 87SFr/76SFr); **Zurich** (6:44am-10:34pm, 62SFr). **Jungfraubahnen,** Harderstr. 14 (☎828 72 33; www.jungfraubahn.ch) runs all trains to the small towns on the way up to the Jungfrau. SwissPass valid for Wengen, Mürren, and Grindelwald; 25% discount at higher stops. Eurail 25% discount on the Jungfraubahnen. Trains leave June-Sept. every 30min., and Sept.-May every hr. from the Ostbahnhof to: **Grindelwald** (6:35am-10:35pm, 9.80SFr) and **Lauterbrunnen** (6:35am-10:35pm, 6.60SFr); with connections to **Kleine Scheidegg** (6:35am-4:35pm, 36.40SFr), **Mürren** (6:35am-7:35pm, 16.40SFr), **Wengen** (6:35am-10:35pm, 12.40SFr), and the **Jungfraujoch** (6:35am-3:35pm; round-trip 163.80SFr, with Good Morning Ticket 125.80SFr; see **The Jungfraujoch,** p. 352).

Taxis: Interlaken Ost, ☎822 80 80. **West,** ☎822 50 50.

Luggage: Lockers at train station 3SFr.

Parking: Parking is 7SFr per day at the train stations, behind the casino on Centralstr.

Bike Rental: At either **train station,** 30SFr per day; 23SFr per half-day. Open 6am-7pm. **Intersport Oberland,** Postg. 16 (☎822 06 61; fax 73 07), rents mountain bikes (30SFr, 20SFr per half-day), and in-line skates (20SFr per day). Open M-F 8am-noon and 1:30-6:30pm, Sa 8am-noon and 1-4pm. AmEx/DC/MC/V. Some hostels also rent bikes.

⎘ PRACTICAL INFORMATION

Tourist Office: Höheweg 37 (☎826 53 00; fax 53 75), in the **Hotel Metropole,** has free maps, courtesy phones to area hotels, and info. Open July-Aug. M-F 8am-7pm, Sa 8am-5pm, Su 10am-noon and 4-6pm; May-June and Sept.-Oct. M-F 8am-6pm, Sa 8am-noon. Nov.-Apr. M-F 8am-noon and 1:30-6pm, Sa 8am-noon.

Currency Exchange: UBS Bank near the Westbahnhof and **Raiffeisen Bank** near the Ostbahnhof have **ATMs,** as do both train stations. Available in the **train station** (☎826 47 36), though rates are 1% better in town. Open daily 8am-6pm.

Bookstore: Buchhandlweg Krebser Haupt, Höheweg 11 (☎822 35 16). Bestsellers, phrasebooks, and travel books. Open M-F 8:30am-6:30pm, Sa 8:30am-4pm.

Library: Marktpl. 4 (☎822 02 12). Novels in English. Open M 3-5pm, Tu 3-4pm, W 9-11am and 3-7pm, Th 3-5pm, F 3-6pm, Sa 10am-noon.

Laundromat: Self-Service Wash & Dry, Beatenbergstr. 5 (☎822 15 66). Cross the bridge to the left of the Westbahnhof and take the 2nd right onto Hauptstr. The manager will do laundry for 12SFr per load M-Sa 8am-noon and 1:30-6pm; Sa closes at 4pm. Self-service open daily 7am-10pm; 6-8SFr. **Backpacker's Villa** (p. 347) has self-service laundry (10SFr, soap included), as does **Balmers** (p. 347) for 8SFr.

Snow and Weather Info: For the Jungfrau, ☎828 79 31.

Emergencies: Police ☎117. **Hospital** ☎826 26 26. **Doctor** ☎823 23 23.

Pharmacy: Grosse Apotheke, Bahnhofstr. 5A (☎822 72 62), and **Pharmacie Internationale,** Höheweg 4 (☎828 34 34), both open M-Sa winter 7:30am-6:30pm; summer until 7pm. AmEx/MC/V.

Internet Access: Many hotels, restaurants, and both train stations have quick access terminals, but the best Internet prices are found in the hostels: **Backpacker's Villa** has 5 computers; **Balmers** has 2 (10SFr per hr.).

Post Office: Marktg. 1 (☎224 89 50). From the Westbahnhof, go left on Bahnhofpl. Open M-F 8am-noon and 1:45-6pm, Sa 8:30-11am.

Postal Code: CH-3800.

ACCOMMODATIONS

Interlaken guest accommodations have a wide range of atmospheres. Those at Balmers and Funny Farm tend to party as late as the city will allow, while Backpackers provides a more low-key but still lively social scene. Farther away from the city, Boltigen's Swiss Adventure Hostel creates its own community and offers guests a respite from the wild "spring break" crowds.

Backpackers Villa Sonnenhof, Alpenstr. 16 (☎826 71 71; www.villa.ch) diagonally across the Höhenmatte from the tourist office. This central but secluded, remodeled villa is friendly and low-key. Calm atmosphere after a tough day of backpacking, but still only a 3min. walk from the roaring nightlife of Balmer's and Funny Farm. Clean, bright rooms have wooden balconies with views of the Jungfrau and Harder Mann. Services include TV with CNN, movies on the villa's big-screen, mountain bike rental (28SFr per day, 18SFr per half-day), laundry (10SFr per load, soap included), free phone for taxis, and **Internet** access (1SFr per 5 min.). The hostel also books **skiing, snowshoe treks, paragliding, skydiving,** and **bungee jumping.** Includes buffet breakfast, kitchen, lockers, towels, sheets, and recreation and meditation rooms. Reception 7:30-11am and 4-10pm. Check-out 7-9:30am, but guests can leave luggage in day lockers for a 2SFr deposit even when reception is closed. No curfew. Call ahead or arrive early in the morning to have a chance at a room. 4- to 7-bed dorms 29-32SFr; doubles 82-88SFr; triples 111-120SFr; quads 132-144SFr. 5SFr per person extra for Jungfrau view, balcony, and in-suite bathroom. AmEx/MC/V. ❷

Swiss Adventure Hostel is an old hotel in the tiny town of Boltigen (☎773 73 73; www.swissadventures.com). Free shuttle to and from Interlaken each day (40min.); call for times and availability. The Adventure Hostel has staked its claim in this quiet valley as a sporty alternative to the party scene in Interlaken. The welcoming community and abundance of sporting opportunities makes a week-long stay attractive. A small adventure company run out of the ancient hostel offers the same activities as Interlaken companies, but with a more personal touch: after your canyoning trip, you eat dinner with your trip leader. **Internet** access (15SFr per hr.), **mountain bike rental** (25SFr per day), a cellar bar and small dance floor (open 9pm-2am), TV, and restaurant (breakfast buffet 7SFr; dinner 12-18SFr, buffet most nights) with accomplished chef. Check-in 10am-11pm. Reservations available online. Spacious 4- to 10-bed dorms with bathroom 20-25SFr; doubles with shower 70-160SFr; quads with shower 100-140SFr. Discount for adventure program participants. AmEx/MC/V. ❷

Happy Inn, Rosenstr. 17 (☎822 32 25; www.happy-inn.com), lives up to its name with a friendly staff and simple style. From Westbahnhof, go left toward the tourist office and right onto Rosenstr. at the Centralpl. The multi-level building houses clean and spacious 4- to 8-person dorms with metal bunks and lockers, and is located above the **Brasserie,** a great bar. Free **parking** in back. **Internet** 5SFr per 25min. Sheets included. Call early for rooms. Breakfast 8SFr. Reception 7am-6pm. Check-out 10am. Dorms 19-22SFr; singles 30-38SFr; doubles 70-76SFr. DC/MC/V. ❷

Balmers Herberge, Hauptstr. 23-25 (☎822 19 61; fax 823 32 61). Walk diagonally across the Höhenmatte from the tourist office and follow signs down Parkstr. Balmers runs a shuttle bus June-Aug. from both stations (every hr. 9-11am and 1-6pm). Switzerland's oldest private hostel (since 1945) is a place to party, not relax. To enjoy the dorms or "Balmers tent" (a huge striped canvas bungalow with no insulation a few blocks from town), you must value camaraderie above comfort. The complex includes an interior courtyard where ping-pong, beer, and sunbathers meet. Services include: **mountain bike rental** (21SFr per half-day, 35SFr per day), nightly movies, TV with CNN and MTV, a mini-department store (open 7:30am-8pm), safety deposit boxes (2SFr; available 6:30am-noon and 4-10:30pm), and **Internet** access (12SFr per hr.). In winter, they offer **free sleds** and a 20% discount on ski and snowboard rental. After 9pm, activity shifts underground to the **Metro Bar.** (Beer 4.50SFr. Happy hour 5-6pm and 9-10pm, 3SFr. Open until 2am.) Breakfast included. Kitchen 1SFr per 20min. Laundry 8SFr per load. Reception summer 6:30am-noon and 4-10pm; winter 6:30-10am and 4:30-10pm. Check-out 9am. Lockout 9:30am-4:30pm. Sign in early, drop off your pack, and return at 4:30pm when beds are assigned (no reservations). Dorms 24-26SFr; singles 40-42SFr; doubles 68-72SFr; triples 90-112SFr; quads 120-128SFr. AmEx/MC/V. ❷

Funny Farm (☎ 652 61 27; www.funny-farm.ch), behind Hotel Mattenhof, down Hauptstr. from Balmers. More frat house than youth hostel, this estate is very accommodating and hopping with people. Currently, Funny Farm offers tennis, basketball, volleyball, an enormous swimming pool with a climbing wall, adventure activities through Alpin Raft, an indoor nightclub with occasional live reggae, and a yard out back, complete with bar, Guinness tent, and volleyball court—in short, a playground for 20-somethings, and the scene of nightly parties. Breakfast included. Dorms 20-25SFr. ❷

Hotel Alphorn, Rugenstr. 8 (☎822 30 51; www.hotel-alphorn.ch). Turn right onto Bahnhofstr., left onto Rugenstr. and right again onto Rothornstr.; it's behind Hotel Eiger. Newly remodeled doubles with clean beds, sparkling bathrooms with showers, balconies, and TV with CNN. Free breakfast, Internet, and parking. Wheelchair accessible. Singles 70-110SFr; doubles 110-150SFr. ❹ For slightly more per night, the 3-star **Hotel Eiger** in front has spacious antique rooms with the same amenities, intricate wooden floors, and in-room tea and coffee. Singles 90-120SFr; doubles 130-180SFr; large family suites (2 adults and 2 children) 180-240SFr. Reception for both 6:30am-10:30pm. Check-out for both 11am. AmEx/MC/V. ❹

Hotel Blume, Jungfraustr. 30 (☎822 71 31; www.hotel-blume.ch), toward the Westbahnhof from the tourist office, leads guests through winding staircases into welcoming rooms in a building decorated with Mexican art. Connecting doors and a central location make this an ideal option for families or groups of travelers. Breakfast included. Reception summer 6am-midnight; winter 7am-midnight. Check-out 11am. Reservations recommended. Singles 55-75SFr, with shower 75-85SFr; doubles 70-100SFr/110-150SFr; family room 150-200SFr. Ask about the unbeatable Jungfraujoch deal—165SFr per person for a double and ticket to the "top of the world." AmEx/DC/MC/V. ❸

Heidi's Hostel (Heidi's Garni-Hotel Beyeler), Bernastr. 37 (☎/fax 822 90 30). Turn right from the Westbahnhof, go left on Bernastr. and walk straight for 300m (5min.). Friendly owners preside over a rambling old house decorated with sleds, bells, old photographs, and carousel horses. Sinks in every room. Private rooms are available with bath and balcony. Common room with TV, kitchen, and laundry (7SFr). **Bikes** 29SFr per day; tours 39SFr. Reception 7am-1am. Check-out 10am. Dorms 23SFr; 2- to 4-bed rooms 60-140SFr; doubles 80-90SFr; quads 135-160SFr; 8-person rooms 250SFr. MC/V. ❷

📷 CAMPING

Camping Sackgut (☎ 079 656 89 58) is closest to town. Head toward town from the Ostbahnhof, turn right across the 1st bridge, and take another right onto the footpath or road. A few choice spots are available by the river, but most of the campground lies in an exposed grassy parking lot. Offers **Internet,** kitchen and laundry (4SFr). Reception July-Sept. 5-7pm. 6.20SFr per person, 16SFr per car, 7SFr per tent; Apr.-June and Sept.-Oct. 4.80SFr/12SFr/6.50SFr. Children 50% off adult price. Tent bungalow 65SFr, parking 3SFr. Electricity 3SFr. Trash 1SFr. ❶

Camping Jungfraublick (☎822 44 14; www.jungfraublick.ch). Take bus #5 from the Westbahnhof toward Widerswil, and continue 5min. past Balmers on Gsteigstr. Has peaceful mountain views and fairly extensive grounds. Pool, cable TV, and a small store. Open May-Sept. Reception summer 7-11am and 2-8pm; winter 8-10am and 4-6pm. 8.40SFr per person high-season, 7.40SFr low-season; 8-28SFr per tent. MC/V. ❶

Lazy Rancho (☎822 87 16; www.lazyrancho.ch). Head past Jungfrau Camping and left onto Lehnweg. This clean campground is equipped with a swimming pool, store, playground, kitchen, and laundry facilities (4-6SFr). Open mid-Apr. to mid-Oct. 7SFr per person high season, low season 6SFr; children half-price; 10SFr/7SFr per tent. Tax 1.60 per person. Electricity 4SFr. MC/V. ❶

◖ FOOD

Generally, the Balmers crowd eats at Balmers (*Bratwurst* and burgers under 10SFr), the hostel crowd eats at the *Jugendherberge* (12.50SFr), those at Backpacker's Villa cook their meals in the hostel's kitchen, and the Funny Farm folks eat from their renovated cable car (wraps 10SFr; burgers and fries 12-15SFr). Most of the restaurants listed here are on Marktg. Head up Aareckstr., the tiny street left from Westbahnhof, and turn left on Spielmatte. **Co-op,** across from the Ostbahnhof or behind the Westbahnhof, houses a restaurant. (Open M-Th 8am-6:30pm, F 8am-9pm, Sa 7:30am-5pm; restaurant additionally Su 9am-5pm.) **Migros,** in front of the Westbahnhof, has a restaurant and keeps the same hours.

Restaurant Goldener Anker, Marktg. 57 (☎822 16 72). This family-run restaurant has many traditional specialties and vegetarian dishes. The California salad (grilled turkey strips on lettuce and fresh fruit; 16.50SFr) is delicious. For dessert try the Crêpe Normandy—it's stuffed with apples and vanilla ice cream (8SFr). Frequently hosts live bands. Billiards available. Open M-W and F-Su 10am-12:30am. MC. ❸

Confiserie Schuh (☎822 94 41), across from the tourist office, has been an Interlaken landmark since the 19th century. A wide array of goodies, including chocolate medallions (1SFr) and strawberry tarts (5SFr). Afternoon tea, complete with chocolates, pastries, and sandwiches, is 19.50SFr. An on-site restaurant (open daily 7:30am-10pm) serves ethnic specialties and many vegetarian options. Open daily 8am-10pm. ❶

El Azteca (☎822 71 31), downstairs from Hotel Blume, serves up excellent Mexican food. Select from numerous entrées (12-20SFr) or choose one of the four daily lunch *Menüs:* Mexican (16.50SFr), international (15SFr), Swiss (14SFr), or vegetarian (14.50SFr), each served noon-1:45pm. Open daily June-Sept. M-Tu and Th-Su 7am-11:30pm; Oct.-May 8am-2pm and 6-11:30pm. Closed Jan. AmEx/MC/V. ❷

Città Vecchia Ristorante and Pizzeria (☎822 17 54), Untere G. 5. From Marktpl., follow Spielmattestr. across the river and turn left onto Untere G. Set off from the hustle of the main street and overlooking a peaceful square, this upscale restaurant offers Italian specialties at reasonable prices. Pizzas (13-19.50SFr) and pastas (13-22SFr) both include a number of vegetarian options. Select from the seasonal menus (22-40SFr) and variety of fine Italian wines (3.50-6SFr per glass). Children's menu available. Open mid-Oct. to Mar. M and W-Su 10am-midnight; Apr. to mid-Sept. M-Sa 10am-2pm and 5-11:30pm; Su 10am-10:30pm. AmEx/MC/V. ❸

BERNESE OBERLAND

⚠ OUTDOORS NEAR INTERLAKEN

❗ Interlaken's adventure sports industry is thrilling and usually safe, but accidents do happen. On July 27, 1999, 19 adventure-seeking tourists were killed by a flash flood while canyoning on the Saxeten River. Be aware that you participate in all adventure sports at your own risk, and if you don't feel comfortable doing something, don't do it.

ADVENTURE SPORTS. Interlaken's steep precipices, raging rivers, and wide-open spaces serve as prime spots for such adrenaline-pumping activities as paragliding, white-water rafting, bungee jumping, and canyoning (a sport in which wet-suited thrill-seekers rappel, dive, and swim through a canyon). **Alpin Raft** (☎ 823 41 00 or 334 62 02; www.alpinraft.com), the most established company in Interlaken, has qualified, personable guides and promises that "unlike some first-time experiences, this one will be great." All prices include transportation to and from any hostel in Interlaken: **paragliding** costs 150SFr, **canyoning** 215SFr, **river rafting** 205SFr, **skydiving** 380SFr, **bungee jumping** 125-295SFr, and **hang gliding** 180SFr. **Outdoor Interlaken** (☎ 826 77 19; www.outdoor-interlaken.ch) offers **rock-climbing** lessons (89SFr per half-day) and **white-water kayaking** tours (155SFr per half-day). **Swissraft** (☎ 823 02 10; www.swissraft.ch.) in Boltingen offers similar adventures, as well as **hydro-speeding** (aided body-surfing down the river; 120SFr), and all-day combinations of multiple activities. **Skydiving Xdream** charges 380SFr per tandem jump. Stefan Heuser, the owner, has been a member of the Swiss skydiving team for 17 years, including two years as a coach, and has over 6000 jumps to his credit. Weekday jumps are from a plane (weekend ones from a helicopter) into waterfall-filled Lauterbrunnen. (☎ 079 75 93 48 3; www.justjump.ch. Open Apr.-Oct.)

The **Swiss Alpine Guides** (☎ 822 60 00; www.swissalpineguides.ch) lead full-day **ice-climbing** clinics (May-Oct., 160SFr), as well as full-day **glacier treks** to the other side of the Jungfrau (June-Oct. 95SFr). Interlaken's winter activities include skiing, snowboarding, ice canyoning, snow rafting, and glacier skiing. Contact the **tourist office** (☎ 826 53 00) for information.

HIKES FROM INTERLAKEN. The towns closer to the mountains offer longer, more strenuous treks, but Interlaken has a few good hikes of its own. The most traversed trail climbs to the **Harder Kulm** (aka Harder Mann; 1310m). Only the Jungfrau can be seen from Interlaken itself, but from the top of this half-day hike, the Eiger and Mönch, a striking mountainscape, are also visible. The easiest starting point is near the Ostbahnhof. From the Ostbahnhof, head toward town, take the first road bridge across the river, and follow the yellow signs to "Harderkulm" that later give way to white-red-white *Bergweg* blazes on the rocks. From the top, signs lead back down to the Westbahnhof. A funicular runs from the trailhead near the Ostbahnhof to the top. (2½hr. up, 1½hr. down; May-Oct. daily. 13.40SFr, round-trip 21SFr; 25% discount with Eurail/SwissPass.)

Flatter trails lead along the lakes that flank the city. Turn left from the train station, then left before the bridge and follow the canal over to the nature reserve on the shore of the Thunersee. The trail (3hr.) winds up the Lombach river, then through pastures at the base of the Harder Kulm back toward town.

🔊 NIGHTLIFE

If you still have energy at the end of the day, Interlaken provides plenty of options for its release. **Balmers** (p. 347) offers live music on most nights, most often reggae. (Beer 4.50SFr. Bar open 9pm-1am.) The **Caverne Bar,** in the basement of the Mattenhof Hotel, in front of the Funny Farm, serves 3.50SFr beer and alternates between live music and techno. Both are filled with English-speaking twenty-somethings. (☎ 821 61 21. Open W-Su 10pm-2:30am.)

If you're feeling adventurous, head beyond the hostel confines to one of the local hangouts. **Buddy's**, Höheweg 33, is a small, crowded English-style pub where the beer is only 3.50-5SFr. Internet access is 12SFr per hr. (☎ 822 76 12. Open daily 10am-12:30am.) **Johnny's Dancing Club**, Höheweg 92, located in the basement of the Hotel Carlton, is Interlaken's oldest disco and serves drinks from 6SFr. (☎ 822 38 21. Open Tu-Su 9:30pm-3am.) For smoky blues try **Brasserie**, Rosenstr. 17, under the Happy Inn, which serves the self-proclaimed "best ribs in town," 22.50SFr. (☎ 822 32 25. Beer from 3.20SFr. Open M-Sa 8:30am-12:30am, Su 3pm-12:30am.) **Positiv Einfach**, Centralstr. 11, is a café by day and a dark cocktail bar by night, complete with a "mood room" in the back and comfortable leather couches. Mixed drinks cost 11.50-12.50SFr, but check for theme days, like Tuesday when almost everything is 6SFr. (☎ 823 40 44; www.positive-einfach.ch. Open Su-Th 5pm-12:30am, F-Sa 5pm-1:30am.) **Hüsi**, Postg. 3, has a local feel. Beers are 5SFr, mixed drinks are 10-13SFr, and pizzas, ordered specially from a neighboring pizzeria, are 14-20SFr. (☎ 822 33 34; www.huesi.ch. Open Tu-Th and Su 4pm-12:30am, F-Sa 4pm-1:30am.)

The apex of Interlaken's cultural life is the outdoor summer production of Friedrich Schiller's **Wilhelm Tell** (in German; English synopsis 2SFr). Lasses with flowing locks and 250 bushy-bearded local men wearing heavy rouge ham up the tale of the Swiss escape from under the Hapsburg thumb. 20 horses gallop by in every scene, and a vaudeville-like stage around the corner from Balmers allows the cast to make real bonfires. (Shows late June to mid-July Th 8pm; mid-July to early Sept. Th and Sa 8pm.) Tickets (22-38SFr) are available at the theater on show nights, or at Tellbüro at the tourist office. (☎ 822 37 22; fax 57 33. Open during run M-F 8am-noon and 1:30-5pm). Children under age 6 not admitted, but free day-care is provided. **Casino Kursaal**, between the Ostbahnhof and the tourist office, houses a newly opened casino and a stage for the **Swiss Folklore Show** in summer. (☎ 827 61 00; www.casino-kursaal.ch. Bar and casino machines open Su-Th noon-2am, F-Sa noon-3am. Roulette and blackjack: Su-Th 6pm-2am, F-Sa 6pm-3am. Shows May-Sept. daily and Oct. M and Th 7:30pm; 20SFr. Include dinner at 7pm for 19-39.50SFr more.)

▶ DAYTRIP FROM INTERLAKEN: ST. BEATUS'S CAVES

To get to the caves, walk 15min. uphill from the Sundlauenen Schiffstation, a 30min. boat ride from Interlaken (every hr. 10:30am-5pm), or take bus #21 (9SFr round-trip from Interlaken Westbahnhof). You can also hike from Interlaken (2hr.) or Beatenberg (1hr.). Just be sure to wear sturdy shoes; the path is rough at times. ☎ 841 16 43; fax 10 64. Caves and museum open Apr.-Oct. daily 10:30am-5pm. 16SFr, students 14SFr, children 9SFr.

At the **Beatushöhlen** (St. Beatus's Caves) in Beatenberg village, it is possible to spelunk through 1000m of glistening stalactites, waterfalls, and grottoes. There are several reflecting pools and neat geological formations, including the limestone sculpture "Virgin with Child," formed by thousands of years of dripping water. At the entrance, a wax St. Beatus (the Irish hermit and dragon-slayer) stares down some cavemen; at the exit, an iron dragon ambushes exiting spelunkers. Even on hot summer days, the cave stays a cool, constant 9°C. Less for outdoor enthusiasts and more for a family adventure, the Caves are accessible only on multi-lingual 1hr. tours which leave every 30min. from the entrance. Admission includes entry to the tiny **Caving Museum**, 5min. downhill, which chronicles the discovery and mapping of Swiss grottoes.

THE JUNGFRAU REGION

A few miles south of Interlaken, the hitherto-middling mountains rear up and become hulking white monsters. This is the Jungfrau Region, home of Europe's largest glacier and some of its steepest crags and highest waterfalls. In summer, the region's hundreds of kilometers of hiking consistently awe a steady stream of travelers with astounding mountain views, wildflower meadows, roaring waterfalls, and pristine forests. The three most famous peaks are the **Jungfrau** (4158m), the **Mönch** (4099m), and the **Eiger** (3970m)—in English, that's the Maiden, the Monk, and the Ogre. Natives say that the monk protects the maiden by standing between her and the ogre. On the other side of these giants, a vast glacial region stretches southward, where six major glaciers, including the **Grosser Aletschgletscher** (at 45km long the largest in Europe) converge at **Konkordiaplatz.**

■ **ORIENTATION.** The Jungfrau is split into two valleys. The first gives access to the glaciers through the town of Grindelwald, while the second, the Lauterbrunnen, holds many smaller towns, including Wengen, Gimmelwald, and Mürren. The valleys are divided by a hikeable ridge; on the end closer to Interlaken

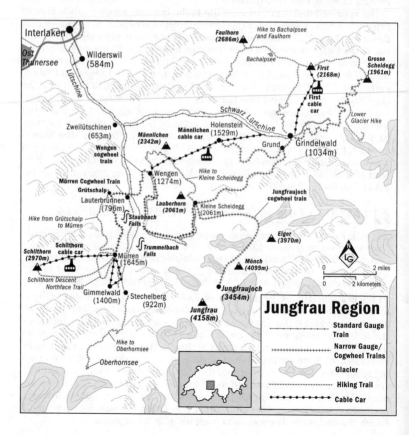

Jungfrau Region

————————	Standard Gauge Train
+++++++++++	Narrow Gauge/ Cogwheel Trains
	Glacier
··············	Hiking Trail
•–•–•–•–•–•	Cable Car

is the Männlichen Peak. At the other end of the ridge, near the Jungfrau, is the train town of Kleine Scheidegg. On either side of Lauterbrunnen, are cliff ledges on which the small towns of Wengen, Mürren, and Gimmelwald are perched; none are accessible by car.

⚡ TRANSPORTATION AND OUTDOOR ACTIVITIES. The **Jungfraubahn** runs throughout the region and includes the cog-railways to the towns above Lauterbrunnen. Because of their proximity, hikes in different towns can frequently be combined, so check out hiking suggestions from other towns regardless of where you're staying. For casual day hikes, the free *Wandern Jungfraubahnen*, available at any tourist office, provides an excellent overview of the region; if you plan on doing any serious hiking, be sure to get a copy of the *Lauterbrunnen/Jungfrau Region Wanderkarte* (15SFr at any tourist office), which gives an overview of all of the hikes.

There are three main ski areas in the Jungfrau region: the **Mürren-Schilthorn** area, the **Kleine Scheidegg-Männlichen** area, and the **Grindelwald-First** area, with over 213km of downhill runs between them. The Mürren-Schilthorn area is much smaller than the other two. Day passes for the individual areas are 42-56SFr. Multiday passes, which include transport on the Jungfraubahn, are available for all 3 ski areas. (☎828 72 33; www.jungfraubahn.ch. 2 days 129SFr, 7 days 318SFr, ages 16-19 96SFr/256SFr, children 6-15 50% discount.) Most towns have separate ski schools. For **snow information** and a **weather report**, dial ☎828 79 31.

GRINDELWALD ☎033

Grindelwald, launching point to the only glaciers in the Bernese Oberland accessible by foot, crouches beneath the north face of the Eiger—a difficult milestone in any climber's career. It is a cold-weather Shangri-la for outdoorsy types, though the tourism can be overwhelming at times. In summertime, inexpensive accommodations make Grindelwald an ideal base for exploring the eastern half of the region.

🚍 TRANSPORT AND PRACTICAL INFORMATION

The Jungfraubahn runs from **Interlaken's** Ostbahnhof (40min., 6:35am-10:30pm; 9.80SFr). Trains to the **Jungfraujoch** (see "The Jungfraujoch," p. 362) and **Kleine Scheidegg** (26SFr, 44SFr round-trip; Eurail or SwissPass 25% discount) leave from the Grindelwald station (every hr. 7:19am-5:19pm, 6:19pm in summer). Balmers hostel in Interlaken also offers a bus (round-trip 15SFr). The **tourist office,** in the Sport-Zentrum to the right of the station, provides a kiosk for hotel reservations, lift information, and a list of free guided excursions. (☎854 12 12; www.grindelwald.ch. Open July-Aug. M-F 8am-noon, 1:30-6pm, Sa 8am-noon, 1:30-5pm, Su 9am-noon, 3:30-5pm. Sept.-June M-F 8am-noon and 2-6pm, Sa 8am-noon and 2-5pm.) Services include: **laundry** at **Wash & Dry** on Haupstr. (Wash 4SFr, dry 1SFr per 10min.; open 24hr.); **weather forecast** ☎162; **medical assistance** ☎853 11 53; **police** ☎117; **emergency** ☎144; **bike Rental** at **Mad House,** 100m to the left of the station, (☎659 17 33. 40SFr full day, 25SFr half-day. Open Tu-F 9-noon, 1:30-6:30. Sa 9-noon, 1:30-5pm); **Pharmacy Eiger** on the main street. (☎853 44 66; emergency also ☎425 68 84. Open M-F 8am-noon and 2-6:30pm, Sa 8am-noon and 2-5pm. AmEx/MC/V.); **Internet** (15SFr per hr.) at the tourist office or **Ernst Schudel's Photo Shop,** across the street. (Open M-F 9am-noon and 2-6pm, Sa 9am-noon and 2-6pm.) The **post office** is opposite the station. (Open M-F 8am-noon and 1:45-6pm, Sa 8-11am.) **Postal Code:** CH-3818.

BERNESE OBERLAND

ACCOMMODATIONS AND CAMPING

When checking into a hotel, be sure to ask for a visitor's card for reduced entrance prices to the sports center, cable cars, and other facilities.

Hotel Hirschen (☎854 84 84; www.hirschen-grindelwald.ch), in the center of town. Turn right from the tourist office. Offers clean, bright rooms with comfortable beds and a bowling alley. All rooms have satellite TV, telephone, and safe, and many have balconies, although the view from the lower floors is partially obstructed. Breakfast and entrance to sports center swimming pool and ice-skating rink included. The hotel also offers currency exchange and bowling. Wheelchair accessible. Reception 8am-10pm. Singles 90-135SFr; doubles 150-220SFr. ❹

Jugendherberge (HI) (☎853 10 09; www.youthhostel.ch/grindelwald). Exit the train station and turn left. Go straight for 400m, then cut uphill to the right just before "Chalet Alpenblume" and follow the steep trail all the way up the hill (400m). It's a hike from town, but the enormous wooden chalet is beautiful. Wood-paneled living rooms have fireplaces and many rooms have balconies facing the Eiger. Laundry (5SFr), **Internet** (15SFr per hr.), TV and game room. Buffet breakfast included. Lunch 8.50-11.50SFr. 3-course dinner 12.50SFr. Vegetarian meals available on request. Lockers and sheets included. Wheelchair accessible. Reception 7:30-10am and 3pm-midnight. No lockout. Quiet time 10pm. Open May-Oct. and mid-Dec. to Apr. Dorms 28-30SFr; 4-bed rooms 30-35SFr; doubles 35SFr per person, with toilet and shower 51SFr. Non-members add 6SFr per person. AmEx/DC/MC. ❷

Lehmann's Herberge (☎853 31 41). Follow the main street past the tourist office and take the first right (5min.). Enjoy the comfort of a renovated home as well as a hearty homemade breakfast (included). Self-serve kitchen. Parking included. Reception 7am-10pm. Dorms and doubles 45SFr per person; after 1st night dorms 40SFr. 4-bed apartments 120-130SFr with one week minimum stay. ❸

Gletscherdorf Camping (☎853 14 29; www.gletscherdorf.ch). Take a right from the station along the main road; at the ski school, take another right downhill and follow the path marked "Wandersteg." Follow the road. The small grounds are the closest campground to Grindelwald and have a phenomenal view. Showers included. Open May-Oct. Reception 8-10am and 5-8pm; come anytime. 6.90SFr per person, 3.50SFr per child; 6-12SFr per tent. Electricity 4SFr. ❶

FOOD

There is a **Co-op,** on Hauptstr. across from the tourist office (open M-F 8am-noon and 1:30-6:30pm, Sa 8am-6pm) and a **Migros** on the main road, 10 min. to the right of the station just past the Eiger Hotel. (Same hours as Co-op.)

Hotel Eiger (☎854 31 31; www.eiger-grindelwald.ch), past the tourist office on the left, contains a variety of eateries. **Memory Bistro** (open 8:30am-11:30pm) and **Barry's Restaurant** upstairs (open 6pm-12:30am) offer cheap burgers (9SFr) and veggie *Rösti* (13SFr). Hosts yodelers and hand-organists for Swiss music night on W. Later at night head across the hallway for the **Gepsi Bar.** Beers from 3.50SFr. Open 5:30pm-1:30am. In the main restaurant, "American" breakfast (potatoes, bacon, eggs, toast, tea, and coffee) served all day. 15SFr. ❷

Ye Olde Spotted Cat (☎853 12 34), on Hauptstr. just past Hotel Hirschen. Scratch a few wooden cats' heads and sip cheap beer (3.80SFr) at this old haunt of Winston Churchill. Lunch menus (15-30SFr). Kitchen closes around 9pm. Open Su-M 11am-5pm, Tu-Sa 11am-12:30am; summer F-Sa until 1:30am. ❶

Pizzeria Da Salvi (☎853 89 99), in Hotel Steinbock at the base of the First Bahn cable car station (see Hiking, below). Offers a hearty meal in a romantic Italian atmosphere. Large pizzas (15-23SFr) and a gamut of pastas (16-18.50SFr) don't overshadow the variety of unique entrées (24-41SFr). Try the oven-baked lamb (31SFr) or mushroom risotto (23SFr) and select from a number of delectable ice cream creations for dessert (8-9.50SFr). Wheelchair accessible. Open daily 11:30am-11:30pm. ❸

Tea Room Riggenburg (☎853 10 59), past the tourist office away from the station, offers soups, salads, lasagnas, pastas, and fresh-baked desserts in a typical tea-room fashion. Drink a huge hot cocoa (3.40SFr) or have a hearty *Birchermüsli* (7SFr) on the heated terrace. Open Tu-Sa 7am-10pm, Su 8am-6pm. ❶

◈ HIKING

Hiking possibilities in Grindelwald run the gamut from easy valley walks to challenges for top climbers. The greatest allure for the hiker is the proximity of glaciers. While most hikes are possible without the aid of expensive trains and cable cars, these means of transportation allow access to some fantastic hikes. The **First Bahn** leaves from the center of town and climbs the eastern side of the valley. (☎854 50 51; www.gofirst.ch. Runs 8:30am-4:30pm; 29SFr, round-trip 46SFr.) The **Männlichen Gondelbahn**, the **longest cable car route in Europe**, is on the other side of the valley. (☎854 80 80. Runs 8am-4pm, until 5:15pm in summer; 32.80SFr, round-trip 52.40SFr. 25% discount with SwissPass; 50% with Eurail.) The **Bergführerbüro** (Mountain Guides Office), located in the sports center next to the tourist office, sells hiking maps (9.80SFr) and coordinates activities like glacier walks, ice climbing, and mountaineering. (☎853 12 00; www.gomountain.ch. Open June-Oct. M-F 9am-noon and 2-5pm. 1-day activities 100-600SFr. Reserve ahead for multi-day expeditions.)

Lower Glacier (*Untere Grindelwaldgletscher*, 5hr. circular hike without funicular). Although conquerable in sneakers, this hike is moderately steep, and becomes steeper the farther the trail proceeds. To find the trailhead, walk up the main street away from station until signs point downhill to "Pfinstegg." Hikers can either walk the first section of the trail (1hr.), following signs up to Pfinstegg, or take a funicular to the Pfinstegg hut. (8am-4pm; July to mid-Sept. 8am-7pm. 9.80SFr.) From the hut, signs lead up the glacier-filled valley to "Stieregg," a hut that offers food.

The Faulhorn via the Bachalpsee (7hr.; shorter options available if cable cars are used). This is the most dramatic strenuous hike away from the glaciers. The HI hostel is the easiest starting point. Head uphill on the road (left at the Y) until signs lead upwards to Allflue, which provides clear views down into town. From Allflue, the trail leads uphill for more than 1hr. to Waldspitz. The final hike from Waldspitz to Bachsee and the Faulhorn travels through highland meadows (5hr.). On the way down, go to **Bussalp** (2hr.), where a bus goes back to Grindelwald. For those with a little less stamina and a bit more money, the **First Bahn** goes straight from town to a station only 1hr. away from the Bachsee, knocking 2-3hr. off the hike. Another level, easy 1hr. hike offering great views of the glaciers runs from the top of the First Bahn to Grosse Scheidegg, where it is possible to catch a bus to Grindelwald.

The Männlichen (1hr.). Access another easy (though more expensive) hike on the other side of the valley by taking the **Männlichen Gondalbahn.** From the Männlichen station, a quick circular hike scales the **Männlichen** peak, which divides Grindelwald from the Lauterbrunnen Valley, before continuing as a flat, 1hr. hike to Kleine Scheidegg and its intimate views of the Eiger, Mönch, and Jungfrau. Hop a train back to Grindelwald from here. This hike is easier (and free or at least with cheaper mechanical access) as part of the hike from **Wengen** (see p. 358).

LAUTERBRUNNEN ☎ 033

The 72 waterfalls plummeting down the sheer walls of the narrow, glacier-cut valley give Lauterbrunnen its name, "loud springs." The town of Lauterbrunnen, which lies in the middle of the valley of the same name, adjoins Switzerland's highest waterfall, **Staubbach Falls** (280m), which inspired Goethe's poem "Song of the Spirit over the Waterfall" (later set to music by Franz Schubert). Mendelssohn composed some of his "Songs without Words" in Lauterbrunnen. The town's abundant accommodations and easy accessibility by car and train make the town an ideal base for those hiking and skiing the Jungfrau region.

TRANSPORTATION AND PRACTICAL INFORMATION

Trains leave every 30min. to: Interlaken Ost (20min., 6:05am-10:05pm, 6.60SFr); Jungfraujoch (1¾hr.; 7:08am-4:10pm; round-trip 145.60SFr, "Good Morning" ticket 108.20SFr); Kleine Scheidegg (45min.; 6:10am-5pm, summer until 6:05pm; 26.80SFr); Mürren (20min.; 6:42am-8pm, summer until 9pm; 9.80SFr); and Wengen (6:10am-midnight, 5.80SFr). The **tourist office,** next to the train station, provides binders of information about activities and large tables to plan your stay. (☎856 85 68; www.wengen-muerren.ch. Open July-Aug. M-F 8am-7pm, Sa 9am-12:30pm and 1:30-5pm, Su 9am-12:30pm and 1:30-4pm; June and Sept. M-F 8am-6pm, Sa-Su 9am-12:30pm and 1:30-4pm; Oct. M-F 8am-12:30pm and 1:30-5pm, Sa 9am-12:30pm and 1:30-4pm; Nov.-May M-F 8am-12:30 and 1:30-5pm.) Other services include: **currency exchange,** small **lockers** and **luggage** storage (3SFr) at the station; **ski rental** at **Crystal Sports** (☎856 90 90); and **bike rental** at **Bike Imboden.** (☎855 21 14. Open M-F 9am-6:30pm, Sa-Su 9am-6pm. 35SFr full day, 25SFr for 4hr.) For **medical assistance** call ☎856 26 26; for **Internet** access visit the **Valley Hostel** (12SFr per hr.), the tourist office (1SFr per 6min.), or the Horner Pub (20SFr per hr.). **Laundry** (wash 5SFr, dry 5SFr) is available at the Valley Hostel. The **post office** is across from the station. (Open M-F 7:45-11:45am and 2-6pm, Sa 7:45-11am.) **Postal Code:** CH-3822.

ACCOMMODATIONS

■ **Valley Hostel** (☎855 20 08; www.valleyhostel.ch). Head left on the main street, past the Co-op on the left. The hostel is down a driveway on the left side of the street. Martha, the owner, offers a pristine environment and a big kitchen. The large windows allow breezes to blow over the comfortable wooden bunks (with fuzzy, cow-patterned sheets) in the large, clean rooms, and have views of Staubbach Falls. A peaceful garden, complete with a barbecue grill, invites guests to relax after a day of hiking. Showers and sheets included. Laundry (5SFr wash, 5SFr dry, but on a nice day use the free clothes line) and **Internet** (4SFr per 20min.) open 8am-10pm. You can request fondue (in advance) for 16SFr. Breakfast 5SFr. Reception 8am-noon and 2-9pm. Dorms 23-26SFr; singles 30SFr; doubles 56-64SFr. ❷

■ **Hotel Staubbach** (☎855 54 54; www.staubbach.ch). Turn left on the main street, 400m from the station on the left. Built in the 19th century, this was one of the oldest hotels in town until it was converted by Craig and Corinne Rochin-Müller into a pleasant and affordable bed and breakfast. Worn Oriental rugs lead the way to multiple rooms—each is a little different, but all are clean and comfortable, with running water. The dark-paneled parlor comes equipped with games, comfortable couches, cable TV, and a kids' corner. Balconies in most rooms. All have beautiful views of the mountains. Parking and breakfast buffet included. Reception 8am-10:30pm. Check-in 3-10pm. Check-out 11am. Call early to reserve a room. Wheelchair accessible. Singles 50SFr, with shower 60SFr; doubles 80SFr/110SFr; 3- to 6-bed family suites 30-50SFr per person. Children in parents' bed 20SFr. 10SFr surcharge for 1-night stays. MC/V. ❸

Hotel-Restaurant Schützen (☎ 855 30 26; www.hotelschuetzen.com). Turn left on the main street, on the right. Slightly more expensive, Schützen provides comfortable beds with wooden headboards. Spacious rooms come fully equipped with telephones, couches, showers, and toilets, some with balconies. Breakfast included. A restaurant on a heated terrace in front of the hotel serves pizzas (18SFr) and traditional Swiss food. Reception 7am-midnight. Check-out 11am. Singles 70-100SFr, low-season 60-90SFr; doubles 130-170SFr/120-150SFr; triples 150-225SFr; quads 180-240SFr. ❹

Camping Schützenbach (☎ 855 12 68; www.schutzenbach-retreat.ch). Take a left on the main road, a left over the river by the church, and follow the street as it curves right (15min.; follow the signs). This camping complex has several lodging options, a small restaurant, and a convenience store. Reception 7:30am-noon and 2-7pm. 6SFr per adult; 3SFr per child; 6-10SFr per tent. Dorms 16.50SFr; doubles with sink 64SFr; 4-bed "tourist rooms" in barracks-like huts 28SFr per person. MC/V. ❶

🍴 FOOD

Crystal Restaurant ❸, on the main street, has a short menu full of Swiss classics. Try *Älpler-Rösti* for 15SFr, cheese fondue for 20.50SFr, or a daily *Menü* including salad and entree for 15-29SFr. A breakfast buffet is available for 12SFr. (☎ 856 90 90. Open daily 8-11am and 5:30-9pm. AmEx/MC/V.) **Horner Bar ❶**, farther down the street, has beer (3.20SFr), pizza (8SFr), and **Internet** access for 12SFr per hr. (☎ 855 16 73. Open 9am-12:30am, disco upstairs open until 2:30am.) A **Co-op** is near the hostel on the main road. (Open M-F 8am-noon and 2-6:30pm, Sa 8am-noon and 1:30-4pm.)

⛰ OUTDOORS

Lauterbrunnen's best hike is the flat trail that leads up the valley (about 7km). The trail below leads to a number of hiking destinations. To reach the trailhead, follow the right branch of the main road as it leaves town (toward Camping Jungfrau). It dwindles slowly to a narrow path before becoming a dirt trail through the woods. **Crystal Sport** (☎ 856 90 90; www.crystal-lauterbrunnen.ch) rents hiking boots for 16SFr (light) or 20SFr (heavy). per day. (Open M-F 8:30am-noon and 2-6:30pm, Sa 8:30am-noon and 2-5pm, Su 9-11am, 4-6pm.)

HIKE DOWN THE LAUTERBRUNNEN VALLEY. The first, and hence most touristed, segment of the trail (45min.) leads to the 🏳Trümmelbach Falls. These 10 glacier-bed chutes are the only drains for the glacial run-off of the Eiger, Mönch, and Jungfrau glaciers and pour up to 20,000L of water per second. An underground elevator takes visitors to just below the highest falls and lets them descend through the cave-canyon via misty tunnels and small bridges. The water is cold: bring warm clothes even during the summer. (Open daily July-Aug. 8:30am-6pm; May-June and Sept.-Oct. 10am-4pm. 10SFr, with Jungfrau region visitor's card 9SFr.) The falls can also be reached by **bus** from Lauterbrunnen (to "Trümmelbach," every hr., 3SFr).

The flat and calm trail leading to the Trümmelbach Falls passes the Staubbach Falls, Spissbach Falls, Agertenbach Falls, and Mümenbach Falls. After the turn-off for the Trümmelbach Falls, the trail becomes less busy as it makes its way toward **Stechelberg**, passing even more waterfalls (1½hr.). Stechelberg, a tiny village with a grocery store, is the last place to catch a bus back to Lauterbrunnen (4.40SFr). From Stechelberg, the trail climbs and enters the end of the valley, accessible only by dirt road. The trail runs through Stechelberg and its one road to the end of town. The **Schilthorn Bahn cable car** runs from Stechelberg to Birg (36.60SFr), Gimmelwald (7.80SFr), Mürren (15.20SFr), and the Schilthorn (53.80SFr). The last cars to Birg leave Stechelber at 4:25pm, and to Gimmewald, Mürren, and Schilthorn at 11:35pm. The trips to Gimmelwald and Mürren are free with SwissPass; Eurail offers a 25% reduction on all destinations. Gimmelwald and Mürren are carless by law. Leave cars at the parking lot near the cable car (day 5SFr, week 21SFr, mo. 30SFr).

Trachsellauenen, a two-building enclave 50min. from Stechelberg, is the next destination on the trail. This is the departure point for the trail leading into the **nature reserve.** A 2½hr. strenuous mountain hike leads to the tiny Oberhornsee, a lake which lies beneath the Tschingel glacier.

BICYCLING. Imboden Bike Adventures, on the main street, rents mountain bikes for 25SFr per 4hr. or 35SFr per day and lends out free maps and helmets. (☎855 21 14. Open daily May-Oct. 8:30am-6:30pm; Nov.-Apr. 9am-noon and 2-6:30pm. AmEx/DC/MC/V.) On the Mürren Loop, go via funicular to Grütschalp (7.80SFr), bike to Mürren and Gimmelwald, and go downhill to Stechelberg and Lauterbrunnen.

WENGEN   ☎ 033

Wengen (pop. 1100), which occupies a ledge on the cliff-curtained Lauterbrunnental, is accessible only by train. Hotel golf carts and a few taxis provide all the transportation around the peaceful town. Despite its seclusion and emptiness in summer, Wengen retains a modern feel and attracts crowds of out-of-town skiers to its top resorts during the peak winter months. Because Eurail does not cover the train ride to Wengen, it is an ideal destination for summer travelers looking for a quiet break from the backpacker social scene of many nearby towns.

■? TRANSPORTATION AND PRACTICAL INFORMATION

Wengen is accessible by **train** from Interlaken Ost (45min., every hr. 6:35am-10:35pm, 12.40SFr) and from Lauterbrunnen (15min., every 25min. 6:10am-midnight, 5.80SFr). After stopping in Wengen, the train continues toward Kleine Scheidegg (7:25am-5:20pm, summer 7:25am-6:25pm; 21SFr) and the Jungfraujoch (7:25am-4:30pm; winter only until 2:30pm; 134SFr, morning ticket 97SFr). Cars can be parked in the Lauterbrunnen **parking garage** (8-16SFr per day depending on season and day of the week). The **tourist office,** right and then an immediate left from the station past the post office, offers **Internet** access (15SFr per hr.), doles out information on local hikes and sells maps for 4SFr (walking) or 15SFr (hiking). (☎855 14 14; fax 30 60. Open daily 9am-6pm.) Services include: **currency exchange, lockers** (3-5SFr), and hotel reservations at the train station; **pharmacy** (☎855 12 46) and **emergency** services (☎280 55 40) to the left out of the station and 2min. past the tourist office (Open M-F 8am-noon and 2-6:30pm, Sa 8am-noon and 2-5pm in the summer, later in the winter); **hospital** in Interlaken (☎826 26 26); **doctor** (☎856 28 28); **Internet** at the station (15SFr per hr.), tourist office (15SFr per hr.), **Rock's** next to the post office (Free for 30 min. with a purchase of a drink. Open 9am-11pm.), or **Hot Chili Peppers** (5SFr per 15min.). The **post office** is next to the tourist office. (Open M-F 8am-noon and 2-6pm, Sa 8:30-11am.) **Postal Code:** CH-3823.

ACCOMMODATIONS AND FOOD

Although it is not one of Switzerland's more glamorous ski resorts, lodging in Wengen does not cater to the budget traveler. Visitors get the best deal by staying in one of the hostels or hotels in Lauterbrunnen. The sole budget option in Wengen, **Wengen Backpacker Lodge ❷** (www.wengenlodge.ch) lies down the hill on the outer edges of town. From the station, turn right and follow the road past the Co-op under the railroad tracks as it makes switchbacks toward the large yellow building with the green shutters (10min.). Once a hotel and then a schoolhouse, this building now offers holiday flats, private rooms, and dorms. The Lodge offers bright and clean rooms with fantastic views. (☎ 745 58 50. Kitchen, free laundry, cable TV, BBQ and table tennis available. Dorms 25SFr. Private rooms 30SFr per person; 40SFr winter). Holiday flats same price, but require 1 week minimum stay. Discounts for groups and long stays.) On the way down the hill, turn right at the bakery for more luxurious accommodations at **Hotel Edelweiss ❹**. This chalet-style hotel has pristine, bright wooden accommodations and a peaceful garden out front. Each spacious room comes equipped with shower and either a balcony or TV. Breakfast, sauna, TV/video room, table tennis, foosball, and access to a small reading room included. Reception all day. (☎ 855 23 88; www.edelweisswengen.ch. June-Oct. 65-75SFr per person; mid-Dec. until Apr. 70-85SFr per person. MC/V.)

Hot Chili Peppers ❶, left from the station past the tourist office, is centrally located and one of Wengen's main social highlights, offering beer (3.50SFr) and snacks (mostly sandwiches; 7-9.50SFr) as well as **Internet** access (5SFr per 15min), billiards, and darts. (☎ 855 50 20; chilis@wengen.com. Open daily 8:30am-2am.) 🗗**Ristorante da Sina ❹**, up the hill from Hot Chili Peppers, has intimate, candle-lit tables inside and a peaceful terrace outside. The menu, which includes an extensive wine selection (from 6SFr per glass), is quite pricey, but you get what you pay for. There are some more affordable options: a large pizza margherita is 15SFr.; with added goodies like asparagus, artichokes, and spinach, it's 19SFr. Take-out and smaller portions (11-19SFr) available. Steaks 36-49SFr. (Open daily 11:30am-2pm and 6-11:30pm. AmEx/DC/MC/V.) Next door is **da Sina's Pub,** which hosts a variety of discos, live music, and karaoke. (Beer 4SFr; 0.5L 6.50SFr. Happy Hour 9-10pm and midnight-1am has a 2 beers for 4.50SFr deal. Open 6pm-2:30am.) A **Co-op** supermarket sits quite visibly opposite the station. (Open M-F 8am-6:30pm, Sa 8am-4pm.)

OUTDOOR ACTIVITIES

Wengen's elevation above the valley floor puts it close to the treeline and provides spectacular views. For bike (35SFr per day; 25SFr per half day), hiking boot, and ski (38SFr) rentals, head to **Sports Inter** across from the tourist office. Open M-F 8am-noon, 2-6:30pm. Sa 8-noon, 2-6pm, Su 10am-noon, 3-5pm. The following 7hr. **hike** from Wengen traverses the ridge above the tree line which divides the two valleys of the Jungfrau Region. Several cable car stops along the way can shorten the journey.

HIKE TO MÄNNLICHEN AND KLEINE SCHEIDEGG. (7hr.) The hike begins with an ascent of **Männlichen.** Walk up the main street, away from the tourist office, and towards the end of town; follow signs upward to "Männlichen" (red-and-white marked trail). The trail wanders upwards through a meadowed lane kept neatly trimmed by grazing cows. As is true for the whole ascent of Männlichen, there are views of the glacier-laden side of the Jungfrau and the cliff-curtained

Lauterbrunnen valley. Toward the top, be sure to turn left when another unmarked trail merges in. The climb to the Männlichen saddle steeply zigzags upwards for about 3hr. The cable car from Grindelwald stops at the saddle, a 15min. stroll from the peak, a vertical promontory with a 360° view of the Bernese Oberland. Walk back down to the Männlichen cable car station and restaurant, then follow the signs to **Kleine Scheidegg.** This highly populated trail curves, without climbing, around the contour of the ridge, all the while looking down on the Grindelwald valley and up to the towering Eiger, Mönch, and Jungfrau. It is possible to take the train from Kleine Scheidegg down to Wengen (21SFr) or Grindelwald (28SFr), or hike back to Wengen on a trail alongside the tracks (2hr). For a quieter hiking option cross over the train tracks and follow the red-and-white trail. The trail passes the Mönch and Jungfrau as closely as is possible on foot, then swings toward Wengen (2½hr. downhill).

SKIING. Ski emergencies call (☎855 13 13 or 853 26 60). The **Swiss Ski School,** beside the Co-op, is the cheaper of the town's two schools. (☎/fax 855 20 22; www.wengen.com/sss. 48SFr for a 3hr. lesson; 5 lessons for 205SFr. Private lessons 325SFr for 5hr. Open from late Dec. to early Apr. Su-F 8:30am-1:30pm and 3:30-6:30pm, Sa 8:45-11am and 4:30-7pm.) As its name suggests, **Privat Ski and Snowboard School,** past the post office from the station 5 min. to the right, offers lessons to smaller groups. (☎/fax 855 50 05 or ☎448 71 24; www.wengen.com/privat. 1-2 people 65SFr per hour; 3-4 70SFr per hr. Office open daily 5-6:30pm.) Every January, Wengen hosts the skiing World Cup's longest and most dangerous downhill race, the **Lauberhorn.** Hotels generally won't allow tourists to book rooms until about a week in advance so that they can guarantee a room for all the racers and support crews. The downhill course starts 2315m above Kleine Scheidegg, curls around Wengernalp, and ends at Ziel (1287m) at the eastern end of the village, a drop of nearly 1200m in 2½min.

MÜRREN ☎033

The quiet, car-free streets of Mürren (pop. 430) are frequented mostly by tractors and tourists. This gem of a town is lined with hotels and guest houses that sprouted up when Mürren invented slalom skiing. Mürren's most popular attraction is the Schilthorn, which Hans Castorp scaled in *The Magic Mountain,* a novel by Thomas Mann, and which 007, the British secret agent James Bond, made famous with a ski scene in *The Spy Who Loved Me.* While Mürren's hikes and proximity to higher towns make it an attractive summer destination, Mürren is busiest during the winter months, when skiers and snowboarders gather on its famous slopes.

TRANSPORTATION AND PRACTICAL INFORMATION

Mürren can be reached by **cogwheel train** from **Lauterbrunnen** (every 30min. 6:25am-8:30pm, 9.80SFr), or by **cable car** from Gimmelwald (7.40SFr) or Stechelberg (15.60SFr). Alternatively, **hike** from Gimmelwald (40min. uphill). From the station, the road leading into town forks in two; nearly everything except the tourist office is on the lower, left fork. The cable car is at the opposite end of town from the train station. The **tourist office,** in the sports center 100m from the station, off the right fork, has information about private rooms, hiking trails and skiing prices. (☎856 86 86; fax 86 96. Open July-Aug. M-Su 8:30am-7pm, Th until 9pm; June M-F 9am-noon and 2-6:30pm.) There are lockers (2SFr) at the train and cable car stations. **Stäger Sport,** across from the tourist office, rents mountain **bikes** for 35SFr. (☎855 23 55. Open Dec.-Apr. and June-Oct. daily 9am-noon and 1:30-5pm.) For **police,** call ☎855 76 11; for **medical assistance,** ☎855 17 10. The Eiger Guest House provides **Internet** access (12SFr per hr.) all day, or try the **Feuz** souvenir shop down the main road near the Co-op. (10SFr per hr. Open daily 11am-6pm.) An **ATM** is available next to the Co-op, down the left fork. The **post office** is on the station side of the main street. (Open M-F 8:15-11:30am and 3:30-5pm, Sa 8:15-10:15am.) **Postal Code:** CH-3825.

ACCOMMODATIONS AND FOOD

Mürren's accommodations are quiet and comfortable in comparison to the alternatives down the hill in Gimmelwald (see p. 362), but they're also less fun. An enthusiastic British woman at the **Chalet Fontana ❸** offers traditional Swiss lodging in seven private rooms. (☎855 26 86 or 642 34 85. Breakfast included. Reservations recommended. Singles 40SFr; doubles 70-90SFr; triples 115SFr. 2-person apartment, including kitchen and breakfast 110SFr. 4-person apartment, same amenities, 185SFr. 2-night min. stay for apts.) The **Eiger Guesthouse ❸,** across the street from the train station, is pristine and comfortable. A small bar, projector room and pool table add to a relaxed atmosphere. (☎856 54 60; www.muerren.ch/eigerguesthouse. Breakfast included. Free access to pool and skating rink at Sports Zentrum. **Internet** access for 12SFr per hr. Reception M-F 8am-11:30pm, Sa-Su 8am-12:30am. Summer dorms 45-55SFr; doubles 100-120SFr, with shower 130-140SFr. 1-night stays 5SFr extra per person. Winter 5SFr surcharge per person per night. Children half-price. AmEx/DC/MC/V.) The **Alpina Hotel ❹,** down the left fork in the main road, also provides its guests with access to the sports center pool and skating rink. The hotel offers chalet-style rooms with fluffy comforters and stunning balconies; ask for a view of the Eiger, Monch and Jungfrau. (☎855 13 61; www.muerren.ch/alpina. Breakfast included. Singles 75-100SFr; doubles 130-170SFr. AmEx/DC/MC/V.)

Eating out in Mürren is pretty reasonable. Almost all of the town's restaurants are in hotels. *Raclette* and an unobstructed view of the snow-capped mountains are available for 14.50SFr at **Alpina Hotel ❸.** Try the house *Rösti* for 17SFr. (☎855 13 61. Wheelchair accessible. AmEx/DC/MC/V.) The **Eiger Guesthouse ❸** also offers specialties such as fondue (21SFr; min. 2 people) and burgers (10.50-17.50SFr) as well as beer (5.20SFr for 0.5L) in a bar environment. (AmEx/DC/MC/V.) **Tham Chinese Restaurant ❷,** down the left fork from the train station right before the Post, serves cheap pan-fried noodles and offers take-away dishes of chicken (21SFr) and duck (27.50SFr). Wonton noodles are 11.50SFr; vegetable fried rice is 12.50SFr. (☎856 01 10. Open daily June to late Oct. 11:30am-9:30pm; mid-Dec. to Apr. noon-11pm.)

Mürren's **Co-op,** which comes in handy for trips to nearby Gimmelwald, is 15min. down the right fork of the main walkway. (Open M-F 8am-noon and 1:45-6:30pm, Sa 8am-noon and 1:45-4pm.) For a more local feel, **Beck,** across from the Post down the left fork, sells the necessities of any good trip: chocolate, wine, and bread. (Open M-F 7:45-11:45am and 2-5:30pm, Sa 7:45-11am and 2-5pm, Su 8-10am and 3-5pm.)

HIKING

Mürren's location on the ledge above Lauterbrunnen makes it the ideal starting point for numerous higher-elevation hikes around the Lauterbrunnen Valley. From Mürren (1645m) the trails leading to Gimmelwald, Stechelberg, and the Trümmelbach Falls provide unparalleled views of the Eiger, Mönch, and Jungfrau. Ask at the tourist office for maps and suggestions.

Grütschalp (top of funicular from Lauterbrunnen) to Mürren (1-2hr.). A flat, 1hr. hike follows the train tracks to Mürren and is well-touristed on sunny days. A more isolated mountain route takes twice as long, but has better views and fewer people. Both trails start across the tracks from the station balcony. A yellow sign to Mürren marks the easier trail, while the red-white-red "Mürren Höhenweg" sign marks the mountainous hike. After an initially steep ascent, the trail wanders through buttercup meadows that stretch before the rising peaks of the Eiger, Mönch, and Jungfrau. When the trail splits, head to "Allmenhubel," then down to Mürren.

Shark's Fin via Stechelberg and Obersteinberg (1½-5hr.). This hike is a steep descent from the Mountain Hostel in Gimmelwald that gives continual views of the sheer rock slabs lining the Lauterbrunnen Valley. It's a grand approach to the **Trümmelbach Falls** (1½hr.), with a return possible by cable car. Alternatively, for a challenging approach to the finish, hikers may take a trail that forks right 5min. after the river crossing on the Stechelberg path. This route crosses the river, climbing steeply and without pause along the flank of the unsettled Lauterbrunnen valley head. After passing **Obersteinberg hut** (1½hr. more), the trail tops out at Tanzboden (1978m), where there is an inspiring panorama of the wall leading to the Jungfrau, and then gradually descends to **Hotel Obersteinberg** (1778m), before continuing to the **Oberhornsee** (2065m, 2hr.).

Schilthorn descent (3-4hr.). For fit and experienced hikers. Head downhill along the secured ridge to **Roter Herd.** At the signpost, backtrack on the left toward the Schilthorn, then take the steep descent to the Rotstock Hut on **Poganggenalp.** Continue to **Bryndli** where a steep narrow trail connects to **Spielbodenalp.** From there a mountain road descends gently to Mürren. An ascent is a longer, harder alternative for those wishing to bypass the expenses of the cable-car. For a different route, head via Allmenhubel to Schilthornhutte for lunch (*Rosti* with *Bratwurst* 13SFr) and a break before the final steep climb to the Schilthorn.

▓ OTHER OUTDOOR ACTIVITIES

UP THE SCHILTORN. The most popular journey this side of the Lauterbrunnen Valley is the short, albeit expensive, cable car trip to the *Schilthorn* (2970m) made famous by the exploits of 007 in *On Her Majesty's Secret Service.* (☎823 14 44; www.schilthorn.ch. From Mürren 38.60SFr, round-trip 63.80SFr; morning ticket 46.80SFr round-trip.) The **Piz Gloria Restaurant ❸** spins at its apex. Settle down for a meal (entrees around 20SFr) and take in the 360° panorama from the Schilthorn station's deck. Bear in mind that there is very little to do at the top when it's cloudy (there tends to be clearer weather earlier in the morning).

The ski school (☎/fax 855 12 47) has classes for downhill, slalom, and snowboarding. Six half-day group lessons run 140SFr. For ski pass information see the **Jungfrau Region** introduction, p. 352. The **Inferno Run** seeks volunteers every January (usually for 3 days from the 20th) for the Inferno downhill ski, which descends 2170m. The Inferno Triathlon is in August; the Mürren-Schilthorn stretch is last.

GIMMELWALD ☎033

Gimmelwald is a farming town of slightly over 100 people that was stopped in its tracks over 50 years ago when it was labeled an avalanche zone. While this warning has ensured that the pristine and rural environment of the town is preserved, it has not frightened away backpackers, who often outnumber the locals and inhabit the lower end of town. Gimmelwald feels secluded, but it is easily accessible by cable car and by foot. The lack of late-night hangouts has fostered a lively atmosphere at the hostel. In the winter, Gimmelwald's tourism industry slows to a crawl as the main road is turned into part of a ski trail.

Splitting to the left after the post office, the lower road in Mürren leads downhill (30min.) to Gimmelwald, as does the **cable car** (to the right of the fork; 7.80SFr, with Swisspass free, Eurail 25% off) from either Mürren or Stechelberg (just up the valley from Lauterbrunnen). Gimmelwald has **no supermarket**, so stock up in Mürren. Fresh-baked bread (2.50-4.50SFr), fresh milk, and yogurt (both 1.20SFr) are available at Esther's Bed and Breakfast and the Mountain Hostel (see below). Some farm stands offer meat and dairy products.

All the beds in Gimmelwald lie along the small trail that rises from the cable car station. At the bottom of the trail, the social **Mountain Hostel ❷** is run by a laid-back couple, Petra and Walter, who offer a communal kitchen and access to life's essentials—fresh bread (3SFr), milk (2SFr), chocolate (2SFr), **Internet** (12SFr per hr.), billiards, and guitars. The hostel bar is also the local hangout, so every night sees a lively mix of travelers and villagers alike relaxing at the bar (beer 3.50SFr; hot chocolate 2.50SFr, with peppermint liquor 3.50SFr), by the pool table, or on the benches outside (☎855 17 04; mountainhostel@tcnet.ch. Showers 1SFr. Reception 8:30-11am and 6-10:30pm. Lockout 9:30-11am. Dorms 20SFr.) At **Hotel Mittaghorn (Walter's B & B) ❷**, at the trail's summit, host Walter makes Glühwein (mulled wine) and Heidi cocoa (with peppermint schnapps). He also cooks a three-course dinner for guests (15SFr; order in advance). The century-old hotel offers clean and unique rooms complete with spectacular views. (☎855 16 58. Showers 1SFr for 5min. Open Apr.-Nov. Old, wooden beds in the attic 25SFr; doubles 70-80SFr; triples 100SFr; quads 125SFr. Add 6SFr for a 1-night stay.) At **Esther's Guesthouse ❷**, a short walk up the street from the cable car station, travelers can sleep in the hay in a barn or in a guest house with more comfortable rooms. (☎855 54 88. Kitchen access included only for those in the guest house. Breakfast 12SFr. Place in the hay 20SFr. No reservations or check-in required. Staff will collect money in the evening. Singles 40SFr; doubles 80-95SFr; triples 100SFr; quads 160SFr.) The **Gimmelwald Guest House ❸**, directly across from the post office, provides the only conventional restaurant, serving *Bratwurst* with *Rösti* for 16.50SFr and other tasty country victuals. (Breakfast 12:30-2:30pm. Dinner served after 6:30pm; reserve early.)

WESTERN BERNESE OBERLAND

KANDERSTEG ☎033

Kandersteg sits at the head of the Kander valley, which extends north to Spiez, and against the imposing peaks of the Doldenhorn (3643m) to the southeast and the Bonderspitz (2546m) to the west. It is the northern terminus of the Lotschberg tunnel, the only connection between the Valais and Bern that doesn't make a large detour to the east or west. Visitors to Kandersteg are greeted with isolated farmhouses and fields rather than big tourist hotels. Devoid of crowds of English-speaking backpackers, Kandersteg retains a more authentically Swiss flair than its rivals in the Jungfrau. Short day hikes lead to isolated glacial lakes, mountain passes with views of the Bernese Alps, and some of Europe's largest glaciers.

◼◪ TRANSPORTATION AND PRACTICAL INFORMATION

Trains connect Kandersteg north to Spiez (30min., every hr. 5:23am-10:39pm, 16.20SFr) and then Interlaken Ost (1hr., 22SFr), or south to Brig (35min., every hr. 6:46am-12:38am, 18.80SFr). To reach the center of town, follow the road perpendicular to and right of the train station 75m until the road crosses a small river and meets the main road at the center of the village. The **tourist office,** left along the main road, offers **Internet access** (10SFr per hr.) and **hiking information.** (☎675 80 80; www.kandersteg.ch. Open July-Sept. and Jan.-Mar. M-F 8am-noon and 1:30-6pm, Sa 8:30am-noon and 1:30-4:30pm; Oct.-Dec. and Apr.-June M-F 8am-noon and 2-5pm.) The **Kandersteg Wanderkarte** (topographical hiking map; 16.80SFr), an invaluable resource for any hike, is sold at the tourist office and at most stores. The tourist office also offers an online description of several hikes and a free **Kandersteg Panorama** map. Other services include: **currency exchange, lockers** (4-5SFr), **luggage storage** (5SFr), and **bike rentals** (30SFr per day, 23SFr per half-day) at one counter of the train station (open daily 7:10am-7:30pm); **taxis** (☎671 23 77 or 07 93 33 39 33); **medical assistance** (☎675 14 24); **helicopter rescue** (☎14 14); and **weather report** (☎162). A **post office** is next to the Co-op. (Open M-F 8-11:30am and 2:30-6pm, Sa 8-11am.) **Postal Code:** CH-3718.

■ ACCOMMODATIONS

Kandersteg International Scout Center (☎675 82 82; reception@kandersteg.sout.org). Bus from the train station (5min., every hr. 7:20am-6:40pm, 2SFr) to "Pfadfinderzentrum," or head right on the main road until it goes under the railroad tracks. The Center is on the right (20min.). The cheerful, multilingual volunteer staff prepares beds in the institutional chalet and some of the campsite. The area can often be overrun with groups of scouts, and the train runs audibly nearby, but other amenities compensate. The Center has extensive summer-camp-reminiscent facilities, and organizes a comprehensive array of outdoor activities, including **mountain biking** (35SFr per person), **canyoning** (86-110SFr), **rock climbing** (8SFr per person, with a group lesson 23-25SFr), and **river rafting** (46-69SFr), and offers discounts on train rides and nearby tourist attractions. Breakfast 6SFr, lunch 11SFr, dinner 13SFr; order in advance. Kitchen included. Bread, milk, camping supplies, and other staples available at the reception. Finnish sauna 9SFr. Sheets 3SFr. Laundry 6SFr. **Internet** access 10SFr per hr. Reception M-Sa 8:15-11:45am and 2-5:30pm, Su 9:15-11:45am and 2-5:30pm. Longer hours in summer. Call if arriving mid-day. Guests who stay for more than 1 night may be required to clean the facilities. Call at least 1 wk. in advance for reservations. Bed in the chalet 21SFr, 16SFr for scouts; campsite 10.50SFr/8.50SFr. ❷

Hotel Garni Alpenblick (☎675 11 29; www.aplenblick.be), left on the main road; 10min. from the station. Clean rooms come with balconies and comforters. Small TV room. Buffet breakfast included. Free pick-up from train station. Reception 8am-midnight. Check-out noon. Reservations recommended. Rooms 50-55SFr per person, with shower 55-65SFr. AmEx/DC/MC/V. ❸

■ FOOD

Most restaurants in Kandersteg are in hotels. Don't be shy, but consider removing your hiking boots before dining. ■**Café Schweizerhof** ❸, on the riverfront at the intersection of the main road and the street leading to the train station, is a gastronomic gem. The wooden-shingled pagoda on the edge of a manicured garden with views of the nearby mountains is an ideal place to enjoy a variety of meals. Pastas run 12.50-17.50SFr, salads 7-18SFr, and traditional *Käseschnitte* 13-17.50SFr. Follow any meal with a crêpe (7-15.50SFr) or one of the delectable ice cream options for 8-9.50SFr. (☎675 22 00. Wheelchair accessible. Open daily 9am-7pm, until 10pm in good weather. MC.) The **Hotel Victoria Ritter** ❸, at the intersection of the main road and the street leading to the station, serves elaborate Swiss specialties (18-33SFr) as well as different "Fitness" *Menüs* (23-28SFr) in a classy dining room. Try the *Bärner Gnusch*, a hearty one-pot mix of meats and vegetables (27SFr), or order from a variety of sandwiches for 8-17.50SFr. (Wheelchair accessible. Open June to late Oct. and mid-Dec. to Apr. daily 9am-midnight; kitchen closes 10:30pm. AmEx/DC/MC/V.)

Pizzeria Antico ❷, to the right on the main street, about 5min. past Hotel zur Post, offers varieties of pizza (11.50-20SFr) and numerous pastas (11-18SFr). A terrace with climbing vines and roses offers a peaceful and beautiful dining venue. (☎675 13 13. Wheelchair accessible. Open noon-2pm and 6-9pm.) A **Co-op** is between the station and town. (Open M-F 8am-noon and 2-6:30pm, Sa 8am-noon and 2-5pm.)

⬛ HIKING

Around Kandersteg, you'll pant up the mountain, then lose your breath again when you catch the views that await hikers. Some of the longest glaciers in Europe, most notably the **Kanderfirm,** are east of town, while the **Öschinensee** is surrounded by steep cliffs that rise to jagged peaks. The **Bergsteigschule,** a climbing school, also offers guided trips into the mountains. (☎675 80 89; www.bs-k.ch.)

Öschinensee (20-90min.). The most easily accessible trails in Kandersteg cover the area around the spectacular Öschinensee. The **Öschinenseebahn** departs from near the tourist office and runs to trailheads. Open daily mid-June to Aug. 7:30am-6:30pm; early to mid-Sept. 7:30am-5pm; early May to mid-June and mid-Sept. to mid-Oct. 8:45am-5pm. 12.60SFr, round-trip 17.10SFr; children 6.30SFr/8.60SFr. From the top, a 20min. trail rolls to the edge of the blue lake bordered on all sides by sheer rock walls. The low ropes that the trail crosses separates the Öschinensee from civilization. The **Öschinensee hut ❷** (www.oeschinensee.ch) is a perfect base for exploring the lake's shore. Its army camp beds adjoin a living room and TV room. Breakfast included. Open daily mid-June to Aug. 7:30am-6:30pm; early to mid-Sept. 7:30am-5pm; early May to mid-June and mid-Sept. to mid-Oct. 8:45am-5pm. Dorms 35-40SFr; doubles 120-160SFr. A small dock with paddleboats and rowboats allows excursions on the lake. Open May-Oct. and Jan.-Apr. Paddleboats 22SFr per hr., rowboats 16SFr per hr.

Blümlisalp Glacier from the Öschinensee (3-4hr.). A steep, rocky trail (3hr.)—to be attempted only with hefty boots—shoots upwards from the cabin to **Fründenhorn hut ❷.** (☎675 14 33. Open June-Oct. 25SFr per night, children 16SFr.) A longer, more gradual trail probes the glacial region between the Kandersteg Valley and the Jungfrau Region. A trail (4hr.) connects the Öschinensee to the **Blümlisalp hut ❷,** a stone fortress-like structure nestled beneath the Blümlisalp glacier. (Open late June to mid-Oct. 27SFr, children 15SFr.)

GSTAAD AND SAANEN ☎033

At the juncture of four Alpine valleys, Gstaad and its earthier sister, Saanen (combined pop. 6500), are at the heart of Swiss skiing country. Only a few kilometers apart, these two towns share little aside from their similar dark wood structures and chalet roofs. Saanen inhabits the mountainous scenery with contented ease, while Gstaad trades goats for Gucci—its five-star hotels and fur-draped tourists make it a glamorous gem surrounded by placid farmland.

▐▀ TRANSPORTATION

Gstaad is accessible by **train** from Interlaken via Spiez (2hr., every hr. 7:22am-8:40pm, 30SFr) or Montreux (1½hr., every hr. 6:30am-9:30pm, 22SFr). Saanen can be reached from Gstaad by train (5min., almost every hr., 2.60SFr), **Post Bus** (10min.; almost every hr. M-Sa 6:35am-7:33pm, Su 7:50am-7:33pm; 3SFr) or a 40min. walk along the Yehudi Menuhin Philosophy Path (signs to Saanen lead the way from the station). **Buses** also run to Les Diablerets (50min.; every hr. 8:33am-1:33pm, summer and winter high-season also 3:50pm; 12.40SFr, half-price with SwissPass).

✈ 𝕚 ORIENTATION AND PRACTICAL INFORMATION

Turn right from the train station and take the main road just past the railway bridge to reach Gstaad's **tourist office** and pick up a useful area map. (☎ 748 81 81, room reservations and package deals 748 81 84; www.gstaad.ch. Open mid-June to late Aug. and mid-Dec. to mid-Mar. M-F 8:30am-6:30pm, Sa 9am-5pm, Su 9am-noon and 1:30-5pm; late Mar. to early June and early Sept. to early Dec. 8:30am-noon and 1:30-6pm, Sa 10am-noon and 1:30-5pm.) Saanen's **tourist office,** labeled *Vehrkehrsbüro*, is on the main street. From the station go straight ahead, then right on the main road 70m. (☎ 748 81 60; saanen@gstaad.ch. Open early Mar. to June and mid-Sept. to mid-Dec. M-F 8:30am-noon and 2-5pm; July to mid-Sept. and mid-Dec. to early Mar. also Sa 9am-noon and 2-5pm.) Gstaad train station services include: **currency exchange; Western Union** (open daily 7am-10:30pm); **ticket counter** (open M-F 5am-9pm, Sa-Su 6am-9pm); **lockers** (3-5SFr); **luggage storage** (M-F 5am-9:30pm, Sa-Su 6am-9:30pm; 3SFr); **bike rental** (30SFr per day, 23SFr per half-day; open daily 8am-noon and 1:30-6pm). Both the Gstaad and Saanen stations have **ski storage** (1SFr deposit). Next door to the Saanen post office, the Saanen Bank **exchanges currency** and cashes traveler's checks; it also has an **ATM.** (Wheelchair accessible. Open M-F 8am-noon and 1:45-5:30pm, Sa 8-11am.) For taxis in Gstaad call ☎ 744 80 80; in both Gstaad and Saanen, ☎ 744 33 33. **Internet access** is available at Public Web (inside Hotel Christiania), across from the Co-op (☎ 744 29 65; 12SFr per hr.; open Tu-Sa 10am-1:30pm and 3-8pm, Su 3-8pm) and Café Pernet, in front of Richi's Pub in Gstaad. (5SFr per 20min. Open 8am-11pm.) Saanen has a **pharmacy,** the Jaggi Drogerie, down the street from the tourist office, on the corner. (☎ 744 13 21. Open M-F 8am-noon and 1:30-6:30pm, Sa 8am-noon and 1:30-4pm.) To get to the **pharmacy** in Gstaad, turn right out of the station and head under the railroad bridge. (☎ 748 86 26. Open M-F 8am-12:15pm and 1:30-6:30pm, Sa 8am-5pm. AmEx/MC/V.) For **medical emergencies,** call ☎ 744 86 86. Gstaad's **post office** has a **24hr. ATM** and Swisscom **payphones.** (Open M-F 8am-noon and 2-6pm, Sa 8:30-11am.) Saanen's **post office,** 50m straight ahead of its station on the left, has a **wheelchair-accessible pay phone.** (Open M-F 8-11:30am and 2-5:30pm, Sa 8-11am.) **Postal Code:** Gstaad: CH-3780; Saanen: CH-3792.

𝕟 ACCOMMODATIONS AND CAMPING

Gstaad proper has few hotels for the budget-conscious, but the tourist office publishes a list of all the hotels and the cheaper *Privatzimmer*, which are further from town. If you're looking to stay closer, a few hotels on the outskirts of town offer reasonable rates. From the tourist office, head right down the Promenade and in the direction of Gsteig. At the intersection next to the river, turn left. About a 10min. walk from Gstaad's center are two comparable hotels. **Sport-Hotel Rütti ❹** is farther down the road on the right and offers bright, spacious rooms right above a pizzeria. (☎ 744 29 21; www.hotelruetti.ch. Prices depend on season. Singles 100-338SFr; doubles 110-143SFr. AmEx/DC/MC/V.) Across the street, the **Hotel Alphorn ❹** provides rooms with TV, minibar, and a family-friendly atmosphere. (☎ 748 45 45; www.gstaad-alphorn.ch. **Internet** 1SFr per 5min. Breakfast included. Reception 7am-midnight. Check-in 2pm. Check-out 11am. Rates vary seasonally, with lowest prices Apr.-May and Oct. to mid-Dec. Singles 88-112SFr; doubles 172-272SFr. AmEx/DC/MC/V.) In the center of town just before the tourist office when walking from the station lies Gstaad's oldest hotel, **Posthotel Rössli ❹.** Here, the Widmer-Spötig family welcomes visitors by providing them with a wealth of advice about Gstaad. Special packages (week-long guided hikes

1261SFr and local music 1010SFr) are favorites. (☎748 42 42. Rates vary seasonally. Singles 110-160SFr; doubles 95-145SFr. AmEx/MC/V.) The cheapest and most picturesque option in Saanen is the **Jugendherberge** (HI) ❷. From Saanen's station, go straight about 100m, turn right on the main street and walk 10min. until it dead-ends near the gas station. Cross over the busy road and follow hostel signs up the hill straight ahead, past the hospital and toward Hotel Spitzhorn. After 5min. uphill, the hostel will be on your left. Rustic rooms upstairs contrast oddly with the brightly-colored kitchen, but the hostel offers **bike rental** (15SFr per day, 10SFr per half-day), TV and game room, and a decent library. (☎744 13 43; www.youthhostel.ch/saanen. Breakfast and sheets included. Dinner 12.50SFr, lunch 9SFr. Laundry 11SFr. Reception 8-10am and 5-9pm; summer 4-10pm. 24hr. access code. Check-out 8-10am. Reservations recommended year-round. Closed in Nov. Dorms 31SFr (ask for a balcony); doubles 74SFr; triples 108SFr. Quads available. Prices do not include tax. Non-HI members 6SFr extra. Children ages 2-6 half-price, under age 2 free. AmEx/DC/MC/V.)

Camping Bellerive ❶ lies off the road between Gstaad and Saanen, a 5min. walk from both. From the Saanen train station, walk past the tourist office to the intersection and follow the camping sign. The site sits in a valley near the river, with mountain views. (☎744 63 30; bellerive.camping@bluewin.ch. May-Oct. 6.40SFr per adult, 3.20SFr per child, 5.30SFr per tent; Nov.-Apr. 7.50SFr/3.20SFr/5.30SFr. Tax 2.50SFr per person, 1.20SFr per child. 20% reduction May to mid-June and Oct. to mid-Dec. Electricity 2.70SFr.) The **Beim Kappeli** ❶, the Saanen campsite, is near the river on the edge of town toward Gstaad. Cross the tracks behind the station and head left along the river for a packed but friendly campsite next to the rushing water. (☎744 61 91; fax 61 84. Office open 6-7pm. 5.20SFr per person, 8SFr per tent, 15SFr per car. MC/V.)

🍴 FOOD

To get to **Richi's Pub** ❷, turn right from the Gstaad station and walk 5min. down the central promenade. Chow down on a burger and a beer (14-18SFr) or soup and salad (14SFr) in a no-frills environment. Vegetarian options are slim: try the pasta (14.50-15.50SFr). Steak comes in three cuts: ladies', men's, or the Sitting Bull (36-54SFr). (☎744 57 87; fax 99 87. 18+. Open daily noon-1:30am.) Meanwhile, the front of the building houses **Café Pernet** ❷, which shares the same menu as Richi's but allows guests of all ages; **Internet access** available for 5SFr per 20min. (Open 8am-11pm.) **Apple-Pie** ❸, at the intersection past the tourist office on the left, serves tasty pizzas (15-21SFr) large enough for two and crêpes (10.40SFr) amidst cowbells and carved wood. (☎744 46 48; apple-pie@gstaad.ch. Ground- level seating is wheelchair accessible. Open daily 8:30am-11pm; kitchen open noon-10pm. No credit cards.)

In Saanen, try Swiss specialties like cheese fondue (23SFr per person) or sautéed veal with *Rösti* (16-20SFr) at the **Saanerhof Restaurant** ❸, across from the train station. (☎744 15 15; www.saanerhof.ch. Open M-F 7:30am-11:30pm, Sa-Su 7:30am-12:30am.) For a more elaborate meal with a spectacular view of the foothills surrounding town, head to **Restaurant Sonnenhof** ❸, 30min. from the station, and follow signs up the hill past the church. The French-influenced menu includes veal with mushroom sauce and roasted duck (both 39SFr). For dessert, try the *crème brulée*. (☎744 10 20. Hours vary based on season; call ahead.)

The **Co-op**, straight ahead from the Gstaad station and left on the main road, sells groceries and cafeteria meals (100g of salad 2.40SFr; chicken nuggets, fries, and a drink 6.50SFr) in a pleasant atmosphere. (Wheelchair accessible. Open M-Th 8am-6:30pm, F 8am-8pm, Sa 8am-5pm. Cafeteria also open Su 9am-5pm. MC/V.)

⚠ OUTDOOR ACTIVITIES

ADVENTURE SPORTS. Three main adventure companies, **Alpinzentrum** (☎748 41 61; www.alpinzentrum.ch) in Gstaad, and **Swissraft** (☎744 50 80; www.swissraft.ch) and **Absolut Activ** (☎748 14 14; www.abslout-activ.ch) in Saanen, arrange adventure activities in the area in both summer and winter. All three companies, in addition to **H₂O Experience** (☎026 928 19 35) in Gstaad, lead **rafting** trips. (Alpinzentrum: 108SFr for 4hr., children ages 8-12 78SFr. H₂O Experience: 90SFr for 3hr., ages 10-15 70SFr. Swissraft: 105SFr for 3hr.; English-speaking guides. Absolut Activ: 98SFr for 4hr.) Absolut Activ also offers **skydiving** (390SFr), **paragliding** (140SFr), and **glacier outings** (388SFr); Swissraft offers **ballooning** (370-580SFr); and both have **canyoning** and **mountain biking** trips (60-370SFr). Alpinzentrum also offers **climbing**, **glacier tours**, and **jeep safari** (98-150SFr); there's even an organized team event where participants compete in traditional Swiss games (call ahead). Hans Büker's **Ballonhafen Gstaad** has been launching balloon excursions for over 25 years. (☎026 924 54 85; www.gstaadballon.ch. 485SFr, children half-price.) **Paragliding Gstaad** can also send you into the stratosphere. (☎079 224 42 70; www.paragstaad.com. Tandem flight 190SFr; helicopter jump 590SFr.)

The tourist office publishes a guide of **mountain bike** trails and sells various maps of the area (basic map free, others 8-15SFr). **Mountain bikes** can be rented in Gstaad at **Stauffer Radsport**. (☎744 42 61. 15SFr per hr., 38SFr per day.) Go past the tourist office to the intersection at the river and head right on Geschwendstr. (10min.) In Saanen, the family-operated **Reuteler Velos and Mofas** is just left on the main road and has about the same prices. (☎1744 51 33; fax 89 62. Open M-F 8am-noon and 1:30-6:30pm, Sa 8am-noon and 1:30-5pm. AmEx/MC/V.) **Horse-trekking** (☎744 24 60; 30min. lesson 40SFr) or riding in a **horse-drawn cart** (☎765 30 34; 1hr. ride 25SFr per person) are novel options. Ask about the *Easy Access* card at overnight accommodations or the tourist office. A two-night stay in the area makes you eligible for a cheap three-day pass to gondolas, admittance to pools, and discounts on guided adventures. It also gives free rides on the region's trains, some mountain railways, and Postauto buses; as well as a 40% discount on the gondola to Glacier 3000, the highest point in the area, and a 25% reduction for the first-class train to Montreux. (3-day pass 28.50SFr, children 15SFr; each additional day 9.50SFr.)

HIKING. The tourist offices have free hiking maps and descriptions of local hikes. A challenging panoramic hike up the Giferspitz horseshoe will take your breath away. From Gstaad station, turn right on the main road, left on the main road just before the river, and take the second big road on the right over the river (signs to "Bissen;" the turn is 1km from Gstaad). Follow the yellow *Wanderweg* signs for "Wasserngrat" up the hill to the top cable car station (1936m). The more fit and adventurous might continue to the Laünehorn (2477m) and, after a rocky scramble, farther to the Giferspitz (2541m), Gstaad's tallest peak. The path circles down to Bissen, but a bus can ease the descent. (1800m ascent. In perfect weather only. Allow 1 day.) A shorter, more accessible hike starts with a cable car ascent to Wispile and continues with a 2-3hr. one-way hike to Laünensee (a lake) and a waterfall nature reserve. (Information: ☎748 82 32. Cable car open May-Oct. One-way 20SFr, children 12SFr.)

SKIING. In winter, Gstaad offers 250km of ski runs and 69 lifts. Experts will not be challenged, but intermediate skiers will find the runs ideal. Of the area's six sectors, #4 is the highest and contains the Tsanfleuron Glacier ("Glacier 3000"). For general information and weather conditions, visit www.skigstaad.ch. The largest sector and the one most commonly used by skiers of moderate skill is #1. For information on opening times of the various lifts, runs, and mountains in the area, contact the Ski Gstaad Bergbahnenbüro (☎748 82 82; www.skigstaad.ch). The **Top Card ski pass** costs 27-52SFr per day for one sector. A two-day pass for 101SFr covers all sectors. A week of skiing costs between 151SFr and 296SFr, depending on age. **Season ski passes** (790SFr) from the Gstaad region allow skiing in Oberengadin/St. Moritz, Kitzbühel/Tirol, Adelboden-Lenk, Alpes Vaudoises, Ordino-Arcalis, and Pal Arinsal (Andorra). The tourist office prints a contact information sheet and compares prices for all the **winter ski equipment rental** outlets in the area. **Ski and snowboard schools** include Alpinzentrum and Absolut-Activ (see Adventure Sports) in Gstaad, as well as Snowsports Saanenland in Saanen (☎744 36 65; www.snow-sports.ch). The Gstaad Snowsports company specializes in classes for children. (☎744 18 65; www.gstaadsnowsports.ch. Office open M-Sa 8am-noon and 2-6pm.) Consult the tourist office for details on **heliskiing, curling, and skating.** Three snowboarding parks and a glacier offer year-round skiing. Summer runs are open June to early August daily 8:30am-2pm. Local boarders report that even in summer, the runs are of fairly good quality—go in the morning for the best snow. **Summer ski rental** is at the top of the glacier. (☎024 492 33 77; www.glacier3000.ch. 20SFr snowsuit, 53SFr skis and boots. Shop open daily 8:30am-4pm.)

SPECIAL EVENTS. The **FIVB Beach Volleyball World Tour** rolls through town at the end of June. (☎744 06 40; www.beachworldtour.ch. Free.) The **Allianz Suisse Open Gstaad tennis tournament** brings professional clay court action to Gstaad's city center. (☎748 83 83, for tickets 0900 61 62 63; hotline costs 1.49SFr per min. Early July. Tickets 40-100SFr.) For a touch of high culture, the Gstaad Polo Club hosts the **Cartier Polo Silver Cup** tournament in mid-August (☎744 07 41; www.pologstaad.ch). **Country Night Gstaad,** an orgy of country music in late September, brings in well-known artists like LeeAnn Womack, Mark Chesnutt, and Joe Diffie. (☎744 88 22; www.countrynight-gstaad.ch. Tickets 55-125SFr.) The **Menuhin Festival Gstaad** is a late-summer musical celebration created by Gstaad resident and violinist Yehudi Menuhin. (☎748 83 33; www.menuhinfestivalg-staad.com. Usually mid-July early Sept.)

CENTRAL
SWITZERLAND

Central Switzerland boasts exciting nightlife as well as beautiful hikes through tiny mountain settlements. While the mountains here aren't quite as spectacular as those in the Engadine and elsewhere, they nonetheless offer breathtaking views of their own. A cosmopolitan area, central Switzerland is considerably more popu-

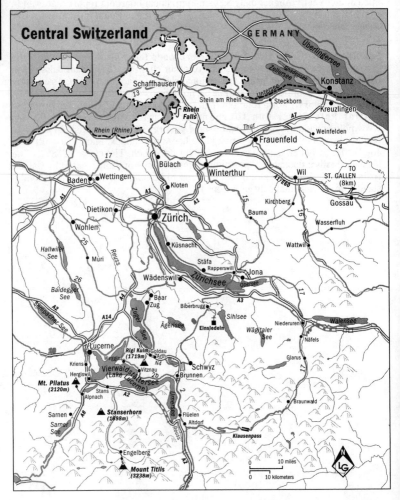

lous than the mountainous cantons to the south. The greater population density and diversity brings a greater mass of cultural artifacts, as evidenced by innovative museums, enchanting castles, and medieval *Altstädte* in Zurich, Lucerne, and other towns along the shores of the region's lakes.

HIGHLIGHTS OF CENTRAL SWITZERLAND

Shock your artistic sense at Zurich's unconventional **Kunsthaus** (p. 382).

Bathe in multicolored light from the incredible stained-glass windows in Zurich's cathedrals, the **Fraumünster** and the **Großmünster** (p. 380).

Cruise the **Vierwaldstättersee** from Lucerne to Alpnachstad, where you can ascend the world's steepest cog railway to blue-shadowed **Mt. Pilatus** (p. 397).

ZURICH (ZÜRICH) ☎ 01

Battalions of briefcase-toting, Armani-suited executives charge daily through the world's largest gold exchange and fourth-largest stock exchange, pumping enough money into the economy to keep Zurich's upper-crust boutiques and posh restaurants thriving. But there is more to Zurich than money; the city was once the focal point of the Reformation in German Switzerland, led by the anti-Catholic firebrand Ulrich Zwingli. The 20th century brought an avant-garde artistic and philosophical radicalism that overwhelmed Zurich's Protestant traditionalism and attracted diverse and progressive thinkers. While James Joyce toiled away at *Ulysses* in one corner of the city, Russian exile Vladimir Lenin read Marx and dreamt of revolution in another. Meanwhile, a group of raucous young artists calling themselves the Dadaists founded a proto-performance art collective, the Cabaret Voltaire, promoting art that challenged traditional aesthetic norms. A walk through Zurich's *Altstadt* and student quarter will immerse you in the energetic youth counterculture that spawned subversive thinkers, only footsteps away from the rabid capitalism of the famous Bahnhofstr. shopping district. Zurich comes alive at night, when travelers and locals alike fill the bars and nightclubs of this hopping city.

⊠ INTERCITY TRANSPORTATION

Because PTT buses cannot go into Zurich proper, the easiest way into the city is by plane, train, or car.

Flights: Kloten Airport (☎816 25 00) is a major stop for **Swiss International Airlines** (☎084 885 20 00), which resulted from the merger between Swissair and Crossair. Daily connections to **Frankfurt, Paris, London,** and **New York.** Trains connect the airport to the Hauptbahnhof in the city center (every 10-20min.; 5:02am-12:15am; 5.40SFr, Eurail and SwissPass valid), where trains arrive from all over Europe.

Trains: Bahnhofpl. To: **Basel** (1hr., 1-2 per hr. 3:30am-2am, 30SFr); **Bern** (1¼hr., 1-2 per hr. 3:30am-2am, 45SFr); **Geneva** via **Bern** (3hr., every hr. 5:26am-10:04pm, 76SFr); **Lucerne** (1hr., 2 per hr. 5:35am-12:07am, 19.80SFr); **Lugano** (3hr., 1-3 per hr. 6:30am-10:07pm, 60SFr); **Milan** (4hr., every hr. 6:30am-10:07pm, 72SFr); **Munich** (5hr., every hr. 6:05am-10:33pm, 86SFr); **Paris** (5hr., every hr. 6:30am-midnight, 133SFr); **Salzburg** (5hr., every hr. 6:11am-7:10pm, 97SFr); **Vienna** (9hr., every hr. 6:07am-6:18pm, 124SFr); and **Winterthur** (25min., every 15min. 5:02am-12:15am, 10.60SFr). Under age 26 discount on international trains.

Ferries: Boats on the **Zürichsee** leave from Bürklipl. and range from a 1½hr. cruise between isolated villages (every 30min. 11am-7pm; 5.40SFr, children 2.90SFr) to a "grand tour" (4-5hr.; every hr. 9:30am-5:30pm; 20SFr, children 10SFr). Ferries also leave from the top of

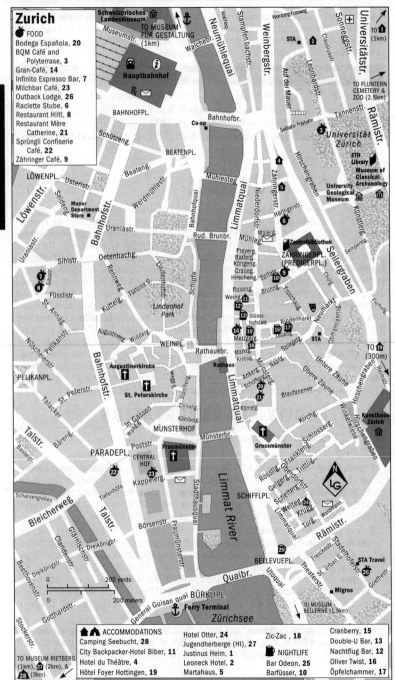

Zurich

🍎 FOOD

Bodega Española, **20**
BQM Café and Polyterrasse, **3**
Gran-Café, **14**
Infinito Espresso Bar, **7**
Milchbar Café, **23**
Outback Lodge, **26**
Raclette Stube, **6**
Restaurant Hiltl, **8**
Restaurant Mère Catherine, **21**
Sprüngli Confiserie Café, **22**
Zähringer Café, **9**

🏠🏕 ACCOMMODATIONS

Camping Seebucht, **28**
City Backpacker-Hotel Biber, **11**
Hotel du Théâtre, **4**
Hôtel Foyer Hottingen, **19**
Hotel Otter, **24**
Jugendherberge (HI), **27**
Justinus Heim, **1**
Leoneck Hotel, **2**
Martahaus, **5**

Zic-Zac, **18**

🍺 NIGHTLIFE

Bar Odeon, **25**
Barfüsser, **10**

Cranberry, **15**
Double-U Bar, **13**
Nachtflug Bar, **12**
Oliver Twist, **16**
Öpfelchammer, **17**

the Bahnhofstr. harbor (every 30min. 10:05am-9:05pm, 3.60SFr) for a cruise of the Limmat River. The Zürichsee authorities (☎01 487 13 33) offer themed tours—there's even a chance for an "Oldies Night" on the Zürichsee with 50s, 60s, and 70s hits (July-Aug. F 7:30pm, 22SFr) or a ride on the "Salsa-Cruise" (June-Aug. Sa 8pm, 27SFr, dance lesson begins at 7:40pm). In late Oct., the "Cheese Fondue Dreamboat" sets sail. (Tu and W 7:30pm, call for prices.) Eurail and *Tageskarten* valid on all boats.

By Car: A1 connects **Bern, Austria,** and southern Switzerland to **Zurich.** From **Basel,** A2 connects to Zurich. From **Geneva,** take A1 to Lausanne, A9 to Vevey, and A12 to Zurich.

■: ORIENTATION

Zurich sits in the middle of north central Switzerland, close to the German border, on some of the lowest land in the whole country. The **Limmat River** splits the city down the middle on its way to the **Zürichsee.** On the west side of the river are the **Hauptbahnhof** and **Bahnhofstraße.** Bahnhofstr. begins outside the Hauptbahnhof and runs parallel to the Limmat River to the head of the Zürichsee. This street forms the center of consumerism, lined with every type of store from H&M to Swarovski. Two-thirds of the way down Bahnhofstr. lies **Paradeplatz,** the town center, under which Zurich's banks reputedly keep their gold reserves. **Bürkliplatz** is at the Zürichsee end of Bahnhofstr., and grassy quais surrounding the lake provide a great spot for sunbathing and afternoon strolls. On the east side of the river lies the University district. Stretching above the narrow **Niederdorfstraße,** it pulses with bars, hip restaurants, and hostels. Stately bridges, offering elegant views of the stately old buildings that line the river, bind the two sectors together.

■ LOCAL TRANSPORTATION

Public Transportation: Trams criss-cross the city, originating at the Hauptbahnhof. Tickets for rides longer than 5 stops cost 3.60SFr and are valid for 1hr. (press the blue button on automatic ticket machines); rides shorter than 5 stops cost 2.10SFr (yellow button). Be aware that the city is small enough that rides of more than 5 stops are unlikely. Purchase a ticket before boarding and validate it by inserting it into the ticket machine. Policemen will fine you (60SFr) if you travel as a *Schwarzfahrer* (Black Rider) and ride for free. If you plan to ride several times, buy a 24hr. **Tageskarte** (7.20SFr), valid on trams, buses, and ferries. *Tageskarten* are available at the tourist office, a few hotels and hostels, the automatic ticket machines, or the **Ticketeria** under the train station in Shop-Ville. (Follow the signs near the train station's escalators. Open M-Sa 6:30am-7pm, Su 7:30am-7pm.) The Ticketeria also offers 6-day cards (36SFr, under age 25 27SFr). All public **buses, trams,** and **trolleys** run 5:30am-midnight. **Night buses** run from the city center to outlying areas (F-Su 1-4am). **Night trains** have recently started running. Pick up a copy of *Nachtnetz* from the tourist office for specific timetables.

Taxis: ☎777 77 77, 444 44 44, or 222 22 22. **TIXI (Transportation Service for the Disabled),** Mühlezelgstr. 15 (☎493 11 44; www.tixi.ch), requires reservations. Services include taxis as well as information on trains, trams, and other forms of transport outfitted for the disabled.

Car Rental: The tourist office maintains a special 20% discount and free upgrade deal with **Europcar** (☎271 56 56; www.europcar.ch). Prices start at 149SFr per day for 1-2 days with unlimited mileage. 20+. **Branches** at the airport (☎813 20 44; fax 813 49 00); Josefstr. 53 (☎271 56 56); Lindenstr. 33 (☎383 17 47). Try to rent in the city, as renting at the airport comes with a 40% tax.

Parking: Metropolitan Zurich has many public parking garages, but prices are often high. Consider taking a tram or train to minimize time lost to traffic congestion (a real issue) and to cut down on parking expenses. If you choose to park, **Universität Irchel,** near the large park on Winterthurstr. 181, is the cheapest option (12.50SFr max.); it and **Engi-Märt,** Seestr. 25, are both suburban lots. In the city, try garages at major department stores: **Jelmoli,** Steinmühlepl., **Migros Limmatplatz,** Limmatstr. 152, and **Globus** at Löwenstr. (All open M-F 8am-8pm, Sa 8am-5pm; prices vary but expect to pay 2SFr every 15min. during peak shopping hours.) City parking 2SFr for first hr. "Blue-Zone" 24hr. parking 10SFr. Suburbs 0.50SFr per hr.

Bike Rental: Bike loans are free at **Globus** (☎079 336 36 10); **Enge** (☎079 336 36 12); and **Hauptbahnhof** (☎210 13 88), at the very end of track 18. Passport and 20SFr deposit. Same day return. Open May-Oct. daily 7am-9:30pm.

⚡ PRACTICAL INFORMATION

TOURIST AND FINANCIAL SERVICES

Tourist Offices: Main office (☎215 40 00, free hotel reservation service 215 40 40; www.zuerich.com), in the main station, offers concert, movie, and bar information, as well as helpful publications. *Zürich News* prints restaurant and hotel listings. German-language *ZüriTipp* provides tips on nightlife. The **electronic hotel reservation board** is at the front of the station near the post office. The tourist office will book hotel rooms during regular hours. Open May-Oct. M-Sa 8am-8:30pm, Su 8:30am-6:30pm; Nov.-Apr. M-Sa 8:30am-7pm, Su 9am-6:30pm. For bikers and backpackers, the **Touring Club des Schweiz (TCS),** Alfred-Escher-Str. 38 (☎286 86 86), offers maps and travel info.

Tours: The tourist office leads frequent tours: the "Stroll through the Old Town" (2hr.; Apr.-Oct. M-F 3pm, Sa-Su 11am and 3pm; Nov.-Mar. W and Sa 11am; 20SFr, 50% discount for children 6-16 and with a ZurichCard); a trolley tour of major sites (2hr.; daily 9:45am, noon, 2pm; 32SFr, children 6-16 16SFr); and a 4hr. tour of the area surrounding Zurich (year-round daily 1pm; 45SFr, children ages 6-16 22.50SFr). Special Christmas-themed tours added in the winter months. Tours available in 8 languages. Zurich by Bike offers guided bicycle tours of the city, including a night tour leaving from platform 18 of the main station. (☎763 08 70; www.zurichbybike.ch. Tour Sa 8:30pm. Reserve in advance. 25SFr including bike, students 17SFr.)

Budget Travel: STA Travel, Leonhardtstr. 10 (☎41 58 450 43 30). Open M-W and F 10am-6:30pm, Th 10am-8pm, Sa 10am-2pm. **Branch** offices at Bäckerstr. 40 (☎297 17 17). Student package tours, STA travel help, ISIC cards. Open M-F 10am-6:30pm, Sa 10am-4pm. Also at Örlikon on Schulstr. 44 (☎058 450 43 00). Open M-F 9am-6:30pm, Sa 10am-2pm. **Globe-Trotter Travel Service AG,** Rennweg 35, 4th fl. (☎213 80 80; fax 213 80 88), specializes in overseas travel. Caters to individual travelers. Student discounts, tickets, and ISIC cards available. Open M-W and F 9am-6pm, Th 10am-6pm, Sa 9am-2pm; must have an appointment for Sa.

Consulates: UK, Hegibachstr. 47 (☎383 65 60). Open M-F 9am-noon. For visas and passports, UK citizens should contact the consulate in Geneva. **US Consulary Office,** Dufourstr. 101 (☎422 25 66). Visas and passports available only at the embassy in Bern. Open M-F 10am-1pm. **Australian, Canadian,** and **Irish** citizens should contact their embassies in Bern. **New Zealand's** consulate is in Geneva.

Currency Exchange: At the main train station. Cash advances with DC/MC/V with photo ID, 200SFr minimum. Open daily 6:30am-10pm. **Crédit Suisse,** Paradepl. 2.50SFr commission. Open M-W and F 8:15am-4:30pm, Th 8:15am-6pm. **Swiss Bank,** Bahnhofstr. 45 and 70, also charges 2.50SFr with MC/V. Branches at Paradepl. and Bellevuepl. Both have currency exchange machines next to ATMs. Open M-F 9am-5pm. **ATMs** accepting all cards are everywhere in Zurich.

LOCAL SERVICES

Luggage Storage: At the station 1 level below ground. Lockers 5SFr and 8SFr per day. 72hr. maximum. Luggage watch 7SFr at the *Gepäck* counter. Open daily 6am-10:50pm.

Bookstores: Orelli Fussli, Bahnhofstr. 70 (☎211 04 44; www.books.ch), has an entire English bookstore right on busy Bahnhofstr. Also at Fusslistr. 4 (☎084 884 98 48). Open M-F 9am-8pm, Sa 9am-5pm. **Travel Bookshop,** Rindermarkt 20 (☎252 38 83; www.travelbookshop.ch), has a wide assortment of travel guides (including *Let's Go*) and maps. Open M 1-6:30pm, Tu-F 9am-6:30pm, Sa 9am-4pm.

Libraries: Zentralbibliothek, Zähringerpl. 6 (☎268 31 00). Open M-F 10am-6pm, Sa 10am-4pm. **Pestalozzi Bibliothek,** Zähringerstr. 17 (☎261 78 11), has foreign magazines and newspapers. **Internet** 1SFr per 10min. Open M-F 10am-7pm, Sa 10am-4pm.

GLBT Organizations: Homosexuelle Arbeitsgruppe Zürich (HAZ), Sihlquai 67 (☎271 22 50; www.haz.ch), P.O. Box 7088, CH-8023, offers a library, meetings, and the free newsletter *InfoSchwül.* Open W 2-6pm. **Frauenzentrum Zürich,** Matteng. 27 (☎272 85 03), provides information for lesbians and a library of magazines and other resources, open Tu and Th 6-8pm. The connected restaurant is open Tu-F 5-11pm.

Laundromat: Speed Wash Self Service Wascherei, Weinbergstr. 37 (☎242 99 14). Wash and dry 10.20SFr for 5kg. Open M-Sa 7am-10pm, Su 10:30am-10pm.

Public Showers and Toilets: McClean Toiletten, at the train station 1 level below ground, Toilets 1-2SFr. Showers 12SFr for 20min., including 2 towels and shower gel. Wheelchair accessible. Open 6am-midnight.

Camping Supplies: TrottoMundo, Rindermarkt 6 (☎252 80 00; fax 252 01 82), located on the 2nd fl. above Oliver Twist Pub. Sells hiking, trekking, and camping gear and travel books. Tents from 300SFr. Open M-F 9am-6:30pm, Sa 11am-4pm.

EMERGENCY AND COMMUNICATIONS SERVICES

Emergencies: Police ☎117. **Fire** ☎118. **Ambulance** ☎144. **First Aid** ☎360 44 44.

24hr. Pharmacy: Bellevue Apotheke, ☎266 62 22, on Bellevuepl..

General Crisis Lines: Sorgen Telefon, ☎286 21 21. **Dargebotene Hand** ☎143.

Rape Crisis Line: ☎291 46 46.

Internet Access: The **ETH Library,** Ramistr. 101 (☎632 21 35; info@library.ethz.ch), in the *Hauptgebäude,* has lots of free computers, but visitors must agree to use them only for educational purposes (no chat, e-mail, or web-surfing). Take tram #6, 9, or 10 to "ETH," enter the large main building, and take the elevator to floor H. Open M-F 8:30am-9pm, Sa 9am-2pm. Internet and more at **Quanta Virtual Fun Space,** Limmatquai 94 (☎260 72 66), at the corner of Mühlg. and the busy Niederdorfstr. Must be 16+ to enter. 3SFr for 15min., 5SFr per 30min. Open daily 9am-midnight. **Internet Café,** Uraniastr. 3 (☎210 33 11; fax 210 33 13), in the Urania Parkhaus. 5SFr per 20min. Open M-Sa 9am-midnight, Su 11am-11pm. **Telefon Corner,** downstairs in the station next to Marché Mövenpick, has 15 PCs. 2SFr per 15min. Open daily 8am-10pm.

Post Office: Main office, Sihlpost, Kasernestr. 95-97, just behind the station. Open M-F 6:30am-10:30pm, Sa 6am-8pm, Su 11am-10:30pm. *Poste Restante:* Sihlpost, Postlagernde Briefe, CH-8021 Zurich. **Branches** throughout the city.

Postal Code: CH-8021.

ACCOMMODATIONS AND CAMPING

The few budget accommodations in Zurich are easily accessible by foot or via public transportation. Reserve at least a day in advance, especially during the summer.

Martahaus, Zähringerstr. 36 (☎251 45 50; www.martahaus.ch). Looking out of the station down Bahnhofstr. and at the large statue, turn left, cross Bahnhofbr., and take the 2nd (sharp) right after Limmatquai at the Seilgraben sign. 3 walls and a thick curtain separate you from your neighbors, who are probably American college students. All rooms have telephone and TV. Clean beds and showers, large lockers, night-lights, and towels. Breakfast 7:30-10am included. Airport shuttle every hr. after 6:20am, 20SFr. **Internet** access included. Lockers (5SFr deposit) in each partitioned alcove. Free luggage storage on days of arrival and departure; 5SFr per day past that. Laundry 10SFr. Reception 24hr. Rooms usually ready between 1 and 2pm. Wheelchair accessible. Dorms 38SFr; singles 75-85, with shower 115SFr; doubles 98-114SFr/150-160SFr; triples 135SFr; quads 200SFr; studio with kitchen for 1-2 people 150SFr, 3 people 185SFr. AmEx/DC/MC/V. ❸ The owners of Martahaus run the nearby **Luther Pension,** a **women-only** residence that shares reception with Martahaus and is cheaper. Breakfast included. Call Martahaus to reserve. Dorms 30SFr, singles 50SFr.❸

Hôtel Foyer Hottingen, Hottingenstr. 31 (☎256 19 19; www.foyer-hottingen.ch). Take tram #3 (dir: Kluspl.) to "Hottingerpl." It's at the corner of Hottingenstr. and Cäcilianstr. Families and student backpackers fill this newly-renovated house a block from the Kunsthaus. Sleek modern facilities, an in-house chapel, and an English-speaking staff make this hostel a good value. The heart of the city is 20min. by foot, far enough to be removed from the noisy and chaotic nightlife. Only women are allowed in the partitioned dorms during summer, but both sexes can rent other rooms. The dorm room lets out onto a rooftop terrace overlooking the city. Breakfast (7-9:30am), lockers, and kitchen included. Free luggage storage. Laundry 5SFr. Reception 7am-11pm. No lockout. Wheelchair accessible. Check-out 11am. 11-bed dorm, partitioned into 2- and 3-bed sections 35SFr; singles 70-85SFr, with bath 105SFr; doubles 110SFr/150-165SFr; triples 140SFr/190SFr; quads 180SFr. MC/V. ❷

Justinus Heim Zürich, Freudenbergstr. 146 (☎361 38 06; justinuszh@bluewin.ch). Take tram #9 or 10 (dir: Haldenegg) to "Seilbahn Rigiblick," then take the hillside funicular (by the Migros) uphill to the end. The hostel awaits across the street from the stop. Home to students from the nearby university, Justinus is ideal for those seeking a little extra privacy and quiet. With the funicular stopping at 12:40am, however, it's not ideal for catching the nightlife of Zurich. Picturesque views of Zurich make the trip up the hill worthwhile. English-speaking staff. Breakfast and kitchen included. Laundry available for the cost of the electricity (0.50-1SFr). Reception 8am-noon and 5-9pm. Check-out 10am. Singles 35-50SFr, with shower 60SFr; doubles 85SFr/100SFr; triples 120-140SFr. Rates reduced for multiple-week stays. V. ❸

The City Backpacker-Hotel Biber, Niederdorfstr. 5 (☎251 90 15; www.city-backpacker.ch). Cross Bahnhofbr. in front of station, then turn right onto Niederdorfstr. Tucked away down Schweizerhofg. (right after Weingasse) and up 3 flights of spiral stairs, this high-traffic hostel is popular among students and those looking for a cheap place to crash. With bustling Niederdorf nightlife just outside the window, you may not even make it back in time to use your bunkbed (or be able to sleep if it's a noisy weekend night). Kitchen available. Pick up a free copy of "Swiss Backpacker News" in the lobby. Small lockers available, but bring a lock. Reception watches bags. Sheets 3SFr, towels 3SFr, blanket provided. Laundry next-day service 10SFr. **Internet** 12SFr per hr. Key deposit 20SFr or passport. Reception 8-11am and 3-10pm. Check-out 10am, strictly enforced. 4- to 6-bed dorms 31SFr; singles 66SFr; doubles 92SFr. All rooms non-smoking. MC/V. ❷

Hotel Otter, Oberdorfstr. 7 (☎251 22 07; www.wueste.ch), and the swanky Wuste Bar below it attract an eclectic and artsy student crowd. Hip and slightly unconventional, as evidenced by the creative decor of the individually-themed rooms (think "Heaven and Hell" and "African Lodge"), Otter is an oasis for not-so-starving artists. Floor bathrooms. Breakfast served from 9:15am (10am on weekends) until there is no more bread. Laundry next-day service 15SFr. TV, phone, fridge, towels, and sheets included. Sink in room. Nearby parking open daily 6am-2am. Reception 8am-6pm in hotel, and until midnight in bar. Check-out noon. Singles 100SFr; doubles 130-160SFr; apartment with shower and kitchen 180SFr. AmEx/MC/V. ❹

Jugendherberge Zürich (HI), Mutschellenstr. 114 (☎399 78 00; www.youthhostel.ch/zuerich). From the station, walk out past the fountain down Bahnhofstr. about 100m. On the right side of the street, take tram #7 (dir: Wollishofen) to "Morgental" and walk 5min. back toward the Migros along Mutschellenstr. Pass a 2nd Migros (on the right) and you'll see the gigantic hostel on the left. The hostel completed a huge expansion in July 2003, adding a 24hr. snack bar, beer on tap, and a projection screen for movies and sporting events. A TV corner, small conference rooms, and a large common area make it a prime spot to catch up with other backpacking hostelers. Breakfast and sheets included. Buffet-style lunch and dinner 15SFr. Rooms equipped with sink. Ask for towels at reception. Lockers available for day storage and nightly, in-room storage (2SFr deposit). **Internet** 1SFr per 4min. Reception 24hr. Check-in 2pm. Check-out 10am. Wheelchair accessible. Singles with shower 99SFr; doubles with shower 116SFr; triples 135SFr, with shower 150SFr; quads with shower 172SFr; family room with 6 beds and sink 210SFr. Under age 6 half-price. Non-members add 6SFr. AmEx/MC/V. ❷

Zic-Zac Rock-Hotel, Marktg. 17 (☎261 21 81; www.ziczac.ch). Each room in this hostel is named after a singer or a band and is decorated with bright colors and funky paintings. This hotel's convenient locale is complemented by rooms with TV, phone, sheets, towels, and sink. Light breakfast 5SFr. Receptionist will watch luggage. Laundry same-day service 12SFr. **Internet** 1SFr per 4min. Reception 24hr. Check-out 11am. Singles 75SFr, with shower 90SFr; doubles 120SFr/135SFr; triples 156SFr/168SFr; quads with shower 260SFr. ISIC 10% off. AmEx/DC/MC/V. ❹

Leoneck Hotel, Leonhardstr. 1 (☎254 22 22; www.leoneck.ch). From train station, take tram #6 or 8 to Haldenegg. and turn left onto Leonhardstr. An obsession with cows and bright colors must have inspired this divinely bovine hotel, which sits above the appropriately named Crazy Cow restaurant. Serving a mixed crowd of families and business people, all rooms include bath, phone, TV, hair dryer, and of course, plenty of cows. Handpainted scenes of Swiss life adorn bathroom walls. **Internet** (5SFr per 15min.) and **currency exchange** available. Laundry next-day service available. Shuttle to airport hourly (6:15-10:15pm, 20SFr per person). Some non-smoking floors. Reception 24hr. Singles 80-140SFr; doubles 130-185SFr; triples 160-240SFr; 4-bed family room 200-290SFr. AmEx/DC/MC/V. ❹

Hôtel du Théâtre, Seilergraben 69, Centralplatz. (☎267 26 70; www.hotel-du-theatre.com). Mainly geared toward businesspeople, this elegant and recently renovated hotel within view of the train station offers discounted rates on weekends. Modern facilities including keycard access. High cleaning standards result in attractive rooms. All rooms, decorated with backlit scenes from classic movies on the walls and funky furniture, include bathroom, TV, phone, hair dryer, minibar, safe, and modem connection. Non-smoking floors available. English-speaking staff. Free **Internet**. Breakfast 15SFr. Laundry service available. Singles M-Th 150-220SFr, F-Su 135-180SFr; doubles 240-260SFr/195-210SFr. 2 mini-suites 290SFr/235SFr. AmEx/DC/MC/V. ❺

Camping Seebucht, Seestr. 559 (☎482 16 12; www.camping-zurich.ch). Take tram #11 to "Bürklipl."; catch bus #161 or 165 to "Stadtgrenze," and the site will be across from the Esso station. Lakeside location makes up for the trek. Market, terrace, café, and restaurant on-site. **Internet** 0.25SFr per min. Reception daily 8am-noon and 3-9pm. Open May-Sept. 8SFr per person, 5SFr per child ages 4-16, 12SFr per 3-person tent, 14SFr per caravan. Tax 1.50SFr. Showers 2SFr. Electricity 4SFr. ❶

◘ FOOD

Zurich's 1300+ restaurants cover every imaginable dietary preference. The cheapest meals in Zurich are available at *Würstli* stands for about 5SFr. For heartier appetites, Zurich prides itself on *Geschnetzeltes mit Rösti*, thinly sliced veal (often kidney or liver) in cream sauce with hash-brown potatoes. Check out the *Swiss Backpacker News* (at the tourist office, Hotel Biber, and Martahaus) for info on budget meals in Zurich. Cheap kebab stands and take-out burger joints on Niederdorfstr. offer meals for around 6SFr. The **Manor** department store off Bahnhofstr. 75 (corner of Uraniastr.) has a gourmet self-service restaurant on the fifth floor. (Open M-F 9am-8pm, Sa 9am-4pm.)

▨ **Bodega Española,** Münsterg. 15 (☎251 23 10). Catalan delights served by charismatic waiters amidst dark wood beams and long tables since 1874. The delicate but filling egg-and-potato tortilla dishes (15.50SFr) and authentic tapas served all day (from 4.80SFr per serving) can easily feed 2 for under 45SFr. Wheelchair accessible. Open daily 10am-midnight. Kitchen open noon-2pm and 6-10pm. AmEx/DC/MC/V. ❷

Restaurant Hiltl, Sihlstr. 28 (☎227 70 00; www.hitl.ch). Munch carrot sticks with the vegetarian crowd at this swank restaurant, where the lack of meat makes things surprisingly cheap. Highlights include the all-day salad buffet (3.60SFr per 100g take-out, 4.60SFr to eat there), and the Indian buffet at night (same price). No smoking. Large salad 15SFr. Open M-Sa 7am-11pm, Su 11am-11pm. AmEx/DC/MC/V. ❷

Outback Lodge, Stadelhoferstr. 18 (☎252 15 75; http://outback-lodge.ch). This Aussie-themed restaurant is located just after STA Travel in Stadelhofer Passage. The atmosphere gleans some authenticity from its cheap Foster's beer on tap (4.20SFr), and dishes like Kangaroo Island (29.50SFr) and Crocodile Dundee (34.50SFr) made from the real thing. Menu includes vegetarian options. 18+ after 6pm. Wheelchair accessible. Open M-F 9am-midnight, Sa-Su 11:30am-2am. AmEx/MC/V. ❹

BQM Café and Polyterrase at Universität Zürich, behind Rämistr. 101. Take streetcar #6 to "ETH Zentrum" from Bahnhofpl. or take the red Polybahn uphill from Central Station. At the university's self-service café Polyterrase or the hip, student-filled BQM Café, sandwiches (2.80-6SFr), salads (1.90SFr), chips, and beer (3.50SFr and up) make for a nice lunch break. The view from the open terrace, with the city's church steeples at eye level, makes the climb worthwhile. Closed during winter recess. Polyterrase open M-F 6:45am-7:45pm. BQM open M-Tu 11:30am-11pm, W-Th 1:30am-midnight, F 11:30am-9pm. No smoking until 6pm. ❷

Restaurant Mère Catherine, Nägelihof 3 (☎250 59 40; www.commercio.ch). Hordes of locals find their way to this yuppie restaurant even though it is hidden away in a small street near the Großmünster, in a building constructed in 1565. Serving mainly Provençal French dishes (starting at 21.50SFr) with a lot of wine, this bustling place exudes ambience, with a rushing fountain and shady outdoor seating to accompany your meal. On Su, families with children can enjoy the Kid's Corner of toys and games. Vegetarian options. Daily fish specials from the Zürichsee 28.50-33.50SFr. English language menu and children's menu available. Wheelchair accessible. Open Su-W 11:30am-10pm, Th-Sa 11:30am-10:30pm. AmEx/DC/MC/V. ❸

Gran-Café, Limmatquai 66 (☎01 252 31 19). Across the street from the rushing Limmat river, the outdoor seating for this popular restaurant is often filled on warm days. Enjoy the inexpensive *Menüs* (from around 16.50SFr) or try one of their tasty dishes (from 14.80SFr) while admiring the Great Gatsby-esque decor. Save room for one of the sundaes (7.50-9.50SFr), or enjoy a creamy iced cappuccino (5.60SFr). Open M-Th 6am-11:30pm, F 6am-midnight, Sa 7am-midnight, Su 7:30am-11:30pm. AmEx/MC/V. ❷

Raclette Stube, Zähringerstr. 16 (☎251 41 30). Serving a limited but high-quality menu of classic Swiss fare, this quaint, family-oriented restaurant opens onto the street and offers a good opportunity to lounge for an extended period of time surrounded by English-speakers. Large *raclette* appetizer 12.50SFr. *Fondue Käse* (cheese fondue) 24.50-28.50SFr per person. *Fondue chinoise* (meat fondue) 39.50SFr per person. All-you-can-eat *raclette* 32.50SFr per person. Open daily 6pm to about 11pm. ❹

CAFÉS

🔲 **Sprüngli Confiserie Café,** Paradepl. (☎224 47 11), is a Zurich landmark, founded by one of the original Lindt chocolate makers who sold his shares to his brother. Women in matching red business suits assist customers in purchasing just the right chocolate from the confectionery. A sweet-tooth heaven, the Confiserie-Konditorei concocts peerless confections (most for around 3SFr) and delicious desserts, including an eye-popping mocha sundae (10.50SFr) with homemade ice cream and sherbet, served on the Bahnhofstr. patio. Pick up a handful of the bite-size *Luxemburgerli* (in flavors including caramel, amaretto, and even champagne) for 8.20SFr per 100g. Lunch *Menüs* 19-28SFr. Salads 6-9.50SFr. Omelettes 12-15.50SFr. Wheelchair-accessible outdoor seating. Confectionery open M-F 7:30am-8pm, Sa 8am-4pm. Café open M-F 7:30am-6:30pm, Sa 8am-6pm, Su 9:30am-5:30pm. AmEx/DC/MC/V.

Zähringer Café, Zähringerpl. 11 (☎252 05 00; www.cafe-zaehringer.com), across the square from the library, at the end of Spitalg., above the *Altstadt*. Enjoy light and healthy fare in this vibrant café with a hippie feel. Try the hummus platter, served with pickles, olives, and salad (11.50SFr), or an assortment of organic salads (3.50 per 100g). Sandwiches (7.50-10.50SFr) and stir-fries (15.50-26.50SFr) are also popular choices. Wheelchair accessible. Open M 6pm-midnight, Tu-Su 8am-midnight.

Milchbar Café, Kappelerg. 16 (☎211 90 13), right behind the Fraumünster, is a popular lunch stop. Simple *Menüs* (15.50-19.50SFr), soups (7SFr), quiches (3-5SFr), and a limited salad bar (3.30SFr per 100g) make Milchbar a convenient place to grab a quick meal between shopping and sightseeing. Full vegetarian menu available. Open M-F 5am-6pm, Sa 6am-5pm.

Infinito Espresso Bar, Sihlstr. 20 (☎01 260 55 35; fax 01 260 55 34), is a chic, minimalist venue that serves a wide coffee selection and other yuppie drinks. Large selection of fruit shakes, including Melon-Passionfruit (7SFr). Espresso from 4SFr. Beer from 6SFr. Sandwiches and snacks 4.50-9SFr. Open M-F 7am-10pm, Sa 8am-7pm.

ON THE MENU

RACLETTE, ANYONE?

You can find it in Alpine huts, restaurants, packaged in TV dinners at the grocery store, and even on sale from street vendors at Basel's Herbschtmaeß (fall festival). It's raclette, a Swiss culinary specialty originally from the Wallis region, which has now spread through the nation. Raclette is older than fondue—Alpine farmers were enjoying it well over 500 years ago. It is a dish that sprang from the mountain farmer's life, like many Swiss specialties, and therefore involves massive amounts of mountain cheese (*Raclettekäse*), along with a few home-grown vegetables.

A large amount of *Raclettekäse*, which melts more easily than regular cheese, is melted in a fondue-like set-up at the center of the table, with a fire blazing cheerily beneath. For the dishes and silverware, a *raclette* set (similar to a fondue one) is used. Once the cheese is melted, it is ladled out to each person at the table. A few hot baked potatoes are given to each person, along with sour pickles (*Gurken*) and small, sweet onions (*Silberzwiebeln*). The diner mixes the garnishes with the cheese and potatoes, adds some black pepper to taste, and enjoys the same, simple yet hearty meal that the Swiss have been enjoying year-round for centuries.

MARKETS AND BAKERIES

Two bakery chains, **Kleiner** and **Buchmann**, are everywhere in Zurich, offering freshly baked bread, sweets (apricot pies 10-12SFr), and *Küchen* (*Bürli* rolls 0.85SFr, *Chäschüchli* 2SFr) for reasonable prices. (Open M-F 6:30am-6:30pm.) The 24hr. **vending machine** in the Shop-Ville beneath the train station has pasta and juice, but you may feel uncomfortable heading over there alone at night.

Farmer's Market, at Burklipl. and Helvetiapl., sells fruit, flowers, and veggies Tu and F 6am-11am. At Rosenhof, fruit, vegetables, and wares are sold Mar.-Dec. Th 10am-8pm and Sa 10am-5pm.

Co-op Super-Center, right on Bahnhofbr., is the Co-op to end all Co-ops, visible from almost everywhere. Open M-F 7am-8pm, Sa 7am-4pm.

Migros, Stadelhoferpl. 16, right off Theaterstr. Open M-F 7am-8pm, Sa 8am-5pm. The adjoining restaurant has the same hours.

🔘 SIGHTS

It's virtually inconceivable to start your tour of Zurich anywhere except the stately **Bahnhofstraße.** The famous causeway of capitalism gets more expensive the further shoppers wander from the train station, and the stretch closest to the lake has shoppers peering into the windows of Cartier, Rolex, Chanel, and Armani. Filled with businessmen and well-dressed shoppers during the day, these last few blocks fall dead quiet when the shops and banks close at 6pm. At the Zürichsee end of Bahnhofstr., **Bürkliplatz** is a good place to begin exploring the lake shore or to just enjoy the cool breeze and shimmering water. The Platz itself hosts a colorful Saturday **flea market** (May-Oct. 6am-3pm). On the other side of the river, the pedestrian zone continues on Niederdorfstr. and Münsterg., and is made up of a wider range of shops, from the ritzy to the erotic. From Niederdorfstr. turn right onto **Spiegelgasse,** Zurich's memory lane, with plaques honoring former residents Goethe, Buchner, and Lenin. A view of Zurich from overhead points to its three largest sights, **Fraumünster, Grossmünster,** and **St. Peterskirche,** all tightly packed and straddling the Limmat river.

FRAUMÜNSTER. This 13th-century cathedral's classic Gothic style is juxtaposed with **Marc Chagall's** less ancient stained-glass windows; the fusion attracts numerous admirers. The five choir windows depict Chagall's interpretations of stories from the Old and New Testament. (See if you can find Chagall's trademark goat worked into each window.) A more subdued window called "the heavenly Paradise" designed by Augusto Giacometti in 1930, decorates the northern transept. Outside the church on Fraumünsterstr., a mural decorating the courtyard's Gothic archway pictures Felix and Regula (the decapitated patron saints of Zurich) with their heads in their hands. Legend has it that they just plucked their heads from the ground and marched on over to where they wanted to be buried. *(Right off Paradepl. Open daily May-Nov. 9am-6pm; Nov.-Apr. 10am-4pm. Free.)*

GROSSMÜNSTER. The twin Neo-Gothic towers of this mainly Romanesque church can be best viewed on the bridge near the Fraumünster. Considered to be the mother church of the Swiss-German Reformation movement begun by Zwingli, it has come to be a symbol of Zurich. The stained-glass windows, depicting the Biblical Christmas narrative, were designed in 1933 by Augusto Giacometti. Below the windows, one of Zwingli's Bibles lies in a protected case near his pulpit. Venture downstairs to the cavernous 12th-century crypt to see the forbidding statue of Charlemagne and his 2m-long sword. If you're feeling energetic, head up the many twisting stairs to the top of one of the towers: the climb is about

10min. and offers a wide view over the city's tiled rooftops and landmarks, as well as shots of the Zürichsee. Guides to glance through or buy (0.30SFr) are available in a variety of languages including English. *(Follow Niederdorfstr., which becomes Münsterg., to the end. Church open daily mid-Mar. to Oct. 9am-6pm; steeple access 9:15am-5pm. Nov. to early Mar. 10am-5pm. Tower open Mar.-Oct. daily 9am-5pm; Nov.-Feb. Sa-Su 9:15am-5pm. Entrance to the tower 2SFr.)* In the same building is the small **Zwingli museum** and monastery. *(Open M-F 9am-4:30pm.)*

ST. PETERSKIRCHE. St. Peterskirche stakes its claim to having the largest clock face in Europe. Find it near the Fraumünster, or just look up. *(Open M-F 8am-6pm, Sa 8am-4pm, Su 11am-5pm.)* Recently excavated Roman baths dating from the first century are visible beneath the iron stairway. *(Down Thermeng. from St. Peter's.)*

LINDENHOF. The original site of **Turricum**, the Roman border control and checkpoint for the ancient city, the park provides refuge from the daily grind. It has a giant chess board and views of the river and the *Altstadt*. *(Follow Strehlg., Rennweg, or Glockeng. uphill to the intersection of the 3 streets.)*

GARDENS AND PARKS. The lush, perfect-for-a-picnic **Rieter-Park**, overlooking the city, creates a romantic backdrop for the Museum Rietberg. *(Take tram #7 to "Museum Rietberg." Head in the direction of the tram to the 1st intersection. Turn right onto Sternenstr. and follow the signs uphill to the museum. Free.)* The **Stadtgärtnerei** attracts botanists and ornithologists alike to the moist Palmhouse/Aviary, complete with an artificial pond and 17 species of tropical birds swooping overhead. In a tropical greenhouse next door, dozens of orchids are nestled amongst a backdrop of ferns and twisting vines, while the outdoor garden includes a display of desert plants and a turtle and goldfish filled man-made stream. *(Sackzelg 25-27. Take tram #3 to "Hubertus" and head down Gutstr. ☎492 14 23; www.stadt-gaertnerei.ch. Open daily 9-11:30am and 1:30-4:30pm. Free.)* When the weather heats up, a visit to the bathing parks along the Zürichsee can offer a cool respite. *Strandbad Mythenquai* is a popular swimming spot on the western shore. *(Take tram #7 to "Brunaustr." and walk in the same direction, cross to the left side of the street, and continue 2min. until you see a set of stairs. Signs lead the way. ☎201 00 00. Open daily June to mid-Aug. 9am-8pm; May and mid-Aug. to early Sept. 9am-7pm. 6SFr, youth 16-20 4SFr, children 6-16 2SFr. Check out www.badi-info.ch for water quality information and other bathing locations.)*

ÜTLIBERG. A 10min. hike from the Ütliberg train station brings visitors to the "top of Zurich," where the metropolis sprawls out to one side, and gently sloping hills and farmland stretch to the other. The flat walk from Ütliberg to Felsenegg provides a peaceful escape from the city's bustle. From Zurich's Hauptbahnhof, take the S10 train to "Ütliberg" *(15min.; 30min; 14.40SFr, discount with Tageskarte)*, then follow the yellow signs to Felsenegg *(1½hr.)*. A cable car runs from Felsenegg to Adliswil, where a train returns to Zurich. *(Buy tickets at any train or cable car station or at most hotels; free with Eurail.)*

OTHER SIGHTS. Upon pushing open the gate to enter the peaceful, flower-filled **Fluntern Cemetery**, visitors are greeted by a map pointing out the graves of such famous "residents" as James Joyce and Elias Canetti. The **Zurich Zoo**, beside the cemetery, has over 250 animal species. Boasting one of the best bear enclosures around, the zoo is a much-frequented cultural treasure, entertaining school groups, families, and art students alike with the antics of its animals. The expansive Masoala Rainforest, a living biosphere of tropical life, just opened in 2003. Get there early to avoid long lines. *(Zürichbergstr. 221. Take tram #6 uphill to "Zoo." From the station, head uphill 100m to find the cemetery on your left; for the zoo, walk past the cemetery and the track, then about 200m more. ☎254 25 05; www.zoo.ch. Open daily Mar.-Oct. 9am-6pm; Nov.-Feb. 9am-5pm. 22SFr; ages 6-16, students and seniors 11SFr; ages 6 and under free.)*

🏛 MUSEUMS

Zurich has channeled much of its banking wealth into universities and museums, which boast outstanding collections. The larger institutions hold the core of the city's artistic and historical wealth, but many smaller museums are equally spectacular. The tourist office in the main station has a helpful listing of all area museums' current exhibits. Colorful posters also coat the city, advertising upcoming museum events. During the first weekend in September each year, 30 of the city's 50+ museums are open from 7pm to 5am. Free entry at all museums listed (and some others) is available with the **Zürich Card,** available through the tourist office.

■ **KUNSTHAUS ZÜRICH.** The Kunsthaus, the largest privately funded museum in Europe, houses a collection ranging from 21st-century American pop art to religious works by the Old Masters. Works by Picasso, van Gogh, Gaugin, Dalí, Rubens, Rembrandt, Renoir, Chagall, and Dégas, and the largest Munch collection outside of Norway are highlights of a museum that, by itself, is a compelling reason to come to Zurich. The collection is continually expanding: a new wing devoted to Alberto Giacometti and his artistic kin opened in May 2002. *(Heimpl. 1. Take tram #3, 5, 8, or 9 to "Kunsthaus."* ☎ *253 84 84; www.kunsthaus.ch. English audio tours and brochures available. Bag storage required. Call ahead for wheelchair access. After 2005, fully accessible without prior arrangements. Open Tu-Th 10am-9pm, F-Su 10am-5pm. 12SFr, students and seniors 6SFr; W free. Special exhibits 10-17SFr more. Free tours W 6:30pm, Sa 3pm.)*

■ **MUSEUM RIETBERG.** In contrast to the Kunsthaus, Rietberg presents an exquisite collection of Asian, African, and other non-European art, housed in two spectacular mansions in the Rieter-Park. Sprung from the well-known collection of Baron von der Heyt, the 50-year-old museum has firmly established itself as one of the best museums in Zurich. Park-Villa Rieter features internationally acclaimed exhibits of Chinese, Japanese, and Indian drawings and paintings. Villa Wesendonck stores most of the permanent collection of non-Western sculpture, with Bodhisattvas from India, China, Japan, Tibet, and Nepal. *(Gablerstr. 15. Take tram #7 to "Museum Rietberg." See directions to Rieter Park ("Gardens and Parks," p. 381).* ☎ *202 45 28; www.rietberg.ch. Villa Wesendonck open Apr.-Sept. Tu and Th-Su 10am-5pm, W 10am-8pm; Oct.-Mar. 10am-5pm. Audioguide (5SFr) and literature available in English and French. Wheelchair accessible. Park-Villa Rieter open Tu-Su 10am-5pm. 6SFr, students 3SFr, under 16 free. Special exhibits and permanent collections 12SFr, students 6SFr. MC/V only at Wesendonck.)*

SCHWEIZERISCHES LANDESMUSEUM. Housed in a castle right next to the Hauptbahnhof, the Landesmuseum provides fascinating insight into Swiss history with its careful reconstructions and preservation of Swiss artifacts. The generic first floor contains medieval artifacts, but the castle rooms have 16th-century astrological instruments, Ulrich Zwingli's weapons from the Battle of Kappel (1531), in which he died, an extensive display of clothes and reconstructed rooms from the 18th to 20th centuries, and a tiny bejeweled clock with a golden skeleton morbidly indicating the hour. Unique, creatively presented special exhibits change every few months. Check www.musee-suisse.com for upcoming events.

MUSEUM OF CLASSICAL ARCHAEOLOGY. As impressive as the collection of Greek and Roman vases and busts filling the first floor lecture hall is, it seems little more than a foil for the astonishing basement, which houses replicas of nearly every great statue of the ancient world from 800 BC on. *(Rämistr. 73. Take tram #6, 9, or 10 to "ETH."* ☎ *01 257 28 20; www.archinst.uniz.ch. Coming to the city center, walk in the direction of the tram 3min. The main ETH building is on your left. Wheelchair-accessible entrance on nearby Karl-Schmiedstr. Signs in German. Open Tu-F 1-6pm, Sa-Su 11am-5pm. Free.)*

MUSEUM FÜR GESTALTUNG (DESIGN MUSEUM). This museum's enormous spaces, adjoining the School of Design, display student work, a collection of vintage advertising posters, and temporary exhibits on subjects such as steam shovel art, female power stations, and giant corn. An exhibit on Sportdesign is on display until early Feb. 2005. *(Ausstellungsstr. 60. Take tram #4 or 13 to "Museum für Gestaltung" or walk 5min. from the main station. ☎336 22 11; www.museum-gestaltung.ch. Open Tu-Th 10am-8pm, F-Su 11am-6pm; graphics, poster, and design collections by appointment. Hall and gallery 10SFr, students 6SFr. Tours every W 6:30pm.)*

LINDT AND SPRÜNGLI CHOCOLATE FACTORY. While visitors won't get to see the factory itself, they are welcomed into a one-room exhibit on chocolate making and the history of the Lindt company. Stock up on cheap chocolate if you're lucky enough to catch a monthly sale, or just browse the displays (mostly in German). *(Seestr. 204. Take train S1 (dir: Zug) or S8 (dir: Pfäffikon) to "Kilchberg" (15min., 2 per hr., round-trip 10.80SFr.) From the station, take the once-per-hour bus #163 to "Lindt-Sprüngli" or walk down the sidewalk path to Seestr., where you continue in the direction of the train for 10min. The factory is on your right. ☎01 716 22 33. Open W-F 10am-noon and 1-4pm. Free.)*

MUSEUM BELLERIVE. Museum Bellerive specializes in constantly changing "out-of-the-ordinary" exhibits, each lasting three months with a one month break between them. The displays may sound tame, but the museum takes them in unexpected directions—one past exhibition included "Illusion and Imagination" (surreally large chairs that people can climb into to watch various bits of movies.) An exhibit on Swiss design fills the rooms until early January 2005. *(Höschg. #3. Take tram #2 or 4 (dir: Tiefenbrunnen) or bus #33 to "Höschg." and walk right; it's by the lake. ☎446 44 69. Closed between exhibits, so call ahead. Wheelchair accessible. Open Tu-W 11am-6pm, Th 10am-8pm, F-Sa 11am-5pm, Su 10am-6pm. 6SFr, students and children 3SFr.)*

🎭 🎬 ENTERTAINMENT AND NIGHTLIFE

For information on after-dark goings-on, check ZüriTipp (www.zueritipp.ch), the free *20 Minutes* newspaper available throughout the city, or the posters that decorate the streets and cinemas at Bellevuepl. or Hirschenpl. Niederdorfstraße rocks as the epicenter of Zurich's nightlife. Beware: many establishments that claim to be "night clubs" are actually strip clubs. As with any nightlife center, women should be cautious about walking alone at night. On Friday and Saturday nights during the summer, **Hirschenpl.** on Niederdorfstr. hosts street performers from around the world. Other hot spots include **Münsterg.** and **Limmatquai,** both of which are lined with cafés and bars that overflow with people into the wee hours of the morning. Beer in Zurich is pricey (from 6SFr), but a number of cheap **bars** have established themselves on Niederdorfstr. near Muhleg. **Cinemas** are another popular option. Most movies are screened in English with German and French subtitles (marked E/d/f). Films generally cost 15SFr and up, less on Mondays. From mid-July to mid-August, the Orange Cinema, an open-air cinema at Zürichhorn (take tram #4 or 2 to "Fröhlichstr."), attracts huge crowds to its lakefront screenings. They sell out quickly, so reserve a seat (18-25SFr) early at www.orangecinema.ch or at the ticket counter at the Bellevue tram station. Film am See and Filmfluss, both by the lake, are two other outdoor cinemas, both running from mid-July to late August. Check www.cineman.ch/kinoprogramm/openair for schedules. Every August, the Street Parade brings together ravers from all over the world for a giant techno party, while "Fasnacht" (Carnival) fills the city with bright costumes and revelry at the end of February.

DO YOU SCHWING?

A summer in Switzerland would not be complete without the institution that is the annual *Schwingfest*, an event dedicated to the arcane sport of *Schwingen*. A form of wrestling, *Schwingen* features two male *Schwingers* faced off in a *Sägemuhlring* (a ring of sawdust). The men wear leather over-shorts with loops on the back, which the other *Schwinger* must grip for leverage at all times. As a *Schwinger*, your goal in life is to throw your opponent down on his back and to stay within the circle while doing so. Matches last around 5min.

The earliest known reference to the sport is a 13th-century stone carving in the cathedral of Lausanne, which depicts two over-short-wearing strongmen at loggerheads. The sport's origins lie in Alpine farming regions, where farmhands competed to see who was the strongest, and where everyone presumably wore suspenders. Today, the men are still distinguished by the roots of their training: *Sennen* are farmers and wear traditional blue workshirts; *Turnen* are gym-trained athletes and wear only white.

The *Schwingfest* itself includes more Swiss tradition than just wrestling. Normally, the playing of an *Alphorn* kicks off the first bout, and flag throwers, yodel choirs, and a beer-and-sausage tent provide entertainment on the sidelines. Check www.esv.ch for information on the *Fest* near you.

Nelson, Beateng. 11 (☎212 60 16). Ex pats, locals, backpackers, and businessmen alike converge on this large and vibrant bar/club. Music blares while people of all ages sip cognac and chug beers before heading onto the jam-packed dance floor. Basic bar food and an international selection of ciders and beers, most around 8.50SFr for a pint. Upstairs, **Lady Hamilton's** maintains the pub atmosphere of **Nelson's** but with a slightly classier feel. Wine and whiskey are preferred to brews. (Both 20+. Nelson's open M-W 11:30am-2am, Th 11:30am-3am, F 11:30am-5am, Sa 3pm-5am, Su 3pm-2am. Lady Hamilton's open M-W 5pm-midnight, Th 5pm-1am, F-Sa 5pm-4am.)

Double-U (W) Bar, Niederdorfstr. 21 (☎251 41 44), on the 1st floor of Hotel Schafli. On the busy Niederdorfstr., this spot is popular with locals and students who crowd the terrace. Comes complete with palm trees, inflatable beer bottles and an occasional live DJ. Beer (5SFr and up) and cocktails (14SFr and up) rise 2SFr in price after midnight. Wheelchair accessible. Open Su-F 4pm-2am, Sa 4pm-4am. AmEx/DC/MC/V.

Oliver Twist, Rindermarkt 6 (☎252 47 10; www.pickwick.ch), welcomes soccer fans, tourists, and other assorted ex pats ready for a pint of English brew (8.50SFr) with the occasional Budweiser thrown in. Traditional fare such as fish and chips (17.50 SFr) is served in a crowded but polite pub atmosphere that's only somewhat contrived. Pub grub available noon-10pm. Open M-Sa 11:30am-midnight, Su 1pm-midnight.

Barfüsser, Spitalg. 14 (☎01 251 40 64), off Zähringerpl., Switzerland's oldest gay bar, provides a lively spot to meet people and chat with the entertaining staff. Chill house and electric pop beats serenade a youngish crowd in their 20s and 30s. Barfüsser specializes in sushi during the day (M-Sa 11:30am-10:30pm, Su 5-10:30pm). At night, cocktails (14-17SFr), wine (6-9SFr), and changing daily concoctions flow freely. Wheelchair accessible. Open M-Th and Su 11am-1am, F-Sa 11am-3am. AmEx/DC/MC/V.

Nachtflug Bar, Café, and Lounge, Stüssihofstaff 4 (☎01 261 99 66; www.nachtflug.ch), boasts a popular outdoor bar when the weather behaves. A crowd of laid-back locals and the odd backpacker fill the Rosenhof. Wine from 7SFr. Beer from 4.90SFr. Mixed drinks 13.50-16.50SFr. Also serves cold tapas (7-9SFr), a wide selection of teas, including Blood Orange (4.50SFr), and fresh-squeezed juices (6SFr) all day. Wheelchair accessible via Niederdorfstr. Open Su-Th 11am-midnight, F-Sa 11am-1:30am. Outdoor bar Th-Su 10pm-midnight.

Öpfelchammer, Rindermarkt 12 (☎ 01 251 23 36). This popular Swiss wine bar (3-5SFr per glass) has low ceilings and wooden crossbeams covered with initials and messages from 200 years of merry-making. Those who climb the rafters and drink a free glass of wine from the beams get to engrave their names on the furniture. It's harder than it looks. Open mid-Aug. to mid-July Tu-Sa 11am-12:30am. AmEx/DC/MC/V.

Cranberry, Metzgerg. 3, (☎/fax 261 27 72) right off Limmatquai, attracts a primarily gay clientele with funky lights, peppy music, and an endless selection of mixed drinks (around 13SFr). Wheelchair accessible. Open Su-W 5pm-12:30am, Th 5pm-1am, F-Sa 5pm-2am. AmEx/DC/MC/V.

Bar Odeon, Limmatquai 2 (☎ 251 16 50), Bellevuepl. This posh, artsy, gay-friendly joint has served the likes of Vladimir Lenin, but is more commonly frequented by a relaxed, slightly older crowd. Great street-side seating. During the day, patrons enjoy espresso, *aperos,* and desserts (from 6.50SFr.) in this classy bar with an old-world feel. Beers from 6SFr. Open Su-Th 7am-2am, F-Sa 7am-4am. AmEx/DC/MC/V.

🔀 DAYTRIP FROM ZURICH

EINSIEDELN
☎ 055

Trains leave Zurich for Wädenswil (dir: Chur, 1-2 per hr. every 20min. 6:10am-10:16pm, 16.20SFr), where trains run to Einsiedeln (30min.). Alternatively, trains leave Lucerne for Biberbrugg (1hr., 1-2 per hr.), where trains run to Einsiedeln (14min., 1-2 per hr., 8.20SFr).

Just 1hr. by train from Zwingli's Protestant pulpit in Zurich, tiny Einsiedeln attracts pilgrims from all over Europe to drink the purported healing waters of its fountain and gaze at its massive cathedral and legendary Black Madonna. To find the **Klosterkirche** (cathedral), exit the station, cross the street to the left, turn right on the small lane behind "Doc Holliday's" restaurant, and turn left uphill on Hauptstr. From there it is a 10min. walk straight ahead. Consecrated in 1735, the cathedral's Milanese exterior dominates the surrounding hills with its twin lemon-shaped domes. Frescoes of cherubs floating on a background of lavender, green, gold, and pink cover every inch of the Baroque ceiling. After Vespers each day (except Sunday) from 4:30-5pm, the group of Benedictine monks who live and work at the monastery chant the "Salve Regina," which has been performed daily at the monastery since 1547. Visitors are welcome, but meditative silence and a ban on photography and videotaping are strictly observed. The 1m-high **Black Madonna** is the cathedral's centerpiece. Years of smoky candlelight and underground storage during the French invasion darkened the figure. When she was brought out of hiding, an Austrian craftsman cleaned off the soot to restore her natural linden-wood color. Refusing to accept the change, the townspeople immediately painted her black again. (Open daily 5:30am-8:30pm. For a schedule of worship activities call ☎ 418 61 11 or see the tourist office website, www.kloster-einsiedeln.ch.) The **monastery** that stretches back from the cathedral offers 1hr. tours of its horse stables and renowned library. (M-Sa 2-3pm. 12SFr. Reserve and buy tickets at the tourist office. Conducted in German; tours in other languages available by appointment.) The gates to the monastery are usually open. To the right of the cathedral, signposts list strolls of the grounds, varying from 10min. to 1hr. Behind the monastery, short trails lead into the hills where its horses graze.

Town bakeries serve the traditional *Einsiedeln Lebkuchen.* These sweet honey- and-nut-filled cakes, unique to the town, come in white and brown varieties. The **Goldapfel Bakery,** Hauptstr. 67, in business for seven generations, and the attached **Lebkuchen Museum,** Kronenstr. 1, give an in-depth view of the history and methods surrounding the creation of these famous sweets. (Open daily Jan. to Easter 1:30-4:30pm; Easter to Dec. 1:30-6pm. Closed Dec. 25 and 26. Free. Bakery ☎ 055 412 23 30. Open M-F 7:45am-6:30pm, Sa 7:45am-5:30pm, Su 9am-5:30pm.)

The town's **tourist office** sits below the cathedral at Hauptstr. 85, Klosterpl. (☎ 418 44 88; www.einsiedeln.ch). A helpful staff can book tours for you and advise you on **hiking** opportunities in the lush hills surrounding the cathedral, as well as provide a schedule of *Klosterkirche* **concerts,** services, and events. They also offer **Internet** access (5SFr per 30min., 10SFr per hr.) on one computer. (Open M-F 10am-noon and 1:30-5pm, Sa 9am-noon and 1:30-4pm, Su and holidays 10am-noon.) A **24hr. ATM** and a Crédit Suisse **bank** (open M-F 8:30am-noon and 1:30-5pm, W until 6pm) are next to the tourist office. Limited **parking** is in front of the monastery. To reach the **police** station and **lost-and-found** office, call ☎ 055 418 74 44.

WINTERTHUR ☎ 052

Once the country home of eastern Switzerland's wealthy industrialists, Winterthur (VIN-ter-tur) today houses the fruits of their labor. The city's 17 museums, mostly endowed by those deceased wealthy industrialists, draw art connoisseurs, history buffs, and science fanatics from around the world.

■♂ TRANSPORT AND PRACTICAL INFORMATION

Trains run to Zurich (4 per hr. 6:22am-11:52pm, 10SFr) and connect there to Basel, Geneva, and St. Gallen (45min., 4 per hr. daily, 18.80SFr). Almost all **buses** leave from just right of the station. Winterthur's museums are closed Mondays. The **tourist office,** within the train station, provides brochures with excursion ideas and museum information. It offers free hotel reservations and a busy **Internet** terminal, free for the first 15min. and 2SFr per 15min. after that. (☎ 267 67 00; www.winterthur-tourismus.ch. Open M-F 8:30am-6:30pm, Sa 8:30am-4pm.) Next to the ticket counters in the information center, you'll find **currency exchange.** (Open daily 6am-8:30pm.) Down the hall from the info center, there's **bike rental** (open M-Sa 8:30am-7:30pm, Su 9am-noon and 2:40-7:30pm; 30SFr per day, under 16 25SFr; add 6SFr if returning to another station), and **luggage storage** (7SFr; same hrs. as bike rental). **Lockers** with 24hr. access (4-6SFr) and a **pharmacy** are also in the train station. The **post office** with a **24 hr. ATM** in the lobby is opposite the train station. (Open M-F 7:30am-7pm, Sa 8:30am-8pm, Su 8am-5pm.) **Postal Code:** CH-8401.

♠♥ ACCOMMODATIONS AND FOOD

Budget accommodations are hard to find in Winterthur. One solid choice is **Jugendunterkunft Winterthur ❷**, 18 Wildbach Str. From the train station, walk 7min. down Tecknikumstr. and turn right onto Zeughaus Str. You'll immediately see a fork in the road; take the right fork (Wildbachstr.) and the hostel will be on the left at the next intersection. Enter the hostel through the back of the building, up a flight of stairs. These clean and spacious rooms lack the typical bunk-bed arrangement and have their own sinks. Spacious, lodge-style rec room and convenient location make this hostel an excellent value. (☎ 267 48 48; fax 267 48 49. Breakfast 7:30am-9am 10SFr. Kitchen, TV room, sheets, and towels. Luggage watch during reception hours. Reception 7-10:30am and 4-9pm. Check-out 10am. Guests have 24hr. access. Quiet hours 10pm-6am. Open Apr.-Sept. 3- to 4-bed rooms 30SFr; singles 38SFr; doubles 38SFr.)

Food stands serve quick and cheap sandwiches throughout the downtown, particularly on Marktg. Locals on lunch break congregate at **Manta Sandwich-Bar ❷**, Untertor 17, near the train station. Filling gourmet sandwiches such as tomato, mozzarella, and eggplant go for 5-12SFr. (☎52 212 43 23; fax 52 212 43 18. Wheelchair accessible. Open M-W and F 6am-6:30pm, Th 6am-9pm, and Sa 6am-5pm.) For a slightly more upscale dining option, check out **National Bistro, Brasserie, and Bodega ❷**, Stadthausst. 24 ☎212 24 24, across from the train station. Lighter fare including a refreshing melon and port wine soup ranges from 8-16SFr, while heartier meat dishes go for 29-36SFr. Pasta falls in the middle of the price range and includes quite a few vegetarian options. Fruit and vegetable markets invade the streets of the *Altstadt* on Tuesdays and Fridays from 6am to 11am. A huge **Co-op** supermarket is behind the post office, attached to the Manor department store. A **Migros** supermarket is on Marktg. and Unterer Graben in the *Altstadt*.

👁 SIGHTS

Since museums are Winterthur's biggest draw, two options save you time and money: buying both a **Tageskarte** (7.20SFr) at the train station for public transportation (biking is also a popular option), and a **museum pass** (16SFr per day without Technorama, 2 days 25SFr, 3 days 28SFr.)

OSKAR REINHART COLLECTION. Winterthur's most generous art patron was Oskar Reinhart, as the two museums housing his collection demonstrate. The smaller but more impressive branch of the collection is just outside of town in the 🖼**Sammlung Oskar Reinhart am Römerholz.** Reinhart's gift to the Swiss Federation, the collection is valued at about three billion Swiss francs, and includes works by those Reinhart considered the "fathers of modern art," like El Greco, Goya, Holbein, and Rubens. The museum also showcases 19th-century masterpieces by Cézanne, Renoir, Manet, van Gogh, and Picasso, including paintings of Arles by van Gogh, completed the year before he passed away. Stop to gaze into the soft eyes of the lady in Manet's "At the Café." (*Haldenstr. 95. Take bus #10 to "Haldengut" (3 per hr. 6am-7pm; turn left and head up Haldenstr. for a steep 10min. walk. The museum sponsors a shuttle service, which runs from the train station to the villa every hr. Tu-Sa 9:45am-4:45pm, round-trip 5SFr. ☎269 27 40; www.kulturschweiz.admin.ch/sor. English audioguides available for 5SFr. Parking right outside the museum. Wheelchair accessible. Open Tu-Su 10am-5pm. 8SFr, students 6SFr. Combination ticket for both Reinhardt museums 12SFr/8SFr.)*

The larger collection is housed in the center of town at 🖼**Museum Oskar Reinhart am Stadtgarten.** The museum focuses on the work of Swiss, German, and Austrian painters, particularly portraits and landscapes. Stainless steel and glass steps lead to the remodeled fourth floor, which houses temporary exhibits. (*Stadthausstr. 6. Turn right out of the station, then go left on Stadthausstr. for 2 blocks. ☎52 267 51 72; fax 52 267 62 28. Open W-Su 10am-5pm, Tu 10am-8pm. 8SFr, students 6SFr.)*

TECHNORAMA. The **Swiss Technology Museum** houses interactive science experiments particularly popular with school groups and families. Explore the amazing properties of water, the power of magnetism, or the magic behind optical illusions. Train lovers will appreciate the tin toy train collection of Dr. Bommer, considered one of the world's most impressive. Play a water-powered drum set, or freeze your shadow in a "shadow box." Most displays are printed in German, French, Italian, and English. (*Technoramastr. 1. Take bus #5 (dir: Technorama) to the last stop (3 per hr. when museum is open). ☎244 08 44; www.technorama.ch. Wheelchair accessible. Open Tu-Su and public holidays 10am-5pm. 19SFr, students 15SFr, seniors 17SFr, ages 6-15 10SFr.)*

KUNSTMUSEUM. Winterthur's *Kunstmuseum* houses renowned Impressionist pieces by the likes of Van Gogh and Monet, but its specialty is Modernist art by Arp, Kandinsky, Klee, Léger, and Mondrian. In the summer, the museum features rotating exhibits of contemporary art. *(Museumstr. 52. Turn left from the station, right on Museumstr., and left on Lindstr. ☎ 267 51 62, automated information 267 58 00; www.kmw.ch. Open Tu 10am-8pm, W-Su 10am-5pm. 10SFr, students 7SFr.)* The **city library** and the **Museum of Natural Science** are in the same building. **Free Internet** is available at the library. *(☎ 267 51 66; www.kmw.ch. Library open M 10am-6pm, Tu-F 9am-8pm. Museum of Natural Science open Tu-Su 10am-5pm. Free.)*

FOTOMUSEUM. Among Winterthur's smaller museums is the unique Fotomuseum, housed in a former factory. The museum, which serves as the center of the counter-culture crowd in Winterthur, hosts exhibitions of photography, lectures, and discussions. *(Grüzenstr. 44. Take bus #2 (dir: Seen) to "Schleife." Follow the signs to the museum; at the fork in the road, stay right. ☎ 52 233 60 86; www.fotomuseum.ch. Open Tu and Th-F noon-6pm, W noon-7:30pm, Sa-Su 11am-5pm. 8SFr, students 5SFr.)*

STADTKIRCHE. While wandering around the *Altstadt,* visit the nearly hidden *Stadtkirche* (city church) on Kirchpl. The church was built in 1180, renovated in the late Gothic style between 1501 and 1515, and now blazes with Alberto Giacometti's stained-glass windows and Paul Zehnder's 1925 murals of brightly colored Bible stories. Check schedules at the church for frequent organ concerts of masterworks. *(Turn right off of Marktg. onto Unt. Kirchg.)*

LUCERNE (LUZERN) ☎ 041

Nestled among the foothills of the Alps, Lucerne (pop. 60,000) lies on a picturesque lake that has inspired poets and composers. A panorama stretching from Mount Rigi to Mount Pilatus shifts from glittering cobalt to foreboding gray as the weather changes. Visits to museums, cruises on the placid **Vierwaldstättersee,** and hikes up the peaks of Mount Pilatus and Rigi Kulm draw hordes of visitors to this city. Lucerne is both the capital of its canton and one of most popular vacation cities in Switzerland.

▣ TRANSPORTATION

Trains: To: **Basel** (1hr., 1-2 per hr.); **Engelberg** (1hr., 1-3 per hr.); **Geneva** (1 every 2-3hr.); **Zurich** (1hr., 1-3 per hr.).

Buses: Typically run every 10min. and leave from in front of the train station. 3-day pass for hotel guests 12SFr. 8-day pass for guests 30SFr.

Taxis: In front of the station and Municipal Theater and at Pilatuspl. and Schwanenpl. **SNG Seetaxi** (lake "taxis;" ☎ 041 368 08 09) leave from piers by the station.

✳ ▟ ORIENTATION AND PRACTICAL INFORMATION

The **Reuss River,** draining from the Vierwaldstättersee (Lake Lucerne), narrows steadily through the center of Lucerne. The train station, tourist office, and post office line the edges of Bahnhofpl. on the bank south of the Reuss, while the streets of the *Altstadt* twist through the northern bank. The **Kapellbrücke** in the east and the **Spreuerbrücke** in the west are the two ancient wooden bridges that span the Reuss, with three bridges between them.

TOURIST AND FINANCIAL SERVICES

Tourist Office: In the train station (☎ 227 17 17; www.luzern.org). Offers free city guide and hotel reservation service. Ask about the **Visitor's Card,** which, in conjunction with a hotel or hostel stamp, provides discounts (usually about 10-20%) at museums, bars, car rental places, and stores. **Internet** terminal in the office (4SFr per 10min.). The

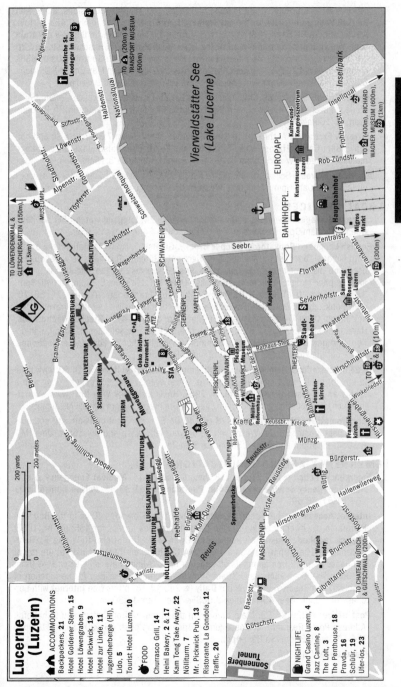

CENTRAL
SWITZERLAND

Lucerne (Luzern)

ACCOMMODATIONS
Backpackers, 21
Hotel Goldener Stern, 15
Hotel Löwengraben, 9
Hotel Pickwick, 13
Hotel zur Linde, 11
Jugendherberge (HI), 1
Lido, 5
Tourist Hotel Luzern, 10

FOOD
Churrasco Grill, 14
Heini Bakery, 2 & 17
Kam Tong Take Away, 22
Nöliturm, 7
Mr. Pickwick Pub, 13
Ristorante La Gondola, 12
Traffic, 20

NIGHTLIFE
Grand Casino Luzern, 4
Jazz Cantine, 8
The Loft, 3
The Penthouse, 18
Pravda, 16
Schüür, 19
Ufer-los, 23

office also sells tickets for Mt. Pilatus, Rigi Kulm, and Mt. Titlis excursions, along with the **Tell-Pass** and tickets for the city **walking tour** (2hr.; May-Oct. daily 9:45am, Nov.-Apr. W and Sa 9:45am; 18SFr.) The city tour may be combined with the new city **train tour**, which departs from the front of the Schweizerhof Hotel on Hirschmattstr. (☎220 11 00; www.citytrain.ch. 35min.; 1 per hr. M-F from 11am, Sa-Su from 10am; 8SFr, children ages 5-12 5SFr) in a combination ticket for 24SFr. Open May-Oct. M-F 8:30am-6:30pm, Sa 9am-6:30pm; Nov.-Apr. M-F 8:30am-5:30pm, Sa-Su 9am-1pm.

Budget Travel: STA Travel, Grabenstr. 8 (☎412 23 23; www.statravel.ch), offers ISICs, student travel deals, and discount flights. Open M-W and F 9:30am-6pm, Th 9:30am-8pm, Sa 10am-4pm.

Currency Exchange: At the station. Open May-Oct. M-F 7:30am-7:30pm, Sa-Su and holidays 8am-6pm. **Migros bank,** Seidenhofstr. 6, off Bahnhofstr., has an exchange machine. Open M-W and F 9am-5:15pm, Th 9am-6:30pm, Sa 8:15am-noon.

American Express: Schweizerhofquai 4 (☎419 99 00). Checks cashed. Travel services open M-F 8:30am-6pm. Also offers **Western Union** services.

LOCAL SERVICES

Luggage Storage: Downstairs at the station, window 24. **Luggage watch** 5SFr per item. Open daily 6am-9pm. **Lockers** in a well-lit area with 24hr. access 4-6SFr.

English-Language Bookstores: Bücher Brocky, Güterstr.1. From the station take a right onto Iselquai, bear left on Werfstr., then right onto Güterstr. This massive warehouse of used and discount books has only a few English shelves, but the selection is unique and the price is right (1SFr for paperbacks). Open M-F 10:30am-6:30pm, Th until 8pm, Sa 9am-4pm. **Orell Füssli Raeber Bücher,** on Frankenstr. 7-9 (☎229 60 20; www.books.ch) off Zentralstr. Sophisticated selection of English literature, travel books, and maps. Open M-F 9am-6:30pm, Th 9am-8pm, Sa 9am-4pm. **Stocker Bücherhaus,** Hertensteinstr. 44 (☎417 25 25; www.buchhaus.ch). Large selection of fiction, non-fiction, and new release paperback and hardcover English books. For English magazines, check out the kiosk in the basement of the train station.

GLBT Organizations: Homosexuelle Arbeitsgruppe Luzern (HALU; ☎360 14 60; www.halu-luzern.ch) publishes a monthly calendar of social events, available online. Along with a library and a disco (see **Nightlife,** p. 395), HALU also runs **Why Not** (www.whynot-luzern.ch), a discussion group for young gays, which meets Tu 9pm at local restaurants.

Laundromat: Jet Wasch, Bruchstr. 28 (☎240 01 51), turn right off Pilatusstr. and continue past Kloster Str. Jet Wasch will be on your left. Wash and dry 16SFr. Open M-F 8:30am-12:30pm and 2:30-6:30pm, Sa 9am-2pm.

EMERGENCY AND COMMUNICATIONS

Emergency: Police ☎117. **Fire** ☎118. **Ambulance** ☎144. **Medical Emergency** ☎111. **Auto Emergency Service** ☎140. **24hr. Pharmacy** ☎211 33 33. **Poison Control** ☎01 251 51 51/66 66.

Internet Access: The best deal, **Stadtbibliothek** (City Library), 1 fl. up in the Bourbaki Panorama at Lowenpl. by the Glacier Garden, provides access for 4SFr per hr. 10SFr deposit required. Wheelchair accessible. Open M 1:30-6:30pm, Tu-W and F 10am-6:30pm, Th 10am-9pm, Sa 10am-4pm. **C+A Clothing,** on Hertensteinstr. at the top of the *Altstadt,* has 2 free terminals on its lower floor. 20min. time limit. Open M-W 9am-6:30pm, Th-F 9am-9pm, Sa 8:30am-4pm. Wheelchair accessible. At the junction of Bruchstr. and Baselstr. the drink bar **Daily** (☎240 14 18) offers **free Internet** with purchase of a drink. Beer 4SFr. Coffee 3.50SFr. Open 7am-11:30pm.

Post Office: ☎229 95 23. Main branch on the corner of Bahnhofstr. and Bahnhofpl. Address *Poste Restante* to: Postlagernde Briefe, Hauptpost; CH-6000 Luzern 1. Open M-F 7:30am-6:30pm, Sa 8am-4pm.

Postal Code: CH-6000.

▚ ACCOMMODATIONS AND CAMPING

Relatively inexpensive beds are available only in limited numbers in Lucerne, so call ahead in order to ensure a roof over your head.

☒ Backpackers, Alpenquai 42 (☎360 04 20; www.backpackerslucerne.ch). Turn right out of the station, following the lake around the corner past the Europapl. fountain. Cross the street and walk straight ahead through the tour bus parking lot to the concrete pedestrian bridge. When the walkway ends (10min.), follow the sidewalk straight ahead 5min. past the park. The hostel is at the end of the road on the right. The long walk can be a hassle, but the path is lit. Dorm rooms with large balconies, a comfortable dining room, a sitting room, and tons of students from around the world make this hostel a pleasant spot. The store sells "survival kits" of pasta, sauce, and wine for 9SFr, and many use the 2 kitchens, each with a refrigerator, oven, and lots of cooking utensils. Tickets sold for cable cars on local mountains. Breakfast 7SFr (M-F 6:30-8:30am). Bike rental 16SFr per day. Ping pong, badminton, roller blades, and scooters available. **Internet** 10SFr per hr., available when reception is open. The staff will wash, dry, and fold laundry for 9SFr. Towel 1SFr. Sheets included (sleeping bags strictly forbidden). Key deposit of 50SFr, passport, or driver's license. Reception 7:30-10am and 4-11pm. 10am check-out strictly enforced. 4-bed dorms 28SFr; 2-bed dorms 34SFr. 2SFr cheaper in winter. ❷

Tourist Hotel Luzern, St. Karliquai 12 (☎410 24 74; www.touristhotel.ch), on the *Altstadt* side of Spreuerbrücke. Manned by an amiable staff, the hotel offers cheap, clean rooms with views of the river at Mt. Pilatus. Very close to the *Altstadt*'s center. Hertz car rentals, Mt. Pilatus tickets, and tickets for other excursions can be booked here. Currency exchange available. No smoking. **Internet** 10SFr per hr. while reception is open. Breakfast included (7-10am). TV room. Free luggage storage. Lockers in dorms are small; bring your own lock. Laundry 10SFr. Reception 7am-10pm. Check-out 11am. Wheelchair accessible. Apr.-Oct. dorms 35-40SFr; singles 69-75SFr; doubles 98-112SFr; triples 120-138SFr. Nov.-Mar. dorms 33SFr; singles, doubles, and triples 10-30SFr cheaper than Apr.-Oct. Add 10-25SFr per person for private shower. AmEx/MC/V. Traveler's checks accepted. Dorms must pay with cash. ❸

Hotel Löwengraben, Löwengraben 18 (☎417 12 12; www.loewengraben.ch). Until November 1998, Hotel Löwengraben was a prison providing full services to the miscreants of Lucerne. In only 7 months the building was converted into a trendy hostel, swathed in black. The ground floor hosts a bar and several theme restaurants. Ask about daily events and tours. Löwengraben's attached club, **Alcatraz,** provides a popular spot for drinks and socializing and also hosts a few city-wide events. No smoking. Breakfast 15SFr. Locked storage room for luggage. Sheets included. Reception 24hr. Check-in after 3pm. Check-out 11am. Quiet hours midnight-7am. Singles with shower 105-150SFr, without shower 84SFr; triples 155SFr; quads 150SFr. Suites 250-300SFr, including breakfast. Reduced rates in winter. AmEx/DC/MC/V. ❷

Hotel Goldener Stern, Burgerstr. 35 (☎227 50 60; www.goldener-stern.ch). From the station head left on Pilatusstr., turn right onto Hirscheng., and veer right onto Burgerstr. The hotel is a short walk from the train station, and all rooms are equipped with shower, toilet, TV, and telephone. Public parking lot across from the hotel. Breakfast included. Reception M-Sa 6am-midnight, Su 6am-10pm. Check-in M-Sa 11am. Check-out 10am. Singles 90-100SFr; doubles 130-155SFr. Reduced rates in winter. AmEx/DC/MC/V. ❹

Jugendherberge Luzern (HI), Sedelstr. 12 (☎420 88 00; www.youthhostel.ch/luzern). During the day, take bus #18 to "Jugendherberge." In a white concrete building, near the Rotsee, with a beautiful valley view. Beds have clean sheets and night lights. Parking and covered bike shed available. 24hr. **Internet** access 2SFr per 10min. Buffet breakfast 7-9:30am. Dinner (and lunch on request) 12.50SFr. Showers, lockers, and sheets included. Quiet hours 10:30pm-7am. Laundry service 15SFr. Reception Apr.-Oct. daily 7-10am and 2pm-midnight; Nov.-Mar. 7-10am and 4pm-midnight. Call ahead in summer. Dorms 32SFr; doubles 78SFr, with shower 108SFr. Children 2-6 half-price, under 2 free. Non-members 6SFr extra. AmEx/DC/MC/V. ❷

Hotel zur Linde, Metzgerrainie 3 (☎410 31 93; fax 32 05). Centrally located on Weinmarkt in the *Altstadt.* Offers basic rooms with communal showers and toilet. Sinks in room. Reception M-Sa 11:30am-2:30pm and 6pm-12:30am. Check-out 10am. Open Apr.-Oct. Singles 54SFr; doubles 100SFr. AmEx/MC/V. ❸

Hotel Pickwick, Rathausquai 6 (☎410 59 27; www.hotelpickwick.ch). Conveniently located in the *Altstadt* between the Kapellbrücke and *Rathaus* Steg bridge. Comfortable rooms with TV. No breakfast, but bar and restaurant downstairs (see **Food,** p. 392). Reception in bar 11:30am-12:30am. Check-out 11am. Singles 75-85SFr, with shower 85-100SFr; doubles 85-120SFr/100-150SFr. Winter prices reduced by 10-20SFr. AmEx/MC/V. ❹

Lido, Lidostr. 8 (☎370 21 46; www.camping-international.ch), 35min. along Nationalquai, or take bus #6 or 8 (dir: Würzenbach) to "Verkehrshaus." A campsite near the lake with all the amenities, including free shower. Reception and snack bar daily 8:30-11:30am and 3-8pm. Open Mar.-Oct. 15.70SFr per person with tent, 20.70SFr with car.

▐ FOOD

Markets along the river sell cheap fresh goods on Tuesday and Saturday mornings, and there is a **fresh fruit market** every morning outside the *Rathaus,* in the *Altstadt.* Supermarkets and department stores offer the cheapest restaurant meals. A 24hr. vending machine is also available on the lower level of the main train station.

Churrasco Grill, Rösslig. 2 (☎410 74 00) offers Argentine specialties such as empanadas (12.80SFr) and grilled meats with chimichurri (32.50-36SFr). Wooden beams and cow-hide-covered booths give the dining room a ranch-like feel. A terrace in the back offers summer seating. ❸

Kam Tong Chinese Take Away, Inselquai 10 (☎218 58 50 or 532 31 54). Turn right in front of the station and right on Inselquai (10min. from Backpackers hostel) to reach this small family-run restaurant housed in a Chinese grocery store. Enjoy cheap and relatively authentic Asian fare at the 2 tables at the store, or take your food to go and relax by the side of the river. The affable staff serve up most meals for 12-17SFr. Chicken with cashews 16SFr. Vegetable lo mein 12SFr. Wheelchair accessible. Open M-W 9am-6:30pm, Th-F 9am-9pm, Sa 9am-4pm. ❷

Heini Bakery, at Löwenpl. and Falkenpl. (☎412 20 20; www.heini.ch). Famous for the seasonal varieties of dense, flaky-crusted tarts it prepares daily (4.10-4.90SFr), good for meals or desserts. Try the *Älplermakkronen* (Swiss mac 'n cheese, 13.30SFr) or the *Heini* plate with vegetable *Strudel* and salad (13.90SFr). Wheelchair accessible. At Löwenpl., open M-F 6am-6:30pm, Sa 6am-5pm, Su 9am-6pm. At Falkenpl., M-F 7am-6:30pm (Th until 10pm), Sa 9am-6pm. AmEx/DC/MC/V only at Falkenpl. ❷

Mr. Pickwick Pub, Rathausquai 6 (☎410 59 27), in the *Altstadt* between the Kapellbrücke and *Rathaus* Steg bridge, offers some of the cheapest fare of the restaurants lining the Reuss. Order fish 'n' chips (17.50SFr) or an English chicken curry sandwich (8.50SFr) at the bar. BBC sports on the television. Hotel upstairs. Burgers from 8.50SFr. Sandwiches 6.50-8.50SFr. Large selection of beer on tap and in bottles starting at 4.50SFr (Guiness 5SFr). Open daily 11:30am-12:30am. AmEx/DC/MC/V. ❷

Traffic, the train station cafeteria, provides a large selection in an atmosphere that is surprisingly clean and pleasant. Dishes from 10.80SFr. Salad bar 2.70SFr per 100g. Many a la carte items are also available (sandwich 4.50SFr, cookies and pastries from 2SFr). Wheelchair accessible. Open daily 6:30am-9:15pm. ❶

Ristorante La Gondola, Weinmarkt 3 (☎410 61 15). Offers fine Italian cuisine in the heart of Lucerne's *Altstadt*. Feast on pizza (13.50-26SFr) and pasta (14.50-29.50SFr) amidst huge murals of Venice. Soups 7-11SFr. Risottos 17-26SFr. Open Tu-F 11:30am-2:30pm and 6pm-midnight, Sa-Su 11:30am-midnight. AmEx/DC/MC/V. ❸

Nölliturm, St. Karlistr. 2 (☎240 28 66), on the *Altstadt* side of the Geissmatt bridge. Cheap, hearty Swiss specialties in this restaurant just outside the *Altstadt. Rösti Bernois* (with bacon and onions) 15.50SFr. *Gnocchis* 16.50SFr. Meat dishes 19.80-28.50SFr. Open daily 8am-12:30am. AmEx/MC/V. ❷

MARKETS

Migros, at the station and at Hertensteinstr. 44. Station location open M-Sa 6:30am-9pm, Su 8am-9pm. Hetensteinstr. location open M-W 8:30am-6:30pm, Th-F 8:30am-9pm, Sa 8am-4pm. Cafeteria-style restaurant in Hertensteinstr. location has inexpensive pizza, pasta, and grill options, as well as a salad and ovo-vegetarian buffet for 2.30SFr per 100g. Open M-F 8:30am-6:30pm, Sa 8am-4pm.

Müller Reformhaus, at the corner of Weinmark and Kornmarkt near the Picasso Museum, sells a large selection of organic foods. Open M and W-F 9am-6:30pm, Tu 8:30am-6:30pm, Sa 8:30am-4pm.

❻ 🏛 SIGHTS AND MUSEUMS

THE OLD CITY. The *Altstadt* is famous for its frescoed houses, especially those of Hirschenpl. and Weinmarkt. It is also known for the gorgeous bridges over the river. The **Kapellbrücke,** a 660-year-old wooden-roofed bridge, connects the *Altstadt* to Bahnhofstr. Its entire center section burned in 1993 (the cause is still unknown, but theories include arson and a burning barge), but proud citizens restored it within a few months. Over the years, its octagonal tower has served as a watchtower, jail, torture chamber, and guildhall. Farther down the river, the **Spreuerbrücke** offers an image of what the *Kapellbrücke* looked like before the fire. Both bridges have painted triangle ceiling supports; those on the Spreuer allow you to confront your mortality in Kaspar Meglinger's eerie *Totentanz* (Dance of Death) paintings. On the hills above the river, the **Museggmauer** and its towers are all that remain of the medieval city's ramparts. They still define the city skyline, especially when illuminated at night. The *Schirmerturm, Männliturm,* and *Zeitturm* towers are accessible to visitors. *(Open summer daily 8am-7pm.)* The **Zeitturm** (clock tower) provides a particularly pleasing panorama of the city. *(From the station head left along the river and cross the Spreuerbrücke, the 2nd wooden bridge. Walk left along St. Karli-Quai, turn right going uphill, and follow the brown castle signs.)*

⬛ PICASSO MUSEUM. A stroll through the museum's three floors reveals an intimate and often humerous side of Picasso's daily life, as captured in over 200 photographs by his longtime friend David Duncan. Through snapshots of the artist getting dressed, painting alongside his children, and lunching with Simone Signoret, visitors to the museum begin to feel that they know this fascinating artist. A large collection of unpublished Picasso lithographs, drawings, and paintings are also on display in this 16th-century home-turned-museum. *(Am Rhyn Haus, Furreng. 21. From Schwanenpl., take Rathausquai to Furreng. Next to the Rathaus. ☎410 17 73 or 410 35 33; fax 10 45. Guidebooks in English and French. Open daily Apr.-Oct. 10am-6pm; Nov.-Mar. 11am-5pm. 8SFr, with guest card 6SFr, students 5SFr. Inquire about the Combi-ticket with the Sammlung Rosengart.)*

⬛ VERKEHRSHAUS DER SCHWEIZ (TRANSPORT MUSEUM). With everything from a fighter jet simulation to a real spaceship open for exploration (The Columbus), to an exhibit allowing visitors to create their own TV program or radio show, to displays of cars from as early as 1898, to a modern art gallery, a trip to this museum can easily fill an entire day. Learn about balloon flight and get a view of the city on the *Hiflyer*, or plan your next day in Switzerland on the largest aerial photograph of the country. Call ahead or pick up an exhaustive brochure with a schedule of special tours, lectures, and exhibitions, including a ride through the inner workings of tunnel construction. The museum also has a planetarium and Switzerland's only IMAX theater. *(Lidostr. 5. ☎227 17 17; www.verkehrshaus.org. Take bus #6, 8, or 24 to "Verkershaus" or walk along the Nationalquai for 20min. IMAX reservations ☎375 75 75; www.imax.ch. Wheelchair accessible. Open daily Apr.-Oct. 10am-6pm; Nov.-Mar. 10am-5pm. Museum 26SFr, guest card holders and students 22SFr, children 6-16 12SFr, with SwissPass 16SFr, with Eurail 14SFr. IMAX 16SFr. Both 32SFr, children under 16 21SFr, families 90SFr. Hiflyer daily 11am-5pm and night flights June-Aug. F-Sa 7-10pm. 16SFr, children under 16 12SFr, families 50SFr.)*

LÖWENDENKMAL AND GLACIER GARDEN. Danish sculptor Bertel Thorvaldesen carved the magnificent *Löwendenkmal* (Lion Monument), the dying lion of Lucerne, out of a cliff on Denkmalstr. The 9m monument honors the Swiss Guard who defended Marie Antoinette to the death at the Tuileries in 1792. Mark Twain described it as "the saddest and most moving piece of rock in the world." At the *Gletschergarten* (Glacier Garden), visitors follow a paved walkway over glacial "potholes" and striations in the smooth rock. A jumbled but interesting museum takes you through a mishmash of glacial science, geology displays, and Lucerne history from the time of the glaciers to today. Next door, the disorienting *Spiegellabyrinth* (mirror maze) strands young and old alike in a Middle Eastern oasis. Just one wrong step leaves friends faced by thousands of reflections of each other, completely unsure of which is the real person. The maze has been called "the finest mirror maze in the world today" by World Mazes Magazine. *(☎410 43 40; fax 43 10. From the station, take bus #1 to Lowenpl., or walk across Seebrücke to Schwanenpl., follow Schweizerhofquai to the right, and turn left on Denkmalstr. Parking available. Ask at desk for wheelchair-accessible entrance. Open daily Apr.-Oct. 9am-6pm; Nov.-Mar. 10am-5pm. 9SFr, with guest card 7.50SFr, students 7SFr, children under 16 5.50SFr. AmEx/MC/V.)*

RICHARD WAGNER MUSEUM. The famous composer's once-secluded lakeside home is now an exhibit of original letters, scores, and antique musical instruments. His years in Lucerne, the "Tribschen years" (1866-1872), were marked by productivity and personal happiness—it was here that he married Cosima von Bülow and entertained the likes of King Ludwig II of Bavaria, Franz Liszt, and Nietzsche. *(Wagnerweg 27. Take bus #6, 7, or 8 to "Wartegg." or turn right from the station and follow directions to Backpackers hostel. Walk 10min. past Backpackers along the lake until you reach the small marina. Go past the marina building to the right and walk uphill on the wooded trail (Tribschenhornweg) 5min., following the brown signs. Parking available. ☎360 23 70; www.richard-wagner-museum.ch. Displays in English, French, and German. Open mid-Mar. to Nov. Tu-Su 10am-noon and 2-5pm. 6SFr, students and guest card holders 4SFr.)*

KUNSTMUSEUM LUZERN. Housed within the futuristic Lucerne Culture and Conference Center, the Lucerne Museum of Art is home to temporary art exhibits spanning all genres and time periods. 2004 saw everything from Romantic-era landscapes to comic book and video installations. A modern 2D art installation will be on display through the beginning of 2005, and an exhibition by artists from the Lucerne area will last through January 2005. *(Europapl. 1, next to the train station. ☎226 78 00; www.kunstmuseumluzern.ch. Literature in English. Wheelchair accessible. Open Tu-Su 10am-5pm, W 10am-8pm. 10SFr, students and guest card holders 8SFr. AmEx/MC/V.)*

SAMMLUNG ROSENGART LUZERN. The newest addition to Lucerne's cultural offerings. This three-story collection displays works of 20th-century artists Miró, Renoir, Kandinsky, Chagall, and Matisse. The entire entry floor is devoted to Picasso's work, while the basement features works by Klee. Museum staff suggests visiting the Picasso Museum first, "to get to know him," followed by the Rosengart Collection. *(Pilatusstr. 10, left from the train station. ☎ 220 16 60; www.rosengart.ch. Open daily Apr.-Oct. 10am-6pm; Nov.-Mar. 11am-5pm. 14SFr, students 9SFr, children 5SFr. Save 2SFr with guest card. Inquire about Combi-ticket with the Picasso Museum.)*

JESUITENKIRCHE. Left from the station down Bahnhofstr., after the Kapellbr. The twin steeples of the Jesuit Church stand out in the Lucerne skyline. Within the church, ornate pink-and-white frescoes and a lavish marble-and-gold front altar are accented by eight equally elaborate side altars, all Baroque pieces telling a different Biblical story. *(www.jesuitenkirche-luzern.ch. Open daily 7am-7pm.)*

CHÂTEAU GÜTSCH AND GÜTSCHWALD. Head left down Bahnhofstr. until it becomes Baselstr. About 50m past the Daily Internet Café, take a left onto Gibraltarstr. and an immediate right onto Gütschweg. This takes you by foot (10min.) up the hill to Château Gütsch, a Cinderella's castle/hotel with gardens and fountains, though its main selling point is a great view of Lucerne below. An alternate way to the top is a 15min. ride on the Gütschbahn funicular. *(Official transportation passes not applicable. Check with the tourist office to see if tours of the grounds are available; the hotel closed in summer 2003. 3SFr, children 2SFr.)*

🎵 ENTERTAINMENT

The city of Lucerne comes alive in the summer with a full calendar of concerts, festivals, and sporting events. Get a monthly schedule at the tourist office. In the third week of July, Lucerne attracts big names for its summer **Blue Balls Festival** (yup) and fall **Blues Festival** (2nd week in Nov.). Past performers include Bonnie Raitt, Herbie Hancock, and Van Morrison. (☎/fax 227 10 58; www.blueballs.ch.) The **Lucerne Festival** runs mid-August to mid-September, attracting famous classical orchestras and featuring contemporary world music. (Hirschmattst 13, Postfach 6002, Luzern. ☎ 226 44 00; www.lucernefestival.ch. Tickets 20-220SFr.) Up to 50,000 people flood the city for the June **Altstadtfest.** Bands perform everything from salsa to covers of American songs to original music in pavilions scattered throughout the old city, while spectators fill up on *Wurst* and beer. The **Nationalquai** is the scene for free summertime **Pavilion Musik** concerts, featuring brass and jazz bands playing Hollywood tunes, Gershwin, and Duke Ellington. (May-Sept. Tu and F 8:15pm, Su 10:15pm.) **Open Air Kino Luzern** (www.open-air-kino.ch), at the outdoor theater in the Seepark near Backpackers Hostel, shows movies (15SFr), mostly in English, every night mid-July to mid-August. Pick up a schedule at the tourist office. In mid-June, the International Rowing Regatta brings the world's elite crews together for the **World Cup Finals** on the Rotsee. On Saturdays 8am-noon, catch the **flea market** (May-Oct.) along Burgerstr. and Reussteg.

🌙 NIGHTLIFE

Locals hang at clubs clustered around Pilatuspl. and down Pilatusstr. (the more modern section of town). Across the river and down Nationalquai, a few other spots around the Casino on Haldenstr. bustle with activity. **Ufer-los,** Geissensteinring 14, a Saturday-night-only disco in conjuction with HALU (p. 390), is Lucerne's only self-proclaimed GLBT option. Check the monthly calendar—the events range from women-only nights to themed parties.

The Loft, Haldenstr. 21 (☎410 92 64; www.theloft.ch). A trendy new club with high ceilings, disco lights, and a young crowd in their 20s and 30s. Hosts special DJs and theme nights. Beer 8-9SFr. Cocktails 12-18SFr. W salsa night. Th pure R&B and house. Half-price happy hour Th 10pm-11pm; W all drinks around 2SFr cheaper; Su women get 1 free drink until 11:30. No cover W, Th 10SFr (5 of which goes towards drink vouchers), F and Sa 15SF, Su 7SFr (all of which goes toward drink vouchers). Open W 9pm-2am, Th-Su 10am-4pm. Across the street, the recently-opened **Grand Casino Luzern,** Haldenstr. 6 (☎418 56 56; www.casinoluzern.ch), offers poker, craps, and 217 slot machines (from 0.05SFr per go). Jacket and tie required after 7pm. 18+. Bring a passport. 10SFr admission after 4pm, 5SFr of which include "Lucky Chips." Open daily noon-4am.

Jazz Cantine, Grabenstr. 8 (☎410 73 73). Affiliated with the Jazz School of Lucerne. Features an almost-daily selection of diploma concerts and jam sessions (usually starting at 7pm). Outdoor seating. Sandwiches 6-8SFr. Thai noodles 15SFr. Coffee 3.20SFr. Beer 3.70SFr. Wheelchair accessible. Open M-Sa 7am-12:30am, Su 4pm-12:30am; food served 11:30am-2pm and 6:30-10pm.

Pravda (☎226 88 88; www.pravda.ch). Left off Pilatusstr. on Winkleriedst. R&B, hip-hop, and house. Cover charges vary with the nightly event (usually 10-20SFr). Free entry and half-price drinks W 10pm-2:30am. R&B Th 10pm-2:30am with free entry. F-Su opening times vary but are typically around 10 or 11pm; open Sa until 4am.

The Penthouse (☎226 88 88; www.astoria-luzern.ch), in the Hotel Astoria, 7 floors up and eye-to-eye with Lucerne's steeples. The sleek rooftop bar hosts a casual, international crowd. Younger folks relax in the couches surrounded by palm trees while an older crowd fills the bar. Beer (5-8SFr) and other drinks rise in price by 2-4SFr after 9pm. DJs spin Th-Sa 9:30pm-2:30am (often tunes from the 70s and 80s). No cover. Open Su-Tu 5pm-12:30am, W-Sa 5pm-2:30am. AmEx/DC/MC/V.

Schüür, Tribschenstr. 1 (☎368 10 30; www.schuur.ch). Follow Zentralstr. along the train tracks, turn left onto Lagensandbr. The club is on the left, on the other end of the bridge. Hosts a variety of theme nights and concerts, ranging from "Noche Cubana" to "Kick'n'Rush Party." Covers and starting times depend on the event. Check the website for exact times and prices. Beer 5SFr. Open Th 8:30pm-2:30am, F-Sa 8:30pm-3:30am.

⚠ OUTDOOR ACTIVITIES

The cheapest option for getting out on the **Vierwaldstättersee** (Lake Lucerne) is to take one of the **ferries** that serve the tiny villages around the lake. Not only can you enjoy the magnificent scenery without exerting yourself, but you can also disembark at the lakeside villages to explore further. The tourist office in the station has a much more user-friendly timetable than the one the ship office provides; it includes information on round-trip tours ranging 1-5hr. A daypass for unlimited boat travel costs 45SFr. In the shadow of Mt. Pilatus, the glass-blowers at **Hergiswil** have been fashioning works of art in their boiling-hot oven room since 1817. At the **Glasi Hergiswil** complex, stroll through the museum and exhibits devoted to glass musical instruments and physics experiments, or take a "guided" audio tour that traces the history of glass-making and the Hergiswil factory. Around the lake, glass art objects and water toys can entertain kids while adults sip beer from foot-tall Hergiswall glass flutes. (1hr. boat ride from Luzern, 10min. by train. ☎632 32 32; www.glasi.ch. Complex open M-F 9am-6pm, Sa 9am-4pm. Glass exhibitions M-F 9:30am-5pm and 5:30-6pm, Sa 9:30am-noon. Free.) A short scenic hike at **Bürgenstock** via **Kehrsiten** (round-trip 2hr., 44SFr) is popular with families. Visitors will find five of central Switzerland's lakes at their feet. For an easy walk along the lake, get off the ferry at **Weggis** (round-trip 2hr., 24SFr). **SGV** boats depart from the piers in front of the train station. (☎367 67 67; www.lakelucerne.ch. SwissPass and Eurail valid.) Catch one of the five fully operational steamships, the internal workings of which are on display. On the **Wilhelm Tell Express,** a bugle-playing sailor may accompany your journey with a jaunty rendition of the famous overture.

Outventure (☎611 14 41; www.outventure.ch) provides outdoor thrills with local flair. The company has grown from the original Mountain Guides Office to a full-service adventure company with **paragliding** (150SFr), **canyoning** (from 170SFr), **glacier hiking** (from 170SFr), and **bungee jumping** (160SFr). Outventure is a member of the Swiss Outdoors Association, a group that maintains safety and training standards. (Daily shuttle from the tourist office at 8:30am. Book in advance.) In winter, ski-loving locals flock to the Engelberg-Titlis slopes to **snowboard** and **ski.** A few slopes are open year-round. See **Engleberg-Titlis** (p. 398) for more information.

◪ DAYTRIPS FROM LUCERNE

Lucerne's most renowned daytrips are excursions to the mountains that haunt the city's skyline. The trip up is as memorable as the view from the top. Don't expect true Swiss countryside on these trips—you'll see few cows—but routes are packed with visitors for good reason: Mt. Titlis is the highest point in central Switzerland, and Pilatus has the highest vista, though views from nearby Rigi are almost as rewarding. If you want to do two or more mountain excursions, consider the **Tell-Pass** (two days of free travel and half-price for another five 135SFr, with Swiss-Pass 108SFr; or five days of free travel, plus 10 at half-price 184SFr/147SFr), sold at the tourist office and at Pier 1. Children up to age 16 travel free provided they are accompanied by a parent and have a Junior Pass. It is also valid for all cable cars, cogwheel trains, boats, buses, and regular trains in central Switzerland. One section of the Titlis route is only half-price for Tell-Pass holders (25SFr).

MOUNT PILATUS

*This memorable travel route begins with the 1½hr. boat ride from Lucerne to Alpnachstad, followed by an ascent on the steepest **cogwheel train** in the world (48° gradient), a descent by cable car to Krienz, then a bus ride back to Lucerne (entire trip 3hr.; 78.40SFr, with Eurail 43SFr, with SwissPass 40.60SFr). Be sure to call the cable car company first because they won't run in windy or stormy conditions. It is slightly cheaper if riding the cable car both ways. Save money by hiking: take the train or boat to Hegiswil and hike 3hr. up the hillside to Fräkmüntegg, a half-way point on the cable car. (23SFr to Hergiswill, SwissPass and Eurail valid. 22SFr round-trip*

THE LOCAL STORY

DA, DA, DA

The silent walls of Spiegalg. 3 in Zurich's *Altstadt* witnessed one of the most rebellious movements in the history of art and theater. The years between the World Wars offered no lull for the city's citizens, as a group of angry young artists spilled their creativity into the craziest forms of art. The result was Dadaism, an art that refused to be art, whose guiding principle was confusion and paradoxical humor. Dada's aim was to provoke a rude awakening from standard thinking and bourgeois preconceptions. Dada is said to have taken its name either from the French word for "hobby-horse," which Hugo Ball selected by sticking a pen-knife into a German-French dictionary, or from the refrain of two Romanian founders of the movement, who used to mutter, "Da, da" ("yes, yes" in Romanian). Distinguished painter/sculptor Alberto Giacometti entered the fray during a sojourn in Zurich—it is said that one day, he opened the door of Cabaret Voltaire, stepped out, shouted, "Viva Dada!" at the top of his lungs, and disappeared, as promenadeurs on the Limmatquai stopped in their tracks. Today Cabaret Voltaire is preserved in the entrails of the disco/bar Castel Dada.

from Fräkmuntegg to the top.) The hike offers views of the lake and Lucerne. In the summer, Fräkmüntegg operates central Switzerland's longest Rodelbahn course. For 7SFr, you can whizz down the hillside on a metal track, riding a plastic slide that achieves surprisingly high speeds. Half the fun is being hauled back up to the top by a ski-lift-type device. The tourist office also offers round-trip guided excursions from May-Oct. at 12:10pm (92SFr). For more information on the Pilatus excursions, contact the Pilatus Railway (☎ 329 11 11; www.pilatus.com).

As hulking as the enormous dragons allegedly spotted here in the 15th century, **Mt. Pilatus** stretches 2132m to the top of Lucerne's southern sky. Numerous quick jaunts to the various craggy promontories are possible from the station and restaurant at the top. The easy and popular "Dragon Trail" tunnels in and out of the mountain and has displays in English that explain Mt. Pilatus's religious and dragon-related history. The trip up the mountain, which can require up to four different types of transportation, is at least half the fun.

RIGI KULM

Start your trip on a ferry to Vitznau (1hr.; round-trip 30SFr). Then hike up (5hr.) or take a cogwheel train ride (30min.; 32SFr) to the top. For a less strenuous hike, take the train partway to Rigi Kaltbad (23SFr) and hike from there (1½hr.). To descend, take the train down, the cable car from Rigi Kaltbad to Weggis, and return to Lucerne by ferry. Alternatively, the tourist office offers a special round-trip deal for 88SFr.

Rigi Kulm (1800m), with a view of Lake Lucerne, rises across the water from Mt. Pilatus. The least-visited of the three peaks, probably because it is a bit harder to reach, Rigi Kulm has wide walking paths and an elegant restaurant at the top. Displays and free viewfinders help you locate all of the area's major geographic features, along with Switzerland's major cities. On a clear day, France and Germany are also visible. Watching the sunrise from the summit is a Lucerne must, and sunsets are spectacular as well (see Mark Twain's 1879 travelogue *A Tramp Abroad*). Staying at **Massenlager Rigi Kulm ❷** on the summit facilitates early morning viewing and also allows for nighttime vistas of thousands of city lights glittering far below. Part of Hotel Rigi Kulm, this dormitory has 18 simple bunks, arrived at only through the hotel's eerie underground tunnel, which winds through the damp, cold stone and past an old bowling lane. (☎855 03 03; fax 00 55. Breakfast 14SFr, but money is better spent at a bakery. Reception 8:30am-6pm. Check-out by noon. Call ahead for weekend availability. Dorms 18SFr. AmEx/DC/MC/V.)

ENGELBERG AND MOUNT TITLIS ☎041

Take the train from Lucerne to Engelberg (1hr., 6:30am-11:32pm, 15.40SFr) and the cable car from Engelberg to Titlis. AmEx/DC/MC/V accepted at ticket counter. ☎639 50 50; www.titlis.ch. First ascent from Engelberg 8:30am, last ascent 3:40pm; last descent from Titlis varies, usually around 4:50pm. Round-trip 86SFr, with Eurail 69SFr, with SwissPass 65SFr. Families with children up to age 15 111SFr. Guided tours available from Lucerne including round-trip rail and Titlis fares (95SFr, discounts with Eurail or SwissPass). The mountain is completely wheelchair-accessible.

Near the small town of **Engelberg,** south of Lucerne, the world's first revolving cable car climbs to the crest of **Mt. Titlis** (3020m), the highest outlook point in central Switzerland. The ride gives views of the crevasses below and peaks above. If a revolving car at 10,000 ft. gives you chills, don't worry—the cabin makes only one complete rotation during the trip. Stop halfway up (your ticket does not go bad) at Trübsee and stroll along the easy walking paths with rustic scenery, a gushing waterfall, and magnificent reflections of the mountains in the lake. Then continue to the summit, which has an active glacial outpost, with observation deck and restaurant, glacial grotto, and a chair-lift (10SFr) that takes visitors over glacial scenery to the Glacier Park, which offers free tube and scooter rides down an ice slide. To avoid uncomfortably crowded cable car rides, plan your ascent and descent for off-peak hours—ascend early in the morning (before 10 or 11am), and try to avoid the last two descending rides of the day. Wear layers and appropriate footwear. The photo shop on the fourth floor of the outpost on the peak rents shoes and jackets (8SFr each). Titlis has snow year-round, and a few runs are maintained for skiing and snowboarding during the summer. For winter activities, get the comprehensive *Winterfaszination* guide from the tourist office, which outlines the locations, prices, and opening hours of the region's slopes.

The Engelberg **tourist office** (☎ 639 77 77; www.engelberg.ch) has **parking** (M-Sa first 45min. free, 10SFr for 24hr.), an **ATM,** and information desk. Turn left out of the train station. At the first intersection, turn right, and then right again at the next street. You'll see the tourist center ahead on the left. The tourist desk sells lift tickets and ski packages and has information on festivals (including their summer festival usually held in June) and events. They also take care of hotel and holiday home reservations and offer hiking maps. (Open M-Sa 8am-6:30pm, Su 9am-1pm.)

NORTHEASTERN SWITZERLAND

Encompassing the cantons of Schaffhausen, St. Gallen, Thurgau, Glarus, and Appenzell, northeastern Switzerland contains some of the country's best-preserved towns. Stein am Rhein invites visitors to its medieval *Altstadt*, while Appenzell still has the farmhouses and agricultural lifestyle that made Switzerland what it is. From snow-covered mountain peaks in Appenzell to gushing waterfalls near St. Gallen, this region is as geographically diverse as it is historically rich.

HIGHLIGHTS OF NORTHEASTERN SWITZERLAND

Experience Switzerland at its small-town quaintest in **Stein am Rhein** (see p. 403).

Sample **Appenzell's** uniquely pungent and potent local *Bitter* liqueur (see p. 411).

Go medieval, browsing priceless tomes in **St. Gallen's** *Stiftsbibliothek* (see p. 409).

SCHAFFHAUSEN   ☎ 052

In this region, the Untersee serves as the border between Germany and Switzerland. The U. S. accidently bombed unlucky Schaffhausen during WWII because it is on the German side of the lake. Remarkably, much of the medieval *Altstadt* survived the bombardment. Frescoes, architecture, and fountains dating to the 15th century decorate much of the town. The **Munot Fortress,** built in the 1500s, stands tall and valiant above the city, though a complete absence of attacks proved it

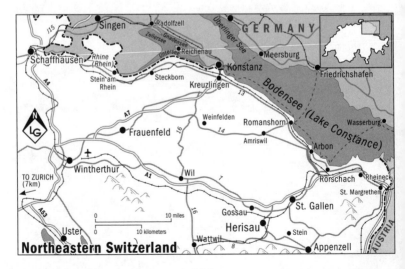

Northeastern Switzerland

rather unnecessary. The citizens apparently used the time spared from military operations to kick back: the local *Falkenbier* is reputedly the best in the canton. A mug of the bold brew will put you in the mood to enjoy Schaffhausen's ambience.

⊡ TRANSPORTATION. If you're the mood for exploration, consider a **Tageskarte** (29SFr), which allows one day of unlimited travel on Bodensee area railways, waterways, and roadways. **Trains** depart from Schaffhausen to Kreuzlingen (50min., 1-2 per hr. 6am-11:05pm, 16.20SFr); St. Gallen (1½hr., 1-3 per hr. 5:45am-10:45pm, 26SFr); Winterthur (30min., 1-3 per hr. 5:27am-11:09pm, 17.20SFr); Zurich (25min., 1-3 per hr. 5:27am-12:18am, 17.20SFr). **Ferries** navigate the Bodensee, departing from Schaffhausen (from Freiepl., below Festung Munot) to Konstanz and Stein am Rhein (4 per day; May to early July and early Sept. to early Oct. 9:10am-3:10pm, early July to early Sept. 1 per day to Konstanz; 19.60SFr). **Parking** is in the garage off Rheinstr., in lots near the cathedral, off Moeratz, and behind the station on Spitalg. (5SFr per day). **Maps** are available at the main station.

🛈 PRACTICAL INFORMATION. The **tourist office,** Herrenaker 15, provides maps and info on the town and surrounding area. From the station, head down Schwertstr. (the narrow street to the right of the post office) and turn right at the fountain of the main square. Keep walking straight, out of the square onto a smaller street (Tanne). Continue for about 150 yards. Tanne will open into a small square, and the tourist office is on your right. (☎632 40 20; fax 632 40 20; www.schaffhausen-tourism.ch. Open Oct.-May M-F 9:30am-12:30pm and 1:30-5pm, Sa 9:30am-5:30pm.) Services include: **Currency exchange** in train station and at **Crédit Suisse** (open M-F 9am-12:15pm and 1:15-4:30pm; Th until 6); 24hr. **ATM** outside the bank; **bike rental** (30SFr per day with photo ID, 25SFr with SwissPass; 6SFr extra to return bike at another station) and **luggage storage** (open M-F 8am-7pm, Sa-Su 9am-12:15pm and 1:15-6pm; 5SFr) on the far left side of the station; **lockers** at station (4-6SFr); **police station,** Berkenstube 1 (emergency ☎117, non-emergency 624 24 24); **Internet** at Energie Punkt, Vorderg. 38 , right across from St. Johannkirche. (☎052 635 11 00. Open M-F 9am-7pm, Sa 10am-2pm.) The **post office** faces the station on Bahnhofstr. (Open M-F 7:30am-6:30pm, Sa 8am-5pm.) **Postal Code:** CH-8200.

🛌🍴 ACCOMMODATIONS AND FOOD. Jugendherberge Belair (HI) ❷, Randenstr. 65, lies in the newer (i.e. early 19th-century) section of Schaffhausen. Take bus #6 (dir: Neuhasen SBB) to "Hallenbad" and find the hostel across the street from the bus stop (2-6 per hr. M-F 5:30am-11:30pm, Sa-Su 1-3 per hr.). Once the rich Maier family hosted writer Herman Hesse here. Now, school groups, families, and backpackers fill its shady paths and volleyball court. Two horses graze in the backyard. Enjoy lunch (on request) and dinner (both 13SFr) on the picnic tables in the large yard. (☎625 88 00; www.youthhostel.ch/schaffhausen. Breakfast and sheets included. Free lockers. Kitchen available. Keys available. Parking lot next to the bus stop. No smoking. Reception 8-10am and 5-9pm. Checkout 9:30am. Open early Mar. to mid-Nov. Dorms 25SFr; family rooms 31.50SFr per person, with sink 34.50SFr. Non-members add 6SFr. Children under age 2 free, ages 2-6 half-price.) Those seeking a restful night away from town should head to **Lowen ❹,** Tremdenzimmer 2, a small guesthouse just outside of Schaffhausen. Take bus #5 (dir: Herblingen) to the last stop, "Herblingen Hirschen." Facing the same direction, turn right and head uphill for 3min. The hotel is the peach building with white shutters on your right. (☎643 22 08. Breakfast, towels, and sheets included. Showers in room. Call ahead to book one of the six rooms or have the tourist office do it for you. Singles 75SFr; doubles 120SFr.) **Camping Rheinwiesen ❶** stands at the edge of the Rhine, 2.5km from Schaffhausen. Take the train (dir: Kreuzlingen) to "Langwiesen." You'll be able to see the camp on the far left along the waterfront. It's about a 10min. walk from there. (☎659 33 00; www.campingtcs.ch. Late Apr. to late Sept., 4.60SFr per adult, 2.30SFr per child, 6.50SFr per tent. Late June to late Aug. 6.60SFr/ 3.30SFr/8.50SFr. Prices may vary; check web. AmEx/DC/MC/V.)

The Fronwagpl. comes alive during the day with outdoor cafés, inexpensive food vendors, restaurants, and live entertainment ranging from mimes to fire-breathers. The blue-shuttered **Restaurant Thiergarten ❸**, on Münsterpl. across from the Allerheiligen Monastery, offers a traditional appetizer, entrée, or dessert from each of the nation's 26 cantons. Their typical Swiss dinners range in price from 18.50 to 29.50SFr and include St. Gallen Bratwurst (a grilled white sausage) and Emmental Schnitzel. They also offer vegetarian dishes, mainly different kinds of *Rösti* (shredded potato shaped into a thick pancake), from 17 to 22SFr. A changing array of ethnically-themed dishes ranging from Thai to Mexican rounds out the menu. (☎625 32 88; www.thiergarten.ch. Wheelchair accessible. Dish descriptions in English. Parking across the street. Open M and W-Su 10am-11pm. AmEx/DC/MC/V.) For take-out, try **Chinatown ❷**, Vorstadt 36, ideal for a quick bite in a sunny outdoor seating. Dishes are 17.50SFr and under. Add 1-4SFr for dining in. (☎624 46 77; fax 47 44. Open daily 11am-11pm.) **Migros**, Bahnhofstr. 58, to the left of the station, has a restaurant as well. (Open M-W and F 8:15am-6:30pm, Th 8:15am-8pm, Sa 8am-4pm.) Stock up on produce at the **farmer's market** at the corner of Kirchhofpl. near Johannkirche (F 9am-noon and 1:30-5:30pm, Sa 8-noon.) There's also **Aperto,** in the station, for basic conveniences. (Open M-Sa 6am-9:30pm, Su 7am-9:30pm.)

◪ SIGHTS. Throughout the *Altstadt*, Schaffhausen's classically Swiss streets, narrow and winding, are lined with frescoes, fountains, and woodcarvings. The **Haus Zum Ritter,** Vorderg 65, now home to a pharmacy, has one of the best Renaissance fresco façades in Switzerland. A military installment dating from the 10th century, **Festung Munot** (Munot Fortress) now hosts tourists and school groups. After climbing a steep flight of stone steps from the town, you are treated to views of the Rhine and of Schaffhausen's rooftops. The surrounding vineyard and Swiss rose garden (which blossoms throughout the summer) offer benches for resting. (☎625 42 25. Turn right at the head of Schwertstr., then left onto Vorderg., continuing until you see signs to the fortress. Wheelchair accessible, but steep. Open daily May-Sept. 8am-8pm; Oct-Apr. 9am-5pm. Free.) The nearby **Allerheiligen Monastery**, features the **Kloster Allerheiligen** (All Saints Monastery), whose arched passageways enclose a well-manicured herb garden and serene courtyard filled with lush shrubs and rosebushes. Enter from the corner of Gartenst. and Goldsternst. Modern minimalist art and the remnants of medieval murals meet in the **Münster Allerheiligen,** a Romanesque church built around 1100 and restored in the 1970s. Within the cloister, you'll find the **Museum zum Allerheiligen,** which encompasses a **Natural History Museum** and exhibits in the **Kunstverein Schaffhausen** (Art Museum). Face off with a stuffed boar, stroll through a Victorian parlor or Medieval Hall, examine thousand-year-old illuminated manuscripts, admire stained glass, and much more, all the while learning about the rich history of this area. (☎633 07 77; www.allerheiligen.ch. From the station, take Schwertstr. up to Vorderg., then turn right onto Münsterg. Signs in German only. Open Tu-Su 11am-5pm. Free.) An old warehouse converted into four floors of permanent gallery space for 14 avant-garde artists, the **Hallen Für Neue Kunst** (Hall for Modern Art), Baumgartenstr. 23, across the street from Kloster Allerheiligen, is littered with massive, seemingly indecipherable shapes, colors, and sounds. (☎052 625 25 15; www.modern-art.ch. Guidebook available in English. Open daily Tu-Sa 3-5pm, Su 11am-5pm. Tours Su 11:30am. 14SFr, students 8SFr.)

🢒 DAYTRIP FROM SCHAFFHAUSEN

RHEINFALLS

The Rheinfalls are just a 10min. train ride from Schaffhausen. Take the train headed for Winterthur to Schloß Laufen am Rheinfall (2 stops on Schaffhausen). From the train stop, walk up the stairs to the left. At the immediate fork in the stairs, continue up to the right, walking through the village and following the signs to the falls. Take the left fork and walk downward to see the falls to avoid the 1SFr charge at the village entrance.

The Rheinfalls is one of Europe's largest sets of waterfalls, though its scope isn't nearly as grand as that designation might lead you to expect. They are no Niagara, but the falls still offer a grand display of natural power. 23m in height, they gush at a rate of 600m^3 per second in the summer (250m^3 per second in the winter). Marvel at the torrents while strolling through winding, wild rose-lined paths. Tourists fill the ample viewing platforms to snap photos and quietly enjoy the awe-inspiring view. Boats operated by Rhyfall-Mändli offer an up-close-and-personal view of the falls, crossing the river from Schloß Laufen to Neuhaussen. From this second stop, they offer four different routes around the falls, including one to a rock outcropping right in the middle of the action, where the falls literally crash at your feet. (☎672 48 11. www.maendli.ch. Ferries leave every 10min. from Neuhausen daily Apr., Oct. 11am-5pm; May, Sept. 10am-6pm; June-Aug. 9:30am-6:30pm. 2.50-11SFr, children 1.50-5.50SFr.) A bridge over the falls leads to where, for 1SFr, you can follow winding stairs down the steep face of the hill to the foot of the falls.

In the turrets of Schloß Laufen, **Jugendherberge Schloß Laufen am Rheinfalls (HI)** ❷ shelters backpackers and occasional student groups. Take the stairs to the left of the train station, then head right on the winding path. At the road, follow the signs to the falls. Once in the small plaza, the hostel will be on your right. Simple rooms recall the castle's 12th-century origins and offer splendid views of the Rhine. The welcoming couple running the hostel lives in one turret. Reserve a bed in advance: the hostel often fills up with school groups. (☎659 61 52; fax 60 39. Bedding and breakfast included 7:30-8:30am, lunch (on request) and dinner 13SFr. Kitchen facilities 2SFr. Shower, sinks, and toilets on floor. Small lockers for day storage. Reception 8-9:30am and 5-9pm. Check-out 10am. Open Mar.-Oct. Dorms 25SFr; 4-person family rooms 35SFr per person. Non-members add 6SFr.) Restaurant **Schloß Laufen** ❷, in the same building as the hostel, serves reasonably priced dishes, including soups from 6SFr, vegetarian pasta options and lighter dinners under 18.50SFr, and filling meat dishes 23-40SFr. For a hearty meal, try the *Füürtopf Plausch* (59SFr per person), an all-you-can-eat meat fondue served with salad and wine. (☎659 67 67; www.schlosslaufen.ch. Open M-Th and Su 11:30am-11pm, Sa 11:30am-midnight, Su brunch 9am-noon. 32SFr, children 16SFr.)

STEIN AM RHEIN ☎052

The tiny medieval *Altstadt* of Stein am Rhein is postcard-perfect. Houses in the central square date from the 15th century and are marked by detailed façades painted to depict the animal or scene after which each house is named. The traditional Swiss architecture is framed by verdant hills and a sparkling river. Once mainly an agricultural town, Stein am Rhein now thrives on a rich tourism industry. The town's proximity to Germany makes it a popular daytrip destination.

🎫🢒 TRANSPORTATION AND PRACTICAL INFORMATION. Trains connect
Stein am Rhein to: Konstanz via Kreuzlingen (40min., 1 per hr. 6:24am-midnight, 9.80SFr); Schaffhausen (1-2 per hr. 5:28am-10:30pm, 7.20SFr); St. Gallen (1½hr., 1 per hr. 6:56am-5:56pm, 22SFr); Winterthur (45min., 1 per hr. 5:07am-11:07pm,

THE LOCAL STORY

NO E WILI

Around 1457, the people of Stein am Rhein broke free of their feudal landlords. The question then arose as to which larger group they would cast their lot with—would they join the Austrian Hapsburgs or the burgeoning confederation of city-state cantons then forming into Switzerland? The mean-spirited mayor of the town, Laitzer, opted for the former, and invited the Hapsburgs to take control of his town.

As the legend goes, one night, ships full of Hapsburg soldiers came sailing into the city. An apprentice working the graveyard shift at the bakery saw the lights along the Rhein. When the Austrians called on him to surrender, he responded with "No e Wili" ("just a moment"), and alerted everyone in the town to the impending invasion. The townsfolk somehow managed to fend off the Austrians, and later happily joined the new Eidgenossenschaft of Switzerland. To get rid of the bad Bürgermeister, they decided to make him "Drink the Rhein," i.e., be put in a sack and tossed into the river.

Though the story is probably a little apocryphal—it is a common mordnacht (murder night) narrative similar to that of Zürich—and was most likely invented by local Heinrich Waldvogel during the Depression, the event is re-enacted every few years by a cast of several hundred.

www.steinamrhein.ch. The next performance is in 2007.

12.40SFr). **Buses** connect the city to small towns in the area and Germany. **Boats** depart four times per day for Schaffhausen (1¼hr., 19.60SFr), Konstanz (2½hr., 24SFr), and other Bodensee towns. (☎634 08 88; www.urh.ch.) An hour-long cruise on the **St. Georg Ferry**, named after Stein am Rhein's patron saint, can be arranged through the Hotel Rheinfels. (☎741 21 44; www.rheinfels.ch.)

To reach the city, head straight out of the station onto Bahnhofstr., first bearing right on Wagenhauserstr., and then left on Charreg., which goes over a bridge and into the Rathauspl. in the *Altstadt*'s center. Once you turn left and continue walking, Rathauspl. becomes Understadt, the town's main drag. **Parking** is available on all streets skirting the *Altstadt*, and along Hemishoferstr., off Untertor. (0.50SFr per hr., 3SFr per day.) Stein am Rhein's **tourist office**, Oberstadt 3, lies on the other side of the *Rathaus*. (☎742 20 90; fax 052 742 20 91. Open Sept.-June M-F 9:30am-noon and 1:30-5pm; July-Aug. also Sa 9:30am-noon and 1:30-4pm.) Other services include: **currency exchange** in the station (open early Apr. to Sept. M-F 6:15am-7:10pm, Sa 6:50am-6:35pm, Su 7:15am-7:35pm; Oct. to early Apr. M-F 6:15am-7:10pm, Sa 6:50am-12:10pm and 12:50-5:10pm, Su 8:15-11:35am and 12:50-6:35pm); **bike rental** in the station (open early Apr. to mid-Oct. M-F 6:15am-7:35pm, Sa 6:15am-6:35pm, Su 7:15am-7:35pm; mid-Oct. to Mar. M-F 6:15am-7:10pm, Sa 6:50am-12:10pm and 12:50-5:10pm, Su 8:15-11:35am and 12:50-6:35pm; 30SFr per day); **24hr. ATM** at the corner of Schwarzhorng. and Rathauspl.; **lockers** in the train station (3SFr); **Internet** at **Kiosk Charregass** (which also serves cheap pizza), Oberstadt 16, past the tourist office coming from Rathauspl., at the end of the street on your right (open Tu-F 9am-6:30pm, Sa 9am-4pm; 1SFr per 5min.) Exiting the station, the **post office** is on your right. (Open M-F 7:30-11am and 3-6pm, Sa 8:30-10:30am.) Branch **post office** is at the corner of Brodlaubegass and Obergass in the *Altstadt*. (Open M-F 8am-noon and 2-5:30pm, Sa 8am-noon.) **Postal Code:** CH-8260.

┌┐┌┐ ACCOMMODATIONS AND FOOD. The family-oriented **Jugendherberge (HI) ❷** is at Hemishoferstr. 87. From the train station, take bus #7349, dir: Singen; on the hr. M-F 7am-10pm, Sa-Su every 1-2hr.) to "Strandbad" and head about 5min. farther in the same direction, walking directly on the road for the last few minutes (watch out for the traffic). The hostel is on your left. By foot, follow the directions to the *Altstadt;* once you cross the bridge, turn left and follow the river for 20min. The hostel fills up quickly, so call ahead. It has clean, if small, rooms, many of which over-look the Rhine. Trench-style sinks give the bathrooms a utilitarian air. (☎052 741 12 55; fax 741 51 40. Breakfast, showers, and sheets included. Kitchen access 2SFr. Access to outdoor grill 2SFr. Lunch and dinner by reservation 13SFr, packed lunch 10SFr. No smoking or eating in rooms. Reception 8-10am and 5-10pm. Check-out by 10am. Curfew 10:30pm; keys available. Open Mar.-Nov. Dorms 25SFr; singles 40SFr; doubles 68SFr; family rooms 34SFr per person. Children ages 6-16 accompanied by an adult half-price. 3SFr low-season discount. Non-members add 6SFr. AmEx/DC/MC/V.)

The team of waitresses at the **Rothen Ochsen Wine Bar ❶**, Rathauspl. 9, are dedicated to preserving the tradition connected with their hall, the oldest pub-lic house in the town, built in 1466. A menu of changing daily food specials includes light fare for under 20SFr. The restaurant's wooden seating and tradi-tional Swiss oven keep the ambience decidedly from another century. (☎052 741 23 28; weinstube@rothenochsen.ch. Wheelchair-accessible outdoor seating. Open Tu-Sa 11:30am-late, Su 10:30am-6pm.) For a sweet afternoon pick-me-up or light meal visit the friendly staff at **La P'tite Crêperie ❶**, Unterstadt 10. The cozy restaurant lives up to its name by serving nearly any kind of crêpe you could imagine (7-13SFr.) Sit at one of the indoor tables to listen to French music while watching your food being prepared, or enjoy the fresh air in the outdoor seating. (☎741 59 55. Open W-Su 11am-9pm.) **The Spaghetteria ❷**, Schif-flände 8, sits directly on the Rhine and serves cheap and tasty Italian fare to tourists, families with children, and locals. An all-you-can-eat spaghetti plate with a turntable of six different sauces (25SFr per person) is the restaurant's special. (☎741 22 36; www.wasserferls.ch. English menu and children's menu available. Wheelchair accessible. Open mid-Mar. to second Su in Nov. M-Th and Su 9am-11pm, F and Sa 9am-midnight. AmEx/DC/MC/V.) The delicious aroma wafting from **Café Spath ❶**, Rathauspl. 21, offers only a hint of the goodies inside. A wide assortment of chocolates, cakes, breads, and marzipan fill the windows and display case of this pastry shop. (☎741 21 82. Open Tu-S. 8am-6pm, Su 9am-6pm.) Picnickers can fill their baskets at the small **Volg** supermar-ket, Rathauspl. 17, at the corner of Rathauspl. and Schwarzhorng. (Open M-F 8:30am-6:30pm, Sa 8am-5pm. AmEx/DC/MC/V.)

◎♬ SIGHTS AND ENTERTAINMENT. The 12th-century establishment of the **Kloster St. George** first made Stein am Rhein prominent. You can reach the Benedic-tine monastery by heading up Chirchhofpl. from the Rathauspl. The rooms are pre-served in their 16th-century state, just as the five-foot-tall monks (judging by the doors) left them. Try to find St. George in the wooden engravings. Less austere is the vibrant **Festsaal**, whose yellow-and-green tiled floor is off-limits to feet. As lights are few and dim, try to go when it is bright outside for the best view of deli-cate paintings and engravings. (☎741 21 42. Information on the museum available in English, although displays are in German only. Open Mar.-Oct. Tu-Su 10am-5pm. 3SFr, students 1.50SFr.) Admire the ornate and well-preserved frescoes adorning the stately **Rathaus,** at the corner of Rhig. and Rathauspl.

Museum Lindwurm, Understadt 18, reconstructs 19th-century Swiss life in this bourgeois house and attached barn. Wander through the richly-furnished abode, examining displays of old letters, cards, and other remnants of the family who once walked the halls. The adjoining barn houses servants' chambers, where visi-tors are encouraged to try on the clothes in the room, lie on the bed, and play with the toys. (☎741 25 12. Exhibit placards in multiple languages, including English. Group tours available in English and French with prior reservation. Open Mar.-Oct. M and W-Su 10am-5pm. 5SFr, students 3SFr.)

SLEEP IN STRAW

If crisply-made Swiss hotel beds and immaculate hostels have grown a little bland, consider making like Heidi (or Frankenstein's monster) and bedding down for a night in the comfortable straw of an authentic Swiss barn. Started in the Jura some ten years ago to provide novel, back-to-the-roots lodging for cost-conscious Swiss families on their vacations, the *Schlaf im Stroh* ('sleep in straw') program now involves some 240 farms in rural northeastern Switzerland, all of which set aside barn space for travelers eager for a different way to spend their night.

Though, as a rule, all *Schlaf im Stroh* plots are as well-tended and hygienic as everything else in Switzerland, bring bug spray to combat mosquitoes and a thick jacket to ward off any pre-dawn alpine chill. Call ahead to make sure there's space for you, and tell the host farmer about any allergies you may have (believe it or not, substantial accommodations can be made). Amenities ranging from donkey rides to craft demonstrations vary from farm-to-farm, but the chances of a riveting Swiss sunrise are the same anywhere. For information on other *Schlaf im Stroh* barns, surf to http://www.abenteuer-stroh.ch/en/ or consult brochures available in regional tourist offices.

In the vicinity of Stein am Rhein, *Let's Go* recommends the *Schlaf im Stroh* barn run by Frau

A 30min. hike will take you up the mountain to the castle on **Hohenklingen**. From Rathauspl., follow Brodlaubeg. out of town; signs point the rest of the way. The trail will meet a parking lot near the top. Continue following the trail left. Within a couple minutes, stairs will lead off to the right to the castle. The steep trek takes you along a relatively treacherous road with beautiful views of the town and then splits off as zig-zagging stairs lead through farm fields and a dense forest. Visitors aren't allowed to explore much of the small fortress itself, now a restaurant, but if you continue left on the path leading around the castle you'll be rewarded with a bird's-eye view of Stein am Rhein and the Bodensee and surrounding area.

ST. GALLEN ☎ 071

Though it lacks the medieval charm of Schaffhausen, St. Gallen's easy access to Zurich, Germany, Austria, the Bodensee, and small mountain villages makes it a popular stopover for travelers. Quiet during the week, the modern *Altstadt* livens up on weekends when students from the university descend from the hill. During the day, the *Altstadt* is a window shopper's dream but a spender's nightmare. St. Gallen has a few cultural gems to share, particularly the *Stiftsbibliothek*, the Baroque library named a World Heritage Treasure by UNESCO.

▐ TRANSPORTATION

Trains: To: **Appenzell** (30min., 1-3 per hr. 5:42am-11:40pm, 10.40SFr); **Bern** (2½hr., 4:36am-11:32pm, 63-65SFr); **Geneva** (4½hr., 4:36am-7:47pm, 94SFr); **Lugano** (4hr., 5:10am-7:02pm, 72-76SFr); **Munich** (3hr.; 4 per day 8:37am-6:37pm; 70SFr, under 26 51SFr); **Zurich** (1hr., 4:36am-11:42pm, 26-34SFr).

Buses: 2.20SFr, ages 6-16 1.30SFr; *Tageskarte* (day pass) 7SFr, ages 6-16 5SFr; 12 rides 22SFr. Buy tickets at each stop or on some buses; passes and Tageskarten available at large kiosks or **VBSG Transit Authority** across from train station.

Taxis: Sprenger AG, Rohrschacherstr. 281 (local ☎333 33 33, toll free 08 00 55 10 30). **Herold Taxi AG,** Poststr. 11 (☎08 00 82 27 77). **Tixi,** wheelchair-accessible taxis (☎244 14 34).

Car Rental: Herold Autovermietung AG, Molkenstr. 7 (☎07 12 28 64 28; fax 64 25). 77SFr per day, 195SFr per weekend. **Europcar,** Neumarkt 1, St.-Leonhardstr. 35 (☎222 11 14; fax 01 57). From 78SFr per day.

Parking: **Neumarkt Parking Garage,** near the Neumarkt Supermarket on St. Leonhardstr. (☎222 11 14). 5am-9pm 2SFr per hr., 9pm-5am 1SFr per hr. Open M-Sa 5am-12:30am. Park in one of the city's **blue zones** M-F for 5.50SFr per day, Sa-Su free.

⚡ PRACTICAL INFORMATION

Tourist Office: Bahnhofpl. 1a (☎227 37 37; www.st.gallen-bodensee.ch). From the train station, walk to the left of the post office, crossing the street with the bus stop on your left. Pass the fountain on the left. The tourist office is on the right. Maps, brochures, hotel booking, and **city tours** available. (June-Oct. M and W-F 2-4pm, Sa 11am-1pm. 15SFr, museum admissions included.) Special night tour around Christmas. (M, W, F, 5-6:30pm. 15SFr, children 10SF. Includes punch and pastries.) Open M-F 9am-6pm, Sa 9am-noon. Phone calls taken M-F 8am-noon and 1:30-5:40pm, Sa 9am-noon.

Currency Exchange: At the station. Open M-F 9am-7pm, Sa 9am-5pm, Su 1-5pm. Services include **Western Union.**

Luggage Storage: At the station. Lockers with 24hr. access 4-7SFr. Luggage watch 7SFr. Open M-F 8am-7:45pm, Sa-Su 9am-noon and 1:30-7pm. A few cheaper lockers (3SFr) at the Appenzeller/Trogen station, across from luggage watch.

Internet Access: Media Lounge, Katherineng. 10 (☎244 30 90; fax 244 30 91). Facing away from the bus stop at Marktpl., cross at far right onto Katerineng. This hip lounge with pop music offers cheap Internet access. 2SFr minimum. After 10min. 1SFr per 5min., 12SFr per 1hr. Open M-F 9am-7pm or 8pm, Sa-Su sporadic hours.

Budget Travel: STA Travel, Metzgerg. 10 (www.statravel.ch). From Markpl. bus station walk to the left of Scala Kino down Metzgerg. STA Travel is on your right, across from Hotel Elite. Open M-W and F 9am-6:30pm, Th 9am-9pm, Sa 10am-4pm.

Pharmacy: In the train station. Open M-F 7:30am-6:30pm, Sa 7:30am-5pm.

Post Office: On Bahnhofpl., across the street to the left of the train station. Open M-W and F 7am-7:30pm, Th 7am-8pm, Sa 7:30am-4pm, Su 3-6pm.

Postal Code: CH-9001.

🏠 ACCOMMODATIONS

🏠 **Jugendherberge St. Gallen (HI),** Jüchstr. 25 (☎245 47 77; www.youthhostel.ch/st.gallen). Next to the train station, you'll find the small Appenzeller/Trogener station with 2 tracks (#12 and 13). Take the orange train

Ullman, her son, Christian, and their amiable St. Bernard, Leila, who tends the chicken coop. Sleep earthily yet comfortably covered in fresh straw on a working farm that includes its own apple orchard, grazing cows and cheery barn wih a massive door.

Contact Fra Ullman through the Stein am Rhein tourist office. To get to her barn, ride the local train to the sleepy hamlet of Eschenz (pop. 1600). Press the button to signal that you want to get off—the train won't stop if you don't. From the station, make a left until you hit a bike path. Travel along the path and then follow the arrows on the Schlaf im Stroh signs. A stay with the Ullmans covers a 'farmer's breakfast' that often includes tea made from an on-premise lindenberry tree, and chocolate milk courtesy of the family's ever-obliging cows. Shower 2SFr. Guests 16+ 20SF; children 10-15 pay by the year; 10 and under 10SFr. Expect a 2-3SFr visitor's tax. For a small fee, the Ullmans will also groom your horse, if you have one.)

from track #12 (dir: Speichen and Trogen) to "Schülerhaus" (10min., 1-4 per hr. 5:32am-12:32am, 2.60SFr). From the stop, walk uphill 6min. on the right. Turn left across the train tracks at the sign for the hostel. You can see it at the bottom of the hill; walk another 2min. and the entrance is around the building on the left. This friendly hostel on a hill attracts an international crowd. Though it's a bit of a hike to get here, the relaxing atmosphere and superb view make up for it. Perks include a breakfast room, terrace, barbecue pit, lawn, library, board games, laundry room, and TV room. Breakfast, sheets, and shower included. Dinner 12.50SFr. Lockers 2SFr deposit. Laundry 6SFr wash, 4SFr dry. Parking available. Reception 7-10am and 5-10:30pm. Call ahead. Check-out 10am. 24hr. keycard access. Quiet hours 10pm-7am. Closed Dec.-Feb. Children ages 2-6 half-price. 6-bed dorms 27SFr; 4-bed dorms 32SFr.; 3-bed rooms 35SFr; 6-bed "family room" with toilet and shower 35SFr per person; singles with sink 48SF, with shower 49.50SFr; doubles 74SFr/78SFr. Non-members add 6SFr. AmEx/DC/MC/V. ❷

Hotel Weisses Kreuz, Engelg. 9 (☎/fax 223 28 43; www.a-o.ch/9000-weisseskreuz). Follow directions to Hotel Elite; Engelg. is 1 street left from Metzgerg. Weisses Kreuz sits atop a lively and smoky bar run by a cheerful staff. The location makes this hotel ideal for late-night pub crawlers in the *Altstadt*. Beware, however: the town's spirited nightlife makes for a noisy stay on the weekends. Breakfast included. Reception M-Th 7am-2pm and 5-11pm, F 7am-2pm and 5pm-midnight, Sa 7am-1pm and 5pm-midnight, Su 9-11am. Lockout at 10pm; keys available upon request. TV and phone in all rooms. Check-out 10am. All singles with shower 61SFr; doubles 115SFr, with shower 135SFr. Children ages 4-12 25SFr per night. Reductions for multiple-night stays. MC/V. ❸

Hotel Elite, Metzgerg. 9-11 (☎227 99 33; www.hotel-elite-sg.com). Exit bus station and turn left, staying on the road closest to the train tracks. This road will become Bahnhofst. and then Marktpl. Turn left onto Metzgerg. directly opposite the bus stop. Located near the *Altstadt* and Marktpl., and within walking distance from Museumstr., this hotel offers simple rooms, most with a sink, TV, and chocolate on each pillow. Again, beware of noisy nightlife. Breakfast included. Doors lock and reception closes at 11pm. Check-out 11am. Internet available (10SFr per hr.). Singles with shower 75-80SFr, with toilet and shower 93-110SFr; doubles 124-134SFr/146-165SFr. Children ages 6-12 half-price, ages 12-16 30% off. AmEx/MC/V. ❹

Hotel am Ring, Unterer Graben 9 (☎223 27 47; hotelamring@bluemail.ch). Situated in a centrally located and historic building, the Hotel am Ring's rooms are as ornate and unique as the extravagantly decorated café downstairs. Breakfast included.Reception open 7:30am-1pm and 5-9:30pm. Reservations by fax encouraged. All rooms with shower, toilet, and TV. Singles 90SFr; doubles 130SFr; triples 180SFr. ❹

◘ FOOD

Migros, St. Leonhardstr., one block behind the train station, has a buffet restaurant in a separate building behind the market. (Market open M-W 9am-7:30pm, Th 9am-9pm, F 9am-6:30pm, Sa 9am-5pm. Restaurant open M-W and F 6:30am-6:30pm, Th 6:30am-9pm, Sa 6:30am-5pm. Wheelchair accessible.) A **public market** on Marktpl. bustles with fresh flowers, produce, bread, and meat. (Open M-Sa 8am-8pm.)

▨ **Restaurant Scheitlinsbüchel,** Scheitlinsbüchelweg 10 (☎/fax 071 244 68 21). Follow the directions to the youth hostel. After walking uphill about 6min., turn right into a small parking lot instead of left at the youth hostel sign. As the road enters the woods, turn left onto the uphill trail and walk on a gradual uphill wooded path about 6min. When you reach the road again, go left and you will be able to see the farmhouse restaurant. The restaurant's terrace provides an amazing view of the surrounding countryside, St. Gallen, and even the Bodensee. Family-oriented in its style. Small cheese and meat plates 19SFr. Vegetarian dishes from 19SFr. Meat entrées 23-33SFr. Large ice cream desserts. The terrace is wheelchair accessible. Parking 2min. down the street. Open Tu-Su 9am until everyone leaves. MC/V. ❸

Christina's, Weberg. 9 (☎223 88 08). Wooden tables and colorful walls provide a suitable backdrop for this modern eatery. Weekly specials, American music, and a bar and dance club that opens up on the weekend (F-Sa 8:30pm-1am). They offer a large variety of fish, vegetarian, and meat dishes from 20SFr. Soup or salad with lunch entrentréee 15-21SFr. Reservations suggested in the winter. Open M-Th 9:30am-11:30pm, F-Sa 9:30am-12:30am. AmEx/MC/V. ❸

Weinstube zum Bäumli, Schmiedg. 18 (☎071 222 11 74). Offers Swiss dishes in an intimate setting where locals sit for hours. Occupying one of the oldest buildings in St. Gallen, this restaurant serves schnitzel and *Wurst* (11-40SFr). Cold food including salads and traditional dried meat platters starts at 9SFr. Open daily 9am-11pm. MC/V. ❹

Roggwiller Confiserie and Tea Room, Multerg. 17 (☎222 50 92; www.roggwiller.ch). A traditional confectionery selling rows of chocolates and tempting pastries, including St. Gallen Biber. In the attached tea room, shoppers and tourists take an afternoon break to sip espresso and polish off tall sundaes. Wheelchair accessible. Open M 10:30am-6:30pm, Tu-F 8:30am-6pm, Sa 8:30am-5pm. AmEx/MC/V. ❷

◙ SIGHTS

Aside from the aptly named Museumstraße, where St. Gallen's four museums are located, the city's main attractions are found within the grounds of the St. Gallen Abbey Precinct. Most noteworthy of these attractions are the magnificent *Stiftsbibliothek* and the Kathedrale St. Gallen. From the far left of the station, walk up Bahnhofstr. to Marktpl., then left on Marktg. to reach the abbey.

STIFTSBIBLIOTHEK. Anyone who loves books and medieval culture will marvel at St. Gallen's main attraction, the *Stiftsbibliothek*, the library of the Benedictine abbey at St. Gallen. You'll glide in on huge gray felt slippers (provided by the library to protect the inlaid wood floors) to a chorus of *oohs* and *aahs* at the library's lavishly carved and polished exotic Baroque and Rococo-style wood shelves, filled with rows of centuries-old, gilt-spined books. The library maintains a collection of 140,000 volumes and 2000 manuscripts, 500 of which date from before AD 1200, including 3rd- and 5th-century texts from Virgil and early Bibles. Although the appearance of the resident death-blackened mummy might indicate otherwise, the *Stiftsbibliothek* is a living, lending library serving scholars from around the globe. (☎227 34 16; www.stibi.ch. Wheelchair accessible. Pamphlets available in English though all displays are in German. Open Apr.-Nov. M-Sa 10am-5pm, Su 10am-4pm; Dec.-Mar. M-Sa 10am-noon and 1:30-5pm, Su 10am-noon and 1:30pm-4pm. Tours in German daily Apr.-May and Oct. 2pm; June, Sept. 10:30am, 2pm; July-Aug. 10:30am, 2, 3pm. English tours available through the tourist office. 7SFr, students 5SFr, under age 16 free. AmEx/DC/MC/V.)

Other attractions of the abbey include the **Kathedrale St. Gallen,** a part of the abbey founded in the 8th century and reconstructed in the mid-18th. The cathedral, having undergone a massive renovation in 2003, now has large, clear windows that bathe the Baroque interior in light. The intricate carvings of the confessionals and the details of the murals are not to be missed. Also check a schedule inside for organ concerts. (☎227 33 81. Open daily 9am-6pm, except during Mass: M-Sa 6:30am and 8:15am, Tu 5:30pm, W 9am, F 6:30pm, Sa 5:30pm, Su 9, 11am, 7:30pm.) The abbey's bright courtyard is ideal for picnicking or sunning. On the far side of the abbey from the library sits the smaller **St. Laurenzenkirche (Evangelical Church of St. Lawrence),** founded in the 9th century. Its interior showcases organ pipes and intricate wall patterning. On a sunny day, the stained-glass windows create shadows in the church that are worth a visit. Its ornate tower offers visitors a view of most of the city. (☎222 67 92. *Open M 9:30-11:30am and 2-4pm, Tu-Sa 9:30am-4pm, Th until 7pm, Su service at 10am. Tower open M-Sa 9:30-11:30am and 2-4pm)*

MUSEUMSTRAßE. Two buildings side by side hold most of St. Gallen's museum-worthy relics. Though all the information is in German, impressive displays and varied themes make a trip to Museumstr. perfect for kids and adults. The small **Natural History Museum** (☎242 06 70; *www.naturmuseumsg.ch*) rotates thoughtful and interactive exhibits of all Mother Nature's creations. Housed in the same building, the four-room **Kunstmuseum** (☎242 06 71; fax 242 06 72) has a small collection that juxtaposes modern and traditional art with constantly changing exhibits that have featured works by Klee, Tinguely, Warhol, and Picasso. St. Gallen's enormous **Historisches Museum** (☎242 06 42; fax 06 44) traces Swiss culture from pre-history through the 20th century. Displays include ancient kitchens, an old barber shop, and children's toys. The **Ethnology Collection** (☎242 06 43; fax 06 44) presents various foreign cultures by avoiding overinterpretation and allowing authentic artifacts to speak for themselves. *(Museumstr. 32-50. From Marktpl., with your back to the bus stop, walk right on Bohl to get to Museumstr. All museums open Tu-F 10am-noon and 2-5pm, Sa-Su 10am-5pm, though Kunstmuseum open W until 8pm. 6SFr, students 2SFr. 1 ticket grants admission to all 4 museums, except special exhibits in the Kunstmuseum.)*

OTHER SIGHTS. For a view of the St. Gallen valley (and a glimpse of some native mountain animals including some endangered species), visit the **Peter and Paul Wildpark,** on Kirchlistr. in Rotmonten. Take bus #5 (dir: Rotmonten) to "Sonne." Walk in the opposite direction of the bus, turn left at the first intersection onto Kirchlistr. and walk uphill about 5min. until you reach Sandrainst. Take a left here and then an immediate right onto the Wanderweg, Konstanzerst. Bear right at the fork, following signs to the Wildpark. A well-tended trail leads through the park, ensuring that you don't miss the ibex, which have made a comeback from near extinction. (☎222 67 92 or 244 51 13. *Open 24hr. Free.)* For a tamer excursion, explore the campus of the **St. Gallen University.**

♫ 🎭 ENTERTAINMENT AND NIGHTLIFE

Birreria, Brühlg. 45 (☎223 25 33). Homesick travelers longing for familiar alcohol will definitely find it in this lively, crowded bar. With 240 types of beer, from plain American Budweiser to the African Castle Lager, Birreria has everyone's beer cravings covered. Try Kloster Bräu, a local favorite made in St. Gallen. Also head into the connecting room for your choice of more than 300 types of whiskey. Open M-Th and Su noon to around midnight, F and Sa noon-1am.

Metzgertor, (☎222 25 10) corner of Metzgerg. and Augustinerg. Peach stuccoed walls, an ivy-covered bar, and faux animal skin-covered lounge tables lend a distinctly island feel to this bar. During the week, university students sip coffees and cocktails to a background of modern jazzy music, while the weekends bring people looking for a drink before they hit up the 2 clubs across the street. Open daily 5pm to around 1am.

Seeger Bar, Oberer Graben 2 (☎222 97 90). A red velvet rope separates the bar from the passing cars and pedestrians at the Seeger Bar, where fashionable couples and groups go out for an early drink and to while away the hours. The **Seeger Lounge,** upstairs from the bar, is a more intimate setting, with silver velvet couches and pillows. Try the *Panache* (4.25SFr), a smooth, sweet beer with a squirt of lemon added. Open M-W 8:45pm-midnight, Th 8:45pm-1am, F-Sa 8:45pm-3am, Su 10pm-midnight.

The Church, 7 Linsebühlst. (☎223 24 84). This tiny gay bar turns into a lively disco on the weekends, when tourists and locals fill the basement dance club to tunes played by various DJs. Cocktails run 10-12 SFr, while shots and non-alcoholic drinks hover around 5SFr. Open daily 7pm until everyone leaves.

Each year, the **Stadttheater**, Museumstr. 24 (☎242 06 66; www.theaterst-gallen.ch) hosts over 200 concerts and plays by renowned artists and musicians. There are also several **movie theaters** at Marktpl. The largest is the **Scala Kinocenter and Bar** (☎228 08 60), on the corner of Marktpl. and Goliathg., with five screens. Every year in late July and early August, the **Open-Air Kino** at Kantonschulpark on Burggraben (www.open-air-kino.ch) screens mostly American films (15SFr).

The **Open Air St. Gallen Music Festival** is the oldest open-air music festival in Europe, and features over 20 live bands performing in St. Gallen's field during late June or early July. Past headliners have included Metallica, the Red Hot Chili Peppers, the Roots, B.B. King, and James Brown. Tickets 69SFr per day, 2 days 99SFr, 3 days 143SFr. Bring a tent (showers and toilets available), or stay in St. Gallen and take the shuttle bus to the concert grounds. (☎084 880 0800; www.openairsg.ch.)

APPENZELL ☎071

Appenzell, Switzerland's smallest canton, is world-renowned for its *Appenzeller Käse* (cheese) and its strong connection with its historical traditions. Its inhabitants maintain the traditional agrarian lifestyle, herding animals and running tiny dairies just as their ancestors have for centuries. The canton is dotted with small villages, but the town of Appenzell is the gathering place for cantonal meetings and agricultural shows. Appenzell is best explored on foot: over centuries, local herdsmen have developed an extensive network of trails in the hills. These trails are frequented by herders and are sprinkled with *Gasthäuser* (guest houses).

▉▐ TRANSPORTATION AND PRACTICAL INFORMATION. The rattling *Appenzellerbahn* chugs between Appenzell and St. Gallen (45min., 2 per hr. 6:11am-10:46pm, 10.40SFr). From St. Gallen and Gossau, there is a regular **train** to Zurich (1hr., 32SFr). The train from St. Gallen continues from Appenzell to Wasserauen, a tiny hamlet that serves as a gateway to the Alpenteil valley and its hikes (10min., 3.80SFr). The Appenzell **tourist office,** Hauptg. 4, down Poststr. from the station and right at the intersection with Hauptg., makes hotel reservations, sells detailed hiking maps, and lists upcoming events. The tourist office also has information on free tours of the local Appenzeller Alpenbitter factory, in which the alcoholic drink has been made for over 100 years. The tour is usually offered at 10am on Wednesday mornings. Call to arrange other times for groups. Ask about the cheese factories that offer tours. There is one free 45min. tour in Stein, accessible by bus. (☎788 96 41; www.appenzell.ch. Open May to mid-Oct. M-F 9am-noon and 1:30-6pm, Sa-Su 10am-noon and 2-5pm; mid-Oct. to Apr. M-F 9am-noon and 2-5pm, Sa 2-5pm.) **Internet** access is available at the library, or sporadically at the tourist office when the library is closed and they are not too busy. (Library open Tu-W 2-5pm, Th 2-4pm, F 5-8pm and Sa 9:30-11:30am.) The train station offers **lockers** (3SFr) and **luggage storage** (5SFr). The **post office** is across the street from the train station. (Open M-F 7:30am-noon and 1:30-6pm, Sa 8-11am.) **Postal Code:** CH-9050.

▉▢ ACCOMMODATIONS AND FOOD. Picturesque lodgings await at **Haus Lydia ❸**, Eggerstrandstr. 53. From the tourist office turn left onto Hauptg., turn left on Gaiserstr., and walk up the bridge. Head uphill 5min. and turn right after the Mercedes-Esso station onto Eggerstrandenstr. Alternatively take the train one stop toward St. Gallen to Hirschberg, turn right onto Hirschbergstr., again under the bridge and once more onto Eggerstrandstr. (3min.). The short walk is worth it. Run by a friendly English- and French-speaking family, Haus Lydia boasts large rooms, Alpine views, and an elegant sitting room. Since a fire destroyed much of the house in recent years, all wood panelling and bathrooms are newly-installed. The atmosphere provides an excellent way to experience Swiss family life. All rooms include a private bathroom. (☎787 42 33; www.haus-lydia.ch. Breakfast included. Barbecue grill open to guests. Reserve rooms two weeks in advance. Singles 45SFr; doubles 90SFr; triples 135SFr. V.) The bustling family-run hotel and restaurant **Gasthaus Hof** ❹, on Landsgemeindepl. in the center of town provides guests with comfortable beds in cozy, low-ceilinged rooms. (☎787 40 30; info@gathaus-hof.com. All rooms with shower and TV. Breakfast included. Restaurant open 8am-10pm. Reception open 7am-11pm. Reserve one week in advance Aug. to mid-Oct. Singles 85SFr; doubles 130SFr; triples 180SFr; 4- and 5-person rooms 55SFr per person and 50SFr per person. AmEx/MC/V.) The tourist office provides a list of **Privatzimmer**. The **Gasthöfe** (guest houses) lining the trail are comfortable overnight stops (see **Hiking**, p. 412).

 Restaurant Traube ❸, Marktg. 7, near the Landsgemeindepl. in Hotel Traube, serves Appenzeller specialties by candlelight on hand-embroidered placemats. *Appenzeller Chäshörnli* (macaroni and cheese) or *Käseschnitte* with ham, egg, or pineapple run 13-14SFr. (☎787 14 07; www.hotel-traube.ch. Open Mar.-Jan. Tu-Sa 9am-midnight, Su 9am-10pm. Meat entrées 21-37SFr, Appenzeller beer 2.60SFr. AmEx/DC/MC/V.) The **Co-op** (with a restaurant) and **Migros** are across from one another on Zielstr. off Landsgemeindepl. (Both wheelchair accessible. **ATM** outside the Co-op entrance. Both open M-Th 8am-6:30pm, F 8am-8pm, Sa 8am-4pm.)

◙ SIGHTS. The **Rathaus**, Hauptg. 4, houses the museum, town hall, cantonal library, and tourist office. The *Großratssaal*, with intricately carved wooden walls and 16th-century frescoes of giants supporting the central beam, is particularly remarkable. (Ask in the tourist office or in the museum to have a look inside.) Inside the *Rathaus* and the adjoining *Haus Buherre Hanisefs*, the **Museum Appenzell**, Hauptg. 4, chronicles local culture in displays of clothing and tools that weave throughout the wooden-raftered house. Take the elevator to the top floor and work your way down through displays of traditional Appenzeller dress, handicraft, furniture, farm tools, and even an Egyptian mummy coffin. A video on hand embroidery (in English, French, and German) is surprisingly captivating and exposes the harsh realities of often-idealized traditional Swiss life. (☎788 96 31; www.museum.ai.ch. Open Apr.-Oct. daily 10am-noon and 2-5pm; Nov.-Mar. Tu-Su 2-5pm. 5SFr, students 3SFr, children under 6 free. Group rates and special tours available. Wheelchair accessible.) Next door, the unassuming exterior of **Pfarrkirche St. Mauritius** hides an impressive Rococo interior, complete with ceiling frescoes, 14 stained-glass windows, and a magnificent golden chandelier.

HIKES IN THE APPENZELL REGION

Deep in the heart of the Alpstein, Appenzell offers great countryside hiking without the altitude or temperature extremes of the Zermatt or Ticino regions. The tourist office offers the **Panorama-Wanderkarte** (8.20SFr), a detailed map showing all trails and rest areas. A comprehensive topographical map is available at the bookstores. There are a number of themed hikes; acquire a *Wandern* brochure from the tourist office for further information. Hiking options range from easy strolls through pastures to strenuous overnight treks.

EASIER HIKES

Gontenbad Hike (2hr. round-trip). A relaxing walk known as the *Barfußweg* begins in the nearby town of Gonten (10min. by train from Appenzell; 3SFr). Stroll barefoot along a special trail over the meadows to Gontenbad (45min.), where you can rest and wash your feet (towels 2SFr) in the garden of the Bad Gonton Hotel and Restaurant before heading back to Appenzell (45min.).

Kapellenweg Hike (4-5hr. round-trip). The Kapellenweg provides a close look at local rural life by passing several country chapels. Cross under the train tracks, take a left, then a right at the major intersection to get to the trailhead; from there, brown "Kapellenweg" signs point the way. For the first 45min., the flat trail winds through local farms. For the adventurous, the trail veers from the paved road at times, leading through sheep and cow pastures. The trail splits in several places, but all paths eventually lead to the **Kapelle Maria** (1½hr.) and the larger and more ornate **Ahornkapelle** (2½hr.). The paved road is the easiest route to follow, passing a series of small painted Stations of the Cross. For a more challenging version of the hike (*sans* paintings, but with chapels), follow the "Kapellenweg" signs that lead uphill. Both trails lead back to Appenzell.

DIFFICULT HIKES

For more difficult hikes, start from tiny **Wasserauen**, the last stop on the Appenzellerbahn (10min. from Appenzell, 1-2 per hr., 3.80SFr). The best way to experience the area is to hike between guesthouses. Several hikes listed below leave from the top of **Ebenalp Cable Car,** across the street from the small train station in Wasserauen. (Cable car runs 7:40am-7pm. 18SFr, round-trip 24SFr; students 14SFr/18.50SFr; SwissPass or Eurail holders half-price.) For those looking to travel and use cable cars daily, consider the **Appenzell Card,** which provides free access to three of the area's four cable cars (Säntis cable car not included) and bus and train lines as far as St. Gallen (1 day 31SFr, 3 days 52SFr, 5 days 84SFr; with SwissPass 22SFr/42SFr/68SFr). The **Berggasthaus Ebenalp,** 100m uphill from the top of the cable car, is a good base from which to explore the mountains, with more amenities than other guesthouses and a spectacular view of the area. (☎799 11 94; www.ebenalp.ch. Breakfast included. Showers 4SFr. Optional sleeping bag 5SFr. Reception 7:30am-10pm. Reserve 2-3 months in advance for Sa stays. Open May-Nov. Dorms 30SFr; singles with sink 52SFr; doubles with sink 104SFr. MC/V.) The last two hikes listed can be done without recourse to cable cars.

Wasserauen to Wildkirchli (30min. round-trip). This quick, popular hike leads down from the Ebenalp (top station) through a cave and a tiny 3-room hut displaying a brief history of the area to the **Wildkirchli,** a 400-yr.-old chapel built into a cliff face and manned until recently by a hermit priest. **Berggasthaus Äscher ❷** lies just beyond Wildkirchli. At 150 yrs., Äscher is the oldest *Gasthaus* around. Tucked into the sheer cliff face at 1454m, one interior wall is the mountain. (☎799 11 42; www.aescher-ai.ch. Breakfast included. No showers. Reception 10am-midnight. Open May to late Oct. 35SFr per person, children under 12 20SFr.)

Schäfler to Meßmer (1½hr.). This exceedingly steep and rickety downhill trail leads from a *Gasthaus* called Schäfler to **Berggasthhaus Meßmer ❸.** A couple sections of the trail have a metal cable for balance, but this trail still should not be attempted after rain or snow. From Schäfler, follow the signs to "Meßmer," which will lead along a path called the Höheweg (30min.). The trail then turns left and descends even more steeply, for a view of the blue-green Seealpsee below. A steep uphill climb through cow pastures (10min.) leads to the final destination. The braying of livestock and clanging of cowbells signal the end. (☎799 12 55, winter 799 10 77; www.mesmer-ai.ch. Breakfast included. No running water, but a well outside. Reception 24hr. Reserve 1-2 mos. ahead for Sa-Su. Open May to late Oct. Dorms 24SFr, children under 17 17SFr.)

Seealpsee to Säntis (4hr.). The climb to **Säntis** (2503m), the highest mountain in the region, is a good hike from Seealpsee. From Seealpsee, hike to **Meglisalp** (1hr.), a cozy cluster of 6 farmhouses tucked beneath the peak. ■ **Berggasthaus Meglisalp ❷** is a great place to stay for a night with cows and the people who tend them. A local farmer calls out a prayer with a wooden megaphone every night for the benefit of neighbors and their cattle. (☎071 799 11 28; www.meglisalp.ch. Breakfast included. Reception 24hr. Reserve 1-2 weeks ahead. Open May-Oct. Dorms 34SFr; singles 52SFr; doubles 104SFr.) To get to Säntis from Meglisalp, head either to Rothsteinpass (more difficult) or Wagenlücke (easier), and then up to Säntis (both trips 3hr.). Both paths have snow through the end of June and contain rock fields where the "trail" is rather do-it-yourself. Two guest houses sit on top of Säntis. **Gasthaus Säntis ❷** is older and more personalized. (☎071 799 11 60, winter 14 11; www.berggasthaus-saentis.ch. Breakfast included. Dorms 38SFr; singles, doubles, and 1 quad available, all 60SFr per person.) There are numerous routes from Säntis back to Wasserauen. The weary can take the cable car down to the **Schwägalp** and travel to Appenzell via Urnäsch. (Cable car every 30min. early June to late Oct. 7:30am-6:30pm; late Oct. to early Jan. and late Jan. to early June 8:30am-5pm. 24SFr, round-trip 34SFr; ages 6-16 12SFr/17SFr; under 6 free. Yellow Postauto bus to Urnäsch behind the Berggasthaus Schwägalp: 30min., 1 per hr., about 5SFr; buy your tickets in Urnäsch. Train to Appenzell: 20min., 1-3 per hr. 6:14am-11:36pm, 5.80SFr; buy tickets at the magazine kiosk at the Urnäsch station.)

GRAUBÜNDEN

The largest, least populous, and most Alpine of the Swiss cantons, Graubünden (*Grischun* in Romansch) is made up of rugged gorges twisting through snow-clad peaks and forests of larch and fir. The various towns ranging from the capital, Chur, to Portein (pop. 22) are scattered throughout the canton and dwarfed by the grandeur of their surroundings. The Swiss National Park in the Lower Engadine is the most protected Alpine landscape in Europe, and communities such as Zuoz and Scuol are equally unspoiled. Glitzy St. Moritz and Davos have sprung up as glamorous ski resorts.

The **Graubünden Total Regional Pass** allows three, five, seven, or 10 consecutive days of free travel on trains, buses, and cable cars in the region and a 50% discount on other days (140SFr, 190SFr, 240SFr, and 290SFr, respectively). The Regional Pass can be issued in Switzerland only from May to October, and is distributed by the **Rhätische Bahn** (**Viafer Retica** in Romansch), Graubünden's own train company. SwissPass and Eurail are also valid.

Graubünden

Plan your trip to Graubünden carefully—in ski season, calling ahead is a necessity. Also be aware that many establishments close for vacation in May and June.

HIGHLIGHTS OF GRAUBÜNDEN

Delve into the psychological underworld of Expressionist Ernst Kirchner at his eponymous museum in **Davos** (p. 426).

Gasp at towering aqueducts and Alpine scenery on the **Rhätische Bahn** (p. 424).

Window-shop with the rich and famous in **St. Moritz** (p. 441).

CHUR (COIRA)   ☎081

Surrounded by snowy peaks and filled with medieval fountains and elaborately-painted façades, Chur has managed to escape the tourists flooding so many other towns. Boasting the oldest settlement in Switzerland (13,000 years and counting), this town proves that it can keep up with modern times with its vibrant nightlife.

▐ TRANSPORTATION

Chur serves as a transportation hub for excursions into Graubünden. **Trains** connect to: Arosa (1hr., 1-2 per hr. 5:35am-10:52pm, 13.40SFr); Basel (2¾hr., 1-2 per hr. 4:48am-10:16pm, 60SFr); Disentis (1¼hr., 1-2 per hr. 6:15am-10:10pm, 25SFr) for the Furka-Oberalp line; St. Gallen (1½hr., every hr. 4:48am-10:16pm, 31SFr); St. Moritz (2hr., every hr. 5:10am-10:16pm, 38SFr); Zurich (1½hr., 1-2 per hr. 4:48am-10:16pm, 35SFr). Postal **buses** run to Ticino via Bellinzona (2½hr., 6 per day 8am-6pm, 50SFr). A new high-speed train line to Zurich should be ready in 2005.

▐ PRACTICAL INFORMATION

Most directions begin at Postpl., which lies two blocks from the station on Bahnhofstr. Chur's **tourist office,** Grabenstr. 5, left on Grabenstr. off Postpl., makes reservations (2SFr) and distributes city maps, as well as guides to the city walking tours. (☎252 18 18; fax 90 76. Open M 1:30-6pm, Tu-F 8:30am-noon and 1:30-6pm, Sa 9am-noon.) Graubünden's **regional tourist office,** Alexanderstr. 24, on the second floor of the Media Café building, to the left of Bahnhofstr., stocks brochures and maps. (☎254 24 24; www.graubuenden.ch. Open M-F 8am-noon and 1:30-5:30pm.)

Train station services include: **currency exchange** (with Western Union services; open Su-F 6am-8pm, Sa 6am-7pm); **lost and found** (daily 9am-noon and 1-7pm); **luggage storage** (7SFr; open M-F 7am-7:45pm, Sa 7am-7:15pm, Su 9am-noon and 1-6:45pm); kiosk for **hotel reservations** outside the station; and **bike rental** (30SFr per day, 23SFr per half-day at baggage check; 6SFr to return to another station. Open M-F 7am-7:45pm, Sa 7am-7:15pm, Su 9am-noon and 1-6:45pm. General ticket counter open Su-F 5:45am-8:15pm, Sa until 7:15pm.) **Lockers** are 2SFr; larger ones can be found at the Post Bus station above (3-5SFr). A **24hr. ATM** is downstairs.

Taxis are available at the train station and by calling **Taxi Rosamilia** (☎252 15 22), **Taxi Giulo** (☎252 51 51) or **A-ABA Taxi** (☎284 55 55). A **pharmacy** is located on Bahnhofstr. 14 near Postpl. (Open M-F 7:30am-6:30pm, F 7:30am-9pm, Sa 7:30am-5pm AmEx/MC/V.) The **police station** (☎081 254 43 41) is located in Karlihofspl. Head down Reichsg. until it turns into Süsswinkelg. on the left in the plaza. Open M-F 8am-5pm. **Lost and Found** in station. **Parking** (☎257 18 18 or 250 24 70) is located mainly down Grabenstr. near Lindenquai. From Postpl., head right down Grabenstr. until it becomes Lindenquai; follow it along until you reach the Arosabahn train tracks. **Buchhandlung Strub**, Poststr. 22. (☎353 23 53, fax 253 30 50; info@buchhandlung.ch), carries a small selection of **English books**. Open M 1-6:30pm, Tu-F 9am-noon and 1-6:30pm, Friday until 8pm, Sa 9am-4pm. **STA Travel**, Untereg. 20 (www.statravel.ch) is open M-F 10am-6:30pm, Sa 10am-2pm. **Internet** access is available at **The Street Café**, Grabenstr. 47. (☎253 79 14. Open M-Th 9am-midnight, F-Sa 9am-2am. 5SFr per 20min.) For the cheapest and quietest spot, try the **Kantonsbibliothek** (☎257 2828; fax 21 53; www.kbchur.ch) at Karlihofpl., 10min. down Reichsg. (Open Tu and Th 9am-5:45pm, W and F 9am-6:45pm, Sa 9am-3:45am. First 15min. free. 2SFR per 15min. thereafter. Printing 0.20SFr/pg. Wheelchair accessible.) **Laundry** (accompanied by pop music) is available at **Malteser's Wash Self-Service**, Grabenstr. 49 in Malteserturm. (Open daily 9am-midnight. Wash 7-10SFr, dry 4-6SFr. Laundry detergent 0.50-2SFr.) The **post office** is just right of the train station in the Post Bus station complex. (Open M-F 7:30am-noon and 1:30-7:30pm, Sa 8am-noon, Su and holidays 4:30-6pm.) Postpl. is a secondary office. (Open M-F 7:30am-6:30pm, Sa 8am-noon.) **Postal Code:** CH-7000/7002.

ACCOMMODATIONS

Budget options are hard to come by in Chur, and those that exist are spartan. The nearest hostel is in **Arosa** (p. 421). **Hotel Drei Könige ❷** has been family-run since 1911. From the tourist office, head right down Grabenstr. and turn right on Reichsg. The "Backpacker's Lodge" is tucked in the attic of this ancient house, lined with comfortable beds, old children's toys, and mismatched furniture. Cooing pigeons nest in the rafters outside, lulling guests to sleep with their song. A generous breakfast, central location, and free 24-hour Internet access make this hotel a definite deal. The restaurant downstairs offers a limited menu of Swiss classics, along with a "Backpacker's Special" dinner for 15SFr. (☎252 17 58; www.dreikoenige.ch. Breakfast and sheets included. 24hr. parking 12SFr. Luggage storage and a safe for valuables available. Cooking allowed in hotel kitchen 6pm-9pm. 20SFr deposit for key gives you 24hr. access. Quiet hours midnight-7am. Non-smoking. Reception 7am-11pm. Check-out 11am. Dorms 25SFr; singles 60-70SFr, with shower 75-95SFr; doubles 100-120SFr/120-160SFr. AmEx/DC/MC/V.)

The **Post Hotel ❹**, Poststr. 11 off Postpl., is located in the pedestrian zone with plant-lined hallways and large, clean rooms. (☎252 68 44; www.comforthotel-post.ch. Breakfast, TV, and telephone included. Reception 7am-11pm. Check-out 11am. Doors lock at midnight. Room keys open the front door. Some non-smoking rooms. Wheelchair accessible. Safe, hair-dryer, telephone, and TV in all rooms. Parking available. Singles 75SFr, with shower 90-120SFr; doubles 130-150, with shower 150-190SFr. Children under 2 free, 3-5 20SFr, 5-12 40SFr. 10% discount for stays of 4 or more nights. AmEx/DC/MC/V.) **Camp Au ❶**, Felsensustr. 61, is a green and grassy campsite on the Rhine. Take bus #2 to "Obere Au" past the sports complex; it's on the left, on the gravel path. Equipped with kiosks and a restaurant, as well as toilets, dish-washing facilities, and waste disposal, Camp Au is a solid option. (☎284 22 83; www.camping-chur.ch. No entry between noon-2pm and 10pm-7am. 6.70SFr per person, ages 6-12 3.30SFr; 6.50-8.60SFr. per tent. Electricity 3.50SFr. 5 nights 505/472/345, with shower and bath 564/527/425. 4SFr per car.)

FOOD AND NIGHTLIFE

Wander around the squares of the old city to find a variety of cuisines, including Spanish, Thai, Greek, and lots of places serving good old *Rösti*. The **Co-op** at the intersection of Quaderstr. and Masanserstr sells groceries, and the restaurant one floor up has a fresh salad bar and menus from 11SFr. Open M-Th 8:30am-6:30pm, F

8:30am-9pm, Sa 8am-5pm. Fresh farmer's market every Sa 7:30am-noon, May-Oct. **Rägawurm**, Comanderg. 3 next to *Martinskirche* (☎252 16 95) is stocked with organic produce. Open M 1:30-6:30pm, Tu-F 9am-12:15pm and 1:30-6:30pm, Sa 9am-4pm. At night, head down to Untereg. to try out Chur's bar and club scene.

Valentino's Grill, Untereg. 5 (☎252 73 22), the "1st Original Swiss Shwarma," right on Grabenstr. from Postpl. and left under the arches. Kebabs 9-10SFr. Falafel in pita 8SFr. Hummus from 11SFr. Beer and wine from 4SFr. Open M-Th 11:45am-2pm and 5-midnight, F 11:45am-2pm and 5pm-2am, Sa 11:45am-2am. ❶

Restaurant Falkner, at the intersection of Reichg and St. Martinspl, next to Martinskirche. Small but delicious selection of salads and entrées. All food is "bio" (organic). Features salad with sprouts, avocado, pear, walnuts, and ginger (small 10SFr, large 16SFr). Daily specials may include "bio-wurst" and typically range from 16-19SFr.

Evviva, Untereg. 11 (☎252 40 21), an Italian gelateria and food store complete with ciabatta sandwiches (around 7.50SFr) and antipasti plates (16.50SFr). Mouth-watering selection of gelato (3SFr single, 5SFr double). Open Tu-Su 11am-midnight.

Restaurante Controversa, Steinbruchstr. 2 (☎252 99 44; fax 99 43), on the corner of Grabenstr. and Reichsg. Artsy decor, Louis XIV drapes, black coffee tables, and neon lights. Enjoy pasta (13-25SFr), meat dishes (28-32SFr), and a salad bar. Wine 4-8SFr. Wheelchair accessible. Open Tu-Sa 11am-2pm and 5pm-midnight. ❸

La Pasteria Otello, Ottopl. (☎250 55 15; www.otello.ch). From the station, turn left onto Ottostr. Secluded from the busy town center, this candlelit restaurant is perfect for an elegant night out. Pastas and pizzas are reasonable (14.50-26SFr), but fish entrées (25-40SFr) are a splurge. Wheelchair accessible. Open daily 10am-midnight, with warm dishes available 11:30am-2pm and 6-10pm. AmEx/DC/MC/V. ❹

China Restaurant Han Kung, Rabeng. 6 (☎252 24 58; fax 31 98). Walk down Reichsg., then turn left onto Rabeng. before St. Martin's Church, to find a bit of China in Haus Pestalozza. Pink arched ceilings and hanging Chinese lanterns transport diners into a different world altogether. 3-course lunch specials 15.50SFr, served noon-2pm. Chicken dishes 19.50-23.50SFr. Ask about sushi options. Open Tu-Su 11:30am-1:45pm and 6-9:45pm. AmEx/DC/MC/V. ❸

Q-Bar, near the laundromat on Grabenstr., with entrances on Untereg. and Engadinstr. Attracts an international mix. Chicly decorated with exposed stone walls and block furniture. The music is as varied as the crowd, but weekends bring familiar hits. Beer 5SFr. Prosecco 7.50SFr. Open M-Th 4pm-midnight, F and Sa 4pm-2am. AmEx/MC/V. ❶

Falsen Bar, Welschdorfli 1, across the Obertorer bridge just few minutes from the hopping Untereg. A chandelier resembling Medusa's tentacles extends from the bar, lighting minimalist black tables and bar stools. DJ fills the dance floor with tunes from the 50's through today every night starting at 10pm. Beer from 5.50SFr. Cocktails from 13.50SFr. 20+, no cover. Open M-F 9:30pm-2am, Sa-Su 9:30pm-4am. AmEx/MC/V.

Street Café, Grabenstr. 47 (☎253 79 14). Filled with a young local crowd grooving to techno-jazz among mirrors, crystal chandeliers, and a metal bar. Beers from 3.90SFr, 1SFr more after 8pm. Panini sandwiches and pasta dishes 10.50SFr. **Internet** 15SFr per hr. 18+ after 8pm. Open M-Th 9am-midnight, F-Sa 9am-2am. AmEx/MC/V. ❶

◙ SIGHTS

Red and green footpaths throughout the town lead visitors past Chur's sights, most of which are located in the city's expanding car-free zone. The cavernous 12th-century **Kathedral St. Mariä Himmelfahrt** at the top of the old town is being restored until 2006 at a cost of nearly 1.5 million Euros. Only a small portion of its impressive Gothic and Romanesque interior is visible, with a small side chapel still open to the public. A display on the history of the church, its art and artifacts, and the restoration project, is translated into English. (From St. Martinspl., go left on Kirchg. and head up the stairs.) Downhill, the **Martinskirche** (St. Martin's Church, built in 1491) offsets the cathedral's looming presence with a simple interior dominated by a pipe organ and three Giacometti stained-glass windows.

Chur's **Bündner Kunstmuseum**, Bahnhofstr. 35, at the corner of Bahnhofstr. and Grabenstr., blazes with the art of the Giacomettis: Giovanni, Alberto, and Augusto. Works by Swiss artists Angelika Kauffman and Ferdinand Hodler occupy the ground floor, while modern exhibits enliven the black-and-white basement, a work of art itself. (☎257 28 68; info@bkm.gr.ch. Open Tu-W and F-Su 10am-noon and 2-5pm, Th 10am-noon and 2-8pm. 8SFr, students 6SFr, under 16 free. During the summer exhibition (usually late June to mid-Sept.), the museum is open without an afternoon break. German tours of special exhibits Th 7pm. Ground and second floors wheelchair-accessible. 12SFr, students 10SFr.) The **Rätisches Museum**, Hofstr. 1, in a former arsenal erected over the cemetery of St. Martin, documents the history of Graubünden since ancient times. Trace the progression of civilization in this area from a collection of archaeological artifacts in the basement through displays of weapons, tapestries, jewel-encrusted ecclesiastical pieces, and more, ending in the rafters of the building with a group of traditional farming tools still occasionally used today. An English guide to the exhibits is available for 6SFr. (☎257 28 88; www.rm.gr.ch. Open Tu-Su 10am-noon and 2-5pm. 5SFr. Students 2SFr, seniors and groups 3SFr, under 16 free.) **Brambrüesch,** a mountain accessible from Chur by cable car, provides hiking in the summer and skiing in the winter. Call 250 55 90, visit www.brambuesch.ch, or check the tourist office for more information. This mountain also hosts the Alpine beard-growing contest every August.

BAD RAGAZ   ☎081

A massage at Bad Ragaz's thermal baths (34°C) will relax weary muscles, though for a hefty price. Thankfully, the laid-back atmosphere of this tree-lined suburb is just as soothing, but free. Bad Ragaz lies in the heart of the region famous as the home of Heidi. Short hikes from the top of mountains allow exploration of the area immortalized by Johanna Spyri's beloved tale. The 1½hr. pass to the **Tamina Therma** (thermal baths) grants access to the town spa's, three pools, waterfalls, watery lounges, and grottoes. (☎303 27 41; fax 20 02; www.resortragaz.ch. Open daily 7:30am-9pm. 17SFr, children 3-11 12SFr. 10SFr key deposit, solarium 12SFr extra for 15 min. Bath and 20-min. massage combo 58SFr.) A popular 1½hr. *Heidi* self-guided walking tour originates from the nearby hamlet of Maienfeld. Take the train to Maienfeld, 1 stop before Bad Ragaz, or ride the yellow Postauto bus from the Bad Ragaz Bahnhof to the Maienfeld Post. (20min., 1 per hr., 3SFr one-way.) The red **"Heidiweg"** markers take you from the town center, through the surrounding hills and vineyards, to **Heididork** and **Heidihaus.** Composed of a small set of buildings and barns, and replete with farm animals, the village was designed to replicate Heidi's 19th-century way of life. This is a great hike even for those who have never read the book, guiding visitors through the ancient streets of Maeienfeld and past spectacular views of the area's vineyards and surrounding mountains. (☎330 19 12; fax 19 13; www.heidi-swiss.ch.; www.heidihaus.ch. Open mid-Mar. to mid-Nov. daily 10am-5pm. 5SFr, children 2SFr.)

Bad Ragaz is accessible by **train** from Chur (15min., every 30min. 4:48am-11:16pm, 7.80SFr) and St. Gallen (1¼hr., every hr. 5:59am-10:21pm, 25SFr). (Train station open for ticketing M-Sa 6am-8pm, Su 7am-8pm.) To get to the **tourist office,** Maienfelderstr. 5, exit the station and head left at the fork, onto Kirchg. (Hotel Bristol will be on your left). This street turns into Fläscherstr. and meet up with the river. Walk 5min. along the river, and then turn right onto Maienfelderstr. The office offers hiking and biking suggestions, along with guided tours through the surrounding "Heidiland," and information about local cheesemakers and popular house-and-carriage rides. (☎302 10 61; fax 62 90; www.badragaz-tourismus.ch. Wheelchair accessible. Open Nov.-May M-F 8:30am-6pm, Sa 8:30am-noon and 1-4pm; June-Oct. M-F 8:30am-7pm, Sat. 8:30am-noon and 1-4pm.) **Currency exchange** (M-F 8:30am-11:30am, and 2pm-6pm, Sa 8:30am-11:30am and 1:30-5:30pm, Su 9:30am-11:30am and 1:30-5:30pm) and 24hr. **lockers** (2-5SFr) are at the train station. **24hr. ATM** available across the street from the tourist office. Get lunch items at the **Co-op** just behind the tourist office. (Wheelchair accessible. Open M-F 8am-6:30pm, Sa 8am-4pm.) **Bike rental** available through the Bristol Hotel, across from the train station. (☎303 77 77; fax 78; www.bristolhotel.ch. 15SFr per 3hr., 23 SFr per 6hr., 30SFr per day.) Hotel also offers **Internet.** (5SFr per 20min.) **Police emergency** (117) **Non-emergency and Lost and Found** (☎302 42 22).

AROSA   ☎081

A squeaking train ride from Chur (1hr.) twists and turns through rugged peaks, past waterfalls, and over lush valleys to reach the secluded town of Arosa. Bounded by two main lakes—Obersee by the train station, and Untersee below the town—Arosa is an outdoor-lover's paradise. Visitors to this small town can gaze in awe at the panorama stretching before them from the top of the 2653m Weißhorn, go for a swim in the Untersee, and hike through wildflower-filled meadows and craggy mountain passes, all before dinnertime. During winter months, ski schools and slopes offer endless entertainment of their own. A popular and lucrative resort area, Arosa also remains accessible to budget travelers, thanks to well-equipped dormitories.

When planning your visit, be aware that Arosa lives by its seasons: *Winter* is from December to April, *Sommer* is from mid-June to mid-October, and the *Zwischen* or *Sonder* seasons are the weeks in between. Hotels break down the year further by defining low, middle, peak, and off-seasons. Be sure to call ahead to make sure your hotel, huts, and activities will be open during your stay.

The Arosa **All-Inclusive Card,** first offered in 2003, is free to travelers staying overnight in an Arosa hotel or hostel and 8SFr for daily visitors. The summer-only pass gives free access to pedal boats on the Obersee, swimming in the Untersee, the ice rink, the Weisshorn cable car, the Hörnli Express, and the Arosa bus system. The tourist office, post office, train station, and hotels give out the cards. A 5SFr deposit is required for the card, which can be returned at hotels, the post office, the train station, and the tourist office.-Check out www.all-inclusive.ch.

⎚ ⑦ TRANSPORTATION AND PRACTICAL INFORMATION

Arosa is accessible by scenic **train** from Chur (1hr., every hr. 5:35am-11:02pm, 13.40SFr). A **free shuttle bus** (summer every 30min., winter every 10min. 7am-7pm; 3SFr in winter, free in summer with the Arosa Card) transports visitors in town, between ski lifts, and along the 10min. walk from the train station to the tourist office (stop: "Casino"). A **night bus service** operates late December-late April (1 per hr. 7pm-2am). The **tourist office,** right out of the station and right uphill 5min. on Poststr., arranges hiking trips and, while they don't book hotels, they can call them and help connect visitors with rooms. Both services are free. (☎378 70 20; www.arosa.ch. Open early Dec. to mid-Apr. M-F 9am-6pm, Sa 9am-5:30pm, Su 4-6pm; mid-Apr. to early Dec. M-F 8am-noon and 1:30-5:30pm, Sa 9am-1pm, late June 29 to mid-Aug. also open Sa 2-4pm.) While parking in central Arosa's is forbidden, **parking** is free in summer with the Arosa Card at city parking garages and in other parts of the city. A strict traffic ban is imposed nightly midnight-6am. The **train station** has **currency exchange** at the ticket counter (☎377 14 90; www.rhb.ch; open daily

6am-9pm), and **luggage storage** (M-F 6am-8pm, Sa-Su 6:30am-8pm; 5SFr). Electronic **lockers** that don't give change are available at the end of the station for luggage (3-5SFr) and skis (2SFr deposit). Crédit Suisse, right out of the train station, offers a **24hr ATM. Bike Rental** is available from the boat-rental building across the lake from the train station. (30SFr per half-day, 40SFr per day. Open daily 10am-5pm.) **Internet** access is available at café Bar Los, across the street from the tourist office. (15SFr per hour. Open summer 2pm-2am, winter till 3am.) Montana Apotheke on Oberseepl. is the **pharmacy**. (☎377 15 22. Open M-F 8 am-noon and 2-6:30pm, Sa 8am-noon and 2-4pm.) The **police station** on Poststr. also houses the lost-and-found office (☎378 67 17. Open M-F 8am-noon and 2-5pm). **Express Taxi** almost always has a car or two at the train station. The **post office** is in the main square, right of the train station. (Open M-F 8am-noon and 2-6pm, Sa 8:30-11am.) **Postal Code: CH-7050.**

ACCOMMODATIONS

Haus Florentinum (www.arosabergbahnen.ch). Follow the right-hand sidewalk of Poststr. past the tourist office. Then make an extreme right and head uphill 10min. on Murasteig, the zig-zagging paved path. At the top, continue right toward Hotel Hohe Promenade, turn left at the gravel path for Pension Suveran, and right at the dirt path in front of the sign. Run by the ski-lift company Arosa Bergbahnen, Florentinum provides cheap and convenient housing in winter (Dec.-Apr.) only (summer is reserved for groups). This enormous former convent in the woods is now a 150-bed party house with large lounges, balconies, and a chapel-turned-disco. Breakfast included. Dinner 15SFr. **Internet**, TV, ping-pong, and washing facilities available. Parking 7SFr per day. In the winter, 2-night min. stay on weekends. Reception open 8:30-11:30am and 4:30-10pm. Dec.-Apr. 2-night stay with 2-day ski pass adults 246SFr, youth and seniors 246SFr, children 175SFr; with shower 270SFr, youth and seniors 253SFr, children 187SFr; 5-night stay 505SFr/472SFr/345SFr, with shower and toilet 564SFr/527SFr/42SFr5. AmEx/DC/MC/V. ❷

Jugendherberge (HI), Seewaldstr. (☎377 13 97; www.backpackers-arosa.ch), past the tourist office down the hill (follow the signs). Friendly English- and Russian-speaking staff. Renovations fall of 2004 to add bathrooms to many of the rooms. Attracts families, school groups, and the occasional sports team. Dorms have balconies overlooking the Untersee or the Engadine slopes. Breakfast (8am) and sheets included. Bag lunch 9SFr; dinner 13SFr. Showers 0.50SFr per 3min. In winter, 2-night stay required on weekends. Reception summer 7-10am and 5-10pm; winter 7am-noon and 4-10pm. Check-out 9am, strictly enforced. Curfew 10pm, 11pm in winter; key provided. Open mid-June to mid-Oct. and mid-Dec. to mid Apr. Summer dorms 32-38SFr; doubles 70SFr. In winter required half-pension included; dorms 153SFr including 2 day ski pass. Children under 16 100SFr, youth under 19 and seniors over 60 137SFr. Single with shower including 2 day ski pass 171/118/155, quads and doubles 163/110/147.) ❸

Pension Suveran (☎377 19 69 or 079 640 49 93; www.suveran.ch), on the way to the Haus Florentium. Wood-paneled chalet in the woods above Arosa. Breakfast included. Dinner on request 15SFr. Sinks in rooms. Hall bathrooms. Reception 7am-9pm. Check-in 3pm. Check-out 10am. Open June-Oct. and Dec.-Apr. Sometimes closed in May and Nov; call to double-check. June-Oct. singles 47-52SFr; doubles 94-104SFr. Dec.-Apr. singles 49-57SFr; doubles 98-114SFr. 10% reduction for stays over 3 days. ❸

Hotel Garni Haus Am Wald (☎/fax 377 31 38; hausamwald@bluewin.ch). Turn right out of station then take the first right, after Crédit Suisse. Bright, modern rooms in a central location. A few minutes from train station, bus stop and Weisshorn cable car, this hotel makes up in convenience and price for what it lacks in charm. All rooms have at least a sink in the room. Many have full bathrooms, and some have kitchens. "Pop Corn" restaurant downstairs. Breakfast included. Check-in until 10pm at bar. Dec.-Apr. singles with shared bathroom 70-80SFr, doubles 120-150SFr, with bath 150-180SFr. May-Nov. 45-55/90-104/110-120. AmEx/MC/V.

Camping Arosa (☎377 17 45; sportanlagen@arosa.ch), about 15min. downhill from the hostel, with signs pointing the way. Cooking facilities available. The caretaker is on location 4:45-5:15pm.l Payment is on the honor system. 9SFr per person, ages 6-12 5SFr, tents 5SFr., cars 3SFr, camper 11SFr, Electricity 3SFr. Showers 0.50SFr per 3min. ❶

🍴 FOOD

There are several quality food options in Arosa. In **café Kaiser,** on Poststr. in the Apparthotel, tourists and locals gather for a drink, light meal, or elaborate ice cream dish. With amazing views of the surrounding mountains (and a legend at each table labeling the peaks), the outdoor terrace provides a sunny alternative to the elegant pink-tableclothed interior. Coffee, tea, and hot chocolate 3-4.50SFr, ice cream 9-10SFr, soups 9SFr, warm meals (served after 11am) 11-16SFr. (☎377 34 54. Children's menu available. Open daily 8am-6pm.) **Hotel Central Arve ❸**, Hubelstr., is down the hill from the tourist office just before the youth hostel on the right. The *Arvenstube* at the hotel serves season-specific *Menüs* for 16.50-21SFr in a cozy den. The "soup trilogy" gets you a small portion of three different soups for 11SFr; the house speciality beef *tartare* (29/38SFr) is prepared at your table. (☎378 52 52; www.arve-central.ch. English menu and parking available. Closed late Apr. to late May. Open daily 11:30am-2pm and 6-10pm. Reservations recommended for summer weekends and in winter. AmEx/MC/V.) At **Orelli's Restaurant ❷**, Poststr., down the hill from the tourist office on the left, families eat Swiss cuisine in a kid-friendly restaurant decorated with Mickey Mouse images. The thrifty can get the soup du jour and bread for 5-8SFr or 2 *Wurstli* (sausages) for 10SFr. A salad buffet (8-12SFr), vegetarian and pasta options (16-20SFr), and meat entrées (18-20SFr) round out the options. (☎377 12 08; www.hotelorelli.ch. English menu available. Open mid-June to mid-Apr. Su-Th 7:30am-9pm, F-Sa 7:30-10pm. MC/V.)

Get groceries at the **Co-op,** on Poststr. (wheelchair accessible; open M-F 8am-12:30pm and 2-6:30pm, Sa 8am-4pm), or at **Denner Superdiscount** (which boasts a massive amount of chocolate), near the station (wheelchair accessible; open M-W and F 8am-12:15pm and 2:30-6:30pm, Sa 8am-12:15pm and 1:15-4pm. Sa winter hours 8am-5pm; summer closed Th).

🅰 🅱 OUTDOOR ACTIVITIES AND ENTERTAINMENT

SKIING. Separate passes for the 15 ski lifts and cableways that hoist skiers to the 70km network of slopes in the Arosa-Tschuggen ski area B are available for tourists not staying in the dorms. The mountains are covered with slopes for all levels, but the easier paths are concentrated on the lower Tschuggen area. Ticket offices in Arosa (at the tourist office and at the main "Arosa Bergbahnen" office behind the train station) offer myriad passes. (Day, morning, afternoon, 1½-day, "choose-your-day" etc. 54SFr per day; 271SFr per week; 410SFr for 2 weeks. AmEx/DC/MC/V.) The smaller Tschuggen-sector day-pass is 34SFr. Children under 15 get a 50% discount; ages 16-19 and seniors get a 10-15% discount. Save 20% by going in the low-season (2nd week of Dec., first 2 weeks of Apr.) or in the first week of December, though only limited runs are open (20SFr for 1 day, children 15SFr).

HIKING. When the snow melts, it uncovers over 200km of flower-covered hiking paths. Retus Schmid offers **guided Alpine hikes**. Call him to arrange times and check prices (☎377 12 08). Two cable cars operate in summer. The **Weisserhornbahn cable**

car, above the train station, whisks travelers to the top of the Weisserhorn (2653m; mid-June to mid-Oct. every 20min. 9am-5pm). The summit allows views of the whole Engadine valley. The **Hörnli-Express** (free with Arosa Card; daily early July to mid Oct. 9am-5pm) at the other end of town is accessible by bus. A 1½hr. hike follows the ridge between lifts; sign-posts on the peaks point the way for longer hikes that wind into the valleys opposite the town. Most hikes that do not involve cable cars start from the Untersee (at the very end of the street on which the hostel is located). A number of hiking maps are available at the tourist office. The "Arosa und Umgebung" map (19.80SFr) comes with a list of suggested trails and lengths.

Alteiner Wasserfällen Hike (2hr. 1-way). This easy-to-medium trail begins at the Untersee and starts out flat, winding through the Hintern Wald and fields of wildflowers before crossing over a stream several times. At the end of a climb, the trail splits, leading to the Kleiner Wasserfall or the impressive Großer Wasserfall. Take the same path to Arosa. To lengthen the hike, climb along the steep trail from the waterfalls to the Atteinsee (5hr. round-trip). This continues to the other side of the ridge and on to Davos.

Ochsenalp to Tschiertschen Hike (5hr. round-trip). After first taking the Arosa bus to Prätschli or Maran, this hike of medium difficulty climbs along the Rot-Tritt trail 2hr. and peaks at Ochsenalp. At 1936m, Ochsenalp offers great views of the surrounding rocky peaks and is home to a traditional Alpine restaurant. The hike then winds down the other side of the mountain 1½hr. to the unpronounceable Tschiertschen. A bus from Tschiertschen to Chur leaves hourly, but check the schedule to be sure of any seasonal changes. Then ride the train from Chur to Arosa (1hr., 1 per hr., 13.60SFr).

OTHER ACTIVITIES. The Untersee's **free beach** is open daily 10am to 7pm, though people often continue to swim after that. Outdoor grills, volleyball nets, and pedal boats are for rent on the Obersee. (10am-5pm. Free with Arosa Card.) The outdoor **ice rink** is open November-April for ice skating, curling, and hockey. An indoor rink, open mid July-April, offers more options for skating fanatics. (☎13 77 17 45. Winter open daily 10am-5pm. Free entry with Arosa Card; skate rental 6SFr. Call ahead in July and Aug., because camps fill up indoor ice time.) **Stall Weierhof** gives **pony rides** for children ages 4-9 (10-18SFr per 30min), and also offers larger horses for 26SFr/hr. (☎377 41 96; www.arosa.com/weiserhof. July-Aug. M-F.) **Cheese tasting** is available at the Alpkäserei Maran (☎377 22 77. near bus stop at Maran). Contact the tourist office the day before by 5:30pm for reservations (June-Sept. Th. 1hr. long. 5SFr, under 12 free.) Don't miss the picturesque area of **Innerarosa,** the town only 20min. from the Arosa city center heading toward the Hörnli Express (by Arosa bus, just 5min.) There, a grassy path leads through lush green hills and brilliantly-colored wildflowers to the **Bergkirchli.** Normally closed to visitors, this church opens its doors for regular organ concerts and traditional music nights. The **Arosa Jazztage** in mid-July grants free admission to local venues. The festival features New Orleans jazz played by a small number of international bands. Contact the tourist office for exact days and locations. For 10 days every mid-December, the **Humorfestival** gets Arosa laughing by hosting comedy shows performed by artists from all over the world. (Tickets 10SFr in afternoon, 35SFr in the evening; available at the tourist office. Ask for a schedule of English-speaking performers.)

DAVOS ☎081

Davos (pop. 12,000) sprawls along the valley floor under seven mountains laced with the wires of chairlifts and cable cars. Originally a health resort for consumptives, the city catered to such fin de siècle celebrity guests as Robert Louis Stevenson and Thomas Mann, who, while in Davos, wrote *Treasure Island* and *The Magic Mountain*, respectively. Davos now relies on its world-famous skiing to lure visitors. Built around tourism, Davos lacks the charm of other Graubünden towns. On the upside, it offers more services and activities geared towards travelers. While summers can be a bit quiet, winters find the town swarming with people of all ages from around the globe. MTV is even interested in this popular resort town, planning winter parties at local clubs and five snowboarding events.

⊏ TRANSPORTATION

Davos is accessible by **train** from Chur via Landquart (1½hr., every hr. 4:57am-10:08pm, 25SFr) or from Klosters (25min.; 2 per hr.; free with guest card from either city, otherwise 8.60SFr) on the Rhätische Bahn lines. The town is divided into two areas, Davos-Dorf and Davos-Platz, each with a train station, linked by the 3km **Promenade.** Platz is the site of the tourist office, main post office, and most other places of interest to budget travelers. Dorf is closer to the quiet and picturesque Davosersee. A convenient system of **buses** (free with guest card or 2.70SFr) runs frequently between the two train stations and stops near major hotels. **Parking lots** line the Promenade and Talstr. (1-2SFr per hr.). Parking is also available at the train station (5SFr per day; additional days 3SFr.)

🚺 PRACTICAL INFORMATION

The high-tech main **tourist office,** Promenade 67, in Platz, up the hill and to the right of the train station, caters mostly to those staying in hotels, but has free **Internet** access and a weekly bulletin of events and general info. A smaller **branch office** sits across from the Dorf train station. (☎415 21 21; www.davos.ch. Both offices open Dec. to mid-Apr. and mid-June to mid-Oct. M-F 8:30am-6:30pm, Sa 9am-5pm, Platz location also open Su 10am-noon and 3-5:30pm; mid.-Oct. to Nov. and mid-Apr. to mid-June M-F 8:30am-noon and 1:45-5pm, Su 8:30am-noon, Platz location also M-F noon-1:45pm.) The stations **store luggage** (*5SFr*), rent **lockers** (3-5SFr), and provide **Western Union** services and **currency exchange.** (Platz station open M-Sa 4:50am-10pm, Su and holidays 5:30am-10pm, luggage storage daily 5am-midnight; Dorf station open daily 6:45am-7:10pm.) **Expert Roro,** in Dorf, Promenade 123, across from the blue-and-pink Hotel Concordia, offers **Internet** access at more terminals than the tourist office. (☎420 11 11. Open M 2-6:30pm, Tu-F 8:30am-noon and 2-6:30pm, Sa 8:30am-noon and 2-5pm. 5SFr per 20min., 12SFr per hr.) **After Hours,** Promenade 64, the first certified MTV 24hr. shop in Switzerland, offers **Internet,** hot food (small pizzas 7-8SFr), DVD and video rental, and other "emergency" supplies and groceries 24 hours per day Nov.-May and July-Aug. Sept.-Oct. and June open M-Th and Su 10:30am-3:30am, F-Sa til 5:30am (☎413 63 76). **Laundry** available at self-service **Waschsalon,** Promenade 102, below the yellow-painted Walhalla Bar. (☎416 32 70. Open M-F 8am-8pm, Sa 9am-5pm. Wash 3-6SFr per load, dry 2-5 SFr.) The main **post office** is in Davos-Pl. at Promenade 43, in the shopping center across from the train station. (Open M-F 7:45am-6:30pm, Sa 8:30am-10am.) **Post office** in Dorf, across from the train station. (Open M-F 8:30am-noon and 2-6pm, Sa 8:30-11am.) **Postal Code:** CH-7270.

▟ ACCOMMODATIONS AND CAMPING

In the summer, or for a more relaxing hostel atmosphere, head to Klosters (see p. 427). Always ask for the Davos **visitor's card,** which grants free unlimited travel on the city's buses and discounts on attractions. The closest campgrounds are at **Caravan & Mobilhome Rinerlodge** in nearby Rinerhorn on bus line #7 from the train station, about 15min., stop "Davos Glaris." (☎401 12 52, www.rinerhorn.ch. Breakfast, hot water, communal showers, and toilets provided. 26SFr with a mobile home, 16SFr with a tent, 6SFr for electricity.)

Youthpalace Davos (HI),Horlaubenstr. 27 (☎420 11 20, fax 21, www.youthhostel.ch/
davos), situated in what used to be the "Beau Site" Sanotorium. 5 min. walk from the
Davos Dorf train station. Turn left onto Bahnhofstr, and left again onto Promenade by
the Arabella Sheraton Hotel. Continue past the Meierhof Hotel and turn right onto Jörg-
Jenatschstr. Follow this until it meets up with Horlaubenstr. Continue until you see the
hostel on your left. Alternatively, take the bus to the Schiabach stop and follow signs
5min. to the hostel. Sun terraces, sitting rooms, TV rooms, bike rental, storage rooms
for bicycles and skis, and a taste of luxury. Breakfast and dinner included. No lock-out.
Wheelchair accessible. Parking available. Dec.-Mar. dorm 55SFr, single 139SFr, double
218SFr. June-Oct. dorm 45SFr, single 75SFr, double 150SFr. Mar.-June and Nov. dorm
30SFr, single 60SFr, double 120SFr, dinner not included.

Jacobshorn Ski Mountain (☎414 90 20; www.fun-mountain.ch). The folks here have
made their youth-oriented mountain accessible to travelers with dorms for winter thrill-
seekers, sold as a package with ski passes for Jacobshorn mountain. ❷

  Snowboarder's Palace, Oberestr. 45-47. Located right above the main tourist office, the Palace
has a lounge and bar. 2- to 6-bed rooms. Breakfast included. 1-night, 2-day ski pass 175-
185SFr; 6-night, 7-day ski pass 570-630SFr, whole region 640-700SFr.

  Guest House Bolgenhof, Brämabülstr. 4A, is convenient, right beside the Davos-Pl. train station,
next to Jakobshorn office near the ski lifts. Prices same as Snowboarder's Palace.

  Snowboardhotel Bolgenschanze, Skistr. 1. The most hopping house is conveniently located over a
bar oodles of post-skiing partying occurs. 18+. 2- to 5-bed dorms. 1-night, 2-day ski-pass 145-
195SFr; 6-night, 7-day ski pass 690SFr, whole region 760SFr.

Hotel Herrmann, Dorfstr. 23 (☎416 17 37; fax 35 73), behind the tourist office and to
the right in Dorf, provides a peaceful respite for those looking to enjoy the resort town
off the slopes. The soothing sounds of the brook beside the house, hardwood floors with
rugs, and a bathtub on the floor make this spot friendlier than most. Parking 10SFr per
day. Reception 7:30am-10pm. Open July-Sept. and Dec.-Apr. Winter singles with breakfast 75-85SFr, with shower 90-100SFr; doubles 150-170/180-200. Summer singles
52/68; doubles 104/136. MC/V. ❹

🍴 FOOD

Grand Café Latino, Promenade 40, right uphill from the Platz train station, brings
a bit of South America to Davos with potted ferns and palms and bright orange
walls. Tapas are 5SFr per serving and can make a complete meal when coupled
with a bowl of soup (7-10SFr). Meat dishes (including ostrich filets and chicken
stuffed with plantains - both 23SFr) and an extensive selection of fish specialties
(fried calamari 19SFr, Red Snapper in mango-pepper sauce 27SFr) round out the
menu, with plenty of vegetarian options thrown in as well (pastas and vegetarian
enchiladas and tortillas 17-19SFr). This Latin bistro is a popular bar for a primarily older crowd after it stops serving warm food at 11pm (9pm on Su). The drink
menu includes beers (3-7SFr), tropical cocktails (16SFr), 6 types of Daquiries and
Margaritas, 14 types of whiskey, mojitos, brandies, cognacs, and more. (☎413 13
83, Open M-Th8am-1am, F-Sa 8am-2am, Su 2pm-midnight. AmEx/MC/V.) **Romeo
& Juliá/Belvedere Tratorria ❹,** Promenade 89 (500m toward Dorf from Platz; bus
stop: "Kirchner Museum") lives up to its name in romance in the white table-
clothed and crystal chandelier-lit dining room in the five-star Hotel Steigen-
berger Belvedere. Gourmet meals served in these elegant surroundings are surprisingly inexpensive. Enjoy a salmon filet with lemon sauce and vegetables for
22.50SFr, or a house-made pasta dish for 18-22.50SFr. Vegetarian options,
including risotto with grilled mushrooms, arugula, and parmesan cheese are 18-
21SFr. Soups 8-9SFr. (☎415 60 00; www.davos.steigenberger.ch. Reservations
suggested in summer; necessary 2-3 days ahead in winter. Open 6pm-midnight.

GRAUBÜNDEN

AmEx/D/MC/V.) Alternatively, grab a Bud and a bar stool, American style, at **Café Carlos ❷**, Promenade 58, which is fittingly located in a mall opposite the main tourist office. This restaurant feeds a friendly local crowd with American standards, including burgers and sandwiches from 7SFr, burritos 8-10SFr, and omelettes for 11SFr. Beers from 5SFr. (☎413 17 22. Wheelchair accessible. English menu available. Open daily except W in summer 10am-midnight, with hot food served 11am-9pm, winter daily 11:30am-10:30pm. AmEx/D/MC/V.)

Haven't had your *Rösti* fix yet? **Röstizzeria ❸**, in Dorf, Promenade 128, downstairs from the Hotel Dishma, can satisfy a craving with 11 variations (18-23SFr), pastas (14-17SFr), and pizza (from 13SFr) in a dining room decorated with carved wood and fake grapevines. A variety of salads supplement their menu in the summer (17-24SFr). (☎416 12 50. Take most any bus to Dischmastr. Open daily 6am-11pm. AmEx/D/MC/V.) **Co-op** (cafeteria-style restaurant inside features weekly *Menüs* 10SFr) across from the Platz station. (Open M-Th 8:30am-6:30pm, F 8:30am-8pm, Sa 8:30am-5pm; restaurant open M-Th 8am-6:30pm, F 8am-8pm, Sa 8am-5pm, Su 10am-6pm.)

🏛 🏔 MUSEUMS AND OUTDOOR ACTIVITIES

Although surprisingly small, Davos's rink holds the title of Europe's largest natural **ice rink** (22,000 sq. m). Located by the sports center between Platz and Dorf, it has figure skating, ice dancing, hockey, speed skating, and curling. (☎415 36 04. Open weather permitting mid-Dec. 15-Feb. 15. M-W and F-Su 10am-4pm, Th 8-10pm. 5SFr, 4SFr with visitors card; skate rental 6.50SFr with 20SFr deposit.)

For joggers, birdwatchers, and aspiring windsurfers, the **Davosersee** is the place to be. A 10min. bus ride from the city, this lake claims to be "the windiest Alpine lake in the world." (Take bus #1 (dir: Stilli) to "Flueelastr." and follow the yellow signs to the lake.) At the **Davosersee Surfcenter,** board rentals are 30SFr for 1hr., 60SFr for the day. (Open mid-June to mid-Sept. daily 11am-6:30pm, weather permitting.) Runners, strollers, and picnickers use the facilities around the lake. **Swissraft** (☎911 52 50) provides **canyoning** and **rafting** excursions, while **School Centre** (☎414 32 65) offers climbing possibilities for 30SFr per half day. Make a reservation at least 2 days in advance. On the Schatzalp, the adventurous are greeted with a 500m-long summer **sledge ride**. Open only in good weather, 10am-5pm. Call ahead if in doubt (☎415 51 51. 1 ride 3.50SFr, 10 for 28SFr)

KIRCHNER MUSEUM. The frosted glass structure opposite the Hotel Belvedere on the Promenade houses an extensive collection of paintings, sculptures, and tapestries by Ernst Ludwig Kirchner, whose harsh colors and long figures reveal troubled visions. This seminal figure of 20th-century German Expressionism lived in Davos for 21 years before committing suicide, perhaps due to a combination of poor health and upset over political turmoil. Curators oversee an ever-changing exhibit that places Kirchner's work alongside that of related artists. (☎413 22 02; kirchnermuseum@spin.ch. Take the bus to "*Sportszentrum/*Kirchner Museum" or *Kongreszentrum*. Open Dec. 25-Easter and mid July-Aug. Tu-Su 10am-6pm; Easter-mid-July Tu-Su 2-6pm. 8SFr, students and children under 16 5SFr.)

SKIING. Davos provides direct access to two main mountains—the Parsenn and Jakobshorn—and four **skiing areas,** covering every degree of difficulty. Parsenn, with long runs and fearsome vertical drops, is the mountain around which Davos built its reputation. Unfortunately, Parsenn's fame has brought hordes of tourists. (www.fun-mountain.ch. Day pass 60SFr.) Jacobshorn has found a niche with the younger crowd since the opening of a snowboarding "fun-park" with two half-pipes (day pass 52SFr). The **Pischa** and **Rinerhorn** are smaller resorts within the Davos area. The **regional ski pass** covers all six mountains in the Davos-Klosters area, including unlimited travel on most transport facilities, and doesn't cost much more than individual tickets (2 days 121SFr). If you're going to be doing a lot of skiing in the area, a season **Snow-Pass** is available for all Graubünden slopes. (www.snowpass.ch. 1200SFr, ages 13-17 800SFr, 6-12 400SFr.) Info and maps can be found at the tourist office. In addition to downhill runs, Davos boasts 75km of **cross-country trails** throughout the valley, including a night-lit trail. **The Swiss Ski School of Davos,** Promenade 157, offers lessons starting at 40SFr per half-day group lesson. (☎416 44 55; www.ssd.ch.) **Fullmoons,** Promenade 110, provides telemark lessons and tours. (☎/fax 240 14 77; www.fullmoons.ch. Half-day 170SFr.)

HIKING. One main ski lift on each mountain is open in summer, and many of the area's trails require these expensive lifts to bring hikers out of the dense valley. The tourist office has a variety of hiking maps, ranging from a free one listing operating hours and hiking routes/lengths to a very detailed contour-map for 29.50SFr.

Panoramaweg (2hr.). A relatively flat trail follows the contours of the broad hills above town, following views of the valley and the Swiss Alps. The route stretches from the Gotschnabahn (from Klosters) to Strelapass above Davos (5hr.). After the renovation, visitors will be able to easily traverse between the "Panoramaweg" stop and Klosters's cable car. (☎417 67 67; www.parsenn.ch.)

Davos-Platz to Monstein (5hr.). A more isolated and difficult hike into an adjoining valley that requires no cable car. Take Bus #8 from Platz to the trailhead at Sertig-Dörfli. Signs lead to "Fenezfurgga," which passes waterfalls and a valley that divides the Hoch Duncan and the Alpihorn. A stone wall separates the trail from the resorts beyond. The trek ends in Monstein, where buses connect to Glaris and then Davos.

KLOSTERS ☎081

Davos's sister resort, Klosters, lies across the Gotschna and Parsenn mountains. Though Klosters is 25 minutes from Davos by train, it retains a distinctly less built-up feel. This small, quiet town attracts mainly British tourists and is frequented by Prince Charles in the Winters. Most ski packages include mountains from both towns, and Klosters's main ski lift leads to a mountain pass where one may ski to either town. Klosters also has better access to fantastic biking trails.

▐ TRANSPORTATION. Klosters-Platz and Klosters-Dorf are connected to Chur by **train** through Landquart (1¼hr., every hr. 5:19am-9:31pm, 18.80SFr) and St. Moritz (1½hr., every hr., 31SFr). The same line connects Klosters and Davos (30min., every hr. 5:34am-11:32pm, 9.20SFr or free with guest card). Local **buses** connect Dorf, Platz, local towns, and the major ski lifts (1-6 stops 1SFr, 7-10 stops 2SFr, more than 10 stops 3SFr; guest card holders and children under 16 free).

▐ PRACTICAL INFORMATION. Like Davos, Klosters is divided into Klosters-Platz and Klosters-Dorf, connected by bus and train; most activity occurs in Platz. Platz and Dorf both have tourist offices, but the main **tourist office** is in Platz right from the train station (follow the signs). Detailed area hiking (15.50SFr) and biking (7.50SFr) maps are available. They also have information on the **Guest Card**, available during the summer to those staying overnight in one of the town's hotels or apartments. The card offers free travel on the local bus lines and the train between Klosters and Davos as well as discounts on mountain railways and various activities from bowling to hang gliding. **Currency exchange** is available on weekends. (☎410 20 20; fax 10; www.klosters.ch. Platz office open May-Nov. M-F 8:30am-noon and 2-6pm, Sa 8:30am-noon and 2-4pm, July-mid Aug. also Su 9-11am; Dec.-Apr. M-Sa 8:30am-noon and 2-6pm, Su 9-11:30am and

4-6pm) Dorf tourist office open late June to mid-Oct M-F 8:30-11:30am) The weekly Klosters newspaper publishes events and other town information (printed every Th; free from tourist office). Services at the Platz station include: **tickets** and **currency exchange** (open daily 6am-8:30pm), **lockers** (2SFr), **luggage storage** (open M-F 6:15am-7pm, Sa-Su 7:15am-7pm; pick up until 10:40pm; 3SFr), **scooter rental** (inquire for prices). **Internet** access in the **Silvretta Park Hotel**, Landstr. 190, is available 24hr. (Wheelchair accessible. 15SFr per hr., 9SFr per half hour for a wireless card for your laptop.) A **bike rental** service is at **Andrist Sport** on Gotschnastr. (☎410 20 80. Open M-F 9am-noon and 2-6:30pm, Sa 8am-noon and 2-4pm. 38SFr per day, 130SFr for 6 days. AmEx/MC/V.) Daily 24hr. **taxi service** is offered by **Cowboy's Taxi** (☎422 20 84 or 079 232 60 60; www.cowboystaxi.ch). The **post office** is to the right of the station. (Open M-F 7:30am-noon and 1:45-6:15pm, Sa 8:30am-noon.) **Post office** on Landstr. 17A in Klosters Dorf open M-F 8-11am and 2-6pm. **Postal Code:** CH-7250.

⌂⌂ ACCOMMODATIONS AND FOOD. Jugendherberge Soldanella (HI) ❷, Talstr. 73, provides a pleasant retreat with a fantastic view of the Alps. From the station, go left uphill past the Hotel Alpina to the church, then cross the street and head up the alleyway to the right of the Kirchplatz bus station sign. Walk 10min. along the street and admire the views as you come upon this massive, renovated chalet with wood paneling, a comfortable reading room, and small playground beside a flagstone terrace. The owners are friendly English-speakers full of hiking suggestions and tips. (☎422 13 16; www.youthhostel.ch/klosters. Breakfast (7-9am) and sheets included. Dinner and lunch on request 13SFr. All rooms non-smoking. Internet 2SFr per 10 min. Free parking. Reception 7-10am and 5-10pm. Check-out 10am. No lockout or curfew. Quiet hours 10pm-7am. Open late June to mid-Oct. and mid-Dec. to mid-Apr. Summer dorms 28SFr; singles 38SFr; doubles with sink 76SFr. Both include sinks. Family rooms 38SFr per person. Winter prices include dinner: 41/52/104/52SFr. children 2-6 halfprice. Tourist tax 2.70SFr per day June-Sept., 2.20SFr Oct.-May; 6SFr non-member surcharge. AmEx/D/MC/V.)

Some great deals await in *Privatzimmer* from 25SFr; a list is available at the tourist office. The tourist office can offer details on **mountain huts** in the Klosters area. Two of them, the **Silvrettahütte** (2341m) ❷ and the **Vereina-Berghaus** (1945m) ❸ are serviced by shuttle buses transporting visitors to and from Klosters. (Silvrettahütte: ☎422 13 06; www.silvrettahuette.ch. Breakfast and dinner included. Open mid-June to mid-Oct. and mid-Feb. to May. Hut 61SFr. Vereina-Berghaus: ☎422 12 16 or 422 11 97. Breakfast and dinner included. Open July to mid-Oct. Dorms 60SFr (includes breakfast and dinner; rooms 80SFr.) For Silvrettahütte, a taxibus provides access to Alp Sardasca, from which the hut is a 2hr. hike. Call ahead for reservations. (☎422 29 72. 1-way 30SFr per person, 60SFr minimum.) A **shuttle bus** for Vereina-Berghaus leaves from Sport Gotschna. (see "Outdoor Activities", below. Call ☎422 11 97. 12 SFR one-way, 24SFr round-trip).

Visitors to **Restaurant Höhwald**, in Monbiel, find Graubünden specialties served in a small cluster of Alpine huts. A limited selection of hearty food including soups (10SFr) and Rosti (16-19SFr) is served all day in the cozy "Stübli" (bar), a century-old wood-panelled room lined with deer antlers and stuffed goats' heads. A more extensive lunch and dinner menu, including a selection of wild game (rabbit and venison from 30SFr) and regional specialties (19-31SFr) awaits guests in the larger dining room. In nice weather, the terrace offers a not-to-be-missed vista of the entire valley and surrounding snow-capped mountains. (Take the bus #2, dir: Monbiel, to Höhwald. 10min. 1 per hour, 1SFr, free with Kloster guest card. The restaurant is about two minutes down the hill on the right. ☎422 30 45. Children's menu. English menu available. Open M and W-Su 10am-11pm;

closed mid-April to mid-May) **Gasthaus Casanna ❸**, Landstr. 171, offers cheap and simple food in a homey atmosphere. Rösti from 9SFr and tasty cheese-filled omelettes starting at 9.50SFr. Soups 5-8.50SFr. (☎422 12 29; fax 422 20 29. Open M-F 7:30am-12:30am, Sa 9am-6pm; closed early-mid May.) **Hotel Rustico ❹**, Landstr. 194 past the Park Hotel, serves fish, vegetarian dishes, and other fresh entrées (avocado salad with Zanderfilet 25SFr) in a bright interior with colorful paintings of wildlife. (☎422 12 46. Open M-W and F-Su 11:30am-1:30pm and 6-9:30pm.) A small **Co-op** grocery store is about 3 minutes from the train station. Take a right on Bahnhofstr. (Wheelchair accessible. Open M-F 8am-12:30pm and 2-6:30pm, Sa 8am-4pm.)

🎿 **OUTDOOR ACTIVITIES. Ski passes** for the Klosters-Davos region run 121SFr for two days and 279SFr for six days (including public transportation). Guests of Klosters and/or Davos hotels get 20% off single rides with a guest card. The **Madrisabahn** leaves from Klosters-Dorf. (1 ride 18SF, 1-day pass 33SFr.)The **Grotschnabahn** gives access to Parsenn and Strela in Davos and Madrisa in Klosters (1-day pass 60SFr, 6-day pass 324SFr). The **ski school**, located on Bahnhofstr. 4, offers ski and snowboard lessons. (☎410 28 28; www.ssk.ch. Ski school/guiding mid Nov. to mid-Dec 415SFr for 5 days (youth 350SFr, children 280SFr) mid-Dec. to early May 435/365/290SFr.) **Swiss Ski and Snowboard School Saas,** operated out of Dörfji Sport at Landstr. 15, has cheaper instruction. (☎420 22 33; www.sss-saas.ch. Open daily 8:15-11:30am, 2:15-6pm; phone 8am-8pm. 75SFr per hr.; 295SFr per day. **Bananas,** operated out of Duty Boardsport, Bahnhofstr. 16, gives snowboard lessons. (☎422 66 60; www.bananas.net. 70SFr per 4hr.; private lessons 80SFr per hr.; board 38SFr per day, boots 18SFr per day for the general public; check for reduced rates for students.) **Ski rental** is available at **Sport Gotschna** across from the tourist office. (☎422 11 97. Open M-F 8am-noon and 2-6:30pm, Sa 8am-12:30pm and 2-6pm, Su 9am-noon and 3-6pm. Skis and snowboards 28-50SFr per day plus 10% insurance, 5 days 95-165SFr; boots 15-19SFr/49-69SFr.)

Summer cable car passes (valid on Parsenn Klosters, Jakobshorn, Rinerhorn, and Madrisabahnen) are also available (4-day pass 80SFr, with guest card 70SFr, teens 13-17 54/50SFr, children 6-13 27/25SFr). On the green valley floor, hikers make a large loop (about 4 hours), from Klosters's Protestant church on Monbielstr. to Monbiel. The route continues to an elevation 1488m and turns left, passing through **Bödmerwald, Fraschmardintobel,** and **Monbieler**

ON THE MENU

GRAUBUNDEN GRUB

Chances are that most visitors to Graubünden will find themselves surrounded by a mouth-watering aroma, but unable to locate its source. Here is a cheat-sheet that will help you to match names to the delicious fragrances.

Bündner Gerstensuppe is a creamy soup made from vegetables, ham, and barley. *Bündner Hochzeitsuppe* is the same thing, but without the barley.

Bündner Fleisch is thinly-sliced air-dried meat served with pickles and thick slices of fresh bread. Diners share a plate of this as an appetizer, although it could be a light meal for one person.

Pizzocheri is a type of pasta made from whole-grain flour, commonly served in a cheesy sauce mixed with cubed potatoes and kale. The Swiss also often top it with ham and butter, melted cheese, or a creamy sauce. Tomato sauce is another option.

Capuns are leaves of kale wrapped around a cheesy, doughy filling with small pieces of *Bündner Fleisch* mixed in, typically covered with a creamy sauce.

Nüsstorte is a Swiss version of pecan pie: nuts in a caramel sauce sandwiched between sweet, rich pie dough.

Birnbrot is a small, sweet loaf vaguely similar to Fig Newtons, with a thin layer of dough wrapped around a paste of dried pear and sometimes nuts.

Wald before climbing to 1634m and returning to Klosters via **Pardels.** Another popular hike is through **Berg** to **Monbiel** and from there up to **Garfium** (1373m; about 2 hours). A narrow path through waist-high grass, meadows bursting with wildflowers, gurgling brooks, and tiny mountain huts, this walk offers spectacular views. "Wanderweg" signs throughout the town point the way to Monbiel, although you can also take the road. A bus running from Klosters to Monbiel cuts the time of the hike in about half. Several adventure companies offer a variety of activities like **river rafting, canoeing, horseback riding, paragliding,** and **glacier trekking.**

LOWER ENGADINE VALLEY

The Engadine Valley takes its name from the Romansch name *(En)* for the Inn River, which flows through the valley and on through Innsbruck, Austria. The transportation line runs from Maloja at the far west end of the valley to Scuol at the far east, connecting all towns by train or short bus rides. The region is divided into the Upper and Lower Engadine, with the town of Brail, just west of Zernez and the Swiss National Park, on the border separating them.

The Lower Engadine valley is Graubünden at its purest. Unaltered by the torrent of change brought by the ski industry elsewhere, the people maintain a strong connection to their land and culture. It is a stronghold of the **Romansch language,** with nearly every sign printed in it. The region may not be a skier's paradise, but **hikers** revel in the untouched Alpine beauty of the **Swiss National Park.**

THE SWISS NATIONAL PARK

Encompassing a mere 172km^2, the Swiss National Park still manages to offer a rich variety of landscapes and wildlife. Paths covered with snow well into the summer stretch to mountain peaks nearly 3000m high before guiding visitors through sweet-smelling pine forests, verdant meadows, and rocky stream beds. Hikers commonly catch a glimpse of marmot, deer, ibexes, eagles, bearded vultures, and other mountain animals, while edelweiss and brilliantly-colored wildflowers fill the meadows and mountainsides of this park. Stringent rules allowing visitors only on the marked paths take away from the fun of exploring on your own, but an extensive route of well-marked paths ensures spectacular views.

◼◼ ◼ ORIENTATION AND PRACTICAL INFORMATION

The Swiss National Park is a kidney-shaped area of land stretching from S-chanf in the southwest to Scuol in the northeast. The wilderness extends southeast from the towns. Thick pine forests and rocky peaks are arrayed around glacial streams. **Munt La Schera** and Chamanna Cluozza, the one alpine hut in the park, lie in the center. The northern regions' grassland is a habitat for red deer and marmots.

Camping and campfires are prohibited in the park, as is collecting flowers, plants, or insects. A team of wardens patrols the park at all times, slapping fines of up to 500SFr on rule-breakers. The park's central office is in Zernez. The names of the park's geographical features are all in Romansch, and a glossary of terms can be found in the back of the park's official trail guide. A few common terms: **piz** and **munt** mean "point" and "mountain," respectively; **val** is "valley;" **ova** is "stream;" **pra** is "meadow;" and **chamanna** means "mountain hut." Bird-watching is best mid-June to mid-July. Deer, chamois, and ibex are most active in September; deer buck for mates during October. The park is closed after the first snowfall (usually sometime between Oct. and Nov.) and reopens at the beginning of June.

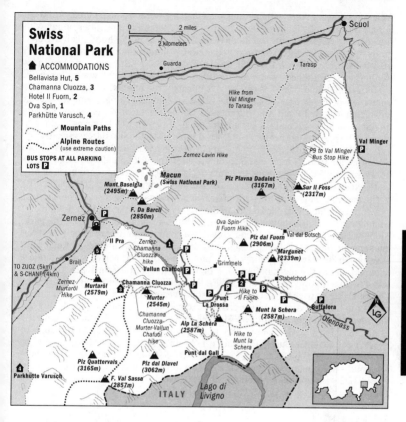

Swiss National Park

ACCOMMODATIONS
Bellavista Hut, **5**
Chamanna Cluozza, **3**
Hotel Il Fuorn, **2**
Ova Spin, **1**
Parkhütte Varusch, **4**

---- **Mountain Paths**

······ **Alpine Routes**
(use extreme caution)

BUS STOPS AT ALL PARKING LOTS P

TRANSPORTATION

The towns of Scuol, Zernez, and S-chanf lie just north of the park along the **Rhätische Bahn train** line. **Post buses** wind along the three major roads that skirt the park. The **Ofenpass** bisects the park from Zernez; nine parking lots sit along it at regular intervals. The buses make almost hourly stops at nearly all of the parking lots and other popular trailheads. If you plan on using them for more than three days, then buy a **Mehrfahrtenkarte.** Cards are available at the Zernez train station or any bus, and provide six rides for 20% off. Roads from S-chanf and Scuol skirt the western and eastern edges of the park. The most manageable hike between the villages surrounding the park is from S-chanf to Zernez, and makes use of the Chamanna Cluozza hut as an overnight resting spot (see **Hiking**, p. 432).

ACCOMMODATIONS

Camping is not allowed in the park, but Zernez, Scuol, and S-chanf have campsites outside the park boundaries. Many hikes leave from around **Hotel Il Fuorn ②,** on the Ofenpass, a short bus ride from Zernez (20min., every hr. 7:10am-7:10pm, 8.40SFr). A friendly crowd fills the **hiker's lodge,** which sits at the base of several peaks and welcomes weary hikers with inviting foam mattresses on wooden bunks. Although across the street from showers and sinks, use of the hotel's facilities, along with the scenery, makes up for the inconvenience. Rooms in the hotel itself are spacious and comfortable. The food is delicious, though the menu is limited and pricey. (*Spätzle* 20SFr. *Rösti* 23SFr. Spaghetti 15-18SFr.) But you don't have a lot of alternatives; the next restaurant is 10km away. (☎856 12 26; www.ilfuorn.ch. Breakfast included, 18SFr if you stay in dorms. Free **Internet** available in office upon request. Reception 7:15am-10pm. Check-in 2pm. Check-out 10am. Reserve in advance mid-June to mid-Aug. during peak hiking season, and Oct., when crowds fill the hotel to watch male deer buck for mates. Open May-Oct. Dorms 19SFr; singles 72-79SFr, with shower 103-112SFr; doubles 134-150SFr/190-208SFr; triples 171-195SFr; quads 204-232SFr.) The simple **Naturfreundehaus Ova Spin ❷**, is before Il Fuorn, 7km from Zernez, just outside the western park boundary. (☎/fax 852 31 42. Dorms 15SFR.) **Wegerhaus Ova Spin ❸**, is slightly more modern and slightly more expensive. (☎/fax 856 10 52 or 079 406 73 33; www.stimer.ch. Dorms 20SFr.)

The **mountain huts** near the park offer instant access to the forest. The shortest way to reach **Chamanna Cluozza ❷**, in the western part of the park, is to hike 3hr. from Zernez. It is the only mountain hut within park limits operated by the park. Along with a happy-but-tired hiker crowd, welcoming family staff members at the hut serve up piping hot, filling meals at 1882m. (☎856 12 35; cluozza@hotmail.com. Breakfast 6:30-7:30am and dinner 6:30-8pm, 31SFr for both. You can order modest packed lunches the night before for 8 or 16SFr. Reception 7am-10pm. Open last week of June to mid-Oct. Rooms 27SFr, under 20 and students under 26 11SFr.) The **Parkhütte Varusch ❷**, just outside the southwestern border of the park, is a 1hr. hike from S-chanf. A solar-powered hut with rooms for two to 10 people, the hut includes a garden restaurant. (☎854 31 22. Breakfast included; lunch and dinner available. Open May-Oct. Dorms 28SFr, ages 13-16 23SFr, under 12 17SFr; doubles 80SFr.) The **Bellavista hut ❷** (2000m), a 1½hr. hike from Zernez along the trail to the Murtaröl and the Chamanna Chuozza, has five beds, a wood stove, a kitchenette, outhouse, and a clear view of Zernez and Piz Linard from the front porch. (☎856 17 21. Bring drinking water. Call 1 week in advance for reservations and to get the key. Sleep sack 5SFr. Summer beds 18SFr; winter 20SFr.)

🔰 HIKING

A network of 21 hiking trails (80km) runs throughout the park, concentrated in the central 100km^2. Trails are clearly marked, and it is illegal to stray from them. Most hikes involve a lot of elevation gain, occasionally into snow-covered areas. The **Parkhouse** in Zernez lists which trails are navigable, though they all almost always are. Available at the Parkhouse are fantastic trail maps (14SFr) and a five-language trail description guide that teeters on the line between helpful and hysterical. (10SFr, 20SFr for both map and guide). The Parkhouse also sells a geological map and a vegetation map of the park. Trails that require no mountaineering gear are marked with white-red-white blazes, but even some of them are tricky. The most challenging trails are marked white-blue-white and require mountain-hiking gear.

Buffalora (1968m) **to Munt la Schera** (2587m) **to Il Fuorn** (1794m) (5½hr.). With this hike, you get a lot of bang for your buck—it can be done in ½ a day and is fairly easy, save the Munt la Schera ascent (which can be easily deleted from the route if so desired). From the **Buffalora** bus stop, a wide cowpath (20min.) heads uphill to **Alp Buffalora** (2038m). The path then becomes deceptively steep through lightly forested cow pastures (30min.). A pleasant amble through flat, meadowy land encompasses most of the 1st 2hr. of this hike. The walk is worth it, however, as you are walking through a postcard-perfect view of the park's eastern range of rocky and snowy peaks.

The climb to **Munt la Schera** passes through marmot country and finally reaches the windy, barren peak (1hr.). Glimpses of the **Lago di Livigno** reservoir and the **Italian Alps** complete the panorama. The descent goes through a larch forest to **Alp la Schera** (2091m), a park ranger hut with drinking water. From here, one can decide to head south toward Italy to the **Vallun Chafuol,** traversing the Spöl many times and catching sights of waterfalls, or head back to **Il Fuorn** along the forested **God la Drossa** (both routes 2hr.; Vallun Chafuol is at the P3 bus stop).

Zernez (1471m) **to Chamanna Cluozza** (1882m) (3hr.). The way to Chamanna Cluozza is a popular hike of easy to moderate difficulty. For the most part, the path is a wide, gravelly trail through the woods, leading through farmland, forest, meadows, and along a rocky ridge, with plenty of mountain views in the last half. It is a great introduction to the park and short enough for a leisurely pace. The trail begins across the wooden bridge over the Spöl river, 100m past the Park House. After a flat walk through a meadow, the path enters the forest, where it turns into an uphill climb. The path turns right at the Fritz Sarasin commemorative stone and quickly splits at **Il Pra** to **Cluozza** or **Bellavista** (1hr.). Take the left fork to Cluozza. From here, the trail opens up into the Cluozza Valley (2100m) and travels along a flat ridge (45min.). Afterwards, the descent to the river offers an opportunity to linger in the **Il Grass** meadows to see the occasional ibex or red deer. After descending to the bridge over the **Ova da Cluozza** with **Piz Linard** in the background (45min.), a final climb awaits **Chamanna Cluozza** overnighters (30min.). With a set of binoculars, you can see tracks of the **Theropod** on the western flank of the Piaz dal Diavel. This 5m-long herbivorous dinosaur roamed the area over 200 million years ago and left footprints 30cm across.

Chamanna Cluozza (1882m) to Murter (2505m) to Vallun Chafuol (1640m) (3.5hr.). A classic route for those who hiked to Cluozza the day before. The 1st 2hr. consist of a steep, zig-zagging ascent of 700m to the peak through the meadowy western face of Murter. Ibex and chamois populate these peaks and are especially active in the early morning around sunrise. The Murter summit provides glimpses of the blue-green Ova Spin reservoir below and the snowy peaks of the closed-off western portion of the park. A steep descent of 1000m on a rocky trail turns into a soft wooded trail, ending at the Plan Praspöl. From there, a 30min. hike across a wooden bridge and up 80m more leads to P3 and Vallun Chafuol. The more motivated hiker can continue for another 2hr. over easy, wooded terrain past Alp Grimmels and on to Il Fuorn.

Zernez (1471m) **to Murtaröl** (2579m) **and back** (6hr.). This hike of moderate difficulty couples an ascent of over 1000m with a fair number of panoramic views as a reward. It begins at the same spot as the Chamanna Cluozza hike and follows the same trail until the path splits at Il Pra (about 1hr.). Take the right-hand fork. After passing the Bellavista hut (see **Accommodations,** p. 431), the trail rises above the tree line and offers wide views of Zernez below. The path passes a set of stone walls (2300m), built during the 19th century in an effort to prevent avalanches, and offers a panoramic view of the Val Tantermozza (inaccessible to visitors) and the mountain chain that surrounds it. The **Murtaröl** crest (3½hr.), with views of the Engadine, Cluozza, and Tantermozza valleys, is only a short climb. Sometimes herds of chamois and ibexes are visible. The route back to Zernez passes bizarre rock formations before plunging into the forest to rejoin the original path at the point where it splits from the Chamanna Cluozza trail.

Val Minger to Tarasp (5hr.). Take the bus from Scuol (dir: Scharl) to "Val Minger" (9.40SFr; with Eurail or SwissPass 4SFr). A more difficult hike. From the bus stop, cross the bridge and turn left on the trail, which begins with a slow and steady climb up rocky stream beds. As you walk, turn around often for magnificent views of **Piz Pradatsch.** When the trail moves above the tree line it enters a half-pipe-shaped valley, at the end of which lies the solitary, majestic **Piz Plavna Dadaint.** The **Sur il Foss pass,** with its intimate view of nearby mountains, lies at the valley's end. From Sur il Foss, a trail leads around the head of the valley to the **Val dal Botsch pass,** which then leads to Il

GRAUBÜNDEN

Fuorn in the center of the park. This route is only safe in later summer, when the snow has melted, and even then should only be attempted with hiking poles and sturdy boots. Check at the National Park House in Zernez for up-to-date conditions. An easier route leads right, toward "Tarasp Fontana." The initial descent can be tricky, depending on recent rock slides. The trail moves into a wide rocky plain, bordered by cliffs that create a visual tunnel, toward the mountain range over Scuol, and backward to Piz Nair and the peaks in front of it. The trail goes through the woods to **Tarasp**, where a bus returns to Scuol (every hr. M-F 6:13am-8:10pm, Sa-Su 8:10am-8:10pm; 4.60SFr).

Nature Route: P8 (1887m) **or P9** (1906m) **to Margunet** (2328m) **to Il Fuorn** (1794m) (3-3½hr.). This is the park's only nature trail, with information about the surrounding flora and fauna provided in 5 languages, and an easier hike that still provides a summit of sorts from which to view the Val dal Botsch and Val da Stabelchod. From P8, the route goes through thick pine forest and then an overgrown meadow to the Stabelchod hut (1958m), a residence for park rangers (30min.). The trail then travels along a gorge and a rushing stream, climbing slowly to an outlook point before the 400m ascent to Margunet (1hr.). Marmot families and a recently re-introduced flock of bearded vultures are sometimes spotted on Margunet's eastern slope. In July, some hikers glimpse the young, which are just learning how to fly during this time. Arriving at the Margunet panorama, the hike quickly descends on the other side of the saddle into the Val dal Botsch (1hr.). A fairly flat path leads back to the Ofenpass and finishes at the Il Fuorn estate.

P9 (1906m) **to Val Minger bus stop** (1794m) (7hr.). Due to the 800m rapid elevation gain over 2 ridges, plus the length of the Val Minger, this route is one of the more difficult hikes. As always, the reward is the views: summitting Marguent (2339m), Val dal Botsch (2677m), and Sur il Foss (2317m) provides views of the northern region of the park, including Piz Tavru (3168), its highest peak. This route follows the 1st half of the Margunet route, then continues north and climbs steeply up to the Val dal Botsch outlook point. From there, the path descends 400m over slippery scree (the bits of rock left behind by a glacier; pick your path carefully). It climbs again, though less steeply, to Sur il Foss. The descent from Sur il Foss lands in the Val Minger, a long stretch of relatively flat meadowland all the way to the bus stop. Val Minger is fairly dry in the summer, so bring plenty of water.

> **■TIP■ HIGHS AND LOWS.** The high altitudes of many of Switzerland's famous peaks bring gorgeous vistas but also the potential for a host of problems. Even if altitude sickness isn't a concern, the lack of oxygen at higher elevations affects all sea-level dwellers, causing fatigue. A day of easy hikes and strolls not only helps lowland folk get acclimated, it also helps you get a feel for how strenuous action at that altitude is, allowing you to gauge the sort of hike you're ready for. Plus, it's better to get some serious altitude sickness on a stroll through a wildflower-filled meadow than on the edge of a cliff.

TOWNS NEAR THE NATIONAL PARK

TRANSPORT HUB: ZERNEZ ☎081

Zernez (pop. 1100) is the main gateway to the **Swiss National Park** and home to the park headquarters, the **National Parkhouse. Trains** depart for Samedan (30min., every hr. 5:53am-11:03pm, 13.40SFr) and Scuol (40min., every hr. 6:52am-10:49pm, 12.40SFr) with connections to the rest of Switzerland, including St. Moritz (45min., 16.60SFr). **Currency exchange** (2SFr fee) and **luggage storage** (3SFr) are available at the train station. (Open M-F 5:30-7:10am and 7:40am-8:10pm, Sa 5:30-7:10am and 7:40am-7:10pm, Su 7:45am-12:10pm and 1:40-5:10pm.) **Banca Chantunella,** directly before the tourist office from the station, offers **currency exchange** as well as a **24hr. ATM.** (Bank open M-F 8am-noon and 2-5pm.) **Internet** access is available at the tourist office. (4SFr for 15min., 2SFr per 15min. thereafter. Printing and disk entry available.) The National Parkhouse also has a free Internet kiosk at the entrance (same hours as the house). The **post office** is across from the train station. (Open M-F 8-11:30am and 2-6pm, Sa 8:30-11am.) **Postal Code:** CH-7530.

From the train station, take the main road (Röven) to the left uphill 6min. to the **tourist office**. (☎ 856 13 00; fax 11 55. Open June-Oct. M-F 9am-noon and 2-6:30pm, Sa 9am-noon and 2-5pm; Nov.-May M-F 9am-noon and 3-5pm.) The **National Parkhouse,** reached by walking from the station uphill 10min., then turning right after the tourist office and heading toward the park 10min. (follow brown signs for "Parc Nazinual Svizzer"), provides information about trail safety and has an extensive selection of maps and souvenirs. They can also arrange for private guided walks. (☎ 856 13 78; www.nationalpark.ch. Open June-Oct. M and W-Su 8:30am-6pm, Tu 8:30am-10pm.) It also houses a small free **museum** about the park; the exhibit is mainly geared toward children. **Sport Sarsura,** in the same building as the tourist office, provides expensive outdoor gear and rents bicycles for 30SFr per day. (☎ 856 14 34. Open M-F 8am-noon and 2-6:30pm, Sa 8am-noon and 2-5pm.) The **Co-op** is across the street from the tourist office. (Open M-F 8am-noon and 2-6:30pm, Sa 8am-noon and 2-4pm.) The smaller **Denner** grocery store, with **Heini Bakery** connected, is left from the train station, about three quarters of the way to the tourist office. Open M-F 7:15am-noon and 1:30-6:30pm, Sa 7:15am-noon and 1:30-4pm. The tourist office lists **private rooms** from 25SFr. **Hotel Bär-Post ❷,** left and within sight of the main intersection past the tourist office, is a classy hotel that offers less classy rooms in a back building. The dorms are small and in need of fresh paint. (☎ 851 55 00; www.baer-post.ch. Breakfast 12SFr. Sleepsack 5SFr. Reception 9am-10pm. Quiet hours after 10pm. Open mid-Dec. to Oct. Dorms 18SFr. AmEx/DC/MC/V.) Just past the National Parkhouse, **Touristenlager Hummel ❶** offers simple lager-style accommodations. The friendly owners, sitting/game room, and well-stocked kitchen (every spice your heart could desire, plus cupboards filled with pans and utensils) make up for the rough wood-planked floors and makeshift bunks. (☎ 856 18 74; fax 19 60. Sheets available on request. Dorms 15SFr; doubles 50.) There is camping at **Camping Cul ❶,** across the train tracks from town, in a quiet spot by the river Inn. The friendly staff speaks German, French, English, and Italian. Turn right out of the station and follow the signs. (☎/fax 856 14 62; www.camping-cul.ch. Showers and toilets included. Breakfast 5.50SFr. Fresh bread (order ahead of time) 0.80-3.20SFr. Washing machine, phone, and fax available. Kiosk sells staple foods and drinks. Reception July-Aug. 8-11am and 2-7pm; Sept.-June times vary. Open May to mid-Oct. 7SFr per adult, 4SFr per child, 6SFr per tent, 3SFr per car. Visitor and trash tax not included. AmEx/MC/V.)

Hotel Filli Restaurant and café ❶, left from the train station on the way to the tourist office, serves cheap and filling Swiss and Italian specialties. Pizzas start at 11SFr, while a steaming-hot plate of the whole-grain pizzocherri pasta with tomato sauce is 10SFr. Hot food served daily 11:30am-9pm. **Grotia Pizzeria Mirta ❸,** downhill around the corner from the bank at the main intersection, is purported to have the best wood-oven pizza (15-19SFr) in Graubünden. (☎ 856 17 35. Hot food served June-Oct. and Dec.-Apr. Tu-Su noon-2pm and 6-10pm. V.) While nights in Zernez are far from lively, **Cruz Alba,** in the Weisses Cruz Hotel, left out of the train station before the tourist office, has a tiny bar packed with boisterous locals. Visitors here can get a drink (beer from 4SFr) and a taste of small-town Swiss life. (Open daily until 2am.) Just 10min. uphill from the main intersection, the **Evangelische Pfarrkirche** and smaller **Kapelle St. Sebastian** overlook the town from a wildflower-filled

GRAUBÜNDEN

meadow. The austere exterior of the larger church hides an ornate Baroque interior, filled with scrolling white reliefs contrasted against a background of bright blue. A few yards away, the 16th-century chapel houses ancient frescoes.

ZUOZ ☎ 081

Though located in the Upper Engadine, Zuoz's (pop. 1300) adherence to architectural and Romansch linguistic traditions, as well as the warmth of its citizens, mark it as a Lower Engadine town. Its position on the border of both regions makes it a good point from which to explore both sides of the Engadine Valley. Burned to the ground by residents in 1499 to keep it out of Austrian hands, Zuoz was rebuilt in the early 16th century and has changed little since. Narrow cobblestone streets wind between centuries-old houses marked by arching carved-wood doors and elaborately-decorated façades. A certain hush pervades the village in spite of its numerous hotels and renowned boarding school.

▐▌ TRANSPORTATION AND PRACTICAL INFORMATION. Zuoz is a **train** ride from St. Moritz (30min., every hr. 6:12am-11:22pm, 9.20SFr) via Samedan (20min., 5.80SFr); and Zernez (20min., every hr. 5:17am-10:26pm, 8.40SFr). The train station provides **luggage storage** (3SFr) and **bike rental.** (30SFr per day, 23SFr per halfday. Open M-Sa 7:50am-noon and 2-5:30pm, Su and holidays 3:45-5:45pm.) **La Passarella,** which extends directly opposite the station (right off the Co-op), leads to the main street in town, **San Basiaun,** which heads right and turns into Via Maestra. The **tourist office,** right on Via Maestra (5min.), provides guides to the local sights and suggests hikes. (☎ 848 986 946; www.zuoz.ch. Open June to mid-Oct. M-F 9am-noon and 1:15-6:30pm, Sa 10am-noon and 4-6:30pm; Aug. to mid-Oct. Su 4-6:30pm; mid-Oct. to Nov. and mid-Apr. to May M-F 9am-noon and 2-5pm.) The **Kantonalbank,** past the tourist office, **exchanges currency** and has a **24hr. ATM.** (Bank open M-F 9am-noon and 2-5pm.) Zuoz has two **public telephones,** one at the station and one at the tourist office. The **post office** is in the train station. (Open M-F 8am-noon and 2:15-5:45pm, Sa 8-11am.) **Postal Code:** CH-7524.

▐▌ ACCOMMODATIONS AND FOOD. The cheapest lodgings are located in the center of town at **Ferienlager Sonder ②.** Head down Via Maestra from the tourist office and turn right onto tiny Chanels at the sign for "Ferienlager" for simple rooms in a 16th-century building with kitchen and ping pong. (☎ 854 07 73; www.engadina.ch. Dorms 19-20SFr.) At the 400-year-old **Chesa Walther ❸,** opposite Willy's Sports near the tourist office, the friendly German-, Italian-, and Spanish-speaking matron warmly welcomes guests into rooms comfortably decorated with plush red furniture and gold-trimmed mirrors. (☎ 854 13 64. Partial kitchen facilities 5SFr. Rooms with communal bathroom 40SFr.)

Restaurant Dorta ❸, from the station, left to the end of the parking lot, then again under the bridge, is a farmhouse-turned-restaurant and bar that defines rustic. The bar stools are tree stumps, and the 400-year-old door is held open with a rope. While locals chat in the candlelit bar, fresh flowers and an impressive menu of Engadine specialties await diners. *Zuozer Krautpizokel,* a large plate of *Spätzli* (a German cross between noodles and gnocchi) with ham, bacon, and cream sauce, is 23SFr. Vegetarians can try the *Maluns,* shredded potatoes with applesauce and plum compote. (☎ 854 20 40; www.dorta.ch. Kids menu available. Open Dec. to Christmas and Easter to June W-F 6-10pm, Sa-Su 11:30am-10pm; Christmas-Easter and June-Oct. Tu-Su 11:30am-10pm. Kitchen open 11:30am-2pm and 6-10pm. Reservations recommended. AmEx/D/MC/V.) The popular **Dorta Bar** runs changing specials and hosts ladies' nights. (Open W-Su 6pm-1am, also Tu in high-season.) **Café-Restorant Klarer ❹,** in the center of town, offers pasta (14-20SFr), along with lighter dishes with an Italian and French flair. At lunch, *Menüs* (20-25SFr) come with soup, salad, and the daily chef's special. Meat entrées (29-45SFr), like grilled Forelle with spinach (29SFr), are available in the evening. Fondue is 22SFr; *pizzoccheri* is 16SFr. Wine enthusiasts can view the extensive cellar. Ask the waiter for a quick tour. (☎851 34 34; www.klarerconda.ch. Wheelchair accessible. Open daily June-Apr. 7:30am-11pm; May 7:30am-noon. AmEx/D/MC/V.) The **Co-op** supermarket is opposite the station. (Open M-F 8am-12:15pm and 2-6:30pm, Sa 8am-5pm.) **Primo** is uphill from the tourist office. (Open M-W and F 7:30am-noon and 2-6:30pm, Th 7:30am-noon, Sa 7:30am-noon and 2-4pm.)

■ ☒ **SIGHTS AND HIKING.** The small **Church San Luzius** on Via Maestra has sweet-smelling pine pews and Romansch hymnals with brilliantly colored stained-glass windows above the altar. The **prison tower** next door is preserved as the last prisoner left it—a dark, dank chamber, filled with terrifying implements of torture and chilling dungeon cells (descriptions only in German). Farther from the tourist office toward the station, on the corner of Via Dorta, lies the tiny **San Bastiaun** chapel with fading frescoes. (Ask the tourist office for the keys to all sights; hours are the same as those of the tourist office; San Luzius open sometimes without the key.)

Zuoz woos **bikers** with 37km of marked trails. **Rental** available at the train station, or for less across the river at the **Inline Shop** operated by Willi Sport. (☎854 08 06. Open July-Aug. and Sept.-May M-W and F 8am-noon and 2-6:30pm, Th and Sa 8am-noon; June and Sept. until 5pm. 25-29SFr per day; children 15-21SFr; 18-20SFr per half-day.) For **hikers,** the National Park is right next door, but Zuoz offers a few distinctive hikes of its own. The **Via Segantini** eventually leads to the **Piz Bernina** (4049m). The path begins past the Hotel Engiadina, on Via Maestra. Turn right onto Chröntschet, then walk along the private driveway, which leads to the gravel path labeled "Castell." The path leads to the historic Alpenschloßhotel Castell; from there, follow signs for "Via Segantini." The easy trail leads from Zuoz to La Punt (2hr.) and Bever (4hr.), where the train runs back to Zuoz.

For a more rugged afternoon, the **Ova d'Arpiglia** leads to a crashing 20m waterfall. To find the trail, turn left from the train station and go through the underpass toward the river. Cross the river on the smaller bridge, head under the road, and turn left, following the yellow "Wanderweg" signs on the dirt road heading into the woods. Stay on the right side of the stream following signs for "Munt Seja," to the waterfall. The path then climbs steeply to a meadow to the right of the falls, known locally as the "Stairway to Heaven." Signs point the way from this picnic haven to Zuoz (round-trip 1½hr.).

UPPER ENGADINE VALLEY

About 350km of ski trails and 60 ski lifts crisscross the Upper Engadine Valley. Unlike Zermatt and Grindelwald, which are filled with Japanese and American tourists, the Upper Engadine attracts mostly German, Italian, and Swiss visitors. Connoisseurs rate the downhill skiing in the Upper Engadine just below the Jungfrau and Matterhorn regions. The summer sun clears the snow from the region's ample hiking trails. The most unique hiking skirts the melting glaciers flowing down from **Piz Bernina** (4049m, the highest in the region) and its neighbors.

Ski, snowboard, and hiking equipment rental is available in multiple shops throughout the towns. Although not standardized, prices tend to be similar. (Top-of-the-line skis 50-70SFr per day, ages 16-20 30-37SFr, ages 6-16 21-24SFr; snowboards 28-38SFr; boots 9-19SFr. Some smaller shops rent basic skis from 28SFr.) Ask at the local tourist office about **ski schools**—many have well-devel-

GRAUBÜNDEN

oped programs for children, including weekly races for novices on Alp Languard (Pontresina). Novices should head for Zuoz or Corviglia (St. Moritz), or Alp Languard (Pontresina); experts, for Diavolezza (Pontresina), Piz Nair (St. Moritz), or Piz Lagalb (Pontresina). One-day passes are available for each town. (St. Moritz and Celerina passes are sold together.) Prices vary according to time in the season. (40-61SFr, ages 16-20 36-55SFr, ages 6-15 20-30SFr. St. Moritz is the most expensive area.) Multiple-day passes are available only for the entire Engadine region—they're not much more expensive and cover most trains and buses as well. (5-day pass 225-277SFr, youth 203-249SFr, children 114-139SFr.) Cross-country fanatics should glide to **Pontresina**, where hundreds train for the grueling **Engadine Ski Marathon,** which stretches from Maloja to S-chanf. The race is on the second Sunday in March. (☎081 850 55 55; www.engadin-skimarathon.ch for application/registration. Ages 16 and up. Entry fee 80SFr.) The weekend before hosts the 17km **Frauenlauf** solely for women. (6th Annual Frauenlauf Mar. 6, 2005. See above for registration. Entry fee 40SFr.) **Ski schools** in almost every village offer private lessons. (General information ☎081 830 00 00; www.skiengadin.ch.)

PONTRESINA   ☎081

Away from the bustle of the rest of the Upper Engadine, Pontresina is nestled in one of the highest wind-sheltered valleys of the region at the head of two major rivers. The resort has glitzy aspirations, with luxury hotels and a modern main street, and the proximity of three major peaks makes Pontresina a favorite mountaineering destination. Every morning, the famous Diavolezza glacier tour draws hordes of hikers. In winter, Pontresina becomes the cross-country skiing center of the Upper Engadine and offers a cheaper downhill alternative to St. Moritz.

TRANSPORTATION. Trains run to: Chur (2hr., every hr. 5:49am-8:04pm, 38SFr) via Samedan and St. Moritz (10min., every hr. 6:52am-7:52pm, 4.60SFr). The **Engadine Bus** connects Pontresina to the villages of the Upper Engadine Valley all the way to Maloja. One route also runs from the left of the train station to the post office, the tourist office, and other important spots in town. (High-season every 30min., low-season every hr. 6:55am-8:36pm; 2.60SFr.)

PRACTICAL INFORMATION. Via de la Staziun winds over two rivers and uphill to the center of town (20min.). The **tourist office,** in the modern "Rondo" building where the Via de la Staziun meets the town, plans free excursions (see p. 441), gives hiking advice, provides information on weekly events, and finds private rooms from 28SFr. (☎838 83 00; www.pontresina.com. Open Easter to mid-June and Oct. to mid-Dec. M-F 8:30am-noon and 2-6pm, Sa 8:30am-noon and 4-6pm; mid-June to Sept. and mid-Dec to Easter also Su 4-6pm.) The **Ferienregion Engadin,** the regional tourist office, answers questions and offers information about the region via telephone. (☎842 65 73. Open Apr. to mid-July and mid-Aug. to Christmas M-F 8:30am-noon and 2-6pm; mid-July to mid-Aug. and Christmas to Mar. also Sa 9am-noon.) Services at the train station include: **luggage storage** (3SFr), **bike rental** (30SFr per day), and **lockers** (2SFr). **Currency exchange, Western Union, and Lost and Found** are also in the station. (All three open 8am-6pm.) (Station ☎842 63 37. Open high season daily 5:40am-7pm; low-season M-F 5:40am-7pm, Sa-Su 6:40am-7pm. The best deal on **Internet** is in the Hotel Saratz, across the street from the tourist office. (☎839 40 00. 5SFr plus 20SFr deposit for a 30min. card. CD-rom drive and printing. Wheelchair accessible.) Take a **taxi** with Bernina Taxi (☎842 01 36). There's a **free telephone** at the station.) The **post office** is 6min. uphill from the tourist office on the corner of Via Maestra and Via da Mulin. (Open M-F 7:45am-noon and 1:45-6:15pm, Sa 8:30am-4pm.) **Postal Code:** CH-7504.

⌗ ACCOMMODATIONS. The **Jugendherberge Tolais (HI) ❸**, in the modern, salmon-colored building across from the train station, is convenient for early-morning ski ventures and connections throughout the Engadine Valley in the winter. In summer, families, young backpackers, and older hikers fill the six-bed dorms. Dinner is required and usually simple but decent, including soup, a main course with salad, and dessert. The hostel also has a restaurant, ping-pong, swings, a large ski room, and a soccer field. (☎ 842 72 23; www.youthhostel.ch/pontresina. Breakfast, lockers, and sheets included. Buffet dinner 6:30pm included; later times and vegetarian options on request. Board 7SFr less if you do not want one meal; cancel before 9am for dinner. Laundry 10SFr. Rent a hiking map for 4SFr with 10SFr deposit. Internet 3SFr per 15min. Towels 3SFr. Copy and fax 0.30SFr per page. Free parking. All rooms non-smoking. Reception 7:30-9:30am, 4-6:30pm, 7:30-9pm. Check-out 9:30am. Doors lock 11pm; entrance code given. Quiet time 10pm-7am. Open Dec.-Apr. and June-Oct. 6-bed dorms 44SFr; doubles 138SFr; quads 220SFr. Nonmembers add 6SFr, families add 12SFr total. Prices do not include tax. AmEx/D/MC/V.) The friendly Hauser family welcomes guest in their **Pension Hauser ❸**, on Giarsun, toward the outskirts of town and just a few minutes from the start of most hiking paths at Kirche Maria. Relatively plain, bright rooms, all with a sink and some with a shower and toilet fill this house-turned-hotel. (☎ 842 63 26; www.hotelpension-hauser.ch. Open Dec. to mid-Apr. and June to mid-Oct. Free parking. Breakfast included. Singles 55-65SFr, with shower 65-75SFr; doubles 110-130SFr/130-150SFr, with shower and toilet 150-180SFr. Optional half-board 25SFr per person per day for stays of 3 nights or more.) In the heart of town (5min. uphill from the tourist office, across from Papeterie Schocher) at **Pension Valtellina ❹**, Mariuccia Della Briotta, a gentle Italian grandmother, furnishes her cozy, mountain-view rooms with warm down comforters. The Pension's triple has a balcony overlooking the Piz Bernina; pink bathrooms are down the hall. (☎ 842 64 06. Breakfast included. Open Dec. 26-May and June-Nov. Singles 55SFr; doubles 110SFr; triples 165SFr.)

The lovely **Camping Plauns ❶**, in Morteratsch (train dir: Tirano; 4SFr), offers laundry (3-4SFr), a basic foods shop, and a grill after 5pm. Campers walk the 3km from the trail head above the train station to the Bernina Pass. (☎ 842 62 85; www.pontresina.com, www.mypage.bluewin/ch/campingplauns. Open June to mid-Oct. and mid-Dec. to mid-Apr. 8.50SFr; ages 12-15 5.50SFr, ages 6-11 4SFr; tents 9SFr; car 4SFr. Electricity 3-4:50SFr.)

❏ FOOD. The **Puntschella Café-Restaurant ❸**, on v. da Mulin, off v. Maestra before the post office, is the birthplace of the **Engadiner Torte** (a local delicacy made from candied almonds, raisins, layers of cream and nut purée, and crunchy crust; 4SFr). A dazzling array of glazed chocolate and fruit delicacies fills the bakery; the restaurant offers local specialties, pasta, and vegetarian dishes (entrées 13-25SFr). Locals fill the bar (beer from 4SFr), while families frequent the red-velvet restaurant area or the outdoor terrace. A wide variety of fancy coffee drinks and ice cream make this a popular afternoon-snack destination, too. (☎ 838 80 30. Open daily June-Oct. 7:30am-10pm; Dec.-Feb. 7:30am-9pm. Closed May and Nov. AmEx/MC/V.) The **Pizzeria Sportpavillon ❷**, 400m downhill from the tourist office near the bus stop "Sportpavillon," looks out on tennis courts and Piz Bernina. The cheerful waitstaff serves pizzas (14-20SFr, 10-11pm all pizzas 11SFr, 2SFr extra for a large pizza) and pasta (from 14SFr). A family special (38SFr) is enough pizza for two adults and two children. A large salad served with bread is 9SFr. Soups run 8SFr. Meat and fish dishes cost 14-28SFr. (☎ 842 63 49. Kitchen open daily noon-2pm and 6-11pm. Reservations suggested 6-8pm.) **Pitschna Scena ❸,** downhill 5min. from the tourist office on Via Maestra and downstairs in the Hotel Saratz, is run by chic waiters dressed in black. *Pitschna* means "little" in Romansch; the restaurant and bar boast several different "little scenes." In the wood-paneled upstairs, get tofu curry (22-28SFr) or a burger (18SFr). Locals fill the bar and connected smoking and billiards rooms, enjoying inexpensive drinks (beer from 4SFr) and an incredibly varied mix of music. Every Thursday in the summer, no-cover concerts fill the bar until the wee hours, featuring bands playing everything from Irish folk tunes to Merengue. People of all ages crowd together, and the price of drinks rises by about 2SFr. (☎ 839 45 80. Concerts start at 10pm; check www.saratz.ch for schedule. Open Dec.-Apr. and mid-June to Oct. daily 11am-2am. Hot food served 11am-11pm; snack menu available after that. AmEx/MC/V.) The **Co-op** is at the corner of Via Maestra and Via da Mulin. (Open M-F 8am-12:15pm and 2-6:30pm, Sa 8am-5pm.)

◉ **SIGHTS.** In a well-preserved 17th-century farmhouse, the **Museum Alpin,** Chesa Delnon, up the street to the left of the tourist office, presents life in the Engadine as it used to be, complete with nearly 400-year-old furniture. The brilliantly lit mineral collection is a highlight, as is the collection of over 100 stuffed Engadine fowl. (☎ 842 72 73. Open Dec.-Apr. and June-Oct. M-Sa 4-6pm, in bad weather 3-6pm. 5SFr, under 16 free. Free short English description of the displays.) At the highest point of the village, the bare exterior of the **Church of Santa Maria** conceals a number of well-preserved frescoes, including the 1495 **Mary Magdalene cycle.** Look closely at the back wall to see where the original frescoes from 1230 were painted over. Don't go during a tour if you want to look around on your own—the church is very small. Check with the tourist office for a schedule of concerts. (Open mid- to late June M, W, F and July-Oct. daily 3:30-5:30pm. German tours W 5pm; July-Aug. also F 5pm. English guide 2SFr.) For an enchanting hour of music, attend the daily *Kurkonzerte* held in the **Taiswald** pavilion in the woods. (Concerts mid-June to mid-Sept. daily 11am-noon. Trail by train station; signs point the way.)

⚑ **OUTDOOR ACTIVITIES.** In winter, Pontresina is a center for **cross-country skiing.** The youth hostel is the *Langlaufzentrum* (cross-country center); trails are not monitored by rescue personnel, and therefore free to all. **Swiss Ski and Snowboard School Pontresina** (☎ 838 83 83) offers ski and snowboard lessons of all types for all ages. The tourist office sells the helpful *Oberengadia Bergell* hiking and mountain biking map (15SFr), which covers the Upper Engadine. A number of trails stretch between the **Piz Languard,** the cable car below it, and **Muottas Maragl cable car.** (Base accessible by post bus, dir: St. Moritz. ☎ 842 83 08. July-Aug. one-way 18SFr, round-trip 26SFr; June and Sept.-Oct. 18SFr/26SFr, children 6-15 half price.) The level "Hohenweg" meanders above the valley between the cable cars (2.5hr.). A more demanding route (1½hr.) leads from the Muottas Muragl to the **Chamanna Segantini,** where the painter Giovanni Segantini spent his last years. The trail then climbs to Piz Languard (3hr.), with photographic views up the snaking Morteratsch glacier to the 4049m **Piz Bernina.** To reach the Piz Languard more quickly, take the **Alp Languard chairlift** from town. (☎ 842 62 55. 13SFr, round-trip 19SFr, children under 16 5SFr/10SFr.) From the top of the lift, follow signs to the steep 2½hr. hike to the peak and restaurant.

For more intimate contact with the surrounding five glaciers, it is possible to take the train (dir: Tirano) to "Diavolezza" (6.20SFr) and then the cable car to the top of the Diavolezza glacier (Call the region cable car office at ☎ 830 00 00 or 0844 844 944 with questions; www.bergbahnengadin.ch. Diavolezza costs 20SFr, round-trip 28SFr, children ages 6-15 half-price.), which sits just above the valley between Piz Palu and Bernina. Bring sunglasses: the snow makes the view nearly blinding to the naked eye. The **Mountaineering School of Pontresina,** Switzerland's largest, leads a popular 5hr. hike from the Diavolezza down the Morteratsch glacier for

30SFr (children ages 9-16 15SFr). A more expensive glacier trek is also offered and requires pre-registration. (☎ 838 83 33; www.bergsteiger-pontresina.ch. Hikes daily June-Aug. and Sept. to mid-Oct. Su, Tu-W, F. Meet at the top of the cable car, or the bottom in questionable weather. Glacier trek 6hr. July-Sept. Th and Su; meet at 8am in the tourist office building; 110SFr; special equipment provided.) Trails also attack the glacier from the bottom, which is significantly cheaper. Take the train from Pontresina (dir: Tirano) to "Morteratsch" (3.80SFr) and walk up to and alongside the Morteratsch glacier. From the train stop it is a 30min. walk to the glacier and a 3hr. hike to the highest hut on the glacier. Signs mark the glacier's recession since the turn of the century. The tourist office has free beach volleyball and fishing, tours, botanical and wildlife observation excursions, and a guided trip to the Swiss National Park. (All available in English. Free only to those staying overnight in Pontresina; for day visitors, certain fees may apply. National Park Excursion 5hr. June-Oct.; 10SFr, children under 11 5SFr.) For canyoning (170SFr), house running (rapelling frontwards; prices vary), or dogsled rides (winter only; 95SFr), call **Pontresina Events** (☎ 842 72 57 or 834 54 32; www.pontresinaevents.ch). For more moderately priced excursions, try **Fähndrich Sport** (part of Pontresina Events). The company offers a weekly summer bulletin at the tourist office, listing canoe trips, mountain biking, inline skating, nordic walking, and other activities that include transportation, equipment rental, and a guide. (☎ 842 71 55; www. faehndrich-sport.ch. Reserve your spot the day before by 6pm. 15-45SFr.)

ST. MORITZ
☎ 081

Chic, elegant, and exclusive, St. Moritz is one of the world's most famous ski resorts, but offers little of substance for the backpacker. A playground for the rich and famous, this "Resort at the Top of the World" will turn almost anyone into a window-shopper. As host to the Winter Olympics in 1928 and 1948, St. Moritz was catapulted into the international spotlight. Today, it offers a wide selection of outdoor activities from world-class skiing and bobsledding to golf, polo, greyhound racing, cricket on the frozen lake, and *Skikjöring*—a sport similar to water skiing in which the water is replaced by snow and the motorboat by a galloping horse.

▐ TRANSPORTATION

Trains run every hour to: Celerina (5min., 4:56am-11:45pm, 2.60SFr); Chur (2hr., 4:56am-8:02pm, 38SFr); Pontresina (10min., 7:14am-8:20pm, 4.60SFr); Zuoz via Samedan (30min., 4:56am-8:02pm, 9.20SFr); Zernez (40min., 4:56am-9:13pm); Scuol-Tarasp (2¼hr., 4:56am-9:02pm). **PostAuto Buses** and the **Engadin Bus** provide similar routes and the only public access to the Engadine Valley west of St. Moritz. Buses depart from the station and run every hr. (6:38am-12:04am; add 5SFr after 9:36pm) to: Maloja (40min., 9.80SFr); Sils (20min., 6.60SFr); Silvaplana (15min., 3.80SFr).

Several scenic train routes originate in St. Moritz. The legendary **Glacier Express** covers the 290km to Zermatt in a leisurely 7½hr., crossing 291 bridges and going through 91 tunnels. (Departs daily mid-Oct. to mid-Dec. 9:02am; late May to mid-Oct. 9:25am; 131SFr; SwissPass valid, Eurail valid until Disentis.) The **Bernina Express,** the only Swiss train that crosses the Alps without entering any tunnels, journeys to Tirano, Italy (2½hr.; every hr. 7:14am-4:45pm; 26SFr, 7SFr booking fee, Eurail and SwissPass valid).

▐ PRACTICAL INFORMATION

The **tourist office,** Via Maistra 12, makes hotel reservations. Follow the signs from the top of Truoch Serlas across from the train station and turn right across the street and up the stairs after the last sign. (☎ 837 33 33; www.stmoritz.ch. Open mid-July to

BUNA SAIRA!

Switzerland's oft-forgotten fourth national language, Romansch, is spoken only in the province of Graubünden. A Romance language like French and Italian, Romansch is descended from Latin. Romansch didn't become a written language until the 16th century, when Biblical texts and historical ballads were first translated. Now, Romansch has a small literature of its own, and its speakers support five different Romansch newspapers, TV news broadcasts, and 100hr. of radio time per week. Today, many schools in Lower Engadine teach strictly in Romansch until students are 10 years old. At this time, students elect to continue their education in either German or Romansch, with continued study of the other language.

Until about 1850, it was the most spoken language in the canton. By 1880, Romansch speakers dropped to 39.8% of the population, a percentage that kept sinking, finally leveling out around 22%. Today, in some small villages like S-chanf, Romansch speakers remain in the majority. Even in larger towns like Chur they make up as much as a quarter of the population. The language is supported by the Swiss government, but its survival is threatened by the fact that at least four different dialects have arisen in isolated mountain villages.

early Sept. and mid-Dec. to Apr. M-F 9am-6:30pm, Sa 9am-6pm, Su 4-6pm; May-June and Nov. M-F 8am-noon and 2-6pm, Sa 9am-noon. Questions answered by phone 1hr. before counter opens.) The **train station** (☎833 55 52 or 833 59 12) has **currency exchange, Western Union services, tickets,** and **information** (daily 6:45am-7pm; Western Union 8am-6pm). At a different counter are **luggage storage** (3SFr), a kiosk for **hotel reservations,** and **bike rental** (30SFr per day, 6SFr extra to return to a different train station; 23SFr per half-day. Open daily 8am-noon and 1:30-5:30pm.) **Lockers** are 3-5SFr. **Taxi** services are available from **Erich's Taxi** (☎833 35 55). **Swisscom,** in the post office, on Via Serlas on the way to the tourist office, offers **Internet** access. (5SFr per 30min. Open M-F 7:45am-noon and 1:45-6:15pm.) **American Bar,** Via dal Bagn 50a, past Galerie Apotheke, has more terminals, two with disk entry (CD, floppy, zip). (☎834 42 83; www.substation.ch. 15SFr per hr. Open daily noon-8pm.) The **Post office** is at Via Serlas 23 and has Swisscom. (Open M-F 7:45am-noon and 1:45-6:15pm, Sa 8:30am-noon.) **Postal Code:** CH-7500.

ACCOMMODATIONS

With a cappuccino maker in the main lobby, the **Jugendherberge Stille (HI) ❸,** Via Surpunt 60, provides luxury on a backpacker's budget. Breakfast and cafeteria-style dinner are required, which adds to the price, but the salad bar and all-you-can-eat entrées are worth it—and probably save you money, all told. Follow signs around the lake left of the station (30min.), or take the Ortsbus #3 (dir: St. Moritz Bad, Signal) to "St. Moritz Bad, Sonne" (10min.; 2-4 per hr. 8am-8pm, after 9pm take the night bus dir: Celerina-Samadan; 2.60SFr) and go left on Via Surpunt (10min.). Perks include: four-bed dorms, semi-private showers, a pool table (2SFr), ping-pong, a game room, **currency exchange** at reception, **Internet** (4SFr per 15min.), and cheap **mountain bike rental** (15SFr per day, 10SFr after 4pm). The hostel can be overrun by sports teams in summer; call in advance. (☎833 39 69; www.youthhostel.ch/st.moritz. Breakfast, dinner, lockers, and sheets included. Towels 3SFr with 10SFr deposit. Lunch 5-9.50SFr, order in advance. Laundry 4SFr wash, 3.60SFr dry. Reception daily June-Oct. and Dec.-Apr. 7-10am and 4-9:45pm; May and Nov. shortened hours. Check-out 9:45am. Door locked at 11pm; entrance code given. May-Oct. dorms 45.50SFr; doubles 117SFr, with shower 140SFr. Nov.-Apr. dorms 52SFr; doubles 130SFr-150SFr/170SFr. Nonmembers add 6SFr. AmEx/D/MC/V.) **Hotel Sonne ❹,** Via Sela 11 (take bus #3 to "St. Moritz Bad, Sonne"), offers luxury lodgings with shower, balcony, safe, TV, and minibar. Attached restaurant serves Italian and Swiss specialties 11:30am-11pm. (☎ 833 03 63; www.sonne-stmoritz.ch. Non-smoking floors. Breakfast included. Reception 6:30am-11pm. Check-out 11am. Mid-Apr. to late Dec. singles 70-105SFr; doubles 110-120SFr, with shower 140-190SFr; triples 150-165SFr, with shower 195-240SFr. Late Dec. to mid-Apr. singles 75-165SFr; doubles 140-150SFr/160-240SFr; triples 165-195SFr/225-300SFr. AmEx/MC/V.) For **Camping Olympiaschanze ❶**, catch the Post Bus (dir: Sils-Maloja) to "St. Moritz Campingplatz" (3SFr). Run by friendly English speakers, this campsite provides an affordable option for escaping the glitz of St. Moritz. (☎ 833 40 90; www.campingtcs.ch. Washing machine available. Bathrooms and showers included. Reception 8:30-11:30am and 3-7pm. Open mid-May to Sept. 7.20SFr per adult, 3.90SFr per child; 8SFr per tent; 3SFr per car. Electricity 4SFr.)

🍴🍺 FOOD AND NIGHTLIFE

In the small convenience store **Die Not ❶**, on Via Serlas, across the street from The Piano Bar, the friendly Italian-speaking staff make hearty Italian-style sandwiches for a great price. Freshly-baked panini bread is filled with your choice of cheese, prosciutto, tuna fish, hard-boiled eggs, pickles, lettuce, tomatoes, and more. A "small" (quite filling) sandwich costs 4.50SFr, while a larger one is 9.50SFr. (Pizza 5SFr. Wurst 7SFr. Open daily 11am-3am.) **Boccalino Pizza ❸**, Via dal Bagn 6, on the Western side of the lake, offers filling and relatively inexpensive Italian food. Pizzas (10-18SFr, small 8-14SFr), include the Boccalino special, which has tomato, mascarpone cheese, prosciutto, and arugula. entrées range 16-35SFr, with soups running 6-9SFr. (☎ 832 11 11. Open M-Th and Su noon-2pm and 6pm-midnight, F-Sa noon-2pm and 6pm-1am.) **Acla ❺**, Via dal Bagn 54, in the Schweizerhof Hotel, has an intimate atmosphere for fine dining. Pastas and vegetarian options are 16-26SFr, while chicken curry is 26SFr. Tempting desserts for around 15SFr include a piña colada parfait with grilled pineapples and a special "pesto." (☎ 837 07 01. Complete lunch menus from 20.50SFr. Salad buffet 12.50SFr. Open daily 11:30am-2pm and 6:30-8:30pm. Reservations recommended. AmEx/DC/MC/V.) For après-skiing action, head downstairs in the Schweizerhof Hotel and try out the three bars. The locals flock to the **Stübli** for a relatively cheap drink in a dark and cozy wood-panelled den. (Beer from 5.50SFr. Live pop and rock music Tu-Su.) The **PianoBar** is just that, a laid-back and sophisticated bar geared towards an older crowd. (One beer available for 8SFr, otherwise pricier aperitifs and champagnes.) The **Muli Bar** pays homage to country music with a young crowd and a grinning mule behind the bar. (☎ 837 07 07 or www.schweizerhofstmoritz.ch for all three. Beer from 4.50SFr. Open daily summer 8pm-2am; winter 4pm-2am.) The leather ceiling, silver bar, crystal dance-floor lighting and red velvet VIP lounge of the **Vivai Dance Club**, under Le Mandarin on Via Traunter Plazzas, lie just across the street from Schweizerhof, yet seem a world apart. A chic and trendy disco filled with regulars and tourists alike, Vivai pulses to hip hop, R&B, Latin, soul, a bit of rock, and special house mixes, all spun by live DJs. Faux ice crystals accent the bar, which serves beer from 10SFr, mixed drinks (12-15SFr), and champagne from 10-750SFr. (☎ 833 69 39; www.vivai. ch. 18+. Dec.-Apr. 20SFr cover; open daily 10pm-5am. June-Dec. 10SFr cover; open Th-Sa 10pm-5am. May open F and Sa only.)

Get groceries at the **Co-op Center,** up from the tourist office or at Via dal Bagn 20, the main road between Dorf and Bad, on the way to the youth hostel. (Open M-F 8am-12:15pm and 2-6:30pm, Sa 8am-5pm. The location on Via dal Bagn is wheelchair accessible. Open during lunchtime and F until 8pm.) The **After Hours** grocery store, Via Maistra 2, under the kiosk, is open Dec.-Apr. and June-Oct. 24hr. (☎ 834 99 00. Open May and Nov. daily 6am-11pm. AmEx/MC/V.) In late Jan., sample culinary delights at the **St. Moritz Gourmet Festival.** Sponsored by the World Gourmet Club, the event brings chefs from around the world, hosts classes, and offers package deals through St. Moritz Tourism. (www.stmoritz.ch. Jan. 31-Feb. 5, 2005.)

🏛 MUSEUMS AND EVENTS

The **Giovanni Segantini Museum,** Via Somplaz 30, is a 15min. uphill walk from the "Aruons" stop on the #3 Ortsbus route or directly next the "Segantini Museum" stop on the #2. The walk is worth it: the domed structure on the hill is both a museum and a memorial to the Art Nouveau painter designed for himself before his death in nearby Maloja. The dome was made to house the exhibit's highlight, the alpine trilogy "Life, Nature, and Death," (also known as "Becoming, Being, and Passing"). On its lower level, the museum displays two rooms full of Segantini originals. (☎ 833 44 54; www.segantini-museum.ch. Pamphlets on the special exhibits in English, German, and French. Open early June to late Oct. and Dec.-Apr. Tu-Su 10am-noon and 3-6pm. 10SFr, students 7SFr, children 3SFr.) The **Engadiner Museum,** Via dal Bagn 39, between Bad and Dorf, displays reconstructions of Engadine rooms from the past 500 years, including a peasant's parlor and Visconti Venosta's hall, and showcases examples of Engadine *sgraffiti* architecture, where designs are carved into plaster on the exterior of buildings to reveal a darker base color. The house features tiny doorways, *Chuchichästlis* (cupboards), and a macabre plague-era four-poster sickbed with a skeleton on the ceiling. The inscription translates, "As you are, I would like to be." (☎ 833 43 33. English guides 1SFr. Open June-Oct. M-F 9:30am-noon and 2-5pm, Su 10am-noon; Dec.-Apr. M-F 10am-noon and 2-5pm, Su 10am-noon. Closed May and Nov. 5SFr, students 4SFr, ages 6-12 2.50SFr.) July brings the **Opern Festival** to the legendary Badrutt's Palace Hotel. (☎ 833 01 10; www.opernfestival-engadin.ch. Tickets 90-170SFr.)

🏔 OUTDOOR ACTIVITIES

St. Moritz's **skiing** is world-famous. Two main areas, Corviglia and Corvatsch, are packed with easy runs, although tougher runs pepper each. The third area, Diavolezza, offers some more difficult slopes. (☎ 830 00 00 for regional ski packages; www.skiengadine.ch. Ski day passes 49-61SFr, ages 16-20 45-55SFr, ages 6-15 26-30SFr. Equipment rental available at several shops throughout town.) The St. Moritz Sports Office, housed in the tourist office, has a listing of all major events throughout the year. Highlights in 2005 include the annual **Polo on Snow** tournament, played on the frozen St. Moritz Lake (Jan. 27-30); and the 77th **White Turf: Running of the Horses,** a similar event where horses race across the ice (Feb. 6, 13, 28). Each year the 1.6km **bobsled** run from the '28 and '48 Olympics is rebuilt by 14 skilled laborers for the **Olympia Bobrun.** (☎ 830 02 00; www.olympia-bobrun.ch. Open Dec. 210SFr for 1 run, diploma, and photo; call ahead, as slots fill up quickly. No experience necessary.)

In the summer, visitors take advantage of the area by **hiking** (the tourist office sells a map for 17SFr). A flat trail cuts its way from St. Moritz to Pontresina (1½hr.). The trailhead is on the other side of the train station (the "See" exit), across the bridge. For a more demanding trip (3hr.), ride from St. Moritz up to **Piz Nair** for a rooftop view of the Engadine. (3075m. ☎ 833 43 44.) From here, a train goes to **Suvretta Lake** (2580m) in the shadow of majestic **Piz Julier** (3380m). Follow the Ova da Suvretta back down to the Signalbahn or St. Moritz (3½hr.). **The St. Moritz Experience** (☎ 833 77 14; www.stmoritz-experience.ch) provides **canyoning** (W and F; 180SFr) and **glacier adventures** (M and Th; 120SFr). Other summer activities include **river rafting** (☎ 861 14 19; www.engadin-adventure.ch; 85-95SFr per half-day, 160SFr per day) and **horseback riding.** (☎ 833 57 33. 60SFr per hr., 90SFr per private lesson.)

ITALIAN SWITZERLAND (TICINO, TESSIN)

Ticino (*Tessin* in German and French), nestled below the Alps, is renowned for its mix of Swiss efficiency and Italian *dolce vita*—no wonder the rest of Switzerland vacations here. Jasmine-laced villas painted bright colors and traditional stone huts replace the charred-wood chalets of northern Switzerland, while the landscape charms with its tropical vegetation and emerald-green lakes. Bellinzona's pastel church façades spill out onto the cities' piazzas, and castles abound. Culture-seekers flock to the annual film festival in Locarno. Farther south in the canton, the financial capital of Lugano serves as a center for budget travelers.

HIGHLIGHTS OF TICINO

Marvel at Marianne Werefkin's modern works at the **Museo Comunale d'Arte Moderna** in Ascona (p. 458).

Groove to bass-heavy beats at the **Bellinzona Blues Festival** (p. 448).

Couldn't crash Cannes? Try the **International Film Festival** in Locarno (p. 455).

BELLINZONA   ☎091

Three impressive medieval castles peer from the heights above Bellinzona (pop. 18,000), reminding visitors that the city was once a strategic Milanese fort guarding trade routes through the San Bernadino and St. Gotthard passes. Today, Bellinzona is the capital of Ticino, and an important crossroads for those heading to lake resorts farther south. Vineyards in the surrounding hills cast a pastoral calm over the city, (melodically disrupted every year by the beats of the Blues Festival).

▄ TRANSPORTATION

Bellinzona is the main train hub for Ticino, with **trains** to: Basel (4hr., every 30min. 6:05am-8:15pm, 72SFr); Locarno (20min., 2 per hr. 5:38am-12:38am, 7.20SFr); Lucerne (2¼hr., 6:05am-9:06pm, 50SFr); Lugano (30min., every 30min. 5:47am-1:34am, 11.40SFr); Milan (2hr., every hr. 5:06-9:25pm, 29SFr); Rome (7hr., every hr. 6:46am-7:36pm, 90SFr); Zurich (2½hr., every hr. 6:26-9:25am and every 30min. 10:26am-9:06pm, 54SFr). Travelers under age 26 save on Milan (23SFr) and Rome (68SFr). Trains to and from Geneva and Zurich require a change in Domodossola, Italy (5-6hr., 90-115SFr). **Post Buses** leave from the station for Chur (Coira) via Thusis (3hr., every hr. 6:07am-6:07pm, 50SFr), San Bernadino (1¼hr., every hr. 6:07am-9:07pm, 19.80SFr), and elsewhere in eastern Switzerland. By **car**, arrive from the north on N2/E35 or N13/E43; from Lugano or the south on N2/E35 north; from Locarno or the west on N13.

▄ PRACTICAL INFORMATION

The town is small and easily navigable; v. Stazione is the main street, leading to Piazza Collegiata, p. Nosetto, and p. Independenza. To reach Bellinzona's **tourist office** on v. Camminata 2 in Palazzo Civico, turn left from the train station and follow the main road past p. Collegiata; it's in the beautiful old **municipal government** building. (☎825 21 31; www.bellinzona.ch. Open M-F 9am-6:30pm, Sa 9am-noon. Closed midday in win-

Italian Switzerland (Ticino)

ter.) Services at the train station (open M-Sa 6:10am-7pm, Su 7:30am-7pm) include: **hotel reservations** (free), **currency exchange, luggage storage** (5SFr at baggage check), **lockers** (3-5SFr), and **bike rental** (at baggage check; reserve ahead; 30SFr per day, 23SFr per half-day; additional 6SFr to return at another station); public **parking** at the station (1SFr per 30min.; 8SFr per day) or covered parking in the Colletivo at p. del Sole, off v. Stazione to the right, down Largo Elvetica. (Open 24hr.; 7am-10pm 1SFr per 45min; 10pm-7am 1SFr per hr.) For **taxis,** call ☎ 825 44 44 or 825 11 51. **Banks** on v. Stazione have 24hr. **ATMs.** (Open 8:30am-noon and 1-4:30pm.) **Farmacia Internazionale,** v. Stazione 2, posts information on after-hours prescriptions. (Open M 9am-noon and 2:30-8:30pm, Tu-Sa 9am-noon and 1:30-8pm.) The **post office,** v. Stazione 18, left from the station, is open M-F 7:30am-6:30pm, Sa 9am-noon. **Postal Code:** CH-6500.

ACCOMMODATIONS AND CAMPING

Youth Hostel Montebello (HI), v. Nocca 4 (☎ 825 15 22; www.youthhostel.ch/bellinzona), occupies the former Instituto Santa Maria just below the Castello di Montebello. Left from the station and then left onto P. Indipendenza. Retains an office-building look; some halls still have historical artifacts in display cases, which rattle every time a train passes. 2 sponge-painted TV rooms with VCR add character. Laundry (6SFr), **Internet** (5SFr per hr.). Ping-pong, billiards, and free movies. Breakfast and sheets included. Dinner 13SFr. Reception 8-10am and 3-10pm. Check-out 10am. Wheelchair accessible. Dorms 30-35SFr; 4- to 5-bed rooms 34-39SFr; singles 45-50SFr; doubles 80-90SFr. Non-members 6SFr extra. MC/V. ❷

Hotel Garni Moderno, v. Stazione 17b (☎/fax 825 13 76). Go left from the station, right on v. Claudio Pelladini, and right on v. Cancelliere Molo. Rooms live up to their name with plush carpeting, sinks, and large windows. Sleek shared baths. Breakfast included. Reception in hotel café M-Sa 6:30am-10:30pm. Singles 55SFr, with bath 90SFr; doubles 90SFr; triples with bath 150SFr; quads with bath 180SFr. MC/V. ❸

Albergo Internazionale, p. Stazione (☎825 43 33; www.ticino.com/hotel-international), across from the train station. A red-carpeted staircase leads to cozy rooms with hall showers. Breakfast buffet included. Reception 8am-noon and 2-6pm. Singles 100SFr; doubles 130-170SFr. AmEx/DC/MC/V. ❹

Camping Bosco de Molinazzo (☎829 11 18; www.campingtcs.ch). Take bus #2 (dir: Castione) to "Arbedo Posta Vecchia" (2.20SFr), then walk under the overpass to the river. Sandwiched between the railroad tracks and the river, the campground has a café, laundry services (wash or dry 0.50SFr per 22min.), and a pool. Reception 9am-noon and 5pm-midnight. Open Apr. to mid-Oct. 6.40-7.40SFr per person, 3.20-3.70 per child ages 6-14; 7-8SFr per tent. Electricity 3-4SFr. Kurtax 1.35SFr per person. ❶

🍴 FOOD

Bellinzona is full of cafés that serve hot and cold panini (sandwiches) for 5-10SFr. Local confectionery shops carry **Bissolo,** chocolate-covered chestnuts inspired by the insignia on the coins minted in Bellinoza. **Migros** is in p. del Sole, across from the Castelgrande entrance. (Open M-F 8am-6:30pm, Sa 7:30am-5pm. Restaurant open M-F 7am-6:30pm, Sa 7am-5pm.) A huge **outdoor market** along v. Stazione lays out everything from fruits and breads to incense and rugs (Sa 7am-noon).

Croce Federale, v. Stazione 12 (☎825 16 67), offers Italian dining on a terrace overlooking the main road, in the dining room with a stone oven, or in a back room decorated with floral watercolors. Enjoy pasta (13-19SFr), pizza (12-18SFr), or meat entrées (21-35SFr) with an inexpensive bottle of local wine. Kitchen open M-Sa 11:30am-2pm and 6-10pm; pizza 11:30am-11pm. ❸

Birreria Corona, v. Camminata 5 (☎825 28 44), on the far end of town before p. Nosetto, also offers solid Italian fare and the option of dining outside on a cobblestone street. Pasta in 2 sizes (10-16SFr), pizza (11-16SFr) and daily Menùs (20SFr) available noon-2pm and 6:30-10pm. Wheelchair accessible. Open M-Th 7am-midnight; F-Sa 7am-1am. Kitchen open noon-2pm and 6:30-10pm; pizza all day. AmEx. ❷

Peverelli Panetteria Tea Room Pasticceria (☎825 60 03), in p. Collegiata off v. Stazione. Serves a selection of teas (3-4SFr), panini (5-6SFr), and pizza (5SFr) to a crowd spilling out onto the piazza. Open M-F 7am-7pm, Sa 7am-6pm. ❶

🎫 SIGHTS

Stone walls once enclosed the three castles of Bellinzona; they became separate entities only after the city joined the Swiss Confederation and the three original cantons Uri, Schwyz, and Nidwalden each claimed one of the battlements. Today the **Castelgrande, Castello di Montebello,** and **Castello di Sasso Corbaro** remain linked through their membership in the UNESCO World Heritage list.

The **Castelgrande** rises 50m above p. del Sole on a huge outcropping of solid rock. To reach it, take the free elevator (runs daily 9am-midnight) or the winding uphill path from the piazza. The castle occupies a site inhabited since the Neolithic period (5500-5000 BC) and fortified since the 4th century. Construction on the current fortress began in the 13th century with the Milanese Visconti family; major changes were introduced between 1473 and 1486 as stone walls were built enclosing the entire valley. The *bianca* (white) and *nera* (black) towers, rising 28 and 27m high respectively, date from the 13th and 14th centuries. The top of the **Torra Bianca** offers panoramic views of Bellinzona and of the large, grassy castle courtyard. The **museum** exhibits unique painted panels from the house of a Bellinzonan noble and a collection of Swiss coins, from the Renaissance years when Bellinzona served as a mint. (Castle grounds open daily 9am-8pm. Free. Tower open 10am-6pm. Free. Museum open daily 10am-6pm. 4SFr, students 2SFr.)

The smaller but more satisfyingly dank **Castello di Montebello,** on the hill opposite Castelgrande, has working drawbridges, ramparts, dungeons, and views as far as Lake Maggiore on a clear day. The castle can be reached on foot from p. Collegiata up the slippery steps of Sallita alla Motta or by bus from v. Stazione. The tower and former residential quarters now house an **archaeological and civic museum** containing vases, jewelry, and ceramics, as well as ancient bric-a-brac and ceremonial arms. (☎825 13 42. Open Feb.-Dec. Castle grounds open daily 8am-8pm. Free. Museum open daily 10am-6pm. 4SFr, students 2SFr.)

Castello di Sasso Corbaro is the smallest of the three, though it commands the best view of the valley from its 230m hilltop. From Castello Montebello, hike 30min. up v. Artore. Despite immensely thick 4.7m (14-ft.) walls, the castle was completed in just six months in 1479. It is now home to a gallery hosting rotating exhibits ranging from the mixed-media constructions of artist Mimmo Rotella to butterfly-related art. (Open daily Mar.-Nov. 10am-6pm. 4SFr, students 2SFr.)

Several notable churches grace Bellinzona, tucked away among the villas and hotels. The gorgeous **Chiesa Collegiata dei SS Pietro e Stefano,** on the p. Collegiata, bears an early Renaissance façade flanked by trumpeting heralds. The breathtakingly ornate stone interior features numerous paintings and frescoes (attributed to Simone Peterzano), overhung by a gilded canopy. Other interesting features include the *scagliola* (a painted plaster imitation of marble) pulpit that dates from 1784 and the holy water stoup, named the "Fontana Trivulziana" after a nobleman from Messocco who owned it in the 15th century. (Open daily 8am-6pm.) To reach the 16th-century **Chiesa di San Biagio** from the station, walk 15min. to the left to v. Pedotti. The church exhibits a gigantic painting of St. Christopher on its exterior and a flock of saints in its columned interior. Tombstones and a beautifully carved granite font are displayed on the south and west walls. (Open daily 9-11am.)

◪ OUTDOOR ACTIVITIES AND ENTERTAINMENT

The **Ticino River** is perfect for idle strollers. A 45min. hike with grand views of Sasso Corbaro starts in Monti di Ravecchia, a short bus ride from Bellinzona. The trail begins at the hospital and follows an ancient mule path, leading to now-deserted **Prada,** an ancient trading post possibly dating from pre-Roman times. The **Blues Festival** (June 22-25, 2005) draws a variety of musicians. Entrance 10SFr per night.

LOCARNO   ☎091

On the shores of **Lago Maggiore,** Locarno's (pop. 30,000) cypress and magnolia bask in warm breezes. The area is heavily touristed, thanks to its sub-tropical climate (at over 2200 hours of sunlight per year, it's the sunniest spot in Switzerland), A lake and mountains provide pristine natural beauty only minutes away. During its famous **film festival** in August, Locarno swells with cinephiles.

▐ TRANSPORTATION

"Holiday" passes, available at the tourist office, the Travel Office at the train station, or at **Viaggi FART** on p. Grand, offer free travel on most bus, ferry and train lines in the Lago Maggiore region. (☎751 87 31; fax 40 77. 3-day pass 46SFr, children 23SFr; 1 week 66SFr/33SFr.)

Trains: p. Stazione (☎743 65 64, rail info 0900 30 03 00). To: **Bellinzona** (25min., every 30min. 5:24am-1:14am, 7.20SFr), connecting north to **Lucerne** (2½hr., every 30min., 54SFr) and **Zurich** (2½hr., 58SFr), and south to **Lugano** (50min., 16.60SFr) and **Milan** via Bellinzona (34SFr). For **Geneva** (5¾hr., 90SFr), **Montreux** (4¾hr., 76SFr), or **Zermatt** (4hr., 86SFr), change trains in **Domodossola, Italy** (1¾hr., every hr. 7:55am-7:12pm, 41SFr).

Buses: FART (Ferrovie Autolinee Regionali Ticinesi; the local transport system) buses leave the train station or p. Grande for **Ascona** (#31, 15min., every 15min. 5:04am-11:46pm, 3.20SFr), and other nearby towns. Buses also run through the **San Bernardino Pass** to eastern Switzerland.

Ferries: Navigazione Lago Maggiore, Largo Zorzi 1 (☎0848 81 11 22), conducts tours of the entire lake, all the way into Italy. A full day on the northernmost part of the lake costs 11SFr, and for the entire Swiss side 18SFr. Sail to **Ascona** (15-45min., 9 per day 9:30am-5:15pm, day pass 11SFr) or **Brissago** farther south (1¼hr., 9 per day 8:05am-6:20pm, day pass 18SFr). "Holiday" cards offer 50% off on Lago di Lugano (p. 449).

By Car: Locarno is accessible from motorway A2 (Exit: Bellinzona-Süd).

Taxi: EcoTaxi (☎08 00 32 13 21) offers hybrid cars and reasonable rates.

Car Rental: Hertz SA, Garage Starnini SA, v. Sempione 12, Muralto (☎743 50 50). Subcompacts from 150SFr for 1 day; 455SFr per wk. Open M-F 8am-noon and 1:30-5:30pm, Sa 8am-noon. AmEx/DC/MC/V.

Parking: Metered parking on v. della Posta and major streets (1SFr per 30min.; max 1½hr.). The 24hr. parking garage, **Autosilo Largo SA** (☎751 96 13), beneath the *Kursaal,* accessible from v. Cattori, has the same rates 7am-10pm (1SFr per hr.).

Bike Rental: At the train station. Bikes 30SFr per day, 23SFr per half-day. Open 9am-1pm and 2:30-6:45pm. Call ☎743 65 64 to reserve.

▐ ▐ ORIENTATION AND PRACTICAL INFORMATION

Piazza Grande, home of Locarno's International Film Festival, is the city's anchor; social life centers around its arcades. Just above p. Grande, the *Città Vecchia* (old town) is home to 16th- and 17th-century architecture. **Via Ramogna** connects the p. Grande to the train station, and Largo Zorzi connects it to the waterfront. **Via Rusca** extends from its other side to the Castello Visconteo.

Tourist Office: Largo Zorzi (☎791 00 91; www.maggiore.ch), on p. Grande in the *Kursaal* (casino). Office makes hotel reservations. Open Apr.-Oct. M-F 9am-6pm, Sa 10am-6pm, Su 10am-1:30pm and 2:30-5pm; Nov.-Mar. closed Su.

Currency Exchange: Banks line p. Grande; open M-F 9am-4pm. Also, location at train station open daily 7:30am-7pm. **Western Union** at station open daily 9am-6pm.

Luggage Storage: At the train station. 7SFr per piece. Open 9am-1pm and 2:30-6:45pm. **Lockers** 4-7SFr.

Bookstore: Libriarte Internationale (☎/fax 743 03 33), p. Stazione 2, around the corner from the train station, houses maps, travel books, and a small selection of English novels. Open M-Sa 7am-8pm, Su 7am-7pm.

ITALIAN SWITZERLAND

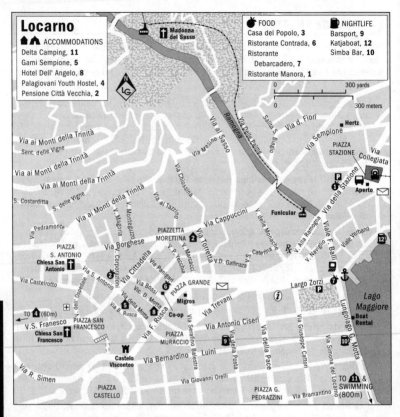

Locarno

■▲⌂ ACCOMMODATIONS
Delta Camping, **11**
Garni Sempione, **5**
Hotel Dell' Angelo, **8**
Palagiovani Youth Hostel, **4**
Pensione Città Vecchia, **2**

🍎 FOOD
Casa del Popolo, **3**
Ristorante Contrada, **6**
Ristorante
Debarcadero, **7**
Ristorante Manora, **1**

🍸 NIGHTLIFE
Barsport, **9**
Katjaboat, **12**
Simba Bar, **10**

Internet Access: Visitors' Center booth on v. Balli (☎/fax 751 84 08), across the street and uphill from the dock (10SFr per hr.). Open daily June-Oct. 10am-6pm.

Emergencies: Police ☎117. **Fire** ☎118. **Road information** ☎021 163. **Weather** ☎021 162. **Medical Assistance** ☎111. **Ambulance** ☎144.

Post Office: p. Grande. Open M-F 7:30am-6:30pm, Sa 8:30am-noon.

Postal Code: CH-6600.

🏠 ACCOMMODATIONS AND CAMPING

A display board by the train station allows free phone calls to hotels and pensions. Reserve a week in advance Mar.-Oct.; 6 months in advance during the film festival.

Palagiovani Youth Hostel (HI), v. Varenna 18 (☎756 15 00; www.youthhostel.ch/locarno). From p. Grande, turn right on v. della Motta. Take the left fork (v. B. Rusca) past p. San Francesco, then take v. S. Francesco, which turns into v. Varenna (HI signs point the way from v. Varenna on). High hedges and floral bushes conceal this establishment. Most of the 2- to 6-bed rooms include balconies, sinks, and lockers. Huge buffet breakfast and sheets included. 3-course lunch and dinner 15SFr each. Laundry 8SFr, towels 2SFr. **Internet** 15SFr per hr. **Mountain bikes** 15SFr per day, 10SFr per half-day. Reception Apr.-Oct. 8-10am and 3-11:30pm; Nov.-Mar. 8-10am and 5-10:30pm. The hostel can be overrun by families and school groups July-Aug., so call ahead. 40-bed dorms 33SFr; 6- to 7-bed dorms with sinks 39SFr; 2- to 4-bed rooms with bath 47SFr; twins 39.50SFr. Non-members 6SFr extra. MC/V. ❷

Pensione Città Vecchia, v. Toretta 13 (☎751 45 54; www.cittavecchia.ch). From p. Grande, turn right onto v. Toretta. Utilitarian co-ed dorms; glass shower doors in co-ed bathrooms don't promote privacy. Sheets and breakfast included. Reception 8am-9pm. Check-in 1-6pm, call ahead if arriving after 6pm. Dorms 29-40SFr; doubles 70-80SFr; triples 120SFr. ❷

Garni Sempione, v. Rusca 6 (☎751 30 64; garni.sempione@ticino.com). Walk to the end of the p. Grande, turn right onto v. della Motta, and then take the left fork onto v. B. Rusca. This hotel brings the outside in with an enclosed courtyard leading to a variety of rooms (some with shower, balcony, or TV). Wood paneling, tile along the walls, and colorful comforters add atmosphere. Breakfast included. Reception 8am-9pm. Check-out 11am. Wheelchair accessible. Singles 60SFr, with shower 65SFr; doubles 100SFr/120SFr; triples 150SFr/165SFr. Prices drop in winter. AmEx/DC/MC/V. ❸

Hotel Dell' Angelo, p. Grande (☎751 81 75; www.hotel-dell-angelo.ch). On the far side of p. Grande. Winding marble staircases and halls containing the remains of frescoes lead to modern hotel rooms with bathroom, TV, and telephone. **Parking** 16SFr. Breakfast included. Reception 7am-1am. Wheelchair accessible. Singles 70-135SFr; doubles 110-210SFr; triples 150-260SFr; quads 180-300SFr. AmEx/DC/MC/V. ❸

Delta Camping, v. Respini 7 (☎751 60 81; www.campingdelta.com). A 30min. walk along the lakeside. Shuttle runs from the campground to Locarno on request (2SFr per person). Like camping, but with all the amenities of home: shady birch trees, rocky swimming beach, a restaurant (entrées 9.50-19.50SFr), market, workout room, **Internet** access (5SFr per 30min.) and **bike** and **kayak rental** (20SFr per day, 12SFr per half-day). Reception July-Aug. 8am-10pm; Mar.-June and Sept.-Oct. 8am-8pm. 100SFr reservation fee July-Aug., 50SFr of which is returned. Open Mar.-Oct.; prices highest July-Aug. 11-18SFr per person, 6SFr per child, 21-47SFr per tent plot, 31-57SFr per waterside tent plot, rental caravans 56-100SFr. Children 6SFr. Electricity 5SFr. ❷

🍴 FOOD

Though Locarno's restaurants have inflated prices, it's possible to get a panini, pasta, or pizza for 10-20SFr, leaving a few extra francs for gelato. Picnickers should visit the **Co-op** at p. Grande (open M-W and F-Sa 8am-6pm, Th 8am-8pm) or **Aperto,** at the station. (Open daily 6am-10pm.) A **market** fills the streets of the *Città Vecchia.* (Apr.-Sept. Sa 9am-1:30pm.)

Ristorante Contrada, p. Grande 26 (☎751 48 15). The specialties are traditional northern Italian dishes like *polenta con funghi porcini* (corn porridge with mushrooms; 21SFr) and *osso bucco* (roasted veal; 28SFr), but the theme here is cats. Felines, rendered in every imaginable artistic medium, line the walls. Pizza (11-19SFr) served all-day long. Wheelchair accessible. Open daily 7am-midnight. AmEx/MC/V. ❷

Casa del Popolo, p. Corporazioni, above p. Grande (☎091 751 12 08). Go northern Italian with *funduta* (cheese fondue; 36SFr) or gnocchi with gorgonzola sauce (17SFr), or go cheap with pizza (15-18SFr) or 1 of 5 kinds of spaghetti (14-19SFr). Piazza-side seating next to fountains. Open daily noon-2:30pm and 7-10:30pm. AmEx/MC/V. ❸

Ristorante Manora, v. della Stazione 1 (☎743 76 76), left of the station. High-quality self-service and tons of options. Breakfast 6SFr. Pasta buffet 9-10SFr. Meat *menùs* 11-17SFr. Wheelchair accessible. Open Mar.-Oct. M-Sa 7:30am-10pm, Su 8am-9m; Nov.-Feb. M-Sa 7:30am-9pm, Su 8am-9pm. ❶

JTTER AND LONG LIFE: THE ALPHORN

*Dani Schlaepfer has been
ɔlaying the Alphorn, the tradi-
ional Swiss wooden instrument,
ɔr the last 10 years as a part of
he Spitzli Trio. The group is
ɔased in Urnäesch, in the Appenzell region, famous for its reverence for traditional Swiss culture,
ɑs well as a population of cows
hat far outnumber the humans.
He stopped during a concert in
Schwaegalp, below Mt. Saentis,
ɔ talk with Let's Go.*

.G: When did you start playing
he alphorn?

A: I started when I was twelve. My
ather taught me.

.G: And his father taught him?

A: No, he just tried it—and ended
ɹp teaching himself.

.G: Tell me a little bit about the
nstrument itself.

A: Well, my alphorn is 2.5m
ong; it's a G flat. They come in
ɑll different keys—F, A sharp, A
lat, etc. The difference in key is
nade by the difference in length
ɔf the horn. The horns are so
ong, they come apart into three
ɔieces so that you can actually
ɕarry them around to practice
ɑnd to different events.

.G: How are they made?

A: There are some Alphorn facto-
ies now, where the entire instru-
nent is made by machines. But I
ɔrdered my horn specially from a
nan who still does it all by hand.

Ristorante Debarcadero (☎ 751 05 55), on Largo Zorzi
by the ferry dock, is one of the very few affordable
spots on the lake. Tourists snap up pizza (12-19SFr)
and homemade pasta (13-17SFr). The crowds come
for gelato (3.20SFr), among the cheapest in town.
Daily *menùs* from 15SFr. Wheelchair accessible. Open
daily 9am-midnight. ❷

⊙ SIGHTS

For centuries, visitors have journeyed to Locarno
solely to see the church of **Madonna del Sasso**
(Madonna of the Rock), founded over 500 years ago
when a Franciscan monk, Bartolomeo d'Ivrea, had a
vision of Mary telling him to build a church high
above the city. Its orange-yellow hue renders it
immediately recognizable from anywhere in town. It
is accessible by a **funicular** that leaves from a small
station near the train station (July-Aug. every 15min.
7am-midnight, Sept.-June until 8pm; 4.50SFr, round-
trip 6.60SFr, with SwissPass 5SF). A 20min. walk up
the cobblestone v. al Sasso (off the v. Cappuccini in
the *Città Vecchia*), where capricious lizards scuttle
across the path, also leads to the top; the stations of
the cross, sequencing Christ's passion, line the trail.
A less religious but equally inspiring path heads past
the turn-off along a shaded, tropical path to the back
of the church. The courtyard houses life-size wooden
niche statues depicting scenes of Christ, including a
Pietà, a Pentecost, and a life-size, room-filling Last
Supper from 1650. Bramartino's *Fuga in Egitto*, Ciseri's *Trasporto di Cristo al Sepolcro*, and a statue
of Mary, sculpted for the church's consecration,
adorn the **sanctuary**. Hundreds of silver heart-shaped
medallions on the walls commemorate Mary's inter-
ventions in the lives of those who have made pilgrim-
ages here. Also on display are paintings
commissioned by survivors of disasters, thanking the
Madonna for answering their prayers. Alongside dozens of sickbeds are arrestingly modern images,
including car crashes and a robbery at machine gun
point. (☎743 62 65; www.cappuccini.ch. Grounds
open daily 6:30am-7pm. English guidebooks for the
entire complex are available at the devotions shop
for 7SFr. Open daily 9am-7pm.)

To reach the **Chiesa San Francesco** (wheelchair
accessible) from p. Grande, turn right onto v. B.
Rusca and left onto v. S. Francesca . The church
was built in the 14th century on top of an older parish founded by the Franciscans shortly after the
death of St. Francis of Assisi in 1226. Built of
stones scavenged from a demolished castle, the
exterior bears incongruous inscriptions from the
material's original incarnation. A vanished ceme-

tery, the only remnant of which is a curious skull-and-crossbones from the Orelli family monument, once surrounded the building.

Follow v. Marcacci from the p. Grande and turn left on v. Borghese to reach the cavernous **Chiesa San Antonio** (wheelchair accessible), which presides over the outskirts of the *Città Vecchia*. (San Antonio is 1 block up from p. San Antonio.) Built between 1668 and 1674, it was renovated in 1863 after the roof and front façade collapsed, killing 45 people. Circular patches of sunlight illuminate a large fresco, *Cristo Morto* (Dead Christ) by G.A. Felice Orelli.

A Milanese duke built the **Castello Visconteo,** down v. F. Rusca from p. Grande, in the 13th century. Visitors can wander through dungeons and towers where soldiers poured boiling oil on attackers. The second floor houses an exhibit on the 1925 Treaty of Locarno, one of many ill-fated attempts to avoid another war; the political cartoons it spawned speak volumes. The castle also houses the **Museo Civico e Archeologico,** which exhibits Roman artifacts. (☎756 31 61. Open Apr.-Oct. Tu-Su 10am-5pm. Combined admission 7SFr, students 5SFr, children 1SFr.)

🏞 OUTDOOR ACTIVITIES

ON THE LAKE. The deep blue water of Lago Maggiore is a delightful sight. A **ferry** ride to points on both the Swiss and Italian shores offers more intimate contact with the lake (p. 449). The tropical **Isole di Brissago,** at the lowest point in Switzerland (193m), was cultivated in 1885 by a utopian-minded baroness hoping to create an earthly paradise. Exotic plants from four continents mingle with delicate stands of bamboo, which conceal brightly colored exotic birds. An early 20th-century villa occupies one end of the island. (☎791 43 61 or 00 91; www.isolebrissago.ch. Wheelchair accessible. Open Mar.-Oct. daily 9am-5pm. 7SFr.) **Marco Brusa,** along the water towards Delta Camping, rents **boats.** (☎07 92 14 62 57. Pedal boats 15-20SFr per hr., 8-12SFr per 30min.; motor boats 45SFr/25SFr). **Bagno Pubblico La Lanca,** 2min. farther along the lake, has the cheapest beach in town. (☎752 12 95. Open 10am-7:30pm. 3SFr, children 6-15 2SFr.) Bathe for free at the **Fiume Maggia,** the rocky river that feeds into the lake. Hop the #10 bus to any point in the Maggia Valley. Take care, as the river can rise rapidly during rain.

VAL VERZASCA HIKE. To escape the city, head out on Post Bus #630 to **Sonogno** (1¼hr.; 7:35am-6:15pm; 16.60SFr, round-trip 33.20SFr) and hike amid the extraordinary peaks at the end of **Val Verzasca.** From

You have to wait 12-14 months for the horn to be made. They cost 3500SFr. He paints a scene from Swiss farm life on the top, and burns his name into the bottom, along with where it was made.

LG: What sort of events do you play?

A: Outside of practice with the trio three times a week, we play at a lot of traditional festivals and events throughout the year.

LG: Tell me a little bit about your clothing.

A: I am wearing the traditional Appenzeller dress from the 19th century. All of the embroidery is done by hand, along with the tanning of the leather for the belts and suspenders. The gold cows on the belt are also hammered out by hand.

LG: And what's with the earring?

A: All Appenzeller men wear this earring. I got mine when I was five. On the top, there's a horseshoe, which means good and long life. The thing that dangles down on the bottom is a *Rahmkette;* it's what the farmer uses to skim the cream off the top of the milk, which then is made into butter.

LG: Why are they together?

A: It's a symbol—it means that through butter, milk, the cows, and the ways of farming, you will enjoy a long and healthy life.

LG: Do you always wear this symbolic earring?

A: No; normally it is just a cow.

THE 200M SCREAM

I went to the Val Verzasca Dam knowing everything. At 220m nearly 700 ft.) above the floor of he Verzasca Valley, it's home to he world's highest fixed-point bungee jump. I knew that it took seven ears of lobbying before the Swiss Government granted Trekking eam AG a license to install jumping equipment there, that James Bond, played by Pierce Brosnan, made it famous in the movie Goldeneye, and that I had heard it had a perfect safety record. Then I saw he dam. It's huge. Simple physics suggests that a falling body should cover the distance in about 6½s, but until the kid standing next to me on the bridge threw a rock into he oblivion, I had no idea how ong that seemed.

After jumps by eight others, none of whom flinched, I found myself at the edge. One second I was standing with my toes curled around the end of a metal platform, with a staff member hanging onto my vest, then there was a 3s countdown and the hand was gone. The sensation of jumping felt like the most natural thing in the world.

Contact Trekking Team at 848 308 007; www.trekking.ch. Open Apr.-Oct. Sa-Su; Jul-Aug W-Su. Reservations required. 255SFr, students 195SFr; additional jumps on the same day 125SFr. Night jumps possible. To reach he dam take the Post Bus (dir: Sonogno) to Diga Verzasca.

—Tom Miller

the bus stop, take the first left and follow the yellow signs to **Lavertezzo.** The mostly flat trail is marked by yellow signs with directions and town names, and white-red-white blazes. It passes through cool, shady glens and rocky riverbeds as it follows the Verzasca river through the valley. Close to **Lavertezzo,** the river eases its rapid pace, making swimming possible. Pick a swimming hole carefully, as the water can be quite cold and the undercurrents strong. Climb the **Ponte dei Salti,** a 17th-century double-arched bridge, and gaze into the clear green ponds. From Sonogno to Lavertezzo is a 6hr. walk, while Lavertezzo to Tenero requires another 5hr., but the Post Bus stops along the trail in the valley. A 4.5km **art trail** also runs from Ganne to Lavertezzo, winding past sculptures, galleries and installations, all free and open to the public.

ADVENTURE SPORTS. The Verzasca Dam has allowed scores of visitors to break speeds of 100km per hr., courtesy of its famous ■**bungee jump,** the highest in the world. The 220m jump, conquered with panache by James Bond in *Goldeneye,* costs 255SFr (students 195SFr), 125SFr for subsequent leaps on the same day. Night jumps are possible. Reservations are required. **Trekking Team** (☎ 0848 80 80 07; www.trekking.ch.), runs Verzasca Dam jump, plus a 70m bridge jump (125SFr, students 95SFr, additional jumps 75SFr), **canyoning** (125-195SFr, students 86-134SFr), **snorkeling** (85-100SFr), **climbing** (125-190SFr, students 86-134SFr) and **spelunking** (98SFr, children 78SFr, students 48SFr) in **Centovalli.** The **Visitors Center** (☎751 84 08; www.visitorscenter.ch) on Vaile Bali, 25m uphill from the ferry dock, books the above activities with Trekking Team, as well as **skydiving** (395SFr for 3500m jump with 30sec. free-fall), **paragliding** (165SFr), **windsurfing lessons** (60SFr per hr.), **waterskiing** and **wakeboarding** (45SFr per 10min.), **rock climbing** (250SFr per day), **rafting** (65-105SFr half-day, 150SFr full day), and **sailing lessons** (2.5hr.; 190SFr, 2-4 people). **Bike rentals** cost 18SFr per half-day, 25SFr per day. (Open daily Mar.-Oct. 10am-6pm.)

🎵 📷 ENTERTAINMENT AND NIGHTLIFE

■**Simba Bar,** toward Camping Delta, appeals to Locarno's wealthier 20-something crowd. Ignore the Lion King mosaic out front: this place is about its mesmerizing aquarium, hanging mirrors, green lights, and lakeside views. (☎752 33 88; www.bar-simba.com. Beers 4.50SFr. Drinks 9-14.50SFr. Music nightly from 8pm; live DJ from 10pm. 18+. Open Apr.-Sept. daily 5pm-1am; Oct.-Mar. Tu-Sa 5pm-1am.) Along v. B. Luini four blocks from the lakeside, **Barsport** caters to a slightly older local crowd with pool, foosball, and a mix of techno and jazzy world music. (☎751 29 31. Beers from 3.70SFr. Sangria 4SFr. Wheelchair accessible. Open Su-Th 8pm-1am, F-Sa 10pm-2am.) For the price of a drink (beer 7SFr, cocktails 11SFr), the young-at-heart can enjoy a 20min. cruise aboard the **Katjaboat**, a yellow vessel that departs from the Hotel Rosa. A soundtrack of sappy love songs ensures that things stay G-rated. (☎ 079 686 39 90. Boat runs 11am-2am, roughly twice per hr.)

For 11 midsummer days (August 3-13, 2005), everything in Locarno halts for the **International Film Festival,** one of the most important cinema events in the world. Unlike Cannes, no invitations are required. Over 150,000 big-screen enthusiasts descend upon the town, so book a room six months to a year ahead. The centerpiece of the festival is a giant 26m by 14m outdoor screen, the largest outdoor screen in Europe, set up in p. Grande for big-name premieres by the likes of Jean-Luc Godard, Woody Allen, Spike Lee, and Bernardo Bertolucci. Smaller screens highlight young experimental filmmakers. (☎756 21 21; www.pardo.ch. Unlimited access 270SFr. For daily ticket prices and more info, write to: International Film Festival, v. Luini 3a, CH-6601 Locarno.)

In the second half of July, Locarno hosts **Ticino Musica,** a classical-music festival focusing on young musicians and students. It features concerts, operas, and master classes at venues throughout Ticino. Tickets (30SFr, students 15SFr) are available at the tourist office and at the door of any event. Free events occur as well. (☎980 09 70; www.ticinomusica.com.)

AURIGENO ☎091

Nestled in the Valle Maggia ("Magic Valley"), Aurigeno offers its own charms with stone-shingled buildings and grapevines galore. An excellent side-trip from Locarno, this out-of-the-way village is a great place to enjoy traditional Swiss-Italian culture and a perfect spot to begin numerous hikes.

▐▀ TRANSPORTATION AND PRACTICAL INFORMATION

Take **bus** #10 from Locarno (30min., every hr. 7:02am-8:10pm and 11:35pm, 7.80SFr). It stops in Rocchini, Aurigeno and Maggia. The **tourist office** for the area is at the bus stop in Maggia beside the Co-op. (☎753 18 85; fax 22 12. Open M-F 9am-noon and 2-5pm; June-Sept. also Sa 9am-noon.) For **taxis,** call ☎079 423 69 (7am-7pm); for **police** ☎117, for an **ambulance** ☎144, and for **helicopter rescue** ☎14 14. The **post office** is on the road between Aurigeno and Moghegno. (Open M-F 7:30-8:30am and 3:45-4:45pm, Sa 8-10am.) **Postal Code:** CH-6677.

▐▌▐▐ ACCOMMODATIONS AND FOOD

Accommodations in Aurigeno are scarce, but Maggia up the road offers a few hotels. ▨**Baracca Backpacker** ❷ is an ideal starting point in Aurigeno. From the Locarno train station, take bus #10 (dir: Valle Maggia) to "Ronchini" (25min., every hr. 7:02am-8:30pm and 11:35pm, 7.20SFr). Cross the street and turn right from the bus stop; follow hostel signs through the forest over the bridge, and into the town (15min.); the hostel is beside the church. Monika and Reto create a homey environment with 12 beds, fresh herbs for cooking and a wood shop for tinkering. Look in the game room for the best map in the area, and for hundreds of **hiking, biking,** and **swimming** suggestions. (☎079 207 15 54. **Bike rental** 10SFr per day. Sleep sack 2SFr per day. Reception 9-11am and 5-8pm. Open Apr.-Oct. Dorms or campsite 25SFr; doubles 30SFr per person.) At the junction of the main road and the bridge, the Pedroni couple offers the opportunity of **Sleeping in the Straw** ❷. (☎753 24 62. Open May-Oct. 20SFr Breakfast included. Call ahead. 20SFr.)

Trattoria Giovanetti ❶, in the center of town along the main road (2min.) is the closest thing to a restaurant in town, with cold plates of meat and cheese (6-15SFr) and minestrone soup (6.50SFr). For warm meals, order ahead. (☎753 11 33. Open M-W and F-Sa 8:30am-11pm, Su 9am-11pm.) Opposite the Aurigeno/Mogheno bus stop on the east side of the main bridge, the simple **Osteria del Ponte ❷** serves pasta and gnocchi (10-13SFr) and beer (3.20SFr) by the stone hearth inside or on the balcony terrace overlooking the river. (☎753 31 95. Open M and W-Su 8:30am-midnight.) There are no grocery stores in Aurigeno, so stock up in Locarno or head to the **Co-op** in Maggia. (Open July to mid-Aug. M-F 8:30am-6:30pm, Sa 8am-5pm; mid-Aug. to June M-F 8:30-noon and 2-6:30pm, Sa 8am-12:15pm and 2-5pm) Baracca Backpacker provides two free bikes daily for grocery runs.

👁 🏔 SIGHTS AND OUTDOOR ACTIVITIES

Just north of the bridge on the east side of the river lies one of Maggia Valley's oldest churches. View the frescoes and votive paintings of Giovanni A. Vanoni in the **Sanctuario Madonna delle Grazie.** (Open May to mid-Oct. Tu-Sa 2-4pm.) Vanoni's work is common throughout the valley and can be seen on buildings in Aurigeno as well as in grottoes along several forest paths; look for liberal use of bright blues. In late June and July a different sort of blues paint the valley, as several villages play home to **Vallemaggia Blues Nights.** The tourist office provides a list of events.

SWIMMING. Aurigeno is home to two amazing swimming holes. The first is a pool hollowed out by a picturesque **waterfall,** surrounded by boulders. To reach it, head left from Baracca's toward town and take the left fork in the main road. Pass a large villa surrounded by a stone wall and follow the small path through the woods (5min.). In the summer, swimming in the fall's Alpine waters is best in the early afternoon, when the water is less frigid. The second one is a secluded lagoon, behind an **old Roman arch bridge,** a wonder in and of itself. From the hostel, turn right and follow the brown signs to the Ponte Romana (10min.). Locals also swim up and down the Maggia River and sunbathe on the white, rocky shores. Take care, as the river can become dangerous after heavy rains in the mountains.

HIKING. Though Auregino's hiking options are mild, it's easy to get lost. Maps are available at Baracca (24SFr) or the tourist office in Maggia (21SFr).

Passon della Garina (4-6hr. round-trip). Made famous by author Max Frisch, the hike over the Passo della Garina (1076m) into Loco in the neighboring Valle Onsernone offers amazing views for hikers. Head south along the main road and follow the signs toward Chiazza. The steep and narrow path follows traditional red-and-white signs to the pass (2hr.). At the pass, hikers have the opportunity to continue upwards along well-marked trails to the summit of Salmone (1559m) and an overview of Lago Maggiore (1hr.). Beyond the pass, the trail continues along to Loco (2hr.). To return, take a Post Bus from Loco to Cavigliano, Bivio Onsernone (4.60SFr), then the train to Ponte Brolla (2.60SFr). From Ponte Brolla, bus #10 from Locarno takes travelers back to Aurigeno (5.20SFr). The last bus from Loco runs at 5:05pm.

Giro Valle del Salto (1hr. round-trip). An easier hike begins from Maggia's main square (marked with red-and-white painted signs). Climb the flight of stairs to the Chapelle della Pioda (476m), which offers panoramas of the valley towns. Proceed into Valle del Salto (746m), then descend toward Maggia on the other side of the mountain. Stop in Braià along the way and view a chapel rich with frescoes by Giovanni A. Vanoni.

BIKING. The 11km village tour through Maggia, Lodano, Moghegno, and Aurigeno follows footpaths and side streets throughout the Maggia Valley. Those looking for a more challenging route should head toward Prato Sornica; a path starts at the ice rink and goes through neighboring villages. The moderate route is accented by an excruciating 260m technical climb from Broglio to Monti di Rima, providing a breathtaking panorama (14km).

ASCONA ☎091

Ascona (pop. 5000), lies on the Côte d'Azure, boasting beautiful Riviera beaches. History buffs can trace the steps of the leftist thinkers and Bohemian artists who tried, around the turn of the century, to establish a utopian community on the mountain above—a venture dubbed **Monte Verità** (Mountain of Truth; p. 458). Others can enjoy it as a respite from the crowds of Locarno.

☐❼ TRANSPORTATION AND PRACTICAL INFORMATION

Travel by **bus** #31 from Locarno (15min., every 15min. 5:04am-11:46pm, 2.60SFr) or by **ferry** (15-45min., 9 per day 9:10am-5:15pm, round-trip 12SFr). The bus stops at "Ascona Posta" on v. Papio. Behind the bus stop the main road of the old city, v. Borgo, stretches to the lake. P. Guiseppe Motta, where the ferry docks, is lined with lakeside hotels and restaurants. For **currency exchange** or an **ATM,** try any of the banks along v. Papio. (All open M-F 9am-12:30pm and 1:30-4:30pm.) The **tourist office,** in the Casa Serodine behind the Chiesa SS Pietro e Paolo, provides a guide of the area sights and services in four languages and also **exchanges currency.** (☎791 00 91; www.maggiore.ch. Open Apr.-Oct. M-Sa 9am-6pm, Su 2:30-5pm; Nov.-Mar. M-F 9am-noon and 1-5pm.) A tiny **sightseeing train** leaves from the ferry docks for tours of the town with commentary. (☎079 240 18 00 or 859 29 57. 30min., daily starting at 11am. 7SFr, children 3SFr.) Other local services include: **taxis** ☎791 46 46 or 41 41; **parking** at the **Autosilo** at the corner of v. Papio and v. Buonamno (1SFr for 30min., 18SFr per 24hr.) or down v. Papio in the covered **parking garage** (☎751 17 07; 1SFr per hr., 18SFr per 24hr.); and **bike rental** at **Bike Cicli Chiandussi,** v. Circonvallazione 14, down v. Papio and a right turn before the Migros. (☎079 337 11 62. 20-25SFr per day, 15-18SFr per half-day. Open M and W-F 9am-noon and 2-7:30pm, Sa until 5pm. MC/V.) A **24hr. accommodations board** across from the **post office,** 25m down from the bus stop, has a list of hotels and a free phone for reservations. (Open M-F 7:30am-6pm, Sa 8:30-10:45am.) **Postal Code:** CH-6612.

⋔◗ ACCOMMODATIONS AND FOOD

Few of the city's beds fall into the budget range. Luckily, Ascona is an easy daytrip from Locarno. Those who stay can try rooms above the **Ristorante Verbano ❸,** v. Borgo, near the modern art museum. The rooms are simple but clean, and are the only affordable choice downtown. (☎791 12 74. Breakfast included. Closed Su. 45SFr per person.) The tourist office has a list of *affitacamere* (private rooms), most of which start from 35SFr per person and require a 2-night minimum stay.

Otello ❸, v. Papio 8, just downhill from the bus stop, offers a taste of Ticino. Diners eat Italian pasta (13-22 SFr), savor selected cheeses (9SFr), or enjoy chocolate mousse (7SFr) surrounded by pillars and Mediterranean murals. (☎791 54 10. Wines from 3.30SFr. Open daily 9am-9:30pm. MC/V.) The prime lake views at **Ristorante La Torre ❸,** p. Motta 61, come at a price, but its bowls of homemade gelato (11.50SFr) just might be worth it. (☎791 54 55; fax 792 27 97. Pizza from 12.80SFr; daily *menùs* 21.50SFr. Open mid-Dec. to Oct. daily 10am-midnight; closed Nov. to mid-Dec. AmEx/MC/V.) Picnicking next to the lake is a far more affordable option. Look for the **Co-op**'s orange sign shining down v. Papio from the bus stop. (Open

July-Aug. M-F 8am-7pm, Sa 8am-6pm; Sept.-June M-F 8:15-12:30pm and 2-6:30pm, Sa 8:15am-5pm.) Or try the **Migros** 200m down the street. (Open M-F 8am-noon and 2-6pm, Sa 8am-5pm.) A weekly **market** fills p. G. Motta. (May-Oct. Tu 9am-4pm.)

◎ SIGHTS

The Post Bus stop at the corner of v. Borgo and v. Papio, at the edge of the old city, is within walking distance of all the sights and the waterfront. The *Città Vecchia* stretches from the lake to v. Papio with banner-hung streets and wrought-iron balconies. The sole remaining tower of the 13th-century **Castello del Ghiriglion,** 26 p. G. Motto, is at the eastern end of the boardwalk. The **Chiesa SS Pietro e Paolo,** V. Cipressi 6, left from where v. Borgo intersects the lake, marks Ascona from the lake with its slender clock tower. The frescoes inside date from the 15th century; canvas paintings such as the "Crowning of the Virgin" (1617) above the altar date from the 17th century. (Open 24hr.) Banana trees and stone coats-of-arms frame the **Collegio Pontifico Papio's** 15th-century courtyard. Enter from V. Papio or V. Capella, one block uphill from the waterfront. Presiding over the still-operating Superior private school (est. 1399), the adjacent church of **Santa Maria della Misericordia** hides 15th-century frescoes by Seregnesi and Antonio da Tradate in a dim interior. Private galleries lining the winding streets promote such artists as Marc Chagall and Georges Braque. **The Museo Comunale d'Arte Moderna,** v. Borgo 34, has an extensive collection of works by Klee, Utrillo, and Jawlensky. One floor is devoted to evocative temperas by Expressionist Marianne Werefkin, a Russian who spent her later years in Ascona. Her wry, sometimes haunting pictures of everyday life in Ticino include mountain landscapes, terminally bored people in cafés, and religious processions. (☎780 51 00; www.cultura-ascona.ch. Open Mar.-Dec. Tu-Sa 10am-noon and 3-6pm, Su 4-6pm. 7SFr, students and seniors 5SFr.)

The **Museo Casa Anatta** immortalizes the dashed dreams of Ascona's utopian thinkers (without English labeling). Walk uphill along the winding Strada della Colina from the bus stop or follow the steep, uneven stone stairs of Scalinata della Ruga off v. Borgo. The one-time "Co-operative vegetarian colony" is now a museum containing photos of a 1930s nudist colony in Brissago, anarchist Ernsy Frick's collection of mystical minerals, and the costumes and crowns worn by members of the "individualistic cooperative." Don't miss the miniature model of one utopian architect's proposed Temple to the Land of Fidus, in which men would pass from the Room of Ambition to the Room of Love and worship a statue of the Woman of the Earth. (☎791 01 81; www.csf-mv.ethz.ch, www.centro-monte-verita.ch. Open July-Aug. Tu-Su 3-7pm; Apr.-June and Sept.-Oct. Tu-Su 2:30-6pm. 6SFr, students and seniors 4SFr.)

♫ ▣ ENTERTAINMENT AND NIGHTLIFE

In late June and early July, Ascona hosts the annual **New Orleans Jazz Ascona.** Musicians play on the waterfront among sculptures and in local cafés. (www.jazzascona.ch. Tickets 10SFr per night, 25SFr for 3 days, 80SFr for 10; children under 16 free.) The **International Horse Jumping Competition** (late July) and the **Settimane Musicali,** held throughout the valley (late-Aug. to mid-Oct.), features classical music performances by young master musicians from around the world. At the corner of P. Motta and V. Borgo, **Mad Wallstreet** puts international DJs on the floor all week long. Everybody gets a nametag with a number upon entering, and then flirts by passing notes via the DJ. ("Hey 967, want to dance? Love, 564.") Drinks cost 6.50SFr. (18+. Open daily 5pm-1am.) Next door, **Disco-Bar Riviera** salsas to a Latin beat into the wee hours. (18+. Open daily 10pm-5am.) Catch a flick at the **Cinema Otello** (☎791 03 23), next to the restaurant of the same name on v. Papio.

LUGANO
☎ 091

Lugano, Switzerland's third-largest banking center, rests on Lago di Lugano in a valley between the San Salvatore and Monte Brè peaks. Cobblestone streets widen into arcade-lined piazzas, where visitors can enjoy a seamless blend of religious beauty, artistic flair, and natural spectacle. There are two extraordinary youth hostels, both built from luxury villas, with swimming pools and magnificent gardens.

⊏ TRANSPORTATION

Trains: p. della Stazione. Most destinations connect through **Bellinzona** (30min., every 30min. 5:36am-12:17am; 11.40SFr), including trains to **Bern** (76SFr), **Locarno** (16.60SFr), **Lucerne** (104SFr), and **Geneva** (104SFr). Direct trains run from Lugano to: **Basel** (4-5hr., every 30min. 5:36am-7:47pm, 79SFr); **Zurich** (3hr.; 5:57am-8:38pm; 60SFr); and **Milan** (45min.; 7:14am-9:48pm; 21SFr).

Public Transportation: Buses run from the neighboring towns to the center of Lugano and also traverse the city. Schedules and ticket machines at each stop. 1.10-1.90SFr per ride. 24hr. "Carta Giorno" (day pass) 5SFr. SwissPass valid.

Taxis: ☎922 88 33, 971 21 21, or 922 02 22.

Car Rental: Avis, 8 v. C. Maraini, in the Hotel Albatro, (☎913 41 51). **Hertz,** 13 v. San Gottardo (☎923 46 75). **Europcar,** 24 v. M. Boglia, at Garage Cassarate (☎971 01 01).

Parking: Autosilo Comunale Balestra, off v. Pioda, on v. S. Balestra. 7am-7pm. 1SFr per hr., overnight parking (7pm-7am) 0.50SFr per hr. Open 24hr.

Bike Rental: At the baggage check in the station (☎923 66 91). 30SFr per day, 23SFr per half-day; 6SFr to return at another station. Open 9am-1pm and 2:30-6:45pm.

■✚ ↗ ORIENTATION AND PRACTICAL INFORMATION

The 15min. downhill walk from the train station to the classically Italian Piazza della Riforma, the town's center, winds through Lugano's large pedestrian zone. For those who would rather avoid the walk, a funicular runs between the train station and the waterfront **Piazza Cioccaro** (5:20am-11:50pm, 1.10SFr).

Tourist Office: (☎913 32 32; www.lugano-tourism.ch). The office is across from the ferry station in the Palazzo Civico, Riva Albertolli, at the corner of p. Rezzonico. Free maps. **Guided city walks** in English May-Oct. M, W, F 9:30am; ask for more info. Open Apr.-Oct. M-F 9am-7pm, Sa 9am-5pm, Su 10am-3pm; Nov.-Mar. M-F 9am-noon and 1-5pm.

Hotel Reservations: 24hr. computer kiosks outside the train station and tourist office list hotels and provide free reservations phones. Tourist office makes reservations (4SFr).

Consulates: UK, 22 v. Sarengo (☎950 06 06; fax 06 09). Open M-F 10am-noon.

Currency Exchange: Western Union in the station (☎923 93 26). Open 9am-1pm and 2:30-6:45pm. Banks open M-F 8:30am-4:30pm, most with **24hr. ATM.**

Luggage Storage: Lockers at station. 4-7SFr. Luggage watch 7SFr per piece. Open 9am-1pm and 2:30-6:45pm.

Lost Property: Check the *Fundbureau* (☎800 80 65) of the Polizei Communale, on the p. Riforma. Open M-F 7:30am-noon and 1:30-5pm.

Emergencies: Police ☎117. **Ambulance** ☎144. **Fire** ☎118. **Medical Services** ☎111. **First Aid** ☎805 61 11. **Pharmacies** are in all major piazzas and along the waterfront.

Internet Access: Biblio-Café Tra, 3 v. A. Vanoni (☎923 23 05). From p. Dante, head down the v. Pretorio (15min.) and turn left onto v. A. Vanoni. Open M-Th 9am-midnight, F 9am-1am, Sa 5pm-1am. 2SFr per 15min. Manor department store in p. Dante has 4 coin-

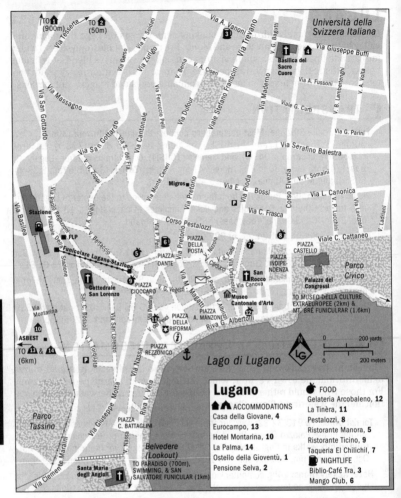

operated terminals on the 3rd floor (10SFr per hr.). Open M-W and F-Sa 8:15am-6:30pm, Th 8:15am-9pm. 1SFr per 6min. Burger King, right from the tourist office, provides 30min. free with purchase of a meal (from 11SFr). Open Su-Th 9am-midnight, F-Sa 9am-1am.

Post Office: v. della Posta, 2 blocks up from the lake near v. al Forte. Open M-F 7:30am-6:15pm, Sa 8am-noon. Traveler's checks cashed. Telephones, telegrams, and faxes at the v. Magatti entrance to the PTT building.

Postal Code: CH-6900; **Postlagerndebriefe** use CH-6901.

🏠 ACCOMMODATIONS AND CAMPING

🏠 **Hotel & Backpackers Montarina,** v. Montarina 1 (☎966 72 72; www.montarina.ch). Walk 200m to the right from the station, cross the tracks, and go 50m uphill. Converted from a luxury villa, this palm-tree-enveloped hostel attracts families and students with its **swimming pool,** well-groomed grounds, ping-pong table, kitchen, and terrace. Laundry 4SFr, soap 1.50SFr. **Internet** 10SFr per hr. Buffet breakfast 12SFr. Sheets 4SFr. Free parking available. Reception 8am-10:30pm. Open Mar.-Oct. Reserve ahead. Dorms 25SFr; singles 70SFR, with bath 80SFR; doubles 100SFr/120SFr. MC/V. ❷

▨ **Ostello della Gioventù (HI),** Lugano-Savosa, v. Cantonale 13 (☎966 27 28; www.luganoyouthhostel.ch). Note: there are 2 streets called v. Cantonale, one in downtown Lugano and one in Savosa, by the hostel. Take bus #5 (walk 350m left from the station, past the parking lot, and cross the street to the bus stop) to "Crocifisso," and then backtrack and turn left up v. Cantonale. A former luxury villa, this sprawling family-run hostel has banana and palm trees in its extensive gardens and a **pool** with a waterslide. Unique, comfortable rooms in several different buildings. Kitchen access 1SFr (after 7pm). **Internet** 5SFr for 20min. Breakfast 8SFr. Sheets included. Towels 2SFr. Parking available. Laundry 5SFr. Reception 6:30am-noon and 3-10pm. Curfew 10pm; keys available with 20SFr deposit. Reserve ahead. Open mid-Mar. to Oct. Dorms 23SFr; singles 40SFr, with kitchenette 47SFr; doubles 60SFr/74SFr; family rooms for 2-6 people 90-120SFr. Apartments for families (1-week min. stay) 100-170SFr per day. Lower rates for extended stays. MC/V. ❷

Pensione Selva, v. Tesserete 36 (☎923 60 17; villaselva@bluewin.ch). Take bus #4 (dir: Ospedale; leaves opposite train station) to "Sassa," then walk along v. Gottardo for 250m and turn right on v. Tesserete. A path overhung with grapes seals this haven from the city noise and leads to the cozily romantic *Pension* with an outdoor pool and terrace. All rooms with bath. Parking available. Breakfast included. Reception 8am-midnight. Closed Nov. Singles 90-110SFr; doubles 120-142SFr. Cash only. ❸

Casa della Giovane, Corso Elvezia 34 (☎911 66 46; fax 66 40), across the street from Basilica Sacro Cuore. Take bus #5 (leaves opposite train station) to "Corso Elvezia." This modern peach and blue building provides rooms (most with balconies) for **women only.** Breakfast 4.50SFr. Lunch or dinner 12SFr. 4-bed dorms 35SFr. Doubles with bath and studio apartment singles available by special request. ❷

Camping: The tourist office provides a complete list of campgrounds. 2 budget lakeside campgrounds are in nearby Agno. To reach them, take the Ferrovia-Lugano-Ponte-Tresa (FLP) tram across from the Lugano train station to Agno (4.60SFr). Exit the tram station and turn left on v. Stazione, then left immediately on to v. Molinazzo. **La Palma** (☎605 25 61) has plenty of waterside plots and reasonably clean shared facilities. Reception 8am-8pm. 7SFr per person, plus 2SFr Kurtax; 8-10SFr per tent; 3SFr per car. Lakeside plots 15-19SFr. Electricity 4SFr. ❶ Down v. Molinazzo 50m farther, **Eurocampo** (☎605 21 14; fax 605 31 87), which has more services, but slightly higher prices, is also right on the lake. Small store, café (pizza from 10SFr), Internet 16SFr per hr, and laundry. 9SFr, plus 2SFr Kurtax; 8SFr per tent, 2.50-4SFr per car. Electricity 3SFr. ❶

▐ FOOD

Outdoor cafés serving similarly priced Italian fare pepper the lakeside piazzas. **Via Pessina,** off p. della Riforma, livens up at midday. The multi-level **Migros,** 15 v. Pretorio, two blocks left from the post office down v. Pretorio, has a food court with slices of pizza from 3SFr and sandwiches from 2.50SFr. (Open M-W and F 8am-6:30pm, Th 8am-9pm, Sa 7:30am-6pm.) A **public market** on p. della Riforma sells seafood, veggie sandwiches (4SFr), and produce. (Open Tu and F 7am-noon.)

La Tinèra, v. dei Gorini 2 (☎923 52 19), behind Crédit Suisse off p. della Riforma, is a romantic, low-lit, underground restaurant, specializing in Lombard cuisine. Daily *Menùs* (13-19SFr) include liver fried with onions and *scaloppina cordon bleu.* Sausage with risotto (14SFr) and vegetarian goulash (4SFr) anchor the regular menu. Open M-Sa 8:30am-3pm and 5:30-11pm. AmEx/DC/MC/V. ❸

ITALIAN SWITZERLAND

Taqueria El Chilicuil, Corsa Pestalozzi 12 (☎922 82 26), down the Corsa Pestalozzi from the p. Indipendenza. The cheese is Swiss, but the rest is authentic Mexican. The snack bar serves tacos (2 for 8SFr), quesadillas and burritos (6-9SFr), and margaritas (7SFr, pitcher 38SFr). Offers takeout. Happy hour M-F 5-7pm (drinks 1-2SFr less). Wheelchair accessible. Open May-Nov. M-Th 11:30am-11pm, F 11:30am-midnight, Sa-Su 7pm-midnight; Dec.-Apr. M-Th 11:30am-10pm, Sa-Su 5pm-midnight. ❶

Ristorante Manora, Manor Department Store in p. Dante, 3rd floor; entrance off Salita Mario e Antonio Chiattone also. The perfect combination of low price, wide selection, and gourmet food cooked before your eyes means budget heaven. Salad bar (4.50-10.20SFr), pasta (7.90-10.90SFr per plate), and beer (1.20-4.50SFr). Hot daily specials 10-15SFr. Wheelchair accessible. Open M-Sa 7:30am-10pm, Su 10am-10pm. ❷

Gelateria Arcobaleno, v. Marconi 2 (☎922 62 18), beside the McDonald's on the waterfront, dishes out creative and unusual gelato desserts. Menu includes gelato pizza (10SFr), *Spiedini* (fruit kebabs and yogurt; 2 for 22SFr), and the "Indonesia," a pineapple filled with yogurt gelato, fruit salsa, and whipped cream (11SFr). 2 scoops 5.50SFr. Open M-F 8:30am-1am, Sa-Su 9am-1am. ❶

Pestalozzi, p. Indipendenza 9 (☎921 46 46), in the Hotel Pesalozzi. Smoke-free, alcohol-free, and serves veggie-friendly, balanced meals. 3-course daily menus offer soup, pasta, and meat for 16-18SFr. Vegetarian pastas with sauce 13-16SFr. Open daily 11am-9:30pm; hot food served 11am-2:30pm and 6-9:30pm. MC/V. ❷

Ristorante Ticino, p. Cioccaro 1 (☎922 77 72; fax 923 62 78). This air-conditioned spot in the center of town offers a dimly lit setting for a special occasion. Chef's recommendations like stuffed pigeon, lobster, or foie gras (54-75SFr) may be featured on the menu, but more reasonably priced meat and fish entrées (22-38SFr) are no less gourmet. Wheelchair accessible. Open M-F noon-2pm and 7-9:30pm, Sa-Su 7-9:30pm. AmEx/DC/MC/V. ❹

🅖 SIGHTS

The ornate frescoes of the 16th-century **Cattedrale San Lorenzo,** downhill from the train station, gleam with still-vivid colors. Marble female angels wielding bronze swords do battle with devils in one side altar. Bernardio Luini's gargantuan fresco, **Crucifixion,** painted in 1529, fills an entire wall in the **Chiesa Santa Maria degli Angioli,** 200m right from the tourist office. In the background of the painting are scenes depicting Christ's trial, bearing of the cross, death, and resurrection, each separated by the crosses in the foreground. The small 14th-century **Chiesa San Rocco,** two blocks to the left of the p. della Riforma, in the p. Maghetti, houses an ornate Madonna altarpiece and a series of 20 frescoes depicting the life of its patron saint. The national monument **Basilica Sacro Cuore,** on Corso Elevezia across from the Casa della Giovane (open M-F 7:45am-5:30pm, Sa-Su 10am-6pm), is more sparing. The large fresco surrounding the altar puts a mountain hiker in the midst of popes, priests and pagans. The **Museo Cantonale d'Arte,** 10 v. Canova, has a permanent collection of 19th- and 20th-century art, including works by Swiss artists Vela, Ciseri, Franzoni, and Klee, though the collection is frequently replaced by special exhibitions and video installations by contemporary artists. (Across from the Chiesa San Rocco. ☎910 47 80; www.museo-cantonale-arte.ch. Wheelchair accessible. Open Tu 2-5pm, W-Su 10am-5pm. Permanent collection 7SFr; special exhibits 10SFr, students 7SFr. MC/V.) An elegant lakeside villa houses the **Museo delle Culture Extraeuropee,** v. Cortivo 24. Over 650 wood-carved masks, statues, and shields from Africa, Oceania and Asia adorn the Neoclassical villa's marble staircases. The collection was the life's work of Surrealist painters Serge and

Graziella Brignoni. (On the footpath to Gandria in the Villa Heleneum. From the tourist office take bus #1 (dir: Castagnola) to "San Domenica" and walk down to the street below. The Villa is 700m on the right. Or take the ferry to the Museo Helenum stop. ☎971 73 53. Captions in Italian. Open Apr.-Oct. W-Su 10am-5pm. 5SFr, students 3SFr.)

🏔 OUTDOOR ACTIVITIES

PARKS AND GARDENS. The **Belvedere** is a sculpture garden with an emphasis on modernist metalwork stretching along riva Caccia and the lakeside promenade. An older statue near the end memorializes American "Giorgio Washington". The serene **Parco Civico** is dotted with flowerbeds. Small beaches offer access to the water. (Open daily Mar.-Oct. 6:30am-11:30pm, Nov.-Feb. 7am-9pm.)

BOATING. The dock for the **Societa Navigazione del Lago di Lugano** (☎923 17 79; www.lakelugano.ch) is across the street from the tourist office. Tours of Lake Lugano pass unspoiled towns along the shore, including Gandria (11.50SFr, round-trip 19.20SFr), Morcote (16.90SFr/28.20SFr), and Paradiso (3SFr/5SFr). A "grand tour" of the lake in English (3½hr.) costs 32.60SFr (19.60SFr with SwissPass); 62SFr/52SFr allows a week of unlimited lake travel.

Various points on the lake rent pedal boats (7-8SFr per 30min.) and motorboats (around 30SFr per 30min.). **Boatcenter Saladin** across from the Chiesa Santa Maria degli Angioli, rents motorboats and outfits waterskiers. (☎923 57 33. Boats from 25SFr per 30min. Waterskiing 30SFr per 10min. Open Apr.-Oct. 9am-midnight.) **Bagno Pubblico,** on riva Caccia toward Paradiso, is good for a swim. (☎994 20 35. Open daily mid-June to Aug. 9:30am-8pm; May to mid-June and Sept. 9:30am-6:30pm. 4SFr, children 8-16 2SFr.) A rope swing is near the Castagnola ferry stop.

HIKING. The tourist office and Ostello della Gioventù have topographical maps and trail guides (15SFr) into the Ticinese mountains. The most rewarding hike is to **Monte Boglio.** The 5hr. round trip can be extended over two days by staying at the Pairolhütte (ask at hostels or the tourist office). Reach the peaks of **Monte Brè** (933m) and **Monte San Salvatore** (912m) by funicular, 20min. down the river to the left of the tourist office, just off of V. Castagnole. The #1, 11 and 12 buses also stop nearby. (☎971 31 71. Open daily 9:10am-6:45pm; July-Aug. until 10:05pm. 13SFr, round-trip 19SFr; ages 6-16 6.50SFr/9.50SFr.) At the top, a 3km educational hike with placards and a walk through olive groves cater to short-distance hikers. The 115-year-old San Salvatore funicular is 20min. from the tourist office in the other direction; from the lakefront, follow V. E. Bosio inland just after the Paradiso ferry dock. (☎985 28 28. Departures every 30min. Mar.-Nov. 8:30am-11pm. One-way 14-17SFr, round-trip 20-14SFr; ages 6-16 7-8.50SFr/10-15.80SFr.) From the summit, a trail leads back down to the village of Carona (Ciona), offering beautiful lake views. Keep an eye open for the pink Daphne Odorosa, a flower found only on the slopes of San Salvatore. Walks along the lake to the east provide access to some beautiful lakeside villages, including romantic **Gandria.**

ADVENTURE SPORTS. The **ASBEST Adventure Company,** v. Basilea 28 (☎966 11 14; www.asbest.ch.), based in the Hotel Continental, provides adventure opportunities. Most require groups; lone travelers should call ahead. In winter, **snowshoe** and **ski** (full-day 90SFr) or **tandem paraglide** over icy crags (165SFr). **Canyoning** (from 90-300SFr) and **river-diving** (with training; 90SFr) are less chilling in Ticino, away from glaciers. In summer, **rock-climb** and **rappel** (90SFr) or **mountain bike** (90SFr).

🎵 📷 ENTERTAINMENT AND NIGHTLIFE

During the first two weekends in July, Lugano's **Festival Jazz** fills the p. della Riforma with free music. Past performers include Miles Davis and Bobby McFerrin. The looser **Blues to Bop Festival** (also free) celebrates R&B, blues, and gospel in late August by hosting international singers and local amateurs. The **Wine Harvest Festival,** in mid-October, drowns those fading summer memories. From late June to early August, **Cinema al Lago** shows international films on a large screen installed on the lake nightly at 9:45pm (after July 15 9:30pm; ☎913 32 32; www.open-air-kino.ch. 15SFr, under age 17 12SFr.)

For a change of pace, head down the v. Pretorio from p. Dante and turn left on v. A. Vanoni for the **Biblio-Café Tra,** v. Vanoni 3, a second home to students from the neighboring university. Have a beer (3.60SFr) and a book from the extensive collection at one of the battered wood tables. (**Internet** 2SFr per 15min. Open M-Th 9am-midnight, F 9am-1am, Sa 5pm-1am.) The Latin American **Mango Club,** 8 p. Dante, mixes live salsa and techno in one of the premier clubs of Lugano.(☎922 94 38. 10SFr admission includes beer. Open W-Su 11pm-5am.)

VALAIS (WALLIS)

Valais occupies the deep, wide glacial gorge traced by the Rhône river. The clefts of the valley divide the land linguistically: in Martigny and Sion, French predominates; in Brig and Zermatt, Swiss-German is used. Whatever the language, the towns share a common penchant for cheese and good wine, and make an industry of shuttling people to the snow-covered peaks on skis or on foot. The region's spectacular skiing, hiking, and climbing opportunities make fighting tourist traffic worth it. Smaller cities like Verbier and Gryon give travelers a relatively more authentic experience, and Zermatt has the most to offer skiers and hikers. Train travelers should note that Eurail is not valid on the regional BVZ train line.

HIGHLIGHTS OF VALAIS (WALLIS)

Gorge yourself on breathtaking views in the hiker's paradise of **Zermatt** (p. 465).
Check out both world-class art *and* traditional alpine cow fights in **Martigny** (p. 478).
Ski in the middle of summer on the slopes surrounding **Sion** (p. 476).

ZERMATT AND THE MATTERHORN   ☎027

A trick of the valley blocks out the great Alpine summits that ring Zermatt, allowing the Matterhorn (4478m) to rise alone above the town. Instantly recognizable and stamped on everything from scarves to pencils, the peak stands as a misshapen monolith that blazes bright orange at dawn and occasionally is clear of clouds long enough to snap a picture. The Bahnhofstraße is populated in equal measure by ruddy outdoors-lovers and their shopping-bag-laden counterparts. The town keeps the peace with *Nachtruhe* (quiet hours) after 10pm and a ban on cars; raucous noise can result in a fine of 200-300SFr. The best way to escape crowds is to take a short hike or cable car ride up to Alpine meadows and splintered icefalls.

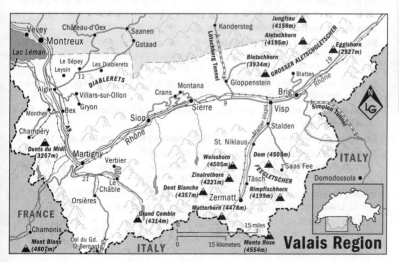

Valais Region

465

▐ TRANSPORTATION

The BVZ (☎ 921 41 11) runs **trains** from Zermatt to: Brig (1½hr.; 6am-9pm; 34SFr, round-trip 67SFr; if coming from Lausanne 73SFr/140SFr or Sion 47.20SFr/ 94SFr) via Visp and Stalden-Saas (1hr.; varying times; 29SFr, round-trip 58SFr; if coming from Saas Fee 41.40SFr/82.80SFr); Täsch (10min.; M-F every hr., Sa-Su every 20min.; 7.80SFr/15.60SFr).

To preserve the Alpine air, Zermatt has outlawed **cars** and **buses.** Locals in toy-like electric buggies alternately dodge and target pedestrians. The town of **Täsch,** one stop before Zermatt, has **parking garages** for 7.50SFr per day. The large out-door lot by the rail station costs 5-6.50SFr per day and has a reservation board for hotels in Zermatt. Zermatt is accessible only by the **HGB** (Matterhorn Gotthard Bahn) rail line (www.mgbahn.ch. SwissPass valid, **Eurail not valid.**) The station and tourist office have free phones to Zermatt's hotels and **hotel taxis,** which wait to round up guests after each train arrives.

▐ ▐ ORIENTATION AND PRACTICAL INFORMATION

Most shops, services, and restaurants stretch along Bahnhofstr. from the train station to the Hotel Weisshorn and the Café du Pont. Halfway between these, Hoffmattstr. heads to the left. Beside the church, Kirchstr. goes down the hill and across the river.

Tourist Office: Bahnhofpl. (☎ 966 81 00; www.zermatt.ch), in the station complex. Dis-tributes the free booklet *Prato Borni* that provides extremely detailed practical info for getting around the city, and the *Wanderkarte* hiking map (25.90SFr). Free **guided tour** W in summer 4:30-5:30pm. Meet at tourist office. Open mid-June to mid-Oct. M-F 8:30am-6pm, Sa 8:30am-6:30pm, Su 9:30am-noon and 4-6pm; mid-Oct. to mid-Dec. and May to mid-June M-F 8:30am-noon and 2-6pm, Sa 9:30am-noon; mid-Dec. to Apr. M-F 8:30am-noon and 2-6pm, Sa 8:30am-6:30pm, Su 9:30am-noon and 4-6pm.

Currency Exchange: Free at the train station (5:45am-8pm). **Banks** are generally open M-F 9am-noon and 2:30-6pm.

Luggage: Lockers for ski equipment downstairs in station (15SFr), at end of the tracks (6-8SFr), or storage at the ticket counter (5SFr per bag). Open daily 5:45am-8pm.

Work Opportunities: The North Wall Bar, ☎ 966 34 12. (See p. 469.)

English-Language Library: Bahnhofstr. 32. In the English Church on the hill behind the post office. Small collection of used novels loaned on the honor system. Open M-Tu and Th-F 4-8pm.

Laundry: Womy Express, inside the Co-op Complex across from the tourist office. 5SFr per kg. Open M-F 8:30am-12:30pm and 1:30-6:30pm, Sa 8:30am-noon.

Weather Conditions: ☎ 162 or check the window of the *Bergführerbüro.* **Winter Ava-lanche Information** ☎ 187.

Emergencies: Police ☎ 117. **Fire** ☎ 118. **Ambulance/24hr. Alpine Rescue** ☎ 144.

Pharmacy: Pharmacie Internationale Zermatt (☎ 966 27 27), Bahnhofstr. to right of station. Open M-Sa 8:30am-noon and 2-6:30pm, Su 11am-noon and 5-6pm. Emer-gency service for 20-30SFr surcharge depending on time.

Internet Access: Ask at the tourist office for a list of public access points. Most cost 15-20SFr per hr. **Stoked** (☎ 967 70 20), on Hoffmatstr. next to the tennis courts, charges 12SFr per hr.

Post Office: Bahnhofstr., in Arcade Mont-Cervin, 5min. to the right of the station. **ATM** and **Western Union.** Open M-F 8:30am-noon and 1:45-6pm, Sa 8:30-11am.

Postal Code: CH-3920.

ACCOMMODATIONS AND CAMPING

Climbers, hikers, and snowboarders raise the demand for budget beds in Zermatt. Finding a dorm bed on the spot can be tough in July and August and mid-February to mid-March. Many hotels in winter and all chalets in summer only accept bookings for a week at a time. Some campers are thus tempted to sleep illegally in the wide-open spaces above town, a practice that can incur fines in the 300SFr range.

Hotel Bahnhof (☎967 24 06; www.hotelbahnhof.com), on Bahnhofstr. to the left of the station, is a climber's hangout. Renovated rooms provide hotel housing at hostel rates. Ask for a view of the Matterhorn. No breakfast, but one of the few places with an extensive kitchen and large dining room. Laundry 6SFr. Dorms 30SFr; singles 60SFr, with shower 71SFr; doubles 88SFr/99SFr; quads 175SFr. MC/V. ❸

Jugendherberge (HI), Winkelmatten (☎967 23 20; www.youthhostel.ch/zermatt). Turn left at the church, cross the river, take the 2nd street to the right (at the Jugendherberge sign) and the left fork in front of Hotel Rhodania. At this recently renovated hostel, tourists get a great deal. Unobstructed views of the Matterhorn from bedroom windows, friendly staff, a giant outdoor chess set, ping-pong, foosball, and **Internet** (5SF per 15min.). Breakfast, hearty dinner (including fondue on Su and vegetarian on request), and sheets included. Laundry 8SFr. Reception 7-10am and 4-10:30pm. Closed May. Dorms 52SFr; 2 doubles 122SFr. Non-members add 6SFr. AmEx/DC/MC/V. ❸

Hotel Mischabel (☎967 11 31; www.zermatt.ch/mischabel), right off of Hofmattstr. This hotel creaks, but reassuringly. Straightforward TV room downstairs. The bedrooms, though plain, are not unpleasant. Rooms with

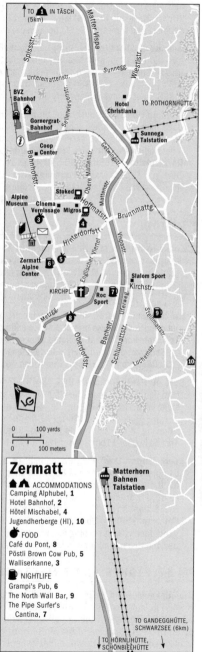

Zermatt

🏠🏕 ACCOMMODATIONS
Camping Alphubel, **1**
Hotel Bahnhof, **2**
Hôtel Mischabel, **4**
Jugendherberge (HI), **10**

🍴 FOOD
Café du Pont, **8**
Pöstli Brown Cow Pub, **5**
Walliserkanne, **3**

🍸 NIGHTLIFE
Grampi's Pub, **6**
The North Wall Bar, **9**
The Pipe Surfer's Cantina, **7**

VALAIS

balconies overlooking the Matterhorn available. Breakfast included. Reception 7:30am-10pm. Check-out 11am. Open mid-June to mid-Oct. and mid-Dec. to late Apr. Singles, doubles, and triples 67-92SFr per person; singles with bath 77-92SFr. MC/V. ❸

Camping Alphubel (☎967 36 35), in Täsch. From the station, cross the parking lot and turn right in front of the tourist office past the river, then right across the railroad tracks. Showers included. Reception 8am-noon and 2-8pm. Open May to mid-Oct. 5SFr per adult, 2.50SFr per child age 6-16, 5.50SFr per tent, 5.50SFr per car, 6.80SFr per caravan. Electricity 3SFr. ❶

Mountain Huts: The tourist office provides a list of private huts in the Zermatt area. A full day's hike from Zermatt, they offer a good deal for serious climbers and hikers. All huts are open July-Aug., are accessible to walkers if there's no snow, and include breakfast unless otherwise noted. Try **Schönbielhütte** (2694m; ☎967 13 54 or 47 62; 35.50SFr), **Rothornhütte** (3198m; ☎967 20 43 or 16 20; fax 16 39; 32SFr; see the **Grandchild Hike,** p. 471), the crowded **Gandegghütte** (3029m; ☎079 607 88 68 or 967 21 12; fax 967 21 49; 26SFr; no breakfast), or **Hörnlihütte,** also called **Berghaus Matterhorn.** (3260m; ☎967 22 64; 43SFr; see **Hörnlihütte Hike,** p. 471.) ❷

⬛ FOOD

It's easy to find an inexpensive meal in Zermatt. Revelers flood the streets after dark, sipping whiskey to warm up after a day in the snow. The **Co-op** is across from the station. (Open M-F 8:15am-12:15pm and 1:45-6:30pm, Sa 8:15am-12:15pm and 1:45-6pm.) A **Migros** is on Hoffmatstr. across from the tennis courts. (Open M-F 8:30am-12:30pm and 2-6:30pm, Sa 8:30am-12:30pm and 2-6pm.)

Walliserkanne (☎966 46 10), Bahnhofstr., next to the post office. Looks upscale inside, but offers filling Swiss fare at down-to-earth prices. The menu includes *Käseschnitte mit Schinken und Tomate* (toasted cheese with ham and tomato; 19SFr) and fondues (23SFr). *Menüs* (28-42SFr) with vegetarian options also available. Pizzas for take out (15-18SFr) from 11:30am-11pm. Open 9am-midnight. MC/V. ❸

Café du Pont, Kirchpl. (☎967 43 43). Zermatt's oldest restaurant, filled with photos from Zermatt's history, attracts a similarly aged clientele. Multilingual menus burnt into slabs of wood hanging on the wall list stick-to-your-ribs Swiss dishes like *Raclette* (7.50SFr), *Rösti* (11-15SFr), and *fondue du Pont* (22SFr). The *Valais Platte* offers a sampling of regional meats (24SFr). Sandwiches 6.50SFr. Open June-Oct. and Dec.-Apr. daily 9am-11pm; food served 11am-10pm. Wheelchair accessible. ❷

Pöstli "Brown Cow" Pub, Bahnhofstr. (☎967 19 31), is in the Great Swiss Disaster complex at the Hotel de la Post. The clientele of lively English-speaking locals comes for the whimsical cow-pattern decor and greasy-spoon food. Try the potato skins (9.50SFr) or chomp on a burger or Vegi Burger (11-15SFr). In the summer cool off with a frappe (6.50SFr) or munch on one of the season's special salads (7-14SFr). Heineken 3.40SFr. Open daily 9am-2am. The rest of the complex offers a 3-story spaghetti factory with evening films and disco, a jazz bar with live music, an underground bar and disco, and a posh hotel. No cover. Discos open until 3:30am. ❷

⬛ ⬛ SIGHTS AND ENTERTAINMENT

The **Alpine Museum,** near the post office, exhibits broken ropes, mangled shoes, and bashed-in lanterns found with the corpses of those who failed to master local peaks, as well as displays of the flora, fauna, and geology of the area. Special attention is given to the first ascent of the Matterhorn on July 14, 1865, when over half the team was killed on the way down. A haunting photograph is all that remains of one victim,

Lord Alfred Douglas (the love of Oscar Wilde's life), whose remains were never found. Remains of the Matterhorn's victims are buried in the cemetery next to the church with picks and ropes carved into their gravestones. The museum also displays relief models of the Matterhorn and the mountain region around Zermatt. (☎967 41 00. Open early July to mid-Aug. daily 10am-noon and 3-6pm; June to early July and mid-Aug. to Oct. daily 10am-noon and 4-6pm; late Dec. to May M-F and Su 4:30-6:30pm. 8SFr, children under 16 2SFr.)

The **Cinema Vernissage** (☎967 66 36), next to Julen Sports on Hoffmattstr., screens one or two nearly new releases per night (M-Sa), usually in English. Mid-August brings the **Alpine Folklore Parade,** when locals take a break from their mountain chores and dust off their *Alphorns* and *Lederhosen*. Pick up a complete program at the tourist office a week before the Parade. The Roman Catholic church hosts **classical music concerts** (25SFr) from mid-July to early August.

■ NIGHTLIFE

▨ The Pipe Surfer's Cantina, on Kirchstr. (☎213 38 07; www.gozermatt.com/thepipe), before the river on the right, is the nightly site of the craziest beach party in the Alps. Owner Nikk, generous with the free shots (stop by in the afternoon for a 2-for-1 coupon or get one at the HI hostel), keeps customers rolling with his hilarious stories of late-night adventures and sound advice on everything Zermatt, and has recently altered the Pipe's image into that of a bistro, with excellent food and a still-lively clientele. The staff are all experts in something, providing a variety of suggested adventure outings and good company (see **Outdoor Activities,** p. 470). Don't leave without downing a shot of Moo, the made-on-the-premises caramel vodka (6SFr). Frozen margaritas 6SFr. Beer 4SFr, 6SFr. In winter, special Bum's Play plate includes beer and entrée. Reggae every night after 11pm. Happy hour daily 6-7pm. Must be over 16 after 8pm. Open daily 3:30pm-2:30am. Food served until 10:30pm.

The North Wall Bar (☎966 34 12). Take the 2nd right past the river on Kirchstr., en route to the youth hostel, to this English-speaking climber's haunt and workman's bar, where skiing and mountaineering videos play every evening alongside the dart games. This is the place to scrounge a job in Zermatt—ask the staff, who also give hiking advice. The kitchen will serve you "the hottest pizza in the Alps" (12SFr, plus 1SFr per fancy topping; options include mussels, corn, broccoli, or egg), while the bar serves "the coldest beer in the Alps" (5SFr for .5L). Open daily mid-June to Sept. and mid-Dec. to Apr. 6:30pm-midnight; later in winter. Pizza served until 10pm.

COW FIGHT!

For centuries, Valaisian breeders have raised cows in hopes of achieving success at the annual cow fights *(Combats de Reines),* a regional spectacle that is the source of much pride. The highest bovine reverence has been accorded to the *Heren* strain, valued for its fine milk, meat, and particularly mountain-adapted nature. *Heren* females have an aggressive streak that reveals itself in their violent eyes. There can only be one alpha female, and the cows battle for the role. When facing off, combatants exhibit a repertoire of well-documented moves and behaviors, from angry mooing, preliminary head movements, and *escarpier* (pawing the ground), to head-on and lateral attacks.

After a mighty struggle, one of the ladies asserts herself, and the other one admits defeat, either by lying down or by running away. The winner receives an extra-special bell and some salt from her owner, along with the distinction of being *la reine* (the queen), the true honor every virtuous cow desires.

Catch the cow fights in mid-October during the first weekend of the Foire du Valais in Martigny.

Grampi's Pub, Bahnhofstr. 70 (☎967 77 75 or 417 99 85; fax 71 13), across from Pöstli Pub. Centrally located bar thumps with pop dance music. Draft beer 4SFr; bottled beer 6-8SFr; "lady killers" 11-13SFr. Pizzas 20SFr. Open 8:30am-2am, downstairs bar until 4am (DJ 9pm-3:30am). Upstairs Italian restaurant 6pm-2am; food until 1am.

◪ OUTDOOR ACTIVITIES

The Zermatt Alpine Center, which houses both the **Bergführerbüro** (Mountain Guide's Office; ☎24 60; www.zermatt.ch/alpincenter) and the **Skischulbüro** (Ski School Office; ☎966 24 66; www.zermatt.ch/skischule), is past the post office from the station. Pick up detailed weather forecasts, ski passes, and information on guided climbing expeditions there. (*Bergführerbüro* open July-Sept. M-F 8:30am-noon and 4-7pm, Sa 3:30-7pm; Su 10am-noon and 3:30-7pm; late Dec. to mid-May daily 5-7pm.) Adventure-seekers looking to take home their vacation should contact the **Freeride Film Factory** (☎213 38 07), operated by the Pipe Surfer's Cantina. Skilled guides offer custom hiking, biking, and climbing expeditions for lower prices (160-250SFr) than the Ski School and also give you a 15-20min. videotape of your expedition. (See **Pipe Surfer's Cantina,** p. 469.) The **Air Taxi Zermatt** (☎967 97 87) sends tandem-paragliders airborne at starting points from 2300m to 4100m (150-190SFr including transportation) and offers a paragliding school. The glitzier hotels have **swimming pools;** Hotel Christiania, Wiestistr., has the biggest one. Follow the right bank of the river to the left past the Rothorn/Sunnegga cable railway station. (Hotel ☎967 80 00. Pool access 10SFr, children 6SFr. Open daily 8-10:30am and 2-8pm, Th until 9pm. Sauna 20SFr.)

SKIING. Seventy-three lifts, 14,200m of combined elevation, and 245km of prepared runs make Zermatt one of the world's most extensive ski centers. Serious skiers will find challenges on **Europe's longest run**—the 13km trail from Klein Matterhorn to Zermatt. The town also has more summer ski trails than any other Alpine ski resort—36km^2 of year-round runs between 2900 and 3900m. In the summer, the **Skischulbüro** (above) offers group five-day skiing (295SFr) and snowboarding (330SFr) classes. Individual, one-day, and summer ski/snowboard lessons are available. **4Synergies** also offers ski instruction privately or in groups. (☎967 70 20; www.4synergies.com. Groups 95SFr per day, 410SFr for 5 days.) **Stoked Swiss Snowboard School** provides qualified instructors for downhill rides. (☎967 87 88; www.stoked.ch. Groups 50SFr per half-day; 200SFr for 5 half-days. Open M-Sa 9am-noon and 2-6pm.) Zermatt's **ski passes** operate on a regional system during the **summer** (late Apr.-Oct.). Passes are available for any of the regions (Matterhorn, Gornergrat, or Sunnegga complexes). The Matterhorn region costs 50SFr per day (children 25SFr). The Klein Matterhorn/Trockener Steg sub-region is now combined with Italy's Mt. Cervinia (1 day 56SFr, children 28SFr). From November to the end of April, a combo pass is available for all three regions (1 day 72SFr, 7 days 338SFr). For **ski and mountain bike rental,** try **Julen Sport** (☎967 43 40), on Hoffmattstr. (Open M-Sa 8:30am-noon and 2-6:30pm. 38-50SFr per day, 28-38SFr per half-day. MC/V.) Its companion, **Roc Sport** (☎967 87 88), on Kirchstr., rents the same equipment, but it's best to head straight to Julen. Rental prices for skis and boots are set throughout Zermatt (skis and snowboards 28-50SFr per day, boots 15-19SFr per day).

CLIMBING. The only company to lead formal expeditions above Zermatt is the **Bergführerbüro.** Groups go up the Breithorn (150SFr), Pollux (260SFr), and Castor (270SFr) daily in summer. Prices do not include equipment, insurance, hut accommodations, or lifts to the departure points. For equipment rental, see **Hiking** below. Climbing the Matterhorn is expensive and requires a guide, perfect skiing condition, a 4am start, and extensive rock-climbing experience (at least PD+).

HIKING. Outstanding walks leave from Zermatt in every direction. Although most paths are well marked, a proper **topographic map** (25.90SFr from the tourist office) is essential for safety and enhances the experience. Available at the tourist office for 2SFr, and at some hotels for free, is a more basic map of hiking routes around Zermatt, which is more than sufficient for most day-hikers. Lifts and railways to the south and east can shorten difficult climbs. (25% discount on many lifts with SwissPass, **Eurail generally not valid.**) Prudent walkers come prepared (see **Health,** p. 20); Zermatt is particularly prone to sudden electrical storms. Check the weather forecast in the Bergführerbüro before departure. Hiking boots can be rented at **Matterhorn Sport,** Bahnhofstr. (☎967 29 56), which also rents out climbing equipment; **Glacier Sport,** Bahnhofstr. (☎967 27 14), across from Walliserkanne; or **Burgener Sport,** on Bahnhofstr., next to Grampi's Pub. (☎967 27 94. 1-day rentals 14SFr, 7 days 52SFr, 14 days 80SFr. All stores open 8am-noon and 2-6:30 or 7pm.)

Hörnlihütte Hike (10hr. round-trip, 5hr. round-trip with cable car). The **Hörnlihütte** serves as the base camp for the most popular route up the Matterhorn and is a good platform for watching climbers claw their way up the ridge. The 1600m ascent to the hut is for the fit and well-booted only (a walking stick is recommended); a **cable car** from the far end of town to the **Schwarzsee** via Furi (2584m) saves 900m of climbing. (Schedule varies throughout the year; ask the tourist office. 20.50SFr, round-trip 33SFr.) Leave Zermatt along the left bank of the Matter Vispa. Approximately 2km from Zermatt, a wide track marked "Zum See, Schwarzsee and Hörnlihütte" leads down and left across the river. Follow the 3hr. path as it zigzags steeply up to the tiny Schwarzsee, passing gorges on the left. From the Schwarzsee, the path becomes rockier and wilder as it joins the true northeast ridge of the Matterhorn, climbing gently at first but ending in a merciless, exposed *arête* (sharp ridge) by the buildings at Hörnli. **Casual hikers *cannot* continue above the hut.** More than 500 people have died above this point. For a different descent, bear right at the *Schwarzsee* to the Furgg cable car terminus and follow path to town. It traverses a steep cliff but has even closer views of the gorges carved by the **Gornergletscher.**

The Gornergrat (numerous hikes possible). The Gornergrat swarms with as many as 5000 visitors per day because it provides the best views of the Matterhorn. The **train,** which departs opposite Zermatt's main station (7am-11pm), ascends to the **Gornergrat** (3090m; 41SFr, round-trip 67SFr) via **Riffelalp** (2211m; 17.20SFr/32SFr), **Riffelberg** (2582m; 27SFr/46SFr), and **Rotenboden** (2815m; 34SFr/58SFr), all of which are trailheads. From the Gornergrat, hikes descend to the wide, flat **Gornergletscher** and along the ridge toward the **Stockhorn** (3532m). A cable car traverses this distance (12SFr each way). Rotenboden is on the other side of Stockhorn. From Rotenboden, hikers can divert to the Monte Rosa hut (5hr. to the hut and back) by following the glacier. Each destination provides a closer encounter with the ice at the cost of losing a fraction of the panorama. Routes from the Riffelalp station descend to Zermatt by following the side of the mountain around to the *Grünsee,* facing the snout of the **Findelngletscher,** then crossing the river and returning to Zermatt by way of the **Moosjesee** and the **Leisee,** 2 small pools that provide a beautiful foreground to the Matterhorn.

Granny Hike, to Zmutt (1hr. round-trip). This easy hike offers the most dramatic encounter with the Matterhorn's north face. The path is wide, clear, and well marked. From Zermatt, follow Bahnhofstr. past the church, then follow the sign to the right. The steady slope climbs through the Arolla pines to the weathered chalets of the hamlet of Zmutt. The path, granting views of the Hörnli ridge and the Matterhorn, levels out as it continues through the meadows above a small reservoir. The Matterhorn's north wall, which drops 200m with an average gradient well over 45°, gradually comes into view above Zmutt.

Grandchild Hike (10hr. round-trip). If you want to make the Granny Hike more challenging (well worth the extra effort, since the views get drastically better as you ascend), the Grandchild Hike continues on to the **Schönbielhütte** (2694m; 4hr. from Zmutt), an ideal spot for lunchtime carbo-loading of pasta or *Rösti,* or an overnight stop. The hike becomes more difficult as it ascends past lakes and waterfalls at the outlet of the rock-strewn **Zmuttgletscher.** On the return, the valley frames the Rimpfischhorn (4199m) and Strahlhorn (4190m). The 25km hike covers 1050m of gentle elevation.

VALAIS

SAAS FEE ☎ 027

Saas Fee, the "Pearl of the Alps," is one of Switzerland's most dramatic sites. The thirteen 4000m peaks that form a semicircle above the town peer down ominously. The glacial ice of the **Feegletscher**, "fairy glacier," comes so low that you can visit the frozen giant on a 30min. evening stroll. To protect its alpine glory, this resort town banned cars from its streets in 1951. Because only the faint whizzing of electrically powered minivans and trucks disturbs the silence, Saas Fee offers visitors a relaxing and quiet Alpine retreat (or else). Town officials prohibit disturbing "the fairy-like charm of Saas Fee" after 10pm (noisemakers are fined 200SFr).

◪ TRANSPORTATION

A **post bus** runs (every hr. 5:35am-7:35pm) to Brig (1¼hr.; 17.20SFr, round-trip 34.40SFr) via Saas Grund (10min.; 3SFr/6SFr); Stalden Saas (40min.; 12.40SFr/24.80SFr), connecting to Zermatt (41.40SFr/82.80SFr, reservations required); and Visp (50min.; 15.20SFr/30.40SFr), where trains connect to Lausanne, Sion, and the rest of Valais. Reserve a seat on all buses starting at Saas Fee at least 2hr. before departure in the high-season. Call ☎958 11 45 or drop by the bus station (open 7:30am-12:35pm and 1:15-6:35pm). For a **taxi**, call ☎958 11 35 57 33 44. **Parking** is available in the lot across the street to the right of the tourist office. (1 day 11SFr, with guest card after 2nd day 7.50SFr; 1 week with guest card 56SFr.)

◪ ❼ ORIENTATION AND PRACTICAL INFORMATION

The **tourist office,** opposite the bus station, dispenses seasonal information, hiking advice, and useful town maps. They also organize free weekly tours of the village. Call for date and times. Outside, a kiosk provides hotel information and a free, direct phone for reservations. (☎958 18 58, reservations 958 18 68; www.saasfee.ch. Open July to mid-Sept. and mid-Dec. to mid-Apr. M-Sa 8:30am-noon and 2-6pm; Su 10am-noon and 4-6pm; closed Su in May.) The bus depot has small **lockers** (2SFr) and **luggage storage** (2SFr). For a **weather report,** call ☎162. In case of **emergency,** call ☎117. **Vallesia Apotheke** pharmacy is down the hill from the tourist office at the main street. (☎957 26 18, for emergencies call 079 417 67 18. Open M-Sa 8:30am-noon and 2-6:30pm, Su 4-6pm.) **Cyber Lion** in Haus Waldrain, left past the Migros, offers **Internet access.** (☎947 39 61. Open daily 8am-11pm. 5SFr per 20min.) There is also access at the **Freizeitzentrun Bielen,** next to the post office. (Open daily 2-9pm. 2.50SFr for 15min.) Or ask at **Hotel Dom** (☎957 51 01), on the main street past the church. There is a **post office** with public **fax** and **ATM** at the bus depot. (Open M-F 8:15am-noon and 2-6pm, Sa 8:15am-noon.) **Postal Code:** CH-3906.

◪ ACCOMMODATIONS

Be sure to request a Saas Valley visitor's card after checking into your hotel for discounts on everything from local bus service to concerts. **Hotel Garni Bergheimat ❸,** in the center of town, offers clean mid-sized rooms at a reasonable rate. Renovated rooms offer all the luxuries: TV, telephone, balcony, and shower. Unrenovated rooms are more charming but lack amenities such as showers. (☎957 20 30; www.bergheimat.ch. Hearty buffet breakfast included. Renovated rooms 85SFr winter; 70SFr summer. Unrenovated rooms 70SFr/55SFr.) Those willing to sacrifice comfort can find bargains in hotel basements. **Hotel Garni Imseng ❷,** across the street from Feehof, has seven rows of three-high bunks, with no space in between. However, the hotel is clean and frequently empty, and there is an impressive breakfast buffet. Rooms upstairs in the hotel have TV and leather couches, but cost more. (☎958 12 58; www.saas-fee.ch/hotel.imseng. Breakfast and lockers included with dorms. All hotel rooms have satellite TV, telephone, and a safe; most have a balcony. Sheets 5SFr. Reception 8:30am-noon and 2-7pm. Dorms 35SFr; singles 108SFr, 123SFr winter; doubles with bath 188/ 219. Hotel wheelchair accessible. Dorms are not.) **Mountain huts** are a bold alternative to staying in Saas Fee proper. Breakfast is always included. The **Mischabel** ❷ (3329m; ☎957 11 17; dinner available, 28SFr), **Hoh-Saas** ❸ (3098m; ☎957 17 13; 36SFr), and **Weissmieshütte** (2726m; ☎957 25 54; 30SFr, dinner included) above Saas Grund are all accessible from July to September. It is a good idea to contact the hut caretaker about vacancies and opening hours before setting out. The Saas Fee tourist office (see **Practical Information,** p. 472) and *Bergführerbüro* (see **Hiking,** below) have more details.

◗ FOOD

Spaghetteria da Rasso ❷, on the main street under the Hotel Britania, has a shady terrace where accordionists occasionally entertain the crowd. Two or more can try the house special with salad, unlimited pasta, and four different sauces for 25SFr. (☎957 15 26. Open Su-M and W-Sa late June to mid-Oct. 9am-11:30pm; mid-Oct. to Apr. 10am-11:30pm. AmEx/MC/V.) Though it's easy to find Swiss specialties around town, the **Restaurant Chämi-Stube** ❸, a little farther down the hill from the church, has a unique, candlelit atmosphere. It serves a variety of *Rösti* for 14-16.50SFr, and a Valaisian fondue for 25SFr. Interestingly, there's also Mexican food (tortillas 17-28SFr). (☎957 17 47. Open Dec.-May and mid-June to Oct. 9am-11:30pm. Warm food 11:30am-2pm and 6-9pm. AmEx/MC/V.) Most of the **supermarkets** in the center of town have the same hours. (M-F 8:15am-12:15pm and 2:15-6:30pm, Sa until 5pm.) Every Thursday mid-July to mid-August (2-6pm), there is a **market** on the main street of Saas Fee.

◢ OUTDOOR ACTIVITIES

SKIING. During the **summer,** two cable cars to **Felskinn** (3000m; 7:30am-4:15pm; 26SFr, round-trip 34SFr) and an underground funicular, the "Metro Alpin," farther to **Allanin** (3500m; 7:45am-4pm; an additional 27SFr, round-trip 36SFr) enable **skiers** to enjoy 20km of runs and a stupendous alpine view. In the winter, an immense network of lifts opens from Allanin (day ski passes 59SFr, children 35SFr; 6 days 27SFr/16SFr; 13 days 480SFr/288SFr). The **Ski School,** across the street from the church, offers group skiing and snowboarding lessons mid-December to April, private lessons for advanced skiers, and snowboarding during the summer. (☎957 23 48; www.saas-fee.ch/skischool. Skiing 46SFr per 3hr., 172SFr per wk.; snowboarding 43SFr per 2hr., 158SFr per wk. Slight reductions available in late Jan. Open M-F 8:30-noon and 2:30-6pm, Sa-Su 4-6pm.) Many stores **rent skis.** Stores in the **Swiss Rent-A-Sport System** (look for the big red "S" logo) offer three grades of equipment (skis and snowboards 28-50SFr per day, 6 days 109-190SFr; boots 15-19SFr/56-80SFr). You can call ahead to reserve equipment; call or fax the main Swiss Rent-A-Sport outlet in town, **Anthamatten Sport Mode,** located across from the Spaghetteria. (☎958 19 18; fax 957 19 70. Open daily May-June and Sept.-Nov. 9am-noon and 2-6pm; July-Aug. 8:30am-noon and 1:30-6:30pm; Dec.-Apr. 8am-7pm. AmEx/DC/MC/V.)

HIKING. The **Bergführerbüro** (Mountain Guides' Office), housed in the same building as the ski school, leads climbs to a number of 4000m summits. (☎/fax 957 44 64; www.rhone.ch/mountainlife. Open July-Apr. M-Sa 9am-noon and 3-6pm.) Day tours run 50-200SFr per person. Hikers have 280km of marked trails from which to

VALAIS

choose. Maps at the tourist office are 26.80SFr, or ask for the free brochure with tour description. The **Saas Valley Hiking Pass** (171SFr, family rate 345SFr), available at the tourist office or any cable car station, provides access for one week to all cable cars and post buses in the valley and entrance to the ice pavilion at **Mittelallanin**, the **Bielen Recreation Center,** and museums. Most lifts close from May to early June and from mid-October to mid-December.

Mischabelhütte Hike (full-day, 1550m ascent, easy). A steep trail leads up to the Mischabelhütte (3329m), the best walking-accessible panorama of Saas Fee's natural amphitheater. From the pharmacy on the main street, turn right after the church and take the right fork after 100m. Check for snow cover before departing, as the last part of the hike is rocky and highly unpleasant with any hint of ice.

Glacier Hike (half-day, moderate). This lovely half-day trek begins with a cable-car ride to **Plattjen** (2570m). From there a path leads to the right and then left after 5min. to views of the Dom and Lezspitze. From the summit, the trail descends for 15min., then heads left around the amphitheater, spiraling slowly down below the **Feegletscher.** The view opens up as the path drops to the **Gletschersee** (1910m) at the glacier tip. From there, the trail gently follows the left bank of the outlet stream back to Saas Fee.

Hannig Hike (round-trip 2½hr.). This easy walk from the church to Hannig follows a trail that begins level (30min.) and gets steeper as it moves into the woods. Follow the "Hannig" signs all the way. On the way up, there are opportunities for close encounters with goats and pigs as the path passes through the small farms on the hill. Stop at the Mannigalp hut for fresh milk and cheese from the cows and goats you saw along the way. After an hour, the path splits into the Hannig trail and the longer, more scenic Hannig Waldweg trail. From the restaurant at the summit, it is possible to continue the trail toward Melchbode and back to Saas Fee or take the **Sonnenbahn Hannig** cable car (15SFr, children 7.50SFr; 25% discount with SwissPass) that descends to a site above the Spaghetteria.

OTHER ACTIVITIES. The **Bielen Recreation Center,** next to the bus station, has a **swimming pool** and **jacuzzi,** and also offers **massages,** indoor **tennis,** a **sauna,** and **badminton.** (☎957 24 75. Open daily June 1-9pm; July-Oct. 10am-9pm. Access to pool, jacuzzi, and steam baths: 13SFr, children 8.50SFr, with guest card 12SFr.) The Mountain Guide Office organizes outings to a nearby gorge every Monday, Wednesday, and Friday in summer, and every Thursday in winter. Scuttle along water-carved rock faces (safety equipment 95SFr). **Feeblitz,** beside the Alpine-Express, offers a self-controlled roller-coaster ride. Riders control single cars that skate along a winding metal track down the mountain. (☎957 31 11. Open daily June noon-5pm; July and Aug. 10am-6pm; Sept.-Oct. Sa-Su 10am-6pm; Nov. F-Su 1-5pm; Dec.-Apr. F-Su noon-6pm. 6SFr, under 16 4SFr, discount with visitors' card.)

For two weeks in mid-August, Saas Fee hosts the **Musica Romantica** classical music festival, which brings artists from all over Europe. (www.saas-fee.ch/romantica. Symphony concert tickets 25-65SFr, recital tickets 16-40SFr, week-long ticket 130-210SFr, children under 16 half-off.) Contact the tourist office for a list of performers and to purchase tickets. Classical music lovers will also appreciate the **International Alpine Music Festival,** a week-long event at the end of July that attracts performers from across the world. Contact the tourist office for 2005 dates.

BRIG ☎027

A simple town, Brig (pop. 11,500) aptly takes its name from the word for "bridge," providing access to the most famous resorts in Valais. Visitors can enjoy a quiet day visiting Brig's many churches and the *Stockalperschloß* (a Baroque castle in the old city), but the best reason to come is to catch a train or cable car to a nearby glacier or mountain peak.

▣ TRANSPORTATION AND PRACTICAL INFORMATION

Brig is accessible by **train** from: Interlaken Ost via Spiez (1½-2hr., every hr. 5:33am-11:37pm, 40SFr); Martigny (50min., every hr. 6:54am-12:54am, 23SFr); Sion (45min., 2 or 3 per hr. 6:04am-1:09am, 17.20SFr). The **BVZ train** runs between Brig and Zermatt (1½hr.; every hr. 5:10am-7:23pm, June-Oct. extra trains and a bus at 8:25pm; 34SFr; Swisspass valid, Eurail not valid). The last return train from Zermatt from June to October is at 9:10pm (Nov.-Apr. 7:52pm). The **Post Bus** leaves for Saas Fee every hr. 6:15am-8:15pm and returns 5:35am-7:35pm. Reservations are required for return trips (1¼hr., 17.20SFr). The **train station** is open Monday through Saturday 6:30am-8:30pm and Su 7:30am-8pm and offers **bike rentals** (30SFr per day, 21SFr per half-day), **luggage storage** (7SFr per bag), **lockers** (4-6SFr), and **currency exchange** (M-F 7am-7pm, Sa 7am-5pm, Su 8-11:30am and 1-5pm). The **tourist information office** is on the second level of the train station. (☎921 60 30; www.brig.ch. Open Oct.-June M-F 8:30am-6pm, Sa 8:30am-1pm; July-Sept. Sa 9am-6pm, Su 9am-1pm.) Other services include: **Internet,** at the Good Night Inn across the river from Sebastians Pl. (1SFr per 10min.); **police** (☎922 41 60); **hospital** (emergencies ☎922 33 33); **taxis** (☎0800 800 608); and a **post office** across the street from the station. (Open M-F 7:45am-noon and 1:30-6:15pm, Sa 8:30-11:30am.) **Postal Code:** 3900.

▌ ACCOMMODATIONS

Budget options in Brig are hard to find. For only a bit more than some hostels, **Pension Post ❷**, Furkastr. 23, is one of the best deals in town. Go right from the station onto Viktoriastr. and then left onto Furkastr., and walk 5min. Spacious, attractive rooms with clean, inviting beds come with or without in-room showers. (☎924 45 54; fax 45 53. Sheets, towels, and breakfast included. Reception M-F 6am-11pm, Sa 7am-6pm. Dorms 35SFr; singles 40SFr, with shower 50SFr; doubles 80SFr/100SFr.) For those with a larger budget, **Hotel Du Pont ❸**, on the far side of Sebastians Pl. adjacent to the river, 5min. up Bahnhofstr. from the station, has aging but clean rooms in its old wing and luxurious doubles in the newer one. (☎923 15 02; dupont.brig@datacomm.ch. Singles 55-75SFr, with shower 95-130SFr; doubles 100-130SFr/150-210SFr. AmEx/DC/MC/V.) **Camping Geschina ❶**, just past the local swimming pool 15min. up Bahnhofstr. on Geshinaweg. off Neue Simplonstr., sports lines of trees between wheel-to-wheel RVs and arranges hikes or visits to cheese makers for its guests. A small grocery store is located near the reception. (☎923 06 88; geshina@campings.ch. Reception 8:30am-noon and 4:30-8pm. Open late Apr. to mid-Oct. 5.50SFr per adult; 3SFr per child; 5SFr per tent.)

▐ FOOD

The main street is dotted with high-priced hotel restaurants, but try **Walliser Weinstube ❷**, Bahnhofstr. 9, for Swiss classics at reasonable prices, including *Käseschnitte* for 14-17SFr and *Rösti* for 11-15SFr. (☎923 14 28; www.walliser-weinstube.ch. Open M-F 6:30am-11pm, Sa-Su 9am-midnight.) Past Sebastians Pl. on Alte Simplonstr., **Tea-Room Bistro Viva ❷** offers traditional fare in a non-traditional setting. Try the *Älpler macaroni* (12SFr) and apple *Strudel* with ice cream (6SFr) in a modern room with that new-car feel. (☎924 56 03. Open Su 8:30am-1pm, M-F 7:30am-6:30pm.) **Molino Pizzeria Ristorante ❸**, at the intersection of Furkastr. and Bahnhofstr., is truly Italian, with Romanesque statues decorating the dining area, an ivy-covered terrace, and 14 kinds of pizza (15.20-25.50SFr), soups, and pastas. (☎923 65 56; fax 924 43 13. Open M-Sa 11:15am-2pm and 5:30-

11pm, F-Sa until midnight, Su 11:15am-11pm. AmEx/MC/V.) **Migros,** left from station and across the street, has a grocery store and restaurant. (Store open M 1:30-6:30pm, Tu-F 8:15am-6:30pm, Sa 7:45am-4pm. Restaurant open M-F 7:30am-6:30pm, Sa 7:30am-4pm.) The **Co-op,** across the river from Sebastians Pl. on Gilserallee offers cheap groceries and a bistro as well. (Open Su 7:30am-4pm, M 1:30-6:30pm, Tu-F 8am-6:30pm.) There's a **farmer's market** every Saturday 8am-noon.

⚑ OUTDOOR ACTIVITIES

Brig provides easy access by bus or train to major ski areas including **Zermatt, Crans-Montana, Riederalp, Bettmeralp and Piesheralp, Rosswald, Belalp,** and **Saas Fee.** In the summer, head to one of the nearby towns for cable-car access to the newly established **Aletsch Nature Reserve** and view 24km of flowing ice, the longest glacier in Switzerland. Ask at the tourist office for more details about the reserve or for suggested **hikes.** Brig lies 2.5km from **Brigerbad,** home to Europe's first Thermal-Grotto pool and the largest **open-air thermal pools** in Switzerland. (Open May-Sept. daily 9:30am-6pm.) The last weekend in August brings the **Schäferwochenende Belalp,** a festival with nearly 2000 sheep herded down from the hills. (☎921 60 40; www.belalp.ch.) If you're spending the day in the city, visit the Baroque **Stockalperschloß** (Stockalper Castle) on Alte Simplonstr. The impressive castle was restored between 1955 and 1961, and now houses a theater and art gallery in its cellar. Visit the museum across the street or walk around the formal garden and park. (☎921 60 30. Open May-Oct. Tu-Su 9:15-11:30am and 1:15-4:30pm. Tours, in German, meet at the museum. Brochures available. Open Oct.-May 9:30am-3:30pm; June-Sept. 9:30am-4:30pm. 7SFr, children 3SFr.) It's also nice to visit the **Kollegiumskirche** for a view of the town. Friday evenings in summer bring live music to Sebastians Pl. Wednesday nights there are open-air movies in the courtyard of the *Stockalperschloß.* (Mid-July to mid-August. Free.)

SION ☎027

Surrounded by the glitz of winter-driven mountain towns, Sion, the capital of Valais canton, is a summer city. Behind the day-to-day business of the main streets lies the cobblestone-lined old city, overlooked by two looming hillside castles and exuding a refreshingly down-to-earth, sunny environment. On the hills surrounding the city lie vineyards, making Sion a wine-lover's paradise. Additionally, Sion's size (large enough for an Olympic bid in 2006) and accessibility make it an ideal base for exploring all of Valais or for a momentary escape from the touring hordes.

⧉ TRANSPORTATION. Trains pass every 30min. in each direction along the Rhône Valley, going west (4:52am-10:52pm) to: Aigle (35min., 17.20SFr); Lausanne (1¼hr., 27SFr); Martigny (15min., 9.20SFr); Montreux (50min., 21SFr); and east (6:04am-1:09am) to: Sierre (10min., 5.80SFr) and Brig (30-45min., 17.20SFr). The **train station** is open Monday to Saturday 6:30am-8pm, and Sunday 6:50am-8pm. Switzerland's largest **Post Bus station** (☎327 34 34; www.poste.ch) is in front of the station. The Sierre-Sion Regional deal offers three days of unlimited travel in the region over one week (48SFr, children 38SFr).

⧉⧉ ORIENTATION AND PRACTICAL INFORMATION. Sion's main artery, ave. de la Gare, runs north up the hill from the train station, passing ave. du Midi on the right, to form the southwest corner of pl. de la Planta with r. de Lausanne. R. du Grand-Pont, a main thoroughfare of the old town, connects to the end of r. de Lausanne east of the plaza. The **tourist office,** off r. de Lausanne in pl. de la Planta, provides 2hr. **guided tours** and room reservations. (☎327 77 27; www.sion-tourism.ch. Open July-Aug. M-F 8am-6pm, Sa 9am-5pm; Sept.-June M-F 8:30am-12:30pm and 1:30-6pm, Sa 9am-1pm. Tours mid-July to Aug. Tu and Th 9:30am, additional group tours on request. 8SFr, children 5SFr.) The train station provides **currency exchange**. Other services include: **lockers** (4-6Fr) and **luggage storage**. (7SFr for 24hr. Open 6:45am-8pm.) **Internet access** is cheapest at **NetOnline**, ave. de la Gare 39, 5min. from the station. (☎321 33 11; www.netonline.ch. 9SFr per hr. Open M-Th 11am-11pm, F-Sa 11am-midnight, Su 2-7pm.) Call ☎117 or ☎144 for an **ambulance**. For a **pharmacy** call ☎111 or head down ave. de la Gare from the train station (where several are located). The **post office**, pl. de la Gare, is left of the train station. (Open M-F 7:30am-6:15pm, Sa 9am-4pm.) **Postal Code:** CH-1950.

ACCOMMODATIONS AND CAMPING. Sion's sole budget-friendly accommodation, the **Auberge de Jeunesse (HI) ❷**, ave. de l'Industrie 2, behind the train station, welcomes guests with brightly colored artwork. The building is vast and institutional, with clean bathrooms, ping pong (10SFr deposit for ball and paddles), bike rental (15SFr per day, 10SFr per half-day), foosball, and a TV room. Rooms are often fully booked from late June to September, so call ahead. (Breakfast included. Lunch on request 12.50SFr. Dinner 12.50SFr; reserve ahead. Kitchen facilities 2.50SFr. Reception open summer 8-10am and 5-9pm; winter 8-10am and 6-9pm. 4-bed dorms 28.80SFr; 3-bed dorms 32.80SFr; 2-bed dorms 35.80SFr. 6SFr surcharge for non-members. DC/MC/V.) Travelers seeking a cheaper bed should try villages outside Sion. **Camping Les Iles ❶**, rte. d'Aproz, boasts five-star riverside campsites 4km from town. Take a short ride on Post Bus #2 to Aproz. (☎346 43 47; fax 68 47. Open Jan.-Oct. and the last 2 weeks in Dec. 8.40SFr per adult; 4.20SFr per child; 9SFr per tent; low-season 6.60SFr/3.30SFr/6SFr.)

FOOD. Cafés and restaurants line the cobblestone streets of the *vieille ville*. The **Café des Châteaux ❸**, behind Hôtel de Ville on r. des Châteaux 3, off r. du Grand Pont, is unpretentious and affordable. Swiss classics like *Raclette* (25SFr) and fondue (19-22SFr) are served alongside *escargots* (15SFr) and *tripe milanaise* (18SFr). (☎322 13 96. Wheelchair accessible. Open Tu-Sa 8am-midnight, Su 10am-midnight. MC/V.) For cheap and filling Turkish delights, head to ave. des Mayennets at ave. du Midi and grab a kebab and drink to go (7-13SFr) at **Kebab Istanbul ❷**. (☎323 79 05. Open M-Th 11am-10pm, F 11am-11pm, Sa 11am-10pm.) **Migros** supermarket is in the Centre Commercial on ave. de France, one block left from the station, and on ave. Ritz, two blocks right from ave. de la Gare. (Ave. de France location open M 1-6:30pm, Tu-Th 8:15am-6:30pm, F 8:15am-7:30pm, Sa 8am-5pm. Ritz location open M 1:30-6:30pm, Tu-F 8:15am-noon and 1:30-6:30pm, Sa 8am-5pm.) The ave. de France location also houses a restaurant.

SIGHTS AND ENTERTAINMENT. Majestically perched on twin hills overlooking Sion are the **Château de Tourbillon** and the **Château de Valère**. The ave. des Châteaux leads upward to the castles from the *Hôtel de Ville*, past **Château de la Majorie et du Vidomnat**, forking to the left toward Tourbillon and to the right to Valère. At night, the hillside castles are set ablaze with floodlamps. Both offer panoramic vistas of Sion and its surroundings.

The **Château de Valère** houses the **Musée Cantonal d'Histoire**, which leads visitors on a tour of the historic building and through Swiss history from early Christian Europe until the present. Highlights include golden engravings from AD 400 and religious art from the 15th century. Beyond the museum, the world's oldest working organ (c. 1390-1430) rests among the faded murals of the **Basilisque du Château de Valère** and can be heard at the annual organ festival every Saturday at 4pm in July and August. (Open June-Sept. daily 11am-6pm; Oct.-May Tu-Su 11am-5pm. Tours in French, English, and German mid-Mar. to mid-Nov. every hour 11:15am-

4:15pm except 3:15pm; additional 5:15pm tour June-Sept. Museum 6SFr, children 3SFr, families 12SFr; basilisque 3SFr/1.50SFr/6SFr; combined ticket 7SFr/4.50SFr/15SFr. Museum open June-Sept. daily 1-6pm; Oct.-May Tu-Su 11am-5pm. Basilisque open June-Sept. M-Sa 10am-6pm, Su 2-6pm; Oct.-May Tu-Sa 10am-5pm, Su 2-5pm.) To the north, the **Château de Tourbillon** is a much simpler edifice made up of old walls ruined by fire and war sitting atop a hill surrounded by terraced vineyards. Admission is free, and a brief hike to the hilltop rewards you with beautiful views and yards perfect for picknicking. (Open mid-Mar. to mid-Nov. Tu-Su 10am-6pm.) Walking down from the castles on r. des Châteaux, to your left is the **Musée d'Archéologie,** r. des Châteaux 12. This museum focuses on the process of archeology, with photos and explanations of digs in the surrounding countryside. (☎606 47 00. Open Tu-Sa 1-5pm. 4SFr, students 2SFr.) At the bottom of the hill, the Château de la Majorie et du Vidomnat houses the **Musée des Beaux-Arts.** Fans of Valaisian art will enjoy the fin de siècle portraiture and the collection of 18th-century Valaisian landscapes. (☎606 46 90. Open Tu-Su Oct.-May 1-5pm; June-Sept. 1-6pm. 5SFr, students 2.50SFr, families 20SFr; tours 8SFr.) Head up the hill 200m to the old **Sion jail** where the **museum** hosts intriguing temporary exhibits, mostly of modern art. (Open daily June-Sept. 1-6pm; Oct.-May 1-5pm.)

Summer evenings bring **free concerts** under the auspices of the **Académie de Musique** (☎322 66 52) and rock, funk, and jazz during **Festiv** (2nd weekend in June). **Open-air cinema** is presented during the last weeks of June and July. The Valais canton produces some of Switzerland's finest wines. Most cafés have terraces where patrons sip whites (*Fendant* or *Johannisberg*) and reds (*Gamay* or *Dole*). Consult the tourist office for organized **wine-tasting excursions** and a list of local cellars. A long-distance path through the vineyards, *le chemin du vignoble,* passes close to Sion. Always call before arriving at a cellar, and try to organize a group if you want the proprietor to be more welcoming. One *centre de dégustation* is **Le Verre à Pied,** ave. du Grand Pont 29, which houses 150 wines from multiple sellers throughout the region. (☎/fax 321 13 80. Open M-Sa 10:30am-1pm and 4-8pm, Su 10:30am-1:30pm and 5:30-8pm, or by reservation. MC/V.)

MARTIGNY   ☎027

French-speaking Martigny (pop. 15,000) serves as one of the major access points to the jagged peak of Mont Blanc (4807m), the highest peak in the Alps, which straddles the French and Italian borders. The oldest town in Valais, Martigny has long been the center of passages across the Alps, serving Hannibal, Caesar, Charlemagne, and Napoleon. The regional architecture thus displays a wide range of cultural influences: a medieval castle towers in the west while a Roman amphitheater stands in the east. The Fondation Pierre Gianadda makes Martigny a center for modern art and classical music.

▌ TRANSPORTATION. Frequent **trains** west to: Aigle (20min.; every 30min. 5am-8pm, every hr. 8-11pm; 9.80SFr); Lausanne (45-60min.; every 30min. 5am-8pm, every hr. 8-11pm; 21SFr); and Montreux (30min.; every 30min. 5am-8pm, every hr. 8-11pm; 15.20SFr); and east to: Sion (15-25min.; 3 per hr. 6:10am-9:10pm, 2 per hr. 9:10pm-12:54am; 9.20SFr). A private line goes to Châtelard (45min.; every hr. 6:42am-7:48pm, less often mid-Sept. to mid-Dec. and mid-Apr. to mid-June; 16.60SFr), where you change for Chamonix in France (one-way 12SFr, round-trip 15SFr), a starting point for the 10- to 14-day Mont Blanc circuit. The line goes to Orsières (30min., every hr. 7:12am-8:11pm, one-way 9.80SFr), where you change for a bus to Aosta in Italy via the St. Bernard Pass (1½hr., 8:35am and 5pm, one-way 19.80SFr). The **information office** is across the street from the station. (☎723 37 01. Open M-F 8am-noon and 1:30-6pm, Sa

8am-noon.) **Buses** run to Champex and the Col de la Forclaz pass, also starting points for Mont Blanc, through the **Post Bus** service (☎ 327 34 34). The **station** has a **travel agency**. (Station open M-F 6:15am-8pm, Sa 6:15am-7:15pm, Su 7:45am-noon and 1:30-7:15pm. Call ☎ 0900 300 300 for schedule information. Travel agency open M-F 9am-noon and 1:30-6pm, Sa 9am-noon and 1:30-5pm.)

█!█ ORIENTATION AND PRACTICAL INFORMATION. The **tourist office**, pl. Centrale 9, is straight down ave. de la Gare at the far corner of pl. Centrale. (☎ 721 22 20; fax 22 24. Open May-Sept. M-F 9am-6pm, Sa 8:30am-12:30pm and 1:30-5:30pm, Su 10am-12:30pm and 4-6pm; Oct.-Apr. M-F 8:30am-noon and 1:30-6:30pm, Sa 8:30am-noon.) In the station, services include: **taxis** (☎ 722 22 00 or 21 17); **currency exchange; lockers** (3-5SFr); **luggage storage** (5SFr); and **bike rental** (30SFr per day, 23SFr per half-day). In an emergency, call ☎ 117 for **police** or ☎ 144 for an **ambulance**. The **hospital** (☎ 603 90 00) can connect you to the late-night doctor and pharmacy. **Internet** access is available at **Cyber Café, Casino, and Cinema,** on the right between the station and pl. Centrale at r. de la Gare 27. (☎ 722 13 93. 4SFr per 15min. Open M-F 6am-midnight, Sa 7am-midnight, Su 9am-11pm.) The **post office**, ave. de la Gare 32, between the station and the tourist office, has a public **fax** and an **ATM**. (☎ 722 26 72. Open M-F 7:30am-noon and 1:30-6:30pm, Sa 8am-noon.) **Postal Code:** CH-1920.

█ ACCOMMODATIONS AND CAMPING. Budget pickings are slim because travelers in Martigny are mainly business types. About a 5min. walk from the train station stands the **Hôtel Grand-Quai ❹,** which offers long, carpeted hallways and sparse, clean rooms. Reservations are suggested for the few single rooms. (☎ 722 20 50 or 55 98; www.grandquai.com. From the train station turn left and go to r. du Simplon. The hotel is on the right. Breakfast included. Singles 70SFr; doubles 100SFr; triples 130SFr.) **Hôtel de la Poste ❸,** r. de la Poste, across from the main post office, offers simple, clean rooms that come with a private bath, TV, and telephone. Dorm rooms (58SFr) are some of the cheapest in town. (☎ 722 14 44. Singles 90SFr; doubles 130SFr. AmEx/MC/V.) **Camping Les Neuvilles ❶,** r. du Levant 68, packs its shaded plot with motor homes. From the station, head straight on ave. de la Gare, take the second left onto ave. des Neuvilles, and turn right onto r. du Levant. Amenities include a **store, laundry,** a **sauna** (7SFr), **miniature golf** (5SFr, children 3SFr), and a **solarium.** (☎ 722 45 44; fax 35 44. Showers included. Reception 8am-noon and 2-8pm. 7.20SFr per person; 9SFr per tent; 19SFr per car or RV. Low-season (Sept.-May) 6.20SFr/7.50SFr/14SFr. AmEx/DC/MC/V.)

█ FOOD. Cafés crowd Martigny's tree-lined pl. Centrale, some with *Menüs* in the 15-25SFr range. For cheaper fare, **Lords' Sandwiches ❶,** ave. du Grand-St. Bernard 15, on a continuation of r. de la Gare past pl. Centrale, serves 36 kinds of sandwiches (3.80-11.80SFr), including a bacon burger with fries, and the "Zeus," an overstuffed roast beef sandwich. Vegetarian options are limited, but the "Socrates," with tomatoes, mushrooms, and cheese, is one good choice. (☎ 723 35 98. Open M-F 8am-10pm, Sa 8:30am-10pm.) **Crêperie Le Rustique ❶,** ave. de la Gare 44, lives up to its name with a dark wood interior and nature scenes painted on stucco. Enjoy savory crèpes (10.50-14.50SFr) or sweet ones (4.50-9.50SFr), washed down with a mug of cider (3.50SFr). (☎ 722 88 33. Lunch special 10SFr. Open M-F 8am-11pm, Sa 10:30am-midnight, Su 1:30-11pm.) For straightforward Italian food, try **Pizzeria au Grotto ❷,** r. du Rhône 3, off r. Marc-Morand to the left of pl. Centrale. Follow one of 22 types of pizza (11-19SFr) with a monster tiramisu (5SFr) and gain a pound or two. (☎ 722 02 46. Open M-Th 8:30am-11pm, F 8:30am-midnight, Sa 10am-midnight, Su 10am-11pm. MC/V.) The **Migros** supermarket at pl. du Manoir 5, just off pl. Centrale, offers all that your picnicking heart might desire, while the popular park behind the market provides the perfect outdoor

VALAIS

dining setting. (Open M-Th 8:15am-6:30pm, F 8:15am-8pm, Sa 8am-5pm. Migros restaurant open M-Th 7:30am-6:30pm, F 7:30am-8pm, Sa 7:30am-5pm.) The **public market**, on ave. de la Gare, sells edible and wearable goods. (Open Th 8am-noon.)

🞇 **SIGHTS.** The **Fondation Pierre Gianadda**, r. du Forum 59, is Martigny's most engaging attraction. Head down the r. Hôtel-de-Ville behind the tourist office and follow the signs. The museum is located off ave. du Grand-St. Bernard. The museum's main building, on the site of a former Gaulois temple, hosts two of the Foundation's permanent exhibits. Head downstairs to the **Automobile Museum** with exhibits of more than 50 vintage cars (1897-1939), including an 1897 Benz, and a Delaunay-Belleville that belonged to Czar Nicholas II. Nearby is the **Louis and Evelyn Franck Collection**, holding a small exhibit of Impressionist art. The garden surrounding the foundation contains Gallo-Roman remains and several modern sculptures. Admission to the park is free on summer nights. Every year from April to October, there is an exhibit on Leonardo da Vinci and his inventions in the **Vieil Arsenal**, held in the gardens behind the Museum. The exhibit includes over 100 facsimiles made from da Vinci's drawings. Models bring some of da Vinci's most treasured ideas—the forerunner of the helicopter, a proposed bridge in Turkey, and a tank—to life. The Museum's big draws are the blockbuster international traveling exhibitions, which have included artists such as Chagall, van Gogh, and da Vinci. (☎ 722 39 78; www.gianadda.ch. Wheelchair accessible. Open daily June-Nov. 9am-7pm; Dec.-May 10am-6pm. Guided tours in French W 8pm or by prior arrangement. 18SFr, students and children 11SFr, seniors 16SFr, family ticket 38SFr.) The foundation hosts classical music concerts and leads 1½hr. **guided tours** of Martigny that include the exhibits. (Mid-July to mid-Aug. 10:30am, 2:30pm; Sept.-June by appointment for groups only. 80SFr plus museum entrance for 2hr.) If you want to explore on your own, the office distributes *Promenade Archéologique*, a brochure detailing a walking tour of Martigny's Roman ruins. Past the railroad tracks, remnants of a Roman road point toward Britannia and, through the pass, Roma. Nearby, the grassy 4th-century **Amphithéâtre Romain** is the spectacular setting for the final contest of the Valais **cowfighting** season.

Le Château de la Bâtiaz, a 13th-century castle, complete with dungeon and tower, once belonged to the bishops of Sion and is now a ruin. From the station, head along ave. de la Gare and turn right at pl. Centrale along r. Marc-Morand. Cross the river via the covered bridge and turn left after the sign. Enter the château via the field. The château is filled with relics from the Middle Ages, including a nail-covered chair and a "stretching" contraption. Climb the massive stone tower extending over an outcropping of bare rock for a bird's-eye perspective of the Rhône. (Open mid-May to late June and late Aug. to mid-Oct. F 4pm-midnight, Sa 10am-midnight, Su 10am-6pm; late June to late Aug. also Th 4pm-midnight. Free.)

FESTIVALS. Martigny hosts the **Foire du Valais**, the trade fair of Valais, in a blue-and-yellow convention center in mid-October. The fair allows local businessmen and farmers to offer everything from shoes to marble sculptures. The first weekend brings two days of all-day **cowfighting**, a must-see event. The **Foire du Lard** (Bacon Fair) has overtaken the pl. Centrale every first Monday in December since the Middle Ages. Traditionally, Valais mountain folk descended on Martigny to stock up on pork products for the winter. Now the festival has expanded to a large open-air market, but the pig still reigns supreme.

VERBIER ☎ 027

Although it may seem like a typical mountain town, Verbier (pop. 2500) is a polished resort, occupying an altitude of 1500-3330m and serving around one million visitors annually. Its transportation system is designed to move skiers and snowboarders between cable cars. Other sports thrive as well, casting an athletic glow over the entire town, though in May and June everything closes (except for the massive sports center) and the streets are virtually silent. Out of some 3000 beds in the area, only about 1000 are found in hotels; the rest are in the chalets that speckle the surrounding hillside.

TRANSPORTATION. Getting to Verbier is a two-step process—from Martigny to Le Châble, then from Le Châble to Verbier, which lies on the high-speed train line that connects Montreux and Lausanne to Sion and Brig. The **St. Bernard Express** runs trains to Le Châble (30min., every hr. 8am-6:53pm, 9.80SFr, Eurail and SwissPass valid). Take the **Post Bus** (25min., every hr. 8:32am-7:30pm, 5.20SFr) or the **cable car** (10min.; runs nonstop Nov.-Apr. 8:30am-6:45pm; 8SFr, round-trip 15SFr) to Verbier. In winter, a **bus** goes directly from Martigny to Verbier. Reservations are crucial; there is only one bus on Friday evenings and three on Saturdays. **Téléverbier** offers **free local bus** service in town (limited between seasons).

ACCOMMODATIONS AND CAMPING. The Bunker ❷ is the world's only youth hostel contained in an atomic bunker. The hostel is housed beneath the city's Centre Polysportif, a 10min. walk down r. de la Poste from the bus station. In the winter, the innovative complex caters to a younger crowd of snowboarders. Concrete walls and steel vault doors have been painted bright pink, but the place retains a military feel, with no windows and up to 45 cramped beds (3-story bunks separated by fireproof curtains) per room. Services include: shuttle bus to ski lifts, vouchers for ski specials, lounge with cable TV and VCR, **Internet** (12SFr per hr.), and free access to skating rinks, indoor and outdoor pools, sauna, squash courts, and beach volleyball courts at the sports center. (☎771 66 04; www.thebunker.ch. Breakfast, 3-course dinner, showers, and lockers included. Reception 9am-9pm. Open mid-June to Apr. Dorms 45SFr. AmEx/D/MC/V, min. 50SFr.) For those who prefer a more traditional hostel arrangement, the new **Summer House ❸** next door has sunny rooms that overlook the pool and free access to the sports center. (☎771 66 04; fax 66 03. Reservations highly recommended. 4- or 8-bed rooms including breakfast and showers at the Sports Center. 58SFr. AmEx/D/MC/V.) The classically Swiss **Les Touristes ❸** is at the bottom of the r. de Verbier in Verbier Village. Heading down the hill, walk past the Catholic Church. Les Touristes will be straight ahead. There are tastefully decorated, if somewhat cramped, rooms and an elegant breakfast room with stunning mountain views. (☎/fax 771 21 47; www.verbier.ch/lestouristes. Reception 9am-8pm. Singles without shower 47-70SFr, low-season 37-55SFr; doubles 86-165SFr/68-100SFr. AmEx/V.) In winter, the **campsite ❶** (☎776 20 51) is outside Le Châble.

FOOD. Though Verbier has achieved major-ski-resort status, many of its restaurants are budget-friendly, and a young international crowd keeps the nightlife jumping and accessible to Anglophones. Restaurants, bars, and clubs pack pl. Centrale and the roads radiating from it. Nightlife slows down during the off-season. **Le Crok No Name Bar ❶** (from pl. Centrale head 2min. up rte. des Creux, on your right, above a bakery), named after its previous building, Aux Croquingnoles, keeps things simple, drawing hip locals and sports-lovers with a tile exterior, terracotta bar, long leather couches, and large porch where *Panini* sandwiches (8SFr) are served. Frequent rock, funk, and jazz concerts heat things up. There is a DJ or live music every night. (☎771 69 34. Open July and Aug. daily noon-2am; May-June and Sept.-Nov. M and Th-Su 5pm-2am; Dec.-Apr. daily 5pm-2am.) **Le Monde des Crêpes ❷** (☎771 28 95), on the right 2min. down r. de la Poste from pl. Centrale, puts an alternative twist on a traditional *crêperie*. (Savory crêpes 6-13SFr. Deserts 6-8SFr.) For Italian specialties, hike up the r. des Creux from pl. Centrale to the **Pizzeria Al Capone ❸.** The restaurant is on the right after ch. de la Morintse.

Shorten the walk by taking the Téléverbier bus to "Brunnet" in the high-season. Try the pizza (14-21SFr), gnocchi (21SFr), or *plats du jour* (18-20SFr). Diners can eat in the rustic cabin or watch snow-capped peaks and neon paragliders on the large terrace. (☎771 67 74. Open daily 8:30am-10pm; food served 11:30am-1:30pm and 6:30-9:30pm. Call in advance for dinner reservations during the high-season.) **Le Caveau ❸,** to the right of the tourist office, serves Swiss and local specialties such as *Raclette*, fondue, and *Rösti*. Try the toast smothered in cheese, or the *assiette du jour* for 17SFr. (☎771 22 26. Open noon-2pm and 6:30-10pm.)

For picnickers, **Denner Superdiscount** is down r. de Verbier from pl. Centrale. (Open M-Tu and Th-F 8:30am-12:15pm and 2:30-6:30pm, Sa 8:30am-12:15pm and 2-5pm.) The **Co-op** is down r. de la Poste. (Open M-W and F 8:30am-12:15pm and 2:30-6:30pm, Th 8:30am-12:15pm, Sa 8:30am-12:15pm and 2:30-5pm.)

OUTDOOR ACTIVITIES AND ENTERTAINMENT. Verbier has a total of 400km of **ski** runs; its best runs are on the **Mont Fort glacier** (3329m), which offers skiing and snowboarding November to April. A behemoth of a cable car, the **Télé-jumbo** can carry 150 passengers at a time to the glacier via Col des Gentianes (also the site of a snowboard half-pipe). From the Médran cable car station (up the r. de Médran from the tourist office), another cable car runs through Les Ruinettes to **Attelas** (2193m), and on to **Mont Gelë** (3023m). Those content with a smaller venue can access Verbier's northern slopes with the **Savoleyres** cable car at the end of rte. des Creux. Beginners can find easier slopes at **Les Moulins** and **Les Esserts.** Ski pass prices and cable car schedules are complicated—make sure to pick up the pertinent info at the tourist or Téléverbier offices. (☎775 25 11; www.televerbier.ch. 2-day pass to the 4-valley region and Mont Fort 115SFr, for the Verbier slopes only 100SFr. 3-day passes 167SFr/145SFr. Photo ID required. Non-skier day pass 38SFr/21SFr. Ages 16-20 15% off, seniors and ages 6-15 30% off; reduced family rates.) Rental shops in Verbier abound, and all offer rentals for the same price, although some stores have deals with certain accommodations. **Medran Sports,** down r. de Verbier from the pl. Centrale, rents equipment. (☎771 60 48. Open M-Sa 9am-noon and 3-5pm. Skis and snowboards 38SFr. Boots 19SFr for adults, 15SFr for children. Bikes 38SFr per day, 30SFr per half-day.)

The tourist office makes recommendations to skiers based on skill level. They do the same for summer **hikers** and offer a map of the trails for 7SFr. For ski lessons contact **La Maison du Sport** (☎775 33 63; www.maisondusport.com), **La Fantastique** (☎771 41 41; www.lafantastique.com), or **Adrenaline** (☎771 74 59; www.adrenaline-verbier.ch). In summer, La Maison du Sport offers multi-day guided excursions, hikes, canyoning and rafting trips, and even a **Kids' Club** (☎775 33 63) for children over age three with daily themes (painting, pottery, and fishing). There also are plenty of opportunities to join the flock of paragliders in Verbier's skies. **Max Biplace** (☎771 55 55 or 079 219 36 55) offers tandem flights—book at La Fantastique. The **Centre de Parapente,** near the Centre Polysportif, offers tandem **paragliding** (☎771 68 18; www.flyverbier.ch. 170SFr.) The multi-level **Centre Polysportif,** downhill from pl. Centrale on r. de la Poste, has a **swimming pool** (open 10am-9pm; 8SFr, children ages 6-16 5SFr), **ice-skating rink** (7SFr; skate rentals 6SFr, children ages 6-16 5SFr), **squash** (15SFr per 30min.), and **tennis courts** (23SFr per hr.) and houses the Bunker and Summer House (p. 481). (Centre Polysportif ☎771 66 01. Open 8am-11pm.)

In summer, Verbier draws an array of talented performers to its **classical music festival** (mid-July to early August), which began in 1994 and has featured musicians such as Bobby McFerrin, and Björk. In 2000 the main sponsor founded the Verbier Youth Orchestra, which performs at the festival under the direction of James Levine. There is also a film weekend at the end of July. Tickets are available by phone or on location. (☎771 82 82; www.verbierfestival.com. Tickets 30-120SFr.) Free events are posted each day of the festival.

GENEVA AND LAC LÉMAN

All around Lac Léman, hills sprinkled with villas and blanketed by patchwork vineyards sewn with garlands of ripening grapes seem tame and settled…until the haze clears. From behind the hills surge rough-hewn mountain peaks, and the lake discards its cultivated urbanity for the promise of unpopulated wilderness and wide lonely expanses. Many travelers suffer financial anxiety when they consider venturing to the refined Lac Léman region, since high prices are the general rule in tourist-infested Geneva, Lausanne, and Montreux. However, adventurers discover that towns along the lake abound with three of Switzerland's cheapest commodities: tranquility is just a short stroll along a tree-lined quai or into vine-laced hills, chocolate is available for a pittance nearly everywhere, and unforgettable views are, as always, free and plentiful.

HIGHLIGHTS OF LAC LÉMAN

Be moved to humanitarian action at Geneva's **Red Cross Museum** (p. 494).

Tiptoe through the dungeon at Montreux's chilling **Chateau Chillon** (p. 508).

Meet thousands of cool cats in mid-July at the **Montreux Jazz Festival (p. 509)**.

GENEVA (GENÈVE, GENF) ☎022

The most international city in Switzerland, Geneva is a brew of 178,000 unlikely neighbors: wealthy businessmen speed past young artists in the streets, while nuclear families share the sidewalks with dreadlocked skaters. Isolated from the rest of Switzerland both ideologically and geographically, Geneva has a sense of independence that unites the city's proudly eclectic group of citizens.

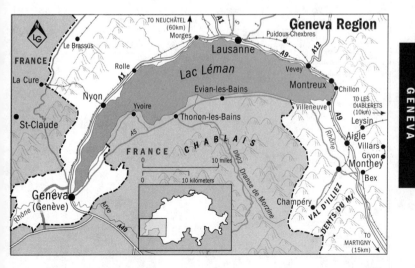

GENEVA

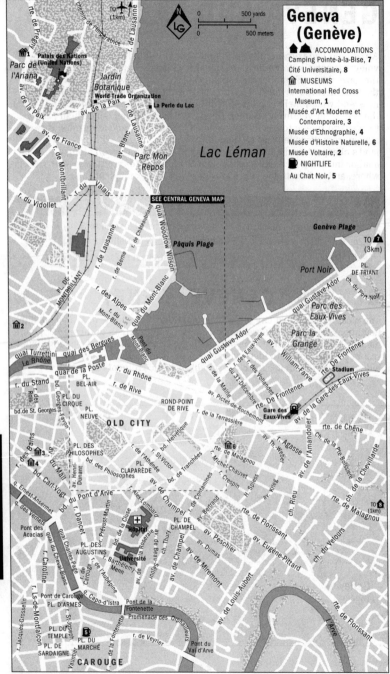

Geneva (Genève)

▲▲ ACCOMMODATIONS
Camping Pointe-à-la-Bise, **7**
Cité Universitaire, **8**

🏛 MUSEUMS
International Red Cross
  Museum, **1**
Musée d'Art Moderne et
  Contemporaire, **3**
Musée d'Ethnographie, **4**
Musée d'Histoire Naturelle, **6**
Musée Voltaire, **2**

🍺 NIGHTLIFE
Au Chat Noir, **5**

GENEVA

0   500 yards
0   500 meters

TO ✈ (1km)

rte. de Pregny

Chemin de l'Impératrice

rte. de Lausanne

🏛1 Palais des Nations
(United Nations)

Parc de l'Ariana

Jardin Botanique

av. de la Paix

World Trade Organization

av. de France

La Perle du Lac

r. de Lausanne

av. Blanc

r. de Montbrillant

Parc Mon Repos

Lac Léman

r. du Valais

r. du Vidollet

SEE CENTRAL GENEVA MAP

quai Woodrow Wilson

r. de Châteaubriand

r. de Lausanne

r. de Berne

Pâquis Plage

Genève Plage

TO 🏕7 (3km)

PL. DE TRIANT

Port Noir

quai du Mont-Blanc

r. des Alpes

r. du Mont-Blanc

PL. DE MONTBRILLANT

ch. du Port-Noir

quai Gustave-Ador

Parc des Eaux-Vives

🏛2

quai Turrettini

quai des Bergues

Le Rhône

Pont du Mont-Blanc

quai Gustave-Ador

av. des Eaux-Vives

av. William-Favre

Parc la Grange

r. de Frontenex

r. du Stand

quai de la Poste

PL. BEL-AIR

r. du Rhône

r. de Rive

r. de la Marne

r. 31-Décembre

rte. De Frontenex

rte. de la Gare-des-Eaux-Vives

Stadium

bd. des Rois

r. des Bains

bd. Georges-Favon

PL. DU CIRQUE

PL. NEUVE

ROND-POINT DE RIVE

r. de la Terrassière

av. Pictet-de-Rochemont

Gare des Eaux-Vives

av. de la Gare-des-Eaux-Vives

rte. de Chêne

bd. de St. Georges

OLD CITY

PL. DES PHILOSOPHES

🏛3

🏛4

r. des Bains

bd. Carl-Vogt

r. Ernest-Ansermet

r. des Verriers

Pont des Acacias

quai Charles-Page

r. du Martin

r. Henri-Dunant

bd. des Philosophes

r. St-Victor

r. de l'Athénée

bd. Helvétique

PL. CLAPARÈDE

av. de Champel

🏛6

r. de Malagnou

r. Michel-Chauvet

r. Crespin

H. Spiess

av. Krieg

av. Th.-Weber

av. Agasse

ch. Rieu

av. de l'Amandolier

rte. de Malagnou

TO 🏕8 (1km)

ch. de la Pte.-Boissière

ch. de la Chevillarde

rte. de Florissant

Université

Hôpital

PL. DES AUGUSTINS

r. Prévost-Martin

r. Dancet

r. de la Cluse

bd. du Pont d'Arve

Alex.-Lombard

av. de Beau-Séjour

ch. Thury

ch. de Beaumont

av. de la Roseraie

r. Barthélemy-Menn

r. Lombard

av. de Champel

av. de Miremont

av. Dumas

av. Peschier

PL. DE CHAMPEL

r. de Contamines

r. Bertrand

rte. de Florissant

av. Eugène-Pittard

av. Louis-Aubert

ch. du Velours

Pont des Acacias

r. Caroline

r. Ls-de-Montfalcon

r. Jacques-Grosselin

quai du Cheval-Blanc

r. de Carouge

r. de l'Aubépine

r. Capo-d'Istra

Pont de Carouge

PL. D'ARMES

r. St-Joseph

PL. DU TEMPLE

PL. DE SARDAIGNE

🍺5

PL. DU MARCHÉ

Pont de la Fontenette

r. de la Fontenette

Promenade des Orphelines

r. de Veyrier

Pont du Val d'Arve

rte. de Florissant

r. de l'Arve

CAROUGE

◼ INTERCITY TRANSPORTATION

Flights: Cointrin Airport (☎ 717 71 11, flight information 799 31 11; fax 798 43 77) is a hub for **Swiss Airlines** (☎ 08 48 85 20 00). Bus #10 runs to the Gare Cornavin (15min., every 5-10min., 2.60SFr). The ticket dispenser requires exact change—large bills can be broken at the "change-o-mat" behind the escalator or at the information desk. For a shorter trip to Gare Cornavin, take the train (6min., every 12min., 2.68-7.40SFr). There are several flights per day to various international hubs. **Air France** (☎ 827 87 87) has 13 flights per day to Paris; **British Airways** (☎ 08 48 80 10 10) 9 per day to London.

Trains: Trains run approximately 4:30am-1am. There are 2 stations:

Gare Cornavin, pl. Cornavin, is the main station. To: **Basel** (2¾hr., every hr. 4:44am-10:44pm, 71SFr); **Bern** (2hr., every hr. 4:34am-10:34pm, 47SFr); **Interlaken** (3hr., every hr. 4:34am-9:30pm, 63SFr); **Lausanne** (40min., every 15-30min. 4:34am-12:21am, 18.80SFr); **Milan** (4hr., 8 per day, 81SFr); **Montreux** (1hr., 2 per hr. 5:16am-11:32pm, 29SFr); **Paris** (3¾hr., 10 per day 5:47am-10:23pm, 103SFr); **Vienna** (10-12hr., 4 per day 6:30am-7:30pm, 189SFr); **Zurich** (3½hr., every 30min., 76SFr). To book a seat on long-distance or international trains, join the throng at the reservation and information counter. Open M-F 8:30am-6:30pm, Sa 9am-5pm. The 24hr. **rail information** number is ☎ 09 00 30 03 00 (1.19SFr per min.).

Gare des Eaux-Vives (☎ 736 16 20), on ave. de la Gare des Eaux-Vives (Tram #12, "Amandoliers SNCF"), connects to France's regional rail lines through **Annecy** (1½hr., 6 per day, 14SFr) or **Chamonix** (2½hr., 4 per day, 24SFr). The ticket machine at the station does not return change. Ticket office open M-F 9am-6pm, Sa 11am-5:45pm.

CGN Ferries: (☎ 312 52 23). To **Lausanne** and **Montreux,** departing from quai du Mont-Blanc. A round-trip ticket (54-74SFr, ages 16-25 half-price, seniors 20% discount) includes the option of returning to Geneva by train. Opens daily at 10am.

By Car: Geneva is more accessible from **France** than from the rest of Switzerland. From the **west,** take A40, which continues on to **Lausanne** and **Montreux.** From the **south** take N201 north. From the **north,** take A40 from France or Switzerland. From the **east,** take A40 west. N1 is the best way to reach Geneva from Lausanne or Montreux. Route numbers are not always visible: follow signs for Geneva.

◼ ORIENTATION

Straddling the Rhône as it opens into Lac Léman, Geneva began as a fortified city on a hill. The *vieille ville* (old city) overlooking the delta remains the city's heart. Just south of the river, the *vieille ville* is characterized by labyrinthine cobbled streets and quiet squares centering around John Calvin's **Cathédrale de St-Pierre;** elsewhere, the city's esplanades coalesce into a more coherent grid. Across the Rhône River to the north, banks and five-star hotels gradually give way to lakeside promenades. To the east of Lake Geneva rises the International Hill, dominated by various UN, Red Cross, and WTO complexes. Across the Arve river to the south lies the village of Carouge, home to many student bars and clubs (take tram #12 or 13 to "pl. du Marché").

◼ LOCAL TRANSPORTATION

Carry your passport at all times; the French border is never more than a few minutes away and buses cross it frequently. Ticket purchasing is largely on the honor system and some backpackers try to get away without paying. *Let's Go* does not recommend fare evasion: fines run 60SFr. The city is easily walkable. Renting a bike is a good way to get around as well (see below).

Public Transportation: Geneva has an efficient bus and tram network. Major hubs are Gare Cornavin, rd.-pt. de Plainpalais, and pl. Bel Air (near the Pont de l'Ile). **Transports Publics Genevois** (☎ 308 34 34), to the left of the exit at Gare Cornavin, provides *Le*

GENEVA

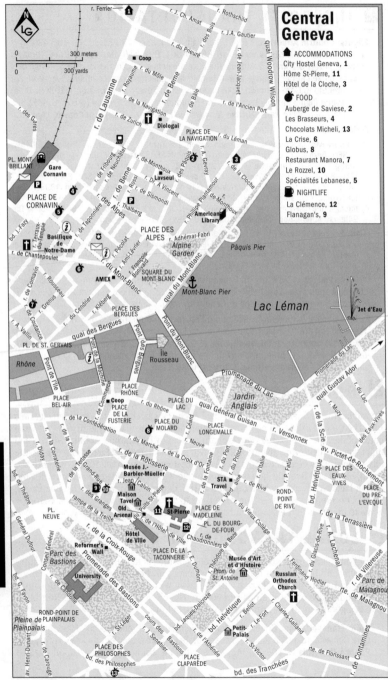

Central Geneva

ACCOMMODATIONS
City Hostel Geneva, **1**
Hôme St-Pierre, **11**
Hôtel de la Cloche, **3**

FOOD
Auberge de Saviese, **2**
Les Brasseurs, **4**
Chocolats Micheli, **13**
La Crise, **6**
Globus, **8**
Restaurant Manora, **7**
Le Rozzel, **10**
Spécialités Lebanese, **5**

NIGHTLIFE
La Clémence, **12**
Flanagan's, **9**

Réseau, a free map of local bus routes. Timetables cost 6SFr but aren't worth it, as buses run frequently and timetables are posted at every stop. Open M-Sa 7am-7pm, Su 9am-5pm. Trips that stay within zone 10 (most of the city) cost 2.20SFr; 3 stops or fewer 1.80SFr. Full-day passes 6SFr for 1 zone, 12SFr for 4. SwissPass valid on all buses; Eurail not valid. **Buses** run roughly 5:30am-midnight. **Noctambus** (3SFr) runs 1:30-4:30am. Buy multi-fare and day tickets at the train station, others at automatic vendors at every stop. Stamp multi-use tickets at the machines before boarding.

Taxis: Taxi-Phone (☎331 41 33). Base fare 6.80SFr, 2.90SFr per km. Taxi from airport to city around 30SFr, max. 4 passengers (15-20min.). There are also taxi phones located on select street corners.

Car Rental: Avis, r. de Lausanne 44 (☎731 90 00). **Europcar,** r. de Lausanne 37 (☎909 69 90). **Budget,** r. de Zurich 36 (☎900 24 00). All have offices at the airport, but beware of possible surcharges.

Parking: On-street 2SFr per hr. The garage under Cornavin station (☎736 66 30) is a convenient option. Enter at pl. Cornavin. 2SFr per hr. 7am-7pm, 6SFr for 2hr.; 1SFr per hr. after 7pm. **Garage Les Alpes,** r. Thalberg. M-F 2SFr per hr., nights and Sa-Su 1SFr per hr. Per-hr. prices decrease as time increases. Digital boards on highways and the main city streets list carparks and the number of vacant spaces remaining in each.

Bike Rental: Pedal-happy Geneva has well-marked bike paths and special traffic lights. For routes, get *Itineraires cyclables* or *Tours de ville avec les vélos de location* from the tourist office. Behind the station, **Geneva Roule,** pl. Montbrillant 17 (☎/fax 740 13 43), rents passable bikes for 7SFr per day and higher-quality bikes for 10SFr per day. 50SFr deposit and photo ID required; hefty fine if bike is lost or stolen. Open summer 7:30am-9:30pm; winter 7:30am-6pm. Geneva Roule kiosks located at Bain des Paquis, pl. du Rhône, and Plaine de Plainpalais offer the same deals.

Hitchhiking: *Let's Go* does not recommend hitchhiking. However, travelers headed to Germany or northern Switzerland have been seen taking bus #4 to "Jardin Botanique." Those headed to France sometimes take bus #4 to "Palettes," then line D to "St-Julien."

◪ PRACTICAL INFORMATION

TOURIST AND FINANCIAL SERVICES

Tourist Offices: At information offices (marked by a blue lower-case "i" sign), the free must-haves are the city map and the booklet *Info Jeunes/Young People.* The **main office,** r. du Mont-Blanc 18 (☎909 70 00; wwww.geneve-tourisme.ch), lies 5min. away from Gare Cornavin toward the pont du Mont-Blanc, within the Central Post Office building. English-speaking staff books hotel rooms (5SFr fee), offers **walking tours,** and provides information on just about everything. The office maintains a free direct phone line to Geneva hotels, as well as a board listing budget accommodations. Open July-Aug. daily 9am-6pm; Sept.-June M-Sa 9am-6pm.

Budget Travel: STA, r. de la Rive 10 (☎818 02 00; www.statravel.ch). Student airfares and the like. Also home to an extensive travel bookstore and a language center (located in the basement). Open M 1-6:30pm, Tu-F 9am-6:30pm, Sa 9am-5pm. AmEx/MC/V.

Consulates: Australia, chemin des Fins 2 (☎799 91 00; fax 91 78); **Canada,** ave. de l'Ariana 5 (☎919 92 00; fax 92 77); **New Zealand,** chemin des Fins 2 (☎929 03 50; fax 03 74); **UK,** r. de Vermont 37 (☎918 24 26; fax 23 22); **US,** r. Versonnex 5 (☎840 51 60, recorded information 51 61; fax 51 62). Call to schedule appointments.

Currency Exchange: ATMs offer the best rates and are easy to find. There are a few at Gare Cornavin, at the top of the escalators from the platforms. For traditional services, Gare Cornavin has good rates and doesn't charge commission on traveler's checks. Advances cash on credit cards (min. 200SFr), and arranges **Western Union** transfers.

GENEVA

Open M-Sa 7am-7:40pm, Su 9:15am-6pm. **Change Cité**, r. du Mont-Blanc 21 (☎901 15 15), offers excellent rates, better than most banks, in a convenient location right by Gare Cornavin. No commission. M-F 8:30am-7pm, Sa 8:30am-5pm. Note that banks are generally open M-Tu and Th–F 8:30am-4:30pm, W 8:30am-5:50pm. Closed Sa-Su.

American Express: r. du Mont-Blanc 7, P.O. Box 1032, CH-1211 Geneva (☎731 76 00; fax 732 72 11). Mail held 2-3 months. All banking services; reasonable exchange rates. Hotel and train reservations (50SFr fee), and tickets for tours (city tour 39SFr, including countryside 68SFr). Open Nov.-Mar. M-F 8:30am-5:45pm; Apr.-Oct. M-F 8:45am-5:45pm, Sa 9am-noon.

TIP Paying by credit card is far less common in Switzerland than in the US, so be sure to have a solid stock of cash on hand. In order to avoid losing money to the lousy exchange rate offered at change counters, use your ATM card. Most machines don't charge you and will give you Swiss Francs using the current exchange rate. Be sure to check with your bank at home about any fees they may impose, though.

LOCAL SERVICES

Luggage Storage: Gare Cornavin. 4-7SFr per day. Open M-F 7am-7:30pm, Sa-Su 8am-12:30pm and 1:30-6:30pm. Lockers 4-7SFr. Open 4:30am-12:30am. For those willing to walk 10min. from the train station, **Auberge de Jeunesse** offers daytime storage (11am-11pm) for 2SFr. Ask the receptionist for a token.

Lost Property: (☎05 12 25 14 33), with the luggage storage. Open M-F 8am-2pm. Or call city's Lost and Found office (☎022 327 60 00). Open M-F 7:30am-4pm.

Bookstores: ELM (English Language and Media) Video and Books, r. Versonnex 5 (☎736 09 45; fax 786 14 29), has a quality range of new books and a book-ordering service. Open M-F 9am-6:30pm, Sa 10am-5pm. AmEx/DC/MC/V. **Librairie des Amateurs,** Grand Rue 15 (☎732 80 97), in the *vieille ville*. Classy secondhand dealer, English titles available. Open M 2-6pm, Tu-F 11am-6pm, Sa 2pm-5pm. **Payot Libraire,** r. de Chantepoulet 5 (☎731 89 50) and r. du Marché 16, is Geneva's largest chain of bookstores, with an excellent stock of English-language books. Open M 10am-6:60pm, Tu-W 9am-6:30pm, Th 9am-7pm, F 9am-6:30pm, Sa 9am-6pm. AmEx/DC/MC/V.

Library: American Library, r. de Monthoux 3 (☎732 80 97), at Emmanuel Church, just steps from the waterfront. Boasts 17,000 titles. 1-month membership (35SFr) allows you to borrow books (6 max.) for 2 weeks. Photocopier available. Open Tu, Th, F 12:30-5pm, W 2-7pm, Sa 10am-4pm, Su 11:30am-1pm. **City Library (Bibliothèque de la Cité),** pl. des Trois Perdrix 5 (☎418 32 22). Open Tu-F 10am-7pm, Sa 10am-5pm.

GLBT Organizations: Diologai, r. de la Navigation 11-13 (☎022 906 40 40; www.diologai.org). From Gare Cornavin, turn left and walk 5min. down r. de Lausanne; turn right onto r. de la Navigation. Resource group with programs from support groups to outdoor activities. Publishes *Diologai*, a guide to French-speaking Switzerland's gay scene. Mostly male, but women welcome. Hosts W gatherings for gay men starting at 6pm; call ahead. **360°,** r. de la Navigation 36 (☎741 00 70; www.360.ch), publishes an eponymous magazine. Walk-in hours Su 4-9pm. **Gay International Group (GIG;** ☎789 18 69; www.360.ch/espace/gig) is for international gay visitors to Geneva. Communal potluck dinners 2nd Sa each month; dinner at restaurant 4th Su each month. **Centre Femmes Natalie Barney,** Chemin Château Bloch 19 (☎797 27 14), offers services similar to those at Diologai, but is smaller and lesbian-oriented. 24hr. answering machine with events listings; live operator W 6-8pm. **Lesbian International Group** is an informal support group. (☎ 583 29 63. Ask for Flo.)

Laundromat: Lavseul, r. de Monthoux 29 (☎735 90 51 or 732 61 46). Wash 5SFr, dry 1SFr per 10min. Does not accept 20-cent pieces. Open daily 7am-midnight.

Public Showers: Point d'Eau, r. Chandieu 4 (☎734 22 40). Take bus #8 to "Canonnière" and turn right onto r. de Vermont; it's on the left. Free hot showers and personal hygiene center. Open M-F 3-7pm, Sa 10am-2pm. Additional location at r. de Fronteneux 48. Open M-F 9am-noon. **McClean,** at the train station, offers showers for 12SFr, urinal access for 1SFr, and toilet access for 2SFr. Open daily 6am-midnight.

EMERGENCY AND COMMUNICATIONS

Emergencies: Fire ☎118. **Ambulance** ☎144.

Police: r. de Berne 6 (☎117, non-emergency 715 38 50), next to post office.

Rape Crisis Hotline: Viol-Secours (☎345 20 20). Open M-Tu 2-6pm, W 4-8pm, Th 9am-1pm, F 9am-noon.

Late-Night Pharmacy: A revolving set of 4 pharmacies is open late (until 9 or 11pm) nightly. Consult the closest pharmacy or *Genève Agenda* for addresses and phone numbers. For urgent deliveries, call ☎144.

Medical Assistance: Hôpital Cantonal, r. Micheli-du-Crest 24 (☎372 33 11). Take bus #1 or 5 or tram #12. Door #2 is for emergency care, door #3 for consultations. For information on walk-in clinics, call the **Association des Médecins** (☎320 84 20).

Internet Access: For less than the cost of doing laundry, **Connections Net World,** r. de Monthoux 58 (☎715 38 28), offers access to the Internet on 20 PCs. 3SFr per 30min., 5SFr per hr. Open M-Sa 9:30am-2:30am, Su 1pm-2am. Copier available. **Point 6,** r. de Vieux-Billard 7a (☎800 26 00), off r. des Bains. 5SFr per hr. Open daily noon-midnight.

Post Office: Poste Centrale, r. de Mont-Blanc 18, a block from Gare Cornavin in the Hôtel des Postes. Counter open M-F 7:30am-6pm, Sa 8:30am-noon. Address Poste Restante to: Genève 1 Mont-Blanc, CH-1211 Geneva. Another branch is located behind the train station at r. des Gares 10-16. 24hr. self-service. Counters open M-F 7:30am-7pm, Sa 8:30am-noon; urgent mail counter open M-F 7am-10pm, Sa-Su noon-8pm.

▐ ACCOMMODATIONS AND CAMPING

Geneva is a cosmopolitan city with a five-star hotel system. Luckily for the budget traveler, however, the seasonal influx of university students and interns has created a secondary network of hostels, pensions, and university dorms moonlighting as summer hotels. *Info Jeunes* lists about 50 options: the highlights are below. The tourist office publishes *Budget Hotels*, stretching the definition of "budget" to 120SFr per person. For longer stays, check *Tribune de Genève's* weekly supplement of apartment classifieds or the tourist office's board.

City Hostel Geneva, r. Ferrier 2 (☎901 15 00; www.cityhostel.ch). From the station, turn left onto r. de Lausanne, left onto r. de Prieuré, and right onto r. Ferrier. 8min. from the station, City Hostel offers snug, clean rooms in a nice neighborhood. The small reception area overflows with friendly backpackers watching the free nightly movies (in English) in the TV room. Beer and Swiss Army knives sold at the desk. Kitchen facilities, book exchange, a comprehensive listing of markets in Geneva, and **Internet** access (8SFr per hr.). Lockers free. Sheets 3.50SFr. Laundry 8.50SFr. 6-night max. stay. Reception 7:30am-noon and 1pm-midnight. Check-out 10am. Single-sex 4-bed dorms 28SFr; singles 58SFr; doubles 85SFr. MC/V. ❷

Hôme St-Pierre, cour St-Pierre 4 (☎310 37 07; info@stpierre.ch). Take bus #5 to "pl. Neuve" or walk 15min. from the train station: cross the Rhône at pont du Mont-Blanc, then go up r. de la Fontaine toward pl. du Bourg-de-Four. Take the stairs up Passage des Degres-de-Poules (after Epicerie Pizzo), walk around to the front of the cathedral. It will be diagonally left with your back to the entrance of the cathedral. Ring the buzzer to be let in. Located in the heart of *vieille ville*, this 150-year-old "home" has comfortable beds and a convivial atmosphere. Although the church bells ring every 15min., the surrounding roads have few cars, and the area is relatively quiet. Breakfast M-Sa 7SFr. Lockers 5SFr. Reception M-Sa 9am-noon and 4-8pm, Su 9am-noon. Check-out 10am. Popular: reserve ahead. Dorms 23SFr; singles 36-45SFr; doubles 50-60SFr. MC/V. ❸

Cité Blueu Universitaire, ave. Miremont 46 (☎839 22 11; fax 22 23). From the right of the station, take bus #3 (dir: Crets-de-Champel) to the last stop; the Cité Universitaire is directly on your right. Institutional college housing in a modern tower has TV rooms, newspapers, a restaurant, a **disco** (all-night dancing Th and Sa, free to residents), ping-pong, tennis courts, a small grocery shop, and great views. Available only July-Oct. Reception M-F 8am-noon and 2-10pm, Sa 8am-noon and 6-10pm, Su 9-11am and 6-10pm. Check-out 10am. Lockout 11am-6pm and curfew 11pm, dorms only. 4 dorms (July-Sept. only) 22SFr, lockers included; singles 55SFr, student price 46SFr; doubles 84SFr; studios with kitchenette and bathroom 75SFr. AmEx/MC/V. ❷

Hôtel de la Cloche, r. de la Cloche 6 (☎732 94 81; fax 738 16 12), off quai du Mont-Blanc across from the Noga Hilton. In this converted mansion with lofty ceilings, most rooms have a chandelier and TV; some have antique mirrors and balconies. Ask for a lake view. Breakfast included. Reception 8am-10pm. Reserve a month in advance in summer. Summer singles 65SFr, winter 50-70SFr; doubles 95SFr/85SFr; triples 110SFr, with bath 130SFr; quads with toilet and shower 140SFr. AmEx/DC/MC/V. ❹

Camping Pointe-à-la-Bise, chemin de la Bise (☎752 12 96). Take bus #8 to "Rive," then bus E (north) to "Bise" and follow the "camping" signs for a 10min. walk down to the lake. The lakefront grounds, far from town, provide a free beach and a lively recreation area, as well as a calmer perspective on Geneva. Reception 8am-noon and 2-9pm. Reservations recommended. Open Apr.-Sept. 6.20SFr per adult, 3.10SFr per child, 9SFr per site (no tents provided). Tax 0.50SFr per visitor. Beds 15SFr. 4-person bungalows 60SFr. Showers free. ❶

◘ FOOD

Boulangeries, pâtisseries, and local open-air markets offer gourmet food at budget prices: 7SFr goes a long way when you combine a fresh loaf of bread with cheese and tomato. There are extensive dining options in the *vieille ville* near the cathedral, but you'll pay for the location. In the Les Paquîs area, bordered by the r. de Lausanne and Gare Cornavin on one side and the quais Mont-Blanc and Wilson on the other, a variety of ethnic foods can be found. Kebab stands are interspersed with Brazilian cafés, and the colorful neighborhood offers better prices than most. To the south, the village of Carouge is known for its lively student population and funky, chic *brasseries.* Dining on the waterfront will cost you; enjoy an ice-cream cone at a lakeside café instead. Around pl. du Cirque and plaine de Plainpalais are cheap, student-oriented "tea rooms," offering bakery fare at good prices.

▨ Chocolats Micheli, r. Micheli-du-Crest 1 (☎329 90 06). Take tram #13 to Plainpalais and walk up bd. des Philosophes until it intersects r. Micheli-du-Crest. Confectionery masterpieces abound in this exquisite Swiss chocolate store and café. The enticing aromas hanging in the air make choosing between the stacks of Swiss chocolate a test of mental toughness. About 1SFR per chocolate. Open Tu-F 8am-7pm, Sa 8am-5pm. MC/V. ❶

Restaurant Manora, r. de Cornavin 4 (☎909 44 10), 3min. from the station on the right, in the Placette department store. This huge self-serve restaurant offers an incredible selection of fresh, high-quality food at excellent prices. Salads (from 3SFr), fruit tarts (3.20SFr), fruit shakes (from 4SFr), main dishes cooked on the spot (from 8SFr), and free tap water (a rare commodity in Geneva). Breakfast 6SFr. Wheelchair accessible. Open M-Sa 7:30am-9:30pm, Su 9am-9:30pm. ❶

Le Rozzel, Grand-Rue 18 (☎312 42 72). Take bus #5 to "pl. Neuve," then walk up the hill past the cathedral on r. Jean-Calvin to Grand-Rue. This small Breton-style *crêperie* with outdoor seating in the *vieille ville* serves salty crêpes (4-18SFr), dessert crêpes (4.50-9SFr), and sangria (5SFr). A restaurant and café as well, Le Rozzel offers elegant salads and meals such as gaspacho and demi-salade-niçoise (15SFr). *Menü* 21SFr. Open M 7am-4pm, Tu-W 7am-7pm, Th-F 7am-10pm, Sa 9am-10pm. AmEx/MC/V. ❷

La Crise, r. de Chantepoulet 13 (☎738 02 64). From the station, turn right onto r. de Cornavin and left onto r. de Chantepoulet. Eat at Mme. LeParc's kitchen for tasty meals at reasonable prices. Quiche and veggies from 9SFr. Soup from 4SFr. Beer or wine from 3SFr. Open M-F 6am-3pm and 5-8pm, Sa 6am-3pm. ❶

Les Brasseurs, pl. Cornavin 20 (☎731 02 06), diagonally left while exiting the station, serves a variety of *flammeküchen,* an Alsatian specialty similar to thin-crust pizza, but topped with cream and onions instead of cheese and tomato sauce (12-23SFr). The main attraction, however, is the beer brewed on location (2L from 31SFr). The *flammeküchen* are served quickly, so be prepared to eat soon after ordering. Open M-W 11am-1am, Th-Sa 11am-2am, Su 5pm-1am. Kitchen open 11:30am-2pm and 6-10:45pm. *Flammeküchen* available daily until midnight. AmEx/V/MC. ❷

Spécialités Lebanese, pl. Cornavin 13 (☎732 02 07), directly in front while exiting the station, serves inexpensive sandwiches (7SFr). Specializes in lamb, chicken, and tabouleh. While perhaps not worth a detour, this authentic restaurant is perfect for budget travelers looking for a quick meal near the station. Open daily 7am-2am. ❶

Auberge de Saviese, r. des Pâquis 20 (☎732 83 30; fax 784 36 23). Take bus #1 to "Monthoux." Or from Gare Cornavin, turn left onto r. de Lausanne, then right on r. de Zurich, until you hit r. des Pâquis. Sip coffee (3SFr) in this English-friendly restaurant frequented by tourists. Excellent *fondue au cognac* (20SFr), *Raclette* with all the trimmings (31SFr), and classic regional perch (29SFr). Open M-Sa 10:30am-3pm and 5pm-12:30am, Su 5pm-12:30am. AmEx/DC/MC/V. ❹

Globus, r. de Rhône 48, on the pl. du Molard. A self-serve establishment that offers fresh fruit, crêpes, and pressed-on-demand orange juice. Other inexpensive gourmet delights include fresh produce, a *fromagerie,* and sushi. Meals 10-27SFr. Daily specials from 11SFr. Open M-W and F 7:30am-6:45pm, Th 7:30am-8pm, Sa 8am-5:45pm. ❷

MARKETS

Co-op, Migros, Grand Passage, and **Orient Express** branches are ubiquitous. On Sundays, the options include Gare Cornavin's **Aperto** (open daily 6am-10pm) and scattered neighborhood groceries and bakeries. A **public market** sells fresh fruits and cheese on **rue de Coutance** (open M-Sa 8am-6pm). A produce market is located on **rd-pt. de Plainpalais** (open Tu and F 8am-1pm, Su 8am-6pm). In Carouge, the **pl. du Marché** offers a market Wednesday and Saturday 8am-1pm. The **place de la Navigation** has markets Thursday and Friday 8am-1pm. **Marché des Eaux-Vives,** blvd. Helvétique, between cours de Rive and r. du Rhône, is a huge dairy, vegetable, and flower market (open M and Th 8am-1pm). City Hostel Geneva posts information on all of the markets in its lobby; the tourist office also has market information.

◉ SIGHTS

For centuries, Geneva was constrained by a belt of fortified walls and trenches. By the mid-19th century, when the fortifications were removed, the city's major historical sites had already been clustered in a dense, easily walkable space. The tourist office offers 2hr. **walking tours** in the summer on all things *genevois.* (Mid-June to Sept. M-Sa 10am, Tu and Th also 6:30pm; Oct. to mid-June Sa 10am. 12SFr, students and seniors 8SFr, children 6SFr. Tour recordings are available in winter for 10SFr plus 50SFr deposit.) Call the tourist office for infomation about themed tours. Tours also depart nightly from the Youth Hostel at 5:15pm and the City Hostel at 5:30pm. (See sign in hostel lobbies. 1½hr. Conducted in English, French, German, Spanish, or Portugese. Includes free boat ride across the lake. 15.80SFr.)

CATHEDRAL. The *vieille ville*'s **Cathédrale de St-Pierre,** the heart of the early Protestant world, is as austere and pure as on the day Calvin stripped the place of its Catholicism. From its altar, Calvin preached to full houses (1536-1564). His chair from those days still remains. The brightly painted **Maccabean Chapel,** restored in flamboyant style, gives a sample of how the cathedral walls might have looked pre-Reformation. Perhaps the most striking part of the cathedral is the silver-plated organ that looms intimidatingly at the rear of the nave. (Concerts Sa 6pm). The 157-step **north tower** provides a commanding view of the old town's winding streets and flower-bedecked homes. *(Open June-Sept. daily 9am-7pm; Oct.-May M-Sa 10am-noon and 2-5pm, Su 11am-12:30pm and 1:30-5pm. Closed Su mornings for services. Tower closes 30min. earlier and costs 3SFr. Bell-ringing July-Aug. Sa afternoon.)* Beneath the cathedral rest the ruins of a Roman sanctuary, a 4th-century basilica, and a 6th-century church. This extensive **archaeological site** includes an ancient version of forced-air heating ducts. *(Open June-Sept. Tu-Sa 11am-5pm, Su 10am-5pm; Oct.-May Tu-Sa 2-5pm, Su 10am-noon and 2-5pm. 5SFr, students 3SFr. Free English audioguide available.)*

OLD CITY. Surrounding the cathedral are the medieval townhouses and mansions of Geneva's *vieille ville*. **Maison Tavel,** a fortified palace and Geneva's oldest residential building, is 1min. from the west end. The 14th-century structure now houses a history **museum** by the same name (see p. 494). The **Old Arsenal** a few steps away has five cannons and a mural depicting the arrival of Huguenot refugees. Across the street is the **Hôtel de Ville** (town hall), whose components date from the 15th through 17th centuries. World leaders signed the first **Geneva Convention,** which governs the treatment of war prisoners, here on August 22, 1864.

Beginning at the *Hôtel de Ville*, the narrow **Grand-Rue** is crammed with medieval workshops and 18th-century mansions, often with hastily added 3rd or 4th floors, the result of the real estate boom following the influx of French Huguenots after Louis XIV repealed the Edict of Nantes. Plaques commemorating famous residents abound, including one at #40 marking the birthplace of philosopher **Jean-Jacques Rousseau.** Shops and galleries line the Grand-Rue, along with restaurants and cafés, whose open-air seating spills out into the cobblestone streets.

Head away from the *vieille ville* on r. de Chaudronniers to reach the nine glittering domes of the **Russian Orthodox Church,** on r. Töpffer, next to the Musée d'Art et d'Histoire. Step inside for the hauntingly lovely icons, stained glass, and opaque, incense-filled air. Hear the choir (Sept.-June Su 4pm). *(Photography, short skirts, and shorts are not allowed. Closed to visitors during the winter.)*

WATERFRONT. Descending from the cathedral toward the lake is like walking forward in time 400 years. Streets widen, buses scuttle back and forth, and nearly every corner sports a chic boutique. On the waterfront, the **Jet d'Eau,** down quai Gustave-Ardor, spews a spectacular plume of water 140m high. The sight, a tourist spectacle, was inspired by a faulty piping jet. The world's highest fountain keeps seven tons of water aloft from March to October and is visible throughout the city.

The floral clock in the nearby **Jardin Anglais,** boasting 6500 plants, including large magnolias and gingko trees, and the world's largest second hand (2.5m), pays homage to Geneva's watch industry. The clock is the city's most overrated sight and was once its most hazardous: almost 1m was cut away from it since tourists, intent on taking the perfect photo, continually backed into oncoming traffic.

The rose-lined *quais* lead to two fun-parks. **Pâquis Plage,** quai du Mont-Blanc 30, is popular with the *Genevois*. (☎732 29 74. Open 9am-8:30pm. 2SFr.) Farther from the city center, **Genève Plage,** on quai Gustave Ador, offers a giant waterslide, an

Olympic-sized pool, volleyball tournaments, and topless sunbathing. (☎734 26 82. 7SFr, children 3.50SFr.) The source of these waters, the Rhône, was consecrated by the pope during a particularly bad outbreak of the bubonic plague as a "burial" ground. Today, the lake and river are crystal clear and free of bodies and pollution. **Ferry tours** leaving from quai du Mont-Blanc provide views of Geneva. **Swiss Boat** (☎732 47 47; 35min. tour 8SFr, children 5SFr; 1¼hr. 12SFr/7SFr; 2hr. 20SFr/15SFr) and **Mouettes Genevoises** (☎732 29 44; 45min. tour 12SFr, children 7SFr, seniors 8SFr; 2hr. 20SFr/15SFr) narrate cruises in English. **CGN** provides a scenic cruise of the shores of Lake Geneva (55min., 12SFr) and has been sending cruises to lakeside towns, including Lausanne, Montreux, and the stupendous Château de Chillon, for the past 125 years. (☎741 52 31 or 741 52 35. Round-trip 54SFr, Eurail and SwissPass valid.)

Travelers with children might also enjoy **STT Train Tours SA**, 36 rue de Mônle. These mini train circuits (35min.) ride around the right bank (depart from Rotonde du Mont-Blanc), the left bank (depart from the English Gardens), or the *vieille ville*. (Depart from the Place du Rhône. ☎781 0404. 7.90SFr, children 4.90SFr.)

PARKS AND GARDENS. Geneva is bedecked with sumptuous gardens scattered strategically throughout the city. Below the cathedral on the r. de la Croix-Rouge, the **Parc des Bastions'** lovely expanse stretches from pl. Neuve to the pl. des Philosophes. On the park's northern corner, *Genevois* can be spotted playing chess with life-sized pieces. **Le Mur des Réformateurs** (Reformers' Wall) displays a sprawling collection of bas-relief narrative panels, an array of multilingual inscriptions, and the towering figures of the Reformers themselves. As the largest statues (Knox, Beze, Calvin, and Farel) jostle each other for "leader of the Protestant pack" bragging rights, Cromwell and Rhode Island's Roger Williams trail behind. The imposing campus of **Geneva University** sits opposite the wall, with sunbathers in between.

Strolling north along the river quais brings you to the lush **Parc Mon-Repos**, off ave. de France, and **La Perle du Lac**, off ave. de la Paix, where panting joggers and playful kids stream along curvy paths painted in various floral hues and lined by massive, ancient trees. The **Jardin Botanique**, situated along r. de Lausanne and opposite the World Trade Organization, is home to three greenhouses that support tropical and Mediterranean plants. This garden is an exhibit in and of itself and merits at least one early morning walkthrough. (Open daily Apr.-Sept. 8am-7:30pm; Oct.-Mar. 9:30am-5pm. Greenhouses open Sa-Th 9:30-11:00am and 3-4:30pm. Free.) Venturing farther uphill brings you to **Parc de l'Ariana**, where impressive grounds surround the UN building and the Ariana pottery museum. On the opposite (south) side of the lake, past the Jet d'Eau on quai Gustave-Ador, **Parc la Grange** features a garden of 40,000 roses, at their peak bloom in June. **Parc des Eaux-Vives**, next to la Grange, is the perfect spot for a picnic or an impromptu frisbee game.

INTERNATIONAL HILL. The parks up the hill behind the train station offer spectacular views of Lac Léman with Mont Blanc in the background (see Jardin Botanique and Parc de l'Ariana, above). For even better vistas, climb up to Geneva's international city, where embassies and multilateral organizations abound. Visit the **International Red Cross**, which contains its own museum (see below). Below it stand the European headquarters of the **United Nations**, filling the building that once sheltered the League of Nations. The guided tour of the UN is quite dull (typical title: "Peace: There is Room for All"), despite some art donated by all the countries of the world and an introductory video recapping the work of the UN in the past year. The constant traffic of international diplomats (often in handsome non-Western dress) provides more excitement than any tour. There's also a not-so-subtle display of Cold War one-upmanship: the armillary sphere depicting the heavens and donated by the US stands next to a monument dedicated to the "conquest of space" donated by the former USSR. (Enter at the Pregny gate across from the Red Cross. Bring a photo ID. ☎917 48 96 or 917 45 38. Open July-Aug. daily 10am-5pm; Apr.-

June and Sept.-Oct. daily 10am-noon and 2-4pm; Nov.-Mar. M-F 10am-noon and 2-4pm. 8.50SFr, seniors and students 6.50SFr, children 4SFr, children under age 6 free. 1hr. tours in any of 15 languages when requested by a sizable group.)

🏛 MUSEUMS

INTERNATIONAL RED CROSS AND RED CRESCENT MUSEUM. A visit to the 🖾International Red Cross and Red Crescent Museum will etch the words of Dostoyevsky into your mind: "Each of us is responsible to all others for everything." The self-guided tour begins with these words and the ensuing passage through the museum's black-walled rooms filled with spotlighted exhibits fixes them firmly on the mind. Built into a hillside, the museum employs photographs and wartime film-clip montages to drive home its emotional narrative of historic humanitarianism. The stark glass and steel building houses a maze of provocative and haunting graphics and audiovisual displays, all through the lens of the life of Henri Dunant, the Red Cross's founder. The Museum also offers a view into the plight of political prisoners by inviting visitors to experience life in a prison cell. *(Ave. de la Paix 17. Take bus #8 or F to "Appia" or bus V or Z to "Ariana." ☎ 748 95 11 or 95 28 or 95 25. Displays in English, French, and German. Open Su-M and W-Sa 10am-5pm. 10SFr, students and seniors 5SFr, under 12 free. Self-guided audio tours in English, French, German, Italian, Japanese, and Spanish 3SFr.)*

ART MUSEUMS. If you visit one art museum in Geneva, the 🖾Petit-Palais should be it. This beautiful mansion has paintings, sculptures, and drawings by Picasso, Renoir, Gauguin, Cézanne, and Chagall. The inventive basement *salles* (rooms) present themed exhibits: the influence of primitive art on modern aesthetes, the nude female form, and radiant meditations on nature. *(Terrasse St-Victor 2, off blvd. Helvétique. Take bus #36 to "Petit Palais" or #1, 3, or 5 to "Claparède." ☎ 346 14 33. Open M-F 10am-6pm, Sa-Su 10am-5pm. 10SFr, students and seniors 5SFr, children under 12 free. V.)*

The **Musée Barbier-Mueller** has one of the world's most respected collections of African art. Photographs of the objects in their original settings put the frequently changing exhibitions in context. There is rarely a crowd. *(R. Jean-Calvin 10. From Grand-Rue in the vieille ville, turn onto r. de la Pélisserie and right onto r. Jean-Calvin. ☎ 312 02 70; musee@barbier-mueller.ch. Open daily 11am-5pm. 5SFr, children under 12 3SFr.)*

For an eclectic collection of 16th-century spears juxtaposed with 18th-century chests of drawers and 20th-century paintings, head to the **Musée d'Art et d'Histoire.** Collections focus on local history. *(2 r. Charles-Galland. ☎ 418 26 00. Heading toward l'Arve, turn right off the bd. Helvetique onto r. Charles-Galland. The museum is on the right. Open Tu-Su 10am-5pm. Free. Temporary exhibits 4.50SFr. Mandatory lockers 2SFr.)*

Featuring everything from creative artistry to the just plain weird, the **Musée d'Art Moderne et Contemporaire** displays the most avant-garde art in Geneva. If you want to see an "I Am Still Alive" telegram exhibit, or huge, clear-plastic mattresses, this is the place to be. Its permanent collections include post-1970s photography, a giant net constructed from rubber bands, and poetry. *(R. des Vieux-Grenadiers 10. Take bus #1 to "Bains." ☎ 320 61 22. From the corner of r. des Bains and r. des Vieux-Grenadiers, turn onto r. des Vieux-Grenadiers. Turn left into a parking lot, then left into the museum. Open Tu-F noon-6pm, Sa-Su 11am-6pm. 9SFr; ages 13-18, students, teachers, artists, and retirees 6SFr; children under 12, scholars, students of art, art history, or architecture, the unemployed, and invalids free. Mandatory lockers 2SFr.)* The museum also houses the **Jean Tua Car and Cycle Museum,** a collection of 70 cars, motorcycles, and bicycles, most pre-WWII. *(R. des Bains 28-30. ☎ 321 36 37. Open W-Su 2-6pm. 9SFr, students 7SFr, children 4SFr.)*

OTHER MUSEUMS. Maison Tavel near the Hôtel de Ville acts as a storehouse for random artifacts typical of daily life in Geneva's past, including the 1799 guillotine from pl. Neuve, a collection of medieval front doors, wallpaper remains, clothing, and a vast zinc and copper model of 1850 Geneva that took 18 years to build. Guidebooks in 12 languages available at the entrance. *(R. du Puits-St-Pierre 6. ☎ 310 29 00. Open Tu-Su 10am-5pm. Free, except for temporary exhibits.)*

The **Musée d'Ethnographie** has a small but varied collection, which includes Japanese Samurai armor, Australian aboriginal paintings, and a Bolivian mummy. *(Blvd. Carl-Vogt 65-67. Take bus #1 to "Ecole-Médecins." ☎ 418 45 50. Open Tu-Su 10am-5pm. Free. Temporary exhibits 4.50SFr, students 2.50SFr, children free.)*

Live boa constrictors and Janus, the two-headed turtle, greet you at the **Musée d'Histoire Naturelle** (Museum of Natural History). The most frequent visitors to the museum are children on school trips, who come to see the extensive exhibits of everything from regional mammals and birds—stuffed and on display—to rocks, crystals, and fossils from all over the world. Be sure to check out the Great Horned Owl on display among a collection of other, more exotic birds. *(Rte. du Malagnou 1. Take bus #1 to "Museum." ☎ 418 63 00. Open Tu-Su 9:30am-5pm. Free.)*

Candide fans should make a pilgrimage to **Musée Voltaire,** located in the witty writer's former home, a chandeliered 18th-century townhouse. *(R. des Délices 25. Take bus #6, 7, 19, or 27 to "Délices." ☎ 344 71 33. Open M-F 2-5pm. Free.)*

🔲 🔲 ENTERTAINMENT AND NIGHTLIFE

FESTIVALS
Summer brings festivals, **free open-air concerts,** and **free organ music** in Cathédrale de St-Pierre. (June-Sept. Sa 6pm. *Carillon* performances Sa 5pm.) In July and August, the **Cinélac** turns Genève Plage into an open-air cinema. (☎ 840 04 04; www.cinelac.ch. 16SFr.) Check the listings in *Genève Agenda* for indoor cinemas. Films marked "v.o." are in their original language with French and sometimes German subtitles, while "st. ang." means that the film has English subtitles.

Geneva hosts the biggest celebration of **American Independence Day** outside the US on July 4 and a firework-filled party for **Swiss National Day** on August 1. The **Fêtes de Genève** in early August feature international music and culminate in a spectacular fireworks display. During this celebration, Roseau Island becomes a carnival for children. **La Bâtie Festival,** traditionally held from late August to early September, draws Swiss music lovers for a two-week orgy of cabaret, theater, and concerts. (☎ 908 69 50; batie@world.com.ch. 10-32SFr, students half-price. Many events free.) **Free jazz concerts** take place in July and August in Parc de la Grange. The best party in Geneva is **L'Escalade,** commemorating the dramatic repulsion of invading Savoyard troops. The revelry lasts for a weekend in early December.

BARS AND NIGHTCLUBS
La Jonction, at the junction of the Rhône and Arve rivers, accessible by the #2, 10-20, and D buses (to "Jonction"), is the home of Artamis and casual bars and concert venues for rockers and ravers. **Place Bourg-de-Four,** in the *vieille ville* below the cathedral, attracts students and professionals to its charming terraces and old-world atmosphere. **Place du Molard,** on the right bank by the pont du Mont-Blanc, has terrace cafés as well as big, loud bars and clubs. **Les Paquis,** near the Gare Cornavin and the pl. de la Navigation, is the red light district, but also appeals to a less prurient appetite with its wide array of rowdy, low-lit bars. **Carouge,** across the River Arve, is a student-friendly locus of nightlife activity, the same place dissidents went to party during Calvin's purification of the city. Some of Geneva's most popular nightlife is semi-underground. **Squats** have become a popular housing option for counter-cultural youth who prefer run-down housing to paying rent and living by rules. The authorities are quite aware of their existence, but rarely break up the parties. Information is generally spread word-of-mouth, but one more official squat is

SAMICHLAUS IS COMING...FOR YOU!

December 5 means one thing for "naughty" children across Switzerland: a day of reckoning. On this day, "Samichlaus" (St. Nicholas) parades through the streets, stopping for a visit at each house along the way. In snowy mountain towns, sleighs bedecked with festive decorations bear the magical man, while a walk on foot must suffice in lower regions. Children frantically tidy themselves up in order to impress their visitor. They have more than just presents at stake here.

Legend (kept alive by aggravated parents) has it that Samichlaus and his helpers cart disobedient children off to the Black Forest for a year of unspeakable horrors. Children tremble to hear Samichlaus's heavy knock on the door and stand wide-eyed as he recounts the worst of their capers for the year. It seems that not a thing escapes the watchful eye of this magical man. (Unbeknownst to the youngsters, the parents hand the visitor a list of their little ones' transgressions for the year when they usher him into the house.) The Black Forest looms closer and closer as the guest recounts mischief after mischief. Luckily, the visit ends in treats all around, and the children return to their old ways, much to their parents' dismay...that is, until December 5 rolls around again.

Le Rhino, blvd. des Philosophes 24, between Plainpalais and pl. Claparède, unmistakable given the oversized red rhino horn that graces it.

🎨 **La Clémence,** pl. du Bourg-de-Four 20 (☎312 24 98). Walk down the stairs at the back of the cathedral, turn right, and walk to the end of pl. du Bourg-de-Four, or take bus #36 to "Bourg-de-Four." Generations of students have eaten at this chic bar, named after the bell atop the Cathédrale de St-Pierre. Come for breakfast (croissant 1.30SFr, coffee 3SFr). Open M-Th 7am-12:30am, F-Sa 7am-1:30am.

Flanagan's, r. du Cheval-Blanc 4 (☎310 13 14), off Grand-Rue in the *vieille ville*. Outside, a sign proclaims, "Irish Parking: All Others Will Be Towed." Inside, friendly bartenders pull a good beer and entertain well in this Irish cellar bar, though you'll be hard-pressed to find an Irish accent among the Anglophones. If you're looking for a dark sports bar replete with televisions that isn't crowded, this is the place. Pint of Guinness 8SFr; 6SFr during happy hour (daily 5-7pm). Open daily 5pm-2am.

Au Chat Noir, r. Vautier 13, Carouge (☎343 49 98). Take tram #12 to "pl. du Marché," turn left upon entering the square, and then left again on r. Vautier; the bar is on the right. The sensuously curved bar and dark red curtains set the mood in this popular jazz, funk, rock, salsa, and blues venue. Live concerts or DJs every night. Has a comprehensive collection of brochures for upcoming concerts and shows. Beer 5SFr. Sangria 6-8SFr. Cover 10-15SFr. Open M-Th 6pm-4am, F 6pm-5am, Sa 9pm-5am, Su 9pm-4am.

LAUSANNE ☎021

Two thousand years ago, Romans came to the little town of Lausanne on the shores of Lac Léman and found it so enticing that they stayed until the collapse of their empire. Later, the city hosted a different sort of visitor, welcoming vacationing novelists Dickens and Thackeray. T.S. Eliot created the wrote *The Waste Land* near the placid Ouchy shoreline and the medieval labyrinth of the *vieille ville*. Today, Lausanne's unique museums, distinctive neighborhoods, winding medieval streets, and magnificent lakefront parks make it worth a stay.

TRANSPORTATION

Trains: pl. de la Gare 9 (☎157 22 22; 1.19SFr per min.). To: **Basel** (2½hr., every hr. 5:27am-11:27pm, 64SFr); **Geneva** (50min., every 20min. 4:55am-12:46am, 19SFr); **Montreux** (20min., every 30min. 5:24am-2:29am, 10SFr); **Paris** (4hr., 4 per day 7:36am-5:52pm, 71SFr); **Zurich** via Biel (2½hr., 3 per hr. 5:27am-10:27pm, 65SFr).

Public Transportation: The 5-stop **Métro Ouchy** runs from the *vieille ville* to the Ouchy waterfront. The **Métro Ouest** runs west to the University of Lausanne and the Federal Institute of Technology. Both *métros* run approximately M-Sa 5am-midnight, Su 6am-midnight. Buses cross the city roughly 6am-midnight (check bus stops for specific lines; the official city map also shows bus lines). Exact change needed. 3-stop ticket 1.50SFr; 1hr. pass 2.40SFr; 24hr. pass 7.20SFr; ages 6-16 1.30SFr/4SFr. Free with Swiss Pass or Lausanne Pass (available at the tourist office).

Ferries: CGN, ave. de Rhodanie 17 (☎614 04 04; for reservations 0 848 822 848). To: **Evian** (4:55am-12:15am; 16SFr, round-trip 27.20SFr); **Geneva** (3½hr.; 9:15am-5:15pm; 34.80SFr, round-trip 54SFr); **Montreux** (1½hr.; 4 per day 9:30am-6:05pm; 20.60SFr, round-trip 35.20SFr). Purchase tickets at dock. Eurail and SwissPass valid. Open M-F 8am-7:30pm.

Taxis: Available at r. Madeleine 1, pl. St-François, pl. de la Navigation, and in front of the station, or call **taxibus** (☎08 00 080 03 12) or **taxiphone** (24hr. ☎08 00 81 08 10).

Car Rental: Avis, ave. de la Gare 50 (☎340 72 00; fax 72 09). **Hertz,** pl. du Tunnel 17 (☎312 53 11). **Europcar,** ave. Ruchonnet 2 (☎323 91 52). **Lococar,** ave. Ruchonnet 30 (☎320 30 80).

Parking: Parking Simplon-Gare, r. du Simplon 2 (☎617 67 44), behind the station (entrance on blvd. de Grancy). 2SFr per 50min., overnight (10pm-7am) 1SFr per hr. Open M-F 8am-7pm, Sa 8am-5pm. MC/V only for 20SFr or more. On city streets, white zones indicate free unlimited parking, while blue zones mark 1½hr. zones. To park on the street, pick up a parking disc from the tourist office. Set the present time and the maximum stay time, and leave the disc displayed on the dashboard.

Bike Rental: (☎0512 24 21 62), at the baggage check in the station. 30SFr per day, 23SFr per half-day. 5SFr discount with Eurail or SwissPass. Return bikes at another station for an additional 6SFr. Helmet and lock included. Open 6:40am-7:40pm. Find bike rental (☎606 27 61) starting from 10SFr at pl. du Port 6, next to the Ouchy Métro exit. Be warned: the winding streets of the old city and the route from Ouchy to the station are extremely hilly.

■ ☐ ORIENTATION AND PRACTICAL INFORMATION

Two-dimensional maps of Lausanne are confusing because the city is on a number of steep hills connected by vaulted bridges. The easiest way to explore the city is on the **Métro Ouchy,** a five-stop cog-rail subway system which runs from the waterfront up to pl. St-François. The *métro*'s Lausanne-CFF stop is across from the station and goes down to Ouchy (the neighborhood on the waterfront) or up to the *vieille ville.* Buses #1, 3, and 5 serve the station; most are routed to pl. St-François. Wheelchair-bound visitors should pay special attention to the city's terrain in planning their visits.

TOURIST AND FINANCIAL SERVICES

Tourist Office: Main office (☎613 73 73 or 73 21; www.lausanne-tourisme.ch), in the main hall of the train station. Open daily 9am-7pm. **Branch office** across from pl. de la Navigation (M: Ouchy or bus #2: Ouchy). Open daily 9am-6pm. Pick up the free *Plan Officiel* (map and public transportation guide) and *Welcome to Lausanne* (booklet listing cheap hotels and private rooms) for free. The staff sells **Lausanne Passes** for 15SFr (p. 502) and makes hotel reservations for 4SFr commission. Wheelchair accessible. AmEx/DC/MC/V.

Budget Travel: STA Travel, blvd. de Grancy 20 (☎617 56 27; www.statravel.ch), 2 streets downhill from the station past the overpass; turn right off of ave. d'Ouchy. Books student tickets, organizes group travel, and sells ISICs for 15SFr. Open M-F 9:15am-6pm, Sa 9am-noon. Another location at 25 r. du Bourg. Open M 1-6:30pm, Tu-F 9am-6:30pm, Su 10am-5pm.

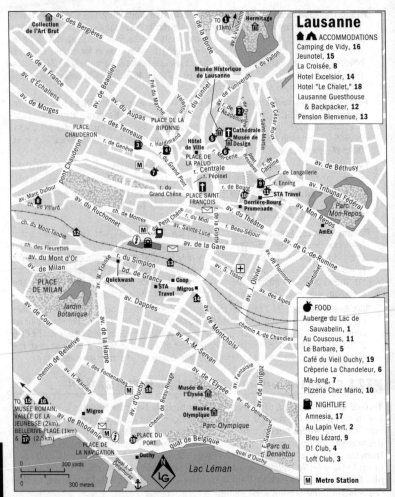

Lausanne

ACCOMMODATIONS
Camping de Vidy, **16**
Jeunotel, **15**
La Croisée, **8**
Hotel Excelsior, **14**
Hotel "Le Chalet," **18**
Lausanne Guesthouse
& Backpacker, **12**
Pension Bienvenue, **13**

FOOD
Auberge du Lac de
Sauvabelin, **1**
Au Couscous, **11**
Le Barbare, **5**
Café du Vieil Ouchy, **19**
Crêperie La Chandeleur, **6**
Ma-Jong, **7**
Pizzeria Chez Mario, **10**

NIGHTLIFE
Amnesia, **17**
Au Lapin Vert, **2**
Bleu Lézard, **9**
D! Club, **4**
Loft Club, **3**

M Metro Station

Currency Exchange: (☎312 38 24), at the station. Good rates. 2SFr commission. No commission on American Express traveler's checks. **Western Union** (☎0 800 007 107) transfers 7am-6:30pm. Cash advances with AmEx/DC/MC/V. Open 6:30am-7:30pm. **24hr. exchange machine** outside offers the same rates for the same commission.

American Express: ave. Mon Répos 14 (☎310 19 00; fax 19 19), across from parking garage. Cashes traveler's checks, sells airline tickets, and holds mail for 2 months. Travel services open M-F 8:30am-5:30pm; financial office open 2-5:30pm.

LOCAL SERVICES
Luggage Storage: (☎0512 24 21 62), at the train station. 7SFr per day. Lockers 4-7SFr per day. Open 6:40am-7:40pm.

Lost Property: At the train station with the luggage storage. Open M-Sa 6:40am-7:40pm.

Bookstore: Payot Librairie, r. Pépinet 4 (☎341 31 31; fax 33 45), down r. Pepinet from pl. St-François. Large English section with contemporary and classic fiction and some nonfiction. Open M-F 9am-6:45pm, Sa 9am-5pm. AmEx/MC/V.

Library: Cantonal and University Palais de Rumine, pl. de la Riponne 6 (☎316 78 80; www.unil.ch/BCU). Borrowing card free with ID. Open for borrowing M-F 10am-6pm, Sa 9am-noon. Reading room open M-F 8am-10pm, Sa 8am-5pm. **Lausanne City Library,** pl. Chauderon (☎ 315 69 15; fax 315 60 07). Take buses #3, 4, 7, or 9 to "Chauderon." Walk down the stairs. Open for borrowing and photocopying services M-Th noon-9pm, F 10am-9pm.

GLBT Organizations: Rainbow Line, chemin des Epinettes 10 (☎0848 80 50 80), near the Lausanne Guesthouse, provides free information Tu 7:30-10pm.

Laundromat: Quick Wash, blvd. de Grancy 44. 2 streets downhill behind the train station; turn right. Wash and dry around 12-14SFr. Open M-F 8:30am-10:30pm, Sa-Su 9am-10:30pm. **Salon Laver du Simplon,** 13 r. du Simplon, a block east of the Co-op. Wash and dry around 15SFr. Open daily 8am-10pm.

Public Showers: McClean, at the train station. Showers 12SFr, urinals 1SFr, toilets 2SFr. Open daily 6am-midnight.

EMERGENCY AND COMMUNICATIONS

Emergency: Police ☎ 117. **Fire** ☎ 118. **Ambulance** ☎ 144. **Crisis Line** ☎ 143.

24hr. Pharmacy: Call ☎ 111 to find out which pharmacy is open all night (they rotate). After-hours emergency service ☎ 613 12 24. 34.30SFr surcharge for after-hours purchases. Pharmacy in the train station open M-F 7:30am-6:45pm, Sa 8am-5pm.

24hr. Medical Service: At the hospital (☎ 314 11 11).

Internet Access: Quanta, ave. de la Gare 4, above the McDonald's and the Lausanne-CFF *métro* stop, and across from the train station. 4SFr per 30min. Open M-F 9am-4:30pm, Sa-Su 9am-1am. **Internet Café,** ave. de Beaulieu 3 (☎312 35 45). 5SFr per hr. Open daily 9am-9pm.

Post Office: Centre Postal, ave. de la Gare 43b (☎344 35 13), on the right exiting the station. Address *Poste Restante* to: 1000 Lausanne 1 Cases, CH-1001, Lausanne. Open M-F 7:30am-6:30pm, Sa 8am-noon. Express mail M-F 6:30am-10pm, Sa noon-4pm, Su 5-9pm. Photocopying service available. To dispatch your postcard from the site where Edward Gibbon wrote *Decline and Fall of the Roman Empire*, visit **Poste St-François,** pl. St-François 15 (☎344 38 31). Open M-F 7:30am-6:30pm, Sa 8am-noon.

Postal Code: CH-1002. Another branch located next to the *métro* station in Ouchy.

▶ ACCOMMODATIONS AND CAMPING

The home of the world's oldest hotel school, Lausanne has a well-deserved reputation for service-industry excellence. It's a good idea to pick up the tourist office's list of cheap hotels, private boarding houses, and *Pensionen,* since innumerable festivals and conferences can make housing scarce. Owners generally prefer stays of at least three nights and often as long as a month. Travelers looking for apartments to rent can turn to the local paper *24 Heures* (free at the tourist office).

🔖 **Lausanne Guesthouse and Backpacker,** chemin des Epinettes 4 (☎601 80 00; info@lausanne-guesthouse.ch). From the train station, head left downhill on ave. W. Fraisse. Take first right on chemin des Epinettes. This elegant guesthouse has a convenient location and comfortable rooms facing the lake. Ask for a room with a balcony to enjoy views of the lake and to distance yourself from the nearby train tracks. Kitchen, BBQ grill, and lockers included. Laundry 5SFr. Night parking 10SFr. Key box available for late arrivals/early departures (1SFr). Reception 7am-noon and 3-10pm. At Backpacker: pillow, blanket, and sheets 5SFr. Locker included. 4-bed dorms 34SFr. At Guesthouse: singles 81SFr, with bathroom 89SFr; doubles 88SFr/100SFr. ❷/❹

La Croisée, ave. Marc Dufour 15 (☎321 09 09; www.hotellacroisee.ch). 10min. from the train station. Walk up ave. du Ruchonnet and continue as it turns into ave. Marc Dufour. This youth hostel and 2-star hotel offers stunning views of Lac Léman (be sure to ask about rooms on the south side), plus TV room, terrace, and cafeteria space. The dormitory quads offer in-room sinks and desks. Breakfast buffet 7.50SFr, dinner around 17SFr. Some showers and bathrooms are in the hall; some are within rooms. Pillow, blanket, and sheets 10.50SFr. Reception M-F 7:30am-9pm, Sa 7:30am-noon and 4-7:30pm, Su 8am-12:30pm. No curfew. Reservations recommended. 4- to 10-bed dorms from 23.50SFr; singles 80-90SFr; doubles 130-150SFr. Children under 6 free, ages 6-11 50% off, ages 12-15 30% off. Special rates for extended stays. MC/V. ❸

Pension Bienvenue, r. du Simplon 2 (☎616 29 86). 5min. from the train station. Exit out the back entrance of the station, cross the street, turn left onto r. du Simplon, and it's 2 blocks further on the left side of the street. **Women only.** This well-worn but recently restored 27-room *Pension* has communal TV rooms and clean, comfortable rooms and beds. Breakfast included. Kitchen available. Laundry 3SFr. Hall showers and bathrooms only. Reception M–F 9-11:30am and 4-8:30pm, Sa-Su 9-11:30am and 5-8:30pm. 52SFr. Special rates for extended stays. ❸

Hôtel "Le Chalet," ave. d'Ouchy 49 (☎616 52 06). Take M: Ouchy to "Jordils" or bus #2 (dir: Bourdonnette) to "Jordils." Built in 1877, this chalet has been run by the same welcoming matron since 1940. Travelers enjoy the homey atmosphere in the individualized rooms, each equipped with a sink. Literati occasionally visit the hotel to commune with the spirit of former resident August Strindberg in the evergreen garden. Breakfast 10SFr. Hall showers. Reception 8am-10pm. Singles 50-63SFr; doubles 92SFr. ❸

Jeunotel (HI), chemin du Bois-de-Vaux 36 (☎626 02 22; www.jeunotel.ch). Take bus #2 (dir: Bourdonnette) to "Bois-de-Vaux." Cross the street and follow the signs. This large industrial hostel is down a long concrete driveway on the right past the Musée Romain de Lausanne-Vidy. Courtyards with ping-pong tables, a bowling alley next door, a bar and a restaurant within the complex, and a backpacker crowd enliven the hostel. Breakfast and sheets included; lunch and dinner available M-F. Small lockers available. Parking available. Reception 24hr. Check-out 10am. Reserve ahead in the summer. Wheelchair accessible. Singles 53SFr, with shower 79SFr; doubles 41SFr/48SFr; triples or quads 31SFr, non-members 39SFr. AmEx/DC/MC/V. ❶

Hôtel Excelsior, chemin du Closelet 6 (☎616 84 51; excelsior@fastnet.ch), 5min. from the train station. Turn right along ave. de la Gare, right on ave. d'Ouchy, and left after the bridge on Closelet. Spacious rooms with televisions, telephones, and desks make up for the cramped, run-down hallways. Breakfast 9SFr. Parking 10SFr. Reception M and Sa 8am-10pm, Tu-F 8am-noon and 2-10pm, Su 8am-noon and 7-10pm. Singles 65-90SFr; doubles 90-130SFr. AmEx/MC/V. ❹

Camping de Vidy, chemin du Camping 3 (☎622 50 00; www.campinglausannevidy.ch). Take bus #2 from M: Ouchy (dir: Bourdonnette) to "Bois-de-Vaux." Cross the street and walk down chemin du Bois-de-Vaux past Jeunotel and under the overpass. The office is straight ahead across rte. de Vidy. Near a swimming pool and minutes from a lively public beach. Restaurant (May-Sept. 7am-11pm), supermarket, and playground. Showers and access to dishwashing facilities included. Laundry and Internet (15SFr per hr.) available. Reception daily July-Aug. 8am-9pm; Sept.-June 8am-12:30pm and 4-8pm. Wheelchair accessible. 6.50SFr per adult, 6SFr per student, 5SFr per child ages 6-15, 8-12SFr per tent. 1- to 2-person bungalows 54SFr; 3- to 4-person bungalows 86SFr. Electricity 3-4SFr. Tax 1.20SFr per tent, 1.30SFr per vehicle.

▶ FOOD

No visit to Lausanne is complete without a taste of Lac Léman's famous perch or *papet vaudois* (a local delicacy made from leeks, potatoes, cabbage, and sausage). Restaurants, cafés, and bars cluster around pl. St-François and the *vieille ville*, while *boulangeries* sell cheap sandwiches on every street. Surprisingly fresh fare and crusty bread await at *métro* stations. Numerous grocery stores, frequent markets, and abundant parks make for affordable and pleasant picnics. While pricey, touristy cafés dominate the culinary scene in Ouchy, crêpes, ice cream, and other sweet fare can be gotten at a number of stands on the waterfront.

Le Barbare, Escaliers du Marché 27 (☎312 21 32), at the top of steps off the far right of the pl. de la Palud. Stop by for lunch or a mid-afternoon treat after trekking to the cathedral. Sandwiches from 5.50SFr. Omelettes 7.50-10SFr. Pizzas 12-16SFr. Try the *Chocolat Maison Viennois avec chantilly*, a rich chocolate drink (5.20SFr), perfect as a reward for the uphill climb. Open M-Sa 8:30am-midnight. AmEx/DC/MC/V. ❶

Crêperie La Chandeleur, r. Mercerie 9 (☎312 84 19). From pl. St-François, head down the r. Pépinet to the pl. de la Palud; with your back to the Hôtel de Ville, r. Mercier is off the far right corner of the pl. de la Palud. Enjoy custom-made crêpes in a tea-room atmosphere or sit outside on the wisteria-covered terrace. Try traditional (butter, sugar, or honey around 6SFr), ice cream (7.30-10.30SFr), or gourmet flambées, with choice of liqueur (10.70-11.70SFr). Open Tu-Th 11:30am-10pm, F-Sa 11:30am-11pm. MC/V. ❶

Au Couscous, r. Enning 2 (☎321 38 40). From pl. St-François, head away from the Zurich Bank sign and turn left up r. de la Paix to r. Enning. Inside this Tunisian/North African restaurant red tablecloths, a mosaic-tiled floor, and sequined pillows are the backdrop for delicious fare. Extensive, veggie-friendly menu (13.90-23SFr). Delicious couscous 23-24SFr. Lunch specials from 17SFr, vegetarian 21SFr. Open M-Tu 11:30am-2:30pm and 6:30pm-midnight, W-Th 11:30am-2:30pm and 6:30pm-1am, F 11:30am-2:30pm and 6:30pm-2am, Sa 6:30pm-2am, Su 6:30pm-1am. ❸

Café du Vieil-Ouchy, pl. du Port 3 (☎616 21 94). Take bus #2 to "Beau-Rivage," walk down the hill to the lake and turn left on r. du Port, on your left. Take in views of the lake and the château while you enjoy a *Rösti* platter (9-23SFr) or cheese fondue (21SFr). Savor a delectable *coupe maison* (10SFr) for dessert. Open M and Th-Su. ❸

Pizzeria Chez Mario, r. du Bourg 28. Head 5min. up r. du Bourg, which lies behind St-François. Mario's offers undeniable atmosphere for those looking for a bite of cheap pizza (from 13SFr) in a funky restaurant filled with local teenagers. A table by the window offers views of the *vieille ville*. Open daily 11:30am-1am. ❷

Auberge du Lac de Sauvabelin (☎647 39 29), at Lac Sauvabelin, 1018 Lausanne. Try this place if you've got a car, or take the infrequent bus #16 to "Lac Sauvabelin." An oasis far from the bustle of Lausanne, this classy, truly authentic Swiss restaurant sits directly on the lake and is next to a deer farm. Traditional Swiss fare (filet of perch 28-36SFr). Taste the high life with escargot (dozen 19SFr). Extensive wine selection. Open daily 11am-3pm and 6pm-midnight. MC/V. ❸

Ma-Jong, escalier du Grand Pont 3 (☎329 05 25). From the Lausanne-Flon *métro* stop, walk up the incline; Ma-Jong will be on the right. Cafeteria-style, pan-Asian dining. Specials from pad thai to roast duck are available for 15SFr (with salad and sometimes rice). For 20SFr, the Japanese fondue lets you simmer raw meat in a pot of heated bouillon. Dim sum and sushi also offered. Vegetarian options (including sautéed tofu, 15SFr) available. Open M-Th 11:30am-10:30pm and F-Sa 11:30am-midnight. ❸

MARKETS

Migros, ave. de Rhodanie 2 (☎613 26 60), right of *métro* Ouchy stop or bus #2 stop "Pl. de la Navigation." Locations throughout city. Open M 9am-9:45pm, Tu-Su 8am-9:45pm.

Co-op (☎ 616 40 66). From the train station, head downhill past the overpass; turn right onto blvd. de Grancy. Open M-F 8am-7pm, Sa 8am-5pm.

Aperto, at the train station. Open daily 6am-10pm.

Produce markets, at pl. de la Palud and the r. de Bourg behind the pl. St-François. W and Sa mornings until around noon.

👁 🏛 SIGHTS AND MUSEUMS

"In Lausanne, people are consuming culture as others swallow vitamins," a tourist brochure proclaims. Perhaps something was lost in the translation, but nevertheless, visitors flock to Lausanne's *vieille ville* and museums each year. For multi-day visits, the **Lausanne Pass** is a great deal, entitling visitors to museum discounts and free public transportation in and around Lausanne (15SFr for 2 days).

THE OLD CITY. The medieval town center is known as the *vieille ville*, but history buffs are quick to point out that the true old city is on the waterfront, where archaeological digs have unearthed 2000-year-old remains of the Vicus de Lousonna. Nonetheless, the *vieille ville* has the charming winding streets, eclectic shops, and beautiful fountains that only a medieval European city possesses. You can stroll through it and see the foundations of a temple, the remains of a basilica, a forum, a few villas, and the traces of a complete Gallo-Roman colony, now overshadowed by gigantic weeds. *(Take bus #2 to "Bois-de-Vaux" and follow signs.)* Those who don't mind a trek from Ouchy can poke around the Musée Romain de Lausanne-Vidy, the excavation site of a Roman house whose wall murals still retain their bright colors. *(Chemin du Bois-de-Vaux 24, next door to the hostel. ☎ 652 10 84. Explanations in French. Open Tu-W and F-Su 11am-6pm, Th 11am-8pm. Wheelchair accessible. 4SFr, seniors 2.50SFr, students free. For walking tours, head to the **Hôtel de Ville.** Guided tours leave M-Sa at 10am and 3pm. 10SFr, seniors 5SFr, students free. In English, German, and French.)*

To explore the Old City, from the train station, head north on r. du Petit Chêne until arriving at pl. St-François. Directly ahead is **Eglise St-François,** a towering church constructed in the 1270s as a convent. Although a 1368 fire gutted much of the original structure, and the Reformation Act forced the monks to leave, the church remains a beautiful landmark *(☎ 312 08 50. Open daily 8am-6pm.)*

In 1275 the **Gothic Cathedral** was consecrated under Holy Roman Emperor Rudolph and Pope Gregory X. From pl. de la Palud, with your back to the Hôtel de Ville, head diagonally right and just off the plaza, climb the two series of medieval covered stairs *(l'escalier du Marché)* which lead to the hilltop, where the cathedral's huge wooden doors open up into the hushed, vaulted space illuminated through stained-glass windows. At the south entrance, 2SFr (children 1SFr) lets you climb the main tower for an impressive view of the lake, the Alps and the surrounding rooftops. *(Cathedral open July to mid-Sept. M-F 7am-7pm, Sa-Su 8am-7pm; mid-Sept. to June closes at 5:30pm. Church services Su 10am, 8:15pm. Free guided tours July to mid-Sept. 10:30, 11:15am, 3, 3:45pm.)*

Next to the Cathedral is the **Musée Historique de Lausanne,** which offers a visual record of Lausanne's history dating back to the Romans. The musical instrument section is particularly strong. *(Pl. de la Cathédrale 6, across from the cathedral. ☎ 312 42 68. Open Tu-Th 11am-6pm, F-Su 11am-5pm. Audioguides available in English, French, Italian, German, and Spanish. Wheelchair accessible. 4SFr, first Sa of each month free. Mandatory 2SFr locker deposit.)* The **Renaissance Hôtel de Ville** (city hall), with its bronze dragon roof, serves as a meeting point for guided tours of the town by local residents. *(On the pl. de la Palud, below the cathedral. Tours M-Sa 10am, 3pm. English available. 10SFr, seniors 5SFr, students free.)* Also below the cathedral is the majestic Palais de Rumine, which houses the Cantonal and University Library, as well as several small archaeological and zoological museums. *(On pl. de la Riponne. Open M-F 11am-10pm, Sa 7am-5pm, Su 10am-5pm.)*

ART MUSEUMS. The ▧**Collection de l'Art Brut** is a must-see. This utterly original gallery filled with disturbing and beautiful sculptures, drawings, and paintings by artists on the fringe—institutionalized schizophrenics, poor and uneducated peasants, and convicted criminals—started as an obsession of Jean Dubuffet. Today, the museum features unorthodox masterpieces, from a prison cell wall painstakingly carved with a broken spoon to intricate junk and sea-shell masks. Equally fascinating are the biographies of the tortured creators, most displayed in English and French and often accompanied by photographic portraits. Don't miss the unforgettable Henry Darger room, the fantasy world of a part-time janitor from Chicago who created an alternate universe on paper. *(Ave. Bergières 11. Take bus #2 or 3 to "Jomini." The museum is across the street. ☎ 647 54 35; www.artbrut.ch. Open July-Aug. daily 11am-6pm; Sept.-June Tu-F 11am-1pm and 2-6pm, Sa-Su 11am-6pm. 6SFr, students and seniors 4SFr, under age 16 free.)*

On a more conventional note, the **Musée de l'Elysée** houses an engaging series of exhibits and photographic archives, ranging from 1820 prints to contemporary film. *(Ave. de l'Elysée 18. Take bus #2 to "Croix d'Ouchy" and go downhill, then left on ave. de l'Elysée. ☎ 316 99 11; www.elysee.ch. Open daily 11am-6pm. 8SFr, seniors 6SFr, students 4SFr.)* North of the *vieille ville*, the **Hermitage** is a magnificent house given over to temporary exhibitions varying from single artists and special themes to individual public and private collections. *(Rte. du Signal 2. From pl. St–François, take bus #16 to "Hermitage". www.foundation-hermitage.ch. Open Tu-W and F-Su 10am-6pm, Th 10am-9pm. 15SFr, seniors 12SFr, students 7SFr, under age 18 free. AmEx/MC/V.)*

MUSÉE OLYMPIQUE. This high-tech temple to Olympians opens with the words "Citius Altius Fortius" (Faster, Higher, Stronger), and a tour through the museum brings these words to life. Displays in English and French detail the history of the Olympics, its athletes, and the politics surrounding this international spectacle from antiquity to the present. An extensive video collection allows visitors to relive any highlight since the games were first filmed, and more recent events can be seen in the 3D cinema. On a busy day beware, though, for the exhibits are frequently swarming with kids. The museum is wheelchair accessible via ave. de l'Elysée. *(Quai d'Ouchy 1. Take bus #2 or M: "Ouchy." ☎ 621 65 11. Open M-W and F-Su 9am-6pm, Th 9am-8pm. Closed M Oct.-Apr. 14SFr, students and seniors 8SFr, ages 10-18 7SFr, families 34SFr max. Audioguide available in 7 languages 3SFr. MC/V.)*

MUSÉE DE DESSIN (MUSEUM OF DESIGN AND CONTEMPORARY APPLIED ARTS). Part contemporary, part traditional, this museum was once dedicated to the decorative arts, but now houses a well-chosen collection of modern, cutting-edge pieces. The overall effect is heady: exhibits of Egyptian and Chinese art in the basement, glass art on the top floor, and temporary exhibits in between. *(Pl. de la Cathédrale 6, next to the cathedral. ☎ 315 25 30; mu.dac@lausanne.ch. Open Tu 11am-9pm, W-Su 11am-6pm. 6SFr, students and seniors 4SFr.)*

WATERFRONT. A sign along the waterfront declares Ouchy to be "a free and independent community," and indeed its slower tempo, indulgent hotels, and eco-modern sculptures set it strikingly apart from the *vieille ville*. Although now somewhat overrun with tourists, Ouchy retains some of the peacefulness of the resort community it once was. Ouchy's main promenades (the **quai de Belgique,** which turns into the **quai d'Ouchy,** and the **place de la Navigation**) are all excellent spots to exercise those calf muscles. Local word has it that Lausanne's citizens have the best-looking legs in Switzerland, the hard-won prize of a life spent hiking the city's hills. (*Let's Go* remains impartial.) Booths along the water rent out pedal boats (10SFr per 30min.) and offer waterskiing or wakeboarding on Lac Léman (30SFr per 15min.). See more of Ouchy's inhabitants at the **Bellerive-Plage,** a beach where locals let their children loose on the lawns while both men and women go topless and take in the sun. *(Take bus #2 to "Bellerive" or walk down ave. de Rhodanie from Ouchy. Open mid-May to early Sept. daily 9:30am until dark or rain. 4.50SFr, students and seniors 3SFr, under age 17 2SFr; discount after 5pm. Lockers 2SFr.)*

PARKS AND GARDENS. The Bellerive Beach is just one of Lausanne's many natural oases. East along the lake from Ouchy, the **park Olympique** and the **Parc du Dena-tou** offer more beautiful views of the lake and well-planned gardens. Farther west, at the **Vallée de la Jeunesse** rose garden, a path of wildflowers bends to reveal a spectacular display of 1000 bushes arranged in a terraced semi-circle around a fountain. *(Take Métro-Ouest to "Renens.")* Exotic birds trill from the aviaries of the downtown **Parc du Mon-Repos.** Centering around a small chateau where Voltaire wrote from 1755 to 1757, the park includes venerable trees, an orange grove, and a small stone temple. *(Take bus #17 (dir: Verdeil) to "Mon-Repos.")* The region's propensity to bloom is channeled at the nearby **Derrière-Bourg Promenade,** where flowers depict events from the canton's history. *(Just off pl. St-François.)* The **Botanical Garden of Lausanne** is in one section of pl. de Milan-Montriond Park. Wander past rose bushes, and visit the observation spot atop the hill next to the gardens for an unobstructed lake panorama. A sign names each peak visible across the water and the date on which it was first conquered. *(Ave. de Cour 14. Just up the hill from the bus #1 stop "Beauregard."* ☎ *616 24 09. Park open daily May-Sept. 10am-12:30pm and 1:30-6:30pm; Mar.-Apr. and Oct. 10am-noon and 1:30-5:30pm.)*

ENTERTAINMENT AND NIGHTLIFE

For every exhibit in Lausanne's museums, there are several performances in progress on stage and screen: the **Béjart Ballet, Lausanne Chamber Orchestra, Cinémathèque Suisse, Municipal Theatre, Opera House,** and **Vidy Theatre** reflect Lausanne's thriving cultural life. For information, reservations, and tickets, call Billetel (☎ 310 16 50). The **Festival de la Cité** (mid-July) brings the *vieille ville* to life with free theater, music, and dance events. Swiss craftwork fills the **Marché des Artisans** in pl. de la Palud from 6am to 7pm on the first Friday of the month from March to December. The **Fête de la Bière** brings more than 200 breweries to the pl. de la Navigation, Ouchy, in early June. **Lunapark** (amusement park) is at Bellerive from mid-May to mid-June.

Lausanne is a clubber's dream and a penny-pincher's nightmare. Bars and clubs line the streets around pl. St-François. Party-goers fill the bars until about 1am (2am Sa-Su) and then move to the clubs, most of which stay open until 4 or 5 in the morning. Unfortunately, the bus and *métro* systems stop running at midnight and cabs can be expensive, especially if you're not staying near the city center. On weekends, cover charges run 15-30SFr, and drinks inside many of the clubs aren't cheap either. For night owls, Lausanne has a "Pyjama" bus service running from about 1:15 to 3:45am, depending on the route (regular fare plus 2SFr supplement).

Loft Club, pl. Bel-Air 1 (☎ 311 64 00; www.loftclub.ch). Up the steps off the right hand side of rte. de Genève, heading toward The Mad. While other clubs may just be warming up, the hordes here are burning with the sounds of house, hip-hop, or techno. Pat-down required for entry. W members-only night. Cover 5-15SFr. Open W-Sa 10:30pm-5am.

Bleu Lézard, r. Enning 10 (☎ 321 38 30). From pl. St-François turn left to r. de Bourg, then head right past Au Couscous. Suits and students alike crowd this bistro, which is decorated by local artists. DJs or live music on weekends. Beer 3.50SFr. Cocktails 13.50SFr. Vegetarian dishes 14.50-19SFr. Open Th 7pm-3am, F-Sa 7pm-2am, Su 9pm-2am. Kitchen open M-Sa 11:30am-2pm and 6:30-10:30pm, Su 10am-5pm and 6:30-10:30pm. AmEx/MC/V.

Amnesia, off allée du Bornan in Esplanade des Cantons. Take bus #2 to "Théâtre de Vidy" and walk toward the lake. This upbeat, popular club features several dance rooms and bars and an outside area with more music and drinks. The clientele is varied too: a jeans and T-shirt crowd mixes with high-rollers coming in off yachts docked at the club's wharf. The club can be expensive, though, as there is a 15SFr cover on weekends, and most drinks are priced 20SFr and up. Open F-Sa 11pm-5am.

Au Lapin Vert (☎312 13 17). On ruelle du Lapin Vert, off r. de l'Académie behind the cathedral, this upscale version of a hole-in-the-wall pub blasts English rock at a local crowd of teenagers, students, and young professionals. Beer 5-8SFr. Mixed drinks 9-10SFr. Open M-Th 8pm-2am, F-Sa 8pm-3am, Su 8pm-2am.

D! Club (☎565 20 13), ruelle de Grand Pont, entrance at pl. Centrale, attracts Lausanne's mature and well-dressed crowd with its wide range of music. Go left out of the Lausanne-Flon *métro* stop, walk under r. de Grand Point bridge, and turn left. Cover F-Sa 23-30SFr, Th free. Open Th 11pm-4am, F-Sa 11pm-5am.

MONTREUX   ☎021

Once the crown jewel of the "Swiss Riviera," Montreux feels like a resort past its heyday—one that could've been frequented by the elegant Jazz Age characters of an F. Scott Fitzgerald novel. The grand hotels and lakefront promenade still emanate wealth and prestige, but the glitz has an air of pleasant decay to it. Music fans descend in early July for the annual **Montreux Jazz Festival.** The festival attracts musicians of all genres and creates an ongoing, city-wide, all-ages party. Luminaries such as Neil Young, Bob Dylan, Stevie Ray Vaughan, and Miles Davis have dropped in. Literary visitors have included Victor Hugo and Fitzgerald himself. Further back in the area's artistic tradition is Lord

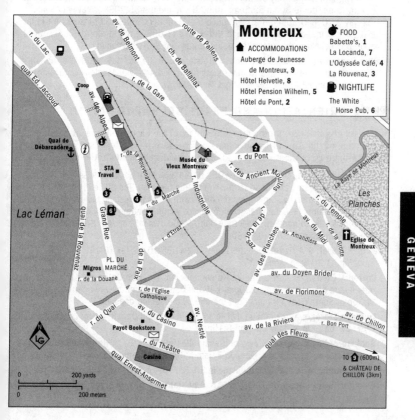

Montreux

▲ ACCOMMODATIONS
Auberge de Jeunesse
de Montreux, **9**
Hôtel Helvetie, **8**
Hôtel Pension Wilhelm, **5**
Hôtel du Pont, **2**

🍎 FOOD
Babette's, **1**
La Locanda, **7**
L'Odyssée Café, **4**
La Rouvenaz, **3**

🍸 NIGHTLIFE
The White
Horse Pub, **6**

GENEVA

Byron's visit to the disturbingly beautiful **Château de Chillon,** a medieval fortress with a checkered history. The empty streets and peeling paint on the hotels attest to the decline of Montreux's prominence, the city's relaxed atmosphere, beautiful mountain vistas, and rich history make a visit well worth it.

TRANSPORTATION

Trains: Ave. des Alpes (☎963 45 15). To: **Bern** (1½hr., 2 per hr. 5:39am-11:05pm, 37SFr); **Geneva** (1hr., 2 per hr. 5:39am-11:39pm, 26SFr); **Lausanne** (20min., 3-5 per hr. 5:29am-12:09am, 9.80SFr). **Direct trains** also go to **Aigle, Brig, Martigny, Sion,** and (literally) through the mountains to **Gstaad.**

Local Transportation: A very helpful map, available at the tourist office in several languages, divides the area into bus zones; your fare is dependent upon the number of zones you cross. 1 zone 2.20SFr, juniors (ages 6-20) 1.60SFr; 2 zones 2.80SFr/2SFr; 3 zones 3.50SFr/2.50SFr; 4 zones 4.20SFr/3SFr. Day-pass 7SFr/5SFr; available at tourist office. SwissPass valid. Late-night buses run during the Jazz Festival, 2-4SFr (buy tickets on the bus); SwissPass valid. Free buses run from **Vevey** through Montreux to **Villeneuve** M-F 6pm-4am, Sa-Su noon-4am during the Jazz Festival.

Boats: CGN (☎963 46 55), on quai du Débarcadère next to the tourist office. To: **Geneva** (4½hr.; 4 per day 9:30am-4:50pm; 40.80SFr, round-trip 63.40SFr); **Lausanne** (1½hr.; 5 per day 9:30am-5:55pm; 20.60SFr, round-trip 35.20SFr); **Vevey** (25min.; 6 per day 9:30am-5:55pm; 9.20SFr, round-trip 16.60SFr). Rides to **Château de Chillon** (7.60SFr, round-trip 13.80SFr) and **Villeneuve** (7.60SFr, round-trip 13.80SFr) available. Buy tickets at the quai or on board. Eurail and SwissPass valid.

Bike Rental: At the baggage check-in the station. 30SFr per day, 23SFr per half-day; 6SFr charge to return bikes to other stations (including Aigle, Martigny, and Sion) by prior arrangement. Open 7:30am-8pm. AmEx/MC/V.

ORIENTATION AND PRACTICAL INFORMATION

Montreux and its surroundings rise rapidly from the eastern shores of Lac Léman to the edge of the Alps at Les-Roches-de-Naye Jardin. The train station is within walking distance of most sights. Hiking up r. du Marché leads to the *vieille ville.*

Tourist Office: Pl. du Débarcadère (☎962 84 84; www.montreux.ch). Descend the stairs opposite the station and head left on Grand Rue for 5min. The office is on the right, by the water. The friendly staff shares the office with desks for festival tickets and bus and train information. Free hotel reservation service within Montreux. They offer 2 free maps. Open mid-June to mid-Sept. M-F 9am-6pm, Sa-Su 10am-5pm; late Sept. to early June M-F 8:30am-5pm, Sa-Su 10am-3pm.

Budget Travel: STA Travel, ave. des Alpes 25 (☎965 10 15; fax 10 19). Open M-F 9am-noon and 1:30-6pm. AmEx/MC.

Currency Exchange: At the station. No commission. **Western Union** does transfers and credit card advances. Open 6:30am-8:45pm. **Banks** in Montreux are open M-F 8:30am-4:30pm. Some close for lunch, but the one by the station does not.

Luggage Storage: At the station. Lockers 4-7SFr, open 5:50am-8:45pm. Luggage watch 7SFr per bag. Open daily 6:30am-8:15pm.

Bookstore: Payot Librairie, ave. du Casino 42 (☎963 06 07). Friendly staff helps you search a multilingual stock. Open M-F 9am-6:30pm, Sa 9am-5pm. AmEx/DC/MC/V.

Laundromat: Salon-Lavoir, r. Industrielle 30. 5SFr per load. Open M-Sa 7am-7pm.

Emergencies: Police ☎117. **Fire** ☎118. **Ambulance** ☎144. **Hospital** ☎966 66 66.

Late-Night Pharmacy: ☎962 77 00.

Internet Access: Internet@Place, Grand Rue 114 (☎966 02 80). 15SFr per hr., includes soft drink. Open M-Sa 10am-8pm.

Post Office: Ave. des Alpes 70. Exit the station, turn left. *Poste Restante:* Montreux 1, CH-1820 Montreux. Open M-F 8am-6pm, Sa 8:30am-noon. **Branch** at r. du Théâtre 8. Open M-F 8am-noon and 2-6pm, Sa 8:30-11am.

Postal Code: CH-1820.

ACCOMMODATIONS AND CAMPING

Cheap rooms are scarce in Montreux and almost nonexistent during the jazz festival. Hotels and hostels are often full before May. Ask at the tourist office for the lists of *Pensions et Petits Hôtels* or studio apartments available during the festival. If you still can't find a room, try the hostels in Vevey (p. 510; free shuttles to and from the festival) or in Gryon (p. 517). Otherwise, take bus #1 to "Villeneuve," 5km away, to a handful of budget hotels, or commute from Lausanne or Martigny.

Auberge de Jeunesse Montreux (HI), passage de l'Auberge 8 (☎963 49 34; fax 27 29). Take bus #1 on Grand Rue (dir: Villeneuve) to "Territet." Head up the street, take 1st right (r. du Bocherex), and go down the stairs (passage de l'Auberge), or walk 20min. along the lake past the Montreux Tennis Club. This modern hostel offers a dining room, TV, Internet, and waterfront location, though it's far from Montreux proper. Light sleepers beware: train tracks run nearby. 112 beds in 6- or 8-bed dorms. Free parking nearby. Wheelchair accessible. Breakfast and sheets included. Dinner 12.50SFr. Lockers 2SFr deposit. Reception 7:30-10am and 5-10pm. Doors lock at 10pm but guests have access. Check-out 10am. Closed mid-Nov. to mid-Feb. Dorms 30.50SFr; doubles 40SFr, with bath 42SFr. Non-members add 6SFr. AmEx/DC/MC/V. ❷

Hôtel Pension Wilhelm, r. du Marché 13-15 (☎963 14 31; hotel.wilhelm@span.ch). From the station, take a left at ave. des Alpes, walk 3min. and take a left onto r. du Marché, uphill past the police station. Clean, bright rooms close to the train station, and a generous staff. A great place to relax and a short walk from *Les Planches.* Many rooms have balconies. Free breakfast. Reception 7am-10pm. Closed Oct.-Feb. Singles 60SFr, with shower 70SFr; doubles 100SFr/120SFr. Cash or traveler's checks only. ❸

Hôtel du Pont, r. du Pont 12 (☎/fax 963 22 49), at the top of the *vieille ville.* From the station, go left on ave. des Alpes (3min.) and then left up r. du Marché. Continue uphill until it becomes r. du Pont; the hotel is on the left (enter through the café). Dark, claustrophobic corridors and the long trek to town are outweighed by bright rooms with bathrooms and TVs. The distance from town may not be a bad thing, however. The trip includes pretty views and the soothing sound of nearby waterfalls. Breakfast included. Dinner 18-25SFr. Reception M 7am-3pm, Tu-F 7am-midnight, Sa-Su 8:30am-midnight. Singles from 70SFr; doubles from 130SFr. Extra bed 40SFr. AmEx/MC/V. ❸

Hôtel Helvetie, ave. du Casino 32 (☎966 77 77; www.montreux.ch/helvetie). From Grand Rue, take bus #1 (dir: Villeneuve) to "Montreux." Rooms with TV, phone, and minibar located a block from the casino. 3 spacious living rooms off the lobby create a homey atmosphere. Private parking. Wheelchair accessible. **Internet** 4SFr per 15min., 12SFr per hr. Breakfast included. Reception 24hr. Check-out noon. Singles 150-180SFr; doubles 200-230SFr. 50SFr discount per night during winter. Children get a discount when sharing a room with an adult: ages 0-6 50%, ages 6-12 30%. ❹

FOOD

Montreux is pricey and most establishments are filled with tourists. Inexpensive markets abound on the Grand Rue and ave. de Casino. **Marché de Montreux,** pl. du Marché, is an outdoor food and flea market. (F 7am-1pm.) There's a **Co-op** at Grand

Rue 80 (open M-F 8am-12:15pm and 2-6:30pm, Sa 8am-5pm), a **Migros** within the *Centre Commercial* near the place du Marché (open M-F 9am-7pm, Sa 7:30am-6pm), and numerous kebab stands lining the waterfront.

L'Odyssée Café, ave. des Alpes 17bis (☎961 38 46). Exiting the station, turn left on ave. Odes Alpes; walk for 3-5min. Cheap café fare off a main road. Terrace in back. Sandwiches 4.50-6.50SFr. Daily *Menüs* 14.50SFr. Open M-F 7am-5pm. ❶

La Rouvenaz, r. du Marché (☎447 21 72), just off Grand Rue. This compact restaurant serves relatively cheap Italian food with a lake view. Pizza from 14.50SFr. Reasonably priced hotel rooms upstairs. MC/V. ❷

Babette's, Grand Rue 60 (☎963 77 96), downstairs from the station to the left. This casual restaurant serves crêpes of all types for lunch (11-14SFr) and dessert (7-10SFr). Great location, but limited seating. Sandwiches to go 7-15SFr. Open daily 7am-7pm. ❷

La Locanda, ave. du Casino 44 (☎963 29 33), is a small restaurant with cozy decor. Large pizzas 15-21SFr. Salads 7-19SFr. Summer specialties 8-28SFr. Open M-Tu and Th-Sa 11:30am-3pm and 6:30pm-midnight, W 6:30pm-midnight. AmEx/MC/V. ❸

🎦 SIGHTS

If you plan to visit more than three area museums, consider purchasing the Montreux-Vevey Museum passport (15SFr), available at the tourist office. The 🎦**Château de Chillon** is the main draw in Montreux and one of Switzerland's most visited attractions. Take the CGN ferry from the quai de Débarcadère (round-trip 13.80SFr) or bus #1 to "Chillon" from anywhere on Grand Rue or ave. de Casino (2.80SFr, ages 6-20 2SFr) or walk 40min. from the station along the lake past elegant villas. Built on an island in the 13th century, Chillon is a fortress with all the comforts of any happy home: prison cells, a torture chamber, armory, and booby traps to fend off attackers who make it past the moat. From the dungeon comes the story of François de Bonivard, a priest who spent four years chained to a dungeon pillar in the 16th century for aiding the Reformation; he was freed in 1536 by Protestant soldiers who seized Montreux from the Catholic Duke of Savoy. Bonivard's captivity inspired Rousseau, Victor Hugo, and Lord Byron, whose poem "The Prisoner of Chillon" is a romanticized version of Bonivard's plight. In the château you can see where Byron etched his name into a pillar, presumably to empathize with poor François. For the less gory-minded there are well-preserved frescos, paintings, and a cavernous Grand Hall. (☎966 89 10; www.chillon.ch. Open daily Apr.-Sept. 9am-6pm; Mar. and Oct. 9:30am-5pm; Nov.-Feb. 10am-4pm. 9SFr, students and seniors 7SFr, ages 6-16 4.50SFr, families 22SFr. Guided tours in English and French available mid-June to mid-Sept. 11:30am. 13SFr, children under 16 6SFr.)

The **Musée de Montreux,** r. de la Gare 40, on the outskirts of the *vieille ville*, chronicles Montreux's history from Roman times through its "colonization" by the resort industry in the late 19th century. The museum is a history buff's dream and has exhibits on everything from ancient local coins to a room filled with hundreds of thimbles. The list of the city's "illustrious guests," including Rousseau, Tolstoy, Hemingway, Hans Christian Andersen, Stravinsky, and Charles Lindberg, is also interesting. (☎963 13 53. Open Apr.-Oct. daily 10am-noon and 2-5pm. 6SFr, students and seniors 4SFr, under 17 free.) From the museum, the *vieille ville* is just a few minutes up the r. du Pont. Worlds away from the bustle of the waterfront, the r. de Temple offers pure views and a quiet walk to the stone Église de Montreux.

♪ ENTERTAINMENT

The **Montreux Jazz Festival** is world-famous for the exceptional musical talent it draws, and for being one of the biggest parties in Europe. Starting the first Friday in July, everything else in town is pushed aside for 15 days, and concerts occur practically non-stop. Past headliners have included B.B. King and Paul Simon. Demand has sent ticket prices into the stratosphere: individual tickets range from 79SFr to 119SFr. Standing-room tickets run 49-79SFr. Write to the tourist office well ahead of time for information and tickets. The easiest way to purchase tickets in advance is at www.montreuxjazz.com. The **jazz hotline** in Montreux, run by the **Jazz Boutique** (☎966 44 36) ticket sellers at Grand Rue 62, is active from mid-March through the summer. In Switzerland, buy tickets from **Ticket Corner** (☎848 80 08 00) and at the **Congress Center** in Montreux or visit www.montreuxjazz.com. Many events sell out before July, some as early as January. If you can't score tickects, come for **Montreux Jazz Under The Sky,** 500hr. of free, open-air concerts. The temporary **Jazz Café** near the mainstage is free for fans to spend entire nights partying.

From late August to mid-September, the **Montreux Voice and Music Festival** takes over with operas, symphonies, and classical recitals performed by musicians from as far away as Moscow and Memphis. (Contact the **Office of the Classical Music Festival**, r. du Théâtre 5, 1st fl., Case Postale 353, CH-1820 Montreux 2. ☎966 80 25; www.montreux-festival.com. Office open M-F 10am-1pm and 2-7pm, Sa 10am-1pm. Extended hrs. 2-3 wks. before the festival. Prices range from 10SFr for student tickets to 160SFr for big-name performers.)

♞ NIGHTLIFE

Montreux caters to all tastes and personalities, from carefree campers to five-star fops. Don't worry about finding "the place to be" in this town—if you're by the water, especially in early July, you're there. The **Casino de Montreux,** r. du Théâtre 9, draws mobs to a ritzy interior and flashy slot machines. From ave. du Casino, turn on r. Igor Stravinsky toward the lake. The charm of the original 1881 establishment (which helped launch Stravinsky's career) is largely gone, but it's worth stopping by to cap off a day with video poker (M-Th and Su 11am-3am, F-Sa 11am-4am) and *boules* (daily from 8:30pm). (☎962 83 83; www.casinodemontreux.ch. 18+. Bring your passport and a bathing suit for the nearby pool (6SFr).) **The White Horse Pub,** Grand Rue 28, has a sign that declares it an "authentic" English pub, but you won't find much inside to bolster the claim, unless crêpes and *caipirinhas* have become English cuisine. What you'll more likely find is a friendly Francophone crowd watching sports on the multiple TVs. (☎963 15 92. Sandwiches 7-9.50SFr. Fish and chips 15.50SFr. Pizza 11-13SFr. Beer 6.20-9.50SFr per pint. Pinball, darts, foosball, and arcade games in back. Open M-F 11am-1am, Sa 11am-2am, Su 3pm-midnight.)

VEVEY ☎021

The upside to its 20th-century decline is that Vevey has avoided the five-star stratification and crowding of nearby Montreux. As a result, it has a less touristy feel. Vevey hit its heyday as a resort town back in the 19th century, when hordes of upper-class Brits made it a virtual colony of the Queen's empire, placing it in countless society novels. Jean-Jacques Rousseau, Victor Hugo, Fyodor Dostoyevsky, Henry James, Le Corbusier, and Graham Greene all worked within

Vevey's borders. Charlie Chaplin fled here from McCarthyism in 1953. The town remains well preserved, and its location along the shore of Lac Léman makes it an ideal base for trips to Lausanne and Montreux or to the nearby mountains.

■ TRANSPORTATION AND PRACTICAL INFORMATION

There are three ways to reach Vevey from Montreux: by **bus** #1 to "Vevey" (20min.; every 10min.; 2.80SFr, children 2SFr); **train** (5min., every 15-30min., 3SFr); or **boat** (20min., 5 per day, 9.20SFr). To get to the **tourist office**, Grand-Place 29, from the station, cross pl. de la Gare, go past ave. de la Gare, and turn left onto ave. Paul Cérésole. At the end of the road, cut across the parking lot toward the columned arcade; the office is inside. (☎962 84 74; www.montreux-vevey.com. Open late June to late Aug. M-F 9am-5:30pm, Sa 9am-6pm; Sept. to mid-June M-F 8:30am-noon and 1:30-6pm, Sa 9:30am-noon.) **Lockers** (4-7SFr) and **bike rental** are available at the train station. (30SFr; children 25SFr; 23SFr/18SFr per half-day. Open 7:30am-7:30pm.) Payot **bookstore**, r. du Conseil 15, has a wide selection. (Open M 1:30-5:30pm, Tu-F 9am-6:30pm, Sa 10:30am-5pm.) Call ☎11 for information about late-night **pharmacies**. In an **emergency**, call ☎117; in case of **fire**, ☎118; for an **ambulance**, ☎144. **Internet** is available at **Cyberworld**, r. de Torrent 4/6. (☎923 78 33. 12SFr per hr. Open daily 1pm-midnight.) The **post office** is across pl. de la Gare and has a 24hr. **ATM.** (Open M-F 7:30am-6pm, Sa 8:30am-noon.) **Postal Code:** CH-1800.

■ ACCOMMODATIONS AND FOOD

Overlooking Grand-Place just off the waterfront is the ⬛**Riviera Lodge ❷**, pl. du Marché 5. Head out of the station on the main road to the open square on the waterfront; the hostel is on the right, with 60 beds in bright rooms and lavish, modern facilities in a converted 19th-century townhouse. The service here is unparalleled: be prepared for a deluge of information and advice on things to do in the region as soon as you check in. The reception desk, manned by owner François and his multilingual staff, shares the 4th floor with a terrace that overlooks the lake and the surrounding mountains. Guests receive a pass for discounts and free activities in the Montreux-Vevey region, such as a ride up the Vevey funicular and free waterskiing. (☎923 80 40; www.rivieralodge.ch. Spotless kitchen. **Internet** 3SFr per 15min., 7SFr per hr. Sheets 5SFr. Laundry up to 7SFr. Reception 8am-noon and 5-8pm, extended during summer season. Reservations strongly recommended. Call if arriving late. 4-, 6-, or 8-bed dorms 26SFr; doubles 80SFr. MC/V.)

Many family homes also house travelers; one is **Pension Bürgle ❸**, r. Louis-Meyer 16, off Grand-Place. Take the first right after the hostel; the *Pension* is on the right. The rooms, though old, are large. Many have balconies and TVs. The *Pension* is the area's only "green" hotel, with wood and solar-power heat. (☎/fax 921 40 23; www.vevey.ch/tourisme/pension-burgle.htm. Breakfast included. Dinner 12SFr. Hall bathrooms and showers. Reception 7am-11pm. Reserve with first night's payment. 42SFr. MC/V.) **Hôtel des Negociants ❹**, r. du Conseil 27, offers modern, wood-paneled rooms with desks. Breakfast is not included, but the hotel is adjacent to a restaurant. (☎922 70 11. July-Aug. singles 105SFr; Apr.-June and Sept.-Oct. 95SFr; Nov.-Mar. 85SFr. Doubles 20SFr more. MC/V.)

Camping is available at the **Plage Camping ❶**. Take the #1 bus from the center of town to "Burier" stop. This beach-side campsite is 2km from town and offers a relaxing and inexpensive option. (4.70SFr per adult, 1.50SFr per child under age 16, 5-10SFr per tent. A place in 1 of their tepees is 12SFr. Laundry available.)

For cheap food, check out the bustling **produce** (and **flea**) **market** at Grand-Place. (Pl. du Marché. Tu and Sa 8:30am-noon.) Do-it-yourself fare is available at **Migros** and the **Co-op**, across ave. Paul Cérésole off Grand-Place. (Both open M 9am-

6:30pm, Tu-W and F 8am-6:30pm, Th 8am-8pm, Sa 7:30am-5pm. Migros restaurant open M-F 30min. earlier.) Café-restaurants with *Menüs* around 12-15SFr line Grand-Place. Snack huts line the lakefront quais, but food is cheaper away from the lakefront. An **Aperto** stands next to the train station. (Open 6am-9:30pm.)

🏛 MUSEUMS

Though not as thrilling as Montreux's Château de Chillon, Vevey's museums are distinctive and well curated. For an excellent deal, pick up a **Montreux-Vevey Museum Passport** (15SFr), which grants entrance to eight museums in the two towns. Many of Vevey's museums can be reached via an eastward stroll along the lake toward the neighboring town of Tour-de-Peilz.

Musée Jenisch, ave. de la Gare 2 (turn left onto ave. de la Gare after exiting the station and walk a block), displays well-constructed, temporary exhibits, filled with paintings and sketches, as well as a room of spontaneous watercolors and pastels by adopted citizen Oskar Kokoschka, who lived in nearby Villeneuve for his last 25 years. (☎921 34 01. Tours available. Open Tu-Su Mar.-Oct. 11am-5:30pm; Nov.-Feb. 2-5:30pm. 12SFr, seniors 10SFr, students 6SFr.)

The **Swiss Museum of Games,** at the end of Quai Roussy in the 13th-century Savoy Château de la Tour-de-Peilzs, chronicles the twin concepts of skill and luck. The museum displays chess pieces, cardboard Cold War games, and Nintendo. Multilingual exhibits wax philosophical on the sociology of games. The museum's final stop is a game room where visitors are invited to try their luck. (☎944 40 50. Open Tu-Su Mar.-Oct. 11am-5:30pm; Nov.-Feb. 2-5pm. 6SFr; students and seniors 3SFr; under age 16 2.50SFr, free when accompanied by an adult. Tours 10SFr, students and seniors 7SFr, under 16 5SFr. AmEx/MC/V.)

The **Nestlé Alimentarium/Food Museum,** on the corner of r. du Léman and quai Perdonnet, three blocks from Grande-Place, tells the story of food, from production to processing in the human body. Nestlé advertisements, an interactive kitchen, a 3D adventure through the digestive tract, and human-sized hamster wheels are some of the highlights of this child-friendly museum. (☎924 41 11. Open Tu-Su 10am-6pm. 10SFr, students and seniors 8SFr, ages 6-16 free. Audioguides in French, German, English, Italian, and Spanish. Lockers for bags 2SFr deposit.)

The **Swiss Camera Museum** features five floors filled with historic photographic equipment from daguerreotypes to early spy cameras and modern digital cameras. The museum ends with several temporary exhibits of photographs. (On the Grande-Place, near the tourist office. Walking from the station, head toward the river to the Grande-Place. The entrance will be to the left. ☎925 21 40; www.cameramuseum.ch. Open Tu-Su Mar.-Oct. 11am-5:30pm; Nov.-Feb. 2-5:30pm. 6SFr, students 4SFr, children free. Wheelchair accessible. Group tours 50SFr by appointment.) The **History Museum of Vevey,** on r. du Château 2, provides a brief cultural, economic, and political history of the city. There are impressive displays of silver, paintings from a range of local artists, and photographs of the city in decades past. From pl. de la Gare, follow r. de Lausanne to r. du Simplon. Take r. du Simplon to its end. Turn left onto r. d'Italie. The museum is one block up on your right. (☎932 07 33. Open daily Mar.-Oct. 10:30am-noon and 2-5:30pm; Nov.-Feb. 2-5:30pm. 6SFr, students 4SFr, under age 6 free.)

🎭 🎵 NIGHTLIFE AND ENTERTAINMENT

Nightlife options are slim in Vevey. If you're in the mood for craziness, head to nearby Montreux or Lausanne. In Vevey, right behind the Riviera Lodge at r. de Torrent 9, the **National** offers quiet meals (from 19SFr) and beers (from 3SFr) among funky decorations on a romantic candlelit terrace. (Open M-Tu 11am-midnight, W-Th 11am-1am, F-Sa 11am-2am, Su 4pm-midnight.) Across the street from the National at r. de Torrent 4-6 lies **Vertigo**, where drinks are served in a fashionable bar atmosphere. (☎922 11 34. Bar open M-Tu 4pm-midnight, W-Th 4pm-1am, F-Sa 4pm-2am, Su 4pm-midnight. Restaurant open M-Sa 6-11pm, Su 6-10pm.)

The **Folklore Market** in pl. du Marché (open July-Aug.) lets you sample all the local wine you can hold for the price of the first glass, sometimes as low as 4SFr. Year-round, the **Winetrain** winds its way through 8km of villages and vineyards in Lavaux. The tourist office has a list of tasting venues, a map of wine centers, and a guide to nearby hiking tours. (From Vevey station take the "Puidoux-Chexbres" train. Every hr. 5:58am-10:08pm, round-trip 10.40SFr. SwissPass and Eurail valid.) The summertime **International Comedy Film Festival**, dedicated to former resident Charlie Chaplin, features comedy competitions by day and screenings by night. The **Theater of Vevey**, r. de Théâtre 4 (☎923 60 55), produces live theater.

LES DIABLERETS   ☎024

Drawing its name from *Quille du Diable*, the tower-shaped rock that looms over the town, Les Diablerets challenges the notion that evil spirits still lurk in the mountains above. Multiple paths throughout the rocky landscape and a skiable glacier welcome adventure seekers year-round. In early summer, the town is filled mainly with locals, but as July and August arrive, summer skiing and extreme sports fill the village with vacationers. Come winter, the town (pop. 1300) holds its own against snootier local rivals Gstaad and Verbier. Because Les Diablerets is more accessible to Geneva and Lausanne than its competitors, the crowd here tends to consist of weekenders looking for an escape from bigger cities.

▐ TRANSPORTATION

Three public transport services connect Les Diablerets to the rest of Switzerland: the **train** to Aigle (50min., every hr. 6:27am-9:28pm, 10.40SFr); the **Post Bus** over the mountains to Gstaad (summer 5 per day 9:39am-5:09pm, 6SFr) via the Col du Pillon, or to Leysin (summer 10 per day M-F 6:27am-5:28pm, 2 per day Sa-Su; 9SFr) via Le Sepey; and to the **BVB bus** to the mountain town of Villars (35min., 3 per day early July to mid-Sept. 10am-5pm, 11.40SFr) via Col de la Croix. Local buses provide access to the Diablerets glacier **cable cars**, which travel to Cabane (21SFr, round-trip 30SFr) and the glacier (34SFr, round-trip 49SFr). The first bus leaves at 9:39am; the last returns at 4:46pm. Plan accordingly or be ready for a 45min. walk. Train station attendants will watch your **luggage** in the small ticket room for free.

▐ PRACTICAL INFORMATION

The **tourist office,** to the right of the station on r. de la Gare, publishes an impressive range of literature, including a list of activities. (☎/fax 492 33 58; www.diablerets.ch. Open early July to late Aug. and mid-Dec. to Apr. daily 8:30am-6:30pm; May-June and Sept.-Nov. M-Sa 8:30am-12:30pm and 2-6pm, Su 9am-12:30pm.) Local services include **taxi** (☎079 205 05 55); **emergency services** (☎144); **ambulance** (☎494 50 30); **police** (☎492 24 88); **mountain rescue** (☎2492 24 88); and **Internet access** at La Diabletine bar and tea room. (☎492 13 55; 3SFr per 15min. Open daily 8am-10pm). The **post office** is right of the train station. (Open M-F 8am-noon and 3-6pm, Sa 8:30-11am.) **Postal Code:** CH-1865.

⌐ ACCOMMODATIONS

Les Lilas, rte. du Col du Pillon (☎492 31 34; fax 31 57). Left out of the train station, after passing the Co-op, turn right on rte. du Pillon; Les Lilas will be on your left. Les Lilas sits above a restaurant and has an interior filled with dark wood. The rooms are well-kept and clean. Double rooms come with full bathroom and TV Most have balconies with beautiful views of the surrounding mountains. Breakfast included. Checkout 11am. Singles 50-60SFr, with bath 85-100SFr; doubles 130-150SFr. AmEx/Mc/V. ❹

Hôtel Mon Abri (☎492 34 81; www.monabri.ch), is on the rte. du Pillon past the Co-op. Under new management intent on improving the hotel's facilities, Mon Abri continues to be a mecca for hard-core snowboarders and skateboarders. In the summer the hotel hosts a massive skateboard camp to which young enthusiasts from all over Europe roll in *en masse,* and Oct.-Nov. it offers snowboard rentals for top-of-the-line test gear as well as special deals on canyoning and biking. Inquire at reception for a full list. Other amenities include **laundry** (3SFr per kg), **free Internet,** a **bar** and **disco, beach volleyball courts,** and **bike rental** in summer. Breakfast included. Reservations recommended in high-season (July-Aug. and Dec.-Apr.), especially on weekends. 48SFr per adult, 28SFr per child. Low-season 40SFr/20SFr. Dormitories 28SFr. ❸

Les Diablotins, rte. du Pillon (☎492 36 33; www.diablotins.ch). A big modern building popular with young snowboarding groups and families. From the station, turn right, bear left around the hairpin turn, and turn left along rte. du Pillon at the top of the hill. Avoid the 30min. uphill walk by calling from the station; the hostel will send a minibus. The 2- to 5-bed rooms are in good shape (all have a private sink and most have a balcony), in spite of the thousands of schoolkids who tramp through the halls and shared showers each year. This huge institution has 4 **dining halls,** several **lounges,** a **bar,** and a **disco.** Breakfast included. Dinner 16SFr. Reception 8am-noon and 2-6pm. Reserve at least 1 wk. ahead in winter. Early to mid-Jan. 54SFr, under 18 38SFr; late Jan. to early Feb. 60SFr/38SFr; mid-Feb. to early Apr. 64SFr/41SFr; mid-Apr. to mid-Dec. 35SFr/33SFr; late Dec. to early Jan. 67SFr/41SFr. AmEx/MC/V. ❸

Camping La Murée (☎079 401 99 15 or 634 52 84; www.camping-caravingvd.ch). Take the Aigle train 1 stop to "Vers l'Eglise," go left past the post office and church, and cross the railroad tracks to camp among the RVs at this quiet site in a tiny valley town. Showers included. Reception 6-7pm. In summer 4.80SFr per person, 9SFr per tent, 9SFr per car; winter 5.30SFr/10SFr/10SFr. ❶

◖ FOOD

Left at the intersection of r. de la Gare and rte. de Colde la Croix, or up the path behind the tourist office, **Pizzeria Locanda Livia** ❷ serves 24 kinds of pizza (15-20SFr, miniature version 2SFr less), including a four-cheese pizza with gruyère called *rêve de souris* (mouse's dream). Chinese food is also available in the evening. (☎492 32 80. Open M-Tu and Th-Su 11:30am-2pm and 6:30-10pm. AmEx/DC/MC/V.) At **Le Muguet** ❶, on the right past the tourist office, try a dessert crêpe (6-10SFr) with *chocolat viennois* (4SFr), a dish of *crème de chantilly* (2SFr), or sandwiches (4-9SFr) and tea or beer. (☎492 26 42. Breakfast 14SFr. Open 6:30am-7pm; food until 5pm. MC/V.) For easy access to the food, ask about renting the apartment upstairs. (☎/fax 492 26 43. Min. 1 wk.) The **Co-op,** left on r. de la Gare from the station, is the perfect place to stock up on cheap cheese, wine, and bread. (Open M-F 8am-12:15pm and 2:30-6:30pm, Sa 8am-12:30pm and 2-5pm.)

▓ OUTDOOR ACTIVITIES

SKIING. Les Diablerets's year-round skiing got better with the addition of a **cable car,** which travels from the Col du Pillon above the village to Cabane, then to the glacier at Scex-Rouge. Diablerets day passes (39SFr), combined Diablerets/Villars passes (46SFr), Alpes Vaudoises transportation and lift passes (54SFr), and other **ski passes** are sold at the cable car's departure point. Book special hotel deals that include stay-and-ski passes, a fondue evening, tobogganing, curling, skating, and babysitting services at the tourist office. **Jacky Sports,** near the tourist office, rents **ski equipment.** (☎492 32 18; www.jackysport.ch. Open daily early July to early Sept. 9am-noon and 2-6:30pm; June and Oct.-Nov. 9am-noon and 2-6pm; Dec.-Apr. 8:30am-6:30pm. Skis and snowboards 28-50SFr per day, boots 15-19SFr; special rates for multi-day rentals. AmEx/DC/MC/V.) **Holiday Sport,** across from the tourist office, is another rental option. (☎492 37 17. Open Tu-Su 8am-noon and 2-6pm. Skis 28-50SFr per day, ski boots 9-15SFr; snowboards 38SFr, boots 15-19SFr.) The **ski and snowboard school,** in the tourist office, offers private lessons. (☎492 20 02; www.diablerets.ch. 6 half-days 142SFr.)

HIKING AND BIKING. Jacky Sports and Holiday Sports rent **mountain bikes.** (Jacky: 35SFr per day, 5 days 110SFr. Holiday: 35-45SFr/135-145SFr. All prices include helmet.) A good hike that can be done in several segments, depending on stamina, starts at the tourist office. Turn right across the river at the pharmacy, then right again so that you are facing the Sommet des Diablerets (3209m) and the glacier. The sides of the valley close in as the level riverside walk progresses and deposits you on the stage of a rugged 200m-high amphitheater at **Creux de Champ.** (1hr., 160m ascent.) The path starts to climb steeply up the sides to the **Refuge de Pierredar** at 2278m. (3hr. above Les Diablerets, 1110m ascent.) The agile can then push up to **Scex Rouge** (2971m), the cable car terminus on the glacier, which affords an unforgettable Alpine view. (1 day. Mid-summer and good weather only. Guide recommended for later sections of the hike.)

ADVENTURE SPORTS. Les Diablerets's adventure sports awaken the death wish within. **Mountain Evasion** (a perplexing misnomer) organizes **canyoning** (80-165SFr), **snow-shoeing** (25-70SFr), **rappeling** (85SFr), and **dirt biking** (35-70SFr), not to mention **luging** for 18SFr, or 36SFr for a nighttime descent with fondue. The office is in a little wooden shack along the river. Turn left across the river by the Co-op and the shack is on the right. Be sure to make reservations several days in advance. (☎492 12 32; fax 22 67. Open daily 8:30-11:30am and 1:30-4:30pm, but best to call ahead. MC.) Left from the train station and past the post office along r. de la Gare, **Centre ParAventure** offers **paragliding** (90-150SFr), **canyoning** (80SFr), and the new **Arapaho mud bike** (40SFr). (☎492 23 82 or 079 435 25 82; www.swissaventure.ch. Open daily 9-9:30am and 5:30-6:30pm. MC/V.)

LEYSIN ☎024

This laid-back town's location, high on the south side of a mountain overlooking the vast Rhone valley, gave it the ideal amount of solar exposure for Dr. August Rollier's tuberculosis treatments in the early years of the 20th century. Patients came in droves for treatment, and by 1930, 3000 of the town's 5698 inhabitants were working on their tans per order of the good doctor. When WWII brought antibiotics and ended faith in the "sun doctor," the town fell into decline. Today, skiers, hikers, and bikers are attracted to the town's sunny days, wide vistas, and white slopes, filling the void created by the departure of the tourist-patients.

🄴🄷 TRANSPORTATION AND PRACTICAL INFORMATION

Leysin can be reached in the summer by **bus** from Les Diablerets (via train to Le Sepey; summer 7 per day M-F 8:28am-5:28pm, only 2 Sa-Su; 9SFr) or year-round by the **cog railway** from Aigle, which chugs passengers up the steep climb at a medium pace (30min., every hr. 6am-10:38pm, SwissPass valid). There are four stops: Leysin-Village (8.40SFr), Versmont (9.80SFr), Feydey (9.80SFr), and Grand-Hôtel (10.40SFr). A free hourly **shuttle** gets you up and down the hillside and stops at the hostel (mid-June to mid-Sept. and mid-Dec. to mid-Apr.). The **tourist office,** located in the Centre Sportif just up the road to the left from pl. du Marché, provides **hiking maps** and general information on the town. (☎494 22 44; fax 16 16; www.leysin.ch. Open M-F 8am-9pm, Sa-Su 9am-9pm.) Other services include: **ATM** at the **Banque Cantonal Vaudous,** just below Hefti Sports; **taxis** (☎493 22 93 or 494 25 55); **bike rental** at the station for 27SFr; **snow report** (☎494 13 01); **emergency services** (☎117); **police** (☎493 45 41). **Pharmacie Leysin** (☎493 45 00; open M-F 9:30-noon and 2-6:30pm, Sa 9am-noon) and the **post office** are both on pl. du Marché. (☎494 12 05. Open M-F 8am-noon and 2:30-6pm, Sa 8:30-11am.) **Postal Code:** CH-1854.

🄵 ACCOMMODATIONS

🄷 **Les Airelles** (☎494 15 08). From the Feydey station, head downhill and bear right at 1st intersection. Hotel is 5min. down the road on the right. Built nearly a century ago as a retreat for a Russian princess, this bed-and-breakfast retains much of the charm and elegance of its illustrious past. Guests are treated to full-service laundry (wash and dry 10SFr), deep bath tubs, a large spotless kitchen, free movies (in French and English), and thoughtfully decorated bedrooms. The welcoming Swiss-American couple that recently bought the hotel have restored the tiles and woodworking of the original house. Outdoor dog-run available for travelers with animals (10SFr extra per day). Breakfast buffet 10SFr. 2- to 3-bed rooms 40SFr; singles 50SFr. Add 10SFr for high-season. ❷

🄷 **Hiking Sheep Guesthouse,** Villa La Joux (☎494 35 35; fax 35 37; www.leysin.net/hikingsheep). From the "Grand Hôtel" turn left on the gravel road. From Feydey, head up the hill for 10min. and follow signs, or catch the shuttle in high season. The Sheep has wooden bunks in crowded but clean dorm rooms, a convivial dining room, balconies, and pristine kitchen facilities. Owner Paul-Henri goes the extra mile by supplying satellite TV, a collection of videos and DVDs, game and meditation rooms, **Internet access** (3SFr per 15min.), fax services (2SFr), and mountain bikes for rent (30SFr per day, 20SFr per half-day). Buffet breakfast 8SFr. Sheets included. Laundry 5SFr wash, 5SFr dry, but on a sunny day ask about free drying rack. Only 2 showers serve the whole house. Reception 8-11am and 5-10pm. Reservations recommended around Christmas and New Year's, and in Feb. and July-Aug. Check-out 10:30am. No curfew. Dorms 30SFr; doubles 80SFr; triples 120SFr. Low-season 3SFr less. Ask about reduced prices for children, extended stays, and groups. MC/V. ❷

Hôtel La Paix (☎/fax 494 13 75), on ave. Rollier opposite the "Versmont" train stop. A doorway decorated with traditional Valais masks open into narrow hallways that connect old-fashioned rooms with fading prints of *Belle Époque* Leysin in this 1901 hotel. Includes beautifully decorated reading, TV, and living rooms. Rooms on the south side cost 15SFr more and include a balcony and a view. Breakfast and in-room showers included. Lunch or dinner 16SFr. Reception 8am-8pm. Singles 57-60SFr; doubles with shower 123SFr. Feb. and Aug. 2SFr less; low-season 5SFr less. AmEx/MC/V. ❸

Camping Semiramis (☎494 39 39; fax 21 21; www.camping-leysin.ch). A large grassy field near an evergreen forest and in the backyard of Hôtel du Soleil (see directions above). Showers included. A small playground is located outside. Summer

ON THE MENU

OMFORT FOOD, SWISS STYLE

Birchermuësli, a chilled oatmeal-and-yogurt porridge, was created by Dr. Maximilian Bircher-Benner a century ago. Convinced that fresh food and clean air made the best medicine, he opened a clinic in Zurich at the turn of the 20th century. It was here that he debuted the recipe that would become a hit around the country. Since then, people have adopted the dish as their own, tweaking it to suit their own needs and tastes.

Traditionally, the Swiss make this popular breakfast item by soaking oats overnight in milk and then adding yogurt, raisins, sugar, sometimes cream, and any variety of seasonal fruits, including apples, bananas, and berries. By the time it is finished, it resembles a runny (and cold) version of oatmeal, and the soft and slightly chewy texture is also similar. It tastes, however, uniquely Swiss: the slight tang of rich yogurt flavored with sweet fruit and rounded out with the mellow earthiness of oats. Children grow up eating the dish, and it remains a favorite and nourishing comfort food for all, particularly in the warm summer months. You can also buy pre-packaged versions in the yogurt section of any grocery store. Typically eaten in the morning, *Birchermuësli* also serves as a quick lunch or filling snack. Beware, however: while it may seem light, this delicious cereal fills you up quickly!

6SFr per person, 3SFr per child, 4SFr per tent. Winter 6.50SFr/4SFr/4SFr/4SFr. Between seasons 5SFr/2.50SFr/3SFr. Electricity 4SFr. Contact for dates of high-season. Tax 3.25SFr per adult, 1.70SFr per child. AmEx/DC/MC/V. ❶

🍴 FOOD

La Prafandaz (☎494 26 27). About 40min. from the Feydey station. Head up the hill. Rather than following signs for the Hiking Sheep Hostel, head straight up the mountain (signs point the way). An off-the-wall chalet decorated with a ticking-udder cow clock and a handmade aquarium. At an elevation of 1600m, the restaurant is surrounded by the romantic tinkling of cowbells. Owner/chef Alex loves mushrooms and makes his own sauce from hand-picked specimens. The menu is short and focuses on the house specialty, *les rosettes,* which consists of meat, vegetables, or salmon rolled into homemade pasta, grilled, and smothered in a rich sauce and cheese for 10-19SFr. Open June-Oct. daily 11am-11pm; Jan. to mid-Apr. M and W-Su only; May Sa-Su only. ❷

La Nonna Restaurant Pizzeria (☎494 21 94), above the Centre Sportif and the tourist office. Feast on hearty pastas (17-22SFr) and risottos (21-27SFr) or try one of the 29 types of pizza (13-20SFr). Open M-Sa 9am-11pm, Su 9:30am-11:30pm; serves food noon-2pm and 6-10:30pm. Closed Th in June. ❸

La Grotta (☎494 15 32), down the hill from the Feyday stop, rewards a stroll to the district. This restaurant offers classic pizzas (12-18SFr) as well as omelettes (9-12SFr) and traditional Swiss fondue (34SFr for 2). The most outstanding feature is the owner's Swatch collection—a dazzling expo of all editions since 1983, including special music alarm, beeper, and ski-pass versions—which are for sale. Open Tu-Su 9am-11pm. ❷

Co-op, just off the big bend in r. Favez, below pl. du Marché and the Centre Sportif, is ideal for groceries. Open M-F 8am-12:15pm and 2-6:30pm, Sa 8am-5pm.

🏔 OUTDOOR ACTIVITIES

A **Leysin Residence Card** (available after paying for 1 night at any hotel or hostel) grants a 10-50% discount at any of Leysin's sports centers, cable cars, and ski lifts. For guided **hiking** and **adventure sports** contact the **Swiss Climbing Club** (☎494 18 46; fax 33 75; www.guideservice.ch). **Tele-Leysin** (☎494 16 35; info@teleleysin.ch) offers a relaxed trip to the top of La Berneuse (2331m); round-trip tickets cost 20SFr, students 18SFr, children 11SFr. At the summit, **Restaurant Tournant Panoramique ❷** (☎494 31

41), provides a self-service meal or more expensive full-service meals upstairs. For more active travelers, a walk begins at the Hiking Sheep and continues past the American School at Leysin to **La Grande Crevasse,** an ideal place to catch the sunset. Follow the path toward the satellite tower for a view of the valley below or continue around to the **Prafandaz** to catch a dinner of rosettes at La Prafandaz (p. 516). The most unusual hike is **La Via Ferrata** (the "iron path"), a series of metal safety cables, steps, and rungs that ascend **La Tour d'Aï,** Leysin's highest peak at 2331m. This is not a hike to be undertaken by the inexperienced. Heed the posted warnings and hike properly equipped—you cannot ascend the peak without the right gear. Inquire at the tourist office. Another option is to ascend La Tour d'Aï from the turnoff past Tête d'Aï. To do this, hike past the tiny collection of huts and turn left after about 10min.; the trail is marked. The 2½hr. hike from the village winds past a cheese farm full of bovine beauties into steep wildflower fields; (small) signs point out the Via Ferrata. The necessary gear (16SFr) is available from **Hefti Sports,** across from the cable car station, or 2min. from the Centre Sportif on pl. du Marché. (Rental ☎494 17 44, shop and office 16 77; www.hefispots.ch. Open M-Sa 8:30am-noon and 2-6:30pm, Su 10am-noon and 3-6pm. MC/V.) **Vieceli Sport,** up the road from the Co-op, has rental deals as well. (☎494 10 05. Open daily 8:30am-noon and 1:30-6:30pm. AmEx/DC/MC/V.) **Ecole Suisse des Sports de Neige,** across from Hefti Sports, offers private ski lessons for 50min for 50SFr. (☎494 12 02. Open in winter only. M/V.)

There are two sports centers. **Centre Sportif,** in the pl. Large, has **squash** and **tennis** courts and **pools.** (☎494 22 44; www.leysin.ch. Open M-F 8am-9pm, Sa-Su 9am-9pm; pools have slightly shorter hours.) Visit the **Tobogganing Park** (20SFr for 1¾hr.) or skate at the **Ice Skating Sports Center,** downhill near the campsite. (☎494 24 42. 7SFr; skate rental 3.50-4.50SFr.) A bus serves this area every 80min. For **paragliding,** call **Ecole Parapante** (☎079 638 26 02; fax 494 26 02), or reach the skies via helicopter. (☎494 34 34. 50SFr per person, min. 5 people.) Horseback riding is available at the **Manège Riding Hall** (☎494 17 07).

GRYON   ☎024

The tiny town of Gryon has experienced a population boom in recent years—from 800 to 1000. Rather than risk a greater unemployment rate, proud locals have an ordinance which allows only one child from each family to stay in the town. The kids have a tendency to come back, though, drawn to Gryon's virtually untouched, tranquil mountain setting within reach of the Dents du Midi and the Les Diablerets glacier. The main draw for world-weary travelers is undoubtedly its popular hostel, the ◪**Swiss Alps Retreat ❷,** housed in the Chalet Martin. From the station, follow the train tracks uphill. You'll see backpacker signs to your left. A gem among Swiss hostels, the Retreat has taken the concept back to its roots and given it a hip twist. New arrivals are immediately sucked into a bohemian, barefoot backpacker community. Owners Bertrand and Robyn (along with a friendly young staff comprised largely of former guests who found the environment too attractive to leave) provide backpackers a temporary family and activities from hiking to chocolate tasting. Happy to "take a vacation from their vacation," travelers passing through Gryon have been known to stay long and return often. In the nine years it took for the hostel to grow from four beds to 87, 10 couples who met here have gotten married. Amenities include discounted **ski rentals, Internet** access (12SFr per hr.), and **video/DVD rental** with free access to the TV (2SFr/4SFr) from a small but entertaining collection. The main chalet features several homey common rooms, one of which provides a stereo and music for your listening pleasure, and funky wood-framed showers. Chalet Martin's real attraction, however, is its prime location for taking advantage of the outdoors. The hostel has daily sign-ups for **cheese farm tours, paragliding, wakeboarding, rock climbing, thermal baths, guided overnight hikes,** and excursions (like a ski trip to Zermatt). They also lend maps to hikers and provide a 40% discount on ski rentals. (☎498 33 21; www.gryon.com. Co-ed dorms and bathrooms. Spotlessly clean large kitchen facilities available. Laundry 3-5SFr. Check-in 9am-9pm. Call ahead. For Christmas and double bookings check the website. Dorms 18-25SFr; doubles 50-75SFr. Discounted prices for multiple-night stays; 110SFr for full week. No credit cards.)

Reach Gryon by **cog railway** from Bex (dir: Villars; 30min.; every hr., last train 8:23pm; 5.80SFr, Eurail and SwissPass valid), which lies on the main rail line connecting the Lac Léman cities (Geneva, Lausanne, Montreux) to Aigle, Martigny, and Sion, or **by foot** from Villars (one stop further on the cog rail; 45min. walk to the hostel). **Buses** connect to Villars, through Col de la Croix to Les Diablerets (35min., 3 per day 9:02am-4:20pm, 10.40SFr), and, from there, a bus runs to Aigle (35min., every 1-2hr. 6:05am-7:45pm, 7.80SFr). The **tourist office,** in neighboring La Barboleuse, is uphill on the route de Villars, about 10min. from the hostel. (☎498 14 22; fax 26 22. Open M-Sa 8am-noon and 2-6pm, Su 9am-noon and 4-6pm.) To reach the small **convenience store** from the station, walk downhill on the road on the right instead of uphill. (Open M-F 7:30am-12:15pm and 2-6:30pm, Sa 7:30am-5pm, Su 8am-noon.)

LAKE NEUCHÂTEL REGION

Almost every town in the Lake Neuchâtel region boasts a sandy beach and a clear view of the Jura mountains. As if this weren't enough, the region also produces some of the richest *Pinot noirs* and spritziest *Chasselas* of the country, a secret well kept by the Swiss. The good wine complements the easygoing local spirit.

HIGHLIGHTS OF LAKE NEUCHÂTEL

Stroll through the vineyards of **Cressier** and sample wine and fresh cheese (p. 523).

Weird yourself out at the eccentric **Château de Gruyères** (p. 529).

Enjoy French-German fusion cuisine in the multilingual **Fribourg** (p. 525).

NEUCHÂTEL ☎ 032

Alexandre Dumas once said that Neuchâtel appeared to be carved out of butter, referring to the unique yellow stone that characterizes many of the city's buildings. But the comment could easily be mistaken for a reference to the calorie-laden treats filling local *pâtisseries*. Beyond tempting desserts, *neuchâteloise* cuisine also prides itself on quality fondue, sausages, and fresh fish from the lake and nearby rivers. Today, students flock to Neuchâtel both to perfect their French with the "pure" speech of the locals and to enjoy the laid-back atmosphere. Despite its small size, Neuchâtel has an impressive range of museums, and the town's winding streets exude historical charm and modern, youth-oriented flair.

◪ TRANSPORTATION AND PRACTICAL INFORMATION

Trains connect Neuchâtel to: Basel (1¾hr., every hr. 5:31am-12:08 am, 34SFr); Bern (45min., every hr. 5:15am-11:24pm, 17.20SFr); Fribourg via Ins-Murten (1hr., every hr. 5:55am-10:00pm, 18SFr); Geneva (1½hr., every hr. 5:57am-10:57pm, 35-40SFr); and Interlaken via Bern (2hr., every hr. 6am-11:21pm, 38SFr). A system of city

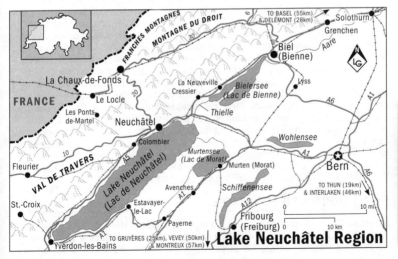

Lake Neuchâtel Region

buses connects downtown to the outskirts. (Short distances 1.70SFr, longer ones 2.50SFr. 1-day pass 7SFr.) An underground **tram** called the *Fun'Ambule* travels from the bottom floor of the train station to the shore area, where you can catch bus #1 to the tourist office and pl. Pury. **Ferries** provide service to Biel (2½hr., 3 per day, 27SFr) and Murten (1¾hr., 6 per day, 16.20SFr), departing from the Port de la Ville, just behind the post office (free with Eurail or SwissPass).

Neuchâtel centers on **place Pury,** a major square and bus line hub. From pl. Pury, face the lake and walk two blocks to the left to find the **tourist office,** in Hôtel des Postes. Check out both the free city maps and the *Terroir Neuchâtelois* guide for a listing of places that produce local goods. (☎889 68 90; www.ne.ch/tourism. Open July-Aug. M-F 9am-6:30pm, Sa 9am-4pm, Su 10am-4pm; Sept.-May M-F 9am-noon and 1:30-5:30pm, Sa 9am-noon.) The train station has **lockers** (4-6SFr), **bike rental** (25SFr per day), and a **free hotel phone.** Other services include: **Internet** at Shogun, Faubourg du Lac 31 (☎721 21 01; 7SFr per hr.); **police** (☎117); **hospital** (☎722 91 11); a **late-night pharmacy** (☎722 22 22); and a **post office.** (Open M-F 7:30am-6:30pm, Sa 8:30am-noon.) **Postal Code:** CH-2001.

ACCOMMODATIONS

In summer, budget travelers should turn to **La Maison de Champréveyres ❷,** r. de la Dime 60. From the station, take bus #7 (dir: Hauterive) to le Châble, and walk 50m toward the lake. An incredible bargain, spacious but simple singles (35SFr) offer views of the lake, a balcony, and a semi-private bath. Unfortunately, during the academic year students occupy most of the spaces; call ahead for availability. (☎753 34 33. Breakfast, sheets, and towel included. Lunch and dinner 10SFr. Laundry 6SFr.) Otherwise, try **Hôtel des Arts ❹,** r. Pourtalès 3 , for a convenient location near the nightlife and the lake. From the *Fun'ambule,* walk a block towards the city center on ave. du Premier-Mars and turn left onto r. Pourtalès for contemporary citrus-colored rooms drenched with sunlight and filled with modern art. Most rooms have TV, and all have a telephone. Ask for a room on the "quiet side" of the building. (☎727 61 61; www.hotel-des-arts.ch. Breakfast included. Reception 24hr. Wireless **Internet** in all rooms 11SFr per hr. Check-out by noon. Wheelchair accessible. Singles 87SFr, with bath 98-126SFr; doubles 112SFr/140-166SFr. 6-person apartments available. AmEx/DC/MC/V.) For a treat, head to the **Hôtel de L'Ecluse ❺,** r. de L'Ecluse 24I. Follow ave. de la Gare downhill until the intersection, then follow the signs; the hotel will be on your right. The hotel combines plush modern rooms featuring the paintings of a local artist, manicured gardens, and an expansive terrace. Perks abound: free wireless **Internet,** recently renovated kitchenettes, and large bathrooms grace every room. Half of the rooms have views of the nearby castle; the others look out onto the garden. (☎729 93 10; www.hoteldelecluse.ch. Breakfast included. Singles 135SFr; doubles 175SFr; triples 210SFr; quads 240SFr. Reductions for longer stays; less expensive on weekends. AmEx/DC/MC/V.) **Paradis Plage campground ❶,** is on the lakefront in nearby Colombier. From pl. Pury, take tram #5 (dir: Boudry) to "Bas des Allées." Cross the tracks at the tram crossing and walk 2min. down the gravel path. The campground has a pool, an on-site restaurant, cooking facilities, mail service, and go-cart rental. (☎841 24 46; www.paradisplage.ch. Reception 8:30am-9pm. Mar.-June and mid-Aug. to Oct. 9SFr per person, 3SFr per child, 8SFr per site; July to early Aug. 9SFr/3SFr/15SFr. Electricity 3.50SFr per night. AmEx/D/MC/V.)

FOOD AND NIGHTLIFE

Neuchâtel lives off tourists in the summer, but the rest of the year it's a university town, which means there's cheap food aplenty. **Crêperie Chez Bach & Buck ❶,** ave. du Premier-Mars 22, across the street from the Jardin Anglais, near the under-

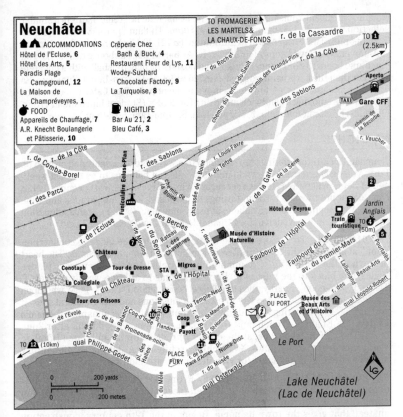

Neuchâtel

▲ ♠ ACCOMMODATIONS	Crêperie Chez
Hôtel de l'Ecluse, 6	Bach & Buck, 4
Hôtel des Arts, 5	Restaurant Fleur de Lys, 11
Paradis Plage	Wodey-Suchard
Campground, 12	Chocolate Factory, 9
La Maison de	La Turquoise, 8
Champréveyres, 1	
	♫ NIGHTLIFE
◆ FOOD	Bar Au 21, 2
Appareils de Chauffage, 7	Bleu Café, 3
A.R. Knecht Boulangerie	
et Pâtisserie, 10	

ground tram exit, counters its laid-back atmosphere with a detailed list of choices. Sit down and enjoy amazing sugar crêpes with fruit or ice cream for 3-8SFr, or meat or cheese ones for 6-11SFr. (☎725 63 53. Wheelchair accessible. Open M-Th 11:30am-2pm and 5:30-10pm, F-Sa 11:30am-2pm and 5:30-11:30pm, Su 6-10pm.) At **A.R. Knecht Boulangerie et Pâtisserie ❶**, situated on the corner of pl. des Halles and r. du Coq d'Inde, locals munch croissants stuffed with spiced ham (3SFr), fruit tarts (3.20-3.60SFr), and *pain noix* (bread with nuts; 3SFr) while enjoying a vibrant atmosphere. (☎725 13 21. Open Tu-Sa 6am-6:30pm.) Further up from pl. Pury on r. du Trésor 8, the inexpensive **La Turquoise ❷** sells grand kebabs (10SFr), enormous Greek salads (16SFr), and Middle Eastern desserts (2SFr). Further up the pl. des Halles, on r. des Moulins, the unassuming bistro **Appareils de Chauffage et de Cuisine ❸** serves an affordable *plat du jour* for 17SFr. (☎721 43 96. Open M-Th 7am-1am, F 7am-2am, Sa 8am-2am, Su 7pm-1am.) This café is the main source of income for the **Centre d'Art Neuchâtel (CAN)** (☎724 01 60; www.can.ch/can) next door, an experimental art center. Those seeking Italian flavor should consider **Restaurant Fleur de Lys ❸**, on the second floor of r. de Bassinof off pl. Numa-Droz. Fleur de Lys offers over 50 kinds of pizza. (Pizza 14-30SFr. Pasta 17-21SFr. AmEx/D/MC/V.) Sample chocolates, fruit tarts (3-4SFr), or cakes (19-22SFr) at the **Wodey-Suchard Chocolate Factory ❶**, r. du Seyon 5, directly behind pl. Pury. (Open M 11am-6:30pm, Tu-F 6:30am-6:30pm, Sa 6:30am-5pm.) In the town center, **Migros**, r. de l'Hôpital 12, has groceries. (Open M-W 8am-6:30pm, Th 8am-10pm, F 7:30am-

6:30pm, Sa 7:30am-7pm. MC/V.) Nearby, the **Co-op,** r. de la Treille 4, offers a similar selection. (Open M 1:30-6pm, Tu-W 8am-6:30pm, Th 8am-8pm, F 8am-6:30pm, Sa 7:30am-5pm.) There's an **Aperto** in the station. (☎721 20 41. Open daily 6am-10pm.)

A university crowd keeps nightlife lively. At **Bar Au 21,** Faubourg de Lac 23, you can nurse beers (3-8SFr) under Pink Floyd posters or play foosball with a clientele younger than the bar's name suggests. (☎725 81 98. M-Th 7pm-1am, F 7pm-2am, Sa 5pm-2am, Su 5pm-1am.) A few doors down is the popular **Bleu Café.** You can catch a flick while enjoying a sandwich and drink for 20SFr. (Student lunch menu 11SFr. Open M-Th 7:15pm-midnight, F 7:45pm-1am, Sa 4pm-1am, Su 4-9pm.)

🔘 SIGHTS

Neuchâtel's cultural offerings are confined to a walkable area centering around pl. Pury. You can traverse the town in minutes, unless it happens to be the last weekend of Sept., when the **Fête des Vendanges** (Wine Harvest Festival) occurs. Then it can take hours to wade through throngs of carousers enjoying parades and wine feasts. A museum passport, available at many museums (30SFr), grants admission to most museums in Neuchâtel, La Chaux-de-Fonds, and nearby La Locle.

THE OLD TOWN. To explore the old town, pick up the free guide "Neuchâtel on Foot," available at the tourist office in English, German, and French. The heart of town is the *vieille ville*, dominated by a cobblestone marketplace (pl. des Halles, one block to the right of pl. Pury) and home to a thrice-weekly market (T, Th, Sa 6:30am-noon). Nearby, the **place Pury** is dedicated to David de Pury, who upon his death left his estate to the city to establish museums and other cultural sites. If you're up for meandering around town in a tourist train, hop aboard at the **Jardin Anglais.** (In English, French, and German, in summer every 30min. after 2pm. 6SFr.) The 1790 **Hôtel de Ville,** at the corner of r. de l'Hôpital and r. de l'Hôtel de Ville, was designed by Louis XVI's chief architects. A detailed 18th-century model of the city is available for viewing on the ground floor.

CHURCHES, CASTLES, AND DUNGEONS. From the pl. des Halles, turn left onto the r. de Château (marked by the red-faced clock, the **Tour de Diesse**) and climb the stairs on your right to reach both the **Collégiale** (a church) and the château that gives the town its name. Begun in the 12th century, construction of the church took so long that architectural styles changed from Romanesque to Gothic during its construction. The golden stars and blue skies of the vaulted ceiling arch harmoniously over stained-glass windows and faded wall murals that were reinstalled after the fervor of the Reformation died down. The garish **Cenotaph,** located in the choir of the church, is a sculptural composition of the Counts of Neuchâtel from 1372 on. The sculpture was covered during the Reformation to prevent destruction and was recently restored. Outside, the Romanesque **cloister** depicts Daniel in the lions' den. *(Open daily Oct.-Mar. 9am-6:30pm; Apr.-Sept. 9am-8pm. Mass Su 10am. Concerts 6:30pm the last F of every mo. Free.)* Next door, the 12th-century **château** served as the seat of the Count of Neuchâtel during the Middle Ages. Look for splotches of red on the old outside walls, remnants of a fire in 1415 that literally baked the yellow stone. Today the bureaucrats of the cantonal government sit behind the striped shutters and flower boxes. *(Guided tours Apr.-Sept. M-F every hr. 10am-noon and 2-4pm, Sa 10-11am and 2-4pm, Su 2-4pm.)* A small garden connects the château to the **Tour des Prisons** (Prison Tower). The 125-step ascent allows you to examine the claustrophobia-inducing wooden cells used until 1848 and to enjoy a view from the top. Models on each level allow visitors to trace the urban development of the city through history. *(On r. Jeanne-de-Hochberg. Open Apr.-Sept. 8am-6pm. 1SFr, coins only.)*

⊠ MUSÉE D'HISTOIRE NATURELLE. The Musée d'Histoire Naturelle (Museum of Natural History) sits atop the r. des Terreaux, to the left off r. de l'Hôpital and features hands-on exhibits about Earth and its creatures. The permanent collection focuses on local natural history, with a well-curated exhibit on the birds native to the region. *(R. des Terreaux 14. Turn right from the pl. des Halles onto the Croix du Marché, which becomes r. de l'Hôpital. ☎ 717 79 60. Open Tu-Su 10am-6pm. 6SFr, students 3SFr.)*

MUSÉE DES BEAUX ARTS ET D'HISTOIRE. The Musée des Beaux Arts et d'Histoire (Museum of Fine Arts and History) is an eclectic collection of paintings, weapons, and textiles telling the history of Neuchâtel. The uncanny 18th-century automatons created by Jacquet-Droz are the museum's pride and joy: two barefoot boys in velvet coats scribble away while a lady plays the harpsichord. Upstairs, the Art Nouveau cupola includes oil paintings capturing the intellectual, agricultural, and commercial life of the city, along with stained glass and sculpted angels that seem to fly out of the walls. *(Esplanade Léopold-Robert 1. From pl. des Halles, walk toward the lake and turn left onto esplanade Léopold-Robert. ☎ 717 79 20; fax 79 29. Wheelchair accessible. Open mid-June to Easter Tu-Su 10am-6pm.; Easter to early June also M 10am-6pm. Presentations by curatorial staff Tu 12:15pm. Automaton performances 1st Su of each month 2, 3, and 4pm. 7SFr, students 4SFr, under 16 free; W free. AmEx/MC/V.)*

OTHER SIGHTS. Further along r. de l'Hôpital, elegant gates and two alluring sphinxes invite a stroll into the Louis XVI-style **Hôtel du Peyrou,** once the home of Rousseau's friend and publisher Alexandre du Peyrou. Fountains and formal 18th-century gardens surround the estate. *(Av. Du Peyrou 1. ☎ 725 11 83. Restaurant open Tu-Th 9am-midnight.)* Gruyère enthusiasts can make a pilgrimage to the **Fromagerie Les Martel** (Cheese Factory) in neighboring Les Ponts-de-Martel for a tour and demonstration. *(Major Benoit 25, Les Ponts-de-Martel. ☎ 937 16 66. 40min. bus ride from train station. Open daily 8am-noon and 5-7pm. Free.)*

⊠ DAYTRIPS FROM NEUCHÂTEL

CRESSIER   ☎ 032

Trains run from Neuchâtel to Cressier (dir: Biel; 10min., every hr. 5:31am-11:08pm, 3.80SFr). Take the regional train (indicated by black writing on the schedule and by the presence of a yellow eye on each train car), as the intercity does not stop in Cressier.

The medieval wine-making hamlet of Cressier is great for a daytrip. Built around a tiny château that houses the local government, the medieval village contains no less than seven *caves* **(wine cellars).** It seems that the entire town is in cahoots to sell the delicious locally produced wine: the water from the street fountains is non-potable. At each cave, friendly local vintners offer tours of their facilities and answer questions about grapes. The finale is *la dégustation,* a sampling of wines poured by the hands that made them. Choose from *chasselas, pinot noir,* or *l'oeil-de-perdrix,* or leave it to the expert by saying "Votre choix" ("you choose").

Caves line the only main street. Of note is the particularly traditional and congenial *cave* of **Jean-Paul Ruedin,** rte. de Troub 4, around the corner from the station. Jean-Paul is the 14th Ruedin son to operate the family vineyards since the first planted grapes in 1614. The *cave* Ruedin, whose white wine (*vin blanc)* has been honored by the *Gerle d'Or* (Golden Cellar) for several years, expresses a philosophical attitude toward the craft: the door declares, *"Aimer le vin c'est aimer la vie"* ("To love wine is to love life"). *(☎ 757 11 51. Open Tu-F 8am-noon and 1:30-5:30pm, Sa 9-11:30am. Call in advance.)* Though sampling is encouraged, it is impolite not to buy afterwards. The cheapest bottles start around 9SFr; 5SFr more can buy fresh baguette, cheese, and chocolate from the **Primo** next to the church on r. Gustave Jeanneret. (Open M-F 7:30am-12:15pm and 2-6:30pm, Sa 8am-2:30pm.)

If the wine has left you feeling too inebriated to return to Neuchâtel, crash at the **Hôtel de la Courone ❸** (☎757 14 58), opposite the station. Simple rooms, including TV and showers, cost 50SFr per person. Or take a 10min. stroll into the vineyards for panoramic views of the valley; follow the yellow *tourisme pédestre* signs off r. de Château. As a side trip, try the Viti Tour (indicated by a red sign with a bunch of grapes) for an educational romp around the vineyards; signs explain the history of the village and the wine it produces. A little extra effort brings you to tiny **Combe**, where the tinkling of cowbells accompanies the lake view.

YVERDON-LES-BAINS   ☎024

Trains to: Basel (2hr., every hr. 5:48am-9:48pm, 45SFr); Geneva (1hr., every hr. 5:51am-12:06am, 30SFr); Lausanne (20min., every hr. 5:51am-11:12am, 13.40SFr); and Neuchâtel (25min., every hr. 5:48am-11:49pm, 12.40SFr). The train station is at ave. de la Gare 1. (☎425 21 15. Open daily 6am-10pm.) The tourist office, 3min. to the left of the train station past the post office, calls itself the office of "thermalisme." (☎423 62 90; www.yverdon-les-bains.ch/tourisme. Open July-Aug. M-F 8am-6pm, Sa-Su 9:30am-3:30pm; Sept.-June M-F 9am-noon and 1:30-6pm, Sa 9am-1pm.)

What's in a name? In the case of Yverdon-les-Bains, it's the essence of the town: its thermal baths. When Roman settlers discovered the hot springs 1500 years ago, they used the mineral-rich waters to ease all sorts of ailments. Tourists and locals flock to the baths, but the city also offers a charming *vieille ville*, a 13th-century château, and Neolithic ruins attesting to the longevity of the locale's appeal.

Yverdon's sights are concentrated in the *centre ville*, a small square flanked by the **Savoy château** to the left and the 18th-century **Baroque church** on the right, with a charming statue of renowned pedagogue Johann Heinrich Pestalozzi standing between the two. The château was built in 1260 by the dukes of Savoy to protect Yverdon on the east, its only exposed side. The square, four-towered edifice houses a museum containing prehistoric artifacts as well as items from Yverdon's days as the Roman camp of Eburondunum. Among its prized possessions is the mummy of an Egyptian priest named Nesshou. (☎425 93 10. Museum open June-Sept. Tu-Su 10am-noon and 2-5pm; Oct.-May Tu-Su 2-5pm. 8SFr, students and seniors 7SFr, children 4SFr.) The château is also home to the **Musée de la Mode**, featuring exhibits on fashion across the ages. (☎425 93 10. Admission included with castle price.) For a total change of pace, visit the inexplicable **Maison d'Ailleurs** (House of Elsewhere), pl. Pestalozzi 14, across pl. Pestalozzi from the château entrance. This treasure trove for sci-fi lovers is the self-proclaimed "only public museum exclusively dedicated to Science Fiction, Utopia, and Extraordinary Journeys." One floor houses a library devoted to the genre. (☎425 64 38. Open W-F 2-6pm, Sa-Su noon-6pm. 7SFr, students 5SFr.)

The ◧**Centre Thermal**, ave. des Bains 22, and its glitzy adjoining hotel entice visitors with three pools and therapeutic treatments ranging from electrotherapy to massage. From the station, head left down ave. de la Gare to ave. Haldimand. Follow the signs, turning right onto r. Cordey and bearing left onto ave. des Bains. Or, take bus #2, Centre Thermal. Plug your nose: the springs produce a sulfurous stench. (☎423 02 32; www.thermes-yverdon.ch. Open M-Sa. Last entry 1hr. before closing. Baths 16SFr, ages 3-16 10SFr. Bathing caps required, 4SFr. Other facilities charge separately.) A large **Co-op** is on the corner of r. d'Orbe and r. de Neuchâtel. From the station, turn left onto ave. de la Gare. Cross the small river and head straight. (Open M-Th 8am-6pm, F 8am-7:30pm, Sa 8am-5pm. Includes a restaurant.) **Internet** access is available at Declic Informatique, r. du Lac 12-14. (☎420 33 44. Open M-F 9am-6:30pm, Sa 9am-5pm.)

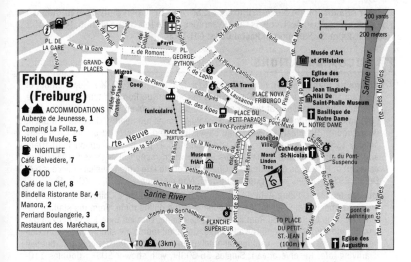

**Fribourg
(Freiburg)**

▲ ▲ ACCOMMODATIONS
Auberge de Jeunesse, 1
Camping La Follaz, 9
Hotel du Musée, 5

NIGHTLIFE
Café Belvedere, 7

FOOD
Café de la Clef, 8
Bindella Ristorante Bar, 4
Manora, 2
Perriard Boulangerie, 3
Restaurant des Maréchaux, 6

FRIBOURG (FREIBURG) ☎ 026

From the train station, Fribourg stretches out toward the river surrounding the *vieille ville*. As the town runs down the hill toward the river, wide paved streets lined by banks and businesses gradually turn into narrow cobblestone paths and twisting alleyways lined by cafés and *pâtisseries*. Founded by the Zähringen dynasty in 1157, the *vieille ville* today boasts beautiful churches, monasteries, and convents, as well as views of the river and the chalky-white gorge that encircles the older part of town. Fribourg has a penchant for modern art, shopping, and fine dining, but its best attractions stem from its history. Fribourg was an isolated bastion of Catholicism during the Reformation, and the city retains that influence today. Besides its churches and monasteries, Fribourg hosts a prestigious Catholic university. Even the local brew, Cardinal beer, celebrates a 19th-century bishop. Fribourg bridges the Swiss linguistic divide: 30% of the population firmly count themselves *Freiburger*, while the remaining 70% are *Fribourgeois*.

TRANSPORTATION AND PRACTICAL INFORMATION

Fribourg sits on the main rail line between Zurich and Geneva. **Trains** to: Basel (1¾hr., every 30min. 5:50am-11:16pm, 45SFr); Bern (25min., every 30min. 5:16am-12:16am, 12.40SFr); Interlaken (1½hr., every hr. 6:42am-9:46pm, 32SFr); Lausanne (50min., every 30min. 4:48am-11:44pm, 21SFr); and Neuchâtel (1hr., every hr. 4:33am-9:33pm, 18SFr). **Budget travel** services are provided at **STA**, 22 r. de Lausanne. (Open M-F 8:30am-6:30pm, Sa 9:30am-12:30pm and 1:30-4pm). A **funicular** train runs up and down the hillside in town. (1SFr). Fribourg's **tourist office** is at ave. de la Gare 1, 100m to the right of the station door. (☎350 11 11; www.fribourg-tourism.ch. Open M-F 9am-6pm, Sa 9am-3pm; closed Oct.-May Sa afternoons.) **Exchange currency** at the train station (open 6am-8pm) or at one of many banks lining r. du Romont. Services at the station include: **lockers** (4-6SFr; open 5:10am-12:45am); **luggage watch** (7SFr per item; open M-F 7:30am-7:40pm, Sa-Su 8am-7:40pm); and **bike rental** (30SFr per day, with ID deposit). **Payot Bookstore**, 19 r. de Lausanne, offers a small English-language section. (Open M 1-6:30pm, Tu-F 9am-6:30pm, Sa 9am-4pm.) For a **taxi**, call ☎079 219 46 10. **Internet** access is available at **Cyber Atlantis,** pl. de Nova-Friburgo. (12SFr per hr. Open daily 1pm-midnight.) The **post office,** ave. de Tivoli, is the skyscraper to the left of the station. (Open M-F 7:30am-6:30pm, Sa 8am-noon.) **Postal Code:** CH-1700.

ACCOMMODATIONS

Auberge de Jeunesse (HI), r. de l'Hôpital 2 (☎323 19 16; fax 19 40). Head left out of the train station on ave. de la Gare, which becomes r. de Romont; turn left onto r. de l'Hôpital. The entrance is at the far end of the building marked #2. This converted hospital has rooms in the basement. Bring earplugs: trains run nearby. Upstairs is a bright dining room. Breakfast, showers, and sheets included. Lunch and dinner (with early notice) 13SFr. TV, laundry (3-5SFr), and kitchen (6SFr per hr.). Reception 7:30-10am and 5-10pm. Check-out 10am. Doors locked when reception is closed. Leave your passport or HI card as a key deposit. Open mid-Feb. to late Nov. Wheelchair accessible. Dorms 29SFr; singles 81SFr; doubles 83SFr. Non-members add 6SFr. MC/V. ❷

Hôtel du Musée, r. Pierre Aeby 11 (☎/fax 322 32 09), above a Chinese restaurant, is right near most of the sights. The reception is in the dining room. From the station, follow ave. de la Gare to r. de Romont to r. de Lausanne. Turn left up r. Pierre Aeby at the end of r. de Lausanne, by pl. Nova-Friburgo. Carpeted rooms are simple and clean. Chinese art graces otherwise institutional hotel. Breakfast 10SFr. Reception 24hr., but call if arriving late. Reserve ahead. Singles 55-60SFr, with shower 80SFr; doubles 110-120SFr/120-130SFr. AmEx/D/MC/V. ❸

Camping La Follaz (☎436 24 95). From the station, take bus #1 to "Marly-Gérines" (2.80SFr). From the stop, backtrack across the bridge, take the 1st right, and follow the signs for 7min. Lakeside plots and showers. Reception 9am-10pm, but call ahead. Open Apr.-Oct. 5.30SFr per person; tents for 1-2 people 5.50SFr, for 4-6 7.50SFr. ❶

FOOD

Small cafés selling quasi-Italian or Swiss-German dishes populate r. de Romont and almost every main street in the *vieille ville*. For kebabs, check out blvd. des Pérolles and other streets around the station. **Produce markets** stand in pl. Georges Python between r. de Romont and r. de Lausanne (open Tu-W 7am-noon) and in pl. Hôtel de Ville (open Sa 7am-noon). Supermarket twins **Co-op** and **Migros** share the same street (r. St-Pierre 6a and 2, respectively, by Grand-Places) and hours (M-W and F 8am-7pm, Th 8am-9pm, Sa 8am-4pm). Co-op also has a restaurant. Migros has a second branch at Pérolles Centre, blvd. de Pérolles 21 (near the station), with a restaurant on the second floor, and a grocery with the same hours as above.

Bindella Ristorante Bar, r. de Lausanne 38 (☎322 49 05). Enjoy a small Swiss breakfast (tea, croissant, and orange juice) for 5SFr. Inventive pasta made in-house (from 13SFr) and other Italian dishes served by ponytailed waiters. A small splurge to people-watch along the popular r. de Lausanne. Live jazz last Th of the month 8:30pm. Open M-Sa 9am-11:30pm; kitchen open noon-2pm and 6:30-10pm. ❷

Café de la Clef, Planche-Supérieure 2 (☎ 322 11 92). Across the Sarine from downtown. After crossing Pont de St-Jean, the café is immediately on the right. While the restaurant has a variety of excellent dishes, including fish specials (28SFr), its primary appeal is its large upstairs terrace. While enjoying *crème brûlée* (8SFr), gaze across the river at the spire of the Cathedral and the Hôtel de Ville. Hours vary; call to check. ❸

Restaurant des Maréchaux, r. des Chanoines 9 (☎322 33 33). In the shadow of the Catholic Cathedral, this Greek restaurant has a relaxed, almost bohemian atmosphere. Greek gourmands will be satisfied with large veggie-friendly plates and soothing Greek music in the background. Feast on spinach pie (10SFr) or souvlaki (23-29SFr) in an airy dining room overlooking the gorge. Open 5pm-midnight; kitchen open 6-11pm. ❸

Perriard Boulangerie, r. de Lausanne 61 (☎322 34 89), will satisfy a sweet tooth with pastries and confectionery delights, such as *noisettines* for 5SFr per 100g, truffles (3SFr), small sandwiches (3.50SFr), and fresh breads (1.50-3.20SFr). Wheelchair accessible. Open Tu-F 7:30am-7pm, Sa 7:30am-6pm, Su 8am-6pm. ❶

Manora, in front of Grand-Place, is a self-service restaurant with a variety of meat and produce, and a worthy array of desserts and drinks. Together they make a fine meal for 8-15SFr. Wheelchair accessible. Open M-Sa 8am-7:30pm, Su 9am-7:30pm. ❷

🔆 SIGHTS

THE OLD TOWN. From the station, head down r. de Romont, past pl. Georges Python, and along r. de Lausanne and its pink-bannered open-air shopping galleries. R. de Lausanne empties into pl. Nova-Friburgo, a busy intersection with a fine view of the **Hôtel de Ville** and its fanciful clock tower. Pantaloon-clad Renaissance automatons chime the hours. A fountain of St. George dominates the courtyard below, near the commemorative **Morat Linden Tree**.

MUSÉE D'ART ET D'HISTOIRE. Off pl. Nova-Friburgo, r. Pierre Aeby leads to the museum, which is itself a historical building: a 16th-century mansion and adjoining slaughterhouse. The haunting historical artifacts are the meat of the collection. Look for the wood carvings of Hans Geiler and Hans Roditzer. The gleefully macabre, bejeweled skeleton of St. Felix, ca. 1755, is in itself a worthwhile reason to visit. Head to the top floor for 20th-century Swiss paintings. The bust of Medusa is also worth a glance. Bring a mirror, of course. *(R. de Morat 12. ☎305 51 40. Wheelchair accessible. Open Tu-W and F-Su 11am-6pm, Th 11am-8pm. Mandatory locker deposit 2SFr. Admission 6-12SFr, depending on special exhibits; students and seniors from 4SFr. MC.)*

JEAN TINGUELY-NIKI DE SAINT-PHALLE MUSEUM. On the other side of the Église des Cordeliers from the Musée d'Art et d'Histoire, the small museum showcases the work of avant-garde Fribourg native Tinguely and his wife, Saint-Phalle. Tinguely's work features bizarre, massive machines made out of rusty metal, while Saint-Phalle's work uses brilliant colors in curvaceous moving sculptures made from antlers, tires, and trees. *(R. de Morat 2. ☎305 51 70. Wheelchair accessible. Open W and F-Su 11am-6pm, Th 11am-8pm. 6SFr, students 4SFr, children under 16 free.)*

THE LOCAL STORY

DEATH, A MAIDEN, AND A LINDEN TREE

Once upon a time (June 22, 1476) in a land far, far away (Fribourg), there lived an old man named Nicholas who declared that he would give his daughter Beatrice's hand in marriage to the man who proved himself most valiant on the battlefield. As the knights went off to fight Charles the Bold in Murten, Beatrice waved a linden branch at Rudolphe, her childhood love. Determined to win her hand, Rudolphe demonstrated the most bravery in battle—at the cost of a mortal wound. Undaunted, he ran back to Fribourg, waving a linden branch and shouting "Victory!" When he finally reached Beatrice's balcony in pl. Hôtel de Ville, he collapsed. Beatrice ran to her love, who could say only "Homeland! Love! To Heaven!" before dying in her arms. The town planted the linden branch as a relic of the victory and the doomed love in the square.

In 1984, a traffic accident uprooted the tree, but the town salvaged a shoot and replanted it in the original spot, where it flourishes today. In memory of the battle and of Rudolphe's plight, runners from Murten and Fribourg race between the two cities every October.

FRI ART. Temporary exhibits of contemporary art attract a trendy crowd in this warehouse-like museum. *(Petites-Rames 22. From the Hôtel de Ville, head down the stairs toward the river. Follow signs.* ☎ *323 23 51; www.fri-art.ch. Open Tu-F 2-6pm, Sa-Su 2-5pm. 6SFr, students 3SFr.)*

MONASTERIES AND CHURCHES. Peeking out from the hills above town are two tiny chapels. There are also a number of other churches worth seeing. At the **Église des Cordeliers,** part of a Franciscan monastery, the unassuming façade masks a colorful, gaudy interior, featuring an elaborate altar that lies in star-studded darkness. *(From the Tinguely museum, backtrack on r. de Morat. Open daily Apr.-Sept. 7:30am-7pm; Oct.-Mar. 7:30am-6pm.)* Down the road is the 18th-century **Basilique de Notre-Dame,** whose dim, incense-laden atmosphere contrasts sharply with the bright, ornate Église des Cordeliers, though its elaborate pulpit does add some elegance. Across pl. Notre-Dame rises the belltower of the **Cathédrale St-Nicolas,** which shoots above the Fribourg skyline. It took over 200 years to erect the Gothic columns, now smoke-blackened, that shoot upward into pointed arches and stained-glass windows. Be sure to admire the intricate designs painted on the cathedral's ceilings. View the town from the 76m, 368-step **tower.** *(Cathedral open M-Sa 7:30am-7pm, Su 8:30am-9:30pm. Free. Tower open June-Oct. M-Sa 10am-noon and 2-5:15pm, Su 2-5:15pm. 3.50SFr, students 2SFr, children 1SFr.)* Although only order members have complete access to the 13th-century **Église des Augustins,** visitors can examine the monastery's huge altarpiece and the intricate altars near the sanctuary. *(From the cathedral, head downhill from r. des Chanoines to r. des Bouchers; take a right onto r. de Zähringen and a left onto Stalden. Take the steps of Stalden down to passage des Augustins and turn left.)*

🎵🍸 ENTERTAINMENT AND NIGHTLIFE

Fribourg's university, music conservatory, art groups, and civic institutions host several festivals throughout the year, including a **Carnival** (a Mardi Gras-type party in the *vieille ville;* Feb. 4-8, 2005), an **International Film Festival** (Mar. 6-13, 2005), an **International Guitar Festival** (late Apr. to early May), and an **International Jazz Parade** (early to mid-June). Musicians, dancers, critics, scholars, and anyone else in the arts gather for the **Belluard Bollwerk International Festival.** (☎ 469 09 00; www.belluard.ch. Late June to early July.) The **Fête du St-Nicolas,** a city-wide parade, is the winter highlight (Dec. 3, 2005). **Open-air cinema,** screens many American films (mid-July to mid-Aug.) get advance tickets from the tourist office. For a relaxed evening, try **█Café Belvedere,** Grande Rue 36, at the top of Stalden down the Grande Rue from the Hôtel de Ville, with comfortably worn couches perfect for intimate conversation. Intellectuals lounge on terraces overlooking the gorge, sampling the wine of the month (3.50-5SFr) while listening to the pleasantly dippy music. (☎ 323 44 07. Open M 2-11:30pm, Tu 1-11:30pm, W-F 1pm-12:30am, F 1pm-2am, Sa 11am-2am, Su 1pm-midnight. Terrace closes at 11pm.)

🏰 DAYTRIP FROM FRIBOURG: GRUYÈRES

(Phone code ☎ *026). To get to Gruyères, buy a ticket (16.80SFr, round-trip 33.20SFr) at the train station in Fribourg and catch a bus from behind the station to Bulle. A 25min. bus ride will land you in Bulle, where you can catch a train to Gruyères (10min., 3SFr). From the station, walk up the hill 10min., following signs, to the historic part of the city. The last train from Gruyères is at 8:17pm, bus at 9:25pm. Buses and trains run approximately every hr.*

Tiny medieval Gruyères (pop. 1600) carries a weighty reputation for its cheese, and it's unlikely that you'll find a cheesier town. The local tourist industry goes to absurd extremes (excessive flower boxes, hostesses in dubiously medieval garb, and suspiciously artificial-smelling smoke permeating a castle whose hearths have been bare and unlit for years), but the towering beauty of the surrounding mountains and the history of the town's buildings partially overcome the kitsch. Despite Gruyères's gourmand reputation, travelers should be sure to pack a lunch, or face eating in the over-priced restaurants that line the old city. (☎ 919 85 00; www.lagruyeres.ch. Open daily 9:30am-12:15pm and 1-5:30pm.)

La Maison du Gruyère, the cheese factory *par excellence*, is located directly across from the train station. The shrill voice of anthropomorphic cow Cherry leads travelers through a well-curated exhibit on the manufacturing of Gruyère cheese. Highlights include demonstrations in the showroom kitchen. Call for times and availability. (☎ 921 84 00; www.lamaisondugruyere.ch. Wheelchair accessible. Open daily Apr.-Sept. 9am-7pm; Oct.-Mar. 9am-6pm. Cheese making three times per day. 5SFr, students and seniors 4SFr, family rate 10SFr. Audioguides available in 6 languages.) The truly cheese-devoted can take a GFM bus (3.80SFr) to "Moléson-sur-Gruyères" to the **Fromagerie d'Alpage.** This 17th-century factory makes cheese the old-fashioned way, over a huge cauldron on the fireplace. After *la Maison,* you'll be amazed at the difference between new and old. (☎ 921 10 44. Open mid-May to mid-Oct. daily 9:30am-10pm. Demonstrations 10am and 3pm.)

Gruyères's only major street, lined by flowerbox-adorned old houses and well-touristed restaurants, leads uphill to the bizarre **Château de Gruyères.** The castle was home to a series of earls from the 12th to 16th centuries, but don't expect to be taken back to its earliest days when you walk in—the mismatched decor of each room reflects many different eras: medieval tapestries are juxtaposed with Louis XV chairs, modern art adorns the walls of the turret, and one room houses **Franz Lizst's** *pianoforte* (he lived here too). The dungeons are all that remain of the original feudal castle—the living quarters burned to the ground in 1493 and were rebuilt as the first Renaissance castle in the northern Alps. Some highlights are walk-in fireplaces, oddly-cobbled floors, and a room displaying dozens of antlers and stuffed game. Adding to the anachronistic confusion, the castle is also now home to the **International Center of Fantastic Art,** an elaborate sci-fi art collection scattered throughout the castle, including a tower of works by artist Patrick Woodroffe. (☎ 921 21 02. Open daily Apr.-Oct. 9am-6pm; Nov.-Mar. 10am-4:30pm. Last admission 30min. before closing. 6.50SFr, students 5.50SFr, ages 6-16 2SFr. Signs in German, French, and English. Information also in Japanese and Italian.)

If you suspect we are not alone in the universe, you can further feed your obsession on the way back to town from the *château* at the freaky **H.R. Giger museum.** Giger, the Academy Award-winning designer of Ridley Scott's *Alien,* constructed this out-of-this-world homage to himself in 1997. There are alien sketches, paintings, and sculptures. Dark curtains hide a glowing red room filled with erotic aliens in compromising positions. (☎ 921 22 00. Open daily Nov.-Apr. 11am-5pm; May-Oct. 10am-6pm. 10SFr, students 7SFr.) If you haven't gotten your extraterrestrial fix by the time you leave, you can enjoy otherworldly music while sipping overpriced drinks from Earth at the **H.R. Giger Bar** across the street. (Open daily 10am-7pm.)

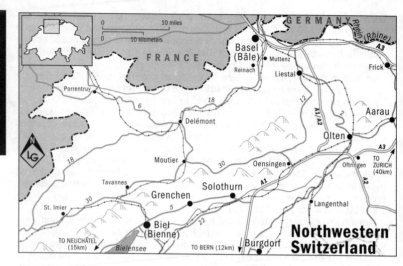

NORTHWESTERN SWITZERLAND

The cantons of Basel-Stadt, Basel-Land, Solothurn, and Aargau inspire peaceful contentment. Odds are, you'll pass through anyway (Basel is a transportation hub for Germany and France), so why not slow down to enjoy excellent museums and a delightful *Altstadt?* Nearby Solothurn offers a stunning Italian cathedral and outdoor activities. Despite their proximity to France and the occasional French town name, the cantons of northwestern Switzerland are German-speaking.

HIGHLIGHTS OF NORTHWEST SWITZERLAND

Catapult yourself into wackiness at the **Museum Jean Tinguely** in Basel (p. 537).

Gaze back in time from the top **St. Ursen Cathedral's dome** in Solothurn (p. 538).

Sip the heavenly *Hell Spezial* with your pretzel in a Basel **Biergarten** (p. 539).

BASEL (BÂLE)   ☎ 061

Basel sits on a spit of land between France and Germany, with most of the city no more than 15min. from either country. The Rhine splits the city into two sectors: *Groß-Basel* and *Klein-Basel*, which share a historical love-hate relationship. Switzerland's third-largest city achieves a balanced identity as both a home of industrial power and a bastion of old-world charm. The University of

Basel, one of the oldest universities in Switzerland and one of the few buildings left untouched after the Thirty Years' War, numbers Erasmus of Rotterdam and Nietzsche among its graduates. On the eastern riverbank, the **Münster** (cathedral) presides over the *Groß-Basel Altstadt* in a towering conglomeration of red sandstone, stained glass, and sprouting spires. And Basel boasts vibrant nightlife—the biggest party of them all being **Fasnacht**, which rivals New Orleans's Mardi Gras in locals' devotion to the pre-Lent event.

TRANSPORTATION

The **Euroairport** (☎267 90 25) serves continental Europe, though most trans-continental flights are routed through Zurich. Shuttle buses run passengers between the airport and the SBB train station on the #50 line (daily 4:55am-11:30pm).

At the crossroads of Switzerland, France, and Germany, Basel has three **train stations:** the French **SNCF** station (www.voyage-sncf.com) is next door to the Swiss **SBB station** (www.sbb.ch) in Centralbahnpl.; trains from Germany arrive at the **DB station** (Badischer Bahnhof; ☎690 11 11; www.bahn.de), across the Rhine down Greifeng. City trams to town depart the SBB station (M-F every 5min, Sa-Su every 15min.). **Buses** to Swiss, French, and German cities depart from their respective stations. **Driving** from France, take A35, E25, or E60; from Germany, E35 or A5; from within Switzerland, Rte. 2 north.

> **Trains: SBB station** (☎157 22 22; 1.19SFr per min.), on Centralbahnpl. To: **Bern** (1¼hr., every hr. 5:50am-11:07pm, 34SFr); **Geneva** (3hr., every hr. 6:24am-8:44pm, 71SFr); **Lausanne** (2½hr., every hr. 5:50am-10:26pm, 60SFr); **Milan** via Lucerne or Bern (4½-6hr., every hr. 6:30am-3:10pm, 91SFr); **Munich** via Zurich or Karlsruhe (5¼hr., every hr. 7am-8:13pm, 116SFr); **Paris** (5-6hr., 12 per day 5:51am-12:28am, 69SFr); **Salzburg** via Zurich (7hr., 5 per day 5:51am-9pm, 122SFr); **Vienna** via Zurich (10-12hr., 5 per day 5:51am-9pm, 149SFr); **Zurich** (1hr., every 15-30min. 12:07am-11:34pm, 30SFr). Make international connections at the French (SNCF) or German (DB) stations. 25% discount on international trips for travelers ages 16-25.

> **Ferries:** 4 ferries cross the Rhine: the **Üli** at St. Johann; the **Vogel Gryff** at Klingental; the **Leu** below the Münster terrace, and the **Wild Maa** at St. Alban (all M-F 7am-7pm, Sa-Su 9am-7pm; 1.20SFr, children 0.60SFr). Rhine **cruises** depart from Schifflände. (☎639 95 00; www.portofbasel.ch. Mar. to late Oct. 2-4 per day. Station open M-F 9am-12:15pm and 1-6pm, Sa 10am-4pm, Su 8am-3pm.) Enjoy "Samba Night" or another special Rhine cruise (varying times and prices; check at the station). Round-trip to Rheinfelden 45SFr, to Waldhaus 23SFr. Tickets available 30min. before departure. Reservations recommended. 25% reduction with Swiss Pass.

> **Public Transportation:** ☎267 90 25. See www.bvb-basel.ch to print door-to-door itineraries and travel plans. Trams and buses run 5:30am-12:30am. Most sights are within zone #10. 1-zone tickets 2.80SFr; ages 6-16 1.80SFr; day ticket 8SFr. Ticket machines at all stops sell tram tickets. Maps and timetables at tourist office or train station. Most have a wheelchair-accessible entrance.

> **Taxis:** In front of the train station, or call ☎271 11 11, 633 33 33, or 271 22 22.

> **Parking: Jelmoli**, Rebg. 20. **Bahnhof SBB**, Güterstr., 2.50SFr per hr.

> **Bike Rental:** At train stations. Open daily 6am-9:40pm. 30SFr per day.

ORIENTATION AND PRACTICAL INFORMATION

Basel sits in the northwest corner of Switzerland, so close to France that the Tour de France sometimes traverses the city. *Groß-Basel* (Greater Basel), where most sights are located, lies on the eastern bank of the Rhine; *Klein-Basel* (Lesser

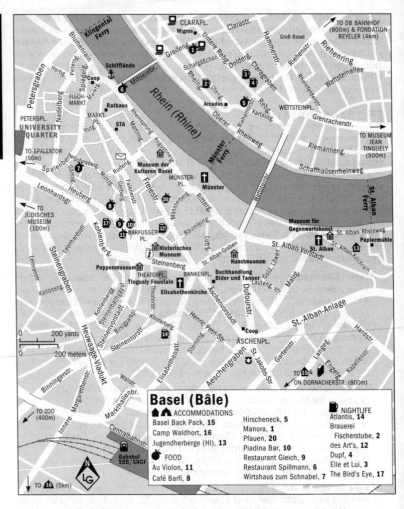

Basel (Bâle)

🏠 🏕 ACCOMMODATIONS
Basel Back Pack, 15
Camp Waldhort, 16
Jugendherberge (HI), 13

🍎 FOOD
Au Violon, 11
Café Barfi, 8

Hirscheneck, 5
Manora, 1
Pfauen, 20
Piadina Bar, 10
Restaurant Gleich, 9
Restaurant Spillmann, 6
Wirtshaus zum Schnabel, 7

🍸 NIGHTLIFE
Atlantis, 14
Brauerei
 Fischerstube, 2
des Art's, 12
Dupf, 4
Elle et Lui, 3
The Bird's Eye, 17

Basel) occupies the western bank and is home to most shops and restaurants. You can pick up a city map (0.50SFr) for motorists and pedestrians at either tourist office, but Basel's easy-to-use pedestrian tourist signs, along with small, free tear-off maps available at the tourist office, hostels, and other sites are very helpful. To reach **Marktplatz** on foot from the SBB and SNCF stations, cross the Centralbahnpl., go left on Elisabethenanlage, right down Elisabethenstr., and left on Freiestr. (20min.) From the DB station, follow Rosentalstr. (which becomes Clarastr., then Greifeng.) over Mittlere Rheinbrücke and around to the left on Eiseng. (15min.).

Tourist Office: Basel Tourismus, Steinenbergstr. (☎268 68 68; www.baseltourismus.ch), in the Stadt Casino building on Barfüsserpl. From the SBB station, take any tram headed to "Barfüsserpl." Guided walking tours are available; they include the old town, art, and history of Basel. (2hr., May-Oct. M-Sa 2:30pm, 15SFr). Hotel reservations 10SFr. Guide to the city in German, French, or English 5.90SFr. Buy a **Basel Card** and get the guided walking tour, admission to all Basel museums, ferries, and the zoo, as well as discounts for some restaurants, clubs, and taxis. Available at tourist office. (24hr. card 20SFr, including public transportation 25SFr; 48hr. 27SFr; 72hr. 35SFr). Open M-F 8:30am-6:30pm, Sa-Su 10am-5pm. **Branch office** (☎271 36 84; hotel@messebasel.ch) at the SBB station open M-F 8:30am-6:30pm, Sa-Su 9am-2pm.

Travel Agency: STA Travel, Freiestr. 15 (☎269 83 00; stabasel@statravel.ch). Open M-F 10am-6:30pm, Sa 10am-4pm.

Currency Exchange: The SBB station bureau, including a **Western Union,** offers currency exchange (2SFr fee) and cash advance with MC/V (min. 200SFr). Open daily 7am-8pm. Same prices and services at the DB station, open daily 6:30am-8:30pm. A **24hr. currency exchange machine** sits next to their office.

Luggage Storage: At all stations. **Lockers** 5SFr, 24hr. access. **Storage** 7SFr per day. Open 6am-9:40pm.

Bookstore: Buchhandlung Bider und Tanner, Bankenpl., Äschenvorstadt 2 (☎206 99 99), is Basel's travel bookshop, with a room of well-selected English-language books. Open M-W and F 9am-6:30pm, Th 9am-8pm, Sa 9am-5pm.

Library: Bibliothek Gundeldinger, Dornacherstr. 192. Located next to the Basel Back Pack hostel. Open M and W 2-6:30pm, Tu and F 10am-noon and 2-6:30pm, Th 2-10pm, Sa 10am-4pm.

GLBT Organizations: Pick up a **doux bole** calendar with all of the month's events, available at the tourist office. **Habs** (*Homosexuelle Arbeitsgruppen Basel;* ☎692 66 55; info@habs.ch), Postfach 1519, CH-4001 Basel, is located on Lindenberg 23 and has general city info. **Arcados,** Rheing. 69 (☎681 31 32; www.arcados.com), at Clarapl., a bookstore, has lots of information on GLBT bars, restaurants, and hangouts. Open Tu-F 1-7pm, Sa noon-4pm.

Public Restrooms and Showers: In the SBB station at McClean. Toilets 1-2SFr. Showers 12SFr per 20min., including towels, and shampoo. Open daily 6am-midnight.

Emergencies: Police ☎117. **Medical** ☎144. **Hospital** ☎265 25 25.

Hotlines: Helping Hand (☎143) for any crisis situation.

Internet Access: Domino, Steinenvorstadt 54. Arcade with Internet coffeebar upstairs. 18+. 10SFr per hr., after 6pm 12SFr per hr. Open M-Th 9:30am-midnight, F-Sa 9am-1am (summer Sa 10am-1am), Su 1pm-midnight. **Jäggi Bucher,** Greifeng. 3/5 has Internet stations in the bookstore. 1SFr per 6 min. Open M, W, F 9am-7pm, Th 9am-8pm, Sa 9am-5pm. **Mausklick,** Klingentalstr. 7. 10SFr per hr. Open M-F 7:30am-5pm. **Manor,** Greifeng. 22. 5SFr per 30min. Open M-W and F 8:30am-7pm, Th 8:30am-9pm, Sa 8am-5pm.

Post Office: Rüdeng 1. Take tram #1 or 8 to "Marktpl." and walk 1 block back from the river. Open M-W and F 7:30am-6:30pm, Th 7:30am-8pm, Sa 8am-noon. Also at the DB Station. Open M-F 7:30am-noon and 2-6pm, Sa 8:30-11:30am. *Poste Restante* address: Postlagernde Briefe, Rüdeng., CH-4001 Basel 1.

Postal Codes: CH-4000 to CH-4059.

ACCOMMODATIONS AND CAMPING

All accommodations in Basel offer a complimentary **Mobility ticket.** The ticket offers free use of public transport for the duration of your stay in zones 10 and 11 (where most sights are located) and of the airport shuttle bus (6.60SFr).

Jugendherberge (HI), St. Alban-Kirchrain 10 (☎272 05 72; www.youthhostel.ch/basel). Tram #2 to "Kunstmuseum." Turn right on St.-Alban-Vorstadt, then follow the signs, or walk 15min. from the SBB station down Äschengraben to St.-Alban-Anlage. At the tower, follow the signs down the hill. This hostel is a mecca for weary travelers. The institutional setup has lockers for every bunk, TV, and phone, but expect long waits for services. The aging facilities are clean and comfortable. Breakfast and sheet included. Also offers **Internet** (5SFr for 25min., after midnight half-price), laundry (7SFr), **currency exchange** (euros and SFr only), and lunch and dinner (12.50SFr). Reception Mar.-Oct. 7am-10am and 2-11:30pm; Nov.-Feb. 2pm-11pm. Check-out 7-10am. Reservations recommended. Wheelchair accessible. 8-bed dorms 30.50SFr; 6-bed dorms 31.50SFr; 4-bed dorms 32.50SFr; singles 80SFr; doubles 100SFr. Non-members add 6SFr. AmEx/MC/V. ❷

Basel Back Pack, Dornacherstr. 192 (☎333 00 37 or 076 538 37 19; www.basel-backpack.ch). Exit the rear of the SBB station, go up the stairs, and turn right onto the gallery that leads to Hochstr. Walk straight down Hochstr., then turn right on Bruderholzstr. Follow Bruderholzstr. until it intersects with Dornacherstr. Enter the gate at #192 and walk all the way to the back of the building. Or ride tram #15 (dir: Bruderholz) to "Bruderholzstr." Follow the signs on the building to the left to find the reception. Though a good distance from the city center, Basel's newest (and only independent) hostel is serviced by a convenient tram. Located in a renovated factory, Back Pack offers new, clean, environmentally friendly facilities. Color-coded rooms include matching lockers and extra-high bunk beds. Couples traveling on the cheap will appreciate queen-size beds in the dorms. Small on-site bar and take-away Thai restaurant. Breakfast 7SFr. Sheets, showers, kitchen, and locker included. **Internet** 1SFr per 5min. Laundry 6SFr. Reception 8am-1pm and 7pm-midnight. Check-out 11am. Online reservations possible. Dorms 30SFr; singles 80SFr; doubles 94SFr; triples 120SFr; quads 150SFr. ❷

Camping: Camp Waldhort, Heideweg 16 (☎71 64 29), in Reinach. Take tram #11 to "Landhof." (3.60SFr). Backtrack 200m toward Basel, cross the main street, and follow the signs for a 10min. walk. Beautiful location in the middle of the woods, but far from Basel. Reception 8am-noon and 2-8pm. Open Mar.-Oct. 7SFr per adult, 4.50SFr per child, 11SFr per tent. ❶

◪ FOOD

Barfüsserpl., Marktpl., and the streets connecting them are full of cheap eats. Don't be alarmed by the local slang for Barfüsserpl.—*Barfi* is no criticism of the food, just an abbreviation. An index of many clubs and restaurants on the web, www.baselrestaurant.ch includes schedules of jazz nights and special events.

RESTAURANTS

Au Violon, Lohnhof 4 (☎269 87 11; www.au-violon.com). Before Gerberg., head left up the tiny Lohnhofgässlein and take the elevator at the top of the stairs to the 1st floor. Moderately priced gourmet food in this French brasserie on the *Barfi*. The leafy terrace is pleasant in the summertime. Entrées include baked lox with saffron sauce and vegetables (32SFr). English menu. Open Tu-Sa 11:30am-12:30am. AmEx/DC/MC/V. ❹

Piadina Bar, Gerberg. 78, on the corner of Gerberg. and Barfüsserpl. This small café serves tasty tortilla breads full of your choice of cheeses, meats, and vegetables (8-12SFr). Open M-Th 10:45am-midnight, F-Sa 10:45am-1am. ❷

Restaurant Gleich, Leonhardsberg 1 (☎281 82 86), off Barfüsserpl. This casual restaurant serves vegetarian dishes popular with locals, including a large salad buffet. Colorful, healthful dishes. Exotic smoothies run 3-5SFr. Open M-F 10:30am-9:30pm. ❸

Restaurant Spillman, Eiseng. 1 (☎261 17 60; fax 16 72), at the foot of Mittlere Rhei-nbr., near Schifflände. An upscale but unpretentious crowd sits above the rushing Rhine in this restaurant with a 2nd-fl. terrace. Lunch Menüs 18SFr. Most dinner entrées 25-35SFr. For a splurge, try the Mediterranean-style king prawns (39SFr). Open M-Sa 8:30am-11pm; kitchen open 8:30am-9:30pm. AmEx/DC/MC/V. ❹

Wirtshaus zum Schnabel, Trillengässlein 2 (☎261 49 09; 49 92). From Marktpl., walk 1 block on Hutg. (by EPA) to Spalenberg.; turn left onto Schnabelg. In this corner ter-race, Italian speakers serve Swiss-German dishes. The Swiss oven in the corner and wood paneling will have you hearkening back to your Alpine farming days, even if you don't really have any. Enjoy wiener schnitzel prepared at your table. Vegetarian Menü available. Pasta 13-20SFr. Open M-Sa 10:30am-midnight. AmEx/DC/MC/V. ❸

Hirscheneck, Lindenberg 23 (☎692 73 33). Cross Wettsteinbr. and turn left onto Kar-tansg. An unabashedly left-of-center restaurant-bar where dreadlocks, piercings, and the hammer and sickle prevail. Features 2 vegetarian and organically grown dishes every day. Menü 12-18.50SFr. Open M-F 11am-midnight, Sa 2pm-1am, Su 10am-mid-night; kitchen open M-F noon-2pm and 6-10pm, Sa 6-10pm, Su 10am-4pm. ❷

Café Barfi, Leonhardsberg 4 (☎261 70 38), to the right of Gerber. from Marktpl. Mostly Italian pizza and pasta with unexpected samosas (7SFr) thrown in. Outdoor din-ers on this tiny, quiet side street sometimes enjoy accordion serenades from street per-formers. Pasta 16-20SFr. Pizza 17-21SFr. Homemade lasagna 20SFr. Open M-Sa 10am-11pm, Su 5-10pm. AmEx/MC/V. ❸

Manora, Greifeng. 22, and **Pfauen,** Freiestr. 75, are both good, cheap self-service res-taurants. Manora is wheelchair accessible. Meals run 5-18SFr. Both open M-W and F 8:30am-6:30pm, Th 8:30am-9pm, Sa 8am-5pm. Manora AmEx/DC/MC/V. ❷

MARKETS

Migros, SBB station and 21 Greifeng., across from Manora. Wheelchair accessible. SBB loca-tion open M-F 6am-10pm, Sa-Su 7:30am-10pm. Greifeng. location open M-W and F 8am-7pm, Th 8am-9pm, Sa 8am-5pm.

Coop, at Schifflände tram stop and on Äschenpl. Wheelchair accessible. Open M-W and F 7am-7pm, Th 7am-9pm, Sa 7:30am-5pm.

Public market, on Marktpl. An impressive array of fresh fruits, vegetables, cheeses, and baked goods every weekday morning. Open M-W until 5:30pm, Th-F until 1:30pm.

◖ SIGHTS

Marktplatz, which sits near the river at the culminating point of Freiestr. and other major shopping avenues, is the center of the *Altstadt*. The tourist office has a bro-chure outlining several well-marked walks through the city, following the lives of famous Basel residents, including Hans Holbein and Erasmus.

THE OLD TOWN. Erected in the early 1500s to celebrate Basel's entry into the Swiss Confederation, the very red **Rathaus** (City Hall) brightens Marktpl. with its blinding façade adorned with gold and green statues. Behind the Marktpl., you can cross the **Mittlere Rheinbrücke.** Built in 1225, the bridge connects *Groß-Basel* to *Klein-Basel*. A block away from Marktpl. in the heart of the *Altstadt*, a colorful Gothic fountain livens up the **Fischmarkt.** Leading off of the Fischmarkt, the tiny **Elftausendjungfern-Gässlein** (Lane of 11,000 Virgins) is famous for St. Ursula's pilgrimage of girls to the Holy Land during the Chil-dren's Crusade. The medieval practice of walking this lane to recoup indul-gences is now defunct, but people still stagger through after overindulging at nearby bars. For a contrasting aesthetic, walk from Marktpl. toward Barfüsserpl. onto Theaterpl. Here, the spectacular ■**Jean Tinguely Fountain,** also known as the **Fasnachtsbrunnen,** captures a moment of modern chaos as iron sculptures spew water. The nearby **Elisabethenkirche** is an impressive structure built between 1857 and 1865. Today, it contains a café.

MÜNSTER (CATHEDRAL). Behind Marktpl. along the Rhine, the **Münster,** Basel's medieval treasure, stands on the site of an ancient Celtic settlement and a Roman fort. The red sandstone façade features hundreds of figures in acts of piety ranging from trumpet-playing to dragon-slaying. Behind the altar, gilded Latin inscriptions memorialize the life of Erasmus, the renowned scholar and staunch Catholic who remained loyal to his faith even after his beloved Basel joined the Reformation in 1529. When he died, the city gave him a proper Catholic burial in its Protestant cathedral, a mark of Basel's religious tolerance. Bernoulli, the mathematician who discovered the science behind flight, rests in the cloister among prominent Basler families. Be sure not to miss the late-Gothic stone pulpit, installed in 1486, and the collection of Bibles in different languages. The **tower** holds the city's best view of the Rhine, *Klein-Basel*, and Black Forest. *(Informational pamphlet available for 2SFr. Open Easter to mid-Oct. M-F 10am-5pm, Sa 10am-4pm, Su 1-5pm; mid-Oct. to Easter M-Sa 11am-4pm, Su 2-4pm. Free. Tower closes 30min. before the church. 3SFr. Due to church policy (and past suicides), you must go up with another person. Services Sa 4:30pm, Su 10am.)*

UNIVERSITY QUARTER. The **University of Basel,** founded in 1406, is Switzerland's oldest university. Its library houses rare volumes by Erasmus, Luther, and Zwingli. The grounds are ideal for picnicking, napping, and tanning. Bargain-hunters head to nearby Petersplatz every Saturday morning for the **flea market,** which starts at 7:30am and lasts until early afternoon. The university's **botanical gardens,** next to the Petersplatz on Petersgraben, showcase plants from around the world. The tropical greenhouse brings a slice of the Amazon to the Alps, complete with birds, vines, and steamy air. *(Open daily Nov.-Mar. 8am-5pm; Apr.-Oct. 8am-6pm.)* Around the corner from the university library, the 700-year-old **Spalentor** (gate tower), one of the original city wall's three remaining towers and one of the most impressive gates in Switzerland, marks the edge of the *Altstadt. (Head down one of the tiny alleys off Fischmarkt to reach Petersgraben, which leads to Peterspl. and the University quarter.)*

ZOO. The *Zoologischer Garten* is a fun stop for the kids after a day of museum browsing. Though animal enclosures are small, ongoing renovations have spruced up many exhibits. Restaurants, picnic areas, and ice cream vendors abound. *(Binningerstr. 40, a 10min. walk down Steinenvorstadt from Barfüsserpl. Follow signs along the wooden path, or take tram #1 or 8 to "Zoo Bachletten."* ☎ *295 35 35. Wheelchair accessible. Open daily May-Aug. 8am-6:30pm; Sept.-Oct. and Mar.-Apr. 8am-6pm; Nov.-Feb. 8am-5:30pm. 14SFr, students and seniors 12SFr, ages 6-16 5SFr; family ticket 30SFr.)*

HIKING. Over 1200km of yellow-blazed trails crisscross the countryside around Basel. Take bus #70 to "Reigoldswil" where the **Gondelbahn** goes to the Jura mountain peak, "Wasserfallen" (937m). "Devil bike" (oversized mountain scooters) rental is available at the top. From the peak you can hike to Waldenburg (2½-3hr.), or to Jägerwegli (1½-2hr.). A steam engine will take you from Waldenburg back to Liestal, where you can connect to Basel (1-3 per hr.).

■ MUSEUMS

Basel's 30 museums may seem overwhelming, but they are worth the time it takes to explore them. The **Kunstmuseum** is deservedly the most famous, but many of the more esoteric galleries are also fascinating. Subjects range from medieval medicine to mechanized mannequins. Pick up the comprehensive museum guide at the tourist office, or visit www.museenbasel.ch. A **Swiss Museum Pass,** valid for one month (all over Switzerland at participating museums) costs 32SFr. A **Basel Card** (p. 532) is good for all museums.

FONDATION BEYELER. The Fondation, which opened its doors in 1997, has quickly emerged as one of Europe's finest private art collections. A dramatic stone and glass building on the outskirts of the city, it includes works from dozens of major artists, including Picasso, Matisse, Klee, van Gogh, Warhol, and Cézanne. The surrounding grounds are lush and were once wrapped in plastic by Christo. The outdoor lily pond is only matched by a massive Monet version within. *(Baselstr. 101, Riehen. Take tram #6 (dir: Riehen Grenze) to "Riehen Dorf," then walk in the direction of the tram 5min. It's on the left after the "Kunstraum Riehen."* ☎ 645 97 00; www.beyeler.com. *Wheelchair accessible. Open daily 9am-6pm, W 9am-8pm. M-F 16SFr, Sa-Su 20SFr; students 5SFr; after 6pm 12SFr. Tours of special exhibits in German, French, and English.)*

KUNSTMUSEUM (MUSEUM OF FINE ARTS). Despite being the first independent public gallery in Switzerland (opened in 1661), the Basel Kunstmuseum still retains its fresh perspective on art. A formidable marble structure that requires at least an afternoon to explore, it houses extensive, outstanding compilations of old and new masters and temporary exhibits. It has a particularly strong collection of local art and Cubist painters (Picasso and Braque). The Picasso collection was begun when a resoundingly affirmative electoral referendum persuaded the city government to grant the museum money to buy two of his works. Touched by such enthusiasm, the artist himself donated four more. *(St. Alban-Graben 16. Accessible by tram #2 or 15.* ☎ 206 62 62; www.kunstmuseumbasel.ch. *Audioguides for temporary exhibits 5SFr. Mandatory 2SFr bag deposit. Wheelchair accessible. Open Tu and Th-Su 10am-5pm, W 10am-7pm. 10SFr, students 8SFr, 1st Su of the mo. free. Includes entrance to Museum für Gegenwartskunst. Special exhibition rates usually 15SFr, students 10SFr. Call ahead to ask about the occasional English guided tours and tours for those in wheelchairs.)*

MUSEUM JEAN TINGUELY. Noise and motion are the preferred modes of expression of this intriguing Swiss sculptor; the hyper-modern pink sandstone façade of this improbable homage to him hides endless amounts of interaction and chaotic entertainment. Tinguely's massive *Grosse Méta Maxi-Maxi Utopia* allows visitors to climb over and experience his crazy futuristic vision. Temporary exhibits focus on the work of Tinguely's contemporaries or of modern artists he inspired. *(Paul-Sacher Anlage 1. Take tram #2 or 15 to "Wettsteinpl." and bus #31 or 36 to "Museum Tinguely." Alternatively, from Wettsteinpl., walk 15min. down Grenzacherstr., turn right and walk through Solitude park. Signs point the way.* ☎ 681 93 20; www.tinguely.ch. *Wheelchair accessible. Open W-Su 11am-7pm. 10SFr, students 7SFr.)*

MUSEUM DER KULTUREN BASEL. A mansion topped by Neoclassical friezes houses elements of non-Western cultures. Particularly notable are the New Guinea *Geisterhern* that stands three floors high, the intricate carvings on canoe paddles from Oceania, and religious sculptures from Tibet. In the same building, you'll find the **Naturhistorisches Museum.** *(Augustinerg. 2.* ☎ 266 55 00. *Wheelchair accessible. Both museums open Tu-Su 10am-5pm. 7SFr, students under age 26 5SFr, under age 16 free, 1st Su of the mo. and Tu-Sa 4-5pm free. Special rates for temporary exhibitions usually 14SFr.)*

MUSEUM FÜR GEGENWARTSKUNST (MODERN ART). Find most of Basel's modern art at this concrete and glass structure that spans a small stream. It is composed largely of temporary exhibition spaces and is located between the youth hostel and the Rhine. *(St. Alban-Rheinweg 60.* ☎ 206 62 62; www.mgkbasel.ch. *Open Tu-Su 11am-5pm. Combined ticket with Kunstmuseum 10SFr, students under 25 8SFr, 1st Su of the mo. free. Special exhibition rates usually 14SFr, students 10SFr.)*

HISTORISCHES MUSEUM: BARFÜSSERKIRCHE. The church collection includes stained-glass windows emblazoned with cantonal coats-of-arms, stunning iconography, fine goldsmithing, and the oldest *crosier* city banner in Switzerland. The early Gothic church, with its pink stone columns and huge windows veiled in transparent linen, was converted into a museum in 1894. Downstairs, recreated rooms showcase medieval and Renaissance furnishings and display a loom used to create silk ribbons. Nearby buildings are dedicated to musical instruments and carriages. *(Steinenberg 4, on Barfüsserpl. ☎ 205 86 00; www.historischesmuseumbasel.ch. Wheelchair accessible. Open M and Th-Su 10am-5pm. 7SFr, students and seniors 5SFr, under 16 and 1st of the mo. free.)*

OTHER MUSEUMS. The **Puppenhausmuseum (Toy Museum) Basel** holds four floors of toys (including over 2000 toy bears) and miniature model towns captured in excruciating detail—this is a museum children will love. *(Steinenvorstadt 1. ☎ 225 95 95; www.pelppenhausmuseum.ch. Wheelchair accessible. Open M-W and F-Su 11am-5pm, Th 11am-8pm. 7SFr, students 5SFr, under age 16 free.)* Learn the art of paper making at the **Papiermühle (Paper Mill)** and try your hand at the printing press. Also enjoy the rustic on-site Mediterranean café with views of the mill. Entrées run 17SFr. *(St. Alban-Tal 37. ☎ 272 96 52. Museum open Tu-Th 2-5pm. Café open Tu-Th and Sa 11:30am-6pm, F 11:30am-midnight, Su 10am-6pm. 12SFr, students 8SFr, families 25SFr.)* The **Jüdisches Museum der Schweiz (Jewish Museum)** contains exhibits on law, the observation of Jewish holidays, and other aspects of Jewish daily life. *(Kornhausg. 8. Take tram #3 to "Lyss." ☎ 261 95 14. Open M and W 2-5pm, Su 11am-5pm. Free.)*

🎵 🎭 ENTERTAINMENT AND NIGHTLIFE

FESTIVALS. In a year-round party town, Basel's carnival, or **Fasnacht** (www.fasnacht.ch), distinguishes itself. The festivities begin on the Sunday after Mardi Gras in Liestal, a town 17km south of Basel, where giant bonfires are floated down the river. The festivities in Basel proper start the following day with the **Morgestraich**, which has occurred annually for the last 600 years. This 4am parade ends precisely 72hr. later with the **Gässle parade.** Fife and drum music plays to revelers in brilliant masks lampooning the year's local scandals. Children wander the streets in costumes on Tuesday, and at night there is an exhibition of the lanterns on Münsterpl., as well as concerts of local *Gugge* music. Spectators should purchase a carnival badge *(Plakete)*—it's not required, but the costumed *Waggis* are mean to those who don't support the event (badges cost 10, 20, and 30SFr, up to 200SFr for specialty designs). The tourist office provides lists of Basel's other cultural offerings—local favorites include **Jazz in the City**, when the city is covered with jazz bands the second weekend in August; the **Klosterbergfest**, which fills the street with international bars, foods, and wares to raise money for Brazilian street children (last week in Aug.); and the 35th annual **ART Basel** fair, an early summer event that brings thousands to gawk at some of the most avant-garde art exhibited today. Basel's fall festival, the **Herbstmesse**, is Switzerland's oldest and largest outdoor market (late Oct.-early Nov.). The **Weihnachtsmarkt** at Christmastime is an impressive display (last week of Nov. until Dec. 23rd). Smaller festivals, like the **Basel Wine Fair** in mid-October and the theater festival **Welt in Basel** (mid-August) are also traditional favorites. Dates are already set for the **International Jazz Festival** (April 19 to May 2, 2005) and the **International Art Fair** (June 15-20, 2005).

BARS AND NIGHTCLUBS. A university town through and through, Basel's nightlife reflects the influence of student patrons. Start bar-hopping at **Barfüsserplatz**, where students sit at outdoor tables and drink wine on the steps of the Barfüsserkirche. When the bars close, kids in black often head for after-hours clubs, where things get rolling around 3-4am. Most places are 21+, but the crowds get younger on weekends. The two most popular beers are **Warteck** and **Cardinal**, though the locally brewed **Üli** is also a favorite.

Atlantis, Klosterberg 10 (☎ 228 96 96; www.atlan-tis.ch). From Bankenpl., it's off Elisa-bethenstr. to the right. Known as "Tis," Atlantis draws a big crowd on weekends. This multi-level, sophisticated bar sways to reggae, jazz, and funk. Bands or DJs play every night the Italian soccer team does not. Doubles as a swank restaurant, serving veggie-friendly specialities (tomato and mozarella salad 15SFr). Wheelchair accessible in bar. Concerts around 35SFr. Club nights F-Sa, cover 15-25SFr. Open Tu-Th 11am-midnight, F 11:30am-4am, Sa 6pm-4am; kitchen open 11am-2pm and 6pm-2am. AmEx/MC/V.

Brauerei Fischerstube, Rheing. 45 (☎ 692 66 35). Cross Mittlere Rheinbr. and take the 1st right. This old-school *Biergarten* is adjacent to Basel's oldest brewery, crafting 4 of the best beers in town. The delectably sharp *Hell Spezial* goes well with the homemade pretzels. Stop by for an early evening *Bier* (3.50-7SFr). Open M-Th 10am-midnight, F-Sa 10am-1am, Su 5pm-midnight; full dinner menu from 6pm. MC/V.

des Art's, am Barfüsserpl. 6 (☎ 273 57 37; www.desarts.ch) to the left of the His-torisches Museum. For over 20 years, this classy café has turned into a hotspot at night, with its locally famous "after-work" party (Tu 6-9pm) and the largest humidor in Basel. Sink into one of the worn leather sofas or a movie theater seat, and you won't want to get back up. Piano player daily from 6pm on. French specialties served until midnight (18-32SFr). Beer from 4.90SFr. Wine 5-7SFr. Cocktails 12-14SFr. Open Su-Th 11am-midnight, F-Sa 11am-3am; kitchen open 11am-2pm and 4-11pm. AmEx/MC/V.

The Bird's Eye, Kohlenberg. 20 (☎ 263 33 41), off Barfüsserpl. on Kohlenberg. This pop-ular club offers live jazz W-Sa nights (10SFr cover) and DJs the rest of the week. Occa-sional free concerts. Open W-Sa 9am-11:30am.

Dupf, Rebg. 43 (☎ 692 00 11). Cross Weittsteinbr. and left onto Rebg. This chic gay and lesbian bar/restaurant welcomes a mixed crowd for low-key evenings out on the terrace and more excitement inside. Beers from 4.50SFr. Open Su-Th 4pm-1am, F-Sa 4pm-late.

Elle et Lui, Rebg. 39 (☎ 691 54 79). Dupf's next-door neighbor caters to a gay and les-bian clientele of all ages. Try the Caipirinha (15SFr) if you brought a friend to carry you home—it's 40% alcohol. Open daily Oct.-Apr. 4pm-3am, May-Sept. 6pm-3am.

SOLOTHURN
☎ 032

Sandwiched snugly between the Jura mountains and the Aare River, Solothurn's charm rubs off on its inhabitants—the friendliness of shopkeepers and restaura-teurs is tangible. Film, music, and literature festivals attest to its love affair with culture. Solothurners unleash their rambunctious sides during the Winter Carni-val, while the peaceful Jura mountains offer endless hiking and biking prospects.

TRANSPORTATION AND PRACTICAL INFORMATION. Trains depart from Solothurn's main station at Hauptbahnhof for: Basel (1hr., 2-4 per hr. 5:50am-11:28pm, 23SFr); Bern (40min., 5 per hr. 5:18am-12:28am, 14SFr); Neu-châtel (45min., 2 per hr. 5:12am-11:50pm, 17.60SFr). For a map or free room res-ervation, head to the **tourist office,** Hauptg. 69. From the train station, take the underpass toward the Zentrum and follow Hauptbahnhofstr. across the river Aare via the Kreuzackerbr. up Kroneng. (☎ 626 46 46; www.solothurn-city.ch. Open M-F 8:30am-noon and 1:30-6pm, Sa 9am-noon.) **Train station** services include: **currency exchange, Western Union,** and **bike rental** (30SFr per day, 36SFr if returned to another station; all open M-F 6:10am-8:50pm, Sa-Su 6:30am-

FROM THE ROAD

GLIDIN' HIGH

"I just leapt off a 2000m mountain peak this morning. But don't worry; I'm still alive." So began an email that I sent to my unsuspecting friends and family members after my tandem paragliding flight. My father asked how many deaths I had died before we took off, my roommate lamented the fact that she'd missed her opportunity for a single, and I glowed for the rest of the day with an I-soared-1000m-over-the-ground grin on my face.

Flight conditions were good that morning, and after a quick ride to the cable car, ascent to the top of the mountain, and 5min. hike to our starting place, I found myself strapped into a parachute, helmet on head, getting instructions on when to run. "Start with your left foot and keep going even after you feel the tug of the sail," the instructor, Lois, explained. On his command, I started running, and within a few steps, I felt us both get lifted off the ground. Thermal updrafts pushed us higher as we soared over the mountainside. Our tiny shadow followed us along the ground below as we swooped through the air. Passing me the handles to steer, he pulled out a camera and started snapping photos before guiding us safely to our landing spot in a small playground. Two little boys ran over to watch Lois repack the gear as I tried to steady my legs after the excitement of the past half-hour.

—Andrea Spillmann

8:50pm); **taxis** (☎622 66 66 or 22 22); **lockers** (3-5SFr, 24hr.); and **luggage storage** (7SFr; open 6:30am-8:50pm). **Internet** is available at Tribe Music, Landhausquai 5, past the hostel on the right. (2SFr per 15min. Open M 1:30-6:30pm, Tu-W and F 10am-6:30pm, Th 10am-9pm, Sa 9am-5pm.) In an emergency, call ☎117 for **police**, ☎118 in case of **fire**, and ☎627 31 21 for the **hospital**. **Post offices** are located both next to the station (open M-F 7:30am-noon and 2-6pm, Sa 9-11am) and past the hostel on Postpl. Turn left off Kreuzackerbr., and onto Landhausquai. (☎625 29 29. Open M-F 7:30am-6pm, Sa 8am-noon). **Postal Code:** CH-4500.

🏠🍴 ACCOMMODATIONS AND FOOD. Overlooking the Aare River on the edge of the *Altstadt*, the **Jugendherberge "Am Land" (HI) ❷**, Landhausquai 23, is a slick, high-tech structure of glass and steel framed by the exterior of a 1642 schoolhouse. From the train station, walk over the Aare via the Kreuzackerbr. and take the first left onto Landhausquai (follow signs to "Landhaus;" street also labelled "Fischerg."). Amenities include a pool table, foosball, roof terrace, large common rooms, and music room. Beds can be close together in dorms, but a few are incredibly spacious. Request a river view. If you are staying here, save money and store your luggage in the free (2SFr deposit) second-floor lockers as opposed to the more expensive train station options before sight-seeing. (☎623 17 06; fax 16 39. Breakfast and sheets included. Lunch and dinner 13SFr; reserve ahead. Reception 7:30-10am and 4:30-10:30pm, but doors open all day. Check-out 10am. Wheelchair accessible. 9-bed dorms 27SFr; 6-bed dorms and 5-bed dorms with sink 30SFr; doubles 86SFr; triples with toilet and shower 114SFr. Tax 2SFr, under age 16 1SFr. Non-members add 6SFr. AmEx/DC/MC/V.) The **Hotel Kreuz ❸**, Kreuzg. 4, offers more privacy but less modernity. Go left off Kreuzackerbr. before the hostel. (☎622 20 20; kreuz@soluet.ch. Breakfast and hall showers included. Free access to kitchen. Reception M-F from 11am, Sa from 9am. Spartan singles 50SFr, larger bed 60SFr; doubles 85SFr for 1 larger bed, 90SFr for 2 twin beds; doubles 110-120SFr; quads 140SFr. Prices drop for multiple nights or group stays.) Although pricey, the **Zunfthaus zu Wirthen ❹**, Hauptg. 41, is worth it for its central location across from the Red Tower and spacious rooms with telephone and TV. (☎626 28 48; www.wirthen.ch. Breakfast included. Reception 6am-midnight. Check-in 2pm. Check-out 11am. Singles 83SFr, with shower 103SFr, with sitting area 135SFr; doubles 115SFr, with shower 138SFr. Children under age 2 free; under 16 30SFr per night. MC.)

Pittaria ❷, at Theaterg. 12, the second left after the bridge from the station, is run by the beaming and talkative Sami Daher. A tiny operation decorated with a camel motif, this spot serves pitas stuffed with vegetables, chicken, and pork for 7-13SFr. (☎/fax 621 22 69. Open Tu-F 10am-9pm, Sa 10am-6pm.) The **Taverna Amphorea ❸**, Hauptg. 51 on Marktpl., serves large vegetarian-friendly Greek and Middle Eastern specialties for 14-27SFr in a simple restaurant near the cathedral. The menu changes daily, and there is outdoor seating in summer. (☎623 67 63. Open Tu and Th 11am-11:30pm, W 9am-11:30pm, F 11am-12:30am, Sa 9am-12:30am.) **Baseltor ❸**, Hauptg. 79, just past the cathedral on the left next to the tower of the same name, is a cooperative with a changing daily menu of creative Italian pasta and meat dishes, mostly organically grown. Salads run 8-12SFr, entrées 19-28SFr. (☎622 34 22; www.baseltor.ch. Open M-Th 8:30am-11:30pm, F-Sa 8:30-midnight, Su 5-11:30pm; kitchen open noon-2pm and 6-10pm. AmEx/MC/V.)

The **Manora** grocery store/self-service restaurant is located on the fourth floor of a department store at Gurzelng. 18 to the left off Marktpl. (Open M-W and F 9am-6:30pm, Th 9am-9pm, Sa 8am-5pm. AmEx/DC/MC/V.) Try the **farmers' market** at Marktpl. (W and Sa 8am-noon). There is an **Aperto** at the train station. (Open M-Sa 6am-10pm, Su 7am-10pm. V.)

🟥 **SIGHTS.** Solothurn's well-preserved Baroque architecture alone justifies a visit to the city. The city's oldest square is **Friedhofplatz**, which contains Roman ruins. Nearby, the **Red Tower** on the Markupl. sports several clock faces and a macabre little skeleton. Built between 1762 and 1773 by a Ticino architect, the Italianate Baroque architecture of the **Kathedrale St. Ursen,** massive for such a small town, dominates Solothurn's *Altstadt* at the end of the Kreuzackerbr. The interior is also impressive and deserves a visit. The cathedral is dedicated to St. Ursus, the patron saint of Solothurn, who lost his head here for refusing to worship Roman gods. Its **tower** provides the *Altstadt's* best view, although the 249 steps are spiralling and can be a tight squeeze. The cathedral hosts classical music concerts during the summer; call for dates and prices. (☎622 37 53. Church open daily Easter-Oct. 8am-noon and 2-7pm; Oct.-Easter 2-6pm. Tower open M-Sa 9:30am-noon and 1:30-5:30pm, Su 1-5:30pm. Tower 2.50SFr, students 1SFr, children under 12 0.50SFr.) Just up the hill from the *Kathedrale*, the four floors of the expansive **Museum Altes Zeughaus,** housed in a 1609 arsenal, trace Swiss military history. Although you might need to be planning an invasion to best appreciate the hundreds of guns, swords, and other instruments of death, the museum provides plenty of historical context for the not-so-bloodthirsty. (Zeughauspl. 1, just uphill to the left of the cathedral. ☎623 35 28. Open May-Oct. Tu-Su 10am-noon and 2-5pm; Nov.-Apr. Tu-F 2-5pm, Sa-Su 10am-noon and 2-5pm. 6SFr, students 4SFr. English brochure free.) On the outskirts of the old town, the **Kunstmuseum,** Werkhofstr. 30, has an extensive collection of post-1850 Swiss works and temporary exhibits. (☎622 23 07; www.kunstmuseum-so.ch. Open Tu-F 10am-noon and 2-5pm, Sa-Su 10am-5pm. Free, but donation suggested.) **Schloß Waldegg** looks over all of Solothurn and the surrounding area. (Take bus #4 (dir: Ruttenen; 10min., 2 per hr.) to "St. Niklaus" 6 stops from the train station, and walk 10min. up Riedholzstr., the road at the intersection in the opposite direction of the bus. Parking available. Wheelchair accessible. Open Mar.-Oct. Tu-Th and Sa 2-5pm, Su 10am-5pm; Nov.-Dec. Su 10am-5pm. 6SFr, students 4SFr.)

🏔 **OUTDOOR ACTIVITIES.** Marked **hiking** and **biking** trails lead through the Jura to nearby Altreu, site of the oldest and best-known stork colony in Switzerland (2hr., trailhead at the corner of Kroneng. and Ritterquai). **Boat tours** leave

Solothurn for Biel and from there run to Murten or Neuchâtel. (☎329 88 11; www.bielersee.ch. Ferries run early May to mid-Oct. 2½hr.; 27SFr, round-trip 46SFr. SwissPass valid.) In the winter, **cross-country skiing** dominates the athletic scene. Weißenstein (1280m) has 7km of trails and chairlifts for downhill skiing on two small slopes best suited to beginners.

🎬 **ENTERTAINMENT.** In 2005, the annual **Swiss Film Festival** will bring celluloid lovers to the city January 25-30. **Fasnacht** is a week-long topsy-turvy carnival intended to drive away winter (Feb. 3-9, 2005). The party involves fantastical masks, raucous *Guggenmusik*, and temporarily renaming the town "Honolulu." Swiss writers gather to read and sit on panels during the **literature festival** (usually in late May). Music fans will enjoy the **Classic: Open Air Fest** (www.classic-openair.ch), July 4-16, 2005 and the **Jazz am Märetplatz** festival, in late August. Concerts fill the Marktpl. for three days, attracting jazz aficionados from far and wide.

MUNICH (MÜNCHEN)

Travelers who step past the stereotypes of *Lederhosen* and pot-bellied conservatives will be pleasantly surprised to discover that Munich is both the sleek southern capital of German affluence and the leafy home of German merriment. The city's cosmopolitan attractions and its long-standing tradition of enjoying beer, life, and nature (in that order) make it both relaxing and stimulating. World-class museums, handsome parks and architecture, and a rambunctious art scene conspire to create a city of astonishing vitality. Müncheners party zealously during *Fasching*, Germany's Mardi Gras (Jan. 7-Mar. 8, 2005), shop with abandon during the *Weinachtsmarkt* (Christmas Market), and imbibe vast quantities of beer during the legendary **Oktoberfest** (Sept. 17-Oct. 2, 2005).

PHONE CODES	The city code for Munich is 089. If calling Austria or Switzerland, dial 00 (int'l dialing prefix); then dial 43 (Austria) or 41 (Switzerland) before dialing the number.

TRANSPORTATION

Flights: Flughafen München (☎ 97 52 13 13). S1 makes the 40min. trip into Munich (sit in the rear of the train), as does S8. Trains between the airport and the train station depart every 10min., costing €8 or 8 stripes on the *Streifenkarte* per person; 2-5 adults can pay a group rate of €15 (see **Public Transportation**, p. 544). A **Lufthansa shuttle bus** runs between the Hauptbahnhof and the airport (45min.), with a stop at the "Nord-friedhof" U-Bahn station in Schwabing. It leaves from Arnulfstr., on the northern side of the train station, every 20min. 5:10am-8:10pm. Buses return from Terminal A *(Zentralbereich)* and Terminal D every 20min. 6:20am-9:50pm. €9.50, round-trip €15.

Trains: Munich's **Hauptbahnhof** (☎ 22 33 12 56) is the transportation hub of southern Germany, with connections to: **Amsterdam** (7-9hr., 1 per hr.); **Berlin** (6½hr., 2 per hr.); **Cologne** (6hr., 2 per hr.); **Frankfurt** (4hr., 2 per hr.); **Füssen** (2hr., every 2hr.); **Hamburg** (6hr., 1 per hr.); **Innsbruck** (2hr., every 2hr.); **Paris** (8-10hr., 6 per day); **Prague** (6-7hr., 4 per day); **Salzburg** (1¾hr., 2 per hr.); **Vienna** (5hr., 1 per hr.); **Zürich** (4½-5½hr., 4-5 per day). For 24hr. schedules, fare information, and reservations (in German), call ☎ 01805 99 66 33. The improved **Bayern-Ticket** (single €15, 2-5 people €22) is now valid for all train transit from 9am (midnight of the previous night on weekends) to 3am the next day, and can take you all the way to Salzburg. **EurAide,** located next to track 11 in the station, provides free train information in English and books train tickets. **Reisezentrum** information counters are open daily 7am-9:30pm.

Public Transportation: MVV, Munich's public transport system (☎ 41 42 43 44), runs Su-Th 5am-12:30am, F-Sa 5am-2am. S-Bahn to the airport starts running at 3:30am. Eurail, InterRail, and German railpasses are valid on the S-Bahn (S) but *not* on the U-Bahn (U), streetcars, or buses. Buy tickets at the blue *MVV-Fahrausweise* vending machines and **validate them** in the blue boxes marked with an "E" **before entering the platform.** Payment is on an honor system, but disguised agents often check for tickets; if you sneak on or don't validate correctly, you risk a €40 fine. Always descend from the right-hand side of the S-Bahn. **Transit maps** and **maps of wheelchair accessible stations** are at the tourist office or EurAide and at MVV counters near the subway entrance in the train station. *Fahrpläne* (schedules) cost €1 at newsstands.

Taxis: Taxi-München-Zentrale (☎ 216 10 or 194 10) has stands in front of the train station and every 5-10 blocks in the city center. Women can request a female driver.

ORIENTATION

Munich's center is encircled by the main **Ring** and quartered by two thoroughfares, which cross at the **Marienplatz** and meet the traffic rings at **Karlsplatz** (a.k.a. **Stachus**) in the west, **Isartorplatz** in the east, **Odeonsplatz** in the north, and **Sendlinger Tor** in the south. The Hauptbahnhof is west of Karlspl. East of the Isartor, the **Isar** river flows south-north by the city center. To get to Marienpl. from the station, go straight on Bayerstr. to Karlspl. and continue through Karlstor to Neuhauser Str., which becomes Kaufingerstr. before it reaches Marienpl. Alternately, take S1-8 (dir: Ostbahnhof; 2 stops from the Hauptbahnhof) to Marienpl.

PRACTICAL INFORMATION

LOCAL SERVICES

EurAide in English (☎ 59 38 89; www.euraide.de), along track 11 (room 3) of the Hauptbahnhof, near the Bayerstr. exit. EurAide is the English-speaking office of the Deutsche Bahn and books train tickets for anywhere in Europe at no extra charge. The website offers

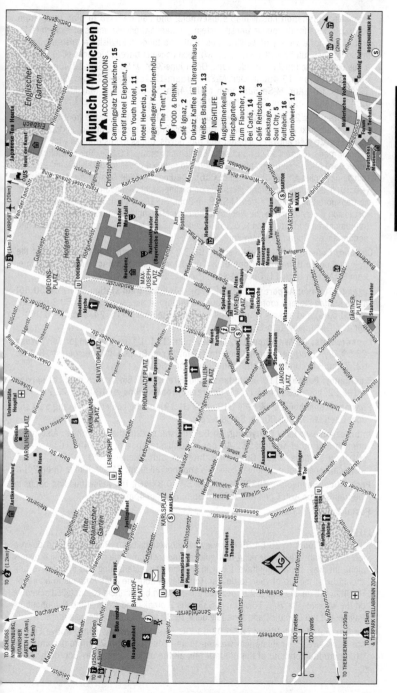

Munich (München)

⌂▲ ACCOMMODATIONS
Campingplatz Thalkirchen, 15
Creatif Hotel Elephant, 4
Euro Youth Hotel, 11
Hotel Helvetia, 10
Jugendlager Kapuzinerhölzl ("The Tent"), 1

FOOD & DRINK
Café Ignaz, 2
Dukatz Kaffee im Literaturhaus, 6
Weißes Bräuhaus, 13

NIGHTLIFE
Augustinerkeller, 7
Hirschgarten, 9
Zum Flaucher, 12
Bei Carla, 14
Café Reitschule, 3
Backstage, 8
Soul City, 5
Kultfabrik, 16
Optimolwerk, 17

MUNICH

extensive information not available elsewhere, and can be used to plan travel from abroad. Tickets for the public transit system (at standard prices), maps of Munich (€1), and tickets for a variety of walking, bus, and bike tours in English are also available, including ones run by EurAide (see below). Also converts traveler's checks (€1). Pick up a free copy of the brochure *Inside Track*. Open June-Sept. M-Sa 7:45am-12:45pm and 2-6pm, Su 7:45am-12:45pm; Oct. M-Sa 7:45am-12:45pm and 2-4pm, Su 7:45am-12:45pm; Nov.-Apr. M-Sa 8am-noon and 1-4pm, Su 8am-noon; May M-Sa 7:45am-12:45pm and 2-4:30pm, Su 7:45am-12:45pm.

Tourist Office: (☎23 39 65 00; www.muenchen.de/Tourismus), on the front side of the train station, next to the SB-Markt on Bahnhofpl. English spoken, but for in-depth questions, EurAide (see above) will better suit your needs. Books rooms (for free with 10-15% deposit made to their office) and sells English city maps (€0.30). The **München Welcome Card** offers free public transportation and reduced prices for 35 sights and services (single-day ticket €6.50, 3-day ticket €16). The English guide *Munich for Young People* (€0.50) lists beer gardens and gives tips on cycling, sightseeing, and navigating the public transportation system. Open M-Sa 9am-8pm, Su 10am-6pm. A large **branch office** just inside the entrance to the *Neues Rathaus* on Marienpl. also books rooms and offers free brochures and city maps (€0.30). A counter to the left sells tickets for concerts and performances. Open M-F 10am-8pm, Sa 10am-4pm.

Currency Exchange: ReiseBank (☎551 08 37; www.reisebank.de), at the front of the train station on Bahnhofpl. Open daily 7am-10pm. Another **branch** around the corner from EurAide at track 11. Open M-Sa 9:15am-12:30pm, 1-4:15pm.

Luggage Storage: Airport (☎97 52 13 75). 24hr. The **train station** (☎13 08 50 36) has a staffed storage room *(Gepäckaufbewahrung)* in the main hall (€0.50-3 per day; max. 3 days) and lockers in main hall and opposite tracks #16, 24, and 28-36. (€1-2 per day. Open daily 4am-12:30am).

Laundromats: SB-Waschcenter, Lindwurmstr. 124. U1 to "Sendlinger Tor." Wash €3.50, dry €0.60 per 10min. Open daily 7am-11pm. **Branch** at Untersbergstr. 8. Take U2, 7 and 8 to "Untersbergstr." Same prices and hours.

Emergency: Police ☎110. **Ambulance** and **Fire** ☎112. **Emergency medical service** ☎192 22, home service 551 771. **Emergency road service** ☎0180 222 22 22.

Pharmacy: Bahnhofpl. 2 (☎59 41 19 or 59 81 19), on the corner outside the train station. Open M-F 8am-6:30pm, Sa 8am-2pm.

Internet Access: Easy Everything, on Bahnhofspl. next to the post office. Also offers printing and other services. €2.40 per hr. Unlimited passes for 24hr. (€4), 7 days (€10), or 30 days (€25). Open 24hr. **Internet Café,** Marienpl. 20 (☎20 70 27 37; www.icafe.spacenet.de), serves cocktails and food all night. €1 per 30min. Open 24hr.

Post Office: Bahnhofpl., 80335 Munich (☎59 90 87 16). The yellow building opposite the train station exit. Open M-F 7:30am-8pm, Sa 9am-4pm.

Postal Code: 80335.

TOURS

▨ **Mike's Bike Tours** (☎25 54 39 88; www.mikesbiketours.com). Bike, swim, and down a few beers with English-speaking tour guides, and pick up some creative Munich history along the way. If you only have 1 day in Munich, this entertaining and informative tour should be at the top of your 'to do' list. Tours leave from the *Altes Rathaus* in Marienpl. The 4hr., 6.5km city tour (€22) includes a *Biergarten* break; there is a detailed schedule on the website. The 7hr., 16km tour (€33) has 2 breaks and stops at the Nymphenburg Palace and the Olympic Park. June-July daily 10:30am. Prices include bike rental.

The Original Munich Walks (☎55 02 93 74; www.munichwalks.com). Native English speakers give 2½hr. historical walking tours of the city with 2 different slants: the 10am introductory tour of the *Altstadt* hits all the major sights (May-Oct. daily; Nov.-

Mar. M, W, Sa), while a more specialized tour traces the history of the Third Reich and important sites from that era (May-Oct. 9:30am, 3pm). €10, students €9, under 14 €5. Discounted combo tickets available for both the walking tours and the Munich Walks guided tour of Dachau. Both walking tours meet at the **EurAide** office next to track 11 10min. before the listed time, or beneath the *Neues Rathaus* at Marienpl. 10min. after the listed time.

ACCOMMODATIONS AND CAMPING

Munich's accommodations seem to fall into one of three categories: seedy, expensive, or booked solid. During Oktoberfest, everything falls into the last category—if you're hoping to participate, begin your search up to a year in advance.

Euro Youth Hotel, Senefelderstr. 5 (☎59 90 88 11; www.euro-youth-hotel.de). From the Bayerstr. exit of the Hauptbahnhof, turn left on Bayerstr., then right on Senefelderstr.; the hotel is on the left. Friendly, English-speaking staff offers loads of information and spotless rooms. Bar serving *Augustinerbräu* (€2.80) open daily 7pm-late. Breakfast buffet €5. Laundry: wash €3, dry €1.30. Reception 24hr. Dorms €20; 3- to 5-person rooms €24 per person; singles without bathroom €45; doubles €55, with private shower, telephone, and breakfast €72; triples €28; and quads €84. Cash only. ❷

Hotel Helvetia, Schillerstr. 6 (☎590 68 50; www.Hotel-Helvetia.de), at the corner of Bahnhofspl., just beyond the Vereinsbank, to the right as you exit the station. Possibly the friendliest hotel in Munich. Recently renovated rooms. **Free Internet.** Breakfast included. Reception 24hr. Singles €30-35; doubles €40-55, with shower €50-65; triples €55-69; quads €75-88; 5-bed rooms separable into 2 rooms €95-110. ❸

Creatif Hotel Elephant, Lämmerstr. 6 (☎55 57 85; www.munich-hotel.net). 300m from the train station. From the Arnulfstr. exit, take a quick right on Pfefferstr., turn left on Hirtenstr., and right on Lämmerstr. All newly renovated rooms with fabulously colorful decor, private bath, telephone, and TV. **Free Internet.** Reception 24hr. Singles €30-40; doubles €40-65; extra bed €10. ❸

Jugendlager Kapuzinerhölzl ("The Tent"), In den Kirschen 30 (☎141 43 00; www.the-tent.de). Streetcar #17 from the Hauptbahnhof (dir: Amalienburgstr.) to "Botanischer Garten" (15min.). Follow the signs straight on Franz-Schrank-Str. and turn left onto In den Kirschen; The Tent is on the right. Night streetcars run at least once per hr. all night. Join 250 fellow international "campers" under a big tent on a wooden floor. Evening campfires. **Internet** €0.50 per 15min. Bike rental €6 per day. Free city tours in German and English. Breakfast and lockers included. Kitchen and laundry facilities available. Wash €2, dry €1.50. Passport required as key deposit. Reception 24hr. Open June-Aug. €8.50 gets you a foam pad, wool blankets, bathrooms, and showering facilities. Actual beds €11. Camping available for €5.50 per campsite plus €5.50 per person. ❶

Campingplatz Thalkirchen, Zentralländstr. 49 (☎723 17 07; fax 724 31 77). U1 or 2 to "Sendlinger Tor," then U3 to "Thalkirchen," change to bus #135 and get off at the "Campingpl." bus stop (20min.). 550 sites on the lush banks of the Isar. Jogging and bike paths nearby. TV lounge and restaurant. Laundry: wash €4, dry €0.50. Reception 7am-11pm. €4.50 per person, €1.30 per child under 14, €3-4 per tent, €4.30 per car. Tent rental €8 per night. Caravan rental €11 per person. Showers €1. ❶

FOOD

The vibrant **Viktualienmarkt,** 2min. south of Marienpl., offers both basic and exotic foods and ingredients, but prices can be steep. (Open M-F 10am-8pm, Sa 8am-4pm.) On every corner, **Biergärten** (beer gardens) serve savory snacks and booze.

▨ **Dukatz Kaffee im Literaturhaus,** Salvatorpl. 1 (☎291 96 00). The center of literary events in Munich, this café is the place to see and be seen. This home for struggling artists serves gourmet food (€6-8) to complement creative drink options (€2-4). Sip a cup of coffee and people-watch—you will unwittingly be observing the city's writers at rest. Open M-F 10am-1pm and 6:30-10:30pm, Sa 10am-3pm and 6:30-10:30pm. ❹

▨ **Schelling Salon,** Schellingstr. 54 (☎272 07 88). Bavarian *Knödel* and billiards since 1872. Rack up at tables where Lenin, Rilke, and Hitler once played (€7 per hr.). Breakfast €3-5.10. German entrées €4-11. Open M and Th-Su 6:30am-1am, kitchen open until midnight. A free **billiard museum** displays a 200-year-old Polish table and the history of pool dating back to the Pharaohs. Museum open Su night or upon request. ❸

▨ **Café Ignaz,** Georgenstr. 67 (☎271 60 93). Take U2 to "Josephspl.," then Adelheidstr. 1 block north and turn right on Georgenstr. Bakery and café serves delicious food to a low-key clientele. Dinners, ranging from crêpes to stir-fry dishes, €5-9. Breakfast buffet M and W-F 8-9am (€5) and 9-11am (€7). Lunch buffet M-F noon-2pm (€5.50). Brunch buffet Sa-Su 9am-1:30pm (€8). Open M-F 8am-10pm, Sa-Su 9am-10pm. ❷

🄶 SIGHTS

RESIDENZ. Down the pedestrian zone from Odeonspl., the richly decorated Residenz is the most visible presence of the Wittelsbach dynasty, whose apartments and state rooms now comprise the **Residenzmuseum.** Highlights include the Rococo **Ahnengalerie,** hung with over 100 "family portraits" tracing the royal lineage, and the spectacular Renaissance **Antiquarium,** the oldest room in the Residenz. Behind the Residenz, the beautifully landscaped **Hofgarten** shelters a small temple. *(Max-Joseph-Pl. 3. Take U3-6 to "Odeonspl." ☎29 06 71. Open Apr. to mid-Oct. M-W and F-Su 9am-6pm, Th 9am-8pm; mid-Oct. to Mar. daily 10am-4pm. Last admission 30min. before closing time. German language tours meet just outside the museum entrance Su 11am. Entrance €6, students €5, children €3.)* The **Schatzkammer** (treasury) contains the most precious religious and secular symbols of Wittelsbach power: crowns, swords, crosses and reliquiaries collected during the Counterreformation to increase the dynasty's Catholic prestige. *(Open same hours as Residenzmuseum. €6; students, seniors, and group members €5; children under 18 free with adult. Combination ticket to Schatzkammer and Residenzmuseum €9, students and seniors €8.)* A collection of **Egyptian art** is also housed on the premises *(☎ 28 92 76 30. Open Tu-F 9am-5pm, Sa-Su 10am-5pm. €4, students and seniors €3.)* Across Max-Joseph-Pl. lies the golden-yellow Baroque **Theatinerkirche,** constructed by Ferdinand Maria from 1663 to 1669 in honor of his son's birth. The crypt houses the bronze coffins of the Wittelsbach clan. *(Church tours June-Sept. Th at 2pm, €3.50. Crypt open M-F 10am-1pm and 1:30-4:30pm, Sa 10am-3pm. €2.)*

MARIENPLATZ. Sacred stone spires tower above the Marienpl., a major S-Bahn and U-Bahn junction and the social nexus of the city. The plaza, formerly known as *Marktplatz,* takes its name from the ornate 17th-century monument to the Virgin Mary at its center, the **Mariensäule,** built in 1638 to celebrate the fact that, during the Thirty Years' War, the city survived both the Swedish army and the plague. At the neo-Gothic **Neues Rathaus** (built in medieval style at the dawn of the 20th century), the **Glockenspiel** chimes with a display of a victorious Bavarian jouster. *(Daily 11am, noon, 3pm; in summer also 5pm.)* On the face of the **Altes Rathaus** tower, to the right of the *Neues Rathaus,* are all of Munich's coats of arms—with the notable exception of the Nazi swastika-bearing shield. *(Tower open M-F 9am-7pm, Sa-Su 10am-7pm. €1.50, under 19 €0.75, under 6 free.)*

FRAUENKIRCHE. The onion-domed towers of the 15th-century Frauenkirche are one of Munich's most notable landmarks. Its towers offer travelers an elevator-accessible view of the old city. Inside is the final resting place of Kaiser Ludwig der Bayer. *(From the Marienpl., walk 1 block toward the Hauptbahnhof on Kaufingerstr.*

ENGLISCHER GARTEN. Three times bigger than New York's Central Park, the Englischer Garten is the largest metropolitan public park in Europe. On sunny days, all of Munich turns out to fly kites, ride horses, or sunbathe. A couple of beer gardens are on the grounds, as is a Japanese tea house, Chinese pagoda, and Greek temple. Nude sunbathing areas are designated *FKK* on signs and park maps: consider yourself warned. Daring Müncheners surf the rapids of the Eisbach, the artificial river that flows through the park. The bridge on Prinzregentenstr., close to the Haus der Kunst, is a great vantage point for these stunts.

SCHLOß NYMPHENBURG. Constructed to celebrate the birth of Max Emanuel in 1662 (after 10 years of failed attempts), the breathtaking Schloß Nymphenburg is an ode to the overambitious hopes of the Wittelsbach dynasty. The gorgeous park was added in 1715 and remodeled in the English style at the beginning of the 19th century. The **Gallery of Beauties** is a fascinating collection of portraits of noblewomen and commoners whom the king fancied or bedded. Particularly famous are **Helene Sedlmayer,** a market girl protected by the king, and **Lola Montez,** an English theatrical dancer with whom Ludwig had an affair well into his 70s and who later led the 1848 revolution that caused his deposition. The faux-ancient **Magdalen hermitage** was meant to provoke penance in the courtiers. See how royalty rode and ate at the **Marstallmuseum** (carriage museum) and the porcelain collection. *(Streetcar #17 (dir: Amalienburgstr.) to "Schloß Nymphenburg." ☎ 17 90 80. Complex open Apr. to mid-Oct. M-W and F-Su 9am-6pm, Th 9am-8pm; late Oct. to Mar. daily 10am-4pm. Museum and Schloß open Tu-Su 9am-noon and 1-5pm. Badenburg, Pagodenburg, and Magdalen hermitage closed in winter. Schloß €5, students €4. Manors €2/€1. Marstallmuseum €4/€3. Entire complex €10/€8; children under 18 free with adult.)*

DACHAU. The first thing prisoners saw as they entered Dachau was the inscription "Arbeit Macht Frei" (work will set you free) on the iron gate of the **Jourhaus,** the only entry to the camp. Dachau was the Third Reich's first concentration camp, opened in 1933 to house political prisoners on the former grounds of a WWI munitions factory. After Hitler visited the camp in 1937, it became a model for the construction of the 3000 other camps throughout Nazi-occupied Europe, and a training-ground for the SS officers who would work at them. Dachau was primarily a work camp, as opposed to extermination camps like Auschwitz; during the war, prisoners made armaments and were hired out to work sites in the area. Many prisoners were worked to death. Those who volunteered for medical experiments in hopes of release were frozen to death or infected with malaria in the name of science. Although Dachau had a gas chamber, it was, for unknown reasons, tested but never put into full use. The tightly packed **barracks,** designed for 6000 prisoners, once held 30,000 men; two have been reconstructed for purposes of remembrance, but the rest were destroyed. Walls, gates, and a crematorium have also been restored since 1962 in a chilling memorial to the victims; a museum further honors their memory. *(From Munich, take S2 (dir: Petershausen) to "Dachau" (20min., €4 or 4 stripes on the Streifenkarte, or use Munich XXL ticket), then bus #724 (dir: Krautgarten) or 726 (dir: Kopernikusstr.) from in front of the station to "KZ-Gedenkstätte" (10min., €1 or 1 stripe on the Streifenkarte). Camp open Tu-Su 9am-5pm. Informative 2½hr. tours of the camp in English leave from the museum June-Aug. daily 1:30pm; Sept.-May Sa-Su 1:30pm. A 30min. introduction takes place M-F at 12:30pm and Sa-Su also at 11am. Tours are free; all donations* *go directly to the Holocaust Survivors' Association. Audio headsets in English and German available inside the entrance to the camp for self-guided tours; €2.50, students and seniors €1.50. Museum guides available in German, English, Dutch, Hebrew, French, Spanish, Hungarian, Polish, and Russian €0.20. Call ☎ 08131 17 41 for more information. Commercial tours also available.)*

▥ MUSEUMS

Munich has been a superb museum city ever since Ludwig I decided to make it into an "Athens on the Isar" in the early 19th century, requiring days for exhaustive perusal. The *Münchner Volkshochschule* (☎ 48 00 62 29) offers tours of many city museums for €6. The tourist office and many larger museums sell day passes for entry to all of Munich's state-owned museums (€15), which are free on Sunday.

▧ **PINAKOTHEK DER MODERNE.** A uniquely rich collection of 20th-century art is on display at this Pinakothek, which opened in 2000. The sleek space designed by *Münchener* Stephan Braunfels is strong on classical modernism: great works of Expressionism, Surrealism, Futurism and Cubism, as well as exciting contemporary sculptural and video installations. The **design section** has something for everyone, from cars to jewelry. The museum's two other departments feature graphic art and architecture. *(Barerstr. 40. U2 to "Königspl." Take a right at Königspl., and a left after 1 block onto Meiserstr. Walk 1½ blocks to the museum. ☎ 23 80 53 60. Open W and F-Su 10am-5pm, Tu-Th 10am-8pm. €9, students €5. Day pass for all 3 Pinakotheken €12/€7.)*

▧ **ALTE PINAKOTHEK.** This world-famous hall contains Munich's finest art from the 14th to 18th centuries, from religious triptychs to portraits and landscapes. Northern European artists are particularly well-represented, including Dürer, Cranach, Brueghel, Rembrandt, and Rubens, but Italian, French, and Spanish masterpieces are also on display. *(Barer Str. 27. ☎ 23 80 52 16. Hours and prices same as Pinakothek der Moderne. Combination ticket for the Alte and Neue Pinakotheken €8/€5.)*

▧ **NEUE PINAKOTHEK.** The 19th century in art, from Jacques-Louis David to Klimt. Special attention given to German art and to overlooked movements such as that of the Nazarenes. The Impressionist rooms are particularly impressive. Look for the iconic portrait of Goethe, by Stiegler of *Schönheitsgalerie* fame. *(Barerstr. 29, next to the Alte Pinakothek. ☎ 23 80 51 95. Open M and W-Su 10am-5pm, Th until 10pm. Tour M noon. Same prices as the Alte Pinakothek.)*

GLYPTOTHEK. Together with the *Antikensammlung*, the Glyptothek is a testament to the enduring German love for all things Greek, as well as Etruscan and Roman sculptures. The brightly painted plaster casts of Grecian sculpture will challenge your notions of classical art. *(Königspl. 3. U2 to "Königspl." Across Luisenstr. from the Lenbachhaus. ☎ 28 61 00. Open W and F-Su 10am-5pm, Th 10am-8pm. Free tour Th at 6pm. €3, students €2; together with Antikensammlung €5/€3.)*

DEUTSCHES MUSEUM. One of the world's largest and best science and technology museums. Exhibits include an early telephone, the work bench upon which Otto Hahn first split an atom, and an underground recreation of mining tunnels. An aerial electrical demonstration takes place daily (11am, 2, 4pm). A walk through the museum's 50+ departments covers over 17km; grab an English guidebook (€4). There's an impressive **flight museum** in a WWI hangar in Schleißheim. *(Effnerstr. 18. S-Bahn to Oberschleißheim, then follow signs. ☎ 315 71 40. Open daily 9am-5pm. €3.50, students and seniors €2.50.)* The **planetarium** shows educational films during the day and music and laser shows at night. *(€7, stu-*

dents €6; combination tickets for planetarium and museum €11.50/€9) The **IMAX screen** shows a variety of 45min. films every hour on the hour, while the **Forum cinema** screens contemporary European comedies and children's movies. *(All attractions located at Museuminsel 1. S1-8 to "Isartor" or streetcar #18 to "Deutsches Museum."* ☎217 91; www.deutsches-museum.de. Open daily 9am-5pm. Cinema €7, students €6, M-Tu €5. Imax 2D €7, students €6; 3D €8.50/€7.50.)

🎭 NIGHTLIFE

A nighttime odyssey begins at Munich's beer gardens and beer halls, and keeps flowing at cafés and bars, which, except on Friday and Saturday nights, shut off their taps at 1am. The dance clubs fill up, and throb relentlessly until 4am. Trendy bars, cafés, cabarets, and discos plugged into **Leopoldstraße in Schwabing** attract tourists from all over Europe. **Münchener Freiheit** (on the U3/6 line) is the most famous (and most touristy) bar/café district. Pick up *Munich Found, in München,* or *Prinz* at any newsstand to find out what's up. Munich's queer scene centers in the **Glockenbachviertel**, stretching from south of the Sendlinger Tor through the Viktualienmarkt/Gärtnerpl. to the Isartor. In adjacent lots lie 🎭**Kultfabrik**, Grafinger Str. 6 (☎49 00 90 70; www.kultfabrik.info), and 🎭**Optimolwerk**, Friedenstr. 10 (☎450 69 20; www.optimolwerke.de) two massive complexes with dozens of nocturnal venues playing all kinds of music. To get there take U5 or S1-8 to "Ostbahnhof," then follow the crowds onto Friedenstr. and then Grafingerstr. Optimolwerk (which contains 13 clubs) is smaller and caters to a slightly older crowd (mid-20s to early 30s) than Kultfabrik (23 clubs; late teens to mid-20s).

🎭 **Café Reitschule,** Königinstr. 34 (☎38 88 76). U3 or 6 to "Giselastr." Above a club, overlooking a horseback-riding school. In the summer, a backyard *Biergarten* teems with students crowding under straw huts and around rose-filled fountains. Breakfast served all day (€7-10). *Weißbier* €3.20. Entrées €7-15. Open daily 9am-1am.

🎭 **Bei Carla,** Buttermelcherstr. 9 (☎22 79 01). S1-8 to "Isartor," then walk 1 block south on Zweibrückenstr., take a right on Rumfordstr., turn left on Klenzestr., then another left onto Buttermelcherstr. This friendly lesbian café and bar is one of Munich's best-kept secrets. Women in their 20s and 30s flock here for pleasant conversation, a few cocktails, and a round or two of darts. Open M-Sa 4pm-1am, Su 6pm-1am.

Backstage, Wilhelm-Hale Str. 16 (☎126 61 00; www.backstage-online.com). Streetcar #16 or 17 to "Steubenpl." or #18 or 19 to "Elsenheimerstr." Plays indie and electronica. Local crowd. *Maß* €2 7-11pm. *Biergarten* shows movies and soccer games. Check online or call for concert listings. Open Su-Th 7pm-3am, F-Sa 7pm-5am.

Soul City, Maximilianspl. 5 (☎59 52 72), at the intersection with Max-Joseph-Str. The biggest gay disco in Bavaria, with music from 70s to Latin to techno. Straight clubbers always welcome. Beer €4 for 0.3L. Cover €5-13. Call for info about live concerts. In the early evening Soul City becomes the theater **KleinKunst Fabrik,** with cabaret, poetry readings and erotic comedy (closed during summer). Club open W 9pm-late, Th and Sa 10pm-late, F 11pm-late, Su 7pm-midnight.

BEER, BEER, AND MORE BEER

The six great Munich labels are *Augustiner, Hacker-Pschorr, Hofbräu, Löwenbräu, Paulaner,* and *Spaten-Franziskaner;* most restaurants will serve only one. The longest beer festival in the world is Munich's **Oktoberfest** (Sept. 17-Oct. 2, 2005) at Theresienwiese (U4 or U5).

■ **Augustinerkeller,** Arnulfstr. 52 (☎59 43 93), at Zirkus-Krone-Str. S1-8 to "Hacker-brücke." Walk left out of the station on the bridge and take a left on Arnulfstr. Founded in 1824, Augustiner is viewed by many as the finest *Biergarten* in town, with dim light-ing beneath 100-year-old chestnut trees, and tasty, enormous *Brez'n*. The real attrac-tion is the delicious, sharp *Augustiner* beer. *Maß* €6. Food €2-14. Open daily 10am-1am; hot food until 10:30pm. *Biergarten* open daily 10:30am-midnight.

■ **Hirschgarten,** Hirschgarten 1 (☎17 25 91). Streetcar 17 (dir: Amalienburgstr.) to "Romanpl." Walk south to the end of Guntherstr. and enter the Hirschgarten. The largest *Biergarten* in Europe (seating 9000) is boisterous and always crowded. Families come for the grassy park and carousel, and to see the deer that are still kept on the premises. entrées €5-15. *Maß* €5.50. Open daily 9am-midnight; kitchen open until 10pm.

APPENDIX

CLIMATE

Average Temperature	January		April		July		October	
	°C	°F	°C	°F	°C	°F	°C	°F
Geneva	0	32	9.5	49	19.5	67	10	50
Interlaken	0	32	10	50	19.5	67	11	51
Zurich	-1	30	8	47	18	64	8	47
Innsbruck	-2.5	28	9.5	49	18	64	9.5	49
Salzburg	-1.5	29	8	47	18	64	9	48
Vienna	-1	30	10	50	20	68	11	51
Munich	0.5	33	9	48	19	66	11	51

Although Austria and Switzerland are at about the same latitude as Newfoundland, their climates are considerably milder. In general, winters are cold and snowy enough for skiing, while summers are warm enough for outdoor cafés. July is usually the hottest month, with temperatures reaching 38°C (100°F) for brief periods, with generally cool evenings. February is the coldest, with temperatures down to -10°C (5°F). Mountainous areas of Austria and Switzerland are cooler and wetter the higher you get; as a rule, temperatures decrease about 1.7°C (3°F) with each additional 300m elevation. Snow cover lasts from late December to March in the valleys, from November to May at about 1800m, and year-round at above 2500m. Switzerland's lake areas, in the temperate swath of plain that extends across from Lake Constance in the northeast through Zurich and Bern down to Geneva, are wet all year—don't forget your umbrella.

TIME ZONES

Austria and Switzerland both use Central European time (abbreviated MEZ in German), which is 6hr. later than Eastern Standard Time in the US and 1hr. later than Greenwich Mean Time. It is 9hr. earlier than Eastern Australia Time and 11hr. earlier than New Zealand Time. Austria and Switzerland use the 24hr. clock for all official purposes, so 19:30 is the same as 7:30pm.

HOLIDAYS AND FESTIVALS

The *International Herald Tribune* lists national holidays in each daily edition. If you plan your itinerary around these dates, you can encounter the festivals that entice you and circumvent the ones that don't. Many services shut down on holidays and could leave you strapped for food and money in the event of an ill-timed arrival. Note also that in Austria, the first Saturday of every month is *Langer Samstag* (long Saturday); most stores stay open until 5pm. In small towns, stores are often closed from noon Saturday until 8am Monday; remember this when stocking up on food for weekends. Check the individual town listings and the index for information on the festivals below.

BOTH COUNTRIES

DATE	FESTIVAL	REGION
January 1	New Year's	National
March 25	Good Friday	National
March 28	Easter Monday	National
May 5	Ascension	National
May 16	Whit Monday	National
December 25	Christmas	National

AUSTRIA

DATE	FESTIVAL	REGION
January 6	Epiphany	National
June 10	Corpus Christi Day	National
May 1	Labor Day	National
Late July to Late August	Salzburg Music Festival	Salzburg
August 15	Feast of the Assumption	National
October 26	Austrian National Day	National
November 1	All Saints' Day	National
December 8	Feast of the Immaculate Conception	National
December 26	Boxing Day	National

SWITZERLAND

DATE	FESTIVAL	REGION
January 2	Berchtold's Day	National
Mid-February	Fasnacht (Carnival)	Basel, Lucerne
Mid-July	International Jazz Festival	Montreux
August 1	Swiss National Day	National
December 26	St. Stephen's Day	National

MEASUREMENTS

Austria and Switzerland use the metric system. Unconventional local units for measuring wine or beer are explained in the text when necessary. Note that gallons in the US are not identical to those across the Atlantic; one US gallon equals 0.83 Imperial gallons.

MEASUREMENT CONVERSIONS

1 inch (in.) = 25.4mm	1 millimeter (mm) = 0.039 in.
1 foot (ft.) = 0.30m	1 meter (m) = 3.28 ft.
1 yard (yd.) = 0.914m	1 meter (m) = 1.09 yd.
1 mile = 1.61km	1 kilometer (km) = 0.62 mi.
1 ounce (oz.) = 28.35g	1 gram (g) = 0.035 oz.
1 pound (lb.) = 0.454kg	1 kilogram (kg) = 2.202 lb.
1 fluid ounce (fl. oz.) = 29.57ml	1 milliliter (mL) = 0.034 fl. oz.
1 gallon (gal.) = 3.785L	1 liter (L) = 0.264 gal.
1 acre (ac.) = 0.405ha	1 hectare (ha) = 2.47 ac.
1 square mile ($mi.^2$) = $2.59km^2$	1 square kilometer (km^2) = 0.386 $mi.^2$

DISTANCE (IN KM)

Distances may vary depending on the type of transportation used and the route traveled. In certain cases, traveling through a neighboring country such as Germany or Italy can be the fastest route.

	Basel	Bern	Geneva	Graz	Innsbruck	Interlaken	Linz	Locarno	Lugano	Salzburg	Vienna	Zermatt
Basel												
Bern	71											
Geneva	187	129										
Graz	597	610	718									
Innsbruck	290	303	418	307								
Interlaken	98	43	230	581	278							
Linz	509	536	658	158	245	517						
Locarno	180	135	204	520	235	92	478					
Lugano	201	158	219	512	233	114	476	21				
Salzburg	410	433	554	200	137	412	108	370	369			
Vienna	658	684	801	138	383	661	151	615	608	249		
Zermatt	169	105	126	602	311	72	555	82	95	447	694	
Zurich	76	98	224	525	216	92	443	135	153	102	591	159

CITY PHONE CODES

CITY TELEPHONE CODES			
Basel	061	Liechtenstein	423
Bern	031	Locarno	091
Bregenz	05574	Lucerne	041
Geneva	022	Lugano	091
Graz	0316	Salzburg	0662
Innsbruck	0512	Vienna	01
Interlaken	033	Zermatt	027
Lausanne	021	Zurich	01

LANGUAGE

Confronted with Switzerland's four official languages and the countless dialects of German spoken throughout Austria and Switzerland, many travelers feel somewhat intimidated by the thought of communicating. Each of the following phrasebooks is designed to help you master your most urgent communication needs in each of the major languages spoken in Austria and Switzerland. Each phrasebook is preceded by a pronunciation guide. Don't be afraid to attempt to use the phrases listed; with a little practice, they'll roll off your tongue.

The first, perhaps most helpful, phrase a traveler should learn is "Sprechen Sie Englisch?," "Parlez-vous anglais?," or "Lei parla inglese?" (for use in the appropriate regions). Even if the person you ask doesn't speak English, she will appreciate your attempt. Most younger Austrian and Swiss urbanites speak at least a smattering of English—usually much more—thanks to the establishment of English as a requirement for high school diplomas. Outside of cities and among older residents, however, English proficiency becomes less common and you may have to rely on phrasebooks or an impromptu translation by the local tourist office.

APPENDIX

If you're unsure in a foreign language, it's best to err on the side of formality. For example, it never hurts to use titles like the German *Herr* (Mr.) or *Frau* (Mrs.), the Italian *Signore* and *Signora*, or the French *Monsieur* and *Madame*. When in doubt, use the formal pronoun "you" (*Sie* in German, *vous* in French, *lei* in Italian) with the appropriate form of the verb. People will let you know when it's time to switch to more familiar language.

GERMAN PRONUNCIATION

In German, consonants are pronounced the same as in English, with the exceptions of C (sometimes pronounced *TS*, but almost never seen outside of diphthongs); J (pronounced *Y*); K (always pronounced, even before N); P (nearly always pronounced, even before F); QU (pronounced *KV*); S (pronounced *Z* at the beginning of a word); V (pronounced *F*); W (pronounced *V*); Z (pronounced *TS*). The ß, or *Ess-tsett*, is simply a double S. An umlaut (Ä, Ö, Ü) theoretically blends the sound of the German vowel *E* with the umlauted vowel (sometimes written AE, OE, UE). Ä is pronounced like the e in "let"; Ö is pronounced like the *oo* in "look;" Ü is pronounced as if you were trying to say *ee* with your mouth positioned to say *ooh*. Pronounce SCH as *SH*. Rs are rolled with the back of the tongue. Unlike in much of Germany, CH in Austria and Switzerland is most often pronounced with the hoarse, throat-clearing sound that people often erroneously associate with High German. Vowels are as follows: A as in "father"; E as the *a* in "hay" or the indistinct vowel sound in "uh"; I as the *ee* in "cheese"; O as in "oh"; U as in "ooh"; Y similar to Ü; AU as in "ouch"; EU as the *oi* in "boil." With EI and IE, pronounce the last letter as a long English vowel.

FRENCH PRONUNCIATION

Learning the pronunciation of French letters is easy; learning when to pronounce them is hard, as many of the letters in a word are silent. In general, do not pronounce any final consonants except L, F, or C. This rule also applies to plural nouns—don't pronounce the final S. An E on the end of the word, however, means that you should pronounce the final consonant sound, e.g., *muet* is mew-AY but *muette* is mew-ET. J is like the S in "pleasure." R is rolled in the front of the mouth even more than in Austria. C sounds like *K* before A, O, and U; like *S* before E and I. G is hard before A, O, and U, and soft before E and I. A ç always sounds like *S*. Vowels are short and precise: pronounce A as the *O* in "mom"; E as in "help" (é becomes the *a* in "hay"); I as the *ee* in "creep"; O as in "oh." UI sounds like the word "whee." U is a short, clipped *oo* sound; hold your lips as if you were about to say "ooh," but say *ee* instead. OU is a straight *oo* sound. With few exceptions, all syllables receive equal emphasis.

ITALIAN PRONUNCIATION

Italian pronounciation isn't too complicated. There are seven vowel sounds in standard Italian: A as in "father," I as the *ee* in "cheese," U as the *oo* in "droop," E either as *ay* in "bay" or *eh* in "set," and O both as *oh* in "bone" and *o* as in "off." Save for a few quirks, Italian consonants are easy. H is always silent, R is always rolled. C and G are hard before A, O, or U, as in "cat" and "goose," but they soften into *CH* and *J* sounds, respectively, when followed by I or E, as in Italian *ciao* (chow; "goodbye"), and *gelato* (jeh-LAH-toh; "ice cream"). CH and GH are pronounced like K and G before I and E, as in *chianti* (ky-AHN-tee; the Tuscan wine), and *spaghetti* (spah-GEHT-tee; the pasta). Pronounce GN like the *ni* in "onion," as in *bagno* (BAHN-yoh; bathroom). GLI is pronounced like the *lli* in *million*, so *sbagliato* ("wrong") is pronounced "zbal-YAH-toh." If followed by A, O, or U, SC is pronounced as *SK*. *Scusi* ("excuse me") yields "SKOO-zee." When followed by an E or I, SC is pronounced SH as in *sciopero* (SHOH-pair-oh; "strike.")

USEFUL PHRASES

ENGLISH	GERMAN	FRENCH	ITALIAN
Hello.	Hallo.	Bonjour.	Ciao/Salve.
Excuse me/Sorry.	Entschuldigung.	Excusez-moi.	Mi scusi/Mi dispiace.
Could you please help me?	Können Sie mir bitte helfen?	Est-ce que vous pouvez m'aider?	Potrebbe aiutarmi?
Good day.	Guten Tag/Grüß Gott (Grüezi/Gruessach).	Bonjour.	Buongiorno.
Good morning.	Guten Morgen.	Bonjour.	Buongiorno.
Good evening.	Guten Abend.	Bonsoir.	Buonasera.
Good night.	Gute Nacht.	Bonne nuit.	Buonanotte.
Good-bye.	Tschüß! (informal); Auf Wiedersehen! (formal)	Au revoir.	Arrivederci/ArrivederLa.
yes/no/maybe	ja/nein/vielleicht	oui/non/peut-être	sì/no/forse
Please.	Bitte.	S'il vous plaît.	Per favore/Per piacere.
Thank you.	Danke.	Merci.	Grazie.
You're welcome.	Bitte.	De rien.	Prego.
Who?	Wer?	Qui?	Chi?
What?	Was?	Comment?	Cosa?
Where?	Wo?	Où?	Dove?
When (what time)?	Wann?	Quand?	Quando?
Why?	Warum?	Pourquoi?	Perche?
My name is...	Ich heiße...	Je m'appelle...	Mi chiamo...
What is your name?	Wie heißen Sie?	Comment vous appelez-vous?	Come si chiama?
Where are you from?	Woher kommen Sie?	D'où venez vous?	Di dov'è?
I'm from...	Ich komme aus...	Je viens de...	Sono di...
How are you?	Wie geht's?	Comment ça va?	Come sta (formal)/stai?
I'm fine.	Es geht mir gut.	Ça va bien.	Sto bene.
I'm not feeling well.	Mir ist schlecht.	J'ai mal.	Sto male.
I have a headache.	Ich habe Kopfweh.	J'ai mal à la tête.	Ho mal di testa.
I need a doctor.	Ich brauche einen Arzt.	J'ai besoin d'un médecin.	Ho bisogno di un medico.
Leave me alone.	Lass mich in Ruhe.	Laissez-moi tranquille.	Lasciami in pace!
I'll call the police.	Ich rufe die Polizei an.	J'appelle la police.	Telefono alla polizia!
Help!	Hilfe!	Au secours!/Aidez-moi, s'il vous plaît.	Aiuto!
Stop/Enough!	Halt!/Genug!	Arrêtez!	Ferma!/Basta!
Do you speak English?	Sprechen Sie Englisch?	Parlez-vous anglais?	Lei parla inglese?
I can't speak _____.	Ich kann kein Deutsch.	Je ne parle pas français.	Non parlo italiano.
I don't understand.	Ich verstehe nicht.	Je ne comprends pas.	Non ho capito.
I understand.	Ich verstehe.	Je comprends.	Ho capito.
Please speak slowly.	Sprechen Sie bitte langsam.	S'il vous plaît, parlez moins vite.	Parla più lentamente, per favore.
Excuse me?	Wie, bitte?	Pardon?	Come?
Please repeat.	Bitte wiederholen Sie.	Répétez, s'il vous plaît.	Potrebbe ripeterlo?
I would like...	Ich möchte...	Je voudrais...	Vorrei...
I'm looking for...	Ich suche...	Je cherche...	Cerco...
How much does that cost?	Wieviel kostet das?	Ça coûte combien?	Quanto costa?

ENGLISH	GERMAN	FRENCH	ITALIAN
Where can I buy something to eat/to drink?	Wo kann ich etwas zu essen kaufen/zu trinken kaufen?	Où est-ce que je peux acheter quelque chose à manger/à boire?	Dove posso comprare qualcosa da bere o mangiare?
OK.	OK/Alles klar.	D'accord.	Va bene.
I don't know.	Ich weiss nicht.	Je ne sais pas.	Boh./Non lo so.
Where is the toilet?	Wo ist die Toilette?	Où sont les toilettes?	Dov'è il gabinetto?
How do you say that in German?/French?...	Wie sagt man das auf Deutsch?	Comment ça se dit en français?	Come si dice...?
What does this mean?	Was bedeutet das?	Qu'est-ce que ça veut dire?	Che significa questo?
Where is the phone?	Wo ist das Telefon?	Où est le téléphone?	Dov'è il telefono?
I am a student (male/female).	Ich bin Student/Studentin.	Je suis étudiant/étudiante.	Sono studente/studentessa.
student discounts	Studentenermässigungen	tarifs réduits pour les étudiants	sconto per gli studenti
No problem.	Kein Problem.	Ce n'est pas grave.	Non c'è problema.

DIRECTIONS AND TRANSPORTATION

(to the) right	rechts	à droite	a destra
(to the) left	links	à gauche	a sinistra
straight ahead	geradeaus	tout droite	sempre diritto
here	hier	ici	qui/qua
there	da	là-bas	lì/là
far	fern	loin	lontano
near	nah	près de	vicino
east/west	Ost/West	est/ouest	est/ovest
north/south	Nord/Süd	nord/sud	nord/sud
I would like a ticket to...	Ich möchte eine Fahrkarte nach...	Je voudrais un billet à...	Vorrei un biglietto per...
Where is this train going?	Wohin fährt dieser Zug?	Quelle est la destination de la train?	Dove va questo treno?
Which bus goes to...	Welcher Bus fährt nach...?	Quel bus va â...?	Qual' è l'autobus che parte per...?
When does the train leave?	Wann fährt der Zug ab?	Quand est-ce que le train part?	A che ora parte il treno?
Please stop.	Bitte halten Sie.	Arrêtez, s'il vous plait.	Ferma, per favore.
Where is...?	Wo ist...?	Où est...?	Dov'è...?
the train station?	der Bahnhof?	la gare?	la stazione?
the tourist office?	das Touristbüro?	le bureau de tourisme?	l'ufficio turistico?
the post office?	die Post?	la poste?	la posta?
the old town?	die Altstadt?	la vieille ville?	il centro storico?
the hostel?	die Jugendherberge?	l'auberge de jeunesse?	l'ostello?
a grocery store?	ein Supermarkt?	un supermarché?	un supermercato?
the bus stop?	die Haltestelle?	l'arrêt d'autobus?	la fermata dell'autobus?
one-way	einfache Fahrt	un billet aller-simple	solo andata
round-trip	hin-und-zurück	un billet aller-retour	andata e ritorno

TIMES AND HOURS

At what time...?	Um welche Uhr...?	À quelle heure?	A che ora...?
What time is it?	Wie spät ist es?	Quelle heure est-il?	Che ore sono?
It is 5 o'clock.	Es ist fünf (5) Uhr.	Il est cinq (5) heures.	Sono le cinque (5).
It's early.	Es ist früh.	Il est tôt.	E presto.
It's late.	Es ist spät.	Il est tard.	E ritardo/tardi.
opening hours	die Öffnungszeiten	Es heures d'ouverture	le ore di apertura
daily	täglich	chaque jour	quotidiano
weekly	wochentlich	chaque semaine	settimanale
monthly	monatlich	chaque mois	mensile
today	heute	aujourd'hui	oggi
tomorrow	morgen	demain	domani
yesterday	gestern	hier	ieri
now	jetzt	maintenant	adesso/ora
immediately	sofort	tout-de-suite	subito
always	immer	toujours	sempre
except	ohne	sauf	ecceto/tranne
January	Januar	janvier	gennaio
February	Februar	février	febbraio
March	März	mars	marzo
April	April	avril	aprile
May	Mai	mai	maggio
June	Juni	juin	giugno
July	Juli	juillet	luglio
August	August	août	agosto
September	September	septembre	settembre
October	Oktober	octobre	ottobre
November	November	novembre	novembre
December	Dezember	décembre	dicembre
open	geöffnet	ouvert	aperto
closed	geschlossen	fermé	chiuso
morning	der Morgen	le matin	mattina
afternoon	der Nachmittag	l'après-midi	pomeriggio
evening	der Abend	le soir	sera
night	die Nacht	la nuit	notte
break time, rest day	die Ruhepause, der Ruhetag	fermeture	pausa, giorno di riposo
Monday	Montag	lundi	lunedì
Tuesday	Dienstag	mardi	martedì
Wednesday	Mittwoch	mercredi	mercoledì
Thursday	Donnerstag	jeudi	giovedì
Friday	Freitag	vendredi	venerdì
Saturday	Samstag	samedi	sabato
Sunday	Sonntag	dimanche	domenica
holidays	Ferien/Urlaub	vacances	giorni festivi/le ferie

APPENDIX

NUMBERS

No.	German	French	Italian
0	null	zéro	zero
1	eins	un	uno
2	zwei or zwoh	deux	due
3	drei	trois	tre
4	vier	quatre	quattro
5	fünf	cinq	cinque
6	sechs	six	sei
7	sieben	sept	sette
8	acht	huit	otto
9	neun	neuf	nove
10	zehn	dix	dieci
11	elf	onze	undici
12	zwölf	douze	dodici
13	dreizehn	treize	tredici
14	vierzehn	quatorze	quattordici
15	fünfzehn	quinze	quindici
16	sechzehn	seize	sedici
17	siebzehn	dix-sept	diciasette
18	achtzehn	dix-huit	diciotto
19	neunzehn	dix-neuf	dicianove
20	zwanzig	vingt	venti
21	ein-und-zwanzig	vingt et un	ventuno
30	dreißig	trente	trenta
40	vierzig	quarante	quaranta
50	fünfzig	cinquante	cinquanta
60	sechzig	soixante	sessanta
70	siebzig	soixante-dix	settanta
80	achtzig	quatre-vingt	ottanta
90	neunzig	quatre-vingt-dix	novanta
100	(ein)hundert	cent	cento
101	hunderteins	cent-et-un	centuno
1000	(ein)tausend	mille	mille

FOOD AND RESTAURANTS

restaurant	das Restaurant	un restaurant	il ristorante
bar	die Bar	un bar	il Bar
meal	das Mahl/das Essen	un repas	il pasto
water	das Wasser	l'eau	l'acqua

breakfast	das Frühstück	le petit déjeuner	la (prima) colazione
lunch	das Mittagessen	le déjeuner	il pranzo
dinner/supper	das Abendessen	le dîner	la cena
I am thirsty/hungry.	Ich habe Durst/Hunger.	J'ai soif/faim.	Ho sete/fame.
waiter(ess)	Kellner(in)/Herr Ober	serveur/euse	cameriere/a
Check, please.	Die Rechnung, bitte.	L'addition, s'il vous plaît.	Il conto, per favore.
Service included.	Bedienung inklusiv.	Service compris.	Servizio compreso.
I would like...	Ich möchte gern...	Je voudrais...	Vorrei...
It tastes good.	Es schmeckt gut.	C'est bon.	Tutto bene.
Do you have vegetarian food?	Haben Sie vegetarisches Essen?	Avez-vous de la nourriture végétarienne?	Ha qualcosa vegeteriana da mangiare?
I am diabetic.	Ich bin Diabetiker.	Je suis diabétique.	Sono diabetico.
milk	das Milch	le lait	il latte
coffee	das Kaffee	le café	il caffè
beer/wine	das Bier/der Wein	la bière/le vin	la birra/il vino
tap water	das Leitungswasser	de l'eau de robinet	acqua di rubinetto
bread	das Brot	le pain	il pane
vegetables	die Gemüse	le légume	le verdure
meat	das Fleisch	la viande	la carne
sausage	die Wurst	le saucisson	la salsiccia
chicken	das Huhn	le poulet	il pollo
pork	das Schweinfleisch	le porc	il maiale
cheese	der Käse	le fromage	il formaggio
pasta	die Nudeln	les pâtes	pasta
dessert	der Nachtisch	le dessert	il dolce

MISCELLANEOUS WORDS AND PHRASES

a single room	ein Einzelzimmer	une chambre simple	una camera singola
money	Geld	l'argent	i soldi
hospital	das Krankenhaus	un hôpital	ospedale
sick	krank	malade	malato/a
smoking	rauchen	fumer`	fumare
good/bad	gut/schlecht	bon/mauvais	buono/cattivo
happy/sad	glücklich, froh/traurig	heureux/triste	felice/triste
hot/cold	heiß/kalt	chaud/froid	caldo/freddo
big/small	groß/klein	grand/petit	piccolo/grande
full/empty	voll/ leer	plein/vide	pieno/vuoto
dangerous/safe	gefährlich/sicher	dangereux/sûr	pericoloso/sicuro
Caution!	Achtung!/Vorsicht!	Attention!	Stai attento!
Fire!	Feuer!	Feu!	Fuoco!
May I buy you a drink?	Darf ich dir ein Getränk kaufen?	Je peux t'offrir quelque chose de boire?	Posso offrirti qualcosa da bere?
I'm waiting for my father/husband/brother.	Ich warte auf meinen Vater/Mann/Bruder.	J'attends mon père/mon mari/mon frère..	Aspetto mio padre/il mio sposo/mio fratello

APPENDIX

INDEX

A

MAP INDEX

MAP LEGEND

✚ Hospital	🏛 Museum	🏨 Hotel/Hostel	▲▲▲ Mountain Peaks
✚ Police	✈ Airport	⛺ Camping	Mountains
✉ Post Office	🚌 Bus Station	🍴 Food & Drink	Glacier
ⓘ Tourist Office	🚉 Train Station	☕ Coffee House	Cliffs
$ Bank	Ⓤ1 U-Bahn Station	★ Entertainment	Tunnel
℞ Pharmacy	⚓ Ferry Landing	Nightlife	Ferry Route
▪ Site or Point of Interest	⛪ Monastery	Theater	Funicular/Cable Car
⚑ Embassy or Consulate	Funicular/Cable Car	Mountain Pass	Pedestrian Zone
Library	Church	Mountain Hut	Stairs
Internet Cafe	Gate or Entrance	Ski Resort	Footpaths/Trails
P Parking	Castle	∫ Waterfall	

Common Map Abbreviations:
Str. & -str.   Straße - street
Pl. & -pl.   Platz - square
G. & -g.   Gasse - lane
r.   Rue - street